£6-00

Edition
1 Volume

1934

PREFACES
BY
BERNARD SHAW

PREFACES BY BERNARD SHAW

LONDON
CONSTABLE AND
COMPANY LIMITED

PUBLISHED BY

Constable and Company Ltd.
LONDON

·

Oxford University Press
BOMBAY CALCUTTA MADRAS

·

The Macmillan Company
of Canada, Limited
TORONTO

·

First published 1934

PRINTED IN GREAT BRITAIN
BY R. & R. CLARK LIMITED EDINBURGH

THE PREFACES

AUTOBIOGRAPHICAL AND PROFESSIONAL

MISCELLANEOUS

TO
INTRODUCE
THE
PREFACES

EVER since the issue of my plays in a single volume in 1931 the demand for a similar collection of my prefaces has been continuous. As these prefaces, forming a series of pamphlets and essays on current political and social problems, are quite journalistic in character, and cover a period of nearly thirty years, most of them should be by this time left completely behind the march of our supposedly progressive civilization. Alas! it is so stationary, not to say stuck-in-the-mud, that the prefaces are still rather ahead of the times than behind them; and I dare say many of their new readers will conclude that I am a daring young innovator of eighteen instead of what I am in fact: a sage of seventyeight who, having long ago given up his contemporaries as hopeless, looks to future generations, brought up quite differently, to make a better job of life than our present respectables and right honorables and reverends can.

My prefaces are not the only ones of which this can be said. The contrast between the wisdom of our literature and the folly of our rulers and voters is a melancholy proof that people get nothing out of books except what they bring to them, and that even when the books explode their prejudices and rebuke their villainies they will read their own dispositions into the books in spite of the authors, and hang up their instruments of torture and their bullet-riddled banners in the very temples of Mercy and Peace. All the preachers and writers who have been anything but mouthpieces and scribes for human vulgarity are still waiting for earnest attention, though their statues and epitaphs are all over the place, and their books in every library. The cross on which Jesus was horribly executed is adopted as an emblem more widely than the eagle, the lion, the swastika, or the fasces; but anyone attempting to take the sayings of Jesus seriously would get into trouble not only with his neighbors but with the law. Thomas More lived so long ago that he might have been the grandfather of Henry Fielding's grandfather; but the name More gave to his proposals for sane and neighborly living is used only to stigmatize all such proposals as impossible. Take up Henry Fielding's Tom Jones. It is divided into several sections; and every section has an admirable preface. For all the effect they have had on the British Constitution or the Church of England they might just as well never have been written. Fielding might have been the great-grandfather of Charles Dickens, whose books, though classed as novels and duly hampered with absurd plots which nobody ever remembers, are really extraordinarily vivid parables. All the political futility which has forced men of the calibre of Mussolini, Kemal, and Hitler to assume dictatorship might have been saved if people had only believed what Dickens told them in Little Dorrit. And Dickens might have been Mussolini's grandfather or my father.

And so it comes about that these prefaces of mine are no more out of date than the Gospels, or Utopia, or Tom Jones, or Little Dorrit, or even the plays of Aristophanes and Euripides and the Socratian dialogues of Plato.

You may well ask me why, with such examples before me, I took the trouble to write them. I can only reply that I do not know. There was no why about it: I had to: that was all.

I hope it is not necessary for me to remind critics unversed in literary tradition that the prefaces to my plays have nothing to do with the theatre. Most of them were written long after the plays to which they are attached had been repeatedly performed. The practice of weighting volumes of plays with political and philosophical disquisitions dates back to Dryden; and I have kept it up in a simple desire to give my customers good value for their money by eking out a pennorth of play with a pound of preface. It has ended, as you see, in this volume, which is all preface and no play.

AYOT ST LAWRENCE
4th December 1933

PREFACES BY BERNARD SHAW

SOCIOLOGICAL

I

GETTING MARRIED

1908

THE REVOLT AGAINST MARRIAGE

There is no subject on which more dangerous nonsense is talked and thought than marriage. If the mischief stopped at talking and thinking it would be bad enough; but it goes further, into disastrous anarchical action. Because our marriage law is inhuman and unreasonable to the point of downright abomination, the bolder and more rebellious spirits form illicit unions, defiantly sending cards round to their friends announcing what they have done. Young women come to me and ask me whether I think they ought to consent to marry the man they have decided to live with; and they are perplexed and astonished when I, who am supposed (heaven knows why!) to have the most advanced views attainable on the subject, urge them on no account to compromise themselves without the security of an authentic wedding ring. They cite the example of George Eliot, who formed an illicit union with Lewes. They quote a saying attributed to Nietzsche, that a married philosopher is ridiculous, though the men of their choice are not philosophers. When they finally give up the idea of reforming our marriage institutions by private enterprise and personal righteousness, and consent to be led to the Registry or even to the altar, they insist on first arriving at an explicit understanding that both parties are to be perfectly free to sip every flower and change every hour, as their fancy may dictate, in spite of the legal bond. I do not observe that their unions prove less monogamic than other people's: rather the contrary, in fact; consequently, I do not know whether they make less fuss than ordinary people when either party claims the benefit of the treaty; but the existence of the treaty shews the same anarchical notion that the law can be set aside by any two private persons by the simple process of promising one another to ignore it.

MARRIAGE NEVERTHELESS INEVITABLE

Now most laws are, and all laws ought to be, stronger than the strongest individual. Certainly the marriage law is. The only people who successfully evade it are those who actually avail themselves of its shelter by pretending to be married when they are not, and by Bohemians who have no position to lose and no career to be closed. In every other case open violation of the marriage laws means either downright ruin or such inconvenience and disablement as a prudent man or woman would get married ten times over rather than face. And these disablements and inconveniences are not even the price of freedom; for, as Brieux has shewn so convincingly in Les Hannetons, an avowedly illicit union is often found in practice to be as tyrannical and as hard to escape from as the worst legal one.

We may take it then that when a joint domestic establishment, involving questions of children or property, is contemplated, marriage is in effect compulsory upon all normal people; and until the law is altered there is nothing for us but to make the best of it as it stands. Even when no such establishment is desired, clandestine irregularities are negligible as an alternative to marriage. How common they are nobody knows; for in spite of the powerful protection afforded to the parties by the law of libel, and the readiness of society on various other grounds to be hoodwinked by the keeping up of the very thinnest appearances, most of them are probably never suspected. But they are neither dignified nor safe and comfortable, which at once rules them out for normal decent people. Marriage remains practically inevitable; and the sooner we acknowledge this, the sooner we shall set to work to make it decent and reasonable.

WHAT DOES THE WORD MARRIAGE MEAN?

However much we may all suffer through marriage, most of us think so little about it that we regard it as a fixed part of the order of nature, like gravitation. Except for this error, which may be regarded as constant, we use the word with reckless looseness, meaning a dozen different things by it, and yet always assuming that to a respectable man it can have only one meaning. The pious citizen, suspecting the Socialist (for example) of unmentionable things, and asking him heatedly whether he wishes to abolish marriage, is infuriated by a sense of unanswerable quibbling when the Socialist asks him what particular variety of marriage he means: English civil marriage, sacramental marriage, indissoluble Roman Catholic marriage, marriage of divorced persons, Scotch marriage, Irish marriage, French, German, Turkish, or South Dakotan marriage. In Sweden, one of the most highly civilized countries in the world, a marriage is dissolved if both parties wish it, without any question of conduct. That is what marriage means in Sweden. In Clapham that is what they call by the senseless name of Free Love. In the British Empire we have unlimited Kulin polygamy, Muslim polygamy limited to four wives, child marriages, and, nearer home, marriages of first cousins: all of them abominations in the eyes of many worthy persons. Not only may the respectable British champion of marriage mean any of these widely different institutions; sometimes he does not mean marriage at all. He means monogamy, chastity, temperance, respectability, morality, Christianity, anti-socialism, and a dozen other things that have no necessary connection with marriage. He often means something that he dare not avow: ownership of the person of another human being, for instance. And he never tells the truth about his own marriage either to himself or anyone else.

With those individualists who in the nineteenth century dreamt of doing away with marriage altogether on the ground that it is a private concern between the two parties with which society has nothing to do, there is now no need to deal. The vogue of "the self-regarding action" has passed; and it may be assumed without argument that unions for the purpose of establishing a family will continue to be registered and regulated by the State. Such registration is marriage, and will continue to be called marriage long after the conditions of the registration have changed so much that no citizen now living would recognize them as marriage conditions at all if he revisited the earth. There is therefore no question of abolishing marriage; but there is a very pressing question of improving its conditions. I have never met anybody really in favor of maintaining marriage as it exists in England today. A Roman Catholic may obey his Church by assenting verbally to the doctrine of indissoluble marriage. But nobody worth counting believes directly, frankly, and instinctively that when a person commits a murder and is put into prison for twenty years for it, the free and innocent husband or wife of that murderer should remain bound by the marriage. To put it briefly, a contract for better for worse is a contract that should not be tolerated. As a matter of fact it is not tolerated fully even by the Roman Catholic Church; for Roman Catholic marriages can be dissolved, if not by the temporal Courts, by the Pope. Indissoluble marriage is an academic figment, advocated only by celibates and by comfortably married people who imagine that if other couples are uncomfortable it must be their own fault, just as rich people are apt to imagine that if other people are poor it serves them right. There is always some means of dissolution. The conditions of dissolution may vary widely, from those on which Henry VIII procured his divorce from Katharine of Aragon to the pleas on which American wives obtain divorces (for instance, "mental anguish" caused by the husband's neglect to cut his toe-nails); but there is always some point at which the theory of the inviolable better-for-worse marriage breaks down in practice. South Carolina has indeed passed what is called a freak law declaring that a marriage shall not be dissolved under any circumstances; but such an absurdity will probably be repealed or amended by sheer force of circumstances before these words are in print. The only question to be considered is, What shall the conditions of the dissolution be?

SURVIVALS OF SEX SLAVERY

If we adopt the common romantic assumption that the object of marriage is bliss, then the very strongest reason for dissolving a marriage is that it shall be disagreeable to one or other or both of the parties. If we accept the view that the object of marriage is to provide for the production and rearing of children, then childlessness should be a conclusive reason for dissolution. As neither of these causes entitles married persons to divorce it is at once clear that our marriage law is not founded on either assumption. What it is really founded on is the morality of the tenth commandment, which Englishwomen will one day succeed in obliterating from the walls of our churches by refusing to enter any building where they are publicly classed with a man's house, his ox, and his ass, as his purchased chattels. In this morality female adultery is malversation by the woman and theft by the man, whilst male adultery with an unmarried woman is not an offence at all. But though this is not only the theory of our marriage laws, but the practical morality of many of us, it is no longer an avowed morality, nor does its persistence depend on marriage; for the abolition of marriage would, other things remaining unchanged, leave women more effectually enslaved than they now are. We shall come to the question of the economic dependence of women on men later on; but at present we had better confine ourselves to the theories of marriage which we are not ashamed to acknowledge and defend, and upon which, therefore, marriage reformers will be obliged to proceed.

We may, I think, dismiss from the field of practical politics the extreme sacerdotal view of marriage as a sacred and indissoluble covenant, because, though reinforced by unhappy marriages as all fanaticisms are reinforced by human sacrifices, it has been reduced to a private and socially inoperative eccentricity by the introduction of civil marriage and divorce. Theoretically, our civilly married couples are to a Catholic as unmarried couples are: that is, they are living in open sin. Practically, civilly married couples are received in society, by Catholics and everyone else, precisely as sacramentally married couples are; and so are people who have divorced their wives or husbands and married again. And yet marriage is enforced by public opinion with such ferocity that the least suggestion of laxity in its support is fatal to even the highest and strongest reputations, although laxity of conduct is winked at with grinning indulgence; so that we find the austere Shelley denounced as a fiend in human form, whilst Nelson, who openly left his wife and formed a *ménage à trois* with Sir William and Lady Hamilton, was idolized. Shelley might have had an illegitimate child in every county in England if he had done so frankly as a sinner. His unpardonable offence was that he attacked marriage as an institution. We feel a strange anguish of terror and hatred against him, as against one who threatens us with a mortal injury. What is the element in his proposals that produces this effect?

The answer of the specialists is the one already alluded to: that the attack on marriage is an attack on property; so that Shelley was something more hateful to a husband than a horse thief: to wit, a wife thief, and something more hateful to a wife than a burglar: namely, one who would steal her husband's house from over her head, and leave her destitute and nameless on the streets. Now, no doubt this accounts for a good deal of anti-Shelleyan prejudice: a prejudice so deeply rooted in our habits that, as I have shewn in my play, men who are bolder freethinkers than Shelley himself can no more bring themselves to commit adultery than to commit any common theft, whilst women who loathe sex slavery more fiercely than Mary Wollstonecraft are unable to face the insecurity and discredit of the vagabondage which is the masterless woman's only alternative to celibacy. But in spite of all this there is a revolt against marriage which has spread so rapidly within my recollection that though we all still assume the existence of a huge and dangerous majority which regards the least hint of scepticism as to the beauty and holiness of marriage as infamous and abhorrent, I sometimes wonder why it is so difficult to find an authentic living member of this dreaded army of convention outside the ranks of the people who never think about public questions at all, and who, for all their numerical weight and apparently invincible prejudices, accept social changes today as tamely as their forefathers accepted the Reformation under Henry and Edward, the Restoration under Mary, and, after Mary's death, the shandygaff which Elizabeth compounded from both doctrines and called the Articles of the Church of England. If matters were left to these simple folk, there would never be any changes at all; and society would perish like a snake that could not cast its skins. Nevertheless the snake does change its skin in spite of them; and there are signs that our marriage-law skin is causing discomfort to thoughtful people and will presently be cast whether the others are satisfied with it or not. The question therefore arises: What is there in marriage that makes the thoughtful people so uncomfortable?

THE NEW ATTACK ON MARRIAGE

The answer to this question is an answer which everybody knows and nobody likes to give. What is driving our ministers of religion and statesmen to blurt it out at last is the plain fact that marriage is now beginning to depopulate the country with such alarming rapidity that we are forced to throw aside our modesty like people who, awakened by an alarm of fire, rush into the streets in their nightdresses or in no dresses at all. The fictitious Free Lover, who was supposed to attack marriage because it thwarted his inordinate affections and prevented him from making life a carnival, has vanished and given place to the very real, very strong, very austere avenger of outraged decency who declares that the licentiousness of marriage, now that it no longer recruits the race, is destroying it.

As usual, this change of front has not yet been noticed by our newspaper controversialists and by the suburban season-ticket holders whose minds the newspapers make. They still defend the citadel on the side on which nobody is attacking it, and leave its weakest front undefended.

The religious revolt against marriage is a very old one. Christianity began with a fierce attack on marriage; and to this day the celibacy of the Roman Catholic priesthood is a standing protest against its compatibility with the higher life. St Paul's reluctant sanction of marriage; his personal protest that he countenanced it of necessity and against his own conviction; his contemptuous "better to marry than to burn" is only out of date in respect of his belief that the end of the world was at hand and that there was therefore no longer any population question. His instinctive recoil from its worst aspect as a slavery to pleasure which induces two people to accept slavery to one another has remained an active force in the world to this day, and is now stirring more uneasily than ever. We have more and more Pauline celibates whose objection to marriage is the intolerable indignity of being supposed to desire or live the married life as ordinarily conceived. Every thoughtful and observant minister of religion is troubled by the determination of his flock to regard marriage as a sanctuary for pleasure, seeing as he does that the known libertines of his parish are visibly suffering much less from intemperance than many of the married people who stigmatize them as monsters of vice.

A FORGOTTEN CONFERENCE OF MARRIED MEN

The late Hugh Price Hughes, an eminent Methodist divine, once organized in London a conference of respectable men to consider the subject. Nothing came of it (nor indeed could have come of it in the absence of women); but it had its value as giving the young sociologists present, of whom I was one, an authentic notion of what a picked audience of respectable men understood by married life. It was certainly a staggering revelation. Peter the Great would have been shocked; Byron would have been horrified; Don Juan would have fled from the conference into a monastery. The respectable men all regarded the marriage ceremony as a rite which absolved them from the laws of health and temperance; inaugurated a life-long honeymoon; and placed their pleasures on exactly the same footing as their prayers. It seemed entirely proper and natural to them that out of every twenty-four hours of their lives they should pass eight shut up in one room with their wives alone, and this, not birdlike, for the mating season, but all the year round and every year. How they settled even such minor questions as to which party should decide whether and how much the window should be open and how many blankets should be on the bed, and at what hour they should go to bed and get up so as to avoid disturbing one another's sleep, seemed insoluble questions to me. But the members of the conference did not seem to mind. They were content to have the whole national housing problem treated on a basis of one room for two people. That was the essence of marriage for them.

Please remember, too, that there was nothing in their circumstances to check intemperance. They were men of business; that is, men for the most part engaged in routine work which exercised neither their minds nor their bodies to the full pitch of their capacities. Compared with statesmen, first-rate professional men, artists, and even with laborers and artisans as far as muscular exertion goes, they were underworked, and could spare the fine edge of their faculties and the last few inches of their chests without being any the less fit for their daily routine. If I had adopted their habits, a startling deterioration would have appeared in my writing before the end of a fortnight, and frightened me back to what they would have considered an impossible asceticism. But they paid no penalty of which they were conscious. They had as much health as they wanted: that is, they did not feel the need of a doctor. They enjoyed their smokes, their meals, their respectable clothes, their affectionate games with their children, their prospects of larger profits or higher salaries, their Saturday half holidays and Sunday walks, and the rest of it. They did less than two hours work a day and took from seven to nine office hours to do it in. And they were no good for any mortal purpose except to go on doing it. They were respectable only by the standard they themselves had set. Considered seriously as electors governing an empire through their votes, and choosing and maintaining its religious and moral institutions by their powers of social persecution, they were a black-coated army of calamity. They were incapable of comprehending the industries they were engaged in, the laws under which they lived, or the relation of their country to other countries. They lived the lives of old men contentedly. They were timidly conservative at the age at which every healthy human being ought to be obstreperously revolutionary. And their wives went through the routine of the kitchen, nursery, and drawing room just as they went through the routine of the office. They had all, as they called it, settled down, like balloons that had lost

their lifting margin of gas; and it was evident that the process of settling down would go on until they settled into their graves. They read old-fashioned newspapers with effort, and were just taking with avidity to a new sort of paper, costing a halfpenny, which they believed to be extraordinarily bright and attractive, and which never really succeeded until it became extremely dull, discarding all serious news and replacing it by vapid tittle-tattle, and substituting for political articles informed by at least some pretence of knowledge of economics, history, and constitutional law, such paltry follies and sentimentalities, snobberies and partisaneries, as ignorance can understand and irresponsibility relish.

What they called patriotism was a conviction that because they were born in Tooting or Camberwell, they were the natural superiors of Beethoven, of Rodin, of Ibsen, of Tolstoy and all other benighted foreigners. Those of them who did not think it wrong to go to the theatre liked above everything a play in which the hero was called Dick; was continually fingering a briar pipe; and, after being overwhelmed with admiration and affection through three acts, was finally rewarded with the legal possession of a pretty heroine's person on the strength of a staggering lack of virtue. Indeed their only conception of the meaning of the word virtue was abstention from stealing other men's wives or from refusing to marry their daughters.

As to law, religion, ethics, and constitutional government, any counterfeit could impose on them. Any atheist could pass himself off on them as a bishop, any anarchist as a judge, any despot as a Whig, any sentimental socialist as a Tory, any philtre-monger or witch-finder as a man of science, any phrase-maker as a statesman. Those who did not believe the story of Jonah and the great fish were all the readier to believe that metals can be transmuted and all diseases cured by radium, and that men can live for two hundred years by drinking sour milk. Even these credulities involved too severe an intellectual effort for many of them: it was easier to grin and believe nothing. They maintained their respect for themselves by "playing the game" (that is, doing what everybody else did), and by being good judges of hats, ties, dogs, pipes, cricket, gardens, flowers, and the like. They were capable of discussing each other's solvency and respectability with some shrewdness, and could carry out quite complicated systems of paying visits and "knowing" one another. They felt a little vulgar when they spent a day at Margate, and quite distinguished and travelled when they spent it at Boulogne. They were, except as to their clothes, "not particular": that is, they could put up with ugly sights and sounds, unhealthy smells, and inconvenient houses, with inhuman apathy and callousness. They had, as to adults, a theory that human nature is so poor that it is useless to try to make the world any better, whilst as to children they believed that if they were only sufficiently lectured and whipped, they could be brought to a state of moral perfection such as no fanatic has ever ascribed to his deity. Though they were not intentionally malicious, they practised the most appalling cruelties from mere thoughtlessness, thinking nothing of imprisoning men and women for periods up to twenty years for breaking into their houses; of treating their children as wild beasts to be tamed by a system of blows and imprisonment which they called education; and of keeping pianos in their houses, not for musical purposes, but to torment their daughters with a senseless stupidity that would have revolted an inquisitor.

In short, dear reader, they were very like you and me. I could fill a hundred pages with the tale of our imbecilities and still leave much untold; but what I have set down here haphazard is enough to condemn the system that produced us. The corner-stone of that system was the family and the institution of marriage as we have it today in England.

HEARTH AND HOME

There is no shirking it: if marriage cannot be made to produce something better than we are, marriage will have to go, or else the nation will have to go. It is no use talking of honor, virtue, purity, and wholesome, sweet, clean English home lives when what is meant is simply the habits I have described. The flat fact is that English home life today is neither honorable, virtuous, wholesome, sweet, clean, nor in any creditable way distinctively English. It is in many respects conspicuously the reverse; and the result of withdrawing children from it completely at an early age, and sending them to a public school and then to a university, does, in spite of the fact that these institutions are class warped and in some respects quite abominably corrupt, produce sociabler men. Women, too, are improved by the escape from home provided by women's colleges; but as very few of them are fortunate enough to enjoy this advantage, most women are so thoroughly home-bred as to be unfit for human society. So little is expected of them that in Sheridan's School for Scandal we hardly notice that the heroine is a female cad, as detestable and dishonorable in her repentance as she is vulgar and silly in her naughtiness. It was left to an abnormal critic like George Gissing to point out the glaring fact that in the collection of life studies of Victorian women to be found in the novels of Dickens, the most convincingly real ones are either vilely unamiable or comically contemptible; whilst his attempts to manufacture admirable heroines by idealizations of home-bred womanhood are not only absurd but not even pleasantly absurd: one has no patience with them.

As all this is corrigible by reducing home life and domestic sentiment to something like reasonable proportions in the life of the individual, the danger of it does not lie in human nature. Home life as we understand it is no more natural to us than a cage is natural to a cockatoo. Its grave danger to the nation lies in its narrow views, its unnaturally sustained and spitefully jealous concupiscences, its petty tyrannies, its false social pretences, its endless grudges and squabbles, its sacrifice of the boy's future by setting him to earn money to help the family when he should be in training for his adult life (remember the boy Dickens and the blacking factory), and of the girl's chances by making her a slave to sick or selfish parents, its unnatural packing into little brick boxes of little parcels of humanity of ill-assorted ages, with the old scolding or beating the young for behaving like young people, and the young hating and thwarting the old for behaving like old people, and all the other ills, mentionable and unmentionable, that arise from excessive segregation. It sets these evils up as benefits and blessings representing the highest attainable degree of honor and virtue, whilst any criticism of or revolt against them is savagely persecuted as the extremity of vice. The revolt, driven under ground and exacerbated, produces debauchery veiled by hypocrisy, an overwhelming demand for licentious theatrical entertainments which no censorship can stem, and, worst of all, a confusion of virtue with the mere morality that steals its name until the real thing is loathed because the imposture is loathsome. Literary traditions spring up in which the libertine and profligate—Tom Jones and Charles Surface—are the heroes, and decorous, law-abiding persons—Blifil and Joseph Surface—are the villains and butts. People like to believe that Nell Gwynne has every amiable quality and the Bishop's wife every odious one. Poor Mr Pecksniff, who is generally no worse than a humbug with a turn for pompous talking, is represented as a criminal instead of as a very typical English paterfamilias keeping a roof over the head of himself and his daughters by inducing people to pay him more for his services than they are worth. In the extreme instances of reaction against convention, female murderers get sheaves of offers of marriage; and when Nature throws up that rare phenomenon, an unscrupulous libertine, his success among "well brought-up" girls is so easy, and the devotion he inspires so extravagant, that it is impossible not to see that the revolt against conventional respectability has transfigured a commonplace rascal into a sort of Anarchist Savior. As to the respectable voluptuary, who joins Omar Khayyám clubs and vibrates to Swinburne's invocation of Dolores to "come down and redeem us from virtue," he is to be found in every suburb.

TOO MUCH OF A GOOD THING

We must be reasonable in our domestic ideals. I do not think that life at a public school is altogether good for a boy any more than barrack life is altogether good for a soldier. But neither is home life altogether good. Such good as it does, I should say, is due to its freedom from the very atmosphere it professes to supply. That atmosphere is usually described as an atmosphere of love; and this definition should be sufficient to put any sane person on guard against it. The people who talk and write as if the highest attainable state is that of a family stewing in love continuously from the cradle to the grave, can hardly have given five minutes serious consideration to so outrageous a proposition. They cannot have even made up their minds as to what they mean by love; for when they expatiate on their thesis they are sometimes talking about kindness, and sometimes about mere appetite. In either sense they are equally far from the realities of life. No healthy man or animal is occupied with love in any sense for more than a very small fraction indeed of the time he devotes to business and to recreations wholly unconnected with love. A wife entirely preoccupied with her affection for her husband, a mother entirely preoccupied with her affection for her children, may be all very well in a book (for people who like that kind of book); but in actual life she is a nuisance. Husbands may escape from her when their business compels them to be away from home all day; but young children may be, and quite often are, killed by her cuddling and coddling and doctoring and preaching: above all, by her continuous attempts to excite precocious sentimentality, a practice as objectionable, and possibly as mischievous, as the worst tricks of the worst nursemaids.

LARGE AND SMALL FAMILIES

In most healthy families there is a revolt against this tendency. The exchanging of presents on birthdays and the like is barred by general consent, and the relations of the parties are placed by express treaty on an unsentimental footing.

Unfortunately this mitigation of family sentimentality is much more characteristic of large families than small ones. It used to be said that members of large families get on in the world; and it is certainly true that for purposes of social training a household of twenty surpasses a household of five as an Oxford College surpasses an eight-roomed house in a cheap street. Ten children, with the necessary adults, make a community in which an excess of sentimentality is impossible. Two children make a doll's house, in which both parents and children become morbid if they keep to themselves. What is more, when large families

were the fashion, they were organized as tyrannies much more than as "atmospheres of love." Francis Place tells us that he kept out of his father's way because his father never passed a child within his reach without striking it; and though the case was an extreme one, it was an extreme that illustrated a tendency. Sir Walter Scott's father, when his son incautiously expressed some relish for his porridge, dashed a handful of salt into it with an instinctive sense that it was his duty as a father to prevent his son enjoying himself. Ruskin's mother gratified the sensual side of her maternal passion, not by cuddling her son, but by whipping him when he fell downstairs or was slack in learning the Bible off by heart; and this grotesque safety-valve for voluptuousness, mischievous as it was in many ways, had at least the advantage that the child did not enjoy it and was not debauched by it, as he would have been by transports of sentimentality.

But nowadays we cannot depend on these safeguards, such as they were. We no longer have large families: all the families are too small to give the children the necessary social training. The Roman father is out of fashion; and the whip and the cane are becoming discredited, not so much by the old arguments against corporal punishment (sound as these were) as by the gradual wearing away of the veil from the fact that flogging is a form of debauchery. The advocate of flogging as a punishment is now exposed to very disagreeable suspicions; and ever since Rousseau rose to the effort of making a certain very ridiculous confession on the subject, there has been a growing perception that child whipping, even for the children themselves, is not always the innocent and highminded practice it professes to be. At all events there is no getting away from the facts that families are smaller than they used to be, and that passions which formerly took effect in tyranny have been largely diverted into sentimentality. And though a little sentimentality may be a very good thing, chronic sentimentality is a horror, more dangerous, because more possible, than the erotomania which we all condemn when we are not thoughtlessly glorifying it as the ideal married state.

THE GOSPEL OF LAODICEA

Let us try to get at the root error of these false domestic doctrines. Why was it that the late Samuel Butler, with a conviction that increased with his experience of life, preached the gospel of Laodicea, urging people to be temperate in what they called goodness as in everything else? Why is it that I, when I hear some well-meaning person exhort young people to make it a rule to do at least one kind action every day, feel very much as I should if I heard them persuade children to get drunk at least once every day? Apart from the initial absurdity of accepting as permanent a state of things in which there would be in this country misery enough to supply occasion for several thousand million kind actions per annum, the effect on the character of the doers of the actions would be so appalling, that one month of any serious attempt to carry out such counsels would probably bring about more stringent legislation against actions going beyond the strict letter of the law in the way of kindness than we have now against excess in the opposite direction.

There is no more dangerous mistake than the mistake of supposing that we cannot have too much of a good thing. The truth is, an immoderately good man is very much more dangerous than an immoderately bad man: that is why Savonarola was burnt and John of Leyden torn to pieces with red-hot pincers whilst multitudes of unredeemed rascals were being let off with clipped ears, burnt palms, a flogging, or a few years in the galleys. That is why Christianity never got any grip of the world until it virtually reduced its claims on the ordinary citizen's attention to a couple of hours every seventh day, and let him alone on week-days. If the fanatics who are preoccupied day in and day out with their salvation were healthy, virtuous, and wise, the Laodiceanism of the ordinary man might be regarded as a deplorable shortcoming; but, as a matter of fact, no more frightful misfortune could threaten us than a general spread of fanaticism. What people call goodness has to be kept in check just as carefully as what they call badness; for the human constitution will not stand very much of either without serious psychological mischief, ending in insanity or crime. The fact that the insanity may be privileged, as Savonarola's was up to the point of wrecking the social life of Florence, does not alter the case. We always hesitate to treat a dangerously good man as a lunatic because he may turn out to be a prophet in the true sense: that is, a man of exceptional sanity who is in the right when we are in the wrong. However necessary it may have been to get rid of Savonarola, it was foolish to poison Socrates and burn St Joan of Arc. But it is none the less necessary to take a firm stand against the monstrous proposition that because certain attitudes and sentiments may be heroic and admirable at some momentous crisis, they should or can be maintained at the same pitch continuously through life. A life spent in prayer and almsgiving is really as insane as a life spent in cursing and picking pockets: the effect of everybody doing it would be equally disastrous. The superstitious tolerance so long accorded to monks and nuns is inevitably giving way to a very general and very natural practice of confiscating their retreats and expelling them from their country, with the result that they come to England and Ireland, where they are partly unnoticed and partly encouraged because they conduct technical schools and teach our girls softer speech and gentler manners than our comparatively ruffianly elementary teachers. But they are still full of the notion that because it is possible for men to attain the summit of Mont Blanc and stay there for an hour, it is possible for them to live there. Children are punished and scolded for not living there; and adults take serious offence if it is not assumed that they live there.

As a matter of fact, ethical strain is just as bad for us as physical strain. It is desirable that the normal pitch of conduct at which men are not conscious of being particularly virtuous, although they feel mean when they fall below it, should be raised as high as possible; but it is not desirable that they should attempt to live above this pitch any more than that they should habitually walk at the rate of five miles an hour or carry a hundredweight continually on their backs. Their normal condition should be in nowise difficult or remarkable; and it is a perfectly sound instinct that leads us to mistrust the good man as much as the bad man, and to object to the clergyman who is pious extra-professionally as much as to the professional pugilist who is quarrelsome and violent in private life. We do not want good men and bad men any more than we want giants and dwarfs. What we do want is a high quality for our normal: that is, people who can be much better than what we now call respectable without self-sacrifice. Conscious goodness, like conscious muscular effort, may be of use in emergencies; but for everyday national use it is negligible; and its effect on the character of the individual may easily be disastrous.

FOR BETTER FOR WORSE

It would be hard to find any document in practical daily use in which these obvious truths seem so stupidly overlooked as they are in the marriage service. As we have seen, the stupidity is only apparent: the service was really only an honest attempt to make the best of a commercial contract of property and slavery by subjecting it to some religious restraint and elevating it by some touch of poetry. But the actual result is that when two people are under the influence of the most violent, most insane, most delusive, and most transient of passions, they are required to swear that they will remain in that excited, abnormal, and exhausting condition continuously until death do them part. And though of course nobody expects them to do anything so impossible and so unwholesome, yet the law that regulates their relations, and the public opinion that regulates that law, is actually founded on the assumption that the marriage vow is not only feasible but beautiful and holy, and that if they are false to it, they deserve no sympathy and no relief. If all married people really lived together, no doubt the mere force of facts would make an end to this inhuman nonsense in a month, if not sooner; but it is very seldom brought to that test. The typical British husband sees much less of his wife than he does of his business partner, his fellow clerk, or whoever works beside him day by day. Man and wife do not, as a rule, live together: they only breakfast together, dine together, and sleep in the same room. In most cases the woman knows nothing of the man's working life and he knows nothing of her working life (he calls it her home life). It is remarkable that the very people who romance most absurdly about the closeness and sacredness of the marriage tie are also those who are most convinced that the man's sphere and the woman's sphere are so entirely separate that only in their leisure moments can they ever be together. A man as intimate with his own wife as a magistrate is with his clerk, or a Prime Minister with the leader of the

Opposition, is a man in ten thousand. The majority of married couples never get to know one another at all: they only get accustomed to having the same house, the same children, and the same income, which is quite a different matter. The comparatively few men who work at home—writers, artists, and to some extent clergymen—have to effect some sort of segregation within the house or else run a heavy risk of overstraining their domestic relations. When the pair is so poor that it can afford only a single room, the strain is intolerable: violent quarrelling is the result. Very few couples can live in a single-roomed tenement without exchanging blows quite frequently. In the leisured classes there is often no real family life at all. The boys are at a public school; the girls are in the schoolroom in charge of a governess: the husband is at his club or in a set which is not his wife's; and the institution of marriage enjoys the credit of a domestic peace which is hardly more intimate than the relations of prisoners in the same gaol or guests at the same garden party. Taking these two cases of the single room and the unearned income as the extremes, we might perhaps locate at a guess whereabout on the scale between them any particular family stands. But it is clear enough that the one-roomed end, though its conditions enable the marriage vow to be carried out with the utmost attainable exactitude, is far less endurable in practice, and far more mischievous in its effect on the parties concerned, and through them on the community, than the other end. Thus we see that the revolt against marriage is by no means only a revolt against its sordidness as a survival of sex slavery. It may even plausibly be maintained that this is precisely the part of it that works most smoothly in practice. The revolt is also against its sentimentality, its romance, its Amorism, even against its enervating happiness.

WANTED: AN IMMORAL STATESMAN

We now see that the statesman who undertakes to deal with marriage will have to face an amazingly complicated public opinion. In fact, he will have to leave opinion as far as possible out of the question, and deal with human nature instead. For even if there could be any real public opinion in a society like ours, which is a mere mob of classes, each with its own habits and prejudices, it would be at best a jumble of superstitions and interests, taboos and hypocrisies, which could not be reconciled in any coherent enactment. It would probably proclaim passionately that it does not matter in the least what sort of children we have, or how few or how many, provided the children are legitimate. Also that it does not matter in the least what sort of adults we have, provided they are married. No statesman worth the name can possibly act on these views. He is bound to prefer one healthy illegitimate child to ten rickety legitimate ones, and one energetic and capable unmarried couple to a dozen inferior apathetic husbands and wives. If it could be proved that illicit unions produce three children each and marriages only one and a half, he would be bound to encourage illicit unions and discourage and even penalize marriage. The common notion that the existing forms of marriage are not political contrivances, but sacred ethical obligations to which everything, even the very existence of the human race, must be sacrificed if necessary (and this is what the vulgar morality we mostly profess on the subject comes to) is one on which no sane Government could act for a moment; and yet it influences, or is believed to influence, so many votes, that no Government will touch the marriage question if it can possibly help it, even when there is a demand for the extension of marriage, as in the case of the recent long-delayed Act legalizing marriage with a deceased wife's sister. When a reform in the other direction is needed (for example, an extension of divorce), not even the existence of the most unbearable hardships will induce our statesmen to move so long as the victims submit sheepishly, though when they take the remedy into their own hands an inquiry is soon begun. But what is now making some action in the matter imperative is neither the sufferings of those who are tied for life to criminals, drunkards, physically unsound and dangerous mates, and worthless and unamiable people generally, nor the immorality of the couples condemned to celibacy by separation orders which do not annul their marriages, but the fall in the birth-rate. Public opinion will not help us out of this difficulty: on the contrary, it will, if it be allowed, punish anybody who mentions it. When Zola tried to repopulate France by writing a novel in praise of parentage, the only comment made here was that the book could not possibly be translated into English, as its subject was too improper.

THE LIMITS OF DEMOCRACY

Now if England had been governed in the past by statesmen willing to be ruled by such public opinion as that, she would have been wiped off the political map long ago. The modern notion that democracy means governing a country according to the ignorance of its majorities is never more disastrous than when there is some question of sexual morals to be dealt with. The business of a democratic statesman is not, as some of us seem to think, to convince the voters that he knows no better than they as to the methods of attaining their common ends, but on the contrary to convince them that he knows much better than they do, and therefore differs from them on every possible question of method. The voter's duty is to take care that the Government consists of men whom he can trust to devize or support institutions making for the common welfare. This is highly skilled work; and to be governed by people who set about it as the man in the street would set about it is to make straight for "red ruin and the breaking up of laws." Voltaire said that Mr Everybody is wiser than anybody; and whether he is or not, it is his will that must prevail; but the will and the way are two very different things. For example, it is the will of the people on a hot day that the means of relief from the effects of the heat should be within the reach of everybody. Nothing could be more innocent, more hygienic, more important to the social welfare. But the way of the people on such occasions is mostly to drink large quantities of beer, or, among the more luxurious classes, iced claret cup, lemon squashes, and the like. To take a moral illustration, the will to suppress misconduct and secure efficiency in work is general and salutary; but the notion that the best and only effective way is by complaining, scolding, punishing, and revenging is equally general. When Mrs Squeers opened an abscess on her pupil's head with an inky penknife, her object was entirely laudable: her heart was in the right place: a statesman interfering with her on the ground that he did not want the boy cured would have deserved impeachment for gross tyranny. But a statesman tolerating amateur surgical practice with inky penknives in school would be a very bad Minister of Education. It is on the question of method that your expert comes in; and though I am democrat enough to insist that he must first convince a representative body of amateurs that his way is the right way and Mrs Squeers's way the wrong way, yet I would not have them assume that Mrs Squeers's amateur way is likely to be the right way because she belongs to the democracy and the Minister to the bureaucracy, or that any other test is to be applied to it except the test of its effect on human welfare.

THE SCIENCE AND ART OF POLITICS

Political Science means nothing else than the devizing of the best ways of fulfilling the will of the world; and, I repeat, it is skilled work. Once the way is discovered, the methods laid down, and the machinery provided, the work of the statesman is done, and that of the official begins. To illustrate, there is no need for the police officer who governs the street traffic to be or to know any better than the people who obey the wave of his hand. All concerted action involves subordination and the appointment of directors at whose signal the others will act. There is no more need for them to be superior to the rest than for the keystone of an arch to be of harder stone than the coping. But when it comes to devizing the directions which are to be obeyed: that is, to making new institutions and scrapping old ones, then you need aristocracy in the sense of government by the best. A military state organized so as to carry out exactly the impulses of the average soldier would not last a year. The result of trying to make the Church of England reflect the notions of the average churchgoer has reduced it to a cipher except for the purposes of a petulantly irreligious social and political club. Democracy as to the thing to be done may be inevitable (hence the vital need for a democracy of supermen); but democracy as to the way to do it is like letting the passengers drive the train: it can only end in collision and wreck. As a matter of fact, we obtain reforms (such as they are), not by allowing the electorate to draft statutes, but by persuading it that a certain minister and his cabinet are gifted with sufficient political sagacity to find out how to produce the desired result. And the usual penalty of taking advantage of this power to reform our institutions is defeat by a vehement "swing of the pendulum" at the next election. Therein lies the peril and the glory of democratic statesmanship. A statesman who confines himself to popular legislation—or, for the matter of that, a playwright who confines himself to popular plays—is like a blind man's dog who goes wherever the blind man pulls him, on the ground that both of them want to go to the same place.

WHY STATESMEN SHIRK THE MARRIAGE QUESTION

The reform of marriage, then, will be a very splendid and very hazardous adventure for the Prime Minister who takes it in hand. He will be posted on every hoarding and denounced in every Opposition paper, especially in the sporting papers, as the destroyer of the home, the family, of decency, of morality, of chastity and what not. All the commonplaces of the modern anti-Socialist Noodle's Oration will be hurled at him. And he will have to proceed without the slightest concession to it, giving the noodles nothing but their due in the assurance "I know how to attain our ends better than you," and staking his political life on the conviction carried by that assurance, which conviction will depend a good deal on the certainty with which it is made, which again can be attained only by studying the facts of marriage and understanding the needs of the nation. And, after all, he will find that the pious commonplaces on which he and the electorate are agreed conceal an utter difference in the real ends in view: his being public, far-sighted, and impersonal, and those of multitudes of the electorate narrow, personal, jealous, and corrupt. Under such circumstances, it is not to be wondered at that the mere mention of the marriage question makes a British Cabinet shiver with apprehension and hastily pass on to safer business. Nevertheless the reform of marriage cannot be put off for ever. When its hour comes, what are the points the Cabinet will have to take up?

THE QUESTION OF POPULATION

First, it will have to make up its mind as to how many people we want in the country. If we want less than at present, we must ascertain how many less; and if we allow the reduction to be made by the continued operation of the present sterilization of marriage, we must settle how the process is to be stopped when it has gone far enough. But if we desire to maintain the population at its present figure, or to increase it, we must take immediate steps to induce people of moderate means to marry earlier and to have more children. There is less urgency in the case of the very poor and the very rich. They breed recklessly: the rich because they can afford it, and the poor because they cannot afford the precautions by which the artisans and the middle classes avoid big families. Nevertheless the population declines, because the high birth-rate of the very poor is counterbalanced by a huge infantile-mortality in the slums, whilst the very rich are also the very few, and are becoming sterilized by the spreading revolt of their women against excessive child-bearing—sometimes against any child-bearing.

This last cause is important. It cannot be removed by any economic readjustment. If every family were provided with £10,000 a year tomorrow, women would still refuse more and more to continue bearing children until they are exhausted whilst numbers of others are bearing no children at all. Even if every woman bearing and rearing a valuable child received a handsome series of payments, thereby making motherhood a real profession as it ought to be, the number of women able or willing to give more of their lives to gestation and nursing than three or four children would cost them might not be very large if the advance in social organization and conscience indicated by such payments involved also the opening up of other means of livelihood to women. And it must be remembered that urban civilization itself, insofar as it is a method of evolution (and when it is not this, it is simply a nuisance), is a sterilizing process as far as numbers go. It is harder to keep up the supply of elephants than of sparrows and rabbits; and for the same reason it will be harder to keep up the supply of highly cultivated men and women than it now is of agricultural laborers. Bees get out of this difficulty by a special system of feeding which enables a queen bee to produce 4000 eggs a day whilst the other females lose their sex altogether and become workers supporting the males in luxury and idleness until the queen has found her mate, when the queen kills him and the quondam females kill all the rest (such at least are the accounts given by romantic naturalists of the matter).

THE RIGHT TO MOTHERHOOD

This system certainly shews a much higher development of social intelligence than our marriage system; but if it were physically possible to introduce it into human society it would be wrecked by an opposite and not less important revolt of women: that is, the revolt against compulsory barrenness. In this two classes of women are concerned: those who, though they have no desire for the presence or care of children, nevertheless feel that motherhood is an experience necessary to their complete psychical development and understanding of themselves and others, and those who, though unable to find or unwilling to entertain a husband, would like to occupy themselves with the rearing of children. My own experience of discussing this question leads me to believe that the one point on which all women are in furious secret rebellion against the existing law is the saddling of the right to a child with the obligation to become the servant of a man. Adoption, or the begging or buying or stealing of another woman's child, is no remedy: it does not provide the supreme experience of bearing the child. No political constitution will ever succeed or deserve to succeed unless it includes the recognition of an absolute right to sexual experience, and is untainted by the Pauline or romantic view of such experience as sinful in itself. And since this experience in its fullest sense must be carried in the case of women to the point of childbearing, it can only be reconciled with the acceptance of marriage with the child's father by legalizing polygyny, because there are more adult women in the country than men. Now though polygyny prevails throughout the greater part of the British Empire, and is as practicable here as in India, there is a good deal to be said against it, and still more to be felt. However, let us put our feelings aside for a moment, and consider the question politically.

MONOGAMY, POLYGYNY, AND POLYANDRY

The number of wives permitted to a single husband or of husbands to a single wife under a marriage system, is not an ethical problem: it depends solely on the proportion of the sexes in the population. If in consequence of a great war three-quarters of the men in this country were killed, it would be absolutely necessary to adopt the Mahometan allowance of four wives to each man in order to recruit the population. The fundamental reason for not allowing women to risk their lives in battle and for giving them the first chance of escape in all dangerous emergencies: in short, for treating their lives as more valuable than male lives, is not in the least a chivalrous reason, though men may consent to it under the illusion of chivalry. It is a simple matter of necessity; for if a large proportion of women were killed or disabled, no possible readjustment of our marriage law could avert the depopulation and consequent political ruin of the country, because a woman with several husbands bears fewer children than a woman with one, whereas a man can produce as many families as he has wives. The natural foundation of the institution of monogamy is not any inherent viciousness in polygyny or polyandry, but the hard fact that men and women are born in about equal numbers. Unfortunately, we kill so many of our male children in infancy that we are left with a surplus of adult women which is sufficiently large to claim attention, and yet not large enough to enable every man to have two wives. Even if it were, we should be met by an economic difficulty. A Kaffir is rich in proportion to the number of his wives, because the women are the breadwinners. But in our civilization women are not paid for their social work in the bearing and rearing of children and the ordering of households: they are quartered on the wages of their husbands. At least four out of five of our men could not afford two wives unless their wages were nearly doubled. Would it not then be well to try unlimited polygyny; so that the remaining fifth could have as many wives apiece as they could afford? Let us see how this would work.

THE MALE REVOLT AGAINST POLGYNY

Experience shews that women do not object to polygyny when it is customary: on the contrary, they are its most ardent supporters. The reason is obvious. The question, as it presents itself in practice to a woman, is whether it is better to have, say, a whole share in a tenth-rate man or a tenth share in a first-rate man. Substitute the word Income for the word Man, and you will have the question as it presents itself economically to the dependent woman. The woman whose instincts are maternal, who desires superior children more than anything else, never hesitates. She would take a thousandth share, if necessary, in a husband who was a man in a thousand, rather than have some comparatively weedy weakling all to herself. It is the comparatively weedy weakling, left mateless by polygyny, who objects. Thus, it was not the women of Salt Lake City nor even of America who attacked Mormon polygyny. It was the men. And very naturally. On the other hand, women object to polyandry, because polyandry enables the best women to monopolize all the men, just as polygyny enables the best men to monopolize all the women. That is why all our ordinary men and women are unanimous in defence of monogamy, the men because it excludes polygyny, and the women because it excludes polyandry. The women, left to themselves, would tolerate polygyny. The men, left to themselves, would tolerate polyandry. But polygyny would condemn a great many men, and polyandry a great many women, to the celibacy of neglect. Hence the resistance any attempt to establish unlimited polygyny always provokes, not from the best people, but from the mediocrities and the inferiors. If we could get rid of our inferiors and screw up our average quality until mediocrity ceased to be a reproach, thus making every man reasonably eligible as a father and every woman reasonably desirable as a mother, polygyny and polyandry would immediately fall into sincere disrepute, because monogamy is so much more convenient and economical that nobody would want to share a husband or wife if he (or she) could have a sufficiently good one all to himself (or herself). Thus it appears that it is the scarcity of husbands or wives of high quality that leads women to polygyny and men to polyandry, and that if this scarcity were cured, monogamy, in the sense of having only one husband or wife at a time (facilities for changing are another matter), would be found satisfactory.

DIFFERENCE BETWEEN ORIENTAL AND OCCIDENTAL POLYGYNY

It may now be asked why the polygynist nations have not gravitated to monogamy, like the latter-day saints of Salt Lake City. The answer is not far to seek: their polygyny is limited. By the Mahometan law a man cannot marry more than four wives; and by the unwritten law of necessity no man can keep more wives than he can afford; so that a man with four wives must be quite as exceptional in Asia as a man with a carriage-and-pair or a motor car is in Europe, where, nevertheless, we may all have as many carriages and motors as we can afford to pay for. Kulin polygyny, though unlimited, is not really a popular institution: if you are a person of high caste you pay another person of very august caste indeed to make your daughter momentarily one of his sixty or seventy momentary wives for the sake of ennobling your grandchildren; but this fashion of a small and intensely snobbish class is negligible as a general precedent. In any case, men and women in the East do not marry anyone they fancy, as in England and America. Women are secluded and marriages are arranged. In Salt Lake City the free unsecluded woman could see and meet the ablest man of the community, and tempt him to make her his tenth wife by all the arts peculiar to women in English-speaking countries. No Eastern woman can do anything of the sort. The man alone has any initiative; but he has no access to the woman; besides, as we have seen, the difficulty created by male license is not polygyny but polyandry, which is not allowed.

Consequently, if we are to make polygyny a success, we must limit it. If we have two women to every one man, we must allow each man only two wives. That is simple; but unfortunately our own actual proportion is, roughly, something like $1\frac{1}{11}$ women to 1 man. Now you cannot enact that each man shall be allowed $1\frac{1}{11}$ wives, or that each woman who cannot get a husband all to herself shall divide herself between eleven already married husbands. Thus there is no way out for us through polygyny. There is no way at all out of the present system of condemning the superfluous women to barrenness, except by legitimizing the children of women who are not married to the fathers.

THE OLD MAID'S RIGHT TO MOTHERHOOD

Now the right to bear children without taking a husband could not be confined to women who are superfluous in the monogamic reckoning. There is the practical difficulty that although in our population there are about a million monogamically superfluous women, yet it is quite impossible to say of any given unmarried woman that she is one of the superfluous. And there is the difficulty of principle. The right to bear a child, perhaps the most sacred of all women's rights, is not one that should have any conditions attached to it except in the interests of race welfare. There are many women of admirable character, strong, capable, independent, who dislike the domestic habits of men; have no natural turn for mothering and coddling them; and find the concession of conjugal rights to any person under any conditions intolerable by their self-respect. Yet the general sense of the community recognizes in these very women the fittest people to have charge of children, and trusts them, as schoolmistresses and matrons of institutions, more than women of any other type when it is possible to procure them for such work. Why should the taking of a husband be imposed on these women as the price of their right to maternity? I am quite unable to answer that question. I see a good deal of first-rate maternal ability and sagacity spending itself on bees and poultry and village schools and cottage hospitals; and I find myself repeatedly asking myself why this valuable strain in the national breed should be sterilized. Unfortunately, the very women whom we should tempt to become mothers for the good of the race are the very last people to press their services on their country in that way. Plato long ago pointed out the importance of being governed by men with sufficient sense of responsibility and comprehension of public duties to be very reluctant to undertake the work of governing; and yet we have taken his instruction so little to heart that we are at present suffering acutely from government by gentlemen who will stoop to all the mean shifts of electioneering and incur all its heavy expenses for the sake of a seat in Parliament. But what our sentimentalists have not yet been told is that exactly the same thing applies to maternity as to government. The best mothers are not those who are so enslaved by their primitive instincts that they will bear children no matter how hard the conditions are, but precisely those who place a very high price on their services, and are quite prepared to become old maids if the price is refused, and even to feel relieved at their escape. Our democratic and matrimonial institutions may have their merits: at all events they are mostly reforms of something worse; but they put a premium on want of self-respect in certain very important matters; and the consequence is that we are very badly governed and are, on the whole, an ugly, mean, ill-bred race.

IBSEN'S CHAIN STITCH

Let us not forget, however, in our sympathy for the superfluous women, that their children must have fathers as well as mothers. Who are the fathers to be? All monogamists and married women will reply hastily: either bachelors or widowers; and this solution will serve as well as another; for it would be hypocritical to pretend that the difficulty is a practical one. None the less, the monogamists, after due reflection, will point out that if there are widowers enough the superfluous women are not really superfluous, and therefore there is no reason why the parties should not marry respectably like other people. And they might in that case be right if the reasons were purely numerical: that is, if every woman were willing to take a husband if one could be found for her, and every man willing to take a wife on the same terms; also, please remember, if widows would remain celibate to give the unmarried woman a chance. These ifs will not work. We must recognize two classes of old maids: one, the really superfluous women, and the other, the women who refuse to accept maternity on the (to them) unbearable condition of taking a husband. From both classes may, perhaps, be subtracted for the present the large proportion of women who could not afford the extra expense of one or more children. I say "perhaps", because it is by no means sure that within reasonable limits mothers do not make a better fight for subsistence, and have not, on the whole, a better time than single women. In any case, we have two distinct cases to deal with: the superfluous and the voluntary; and it is the voluntary whose grit we are most concerned to fertilize. But here, again, we cannot put our finger on any particular case and pick out Miss Robinson's as superfluous, and Miss Wilkinson's as voluntary. Whether we legitimize the child of the unmarried woman as a duty to the superfluous or as a bribe to the voluntary, the practical result must be the same: to wit, that the condition of marriage now attached to legitimate parentage will be withdrawn from all women, and fertile unions outside marriage recognized by society. Now clearly the consequences would not stop there. The strong-minded ladies who are resolved to be mistresses in their own houses would not be the only ones to take advantage of the new law. Even women to whom a home without a man in it would be no home at all, and who fully intended, if the man turned out to be the right one, to live with him exactly as married couples live, would, if they were possessed of independent means, have every inducement to adopt the new conditions instead of the old ones. Only the women whose sole means of livelihood was wifehood would insist on marriage: hence a tendency would set in to make marriage more and more one of the customs imposed by necessity on the poor, whilst the freer form of union, regulated, no doubt, by settlements and private contracts of various kinds, would become the practice of the rich: that is, would become the fashion. At which point nothing but the achievement of economic independence by women, which is already seen clearly ahead of us, would be needed to make marriage disappear altogether, not by formal abolition, but by simple disuse. The private contract stage of this process was reached in ancient Rome. The only practicable alternative to it seems to be such an extension of divorce as will reduce the risks and obligations of marriage to a degree at which they will be no worse than those of the alternatives to marriage. As we shall see, this is the solution to which all the arguments tend. Meanwhile, note how much reason a statesman has to pause before meddling with an institution which, unendurable as its drawbacks are, threatens to come to pieces in all directions if a single thread of it be cut. Ibsen's similitude of the machine-made chain stitch, which unravels the whole seam at the first pull when a single stitch is ripped, is very applicable to the knot of marriage.

REMOTENESS OF THE FACTS FROM THE IDEAL

But before we allow this to deter us from touching the sacred fabric, we must find out whether it is not already coming to pieces in all directions by the continuous strain of circumstances. No doubt, if it were all that it pretends to be, and human nature were working smoothly within its limits, there would be nothing more to be said: it would be let alone as it always is let alone during the cruder stages of civilization. But the moment we refer to the facts, we discover that the ideal matrimony and domesticity which our bigots implore us to preserve as the corner-stone of our society is a figment: what we have really got is something very different, questionable at its best, and abominable at its worst. The word pure, so commonly applied to it by thoughtless people, is absurd; because if they do not mean celibate by it, they mean nothing; and if they do mean celibate, then marriage is legalized impurity, a conclusion which is offensive and inhuman. Marriage as a fact is not in the least like marriage as an ideal. If it were, the sudden changes which have been made on the Continent from indissoluble Roman Catholic marriage to marriage that can be dissolved by a box on the ear as in France, by an epithet as in Germany, or simply at the wish of both parties as in Sweden, not to mention the experiments made by some of the American States, would have shaken society to its foundations. Yet they have produced so little effect that Englishmen open their eyes in surprise when told of their existence.

DIFFICULTY OF OBTAINING EVIDENCE

As to what actual marriage is, one would like evidence instead of guesses; but as all departures from the ideal are regarded as disgraceful, evidence cannot be obtained; for when the whole community is indicted, nobody will go into the witness-box for the prosecution. Some guesses we can make with some confidence. For example, if it be objected to any change that our bachelors and widowers would no longer be Galahads, we may without extravagance or cynicism reply that many of them are not Galahads now, and that the only change would be that hypocrisy would no longer be compulsory. Indeed, this can hardly be called guessing: the evidence is in the streets. But when we attempt to find out the truth about our marriages, we cannot even guess with any confidence. Speaking for myself, I can say that I know the inside history of perhaps half-a-dozen marriages. Any family solicitor knows more than this; but even a family solicitor, however large his practice, knows nothing of the million households which have no solicitors, and which nevertheless make marriage what it really is. And all he can say comes to no more than I can say: to wit, that no marriage of which I have any knowledge is in the least like the ideal marriage. I do not mean that it is worse: I mean simply that it is different. Also, far from society being organized in a defence of its ideal so jealous and implacable that the least step from the straight path means exposure and ruin, it is almost impossible by any extravagance of misconduct to provoke society to relax its steady pretence of blindness, unless you do one or both of two fatal things. One is to get into the newspapers; and the other is to confess. If you confess misconduct to respectable men or women they must either disown you or become virtually your accomplices: that is why they are so angry with you for confessing. If you get into the papers, the pretence of not knowing becomes impossible. But it is hardly too much to say that if you avoid these two perils, you can do anything you like, as far as your neighbors are concerned. And since we can hardly flatter ourselves that this is the effect of charity, it is difficult not to suspect that our extraordinary forbearance in the matter of stone throwing is that suggested in the well-known parable of the woman taken in adultery which some early free-thinker slipped into the Gospel of St John: namely, that we all live in glass houses. We may take it, then, that the ideal husband and the ideal wife are no more real human beings than the cherubim. Possibly the great majority keeps its marriage vows in the technical divorce court sense. No husband or wife yet born keeps them or ever can keep them in the ideal sense.

MARRIAGE AS A MAGIC SPELL

The truth which people seem to overlook in this matter is that the marriage ceremony is quite useless as a magic spell for changing in an instant the nature of the relations of two human beings to one another. If a man marries a woman after three weeks acquaintance, and the day after meets a woman he has known for twenty years, he finds, sometimes to his own irrational surprise and his wife's equally irrational indignation, that his wife is a stranger to him, and the other woman an old friend. Also, there is no hocus pocus that can possibly be devized with rings and veils and vows and benedictions that can fix either a man's or woman's affection for twenty minutes, much less twenty years. Even the most affectionate couples must have moments during which they are far more conscious of one another's faults than of one another's attractions. There are couples who dislike one another furiously for several hours at a time; there are couples who dislike one another permanently; and there are couples who never dislike one another; but these last are people who are incapable of disliking anybody. If they do not quarrel, it is not because they are married, but because they are not quarrel-some. The people who are quarrelsome quarrel with their husbands and wives just as easily as with their servants and relatives and acquaintances: marriage makes no difference. Those who talk and write and legislate as if all this could be prevented by making solemn vows that it shall not happen, are either insincere, insane, or hopelessly stupid. There is some sense in a contract to perform or abstain from actions that are reasonably within voluntary control; but such contracts are only needed to provide against the possibility of either party being no longer desirous of the specified performance or abstention. A person proposing or accepting a contract not only to do something but to like doing it would be certified as mad. Yet popular superstition credits the wedding rite with the power of fixing our fancies or affections for life even under the most unnatural conditions.

THE IMPERSONALITY OF SEX

It is necessary to lay some stress on these points, because few realize the extent to which we proceed on the assumption that marriage is a short cut to perfect and permanent intimacy and affection. But there is a still more unworkable assumption which must be discarded before discussions of marriage can get into any sort of touch with the facts of life. That assumption is that the specific relation which marriage authorizes between the parties is the most intimate and personal of human relations, and embraces all the other high human relations. Now this is violently untrue. Every adult knows that the relation in question can and does exist between entire strangers, different in language, color, tastes, class, civilization, morals, religion, character: in everything, in short, except their bodily homology and the reproductive appetite common to all living organisms. Even hatred, cruelty, and contempt are not incompatible with it; and jealousy and murder are as near to it as affectionate friendship. It is true that it is a relation beset with wildly extravagant illusions for inexperienced people, and that even the most experienced people have not always sufficient analytic faculty to disentangle it from the sentiments, sympathetic or abhorrent, which may spring up through the other relations which are compulsorily attached to it by our laws, or sentiment-ally associated with it in romance. But the fact remains that the most disastrous mar-riages are those founded exclusively on it, and the most successful those in which it has been least considered, and in which the decisive considerations have had nothing to do with sex, such as liking, money, congeniality of tastes, similarity of habits, suitability of class, etc. etc.

It is no doubt necessary under existing circumstances for a woman without pro-perty to be sexually attractive, because she must get married to secure a liveli-hood; and the illusions of sexual attraction will cause the imagination of young men to endow her with every accomplishment and virtue that can make a wife a treasure. The attraction being thus constantly and ruthlessly used as a bait, both by indi-viduals and by society, any discussion tending to strip it of its allusions and get at its real natural history is nervously dis-couraged. But nothing can well be more unwholesome for everybody than the exaggeration and glorification of an in-stinctive function which clouds the reason and upsets the judgment more than all the other instincts put together. The pro-cess may be pleasant and romantic; but the consequences are not. It would be far better for everyone, as well as far honester, if young people were taught that what they call love is an appetite which, like all other appetites, is destroyed for the moment by its gratification; that no profession, promise, or proposal made under its influence should bind anybody; and that its great natural purpose so com-pletely transcends the personal interests of any individual or even of any ten generations of individuals that it should be held to be an act of prostitution and even a sort of blasphemy to attempt to turn it to account by exacting a personal return for its gratification, whether by process of law or not. By all means let it be the subject of contracts with society as to its consequences; but to make marriage an open trade in it as at present, with money, board and lodging, personal slavery, vows of eternal exclusive per-sonal sentimentalities and the rest of it as the price, is neither virtuous, dignified, nor decent. No husband ever secured his domestic happiness and honor, nor has any wife ever secured hers, by relying on it. No private claims of any sort should be founded on it: the real point of honor is to take no corrupt advantage of it. When we hear of young women being led astray and the like, we find that what has led them astray is a sedulously in-culcated false notion that the relation they are temped to contract is so intensely per-sonal, and the vows made under the in-fluence of its transient infatuation so sacred and enduring, that only an atroci-ously wicked man could make light of or forget them. What is more, as the same fantastic errors are inculcated in men, and the conscientious ones therefore feel bound in honor to stand by what they have promised, one of the surest methods to obtain a husband is to practise on his susceptibilities until he is either carried away into a promise of marriage to which he can be legally held, or else into an indis-cretion which he must repair by marriage on pain of having to regard himself as a scoundrel and a seducer, besides facing the utmost damage the lady's relatives can do him.

Such a transaction is not an entrance into a "holy state of matrimony": it is as often as not the inauguration of a lifelong squabble, a corroding grudge, that causes more misery and degradation of character than a dozen entirely natural "desertions" and "betrayals." Yet the number of marriages effected more or less in this way must be enormous. When people say that love should be free, their words, taken literally, may be foolish; but they are only expressing inaccurately a very real need for the disentanglement of sexual relations from a mass of exorbitant and irrelevant conditions imposed on them on false pretences to enable needy parents to get their daughters "off their hands" and to keep those who are already married effectually enslaved by one another.

THE ECONOMIC SLAVERY OF WOMEN

One of the consequences of basing marriage on the considerations stated with cold abhorrence by Saint Paul in the seventh chapter of his epistle to the Corinthians, as being made necessary by the unlikeness of most men to himself, is that the sex slavery involved has become complicated by economic slavery; so that whilst the man defends marriage because he is really defending his pleasures, the women is even more vehement on the same side because she is defending her only means of livelihood. To a woman without property or marketable talent a husband is more necessary than a master to a dog. There is nothing more wounding to our sense of human dignity than the husband hunting that begins in every family when the daughters become marriageable; but it is inevitable under existing circumstances; and the parents who refuse to engage in it are bad parents, though they may be superior individuals. The cubs of a humane tigress would starve; and the daughters of women who cannot bring themselves to devote several years of their lives to the pursuit of sons-in-law often have to expiate their mothers' squeamishness by lifelong celibacy and indigence. To ask a young man his intentions when you know he has no intentions, but is unable to deny that he has paid attentions; to threaten an action for breach of promise of marriage; to pretend that your daughter is a musician when she has with the greatest difficulty been coached into playing three pianoforte pieces which she loathes; to use your own mature charms to attract men to the house when your daughters have no aptitude for that department of sport; to coach them, when they have, in the arts by which men can be led to compromise themselves; and to keep all the skeletons carefully locked up in the family cupboard until the prey is duly hunted down and bagged; all this is a mother's duty today; and a very revolting duty it is: one that disposes of the conventional assumption that it is in the faithful discharge of her home duties that a woman finds her self-respect. The truth is that family life will never be decent, much less ennobling, until this central horror of the dependence of women on men is done away with. At present it reduces the difference between marriage and prostitution to the difference between Trade Unionism and unorganized casual labor: a huge difference, no doubt, as to order and comfort, but not a difference in kind.

However, it is not by any reform of the marriage laws that this can be dealt with. It is in the general movement for the prevention of destitution that the means for making women independent of the compulsory sale of their persons, in marriage or otherwise, will be found; but meanwhile those who deal specifically with the marriage laws should never allow themselves for a moment to forget this abomination that "plucks the rose from the fair forehead of an innocent love, and sets a blister there," and then calmly calls itself purity, home, motherhood, respectability, honor, decency, and any other fine name that happens to be convenient, not to mention the foul epithets it hurls freely at those who are ashamed of it.

UNPOPULARITY OF IMPERSONAL VIEWS

Unfortunately it is very hard to make an average citizen take impersonal views of any sort in matters affecting personal comfort or conduct. We may be enthusiastic Liberals or Conservatives without any hope of seats in Parliament, knighthoods, or posts in the Government, because party politics do not make the slightest difference in our daily lives and therefore cost us nothing. But to take a vital process in which we are keenly interested personal instruments and ask us to regard it, and feel about it, and legislate on it, wholly as if it were an impersonal one, is to make a higher demand than most people seem capable of responding to. We all have personal interests in marriage which we are not prepared to sink. It is not only the women who want to get married: the men do too, sometimes on sentimental grounds, sometimes on the more sordid calculation that bachelor life is less comfortable and more expensive, since a wife pays for her status with domestic service as well as with the other services expected of her. Now that children are avoidable, this calculation is becoming more common and conscious than it was: a result which is regarded as "a steady improvement in general morality."

IMPERSONALITY IS NOT PROMISCUITY

There is, too, a really appalling prevalence of the superstition that the sexual instinct in men is utterly promiscuous and that the least relaxation of law and custom must produce a wild outbreak of licentiousness. As far as our moralists can grasp the proposition that we should deal with the sexual relation as impersonal, it seems to them to mean that we should encourage it to be promiscuous: hence their recoil from it. But promiscuity and impersonality are not the same thing. No man ever yet fell in love with the entire female sex, nor any woman with the entire male sex. We often do not fall in love at all; and when we do we fall in love with one person, and remain indifferent to thousands of others who pass before our eyes every day. Selection, carried even to such fastidiousness as to induce people to say quite commonly that there is only one man or woman in the world for them, is the rule in nature. If anyone doubts this, let him open a shop for the sale of picture post-cards, and, when an enamoured lady customer demands a portrait of her favorite actor or a gentleman of his favorite actress, try to substitute some other portrait on the ground that since the sexual instinct is promiscuous, one portrait is as pleasing as another. I suppose no shopkeeper has ever been foolish enough to do such a thing; and yet all our shopkeepers, the moment a discussion arises on marriage, will passionately argue against all reform on the ground that nothing but the most severe coercion can save their wives and daughters from quite indiscriminate rapine.

DOMESTIC CHANGE OF AIR

Our relief at the morality of the reassurance that man is not promiscuous in his fancies must not blind us to the fact that he is (to use the word coined by certain American writers to describe themselves) something of a Varietist. Even those who say there is only one man or woman in the world for them, find that it is not always the same man or woman. It happens that our law permits us to study this phenomenon among entirely law-abiding people. I know one lady who has been married five times. She is, as might be expected, a wise, attractive, and interesting woman. The question is, Is she wise, attractive, and interesting because she has been married five times, or has she been married five times because she is wise, attractive, and interesting? Probably some of the truth lies both ways. I also know of a household consisting of three families, A having married first B, and then C, who afterwards married D. All three unions were fruitful; so that the children had a change both of fathers and mothers. Now I cannot honestly say that these and similar cases have convinced me that people are the worse for a change. The lady who has married and managed five husbands must be much more expert at it than most monogamic ladies; and as a companion and counsellor she probably leaves them nowhere. Mr Kipling's question

What can they know of England that only
  England know?

disposes not only of the patriots who are so patriotic that they never leave their own country to look at another, but of the citizens who are so domestic that they have never married again and never loved anyone except their own husbands and wives. The domestic doctrinaires are also the dull people. The impersonal relation of sex may be judicially reserved for one person; but any such reservation of friendship, affection, admiration, sympathy and so forth is only possible to a wretchedly narrow and jealous nature; and neither history nor contemporary society shews us a single amiable and respectable character capable of it. This has always been recognized in cultivated society: that is why poor people accuse cultivated society of profligacy, poor people being often so ignorant and uncultivated that they have nothing to offer each other but the sex relationship, and cannot conceive why men and women should associate for any other purpose.

As to the children of the triple household, they were not only on excellent terms with one another, and never thought of any distinction between their full and their half brothers and sisters, but they

had the superior sociability which distinguishes people who live in communities from those who live in small families.

The inference is that changes of partners are not in themselves injurious or undesirable. People are not demoralized by them when they are effected according to law. Therefore we need not hesitate to alter the law merely because the alteration would make such changes easier.

HOME MANNERS ARE BAD MANNERS

On the other hand, we have all seen the bonds of marriage vilely abused by people who are never classed with shrews and wife-beaters: they are indeed sometimes held up as models of domesticity because they do not drink nor gamble nor neglect their children nor tolerate dirt and untidiness, and because they are not amiable enough to have what are called amiable weaknesses. These terrors conceive marriage as a dispensation from all the common civilities and delicacies which they have to observe among strangers, or, as they put it, "before company." And here the effects of indissoluble marriage-for-better-for-worse are very plainly and disagreeably seen. If such people took their domestic manners into general society, they would very soon find themselves without a friend or even an acquaintance in the world. There are women who, through total disuse, have lost the power of kindly human speech and can only scold and complain: there are men who grumble and nag from inveterate habit even when they are comfortable. But their unfortunate spouses and children cannot escape from them.

SPURIOUS "NATURAL" AFFECTION

What is more, they are protected from even such discomfort as the dislike of his prisoners may cause to a gaoler by the hypnotism of the convention that the natural relation between husband and wife and parent and child is one of intense affection, and that to feel any other sentiment towards a member of one's family is to be a monster. Under the influence of the emotion thus manufactured the most detestable people are spoilt with entirely undeserved deference, obedience, and even affection whilst they live, and mourned when they die by those whose lives they wantonly or maliciously made miserable. And this is what we call natural conduct. Nothing could well be less natural. That such a convention should have been established shews that the indissolubility of marriage creates such intolerable situations that only by beglamoring the human imagination with a hypnotic suggestion of wholly unnatural feelings can it be made to keep up appearances.

If the sentimental theory of family relationship encourages bad manners and personal slovenliness and uncleanness in the home, it also, in the case of sentimental people, encourages the practice of rousing and playing on the affections of children prematurely and far too frequently. The lady who says that as her religion is love, her children shall be brought up in an atmosphere of love, and institutes a system of sedulous endearments and exchanges of presents and conscious and studied acts of artificial kindness, may be defeated in a large family by the healthy derision and rebellion of children who have acquired hardihood and common sense in their conflicts with one another. But the small families, which are the rule just now, succumb more easily; and in the case of a single sensitive child the effect of being forced in a hothouse atmosphere of unnatural affection may be disastrous.

In short, whichever way you take it, the convention that marriage and family relationship produce special feelings which alter the nature of human intercourse is a mischievous one. The whole difficulty of bringing up a family well is the difficulty of making its members behave as considerately at home as on a visit in a strange house, and as frankly, kindly, and easily in a strange house as at home. In the middle classes, where the segregation of the artificially limited family in its little brick box is horribly complete, bad manners, ugly dresses, awkwardness, cowardice, peevishness, and all the petty vices of unsociability flourish like mushrooms in a cellar. In the upper class, where families are not limited for money reasons; where at least two houses and sometimes three or four are the rule (not to mention the clubs); where there is travelling and hotel life; and where the men are brought up, not in the family, but in public schools, universities, and the naval and military services, besides being constantly in social training in other people's houses, the result is to produce a set that, in comparison with the middle class, counts as a different and much more sociable species. And in the very poorest class, where people have no homes, only sleeping places crowded with lodgers, and consequently live practically in the streets, sociability again appears, leaving the middle class despised and disliked for its helpless and offensive unsociability as much by those below it as those above it, and yet ignorant enough to be proud of it, and to hold itself up as a model for the reform of the (as it considers) elegantly vicious rich and profligate poor alike.

CARRYING THE WAR INTO THE ENEMY'S COUNTRY

Without pretending to exhaust the subject, I have said enough to make it clear that the moment we lose the desire to defend our present matrimonial and family arrangements, there will be no difficulty in making out an overwhelming case against them. No doubt until then we shall continue to hold up the British home as the Holy of Holies in the temple of honorable motherhood, innocent childhood, manly virtue, and sweet and wholesome national life. But with a clever turn of the hand this holy of holies can be exposed as an Augean stable, so filthy that it would seem more hopeful to burn it down than to attempt to sweep it out. And this latter view will perhaps prevail if the idolaters of marriage persist in refusing all proposals for reform and treating those who advocate it as infamous delinquents. Neither view is of any use except as a poisoned arrow in a fierce fight between two parties determined to discredit each other with a view to obtaining powers of legal coercion over one another.

SHELLEY AND QUEEN VICTORIA

The best way to avert such a struggle is to open the eyes of the thoughtlessly conventional people to the weakness of their position in a mere contest of recrimination. Hitherto they have assumed that they have the advantage of coming into the field without a stain on their characters to combat libertines who have no character at all. They conceive it to be their duty to throw mud; and they feel that even if the enemy can find any mud to throw, none of it will stick. They are mistaken. There will be plenty of that sort of ammunition in the other camp; and most of it will stick very hard indeed. The moral is, do not throw any. If we can imagine Shelley and Queen Victoria arguing out their differences in another world, we may be sure that the Queen has long ago found out that she cannot settle the question by classing Shelley with George IV as a bad man; and Shelley is not likely to have called her vile names on the general ground that as the economic dependence of women makes marriage a money bargain in which the man is the purchaser and the woman the purchased, there is no essential difference between a married woman and the woman of the streets. Unfortunately, all the people whose methods of controversy are represented by our popular newspapers are not Queen Victorias and Shelleys. A great mass of them, when their prejudices are challenged, have no other impulse than to call the challenger names, and, when the crowd seems to be on their side, to maltreat him personally or hand him over to the law, if he is vulnerable to it. Therefore I cannot say that I have any certainty that the marriage question will be dealt with decently and tolerantly. But dealt with it will be, decently or indecently; for the present state of things in England is too strained and mischievous to last. Europe and America have left us a century behind in this matter.

A PROBABLE EFFECT OF GIVING WOMEN THE VOTE

The political emancipation of women is likely to lead to a comparatively stringent enforcement by law of sexual morality (that is why so many of us dread it); and this will soon compel us to consider what our sexual morality shall be. At present a ridiculous distinction is made between vice and crime, in order that men may be vicious with impunity. Adultery, for instance, though it is sometimes fiercely punished by giving an injured husband crushing damages in a divorce suit (injured wives are not considered in this way), is not now directly prosecuted; and this impunity extends to illicit relations between unmarried persons who have reached what is called the age of consent. There are other matters, such as notification of contagious disease and solicitation, in which the hand of the law has been brought down on one sex only. Outrages which were capital offences within the memory of persons still living when committed on women outside marriage, can still be inflicted by men on their wives without legal remedy. At all such points the code will be screwed up by the operation of Votes for Women, if there be any virtue in the franchise at all. The result will be that men will find the more ascetic side of our sexual morality taken seriously by the law. It is easy to foresee the consequences. No man will take much trouble to alter laws which he can evade, or which are either not enforced or enforced on women only. But when these laws take him by the collar and thrust him into prison, he suddenly becomes keenly critical of them, and of the arguments by which they are supported. Now we have seen that our marriage laws will not stand criticism, and that they have held out so far only because they are so worked as to fit roughly our state of society, in which women are neither politically nor personally free, in which indeed women are called womanly only when they regard themselves as existing solely for the use of men. When Liberalism enfranchises them politically, and Socialism emancipates them economically, they will no longer allow the law to take immorality so easily. Both men and women will be forced to behave morally in sex matters; and when they find that this is inevitable they will raise the question of what behavior really should be established as moral. If they decide in favor of our present professed morality, they will have to make a revolutionary change in their habits by becoming in fact what they only pretend to be at present. If, on the other hand, they find that this would be an unbearable tyranny, without even the excuse of justice or sound eugenics, they will reconsider their morality and remodel the law.

THE PERSONAL SENTIMENTAL BASIS OF MONOGAMY

Monogamy has a sentimental basis which is quite distinct from the political one of equal numbers of the sexes. Equal numbers in the sexes are quite compatible with a change of partners every day or every hour. Physically there is nothing to distinguish human society from the farm-yard except that children are more troublesome and costly than chickens and calves, and that men and women are not so completely enslaved as farm stock. Accordingly, the people whose conception of marriage is a farm-yard or slave-quarter conception are always more or less in a panic lest the slightest relaxation of the marriage laws should utterly demoralize society; whilst those to whom marriage is a matter of more highly evolved sentiments and needs (sometimes said to be distinctively human, though birds and animals in a state of freedom evince them quite as touchingly as we) are much more liberal, knowing as they do that monogamy will take care of itself provided the parties are free enough, and that promiscuity is a product of slavery and not of liberty.

The solid foundation of their confidence is the fact that the relationship set up by a comfortable marriage is so intimate and so pervasive of the whole life of the parties to it, that nobody has room in his or her life for more than one such relationship at a time. What is called a household of three is never really of three except in the sense that every household becomes a household of three when a child is born, and may in the same way become a household of four or fourteen if the union be fertile enough. Now no doubt the marriage tie means so little to some people that the addition to the household of half-a-dozen more wives or husbands would be as possible as the addition of half-a-dozen governesses or tutors or visitors or servants. A Sultan may have fifty wives as easily as he may have fifty dishes on his table, because in the English sense he has no wives at all; nor have his wives any husband: in short, he is not what we call a married man. And there are sultans and sultanas and seraglios existing in England under English forms. But when you come to the real modern marriage of sentiment, a relation is created which has never to my knowledge been shared by three persons except when all three have been extraordinarily fond of one another. Take for example the famous case of Nelson and Sir William and Lady Hamilton. The secret of this household of three was not only that both the husband and Nelson were devoted to Lady Hamilton, but that they were also apparently devoted to one another. When Hamilton died both Nelson and Emma seem to have been equally heart-broken. When there is a successful household of one man and two women the same unusual condition is fulfilled: the two women not only cannot live happily without the man but cannot live happily without each other. In every other case known to me, either from observation or record, the experiment is a hopeless failure: one of the two rivals for the really intimate affection of the third inevitably drives out the other. The driven-out party may accept the situation and remain in the house as a friend to save appearances, or for the sake of the children, or for economic reasons; but such an arrangement can subsist only when the forfeited relation is no longer really valued; and this indifference, like the triple bond of affection which carried Sir William Hamilton through, is so rare as to be practicably negligible in the establishment of a conventional morality of marriage. Therefore sensible and experienced people always assume that when a declaration of love is made to an already married person, the declaration binds the parties in honor never to see one another again unless they contemplate divorce and remarriage. And this is a sound convention, even for unconventional people. Let me illustrate by reference to a fictitious case: the one imagined in my own play Candida will do as well as another. Here a young man who had been received as a friend into the house of a clergyman falls in love with the clergyman's wife, and, being young and inexperienced, declares his feelings, and claims that he, and not the clergyman, is the more suitable mate for the lady. The clergyman, who has a temper, is first tempted to hurl the youth into the street by bodily violence: an impulse natural, perhaps, but vulgar and improper, and not open, on consideration, to decent men. Even coarse and inconsiderate men are restrained from it by the fact that the sympathy of the woman turns naturally to the victim of physical brutality and against the bully, the Thackerayan notion to the contrary being one of the illusions of literary masculinity. Besides, the husband is not necessarily the stronger man: and appeal to force has resulted in the ignominious defeat of the husband quite as often as in poetic justice as conceived in the conventional novelet. What an honorable and sensible man does when his household is invaded is what the Reverend James Mavor Morell does in my play. He recognizes that just as there is not room for two women in that sacredly intimate relation of sentimental domesticity which is what marriage means to him, so there is no room for two men in that relation with his wife; and he accordingly tells her firmly that she must choose which man will occupy the place that is large enough for one only. He is so far shrewdly unconventional as to recognize that if she chooses the other man, he must give way, legal tie or no legal tie; but he knows that either one or the other must go. And a sensible wife would act in the same way. If a romantic young lady came into her house and proposed to adore her husband on a tolerated footing, she would say "My husband has not room in his life for two wives: either you go out of the house or I go out of it." The situation is not at all unlikely: I had almost said not at all unusual. Young ladies and gentlemen in the greensickly condition which is called calf-love, associating with married couples at dangerous periods of mature life, quite often find themselves in it; and the extreme reluctance of proud and sensitive people to make any assertion of matrimonial rights, or to condescend to jealousy, sometimes make the threatened husband or wife hesitate to take prompt steps and do the apparently conventional thing. But whether they hesitate or act the result is always the same. In a real marriage of sentiment the wife or husband cannot be supplanted by halves; and such a marriage will break very soon under the strain of polygyny or polyandry. What we want at present is a sufficiently clear teaching of this fact to ensure that prompt and decisive action shall always be taken in such cases without any false shame of seeming conventional (a shame to which people capable of such real marriage are specially susceptible), and a rational divorce law to enable the marriage to be dissolved and the parties honorably re-sorted and re-coupled without disgrace and scandal if that should prove the proper solution.

It must be repeated here that no law, however stringent, can prevent polygamy among groups of people who choose to live loosely and be monogamous only in appearance. But such cases are not now under consideration. Also, affectionate husbands like Samuel Pepys, and affectionate wives of the corresponding temperament, may, it appears, engage in transient casual adventures out of doors without breaking up their home life. But within doors that home life may be regarded as naturally monogamous. It does not need to be protected against polygamy; it protects itself.

DIVORCE

All this has an important bearing on the question of divorce. Divorce reformers are so much preoccupied with the injustice of forbidding a woman to divorce her husband for unfaithfulness to his marriage vow, whilst allowing him that power over her, that they are apt to overlook the pressing need for admitting other and far more important grounds for divorce. If we take a document like Pepys' Diary, we learn that a woman may have an incorrigibly unfaithful husband, and yet be much better off than if she had an ill-tempered, peevish, maliciously sarcastic one, or was chained for life to a criminal, a drunkard, a lunatic, an idle vagrant, or a person whose religious faith was contrary to her own. Imagine being married to a liar, a borrower, a mischief maker, a teaser or tormentor of children and animals, or even simply to a bore! Conceive yourself tied for life to one of the perfectly "faithful" husbands who are sentenced to a month's imprisonment occasionally for idly leaving their wives in childbirth without food, fire, or attendance? What woman would not rather marry ten Pepyses? what man a dozen Nell Gwynnes? Adultery, far from being the first and only ground for divorce, might more reasonably be made the last, or wholly excluded. The present law is perfectly logical only if you once admit (as no decent person ever does) its fundamental assumption that there can be no companionship between men and women because the woman has a "sphere" of her own, that of housekeeping, in which the man must not meddle, whilst he has all the rest of human activity for his sphere: the only point at which the two spheres touch being that of replenishing the population. On this assumption the man naturally asks for a guarantee that the children shall be his because he has to find the money to support them. The power of divorcing a woman for adultery is this guarantee, a guarantee that she does not need to protect her against a similar imposture on his part, because he cannot bear children. No doubt he can spend the money that ought to be spent on her children on another woman and her children; but this is desertion, which is a separate matter. The fact for us to seize is that in the eye of the law, adultery without consequences is merely a sentimental grievance, whereas the planting on one man of another man's offspring is a substantial one. And so, no doubt, it is; but the day has gone by for basing laws on the assumption that a woman is less to a man than his dog, and thereby encouraging and accepting the standards of the husbands who buy meat for their bull-pups and leave their wives and children hungry. That basis is the penalty we pay for having borrowed our religion from the East, instead of building up a religion of our own out of our western inspiration and western sentiment. The result is that we all believe that our religion is on its last legs, whereas the truth is that it is not yet born, though the age walks visibly pregnant with it. Meanwhile, as women are dragged down by their oriental servitude to our men, and as, further, women drag down those who degrade them quite as effectually as men do, there are moments when it is difficult to see anything in our sex institutions except a *police des mœurs* keeping the field for a competition as to which sex shall corrupt the other most.

IMPORTANCE OF SENTIMENTAL GRIEVANCES

Any tolerable western divorce law must put the sentimental grievances first, and should carefully avoid singling out any ground of divorce in such a way as to create a convention that persons having that ground are bound in honor to avail themselves of it. It is generally admitted that people should not be encouraged to petition for a divorce in a fit of petulance. What is not so clearly seen is that neither should they be encouraged to petition in a fit of jealousy, which is certainly the

most detestable and mischievous of all the passions that enjoy public credit. Still less should people who are not jealous be urged to behave as if they were jealous, and to enter upon duels and divorce suits in which they have no desire to be successful. There should be no publication of the grounds on which a divorce is sought or granted; and as this would abolish the only means the public now has of ascertaining that every possible effort has been made to keep the couple united against their wills, such privacy will only be tolerated when we at last admit that the sole and sufficient reason why people should be granted a divorce is that they want one. Then there will be no more reports of divorce cases, no more letters read in court with an indelicacy that makes every sensitive person shudder and recoil as from a profanation, no more washing of household linen, dirty or clean, in public. We must learn in these matters to mind our own business and not impose our individual notions of propriety on one another, even if it carries us to the length of openly admitting what we are now compelled to assume silently, that every human being has a right to sexual experience, and that the law is concerned only with parentage, which is now a separate matter.

DIVORCE WITHOUT ASKING WHY

The one question that should never be put to a petitioner for divorce is "Why?" When a man appeals to a magistrate for protection from someone who threatens to kill him, on the simple ground that he desires to live, the magistrate might quite reasonably ask him why he desires to live, and why the person who wishes to kill him should not be gratified. Also whether he can prove that his life is a pleasure to himself or a benefit to anyone else, and whether it is good for him to be encouraged to exaggerate the importance of his short span in this vale of tears rather than to keep himself constantly ready to meet his God.

The only reason for not raising these very weighty points is that we find society unworkable except on the assumption that every man has a natural right to live. Nothing short of his own refusal to respect that right in others can reconcile the community to killing him. From this fundamental right many others are derived. The American Constitution, one of the few modern political documents drawn up by men who were forced by the sternest circumstances to think out what they really had to face instead of chopping logic in a university class-room, specifies "liberty and the pursuit of happiness" as natural rights. The terms are too vague to be of much practical use; for the supreme right to life, extended as it now must be to the life of the race, and to the quality of life as well as to the mere fact of breathing, is making short work of many ancient liberties, and exposing the pursuit of happiness as perhaps the most miserable of human occupations. Nevertheless, the American Constitution roughly expresses the conditions to which modern democracy commits us. To impose marriage on two unmarried people who do not desire to marry one another would be admittedly an act of enslavement. But it is no worse than to impose a continuation of marriage on people who have ceased to desire to be married. It will be said that the parties may not agree on that; that one may desire to maintain the marriage the other wishes to dissolve. But the same hardship arises whenever a man in love proposes marriage to a woman and is refused. The refusal is so painful to him that he often threatens to kill himself and sometimes even does it. Yet we expect him to face his ill luck, and never dream of forcing the woman to accept him. His case is the same as that of the husband whose wife tells him she no longer cares for him, and desires the marriage to be dissolved. You will say, perhaps, if you are superstitious, that it is not the same—that marriage makes a difference. You are wrong: there is no magic in marriage. If there were, married couples would never desire to separate. But they do. And when they do, it is simple slavery to compel them to remain together.

ECONOMIC SLAVERY AGAIN THE ROOT DIFFICULTY

The husband, then, is to be allowed to discard his wife when he is tired of her, and the wife the husband when another man strikes her fancy? One must reply unhesitatingly in the affirmative; for if we are to deny every proposition that can be stated in offensive terms by its opponents, we shall never be able to affirm anything at all. But the question reminds us that until the economic independence of women is achieved, we shall have to remain impaled on the other horn of the dilemma and maintain marriage as a slavery. And here let me ask the Government of the day (1910) a question with regard to the Labor Exchanges it has very wisely established throughout the country. What do these Exchanges do when a woman enters and states that her occupation is that of a wife and mother; that she is out of a job; and that she wants an employer? If the Exchanges refuse to entertain her application, they are clearly excluding nearly the whole female sex from the benefit of the Act. If not, they must become matrimonial agencies, unless, indeed, they are prepared to become something worse by putting the woman down as a housekeeper and introducing her to an employer without making marriage a condition of the hiring.

LABOR EXCHANGES AND THE WHITE SLAVERY

Suppose, again, a woman presents herself at the Labor Exchange, and states her trade as that of a White Slave, meaning the unmentionable trade pursued by many thousands of women in all civilized cities. Will the Labor Exchange find employers for her? If not, what will it do with her? If it throws her back destitute and unhelped on the streets to starve, it might as well not exist as far as she is concerned; and the problem of unemployment remains unsolved at its most painful point. Yet if it finds honest employment for her and for all the unemployed wives and mothers, it must find new places in the world for women; and in so doing it must achieve for them economic independence of men. And when this is done, can we feel sure that any woman will consent to be a wife and mother (not to mention the less respectable alternative) unless her position is made as eligible as that of the women for whom the Labor Exchanges are finding independent work? Will not many women now engaged in domestic work under circumstances which make it repugnant to them, abandon it and seek employment under other circumstances? As unhappiness in marriage is almost the only discomfort sufficiently irksome to induce a woman to break up her home, and economic dependence the only compulsion sufficiently stringent to force her to endure such unhappiness, the solution of the problem of finding independent employment for women may cause a great number of childless unhappy marriages to break up spontaneously, whether the marriage laws are altered or not. And here we must extend the term childless marriages to cover households in which the children have grown up and gone their own way, leaving the parents alone together: a point at which many worthy couples discover for the first time that they have long since lost interest in one another, and have been united only by a common interest in their children. We may expect, then, that marriages which are maintained by economic pressure alone will dissolve when that pressure is removed; and as all the parties to them will certainly not accept a celibate life, the law must sanction the dissolution in order to prevent a recurrence of the scandal which has moved the Government to appoint the Commission now sitting to investigate the marriage question: the scandal, that is, of a great number of persons, condemned to celibacy by magisterial separation orders, and, of course, refusing to submit to the condemnation, forming illicit connections to an extent which threatens to familiarize the working classes with an open disuse of marriage. In short, once set women free from their economic slavery, and you will find that unless divorce is made as easy as the dissolution of a business partnership, the practice of dispensing with marriage will presently become so common that conventional couples will be ashamed to get married.

DIVORCE FAVORABLE TO MARRIAGE

Divorce, in fact, is not the destruction of marriage, but the first condition of its maintenance. A thousand indissoluble marriages mean a thousand marriages and no more. A thousand divorces may mean two thousand marriages; for the couples may marry again. Divorce only re-assorts the couples: a very desirable thing when they are ill-assorted. Also, it makes people much more willing to marry, especially prudent people and proud people with a high sense of self-respect. Further, the fact that a divorce is possible often prevents its being petitioned for, not only because it puts married couples on their good behavior towards one another, but because, as no room feels like a prison if the door is left open, the removal of the sense of bondage would at once make marriage much happier than it is now. Also, if the door were always open, there would be no need to rush through it as

C

there is now when it opens for one moment in a lifetime, and may never open again.

From this point of view England has the worst civil marriage law in the world, with the exception of silly South Carolina. In every other reasonably civilized country the grounds on which divorce can be granted admit of so wide an interpretation that all unhappy marriages can be dissolved without resorting to the shameful shifts imposed by our law. Yet the figures just given to the Royal Commission shew that in the State of Washington, where there are eleven different grounds of divorce, and where, in fact, divorce can be had for the asking at a negligible cost, the divorce rate is only 184 per 100,000 of the population, which, if we assume that the 100,000 people represent 20,000 families, means less than one per cent of domestic failures. In Japan the rate is 215, which is said to be the highest on record. This is not very alarming: what is quite hideous is that the rate in England is only 2, a figure which, if we assume that human nature is much the same in Walworth as in Washington, must represent a frightful quantity of useless unhappiness and clandestine polygamy. I am not forgetting my own demonstration that the rate is kept down in Washington by the economic slavery of women; but I must point out that this is at its worst in the middle classes only, because a woman of the working class can turn to and support herself, however poorly; and a woman of the upper classes usually has some property. And in all classes we may guess that the object of many divorces is not the resumption of a single life, but a change of partners. As this change can be effected easily under the existing law in the State of Washington it is not certain that the economic emancipation of women would alter the rate there to any startling extent. What is certain is that it could not conceivably raise it to a figure at which even the most panicky alarmist could persuade sensible people that the whole social fabric was tumbling to pieces. When journalists and bishops and American Presidents and other simple people describe this Washington result as alarming, they are speaking as a peasant speaks of a motor car or an aeroplane when he sees one for the first time. All he means is that he is not used to it and therefore fears that it may injure him. Every advance in civilization frightens these honest folk. This is a pity; but if we were to spare their feelings we should never improve the world at all. To let them frighten us, and then pretend that their stupid timidity is virtue and purity and so forth, is simply moral cowardice.

MALE ECONOMIC SLAVERY AND THE RIGHTS OF BACHELORS

It must not be forgotten that the refusal to accept the indignities, risks, hardships, softships, and divided duties of marriage is not confined to our voluntary old maids. There are men of the mould of Beethoven and Samuel Butler, whom one can hardly conceive as married men. There are the great ecclesiastics, who will not own two loyalties: one to the Church and one to the hearth. There are men like Goethe, who marry late and reluctantly solely because they feel that they cannot in honest friendship refuse the status of marriage to any woman of whose attachment to them they have taken any compromising advantage, either in fact or in appearance. No sensible man can, under existing circumstances, advise a woman to keep house with a man without insisting on his marrying her, unless she is independent of conventional society (a state of things which can occur only very exceptionally); and a man of honor cannot advise a woman to do for his sake what he would not advise her to do for anyone else's. The result is that our

Beethovens and Butlers—of whom, in their ordinary human aspect, there are a good many—become barren old bachelors, and rather savage ones at that.

Another difficulty which we always think of in connection with women, but which is by no means without its application to men, is the economic one. The number of men who cannot afford to marry is large enough to produce very serious social results; and the higher the work the man is doing, the more likely he is to find himself in this class until he has reached or passed middle age. The higher departments of science, law, philosophy, poetry, and the fine arts are notoriously starved in youth and early manhood: the marriageable age there, economically speaking, is nearer fifty than twenty. Even in business the leading spirits seldom reach a position of security until they are far beyond the age at which celibacy is tolerable. Account must also be taken of the younger sons of the propertied classes, brought up in households in which the rate of expenditure, though ten times that possible on a younger son's portion, yet represents the only habit of life he has learnt.

Taking all these cases as representing a bachelor class, and bearing in mind that though a man who marries at forty is not called a bachelor, yet he has for twenty years of his adult life been one, and therefore produced all the social problems that arise out of the existence of unmarried men, we must not shrink from asking whether all these gentlemen are celibates, even though we know that the question must be answered very emphatically in the negative. Some of them marry women of property, thereby reproducing the economic dependence of women on men with the sexes reversed. But there are so few women of property available for this purpose in comparison with the number of bachelors who cannot afford to marry, that this resource does not solve the problem of the bachelor who cannot afford a wife. If there were no other resources available, bachelors would make love to the wives and daughters of their friends. This being morally inadmissible, a demand arises for a cheap temporary substitute for marriage. A class of women must be found to protect the wives and daughters of the married by keeping company with the bachelors for hire for as long or as short a time as the bachelor can afford, on the understanding that no claim is to be made on him after the hiring is ended. And such an institution, as we know, exists among us. It is commonly spoken of and thought of as an offence against our marriage morality; but all the experts who write scientific treatises on marriage seem to be agreed that it is, on the contrary, a necessary part of that morality, and must stand and fall with it.

I do not myself think that this view will bear examination. In my play, Mrs Warren's Profession, I have shewn that the institution in question is an economic phenomenon, produced by our underpayment and ill-treatment of women who try to earn an honest living. I am aware that for some reason scientific writers are perversely impatient of this view, and, to discredit it, quote police lists of the reasons given by the victims for adopting their trade, and insist on the fact that poverty is not often alleged. But this means only that the actual word is seldom used. If a prisonful of thieves were asked what induced them to take to thieving, and some replied Poverty, and others Hunger, and others Desire for Excitement, no one would deny that the three answers were really one answer—that poverty means hunger, an intolerable lack of variety and pleasure, and, in short, all sorts of privations. When a girl, similarly interrogated, says she wanted fine clothes, or more fun, or the like, she is really saying that she lacked what no woman with plenty of money need lack. The fact that, according to the testimony of men who profess experience in such matters, you may search Europe in vain for a woman in this trade who has the table manners of a lady, shews that prostitution is not a vocation but a slavery to which women are driven by the miseries of honest poverty. When every young woman has an honorable and comfortable livelihood open to her on reasonable terms, the streets will make no more recruits. When every young man can afford to marry, and marriage reform makes it easy to dissolve unions contracted by young and inexperienced people in the event of their turning out badly, or of one of the pair achieving a position neither comfortable nor suitable for the other, both prostitution and bachelordom will die a natural death. Until then, all talk of "purification" is idle. It is for that reason that I lay little stress on prostitution here, and refer readers who are curious about the psychopathy of bachelordom and spinsterhood to the monumental work of my friend Havelock Ellis.

THE PATHOLOGY OF MARRIAGE

I shall also say as little as possible of the pathology of marriage and its kerbstone breakwater. Only, as there seems to be no bottom to the abyss of public ignorance on the subject, I am compelled to warn my readers that marriage has a pathology and even a criminology. But they are both so frightful that they have been dealt with not only in such treatises as those of Havelock Ellis, Fournier, Duclaux, and many German writers, but in such comparatively popular works as The Heavenly Twins by Sarah Grand, and several of the plays of Brieux: notably Les Avariés, Les Trois Filles de M. Dupont, and Maternité. I purposely pass them by quickly, not only because attention has already been called to them by these devoted writers, but because my mission is not to deal with obvious

horrors, but to open the eyes of normal respectable men to evils which are escaping their consideration.

As to the evils of disease and contagion, our consciences are sound enough: what is wrong with us is ignorance of the facts. No doubt this is a very formidable ignorance in a country where the first cry of the soul is "Dont tell me: I dont want to know," and where frantic denials and furious suppressions indicate everywhere the cowardice and want of faith which conceives life as something too terrible to be faced. In this particular case "I dont want to know" takes a righteous air, and becomes "I dont want to know anything about the diseases which are the just punishment of wretches who should not be mentioned in my presence or in any book that is intended for family reading." Wicked and foolish as the spirit of this attitude is, the practice of it is so easy and lazy and uppish that it is very common. But its cry is drowned by a louder and more sincere one. We who do not want to know also do not want to go blind, to go mad, to be disfigured, to be barren, to become pestiferous, or to see such things happening to our children. We learn, at last, that the majority of the victims are not the people of whom we so glibly say "Serve them right," but quite innocent children and innocent parents, smitten by a contagion which, no matter in what vice it may or may not have originated, contaminates the innocent and the guilty alike once it is launched exactly as any other contagious disease does; that indeed it often hits the innocent and misses the guilty because the guilty know the danger and take elaborate precautions against it, whilst the innocent, who have been either carefully kept from any knowledge of their danger, or erroneously led to believe that contagion is possible through misconduct only, run into danger blindfold. Once knock this fact into people's minds, and their self-righteous indifference and intolerance soon change into lively concern for themselves and their families.

THE CRIMINOLOGY OF MARRIAGE

The pathology of marriage involves the possibility of the most horrible crime imaginable: that of the person who, when suffering from contagious disease, forces the contagion on another person by an act of violence. Such an act occurring between unmarried people would, within the memory of persons now living, have exposed the aggressor to the penalty of death; and it is still punished unmercifully by an extreme term of penal servitude when it occurs, as it sometimes does, through the hideous countryside superstition that it effects a cure when the victim is a virgin. Marriage makes this outrage absolutely legal. You may with impunity do to the person to whom you are married what you may not do to the most despised outcast of the streets. And this is only the extreme instance of the outlawry which our marriage laws effect. In our anxiety to provide for ourselves a little private Alsatia in which we can indulge ourselves as we please without reproach or interference from law, religion, or even conscience (and this is what marriage has come to mean to many of us), we have forgotten that we cannot escape restraints without foregoing rights; that all the laws that are needed to compel strangers to respect us are equally if not more necessary to compel our husbands and wives to respect us; and that society without law, whether between two or two million persons, means tyranny and slavery.

If the incorrigible sentimentalists here raise their little pipe of "Not if they love one another," I tell them, with such patience as is possible, that if they had ever had five minutes' experience of love they would know that love is itself a tyranny requiring special safeguards; that people will perpetrate "for the sake of" those they love, exactions and submissions that they would never dream of proposing to or suffering from those they dislike or regard with indifference; that healthy marriages are partnerships of companionable and affectionate friendship; that cases of chronic lifelong love, whether sentimental or sensual, ought to be sent to the doctor if not to the executioner; and that honorable men and women, when their circumstances permit it, are so far from desiring to be placed helplessly at one another's mercy that they employ every device the law now admits of, from the most stringent marriage settlements to the employment of separate legal advisers, to neutralize the Alsatian evils of the marriage law.

DOES IT MATTER?

A less obviously silly evasion, and one which has a greater air of common sense, is "After all, seeing that most couples get on very well together, does it matter so much?" The same reply might be made by a lazy magistrate when asked for a warrant to arrest a burglar, or by a sleepy fireman wakened by a midnight call for his fire-escape. "After all, very few people have their houses broken into; and fewer still have them burnt. Does it matter?" But tell the magistrate or fireman that it is *his* house that has been broken into, or *his* house that has been burnt; and you will be startled by the change in his attitude. Because a mass of people have shaken down into comfort enough to satisfy them, or at least to cause them no more discomfort than they are prepared to put up with for the sake of a quiet life, less lucky and more sensitive and conscientious people should not be condemned to expose themselves to intolerable wrongs. Besides, people ought not to be content with the marriage law as it is merely because it is not often unbearably uncomfortable. Slaves are very often much more comfortable both in body and mind than fully responsible free men. That does not excuse anybody for embracing slavery. It is no doubt a great pity, from many points of view, that we were not conquered by Napoleon, or even by Bismarck and Moltke. None the less we should have been rightly despised if we had not been prepared to fight them for the right to misgovern ourselves.

But, as I have said, I am content, in this matter of the evils of our marriage law, to take care of the pence and let the pounds take care of themselves. The crimes and diseases of marriage will force themselves on public attention by their own virulence. I mention them here only because they reveal certain habits of thought and feeling with regard to marriage of which we must rid ourselves if we are to act sensibly when we take the necessary reforms in hand.

CHRISTIAN MARRIAGE

First among these is the habit of allowing ourselves to be bound not only by the truths of the Christian religion but by the excesses and extravagances which the Christian movement acquired in its earlier days as a violent reaction against what it still calls paganism. By far the most dangerous of these, because it is a blasphemy against life, and, to put it in Christian terms, an accusation of indecency against God, is the notion that sex, with all its operations, is in itself absolutely an obscene thing, and that an immaculate conception is a miracle. So unwholesome an absurdity could only have gained ground under two conditions: one, a reaction against a society in which sensual luxury had been carried to revolting extremes, and, two, a belief that the world was coming to an end, and that therefore sex was no longer a necessity. Christianity, because it began under these conditions, made sexlessness and Communism the two main practical articles of its propaganda; and it has never quite lost its original bias in these directions. In spite of the putting off of the Second Coming from the lifetime of the apostles to the millennium, and of the great disappointment of the year 1000 A.D., in which multitudes of Christians seriously prepared for the end of the world, the prophet who announces that the end is at hand is still popular. Many of the people who ridicule his demonstrations that the fantastic monsters of the book of Revelation are among us in the persons of our own political contemporaries, and who proceed sanely in all their affairs on the assumption that the world is going to last, really do believe that there will be a Judgment Day, and that it *might* even be in their own time. A thunderstorm, an eclipse, or any very unusual weather will make them apprehensive and uncomfortable.

This explains why, for a long time, the Christian Church refused to have anything to do with marriage. The result was, not the abolition of sex, but its excommunication. And, of course, the consequences of persuading people that matrimony was an unholy state were so grossly carnal, that the Church had to execute a complete right-about-face, and try to make people understand that it was a holy state: so holy indeed that it could not be validly inaugurated without the blessing of the Church. And by this teaching it did something to atone for its earlier blasphemy. But the mischief of chopping and changing your doctrine to meet this or that practical emergency instead of keeping it adjusted to the whole scheme of life, is that you end by having half-a-dozen contradictory doctrines to suit half-a-dozen different emergencies. The Church solemnized and sanctified marriage without ever giving up its original Pauline doctrine on the subject. And it soon fell into another confusion. At the point at which it took up marriage and endeavored to make it holy, marriage was, as it still is, largely a survival of the custom of selling women to men. Now in all trades a marked difference is made in price between a new article and a second-hand one. The moment we meet with this difference in value between human beings, we may know that we are in the slave-market, where the conception of our relations to the persons sold is neither religious nor natural nor human nor superhuman, but simply commercial. The Church, when it finally gave its blessing to marriage, did not, in its innocence, fathom these commercial traditions. Consequently it tried to sanctify them too, with grotesque results. The slave-dealer having always asked more money for virginity, the Church, instead of detecting the money-changer and driving him out of the temple, took him for a sentimental and chivalrous lover, and, helped by its only half-discarded doctrine of celibacy, gave virginity a heavenly value to ennoble its commercial pretensions. In short, Mammon, always mighty, put the Church in his pocket, where he keeps it to this day, in spite of the occasional saints and martyrs who contrive from time to time to get their heads and souls free to testify against him.

DIVORCE A SACRAMENTAL DUTY

But Mammon overreached himself when he tried to impose his doctrine of inalienable property on the Church under the guise of indissoluble marriage. For the Church tried to shelter this inhuman doctrine and flat contradiction of the gospel by claiming, and rightly claiming, that marriage is a sacrament. So it is; but that is exactly what makes divorce a duty when the marriage has lost the inward and spiritual grace of which the marriage ceremony is the outward and visible sign. In vain do bishops stoop to pick up the discarded arguments of the atheists of fifty years ago by pleading that the words of Jesus were in an obscure Aramaic dia-

lect, and were probably misunderstood, as Jesus, they think, could not have said anything a bishop would disapprove of. Unless they are prepared to add that the statement that those who take the sacrament with their lips but not with their hearts eat and drink their own damnation is also a mistranslation from the Aramaic, they are most solemnly bound to shield marriage from profanation, not merely by permitting divorce, but by making it compulsory in certain cases as the Chinese do.

When spiritual revolt broke out in the sixteenth century, and the Church was reformed in several countries, the Reformation was so largely a rebellion against sacerdotalism that marriage was very nearly excommunicated again: our modern civil marriage, round which so many fierce controversies and political conflicts have raged, would have been thoroughly approved of by Calvin, and hailed with relief by Luther. But the instinctive doctrine that there is something holy and mystic in sex, a doctrine which many of us now easily dissociate from any priestly ceremony, but which in those days seemed to all who felt it to need a ritual affirmation, could not be thrown on the scrap-heap with the sale of Indulgences and the like; and so the Reformation left marriage where it was: a curious mixture of commercial sex slavery, early Christian sex abhorrence, and later Christian sex sanctification.

OTHELLO AND DESDEMONA

How strong was the feeling that a husband or a wife is an article of property, greatly depreciated in value at second-hand, and not to be used or touched by any person but the proprietor, may be learnt from Shakespear. His most infatuated and passionate lovers are Antony and Othello; yet both of them betray the commercial and proprietary instinct the moment they lose their tempers. "I found you," says Antony, reproaching Cleopatra, "as a morsel cold upon dead Cæsar's trencher." Othello's worst agony is the thought of "keeping a corner in the thing he loves for others' uses." But this is not what a man feels about the thing he loves, but about the thing he owns. I never understood the full significance of Othello's outburst until I one day heard a lady, in the course of a private discussion as to the feasibility of "group marriage," say with cold disgust that she would as soon think of lending her toothbrush to another woman as her husband. The sense of outraged manhood with which I felt myself and all other husbands thus reduced to the rank of a toilet appliance gave me a very unpleasant taste of what Desdemona might have felt had she overheard Othello's outburst. I was so dumbfounded that I had not the presence of mind to ask the lady whether she insisted on having a doctor, a nurse, a dentist, and even a priest and solicitor all to herself as well. But I had too often heard men speak of women as if they were mere personal conveniences to feel surprised that exactly the same view is held, only more fastidiously, by women.

All these views must be got rid of before we can have any healthy public opinion (on which depends our having a healthy population) on the subject of sex, and consequently of marriage. Whilst the subject is considered shameful and sinful we shall have no systematic instruction in sexual hygiene, because such lectures as are given in Germany, France, and even prudish America (where the great Miltonic tradition in this matter still lives) will be considered a corruption of that youthful innocence which now subsists on nasty stories and whispered traditions handed down from generation to generation of school children: stories and traditions which conceal nothing of sex but its dignity, its honor, its sacredness, its rank as the first necessity of society and the

deepest concern of the nation. We shall continue to maintain the White Slave Trade and protect its exploiters by, on the one hand, tolerating the white slave as the necessary breakwater of marriage; and, on the other, trampling on her and degrading her until she has nothing to hope from our Courts; and so, with policemen at every corner, and law triumphant all over Europe, she will still be smuggled and cattle-driven from one end of the civilized world to the other, cheated, beaten, bullied, and hunted into the streets to disgusting overwork, without daring to utter the cry for help that brings, not rescue, but exposure and infamy, yet revenging herself terribly in the end by scattering blindness and sterility, pain and disfigurement, insanity and death among us with the certainty that we are much too pious and genteel to allow such things to be mentioned with a view to saving either her or ourselves from them. And all the time we shall keep enthusiastically investing her trade with every allurement that the art of the novelist, the playwright, the dancer, the milliner, the painter, the limelight man, and the sentimental poet can devize, after which we shall continue to be very much shocked and surprised when the cry of the youth, of the young wife, of the mother, of the infected nurse, and of all the other victims, direct and indirect, arises with its invariable refrain: "Why did nobody warn me?"

WHAT IS TO BECOME OF THE CHILDREN?

I must not reply flippantly, Make them all Wards in Chancery; yet that would be enough to put any sensible person on the track of the reply. One would think, to hear the way in which people sometimes ask the question, that not only does marriage prevent the difficulty from ever arising, but that nothing except divorce can ever raise it. It is true that if you divorce the parents, the children have to be disposed of. But if you hang the parents, or imprison the parents, or take the children out of the custody of the parents because they hold Shelley's opinions, or if the parents die, the same difficulty arises. And as these things have happened again and again, and as we have had plenty of experience of divorce decrees and separation orders, the attempt to use children as an obstacle to divorce is hardly worth arguing with. We shall deal with the children just as we should deal with them if their homes were broken up by any other cause. There is a sense in which children are a real obstacle to divorce: they give parents a common interest which keeps together many a couple who, if childless, would separate. The marriage law is superfluous in such cases. This is shewn by the fact that the proportion of childless divorces is much larger than the proportion of divorces from all causes. But it must not be forgotten that the interest of the children forms one of the most powerful arguments for divorce. An unhappy household is a bad nursery. There is something to be said for the polygynous or polyandrous household as a school for children: children really do suffer from having too few parents: this is why uncles and aunts and tutors and governesses are often so good for children. But it is just the polygamous household which our marriage law allows to be broken up, and which, as we have seen, is not possible as a typical institution in a democratic country where the numbers of the sexes are about equal. Therefore polygyny and polyandry as a means of educating children fall to the ground, and with them, I think, must go the opinion which has been expressed by Gladstone and others, that an extension of divorce, whilst admitting many new grounds for it, might exclude the ground of adultery. There are, however, clearly many things that make some of our domestic interiors little private hells for children (especially when the children are quite content in them) which would justify any intelligent State in breaking up the home and giving the custody of the children either to the parent whose conscience had revolted against the corruption of the children, or to neither.

Which brings me to the point that divorce should no longer be confined to cases in which one of the parties petitions for it. If, for instance, you have a thoroughly rascally couple making a living by infamous means and bringing up their children to their trade, the king's proctor, instead of pursuing his present purely mischievous function of preventing couples from being divorced by proving that they both desire it, might very well intervene and divorce these children from their parents. At present, if the Queen herself were to rescue some unfortunate child from degradation and misery and place her in a respectable home, and some unmentionable pair of blackguards claimed the child and proved that they were its father and mother, the child would be given to them in the name of the sanctity of the home and the holiness of parentage, after perpetrating which crime, the law would calmly send an education officer to take the child out of the parents' hands several hours a day in the still more sacred name of compulsory education. (Of course what would really happen would be that the couple would blackmail the Queen for their consent to the salvation of the child, unless, indeed, a hint from a police inspector convinced them that bad characters cannot always rely on pedantically constitutional treatment when they come into conflict with persons in high station.)

The truth is, not only must the bond between man and wife be made subject to a reasonable consideration of the welfare of the parties concerned and of the community, but the whole family bond as

C 2

well. The theory that the wife is the property of the husband or the husband of the wife is not a whit less abhorrent and mischievous than the theory that the child is the property of the parent. Parental bondage will go the way of conjugal bondage: indeed the order of reform should rather be put the other way about; for the helplessness of children has already compelled the State to intervene between parent and child more than between husband and wife. If you pay less than £40 a year rent, you will sometimes feel tempted to say to the vaccination officer, the school attendance officer, and the sanitary inspector: "Is this child mine or yours?" The answer is that as the child is a vital part of the nation, the nation cannot afford to leave it at the irresponsible disposal of any individual or couple of individuals as a mere small parcel of private property. The only solid ground that the parent can take is that as the State, in spite of its imposing name, can, when all is said, do nothing with the child except place it in the charge of some human being or another, the parent is no worse a custodian than a stranger. And though this proposition may seem highly questionable at first sight to those who imagine that only parents spoil children, yet those who realize that children are as often spoilt by severity and coldness as by indulgence, and that the notion that natural parents are any worse than adopted parents is probably as complete an illusion as the notion that they are any better, see no serious likelihood that State action will detach children from their parents more than it does at present: nay, it is even likely that the present system of taking the children out of the parents' hands and having the parental duty performed by officials, will, as poverty and ignorance become the exception instead of the rule, give way to the system of simply requiring certain results, beginning with the baby's weight and ending perhaps with some sort of practical arts degree, but leaving parents and children to achieve the results as they best may. Such freedom is, of course, impossible in our present poverty-stricken circumstances. As long as the masses of our people are too poor to be good parents or good anything else except beasts of burden, it is no use requiring much more from them but hewing of wood and drawing of water: whatever is to be done must be done *for* them, mostly, alas! by people whose superiority is merely technical. Until we abolish poverty it is impossible to push rational measures of any kind very far: the wolf at the door will compel us to live in a state of siege and to do everything by a bureaucratic martial law that would be quite unnecessary and indeed intolerable in a prosperous community. But, however we settle the question, we must make the parent justify his custody of the child exactly as we should make a stranger justify it. If a family is not achieving the purposes of a family it should be dissolved just as a marriage should when it, too, is not achieving the purposes of marriage. The notion that there is or ever can be anything magical and inviolable in the legal relations of domesticity, and the curious confusion of ideas which makes some of our bishops imagine that in the phrase "Whom God hath joined," the word God means the district registrar or the Reverend John Smith or William Jones, must be got rid of. Means of breaking up undesirable families are as necessary to the preservation of the family as means of dissolving undesirable marriages are to the preservation of marriage. If our domestic laws are kept so inhuman that they at last provoke a furious general insurrection against them as they already provoke many private ones, we shall in a very literal sense empty the baby out with the bath by abolishing an institution which needs nothing more than a little obvious and easy rationalizing to make it not only harmless but comfortable, honorable, and useful.

THE COST OF DIVORCE

But please do not imagine that the evils of indissoluble marriage can be cured by divorce laws administered on our present plan. The very cheapest undefended divorce, even when conducted by a solicitor for its own sake and that of humanity, costs at least £30 out-of-pocket expenses. To a client on business terms it costs about three times as much. Until divorce is as cheap as marriage, marriage will remain indissoluble for all except the handful of people to whom £100 is a procurable sum. For the enormous majority of us there is no difference in this respect between a hundred and a quadrillion. Divorce is the one thing you may not sue for *in forma pauperis*.

Let me, then, recommend as follows:

1. Make divorce as easy, as cheap, and as private as marriage.

2. Grant divorce at the request of either party, whether the other consents or not; and admit no other ground than the request, which should be made without stating any reasons.

3. Confine the power of dissolving marriage for misconduct to the State acting on the petition of the king's proctor or other suitable functionary, who may, however, be moved by either party to intervene in ordinary request cases, not to prevent the divorce taking place, but to enforce alimony if it be refused and the case is one which needs it.

4. Make it impossible for marriage to be used as a punishment as it is at present. Send the husband and wife to penal servitude if you disapprove of their conduct and want to punish them; but do not send them back to perpetual wedlock.

5. If, on the other hand, you think a couple perfectly innocent and well conducted, do not condemn them also to perpetual wedlock against their wills, thereby making the treatment of what you consider innocence on both sides the same as the treatment of what you consider guilt on both sides.

6. Place the work of a wife and mother on the same footing as other work: that is, on the footing of labor worthy of its hire; and provide for unemployment in it exactly as for unemployment in shipbuilding or any other recognized breadwinning trade.

7. And take and deal with all the consequences of these acts of justice instead of letting yourself be frightened out of reason and good sense by fear of consequences. We must finally adapt our institutions to human nature. In the long run our present plan of trying to force human nature into a mould of existing abuses, superstitions, and corrupt interests, produces the explosive forces that wreck civilization.

8. Never forget that if you leave your law to judges and your religion to bishops you will presently find yourself without either law or religion. If you doubt this, ask any decent judge or bishop. Do *not* ask somebody who does not know what a judge is, or what a bishop is, or what the law is, or what religion is. In other words, do not ask your newspaper. Journalists are too poorly paid in this country to know anything that is fit for publication.

CONCLUSIONS

To sum up, we have to depend on the solution of the problem of unemployment, probably on the principles laid down in the Minority Report of the Royal Commission on the Poor Law, to make the sexual relations between men and women decent and honorable by making women economically independent of men, and (in the younger son section of the upper classes) men economically independent of women. We also have to bring ourselves into line with the rest of

Protestant civilization by providing means for dissolving all unhappy, improper, and inconvenient marriages. And, as it is our cautious custom to lag behind the rest of the world to see how their experiments in reform turn out before venturing ourselves, and then take advantage of their experience to get ahead of them, we should recognize that the ancient system of specifying grounds for divorce, such as adultery, cruelty, drunkenness, felony, insanity, vagrancy, neglect to provide for wife and children, desertion, public defamation, violent temper, religious heterodoxy, contagious disease, outrages, indignities, personal abuse, "mental anguish," conduct rendering life burdensome, and so forth (all these are examples from some code actually in force at present), is a mistake, because the only effect of compelling people to plead and prove misconduct is that cases are manufactured and clean linen purposely smirched and washed in public, to the great distress and disgrace of innocent children and relatives, whilst the grounds have at the same time to be made so general that any sort of human conduct may be brought within them by a little special pleading and a little mental reservation on the part of witnesses examined on oath. When it comes to "conduct rendering life burdensome," it is clear that no marriage is any longer indissoluble; and the sensible thing to do then is to grant divorce whenever it is desired, without asking why.

POSTSCRIPT 1933. A fashion has set in among the theatre critics of declaring that Getting Married, and by implication its preface, are obsolete because all the grievances and difficulties pointed out in them have been removed by recent legislation. This is a striking example of the delusion of progress which saves us from despair. The sole change made in our marriage laws since the Married Women's Property Act created serious male grievances with one hand whilst abolishing some gross female ones with the other, is that by which a wife can now obtain a divorce just as a husband can for adultery alone, instead of having to prove cruelty and desertion as well. In every other respect British marriage is what it was when the play was written: that is, so monstrously unreasonable that it is sustained only by the fact that in most marriages the couples, being ignorant of the law, do not realize the risks they are running, and seldom find them out later on because the unbearably hard cases are exceptional. Meanwhile in countries where marriages can be dissolved at the demand of either party without delay or serious expense, subject only to provision for the children, so that there is no longer any excuse for illicit and dissolute relations, public opinion on questions of sexual behavior is sterner than with us; and none of the disastrous consequences of unimpeded divorce predicted by our upholders of indissoluble marriage are complained of.

II

PARENTS AND CHILDREN (MISALLIANCE)

1910

TRAILING CLOUDS OF GLORY

Childhood is a stage in the process of that continual remanufacture of the Life Stuff by which the human race is perpetuated. The Life Force either will not or cannot achieve immortality except in very low organisms: indeed it is by no means ascertained that even the amoeba is immortal. Human beings visibly wear out, though they last longer than their friends the dogs. Turtles, parrots, and elephants are believed to be capable of outliving the memory of the oldest human inhabitant. But the fact that new ones are born conclusively proves that they are not immortal. Do away with death and you do away with the need for birth: in fact if you went on breeding, you would finally have to kill old people to make room for young ones.

Now death is not necessarily a failure of energy on the part of the Life Force. People with no imagination try to make things which will last for ever, and even want to live for ever themselves. But the intelligently imaginative man knows very well that it is waste of labor to make a machine that will last ten years, because it will probably be superseded in half that time by an improved machine answering the same purpose. He also knows that if some devil were to convince us that our dream of personal immortality is no dream but a hard fact, such a shriek of despair would go up from the human race as no other conceivable horror could provoke. With all our perverse nonsense as to John Smith living for a thousand million eons and for ever after, we die voluntarily, knowing that it is time for us to be scrapped, to be remanufactured, to come back, as Wordsworth divined, trailing ever brightening clouds of glory. We must all be born again, and yet again and again. We should like to live a little longer just as we should like £50: that is, we should take it if we could get it for nothing; but that sort of idle liking is not will. It is amazing—considering the way we talk —how little a man will do to get £50: all the £50 notes I have ever known of have been more easily earned than a laborious sixpence; but the difficulty of inducing a man to make any serious effort to obtain £50 is nothing to the difficulty of inducing him to make a serious effort to keep alive. The moment he sees death approach, he gets into bed and sends for a doctor. He knows very well at the back of his conscience that he is rather a poor job and had better be remanufactured. He knows that his death will make room for a birth; and he hopes that it will be a birth of something that he aspired to be and fell short of. He knows that it is through death and rebirth that this corruptible shall become incorruptible, and this mortal put on immortality. Practise as you will on his ignorance, his fears, and his imagination with bribes of paradises and threats of hells, there is only one belief that can rob death of its sting and the grave of its victory; and that is the belief that we can lay down the burden of our wretched little makeshift individualities for ever at each lift towards the goal of evolution, which can only be a being that cannot be improved upon. After all, what man is capable of the insane self-conceit of believing that an eternity of himself would be tolerable even to himself? Those who try to believe it postulate that they shall be made perfect first. But if you make me perfect I shall no longer be myself, nor will it be possible for me to conceive my present imperfections (and what I cannot conceive I cannot remember); so that you may just as well give me a new name and face the fact that I am a new person and that the old Bernard Shaw is as dead as mutton. Thus, oddly enough, the conventional belief in the matter comes to this: that if you wish to live for ever you must be wicked enough to be irretrievably damned, since the saved are no longer what they were, and in hell alone do people retain their sinful nature: that is to say, their individuality. And this sort of hell, however convenient as a means of intimidating persons who have practically no honor and no conscience, is not a fact. Death is for many of us the gate of hell; but we are inside on the way out, not outside on the way in. Therefore let us give up telling one another idle stories, and rejoice in death as we rejoice in birth; for without death we cannot be born again; and the man who does not wish to be born again and born better is fit only to represent the City of London in Parliament, or perhaps the university of Oxford.

THE CHILD IS FATHER TO THE MAN

Is he? Then in the name of common sense why do we always treat children on the assumption that the man is father to the child? Oh, these fathers! And we are not content with fathers: we must have godfathers, forgetting that the child is godfather to the man. Has it ever struck you as curious that in a country where the first article of belief is that every child is born with a godfather whom we all call "our father which art in heaven," two very limited individual mortals should be allowed to appear at its baptism and explain that they are its godparents, and that they will look after its salvation until it is no longer a child. I had a godmother who made herself responsible in this way for me. She pre-

sented me with a Bible with a gilt clasp and edges, larger than the Bibles similarly presented to my sisters, because my sex entitled me to a heavier article. I must have seen that lady at least four times in the twenty years following. She never alluded to my salvation in any way. People occasionally ask me to act as godfather to their children with a levity which convinces me that they have not the faintest notion that it involves anything more than calling the helpless child George Bernard, without regard to the possibility that it may grow up in the liveliest abhorrence of my notions.

A person with a turn for logic might argue that if God is the Father of all men, and if the child is father to the man, it follows that the true representative of God at the christening is the child itself. But such posers are unpopular, because they imply that our little customs, or, as we often call them, our religion, mean something, or must originally have meant something, and that we understand and believe that something.

However, my business is not to make confusion worse confounded, but to clear it up. Only, it is as well to begin by a sample of current thought and practice which shews that on the subject of children we are very deeply confused. On the whole, whatever our theory or no theory may be, our practice is to treat the child as the property of its immediate physical parents, and to allow them to do what they like with it, as far as it will let them. It has no rights and no liberties: in short, its condition is that which adults recognize as the most miserable and dangerous politically possible for themselves: namely, the condition of slavery. For its alleviation we trust to the natural affection of the parties, and to public opinion. A father cannot for his own credit let his son go in rags. Also, in a very large section of the population, parents finally become dependent on their children. Thus there are checks on child slavery which do not exist, or are less powerful, in the case of manual and industrial slavery. Sensationally bad cases fall into two classes, which are really the same class: namely, the children whose parents are excessively addicted to the sensual luxury of petting children, and the children whose parents are excessively addicted to the sensual luxury of physically torturing them. There is a Society for the Prevention of Cruelty to Children which has effectually made an end of our belief that mothers are any more to be trusted than stepmothers, or fathers than slave-drivers. And there is a growing body of law designed to prevent parents from using their children ruthlessly to make money for the household. Such legislation has always been furiously resisted by the parents, even when the horrors of factory slavery were at their worst; and the extension of such legislation at present would be impossible if it were not that the parents affected by it cannot control a majority of votes in Parliament. In domestic life a great deal of service is done by children, the girls acting as nursemaids and general servants, and the lads as errand boys. In the country both boys and girls do a substantial share of farm labor. This is why it is necessary to coerce poor parents to send their children to school, though in the relatively small class which keeps plenty of servants it is impossible to induce parents to keep their children at home instead of paying schoolmasters to take them off their hands.

It appears then that the bond of affection between parents and children does not save children from the slavery that denial of rights involves in adult political relations. It sometimes intensifies it, sometimes mitigates it; but on the whole children and parents confront one another as two classes in which all the political power is on one side; and the results are not at all unlike what they would be if there were no immediate consanguinity between them, and one were white and the other black, or one enfranchised and the other disenfranchised, or one ranked as gentle and the other simple. Not that Nature counts for nothing in the case and political rights for everything. But a denial of political rights, and the resultant delivery of one class into the mastery of another, affects their relations so extensively and profoundly that it is impossible to ascertain what the real natural relations of the two classes are until this political relation is abolished.

WHAT IS A CHILD?

An experiment. A fresh attempt to produce the just man made perfect: that is, to make humanity divine. And you will vitiate the experiment if you make the slightest attempt to abort it into some fancy figure of your own: for example, your notion of a good man or a womanly woman. If you treat it as a little wild beast to be tamed, or as a pet to be played with, or even as a means to save you trouble and to make money for you (and these are our commonest ways), it may fight its way through in spite of you and save its soul alive; for all its instincts will resist you, and possibly be strengthened in the resistance; but if you begin with its own holiest aspirations, and suborn them for your own purposes, then there is hardly any limit to the mischief you may do. Swear at a child, throw your boots at it, send it flying from the room with a cuff or a kick; and the experience will be as instructive to the child as a difficulty with a short-tempered dog or a bull. Francis Place tells us that his father always struck his children when he found one within his reach. The effect on the young Places seems to have been simply to make them keep out of their father's way, which was no doubt what he desired, as far as he desired anything at all. Francis records the habit without bitterness, having reason to thank his stars that his father respected the inside of his head whilst cuffing the outside of it; and this made it easy for Francis to do yeoman's service to his country as that rare and admirable thing, a Freethinker: the only sort of thinker, I may remark, whose thoughts, and consequently whose religious convictions, command any respect.

Now Mr Place, senior, would be described by many as a bad father; and I do not contend that he was a conspicuously good one. But as compared with the conventional good father who deliberately imposes himself on his son as a god; who takes advantage of childish credulity and parent worship to persuade his son that what he approves of is right and what he disapproves of is wrong; who imposes a corresponding conduct on the child by a system of prohibitions and penalties, rewards and eulogies, for which he claims divine sanction: compared to this sort of abortionist and monster maker, I say, Place appears almost as a Providence. Not that it is possible to live with children any more than with grown-up people without imposing rules of conduct on them. There is a point at which every person with human nerves has to say to a child "Stop that noise." But suppose the child asks why! There are various answers in use. The simplest: "Because it irritates me," may fail; for it may strike the child as being rather amusing to irritate you; also the child, having comparatively no nerves, may be unable to conceive your meaning vividly enough. In any case it may want to make a noise more than to spare your feelings. You may therefore have to explain that the effect of the irritation will be that you will do something unpleasant if the noise continues. The something unpleasant may be only a look of suffering to rouse the child's affectionate sympathy (if it has any), or it may run to forcible expulsion from the room with plenty of unnecessary violence; but the principle is the same: there are no false pretences involved: the child learns in a straightforward way that it does not pay to be inconsiderate. Also, perhaps, that Mamma, who made the child learn the Sermon on the Mount, is not really a Christian.

THE SIN OF NADAB AND ABIHU

But there is another sort of answer in wide use which is neither straightforward, instructive, nor harmless. In its simplest form it substitutes for "Stop that noise," "Dont be naughty," which means that the child, instead of annoying you by a perfectly healthy and natural infantile procedure, is offending God. This is a blasphemous lie; and the fact that it is on the lips of every nurserymaid does not excuse it in the least. Dickens tells us of a nurserymaid who elaborated it into "If you do that, angels wont never love you." I remember a servant who used to tell me that if I were not good, by which she meant if I did not behave with a single eye to her personal convenience, the cock would come down the chimney. Less imaginative but equally dishonest people told me I should go to hell if I did not make myself agreeable to them. Bodily violence, provided it be the hasty expression of normal provoked resentment and not vicious cruelty, cannot harm a child as this sort of pious fraud harms it. There is a legal limit to physical cruelty; and there are also human limits to it. There is an active Society which brings to book a good many parents who starve and torture and overwork their children, and intimidates a good many more. When parents of this type are caught, they are treated as criminals; and not infrequently the police have some trouble to save them from being lynched. The people against whom children are wholly un-

protected are those who devote themselves to the very mischievous and cruel
sort of abortion which is called bringing
up a child in the way it should go. Now
nobody knows the way a child should
go. All the ways discovered so far lead
to the horrors of our existing civilizations, described quite justifiably by
Ruskin as heaps of agonizing human
maggots, struggling with one another
for scraps of food. Pious fraud is an
attempt to pervert that divine mystery
called the child's conscience into an
instrument of our own convenience, and
to use that wonderful and terrible power
called Shame to grind our own axe. It is
the sin of stealing fire from the altar: a
sin so impudently practised by popes,
parents, and pedagogues, that one can
hardly expect the nurserymaids to see
any harm in stealing a few cinders when
they are worried.

Into the blackest depths of this violation of children's souls one can hardly
bear to look; for here we find pious
fraud masking the violation of the body
by obscene cruelty. Any parent or school
teacher who takes a secret and abominable delight in torture is allowed to lay
traps into which every child must fall,
and then beat it to his or her heart's content. A gentleman once wrote to me and
said, with an obvious conviction that
he was being most reasonable and highminded, that the only thing he beat
his children for was failure in perfect
obedience and perfect truthfulness. On
these virtues, he said, he must insist. As
one of them is not a virtue at all, and the
other is the attribute of a god, one can
imagine what the lives of this gentleman's
children would have been if it had been
possible for him to live down to his
monstrous and foolish pretensions. And
yet he might have written his letter to
The Times (he very nearly did, by the
way) without incurring any danger of
being removed to an asylum, or even

losing his reputation for taking a very
proper view of his parental duties. And
at least it was not a trivial view, nor an
ill meant one. It was much more respectable than the general consensus of opinion
that if a school teacher can devize a question a child cannot answer, or overhear
it calling omega omeega, he or she may
beat the child viciously. Only, the
cruelty must be whitewashed by a moral
excuse, and a pretence of reluctance.
It must be for the child's good. The
assailant must say "This hurts me more
than it hurts you." There must be hypocrisy as well as cruelty. The injury to the
child would be far less if the voluptuary
said frankly "I beat you because I like
beating you; and I shall do it whenever
I can contrive an excuse for it." But to
represent this detestable lust to the child
as Divine wrath, and the cruelty as the
beneficent act of God, which is exactly
what all our floggers do, is to add to the
torture of the body, out of which the
flogger at least gets some pleasure, the
maiming and blinding of the child's soul,
which can bring nothing but horror to
anyone.

THE MANUFACTURE OF MONSTERS

This industry is by no means peculiar
to China. The Chinese (they say) make
physical monsters. We revile them for it
and proceed to make moral monsters of
our own children. The most excusable
parents are those who try to correct their
own faults in their offspring. The parent
who says to his child: "I am one of the successes of the Almighty: therefore imitate
me in every particular or I will have the skin
off your back" (a quite common attitude)
is a much more absurd figure than the man
who, with a pipe in his mouth, thrashes
his boy for smoking. If you must hold
yourself up to your children as an object
lesson (which is not at all necessary),
hold yourself up as a warning and not as
an example. But you had much better

let the child's character alone. If you once allow yourself to regard a child as so much material for you to manufacture into any shape that happens to suit your fancy you are defeating the experiment of the Life Force. You are assuming that the child does not know its own business, and that you do. In this you are sure to be wrong: the child feels the drive of the Life Force (often called the Will of God); and you cannot feel it for him. Handel's parents no doubt thought they knew better than their child when they tried to prevent his becoming a musician. They would have been equally wrong and equally unsuccessful if they had tried to prevent the child becoming a great rascal had its genius lain in that direction. Handel would have been Handel, and Napoleon and Peter of Russia *them*selves in spite of all the parents in creation, because, as often happens, they were stronger than their parents. But this does not happen always. Most children can be, and many are, hopelessly warped and wasted by parents who are ignorant and silly enough to suppose that they know what a human being ought to be, and who stick at nothing in their determination to force their children into their moulds. Every child has a right to its own bent. It has a right to be a Plymouth Brother though its parents be convinced atheists. It has a right to dislike its mother or father or sister or brother or uncle or aunt if they are antipathetic to it. It has a right to find its own way and go its own way, whether that way seems wise or foolish to others, exactly as an adult has. It has a right to privacy as to its own doings and its own affairs as much as if it were its own father.

SMALL AND LARGE FAMILIES

These rights have now become more important than they used to be, because the modern practice of limiting families enables them to be more effectually violated. In a family of ten, eight, six, or even four children, the rights of the younger ones to a great extent take care of themselves and of the rights of the elder ones too. Two adult parents, in spite of a house to keep and an income to earn, can still interfere to a disastrous extent with the rights and liberties of one child. But by the time a fourth child has arrived, they are not only outnumbered two to one, but are getting tired of the thankless and mischievous job of bringing up their children in the way they think they should go. The old observation that members of large families get on in the world holds good because in large families it is impossible for each child to receive what schoolmasters call "individual attention." The children may receive a good deal of individual attention from one another in the shape of outspoken reproach, ruthless ridicule, and violent resistance to their attempts at aggression; but the parental despots are compelled by the multitude of their subjects to resort to political rather than personal rule, and to spread their attempts at moral monster-making over so many children, that each child has enough freedom, and enough sport in the prophylactic process of laughing at its elders behind their backs, to escape with much less damage than the single child. In a large school the system may be bad; but the personal influence of the head master has to be exerted, when it is exerted at all, in a public way, because he has little more power of working on the affections of the individual scholar in the intimate way that, for example, the mother of a single child can, than the prime minister has of working on the affections of any individual voter.

CHILDREN AS NUISANCES

Experienced parents, when children's rights are preached to them, very naturally ask whether children are to be allowed to do what they like. The best reply is to ask whether adults are to be allowed to do what they like. The two cases are the same. The adult who is nasty is not allowed to do what he likes: neither can the child who likes to be nasty. There is no difference in principle between the rights of a child and those of an adult: the difference in their cases is one of circumstance. An adult is not supposed to be punished except by process of law; nor, when he is so punished, is the person whom he has injured allowed to act as judge, jury, and executioner. It is true that employers do act in this way every day to their workpeople; but this is not a justified and intended part of the situation: it is an abuse of Capitalism which nobody defends in principle. As between child and parent or nurse it is not argued about, because it is inevitable. You cannot hold an impartial judicial inquiry every time a child misbehaves itself. To allow the child to misbehave without instantly making it unpleasantly conscious of the fact would be to spoil it. The adult has therefore to take action of some sort with nothing but his conscience to shield the child from injustice or unkindness. The action may be a torrent of scolding culminating in a furious smack causing terror and pain, or it may be a remonstrance causing remorse, or it may be a sarcasm causing shame and humiliation, or it may be a sermon causing the child to believe that it is a little reprobate on the road to hell. The child has no defence in any case except the kindness and conscience of the adult; and the adult had better not forget this, for it involves a heavy responsibility.

And now comes our difficulty. The responsibility, being so heavy, cannot be discharged by persons of feeble character or intelligence. And yet people of high character and intelligence cannot be plagued with the care of children. A child is a restless, noisy little animal, with an insatiable appetite for knowledge, and consequently a maddening persistence in asking questions. If the child is to remain in the room with a highly intelligent and sensitive adult, it must be told, and if necessary forced, to sit still and not speak, which is injurious to its health, unnatural, unjust, and therefore cruel and selfish beyond toleration. Consequently the highly intelligent and sensitive adult hands the child over to a nurserymaid who has no nerves and can therefore stand more noise, but who has also no scruples, and may therefore be very bad company for the child.

Here we have come to the central fact of the question: a fact nobody avows, which is yet the true explanation of the monstrous system of child imprisonment and torture which we disguise under such hypocrisies as education, training, formation of character and the rest of it. This fact is simply that a child is a nuisance to a grown-up person. What is more, the nuisance becomes more and more intolerable as the grown-up person becomes more cultivated, more sensitive, and more deeply engaged in the highest methods of adult work. The child at play is noisy and ought to be noisy: Sir Isaac Newton at work is quiet and ought to be quiet. And the child should spend most of its time at play, whilst the adult should spend most of his time at work. I am not now writing on behalf of persons who coddle themselves into a ridiculous condition of nervous feebleness, and at last imagine themselves unable to work under conditions of bustle which to healthy people are cheerful and stimulating. I am sure that if people had to choose between living where the noise of children never stopped and where it was never heard, all the goodnatured and sound people would prefer the incessant noise to the incessant silence. But that choice is not thrust upon us by the nature of things. There is no reason why children and adults should not see just as much of one another as is good for them, no more and no less. Even at present you are not compelled to choose between sending your child to a boarding school (which means getting rid of it altogether on more or less hypocritical pretences) and keeping it continually at home. Most working folk today either send their children to day schools or turn them out of doors. This solves the problem for the parents. It does not solve it for the children, any more than the tethering of a goat in a field or the chasing of an unlicensed dog into the streets solves it for the goat or the dog; but it shews that in no class are people willing to endure the society of their children, and consequently that it is an error to believe that the family provides children with edifying adult society, or that the family is a social unit. The family is in that, as in so many other respects, a humbug. Old people and young people cannot walk at the same pace without distress and final loss of health to one of the parties. When they are sitting indoors they cannot endure the same degrees of temperature and the same supplies of fresh air. Even if the main factors of noise, restlessness, and inquisitiveness are left out of account, children can stand with indifference sights, sounds, smells, and disorders that would make an adult of fifty utterly miserable; whilst on the other hand such adults find a tranquil happiness in conditions which to children mean unspeakable boredom. And since our system is nevertheless to pack them all into the same house and pretend that they are happy, and that this particular sort of happiness is the foundation of virtue, it is found that in discussing family life we never speak of actual adults or actual children, or of realities of any sort, but always of ideals such as The

Home, a Mother's Influence, a Father's Care, Filial Piety, Duty, Affection, Family Life, etc. etc., which are no doubt very comforting phrases, but which beg the question of what a home and a mother's influence and a father's care and so forth really come to in practice. How many hours a week of the time when his children are out of bed does the ordinary bread-winning father spend in the company of his children or even in the same building with them? The home may be a thieves' kitchen, the mother a procuress, the father a violent drunkard; or the mother and father may be fashionable people who see their children three or four times a year during the holidays, and then not oftener than they can help, living meanwhile in daily and intimate contact with their valets and lady's-maids, whose influence and care are often dominant in the household. Affection, as distinguished from simple kindliness, may or may not exist: when it does, it either depends on qualities in the parties that would produce it equally if they were of no kin to one another, or it is a more or less morbid survival of the nursing passion; for affection between adults (if they are really adult in mind and not merely grown-up children) and creatures so relatively selfish and cruel as children necessarily are without knowing it or meaning it, cannot be called natural: in fact the evidence shews that it is easier to love the company of a dog than of a commonplace child between the ages of six and the beginnings of controlled maturity; for women who cannot bear to be separated from their pet dogs send their children to boarding schools cheerfully. They may say and even believe that in allowing their children to leave home they are sacrificing themselves for their children's good; but there are very few pet dogs who would not be the better for a month or two spent elsewhere than in a lady's lap or roasting on a drawing-room hearthrug. Besides, to allege that children are better continually away from home is to give up the whole popular sentimental theory of the family; yet the dogs are kept and the children are banished.

CHILD FANCIERS

There is, however, a good deal of spurious family affection. There is the clannishness that will make a dozen brothers and sisters who quarrel furiously among themselves close up their ranks and make common cause against a brother-in-law or a sister-in-law. And there is a strong sense of property in children, which often makes mothers and fathers bitterly jealous of allowing anyone else to interfere with their children, whom they may none the less treat very badly. And there is an extremely dangerous craze for children which leads certain people to establish orphanages and baby farms and schools, seizing any pretext for filling their houses with children exactly as some eccentric old ladies and gentlemen fill theirs with cats. In such places the children are the victims of all the caprices of doting affection and all the excesses of lascivious cruelty. Yet the people who have this morbid craze seldom have any difficulty in finding victims. Parents and guardians are so worried by children and so anxious to get rid of them that anyone who is willing to take them off their hands is welcomed and whitewashed. The very people who read with indignation of Squeers and Creakle in the novels of Dickens are quite ready to hand over their own children to Squeers and Creakle, and to pretend that Squeers and Creakle are monsters of the past. But read the autobiography of Stanley the traveller, or sit in the company of men talking about their schooldays, and you will soon find that fiction, which must, if it is to be sold and read, stop short of being positively

sickening, dare not tell the whole truth about the people to whom children are handed over on educational pretexts. Not very long ago a schoolmaster in Ireland was murdered by his boys; and for reasons which were never made public it was at first decided not to prosecute the murderers. Yet all these flogging schoolmasters and orphanage fiends and baby farmers are "lovers of children." They are really child fanciers (like bird fanciers or dog fanciers) by irresistible natural predilection, never happy unless they are surrounded by their victims, and always certain to make their living by accepting the custody of children, no matter how many alternative occupations may be available. And bear in mind that they are only the extreme instances of what is commonly called natural affection, apparently because it is obviously unnatural.

The really natural feeling of adults for children in the long prosaic intervals between the moments of affectionate impulse is just that feeling that leads them to avoid their care and constant company as a burden beyond bearing, and to pretend that the places they send them to are well conducted, beneficial, and indispensable to the success of the children in after life. The true cry of the kind mother after her little rosary of kisses is "Run away, darling." It is nicer than "Hold your noise, you young devil; or it will be the worse for you;" but fundamentally it means the same thing: that if you compel an adult and a child to live in one another's company either the adult or the child will be miserable. There is nothing whatever unnatural or wrong or shocking in this fact; and there is no harm in it if only it be sensibly faced and provided for. The mischief that it does at present is produced by our efforts to ignore it, or to smother it under a heap of sentimental lies and false pretences.

CHILDHOOD AS A STATE OF SIN

Unfortunately all this nonsense tends to accumulate as we become more sympathetic. In many families it is still the custom to treat childhood frankly as a state of sin, and impudently proclaim the monstrous principle that little children should be seen and not heard, and to enforce a set of prison rules designed solely to make cohabitation with children as convenient as possible for adults, without the smallest regard for the interests, either remote or immediate, of the children. This system tends to produce a tough, rather brutal, stupid, unscrupulous class, with a fixed idea that all enjoyment consists in undetected sinning; and in certain phases of civilization people of this kind are apt to get the upper hand of more amiable and conscientious races and classes. They have the ferocity of a chained dog, and are proud of it. But the end of it is that they are always in chains, even at the height of their military or political success; they win everything on condition that they are afraid to enjoy it. Their civilizations rest on intimidation, which is so necessary to them that when they cannot find anybody brave enough to intimidate them they intimidate themselves and live in a continual moral and political panic. In the end they get found out and bullied. But that is not the point that concerns us here, which is, that they are in some respects better brought up than the children of sentimental people who are always anxious and miserable about their duty to their children, and who end by neither making their children happy nor having a tolerable life for themselves. A selfish tyrant you know where to have, and he (or she) at least does not confuse your affections; but a conscientious and kindly meddler may literally worry you out of your senses. It is fortunate that only very few parents are capable of doing what they conceive their duty continually or even at all, and that still fewer are tough enough to ride roughshod over their children at home.

SCHOOL

But please observe the limitation "at home." What private amateur parental enterprise cannot do may be done very effectively by organized professional enterprise in large institutions established for the purpose. And it is to such professional enterprise that parents hand over their children when they can afford it. They send their children to school; and there is, on the whole, nothing on earth intended for innocent people so horrible as a school. To begin with, it is a prison. But it is in some respects more cruel than a prison. In a prison, for instance, you are not forced to read books written by the warders and the governor (who of course would not be warders and governors if they could write readable books), and beaten or otherwise tormented if you cannot remember their utterly unmemorable contents. In the prison you are not forced to sit listening to turnkeys discoursing without charm or interest on subjects that they dont understand and dont care about, and are therefore incapable of making you understand or care about. In a prison they may torture your body; but they do not torture your brains; and they protect you against violence and outrage from your fellow-prisoners. In a school you have none of these advantages. With the world's bookshelves loaded with fascinating and inspired books, the very manna sent down from heaven to feed your souls, you are forced to read a hideous imposture called a school book, written by a man who cannot write: a book from which no human being can learn anything: a book which, though you may decipher it, you cannot in any fruitful sense read, though the enforced attempt will make you loathe the sight of a book all the rest of your life. With millions of acres of woods and valleys and hills and wind and air and birds and streams and fishes and all sorts of instructive and healthy things easily accessible, or with streets and shop windows and crowds and vehicles and all sorts of city delights at the door, you are forced to sit, not in a room with some human grace and comfort of furniture and decoration but in a stalled pound with a lot of other children, beaten if you talk, beaten if you move, beaten if you cannot prove by answering idiotic questions that even when you escaped from the pound and from the eye of your gaoler you were still agonizing over his detestable sham books instead of daring to live. And your childish hatred of your gaoler and flogger is nothing to his adult hatred of you; for he is a slave forced to endure your society for his daily bread. You have not even the satisfaction of knowing how you are torturing him and how he loathes you; and you give yourself unnecessary pains to annoy him with furtive tricks and spiteful doing of forbidden things. No wonder he is sometimes provoked to fiendish outbursts of wrath. No wonder men of downright sense, like Dr Johnson, admit that under such circumstances children will not learn anything unless they are so cruelly beaten that they make desperate efforts to memorize words and phrases to escape flagellation. It is a ghastly business, quite beyond words, this schooling.

And now I hear cries of protest arising all round. First my own schoolmasters, or their ghosts, asking whether I was cruelly beaten at school? No; but then I did not learn anything at school. Dr Johnson's schoolmaster presumably did care enough whether Sam learned anything to beat him savagely enough to force him to lame his mind—for Johnson's great mind *was* lamed—by learning

his lessons. None of my schoolmasters really cared a rap (or perhaps it would be fairer to them to say that their employers did not care a rap and therefore did not give them the necessary caning powers) whether I learnt my lessons or not, provided my father paid my schooling bill, the collection of which was the real object of the school. Consequently I did not learn my school lessons, having much more important ones in hand, with the result that I have not wasted my life trifling with literary fools in taverns as Johnson did when he should have been shaking England with the thunder of his spirit. My schooling did me a great deal of harm and no good whatever: it was simply dragging a child's soul through the dirt; but I escaped Squeers and Creakle just as I escaped Johnson and Carlyle. And this is what happens to most of us. We are not effectively coerced to learn: we stave off punishment as far as we can by lying and trickery and guessing and using our wits; and when this does not suffice we scribble impositions, or suffer extra imprisonments—"keeping in" was the phrase in my time—or let a master strike us with a cane and fall back on our pride at being able to bear it physically (he not being allowed to hit us too hard) to outface the dishonor we should have been taught to die rather than endure. And so idleness and worthlessness on the one hand and a pretence of coercion on the other became a despicable routine. If my schoolmasters had been really engaged in educating me instead of painfully earning their bread by keeping me from annoying my elders they would have turned me out of the school, telling me that I was thoroughly disloyal to it; that I had no intention of learning; that I was mocking and distracting the boys who did wish to learn; that I was a liar and a shirker and a seditious little nuisance; and that nothing could injure me in character and degrade their occupation more than allowing me (much less forcing me) to remain in the school under such conditions. But in order to get expelled, it was necessary to commit a crime of such atrocity that the parents of the other boys would have threatened to remove their sons sooner than allow them to be schoolfellows with the delinquent. I can remember only one case in which such a penalty was threatened; and in that case the culprit, a boarder, had kissed a housemaid, or possibly, being a handsome youth, been kissed by her. She did not kiss me; and nobody ever dreamt of expelling me. The truth was, a boy meant just so much a year to the institution. That was why he was kept there against his will. That was why he was kept there when his expulsion would have been an unspeakable relief and benefit both to his teachers and himself.

It may be argued that if the uncommercial attitude had been taken, and all the disloyal wasters and idlers shewn sternly to the door, the school would not have been emptied, but filled. But so honest an attitude was impossible. The masters must have hated the school much more than the boys did. Just as you cannot imprison a man without imprisoning a warder to see that he does not escape, the warder being tied to the prison as effectually by the fear of unemployment and starvation as the prisoner is by the bolts and bars, so these poor schoolmasters, with their small salaries and large classes, were as much prisoners as we were, and much more responsible and anxious ones. They could not impose the heroic attitude on their employers; nor would they have been able to obtain places as schoolmasters if their habits had been heroic. For the best of them their employment was provisional: they looked forward to escaping from it into the pulpit. The ablest and most impatient of them were often so irritated by the awkward, slow-witted, slovenly boys: that is, the ones that required special consideration and patient treatment, that they vented their irritation on them ruthlessly, nothing being easier than to entrap or bewilder such a boy into giving a pretext for punishing him.

MY SCHOLASTIC ACQUIREMENTS

The results, as far as I was concerned, were what might have been expected. My school made only the thinnest pretence of teaching anything but Latin and Greek. When I went there as a very small boy I knew a good deal of Latin grammar which I had been taught in a few weeks privately by my uncle. When I had been several years at school this same uncle examined me and discovered that the net result of my schooling was that I had forgotten what he had taught me, and had learnt nothing else. To this day, though I can still decline a Latin noun and repeat some of the old paradigms in the old meaningless way, because their rhythm sticks to me, I have never yet seen a Latin inscription on a tomb that I could translate throughout. Of Greek I can decipher perhaps the greater part of the Greek alphabet. In short, I am, as to classical education, another Shakespear. I can read French as easily as English; and under pressure of necessity I can turn to account some scraps of German and a little operatic Italian; but these I was never taught at school. Instead, I was taught lying, dishonourable submission to tyranny, dirty stories, a blasphemous habit of treating love and maternity as obscene jokes, hopelessness, evasion, derision, cowardice, and all the blackguard's shifts by which the coward intimidates other cowards. And if I had been a boarder at an English public school instead of a day boy at an Irish one, I might have had to add to these, deeper shames still.

SCHOOLMASTERS OF GENIUS

And now, if I have reduced the ghosts of my schoolmasters to melancholy acquiescence in all this (which everybody who has been at an ordinary school will recognize as true), I have still to meet the much more sincere protests of the handful of people who have a natural genius for "bringing up" children. I shall be asked with kindly scorn whether I have heard of Froebel and Pestalozzi, whether I know the work that is being done by Miss Mason and the Dottoressa Montessori or, best of all as I think, the Eurythmics School of Jacques Dalcroze at Hellerau near Dresden. Jacques Dalcroze, like Plato, believes in saturating his pupils with music. They walk to music, play to music, work to music, obey drill commands that would bewilder a guardsman to music, think to music, live to music, get so clearheaded about music that they can move their several limbs each in a different metre until they become complicated living magazines of cross rhythms, and, what is more, make music for others to do all these things to. Stranger still, though Jacques Dalcroze, like all these great teachers, is the completest of tyrants, knowing what is right and that he must and will have the lesson just so or else break his heart (not somebody else's, observe), yet his school is so fascinating that every woman who sees it exclaims "Oh, why was I not taught like this!" and elderly gentlemen excitedly enrol themselves as students and distract classes of infants by their desperate endeavors to beat two in a bar with one hand and three with the other, and start off on earnest walks round the room, taking two steps backward whenever Monsieur Dalcroze calls out "Hop!" Oh yes: I know all about these wonderful schools that you cannot keep children or even adults out of, and these teachers whom their pupils not only obey without coercion, but adore. And if you will tell me roughly how many Masons and Montessoris and Dalcrozes you think you can pick up in Europe for salaries of from thirty shillings to five pounds a week, I will estimate your chances of converting your millions of little scholastic hells into little scholastic heavens. If you are a distressed gentlewoman starting to make a living, you can still open a little school: and you can easily buy a secondhand brass plate inscribed PESTALOZZIAN INSTITUTE and nail it to your door, though you have no more idea of who Pestalozzi was and what he advocated or how he did it than the manager of a hotel which began as a Hydropathic has of the water cure. Or you can buy a cheaper plate inscribed KINDERGARTEN, and imagine, or leave others to imagine, that Froebel is the governing genius of your little *crèche*. No doubt the new brass plates are being inscribed Montessori Institute, and will be used when the Dottoressa is no longer with us by all the Mrs Pipchins and Mrs Wilfers throughout this unhappy land.

I will go further, and admit that the brass plates may not all be frauds. I will tell you that one of my friends was led to genuine love and considerable knowledge of classical literature by an Irish schoolmaster whom you would call a hedge schoolmaster (he would not be allowed to teach anything now) and that it took four years of Harrow to obliterate that knowledge and change the love into loathing. Another friend of mine who keeps a school in the suburbs, and who deeply deplores my " prejudice against schoolmasters," has offered to accept my challenge to tell his pupils that they are as free to get up and go out of the school at any moment as their parents are to get up and go out of a theatre where my plays are being performed. Even among my own schoolmasters I can recollect a few whose classes interested me, and whom I should certainly have pestered for information and instruction if I could have got into any decent human relationship with them, and if they had not been compelled by their position to defend themselves as carefully against such advances as against furtive attempts to hurt them accidentally in the football field or smash their hats with a clod from behind a wall. But these rare cases actually do more harm than good; for they encourage us to pretend that all schoolmasters are like that. Of what use is it to us that there are always somewhere two or three teachers of children whose specific genius for their occupation triumphs over our tyrannous system and even finds in it its opportunity? For that matter, it is possible, if difficult, to find a solicitor, or even a judge, who has some notion of what law means, a doctor with a glimmering of science, an officer who understands duty and discipline, and a clergyman with an inkling of religion, though there are nothing like enough of them to go round. But even the few who, like Ibsen's Mrs Solness, have "a genius for nursing the souls of little children" are like angels forced to work in prisons instead of in heaven; and even at that they are mostly underpaid and despised. That friend of mine who went from the hedge schoolmaster to Harrow once saw a schoolmaster rush from an elementary school in pursuit of a boy and strike him. My friend, not considering that the unfortunate man was probably goaded beyond endurance, smote the schoolmaster and blackened his eye. The schoolmaster appealed to the law; and my friend found himself waiting nervously in the Hammersmith Police Court to answer for his breach of the peace. In his anxiety he asked a police officer what would happen to him. "What did you do?" said the officer. "I gave a man a black eye" said my friend. "Six pounds if he was a gentleman: two

pounds if he wasnt," said the constable. "He was a schoolmaster" said my friend. "Two pounds" said the officer; and two pounds it was. The blood money was paid cheerfully; and I have ever since advised elementary schoolmasters to qualify themselves in the art of self-defence, as the British Constitution expresses our national estimate of them by allowing us to blacken three of their eyes for the same price as one of an ordinary professional man. How many Froebels and Pestalozzis and Miss Masons and Doctoress Montessoris would you be likely to get on these terms even if they occurred much more frequently in nature than they actually do?

No: I cannot be put off by the news that our system would be perfect if it were worked by angels. I do not admit it even at that, just as I do not admit that if the sky fell we should all catch larks. But I do not propose to bother about a supply of specific genius which does not exist, and which, if it did exist, could operate only by at once recognizing and establishing the rights of children.

WHAT WE DO NOT TEACH, AND WHY

To my mind, a glance at the subjects now taught in schools ought to convince any reasonable person that the object of the lessons is to keep children out of mischief, and not to qualify them for their part in life as responsible citizens of a free State. It is not possible to maintain freedom in any State, no matter how perfect its original constitution, unless its publicly active citizens know a good deal of constitutional history, law, and political science, with its basis of economics. If as much pains had been taken a century ago to make us all understand Ricardo's law of rent as to learn our catechisms, the face of the world would have been changed for the better. But for that very reason the greatest care is taken to keep such beneficially subversive knowledge from us, with the result that in public life we are either place-hunters, anarchists, or sheep shepherded by wolves.

But it will be observed that these are highly controversial subjects. Now no controversial subject can be taught dogmatically. He who knows only the official side of a controversy knows less than nothing of its nature. The abler a schoolmaster is, the more dangerous he is to his pupils unless they have the fullest opportunity of hearing another equally able person do his utmost to shake his authority and convict him of error.

At present such teaching is very unpopular. It does not exist in schools; but every adult who derives his knowledge of public affairs from the newspapers can take in, at the cost of an extra halfpenny, two papers of opposite politics. Yet the ordinary man so dislikes having his mind unsettled, as he calls it, that he angrily refuses to allow a paper which dissents from his views to be brought into his house. Even at his club he resents seeing it, and excludes it if it happens to run counter to the opinions of all the members. The result is that his opinions are not worth considering. A churchman who never reads The Freethinker very soon has no more real religion than the atheist who never reads The Church Times. The attitude is the same in both cases: they want to hear nothing good of their enemies; consequently they remain enemies and suffer from bad blood all their lives; whereas men who know their opponents and understand their case, quite commonly respect and like them, and always learn something from them.

Here, again, as at so many points, we come up against the abuse of schools to keep people in ignorance and error, so that they may be incapable of successful revolt against their industrial slavery. The most important simple fundamental economic truth to impress on a child in complicated civilizations like ours is the truth that whoever consumes goods or services without producing by personal effort the equivalent of what he or she consumes, inflicts on the community precisely the same injury that a thief produces, and would, in any honest State, be treated as a thief, however full his or her pockets might be of money made by other people. The nation that first teaches its children that truth, instead of flogging them if they discover it for themselves, may have to fight all the slaves of all the other nations to begin with; but it will beat them as easily as an unburdened man with his hands free and with all his energies in full play can beat an invalid who has to carry another invalid on his back.

This, however, is not an evil produced by the denial of children's rights, nor is it inherent in the nature of schools. I mention it only because it would be folly to call for a reform of our schools without taking account of the corrupt resistance which awaits the reformer.

A word must also be said about the opposition to reform of the vested interest of the classical and coercive schoolmaster. He, poor wretch, has no other means of livelihood; and reform would leave him as a workman is now left when he is superseded by a machine. He had therefore better do what he can to get the workman compensated, so as to make the public familiar with the idea of compensation before his own turn comes.

TABOO IN SCHOOLS

The suppression of economic knowledge, disastrous as it is, is quite intelligible, its corrupt motive being as clear as the motive of a burglar for concealing his jemmy from a policeman. But the other great suppression in our schools, the suppression of the subject of sex, is a case of taboo. In mankind, the lower the type, and the less cultivated the mind, the less courage there is to face important subjects objectively. The ablest and most highly cultivated people continually discuss religion, politics, and sex: it is hardly an exaggeration to say that they discuss nothing else with fully awakened interest. Commoner and less cultivated people, even when they form societies for discussion, make a rule that politics and religion are not to be mentioned, and take it for granted that no decent person would attempt to discuss sex. The three subjects are feared because they rouse the crude passions which call for furious gratification in murder and rapine at worst, and, at best, lead to quarrels and undesirable states of consciousness.

Even when this excuse of bad manners, ill temper, and brutishness (for that is what it comes to) compels us to accept it from those adults among whom political and theological discussion does as a matter of fact lead to the drawing of knives and pistols, and sex discussion leads to obscenity, it has no application to children except as an imperative reason for training them to respect other people's opinions, and to insist on respect for their own in these as in other important matters which are equally dangerous: for example, money. And in any case there are decisive reasons, superior, like the reasons for suspending conventional reticences between doctor and patient, to all considerations of mere decorum, for giving proper instruction in the facts of sex. Those who object to it (not counting coarse people who thoughtlessly seize every opportunity of affecting and parading a fictitious delicacy) are, in effect, advocating ignorance as a safeguard against precocity. If ignorance were practicable there would be something to be said for it up to the age at which ignorance is a danger instead of a safe-guard. Even as it is, it seems undesirable that any special emphasis should be given to the subject, whether by way of delicacy and poetry or too impressive warning. But the plain fact is that in refusing to allow the child to be taught by qualified unrelated elders (the parents shrink from the lesson, even when they are otherwise qualified, because their own relation to the child makes the subject impossible between them) we are virtually arranging to have our children taught by other children in guilty secrets and unclean jests. And that settles the question for all sensible people.

The dogmatic objection, the sheer instinctive taboo which rules the subject out altogether as indecent, has no age limit. It means that at no matter what age a woman consents to a proposal of marriage, she should do so in ignorance of the relation she is undertaking. When this actually happens (and apparently it does happen oftener than would seem possible) a horrible fraud is being practised on both the man and the woman. He is led to believe that she knows what she is promising, and that he is in no danger of finding himself bound to a woman to whom he is eugenically antipathetic. She contemplates nothing but such affectionate relations as may exist between her and her nearest kinsmen, and has no knowledge of the condition which, if not foreseen, must come as an amazing revelation and a dangerous shock, ending possibly in the discovery that the marriage has been an irreparable mistake. Nothing can justify such a risk. There may be people incapable of understanding that the right to know all there is to know about oneself is a natural human right that sweeps away all the pretences of others to tamper with one's consciousness in order to produce what they choose to consider a good character. But they must here bow to the plain mischievousness of entrapping people into contracts on which the happiness of their whole lives depends without letting them know what they are undertaking.

ALLEGED NOVELTIES IN MODERN SCHOOLS

There is just one more nuisance to be disposed of before I come to the positive side of my case. I mean the person who tells me that my schooldays belong to a bygone order of educational ideas and institutions, and that schools are not now a bit like my old school. I reply, with Sir Walter Raleigh, by calling on my soul to give this statement the lie. Some years ago I lectured in Oxford on the subject of Education. A friend to whom I mentioned my intention said, "You know nothing of modern education: schools are not now what they were when you were a boy." I immediately procured the time sheets of half a dozen modern schools, and found, as I expected, that they might all have been my old school: there was no real difference. I may mention, too, that I have visited modern schools, and observed that there is a tendency to hang printed pictures in an untidy and soulless manner on the walls, and occasionally to display on the mantelshelf a deplorable glass case containing certain objects which might possibly, if placed in the hands of the pupils, give them some practical experience of the weight of a pound and the length of an inch. And sometimes a scoundrel who has rifled a bird's nest or killed a harmless snake encourages the children to go and do likewise by putting his victims into an imitation nest and bottling and exhibiting them as aids to "Nature study." A suggestion that Nature is worth study would certainly have staggered my schoolmasters; so perhaps I may admit a gleam of progress here. But as any child who attempted to handle these dusty objects would probably be caned, I do not attach any importance to such modernities in school furniture. The school remains what it was in my boyhood, because its real object remains what it was. And that object, I repeat, is to keep the children out of mischief: mischief meaning for the most part worrying the grown-ups.

WHAT IS TO BE DONE?

The practical question, then, is what to do with the children. Tolerate them at home we will not. Let them run loose in the streets we dare not until our streets become safe places for children, which, to our utter shame, they are not at present, though they can hardly be worse than some homes and some schools.

The grotesque difficulty of making even a beginning was brought home to me by the lady of the manor in the little village in Hertfordshire where I write these lines. She asked me very properly what I was going to do for the village school. I did not know what to reply. As the school kept the children quiet during my working hours, I did not for the sake of my own personal convenience want to blow it up with dynamite as I should like to blow up most schools. So I asked for guidance. "You ought to give a prize" said the lady. I asked if there was a prize for good conduct. As I expected, there was: one for the best-behaved boy and another for the best-behaved girl. On reflection I offered a handsome prize for the worst-behaved boy and girl on condition that a record should be kept of their subsequent careers and compared with the records of the best-behaved, in order to ascertain whether the school criterion of good conduct was valid out of school. My offer was refused because it would not have had the effect of encouraging the children to give as little trouble as possible, which is of course the real object of all conduct prizes in schools.

I must not pretend, then, that I have

a system ready to replace all the other systems. Obstructing the way of the proper organization of childhood, as of everything else, lies our ridiculous misdistribution of the national income, with its accompanying class distinctions and imposition of snobbery on children as a necessary part of their social training. The result of our economic folly is that we are a nation of undesirable acquaintances; and the first object of all our institutions for children is segregation. If, for example, our children were set free to roam and play about as they pleased, they would have to be policed; and the first duty of the police in a State like ours would be to see that every child wore a badge indicating its class in society, and that every child seen speaking to another child with a lower-class badge, or any child wearing a higher badge than that allotted to it by, say, the College of Heralds, should immediately be skinned alive with a birch rod. It might even be insisted that girls with high-class badges should be attended by footmen, grooms, or even military escorts. In short, there is hardly any limit to the follies with which our Commercialism would infect any system that it would tolerate at all. But something like a change of heart is still possible; and since all the evils of snobbery and segregation are rampant in our schools at present we may as well make the best as the worst of them.

CHILDREN'S RIGHTS AND DUTIES

Now let us ask what are a child's rights, and what are the rights of society over the child. Its rights, being clearly those of any other human being, are summed up in the right to live: that is, to have all the conclusive arguments that prove that it would be better dead, that it is a child of wrath, that the population is already excessive, that the pains of life are greater than its pleasures, that its sacrifice in a hospital or laboratory ex-periment might save millions of lives, etc. etc. etc., put out of the question, and its existence accepted as necessary and sacred, all theories to the contrary notwithstanding, whether by Calvin or Schopenhauer or Pasteur or the nearest person with a taste for infanticide. And this right to live includes, and in fact is, the right to be what the child likes and can, to do what it likes and can, to make what it likes and can, to think what it likes and can, to smash what it dislikes and can, and generally to behave in an altogether unaccountable manner within the limits imposed by the similar rights of its neighbors. And the rights of society over it clearly extend to requiring it to qualify itself to live in society without wasting other people's time: that is, it must know the rules of the road, be able to read placards and proclamations, fill voting papers, compose and send letters and telegrams, purchase food and clothing and railway tickets for itself, count money and give and take change, and, generally, know how many beans make five. It must know some law, were it only a simple set of commandments, some political economy, agriculture enough to shut the gates of fields with cattle in them and not to trample on growing crops, sanitation enough not to defile its haunts, and religion enough to have some idea of why it is allowed its rights and why it must respect the rights of others. And the rest of its education must consist of anything else it can pick up; for beyond this society cannot go with any certainty, and indeed can only go this far rather apologetically and pro-visionally, as doing the best it can on very uncertain ground.

SHOULD CHILDREN EARN THEIR LIVING?

Now comes the question how far children should be asked to contribute to the support of the community. In approach-ing it we must put aside the considerations that now induce all humane and thoughtful political students to agitate for the uncompromising abolition of child labor under our capitalist system. It is not the least of the curses of that system that it will bequeath to future generations a mass of legislation to prevent capitalists from "using up nine generations of men in one generation," as they began by doing until they were restrained by law at the suggestion of Robert Owen, the founder of English Socialism. Most of this legislation will become an insufferable restraint upon freedom and variety of action when Capitalism goes the way of Druidic human sacrifice (a much less slaughterous institution). There is every reason why a child should not be allowed to work for commercial profit or for the support of its parents at the expense of its own future; but there is no reason whatever why a child should not do some work for its own sake and that of the community if it can be shewn that both it and the community will be the better for it.

CHILDREN'S HAPPINESS

Also it is important to put the happiness of the children rather carefully in its place, which is really not a front place. The unsympathetic, selfish, hard people who regard happiness as a very exceptional indulgence to which children are by no means entitled, though they may be allowed a very little of it on their birthdays or at Christmas, are sometimes better parents in effect than those who imagine that children are as capable of happiness as adults. Adults habitually exaggerate their own capacity in that direction grossly; yet most adults can stand an allowance of happiness that would be quite thrown away on children. The secret of being miserable is to have leisure to bother about whether you are happy or not. The cure for it is occupa-

tion, because occupation means pre-occupation; and the preoccupied person is neither happy nor unhappy, but simply alive and active, which is pleasanter than any happiness until you are tired of it. That is why it is necessary to happiness that one should be tired. Music after dinner is pleasant: music before breakfast is so unpleasant as to be clearly unnatural. To people who are not over-worked holidays are a nuisance. To people who are, and who can afford them, they are a troublesome necessity. A perpetual holiday is a good working definition of hell.

THE HORROR OF THE PERPETUAL HOLIDAY

It will be said here that, on the contrary, heaven is always conceived as a perpetual holiday, and that whoever is not born to an independent income is striving for one or longing for one because it gives holidays for life. To which I reply, first, that heaven, as conventionally conceived, is a place so inane, so dull, so useless, so miserable, that nobody has ever ventured to describe a whole day in heaven, though plenty of people have described a day at the seaside; and that the genuine popular verdict on it is expressed in the proverb "Heaven for holiness and Hell for company." Second, I point out that the wretched people who have independent incomes and no useful occupation, do the most amazingly disagreeable and dangerous things to make themselves tired and hungry in the evening. When they are not involved in what they call sport, they are doing aimlessly what other people have to be paid to do: driving horses and motor cars; trying on dresses and walking up and down to shew them off; and acting as footmen and housemaids to royal personages. The sole and obvious cause of the notion that idleness is delightful and that heaven is a place where there is nothing to be done, is our school system and our industrial system. The school is a prison in which work is a punishment and a curse. In avowed prisons, hard labor, the only alleviation of a prisoner's lot, is treated as an aggravation of his punishment; and everything possible is done to intensify the prisoner's inculcated and unnatural notion that work is an evil. In industry we are overworked and underfed prisoners. Under such absurd circumstances our judgment of things becomes as perverted as our habits. If we were habitually underworked and overfed, our notion of heaven would be a place where everybody worked strenuously for twenty-four hours a day and never got anything to eat.

Once realize that a perpetual holiday is beyond human endurance, and that "Satan finds some mischief still for idle hands to do," and it will be seen that we have no right to impose a perpetual holiday on children. If we did, they would soon outdo the Labor Party in their claim for a Right to Work Bill.

In any case no child should be brought up to suppose that its food and clothes come down from heaven or are miraculously conjured from empty space by papa. Loathsome as we have made the idea of duty (like the idea of work) we must habituate children to a sense of repayable obligation to the community for what they consume and enjoy, and inculcate the repayment as a point of honor. If we did that today—and nothing but flat dishonesty prevents us from doing it—we should have no idle rich and indeed probably no rich, since there is no distinction in being rich if you have to pay scot and lot in personal effort like the working folk. Therefore, if for only half an hour a day, a child should do something serviceable to the community.

Productive work for children has the advantage that its discipline is the discipline of impersonal necessity, not that of wanton personal coercion. The eagerness of children in our industrial districts to escape from school to the factory is not caused by lighter tasks or shorter hours in the factory, nor altogether by the temptation of wages, nor even by the desire for novelty, but by the dignity of adult work, the exchange of the humiliating liability to personal assault from the lawless schoolmaster, from which the grown-ups are free, for the stern but entirely dignified pressure of necessity to which all flesh is subject.

UNIVERSITY SCHOOLBOYISHNESS

Older children might do a good deal before beginning their collegiate education. What is the matter with our universities is that the students are school children, whereas it is of the very essence of university education that they should be adults. The function of a university is not to teach things that can now be taught as well or better by University Extension lectures or by private tutors or modern correspondence classes with gramophones. We go to them to be socialized: to acquire the hall mark of communal training; to become citizens of the world instead of inmates of the enlarged rabbit hutches we call homes; to learn manners and become unchallengeable ladies and gentlemen. The social pressure which effects these changes should be that of persons who have faced the full responsibilities of adults as working members of the general community, not that of a rowdy rabble of half emancipated school children and unemancipable pedants. It is true that in a reasonable state of society this outside experience would do for us very completely what the university does now so corruptly that we tolerate its bad manners only because they are better than no manners at all. But the university will always exist in some form as a community of persons desirous of pushing their culture to the highest pitch they are capable of, not as solitary students reading in seclusion, but as members of a body of individuals all pursuing culture, talking culture, thinking culture, above all, criticizing culture. If such persons are to read and talk and criticize to any purpose, they must know the world outside the university at least as well as the shopkeeper in the High Street does. And this is just what they do not know at present. You may say of them, paraphrasing Mr Kipling, "What do they know of Plato that only Plato know?" If our universities would exclude everybody who had not earned a living by his or her own exertions for at least a couple of years, their effect would be vastly improved.

THE NEW LAZINESS

The child of the future, then, if there is to be any future but one of decay, will work more or less for its living from an early age; and in doing so it will not shock anyone, provided there be no longer any reason to associate the conception of children working for their living with infants toiling in a factory for ten hours a day or boys drudging from nine to six under gas lamps in underground city offices. Lads and lasses in their teens will probably be able to produce as much as the most expensive person now costs in his own person (it is retinue that eats up the big income) without working too hard or too long for quite as much happiness as they can enjoy. The question to be balanced then will be, not how soon people should be put to work, but how soon they should be released from any obligation of the kind. A life's work is like a day's work: it can begin early and leave off early or begin late and leave off late, or, as with us, begin too early and never leave off at all, obviously the worst of all possible plans. In any event we must finally reckon work, not as the curse our schools

and prisons and capitalist profit factories make it seem today, but as a prime necessity of a tolerable existence. And if we cannot devize fresh wants as fast as we shorten the process of supplying the old ones, there will come a scarcity of work simultaneously with an excess of leisure. Work may have to be shared out among people who want more of it. Our spurious substitute, exercise, will not serve. A new sort of laziness will become the bugbear of society: the laziness that refuses to face the mental toil and adventure of making work by inventing new ideas or extending the domain of knowledge, and insists on a ready-made routine. It may come to forcing people to retire before they are willing to make way for younger ones: that is, to driving all persons of a certain age out of industry, leaving them to find something experimental to occupy them on pain of perpetual holiday. Men will then try to spend twenty thousand a year for the sake of having to earn it. Instead of being what we are now, the cheapest and nastiest of the animals, we shall be the costliest, most fastidious, and best bred. In short, there is no end to the astonishing things that may happen when the curse of Adam becomes first a blessing and then an incurable habit. And in view of that day we must not grudge children their share of it.

THE INFINITE SCHOOL TASK

The question of children's work, however, is only a question of what the child ought to do for the community. How highly it should qualify itself is another matter. But most of the difficulty of inducing children to learn would disappear if our demands became not only definite but finite. When learning is only an excuse for imprisonment, it is an instrument of torture which becomes more painful the more progress is made. Thus when you have forced a child to learn the Church Catechism, a document profound beyond

D

the comprehension of most adults, you are sometimes at a standstill for something else to teach; and you therefore keep the wretched child repeating its catechism again and again until you hit on the plan of making it learn instalments of Bible verses, preferably from the book of Numbers. But as it is less trouble to set a lesson that you know yourself, there is a tendency to keep repeating the already learnt lesson rather than break new ground. At school I began with a fairly complete knowledge of Latin grammar in the childish sense of being able to repeat all the paradigms; and I was kept at this, or rather kept in a class where the master never asked me to do it because he knew I could, and therefore devoted himself to trapping the boys who could not, until I finally forgot most of it. But when progress took place, what did it mean? First it meant Cæsar, with the foreknowledge that to master Cæsar meant only being set at Virgil, with the culminating horror of Greek and Homer in reserve at the end of that. I preferred Cæsar, because his statement that Gaul is divided into three parts, though neither interesting nor true, was the only Latin sentence I could translate at sight: therefore the longer we stuck at Cæsar the better I was pleased. Just so do less classically educated children see nothing in the mastery of addition but the beginning of subtraction, and so on through multiplication and division and fractions, with the black cloud of algebra on the horizon. And if a boy rushes through all that, there is always the calculus to fall back on, unless indeed you insist on his learning music, and proceed to hit him if he cannot tell you the year Beethoven was born.

A child has a right to finality as regards its compulsory lessons. Also as regards physical training. At present it is assumed that the schoolmaster has a right to force every child into an attempt to become Porson and Bentley, Leibnitz and Newton, all rolled into one. This is the tradition of the oldest grammar schools. In our times an even more horrible and cynical claim has been made for the right to drive boys through compulsory games in the playing fields until they are too much exhausted physically to do anything but drop off to sleep. This is supposed to protect them from vice; but as it also protects them from poetry, literature, music, meditation and prayer, it may be dismissed with the obvious remark that if boarding schools are places whose keepers are driven to such monstrous measures lest more abominable things should happen, then the sooner boarding schools are violently abolished the better. It is true that society may make physical claims on the child as well as mental ones: the child must learn to walk, to use a knife and fork, to swim, to ride a bicycle, to acquire sufficient power of self-defence to make an attack on it an arduous and uncertain enterprise, perhaps to fly. What as a matter of common sense it clearly has not a right to do is to make this an excuse for keeping the child slaving for ten hours at physical exercises on the ground that it is not yet as dexterous as Cinquevalli and as strong as Sandow.

THE REWARDS AND RISKS OF KNOWLEDGE

In a word, we cannot completely educate a child; for its education can end only with its life and will not even then be complete. Compulsory completion of education is the last folly of a rotten and desperate civilization. All we can fairly do is to prescribe definite acquirements and accomplishments as qualifications for citizenship in general, with further specific qualifications for professional employments; and to secure them, not by the ridiculous method of inflicting artificial injuries on the persons who have not yet mastered them, but by the natural co-operation of self-respect from within with social respect from without.

Most acquirements carry their own privileges with them. Thus a baby has to be pretty closely guarded and imprisoned because it cannot take care of itself. It has even to be carried about (the most complete conceivable infringement of its liberty) until it can walk. But nobody goes on carrying children after they can walk lest they should walk into mischief, though Arab boys make their sisters carry them, as our own spoiled children sometimes make their nurses, out of mere laziness, because sisters in the East and nurses in the West are kept in servitude. But in a society of equals (the only reasonable and permanently possible sort of society) children are in much greater danger of acquiring bandy legs through being left to walk before they are strong enough than of being carried when they are well able to walk. Anyhow, freedom of movement in a nursery is the reward of learning to walk; and in precisely the same way freedom of movement in a city is the reward of learning how to read public notices, and to count and use money. The consequences are of course much larger than the mere ability to read the name of a street or the number of a railway platform and the destination of a train. When you enable a child to read these, you also enable it to read this preface, to the utter destruction, you may quite possibly think, of its morals (its docility). You also expose it to the danger of being run over by taxicabs and trains. The moral and physical risks of education are enormous: every new power a child acquires, from speaking, walking, and co-ordinating its vision, to conquering continents and founding religions, opens up immense new possibilities of mischief. Teach a child to write and you teach it how to forge: teach it to speak and you teach it how to lie: teach it to walk and you teach it how to kick its mother to death.

The great problem of slavery for those whose aim is to maintain it is the problem of reconciling the efficiency of the slave with the helplessness that keeps him in servitude; and this problem is fortunately not completely soluble; for it is not in fact found possible for a duke to treat his solicitor or his doctor as he treats his laborers, though they are all equally his slaves: the laborer being in fact less dependent on his favor than the professional man. Hence it is that men come to resent, of all things, protection, because it so often means restriction of their liberty lest they should make a bad use of it. If there are dangerous precipices about, it is much easier and cheaper to forbid people to walk near the edge than to put up an effective fence: that is why both legislators and parents and the paid deputies of parents are always inhibiting and prohibiting and punishing and scolding and laming and cramping and delaying progress and growth instead of making the dangerous places as safe as possible and then boldly taking and allowing others to take the irreducible minimum of risk.

ENGLISH PHYSICAL HARDIHOOD AND SPIRITUAL COWARDICE

It is easier to convert most people to the need for allowing their children to run physical risks than moral ones. I can remember a relative of mine who, when I was a small child, unused to horses and very much afraid of them, insisted on putting me on a rather rumbustious pony with little spurs on my heels (knowing that in my agitation I would use them unconsciously), and being enormously amused at my terrors. Yet when that same lady discovered that I had found a copy of The Arabian Nights and was devouring it with avidity, she was horrified, and hid it away from me lest it should break my soul as the pony might have broken my neck. This way of producing hardy bodies and timid souls is so common in country-houses that you may spend hours in them listening to stories of broken collar bones, broken backs, and broken necks without coming upon a single spiritual adventure or daring thought.

But whether the risks to which liberty exposes us are moral or physical, our right to liberty involves the right to run them. A man who is not free to risk his neck as an aviator or his soul as a heretic is not free at all; and the right to liberty begins, not at the age of 21 years but of 21 seconds.

THE RISKS OF IGNORANCE AND WEAKNESS

The difficulty with children is that they need protection from risks they are too young to understand, and attacks they can neither avoid nor resist. You may on academic grounds allow a child to snatch glowing coals from the fire once. You will not do it twice. The risks of liberty we must let everyone take; but the risks of ignorance and self-helplessness are another matter. Not only children but adults need protection from them. At present adults are often exposed to risks outside their knowledge or beyond their comprehension or powers of resistance or foresight: for example, we have to look on every day at marriages or financial speculations that may involve far worse consequences than burnt fingers. And just as it is part of the business of adults to protect children, to feed them, clothe them, shelter them, and shift for them in all sorts of ways until they are able to shift for themselves, it is coming more and more to be seen that this is true not only of the relation between adults and children, but between adults and adults. We shall not always look on indifferently at foolish marriages and financial speculations, nor allow dead men to control live communities by ridiculous wills and living heirs to squander and ruin great estates, nor tolerate a hundred other absurd liberties that we allow today because we are too lazy to find out the proper way to interfere. But the interference must be regulated by some theory of the individual's rights. Though the right to live is absolute, it is not unconditional. If a man is unbearably mischievous, he must be killed. This is a mere matter of necessity, like the killing of a man-eating tiger in a nursery, a venomous snake in the garden, or a fox in the poultry yard. No society could be constructed on the assumption that such extermination is a violation of the creature's right to live, and therefore must not be allowed. And then at once arises the danger into which morality has led us: the danger of persecution. One Christian spreading his doctrines may seem more mischievous than a dozen thieves: throw him therefore to the lions. A lying or disobedient child may corrupt a whole generation and make human Society impossible: therefore thrash the vice out of him. And so on until our whole system of abortion, intimidation, tyranny, cruelty, and the rest is in full swing again.

THE COMMON SENSE OF TOLERATION

The real safeguard against this is the dogma of Toleration. I need not here repeat the compact treatise on it which I prepared for the Joint Committee on the Censorship of Stage Plays, and prefixed to The Shewing Up of Blanco Posnet. It must suffice now to say that the present must not attempt to schoolmaster the future by pretending to know good from evil in tendency, or protect citizens against shocks to their opinions and convictions, moral, political, or religious: in other words it must not persecute doctrines of any kind, or what is called bad taste, and must insist on all persons facing such shocks as they face frosty weather or any of the other disagreeable, dangerous, or bracing incidents of freedom. The expediency of Toleration has been forced on us by the fact that progressive enlightenment depends on a fair hearing for doctrines which at first appear seditious, blasphemous, and immoral, and which deeply shock people who never think originally, thought being with them merely a habit and an echo. The deeper ground for Toleration is the nature of creation, which, as we now know, proceeds by evolution. Evolution finds its way by experiment; and this finding of the way varies according to the stage of development reached, from the blindest groping along the line of least resistance to conscious intellectual speculation, with its routine of hypothesis and verification, induction and deduction; or even into so rapid and intuitive an integration of all these processes in a single brain that we get the inspired guess of the man of genius and the fanatical resolution of the teacher of new truths who is first slain as a blasphemous apostate and then worshipped as a prophet.

Here the law for the child is the same as for the adult. The high priest must not rend his garments and cry "Crucify him" when he is shocked, nor the atheist clamor for the suppression of Law's Serious Call because it has for two centuries destroyed the natural happiness of innumerable children by persuading pious parents that it is a religious duty to make children miserable. It, and the Sermon on the Mount, and Machiavelli's Prince, and La Rochefoucauld's maxims, and Hymns Ancient and Modern, and De Glanville's apologue, and Dr. Watts's rhymes, and Nietzsche's Gay Science, and Ingersoll's Mistakes of Moses, and the speeches and pamphlets of the people who want us to make war on Germany, and the Noodle's Orations and articles of our politicians and journalists, must all be tolerated not only because any of them may for all we know be on the right track but because it is in the conflict of opinion that we win knowledge and wisdom. However terrible the wounds suffered in that conflict, they are better than the barren peace of death that follows when all the combatants are slaughtered or bound hand and foot.

The difficulty at present is that though this necessity for Toleration is a law of political science as well established as the law of gravitation, our rulers are never taught political science: on the contrary, they are taught in school that the master tolerates nothing that is disagreeable to him; that ruling is simply being master; and that the master's method is the method of violent punishment. And our citizens, all school taught, are walking in the same darkness. As I write these lines the Home Secretary is explaining that he must not release a man who has been imprisoned for blasphemy, as his remarks were painful to the feelings of his pious fellow townsmen. Now it happens that this very Home Secretary has driven many thousands of his fellow citizens almost beside themselves by the crudity of his notions of government, and his simple inability to understand why he should not use and make laws to torment and subdue people who do not happen to agree with him. In a word, he is not a politician, but a grown-up schoolboy who has at last got a cane in his hand. And as all the rest of us are in the same condition (except as to command of the cane) the only objection made to his proceedings takes the shape of clamorous demands that *he* should be caned instead of being allowed to cane other people.

THE SIN OF ATHANASIUS

It seems hopeless. Anarchists are tempted to preach a violent and implacable resistance to all law as the only remedy; and the result of that speedily is that people welcome any tyranny that will rescue them from chaos. But there is really no need to choose between anarchy and tyranny. A quite reasonable state of things is practicable if we proceed on human assumptions and not on academic ones. If adults will frankly give up their claim to know better than children what the purposes of the Life Force are, and treat the child as an experiment like themselves, and possibly a more successful one, and at the same time relinquish their monstrous parental claims to personal private property in children, the rest may be left to common sense. It is our attitude, our religion, that is wrong. A good beginning might be made by enacting that any person dictating a piece of conduct to a child or to anyone else as the will of God, or as absolutely right, should be dealt with as a blasphemer: as, indeed, guilty of the unpardonable sin against the Holy Ghost. If the penalty were death, it would rid us at once of that scourge of humanity, the amateur Pope. As an Irish Protestant, I raise the cry of No Popery with hereditary zest. We are overrun with Popes. From curates and governesses, who may claim a sort of professional standing, to parents and uncles and nurserymaids and school teachers and wiseacres generally, there are scores of thousands of human insects groping through our darkness by the feeble phosphorescence of their own tails, yet ready at a moment's notice to reveal the will of God on every possible subject; to explain how and why the universe was made (in my youth they added the exact date) and the circumstances under which it will cease to exist; to lay down precise rules of right and wrong conduct; to discriminate infallibly between virtuous and vicious character; and this with such certainty that they are prepared to visit all the

rigors of the law, and all the ruinous penalties of social ostracism on those, however harmless their actions may be, who venture to laugh at their monstrous conceit or to pay their assumptions the extravagant compliment of criticizing them. As to children, who shall say what canings and birchings and terrifyings and threats of hell fire and impositions and humiliations and petty imprisonings and sendings to bed and standing in corners and the like they have suffered because their parents and guardians and teachers knew everything so much better than Socrates or Solon?

It is this ignorant uppishness that does the mischief. A stranger on the planet might expect that its grotesque absurdity would provoke enough ridicule to cure it; but unfortunately quite the contrary happens. Just as our ill-health delivers us into the hands of medical quacks and creates a passionate demand for impudent pretences that doctors can cure the diseases they themselves die of daily, so our ignorance and helplessness set us clamoring for spiritual and moral quacks who pretend that they can save our souls from their own damnation. If a doctor were to say to his patients, "I am familiar with your symptoms, because I have seen other people in your condition; and I will bring the very little knowledge we have to your treatment; but except in that very shallow sense I dont know what is the matter with you; and I cant undertake to cure you" he would be a lost man professionally; and if a clergyman, on being called on to award a prize for good conduct in the village school, were to say, "I am afraid I cannot say who is the best-behaved child, because I really do not know what good conduct is; but I will gladly take the teacher's word as to which child has caused least inconvenience" he would probably be unfrocked, if not excommunicated. And yet no honest and intellectually capable doctor or parson can say more. Clearly it would not be wise of the doctor to say it, because optimistic lies have such immense therapeutic value that a doctor who cannot tell them convincingly has mistaken his profession. And a clergyman who is not prepared to lay down the law dogmatically will not be of much use in a village school, though it behoves him all the more to be very careful what law he lays down. But unless both the clergyman and the doctor are in the attitude expressed by these speeches they are not fit for their work. The man who believes that he has more than a provisional hypothesis to go upon is a born fool. He may have to act vigorously on it. The world has no use for the Agnostic who wont believe anything because anything might be false, and wont deny anything because anything might be true. But there is a wide difference between saying, "I believe this; and I am going to act on it," or, "I dont believe it; and I wont act on it," and saying, "It is true; and it is my duty and yours to act on it," or, "It is false; and it is my duty and yours to refuse to act on it." The difference is as great as that between the Apostles' Creed and the Athanasian Creed. When you repeat the Apostles' Creed you affirm that you believe certain things. There you are clearly within your rights. When you repeat the Athanasian Creed, you affirm that certain things are so, and that anybody who doubts that they are so cannot be saved. And this is simply a piece of impudence on your part, as you know nothing about it except that as good men as you have never heard of your creed. The apostolic attitude is a desire to convert others to our beliefs for the sake of sympathy and light: the Athanasian attitude is a desire to murder people who dont agree with us. I am sufficient of an Athanasian to advocate a law for the speedy execution of all Athanasians, because they violate the fundamental proposition of my creed, which is, I repeat, that all living creatures are experiments. The precise formula for the Superman, *ci-devant* The Just Man Made Perfect, has not yet been discovered. Until it is, every birth is an experiment in the Great Research which is being conducted by the Life Force to discover that formula.

THE EXPERIMENT EXPERIMENTING

And now all the modern schoolmaster abortionists will rise up beaming, and say, "We quite agree. We regard every child in our school as a subject for experiment. We are always experimenting with them. We challenge the experimental test for our system. We are continually guided by our experience in our great work of moulding the character of our future citizens, etc. etc. etc." I am sorry to seem irreconcilable; but it is the Life Force that has to make the experiment and not the schoolmaster; and the Life Force for the child's purpose is in the child and not in the schoolmaster. The schoolmaster is another experiment; and a laboratory in which all the experiments began experimenting on one another would not produce intelligible results. I admit, however, that if my schoolmasters had treated me as an experiment of the Life Force: that is, if they had set me free to do as I liked subject only to my political rights and theirs, they could not have watched the experiment very long, because the first result would have been a rapid movement on my part in the direction of the door, and my disappearance therethrough.

It may be worth inquiring where I should have gone to. I should say that practically every time I should have gone to a much more educational place. I should have gone into the country, or into the sea, or into the National Gallery, or to hear a band if there was one, or to any library where there were no schoolbooks. I should have read very dry and difficult books: for example, though nothing would have induced me to read the budget of stupid party lies that served as a text-book of history in school, I remember reading Robertson's Charles V. and his history of Scotland from end to end most laboriously. Once, stung by the airs of a schoolfellow who alleged that he had read Locke On The Human Understanding, I attempted to read the Bible straight through, and actually got to the Pauline Epistles before I broke down in disgust at what seemed to me their inveterate crookedness of mind. If there had been a school where children were really free, I should have had to be driven out of it for the sake of my health by the teachers; for the children to whom a literary education can be of any use are insatiable: they will read and study far more than is good for them. In fact the real difficulty is to prevent them from wasting their time by reading for the sake of reading and studying for the sake of studying, instead of taking some trouble to find out what they really like and are capable of doing some good at. Some silly person will probably interrupt me here with the remark that many children have no appetite for a literary education at all, and would never open a book if they were not forced to. I have known many such persons who have been forced to the point of obtaining university degrees. And for all the effect their literary exercises has left on them they might just as well have been put on the treadmill. In fact they are actually less literate than the treadmill would have left them; for they might now by chance pick up and dip into a volume of Shakespear or a translation of Homer if they had not been driven to loathe every famous name in literature. I should probably know as much Latin as French, if Latin had not been made the excuse for my school imprisonment and degradation.

WHY WE LOATHE LEARNING AND LOVE SPORT

If we are to discuss the importance of art, learning, and intellectual culture, the first thing we have to recognize is that we have very little of them at present; and that this little has not been produced by compulsory education: nay, that the scarcity is unnatural and has been produced by the violent exclusion of art and artists from schools. On the other hand we have quite a considerable degree of bodily culture: indeed there is a continual outcry against the sacrifice of mental accomplishments to athletics. In other words a sacrifice of the professed object of compulsory education to the real object of voluntary education. It is assumed that this means that people prefer bodily to mental culture; but may it not mean that they prefer liberty and satisfaction to coercion and privation. Why is it that people who have been taught Shakespear as a school subject loathe his plays and cannot by any means be persuaded ever to open his works after they escape from school, whereas there is still, 300 years after his death, a wide and steady sale for his works to people who regard his plays as plays, not as task work? If Shakespear, or for that matter, Newton and Leibnitz, are allowed to find their readers and students they will find them. If their works are annotated and paraphrased by dullards, and the annotations and paraphrases forced on all young people by imprisonment and flogging and scolding, there will not be a single man of letters or higher mathematician the more in the country: on the contrary there will be less, as so many potential lovers of literature and mathematics will have been incurably prejudiced against them. Everyone who is conversant with the class in which child imprisonment and compulsory schooling is carried out to the final extremity of the university degree knows that its scholastic culture is a sham; that it knows little about literature or art and a great deal about point-to-point races; and that the village cobbler, who has never read a page of Plato, and is admittedly a dangerously ignorant man politically, is nevertheless a Socrates compared to the classically educated gentlemen who discuss politics in country-houses at election time (and at no other time) after their day's earnest and skilful shooting. Think of the years and years of weary torment the women of the piano-possessing class have been forced to spend over the keyboard, fingering scales. How many of them could be bribed to attend a pianoforte recital by a great player, though they will rise from sick beds rather than miss Ascot or Goodwood?

Another familiar fact that teaches the same lesson is that many women who have voluntarily attained a high degree of culture cannot add up their own housekeeping books, though their education in simple arithmetic was compulsory, whereas their higher education has been wholly voluntary. Everywhere we find the same result. The imprisonment, the beating, the taming and laming, the breaking of young spirits, the arrest of development, the atrophy of all inhibitive power except the power of fear, are real: the education is sham. Those who have been taught most know least.

ANTICHRIST

Among the worst effects of the unnatural segregation of children in schools and the equally unnatural constant association of them with adults in the family is the utter defeat of the vital element in Christianity. Christ stands in the world for that intuition of the highest humanity that we, being members one of another, must not complain, must not scold, must not strike, nor revile nor persecute nor revenge nor punish. Now family life and school life are, as far as the moral training of children is concerned, nothing but the deliberate inculcation of a routine of complaint, scolding, punishment, persecution, and revenge as the natural and only possible way of dealing with evil or inconvenience. "Aint nobody to be whopped for this here?" exclaimed Sam Weller when he saw his employer's name written up on a stage coach, and conceived the phenomenon as an insult which reflected on himself. This exclamation of Sam Weller is at once the negation of Christianity and the beginning and the end of current morality; and so it will remain as long as the family and the school persist as we know them: that is, as long as the rights of children are so utterly denied that nobody will even take the trouble to ascertain what they are, and coming of age is like the turning of a convict into the streets after twentyone years penal servitude. Indeed it is worse; for the convict, having learnt before his conviction how to live at large, may remember how to set about it, however lamed his power of initiative may have become through disuse; but the child knows no other way of life than the slave's way. Born free, as Rousseau says, he has been laid hands on by slaves from the moment of his birth and brought up as a slave. How is he, when he is at last set free, to be anything else than the slave he actually is, clamoring for war, for the lash, for police, prisons, and scaffolds in a wild panic of delusion that without these things he is lost. The grown-up Englishman is to the end of his days a badly brought-up child, beyond belief quarrelsome, petulant, selfish, destructive, and cowardly: afraid that the Germans will come and enslave him; that the burglar will come and rob him; that the bicycle or motor car will run over him; that the smallpox will attack him; and that the devil will run away with him and empty him out like a sack of coals on a blazing fire unless his nurse or his parents or his schoolmaster or his bishop or his judge or his army or his navy will do something to frighten these bad things away. And this Englishman, without the moral courage of a louse, will risk his neck for fun fifty times every winter in the hunting field, and at Badajos sieges and the like will ram his head into a hole bristling with sword blades rather than be beaten in the one department in which he has been brought up to consult his own honor. As a Sportsman (and war is fundamentally the sport of hunting and fighting the most dangerous of the beasts of prey) he feels free. He will tell you himself that the true sportsman is never a snob, a coward, a duffer, a cheat, a thief, or a liar. Curious, is it not, that he has not the same confidence in other sorts of man?

And even sport is losing its freedom. Soon everybody will be schooled, mentally and physically, from the cradle to the end of the term of adult compulsory military service, and finally of compulsory civil service lasting until the age of superannuation. Always more schooling, more compulsion. We are to be cured by an excess of the dose that has poisoned us. Satan is to cast out Satan.

UNDER THE WHIP

Clearly this will not do. We must reconcile education with liberty. We must find out some means of making men workers and, if need be, warriors, without making them slaves. We must cultivate the noble virtues that have their root in pride. Now no schoolmaster will teach these any more than a prison governor will teach his prisoners how to mutiny and escape. Self-preservation forces him to break the spirit that revolts against him, and to inculcate submission, even to obscene assault, as a duty. A

bishop once had the hardihood to say that he would rather see England free than England sober. Nobody has yet dared to say that he would rather see an England of ignoramuses than an England of cowards and slaves. And if anyone did, it would be necessary to point out that the antithesis is not a practical one, as we have at present an England of ignoramuses who are also cowards and slaves, and patriotically proud of it at that, because in school they are taught to submit, with what they ridiculously call Oriental fatalism (as if any Oriental has ever submitted more helplessly and sheepishly to robbery and oppression than we Occidentals do), to be driven day after day into compounds and set to the tasks they loathe by the men they hate and fear, as if this were the inevitable destiny of mankind. And naturally, when they grow up, they helplessly exchange the prison of the school for the prison of the mine or the workshop or the office, and drudge along stupidly and miserably, with just enough gregarious instinct to turn furiously on any intelligent person who proposes a change. It would be quite easy to make England a paradise, according to our present ideas, in a few years. There is no mystery about it: the way has been pointed out over and over again. The difficulty is not the way but the will. And we have no will because the first thing done with us in childhood was to break our will. Can anything be more disgusting than the spectacle of a nation reading the biography of Gladstone and gloating over the account of how he was flogged at Eton, two of his schoolfellows being compelled to hold him down whilst he was flogged. Not long ago a public body in England had to deal with the case of a schoolmaster who, conceiving himself insulted by the smoking of a cigaret against his orders by a pupil eighteen years old, proposed to flog him publicly as a satisfaction to what he called his honor and authority. I had intended to give the particulars of this case, but find the drudgery of raking over such stuff too sickening, and the effect unjust to a man who was doing only what others all over the country were doing as part of the established routine of what is called education. The astounding part of it was the manner in which the person to whom this outrage on decency seemed quite proper and natural claimed to be a functionary of high character, and had his claim allowed. In Japan he would hardly have been allowed the privilege of committing suicide. What is to be said of a profession in which such obscenities are made points of honor, or of institutions in which they are an accepted part of the daily routine? Wholesome people would not argue about the taste of such nastinesses: they would spit them out; but we are tainted with flagellomania from our childhood. When will we realize that the fact that we can become accustomed to anything, however disgusting at first, makes it necessary for us to examine carefully everything we have become accustomed to? Before motor cars became common, necessity had accustomed us to a foulness in our streets which would have horrified us had the street been our drawing-room carpet. Before long we shall be as particular about our streets as we now are about our carpets; and their condition in the nineteenth century will become as forgotten and incredible as the condition of the corridors of palaces and the courts of castles was as late as the eighteenth century. This foulness, we can plead, was imposed on us as a necessity by the use of horses and of huge retinues; but flogging has never been so imposed: it has always been a vice, craved for on any pretext by those depraved by it. Boys were flogged when criminals were hanged, to impress the awful warning on them. Boys were flogged at boundaries, to impress the boundaries

on their memory. Other methods and other punishments were always available: the choice of this one betrayed the sensual impulse which makes the practice an abomination. But when its viciousness made it customary, it was practised and tolerated on all hands by people who were innocent of anything worse than stupidity, ill temper, and inability to discover other methods of maintaining order than those they had always seen practised and approved of. From children and animals it extended to slaves and criminals. In the days of Moses it was limited to 39 lashes. In the early nineteenth century it had become an open madness: soldiers were sentenced to a thousand lashes for trifling offences, with the result (among others less mentionable) that the Iron Duke of Wellington complained that it was impossible to get an order obeyed in the British army except in two or three crack regiments. Such frantic excesses of this disgusting neurosis provoked a reaction against it; but the clamor for it by depraved persons never ceased, and was tolerated by a nation trained to it from childhood in the schools until last year (1913), when, in what must be described as a paroxysm of sexual excitement provoked by the agitation concerning the White Slave Traffic (the purely commercial nature of which I was prevented from exposing on the stage by the Censorship twenty years ago), the Government yielded to an outcry for flagellation led by the Archbishop of Canterbury, and passed an Act under which a judge can sentence a man to be flogged to the utmost extremity with any instrument usable for such a purpose that he cares to prescribe. Such an Act is not a legislative phenomenon but a psychopathic one. Its effect on the White Slave Traffic was, of course, to distract public attention from its real cause and from the people who really profit by it to imaginary "foreign scoundrels," and to secure a monopoly of its organization for women.

And all this evil is made possible by the schoolmaster with his cane and birch, by the parents getting rid as best they can of the nuisance of children making noise and mischief in the house, and by the denial to children of the elementary rights of human beings.

The first man who enslaved and "broke in" an animal with a whip would have invented the explosion engine instead could he have foreseen the curse he was laying on his race. For men and women learnt thereby to enslave and break in their children by the same means. These children, grown up, knew no other methods of training. Finally the evil that was done for gain by the greedy was refined on and done for pleasure by the lustful. Flogging has become a pleasure purchasable in our streets, and inhibition a grown-up habit that children play at. "Go and see what baby is doing; and tell him he mustnt" is the last word of the nursery; and the grimmest aspect of it is that it was first formulated by a comic paper as a capital joke.

TECHNICAL INSTRUCTION

Technical instruction tempts to violence (as a short cut) more than liberal education. The sailor in Mr Rudyard Kipling's Captains Courageous, teaching the boy the names of the ship's tackle with a rope's end, does not disgust us as our schoolmasters do, especially as the boy was a spoiled boy. But an unspoiled boy would not have needed that drastic medicine. Technical training may be as tedious as learning to skate or to play the piano or violin; but it is the price one must pay to achieve certain desirable results or necessary ends. It is a monstrous thing to force a child to learn Latin or Greek or mathematics on the ground that they are an indispensable gymnastic for the mental powers. It

would be monstrous even if it were true; for there is no labor that might not be imposed on a child or an adult on the same pretext; but as a glance at the average products of our public school and university education shews that it is not true, it need not trouble us. But it is a fact that ignorance of Latin and Greek and mathematics closes certain careers to men (I do not mean artificial, unnecessary, noxious careers like those of the commercial schoolmaster). Languages, even dead ones, have their uses; and, as it seems to many of us, mathematics have their uses. They will always be learned by people who want to learn them; and people will always want to learn them as long as they are of any importance in life: indeed the want will survive their importance: superstition is nowhere stronger than in the field of obsolete acquirements. And they will never be learnt fruitfully by people who do not want to learn them either for their own sake or for use in necessary work. There is no harder schoolmaster than experience; and yet experience fails to teach where there is no desire to learn.

Still, one must not begin to apply this generalization too early. And this brings me to an important factor in the case: the factor of evolution.

DOCILITY AND DEPENDENCE

If anyone, impressed by my view that the rights of a child are precisely those of an adult, proceeds to treat a child as if it were an adult, he (or she) will find that though the plan will work much better at some points than the usual plan, at others it will not work at all; and this discovery may provoke him to turn back from the whole conception of children's rights with a jest at the expense of bachelors' and old maids' children. In dealing with children what is needed is not logic but sense. There is no logical reason why young persons should be allowed greater control of their property the day after they are twenty-one than the day before it. There is no logical reason why I, who strongly object to an adult standing over a boy of ten with a Latin grammar, and saying "You must learn this, whether you want to or not," should nevertheless be quite prepared to stand over a boy of five with the multiplication table or a copy book or a code of elementary good manners, and practise on his docility to make him learn them. And there is no logical reason why I should do for a child a great many little offices, some of them troublesome and disagreeable, which I should not do for a boy twice its age, or support a boy or girl when I would unhesitatingly throw an adult on his own resources. But there are practical reasons, and sensible reasons, and affectionate reasons for all these illogicalities. Children do not want to be treated altogether as adults: such treatment terrifies them and overburdens them with responsibility. In truth, very few adults care to be called on for independence and originality: they also are bewildered and terrified in the absence of precedents and precepts and commandments; but modern Democracy allows them a sanctioning and cancelling power if they are capable of using it, which children are not. To treat a child wholly as an adult would be to mock and destroy it. Infantile docility and juvenile dependence are, like death, a product of Natural Selection; and though there is no viler crime than to abuse them, yet there is no greater cruelty than to ignore them. I have complained sufficiently of what I suffered through the process of assault, imprisonment, and compulsory lessons that taught me nothing, which are called my schooling. But I could say a good deal also about the things I was not taught and should have been taught, not to mention the things I was allowed to do which I should not have been

allowed to do. I have no recollection of being taught to read or write; so I presume I was born with both faculties; but many people seem to have bitter recollections of being forced reluctantly to acquire them. And though I have the uttermost contempt for a teacher so ill-mannered and incompetent as to be unable to make a child learn to read and write without also making it cry, still I am prepared to admit that I had rather have been compelled to learn to read and write with tears by an incompetent and ill-mannered person than left in ignorance. Reading, writing, and enough arithmetic to use money honestly and accurately, together with the rudiments of law and order, become necessary conditions of a child's liberty before it can appreciate the importance of its liberty, or foresee that these accomplishments are worth acquiring.   Nature has provided for this by evolving the instinct of docility. Children are very docile: they have a sound intuition that they must do what they are told or perish. And adults have an intuition, equally sound, that they must take advantage of this docility to teach children how to live properly or the children will not survive. The difficulty is to know where to stop. To illustrate this, let us consider the main danger of childish docility and parental officiousness.

THE ABUSE OF DOCILITY

Docility may survive as a lazy habit long after it has ceased to be a beneficial instinct. If you catch a child when it is young enough to be instinctively docile, and keep it in a condition of unremitted tutelage under the nurserymaid, the governess, the preparatory school, the secondary school, and the university, until it is an adult, you will produce, not a self-reliant, free, fully matured human being, but a grown-up schoolboy or schoolgirl, capable of nothing in the way of original or independent action except outbursts of naughtiness in the women and blackguardism in the men. That is exactly what we get at present in our rich and consequently governing classes: they pass from juvenility to senility without ever touching maturity except in body. The classes which cannot afford this sustained tutelage are notably more self-reliant and grown-up: an office boy of fifteen is often more of a man than a university student of twenty. Unfortunately this precocity is disabled by poverty, ignorance, narrowness, and a hideous power of living without art or love or beauty and being rather proud of it. The poor never escape from servitude: their docility is preserved by their slavery. And so all become the prey of the greedy, the selfish, the domineering, the unscrupulous, the predatory. If here and there an individual refuses to be docile, ten docile persons will beat him or lock him up or shoot him or hang him at the bidding of his oppressors and their own. The crux of the whole difficulty about parents, schoolmasters, priests, absolute monarchs, and despots of every sort, is the tendency to abuse natural docility. A nation should always be healthily rebellious; but rulers have yet to be found who will make trouble for themselves by cultivating that side of the national spirit. A child should begin to assert itself early, and shift for itself more and more not only in washing and dressing itself, but in opinions and conduct; yet as nothing is so exasperating and so unlovable as an uppish child, it is useless to expect parents and schoolmasters to inculcate this uppishness. Such unamiable precepts as Always contradict an authoritative statement, Always return a blow, Never lose a chance of a good fight, When you are scolded for a mistake ask the person who scolds you whether he or she supposes you did it on purpose, and follow the question with a blow or an insult or some

other unmistakeable expression of resentment, Remember that the progress of the world depends on your knowing better than your elders, are just as important as those of the Sermon on the Mount; but no one has yet seen them written up in letters of gold in a schoolroom or nursery. The child is taught to be kind, to be respectful, to be quiet, not to answer back, to be truthful when its elders want to find out anything from it, to lie when the truth would shock or hurt its elders, to be above all things obedient, and to be seen and not heard. Here we have two sets of precepts, each of which will spoil an ordinary child if the other be omitted. Unfortunately we do not allow fair play between them. The rebellious, intractable, aggressive, selfish set provoke a corrective resistance, and do not pretend to high moral or religious sanctions; and they are never urged by grown-up people on young people. They are therefore more in danger of neglect or suppression than the other set, which have all the adults, all the laws, all the religions on their side. How is the child to be secured its due share of both bodies of doctrine?

THE SCHOOLBOY AND THE HOMEBOY

In practice what happens is that parents notice that boys brought up at home become mollycoddles, or prigs, or duffers, unable to take care of themselves. They see that boys should learn to rough it a little and to mix with children of their own age. This is natural enough. When you have preached at and punished a boy until he is a moral cripple, you are as much hampered by him as by a physical cripple; and as you do not intend to have him on your hands all your life, and are generally rather impatient for the day when he will earn his own living and leave you to attend to yourself, you sooner or later begin to talk to him about the need for self-reliance, learning to think, and so forth, with the result that your victim, bewildered by your inconsistency, concludes that there is no use trying to please you, and falls into an attitude of sulky resentment. Which is an additional inducement to pack him off to school.

In school, he finds himself in a dual world, under two dispensations. There is the world of the boys, where the point of honor is to be untameable, always ready to fight, ruthless in taking the conceit out of anyone who ventures to give himself airs of superior knowledge or taste, and generally to take Lucifer for one's model. And there is the world of the masters, the world of discipline, submission, diligence, obedience, and continual and shameless assumption of moral and intellectual authority. Thus the schoolboy hears both sides, and is so far better off than the home-bred boy who hears only one. But the two sides are not fairly presented. They are presented as good and evil, as vice and virtue, as villainy and heroism. The boy feels mean and cowardly when he obeys, and selfish and rascally when he disobeys. He loses his moral courage just as he comes to hate books and languages. In the end, John Ruskin, tied so closely to his mother's apron-string that he did not escape even when he went to Oxford, and John Stuart Mill, whose father ought to have been prosecuted for laying his son's childhood waste with lessons, were superior, as products of training, to our schoolboys. They were very conspicuously superior in moral courage; and though they did not distinguish themselves at cricket and football, they had quite as much physical hardihood as any civilized man needs. But it is to be observed that Ruskin's parents were wise people who gave John a full share in their own life, and put up with his presence both at home and abroad when they must sometimes have been very weary of

him; and Mill, as it happens, was deliberately educated to challenge all the most sacred institutions of his country. The households they were brought up in were no more average households than a Montessori school is an average school.

THE COMINGS OF AGE OF CHILDREN

All this inculcated adult docility, which wrecks every civilization as it is wrecking ours, is inhuman and unnatural. We must reconsider our institution of the Coming of Age, which is too late for some purposes, and too early for others. There should be a series of Coming of Ages for every individual. The mammals have their first coming of age when they are weaned; and it is noteworthy that this rather cruel and selfish operation on the part of the parent has to be performed resolutely, with claws and teeth; for your little mammal does not want to be weaned, and yields only to a pretty rough assertion of the right of the parent to be relieved of the child as soon as the child is old enough to bear the separation. The same thing occurs with children: they hang on to the mother's apron-string and the father's coat tails as long as they can, often baffling those sensitive parents who know that children should think for themselves and fend for themselves, but are too kind to throw them on their own resources with the ferocity of the domestic cat. The child should have its first coming of age when it is weaned, another when it can talk, another when it can walk, another when it can dress itself without assistance; and when it can read, write, count money, and pass an examination in going a simple errand involving a purchase and a journey by rail or other public method of locomotion, it should have quite a majority. At present the children of laborers are soon mobile and able to shift for themselves, whereas it is possible to find grown-up women in the rich classes who are actually afraid to take a walk in the streets unattended and unprotected. It is true that this is a superstition from the time when a retinue was part of the state of persons of quality, and the unattended person was supposed to be a common person of no quality, earning a living; but this has now become so absurd that children and young women are no longer told why they are forbidden to go about alone, and have to be persuaded that the streets are dangerous places, which of course they are; but people who are not educated to live dangerously have only half a life, and are more likely to die miserably after all than those who have taken all the common risks of freedom from their childhood onward as matters of course.

THE CONFLICT OF WILLS

The world wags in spite of its schools and its families because both schools and families are mostly very largely anarchic: parents and schoolmasters are goodnatured or weak or lazy; and children are docile and affectionate and very short-winded in their fits of naughtiness; and so most families slummock along and muddle through until the children cease to be children. In the few cases when the parties are energetic and determined, the child is crushed or the parent is reduced to a cipher, as the case may be. When the opposed forces are neither of them strong enough to annihilate the other, there is serious trouble: that is how we get those feuds between parent and child which recur to our memory so ironically when we hear people sentimentalizing about natural affection. We even get tragedies; for there is nothing so tragic to contemplate or so devastating to suffer as the oppression of will without conscience; and the whole tendency of our family and school system is to set the will of the parent and the school despot above conscience as something that must be de-

ferred to abjectly and absolutely for its own sake.

The strongest, fiercest force in nature is human will. It is the highest organization we know of the will that has created the whole universe. Now all honest civilization, religion, law, and convention is an attempt to keep this force within beneficent bounds. What corrupts civilization, religion, law, and convention (and they are at present pretty nearly as corrupt as they dare) is the constant attempts made by the wills of individuals and classes to thwart the wills and enslave the powers of other individuals and classes. The powers of the parent and the schoolmaster, and of their public analogues the lawgiver and the judge, become instruments of tyranny in the hands of those who are too narrow-minded to understand law and exercise judgment; and in their hands (with us they mostly fall into such hands) law becomes tyranny. And what is a tyrant? Quite simply a person who says to another person, young or old, "You shall do as I tell you; you shall make what I want; you shall profess my creed; you shall have no will of your own; and your powers shall be at the disposal of my will." It has come to this at last: that the phrase "she has a will of her own," or "he has a will of his own" has come to denote a person of exceptional obstinacy and self-assertion. And even persons of good natural disposition, if brought up to expect such deference, are roused to unreasoning fury, and sometimes to the commission of atrocious crimes, by the slightest challenge to their authority. Thus a laborer may be dirty, drunken, untruthful, slothful, untrustworthy in every way without exhausting the indulgence of the country-house. But let him dare to be "disrespectful" and he is a lost man, though he be the cleanest, soberest, most diligent, most veracious, most trustworthy man in the county.

Dickens's instinct for detecting social cankers never served him better than when he shewed up Mrs Heep teaching her son to "be umble," knowing that if he carried out that precept he might be pretty well anything else he liked. The maintenance of deference to our wills becomes a mania which will carry the best of us to any extremity. We will allow a village of Egyptian fellaheen or Indian tribesmen to live the lowest life they please among themselves without molestation; but let one of them slay an Englishman or even strike him on the strongest provocation, and straightway we go stark mad, burning and destroying, shooting and shelling, flogging and hanging, if only such survivors as we may leave are thoroughly cowed in the presence of a man with a white face. In the committee room of a local council or city corporation, the humblest employees of the committee find defenders if they complain of harsh treatment. Gratuities are voted, indulgences and holidays are pleaded for, delinquencies are excused in the most sentimental manner provided only the employee, however patent a hypocrite or incorrigible a slacker, is hat in hand. But let the most obvious measure of justice be demanded by the secretary of a Trade Union in terms which omit all expressions of subservience, and it is with the greatest difficulty that the cooler-headed can defeat angry motions that the letter be thrown into the wastepaper basket and the committee proceed to the next business.

THE DEMAGOGUE'S OPPORTUNITY

And the employee has in him the same fierce impulse to impose his will without respect for the will of others. Democracy is in practice nothing but a device for cajoling from him the vote he refuses to arbitrary authority. He will not vote for Coriolanus; but when an experienced demagogue comes along and says "Sir: *you* are the dictator: the voice of the people is the voice of God; and I am only your very humble servant" he says at once "All right: tell me what to dictate" and is presently enslaved more effectually with his own silly consent than Coriolanus would ever have enslaved him without asking his leave. And the trick by which the demagogue defeats Coriolanus is played on him in his turn by *his* inferiors. Everywhere we see the cunning succeeding in the world by seeking a rich or powerful master and practising on his lust for subservience. The political adventurer who gets into Parliament by offering himself to the poor voter, not as his representative but as his will-less soulless "delegate," is himself the dupe of a clever wife who repudiates Votes for Women, knowing well that whilst the man is master, the man's mistress will rule. Uriah Heep may be a crawling creature; but his crawling takes him upstairs.

Thus does the selfishness of the will turn on itself, and obtain by flattery what it cannot seize by open force. Democracy becomes the latest trick of tyranny: "womanliness" becomes the latest wile of prostitution.

Between parent and child the same conflict wages and the same destruction of character ensues. Parents set themselves to bend the will of their children to their own—to break their stubborn spirit, as they call it—with the ruthlessness of Grand Inquisitors. Cunning, unscrupulous children learn all the arts of the sneak in circumventing tyranny: children of better character are cruelly distressed and more or less lamed for life by it.

OUR QUARRELSOMENESS

As between adults, we find a general quarrelsomeness which makes political reform as impossible to most Englishmen as to hogs. Certain sections of the nation get cured of this disability. University men, sailors, and politicians are comparatively free from it, because the communal life of the university, the fact that in a ship a man must either learn to consider others or else go overboard or into irons, and the habit of working on committees and ceasing to expect more of one's own way than is included in the greatest common measure of the committee, educate the will socially. But no one who has ever had to guide a committee of ordinary private Englishmen through their first attempts at collective action, in committee or otherwise, can retain any illusions as to the appalling effects on our national manners and character of the organization of the home and the school as petty tyrannies, and the absence of all teaching of self-respect and training in self-assertion. Bullied and ordered about, the Englishman obeys like a sheep, evades like a knave, or tries to murder his oppressor. Merely criticized or opposed in committee, or invited to consider anybody's views but his own, he feels personally insulted and wants to resign or leave the room unless he is apologized to. And his panic and bewilderment when he sees that the older hands at the work have no patience with him and do not intend to treat him as infallible, are pitiable as far as they are anything but ludicrous. That is what comes of not being taught to consider other people's wills, and left to submit to them or to override them as if they were the winds and the weather. Such a state of mind is incompatible not only with the democratic introduction of high civilization, but with the comprehension and maintenance of such civilized institutions as have been introduced by benevolent and intelligent despots and aristocrats.

WE MUST REFORM SOCIETY BEFORE
WE CAN REFORM OURSELVES

When we come to the positive problem of what to do with children if we are to give up the established plan, we find the difficulties so great that we begin to understand why so many people who detest the system and look back with loathing on their own schooldays, must helplessly send their children to the very schools they themselves were sent to, because there is no alternative except abandoning the children to undisciplined vagabondism. Man in society must do as everybody else does in his class: only fools and romantic novices imagine that freedom is a mere matter of the readiness of the individual to snap his fingers at convention. It is true that most of us live in a condition of quite unnecessary inhibition, wearing ugly and uncomfortable clothes, making ourselves and other people miserable by the heathen horrors of mourning, staying away from the theatre because we cannot afford the stalls and are ashamed to go to the pit, and in dozens of other ways enslaving ourselves when there are comfortable alternatives open to us without any real drawbacks. The contemplation of these petty slaveries, and of the triumphant ease with which sensible people throw them off, creates an impression that if we only take Johnson's advice to free our minds from cant, we can achieve freedom. But if we all freed our minds from cant we should find that for the most part we should have to go on doing the necessary work of the world exactly as we did it before until we organized new and free methods of doing it. Many people believed in secondary co-education (boys and girls taught together) before schools like Bedales were founded: indeed the practice was common enough in elementary schools and in Scotland; but their belief did not help them until Bedales and St George's were organized; and there are still not nearly enough co-educational schools in existence to accommodate all the children of the parents who believe in co-education up to university age, even if they could always afford the fees of these exceptional schools. It may be edifying to tell a duke that our public schools are all wrong in their constitution and methods, or a costermonger that children should be treated as in Goethe's Wilhelm Meister instead of as they are treated at the elementary school at the corner of his street; but what are the duke and the coster to do? Neither of them has any effective choice in the matter: their children must either go to the schools that are, or to no school at all. And as the duke thinks with reason that his son will be a lout or a milksop or a prig if he does not go to school, and the coster knows that his son will become an illiterate hooligan if he is left to the streets, there is no real alternative for either of them. Child life must be socially organized: no parent, rich or poor, can choose institutions that do not exist; and the private enterprise of individual schoolmasters appealing to a group of well-to-do parents, though it may shew what can be done by enthusiasts with new methods, cannot touch the mass of our children. For the average parent or child nothing is really available except the established practice; and this is what makes it so important that the established practice should be a sound one, and so useless for clever individuals to disparage it unless they can organize an alternative practice and make it, too, general.

THE PURSUIT OF MANNERS

If you cross-examine the duke and the coster, you will find that they are not concerned for the scholastic attainments of their children. Ask the duke whether he could pass the standard examination of twelve-year-old children in elementary schools, and he will admit, with an entirely placid smile, that he would almost certainly be ignominiously plucked. And he is so little ashamed of or disadvantaged by his condition that he is not prepared to spend an hour in remedying it. The coster may resent the inquiry instead of being amused by it; but his answer, if true, will be the same. What they both want for their children is the communal training, the apprenticeship to society, the lessons in holding one's own among people of all sorts with whom one is not, as in the home, on privileged terms. These can be acquired only by "mixing with the world," no matter how wicked the world is. No parent cares twopence whether his children can write Latin hexameters or repeat the dates of the accession of all the English monarchs since the Conqueror; but all parents are earnestly anxious about the manners of their children. Better Claude Duval than Kaspar Hauser. Laborers who are contemptuously anti-clerical in their opinions will send their daughters to the convent school because the nuns teach them some sort of gentleness of speech and behavior. And peers who tell you that our public schools are rotten through and through, and that our universities ought to be razed to the foundations, send their sons to Eton and Oxford, Harrow and Cambridge, not only because there is nothing else to be done, but because these places, though they turn out blackguards and ignoramuses and boobies galore, turn them out with the habits and manners of the society they belong to. Bad as those manners are in many respects, they are better than no manners at all. And no individual or family can possibly teach them. They can be acquired only by living in an organized community in which they are traditional.

Thus we see that there are reasons for the segregation of children even in families where the great reason: namely, that children are nuisances to adults, does not press very hardly, as, for instance, in the houses of the very poor, who can send their children to play in the streets, or the houses of the very rich, which are so large that the children's quarters can be kept out of the parents' way like the servants' quarters.

NOT TOO MUCH WIND ON THE HEATH, BROTHER

What, then, is to be done? For the present, unfortunately, little except propagating the conception of Children's Rights. Only the achievement of economic equality through Socialism can make it possible to deal thoroughly with the question from the point of view of the total interest of the community, which must always consist of grown-up children. Yet economic equality, like all simple and obvious arrangements, seems impossible to people brought up as children are now. Still, something can be done even within class limits. Large communities of children of the same class are possible today; and voluntary organization of outdoor life for children has already begun in Boy Scouting and excursions of one kind or another. The discovery that anything, even school life, is better for the child than home life, will become an over-ridden hobby; and we shall presently be told by our faddists that anything, even camp life, is better than school life. Some blundering beginnings of this are already perceptible. There is a movement for making our British children into priggish little barefooted vagabonds, all talking like that born fool George Borrow, and supposed to be splendidly healthy because they would die if they slept in rooms with the windows shut, or perhaps even with a roof over their heads. Still, this is a fairly healthy folly; and it may do something to establish Mr Harold Cox's claim of a Right to Roam as the basis of a much needed law compelling proprietors of land to provide plenty of gates in their fences, and to leave them unlocked when there are no growing crops to be damaged nor bulls to be encountered, instead of, as at present, imprisoning the human race in dusty or muddy thoroughfares between walls of barbed wire.

The reaction against vagabondage will come from the children themselves. For them freedom will not mean the expensive kind of savagery now called "the simple life." Their natural disgust with the visions of cockney book fanciers blowing themselves out with "the wind on the heath, brother," and of anarchists who are either too weak to understand that men are strong and free in proportion to the social pressure they can stand and the complexity of the obligations they are prepared to undertake, or too strong to realize that what is freedom to them may be terror and bewilderment to others, will drive them back to the home and the school if these have meanwhile learned the lesson that children are independent human beings and have rights.

WANTED: A CHILD'S MAGNA CHARTA

Whether we shall presently be discussing a Juvenile Magna Charta or Declaration of Rights by way of including children in the Constitution is a question on which I leave others to speculate. But if it could once be established that a child has an adult's Right of Egress from uncomfortable places and unpleasant company, and there were children's lawyers to sue pedagogues and others for assault and imprisonment, there would be an amazing change in the behavior of schoolmasters, the quality of school books, and the amenities of school life. That Consciousness of Consent which, even in its present delusive form, has enabled Democracy to oust tyrannical systems in spite of all its vulgarities and stupidities and rancors and ineptitudes and ignorances, would operate as powerfully among children as it does now among grown-ups. No doubt the

pedagogue would promptly turn demagogue, and woo his scholars by all the
arts of demagogy; but none of these arts
can easily be so dishonorable or mischievous as the art of caning. And, after
all, if larger liberties are attached to the
acquisition of knowledge, and the child
finds that it can no more go to the seaside
without a knowledge of the multiplication and pence tables than it can be an
astronomer without mathematics, it will
learn the multiplication table, which is
more than it always does at present, in
spite of all the canings and keepings-in.

THE PURSUIT OF LEARNING

When the Pursuit of Learning comes
to mean the pursuit of learning by the
child instead of the pursuit of the child
by Learning, cane in hand, the danger
will be precocity of the intellect, which
is just as undesirable as precocity of the
emotions. We still have a silly habit of
talking and thinking as if intellect were
a mechanical process and not a passion;
and in spite of the German tutors who
confess openly that three out of every
five of the young men they coach for
examinations are lamed for life thereby;
in spite of Dickens and his picture of
little Paul Dombey dying of lessons, we
persist in heaping on growing children
and adolescent youths and maidens tasks
Pythagoras would have declined out of
common regard for his own health and
common modesty as to his own capacity.
And this overwork is not all the effect
of compulsion; for the average schoolmaster does not compel his scholars to
learn: he only scolds and punishes them
if they do not, which is quite a different
thing, the net effect being that the school
prisoners need not learn unless they like.
Nay, it is sometimes remarked that the
school dunce — meaning the one who
does not like—often turns out well afterwards, as if idleness were a sign of ability
and character. A much more sensible

explanation is that the so-called dunces
are not exhausted before they begin the
serious business of life. It is said that boys
will be boys; and one can only add one
wishes they would. Boys really want
to be manly, and are unfortunately
encouraged thoughtlessly in this very
dangerous and overstraining aspiration.
All the people who have really worked
(Herbert Spencer for instance) warn us
against work as earnestly as some people
warn us against drink. When learning is
placed on the voluntary footing of sport,
the teacher will find himself saying every
day "Run away and play: you have
worked as much as is good for you."
Trying to make children leave school
will be like trying to make them go to
bed; and it will be necessary to surprise
them with the idea that teaching is work,
and that the teacher is tired and must go
play or rest or eat: possibilities always
concealed by that infamous humbug the
current schoolmaster, who achieves a
spurious divinity and a witch doctor's
authority by persuading children that
he is not human, just as ladies used
to persuade them that they have no
legs.

CHILDREN AND GAME: A PROPOSAL

Of the many wild absurdities of our
existing social order perhaps the most
grotesque is the costly and strictly enforced reservation of large tracts of
country as deer forests and breeding
grounds for pheasants whilst there is
so little provision of the kind made for
children. I have more than once thought
of trying to introduce the shooting of
children as a sport, as the children would
then be preserved very carefully for ten
months in the year, thereby reducing
their death rate far more than the fusil-
lades of the sportsmen during the other
two would raise it. At present the killing
of a fox except by a pack of foxhounds
is regarded with horror; but you may

and do kill children in a hundred and fifty ways provided you do not shoot them or set a pack of dogs on them. It must be admitted that the foxes have the best of it; and indeed a glance at our pheasants, our deer, and our children will convince the most sceptical that the children have decidedly the worst of it.

This much hope, however, can be extracted from the present state of things. It is so fantastic, so mad, so apparently impossible, that no scheme of reform need ever henceforth be discredited on the ground that it is fantastic or mad or apparently impossible. It is the sensible schemes, unfortunately, that are hopeless in England. Therefore I have great hopes that my own views, though fundamentally sensible, can be made to appear fantastic enough to have a chance.

First, then, I lay it down as a prime condition of sane society, obvious as such to anyone but an idiot, that in any decent community, children should find in every part of their native country, food, clothing, lodging, instruction, and parental kindness for the asking. For the matter of that, so should adults; but the two cases differ in that as these commodities do not grow on the bushes, the adults cannot have them unless they themselves organize and provide the supply, whereas the children must have them as if by magic, with nothing to do but rub the lamp, like Aladdin, and have their needs satisfied.

THE PARENTS' INTOLERABLE BURDEN

There is nothing new in this: it is how children have always had and must always have their needs satisfied. The parent has to play the part of Aladdin's djinn; and many a parent has sunk beneath the burden of this service. All the novelty we need is to organize it so that instead of the individual child fastening like a parasite on its own particular parents, the whole body of children should be thrown not only upon the whole body of parents, but upon the celibates and childless as well, whose present exemption from a full share in the social burden of children is obviously unjust and unwholesome. Today it is easy to find a widow who has at great cost to herself in pain, danger, and disablement, borne six or eight children. In the same town you will find rich bachelors and old maids, and married couples with no children or with families voluntarily limited to two or three. The eight children do not belong to the woman in any real or legal sense. When she has reared them they pass away from her into the community as independent persons, marrying strangers, working for strangers, spending on the community the life that has been built up at her expense. No more monstrous injustice could be imagined than that the burden of rearing the children should fall on her alone and not on the celibates and the selfish as well.

This is so far recognized that already the child finds, wherever it goes, a school for it, and somebody to force it into the school; and more and more these schools are being driven by the mere logic of facts to provide the children with meals, with boots, with spectacles, with dentists and doctors. In fact, when the child's parents are destitute or not to be found, bread, lodging, and clothing are provided. It is true that they are provided grudgingly and on conditions infamous enough to draw down abundant fire from Heaven upon us every day in the shape of crime and disease and vice; but still the practice of keeping children barely alive at the charge of the community is established; and there is no need for me to argue about it. I propose only two extensions of the practice. One is to provide for all the child's reasonable human wants, on which point, if you differ from me, I shall take leave to say that you are socially a fool and personally an inhuman wretch. The other is that these wants should be supplied in complete freedom from compulsory schooling or compulsory anything except restraint from crime, though, as they can be supplied only by social organization, the child must be conscious of and subject to the conditions of that organization, which may involve such portions of adult responsibility and duty as a child may be able to bear according to its age, and which will in any case prevent it from forming the vagabond and anarchist habit of mind.

One more exception might be necessary: compulsory freedom. I am sure that a child should not be imprisoned in a school. I am not so sure that it should not sometimes be driven out into the open—imprisoned in the woods and on the mountains, as it were. For there are frowsty children, just as there are frowsty adults, who dont want freedom. This morbid result of over - domestication would, let us hope, soon disappear with its cause.

MOBILIZATION

Those who see no prospect held out to them by this except a country in which all the children shall be roaming savages, should consider, first, whether their condition would be any worse than that of the little caged savages of today; and second, whether either children or adults are so apt to run wild that it is necessary to tether them fast to one neighborhood to prevent a general dissolution of society. My own observation leads me to believe that we are not half mobilized enough. True, I cannot deny that we are more mobile than we were. You will still find in the home counties old men who have never been to London, and who tell you that they once went to Winchester or St Albans much as if they had been to the South Pole; but they are not so common as the clerk who has been to Paris or to Lovely Lucerne, and who "goes away somewhere" when he has a holiday. His grandfather never had a holiday, and, if he had, would no more have dreamed of crossing the Channel than of taking a box at the Opera. But with all allowance for the Polytechnic excursion and the tourist agency, our inertia is still appalling. I confess to having once spent nine years in London without putting my nose outside it; and though this was better, perhaps, than the restless globe-trotting vagabondage of the idle rich, wandering from hotel to hotel and never really living anywhere, yet I should no more have done it if I had been properly mobilized in my childhood than I should have worn the same suit of clothes all that time (which, by the way, I very nearly did, my professional income not having as yet begun to sprout). There are masses of people who could afford at least a trip to Margate, and a good many who could afford a trip round the world, who are more immovable than Aldgate pump. To others, who would move if they knew how, travelling is surrounded with imaginary difficulties and terrors. In short, the difficulty is not to fix people, but to root them up. We keep repeating the silly proverb that a rolling stone gathers no moss, as if moss were a desirable parasite. What we mean is that a vagabond does not prosper. Even this is not true, if prosperity means enjoyment as well as responsibility and money. The real misery of vagabondage is the misery of having nothing to do and nowhere to go, the misery of being derelict of God and Man, the misery of the idle, poor or rich. And this is one of the miseries of unoccupied childhood. The unoccupied adult, thus afflicted, tries many distractions which are, to say the least, unsuited to children. But one of them, the distraction of seeing the world, is innocent and beneficial. Also it is childish, being a continuation of what nurses call "taking notice," by which a child becomes experienced. It is pitiable nowadays to see men and women doing after the age of 45 all the travelling and sightseeing they should have done before they were 15. Mere wondering and staring at things is an important part of a child's education: that is why children can be thoroughly mobilized without making vagabonds of them. A vagabond is at home nowhere because he wanders: a child should wander because it ought to be at home everywhere. And if it has its papers and its passports, and gets what it requires not by begging and pilfering, but from responsible agents of the community as of right, and with some formal acknowledgment of the obligations it is incurring and a knowledge of the fact that these obligations are being recorded: if, further, certain qualifications are exacted before it is promoted from permission to go as far as its legs will carry it to using mechanical aids to locomotion, it can roam without much danger of gypsification.

Under such circumstances the boy or girl could always run away, and never be lost; and on no other conditions can a child be free without being also a homeless outcast. Parents could also run away from disagreeable children or drive them out of doors or even drop their acquaintance, temporarily or permanently, without inhumanity. Thus both parties would be on their good behavior, and not, as at present, on their filial or parental behavior, which, like all unfree behavior, is mostly bad behavior.

As to what other results might follow, we had better wait and see; for nobody now alive can imagine what customs and institutions would grow up in societies of free children. Child laws and child fashions, child manners and child morals are now not tolerated; but among free children there would certainly be surprising developments in this direction. I do not think there would be any danger of free children behaving as badly as grown-up people do now because they have never been free. They could hardly behave worse, anyhow.

CHILDREN'S RIGHTS AND PARENTS' WRONGS

A very distinguished man once assured a mother of my acquaintance that she would never know what it meant to be hurt until she was hurt through her children. Children are extremely cruel without intending it; and in ninety-nine cases out of a hundred the reason is that they do not conceive their elders as having any human feelings. Serve the elders right, perhaps, for posing as superhuman! The penalty of the impostor is not that he is found out (he very seldom is) but that he is taken for what he pretends to be, and treated as such. And to be treated as anything but what you really are may seem pleasant to the imagination when the treatment is above your merits; but in actual experience it is often quite the reverse. When I was a very small boy, my romantic imagination, stimulated by early doses of fiction, led me to brag to a still smaller boy so outrageously that he, being a simple soul, really believed me to be an invincible hero. I cannot remember whether this pleased me much; but I do remember very distinctly that one day this admirer of mine, who had a pet goat, found the animal in the hands of a larger boy than either of us, who mocked him and refused to restore the animal to his rightful owner. Whereupon, naturally, he came weeping to me, and demanded that I should rescue the goat and annihilate the aggressor. My terror was beyond description: fortunately for me, it imparted such a ghastliness to my voice and aspect as I, under the eye of my poor little dupe, advanced on the enemy with that hideous extremity of cowardice which is called the courage of despair, and said "You let go that goat," that he abandoned his prey and fled, to my unforgettable, unspeakable relief. I have never since exaggerated my prowess in bodily combat.

Now what happened to me in the adventure of the goat happens very often to parents, and would happen to schoolmasters if the prison door of the school did not shut out the trials of life. I remember once, at school, the resident head master was brought down to earth by the sudden illness of his wife. In the confusion that ensued it became necessary to leave one of the schoolrooms without a master. I was in the class that occupied that schoolroom. To have sent us home would have been to break the fundamental bargain with our parents by which the school was bound to keep us out of their way for half the day at all hazards. Therefore an appeal had to be made to our better feelings: that is, to our common humanity, not to make a noise. But the head master had never admitted any common humanity with us. We had been carefully broken in to regard him as a being quite aloof from and above us: one not subject to error or suffering or death or illness or mortality. Consequently sympathy was impossible; and if the unfortunate lady did not perish, it was because, as I now comfort myself with guessing, she was too much preoccupied with her own pains, and possibly making too much noise herself, to be conscious of the pandemonium downstairs.

A great deal of the fiendishness of schoolboys and the cruelty of children to their elders is produced just in this way. Elders cannot be superhuman beings and suffering fellow creatures at the same time. If you pose as a little god, you must pose for better for worse.

HOW LITTLE WE KNOW ABOUT OUR PARENTS

The relation between parent and child has cruel moments for the parent even when money is no object and the material worries are delegated to servants and school teachers. The child and the parent are strangers to one another necessarily, because their ages must differ widely. Read Goethe's autobiography; and note that though he was happy in his parents and had exceptional powers of observation, divination, and story-telling, he knew less about his father and mother than about most of the other people he mentions. I myself was never on bad terms with my mother: we lived together until I was forty-two years old, absolutely without the smallest friction of any kind; yet when her death set me thinking curiously about our relations, I realized that I knew very little about her. Introduce me to a strange woman who was a child when I was a child, a girl when I was a boy, an adolescent when I was an adolescent; and if we take naturally to one another I will know more of her and she of me at the end of forty days (I had almost said of forty minutes) than I knew of my mother at the end of forty years. A contemporary stranger is a novelty and an enigma, also a possibility; but a mother is like a broomstick or like the sun in the heavens, it does not matter which as far as one's knowledge of her is concerned: the broomstick is there and the sun is there; and whether the child is beaten by it or warmed and enlightened by it, it accepts it as a fact in nature, and does not conceive it as having had youth, passions, and weaknesses, or as still growing, yearning, suffering, and learning. If I meet a widow I may ask her all about her marriage; but what son ever dreams of asking his mother about her marriage, or could endure to hear of it without violently breaking off the old sacred relationship between them, and ceasing to be her child or anything more to her than the first man in the street might be?

Yet though in this sense the child cannot realize its parent's humanity, the parent can realize the child's; for the parents with their experience of life have none of the illusions about the child that the child has about the parents; and the consequence is that the child can hurt its parents' feelings much more than its parents can hurt the child's, because the child, even when there has been none of the deliberate hypocrisy by which children are taken advantage of by their elders, cannot conceive the parent as a fellow creature, whilst the parents know very well that the children are only themselves over again. The child cannot conceive that its blame or contempt or want of interest could possibly hurt its parent, and therefore expresses them all with an indifference which has given rise to the term *enfant terrible* (a tragic term in spite of the jests connected with it); whilst the parent can suffer from such slights and reproaches more from a child than from anyone else, even when the child is not beloved, because the child is so unmistakeably sincere in them.

OUR ABANDONED MOTHERS

Take a very common instance of this agonizing incompatibility. A widow brings up her son to manhood. He meets a strange woman, and goes off with and marries her, leaving his mother desolate. It does not occur to him that this is at all hard on her: he does it as a matter of course, and actually expects his mother to receive, on terms of special affection, the woman for whom she has been abandoned. If he shewed any sense of what he was doing, any remorse; if he mingled his tears with hers and asked her not to think too hardly of him because he had obeyed the inevitable destiny of a man

to leave his father and mother and cleave to his wife, she could give him her blessing and accept her bereavement with dignity and without reproach. But the man never dreams of such considerations. To him his mother's feeling in the matter, when she betrays it, is unreasonable, ridiculous, and even odious, as shewing a prejudice against his adorable bride.

I have taken the widow as an extreme and obvious case; but there are many husbands and wives who are tired of their consorts, or disappointed in them, or estranged from them by infidelities; and these parents, in losing a son or a daughter through marriage, may be losing everything they care for. No parent's love is as innocent as the love of a child: the exclusion of all conscious sexual feeling from it does not exclude the bitterness, jealousy, and despair at loss which characterize sexual passion: in fact, what is called a pure love may easily be more selfish and jealous than a carnal one. Anyhow, it is plain matter of fact that naïvely selfish people sometimes try with fierce jealousy to prevent their children marrying.

FAMILY AFFECTION

Until the family as we know it ceases to exist, nobody will dare to analyse parental affection as distinguished from that general human sympathy which has secured to many an orphan fonder care in a stranger's house than it would have received from its actual parents. Not even Tolstoy, in The Kreutzer Sonata, has said all that we suspect about it. When it persists beyond the period at which it ceases to be necessary to the child's welfare, it is apt to be morbid; and we are probably wrong to inculcate its deliberate cultivation. The natural course is for the parents and children to cast off the specific parental and filial relation when they are no longer necessary to one another. The child does this readily enough to form fresh ties, closer and more fascinating. Parents are not always excluded from such compensations: it happens sometimes that when the children go out at the door the lover comes in at the window. Indeed it happens now oftener than it used to, because people remain much longer in the sexual arena. The cultivated Jewess no longer cuts off her hair at her marriage. The British matron has discarded her cap and her conscientious ugliness; and a bishop's wife at fifty has more of the air of a *femme galante* than an actress had at thirty-five in her grandmother's time. But as people marry later, the facts of age and time still inexorably condemn most parents to comparative solitude when their children marry. This may be a privation and may be a relief: probably in healthy circumstances it is no worse than a salutary change of habit; but even at that it is, for the moment at least, a wrench. For though parents and children sometimes dislike one another, there is an experience of succor and a habit of dependence and expectation formed in infancy which naturally attaches a child to its parent or to its nurse (a foster parent) in a quite peculiar way. A benefit to the child may be a burden to the parent; but people become attached to their burdens sometimes more than the burdens are attached to them; and to "suffer little children" has become an affectionate impulse deep in our nature.

Now there is no such impulse to suffer our sisters and brothers, our aunts and uncles, much less our cousins. If we could choose our relatives, we might, by selecting congenial ones, mitigate the repulsive effect of the obligation to like them and to admit them to our intimacy. But to have a person imposed on us as a brother merely because he happens to have the same parents is unbearable when, as may easily happen, he is the sort of person we should carefully avoid if he were any-

one else's brother. All Europe (except Scotland, which has clans instead of families) draws the line at second cousins. Protestantism draws it still closer by making the first cousin a marriageable stranger; and the only reason for not drawing it at sisters and brothers is that the institution of the family compels us to spend our childhood with them, and thus imposes on us a curious relation in which familiarity destroys romantic charm, and is yet expected to create a specially warm affection. Such a relation is dangerously factitious and unnatural; and the practical moral is that the less said at home about specific family affection the better. Children, like grown-up people, get on well enough together if they are not pushed down one another's throats; and grown-up relatives will get on together in proportion to their separation and their care not to presume on their blood relationship. We should let children's feelings take their natural course without prompting. I have seen a child scolded and called unfeeling because it did not occur to it to make a theatrical demonstration of affectionate delight when its mother returned after an absence: a typical example of the way in which spurious family sentiment is stoked up. We are, after all, sociable animals; and if we are let alone in the matter of our affections, and well brought up otherwise, we shall not get on any the worse with particular people because they happen to be our brothers and sisters and cousins. The danger lies in assuming that we shall get on any better.

The main point to grasp here is that families are not kept together at present by family feeling but by human feeling. The family cultivates sympathy and mutual help and consolation as any other form of kindly association cultivates them; but the addition of a dictated compulsory affection as an attribute of near kinship is not only unnecessary, but positively detrimental; and the alleged tendency of modern social development to break up the family need alarm nobody. We cannot break up the facts of kinship nor eradicate its natural emotional consequences. What we can do and ought to do is to set people free to behave naturally and to change their behavior as circumstances change. To impose on a citizen of London the family duties of a Highland cateran in the eighteenth century is as absurd as to compel him to carry a claymore and target instead of an umbrella. The civilized man has no special use for cousins; and he may presently find that he has no special use for brothers and sisters. The parent seems likely to remain indispensable; but there is no reason why that natural tie should be made the excuse for unnatural aggravations of it, as crushing to the parent as they are oppressive to the child. The mother and father will not always have to shoulder the burthen of maintenance which should fall on the Atlas shoulders of the fatherland and motherland. Pending such reforms and emancipations, a shattering break-up of the paternal home must remain one of normal incidents of marriage. The parent is left lonely and the child is not. Woe to the old if they have no impersonal interests, no convictions, no public causes to advance, no tastes or hobbies! It is well to be a mother but not to be a mother-in-law; and if men were cut off artificially from intellectual and public interests as women are, the father-in-law would be as deplorable a figure in popular tradition as the mother-in-law.

It is not to be wondered at that some people hold that blood relationship should be kept a secret from the persons related, and that the happiest condition in this respect is that of the foundling who, if he ever meets his parents or brothers or sisters, passes them by without knowing them. And for such a view there is this to be said: that our family system does unquestionably take the natural bond between members of the same family, which, like all natural bonds, is not too tight to be borne, and superimposes on it a painful burden of forced, inculcated, suggested, and altogether unnecessary affection and responsibility which we should do well to get rid of by making relatives as independent of one another as possible.

THE FATE OF THE FAMILY

The difficulty of inducing people to talk sensibly about the family is the same as that which I pointed out in a previous volume as confusing discussions of marriage. Marriage is not a single invariable institution: it changes from civilization to civilization, from religion to religion, from civil code to civil code, from frontier to frontier. The family is still more variable, because the number of persons constituting a family, unlike the number of persons constituting a marriage, varies from one to twenty: indeed, when a widower with a family marries a widow with a family, and the two produce a third family, even that very high number may be surpassed. And the conditions may vary between opposite extremes: for example, in a London or Paris slum every child adds to the burden of poverty and helps to starve the parents and all the other children, whereas in a settlement of pioneer colonists every child, from the moment it is big enough to lend a hand to the family industry, is an investment in which the only danger is that of temporary over-capitalization. Then there are the variations in family sentiment. Sometimes the family organization is as frankly political as the organization of an army or an industry: fathers being no more expected to be sentimental about their children than colonels about soldiers, or factory owners about their employees, though the mother may be allowed a little tenderness if her character is weak. The Roman father was a despot: the Chinese father is an object of worship: the sentimental modern western father is often a playfellow looked to for toys and pocket-money. The farmer sees his children constantly: the squire sees them only during the holidays, and not then oftener than he can help: the tram conductor, when employed by a joint stock company, sometimes never sees them at all.

Under such circumstances phrases like The Influence of Home Life, The Family, The Domestic Hearth, and so on, are no more specific than The Mammals, or The Man In The Street; and the pious generalizations founded so glibly on them by our sentimental moralists are unworkable. When households average twelve persons with the sexes about equally represented, the results may be fairly good. When they average three the results may be very bad indeed; and to lump the two together under the general term The Family is to confuse the question hopelessly. The modern small family is much too stuffy: children "brought up at home" in it are unfit for society.

But here again circumstances differ. If the parents live in what is called a garden suburb, where there is a good deal of social intercourse, and the family, instead of keeping itself to itself, as the evil old saying is, and glowering at the neighbors over the blinds of the long street in which nobody knows his neighbor and everyone wishes to deceive him as to his income and social importance, is in effect broken up by school life, by out-of-door habits, and by frank neighborly intercourse through dances and concerts and theatricals and excursions and the like, families of four may turn out much less barbarous citizens than families of ten which attain the Boer ideal of being out of sight of one another's chimney smoke.

All one can say is, roughly, that the homelier the home, and the more familiar the family, the worse for everybody concerned. The family ideal is a humbug and a nuisance: one might as reasonably talk of the barrack ideal, or the forecastle ideal, or any other substitution of the machinery of social organization for the end of it, which must always be the fullest and most capable life: in short, the most godly life. And this significant word reminds us that though the popular conception of heaven includes a Holy Family, it does not attach to that family the notion of a separate home, or a private nursery or kitchen or mother-in-law, or anything that constitutes the family as we know it. Even blood relationship is miraculously abstracted from it; and the Father is the father of all children, the mother the mother of all mothers and babies, and the Son the Son of Man and the Savior of his brothers: one whose chief utterance on the subject of the conventional family was an invitation to all of us to leave our families and follow him, and to leave the dead to bury the dead, and not debauch ourselves at that gloomy festival the family funeral, with its sequel of hideous mourning and grief which is either affected or morbid.

FAMILY MOURNING

I do not know how far this detestable custom of mourning is carried in France; but judging from the appearance of the French people I should say that a Frenchwoman goes into mourning for her cousins to the seventeenth degree. The result is that when I cross the Channel I seem to have reached a country devastated by war or pestilence. It is really suffering only from the family. Will anyone pretend that England has not the better of this striking difference? It is such senseless and unnatural conventions as this that make us so impatient of what we call family feeling. Even apart from its insufferable pretensions, the family needs hearty discrediting; for there is hardly any vulnerable part of it that could not be amputated with advantage.

ART TEACHING

By art teaching I hasten to say that I do not mean giving children lessons in freehand drawing and perspective. I am simply calling attention to the fact that fine art is the only teacher except torture. I have already pointed out that nobody, except under threat of torture, can read a school book. The reason is that a school book is not a work of art. Similarly, you cannot listen to a lesson or a sermon unless the teacher or the preacher is an artist. You cannot read the Bible if you have no sense of literary art. The reason why the continental European is, to the Englishman or American, so surprisingly ignorant of the Bible, is that the authorized English version is a great work of literary art, and the continental versions are comparatively artless. To read a dull book; to listen to a tedious play or prosy sermon or lecture; to stare at uninteresting pictures or ugly buildings: nothing, short of disease, is more dreadful than this. The violence done to our souls by it leaves injuries and produces subtle maladies which have never been properly studied by psychopathologists. Yet we are so inured to it in school, where practically all the teachers are bores trying to do the work of artists, and all the books artless, that we acquire a truly frightful power of enduring boredom. We even acquire the notion that fine art is lascivious and destructive to the character. In church, in the House of Commons, at public meetings, we sit solemnly listening to bores and twaddlers because from the time we could walk or speak we have been snubbed, scolded, bullied, beaten and imprisoned whenever we dared to resent being bored or twaddled at, or to express our natural impatience and derision of bores and twaddlers. And when a man arises with a soul of sufficient native strength to break the bonds of this inculcated reverence and to expose and deride and tweak the noses of our humbugs and panjandrums, like Voltaire or Dickens, we are shocked and scandalized, even when we cannot help laughing. Worse, we dread and persecute those who can see and declare the truth, because their sincerity and insight reflects on our delusion and blindness. We are all like Nell Gwynne's footman, who defended Nell's reputation with his fists, not because he believed her to be what he called an honest woman, but because he objected to be scorned as the footman of one who was no better than she should be.

This wretched power of allowing ourselves to be bored may seem to give the fine arts a chance sometimes. People will sit through a performance of Beethoven's ninth symphony or of Wagner's Ring just as they will sit through a dull sermon or a front bench politician saying nothing for two hours whilst his unfortunate country is perishing through the delay of its business in Parliament. But their endurance is very bad for the ninth symphony, because they never hiss when it is murdered. I have heard an Italian conductor (no longer living) take the *adagio* of that symphony at a lively *allegretto*, slowing down for the warmer major sections into the speed and manner of the heroine's death song in a Verdi opera; and the listeners, far from relieving my excruciation by rising with yells of fury and hurling their programs and opera glasses at the miscreant, behaved just as they do when Richter conducts it. The mass of imposture that thrives on this combination of ignorance with despairing endurance is incalculable. Given a public trained from childhood to stand anything tedious, and so saturated with school discipline that even with the doors open and no schoolmasters to stop them they will sit there helplessly until the end of the concert or opera gives them leave to go home; and you will have in great capitals hundreds of thousands of pounds spent every night in the season on professedly artistic entertainments which have no other effect on fine art than to exacerbate the hatred in which it is already secretly held in England.

Fortunately, there are arts that cannot be cut off from the people by bad performances. We can read books for ourselves; and we can play a good deal of fine music for ourselves with the help of a pianola. Nothing stands between us and the actual handwork of the great masters of painting except distance; and modern photographic methods of reproduction are in some cases quite and in many nearly as effective in conveying the artist's message as a modern edition of Shakespear's plays is in conveying the message that first existed in his handwriting. The reproduction of great feats of musical execution is already on the way: the gramophone, for all its wheezing and snarling and braying, is steadily improving in its manners; and what with this improvement on the one hand, and on the other that blessed selective faculty which enables us to ignore a good deal of disagreeable noise if there is a thread of music in the middle of it (few critics of the gramophone seem to be conscious of the very considerable mechanical noise set up by choirs and orchestras) we have at last reached a point at which, for example, a person living in an English village where the church music is the only music, and that music is made by a few well-intentioned ladies with the help of a harmonium, can hear masses by Palestrina very passably executed, and can thereby be led to the discovery that Jackson in F and Hymns Ancient and Modern are not perhaps the last word of beauty and propriety in the praise of God.

In short, there is a vast body of art now within the reach of everybody. The difficulty is that this art, which alone can educate us in grace of body and soul, and which alone can make the history of the past live for us or the hope of the future shine for us, which alone can give delicacy and nobility to our crude lusts, which is the appointed vehicle of inspiration and the method of the communion of saints, is actually branded as sinful among us because, wherever it arises, there is resistance to tyranny, breaking of fetters, and the breath of freedom. The attempt to suppress art is not wholly successful: we might as well try to suppress oxygen. But it is carried far enough to inflict on huge numbers of people a most injurious art starvation, and to corrupt a great deal of the art that is tolerated. You will find in England plenty of rich families with little more culture than their dogs and horses. And you will find poor families, cut off by poverty and town life from the contemplation of the beauty of the earth, with its dresses of leaves, its scarves of cloud, and its contours of hill and valley, who would positively be happier as hogs, so little have they cultivated their humanity by the only effective instrument of culture: art. The dearth is artificially maintained even when there are the means of satisfying it. Story books are forbidden, picture post cards are forbidden, theatres are forbidden, operas are forbidden, circuses are forbidden, sweetmeats are forbidden, pretty colors are forbidden, all exactly as vice is forbidden. The Creator is explicitly prayed to, and implicitly convicted of indecency every day. An association of vice and sin with everything that is delightful and of goodness with everything that is wretched and detestable is set up. All the most perilous (and glorious) appetites and propensities are at once inflamed by starvation and uneducated by art. All the wholesome conditions which art imposes on appetite are waived: instead of cultivated men and women restrained by a thousand delicacies, repelled by ugliness, chilled by vulgarity, horrified by coarseness, deeply and sweetly moved by the graces that art has revealed to them and nursed in them, we get indiscriminate rapacity in pursuit of pleasure and a parade of the grossest stimulations in catering for it. We have a continual clamor for goodness, beauty, virtue, and sanctity, with such an appalling inability to recognize it or love it when it arrives that it is more dangerous to be a great prophet or poet than to promote twenty companies for swindling simple folk out of their savings. Do not for a moment suppose that uncultivated people are merely indifferent to high and noble qualities. They hate them malignantly. At best, such qualities are like rare and beautiful birds: when they appear the whole country takes down its guns; but the birds receive the statuary tribute of having their corpses stuffed.

And it really all comes from the habit of preventing children from being troublesome. You are so careful of your boy's morals, knowing how troublesome they may be, that you keep him away from the Venus of Milo only to find him in the arms of the scullery maid or someone much worse. You decide that the Hermes of Praxiteles and Wagner's Tristan are not suited for young girls; and your daughter marries somebody appallingly unlike either Hermes or Tristan solely to escape from your parental protection. You have not stifled a single passion nor averted a single danger: you have depraved the passions by starving them, and broken down all the defences which so effectively protect children brought up in freedom. You have men who imagine themselves to be ministers of religion openly declaring that when they pass through the streets they have to keep out in the wheeled traffic to avoid the temptations of the pavement. You have them organizing hunts of the women who tempt them— poor creatures whom no artist would touch without a shudder—and wildly clamoring for more clothes to disguise and conceal the body, and for the abolition of pictures, statues, theatres, and pretty colors. And incredible as it seems, these unhappy lunatics are left at large, unrebuked, even admired and revered, whilst artists have to struggle for toleration. To them an undraped human body is the most monstrous, the most blighting, the most obscene, the most unbearable spectacle in the universe. To an artist it is, at its best, the most admirable spectacle in nature, and, at its average, an object of indifference. If every rag of clothing miraculously dropped from the inhabitants of London at noon tomorrow (say as a preliminary to the Great Judgment), the artistic people would not turn a hair; but the artless people would go mad and call on the mountains to hide them. I submit that this indicates a thoroughly healthy state on the part of the artists, and a thoroughly morbid one on the part of the artless. And the healthy state is attainable in a cold country like ours only by familiarity with the undraped figure acquired through pictures, statues, and theatrical representations in which an illusion of natural clotheslessness is produced and made poetic.

In short, we all grow up stupid and mad to just the extent to which we have not been artistically educated; and the fact that this taint of stupidity and madness has to be tolerated because it is general, and is even boasted of as characteristically English, makes the situation all the worse. It is becoming exceedingly grave at present, because the last ray of art is being cut off from our schools by the discontinuance of religious education.

THE IMPOSSIBILITY OF SECULAR EDUCATION

Now children must be taught some sort of religion. Secular education is an impossibility. Secular education comes to this: that the only reason for ceasing to do evil and learning to do well is that if you do not you will be caned. This is worse than being taught in a church school that if you become a dissenter you will go to hell; for hell is presented as the instrument of something eternal, divine, and inevitable: you cannot evade it the moment the schoolmaster's back is turned. What confuses this issue and leads even highly intelligent religious persons to advocate secular education as a means of rescuing children from the strife of rival proselytizers is the failure to distinguish between the child's personal subjective need for a religion and its right to an impartially communicated historical objective knowledge of all the creeds and Churches. Just as a child, no matter what its race and color may be, should know that there are black men and brown men and yellow men, and, no matter what its political convictions may be, that there are Monarchists and Republicans and Positivists, Socialists and Unsocialists, so it should know that there are Christians and Mahometans and Buddhists and Shintoists and so forth, and that they are on the average just as honest and well-behaved as its own father. For example, it should not be told that Allah is a false god set up by the Turks and Arabs, who will all be damned for taking that liberty; but it should be told that many English people think so, and that many Turks and Arabs think the converse about English people. It should be taught that Allah is simply the name by which God is known to Turks and Arabs, who are just as eligible for salvation as any Christian. Further, that the practical reason why a Turkish child should pray in a mosque and an English child in a church is that as worship is organized in Turkey in mosques in the name of Mahomet and in England in churches in the name of Christ, a Turkish child joining the Church of England or an English child following Mahomet will find that it has no place for its worship and no organization of its religion within its reach. Any other teaching of the history and present facts of religion is false teaching, and is politically extremely dangerous in an empire in which a huge majority of the fellow-subjects of the governing island do not profess the religion of that island.

But this objectivity, though intellectually honest, tells the child only what other people believe. What it should itself believe is quite another matter. The sort of Rationalism which says to a child "You must suspend your judgment until you are old enough to choose your religion" is Rationalism gone mad. The child must have a conscience and a code of honor (which is the essence of religion) even if it be only a provisional one, to be revised at its confirmation. For confirmation is meant to signalize a spiritual coming of age, and may be a repudiation. Really active souls have many confirmations and repudiations as their life deepens and their knowledge widens. But what is to guide the child before its first confirmation? Not mere orders, because orders must have a sanction of some sort or why should the child obey them? If, as a Secularist, you refuse to teach any sanction, you must say "You will be punished if you disobey." "Yes," says the child to itself, "if I am found out; but wait until your back is turned and I will do as I like, and lie about it." There can be no objective punishment for successful fraud; and as no espionage can cover the whole range of a child's conduct, the upshot is that the child becomes a liar and schemer with an

E

atrophied conscience. And a good many of the orders given to it are not obeyed after all. Thus the Secularist who is not a fool is forced to appeal to the child's vital impulse towards perfection, to the divine spark; and no resolution not to call this impulse an impulse of loyalty to the Fellowship of the Holy Ghost, or obedience to the Will of God, or any other standard theological term, can alter the fact that the Secularist has stepped outside Secularism and is educating the child religiously, even if he insists on repudiating that pious adverb and substituting the word metaphysically.

NATURAL SELECTION AS A RELIGION

We must make up our minds to it therefore that whatever measures we may be forced to take to prevent the recruiting sergeants of the Churches, free or established, from obtaining an exclusive right of entry to schools, we shall not be able to exclude religion from them. The most horrible of all religions: that which teaches us to regard ourselves as the helpless prey of a series of senseless accidents called Natural Selection, is allowed and even welcomed in so-called secular schools because it is, in a sense, the negation of all religion; but for school purposes a religion is a belief which affects conduct: and no belief affects conduct more radically and often so disastrously as the belief that the universe is a product of Natural Selection. What is more, the theory of Natural Selection cannot be kept out of schools, because many of the natural facts that present the most plausible appearance of design can be accounted for by Natural Selection; and it would be as absurd to keep a child in delusive ignorance of so potent a factor in evolution as to keep it in ignorance of radiation or capillary attraction. Even if you make a religion of Natural Selection, and teach the child to regard itself as the irresponsible prey

of its circumstances and appetites (or its heredity as you will perhaps call them), you will none the less find that its appetites are stimulated by your encouragement and daunted by your discouragement; that one of its appetites is an appetite for perfection; that if you discourage this appetite and encourage the cruder acquisitive appetites the child will steal and lie and be a nuisance to you; and that if you encourage its appetite for perfection and teach it to attach a peculiar sacredness to it and place it before the other appetites, it will be a much nicer child and you will have a much easier job, at which point you will, in spite of your pseudo-scientific jargon, find yourself back in the old-fashioned religious teaching as deep as Dr Watts and in fact fathoms deeper.

MORAL INSTRUCTION LEAGUES

And now the voices of our Moral Instruction Leagues will be lifted, asking whether there is any reason why the appetite for perfection should not be cultivated in rationally scientific terms instead of being associated with the story of Jonah and the great fish and the thousand other tales that grow up round religions. Yes: there are many reasons; and one of them is that children all like the story of Jonah and the whale (they insist on its being a whale in spite of demonstrations by Bible smashers without any sense of humor that Jonah would not have fitted into a whale's gullet—as if the story would be credible of a whale with an enlarged throat) and that no child on earth can stand moral instruction books or catechisms or any other statement of the case for religion in abstract terms. The object of a moral instruction book is not to be rational, scientific, exact, proof against controversy, nor even credible: its object is to make children good. If it makes them sick instead its place is the waste-paper basket. And if it is to be read it must be readable.

Take for an illustration the story of Elisha and the bears. To the authors of the moral instruction books it is in the last degree reprehensible. It is obviously not true as a record of fact; and the picture it gives us of the temper of God (which is what interests an adult reader) is shocking and blasphemous. But it is a capital story for a child. It interests a child because it is about bears; and it leaves the child with an impression that children who poke fun at old gentlemen and make rude remarks about bald heads are not nice children, which is a highly desirable impression, and just as much as a child is capable of receiving from the story. When a story is about God and a child, children take God for granted and criticize the child. Adults do the opposite, and are thereby often led to talk great nonsense about the bad effect of Bible stories on infants.

But let no one think that a child or anyone else can learn religion from a teacher or a book or by any academic process whatever. It is only by an unfettered access to the whole body of Fine Art: that is, to the whole body of inspired revelation, that we can build up that conception of divinity to which all virtue is an aspiration. And to hope to find this body of art purified from all that is obsolete or dangerous or fierce or lusty, or to pick and choose what will be good for any particular child, much less for all children, is the shallowest of vanities. Such schoolmasterly selection is neither possible nor desirable. Ignorance of evil is not virtue but imbecility: admiring it is like giving a prize for honesty to a man who has not stolen your watch because he did not know you had one. Virtue chooses good from evil; and without knowledge there can be no choice. And even this is a dangerous simplification of what actually occurs.

We are not choosing: we are growing. Were you to cut all of what you call the evil out of a child, it would drop dead. If you try to stretch it to full human stature when it is ten years old, you will simply pull it into two pieces and be hanged. And when you try to do this morally, which is what parents and schoolmasters are doing every day, you ought to be hanged; and some day, when we take a sensible view of the matter, you will be; and serve you right. The child does not stand between a good and a bad angel: what it has to deal with is a middling angel who, in normal healthy cases, wants to be a good angel as fast as it can without killing itself in the process, which is a dangerous one.

Therefore there is no question of providing the child with a carefully regulated access to good art. There is no good art, any more than there is good anything else in the absolute sense. Art that is too good for the child will either teach it nothing or drive it mad, as the Bible has driven many people mad who might have kept their sanity had they been allowed to read much lower forms of literature. The practical moral is that we must read whatever stories, see whatever pictures, hear whatever songs and symphonies, go to whatever plays we like. We shall not like those which have nothing to say to us; and though everyone has a right to bias our choice, no one has a right to deprive us of it by keeping us from any work of art or any work of art from us.

I may now say without danger of being misunderstood that the popular English compromise called Cowper-Templeism (unsectarian Bible education) is not so silly as it looks. It is true that the Bible inculcates half-a-dozen religions: some of them barbarous; some cynical and pessimistic; some amoristic and romantic; some sceptical and challenging; some kindly, simple, and intuitional;

some sophistical and intellectual; none suited to the character and conditions of western civilization unless it be the Christianity which was finally suppressed by the Crucifixion, and has never been put into practice by any State before or since. But the Bible contains the ancient literature of a very remarkable Oriental race; and the imposition of this literature, on whatever false pretences, on our children left them more literate than if they knew no literature at all, which was the practical alternative. And as our Authorized Version is a great work of art as well, to know it was better than knowing no art, which also was the practical alternative. It is at least not a school book; and it is not a bad story book, horrible as some of the stories are. Therefore as between the Bible and the blank represented by secular education in its most matter-of-fact sense, the choice is with the Bible.

THE BIBLE

But the Bible is not sufficient. The real Bible of modern Europe is the whole body of great literature in which the inspiration and revelation of Hebrew Scripture has been continued to the present day. Nietzsche's Thus Spake Zoroaster is less comforting to the ill and unhappy than the Psalms; but it is much truer, subtler, and more edifying. The pleasure we get from the rhetoric of the book of Job and its tragic picture of a bewildered soul cannot disguise the ignoble irrelevance of the retort of God with which it closes, nor supply the need for such modern revelations as Shelley's Prometheus or The Niblung's Ring of Richard Wagner. There is nothing in the Bible greater in inspiration than Beethoven's ninth symphony; and the power of modern music to convey that inspiration to a modern man is far greater than that of Elizabethan English, which is, except for people steeped in the Bible from childhood like Sir Walter Scott and Ruskin, a dead language.

Besides, many who have no ear for literature or for music are accessible to architecture, to pictures, to statues, to dresses, and to the arts of the stage. Every device of art should be brought to bear on the young; so that they may discover some form of it that delights them naturally; for there will come to all of them that period between dawning adolescence and full maturity when the pleasures and emotions of art will have to satisfy cravings which, if starved or insulted, may become morbid and seek disgraceful satisfactions, and, if prematurely gratified otherwise than poetically, may destroy the stamina of the race. And it must be borne in mind that the most dangerous art for this necessary purpose is the art that presents itself as religious ecstasy. Young people are ripe for love long before they are ripe for religion. Only a very foolish person would substitute the Imitation of Christ for Treasure Island as a present for a boy or girl, or for Byron's Don Juan as a present for a swain or lass. Pickwick is the safest saint for us in our nonage. Flaubert's Temptation of St Anthony is an excellent book for a man of fifty, perhaps the best within reach as a healthy study of visionary ecstasy; but for the purposes of a boy of fifteen Ivanhoe and the Templar make a much better saint and devil. And the boy of fifteen will find this out for himself if he is allowed to wander in a well-stocked literary garden, and hear bands and see pictures and spend his pennies on cinematograph shows. His choice may often be rather disgusting to his elders when they want him to choose the best before he is ready for it. The greatest Protestant Manifesto ever written, as far as I know, is Houston Chamberlain's Foundations of the Nineteenth Century: everybody capable of it should read it. Probably the History of Maria Monk is at the opposite extreme of merit (this is a guess: I have never read it); but it is certain that a boy let loose in a library would go for Maria Monk and have no use whatever for Mr Chamberlain. I should probably have read Maria Monk myself if I had not had the Arabian Nights and their like to occupy me better. In art, children, like adults, will find their level if they are left free to find it, and not restricted to what adults think good for them. Just at present our young people are going mad over ragtimes, apparently because syncopated rhythms are new to them. If they had learnt what can be done with syncopation from Beethoven's third Leonora overture, they would enjoy the ragtimes all the more; but they would put them in their proper place as amusing vulgarities.

ARTIST IDOLATRY

But there are more dangerous influences than ragtimes waiting for people brought up in ignorance of fine art. Nothing is more pitiably ridiculous than the wild worship of artists by those who have never been seasoned in youth to the enchantments of art. Tenors and prima donnas, pianists and violinists, actors and actresses enjoy powers of seduction which in the middle ages would have exposed them to the risk of being burnt for sorcery. But as they exercise this power by singing, playing, and acting, no great harm is done except perhaps to themselves. Far graver are the powers enjoyed by brilliant persons who are also connoisseurs in art. The influence they can exercise on young people who have been brought up in the darkness and wretchedness of a home without art, and in whom a natural bent towards art has always been baffled and snubbed, is incredible to those who have not witnessed and understood it. He (or she) who reveals the world of art to them opens heaven to them. They become satellites, disciples, worshippers of the apostle. Now the apostle may be a voluptuary without much conscience. Nature may have given him enough virtue to suffice in a reasonable environment. But this allowance may not be enough to defend him against the temptation and demoralization of finding himself a little god on the strength of what ought to be a quite ordinary culture. He may find adorers in all directions in our uncultivated society among people of stronger character than himself, not one of whom, if they had been artistically educated, would have had anything to learn from him or regarded him as in any way extraordinary apart from his actual achievements as an artist. Tartuffe is not always a priest. Indeed he is not always a rascal: he is often a weak man absurdly credited with omniscience and perfection, and taking unfair advantages only because they are offered to him and he is too weak to refuse. Give everyone his culture, and no one will offer him more than his due.

In thus delivering our children from the idolatry of the artist, we shall not destroy for them the enchantment of art: on the contrary, we shall teach them to demand art everywhere as a condition attainable by cultivating the body, mind, and heart. Art, said Morris, is the expression of pleasure in work. And certainly, when work is made detestable by slavery, there is no art. It is only when learning is made a slavery by tyrannical teachers that art becomes loathsome to the pupil.

"THE MACHINE"

When we set to work at a Constitution to secure freedom for children, we had better bear in mind that the children may not be at all obliged to us for our pains. Rousseau said that men are born free; and this dangerous saying, as Rousseau meant it, was and is a great and true saying; yet let it not lead us into the error of supposing that all men long for freedom and embrace it when it is offered to them. On the contrary, it has to be forced on them; and even then they will give it the slip if it is not religiously inculcated and strongly safeguarded.

Besides, men are born docile, and must in the nature of things remain so with regard to everything they do not understand. Now political science and the art of government are among the things they do not understand, and indeed are not at present allowed to understand. They can be enslaved by a system, as we are at present, because it happens to be there, and nobody understands it. An intelligently worked Capitalist system, as Comte saw, would give us all that most of us are intelligent enough to want. What makes it produce such unspeakably vile results is that it is an automatic system which is as little understood by those who profit by it in money as by those who are starved and degraded by it: our millionaires and statesmen are manifestly no more "captains of industry" or scientific politicians than our bookmakers are mathematicians. For some time past a significant word has been coming into use as a substitute for Destiny, Fate, and Providence. It is "The Machine": the machine that has no god in it. Why do governments do nothing in spite of reports of Royal Commissions that establish the most frightful urgency? Why do our philanthropic millionaires do nothing, though they are ready to throw bucketfuls of gold into the streets? The Machine will not let them. Always The Machine. In short, they dont know how. They try to reform Society as an old lady might try to restore a broken down locomotive by prodding it with a knitting needle. And this is not at all because they are born fools, but because they have been educated, not into manhood and freedom, but into blindness and slavery by their parents and schoolmasters, themselves the victims of a similar misdirection, and consequently of The Machine. They do not want liberty. They have not been educated to want it. They choose slavery and inequality; and all the other evils are automatically added to them.

And yet we must have The Machine. It is only in unskilled hands under ignorant direction that machinery is dangerous. We can no more govern modern communities without political machinery than we can feed and clothe them without industrial machinery. Shatter The Machine, and you get Anarchy. And yet The Machine works so detestably at present that we have people who advocate anarchy and call themselves Anarchists.

THE PROVOCATION TO ANARCHISM

The Anarchists are right when they say that Governments, like schoolmasters, try to simplify their task by destroying liberty and glorifying authority, especially their own. But the difficulty of combining law and order with free institutions is not a natural one. It is a matter of inculcation. If people are brought up to be slaves, it is useless and dangerous to let them loose at the age of twentyone and say "Now you are free." No one with the tamed soul and broken spirit of a slave can be free. It is like saying to a laborer brought up on a family income of thirteen shillings a week, "Here is one hundred thousand pounds: now you are wealthy." Nothing can make such a man really wealthy. Freedom and wealth are difficult and responsible conditions to which men must be accustomed and socially trained from birth. A nation that is free at twentyone is not free at all; just as a man first enriched at fifty remains poor all his life, even if he does not curtail it by drinking himself to death in the first wild ecstasy of being able to swallow as much as he likes for the first time. You cannot govern men brought up as slaves otherwise than as slaves are governed. You may pile Bills of Right and Habeas Corpus Acts on Great Charters; promulgate American Constitutions; burn the chateaux and guillotine the seigneurs; chop off the heads of kings and queens and set up Democracy on the ruins of feudalism: the end of it all for us is that already in the twentieth century there has been as much brute coercion and savage intolerance, as much flogging and hanging, as much impudent injustice on the bench and lustful rancor in the pulpit, as much naïve resort to torture, persecution, and suppression of free speech and freedom of the Press, as much war, as much of the vilest excess of mutilation, rapine, and delirious indiscriminate slaughter of helpless non-combatants, old and young, as much prostitution of professional talent, literary and political, in defence of manifest wrong, as much cowardly sycophancy giving fine names to all this villainy or pretending that it is "greatly exaggerated," as we can find any record of from the days when the advocacy of liberty was a capital offence and Democracy was hardly thinkable. Democracy exhibits the vanity of Louis XIV, the savagery of Peter of Russia, the nepotism and provinciality of Napoleon, the fickleness of Catherine II: in short, all the childishnesses of all the despots without any of the qualities that enabled the greatest of them to fascinate and dominate their contemporaries.

And the flatterers of Democracy are as impudently servile to the successful, and insolent to common honest folk, as the flatterers of the monarchs. Democracy in America has led to the withdrawal of ordinary refined persons from politics; and the same result is coming in England as fast as we make Democracy as democratic as it is in America. This is true also of popular religion: it is so horribly irreligious that nobody with the smallest pretence to culture, or the least inkling of what the great prophets vainly tried to make the world understand, will have anything to do with it except for purely secular reasons.

IMAGINATION

Before we can clearly understand how baleful is this condition of intimidation in which we live, it is necessary to clear up the confusion made by our use of the word imagination to denote two very different powers of mind. One is the power to imagine things as they are not: this I call the romantic imagination. The other is the power to imagine things as they are without actually sensing them; and this I will call the realistic imagination. Take for example marriage and war. One man has a vision of perpetual bliss with a domestic angel at home, and of flashing sabres, thundering guns, victorious cavalry charges, and routed enemies in the field. That is romantic imagination; and the mischief it does is incalculable. It begins in silly and selfish expectations of the impossible, and ends in spiteful disappointment, sour grievance, cynicism, and misanthropic resistance to any attempt to better a hopeless world. The wise man knows that imagination is not only a means of pleasing himself and beguiling tedious hours with romances and fairy tales and fools' paradises (a quite defensible and delightful amusement when you know exactly what you are doing and where fancy ends and facts begin), but also a means of foreseeing and being prepared for realities as yet unexperienced, and of testing the feasibility and desirability of serious Utopias. He does not expect his wife to be an angel; nor does he overlook the facts that war depends on the rousing of all the murderous blackguardism still latent in mankind; that every victory means a defeat; that fatigue, hunger, terror, and disease are the raw material which romancers work up into military glory; and that soldiers for the most part go to war as children go to school, because they are afraid not to. They are afraid even to say they are afraid, as such candor is punishable by death in the military code.

A very little realistic imagination gives an ambitious person enormous power over the multitudinous victims of the romantic imagination. For the romancer not only pleases himself with fictitious glories: he also terrifies himself with imaginary dangers. He does not even picture what these dangers are: he conceives the unknown as always dangerous. When you say to a realist "You must do this" or "You must not do that," he instantly asks what will happen to him if he does (or does not, as the case may be). Failing an unromantic convincing answer, he does just as he pleases unless he can find for himself a real reason for refraining. In short, though you can intimidate him, you cannot bluff him. But you can always bluff the romantic person: indeed his grasp of real considerations is so feeble that you find it necessary to bluff him even when you have solid considerations to offer him instead. The campaigns of Napoleon, with their atmosphere of glory, illustrate this. In the Russian campaign Napoleon's marshals achieved miracles of bluff, especially Ney, who, with a handful of men, monstrously outnumbered, repeatedly kept the Russian troops paralyzed with terror by pure bounce. Napoleon himself, much more a realist than Ney (that was why he dominated him), would probably have surrendered; for sometimes the bravest of the brave will achieve successes never attempted by the cleverest of the clever. Wellington was a completer realist than Napoleon. It was impossible to persuade Wellington that he was beaten until he actually was beaten. He was unbluffable; and if Napoleon had understood the

nature of Wellington's strength instead of returning Wellington's snobbish contempt for him by an academic contempt for Wellington, he would not have left the attack at Waterloo to Ney and D'Erlon, who, on that field, did not know when they were beaten, whereas Wellington knew precisely when he was not beaten. The unbluffable would have triumphed anyhow, probably, because Napoleon was an academic soldier, doing the academic thing (the attack in columns and so forth) with superlative ability and energy; whilst Wellington was an original soldier who, instead of outdoing the terrible academic columns with still more terrible and academic columns, outwitted them with the thin red line, not of heroes, but, as this uncompromising realist never hesitated to testify, of the scum of the earth.

GOVERNMENT BY BULLIES

These picturesque martial incidents are being reproduced every day in our ordinary life. We are bluffed by hardy simpletons and headstrong bounders as the Russians were bluffed by Ney; and our Wellingtons are threadbound by slave-democracy as Gulliver was threadbound by the Lilliputians. We are a mass of people living in a submissive routine to which we have been drilled from our childhood. When you ask us to take the simplest step outside that routine, we say shyly, "Oh, I really couldnt," or "Oh, I shouldnt like to," without being able to point out the smallest harm that could possibly ensue: victims, not of a rational fear of real dangers, but of pure abstract fear, the quintessence of cowardice, the very negation of "the fear of God." Dotted about among us are a few spirits relatively free from this inculcated paralysis, sometimes because they are half-witted, sometimes because they are unscrupulously selfish, sometimes because they are realists as to money and unimaginative as to other things, sometimes even because they are exceptionally able, but always because they are not afraid of shadows nor oppressed with nightmares. And we see these few rising as if by magic into power and affluence, and forming, with the millionaires who have accidentally gained huge riches by the occasional windfalls of our commerce, the governing class. Now nothing is more disastrous than a governing class that does not know how to govern. And how can this rabble of the casual products of luck, cunning, and folly, be expected to know how to govern? The merely lucky ones and the hereditary ones do not owe their position to their qualifications at all. As to the rest, the realism which seems their essential qualification often consists not only in a lack of romantic imagination, which lack is a merit, but of the realistic, constructive, Utopian imagination, which lack is a ghastly defect. Freedom from imaginative illusion is therefore no guarantee whatever of nobility of character: that is why inculcated submissiveness makes us slaves to people much worse than ourselves, and why it is so important that submissiveness should no longer be inculcated.

And yet as long as you have the compulsory school as we know it, we shall have submissiveness inculcated. What is more, until the active hours of child life are organized separately from the active hours of adult life, so that adults can enjoy the society of children in reason without being tormented, disturbed, harried, burdened, and hindered in their work by them as they would be now if there were no compulsory schools and no children hypnotized into the belief that they must tamely go to them and be imprisoned and beaten and overtasked in them, we shall have schools under one pretext or another; and we shall have all the evil consequences and all the social hopelessness that result from turning a nation of potential freemen and freewomen into a nation of two-legged spoilt spaniels with everything crushed out of their nature except dread of the whip. Liberty is the breath of life to nations; and liberty is the one thing that parents, schoolmasters, and rulers spend their lives in extirpating for the sake of an immediately quiet and finally disastrous life.

III

OVERRULED

1912

THE ALLEVIATIONS OF MONOGAMY

This piece is not an argument for or against polygamy. It is a clinical study of how the thing actually occurs among quite ordinary people, innocent of all unconventional views concerning it. The enormous majority of cases in real life are those of people in that position. Those who deliberately and conscientiously profess what are oddly called advanced views by those others who believe them to be retrograde, are often, and indeed mostly, the last people in the world to engage in unconventional adventures of any kind, not only because they have neither time nor disposition for them, but because the friction set up between the individual and the community by the expression of unusual views of any sort is quite enough hindrance to the heretic without being complicated by personal scandals. Thus the theoretic libertine is usually a person of blameless family life, whilst the practical libertine is mercilessly severe on all other libertines, and excessively conventional in professions of social principle.

What is more, these professions are not hypocritical: they are for the most part quite sincere. The common libertine, like the drunkard, succumbs to a temptation which he does not defend, and against which he warns others with an earnestness proportionate to the intensity of his own remorse. He (or she) may be a liar and a humbug, pretending to be better than the detected libertines, and clamoring for their condign punishment; but this is mere self-defence. No reasonable person expects the burglar to confess his pursuits, or to refrain from joining in the cry of Stop Thief when the police get on the track of another burglar. If society chooses to penalize candor, it has itself to thank if its attack is countered by falsehood. The clamorous virtue of the libertine is therefore no more hypocritical than the plea of Not Guilty which is allowed to every criminal. But one result is that the theorists who write most sincerely and favorably about polygamy know least about it; and the practitioners who know most about it keep their knowledge very jealously to themselves. Which is hardly fair to the practice.

INACCESSIBILITY OF THE FACTS

Also, it is impossible to estimate its prevalence. A practice to which nobody confesses may be both universal and unsuspected, just as a virtue which everybody is expected, under heavy penalties, to claim, may have no existence. It is often assumed—indeed it is the official assumption of the Churches and the divorce courts—that a gentleman and a lady cannot be alone together innocently. And that is manifest blazing nonsense, though many women have been stoned to death in the east, and divorced in the west, on the strength of it. On the other hand, the innocent and conventional people who regard gallant adventures as crimes of so horrible a nature that only the most depraved and desperate characters engage in them or would listen to advances in that direction without raising an alarm with the noisiest indignation, are clearly examples of the fact that most sections of society do not know how the other sections live. Industry is the most effective check on gallantry. Women may, as Napoleon said, be the occupation of the idle man just as men are the preoccupation of the idle woman; but the mass of mankind is too busy and too poor for the long and expensive sieges which the professed libertine lays to virtue. Still, wherever there is idleness or even a reasonable supply of elegant leisure there is a good deal of coquetry and philandering. It is so much pleasanter to dance on the edge of a precipice than to go over it that leisured society is full of people who spend a great part of their lives in flirtation, and conceal nothing but the humiliating secret that they have never gone any further. For there is no pleasing people in the matter of reputation in this department: every insult is a flattery: every testimonial is a disparagement: Joseph is despised and promoted, Potiphar's wife admired and condemned: in short, you are never on solid ground until you get away from the subject altogether. There is a continual and irreconcilable conflict between the natural and conventional sides of the case, between spontaneous human relations between independent men and women on the one hand and the property relation between husband and wife on the other, not to mention the confusion under the common name of love of a generous natural attraction and interest with the murderous jealousy that fastens on and clings to its mate (especially a hated mate) as a tiger fastens on a carcase. And the confusion is natural; for these extremes are extremes of the same passion; and most cases lie somewhere on the scale between them, and are so complicated by ordinary likes and dislikes, by incidental wounds to vanity or gratifications of it, and by class feeling, that A will be jealous of B and not of C, and will tolerate infidelities on the part of D whilst being furiously angry when they are committed by E.

THE CONVENTION OF JEALOUSY

That jealousy is independent of sex is shewn by its intensity in children, and by the fact that very jealous people are jealous of everybody without regard to rela-

tionship or sex, and cannot bear to hear the person they "love" speak favorably of anyone under any circumstances (many women, for instance, are much more jealous of their husbands' mothers and sisters than of unrelated women whom they suspect him of fancying); but it is seldom possible to disentangle the two passions in practice. Besides, jealousy is an inculcated passion, forced by society on people in whom it would not occur spontaneously. In Brieux's Bourgeois aux Champs, the benevolent hero finds himself detested by the neighboring peasants and farmers, not because he preserves game, and sets mantraps for poachers, and defends his legal rights over his land to the extremest point of unsocial savagery, but because, being an amiable and public-spirited person, he refuses to do all this, and thereby offends and disparages the sense of property in his neighbors. The same thing is true of matrimonial jealousy: the man who does not at least pretend to feel it, and behave as badly as if he really felt it, is despised and insulted; and many a man has shot or stabbed a friend or been shot or stabbed by him in a duel, or disgraced himself and ruined his own wife in a divorce scandal, against his conscience, against his instinct, and to the destruction of his home, solely because Society conspired to drive him to keep its own lower morality in countenance in this miserable and undignified manner.

Morality is confused in such matters. In an elegant plutocracy, a jealous husband is regarded as a boor. Among the tradesmen who supply that plutocracy with its meals, a husband who is not jealous, and refrains from assailing his rival with his fists, is regarded as a ridiculous, contemptible, and cowardly cuckold. And the laboring class is divided into the respectable section which takes the tradesman's view, and the disreputable section which enjoys the license of the plutocracy without its money: creeping below the law as its exemplars prance above it; cutting down all expenses of respectability and even decency; and frankly accepting squalor and disrepute as the price of anarchic self-indulgence. The conflict between Malvolio and Sir Toby, between the marquis and the bourgeois, the cavalier and the puritan, the ascetic and the voluptuary, goes on continually, and goes on not only between class and class and individual and individual, but in the selfsame breast in a series of reactions and revulsions in which the irresistible becomes the unbearable, and the unbearable the irresistible, until none of us can say what our characters really are in this respect.

THE MISSING DATA OF A SCIENTIFIC NATURAL HISTORY OF MARRIAGE

Of one thing I am persuaded: we shall never attain to a reasonably healthy public opinion on sex questions until we offer, as the data for that opinion, our actual conduct and our real thoughts instead of a moral fiction which we agree to call virtuous conduct, and which we then—and here comes in the mischief—pretend is our conduct and our thoughts. If the result were that we all believed one another to be better than we really are, there would be something to be said for it; but the actual result appears to be a monstrous exaggeration of the power and continuity of sexual passion. The whole world shares the fate of Lucrezia Borgia, who, though she seems on investigation to have been quite a suitable wife for a modern British Bishop, has been invested by the popular historical imagination with all the extravagances of a Messalina or a Cenci. Writers of belles lettres who are rash enough to admit that their whole life is not one constant preoccupation with adored members of the opposite sex, and who even countenance La Rochefoucauld's remark that very few people would ever imagine themselves in love if they had never read anything about

it, are gravely declared to be abnormal or physically defective by critics of crushing unadventurousness and domestication. French authors of saintly temperament are forced to include in their retinue countesses of ardent complexion with whom they are supposed to live in sin. Sentimental controversies on the subject are endless; but they are useless, because nobody tells the truth. Rousseau did it by an extraordinary effort, aided by a superhuman faculty for human natural history; but the result was curiously disconcerting because, though the facts were so conventionally shocking that people felt that they ought to matter a great deal, they actually mattered very little. And even at that everybody pretends not to believe him.

ARTIFICIAL RETRIBUTION

The worst of this is that busybodies with perhaps rather more than a normal taste for mischief are continually trying to make negligible things matter as much in fact as they do in convention by deliberately inflicting injuries—sometimes atrocious injuries—on the parties concerned. Few people have any knowledge of the savage punishments that are legally inflicted for aberrations and absurdities to which no sanely instructed community would call any attention. We create an artificial morality, and consequently an artificial conscience, by manufacturing disastrous consequences for events which, left to themselves, would do very little harm (sometimes not any) and be forgotten in a few days.

But the artificial morality is not therefore to be condemned offhand. In many cases it may save mischief instead of making it: for example, though the hanging of a murderer is the duplication of a murder, yet it may be less murderous than leaving the matter to be settled by blood feud or vendetta. As long as human nature insists on revenge, the official organization and satisfaction of revenge by the State may be also its minimization. The mischief begins when the official revenge persists after the passion it satisfies has died out of the race. Stoning a woman to death in the east because she has ventured to marry again after being deserted by her husband may be more merciful than allowing her to be mobbed to death; but the official stoning or burning of an adulteress in the west would be an atrocity, because few of us hate an adulteress to the extent of desiring such a penalty, or of being prepared to take the law into our own hands if it were withheld. Now what applies to this extreme case applies also in due degree to the other cases. Offences in which sex is concerned are often needlessly magnified by penalties, ranging from various forms of social ostracism to long sentences of penal servitude, which would be seen to be monstrously disproportionate to the real feeling against them if the removal of both the penalties and the taboo on their discussion made it possible for us to ascertain their real prevalence and estimation. Fortunately there is one outlet for the truth. We are permitted to discuss in jest what we may not discuss in earnest. A serious comedy about sex is taboo: a farcical comedy is privileged.

THE FAVORITE SUBJECT OF FARCICAL COMEDY

The little piece which follows this preface accordingly takes the form of a farcical comedy, because it is a contribution to the very extensive dramatic literature which takes as its special department the gallantries of married people. The stage has been preoccupied by such affairs for centuries, not only in the jesting vein of Restoration Comedy and Palais Royal farce, but in the more tragically turned adulteries of the Parisian school which dominated the stage until Ibsen put them out of countenance and relegated them to

their proper place as articles of commerce. Their continued vogue in that department maintains the tradition that adultery is the dramatic subject *par excellence*, and indeed that a play that is not about adultery is not a play at all. I was considered a heresiarch of the most extravagant kind when I expressed my opinion, at the outset of my career as a playwright, that adultery is the dullest of themes on the stage, and that from Francesca and Paolo down to the latest guilty couple of the school of Dumas *fils*, the romantic adulterers have all been intolerable bores.

THE PSEUDO SEX PLAY

Later on, I had occasion to point out to the defenders of sex as the proper theme of drama, that though they were right in ranking sex as an intensely interesting subject, they were wrong in assuming that sex is an indispensable motive in popular plays. The plays of Molière are, like the novels of the Victorian epoch or Don Quixote, as nearly sexless as anything not absolutely inhuman can be; and some of Shakespear's plays are sexually on a par with the census: they contain women as well as men, and that is all. This had to be admitted; but it was still assumed that the plays of the nineteenth century Paris school are, in contrast with the sexless masterpieces, saturated with sex; and this I strenuously denied. A play about the convention that a man should fight a duel or come to fisticuffs with his wife's lover if she has one, or the convention that he should strangle her like Othello, or turn her out of the house and never see her or allow her to see her children again, or the convention that she should never be spoken to again by any decent person and should finally drown herself, or the convention that persons involved in scenes of recrimination or confession by these conventions should call each other certain abusive names and describe their conduct as guilty and frail and so on: all these may provide material for very effective plays; but such plays are not dramatic studies of sex: one might as well say that Romeo and Juliet is a dramatic study of pharmacy because the catastrophe is brought about through an apothecary. Duels are not sex; divorce cases are not sex; the Trade Unionism of married women is not sex. Only the most insignificant fraction of the gallantries of married people produce any of the conventional results; and plays occupied wholly with the conventional results are therefore utterly unsatisfying as sex plays, however interesting they may be as plays of intrigue and plot puzzles.

The world is finding this out rapidly. The Sunday papers, which in the days when they appealed almost exclusively to the lower middle class were crammed with police intelligence, and more especially with divorce and murder cases, now lay no stress on them; and police papers which confined themselves entirely to such matters, and were once eagerly read, have perished through the essential dulness of their topics. And yet the interest in sex is stronger than ever: in fact, the literature that has driven out the journalism of the divorce courts is a literature occupied with sex to an extent and with an intimacy and frankness that would have seemed utterly impossible to Thackeray or Dickens if they had been told that the change would complete itself within fifty years of their own time.

ART AND MORALITY

It is ridiculous to say, as inconsiderate amateurs of the arts do, that art has nothing to do with morality. What is true is that the artist's business is not that of the policeman; and that such factitious consequences and put-up jobs as divorces and executions and the detective operations that lead up to them are no essential part

of life, though, like poisons and buttered slides and red-hot pokers, they provide material for plenty of thrilling or amusing stories suited to people who are incapable of any interest in psychology. But the fine artist must keep the policeman out of his studies of sex and studies of crime. It is by clinging nervously to the policeman that most of the pseudo sex plays convince me that the writers have either never had any serious personal experience of their ostensible subject, or else have never conceived it possible that the stage dare present the phenomena of sex as they appear in nature.

THE LIMITS OF STAGE PRESENTATION

But the stage presents much more shocking phenomena than those of sex. There is, of course, a sense in which you cannot present sex on the stage, just as you cannot present murder. Macbeth must no more really kill Duncan than he must himself be really slain by Macduff. But the feelings of a murderer can be expressed in a certain artistic convention; and a carefully prearranged sword exercise can be gone through with sufficient pretence of earnestness to be accepted by the willing imaginations of the younger spectators as a desperate combat.

The tragedy of love has been presented on the stage in the same way. In Tristan and Isolde, the curtain does not, as in Romeo and Juliet, rise with the lark: the whole night of love is played before the spectators. The lovers do not discuss marriage in an elegantly sentimental way: they utter the visions and feelings that come to lovers at the supreme moments of their love, totally forgetting that there are such things in the world as husbands and lawyers and duelling codes and theories of sin and notions of propriety and all the other irrelevancies which provide hackneyed and bloodless material for our so-called plays of passion.

PRUDERIES OF THE FRENCH STAGE

To all stage presentations there are limits. If Macduff were to stab Macbeth, the spectacle would be intolerable; and even the pretence which we allow on our stage is ridiculously destructive to the illusion of the scene. Yet pugilists and gladiators will actually fight and kill in public without shame, even as a spectacle for money. But no sober couple of lovers of any delicacy could endure to be watched. We in England, accustomed to consider the French stage much more licentious than the British, are always surprised and puzzled when we learn, as we may do any day if we come within reach of such information, that French actors are often scandalized by what they consider the indecency of the English stage, and that French actresses who desire a greater license in appealing to the sexual instincts than the French stage allows them, learn English and establish themselves on the English stage. The German and Russian stages are in the same relation to the French and, perhaps more or less, all the Latin stages. The reason is that, partly from a want of respect for the theatre, partly from a sort of respect for art in general which moves them to accord moral privileges to artists, partly from the very objectionable tradition that the realm of art is Alsatia and the contemplation of works of art a holiday from the burden of virtue, partly because French prudery does not attach itself to the same points of behavior as British prudery, and has a different code of the mentionable and the unmentionable, and for many other reasons, the French tolerate plays which are never performed in England until they have been spoiled by a process of bowdlerization; yet French taste is more fastidious than ours as to the exhibition and treatment on the stage of the physical incidents of sex. On the French stage a kiss is as obvious a convention as the thrust under the arm by which Macduff runs Macbeth through. It is even a purposely unconvincing convention: the actors rather insisting that it shall be impossible for any spectator to mistake a stage kiss for a real one. In England, on the contrary, realism is carried to the point at which nobody except the two performers can perceive that the caress is not genuine. And here the English stage is certainly in the right; for whatever question there arises as to what incidents are proper for representation on the stage or not, my experience as a playgoer leaves me in no doubt that once it is decided to represent an incident, it will be offensive, no matter whether it be a prayer or a kiss, unless it is presented with a convincing appearance of sincerity.

OUR DISILLUSIVE SCENERY

For example, the main objection to the use of illusive scenery (in most modern plays scenery is not illusive: everything visible is as real as in your drawing room at home) is that it is unconvincing; whilst the imaginary scenery with which the audience transfigures a platform or tribune like the Elizabethan stage or the Greek stage used by Sophocles, is quite convincing. In fact, the more scenery you have the less illusion you produce. The wise playwright, when he cannot get absolute reality of presentation, goes to the other extreme, and aims at atmosphere and suggestion of mood rather than at direct simulative illusion. The theatre, as I first knew it, was a place of wings and flats which destroyed both atmosphere and illusion. This was tolerated, and even intensely enjoyed, but not in the least because nothing better was possible; for all the devices employed in the productions of Mr Granville Barker or Max Reinhardt or the Moscow Art Theatre were equally available for Colley Cibber and Garrick, except the intensity of our artificial light. When Garrick played

Richard III in slashed trunk hose and plumes, it was not because he believed that the Plantagenets dressed like that, or because the costumiers could not have made him a XV century dress as easily as a nondescript combination of the state robes of George III with such scraps of older fashions as seemed to playgoers for some reason to be romantic. The charm of the theatre in those days was its make-believe. It has that charm still, not only for the amateurs, who are happiest when they are most unnatural and impossible and absurd, but for audiences as well. I have seen performances of my own plays which were to me far wilder burlesques than Sheridan's Critic or Buckingham's Rehearsal; yet they have produced sincere laughter and tears such as the most finished metropolitan productions have failed to elicit. Fielding was entirely right when he represented Partridge as enjoying intensely the performance of the king in Hamlet because anybody could see that the king was an actor, and resenting Garrick's Hamlet because it might have been a real man. Yet we have only to look at the portraits of Garrick to see that his performances would nowadays seem almost as extravagantly stagey as his costumes. In our day Calvé's intensely real Carmen never pleased the mob as much as the obvious fancy ball masquerading of suburban young ladies in the same character.

HOLDING THE MIRROR UP TO NATURE

Theatrical art begins as the holding up to Nature of a distorting mirror. In this phase it pleases people who are childish enough to believe that they can see what they look like and what they are when they look at a true mirror. Naturally they think that a true mirror can teach them nothing. Only by giving them back some monstrous image can the mirror amuse them or terrify them. It is not until they grow up to the point at which they learn that they know very little about themselves, and that they do not see themselves in a true mirror as other people see them, that they become consumed with curiosity as to what they really are like, and begin to demand that the stage shall be a mirror of such accuracy and intensity of illumination that they shall be able to get glimpses of their real selves in it, and also learn a little how they appear to other people.

For audiences of this highly developed class, sex can no longer be ignored or conventionalized or distorted by the playwright who makes the mirror. The old sentimental extravagances and the old grossnesses are of no further use to him. Don Giovanni and Zerlina are not gross: Tristan and Isolde are not extravagant or sentimental. They say and do nothing that you cannot bear to hear and see; and yet they give you, the one pair briefly and slightly, and the other fully and deeply, what passes in the minds of lovers. The love depicted may be that of a philosophic adventurer tempting an ignorant country girl, or of a tragically serious poet entangled with a woman of noble capacity in a passion which has become for them the reality of the whole universe. No matter: the thing is dramatized and dramatized directly, not talked about as something that happened before the curtain rose, or that will happen after it falls.

FARCICAL COMEDY SHIRKING ITS SUBJECT

Now if all this can be done in the key of tragedy and philosophic comedy, it can, I have always contended, be done in the key of farcical comedy; and Overruled is a trifling experiment in that manner. Conventional farcical comedies are always finally tedious because the heart of them, the inevitable conjugal infidelity, is always evaded. Even its consequences are evaded. Mr Granville Barker has pointed out rightly that if the third acts of our farcical comedies dared to describe the consequences that would follow from the first and second in real life, they would end as squalid tragedies; and in my opinion they would be greatly improved thereby even as entertainments; for I have never seen a three-act farcical comedy without being bored and tired by the third act, and observing that the rest of the audience were in the same condition, though they were not vigilantly introspective enough to find that out, and were apt to blame one another, especially the husbands and wives, for their crossness. But it is happily by no means true that conjugal infidelities always produce tragic consequences, or that they need produce even the unhappiness which they often do produce. Besides, the more momentous the consequences, the more interesting become the impulses and imaginations and reasonings, if any, of the people who disregard them. If I had an opportunity of conversing with the ghost of an executed murderer, I have no doubt he would begin to tell me eagerly about his trial, with the names of the distinguished ladies and gentlemen who honored him with their presence on that occasion, and then about his execution. All of which would bore me exceedingly. I should say, "My dear sir: such manufactured ceremonies do not interest me in the least. I know how a man is tried, and how he is hanged. I should have had you killed in a much less disgusting, hypocritical, and unfriendly manner if the matter had been in my hands. What I want to know about is the murder. How did you feel when you committed it? Why did you do it? What did you say to yourself about it? If, like most murderers, you had not been hanged, would you have committed other murders? Did you really dislike the victim, or did you want his money, or did you murder a person whom you did not dislike, and from whose death you had nothing to gain, merely for the sake of murdering? If so can you describe the charm to me? Does it come upon you periodic-ally; or is it chronic? Has curiosity anything to do with it?" I would ply him with all manner of questions to find out what murder is really like; and I should not be satisfied until I had realized that I, too, might commit a murder, or else that there is some specific quality present in a murderer and lacking in me. And, if so, what that quality is.

In just the same way, I want the unfaithful husband or the unfaithful wife in a farcical comedy not to bother me with their divorce cases or the stratagems they employ to avoid a divorce case, but to tell me how and why married couples are unfaithful. I dont want to hear the lies they tell one another to conceal what they have done, but the truths they tell one another when they have to face what they have done without concealment or excuse. No doubt prudent and considerate people conceal such adventures, when they can, from those who are most likely to be wounded by them; but it is not to be presumed that, when found out, they necessarily disgrace themselves by irritating lies and transparent subterfuges.

My playlet, which I offer as a model to all future writers of farcical comedy, may now, I hope, be read without shock. I may just add that Mr Sibthorpe Juno's view that morality demands, not that we should behave morally (an impossibility to our sinful nature) but that we shall not attempt to defend our immoralities, is a standard view in England, and was advanced in all seriousness by an earnest and distinguished British moralist shortly after the first performance of Overruled. My objection to that aspect of the doctrine of original sin is that no necessary and inevitable operation of human nature can reasonably be regarded as sinful at all, and that a morality which assumes the contrary is an absurd morality, and can be kept in countenance only by hypocrisy. When people were ashamed of sanitary problems, and refused to face them, leaving them to solve themselves clandestinely in dirt and secrecy, the solution arrived at was the Black Death. A similar policy as to sex problems has solved itself by an even worse plague than the Black Death; and the remedy for that is not salvarsan, but sound moral hygiene, the first foundation of which is the discontinuance of our habit of telling not only the comparatively harmless lies that we know we ought not to tell, but the ruinous lies that we foolishly think we ought to tell.

IV

MAJOR BARBARA

1905

Before dealing with the deeper aspects of Major Barbara, let me, for the credit of English literature, make a protest against an unpatriotic habit into which many of my critics have fallen. Whenever my view strikes them as being at all outside the range of, say, an ordinary suburban churchwarden, they conclude that I am echoing Schopenhauer, Nietzsche, Ibsen, Strindberg, Tolstoy, or some other heresiarch in northern or eastern Europe.

I confess there is something flattering in this simple faith in my accomplishment as a linguist and my erudition as a philosopher. But I cannot countenance the assumption that life and literature are so poor in these islands that we must go abroad for all dramatic material that is not common and all ideas that are not superficial. I therefore venture to put my critics in possession of certain facts concerning my contact with modern ideas.

About half a century ago, an Irish novelist, Charles Lever, wrote a story entitled A Day's Ride: A Life's Romance. It was published by Charles Dickens in Household Words, and proved so strange to the public taste that Dickens pressed Lever to make short work of it. I read scraps of this novel when I was a child; and it made an enduring impression on me. The hero was a very romantic hero, trying to live bravely, chivalrously, and powerfully by dint of mere romance-fed imagination, without courage, without means, without knowledge, without skill, without anything real except his bodily appetites. Even in my childhood I found in this poor devil's unsuccessful encounters with the facts of life, a poignant quality that romantic fiction lacked. The book, in spite of its first failure, is not dead: I saw its title the other day in the catalogue of Tauchnitz.

Now why is it that when I also deal in the tragi-comic irony of the conflict between real life and the romantic imagination, critics never affiliate me to my countryman and immediate forerunner, Charles Lever, whilst they confidently derive me from a Norwegian author of whose language I do not know three words, and of whom I knew nothing until years after the Shavian *Anschauung* was already unequivocally declared in books full of what came, ten years later, to be perfunctorily labelled Ibsenism? I was not Ibsenist even at second hand; for Lever, though he may have read Henri Beyle, *alias* Stendhal, certainly never read Ibsen. Of the books that made Lever popular, such as Charles O'Malley and Harry Lorrequer, I know nothing but the names and some of the illustrations. But the story of the day's ride and life's romance of Potts (claiming alliance with Pozzo di Borgo) caught me and fascinated me as something strange and significant, though I already knew all about Alnaschar and Don Quixote and Simon Tappertit and many another romantic hero mocked by reality. From the plays of Aristophanes to the tales of Stevenson that mockery has been made familiar to all who are properly saturated with letters.

Where, then, was the novelty in Lever's tale? Partly, I think, in a new seriousness in dealing with Potts's disease. Formerly, the contrast between madness and sanity was deemed comic: Hogarth shews us how fashionable people went in parties to Bedlam to laugh at the lunatics. I myself have had a village idiot exhibited to me as something irresistibly funny. On the stage the madman was once a regular comic figure: that was how Hamlet got his opportunity before Shakespear touched him. The originality of Shakespear's version lay in his taking the lunatic sympathetically and seriously, and thereby making an advance towards the eastern consciousness of the fact that lunacy may be inspiration in disguise, since a man who has more brains than his fellows necessarily appears as mad to them as one who has less. But Shakespear did not do for Pistol and Parolles what he did for Hamlet. The particular sort of madman they represented, the romantic make-believer, lay outside the pale of sympathy in literature: he was pitilessly despised and ridiculed here as he was in the east under the name of Alnaschar, and was doomed to be, centuries later, under the name of Simon Tappertit. When Cervantes relented over Don Quixote, and Dickens relented over Pickwick, they did not become impartial: they simply changed sides, and became friends and apologists where they had formerly been mockers.

In Lever's story there is a real change of attitude. There is no relenting towards Potts: he never gains our affections like Don Quixote and Pickwick: he has not even the infatuate courage of Tappertit. But we dare not laugh at him, because, somehow, we recognize ourselves in Potts. We may, some of us, have enough nerve, enough muscle, enough luck, enough tact or skill or address or knowledge to carry things off better than he did; to impose on the people who saw through him; to fascinate Katinka (who cut Potts so ruthlessly at the end of the story); but for all that, we know that Potts plays an enormous part in ourselves and in the world, and that the social problem is not a problem of story-book heroes of the older pattern, but a problem of Pottses, and of how to make men of

them. To fall back on my old phrase, we have the feeling—one that Alnaschar, Pistol, Parolles, and Tappertit never gave us—that Potts is a piece of really scientific natural history as distinguished from funny story telling. His author is not throwing a stone at a creature of another and inferior order, but making a confession, with the effect that the stone hits each of us full in the conscience and causes our self-esteem to smart very sorely. Hence the failure of Lever's book to please the readers of Household Words. That pain in the self-esteem nowadays causes critics to raise a cry of Ibsenism. I therefore assure them that the sensation first came to me from Lever and may have come to him from Beyle, or at least out of the Stendhalian atmosphere. I exclude the hypothesis of complete originality on Lever's part, because a man can no more be completely original in that sense than a tree can grow out of air.

Another mistake as to my literary ancestry is made whenever I violate the romantic convention that all women are angels when they are not devils; that they are better looking than men; that their part in courtship is entirely passive; and that the human female form is the most beautiful object in nature. Schopenhauer wrote a splenetic essay which, as it is neither polite nor profound, was probably intended to knock this nonsense violently on the head. A sentence denouncing the idolized form as ugly has been largely quoted. The English critics have read that sentence; and I must here affirm, with as much gentleness as the implication will bear, that it has yet to be proved that they have dipped any deeper. At all events, whenever an English playwright represents a young and marriageable woman as being anything but a romantic heroine, he is disposed of without further thought as an echo of Schopenhauer. My own case is a specially hard one, because, when I implore the critics who are obsessed with the Schopenhauerian formula to remember that playwrights, like sculptors, study their figures from life, and not from philosophic essays, they reply passionately that I am not a playwright and that my stage figures do not live. But even so, I may and do ask them why, if they must give the credit of my plays to a philosopher, they do not give it to an English philosopher? Long before I ever read a word by Schopenhauer, or even knew whether he was a philosopher or a chemist, the Socialist revival of the eighteen-eighties brought me into contact, both literary and personal, with Ernest Belfort Bax, an English Socialist and philosophic essayist, whose handling of modern feminism would provoke romantic protests from Schopenhauer himself, or even Strindberg. As a matter of fact I hardly noticed Schopenhauer's disparagements of women when they came under my notice later on, so thoroughly had Bax familiarized me with the homoist attitude, and forced me to recognize the extent to which public opinion, and consequently legislation and jurisprudence, is corrupted by feminist sentiment.

Belfort Bax's essays were not confined to the Feminist question. He was a ruthless critic of current morality. Other writers have gained sympathy for dramatic criminals by eliciting the alleged "soul of goodness in things evil"; but Bax would propound some quite undramatic and apparently shabby violation of our commercial law and morality, and not merely defend it with the most disconcerting ingenuity, but actually prove it to be a positive duty that nothing but the certainty of police persecution should prevent every right-minded man from at once doing on principle. The Socialists were naturally shocked, being for the most part morbidly moral people; but at all events they were saved later on from the delusion that nobody but Nietzsche had ever challenged our mercanto-Christian morality. I first heard the name of Nietzsche from a German mathematician, Miss Borchardt, who had read my Quintessence of Ibsenism, and told me that she saw what I had been reading: namely, Nietzsche's Jenseits von Gut und Böse. Which I protest I had never seen, and could not have read with any comfort, for want of the necessary German, if I had seen it.

Nietzsche, like Schopenhauer, is the victim in England of a single much quoted sentence containing the phrase "big blonde beast." On the strength of this alliteration it is assumed that Nietzsche gained his European reputation by a senseless glorification of selfish bullying as the rule of life, just as it is assumed, on the strength of the single word Superman (Übermensch) borrowed by me from Nietzsche, that I look for the salvation of society to the despotism of a single Napoleonic Superman, in spite of my careful demonstration of the folly of that outworn infatuation. But even the less recklessly superficial critics seem to believe that the modern objection to Christianity as a pernicious slave-morality was first put forward by Nietzsche. It was familiar to me before I ever heard of Nietzsche. The late Captain Wilson, author of several queer pamphlets, propagandist of a metaphysical system called Comprehensionism, and inventor of the term "Crosstianity" to distinguish the retrograde element in Christendom, was wont thirty years ago, in the discussions of the Dialectical Society, to protest earnestly against the beatitudes of the Sermon on the Mount as excuses for cowardice and servility, as destructive of our will, and consequently of our honor and manhood. Now it is true that Captain Wilson's moral criticism of Christianity was not a historical theory of it, like Nietzsche's; but this objection cannot be made to Stuart-Glennie, the successor of

Buckle as a philosophic historian, who devoted his life to the elaboration and propagation of his theory that Christianity is part of an epoch (or rather an aberration, since it began as recently as 6000 B.C. and is already collapsing) produced by the necessity in which the numerically inferior white races found themselves to impose their domination on the colored races by priestcraft, making a virtue and a popular religion of drudgery and submissiveness in this world not only as a means of achieving saintliness of character but of securing a reward in heaven. Here was the slave-morality view formulated by a Scotch philosopher of my acquaintance long before we all began chattering about Nietzsche.

As Stuart-Glennie traced the evolution of society to the conflict of races, his theory made some sensation among Socialists — that is, among the only people who were seriously thinking about historical evolution at all—by its collision with the class-conflict theory of Karl Marx. Nietzsche, as I gather, regarded the slave-morality as having been invented and imposed on the world by slaves making a virtue of necessity and a religion of their servitude. Stuart-Glennie regarded the slave-morality as an invention of the superior white race to subjugate the minds of the inferior races whom they wished to exploit, and who would have destroyed them by force of numbers if their minds had not been subjugated. As this process is in operation still, and can be studied at first hand not only in our Church schools and in the struggle between our modern proprietary classes and the proletariat, but in the part played by Christian missionaries in reconciling the black races of Africa to their subjugation by European Capitalism, we can judge for ourselves whether the initiative came from above or below. My object here is not to argue the historical point, but simply to make our theatre critics ashamed of their habit of treating Britain as an intellectual void, and assuming that every philosophical idea, every historic theory, every criticism of our moral, religious, and juridical institutions, must necessarily be either a foreign import, or else a fantastic sally (in rather questionable taste) totally unrelated to the existing body of thought. I urge them to remember that this body of thought is the slowest of growths and the rarest of blossomings, and that if there be such a thing on the philosophic plane as a matter of course, it is that no individual can make more than a minute contribution to it. In fact, their conception of clever persons parthenogenetically bringing forth complete original cosmogonies by dint of sheer "brilliancy" is part of that ignorant credulity which is the despair of the honest philosopher, and the opportunity of the religious impostor.

THE GOSPEL OF ST ANDREW UNDERSHAFT

It is this credulity that drives me to help my critics out with Major Barbara by telling them what to say about it. In the millionaire Undershaft I have represented a man who has become intellectually and spiritually as well as practically conscious of the irresistible natural truth which we all abhor and repudiate: to wit, that the greatest of our evils, and the worst of our crimes is poverty, and that our first duty, to which every other consideration should be sacrificed, is not to be poor. "Poor but honest," "the respectable poor," and such phrases are as intolerable and as immoral as "drunken but amiable," "fraudulent but a good after-dinner speaker," "splendidly criminal," or the like. Security, the chief pretence of civilization, cannot exist where the worst of dangers, the danger of poverty, hangs over everyone's head, and where the alleged protection of our persons from violence is only an accidental result of the existence of a police force whose real business is to force the poor man to see his children starve whilst idle people overfeed pet dogs with the money that might feed and clothe them.

It is exceedingly difficult to make people realize that an evil is an evil. For instance, we seize a man and deliberately do him a malicious injury: say, imprison him for years. One would not suppose that it needed any exceptional clearness of wit to recognize in this an act of diabolical cruelty. But in England such a recognition provokes a stare of surprise, followed by an explanation that the outrage is punishment or justice or something else that is all right, or perhaps by a heated attempt to argue that we should all be robbed and murdered in our beds if such stupid villainies as sentences of imprisonment were not committed daily. It is useless to argue that even if this were true, which it is not, the alternative to adding crimes of our own to the crimes from which we suffer is not helpless submission. Chickenpox is an evil; but if I were to declare that we must either submit to it or else repress it sternly by seizing everyone who suffers from it and punishing them by inoculation with smallpox, I should be laughed at; for though nobody could deny that the result would be to prevent chickenpox to some extent by making people avoid it much more carefully, and to effect a further apparent prevention by making them conceal it very anxiously, yet people would have sense enough to see that the deliberate propagation of smallpox was a creation of evil, and must therefore be ruled out in favor of purely humane and hygienic measures. Yet in the precisely parallel case of a man breaking into my house and stealing my wife's diamonds I am expected as a matter of course to steal ten years of his life, torturing him all the time. If he tries to defeat that monstrous retaliation by shooting me, my survivors hang him. The net result suggested by the police statistics is that we inflict atrocious injuries on the burglars we catch in order to make the rest take effectual precautions against detection; so that instead of saving our wives' diamonds from burglary we only greatly decrease our chances of ever getting them back, and increase our chances of being shot by the robber if we are unlucky enough to disturb him at his work.

But the thoughtless wickedness with which we scatter sentences of imprisonment, torture in the solitary cell and on the plank bed, and flogging, on moral invalids and energetic rebels, is as nothing compared to the silly levity with which we tolerate poverty as if it were either a wholesome tonic for lazy people or else a virtue to be embraced as St Francis embraced it. If a man is indolent, let him be poor. If he is drunken, let him be poor. If he is not a gentleman, let him be poor. If he is addicted to the fine arts or to pure science instead of to trade and finance, let him be poor. If he chooses to spend his urban eighteen shillings a week or his agricultural thirteen shillings a week on his beer and his family instead of saving it up for his old age, let him be poor. Let nothing be done for "the undeserving": let him be poor. Serve him right! Also —somewhat inconsistently—blessed are the poor!

Now what does this Let Him Be Poor mean? It means let him be weak. Let him be ignorant. Let him become a nucleus of disease. Let him be a standing exhibition and example of ugliness and dirt. Let him have rickety children. Let him be cheap, and drag his fellows down to his own price by selling himself to do their work. Let his habitations turn our cities into poisonous congeries of slums. Let his daughters infect our young men with the diseases of the streets, and his sons revenge him by turning the nation's manhood into scrofula, cowardice, cruelty, hypocrisy, political imbecility, and all the other fruits of oppression and malnutrition. Let the undeserving become still less deserving; and let the deserving lay up for himself, not treasures in heaven, but horrors in hell upon earth. This being so, is it really wise to let him be poor? Would he not do ten times less harm as a prosperous burglar, incendiary, ravisher or murderer, to the utmost limits of humanity's comparatively negligible impulses in these directions? Suppose we were to abolish all penalties for such activities, and decide that poverty is the one thing we will not tolerate—that every adult with less than, say, £365 a year shall be painlessly but inexorably killed, and every hungry half naked child forcibly fattened and clothed, would not that be an enormous improvement on our existing system, which has already destroyed so many civilizations, and is visibly destroying ours in the same way?

Is there any radicle of such legislation in our parliamentary system? Well, there are two measures just sprouting in the political soil, which may conceivably grow to something valuable. One is the institution of a Legal Minimum Wage. The other, Old Age Pensions. But there is a better plan than either of these. Some time ago I mentioned the subject of Universal Old Age Pensions to my fellow Socialist Cobden-Sanderson, famous as an artist-craftsman in bookbinding and printing. "Why not Universal Pensions for Life?" said Cobden-Sanderson. In saying this, he solved the industrial problem at a stroke. At present we say callously to each citizen "If you want money, earn it" as if his having or not having it were a matter that concerned himself alone. We do not even secure for him the opportunity of earning it: on the contrary, we allow our industry to be organized in open dependence on the maintenance of "a reserve army of unemployed" for the sake of "elasticity." The sensible course would be Cobden-Sanderson's: that is, to give every man enough to live well on, so as to guarantee the community against the possibility of a case of the malignant disease of poverty, and then (necessarily) to see that he earned it.

Undershaft, the hero of Major Barbara, is simply a man who, having grasped the fact that poverty is a crime, knows that when society offered him the alternative of poverty or a lucrative trade in death and destruction, it offered him, not a choice between opulent villainy and humble virtue, but between energetic enterprise and cowardly infamy. His conduct stands the Kantian test, which Peter Shirley's does not. Peter Shirley is what we call the honest poor man. Undershaft is what we call the wicked rich one: Shirley is Lazarus, Undershaft Dives. Well, the misery of the world is due to the fact that the great mass of men act and believe as Peter Shirley acts and believes. If they acted and believed as Undershaft acts and believes, the immediate result would be a revolution of incalculable beneficence. To be wealthy, says Undershaft, is with me a point of honor for which I am prepared to kill at the risk of my own life. This preparedness is, as he says, the final test of sincerity. Like Froissart's medieval hero, who saw that "to rob and pill was a good life," he is not the dupe of that public sentiment against killing which is propagated and endowed by people who would otherwise be killed themselves, or of the mouth-honor paid to poverty and obedience by rich and insubordinate do-nothings who want to rob the poor without courage and command them without superiority. Froissart's knight, in placing the achievement of a good life before all the other duties—which indeed are not duties at all when they conflict with it, but plain wickednesses — behaved bravely, admirably, and, in the final analysis, public-spiritedly. Medieval society, on the other hand, behaved very badly indeed in organizing itself so stupidly that a good life could be achieved by robbing and pilling. If the knight's contemporaries had been all as resolute as he, robbing and pilling would have been the shortest way to the gallows, just as, if we were all as resolute and clearsighted as Undershaft, an attempt to live by means of what is called "an independent income" would be the shortest way to the lethal chamber. But as, thanks to our political imbecility and personal cowardice (fruits of poverty, both), the best imitation of a good life now procurable is life on an independent income, all sensible people aim at securing such an income, and are, of course, careful to legalize and moralize both it and all the actions and sentiments which lead to it and support it as an institution. What else can they do? They know, of course, that they are rich because others are poor. But they cannot help that: it is for the poor to repudiate poverty when they have had enough of it. The thing can be done easily enough: the demonstrations to the contrary made by the economists, jurists, moralists, and sentimentalists hired by the rich to defend them, or even doing the work gratuitously out of sheer folly and abjectness, impose only on those who want to be imposed on.

The reason why the independent income-tax payers are not solid in defence of their position is that since we are not medieval rovers through a sparsely populated country, the poverty of those we rob prevents our having the good life for which we sacrifice them. Rich men or aristocrats with a developed sense of life—men like Ruskin and William Morris and Kropotkin—have enormous social appetites and very fastidious personal ones. They are not content with handsome houses: they want handsome cities. They are not content with bediamonded wives and blooming daughters:

they complain because the charwoman is badly dressed, because the laundress smells of gin, because the sempstress is anemic, because every man they meet is not a friend and every woman not a romance. They turn up their noses at their neighbor's drains, and are made ill by the architecture of their neighbor's houses. Trade patterns made to suit vulgar people do not please them (and they can get nothing else): they cannot sleep nor sit at ease upon "slaughtered" cabinet makers' furniture. The very air is not good enough for them: there is too much factory smoke in it. They even demand abstract conditions: justice, honor, a noble moral atmosphere, a mystic nexus to replace the cash nexus. Finally they declare that though to rob and pill with your own hand on horseback and in steel coat may have been a good life, to rob and pill by the hands of the policeman, the bailiff, and the soldier, and to underpay them meanly for doing it, is not a good life, but rather fatal to all possibility of even a tolerable one. They call on the poor to revolt, and, finding the poor shocked at their ungentlemanliness, despairingly revile the proletariat for its "damned wantlessness" (*verdammte Bedürfnislosigkeit*).

So far, however, their attack on society has lacked simplicity. The poor do not share their tastes nor understand their art-criticisms. They do not want the simple life, nor the esthetic life; on the contrary, they want very much to wallow in all the costly vulgarities from which the elect souls among the rich turn away with loathing. It is by surfeit and not by abstinence that they will be cured of their hankering after unwholesome sweets. What they do dislike and despise and are ashamed of is poverty. To ask them to fight for the difference between the Christmas number of the Illustrated London News and the Kelmscott Chaucer is silly: they prefer the News. The difference between a stockbroker's cheap and dirty starched white shirt and collar and the comparatively costly and carefully dyed blue shirt of William Morris is a difference so disgraceful to Morris in their eyes that if they fought on the subject at all, they would fight in defence of the starch. "Cease to be slaves, in order that you may become cranks" is not a very inspiring call to arms; nor is it really improved by substituting saints for cranks. Both terms denote men of genius; and the common man does not want to live the life of a man of genius: he would much rather live the life of a pet collie if that were the only alternative. But he does want more money. Whatever else he may be vague about, he is clear about that. He may or may not prefer Major Barbara to the Drury Lane pantomime; but he always prefers five hundred pounds to five hundred shillings.

Now to deplore this preference as sordid, and teach children that it is sinful to desire money, is to strain towards the extreme possible limit of impudence in lying and corruption in hypocrisy. The universal regard for money is the one hopeful fact in our civilization, the one sound spot in our social conscience. Money is the most important thing in the world. It represents health, strength, honor, generosity, and beauty as conspicuously and undeniably as the want of it represents illness, weakness, disgrace, meanness, and ugliness. Not the least of its virtues is that it destroys base people as certainly as it fortifies and dignifies noble people. It is only when it is cheapened to worthlessness for some and made impossibly dear to others, that it becomes a curse. In short, it is a curse only in such foolish social conditions that life itself is a curse. For the two things are inseparable: money is the counter that enables life to be distributed socially: it *is* life as truly as sovereigns and bank notes are money. The first duty of every citizen is to insist on having money on reasonable terms; and this demand is not complied with by giving four men three shillings each for ten or twelve hours' drudgery and one man a thousand pounds for nothing. The crying need of the nation is not for better morals, cheaper bread, temperance, liberty, culture, redemption of fallen sisters and erring brothers, nor the grace, love, and fellowship of the Trinity, but simply for enough money. And the evil to be attacked is not sin, suffering, greed, priestcraft, kingcraft, demagogy, monopoly, ignorance, drink, war, pestilence, nor any other of the scapegoats which reformers sacrifice, but simply poverty.

Once take your eyes from the ends of the earth and fix them on this truth just under your nose; and Andrew Undershaft's views will not perplex you in the least. Unless indeed his constant sense that he is only the instrument of a Will or Life Force which uses him for purposes wider than his own, may puzzle you. If so, that is because you are walking either in artificial Darwinian darkness, or in mere stupidity. All genuinely religious people have that consciousness. To them Undershaft the Mystic will be quite intelligible, and his perfect comprehension of his daughter the Salvationist and her lover the Euripidean republican natural and inevitable. That, however, is not new, even on the stage. What is new, as far as I know, is that article in Undershaft's religion which recognizes in Money the first need and in poverty the vilest sin of man and society.

This dramatic conception has not, of course, been attained *per saltum*. Nor has it been borrowed from Nietzsche or from any man born beyond the Channel. The late Samuel Butler, in his own department the greatest English writer of the latter half of the XIX century, steadily inculcated the necessity and morality of a conscientious Laodiceanism in religion and of an earnest and constant sense of the importance of money. It drives one almost to despair of English literature when one sees so extraordinary a study of English life as Butler's posthumous Way of All Flesh making so little impression that when, some years later, I produce plays in which Butler's extraordinarily fresh, free, and future-piercing suggestions have an obvious share, I am met with nothing but vague cacklings about Ibsen and Nietzsche, and am only too thankful that they are not about Alfred de Musset and Georges Sand. Really, the English do not deserve to have great men. They allowed Butler to die practically unknown, whilst I, a comparatively insignificant Irish journalist, was leading them by the nose into an advertisement of me which has made my own life a burden. In Sicily there is a Via Samuele Butler. When an English tourist sees it, he either asks "Who the devil was Samuele Butler?" or wonders why the Sicilians should perpetuate the memory of the author of Hudibras.

Well, it cannot be denied that the English are only too anxious to recognize a man of genius if somebody will kindly point him out to them. Having pointed myself out in this manner with some success, I now point out Samuel Butler, and trust that in consequence I shall hear a little less in future of the novelty and foreign origin of the ideas which are now making their way into the English theatre through plays written by Socialists. There are living men whose originality and power are as obvious as Butler's and when they die that fact will be discovered. Meanwhile I recommend them to insist on their own merits as an important part of their own business.

THE SALVATION ARMY

When Major Barbara was produced in London, the second act was reported in an important northern newspaper as a withering attack on the Salvation Army, and the despairing ejaculation of Barbara deplored by a London daily as a tasteless blasphemy. And they were set right, not by the professed critics of the theatre, but by religious and philosophical publicists like Sir Oliver Lodge and Dr Stanton Coit, and strenuous Nonconformist journalists like William Stead, who not only understood the act as well as the Salvationists themselves, but also saw it in its relation to the religious life of the nation, a life which seems to lie not only outside the sympathy of many of our theatre critics, but actually outside their knowledge of society. Indeed nothing could be more ironically curious than the confrontation Major Barbara effected of the theatre enthusiasts with the religious enthusiasts. On the one hand was the playgoer, always seeking pleasure, paying exorbitantly for it, suffering unbearable discomforts for it, and hardly ever getting it. On the other hand was the Salvationist, repudiating gaiety and courting effort and sacrifice, yet always in the wildest spirits, laughing, joking, singing, rejoicing, drumming, and tambourining: his life flying by in a flash of excitement, and his death arriving as a climax of triumph. And, if you please, the playgoer despising the Salvationist as a joyless person, shut out from the heaven of the theatre, self-condemned to a life of hideous gloom; and the Salvationist mourning over the playgoer as over a prodigal with vine leaves in his hair, careering outrageously to hell amid the popping of champagne corks and the ribald laughter of sirens! Could misunderstanding be more complete, or sympathy worse misplaced?

Fortunately, the Salvationists are more accessible to the religious character of the drama than the playgoers to the gay energy and artistic fertility of religion. They can see, when it is pointed out to them, that a theatre, as a place where two or three are gathered together, takes from that divine presence an inalienable sanctity of which the grossest and profanest farce can no more deprive it than a hypocritical sermon by a snobbish bishop can desecrate Westminster Abbey. But in our professional playgoers this indispensable preliminary conception of sanctity seems wanting. They talk of actors as mimes and mummers, and, I fear, think of dramatic authors as liars and pandars, whose main business is the voluptuous soothing of the tired city speculator when what he calls the serious business of the day is over. Passion, the life of drama, means nothing to them but primitive sexual excitement: such phrases as "impassioned poetry" or "passionate love of truth" have fallen quite out of their vocabulary and been replaced by "passional crime" and the like. They assume, as far as I can gather, that people in whom passion has a larger scope are passionless and therefore uninteresting. Consequently they come to think of religious people as people who are not interesting and not amusing. And so, when Barbara cuts the regular Salvation Army jokes, and snatches a kiss from her lover across his drum, the devotees of the theatre think they ought to appear shocked, and conclude that the whole play is an elaborate mockery of the Army. And then either hypocritically rebuke me for mocking, or foolishly take part in the supposed mockery!

Even the handful of mentally competent critics got into difficulties over my demonstration of the economic deadlock in which the Salvation Army finds itself. Some of them thought that the Army would not have taken money from a distiller and a cannon founder: others thought it should not have taken it: all assumed more or less definitely that it reduced itself to absurdity or hypocrisy by taking it. On the first point the reply of the Army itself was prompt and conclusive. As one of its officers said, they would take money from the devil himself and be only too glad to get it out of his hands and into God's. They gratefully acknowledged that publicans not only give them money but allow them to collect it in the bar—sometimes even when there is a Salvation meeting outside preaching teetotalism. In fact, they questioned the verisimilitude of the play, not because Mrs. Baines took the money, but because Barbara refused it.

On the point that the Army ought not to take such money, its justification is obvious. It must take the money because it cannot exist without money, and there is no other money to be had. Practically all the spare money in the country consists of a mass of rent, interest, and profit, every penny of which is bound up with crime, drink, prostitution, disease, and all the evil fruits of poverty, as inextricably as with enterprise, wealth, commercial probity, and national prosperity. The notion that you can earmark certain coins as tainted is an unpractical individualist superstition. None the less the fact that all our money is tainted gives a very severe shock to earnest young souls when some dramatic instance of the taint first makes them conscious of it. When an enthusiastic young clergyman of the Established Church first realizes that the Ecclesiastical Commissioners receive the rents of sporting public houses, brothels, and sweating dens; or that the most generous contributor at his last charity sermon was an employer trading in female labor cheapened by prostitution as unscrupulously as a hotel keeper trades in waiters' labor cheapened by tips, or commissionaires' labor cheapened by pensions; or that the only patron who can afford to rebuild his church or his schools or give his boys' brigade a gymnasium or a library is the son-in-law of a Chicago meat king, that young clergyman has, like Barbara, a very bad quarter hour. But he cannot help himself by refusing to accept money from any-body except sweet old ladies with in-dependent incomes and gentle and lovely ways of life. He has only to follow up the income of the sweet ladies to its in-dustrial source, and there he will find Mrs Warren's profession and the poisonous canned meat and all the rest of it. His own stipend has the same root. He must either share the world's guilt or go to another planet. He must save the world's honor if he is to save his own. This is what all the Churches find just as the Salvation Army and Barbara find it in the play. Her discovery that she is her father's ac-complice; that the Salvation Army is the accomplice of the distiller and the dyna-mite maker; that they can no more escape one another than they can escape the air they breathe; that there is no salvation for them through personal righteousness, but only through the redemption of the whole nation from its vicious, lazy, com-petitive anarchy: this discovery has been made by everyone except the Pharisees and (apparently) the professional play-goers, who still wear their Tom Hood shirts and underpay their washerwomen without the slightest misgiving as to the elevation of their private characters, the purity of their private atmospheres, and their right to repudiate as foreign to themselves the coarse depravity of the garret and the slum. Not that they mean any harm: they only desire to be, in their little private way, what they call gentle-men. They do not understand Barbara's lesson because they have not, like her, learnt it by taking their part in the larger life of the nation.

BARBARA'S RETURN TO THE COLORS

Barbara's return to the colors may yet provide a subject for the dramatic his-torian of the future. To go back to the Salvation Army with the knowledge that even the Salvationists themselves are not saved yet; that poverty is not blessed, but a most damnable sin; and that when General Booth chose Blood and Fire for the emblem of Salvation instead of the Cross, he was perhaps better inspired than he knew: such knowledge, for the daughter of Andrew Undershaft, will clearly lead to something hopefuller than distributing bread and treacle at the ex-pense of Bodger.

It is a very significant thing, this in-stinctive choice of the military form of organization, this substitution of the drum for the organ, by the Salvation Army. Does it not suggest that the Salvationists divine that they must actu-ally fight the devil instead of merely praying at him? At present, it is true, they have not quite ascertained his cor-rect address. When they do, they may give a very rude shock to that sense of security which he has gained from his experience of the fact that hard words, even when uttered by eloquent essayists and lecturers, or carried unanimously at enthusiastic public meetings on the motion of eminent reformers, break no bones. It has been said that the French Revolution was the work of Voltaire, Rousseau, and the Encyclopedists. It seems to me to have been the work of men who had observed that virtuous indignation, caustic criticism, conclusive argument, and instructive pamphleteer-ing, even when done by the most earnest and witty literary geniuses, were as use-less as praying, things going steadily from bad to worse whilst the Social Con-tract and the pamphlets of Voltaire were at the height of their vogue. Eventually, as we know, perfectly respectable citizens and earnest philanthropists connived at the September massacres because hard experience had convinced them that if they contented themselves with appeals to humanity and patriotism, the aristo-cracy, though it would read their appeals with the greatest enjoyment and appreciation, flattering and admiring the writers, would none the less continue to conspire with foreign monarchists to undo the revolution and restore the old system with every circumstance of savage vengeance and ruthless repression of popular liberties.

The nineteenth century saw the same lesson repeated in England. It had its Utilitarians, its Christian Socialists, its Fabians (still extant): it had Bentham, Mill, Dickens, Ruskin, Carlyle, Butler, Henry George, and Morris. And the end of all their efforts is the Chicago described by Mr Upton Sinclair, and the London in which the people who pay to be amused by my dramatic representation of Peter Shirley turned out to starve at forty because there are younger slaves to be had for his wages, do not take, and have not the slightest intention of taking, any effective step to organize society in such a way as to make that everyday infamy impossible. I, who have preached and pamphleteered like any Encyclopedist, have to confess that my methods are no use, and would be no use if I were Voltaire, Rousseau, Bentham, Marx, Mill, Dickens, Carlyle, Ruskin, Butler, and Morris all rolled into one, with Euripides, More, Montaigne, Molière, Beaumarchais, Swift, Goethe, Ibsen, Tolstoy, Jesus and the prophets all thrown in (as indeed in some sort I actually am, standing as I do on all their shoulders). The problem being to make heroes out of cowards, we paper apostles and artist-magicians have succeeded only in giving cowards all the sensations of heroes whilst they tolerate every abomination, accept every plunder, and submit to every oppression. Christianity, in making a merit of such submission, has marked only that depth in the abyss at which the very sense of shame is lost. The Christian has been like Dickens' doctor in the debtor's prison, who tells the newcomer of its ineffable peace and security: no duns; no tyrannical collectors of rates, taxes, and rent; no importunate hopes nor exacting duties; nothing but the rest and safety of having no farther to fall.

Yet in the poorest corner of this soul-destroying Christendom vitality suddenly begins to germinate again. Joyousness, a sacred gift long dethroned by the hellish laughter of derision and obscenity, rises like a flood miraculously out of the fetid dust and mud of the slums; rousing marches and impetuous dithyrambs rise to the heavens from people among whom the depressing noise called "sacred music" is a standing joke; a flag with Blood and Fire on it is unfurled, not in murderous rancor, but because fire is beautiful and blood a vital and splendid red; Fear, which we flatter by calling Self, vanishes; and transfigured men and women carry their gospel through a transfigured world, calling their leader General, themselves captains and brigadiers, and their whole body an Army: praying, but praying only for refreshment, for strength to fight, and for needful MONEY (a notable sign, that) preaching, but not preaching submission; daring ill-usage and abuse, but not putting up with more of it than is inevitable; and practising what the world will let them practise, including soap and water, color and music. There is danger in such activity; and where there is danger there is hope. Our present security is nothing, and can be nothing, but evil made irresistible.

WEAKNESSES OF THE SALVATION ARMY

For the present, however, it is not my business to flatter the Salvation Army. Rather must I point out to it that it has almost as many weaknesses as the Church of England itself. It is building up a business organization which will compel it eventually to see that its present staff of enthusiast-commanders shall be succeeded by a bureaucracy of men of business who will be no better than bishops, and perhaps a good deal more unscrupulous. That has always happened sooner or later to great orders founded by saints; and the order founded by St William Booth is not exempt from the same danger. It is even more dependent than the Church on rich people who would cut off supplies at once if it began to preach that indispensable revolt against poverty which must also be a revolt against riches. It is hampered by a heavy contingent of pious elders who are not really Salvationists at all, but Evangelicals of the old school. It still, as Commissioner Howard affirms, "sticks to Moses," which is flat nonsense at this time of day if the Commissioner means, as I am afraid he does, that the Book of Genesis contains a trustworthy scientific account of the origin of species, and that the god to whom Jephthah sacrificed his daughter is any less obviously a tribal idol than Dagon or Chemosh.

Further, there is still too much other-worldliness about the Army. Like Frederick's grenadier, the Salvationist wants to live for ever (the most monstrous way of crying for the moon); and though it is evident to anyone who has ever heard General Booth and his best officers that they would work as hard for human salvation as they do at present if they believed that death would be the end of them individually, they and their followers have a bad habit of talking as if the Salvationists were heroically enduring a very bad time on earth as an investment which will bring them in dividends later on in the form, not of a better life to come for the whole world, but of an eternity spent by themselves personally in a sort of bliss which would bore any active person to a second death. Surely the truth is that the Salvationists are unusually happy people. And is it not the very diagnostic of true salvation that it shall overcome the fear of death? Now the man who has come to believe that there is no such thing as death, the change so called being merely the transition to an exquisitely happy and utterly careless life, has not overcome the fear of death at all: on the contrary, it has overcome him so completely that he refuses to die on any terms whatever. I do not call a Salvationist really saved until he is ready to lie down cheerfully on the scrap heap, having paid scot and lot and something over, and let his eternal life pass on to renew its youth in the battalions of the future.

Then there is the nasty lying habit called confession, which the Army encourages because it lends itself to dramatic oratory, with plenty of thrilling incident. For my part, when I hear a convert relating the violences and oaths and blasphemies he was guilty of before he was saved, making out that he was a very terrible fellow then and is the most contrite and chastened of Christians now, I believe him no more than I believe the millionaire who says he came up to London or Chicago as a boy with only three half-pence in his pocket. Salvationists have said to me that Barbara in my play would never have been taken in by so transparent a humbug as Snobby Price; and certainly I do not think Snobby could have taken in any experienced Salvationist on a point on which the Salvationist did not wish to be taken in. But on the point of conversion all Salvationists wish to be taken in; for the more obvious the sinner the more obvious the miracle of his conversion. When you advertize a converted burglar or reclaimed drunkard as one of the attractions at an experience meeting, your burglar can hardly have been too burglarious or your drunkard too drunken. As long as such attractions are relied on, you will have your Snobbies claiming to have beaten their mothers when they were as a matter of prosaic fact habitually beaten by them, and your

Rummies of the tamest respectability pretending to a past of reckless and dazzling vice. Even when confessions are sincerely autobiographic we should beware of assuming that the impulse to make them was pious or that the interest of the hearers is wholesome. As well might we assume that the poor people who insist on shewing disgusting ulcers to district visitors are convinced hygienists, or that the curiosity which sometimes welcomes such exhibitions is a pleasant and creditable one. One is often tempted to suggest that those who pester our police superintendents with confessions of murder might very wisely be taken at their word and executed, except in the few cases in which a real murderer is seeking to be relieved of his guilt by confession and expiation. For though I am not, I hope, an unmerciful person, I do not think that the inexorability of the deed once done should be disguised by any ritual, whether in the confessional or on the scaffold.

And here my disagreement with the Salvation Army, and with all propagandists of the Cross (which I loathe as I loathe all gibbets) becomes deep indeed. Forgiveness, absolution, atonement, are figments: punishment is only a pretence of cancelling one crime by another; and you can no more have forgiveness without vindictiveness than you can have a cure without a disease. You will never get a high morality from people who conceive that their misdeeds are revocable and pardonable, or in a society where absolution and expiation are officially provided for us all. The demand may be very real; but the supply is spurious. Thus Bill Walker, in my play, having assaulted the Salvation Lass, presently finds himself overwhelmed with an intolerable conviction of sin under the skilled treatment of Barbara. Straightway he begins to try to unassault the lass and deruffianize his deed, first by getting

punished for it in kind, and, when that relief is denied him, by fining himself a pound to compensate the girl. He is foiled both ways. He finds the Salvation Army as inexorable as fact itself. It will not punish him: it will not take his money. It will not tolerate a redeemed ruffian: it leaves him no means of salvation except ceasing to be a ruffian. In doing this, the Salvation Army instinctively grasps the central truth of Christianity and discards its central superstition: that central truth being the vanity of revenge and punishment, and that central superstition the salvation of the world by the gibbet.

For, be it noted, Bill has assaulted an old and starving woman also; and for this worse offence he feels no remorse whatever, because she makes it clear that her malice is as great as his own. "Let her have the law of me, as she said she would," says Bill: "what I done to her is no more on what you might call my conscience than sticking a pig." This shews a perfectly natural and wholesome state of mind on his part. The old woman, like the law she threatens him with, is perfectly ready to play the game of retaliation with him: to rob him if he steals, to flog him if he strikes, to murder him if he kills. By example and precept the law and public opinion teach him to impose his will on others by anger, violence, and cruelty, and to wipe off the moral score by punishment. That is sound Crosstianity. But this Crosstianity has got entangled with something which Barbara calls Christianity, and which unexpectedly causes her to refuse to play the hangman's game of Satan casting out Satan. She refuses to prosecute a drunken ruffian; she converses on equal terms with a blackguard to whom no lady should be seen speaking in the public street: in short, she imitates Christ. Bill's conscience reacts to this just as naturally as it does to the old woman's threats. He is placed in a position of unbearable moral inferiority, and strives by every means in his power to escape from it, whilst he is still quite ready to meet the abuse of the old woman by attempting to smash a mug on her face. And that is the triumphant justification of Barbara's Christianity as against our system of judicial punishment and the vindictive villain-thrashings and "poetic justice" of the romantic stage.

For the credit of literature it must be pointed out that the situation is only partly novel. Victor Hugo long ago gave us the epic of the convict and the bishop's candlesticks, of the Crosstian policeman annihilated by his encounter with the Christian Valjean. But Bill Walker is not, like Valjean, romantically changed from a demon into an angel. There are millions of Bill Walkers in all classes of society today; and the point which I, as a professor of natural psychology, desire to demonstrate, is that Bill, without any change in his character or circumstances whatsoever, will react one way to one sort of treatment and another way to another.

In proof I might point to the sensational object lesson provided by our commercial millionaires today. They begin as brigands: merciless, unscrupulous, dealing out ruin and death and slavery to their competitors and employees, and facing desperately the worst that their competitors can do to them. The history of the English factories, the American Trusts, the exploitation of African gold, diamonds, ivory and rubber, outdoes in villainy the worst that has ever been imagined of the buccaneers of the Spanish Main. Captain Kidd would have marooned a modern Trust magnate for conduct unworthy of a gentleman of fortune. The law every day seizes on unsuccessful scoundrels of this type and punishes them with a cruelty worse than their own, with the result that they come out of the torture house more dangerous than they went in, and renew their evil doing (nobody will employ them at any-thing else) until they are again seized, again tormented, and again let loose, with the same result.

But the successful scoundrel is dealt with very differently, and very Christianly. He is not only forgiven: he is idolized, respected, made much of, all but worshipped. Society returns him good for evil in the most extravagant over-measure. And with what result? He begins to idolize himself, to respect himself, to live up to the treatment he receives. He preaches sermons; he writes books of the most edifying advice to young men, and actually persuades himself that he got on by taking his own advice; he endows educational institutions; he supports charities; he dies finally in the odor of sanctity, leaving a will which is a monument of public spirit and bounty. And all this without any change in his character. The spots of the leopard and the stripes of the tiger are as brilliant as ever; but the conduct of the world towards him has changed; and his conduct has changed accordingly. You have only to reverse your attitude towards him—to lay hands on his property, revile him, assault him, and he will be a brigand again in a moment, as ready to crush you as you are to crush him, and quite as full of pretentious moral reasons for doing it.

In short, when Major Barbara says that there are no scoundrels, she is right: there are no absolute scoundrels, though there are impracticable people of whom I shall treat presently. Every reasonable man (and woman) is a potential scoundrel and a potential good citizen. What a man is depends on his character; but what he does, and what we think of what he does, depends on his circumstances. The characteristics that ruin a man in one class make him eminent in another. The characters that behave differently in different circumstances behave alike in similar circumstances. Take a common English character like that of

F

Bill Walker. We meet Bill everywhere: on the judicial bench, on the episcopal bench, in the Privy Council, at the War Office and Admiralty, as well as in the Old Bailey dock or in the ranks of casual unskilled labor. And the morality of Bill's characteristics varies with these various circumstances. The faults of the burglar are the qualities of the financier: the manners and habits of a duke would cost a city clerk his situation. In short, though character is independent of circumstances, conduct is not; and our moral judgments of character are not: both are circumstantial. Take any condition of life in which the circumstances are for a mass of men practically alike: felony, the House of Lords, the factory, the stables, the gipsy encampment or where you please! In spite of diversity of character and temperament, the conduct and morals of the individuals in each group are as predicable and as alike in the main as if they were a flock of sheep, morals being mostly only social habits and circumstantial necessities. Strong people know this and count upon it. In nothing have the master-minds of the world been distinguished from the ordinary suburban season-ticket holder more than in their straightforward perception of the fact that mankind is practically a single species, and not a menagerie of gentlemen and bounders, villains and heroes, cowards and daredevils, peers and peasants, grocers and aristocrats, artisans and laborers, washerwomen and duchesses, in which all the grades of income and caste represent distinct animals who must not be introduced to one another or intermarry. Napoleon constructing a galaxy of generals and courtiers, and even of monarchs, out of his collection of social nobodies; Julius Cæsar appointing as governor of Egypt the son of a freedman—one who but a short time before would have been legally disqualified for the post even of a private soldier in the Roman army; Louis

XI making his barber his privy councillor: all these had in their different ways a firm hold of the scientific fact of human equality, expressed by Barbara in the Christian formula that all men are children of one father. A man who believes that men are naturally divided into upper and lower and middle classes morally is making exactly the same mistake as the man who believes that they are naturally divided in the same way socially. And just as our persistent attempts to found political institutions on a basis of social inequality have always produced long periods of destructive friction relieved from time to time by violent explosions of revolution; so the attempt—will Americans please note—to found moral institutions on a basis of moral inequality can lead to nothing but unnatural Reigns of the Saints relieved by licentious Restorations; to Americans who have made divorce a public institution turning the face of Europe into one huge sardonic smile by refusing to stay in the same hotel with a Russian man of genius who has changed wives without the sanction of South Dakota; to grotesque hypocrisy, cruel persecution, and final utter confusion of conventions and compliances with benevolence and respectability. It is quite useless to declare that all men are born free if you deny that they are born good. Guarantee a man's goodness and his liberty will take care of itself. To guarantee his freedom on condition that you approve of his moral character is formally to abolish all freedom whatsoever, as every man's liberty is at the mercy of a moral indictment which any fool can trump up against everyone who violates custom, whether as a prophet or as a rascal. This is the lesson Democracy has to learn before it can become anything but the most oppressive of all the priesthoods.

Let us now return to Bill Walker and his case of conscience against the Salvation Army. Major Barbara, not being a modern Tetzel, or the treasurer of a hospital, refuses to sell absolution to Bill for a sovereign. Unfortunately, what the Army can afford to refuse in the case of Bill Walker, it cannot refuse in the case of Bodger. Bodger is master of the situation because he holds the purse strings. "Strive as you will," says Bodger, in effect: "me you cannot do without. You cannot save Bill Walker without my money." And the Army answers, quite rightly under the circumstances, "We will take money from the devil himself sooner than abandon the work of Salvation." So Bodger pays his conscience money and gets the absolution that is refused to Bill. In real life Bill would perhaps never know this. But I, the dramatist whose business it is to shew the connexion between things that seem apart and unrelated in the haphazard order of events in real life, have contrived to make it known to Bill, with the result that the Salvation Army loses its hold of him at once.

But Bill may not be lost, for all that. He is still in the grip of the facts and of his own conscience, and may find his taste for blackguardism permanently spoiled. Still, I cannot guarantee that happy ending. Walk through the poorer quarters of our cities on Sunday when the men are not working, but resting and chewing the cud of their reflections. You will find one expression common to every mature face: the expression of cynicism. The discovery made by Bill Walker about the Salvation Army has been made by everyone there. They have found that every man has his price; and they have been foolishly or corruptly taught to mistrust and despise him for that necessary and salutary condition of social existence. When they learn that General Booth, too, has his price, they do not admire him because it is a high one, and admit the need of organizing society so that he shall get it in an honorable way: they conclude that his character is un-

sound and that all religious men are hypocrites and allies of their sweaters and oppressors. They know that the large subscriptions which help to support the Army are endowments, not of religion, but of the wicked doctrine of docility in poverty and humility under oppression; and they are rent by the most agonizing of all the doubts of the soul, the doubt whether their true salvation must not come from their most abhorrent passions, from murder, envy, greed, stubbornness, rage, and terrorism, rather than from public spirit, reasonableness, humanity, generosity, tenderness, delicacy, pity, and kindness. The confirmation of that doubt, at which our newspapers have been working so hard for years past, is the morality of militarism; and the justification of militarism is that circumstances may at any time make it the true morality of the moment. It is by producing such moments that we produce violent and sanguinary revolutions, such as the one now in progress in Russia and the one which Capitalism in England and America is daily and diligently provoking.

At such moments it becomes the duty of the Churches to evoke all the powers of destruction against the existing order. But if they do this, the existing order must forcibly suppress them. Churches are suffered to exist only on condition that they preach submission to the State as at present capitalistically organized. The Church of England itself is compelled to add to the thirtysix articles in which it formulates its religious tenets, three more in which it apologetically protests that the moment any of these articles comes in conflict with the State it is to be entirely renounced, abjured, violated, abrogated and abhorred, the policeman being a much more important person than any of the Persons of the Trinity. And this is why no tolerated Church nor Salvation Army can ever win the entire confidence of the poor.

It must be on the side of the police and the military, no matter what it believes or disbelieves; and as the police and the military are the instruments by which the rich rob and oppress the poor (on legal and moral principles made for the purpose), it is not possible to be on the side of the poor and of the police at the same time. Indeed the religious bodies, as the almoners of the rich, become a sort of auxiliary police, taking off the insurrectionary edge of poverty with coals and blankets, bread and treacle, and soothing and cheering the victims with hopes of immense and inexpensive happiness in another world when the process of working them to premature death in the service of the rich is complete in this.

CHRISTIANITY AND ANARCHISM

Such is the false position from which neither the Salvation Army nor the Church of England nor any other religious organization whatever can escape except through a reconstitution of society. Nor can they merely endure the State passively, washing their hands of its sins. The State is constantly forcing the consciences of men by violence and cruelty. Not content with exacting money from us for the maintenance of its soldiers and policemen, its gaolers and executioners, it forces us to take an active personal part in its proceedings on pain of becoming ourselves the victims of its violence. As I write these lines, a sensational example is given to the world. A royal marriage has been celebrated, first by sacrament in a cathedral, and then by a bullfight having for its main amusement the spectacle of horses gored and disembowelled by the bull, after which, when the bull is so exhausted as to be no longer dangerous, he is killed by a cautious matador. But the ironic contrast between the bullfight and the sacrament of marriage does not move anyone. Another contrast—that between the

splendor, the happiness, the atmosphere of kindly admiration surrounding the young couple, and the price paid for it under our abominable social arrangements in the misery, squalor, and degradation of millions of other young couples —is drawn at the same moment by a novelist, Mr Upton Sinclair, who chips a corner of the veneering from the huge meat packing industries of Chicago, and shews it to us as a sample of what is going on all over the world underneath the top layer of prosperous plutocracy. One man is sufficiently moved by that contrast to pay his own life as the price of one terrible blow at the responsible parties. His poverty has left him ignorant enough to be duped by the pretence that the innocent young bride and bridegroom, put forth and crowned by plutocracy as the heads of a State in which they have less personal power than any policeman, and less influence than any Chairman of a Trust, are responsible. At them accordingly he launches his sixpennorth of fulminate, missing his mark, but scattering the bowels of as many horses as any bull in the arena, and slaying twentythree persons, besides wounding ninetynine. And of all these, the horses alone are innocent of the guilt he is avenging: had he blown all Madrid to atoms with every adult person in it, not one could have escaped the charge of being an accessory, before, at, and after the fact, to poverty and prostitution, to such wholesale massacre of infants as Herod never dreamt of, to plague, pestilence, and famine, battle, murder, and lingering death—perhaps not one who had not helped, through example, precept, connivance, and even clamor, to teach the dynamiter his well-learnt gospel of hatred and vengeance, by approving every day of sentences of years of imprisonment so infernal in their unnatural stupidity and panic-stricken cruelty, that their advocates can disavow neither the dagger nor the bomb without stripping the mask of justice and humanity from themselves also.

Be it noted that at this very moment there appears the biography of one of our dukes, who, being a Scot, could argue about politics, and therefore stood out as a great brain among our aristocrats. And what, if you please, was his grace's favorite historical episode, which he declared he never read without intense satisfaction? Why, the young General Bonaparte's pounding of the Paris mob to pieces in 1795, called in playful approval by our respectable classes "the whiff of grapeshot," though Napoleon, to do him justice, took a deeper view of it, and would fain have had it forgotten. And since the Duke of Argyll was not a demon, but a man of like passions with ourselves, by no means rancorous or cruel as men go, who can doubt that all over the world proletarians of the ducal kidney are now revelling in "the whiff of dynamite" (the flavor of the joke seems to evaporate a little, does it not?) because it was aimed at the class they hate even as our argute duke hated what he called the mob.

In such an atmosphere there can be only one sequel to the Madrid explosion. All Europe burns to emulate it. Vengeance! More blood! Tear "the Anarchist beast" to shreds. Drag him to the scaffold. Imprison him for life. Let all civilized States band together to drive his like off the face of the earth; and if any State refuses to join, make war on it. This time the leading London newspaper, anti-Liberal and therefore anti-Russian in politics, does not say "Serve you right" to the victims, as it did, in effect, when Bobrikoff, and De Plehve, and Grand Duke Sergius were in the same manner unofficially fulminated into fragments. No: fulminate our rivals in Asia by all means, ye brave Russian revolutionaries; but to aim at an English princess!

monstrous! hideous! hound down the wretch to his doom; and observe, please, that we are a civilized and merciful people, and, however much we may regret it, must not treat him as Ravaillac and Damiens were treated. And meanwhile, since we have not yet caught him, let us soothe our quivering nerves with the bullfight, and comment in a courtly way on the unfailing tact and good taste of the ladies of our royal houses, who, though presumably of full normal natural tenderness, have been so effectually broken in to fashionable routine that they can be taken to see the horses slaughtered as helplessly as they could no doubt be taken to a gladiator show, if that happened to be the mode just now.

Strangely enough, in the midst of this raging fire of malice, the one man who still has faith in the kindness and intelligence of human nature is the fulminator, now a hunted wretch, with nothing, apparently, to secure his triumph over all the prisons and scaffolds of infuriate Europe except the revolver in his pocket and his readiness to discharge it at a moment's notice into his own or any other head. Think of him setting out to find a gentleman and a Christian in the multitude of human wolves howling for his blood. Think also of this: that at the very first essay he finds what he seeks, a veritable grandee of Spain, a noble, high-thinking, unterrified, malice-void soul, in the guise—of all masquerades in the world!—of a modern editor. The Anarchist wolf, flying from the wolves of plutocracy, throws himself on the honor of the man. The man, not being a wolf (nor a London editor), and therefore not having enough sympathy with his exploit to be made bloodthirsty by it, does not throw him back to the pursuing wolves—gives him, instead, what help he can to escape, and sends him off acquainted at last with a force that goes deeper than dynamite, though you cannot buy so much of it for sixpence. That righteous and honorable high human deed is not wasted on Europe, let us hope, though it benefits the fugitive wolf only for a moment. The plutocratic wolves presently smell him out. The fugitive shoots the unlucky wolf whose nose is nearest; shoots himself; and then convinces the world, by his photograph, that he was no monstrous freak of reversion to the tiger, but a good looking young man with nothing abnormal about him except his appalling courage and resolution (that is why the terrified shriek Coward at him): one to whom murdering a happy young couple on their wedding morning would have been an unthinkably unnatural abomination under rational and kindly human circumstances.

Then comes the climax of irony and blind stupidity. The wolves, balked of their meal of fellow wolf, turn on the man, and proceed to torture him, after their manner, by imprisonment, for refusing to fasten his teeth in the throat of the dynamiter and hold him down until they came to finish him.

Thus, you see, a man may not be a gentleman nowadays even if he wishes to. As to being a Christian, he is allowed some latitude in that matter, because, I repeat, Christianity has two faces. Popular Christianity has for its emblem a gibbet, for its chief sensation a sanguinary execution after torture, for its central mystery an insane vengeance bought off by a trumpery expiation. But there is a nobler and profounder Christianity which affirms the sacred mystery of Equality, and forbids the glaring futility and folly of vengeance, often politely called punishment or justice. The gibbet part of Christianity is tolerated. The other is criminal felony. Connoisseurs in irony are well aware of the fact that the only editor in England who denounces punishment as radically wrong, also repudiates Christianity; calls his paper The Freethinker; and has been imprisoned for "bad taste" under the law against blasphemy.

SANE CONCLUSIONS

And now I must ask the excited reader not to lose his head on one side or the other, but to draw a sane moral from these grim absurdities. It is not good sense to propose that laws against crime should apply to principals only and not to accessories whose consent, counsel, or silence may secure impunity to the principal. If you institute punishment as part of the law, you must punish people for refusing to punish. If you have a police, part of its duty must be to compel everybody to assist the police. No doubt if your laws are unjust, and your policemen agents of oppression, the result will be an unbearable violation of the private consciences of citizens. But that cannot be helped: the remedy is, not to license everybody to thwart the law if they please, but to make laws that will command the public assent, and not to deal cruelly and stupidly with lawbreakers. Everybody disapproves of burglars; but the modern burglar, when caught and overpowered by a householder, usually appeals, and often, let us hope, with success, to his captor not to deliver him over to the useless horrors of penal servitude. In other cases the lawbreaker escapes because those who could give him up do not consider his breach of the law a guilty action. Sometimes, even, private tribunals are formed in opposition to the official tribunals; and these private tribunals employ assassins as executioners, as was done, for example, by Mahomet before he had established his power officially, and by the Ribbon lodges of Ireland in their long struggle with the landlords. Under such circumstances, the assassin goes free although everybody in the district knows who he is and what he has done. They do not betray him, partly because they justify him exactly as the regular Government justifies its official executioner, and partly because they would themselves be assassinated if they betrayed him: another method learnt from the official government. Given a tribunal, employing a slayer who has no personal quarrel with the slain; and there is clearly no moral difference between official and unofficial killing.

In short, all men are anarchists with regard to laws which are against their consciences, either in the preamble or in the penalty. In London our worst anarchists are the magistrates, because many of them are so old and ignorant that when they are called upon to administer any law that is based on ideas or knowledge less than half a century old, they disagree with it, and being mere ordinary homebred private Englishmen without any respect for law in the abstract, naïvely set the example of violating it. In this instance the man lags behind the law; but when the law lags behind the man, he becomes equally an anarchist. When some huge change in social conditions, such as the industrial revolution of the eighteenth and nineteenth centuries, throws our legal and industrial institutions out of date, Anarchism becomes almost a religion. The whole force of the most energetic geniuses of the time in philosophy, economics, and art concentrates itself on demonstrations and reminders that morality and law are only conventions, fallible and continually obsolescing. Tragedies in which the heroes are bandits, and comedies in which law-abiding and conventionally moral folk are compelled to satirize themselves by outraging the conscience of the spectators every time they do their duty, appear simultaneously with economic treatises entitled "What is Property? Theft!" and with histories of "The Conflict between Religion and Science."

Now this is not a healthy state of things. The advantages of living in society are proportionate, not to the freedom of the individual from a code, but to the complexity and subtlety of the code he is prepared not only to accept but to uphold as a matter of such vital importance that a lawbreaker at large is hardly to be tolerated on any plea. Such an attitude becomes impossible when the only men who can make themselves heard and remembered throughout the world spend all their energy in raising our gorge against current law, current morality, current respectability, and legal property. The ordinary man, uneducated in social theory even when he is schooled in Latin verse, cannot be set against all the laws of his country and yet persuaded to regard law in the abstract as vitally necessary to society. Once he is brought to repudiate the laws and institutions he knows, he will repudiate the very conception of law and the very groundwork of institutions, ridiculing human rights, extolling brainless methods as "historical," and tolerating nothing except pure empiricism in conduct, with dynamite as the basis of politics and vivisection as the basis of science. That is hideous; but what is to be done? Here am I, for instance, by class a respectable man, by common sense a hater of waste and disorder, by intellectual constitution legally minded to the verge of pedantry, and by temperament apprehensive and economically disposed to the limit of old-maidishness; yet I am, and have always been, and shall now always be, a revolutionary writer, because our laws make law impossible; our liberties destroy all freedom; our property is organized robbery; our morality is an impudent hypocrisy; our wisdom is administered by inexperienced or malexperienced dupes, our power wielded by cowards and weaklings, and our honor false in all its points. I am an enemy of the existing order for good reasons; but that does not make my attacks any less encouraging or helpful to people who are its enemies for bad reasons. The existing order may shriek that if I tell the truth about it, some foolish person may drive it to become still worse by trying to assassinate it. I cannot help that, even if I could see what worse it could do than it is already doing. And the disadvantage of that worst even from its own point of view is that society, with all its prisons and bayonets and whips and ostracisms and starvations, is powerless in the face of the Anarchist who is prepared to sacrifice his own life in the battle with it. Our natural safety from the cheap and devastating explosives which every Russian student can make, and every Russian grenadier has learnt to handle in Manchuria, lies in the fact that brave and resolute men, when they are rascals, will not risk their skins for the good of humanity, and, when they are not, are sympathetic enough to care for humanity, abhorring murder, and never committing it until their consciences are outraged beyond endurance. The remedy is, then, simply not to outrage their consciences.

Do not be afraid that they will not make allowances. All men make very large allowances indeed before they stake their own lives in a war to the death with society. Nobody demands or expects the millennium. But there are two things that must be set right, or we shall perish, like Rome, of soul atrophy disguised as empire.

The first is, that the daily ceremony of dividing the wealth of the country among its inhabitants shall be so conducted that no crumb shall, save as a criminal's ration, go to any able-bodied adults who are not producing by their personal exertions not only a full equivalent for what they take, but a surplus sufficient to provide for their superannuation and pay back the debt due for their nurture.

The second is that the deliberate infliction of malicious injuries which now goes on under the name of punishment be abandoned; so that the thief, the ruffian, the gambler, and the beggar may without inhumanity be handed over to the law, and made to understand that a State which is too humane to punish will also be too thrifty to waste the life of honest men in watching or restraining dishonest ones. That is why we do not imprison dogs. We even take our chance of their first bite. But if a dog delights to bark and bite, it goes to the lethal chamber. That seems to me sensible. To allow the dog to expiate his bite by a period of torment, and then let him loose in a much more savage condition (for the chain makes a dog savage) to bite again and expiate again, having meanwhile spent a great deal of human life and happiness in the task of chaining and feeding and tormenting him, seems to me idiotic and superstitious. Yet that is what we do to men who bark and bite and steal. It would be far more sensible to put up with their vices, as we put up with their illnesses, until they give more trouble than they are worth, at which point we should, with many apologies and expressions of sympathy, and some generosity in complying with their last wishes, place them in the lethal chamber and get rid of them. Under no circumstances should they be allowed to expiate their misdeeds by a manufactured penalty, to subscribe to a charity, or to compensate the victims. If there is to be no punishment there can be no forgiveness. We shall never have real moral responsibility until everyone knows that his deeds are irrevocable, and that his life depends on his usefulness. Hitherto, alas! humanity has never dared face these hard facts. We frantically scatter conscience money and invent systems of conscience banking, with expiatory penalties, atonements, redemptions, salvations, hospital subscription lists and what not, to enable us to contract-out of the moral code. Not content with the old scapegoat and sacrificial lamb, we deify human saviors, and pray to miraculous virgin intercessors. We attribute mercy to the inexorable; soothe our consciences after committing murder by throwing ourselves on the bosom of divine love; and shrink even from our own gallows because we are forced to admit that it, at least, is irrevocable—as if one hour of imprisonment were not as irrevocable as any execution!

If a man cannot look evil in the face without illusion, he will never know what it really is, or combat it effectually. The few men who have been able (relatively) to do this have been called cynics, and have sometimes had an abnormal share of evil in themselves, corresponding to the abnormal strength of their minds; but they have never done mischief unless they intended to do it. That is why great scoundrels have been beneficent rulers whilst amiable and privately harmless monarchs have ruined their countries by trusting to the hocus-pocus of innocence and guilt, reward and punishment, virtuous indignation and pardon, instead of standing up to the facts without either malice or mercy. Major Barbara stands up to Bill Walker in that way, with the result that the ruffian who cannot get hated, has to hate himself. To relieve this agony he tries to get punished; but the Salvationist whom he tries to provoke is as merciless as Barbara, and only prays for him. Then he tries to pay, but can get nobody to take his money. His doom is the doom of Cain, who, failing to find either a savior, a policeman, or an almoner to help him to pretend that his brother's blood no longer cried from the ground, had to live and die a murderer. Cain took care not to commit another murder; but had he been allowed to pay off his score, he might possibly have killed Adam and Eve for the mere sake of a second luxurious reconciliation with God afterwards. Bodger, you may depend on it, will go on to the end of his life besotting people, because he can always depend on the Churches to negotiate his redemption for a trifling percentage of his profits.

There is a third condition too, which must be fulfilled before the great teachers of the world will cease to scoff at its religions. Creeds must become intellectually honest. At present there is not a single credible established religion in the world. That is perhaps the most stupendous fact in the whole world-situation. This play of mine, Major Barbara, is, I hope, both true and inspired; but whoever says that it all happened, and that faith in it and understanding of it consist in believing that it is a record of an actual occurrence, is, to speak according to Scripture, a fool and a liar, and is hereby solemnly denounced and cursed as such by me, the author, to all posterity.

POSTSCRIPT 1933. In spite of the emphasis laid both in this preface and in the play on the fact that poverty is an infectious pestilence to be prevented at all costs, the lazy habit still prevails of tolerating it not only as an inevitable misfortune to be charitably patronized and relieved, but as a useful punishment for all sorts of misconduct and inefficiency that are not expressly punishable by law. Until we have a general vital hatred of poverty, and a determination to "liquidate" the underfed either by feeding them or killing them, we shall not tackle the poverty question seriously. Long ago I proposed to eradicate the dangerous disease of hunger among children by placing good bread on public supply like drinking water. No Government nor municipality has yet taken up that very sensible proposal.

V

FANNY'S FIRST PLAY

1911

Fanny's First Play, being but a pot-boiler, needs no preface. But its lesson is not, I am sorry to say, unneeded. Mere morality, or the substitution of custom for conscience, was once accounted a shameful and cynical thing: people talked of right and wrong, of honor and dishonor, of sin and grace, of salvation and damnation, not of morality and immorality. The word morality, if we met it in the Bible, would surprise us as much as the word telephone or motor car. Nowadays we do not seem to know that there is any other test of conduct except morality; and the result is that the young had better have their souls awakened by disgrace, capture by the police, and a month's hard labor, than drift along from their cradles to their graves doing what other people do for no other reason than that other people do it, and knowing nothing of good and evil, of courage and cowardice, or indeed anything but how to keep hunger and concupiscence and fashion-able dressing within the bounds of good taste except when their excesses can be concealed. Is it any wonder that I am driven to offer to young people in our suburbs the desperate advice: Do something that will get you into trouble? But please do not suppose that I defend a state of things which makes such advice the best that can be given under the circumstances, or that I do not know how difficult it is to find out a way of getting into trouble that will combine loss of respectability with integrity of self-respect and reasonable consideration for other people's feelings and interests on every point except their dread of losing their own respectability. But when there's a will there's a way. I hate to see dead people walking about: it is unnatural. And our respectable middle-class people are all as dead as mutton. Out of the mouth of Mrs Knox I have delivered on them the judgment of her God.

VI

KILLING FOR SPORT

MARCH 1914

Sport is a difficult subject to deal with honestly. It is easy for the humanitarian to moralize against it; and any fool on its side can gush about its glorious breezy pleasures and the virtues it nourishes. But neither the moralizings nor the gushings are supported by facts: indeed they are mostly violently contradicted by them. Sportsmen are not crueller than other people. Humanitarians are not more humane than other people. The pleasures of sport are fatigues and hardships: nobody gets out of bed before sunrise on a drizzling wintry morning and rides off into darkness, cold, and rain, either for luxury or thirst for the blood of a fox cub. The humanitarian and the sportsman are often the self-same person drawing altogether unaccountable lines between pheasants and pigeons, between hares and foxes, between tame stags from the cart and wild ones from the heather, between lobsters or *paté de foie gras* and beefsteaks: above all, between man and the lower animals; for people who are sickened by the figures of a *battue* do not turn a hair over the infantile death-rate in Lisson Grove or the slums of Dundee.

Clearly the world of sport is a crystal palace in which we had better not throw stones unless we are prepared to have our own faces cut by the falling glass. My own pursuits as a critic and as a castigator of morals by ridicule (otherwise a writer of comedies) are so cruel that in point of giving pain to many worthy people I can hold my own with most dentists, and beat a skilful sportsman hollow. I know many sportsmen; and none of them are ferocious. I know several humanitarians; and they are all ferocious. No book of sport breathes such a wrathful spirit as this book of humanity. No sportsman wants to kill the fox or the pheasant as I want to kill him when I see him doing it. Callousness is not cruel. Stupidity is not cruel. Love of exercise and of feats of skill is not cruel. They may and do produce more destruction and suffering than all the neuroses of all the Neros. But they are characteristic of quite amiable and cheerful people, mostly lovers of pet animals. On the other hand, humane sensitiveness is impatient, angry, ruthless, and murderous. Marat was a supersensitive humanitarian, by profession a doctor who had practised successfully in genteel circles in England. What Marat felt towards marquesses most humanitarians feel more or less towards sportsmen. Therefore let no sportsman who reads these pages accuse me of hypocrisy, or of claiming to be a more amiable person than he. And let him excuse me, if he will be so good, for beginning with an attempt to describe how I feel about sport.

To begin with, sport soon bores me when it does not involve killing; and when it does, it affects me much as the murder of a human being would affect me, rather more than less; for just as the murder of a child is more shocking than the murder of an adult (because, I suppose, the child is so helpless and the breach of social faith therefore so unconscionable), the murder of an animal is an abuse of man's advantage over animals: the proof being that when the animal is powerful and dangerous, and the man unarmed, the repulsion vanishes and is replaced by congratulation. But quite humane and cultivated people seem unable to understand why I should bother about the feelings of animals. I have seen the most horrible pictures published in good faith as attractive in illustrated magazines. One of them, which I wish I could forget, was a photograph taken on a polar expedition, shewing a murdered bear with its living cub trying to make it attend to its maternal duties. I have seen a photograph of a criminal being cut into a thousand pieces by a Chinese executioner, which was by comparison amusing. I have also seen thrown on a screen for the entertainment of a large audience a photograph of an Arctic explorer taking away a sledge dog to shoot it for food, the dog jumping about joyously without the least suspicion of its human friend's intentions. If the doomed dog had been a man or a woman, I believe I should have had less sense of treachery. I do not say that this is reasonable: I simply state it as a fact. It was quite evident that the lecturer had no suspicion of the effect the picture was producing on me; and as far as I could see, his audience was just as callous; for if they had all felt as I felt there would have been at least a very perceptible shudder, if not an articulate protest. Now this was not a case of sport. It was necessary to shoot the dog: I should have shot it myself under the same circumstances. But I should have regarded the necessity as a horrible one; and I should have presented it to the audience as a painful episode, like cannibalism in a crew of castaways, and not as a joke. For I must add that a good many people present regarded it as a bit of fun. I absolve the lecturer from this extremity of insensibility. The shooting of a dog was a trifle to what he had endured; and I did not blame him for thinking it by comparison a trivial matter. But to us, who had endured nothing, it might have seemed a little hard on the dog, and calling for some apology from the man.

I am driven to the conclusion that my sense of kinship with animals is greater than most people feel. It amuses me to talk to animals in a sort of jargon I have invented for them; and it seems to me that it amuses them to be talked to, and that they respond to the tone of the conversation, though its intellectual content may to some extent escape them. I am quite sure, having made the experiment several times on dogs left in my care as part of the furniture of hired houses, that an animal who has been treated as a brute, and is consequently undeveloped socially (as human beings remain socially undeveloped under the same circumstances), will, on being talked to as a fellow-creature, become friendly and companionable in a very short time. This process has been described by some reproachful dog owners as spoiling the dog, and sincerely deplored by them, because I am glad to say it is easier to do than to undo except by brutalities of which few people are capable. But I find it impossible to associate with animals on any other terms. Further, it gives me extraordinary gratification to find a wild bird treating me with confidence, as robins sometimes do. It pleases me to conciliate an animal who is hostile to me. What is more, an animal who will not be conciliated offends me. There is at the Zoo a morose maned lion who will tear you to pieces if he gets half a chance. There is also a very handsome maneless lion with whom you may play more safely than with most St Bernard dogs, as he seems to need nothing but plenty of attention and admiration to put him into the best of humors. I do not feel towards these two lions as a carpenter does towards two pieces of wood, one hard and knotty, and the other easy to work; nor as I do towards two motor bicycles, one troublesome and dangerous, and the other in perfect order. I feel towards the two lions as I should towards two men similarly diverse. I like one and dislike the other. If they got loose and were shot, I should be distressed in the one case whilst in the other I should say "Serve the brute right!" This is clearly fellow-feeling. And it seems to me that the plea of the humanitarian is a plea for widening the range of fellow-feeling.

The limits of fellow-feeling are puzzling. People who have it in a high degree for animals often seem utterly devoid of it for human beings of a different class. They will literally kill their dogs with kindness whilst behaving to their servants with such utter inconsideration that they have to change their domestic staff once a month or oftener. Or they hate horses and like snakes. One could fill pages with such inconsistencies. The lesson of these apparent contradictions is that fellow-feeling is a matter of dislikes as well as of likes. No man wants to destroy the engine which catches him in its cog-wheels and tears a limb from him. But many a man has tried to kill another man for a very trifling slight. The machine, not being our fellow, cannot be loved or hated. The man, being our fellow, can.

Let us try to get down to the bottom of this matter. There is no use in saying that our fellow-creatures must not be killed. That is simply untrue; and the converse proposal that they must be killed is simply true. We see the Buddhist having his path swept before him lest he should tread on an insect and kill it; but we do not see what that Buddhist does when he catches a flea that has kept him awake for an hour; and we know that he has to except certain poisonous snakes from his forbearance. If mice get into your house and you do not kill them, they will end by killing you. If rabbits breed on your farm and you do not exterminate them, you will end by having no farm. If you keep deer in your park and do not thin them, your neighbors or the authorities will finally have to save you the trouble. If you hold the life of a mosquito sacred, malaria and yellow fever will not return the compliment. I have had an interview with an adder, in the course of which it struck repeatedly and furiously at my stick; and I let it go unharmed; but if I were the mother of a family of young children, and I found a cobra in the garden, I would vote for "*La mort sans phrase*," as many humane and honorable persons voted in the case, not of a serpent, but of an anointed king.

I see no logical nor spiritual escape from the theory that evolution (not, please observe, Natural Selection) involves a deliberate intentional destruction by the higher forms of life of the lower. It is a dangerous and difficult business; for in the course of natural selection the lower forms may have become necessary to the existence of the higher; and the gamekeeper shooting everything that could hurt his pheasants or their chicks may be behaving as foolishly as an Arab lunatic shooting horses and camels. But where Man comes, the megatherium must go as surely as where the poultry farmer comes the fox must go unless the hunt will pay for the fox's depredations. To plead for the tiger, the wolf, and the poisonous snake, is as useless as to plead for the spirochete or the tetanus bacillus: we must frankly class these as early and disastrous experiments in creation, and accept it as part of the mission of the later and more successful experiments to recognize them as superseded, and to destroy them purposely. We should, no doubt, be very careful how we jump from the indisputable general law that the higher forms of life must exterminate or limit the lower, to the justification of any particular instance of the slaughter of non-human animals by men, or the slaughter of a low type of man by a high type of man. Still, when all due reservations are made, the fact remains that a war of extermination is being waged daily and necessarily by man against his rivals for possession of the earth, and that though an urban humanitarian and vegetarian who never has occasion to kill anything but a microbe may shudder at the callousness with which a farmer kills rats and rabbits and sparrows and moles and caterpillars and ladybirds and many more charming creatures, yet if he were in the farmer's place he would have to do exactly the same, or perish.

In that case why not make a pleasure of necessity, and a virtue of pleasure, as the sportsmen do? I think we must own that there is no objection from the point of view of the animals. On the contrary, it is quite easy to shew that there is a positive advantage to them in the organization of killing as sport. Fox hunting has saved the existing foxes from extermination; and if it were not for the civilization that makes fox hunting possible, the fox would still be hunted and killed by packs of wolves. I am so conscious of this that I have in another place suggested that children should be hunted or shot during certain months of the year, as they would then be fed and preserved by the sportsmen of the counties as generously and carefully as pheasants now are; and the survivors would make a much better nation than our present slum products. And I go further. I maintain that the abolition of public executions was a very bad thing for the murderers. Before that time, we did exactly as our sportsmen now do. We made a pleasure of the necessity for exterminating murderers, and a virtue of the pleasure. Hanging was a popular sport, like racing. Huge crowds assembled to see it and paid large prices for seats. There would have been betting on the result if it had been at all uncertain. The criminal had what all criminals love: a large audience. He had a procession to Tyburn: he had a drink: he was allowed to make a speech if he could; and if he could not, the speech was made for him and published and sold in great numbers. Above all, such fair play as an execution admits of was guaranteed to him by the presence of the public, whereas now he perishes in a horrible secrecy which

lends itself to all the abuses of secrecy. Whether the creature slain be man or what we very invidiously call brute, there is no case to be made against sport on its behalf. Even cruelty can justify itself, as far as the victim is concerned, on the ground that it makes sport attractive to cruel people, and that sport is good for the quarry.

The true objection to sport is the one taken by that wise and justly famous Puritan who objected to bear baiting not because it gave pain to the bear but because it gave pleasure to the spectators. He rightly saw that it was not important that we should be men of pleasure, and that it was enormously important that we should be men of honor. What the bear would have said if it had had any say in the matter can only be conjectured. Its captors might have argued that if they could not have made money by keeping it alive whilst taking it to England to be baited, they would have killed it at sight in the Pyrenees; so that it owed several months of life, with free board and lodging, to the institution of bear baiting. The bear might have replied that if it had not been for the bear pit in England they would never have come to hunt for it in the Pyrenees, where it could have ended its days in a free and natural manner. Let us admit for the sake of a quiet life that the point is disputable. What is not disputable by any person who has ever seen sport of this character is that the man who enjoys it is degraded by it. We do not bait bears now (I do not quite know why); but we course rabbits in the manner described in one of the essays in this book. I lived for a time on the south slope of the Hog's Back; and every Sunday morning rabbits were coursed within earshot of me. And I noticed that it was quite impossible to distinguish the cries of the excited terriers from the cries of the sportsmen, although ordinarily the voice of a man is no more like the voice of a dog than like the voice of a nightingale. Sport reduced them all, men and terriers alike, to a common denominator of bestiality. The sound did not make me more humane: on the contrary, I felt that if I were an irresponsible despot with a park of artillery at my disposal, I should (especially after seeing the sportsmen on their way to and from their sport) have said: "These people have become subhuman, and will be better dead. Be kind enough to mow them down for me."

As a matter of fact there is always a revulsion against these dehumanizing sports in which the killing can be seen, and the actual visible chase shared, by human beings: in short, the sports in which men revert to the excitements of beasts of prey. Several have been abolished by law: among them bear baiting and cock fighting: both of them sports in which the spectators shared at close quarters the excitement of the animals engaged. In the sports firmly established among us there is much less of this abomination. In fox hunting and shooting, predatory excitement is not a necessary part of the sport, and is indeed abhorred by many who practise it. Inveterate foxhunters have been distressed and put off their hunting for days by happening to see a fox in the last despairing stage of its run from the hounds: a sight which can be avoided, and often is, by the hunters, but which they may happen upon some day when they are not hunting. Such people hunt because they delight in meets and in gallops across country as social and healthy incidents of country life. They are proud of their horsemanship and their craftiness in taking a line. They like horses and dogs and exercise and wind and weather, and are unconscious of the fact that their expensive and well equipped hunting stables and kennels are horse prisons and dog prisons. It is useless to pretend that these ladies and gentlemen are fiends in human form: they

clearly are not. By avoiding being in at the death they get all the good out of hunting without incurring the worst of the evil, and so come out with a balance in their favor.

Shooting is subtler: it is a matter of skill with one's weapons. The expert at it is called, not a good chicken butcher, but a good shot. When I want, as I often do, to pick him off, I do so not because I feel that he is cruel or degraded but because he is a nuisance to me with the very disagreeable noise of his explosions, and because there is an unbearable stupidity in converting an interesting, amusing, prettily colored live wonder like a pheasant into a slovenly unhandsome corpse. But at least he does not yap like a terrier, and shake with a detestable excitement, and scream out frantic bets to bookmakers. His expression is that of a man performing a skilled operation with an instrument of precision: an eminently human expression, quite incompatible with the flush of blood to the eyes and the uncovering of the dog-tooth that makes a man like a beast of prey. And this is why it is impossible to feel that skilled shooting or foxhunting are as abominable as rabbit coursing, hare-hunting with beagles, or otter-hunting.

And yet shooting depends for its toleration on custom as much as on the coolness with which it has to be performed. It may be illogical to forgive a man for shooting a pheasant and to loathe him for shooting a seagull; but as a matter of plain fact one feels that a man who shoots seagulls is a cad, and soon makes him feel it if he attempts to do it on board a public ship, whereas the snipe shooter excites no such repulsion. And "fair game" must be skilfully shot if the maximum of toleration is to be enjoyed. Even then it is not easy for some of us to forget that many a bird must have been miserably maimed before the shooter perfected his skill. The late King Edward the Seventh, immediately after his recovery from a serious operation which stirred the whole nation to anxious sympathy with him, shot a stag, which got away to die of just such internal inflammation as its royal murderer had happily escaped. Many people read the account without the least emotion. Others thought it natural that the King should be ashamed, as a marksman, of his failure to kill, but rejected as sentimental nonsense the notion that he should feel any remorse on the stag's behalf. Had he deliberately shot a cow instead, everyone would have been astounded and horrified. Custom will reconcile people to any atrocity; and fashion will drive them to acquire any custom. The English princess who sits on the throne of Spain goes to bullfights because it is the Spanish fashion. At first she averted her face, and probably gave offence by doing so. Now, no doubt, she is a *connoisseuse* of the sport. Yet neither she nor the late King Edward can be classed as cruel monsters. On the contrary, they are conspicuous examples of the power of cruel institutions to compel the support and finally win the tolerance and even the enjoyment of persons of full normal benevolence.

But this is not why I call shooting subtle. It fascinates even humane persons, not only because it is a game of skill in the use of the most ingenious instrument in general use, but because killing by craft from a distance is a power that makes a man divine rather than human.

Oft have I struck
Those that I never saw, and struck them dead

said the statesman to Jack Cade (who promptly hanged him); and something of the sense of power in that boast stimulates every boy with a catapult and every man with a gun. That is why there is an interest in weapons fathoms deeper than the interest in cricket bats and golf clubs. It is not a question of skill or risk. The men who go to Africa with cameras and obtain photographs and even cinematographs of the most dangerous animals at close quarters, shew much more skill and nerve than the gentlemen who disgust us with pictures of themselves sitting on the body of the huge creatures they have just killed with explosive bullets. Shooting "big game," like serving as a soldier in the field, is glorified conventionally as a proof of character and courage, though everyone knows that men can be found by the hundred thousand to face such ordeals, including several who would be afraid to walk down Bond Street in an unfashionable hat. The real point of the business is neither character nor courage, but ability to kill. And the greater cowards and the feebler weaklings we are, the more important this power is to us. It is a matter of life and death to us to be able to kill our enemies without coming to handgrips with them; and the consequence is that our chief form of play is to pretend that something is our enemy and kill it. Even to pretend to kill it is some satisfaction: nay, the spectacle of other people pretending to do it is a substitute worth paying for. Nothing more supremely ridiculous as a subject of reasonable contemplation could be imagined than a sham fight in Earl's Court between a tribe of North American Indians and a troop of cowboys, both imported by Buffalo Bill as a theatrical speculation. To see these grown-up men behaving like children, galloping about and firing blank cartridges at one another, and pretending to fall down dead, was absurd and incredible enough from any rational point of view; but that thousands of respectable middle-aged and elderly citizens and their wives, all perfectly sober, should pay to be allowed to look on, seems flat madness. Yet the thing not only occurred in London, but occurs now daily in the cinema theatres and yearly at the Military Tournaments. And what honest man dare pretend that he gets no fun out of these spectacles? Certainly not I. They revived enough of my boyish delight in stage fights and in the stories of Captain Mayne Reid to induce me to sit them out, conscious as I was of their silliness.

Please do not revile me for telling you what I felt instead of what I ought to have felt. What prevents the sport question and every other question from getting squarely put before us is our habit of saying that the things we think should disgust us and fill us with abhorrence actually do disgust us and fill us with abhorrence, and that the persons who, against all reason and decency, find some sort of delight in them, are vile wretches quite unlike ourselves, though, as everyone can see, we and they are as like as potatoes. You may not agree with Mr Rudyard Kipling about war, or with Colonel Roosevelt about sport; but beware how you pretend that war does not interest and excite you more than printing, or that the thought of bringing down a springing tiger with a well-aimed shot does not interest you more than the thought of cleaning your teeth. Men may be as the poles asunder in their speculative views. In their actual nervous and emotional reactions they are "members one of another" to a much greater extent than they choose to confess. The reason I have no patience with Colonel Roosevelt's tedious string of rhinoceros murders in South Africa is not that I am not interested in weapons, in marksmanship, and in killing, but because my interest in life and creation is still greater than my interest in death and destruction, and because I have sufficient fellow-feeling with a rhinoceros to think it a frightful thing that it should be killed for fun.

Consider a moment how one used to feel when an Irish peasant shot his landlord, or when a grand duke was blown to pieces in Russia, or when one read of how Charlotte Corday killed Marat. On the one hand we applauded the courage, the skill, the resolution of the assassin; we exulted in the lesson taught to tyrants and in the overthrow of the strong oppressor by the weak victim; but we were horrified by the breach of law, by the killing of the accused at the decree of an irresponsible Ribbon Lodge under no proper public control, by the execution of the grand duke without trial and opportunity of defence, by the suspicion that Charlotte Corday was too like Marat in her lust for the blood of oppressors to have the right to kill him. Such cases are extremely complicated, except for those simple victims of political or class prejudice who think Charlotte Corday a saint because she killed a Radical, and the Ribbonmen demons because they were common fellows who dared to kill country gentlemen. But however the cases catch us, there is always that peculiar interest in individual killing, and consequently in the means and weapons by which individuals can kill their enemies, which is at the root of the sport of shooting.

It all comes back to fellow-feeling and appetite for fruitful activity and a high quality of life: there is nothing else to appeal to. No commandment can meet the case. It is no use saying "Thou shalt not kill" in one breath, and in the next "Thou shalt not suffer a witch to live." Men must be killed and animals must be killed: nay, whole species of animals and types of men must be exterminated before the earth can become a tolerable place of habitation for decent folk. But among the men who will have to be wiped out stands the sportsman: the man without fellow-feeling, the man so primitive and uncritical in his tastes that the destruction of life is an amusement to him, the man whose outlook is as narrow as that of his dog. He is not even cruel: sport is partly a habit to which he has been brought up, and partly stupidity, which can always be measured by wastefulness and by lack of sense of the importance and glory of life. The horrible murk and grime of the Pottery towns is caused by indifference to a stupid waste of sunlight, natural beauty, cleanliness, and pleasant air, combined with a brutish appetite for money. A *battue* is caused by indifference to the beauty and interest of bird life and song, and callousness to glazed eyes and blood-bedabbled corpses, combined with a boyish love of shooting. All the people who waste beauty and life in this way are characterized by deficiency in fellow-feeling: not only have they none of St Francis's feeling that the birds are of our kin, but they would be extremely indignant if a loader or a gamekeeper asserted any claim to belong to their species. Sport is a sign either of limitation or of timid conventionality.

And this disposes of the notion that sport is the training of a conquering race. Even if such things as conquering races existed, or would be tolerable if they did exist, they would not be races of sportsmen. The red scalp-hunting braves of North America were the sportingest race imaginable; and they were conquered as easily as the bisons they hunted. The French can boast more military glory to the square inch of history than any other nation; but until lately they were the standing butt of English humorists for their deficiencies as sportsmen. In the Middle Ages, when they fought as sportsmen and gentlemen, they were annihilated by small bodies of starving Englishmen who carefully avoided sportsmanlike methods and made a laborious business (learnt at the village target) of killing them. As to becoming accustomed to risks, there are plenty of ways of doing that without killing anything except occasionally yourself. The motor cyclist takes more trying risks than the fox-hunter; and motor cycling seems safety itself compared to aviation. A dive from a high springboard will daunt a man as effectually as a stone wall in the hunting field. The notion that if you have no sportsmen you will have no soldiers (as if more than the tiniest fraction of the armies of the world had ever been sportsmen) is as absurd as the notion that burglars and garrotters should be encouraged because they might make hardier and more venturesome soldiers than honest men; but since people foolishly do set up such arguments they may as well be mentioned in passing for what they are worth.

The question then comes to this: Which is the superior man? the man whose pastime is slaughter, or the man whose pastime is creative or contemplative? I have no doubt about the matter myself, being on the creative and contemplative side by nature. Slaughter is necessary work, like scavenging; but the man who not only does it unnecessarily for love of it but actually makes as much of it as possible by breeding live things to slaughter, seems to me to be little more respectable than one who befouls the streets for the pleasure of sweeping them. I believe that the line of evolution leads to the prevention of the birth of creatures whose lives are not useful and enjoyable, and that the time will come when a gentleman found amusing himself with a gun will feel as compromised as he does now when found amusing himself with a whip at the expense of a child or an old lame horse covered with sores. Sport, like murder, is a bloody business; and the sportsmen will not always be able to outface that fact as they do at present.

But there is something else. Killing, if it is to give us heroic emotions, must not be done for pleasure. Interesting though the slaying of one man by another may be, it is abhorrent when it is done merely for the fun of doing it (the sportsman's way) or to satisfy the envious spite of the worse man towards the better (Cain's way). When Charlotte Corday stabbed Marat, and when Hamilton of Bothwellhaugh shot the Regent Murray, they were stung by intolerable social wrongs for which the law offered them no redress. When Brutus and his fellow-conspirators killed Cæsar, they had persuaded themselves that they were saving Rome. When Samson slew the lion, he had every reason to feel convinced that if he did not, the lion would slay him. Conceive Charlotte Corday stabbing Marat as an exercise of manual and anatomical skill, or Hamilton bringing down the Regent as a feat of marksmanship! Their deeds at once become, not less, but more horrifying than if they had done them from a love of killing. Jack the Ripper was a madman of the most appalling sort; but the fascination of murder for him must have been compounded of dread, of horror, and of a frightful perversion of an instinct which in its natural condition is a kindly one. He was a ghastly murderer; but he was a hot-blooded one. The perfection of callousness is not reached until a life is sacrificed, and often cruelly sacrificed, solely as a feat of skill. Peter the Great amusing himself by torturing his son to death was a revolting monster; but he was not so utterly inhuman in that crime as he was when, on being interested by a machine for executing criminals which he saw in a museum on his travels, he proposed to execute one of his retinue to see how the machine worked, and could with difficulty be brought to understand that there was a sentimental objection to the proceeding on the part of his hosts which made the experiment impossible. When he tortured his son he knew that he was committing an abomination. When he wanted to try an experiment at the cost of a servant's life he was unconscious of doing anything that was not a matter of course for any nobleman. And in this he was worse than abominable: he was deficient, imbecile, less than human. Just so is the sportsman, shooting quite skilfully and coolly without the faintest sense of any murderous

excitement, and with no personal feeling against the birds, really further from salvation than the man who is humane enough to get some sense of wickedness out of his sport. To have one's fellow-feeling corrupted and perverted into a lust for cruelty and murder is hideous; but to have no fellow-feeling at all is to be something less than even a murderer. The man who sees red is more complete than the man who is blind.

The triviality of sport as compared with the risk and trouble of its pursuit and the gravity of its results makes it much sillier than crime. The idler who can find nothing better to do than to kill is past our patience. If a man takes on himself the heavy responsibility of killing, he should not do it for pastime. Pastimes are very necessary; for though a busy man can always find something to do, there comes a point at which his health, his sanity, his very existence may depend on his doing nothing of the smallest importance; and yet he cannot sit still and twiddle his thumbs: besides, he requires bodily exercise. He needs an idle pastime. Now "Satan finds some mischief still for idle hands to do" if the idler lets his conscience go to sleep. But he need not let it go to sleep. There are plenty of innocent idle pastimes for him. He can read detective stories. He can play tennis. He can drive a motor car if he can afford one. He can fly. Satan may suggest that it would be a little more interesting to kill something; but surely only an outrageous indifference to the sacredness of life and the horrors of suffering and terror, combined with a monstrously selfish greed for sensation, could drive a man to accept the Satanic suggestion if sport were not organized for him as a social institution. Even as it is, there are now so many other pastimes available that the choice of killing is becoming more and more a disgrace to the chooser. The wantonness of the choice is beyond excuse. To kill as the poacher does, to sell or eat the victim, is at least to act reasonably. To kill from hatred or revenge is at least to behave passionately. To kill in gratification of a lust for death is at least to behave villainously. Reason, passion, and villainy are all human. But to kill, being all the time quite a good sort of fellow, merely to pass away the time when there are a dozen harmless ways of doing it equally available, is to behave like an idiot or a silly imitative sheep.

Surely the broad outlook and deepened consciousness which admits all living things to the commonwealth of fellow-feeling, and the appetite for fruitful activity and generous life which come with it, are better than this foolish doing of unamiable deeds by people who are not in the least unamiable.

MAN AND SUPERMAN

1901–3

EPISTLE DEDICATORY

TO ARTHUR BINGHAM WALKLEY

My dear Walkley

You once asked me why I did not write a Don Juan play. The levity with which you assumed this frightful responsibility has probably by this time enabled you to forget it; but the day of reckoning has arrived: here is your play! I say your play, because *qui facit per alium facit per se.* Its profits, like its labor, belong to me: its morals, its manners, its philosophy, its influence on the young, are for you to justify. You were of mature age when you made the suggestion; and you knew your man. It is hardly fifteen years since, as twin pioneers of the New Journalism of that time, we two, cradled in the same new sheets, began an epoch in the criticism of the theatre and the opera house by making it the pretext for a propaganda of our own views of life. So you cannot plead ignorance of the character of the force you set in motion. You meant me to épater le bourgeois; and if he protests, I hereby refer him to you as the accountable party.

I warn you that if you attempt to repudiate your responsibility, I shall suspect you of finding the play too decorous for your taste. The fifteen years have made me older and graver. In you I can detect no such becoming change. Your levities and audacities are like the loves and comforts prayed for by Desdemona: they increase, even as your days do grow. No mere pioneering journal dares meddle with them now: the stately Times itself is alone sufficiently above suspicion to act as your chaperone; and even the Times must sometimes thank its stars that new plays are not produced every day, since after each such event its gravity is compromised, its platitude turned to epigram, its portentousness to wit, its propriety to elegance, and even its decorum into naughtiness by criticisms which the traditions of the paper do not allow you to sign at the end, but which you take care to sign with the most extravagant flourishes between the lines. I am not sure that this is not a portent of Revolution. In eighteenth century France the end was at hand when men bought the Encyclopedia and found Diderot there. When I buy the Times and find you there, my prophetic ear catches a rattle of twentieth century tumbrils

However, that is not my present anxiety. The question is, will you not be disappointed with a Don Juan play in which not one of that hero's *mille e tre* adventures is brought upon the stage? To propitiate you, let me explain myself. You will retort that I never do anything else: it is your favorite jibe at me that what I call drama is nothing but explanation. But you must not expect me to adopt your inexplicable, fantastic, petulant, fastidious ways: you must take me as I am, a reasonable, patient, consistent, apologetic, laborious person, with the temperament of a schoolmaster and the pursuits of a vestryman. No doubt that literary knack of mine which happens to amuse the British public distracts attention from my character; but the character is there none the less, solid as bricks. I have a conscience; and conscience is always anxiously explanatory. You, on the contrary, feel that a man who discusses his conscience is much like a woman who discusses her modesty. The only moral force you condescend to parade is the force of your wit: the only demand you make in public is the demand of your artistic temperament for symmetry, elegance, style, grace, refinement, and the cleanliness which comes next to godliness if not before it. But my conscience is the genuine pulpit article: it annoys me to see people comfortable when they ought to be uncomfortable; and I insist on making them think in order to bring them to conviction of sin. If you dont like my preaching you must lump it. I really cannot help it.

In the preface to my Plays for Puritans I explained the predicament of our contemporary English drama, forced to deal almost exclusively with cases of sexual attraction, and yet forbidden to exhibit the incidents of that attraction or even to discuss its nature. Your suggestion that I should write a Don Juan play was virtually a challenge to me to treat this subject myself dramatically. The challenge was difficult enough to be worth accepting, because, when you come to think of it, though we have plenty of dramas with heroes and heroines who are in love and must accordingly marry or perish at the end of the play, or about people whose relations with one another have been complicated by the marriage laws, not to mention the looser sort of plays which trade on the tradition that illicit love affairs are at once vicious and delightful, we have no modern English plays in which the natural attraction of the sexes for one another is made the mainspring of the action. That is why we insist on beauty in our performers, differing herein from the countries our friend William Archer holds up as examples of seriousness to our childish theatres. There the Juliets and Isoldes, the Romeos and Tristans, might be our mothers and fathers. Not so the English actress. The heroine she impersonates is not allowed to discuss the elemental relations of men and women: all her romantic twaddle about novelet-made love, all her purely legal dilemmas as to whether she was married or "betrayed," quite miss our hearts and worry our minds. To console ourselves we must just look at her. We do so; and her beauty feeds our starving emotions. Sometimes we grumble ungallantly at the lady because she does not act as well as she looks. But in a drama which, with all its preoccupation with sex, is really void of sexual interest, good looks are more desired than histrionic skill.

Let me press this point on you, since you are too clever to raise the fool's cry of paradox whenever I take hold of a stick by the right instead of the wrong end. Why are our occasional attempts to deal with the sex problem on the stage so repulsive and dreary that even those who are most determined that sex questions shall be held open and their discussion kept free, cannot pretend to relish these joyless attempts at social sanitation? Is it not because at bottom they are utterly sexless? What is the usual formula for such plays? A woman has, on some past occasion, been brought into conflict with the law which regulates the relations of the sexes. A man, by falling in love with her, or marrying her, is brought into conflict with the social convention which discountenances the woman. Now the conflicts of individuals with law and convention can be dramatized like all other human conflicts; but they are purely judicial; and the fact that we are much more curious about the suppressed relations between the man and the woman than about the relations between both and our courts of law and private juries of matrons, produces that sensation of evasion, of dissatisfaction, of fundamental irrelevance, of shallowness, of useless disagreeableness, of total failure to edify and partial failure to interest, which is as familiar to you in the theatres as it was to me when I, too, frequented those uncomfortable buildings, and found our popular playwrights in the mind to (as they thought) emulate Ibsen.

I take it that when you asked me for a Don Juan play you did not want that sort of thing. Nobody does: the successes such plays sometimes obtain are due to the incidental conventional melodrama with which the experienced popular author instinctively saves himself from failure. But what did you want? Owing to your unfortunate habit—you now, I hope, feel its inconvenience—of not explaining yourself, I have had to discover this for myself. First, then, I have had to ask myself, what is a Don Juan? Vulgarly, a libertine. But your dislike of vulgarity is pushed to the length of a defect (universality of character is impossible without a share of vulgarity); and even if you could acquire the taste, you would find yourself overfed from ordinary sources without troubling me. So I took it that you demanded a Don Juan in the philosophic sense.

Philosophically, Don Juan is a man who, though gifted enough to be exceptionally capable of distinguishing between good and evil, follows his own instincts without regard to the common, statute, or canon law; and therefore, whilst gaining the ardent sympathy of our rebellious instincts (which are flattered by the brilliancies with which Don Juan associates them) finds himself in mortal conflict with existing institutions, and defends himself by fraud and force as unscrupulously as a farmer defends his crops by the same means against vermin. The prototypic Don Juan, invented early in the XVI century by a Spanish monk, was presented, according to the ideas of that time, as the enemy of God, the approach of whose vengeance is felt throughout the drama, growing in menace from minute to minute. No anxiety is caused on Don Juan's account by any minor antagonist: he easily eludes the police, temporal and spiritual; and when an indignant father seeks private redress with the sword, Don Juan kills him without an effort. Not until the slain father returns from heaven as the agent of God, in the form of his own statue, does he prevail against his slayer and cast him into hell. The moral is a monkish one: repent and reform now; for tomorrow it may be too late. This is really the only point on which Don Juan is sceptical; for he is a devout believer in an ultimate hell, and risks damnation only because, as he is young, it seems so far off that repentance can be postponed until he has amused himself to his heart's content.

But the lesson intended by an author is hardly ever the lesson the world chooses to learn from his book. What attracts and impresses us in El Burlador de Sevilla is not the immediate urgency of repentance, but the heroism of daring to be the enemy of God. From Prometheus to my own Devil's Disciple, such enemies have always been popular. Don Juan became such a pet that the world could not bear his damnation. It reconciled him sentimentally to God in a second version, and clamored for his canonization for a whole century, thus treating him as English journalism has treated that comic foe of the gods, Punch. Molière's Don Juan casts back to the original in point of impenitence; but in piety he falls off greatly. True, he also proposes to repent; but in what terms! "Oui, ma foi! il faut s'amender. Encore vingt ou trente ans de cette vie-ci, et puis nous songerons à nous." After Molière comes the artist-enchanter, the master beloved by masters, Mozart, revealing the hero's spirit in magical harmonies, elfin tones, and elate darting rhythms as of summer lightning made audible. Here you have freedom in love and in morality mocking exquisitely at slavery to them, and interesting you, attracting you, tempting you, inexplicably forcing you to range the hero with his enemy the statue on a transcendent plane, leaving the prudish daughter and her priggish lover on a crockery shelf below to live piously ever after.

After these completed works Byron's fragment does not count for much philosophically. Our vagabond libertines are no more interesting from that point of view than the sailor who has a wife in every port; and Byron's hero is, after all, only a vagabond libertine. And he is dumb: he does not discuss himself with a Sganarelle-Leporello or with the fathers or brothers of his mistresses: he does not even, like Casanova, tell his own story. In fact he is not a true Don Juan at all; for he is no more an enemy of God than any romantic and adventurous young sower of wild oats. Had you and I been in his place at his age, who knows whether we might not have done as he did, unless indeed your fastidiousness had saved you from the empress Catherine. Byron was as little of a philosopher as Peter the Great: both were instances of that rare and useful, but unedifying variation, an energetic genius born without the prejudices or superstitions of his contemporaries. The resultant unscrupulous freedom of thought made Byron a bolder poet than Wordsworth just as it made Peter a bolder king than George III; but as it was, after all, only a negative qualification, it did not prevent Peter from being an appalling blackguard and an arrant poltroon, nor did it enable Byron to become a religious force like Shelley. Let us, then, leave Byron's Don Juan out of account. Mozart's is the last of the true Don Juans; for by the time he was of age, his cousin Faust had, in the hands of Goethe, taken his place and carried both his warfare and his reconciliation with the gods far beyond mere lovemaking into politics, high art,

schemes for reclaiming new continents from the ocean, and recognition of an eternal womanly principle in the universe. Goethe's Faust and Mozart's Don Juan were the last words of the XVIII century on the subject; and by the time the polite critics of the XIX century, ignoring William Blake as superficially as the XVIII had ignored Hogarth or the XVII Bunyan, had got past the Dickens-Macaulay Dumas-Guizot stage and the Stendhal-Meredith-Turgenieff stage, and were confronted with philosophic fiction by such pens as Ibsen's and Tolstoy's, Don Juan had changed his sex and become Doña Juana, breaking out of the Doll's House and asserting herself as an individual instead of a mere item in a moral pageant.

Now it is all very well for you at the beginning of the XX century to ask me for a Don Juan play; but you will see from the foregoing survey that Don Juan is a full century out of date for you and for me; and if there are millions of less literate people who are still in the eighteenth century, have they not Molière and Mozart, upon whose art no human hand can improve? You would laugh at me if at this time of day I dealt in duels and ghosts and "womanly" women. As to mere libertinism, you would be the first to remind me that the Festin de Pierre of Molière is not a play for amorists, and that one bar of the voluptuous sentimentality of Gounod or Bizet would appear as a licentious stain on the score of Don Giovanni. Even the more abstract parts of the Don Juan play are dilapidated past use: for instance, Don Juan's supernatural antagonist hurled those who refuse to repent into lakes of burning brimstone, there to be tormented by devils with horns and tails. Of that antagonist, and of that conception of repentance, how much is left that could be used in a play by me dedicated to you? On the other hand, those forces of middle class public opinion which hardly existed for a Spanish nobleman in the days of the first Don Juan, are now triumphant everywhere. Civilized society is one huge bourgeoisie: no nobleman dares now shock his greengrocer. The women, "marchesane, principesse, cameriere, cittadine" and all, are become equally dangerous: the sex is aggressive, powerful: when women are wronged they do not group themselves pathetically to sing "Protegga il giusto cielo": they grasp formidable legal and social weapons, and retaliate. Political parties are wrecked and public careers undone by a single indiscretion. A man had better have all the statues in London to supper with him, ugly as they are, than be brought to the bar of the Nonconformist Conscience by Donna Elvira. Excommunication has become almost as serious a business as it was in the tenth century.

As a result, Man is no longer, like Don Juan, victor in the duel of sex. Whether he has ever really been may be doubted: at all events the enormous superiority of Woman's natural position in this matter is telling with greater and greater force. As to pulling the Nonconformist Conscience by the beard as Don Juan plucked the beard of the Commandant's statue in the convent of San Francisco, that is out of the question nowadays: prudence and good manners alike forbid it to a hero with any mind. Besides, it is Don Juan's own beard that is in danger of plucking. Far from relapsing into hypocrisy, as Sganarelle feared, he has unexpectedly discovered a moral in his immorality. The growing recognition of his new point of view is heaping responsibility on him. His former jests he has had to take as seriously as I have had to take some of the jests of Mr W. S. Gilbert. His scepticism, once his least tolerated quality, has now triumphed so completely that he can no longer assert himself by witty negations, and must, to save himself from cipherdom, find an affirmative position. His thousand and three affairs of gallantry, after becoming, at most, two immature intrigues leading to sordid and prolonged complications and humiliations, have been discarded altogether as unworthy of his philosophic dignity and compromising to his newly acknowledged position as the founder of a school. Instead of pretending to read Ovid he does actually read Schopenhauer and Nietzsche, studies Westermarck, and is concerned for the future of the race instead of for the freedom of his own instincts. Thus his profligacy and his daredevil airs have gone the way of his sword and mandoline into the rag shop of anachronisms and superstitions. In fact, he is now more Hamlet than Don Juan; for though the lines put into the actor's mouth to indicate to the pit that Hamlet is a philosopher are for the most part mere harmonious platitude which, with a little debasement of the word-music, would be properer to Pecksniff, yet if you separate the real hero, inarticulate and unintelligible to himself except in flashes of inspiration, from the performer who has to talk at any cost through five acts; and if you also do what you must always do in Shakespear's tragedies: that is, dissect out the absurd sensational incidents and physical violences of the borrowed story from the genuine Shakespearian tissue, you will get a true Promethean foe of the gods, whose instinctive attitude towards women much resembles that to which Don Juan is now driven. From this point of view Hamlet was a developed Don Juan whom Shakespear palmed off as a reputable man just as he palmed poor Macbeth off as a murderer. Today the palming off is no longer necessary (at least on your plane and mine) because Don Juanism is no longer misunderstood as mere Casanovism. Don Juan himself is almost ascetic in his desire to avoid that misunderstanding; and so my attempt to bring him up to date by launching him as a modern Englishman into a modern English environment has produced a figure superficially quite unlike the hero of Mozart.

And yet I have not the heart to disappoint you wholly of another glimpse of the Mozartian *dissoluto punito* and his antagonist the statue. I feel sure you would like to know more of that statue—to draw him out when he is off duty, so to speak. To gratify you, I have resorted to the trick of the strolling theatrical manager who advertizes the pantomime of Sinbad the Sailor with a stock of second-hand picture posters designed for Ali Baba. He simply thrusts a few oil jars into the valley of diamonds, and so fulfils the promise held out by the hoardings to the public eye. I have adapted this easy device to our occasion by thrusting into my perfectly modern three-act play a totally extraneous act in which my hero, enchanted by the air of the Sierra, has a dream in which his Mozartian ancestor appears and philosophizes at great length in a Shavio-Socratic dialogue with the lady, the statue, and the devil.

But this pleasantry is not the essence of the play. Over this essence I have no control. You propound a certain social substance, sexual attraction to wit, for dramatic distillation; and I distil it for you. I do not adulterate the product with aphrodisiacs nor dilute it with romance and water; for I am merely executing your commission, not producing a popular play for the market. You must therefore (unless, like most wise men, you read the play first and the preface afterwards) prepare yourself to face a trumpery story of modern London life, a life in which, as you know, the ordinary man's main business is to get means to keep up the position and habits of a gentleman, and the ordinary woman's

business is to get married. In 9,999 cases out of 10,000, you can count on their doing nothing, whether noble or base, that conflicts with these ends; and that assurance is what you rely on as their religion, their morality, their principles, their patriotism, their reputation, their honor and so forth.

On the whole, this is a sensible and satisfactory foundation for society. Money means nourishment and marriage means children; and that men should put nourishment first and women children first is, broadly speaking, the law of Nature and not the dictate of personal ambition. The secret of the prosaic man's success, such as it is, is the simplicity with which he pursues these ends: the secret of the artistic man's failure, such as that is, is the versatility with which he strays in all directions after secondary ideals. The artist is either a poet or a scallawag: as poet, he cannot see, as the prosaic man does, that chivalry is at bottom only romantic suicide: as scallawag, he cannot see that it does not pay to sponge and beg and lie and brag and neglect his person. Therefore do not misunderstand my plain statement of the fundamental constitution of London society as an Irishman's reproach to your nation. From the day I first set foot on this foreign soil I knew the value of the prosaic qualities of which Irishmen teach Englishmen to be ashamed as well as I knew the vanity of the poetic qualities of which Englishmen teach Irishmen to be proud. For the Irishman instinctively disparages the quality which makes the Englishman dangerous to him; and the Englishman instinctively flatters the fault that makes the Irishman harmless and amusing to him. What is wrong with the prosaic Englishman is what is wrong with the prosaic men of all countries: stupidity. The vitality which places nourishment and children first, heaven and hell a somewhat remote second, and the health of society as an organic whole nowhere, may muddle successfully through the comparatively tribal stages of gregariousness; but in nineteenth century nations and twentieth century commonwealths the resolve of every man to be rich at all costs, and of every woman to be married at all costs, must, without a highly scientific social organization, produce a ruinous development of poverty, celibacy, prostitution, infant mortality, adult degeneracy, and everything that wise men most dread. In short, there is no future for men, however brimming with crude vitality, who are neither intelligent nor politically educated enough to be Socialists. So do not misunderstand me in the other direction either: if I appreciate the vital qualities of the Englishman as I appreciate the vital qualities of the bee, I do not guarantee the Englishman against being, like the bee (or the Canaanite), smoked out and unloaded of his honey by beings inferior to himself in simple acquisitiveness, combativeness, and fecundity, but superior to him in imagination and cunning.

The Don Juan play, however, is to deal with sexual attraction, and not with nutrition, and to deal with it in a society in which the serious business of sex is left by men to women, as the serious business of nutrition is left by women to men. That the men, to protect themselves against a too aggressive prosecution of the women's business, have set up a feeble romantic convention that the initiative in sex business must always come from the man, is true; but the pretence is so shallow that even in the theatre, that last sanctuary of unreality, it imposes only on the inexperienced. In Shakespear's plays the woman always takes the initiative. In his problem plays and his popular plays alike the love interest is the interest of seeing the woman hunt the man down. She may do it by charming him, like Rosalind, or by stratagem, like Mariana; but in every case the relation between the woman and the man is the same: she is the pursuer and contriver, he the pursued and disposed of. When she is baffled, like Ophelia, she goes mad and commits suicide; and the man goes straight from her funeral to a fencing match. No doubt Nature, with very young creatures, may save the woman the trouble of scheming: Prospero knows that he has only to throw Ferdinand and Miranda together and they will mate like a pair of doves; and there is no need for Perdita to capture Florizel as the lady doctor in All's Well That Ends Well (an early Ibsenite heroine) captures Bertram. But the mature cases all illustrate the Shakespearian law. The one apparent exception, Petruchio, is not a real one: he is most carefully characterized as a purely commercial matrimonial adventurer. Once he is assured that Katharine has money, he undertakes to marry her before he has seen her. In real life we find not only Petruchios, but Mantalinis and Dobbins who pursue women with appeals to their pity or jealousy or vanity, or cling to them in a romantically infatuated way. Such effeminates do not count in the world scheme: even Bunsby dropping like a fascinated bird into the jaws of Mrs MacStinger is by comparison a true tragic object of pity and terror. I find in my own plays that Woman, projecting herself dramatically by my hands (a process over which I assure you I have no more real control than I have over my wife), behaves just as Woman did in the plays of Shakespear.

And so your Don Juan has come to birth as a stage projection of the tragicomic love chase of the man by the woman; and my Don Juan is the quarry instead of the huntsman. Yet he is a true Don Juan, with a sense of reality that disables convention, defying to the last the fate which finally overtakes him. The woman's need of him to enable her to carry on Nature's most urgent work, does not prevail against him until his resistance gathers her energy to a climax at which she dares to throw away her customary exploitations of the conventional affectionate and dutiful poses, and claim him by natural right for a purpose that far transcends their mortal personal purposes.

Among the friends to whom I have read this play in manuscript are some of our own sex who are shocked at the "unscrupulousness," meaning the utter disregard of masculine fastidiousness, with which the woman pursues her purpose. It does not occur to them that if women were as fastidious as men, morally or physically, there would be an end of the race. Is there anything meaner than to throw necessary work upon other people and then disparage it as unworthy and indelicate. We laugh at the haughty American nation because it makes the negro clean its boots and then proves the moral and physical inferiority of the negro by the fact that he is a shoeblack; but we ourselves throw the whole drudgery of creation on one sex, and then imply that no female of any womanliness or delicacy would initiate any effort in that direction. There are no limits to male hypocrisy in this matter. No doubt there are moments when man's sexual immunities are made acutely humiliating to him. When the terrible moment of birth arrives, its supreme importance and its superhuman effort and peril, in which the father has no part, dwarf him into the meanest insignificance: he slinks out of the way of the humblest petticoat, happy if he be poor enough to be pushed out of the house to outface his ignominy by drunken rejoicings. But when the crisis is over he takes his revenge, swaggering as the breadwinner, and speaking of Woman's "sphere" with condescension, even with chivalry, as if the kitchen and the nursery were less important than the office in the city. When his swagger is exhausted he drivels into erotic poetry or sentimental uxoriousness; and the Tennysonian King Arthur posing at Guinevere becomes Don Quixote grovelling before Dulcinea. You must admit that here Nature beats Comedy out of the field: the wildest hominist or feminist farce is insipid after the most commonplace "slice of life." The pretence that women do not take the initiative is part of the farce. Why, the whole world is strewn with snares, traps, gins, and pitfalls for the capture of men by women. Give women the vote, and in five years there will be a crushing tax on bachelors. Men, on the other hand, attach penalties to marriage, depriving women of property, of the franchise, of the free use of their limbs, of that ancient symbol of immortality, the right to make oneself at home in the house of God by taking off the hat, of everything that he can force Woman to dispense with without compelling himself to dispense with her. All in vain. Woman must marry because the race must perish without her travail: if the risk of death and the certainty of pain, danger, and unutterable discomforts cannot deter her, slavery and swaddled ankles will not. And yet we assume that the force that carries women through all these perils and hardships, stops abashed before the primnesses of our behavior for young ladies. It is assumed that the woman must wait, motionless, until she is wooed. Nay, she often does wait motionless. That is how the spider waits for the fly. But the spider spins her web. And if the fly, like my hero, shews a strength that promises to extricate him, how swiftly does she abandon her pretence of passiveness, and openly fling coil after coil about him until he is secured for ever!

If the really impressive books and other art-works of the world were produced by ordinary men, they would express more fear of women's pursuit than love of their illusory beauty. But ordinary men cannot produce really impressive art-works. Those who can are men of genius: that is, men selected by Nature to carry on the work of building up an intellectual consciousness of her own instinctive purpose. Accordingly, we observe in the man of genius all the unscrupulousness and all the "self-sacrifice" (the two things are the same) of Woman. He will risk the stake and the cross; starve, when necessary, in a garret all his life; study women and live on their work and care as Darwin studied worms and lived upon sheep; work his nerves into rags without payment, a sublime altruist in his disregard of himself, an atrocious egotist in his disregard of others. Here Woman meets a purpose as impersonal, as irresistible as her own; and the clash is sometimes tragic. When it is complicated by the genius being a woman, then the game is one for a king of critics: your George Sand becomes a mother to gain experience for the novelist and to develop her, and gobbles up men of genius, Chopins, Mussets, and the like, as mere hors d'œuvres.

I state the extreme case, of course; but what is true of the great man who incarnates the philosophic consciousness of Life and the woman who incarnates its fecundity, is true in some degree of all geniuses and all women. Hence it is that the world's books get written, its pictures painted, its statues modelled, its symphonies composed, by people who are free from the otherwise universal dominion of the tyranny of sex. Which leads us to the conclusion, astonishing to the vulgar, that art, instead of being before all things the expression of the normal sexual situation, is really the only department in which sex is a superseded and secondary power, with its consciousness so confused and its purpose so perverted, that its ideas are mere fantasy to common men. Whether the artist becomes poet or philosopher, moralist or founder of a religion, his sexual doctrine is nothing but a barren special pleading for pleasure, excitement, and knowledge when he is young, and for contemplative tranquillity when he is old and satiated. Romance and Asceticism, Amorism and Puritanism are equally unreal in the great Philistine world. The world shewn us in books, whether the books be confessed epics or professed gospels, or in codes, or in political orations, or in philosophic systems, is not the main world at all: it is only the self-consciousness of certain abnormal people who have the specific artistic talent and temperament. A serious matter this for you and me, because the man whose consciousness does not correspond to that of the majority is a madman; and the old habit of worshipping madmen is giving way to the new habit of locking them up. And since what we call education and culture is for the most part nothing but the substitution of reading for experience, of literature for life, of the obsolete fictitious for the contemporary real, education, as you no doubt observed at Oxford, destroys, by supplantation, every mind that is not strong enough to see through the imposture and to use the great Masters of Arts as what they really are and no more: that is, patentees of highly questionable methods of thinking, and manufacturers of highly questionable, and for the majority but half valid representations of life. The schoolboy who uses his Homer to throw at his fellow's head makes perhaps the safest and most rational use of him: and I observe with reassurance that you occasionally do the same, in your prime, with your Aristotle.

Fortunately for us, whose minds have been so overwhelmingly sophisticated by literature, what produces all these treatises and poems and scriptures of one sort or another is the struggle of Life to become divinely conscious of itself instead of blindly stumbling hither and thither in the line of least resistance. Hence there is a driving towards truth in all books on matters where the writer, though exceptionally gifted, is normally constituted, and has no private axe to grind. Copernicus had no motive for misleading his fellow men as to the place of the sun in the solar system: he looked for it as honestly as a shepherd seeks his path in a mist. But Copernicus would not have written love stories scientifically. When it comes to sex relations, the man of genius does not share the common man's danger of capture, nor the woman of genius the common woman's overwhelming specialization. And that is why our scriptures and other art works, when they deal with love, turn from honest attempts at science in physics to romantic nonsense, erotic ecstasy, or the stern asceticism of satiety ("the road of excess leads to the palace of wisdom" said William Blake; for "you never know what is enough unless you know what is more than enough").

There is a political aspect of this sex question which is too big for my comedy, and too momentous to be passed over without culpable frivolity. It is impossible to demonstrate that the initiative in sex transactions remains with Woman, and has been confirmed to her, so far, more and more by the suppression of rapine and discouragement of importunity, without being driven to very serious reflections on the fact that this initiative is politically the most important of all the initiatives, because our political experiment of democracy, the last refuge of cheap misgovernment, will ruin us if our citizens are ill bred.

When we two were born, this country was still dominated by a selected class bred by political marriages. The commercial class had not then completed the first twentyfive years of its new share of political power; and it was itself selected by money qualification, and bred, if not by political marriage, at least by a pretty rigorous class marriage. Aristocracy and plutocracy still furnish the figureheads of politics; but they are now dependent on the votes of the promiscuously bred masses. And this, if you please, at the very moment when the political problem, having suddenly ceased to mean a very limited and occasional interference, mostly by way of jobbing public appointments, in the mismanagement of a tight but parochial little island, with occasional meaningless prosecution of dynastic wars, has become the industrial reorganization of Britain, the construction of a practically international Commonwealth, and the partition of the whole of Africa and perhaps the whole of Asia by the civilized Powers. Can you believe that the people whose conceptions of society and conduct, whose power of attention and scope of interest, are measured by the British theatre as you know it today, can either handle this colossal task themselves, or understand and support the sort of mind and character that is (at least comparatively) capable of handling it? For remember: what our voters are in the pit and gallery they are also in the polling booth. We are all now under what Burke called "the hoofs of the swinish multitude." Burke's language gave great offence because the implied exceptions to its universal application made it a class insult; and it certainly was not for the pot to call the kettle black. The aristocracy he defended, in spite of the political marriages by which it tried to secure breeding for itself, had its mind undertrained by silly schoolmasters and governesses, its character corrupted by gratuitous luxury, its self-respect adulterated to complete spuriousness by flattery and flunkeyism. It is no better today and never will be any better: our very peasants have something morally hardier in them that culminates occasionally in a Bunyan, a Burns, or a Carlyle. But observe, this aristocracy, which was overpowered from 1832 to 1885 by the middle class, has come back to power by the votes of "the swinish multitude." Tom Paine has triumphed over Edmund Burke; and the swine are now courted electors. How many of their own class have these electors sent to Parliament? Hardly a dozen out of 670, and these only under the persuasion of conspicuous personal qualifications and popular eloquence. The multitude thus pronounces judgment on its own units: it admits itself unfit to govern, and will vote only for a man morphologically and generically transfigured by palatial residence and equipage, by transcendent tailoring, by the glamor of aristocratic kinship. Well, we two know these transfigured persons, these college passmen, these well groomed monocular Algys and Bobbies, these cricketers to whom age brings golf instead of wisdom, these plutocratic products of "the nail and sarspan business as he got his money by." Do you know whether to laugh or cry at the notion that they, poor devils! will drive a team of continents as they drive a four-in-hand; turn a jostling anarchy of casual trade and speculation into an ordered productivity; and federate our colonies into a world-Power of the first magnitude? Give these people the most perfect political constitution and the soundest political program that benevolent omniscience can devise for them, and they will interpret it into mere fashionable folly or canting charity as infallibly as a savage converts the philosophical theology of a Scotch missionary into crude African idolatry.

I do not know whether you have any illusions left on the subject of education, progress, and so forth. I have none. Any pamphleteer can shew the way to better things; but when there is no will there is no way. My nurse was fond of remarking that you cannot make a silk purse out of a sow's ear; and the more I see of the efforts of our churches and universities and literary sages to raise the mass above its own level, the more convinced I am that my nurse was right. Progress can do nothing but make the most of us all as we are, and that most would clearly not be enough even if those who are already raised out of the lowest abysses would allow the others a chance. The bubble of Heredity has been pricked: the certainty that acquirements are negligible as elements in practical heredity has demolished the hopes of the educationists as well as the terrors of the degeneracy mongers; and we know now that there is no hereditary "governing class" any more than a hereditary hooliganism. We must either breed political capacity or be ruined by Democracy, which was forced on us by the failure of the older alternatives. Yet if Despotism failed only for want of a capable benevolent despot, what chance has Democracy, which requires a whole population of capable voters: that is, of political critics who, if they cannot govern in person for lack of spare energy or specific talent for administration, can at least recognize and appreciate capacity and benevolence in others, and so govern through capably benevolent representatives? Where are such voters to be found today? Nowhere. Plutocratic inbreeding has produced a weakness of character that is too timid to face the full stringency of a thoroughly competitive struggle for existence and too lazy and petty to organize the commonwealth co-operatively. Being cowards, we defeat natural selection under cover of philanthropy: being sluggards, we neglect artificial selection under cover of delicacy and morality.

Yet we must get an electorate of capable critics or collapse as Rome and

Egypt collapsed. At this moment the Roman decadent phase of *panem et circenses* is being inaugurated under our eyes. Our newspapers and melodramas are blustering about our imperial destiny; but our eyes and hearts turn eagerly to the American millionaire. As his hand goes down to his pocket, our fingers go up to the brims of our hats by instinct. Our ideal prosperity is not the prosperity of the industrial north, but the prosperity of the Isle of Wight, of Folkestone and Ramsgate, of Nice and Monte Carlo. That is the only prosperity you see on the stage, where the workers are all footmen, parlourmaids, comic lodging-letters, and fashionable professional men, whilst the heroes and heroines are miraculously provided with unlimited dividends and eat gratuitously, like the knights in Don Quixote's books of chivalry. The city papers prate of the competition of Bombay with Manchester and the like. The real competition is the competition of Regent Street with the Rue de Rivoli, of Brighton and the south coast with the Riviera, for the spending money of the American Trusts. What is all this growing love of pageantry, this effusive loyalty, this officious rising and uncovering at a wave from a flag or a blast from a brass band? Imperialism? Not a bit of it. Obsequiousness, servility, cupidity roused by the prevailing smell of money. When Mr Carnegie rattled his millions in his pockets all England became one rapacious cringe. Only, when Rhodes (who had probably been reading my Socialism for Millionaires) left word that no idler was to inherit his estate, the bent backs straightened mistrustfully for a moment. Could it be that the Diamond King was no gentleman after all? However, it was easy to ignore a rich man's solecism. The ungentlemanly clause was not mentioned again; and the backs soon bowed themselves back into their natural shape.

But I hear you asking me in alarm whether I have actually put all this tub thumping into a Don Juan comedy. I have not. I have only made my Don Juan a political pamphleteer, and given you his pamphlet in full by way of appendix. You will find it at the end of the book. I am sorry to say that it is a common practice with romancers to announce their hero as a man of extraordinary genius, and then leave his works entirely to the reader's imagination; so that at the end of the book you whisper to yourself ruefully that but for the author's solemn preliminary assurance you should hardly have given the gentleman credit for ordinary good sense. You cannot accuse me of this pitiable barrenness, this feeble evasion. I not only tell you that my hero wrote a revolutionists' handbook: I give you the handbook at full length for your edification if you care to read it. And in that handbook you will find the politics of the sex question as I conceive Don Juan's descendant to understand them. Not that I disclaim the fullest responsibility for his opinions and for those of all my characters, pleasant and unpleasant. They are all right from their several points of view; and their points of view are, for the dramatic moment, mine also. This may puzzle the people who believe that there is such a thing as an absolutely right point of view, usually their own. It may seem to them that nobody who doubts this can be in a state of grace. However that may be, it is certainly true that nobody who agrees with them can possibly be a dramatist, or indeed anything else that turns upon a knowledge of mankind. Hence it has been pointed out that Shakespear had no conscience. Neither have I, in that sense.

You may, however, remind me that this digression of mine into politics was preceded by a very convincing demonstration that the artist never catches the point of view of the common man on the question of sex, because he is not in the same predicament. I first prove that anything I write on the relation of the sexes is sure to be misleading; and then I proceed to write a Don Juan play. Well, if you insist on asking me why I behave in this absurd way, I can only reply that you asked me to, and that in any case my treatment of the subject may be valid for the artist, amusing to the amateur, and at least intelligible and therefore possibly suggestive to the Philistine. Every man who records his illusions is providing data for the genuinely scientific psychology which the world still waits for. I plank down my view of the existing relations of men to women in the most highly civilized society for what it is worth. It is a view like any other view and no more, neither true nor false, but, I hope, a way of looking at the subject which throws into the familiar order of cause and effect a sufficient body of fact and experience to be interesting to you, if not to the playgoing public of London. I have certainly shewn little consideration for that public in this enterprise; but I know that it has the friendliest disposition towards you and me as far as it has any consciousness of our existence, and quite understands that what I write for you must pass at a considerable height over its simple romantic head. It will take my books as read and my genius for granted, trusting me to put forth work of such quality as shall bear out its verdict. So we may disport ourselves on our own plane to the top of our bent; and if any gentleman points out that neither this epistle dedicatory nor the dream of Don Juan in the third act of the ensuing comedy is suitable for immediate production at a popular theatre we need not contradict him. Napoleon provided Talma with a pit of kings, with what effect on Talma's acting is not recorded. As for me, what I have always wanted is a pit of philosophers; and this is a play for such a pit.

I should make formal acknowledgment to the authors whom I have pillaged in the following pages if I could recollect them all. The theft of the brigand-poetaster from Sir Arthur Conan Doyle is deliberate; and the metamorphosis of Leporello into Enry Straker, motor engineer and New Man, is an intentional dramatic sketch of the contemporary embryo of Mr H. G. Wells's anticipation of the efficient engineering class which will, he hopes, finally sweep the jabberers out of the way of civilization. Mr Barrie has also, whilst I am correcting my proofs, delighted London with a servant who knows more than his masters. The conception of Mendoza Limited I trace back to a certain West Indian colonial secretary, who, at a period when he and I and Mr Sidney Webb were sowing our political wild oats as a sort of Fabian Three Musketeers, without any prevision of the surprising respectability of the crop that followed, recommended Webb, the encyclopedic and inexhaustible, to form himself into a company for the benefit of the shareholders. Octavius I take over unaltered from Mozart; and I hereby authorize any actor who impersonates him, to sing "Dalla sua pace" (if he can) at any convenient moment during the representation. Ann was suggested to me by the fifteenth century Dutch morality called Everyman, which Mr William Poel has lately resuscitated so triumphantly. I trust he will work that vein further, and recognize that Elizabethan Renascence fustian is no more bearable after medieval poesy than Scribe after Ibsen. As I sat watching Everyman at the Charterhouse, I said to myself Why not Everywoman? Ann was the result: every woman is not Ann; but Ann is Everywoman.

That the author of Everyman was no mere artist, but an artist-philosopher,

G

and that the artist-philosophers are the only sort of artists I take quite seriously, will be no news to you. Even Plato and Boswell, as the dramatists who invented Socrates and Dr Johnson, impress me more deeply than the romantic playwrights. Ever since, as a boy, I first breathed the air of the transcendental regions at a performance of Mozart's Zauberflöte, I have been proof against the garish splendors and alcoholic excitements of the ordinary stage combinations of Tappertitian romance with the police intelligence. Bunyan, Blake, Hogarth, and Turner (these four apart and above all the English classics), Goethe, Shelley, Schopenhauer, Wagner, Ibsen, Morris, Tolstoy, and Nietzsche are among the writers whose peculiar sense of the world I recognize as more or less akin to my own. Mark the word peculiar. I read Dickens and Shakespear without shame or stint; but their pregnant observations and demonstrations of life are not co-ordinated into any philosophy or religion; on the contrary, Dickens's sentimental assumptions are violently contradicted by his observations; and Shakespear's pessimism is only his wounded humanity. Both have the specific genius of the fictionist and the common sympathies of human feeling and thought in pre-eminent degree. They are often saner and shrewder than the philosophers just as Sancho Panza was often saner and shrewder than Don Quixote. They clear away vast masses of oppressive gravity by their sense of the ridiculous, which is at bottom a combination of sound moral judgment with lighthearted good humor. But they are concerned with the diversities of the world instead of with its unities: they are so irreligious that they exploit popular religion for professional purposes without delicacy or scruple (for example, Sydney Carton and the ghost in Hamlet!): they are anarchical, and cannot balance their exposures of Angelo and Dogberry, Sir Leicester Dedlock and Mr Tite Barnacle, with any portrait of a prophet or a worthy leader: they have no constructive ideas: they regard those who have them as dangerous fanatics: in all their fictions there is no leading thought or inspiration for which any man could conceivably risk the spoiling of his hat in a shower, much less his life. Both are alike forced to borrow motives for the more strenuous actions of their personages from the common stockpot of melodramatic plots; so that Hamlet has to be stimulated by the prejudices of a policeman and Macbeth by the cupidities of a bushranger. Dickens, without the excuse of having to manufacture motives for Hamlets and Macbeths, superfluously punts his crew down the stream of his monthly parts by mechanical devices which I leave you to describe, my own memory being quite baffled by the simplest question as to Monks in Oliver Twist, or the long lost parentage of Smike, or the relations between the Dorrit and Clennam families so inopportunely discovered by Monsieur Rigaud Blandois. The truth is, the world was to Shakespear a great "stage of fools" on which he was utterly bewildered. He could see no sort of sense in living at all; and Dickens saved himself from the despair of the dream in The Chimes by taking the world for granted and busying himself with its details. Neither of them could do anything with a serious positive character: they could place a human figure before you with perfect verisimilitude; but when the moment came for making it live and move, they found, unless it made them laugh, that they had a puppet on their hands, and had to invent some artificial external stimulus to make it work. This is what is the matter with Hamlet all through: he has no will except in his bursts of temper. Foolish Bardolaters make a virtue of this after their fashion: they declare that the play is the tragedy of irresolution; but all Shakespear's projections of the deepest humanity he knew have the same defect: their characters and manners are lifelike; but their actions are forced on them from without, and the external force is grotesquely inappropriate except when it is quite conventional, as in the case of Henry V. Falstaff is more vivid than any of these serious reflective characters, because he is self-acting: his motives are his own appetites and instincts and humors. Richard III, too, is delightful as the whimsical comedian who stops a funeral to make love to the corpse's son's widow; but when, in the next act, he is replaced by a stage villain who smothers babies and offs with people's heads, we are revolted at the imposture and repudiate the changeling. Faulconbridge, Coriolanus, Leontes are admirable descriptions of instinctive temperaments: indeed the play of Coriolanus is the greatest of Shakespear's comedies; but description is not philosophy; and comedy neither compromises the author nor reveals him. He must be judged by those characters into which he puts what he knows of himself, his Hamlets and Macbeths and Lears and Prosperos. If these characters are agonizing in a void about factitious melodramatic murders and revenges and the like, whilst the comic characters walk with their feet on solid ground, vivid and amusing, you know that the author has much to shew and nothing to teach. The comparison between Falstaff and Prospero is like the comparison between Micawber and David Copperfield. At the end of the book you know Micawber, whereas you only know what has happened to David, and are not interested enough in him to wonder what his politics or religion might be if anything so stupendous as a religious or political idea, or a general idea of any sort, were to occur to him.

He is tolerable as a child; but he never becomes a man, and might be left out of his own biography altogether but for his usefulness as a stage confidant, a Horatio or "Charles his friend": what they call on the stage a feeder.

Now you cannot say this of the works of the artist-philosophers. You cannot say it, for instance, of The Pilgrim's Progress. Put your Shakespearian hero and coward, Henry V and Pistol or Parolles, beside Mr Valiant and Mr Fearing, and you have a sudden revelation of the abyss that lies between the fashionable author who could see nothing in the world but personal aims and the tragedy of their disappointment or the comedy of their incongruity, and the field preacher who achieved virtue and courage by identifying himself with the purpose of the world as he understood it. The contrast is enormous: Bunyan's coward stirs your blood more than Shakespear's hero, who actually leaves you cold and secretly hostile. You suddenly see that Shakespear, with all his flashes and divinations, never understood virtue and courage, never conceived how any man who was not a fool could, like Bunyan's hero, look back from the brink of the river of death over the strife and labor of his pilgrimage, and say "yet do I not repent me"; or, with the panache of a millionaire, bequeath "my sword to him that shall succeed me in my pilgrimage, and my courage and skill to him that can get it." This is the true joy in life, the being used for a purpose recognized by yourself as a mighty one; the being thoroughly worn out before you are thrown on the scrap heap; the being a force of Nature instead of a feverish selfish little clod of ailments and grievances complaining that the world will not devote itself to making you happy. And also the only real tragedy in life is the being used by personally minded men for purposes which you recognize to be base. All the rest is at worst mere misfortune or mortality: this alone is misery, slavery, hell on earth; and the revolt against it is the only force that offers a man's work to the poor artist, whom our personally minded rich people would so willingly employ as pandar, buffoon, beauty monger, sentimentalizer, and the like.

It may seem a long step from Bunyan to Nietzsche; but the difference between their conclusions is merely formal. Bunyan's perception that righteousness is filthy rags, his scorn for Mr Legality in the village of Morality, his defiance of the Church as the supplanter of religion, his insistence on courage as the virtue of virtues, his estimate of the career of the conventionally respectable and sensible Worldly Wiseman as no better at bottom than the life and death of Mr Badman: all this, expressed by Bunyan in the terms of a tinker's theology, is what Nietzsche has expressed in terms of post-Darwin, post-Schopenhauer philosophy; Wagner in terms of polytheistic mythology; and Ibsen in terms of mid-XIX century Parisian dramaturgy. Nothing is new in these matters except their novelties: for instance, it is a novelty to call Justification by Faith "Wille," and Justification by Works "Vorstellung." The sole use of the novelty is that you and I buy and read Schopenhauer's treatise on Will and Representation when we should not dream of buying a set of sermons on Faith versus Works. At bottom the controversy is the same, and the dramatic results are the same. Bunyan makes no attempt to present his pilgrims as more sensible or better conducted than Mr Worldly Wiseman. Mr W. W.'s worst enemies, Mr Embezzler, Mr Never-go-to-Church-on-Sunday, Mr Bad Form, Mr Murderer, Mr Burglar, Mr Co-respondent, Mr Blackmailer, Mr Cad, Mr Drunkard, Mr Labor Agitator, and so forth, can read the Pilgrim's Progress without finding a word said against them; whereas the respectable people who snub them and put them in prison, such as Mr W. W. himself and his young friend Civility; Formalist and Hypocrisy; Wildhead, Inconsiderate, and Pragmatick (who were clearly young university men of good family and high feeding); that brisk lad Ignorance, Talkative, By-ends of Fairspeech and his mother-in-law Lady Feigning, and other reputable gentlemen and citizens, catch it very severely. Even Little Faith, though he gets to heaven at last, is given to understand that it served him right to be mobbed by the brothers Faint Heart, Mistrust, and Guilt, all three recognized members of respectable society and veritable pillars of the law. The whole allegory is a consistent attack on morality and respectability, without a word that one can remember against vice and crime. Exactly what is complained of in Nietzsche and Ibsen, is it not? And also exactly what would be complained of in all the literature which is great enough and old enough to have attained canonical rank, officially or unofficially, were it not that books are admitted to the canon by a compact which confesses their greatness in consideration of abrogating their meaning; so that the reverend rector can agree with the prophet Micah as to his inspired style without being committed to any complicity in Micah's furiously Radical opinions. Why, even I, as I force myself, pen in hand, into recognition and civility, find all the force of my onslaught destroyed by a simple policy of non-resistance. In vain do I redouble the violence of the language in which I proclaim my heterodoxies. I rail at the theistic credulity of Voltaire, the amoristic superstition of Shelley, the revival of tribal soothsaying and idolatrous rites which Huxley called Science and mistook for an advance on the Pentateuch, no less than at the welter of ecclesiastical and professional humbug which saves the face of the stupid system of violence and robbery which we call Law and Industry. Even atheists reproach me with infidelity and anarchists with nihilism because I cannot endure their moral tirades. And yet, instead of exclaiming "Send this inconceivable Satanist to the stake," the respectable newspapers pith me by announcing "another book by this brilliant and thoughtful writer." And the ordinary citizen, knowing that an author who is well spoken of by a respectable newspaper must be all right, reads me, as he reads Micah, with undisturbed edification from his own point of view. It is narrated that in the eighteen-seventies an old lady, a very devout Methodist, moved from Colchester to a house in the neighborhood of the City Road, in London, where, mistaking the Hall of Science for a chapel, she sat at the feet of Charles Bradlaugh for many years, entranced by his eloquence, without questioning his orthodoxy or moulting a feather of her faith. I fear I shall be defrauded of my just martyrdom in the same way.

However, I am digressing, as a man with a grievance always does. And after all, the main thing in determining the artistic quality of a book is not the opinions it propagates, but the fact that the writer has opinions. The old lady from Colchester was right to sun her simple soul in the energetic radiance of Bradlaugh's genuine beliefs and disbeliefs rather than in the chill of such mere painting of light and heat as elocution and convention can achieve. My contempt for belles lettres, and for amateurs who become the heroes of the fanciers of literary virtuosity, is not founded on any illusion of mine as to the permanence of those forms of thought (call them opinions) by which I strive to communicate my bent to my fellows. To younger men they are already outmoded; for though they have

no more lost their logic than an eighteenth century pastel has lost its drawing or its color, yet, like the pastel, they grow indefinably shabby, and will grow shabbier until they cease to count at all, when my books will either perish, or, if the world is still poor enough to want them, will have to stand, with Bunyan's, by quite amorphous qualities of temper and energy. With this conviction I cannot be a belletrist. No doubt I must recognize, as even the Ancient Mariner did, that I must tell my story entertainingly if I am to hold the wedding guest spellbound in spite of the siren sounds of the loud bassoon. But "for art's sake" alone I would not face the toil of writing a single sentence. I know that there are men who, having nothing to say and nothing to write, are nevertheless so in love with oratory and with literature that they delight in repeating as much as they can understand of what others have said or written aforetime. I know that the leisurely tricks which their want of conviction leaves them free to play with the diluted and misapprehended message supply them with a pleasant parlor game which they call style. I can pity their dotage and even sympathize with their fancy. But a true original style is never achieved for its own sake: a man may pay from a shilling to a guinea, according to his means, to see, hear, or read another man's act of genius; but he will not pay with his whole life and soul to become a mere virtuoso in literature, exhibiting an accomplishment which will not even make money for him, like fiddle playing. Effectiveness of assertion is the alpha and omega of style. He who has nothing to assert has no style and can have none: he who has something to assert will go as far in power of style as its momentousness and his conviction will carry him. Disprove his assertion after it is made, yet its style remains. Darwin has no more destroyed the style of Job nor of Handel than Martin Luther destroyed the style of Giotto. All the assertions get disproved sooner or later; and so we find the world full of magnificent débris of artistic fossils, with the matter-of-fact credibility gone clean out of them, but the form still splendid. And that is why the old masters play the deuce with our mere susceptibles. Your Royal Academician thinks he can get the style of Giotto without Giotto's beliefs, and correct his perspective into the bargain. Your man of letters thinks he can get Bunyan's or Shakespear's style without Bunyan's conviction or Shakespear's apprehension, especially if he takes care not to split his infinitives. And so with your Doctors of Music, who, with their collections of discords duly prepared and resolved or retarded or anticipated in the manner of the great composers, think they can learn the art of Palestrina from Cherubini's treatise. All this academic art is far worse than the trade in sham antique furniture; for the man who sells me an oaken chest which he swears was made in the XIII century, though as a matter of fact he made it himself only yesterday, at least does not pretend that there are any modern ideas in it; whereas your academic copier of fossils offers them to you as the latest outpouring of the human spirit, and, worst of all, kidnaps young people as pupils and persuades them that his limitations are rules, his observances dexterities, his timidities good taste, and his emptinesses purities. And when he declares that art should not be didactic, all the people who have nothing to teach and all the people who dont want to learn agree with him emphatically.

I pride myself on not being one of these susceptibles. If you study the electric light with which I supply you in that Bumbledonian public capacity of mine over which you make merry from time to time, you will find that your house contains a great quantity of highly susceptible copper wire which gorges itself with electricity and gives you no light whatever. But here and there occurs a scrap of intensely insusceptible, intensely resistant material; and that stubborn scrap grapples with the current and will not let it through until it has made itself useful to you as those two vital qualities of literature, light and heat. Now if I am to be no mere copper wire amateur but a luminous author, I must also be a most intensely refractory person, liable to go out and to go wrong at inconvenient moments, and with incendiary possibilities. These are the faults of my qualities; and I assure you that I sometimes dislike myself so much that when some irritable reviewer chances at that moment to pitch into me with zest, I feel unspeakably relieved and obliged. But I never dream of reforming, knowing that I must take myself as I am and get what work I can out of myself. All this you will understand; for there is community of material between us: we are both critics of life as well as of art; and you have perhaps said to yourself when I have passed your windows "There, but for the grace of God, go I." An awful and chastening reflection, which shall be the closing cadence of this immoderately long letter from yours faithfully,

G. BERNARD SHAW.

WOKING, 1903.

P.S.—Amid unprecedented critical cerebration over this book of ours—alas! that your own voice should be dedicated to silence! —I find myself warned to prepare a new edition. I take the opportunity to correct a slip or two. You may have noticed (nobody else has, by the way) that I fitted you with a quotation from Othello, and then unconsciously referred it to A Winter's Tale. I correct this with regret; for half its appropriateness goes with Florizel and Perdita: still, one must not trifle with Shakespear; so I have given Desdemona back her property.

On the whole, the book has done very well. The strong critics are impressed; the weak intimidated; the connoisseurs tickled by my literary bravura (put in to please you): the humorists alone, oddly enough, sermonize me, scared out of their profession into the quaintest tumults of conscience. Not all my reviewers have understood me: like Englishmen in France, confidently uttering their own island diphthongs as good French vowels, many of them offer, as samples of the Shavian philosophy, the likest article from their own stock. Others are the victims of association of ideas: they call me Pessimist because my remarks wound their self-complacency, and Renegade because I would have my mob all Cæsars instead of Toms, Dicks, and Harrys. Worst of all, I have been accused of preaching a Final Ethical Superman: no other, in fact, than our old friend the Just Man made Perfect! This misunderstanding is so galling that I lay down my pen without another word lest I should be tempted to make the postscript longer even than the letter.

THE REVOLUTIONIST'S HANDBOOK

"No one can contemplate the present condition of the masses of the people without desiring something like a revolution for the better." *Sir Robert Giffen*, Essays in Finance, vol. ii. p. 393.

FOREWORD

A REVOLUTIONIST is one who desires to discard the existing social order and try another.

The Constitution of England is revolutionary. To a Russian or Anglo-Indian bureaucrat, a general election is as much a revolution as a referendum or plebiscite in which the people fight instead of voting. The French Revolution overthrew one set of rulers and substituted another with different interests and different views. That is what a general election enables the people to do in England every seven years if they choose. Revolution is therefore a national institution in England; and its advocacy by an Englishman needs no apology.

Every man is a revolutionist concerning the thing he understands. For example, every person who has mastered a profession is a sceptic concerning it, and consequently a revolutionist.

Every genuine religious person is a heretic and therefore a revolutionist.

All who achieve real distinction in life begin as revolutionists. The most distinguished persons become more revolutionary as they grow older, though they are commonly supposed to become more conservative owing to their loss of faith in conventional methods of reform.

Any person under the age of thirty, who, having any knowledge of the existing social order, is not a revolutionist, is an inferior.

AND YET

Revolutions have never lightened the burden of tyranny: they have only shifted it to another shoulder.

JOHN TANNER.

I

ON GOOD BREEDING

IF there were no God, said the eighteenth century Deist, it would be necessary to invent Him. Now this XVIII century god was *deus ex machina*, the god who helped those who could not help themselves, the god of the lazy and incapable. The nineteenth century decided that there is indeed no such god; and now Man must take in hand all the work that he used to shirk with an idle prayer. He must, in effect, change himself into the political Providence which he formerly conceived as god; and such change is not only possible, but the only sort of change that is real. The mere transfiguration of institutions, as from military and priestly dominance to commercial and scientific dominance, from commercial dominance to proletarian democracy, from slavery to serfdom, from serfdom to capitalism, from monarchy to republicanism, from polytheism to monotheism, from monotheism to atheism, from atheism to pantheistic humanitarianism, from general illiteracy to general literacy, from romance to realism, from realism to mysticism, from metaphysics to physics, are all but changes from Tweedledum to Tweedledee: *plus ça change, plus c'est la même chose*. But the changes from the crab apple to the pippin, from the wolf and fox to the house dog, from the charger of Henry V to the brewer's draught horse and the racehorse, are real; for here Man has played the god, subduing Nature to his intention, and ennobling or debasing Life for a set purpose. And what can be done with a wolf can be done with a man. If such monsters as the tramp and the gentleman can appear as mere by-products of Man's individual greed and folly, what might we not hope for as a main product of his universal aspiration?

This is no new conclusion. The despair of institutions, and the inexorable "ye must be born again," with Mrs Poyser's stipulation, "and born different," recurs in every generation. The cry for the Superman did not begin with Nietzsche, nor will it end with his vogue. But it has always been silenced by the same question: what kind of person is this Superman to be? You ask, not for a super-apple, but for an eatable apple; not for a super-horse, but for a horse of greater draught or velocity. Neither is it of any use to ask for a Superman: you must furnish a specification of the sort of man you want. Unfortunately you do not know what sort of man you want. Some sort of goodlooking philosopher-athlete, with a handsome healthy woman for his mate, perhaps.

Vague as this is, it is a great advance on the popular demand for a perfect gentleman and a perfect lady. And, after all, no market demand in the world takes the form of exact technical specification of the article required. Excellent poultry and potatoes are produced to satisfy the demand of housewives who do not know the technical differences between a tuber and a chicken. They will tell you that the proof of the pudding is in the eating; and they are right. The proof of the Superman will be in the living; and we shall find out how to produce him by the old method of trial and error, and not by waiting for a completely convincing prescription of his ingredients.

Certain common and obvious mistakes may be ruled out from the beginning. For example, we agree that we want superior mind; but we need not fall into the football club folly of counting on this as a product of superior body. Yet if we recoil so far as to conclude that superior mind consists in being the dupe of our ethical classifications of virtues and vices, in short, of conventional morality, we shall fall out of the fryingpan of the football club into the fire of the Sunday School. If we must choose between a race of athletes and a race of "good" men, let us have the athletes: better Samson and Milo than Calvin and Robespierre. But neither alternative is worth changing for: Samson is no more a Superman than Calvin. What then are we to do?

II

PROPERTY AND MARRIAGE

Let us hurry over the obstacles set up by property and marriage. Revolutionists make too much of them. No doubt it is easy to demonstrate that property will destroy society unless society destroys it. No doubt, also, property has hitherto held its own and destroyed all the empires. But that was because the superficial objection to it (that it distributes social wealth and the social labor burden in a grotesquely inequitable manner) did not threaten the existence of the race, but only the individual happiness of its units, and finally the maintenance of some irrelevant political form or other, such as a nation, an empire, or the like. Now as happiness never matters to Nature, as she neither recognizes flags and frontiers nor cares a straw whether the economic system adopted by a society is feudal, capitalistic, or collectivist, provided it keeps the race afoot (the hive and the anthill being as acceptable to her as Utopia), the demonstrations of Socialists, though irrefutable, will never make any serious impression on property. The knell of that overrated institution will not sound until it is felt to conflict with some more vital matter than mere personal inequities in industrial economy. No such conflict was perceived whilst society had not yet grown beyond national communities too small and simple to overtax Man's limited political capacity disastrously. But we have now reached the stage of international organization. Man's political capacity and magnanimity are clearly beaten by the vastness and complexity of the problems forced on him. And it is at this anxious moment that he finds, when he looks upward for a mightier mind to help him, that the heavens are empty. He will presently see that his discarded formula that Man is the Temple of the Holy Ghost happens to be precisely true, and that it is only through his own brain and hand that this Holy Ghost, formally the most nebulous person in the Trinity, and now become its sole survivor as it has always been its real Unity, can help him in any way. And so, if the Superman is to come, he must be born of Woman by Man's intentional and well-considered contrivance. Conviction of this will smash everything that opposes it. Even Property and Marriage, which laugh at the laborer's petty complaint that he is defrauded of "surplus value," and at the domestic miseries of the slaves of the wedding ring, will themselves be laughed aside as the lightest of trifles if they cross this conception when it becomes a fully realized vital purpose of the race.

That they must cross it becomes obvious the moment we acknowledge the futility of breeding men for special qualities as we breed cocks for game, greyhounds for speed, or sheep for mutton. What is really important in Man is the part of him that we do not yet understand. Of much of it we are not even conscious, just as we are not normally conscious of keeping up our circulation by our heart-pump, though if we neglect it we die. We are therefore driven to the conclusion that when we have carried selection as far as we can by rejecting from the list of eligible parents all persons who are uninteresting, unpromising, or blemished without any set-off, we shall still have to trust to the guidance of fancy (*alias* Voice of Nature), both in the breeders and the parents, for that superiority in the unconscious self which will be the true characteristic of the Superman.

At this point we perceive the importance of giving fancy the widest possible field. To cut humanity up into small cliques, and effectively limit the selection of the individual to his own clique, is to

postpone the Superman for eons, if not
for ever. Not only should every person
be nourished and trained as a possible
parent, but there should be no possibility
of such an obstacle to natural selection as
the objection of a countess to a navvy
or of a duke to a charwoman. Equality is
essential to good breeding; and equality,
as all economists know, is incompatible
with property.

Besides, equality is an essential condition of bad breeding also; and bad
breeding is indispensable to the weeding
out of the human race. When the conception of heredity took hold of the
scientific imagination in the middle of
last century, its devotees announced that
it was a crime to marry the lunatic to the
lunatic or the consumptive to the consumptive. But pray are we to try to
correct our diseased stocks by infecting
our healthy stocks with them? Clearly
the attraction which disease has for diseased people is beneficial to the race.
If two really unhealthy people get
married, they will, as likely as not, have
a great number of children who will all
die before they reach maturity. This is a
far more satisfactory arrangement than
the tragedy of a union between a healthy
and an unhealthy person. Though more
costly than sterilization of the unhealthy,
it has the enormous advantage that in the
event of our notions of health and un-
health being erroneous (which to some
extent they most certainly are), the error
will be corrected by experience instead
of confirmed by evasion.

One fact must be faced resolutely, in
spite of the shrieks of the romantic.
There is no evidence that the best citizens
are the offspring of congenial marriages,
or that a conflict of temperament is not
a highly important part of what breeders
call crossing. On the contrary, it is quite
sufficiently probable that good results
may be obtained from parents who
would be extremely unsuitable com-

panions and partners, to make it certain
that the experiment of mating them will
sooner or later be tried purposely almost
as often as it is now tried accidentally.
But mating such couples must clearly
not involve marrying them. In conjugation two complementary persons may
supply one another's deficiencies: in the
domestic partnership of marriage they
only feel them and suffer from them.
Thus the son of a robust, cheerful,
eupeptic British country squire, with
the tastes and range of his class, and of a
clever, imaginative, intellectual, highly
civilized Jewess, might be very superior
to both his parents; but it is not likely
that the Jewess would find the squire an
interesting companion, or his habits, his
friends, his place and mode of life congenial to her. Therefore marriage, whilst
it is made an indispensable condition of
mating, will delay the advent of the
Superman as effectually as Property, and
will be modified by the impulse towards
him just as effectually.

The practical abrogation of Property
and Marriage as they exist at present will
occur without being much noticed. To
the mass of men, the intelligent abolition
of property would mean nothing except
an increase in the quantity of food,
clothing, housing, and comfort at their
personal disposal, as well as a greater control over their time and circumstances.
Very few persons now make any distinction between virtually complete property
and property held on such highly developed public conditions as to place its
income on the same footing as that of a
propertyless clergyman, officer, or civil
servant. A landed proprietor may still
drive men and women off his land, demolish their dwellings, and replace them
with sheep or deer; and in the unregulated trades the private trader may
still spunge on the regulated trades and
sacrifice the life and health of the nation
as lawlessly as the Manchester cotton

manufacturers did at the beginning of last century. But though the Factory Code on the one hand, and Trade Union organization on the other, have, within the lifetime of men still living, converted the old unrestricted property of the cotton manufacturer in his mill and the cotton spinner in his labor into a mere permission to trade or work on stringent public or collective conditions, imposed in the interest of the general welfare without any regard for individual hard cases, people in Lancashire still speak of their "property" in the old terms, meaning nothing more by it than the things a thief can be punished for stealing. The total abolition of property, and the conversion of every citizen into a salaried functionary in the public service, would leave much more than 99 per cent of the nation quite unconscious of any greater change than now takes place when the son of a shipowner goes into the navy. They would still call their watches and umbrellas and back gardens their property.

Marriage also will persist as a name attached to a general custom long after the custom itself will have altered. For example, modern English marriage, as modified by divorce and by Married Women's Property Acts, differs more from early XIX century marriage than Byron's marriage did from Shakespear's. At the present moment marriage in England differs not only from marriage in France, but from marriage in Scotland. Marriage as modified by the divorce laws in South Dakota would be called mere promiscuity in Clapham. Yet the Americans, far from taking a profligate and cynical view of marriage, do homage to its ideals with a seriousness that seems old fashioned in Clapham. Neither in England nor America would a proposal to abolish marriage be tolerated for a moment; and yet nothing is more certain than that in both countries the progres-

sive modification of the marriage contract will be continued until it is no more onerous nor irrevocable than any ordinary commercial deed of partnership. Were even this dispensed with, people would still call themselves husbands and wives; describe their companionships as marriages; and be for the most part unconscious that they were any less married than Henry VIII. For though a glance at the legal conditions of marriage in different Christian countries shews that marriage varies legally from frontier to frontier, domesticity varies so little that most people believe their own marriage laws to be universal. Consequently here again, as in the case of Property, the absolute confidence of the public in the stability of the institution's name, makes it all the easier to alter its substance.

However, it cannot be denied that one of the changes in public opinion demanded by the need for the Superman is a very unexpected one. It is nothing less than the dissolution of the present necessary association of marriage with conjugation, which most unmarried people regard as the very diagnostic of marriage. They are wrong, of course: it would be quite as near the truth to say that conjugation is the one purely accidental and incidental condition of marriage. Conjugation is essential to nothing but the propagation of the race; and the moment that paramount need is provided for otherwise than by marriage, conjugation, from Nature's creative point of view, ceases to be essential in marriage. But marriage does not thereupon cease to be so economical, convenient, and comfortable, that the Superman might safely bribe the matrimonomaniacs by offering to revive all the old inhuman stringency and irrevocability of marriage, to abolish divorce, to confirm the horrible bond which still chains decent people to drunkards, criminals, and wasters, provided only the complete extrication of conjugation from it were conceded to him. For if people could form domestic companionships on no easier terms than these, they would still marry. The Roman Catholic, forbidden by his Church to avail himself of the divorce laws, marries as freely as the South Dakotan Presbyterians who can change partners with a facility that scandalizes the old world; and were his Church to dare a further step towards Christianity and enjoin celibacy on its laity as well as on its clergy, marriages would still be contracted for the sake of domesticity by perfectly obedient sons and daughters of the Church. One need not further pursue these hypotheses: they are only suggested here to help the reader to analyse marriage into its two functions of regulating conjugation and supplying a form of domesticity. These two functions are quite separable; and domesticity is the only one of the two which is essential to the existence of marriage, because conjugation without domesticity is not marriage at all, whereas domesticity without conjugation is still marriage: in fact it is necessarily the actual condition of all fertile marriages during a great part of their duration, and of some marriages during the whole of it.

Taking it, then, that Property and Marriage, by destroying Equality and thus hampering sexual selection with irrelevant conditions, are hostile to the evolution of the Superman, it is easy to understand why the only generally known modern experiment in breeding the human race took place in a community which discarded both institutions.

III

THE PERFECTIONIST EXPERIMENT AT ONEIDA CREEK

In 1848 the Oneida Community was founded in America to carry out a resolution arrived at by a handful of Perfectionist Communists "that we will devote ourselves exclusively to the establishment of the Kingdom of God." Though the American nation declared that this sort of thing was not to be tolerated in a Christian country, the Oneida Community held its own for over thirty years, during which period it seems to have produced healthier children and done and suffered less evil than any Joint Stock Company on record. It was, however, a highly selected community; for a genuine communist (roughly definable as an intensely proud person who proposes to enrich the common fund instead of to spunge on it) is superior to an ordinary joint stock capitalist precisely as an ordinary joint stock capitalist is superior to a pirate. Further, the Perfectionists were mightily shepherded by their chief Noyes, one of those chance attempts at the Superman which occur from time to time in spite of the interference of Man's blundering institutions. The existence of Noyes simplified the breeding problem for the Communists, the question as to what sort of man they should strive to breed being settled at once by the obvious desirability of breeding another Noyes.

But an experiment conducted by a handful of people, who, after thirty years of immunity from the unintentional child slaughter that goes on by ignorant parents in private homes, numbered only 300, could do very little except prove that Communists, under the guidance of a Superman "devoted exclusively to the establishment of the Kingdom of God," and caring no more for property and marriage than a Camberwell minister cares for Hindoo Caste or Suttee, might make a much better job of their lives than ordinary folk under the harrow of both these institutions. Yet their Superman himself admitted that this apparent success was only part of the abnormal phenomenon of his own occurrence; for when he came to the end of his powers through age, he himself guided and organized the voluntary relapse of the communists into marriage, capitalism, and customary private life, thus admitting that the real social solution was not what a casual Superman could persuade a picked company to do for him, but what a whole community of Supermen would do spontaneously. If Noyes had had to organize, not a few dozen Perfectionists, but the whole United States, America would have beaten him as completely as England beat Oliver Cromwell, France Napoleon, or Rome Julius Cæsar. Cromwell learnt by bitter experience that God himself cannot raise a people above its own level, and that even though you stir a nation to sacrifice all its appetites to its conscience, the result will still depend wholly on what sort of conscience the nation has got. Napoleon seems to have ended by regarding mankind as a troublesome pack of hounds only worth keeping for the sport of hunting with them. Cæsar's capacity for fighting without hatred or resentment was defeated by the determination of his soldiers to kill their enemies in the field instead of taking them prisoners to be spared by Cæsar; and his civil supremacy was purchased by colossal bribery of the citizens of Rome. What great rulers cannot do, codes and religions cannot do. Man reads his own nature into every ordinance: if you devize a superhuman commandment so cunningly that it cannot be misinterpreted in terms of his will, he will denounce it as seditious blasphemy, or else disregard it as either crazy or totally unintelligible. Parliaments and synods may tinker as much as they please with their codes and creeds as circumstances alter the balance of classes and their interests; and, as a result of the tinkering, there may be an occasional illusion of moral evolution, as when the victory of the commercial caste over the military caste leads to the substitution of social boycotting and pecuniary damages for duelling. At certain moments there may even be a considerable material advance, as when the conquest of political power by the working class produces a better distribution of wealth through the simple action of the selfishness of the new masters; but all this is mere readjustment and reformation: until the heart and mind of the people is changed the very greatest man will no more dare to govern on the assumption that all are as great as he than a drover dare leave his flock to find its way through the streets as he himself would. Until there is an England in which every man is a Cromwell, a France in which every man is a Napoleon, a Rome in which every man is a Cæsar, a Germany in which every man is a Luther plus a Goethe, the world will be no more improved by its heroes than a Brixton villa is improved by the pyramid of Cheops. The production of such nations is the only real change possible to us.

IV

MAN'S OBJECTION TO HIS OWN IMPROVEMENT

But would such a change be tolerated if Man must rise above himself to desire it? It would, through his misconception of its nature. Man does desire an ideal Superman with such energy as he can spare from his nutrition, and has in every age magnified the best living substitute for it he can find. His least incompetent general is set up as an Alexander; his king is the first gentleman in the world; his Pope is a saint. He is never without an array of human idols who are all nothing but sham Supermen. That the real Superman will snap his superfingers at all Man's present trumpery ideals of right, duty, honor, justice, religion, even decency, and accept moral obligations beyond present human endurance, is a thing that contemporary Man does not foresee: in fact he does not notice it when our casual Supermen do it in his very face. He actually does it himself every day without knowing it. He will therefore make no objection to the production of a race of what he calls Great Men or Heroes, because he will imagine them, not as true Supermen, but as himself endowed with infinite brains, infinite courage, and infinite money.

The most troublesome opposition will arise from the general fear of mankind that any interference with our conjugal customs will be an interference with our pleasures and our romance. This fear, by putting on airs of offended morality, has always intimidated people who have not measured its essential weakness; but it will prevail with those degenerates only in whom the instinct of fertility has faded into a mere itching for pleasure. The modern devices for combining pleasure with sterility, now universally known and accessible, enable these persons to weed themselves out of the race, a process already vigorously at work; and the consequent survival of the intelligently fertile means the survival of the partizans of the Superman; for what is proposed is nothing but the replacement of the old unintelligent, inevitable, almost unconscious fertility by an intelligently controlled, conscious fertility, and the elimination of the mere voluptuary from the evolutionary process.[1] Even

if this selective agency had not been invented, the purpose of the race would still shatter the opposition of individual instincts. Not only do the bees and the ants satisfy their reproductive and parental instincts vicariously; but marriage itself successfully imposes celibacy on millions of unmarried normal men and women. In short, the individual instinct in this matter, overwhelming as it is thoughtlessly supposed to be, is really a finally negligible one.

V

THE POLITICAL NEED FOR THE SUPERMAN

The need for the Superman is, in its most imperative aspect, a political one. We have been driven to Proletarian Democracy by the failure of all the alternative systems; for these depended on the existence of Supermen acting as despots or oligarchs; and not only were these Supermen not always or even often forthcoming at the right moment and in an eligible social position, but when they were forthcoming they could not, except for a short time and by morally suicidal coercive methods, impose superhumanity on those whom they governed; so, by mere force of "human nature," government by consent of the governed has supplanted the old plan of governing the citizen as a public-schoolboy is governed.

Now we have yet to see the man who, having any practical experience of Proletarian Democracy, has any belief in its capacity for solving great political prob-

---

[1] The part played in evolution by the voluptuary will be the same as that already played by the glutton. The glutton, as the man with the strongest motive for nourishing himself, will always take more pains than his fellows to get food. When food is so difficult to get that only great exertions can secure a sufficient supply of it, the glutton's appetite develops his cunning and enterprise to the utmost; and he becomes not only the best fed but the ablest man in the community. But in more hospitable climates, or where the social organization of the food supply makes it easy for a man to overeat, then the glutton eats himself out of health and finally out of existence. All other voluptuaries prosper and perish in the same way; and this is why the survival of the fittest means finally the survival of the self-controlled, because they alone can adapt themselves to the perpetual shifting of conditions produced by industrial progress.

lems, or even for doing ordinary parochial work intelligently and economically. Only under despotisms and oligarchies has the Radical faith in "universal suffrage" as a political panacea arisen. It withers the moment it is exposed to practical trial, because Democracy cannot rise above the level of the human material of which its voters are made. Switzerland seems happy in comparison with Russia; but if Russia were as small as Switzerland, and had her social problems simplified in the same way by impregnable natural fortifications and a population educated by the same variety and intimacy of international intercourse, there might be little to choose between them. At all events Australia and Canada, which are virtually protected democratic republics, and France and the United States, which are avowedly independent democratic republics, are neither healthy, wealthy, nor wise; and they would be worse instead of better if their popular ministers were not experts in the art of dodging popular enthusiasms and duping popular ignorance. The politician who once had to learn how to flatter Kings has now to learn how to fascinate, amuse, coax, humbug, frighten, or otherwise strike the fancy of the electorate; and though in advanced modern States, where the artizan is better educated than the King, it takes a much bigger man to be a successful demagogue than to be a successful courtier, yet he who holds popular convictions with prodigious energy is the man for the mob, whilst the frailer sceptic who is cautiously feeling his way towards the next century has no chance unless he happens by accident to have the specific artistic talent of the mountebank as well, in which case it is as a mountebank that he catches votes, and not as a meliorist. Consequently the demagogue, though he professes (and fails) to readjust matters in the interests of the majority of the electors, yet stereotypes mediocrity, organizes intolerance, disparages exhibitions of uncommon qualities, and glorifies conspicuous exhibitions of common ones. He manages a small job well: he muddles rhetorically through a large one. When a great political movement takes place, it is not consciously led nor organized: the unconscious self in mankind breaks its way through the problem as an elephant breaks through a jungle; and the politicians make speeches about whatever happens in the process, which, with the best intentions, they do all in their power to prevent. Finally, when social aggregation arrives at a point demanding international organization before the demagogues and electorates have learnt how to manage even a country parish properly much less internationalize Constantinople, the whole political business goes to smash; and presently we have Ruins of Empires, New Zealanders sitting on a broken arch of London Bridge, and so forth.

To that recurrent catastrophe we shall certainly come again unless we can have a Democracy of Supermen; and the production of such a Democracy is the only change that is now hopeful enough to nerve us to the effort that Revolution demands.

VI

PRUDERY EXPLAINED

Why the bees should pamper their mothers whilst we pamper only our operatic prima donnas is a question worth reflecting on. Our notion of treating a mother is, not to increase her supply of food, but to cut it off by forbidding her to work in a factory for a month after her confinement. Everything that can make birth a misfortune to the parents as well as a danger to the mother is conscientiously done. When a great French writer, Émile Zola, alarmed at the sterilization of his nation, wrote an eloquent and powerful book to restore the prestige of parentage, it was at once assumed in England that a work of this character, with such a title as Fecundity, was too abominable to be translated, and that any attempt to deal with the relations of the sexes from any other than the voluptuary or romantic point of view must be sternly put down. Now if this assumption were really founded on public opinion, it would indicate an attitude of disgust and resentment towards the Life Force that could only arise in a diseased and moribund community in which Ibsen's Hedda Gabler would be the typical woman. But it has no vital foundation at all. The prudery of the newspapers is, like the prudery of the dinner table, a mere difficulty of education and language. We are not taught to think decently on these subjects, and consequently we have no language for them except indecent language. We therefore have to declare them unfit for public discussion, because the only terms in which we can conduct the discussion are unfit for public use. Physiologists, who have a technical vocabulary at their disposal, find no difficulty; and masters of language who think decently can write popular stories like Zola's Fecundity or Tolstoy's Resurrection without giving the smallest offence to readers who can also think decently. But the ordinary modern journalist, who has never discussed such matters except in ribaldry, cannot write a simple comment on a divorce case without a conscious shamefulness or a furtive facetiousness that makes it impossible to read the comment aloud in company. All this ribaldry and prudery (the two are the same) does not mean that people do not feel decently on the subject: on the contrary, it is just the depth and seriousness of our feeling that makes its desecration by vile language and coarse humor in-

tolerable; so that at last we cannot bear to have it spoken of at all because only one in a thousand can speak of it without wounding our self-respect, especially the self-respect of women. Add to the horrors of popular language the horrors of popular poverty. In crowded populations poverty destroys the possibility of cleanliness; and in the absence of cleanliness many of the natural conditions of life become offensive and noxious, with the result that at last the association of uncleanliness with these natural conditions becomes so overpowering that among civilized people (that is, people massed in the labyrinths of slums we call cities), half their bodily life becomes a guilty secret, unmentionable except to the doctor in emergencies; and Hedda Gabler shoots herself because maternity is so unladylike. In short, popular prudery is only a mere incident of popular squalor: the subjects which it taboos remain the most interesting and earnest of subjects in spite of it.

VII

PROGRESS AN ILLUSION

Unfortunately the earnest people get drawn off the track of evolution by the illusion of progress. Any Socialist can convince us easily that the difference between Man as he is and Man as he might become, without further evolution, under millennial conditions of nutrition, environment, and training, is enormous. He can shew that inequality and iniquitous distribution of wealth and allotment of labor have arisen through an unscientific economic system, and that Man, faulty as he is, no more intended to establish any such ordered disorder than a moth intends to be burnt when it flies into a candle flame. He can shew that the difference between the grace and strength of the acrobat and the bent back of the rheumatic field laborer is a difference produced by conditions, not by nature. He can shew that many of the most detestable human vices are not radical, but are mere reactions of our institutions on our very virtues. The Anarchist, the Fabian, the Salvationist, the Vegetarian, the doctor, the lawyer, the parson, the professor of ethics, the gymnast, the soldier, the sportsman, the inventor, the political program-maker, all have some prescription for bettering us; and almost all their remedies are physically possible and aimed at admitted evils. To them the limit of progress is, at worst, the completion of all the suggested reforms and the levelling up of all men to the point attained already by the most highly nourished and cultivated in mind and body.

Here, then, as it seems to them, is an enormous field for the energy of the reformer. Here are many noble goals attainable by many of those paths up the Hill Difficulty along which great spirits love to aspire. Unhappily, the hill will never be climbed by Man as we know him. It need not be denied that if we all struggled bravely to the end of the reformers' paths we should improve the world prodigiously. But there is no more hope in that If than in the equally plausible assurance that if the sky falls we shall all catch larks. We are not going to tread those paths: we have not sufficient energy. We do not desire the end enough: indeed in most cases we do not effectively desire it at all. Ask any man would he like to be a better man; and he will say yes, most piously. Ask him would he like to have a million of money; and he will say yes, most sincerely. But the pious citizen who would like to be a better man goes on behaving just as he did before. And the tramp who would like the million does not take the trouble to earn ten shillings: multitudes of men and women, all eager to accept a legacy of a million, live and die without having ever possessed five pounds at one time, although beggars have died in rags on mattresses stuffed with gold which they accumulated because they desired it enough to nerve them to get it and keep it. The economists who discovered that demand created supply soon had to limit the proposition to "effective demand," which turned out, in the final analysis, to mean nothing more than supply itself; and this holds good in politics, morals, and all other departments as well: the actual supply is the measure of the effective demand; and the mere aspirations and professions produce nothing. No community has ever yet passed beyond the initial phases in which its pugnacity and fanaticism enabled it to found a nation, and its cupidity to establish and develop a commercial civilization. Even these stages have never been attained by public spirit, but always by intolerant wilfulness and brute force. Take the Reform Bill of 1832 as an example of a conflict between two sections of educated Englishmen concerning a political measure which was as obviously necessary and inevitable as any political measure has ever been or is ever likely to be. It was not passed until the gentlemen of Birmingham had made arrangements to cut the throats of the gentlemen of St James's parish in due military form. It would not have been passed to this day if there had been no force behind it except the logic and public conscience of the Utilitarians. A despotic ruler with as much sense as Queen Elizabeth would have done better than the mob of grownup Eton boys who governed us then by privilege, and who, since the introduction of practically Manhood Suffrage in 1884, now govern us at the request of Proletarian Democracy.

At the present time we have, instead of the Utilitarians, the Fabian Society, with its peaceful, constitutional, moral, economical policy of Socialism, which needs nothing for its bloodless and benevolent realization except that the English people shall understand it and approve of it. But why are the Fabians well spoken of in circles where thirty years ago the word Socialist was understood as equivalent to cutthroat and incendiary? Not because the English have the smallest intention of studying or adopting the Fabian policy, but because they believe that the Fabians, by eliminating the element of intimidation from the Socialist agitation, have drawn the teeth of insurgent poverty and saved the existing order from the only method of attack it really fears. Of course, if the nation adopted the Fabian policy, it would be carried out by brute force exactly as our present property system is. It would become the law; and those who resisted it would be fined, sold up, knocked on the head by policemen, thrown into prison, and in the last resort "executed" just as they are when they break the present law. But as our proprietary class has no fear of that conversion taking place, whereas it does fear sporadic cutthroats and gunpowder plots, and strives with all its might to hide the fact that there is no moral difference whatever between the methods by which it enforces its proprietary rights and the method by which the dynamitard asserts his conception of natural human rights, the Fabian Society is patted on the back just as the Christian Social Union is, whilst the Socialist who says bluntly that a Social revolution can be made only as all other revolutions have been made, by the people who want it killing, coercing, and intimidating the people who dont want it, is denounced as a misleader of the people, and imprisoned with hard labor to shew him how much sincerity there is in the objection of his captors to physical force.

Are we then to repudiate Fabian methods, and return to those of the barricader, or adopt those of the dynamitard and the assassin? On the contrary, we are to recognize that both are fundamentally futile. It seems easy for the dynamitard to say "Have you not just admitted that nothing is ever conceded except to physical force? Did not Gladstone admit that the Irish Church was disestablished, not by the spirit of Liberalism, but by the explosion which wrecked Clerkenwell prison?" Well, we need not foolishly and timidly deny it. Let it be fully granted. Let us grant, further, that all this lies in the nature of things; that the most ardent Socialist, if he owns property, can by no means do otherwise than Conservative proprietors until property is forcibly abolished by the whole nation; nay, that ballots and parliamentary divisions, in spite of their vain ceremony of discussion, differ from battles only as the bloodless surrender of an outnumbered force in the field differs from Waterloo or Trafalgar. I make a present of all these admissions to the Fenian who collects money from thoughtless Irishmen in America to blow up Dublin Castle; to the detective who persuades foolish young workmen to order bombs from the nearest ironmonger and then delivers them up to penal servitude; to our military and naval commanders who believe, not in preaching, but in an ultimatum backed by plenty of lyddite; and, generally, to all whom it may concern. But of what use is it to substitute the way of the reckless and bloodyminded for the way of the cautious and humane? Is England any the better for the wreck of Clerkenwell prison, or Ireland for the disestablishment of the Irish Church? Is there the smallest reason to suppose that the nation which sheepishly let Charles and Laud and Strafford coerce it, gained anything because it afterwards, still more sheepishly, let a few strongminded Puritans, inflamed by the masterpieces of

Jewish revolutionary literature, cut off the heads of the three? Suppose the Gunpowder plot had succeeded, and set a Fawkes dynasty permanently on the throne, would it have made any difference to the present state of the nation? The guillotine was used in France up to the limit of human endurance, both on Girondins and Jacobins. Fouquier Tinville followed Marie Antoinette to the scaffold; and Marie Antoinette might have asked the crowd, just as pointedly as Fouquier did, whether their bread would be any cheaper when her head was off. And what came of it all? The Imperial France of the Rougon Macquart family, and the Republican France of the Panama scandal and the Dreyfus case. Was the difference worth the guillotining of all those unlucky ladies and gentlemen, useless and mischievous as many of them were? Would any sane man guillotine a mouse to bring about such a result? Turn to Republican America. America has no Star Chamber, and no feudal barons. But it has Trusts; and it has millionaires whose factories, fenced in by live electric wires and defended by Pinkerton retainers with magazine rifles, would have made a Radical of Reginald Front de Bœuf. Would Washington or Franklin have lifted a finger in the cause of American Independence if they had foreseen its reality?

No: what Cæsar, Cromwell, and Napoleon could not do with all the physical force and moral prestige of the State in their mighty hands, cannot be done by enthusiastic criminals and lunatics. Even the Jews, who, from Moses to Marx and Lassalle, have inspired all the revolutions, have had to confess that, after all, the dog will return to his vomit and the sow that was washed to her wallowing in the mire; and we may as well make up our minds that Man will return to his idols and his cupidities, in spite of all "movements" and all revolutions, until his nature is changed. Until then, his early successes in building commercial civilizations (and such civilizations, Good Heavens!) are but preliminaries to the inevitable later stage, now threatening us, in which the passions which built the civilization become fatal instead of productive, just as the same qualities which make the lion king in the forest ensure his destruction when he enters a city. Nothing can save society then except the clear head and the wide purpose: war and competition, potent instruments of selection and evolution in one epoch, become ruinous instruments of degeneration in the next. In the breeding of animals and plants, varieties which have arisen by selection through many generations relapse precipitously into the wild type in a generation or two when selection ceases; and in the same way a civilization in which lusty pugnacity and greed have ceased to act as selective agents and have begun to obstruct and destroy, rushes downwards and backwards with a suddenness that enables an observer to see with consternation the upward steps of many centuries retraced in a single lifetime. This has often occurred even within the period covered by history; and in every instance the turning point has been reached long before the attainment, or even the general advocacy on paper, of the levelling-up of the mass to the highest point attainable by the best nourished and cultivated normal individuals.

We must therefore frankly give up the notion that Man as he exists is capable of net progress. There will always be an illusion of progress, because wherever we are conscious of an evil we remedy it, and therefore always seem to ourselves to be progressing, forgetting that most of the evils we see are the effects, finally become acute, of long-unnoticed retrogressions; that our compromising remedies seldom fully recover the lost ground; above all, that on the lines along which we are degenerating, good has become evil in our eyes, and is being undone in the name of progress precisely as evil is undone and replaced by good on the lines along which we are evolving. This is indeed the Illusion of Illusions; for it gives us infallible and appalling assurance that if our political ruin is to come, it will be effected by ardent reformers and supported by enthusiastic patriots as a series of necessary steps in our progress. Let the Reformer, the Progressive, the Meliorist then reconsider himself and his eternal ifs and ans which never become pots and pans. Whilst Man remains what he is, there can be no progress beyond the point already attained and fallen headlong from at every attempt at civilization; and since even that point is but a pinnacle to which a few people cling in giddy terror above an abyss of squalor, mere progress should no longer charm us.

VIII

THE CONCEIT OF CIVILIZATION

After all, the progress illusion is not so very subtle. We begin by reading the satires of our fathers' contemporaries; and we conclude (usually quite ignorantly) that the abuses exposed by them are things of the past. We see also that reforms of crying evils are frequently produced by the sectional shifting of political power from oppressors to oppressed. The poor man is given a vote by the Liberals in the hope that he will cast it for his emancipators. The hope is not fulfilled; but the lifelong imprisonment of penniless men for debt ceases; Factory Acts are passed to mitigate sweating; schooling is made free and compulsory; sanitary by-laws are multiplied; public steps are taken to house the masses decently; the barefooted get boots; rags become rare; and bathrooms and pianos, smart tweeds and starched collars, reach numbers of people who once, as "the unsoaped," played the Jew's harp or the accordion in moleskins and belchers. Some of these changes are gains: some of them are losses. Some of them are not changes at all: all of them are merely the changes that money makes. Still, they produce an illusion of bustling progress; and the reading class infers from them that the abuses of the early Victorian period no longer exist except as amusing pages in the novels of Dickens. But the moment we look for a reform due to character and not to money, to statesmanship and not to interest or mutiny, we are disillusioned. For example, we remembered the maladministration and incompetence revealed by the Crimean War as part of a bygone state of things until the South African war shewed that the nation and the War Office, like those poor Bourbons who have been so impudently blamed for a universal characteristic, had learnt nothing and forgotten nothing. We had hardly recovered from the fruitless irritation of this discovery when it transpired that the officers' mess of our most select regiment included a flogging club presided over by the senior subaltern. The disclosure provoked some disgust at the details of this schoolboyish debauchery, but no surprise at the apparent absence of any conception of manly honor and virtue, of personal courage and self-respect, in the front rank of our chivalry. In civil affairs we had assumed that the sycophancy and idolatry which encouraged Charles I to undervalue the puritan revolt of the XVII century had been long outgrown; but it has needed nothing but favorable circumstances to revive, with added abjectness to compensate for its lost piety. We have relapsed into disputes about transubstantiation at the very moment when the discovery of the wide prevalence of theophagy as a tribal custom has deprived us of the last excuse for believing that our official religious rites differ in essentials from those of barbarians. The Christian doctrine of the uselessness of punishment and the wickedness of revenge has not, in spite of its simple common sense, found a single convert among the nations: Christianity means nothing to the masses but a sensational public execution which is made an excuse for other executions. In its name we take ten years of a thief's life minute by minute in the slow misery and degradation of modern reformed imprisonment with as little remorse as Laud and his Star Chamber clipped the ears of Bastwick and Burton. We dug up and mutilated the remains of the Mahdi the other day exactly as we dug up and mutilated the remains of Cromwell two centuries ago. We have demanded the decapitation of the Chinese Boxer princes as any Tartar would have done; and our military and naval expeditions to kill, burn, and destroy tribes and villages for knocking an Englishman on the head are so common a part of our Imperial routine that the last dozen of them has not called forth as much pity as can be counted on by any lady criminal. The judicial use of torture to extort confession is supposed to be a relic of darker ages; but whilst these pages are being written an English judge has sentenced a forger to twenty years penal servitude with an open declaration that the sentence will be carried out in full unless he confesses where he has hidden the notes he forged. And no comment whatever is made either on this or on a telegram from the seat of war in Somaliland mentioning that certain information has been given by a prisoner of war "under punishment." Even if these reports are false, the fact that they are accepted without protest as indicating a natural and proper course of public conduct shews that we are still as ready to resort to torture as Bacon was. As to vindictive cruelty, an incident in the South African war, when the relatives and friends of a prisoner were forced to witness his execution, betrayed a baseness of temper and character which hardly leaves us the right to plume ourselves on our superiority to Edward III at the surrender of Calais. And the democratic American officer indulges in torture in the Philippines just as the aristocratic English officer did in South Africa. The incidents of the white invasion of Africa in search of ivory, gold, diamonds, and sport, have proved that the modern European is the same beast of prey that formerly marched to the conquest of new worlds under Alexander, Antony, and Pizarro. Parliaments and vestries are just what they were when Cromwell suppressed them and Dickens derided them. The democratic politician remains exactly as Plato described him; the physician is still the credulous impostor and petulant scientific coxcomb whom Molière ridiculed; the schoolmaster remains at best a pedantic child farmer and at worst a flagellomaniac; arbitrations are more dreaded by honest men than lawsuits; the philanthropist is still a parasite on misery as the doctor is on disease; the miracles of priestcraft are none the less fraudulent and mischievous because they are now called scientific experiments and conducted by professors; witchcraft, in the modern form of patent medicines and prophylactic inoculations, is rampant; the landowner who is no longer powerful enough to set the mantrap of Rhampsinitis improves on it by barbed wire; the modern gentleman who is too lazy to daub his face with vermilion as a symbol of bravery employs a laundress to daub his shirt with starch as a symbol of cleanliness; we shake our heads at the dirt of the middle ages in cities made grimy with soot and foul and disgusting with shameless tobacco smoking; holy water, in its latest form of disinfectant fluid, is more widely used and believed in than ever; public health authorities deliberately go through incantations with burning sulphur (which they know to be useless) because the people believe in it as devoutly as the Italian peasant believes in the liquefaction of the blood of St Januarius; and straightforward public lying has reached gigantic developments, there being nothing to choose in this respect between the pickpocket at the police station and the minister on the treasury bench, the editor in the newspaper office, the city magnate advertizing bicycle tires that do not side-slip, the clergyman subscribing the thirty-nine articles, and the vivisector who pledges his knightly honor that no animal operated on in the physiological laboratory suffers the slightest pain. Hypocrisy is at its worst; for we not only persecute bigotedly but sincerely in the name of the curemongering witchcraft we do believe in, but callously and hypocritically in the name of the Evangelical creed that our rulers privately smile at as the Italian patricians of the fifth century smiled at Jupiter and Venus. Sport is, as it has always been, murderous excitement: the impulse to slaughter is universal; and museums are set up throughout the country to encourage little children and elderly gentlemen to make collections of corpses preserved in alcohol, and to steal birds' eggs and keep them as the red Indian used to keep scalps. Coercion with the lash is as natural to an Englishman as it was to Solomon spoiling Rehoboam: indeed, the comparison is unfair to the Jews in view of the facts that the Mosaic law forbade more than forty lashes in the name of humanity, and that floggings of a thousand lashes were inflicted on English soldiers in the XVIII and XIX centuries, and would be inflicted still but for the change in the balance of political power between the military caste and the commercial classes and the proletariat. In spite of that change, flogging is still an institution in the public school, in the military prison, on the training ship, and in that school of littleness called the home. The lascivious clamor of the flagellomaniac for more of it, constant as the clamor for more insolence, more war, and lower rates, is tolerated and even gratified because, having no moral ends in view, we have sense enough to see that nothing but brute coercion can impose our selfish will on others. Cowardice is universal: patriotism, public opinion, parental duty, discipline, religion, morality, are only fine names for intimidation; and cruelty, gluttony, and credulity keep cowardice in countenance. We cut the throat of a calf and hang it up by the heels to bleed to death so that our veal cutlet may be white; we nail geese to a board and cram them with food because we like the taste of liver disease; we tear birds to pieces to decorate our women's hats; we mutilate domestic animals for no reason at all except to follow an instinctively cruel fashion; and we connive at the most abominable tortures in the hope of discovering some magical cure for our own diseases by them.

Now please observe that these are not exceptional developments of our admitted vices, deplored and prayed against by all good men. Not a word has been said here of the excesses of our Neros, of whom we have the full usual percentage. With the exception of the few military examples, which are mentioned mainly to shew that the education and standing of a gentleman, reinforced by the strongest conventions of honor, *esprit de corps*, publicity and responsibility, afford no better guarantees of conduct than the passions of a mob, the illustrations given above are commonplaces taken from the daily practices of our best citizens, vehemently defended in our newspapers and in our pulpits. The very humanitarians who abhor them are stirred to murder by them: the dagger of Brutus and Ravaillac is still active in the hands of Caserio and Luccheni; and the pistol has come to its aid in the hands of Guiteau and Czolgosz. Our remedies are still limited to endurance or assassination; and the assassin is still judicially assassinated on the principle that two blacks make a white. The only novelty is in our methods: through the discovery of dynamite the overloaded musket of Hamilton of Bothwellhaugh has been superseded by the bomb; but Ravachol's heart burns just as Hamilton's did. The world will not bear thinking of to those who know what it is, even with the largest discount for the restraints of poverty on the poor and cowardice on the rich.

All that can be said for us is that people must and do live and let live up to a certain point. Even the horse, with his docked tail and bitted jaw, finds his slavery mitigated by the fact that a total disregard of his need for food and rest would put his master to the expense of buying a new horse every second day: for you cannot work a horse to death and then pick up another one for nothing, as you can a laborer. But this natural check on inconsiderate selfishness is itself checked, partly by our shortsightedness, and partly by deliberate calculation; so that beside the man who, to his own loss, will shorten his horse's life in mere stinginess, we have the tramway company which discovers actuarially that though a horse may live from 24 to 40 years, yet it pays better to work him to death in 4 and then replace him by a fresh victim. And human slavery, which has reached its worst recorded point

within our own time in the form of free wage labor, has encountered the same personal and commercial limits to both its aggravation and its mitigation. Now that the freedom of wage labor has produced a scarcity of it, as in South Africa, the leading English newspaper and the leading English weekly review have openly and without apology demanded a return to compulsory labor: that is, to the methods by which, as we believe, the Egyptians built the pyramids. We know now that the crusade against chattel slavery in the XIX century succeeded solely because chattel slavery was neither the most effective nor the least humane method of labor exploitation; and the world is now feeling its way towards a still more effective system which shall abolish the freedom of the worker without again making his exploiter responsible for him.

Still, there is always some mitigation: there is the fear of revolt; and there are the effects of kindliness and affection. Let it be repeated therefore that no indictment is here laid against the world on the score of what its criminals and monsters do. The fires of Smithfield and of the Inquisition were lighted by earnestly pious people, who were kind and good as kindness and goodness go. And when a negro is dipped in kerosine and set on fire in America at the present time, he is not a good man lynched by ruffians: he is a criminal lynched by crowds of respectable, charitable, virtuously indignant, high-minded citizens, who, though they act outside the law, are at least more merciful than the American legislators and judges who not so long ago condemned men to solitary confinement for periods, not of five months, as our own practice is, but of five years and more. The things that our moral monsters do may be left out of account with St Bartholomew massacres and other momentary outbursts of social disorder. Judge us by the admitted and respected practice of our most reputable circles; and, if you know the facts and are strong enough to look them in the face, you must admit that unless we are replaced by a more highly evolved animal—in short, by the Superman—the world must remain a den of dangerous animals among whom our few accidental supermen, our Shakespears, Goethes, Shelleys, and their like, must live as precariously as lion tamers do, taking the humor of their situation, and the dignity of their superiority, as a set-off to the horror of the one and the loneliness of the other.

IX

THE VERDICT OF HISTORY

It may be said that though the wild beast breaks out in Man and casts him back momentarily into barbarism under the excitement of war and crime, yet his normal life is higher than the normal life of his forefathers. This view is very acceptable to Englishmen, who always lean sincerely to virtue's side as long as it costs them nothing either in money or in thought. They feel deeply the injustice of foreigners, who allow them no credit for this conditional highmindedness. But there is no reason to suppose that our ancestors were less capable of it than we are. To all such claims for the existence of a progressive moral evolution operating visibly from grandfather to grandson, there is the conclusive reply that a thousand years of such evolution would have produced enormous social changes, of which the historical evidence would be overwhelming. But not Macaulay himself, the most confident of Whig meliorists, can produce any such evidence that will bear cross-examination. Compare our conduct and our codes with those mentioned con-

temporarily in such ancient scriptures and classics as have come down to us, and you will find no jot of ground for the belief that any moral progress whatever has been made in historic time, in spite of all the romantic attempts of historians to reconstruct the past on that assumption. Within that time it has happened to nations as to private families and individuals that they have flourished and decayed, repented and hardened their hearts, submitted and protested, acted and reacted, oscillated between natural and artificial sanitation (the oldest house in the world, unearthed the other day in Crete, has quite modern sanitary arrangements), and rung a thousand changes on the different scales of income and pressure of population, firmly believing all the time that mankind was advancing by leaps and bounds because men were constantly busy. And the mere chapter of accidents has left a small accumulation of chance discoveries, such as the wheel, the arch, the safety pin, gunpowder, the magnet, the Voltaic pile, and so forth: things which, unlike the gospels and philosophic treatises of the sages, can be usefully understood and applied by common men; so that steam locomotion is possible without a nation of Stephensons, although national Christianity is impossible without a nation of Christs. But does any man seriously believe that the chauffeur who drives a motor car from Paris to Berlin is a more highly evolved man than the charioteer of Achilles, or that a modern Prime Minister is a more enlightened ruler than Cæsar because he rides a tricycle, writes his dispatches by the electric light, and instructs his stockbroker through the telephone?

Enough, then, of this goose-cackle about Progress: Man, as he is, never will nor can add a cubit to his stature by any of its quackeries, political, scientific, educational, religious, or artistic. What is likely to happen when this conviction gets into the minds of the men whose present faith in these illusions is the cement of our social system, can be imagined only by those who know how suddenly a civilization which has long ceased to think (or in the old phrase, to watch and pray) can fall to pieces when the vulgar belief in its hypocrisies and impostures can no longer hold out against its failures and scandals. When religious and ethical formulæ become so obsolete that no man of strong mind can believe them, they have also reached the point at which no man of high character will profess them; and from that moment until they are formally disestablished, they stand at the door of every profession and every public office to keep out every able man who is not a sophist or a liar. A nation which revises its parish councils once in three years, but will not revise its articles of religion once in three hundred, even when those articles avowedly began as a political compromise dictated by Mr Facing-Both-Ways, is a nation that needs remaking.

Our only hope, then, is in evolution. We must replace the man by the superman. It is frightful for the citizen, as the years pass him, to see his own contemporaries so exactly reproduced by the younger generation, that his companions of thirty years ago have their counterparts in every city crowd, where he has to check himself repeatedly in the act of saluting as an old friend some young man to whom he is only an elderly stranger. All hope of advance dies in his bosom as he watches them: he knows that they will do just what their fathers did, and that the few voices which will still, as always before, exhort them to do something else and be something better, might as well spare their breath to cool their porridge (if they can get any). Men like Ruskin and Carlyle will preach to Smith and Brown for the sake of preach-

ing, just as St Francis preached to the birds and St Anthony to the fishes. But Smith and Brown, like the fishes and birds, remain as they are; and poets who plan Utopias and prove that nothing is necessary for their realization but that Man should will them, perceive at last, like Richard Wagner, that the fact to be faced is that Man does not effectively will them. And he never will until he becomes Superman.

And so we arrive at the end of the Socialist's dream of "the socialization of the means of production and exchange," of the Positivist's dream of moralizing the capitalist, and of the ethical professor's, legislator's, educator's dream of putting commandments and codes and lessons and examination marks on a man as harness is put on a horse, ermine on a judge, pipeclay on a soldier, or a wig on an actor, and pretending that his nature has been changed. The only fundamental and possible Socialism is the socialization of the selective breeding of Man: in other terms, of human evolution. We must eliminate the Yahoo, or his vote will wreck the commonwealth.

X

THE METHOD

As to the method, what can be said as yet except that where there is a will, there is a way? If there be no will, we are lost. That is a possibility for our crazy little empire, if not for the universe; and as such possibilities are not to be entertained without despair, we must, whilst we survive, proceed on the assumption that we have still energy enough to not only will to live, but to will to live better. That may mean that we must establish a State Department of Evolution, with a seat in the Cabinet for its chief, and a revenue to defray the cost of direct State experiments, and provide inducements to private persons to achieve successful results. It may mean a private society or a chartered company for the improvement of human live stock. But for the present it is far more likely to mean a blatant repudiation of such proposals as indecent and immoral, with, nevertheless, a general secret pushing of the human will in the repudiated direction; so that all sorts of institutions and public authorities will under some pretext or other feel their way furtively towards the Superman. Mr Graham Wallas has already ventured to suggest, as Chairman of the School Management Committee of the London School Board, that the accepted policy of the Sterilization of the Schoolmistress, however administratively convenient, is open to criticism from the national stock-breeding point of view; and this is as good an example as any of the way in which the drift towards the Superman may operate in spite of all our hypocrisies. One thing at least is clear to begin with. If a woman can, by careful selection of a father, and nourishment of herself, produce a citizen with efficient senses, sound organs, and a good digestion, she should clearly be secured a sufficient reward for that natural service to make her willing to undertake and repeat it. Whether she be financed in the undertaking by herself, or by the father, or by a speculative capitalist, or by a new department of, say, the Royal Dublin Society, or (as at present) by the War Office maintaining her "on the strength" and authorizing a particular soldier to marry her, or by a local authority under a by-law directing that women may under certain circumstances have a year's leave of absence on full salary, or by the central government, does not matter provided the result be satisfactory.

It is a melancholy fact that as the vast majority of women and their husbands have, under existing circumstances, not enough nourishment, no capital, no credit, and no knowledge of science or business, they would, if the State would pay for birth as it now pays for death, be exploited by joint stock companies for dividends, just as they are in ordinary industries. Even a joint stock human stud farm (piously disguised as a reformed Foundling Hospital or something of that sort) might well, under proper inspection and regulation, produce better results than our present reliance on promiscuous marriage. It may be objected that when an ordinary contractor produces stores for sale to the Government, and the Government rejects them as not up to the required standard, the condemned goods are either sold for what they will fetch or else scrapped: that is, treated as waste material; whereas if the goods consisted of human beings, all that could be done would be to let them loose or send them to the nearest workhouse. But there is nothing new in private enterprise throwing its human refuse on the cheap labor market and the workhouse; and the refuse of the new industry would presumably be better bred than the staple product of ordinary poverty. In our present happy-go-lucky industrial disorder, all the human products, successful or not, would have to be thrown on the labor market; but the unsuccessful ones would not entitle the company to a bounty and so would be a dead loss to it. The practical commercial difficulty would be the uncertainty and the cost in time and money of the first experiments. Purely commercial capital would not touch such heroic operations during the experimental stage; and in any case the strength of mind needed for so momentous a new departure could not be fairly expected from the Stock Exchange. It will have to be handled by statesmen with character enough to tell our democracy and plutocracy that statecraft does not consist in flattering their follies or applying their suburban standards of propriety to the affairs of four continents. The matter must be taken up either by the State or by some organization strong enough to impose respect upon the State.

The novelty of any such experiment, however, is only in the scale of it. In one conspicuous case, that of royalty, the State does already select the parents on purely political grounds; and in the peerage, though the heir to a dukedom is legally free to marry a dairymaid, yet the social pressure on him to confine his choice to politically and socially eligible mates is so overwhelming that he is really no more free to marry the dairymaid than George IV was to marry Mrs Fitzherbert; and such a marriage could only occur as a result of extraordinary strength of character on the part of the dairymaid acting upon extraordinary weakness on the part of the duke. Let those who think the whole conception of intelligent breeding absurd and scandalous ask themselves why George IV was not allowed to choose his own wife whilst any tinker could marry whom he pleased? Simply because it did not matter a rap politically whom the tinker married, whereas it mattered very much whom the king married. The way in which all considerations of the king's personal rights, of the claims of the heart, of the sanctity of the marriage oath, and of romantic morality crumpled up before this political need shews how negligible all these apparently irresistible prejudices are when they come into conflict with the demand for quality in our rulers. We learn the same lesson from the case of the soldier, whose marriage, when it is permitted at all, is despotically controlled with a view solely to military efficiency.

Well, nowadays it is not the King that rules, but the tinker. Dynastic wars are no longer feared, dynastic alliances no longer valued. Marriages in royal families are becoming rapidly less political, and more popular, domestic, and romantic. If all the kings in Europe were made as free tomorrow as King Cophetua, nobody but their aunts and chamberlains would feel a moment's anxiety as to the consequences. On the other hand a sense of the social importance of the tinker's marriage has been steadily growing. We have made a public matter of his wife's health in the month after her confinement. We have taken the minds of his children out of his hands and put them into those of our State schoolmaster. We shall presently make their bodily nourishment independent of him. But they are still riff-raff; and to hand the country over to riff-raff is national suicide, since riff-raff can neither govern nor will let anyone else govern except the highest bidder of bread and circuses. There is no public enthusiast alive of twenty years' practical democratic experience who believes in the political adequacy of the electorate or of the bodies it elects. The overthrow of the aristocrat has created the necessity for the Superman.

Englishmen hate Liberty and Equality too much to understand them. But every Englishman loves and desires a pedigree. And in that he is right. King Demos must be bred like all other Kings; and with Must there is no arguing. It is idle for an individual writer to carry so great a matter further in a pamphlet. A conference on the subject is the next step needed. It will be attended by men and women who, no longer believing that they can live for ever, are seeking for some immortal work into which they can build the best of themselves before their refuse is thrown into that arch dust destructor, the cremation furnace.

MAXIMS FOR REVOLUTIONISTS

THE GOLDEN RULE

Do not do unto others as you would that they should do unto you. Their tastes may not be the same.

Never resist temptation: prove all things: hold fast that which is good.

Do not love your neighbor as yourself. If you are on good terms with yourself it is an impertinence; if on bad, an injury.

The golden rule is that there are no golden rules.

IDOLATRY

The art of government is the organization of idolatry.

The bureaucracy consists of functionaries; the aristocracy, of idols; the democracy, of idolaters.

The populace cannot understand the bureaucracy: it can only worship the national idols.

The savage bows down to idols of wood and stone: the civilized man to idols of flesh and blood.

A limited monarchy is a device for combining the inertia of a wooden idol with the credibility of a flesh and blood one.

When the wooden idol does not answer the peasant's prayer, he beats it: when the flesh and blood idol does not satisfy the civilized man, he cuts its head off.

He who slays a king and he who dies for him are alike idolaters.

ROYALTY

Kings are not born: they are made by artificial hallucination. When the process is interrupted by adversity at a critical age, as in the case of Charles II, the sub-

ject becomes sane and never completely recovers his kingliness.

The Court is the servants' hall of the sovereign.

Vulgarity in a king flatters the majority of the nation.

The flunkeyism propagated by the throne is the price we pay for its political convenience.

DEMOCRACY

If the lesser mind could measure the greater as a footrule can measure a pyramid, there would be finality in universal suffrage. As it is, the political problem remains unsolved.

Democracy substitutes election by the incompetent many for appointment by the corrupt few.

Democratic republics can no more dispense with national idols than monarchies with public functionaries.

Government presents only one problem: the discovery of a trustworthy anthropometric method.

IMPERIALISM

Excess of insularity makes a Briton an Imperialist.

Excess of local self-assertion makes a colonist an Imperialist.

A colonial Imperialist is one who raises colonial troops, equips a colonial squadron, claims a Federal Parliament sending its measures to the Throne instead of to the Colonial Office, and, being finally brought by this means into insoluble conflict with the insular British Imperialist, "cuts the painter" and breaks up the Empire.

LIBERTY AND EQUALITY

He who confuses political liberty with freedom and political equality with similarity has never thought for five minutes about either.

Nothing can be unconditional: consequently nothing can be free.

Liberty means responsibility. That is why most men dread it.

The duke inquires contemptuously whether his gamekeeper is the equal of the Astronomer Royal; but he insists that they shall both be hanged equally if they murder him.

The notion that the colonel need be a better man than the private is as confused as the notion that the keystone need be stronger than the coping stone.

Where equality is undisputed, so also is subordination.

Equality is fundamental in every department of social organization.

The relation of superior to inferior excludes good manners.

EDUCATION

When a man teaches something he does not know to somebody else who has no aptitude for it, and gives him a certificate of proficiency, the latter has completed the education of a gentleman.

A fool's brain digests philosophy into folly, science into superstition, and art into pedantry. Hence University education.

The best brought-up children are those who have seen their parents as they are. Hypocrisy is not the parent's first duty.

The vilest abortionist is he who attempts to mould a child's character.

At the University every great treatise is postponed until its author attains impartial judgment and perfect knowledge. If a horse could wait as long for its shoes and would pay for them in advance, our blacksmiths would all be college dons.

He who can, does. He who cannot, teaches.

A learned man is an idler who kills time with study. Beware of his false knowledge: it is more dangerous than ignorance.

Activity is the only road to knowledge.

Every fool believes what his teachers tell him, and calls his credulity science or morality as confidently as his father called it divine revelation.

No man fully capable of his own language ever masters another.

No man can be a pure specialist without being in the strict sense an idiot.

Do not give your children moral and religious instruction unless you are quite sure they will not take it too seriously. Better be the mother of Henri Quatre and Nell Gwynne than of Robespierre and Queen Mary Tudor.

MARRIAGE

Marriage is popular because it combines the maximum of temptation with the maximum of opportunity.

Marriage is the only legal contract which abrogates as between the parties all the laws that safeguard the particular relation to which it refers.

The essential function of marriage is the continuance of the race, as stated in the Book of Common Prayer.

The accidental function of marriage is the gratification of the amoristic sentiment of mankind.

The artificial sterilization of marriage makes it possible for marriage to fulfil its accidental function whilst neglecting its essential one.

The most revolutionary invention of the XIX century was the artificial sterilization of marriage.

Any marriage system which condemns a majority of the population to celibacy will be violently wrecked on the pretext that it outrages morality.

Polygamy, when tried under modern democratic conditions, as by the Mormons, is wrecked by the revolt of the mass of inferior men who are condemned to celibacy by it; for the maternal instinct leads a woman to prefer a tenth share in a first rate man to the exclusive possession of a third rate one. Polyandry has not been tried under these conditions.

The minimum of national celibacy (ascertained by dividing the number of males in the community by the number of females, and taking the quotient as the number of wives or husbands permitted to each person) is secured in England (where the quotient is 1) by the institution of monogamy.

The modern sentimental term for the national minimum of celibacy is Purity.

Marriage, or any other form of promiscuous amoristic monogamy, is fatal to large States because it puts its ban on the deliberate breeding of man as a political animal.

CRIME AND PUNISHMENT

All scoundrelism is summed up in the phrase "Que Messieurs les Assassins commencent!"

The man who has graduated from the flogging block at Eton to the bench from which he sentences the garotter to be flogged is the same social product as the garotter who has been kicked by his father and cuffed by his mother until he has grown strong enough to throttle and rob the rich citizen whose money he desires.

Imprisonment is as irrevocable as death.

Criminals do not die by the hands of the law. They die by the hands of other men.

The assassin Czolgosz made President McKinley a hero by assassinating him. The United States of America made Czolgosz a hero by the same process.

Assassination on the scaffold is the worst form of assassination, because there it is invested with the approval of society.

It is the deed that teaches, not the name we give it. Murder and capital punishment are not opposites that cancel one another, but similars that breed their kind.

Crime is only the retail department of what, in wholesale, we call penal law.

When a man wants to murder a tiger he calls it sport: when the tiger wants to murder him he calls it ferocity. The distinction between Crime and Justice is no greater.

Whilst we have prisons it matters little which of us occupy the cells.

The most anxious man in a prison is the governor.

It is not necessary to replace a guillotined criminal: it is necessary to replace a guillotined social system.

TITLES

Titles distinguish the mediocre, embarrass the superior, and are disgraced by the inferior.

Great men refuse titles because they are jealous of them.

HONOR

There are no perfectly honorable men; but every true man has one main point of honor and a few minor ones.

You cannot believe in honor until you have achieved it. Better keep yourself clean and bright: you are the window through which you must see the world.

Your word can never be as good as your bond, because your memory can never be as trustworthy as your honor.

PROPERTY

Property, said Proudhon, is theft. This is the only perfect truism that has been uttered on the subject.

SERVANTS

When domestic servants are treated as human beings it is not worth while to keep them.

The relation of master and servant is advantageous only to masters who do not scruple to abuse their authority, and to servants who do not scruple to abuse their trust.

The perfect servant, when his master makes humane advances to him, feels that his existence is threatened, and hastens to change his place.

Masters and servants are both tyrannical; but the masters are the more dependent of the two.

A man enjoys what he uses, not what his servants use.

Man is the only animal which esteems itself rich in proportion to the number and voracity of its parasites.

Ladies and gentlemen are permitted to have friends in the kennel, but not in the kitchen.

Domestic servants, by making spoiled children of their masters, are forced to intimidate them in order to be able to live with them.

In a slave state, the slaves rule: in Mayfair, the tradesman rules.

HOW TO BEAT CHILDREN

If you strike a child, take care that you strike it in anger, even at the risk of maiming it for life. A blow in cold blood neither can nor should be forgiven.

If you beat children for pleasure, avow your object frankly, and play the game according to the rules, as a fox-hunter does; and you will do comparatively little harm. No fox-hunter is such a cad as to pretend that he hunts the fox to teach it not to steal chickens, or that he suffers more acutely than the fox at the death. Remember that even in child-beating there is the sportsman's way and the cad's way.

RELIGION

Beware of the man whose god is in the skies.

What a man believes may be ascertained, not from his creed, but from the assumptions on which he habitually acts.

VIRTUES AND VICES

No specific virtue or vice in a man implies the existence of any other specific virtue or vice in him, however closely the imagination may associate them.

Virtue consists, not in abstaining from vice, but in not desiring it.

Self-denial is not a virtue: it is only the effect of prudence on rascality.

Obedience simulates subordination as fear of the police simulates honesty.

Disobedience, the rarest and most courageous of the virtues, is seldom distinguished from neglect, the laziest and commonest of the vices.

Vice is waste of life. Poverty, obedience, and celibacy are the canonical vices.

Economy is the art of making the most of life.

The love of economy is the root of all virtue.

FAIRPLAY

The love of fairplay is a spectator's virtue, not a principal's.

GREATNESS

Greatness is only one of the sensations of littleness.

In heaven an angel is nobody in particular.

Greatness is the secular name for

Divinity: both mean simply what lies beyond us.

If a great man could make us understand him, we should hang him.

We admit that when the divinity we worshipped made itself visible and comprehensible we crucified it.

To a mathematician the eleventh means only a single unit: to the bushman who cannot count further than his ten fingers it is an incalculable myriad.

The difference between the shallowest routineer and the deepest thinker appears, to the latter, trifling; to the former, infinite.

In a stupid nation the man of genius becomes a god: everybody worships him and nobody does his will.

BEAUTY AND HAPPINESS, ART AND RICHES

Happiness and Beauty are by-products.

Folly is the direct pursuit of Happiness and Beauty.

Riches and Art are spurious receipts for the production of Happiness and Beauty.

He who desires a lifetime of happiness with a beautiful woman desires to enjoy the taste of wine by keeping his mouth always full of it.

The most intolerable pain is produced by prolonging the keenest pleasure.

The man with toothache thinks everyone happy whose teeth are sound. The poverty stricken man makes the same mistake about the rich man.

The more a man possesses over and above what he uses, the more careworn he becomes.

The tyranny that forbids you to make the road with pick and shovel is worse than that which prevents you from lolling along it in a carriage and pair.

In an ugly and unhappy world the richest man can purchase nothing but ugliness and unhappiness.

In his efforts to escape from ugliness and unhappiness the rich man intensifies both. Every new yard of West End creates a new acre of East End.

The XIX century was the Age of Faith in Fine Art. The results are before us.

THE PERFECT GENTLEMAN

The fatal reservation of the gentleman is that he sacrifices everything to his honor except his gentility.

A gentleman of our days is one who has money enough to do what every fool would do if he could afford it: that is, consume without producing.

The true diagnostic of modern gentility is parasitism.

No elaboration of physical or moral accomplishment can atone for the sin of parasitism.

A modern gentleman is necessarily the enemy of his country. Even in war he does not fight to defend it, but to prevent his power of preying on it from passing to a foreigner. Such combatants are patriots in the same sense as two dogs fighting for a bone are lovers of animals.

The North American Indian was a type of the sportsman warrior gentleman. The Periclean Athenian was a type of the intellectually and artistically cultivated gentleman. Both were political failures. The modern gentleman, without the hardihood of the one or the culture of the other, has the appetite of both put together. He will not succeed where they failed.

He who believes in education, criminal law, and sport, needs only property to make him a perfect modern gentleman.

MODERATION

Moderation is never applauded for its own sake.

A moderately honest man with a moderately faithful wife, moderate drinkers both, in a moderately healthy house: that is the true middle class unit.

THE UNCONSCIOUS SELF

The unconscious self is the real genius. Your breathing goes wrong the moment your conscious self meddles with it.

Except during the nine months before he draws his first breath, no man manages his affairs as well as a tree does.

REASON

The reasonable man adapts himself to the world: the unreasonable one persists in trying to adapt the world to himself. Therefore all progress depends on the unreasonable man.

The man who listens to Reason is lost: Reason enslaves all whose minds are not strong enough to master her.

DECENCY

Decency is Indecency's Conspiracy of Silence.

EXPERIENCE

Men are wise in proportion, not to their experience, but to their capacity for experience.

If we could learn from mere experience, the stones of London would be wiser than its wisest men.

TIME'S REVENGES

Those whom we called brutes had their revenge when Darwin shewed us that they are our cousins.

The thieves had their revenge when Marx convicted the bourgeoisie of theft.

GOOD INTENTIONS

Hell is paved with good intentions, not with bad ones.

All men mean well.

NATURAL RIGHTS

The Master of Arts, by proving that no man has any natural rights, compels himself to take his own for granted.

The right to live is abused whenever it is not constantly challenged.

FAUTE DE MIEUX

In my childhood I demurred to the description of a certain young lady as "the pretty Miss So and So." My aunt rebuked me by saying "Remember always that the least plain sister is the family beauty."

No age or condition is without its heroes. The least incapable general in a nation is its Cæsar, the least imbecile statesman its Solon, the least confused thinker its Socrates, the least commonplace poet its Shakespear.

CHARITY

Charity is the most mischievous sort of pruriency.

Those who minister to poverty and disease are accomplices in the two worst of all the crimes.

He who gives money he has not earned is generous with other people's labor.

Every genuinely benevolent person loathes almsgiving and mendicity.

FAME

Life levels all men: death reveals the eminent.

DISCIPLINE

Mutiny Acts are needed only by officers who command without authority. Divine right needs no whip.

WOMEN IN THE HOME

Home is the girl's prison and the woman's workhouse.

CIVILIZATION

Civilization is a disease produced by

H

the practice of building societies with rotten material.

Those who admire modern civilization usually identify it with the steam engine and the electric telegraph.

Those who understand the steam engine and the electric telegraph spend their lives in trying to replace them with something better.

The imagination cannot conceive a viler criminal than he who should build another London like the present one, nor a greater benefactor than he who should destroy it.

GAMBLING

The most popular method of distributing wealth is the method of the roulette table.

The roulette table pays nobody except him that keeps it. Nevertheless a passion for gaming is common, though a passion for keeping roulette tables is unknown.

Gambling promises the poor what Property performs for the rich: that is why the bishops dare not denounce it fundamentally.

THE SOCIAL QUESTION

Do not waste your time on Social Questions. What is the matter with the poor is Poverty: what is the matter with the rich is Uselessness.

STRAY SAYINGS

We are told that when Jehovah created the world he saw that it was good. What would he say now?

The conversion of a savage to Christianity is the conversion of Christianity to savagery.

No man dares say so much of what he thinks as to appear to himself an extremist.

Mens sana in corpore sano is a foolish saying. The sound body is a product of the sound mind.

Decadence can find agents only when it wears the mask of progress.

In moments of progress the noble succeed, because things are going their way: in moments of decadence the base succeed for the same reason: hence the world is never without the exhilaration of contemporary success.

The reformer for whom the world is not good enough finds himself shoulder to shoulder with him that is not good enough for the world.

Every man over forty is a scoundrel.

Youth, which is forgiven everything, forgives itself nothing: age, which forgives itself everything, is forgiven nothing.

When we learn to sing that Britons never will be masters we shall make an end of slavery.

Do not mistake your objection to defeat for an objection to fighting, your objection to being a slave for an objection to slavery, your objection to not being as rich as your neighbor for an objection to poverty. The cowardly, the insubordinate, and the envious share your objections.

Take care to get what you like or you will be forced to like what you get. Where there is no ventilation fresh air is declared unwholesome. Where there is no religion hypocrisy becomes good taste. Where there is no knowledge ignorance calls itself science.

If the wicked flourish and the fittest survive, Nature must be the God of rascals.

If history repeats itself, and the unexpected always happens, how incapable must Man be of learning from experience!

Compassion is the fellow-feeling of the unsound.

Those who understand evil pardon it: those who resent it destroy it.

Acquired notions of propriety are stronger than natural instincts. It is easier to recruit for monasteries and convents than to induce an Arab woman to uncover her mouth in public, or a British officer to walk through Bond Street in a golfing cap on an afternoon in May.

It is dangerous to be sincere unless you are also stupid.

The Chinese tame fowls by clipping their wings, and women by deforming their feet. A petticoat round the ankles serves equally well.

Political Economy and Social Economy are amusing intellectual games; but Vital Economy is the Philosopher's Stone.

When a heretic wishes to avoid martyrdom he speaks of "Orthodoxy, True and False" and demonstrates that the True is his heresy.

Beware of the man who does not return your blow: he neither forgives you nor allows you to forgive yourself.

If you injure your neighbor, better not do it by halves.

Sentimentality is the error of supposing that quarter can be given or taken in moral conflicts.

Two starving men cannot be twice as hungry as one; but two rascals can be ten times as vicious as one.

Make your cross your crutch; but when you see another man do it, beware of him.

SELF-SACRIFICE

Self-sacrifice enables us to sacrifice other people without blushing.

If you begin by sacrificing yourself to those you love, you will end by hating those to whom you have sacrificed yourself.

POSTSCRIPT 1933. The evolutionary theme of the third act of Man and Superman was resumed by me twenty years later in the preface to Back to Methuselah, where it is developed as the basis of the religion of the near future.

THREE PLAYS BY BRIEUX

1909

FROM MOLIÈRE TO BRIEUX

Since the death of Ibsen, Brieux confronts Europe as the most important dramatist west of Russia. In that kind of comedy which is so true to life that we have to call it tragi-comedy, and which is not only an entertainment but a history and a criticism of contemporary morals, he is incomparably the greatest writer France has produced since Molière. The French critics who take it for granted that no contemporary of theirs could possibly be greater than Beaumarchais are really too modest. They have never read Beaumarchais, and therefore do not know how very little of him there is to read, and how, out of the two variations he wrote on his once famous theme, the second is only a petition in artistic and intellectual bankruptcy. Had the French theatre been capable of offering a field to Balzac, my proposition might have to be modified. But as it was no more able to do that than the English theatre was to enlist the genius of Dickens, I may say confidently that in that great comedy which Balzac called "the comedy of humanity," to be played for the amusement of the gods rather than for that of the French public, there is no summit in the barren plain that stretches from Mount Molière to our own times until we reach Brieux.

HOW THE XIX CENTURY FOUND ITSELF OUT

It is reserved for some great critic to give us a study of the psychology of the XIX century. Those of us who as adults saw it face to face in that last moiety of its days when one fierce hand after another —Marx's, Zola's, Ibsen's, Strindberg's, Turgenieff's, Tolstoy's — stripped its masks off and revealed it as, on the whole, perhaps the most villainous page of recorded human history, can also recall the strange confidence with which it regarded itself as the very summit of civilization, and talked of the past as a cruel gloom that had been dispelled for ever by the railway and the electric telegraph. But centuries, like men, begin to find themselves out in middle age. The youthful conceit of the nineteenth had a splendid exponent in Macaulay, and, for a time, a gloriously jolly one during the nonage of Dickens. There was certainly nothing morbid in the air then: Dickens and Macaulay are as free from morbidity as Dumas *père* and Guizot. Even Stendhal and Prosper Mérimée, though by no means burgess optimists, are quite sane. When you come to Zola and Maupassant, Flaubert and the Goncourts, to Ibsen and Strindberg, to Aubrey Beardsley and George Moore, to D'Annunzio and Echegaray, you are in a new and morbid atmosphere. French literature up to the middle of the XIX century was still all of one piece with Rabelais, Montaigne, and Molière. Zola breaks that tradition completely: he is as different as Karl Marx from Turgot or Darwin from Cuvier.

In this new phase we see the bourgeoisie, after a century and a half of complacent vaunting of its own probity and modest happiness (begun by Daniel Defoe in Robinson Crusoe's praises of "the middle station of life"), suddenly turning bitterly on itself with accusations of hideous sexual and commercial corruption. Thackeray's campaign against snobbery and Dickens's against hypocrisy were directed against the vices of respectable men; but now even the respectability was passionately denied: the bourgeois was depicted as a thief, a tyrant, a sweater, a selfish voluptuary whose marriages were simple legalizations of unbridled licentiousness. Sexual irregularities began to be attributed to the sympathetic characters in fiction not as the blackest spots in their portraits, but positively as redeeming humanities in them.

JACK THE RIPPER

I am by no means going here either to revive the old outcry against this school of iconoclasts and disillusioners, or to join the new reaction against it. It told the world many truths: it brought romance back to its senses. Its very repudiation of the graces and enchantments of fine art was necessary; for the artistic morbidezza of Byron and Victor Hugo was too imaginative to allow the Victorian bourgeoisie to accept them as chroniclers of real facts and real people. The justification of Zola's comparative coarseness is that his work could not have been done in any other way. If Zola had had a sense of humor, or a great artist's delight in playing with his ideas, his materials, and his readers, he would have become either as unreadable to the very people he came to wake up as Anatole France is, or as incredible as Victor Hugo was. He would also have incurred the mistrust and hatred of the majority of Frenchmen, who, like the majority of men of all nations, are not merely incapable of fine art, but resent it furiously. A wit is to them a man who is laughing at them: an artist is a man of loose character who lives by telling lying stories and pandering to the voluptuous passions. What they like to read is the police intelligence, especially the murder cases and divorce cases. The invented murders and divorces of the novelists and playwrights do not satisfy them, because they cannot believe in them; and belief that the horror or scandal actually occurred, that real people are shedding real blood and real tears, is indispensable to their enjoyment. To produce this belief by works of fiction, the writer must disguise and even discard the arts of the man of letters and assume the style of the descriptive reporter of the criminal courts. As an example of how to cater for such readers, we may take Zola's Bête Humaine. It is in all its essentials a simple and touching story, like Prévost's Manon Lescaut. But into it Zola has violently thrust the greatest police sensation of the XIX century: the episode of Jack the Ripper. Jack's hideous neurosis is no more a part of human nature than Cæsar's epilepsy or Gladstone's missing finger. One is tempted to accuse Zola of having borrowed it from the newspapers to please his customers just as Shakespear used to borrow stories of murder and jealousy from the tales and chronicles of his time, and heap them on the head of convivial humorists like Iago and Richard III, or gentle poets like Macbeth and Hamlet. Without such allurements, Shakespear could not have lived by his plays. And if he had been rich enough to disregard this consideration, he would still have had to provide sensation enough to induce people to listen to what he was inspired to say. It is only the man who has no message who is too fastidious to beat the drum at the door of his booth.

RISE OF THE SCIENTIFIC SPIRIT

Still, the Shakespearian murders were romantic murders: the Zolaesque ones were police reports. The old mad heroines, the Ophelias and Lucies of Lammermoor, were rhapsodists with flowers in their hands: the new ones were clinical studies of mental disease. The new note was as conspicuous in the sensational chapters as in the dull chapters, of which there were many. This was the punishment of the middle class for hypocrisy. It had carried the conspiracy of silence which we call decorum to such lengths that when young men discovered the suppressed truths, they felt bound to shout them in the streets. I well remember how when I was a youth in my teens I happened to obtain access to the papers of an Irish crown solicitor through a colleague who had some clerical work to do upon them. The county concerned was not one of the crimeless counties: there was a large camp in it; and the soldier of that day was not the respectable, rather pious, and very low-spirited youth who now makes the King's uniform what the curate's black coat was then. There were not only cases which were tried and not reported: there were cases which could not even be tried, the offenders having secured impunity by pushing their follies to lengths too grotesque to be bearable even in a criminal court—also because of the silly ferocity of the law, which punished the negligible indecencies of drunken young soldiers as atrocious crimes. The effect produced by these revelations on my raw youth was a sense of heavy responsibility for conniving at their concealment. I felt that if camp and barrack life involved these things, they ought to be known. I had been caught by the great wave of scientific enthusiasm which was then passing over Europe as a result of the discovery of Natural Selection by Darwin, and of the blow it dealt to the vulgar Bible worship and redemption mongering which had hitherto passed among us for religion. I wanted to get at the facts. I was prepared for the facts being unflattering: had I not already faced the fact that instead of being a fallen angel I was first cousin to a monkey? Long afterwards, when I was a well-known writer, I said that what we wanted as the basis of our plays and novels was not romance, but a really scientific natural history. Scientific natural history is not compatible with taboo; and as everything connected with sex was tabooed, I felt the need for mentioning the forbidden sub-jects, not only because of their own importance, but for the sake of destroying taboo by giving it the most violent possible shocks. The same impulse is unmistakeably active in Zola and his contemporaries. He also wanted, not works of literary art, but stories he could believe in as records of things that really happen. He imposed Jack the Ripper on his idyll of the railwayman's wife to make it scientific. To all artists and Platonists he made it thereby very unreal; for to the Platonist all accidents are unreal and negligible; but to the people he wanted to get at—the anti-artistic people—he made it readable.

The scientific spirit was unintelligible to the Philistines and repulsive to the dilettanti, who said to Zola: "If you must tell us stories about agricultural laborers, why tell us dirty ones?" But Zola did not want, like the old romancers, to tell a story. He wanted to tell the world the scientific truth about itself. His view was that if you were going to legislate for agricultural laborers, or deal with them or their business in any way, you had better know what they are really like; and in supplying you with the necessary information he did not tell you what you already knew, which included pretty nearly all that could be decorously mentioned, but what you did not know, which was that part of the truth that was tabooed. For the same reason, when he found a generation whose literary notions of Parisian cocotterie were founded on Marguerite Gauthier, he felt it to be a duty to shew them Nana. And it was a very necessary thing to do. If some Irish writer of the seventies had got himself banished from all decent society, and perhaps convicted of obscene libel, by writing a novel shewing the side of camp life that was never mentioned except in the papers of the Crown Solicitor, we should be nearer to a rational military system than we are today.

ZOLAISM AS A SUPERSTITION

It is, unfortunately, much easier to throw the forces of art into a reaction than to recall them when the reaction has gone far enough. A case which came under my own notice years ago illustrates the difficulty. The wife of an eminent surgeon had some talent for drawing. Her husband wrote a treatise on cancer; and she drew the illustrations. It was the first time she had used her gift for a serious purpose; and she worked hard enough at it to acquire considerable skill in depicting cancerous proliferation. The book being finished and published, she resumed her ordinary practice of sketching for pleasure. But all her work now had an uncanny look. When she drew a landscape, it was like a cancer that accidentally looked like a landscape. She had acquired a cancerous technique; and she could not get rid of it.

This happens as easily in literature as in the other arts. The men who trained themselves as writers by dragging the unmentionable to light, presently found that they could do that so much better than anything else that they gave up dealing with the other subjects. Even their quite mentionable episodes had an unmentionable air. Their imitators assumed that unmentionability was an end in itself—that to be decent was to be out of the movement. Zola and Ibsen could not, of course, be confined to mere reaction against taboo. Ibsen was to the last fascinating and full of a strange moving beauty; and Zola often broke into sentimental romance. But neither Ibsen nor Zola, after they once took in hand the work of unmasking the idols of the bourgeoisie, ever again wrote a happy or pleasant play or novel. Ibsen's suicides and catastrophes at last produced the cry of "People dont do such things," which he ridiculed through Judge Brack in Hedda Gabler. This was easy enough:

Brack was so far wrong that people do do such things occasionally. But on the whole Brack was right. The tragedy of Hedda in real life is not that she commits suicide but that she continues to live. If such acts of violent rebellion as those of Hedda and Nora and Rebecca and the rest were the inevitable or even the probable consequences of their unfitness to be wives and mothers, or of their contracting repugnant marriages to avoid being left on the shelf, social reform would be very rapid; and we should hear less nonsense as to women like Nora and Hedda being mere figments of Ibsen's imagination. Our real difficulty is the almost boundless docility and submission to social convention which is characteristic of the human race. What balks the social reformer everywhere is that the victims of social evils do not complain, and even strongly resent being treated as victims. The more a dog suffers from being chained the more dangerous it is to release him: he bites savagely at the hand that dares touch his collar. Our Rougon-Macquart families are usually enormously proud of themselves; and though they have to put up with their share of drunkards and madmen, they do not proliferate into Jack-the-Rippers. Nothing that is admittedly and unmistakeably horrible matters very much, because it frightens people into seeking a remedy: the serious horrors are those which seem entirely respectable and normal to respectable and normal men. Now the formula of tragedy had come down to the nineteenth century from days in which this was not recognized, and when life was so thoroughly accepted as a divine institution that in order to make it seem tragic, something dreadful had to happen and somebody had to die. But the tragedy of modern life is that nothing happens, and that the resultant dulness does not kill. Maupassant's Une Vie is infinitely more tragic than the death of Juliet.

In Ibsen's works we find the old traditions and the new conditions struggling
in the same play, like a gudgeon half
swallowed by a pike. Almost all the
sorrow and the weariness which make
his plays so poignant are the sorrow and
weariness of the mean dull life in which
nothing happens; but none the less he
provides a final catastrophe of the approved fifth-act-blank-verse type. Hed-
wig and Hedda shoot themselves: Rosmer
and Rebecca throw themselves into the
mill-race: Solness and Rubeck are dashed
to pieces: Borkman dies of acute stage
tragedy without discoverable lesions. I
will not again say, as I have said before,
that these catastrophes are forced, because
a fortunate performance often makes
them seem inevitable; but I do submit
that the omission of them would leave
the play sadder and more convincing.

THE PASSING OF THE TRAGIC CATA-
STROPHE AND THE HAPPY ENDING

Not only is the tradition of the catastrophe unsuitable to modern studies of
life: the tradition of an ending, happy or
the reverse, is equally unworkable. The
moment the dramatist gives up accidents
and catastrophes, and takes "slices of
life" as his material, he finds himself committed to plays that have no endings. The
curtain no longer comes down on a hero
slain or married: it comes down when the
audience has seen enough of the life presented to it to draw the moral, and must
either leave the theatre or miss its last
train.

The man who faced France with a
drama fulfilling all these conditions was
Brieux. He was as scientific, as conscientious, as unflinching as Zola without
being in the least morbid. He was no
more dependent on horrors than Molière,
and as sane in his temper. He threw over
the traditional forced catastrophe uncompromisingly. You do not go away from a
Brieux play with the feeling that the affair

is finished or the problem solved for you
by the dramatist. Still less do you go
away in "that happy, easy, ironically
indulgent frame of mind that is the true
test of comedy," as Mr Walkley put it in
The Times of the 1st October 1909. You
come away with a very disquieting sense
that you are involved in the affair, and
must find the way out of it for yourself
and everybody else if civilization is to be
tolerable to your sense of honor.

THE DIFFERENCE BETWEEN BRIEUX
AND MOLIÈRE OR SHAKESPEAR

Brieux's task is thus larger than Molière's. Molière destroyed the prestige of
those conspiracies against society which
we call the professions, and which thrive
by the exploitation of idolatry. He unmasked the doctor, the philosopher, the
fencing master, the priest. He ridiculed
their dupes: the hypochondriac, the academician, the devotee, the gentleman in
search of accomplishments. He exposed
the snob: he shewed the gentleman as the
butt and creature of his valet, emphasizing
thus the inevitable relation between the
man who lives by unearned money and
the man who lives by weight of service.
Beyond bringing this latter point up to a
later date Beaumarchais did nothing. But
Molière never indicted society. Burke said
that you cannot bring an indictment
against a nation; yet within a generation
from that utterance men began to draw
indictments against whole epochs, especially against the capitalistic epoch. It is
true that Molière, like Shakespear, indicted human nature, which would seem
to be a broader attack; but such attacks
only make thoughtful men melancholy
and hopeless, and practical men cynical
or murderous. Le Misanthrope, which
seems to me, as a foreigner perhaps, to be
Molière's dullest and worst play, is like
Hamlet in two respects. The first, which
is that it would have been much better if
it had been written in prose, is merely

technical and need not detain us. The second is that the author does not clearly know what he is driving at. Le Festin de Pierre, Molière's best philosophic play, is as brilliant and arresting as Le Misanthrope is neither the one nor the other; but here again there is no positive side: the statue is a hollow creature with nothing to say for himself; and Don Juan makes no attempt to take advantage of his weakness. The reason why Shakespear and Molière are always well spoken of and recommended to the young is that their quarrel is really a quarrel with God for not making men better. If they had quarrelled with a specified class of persons with incomes of four figures for not doing their work better, or for doing no work at all, they would be denounced as seditious, impious, and profligate corrupters of morality.

Brieux wastes neither ink nor indignation on Providence. The idle despair that shakes its fist impotently at the skies, uttering sublime blasphemies, such as

"As flies to wanton boys are we to the gods:
 They kill us for their sport,"

does not amuse Brieux. His fisticuffs are not aimed heavenward: they fall on human noses for the good of human souls. When he sees human nature in conflict with a political abuse, he does not blame human nature, knowing that such blame is the favorite trick of those who wish to perpetuate the abuse without being able to defend it. He does not even blame the abuse: he exposes it, and then leaves human nature to tackle it with its eyes open. And his method of exposure is the dramatic method. He is a born dramatist, differing from the ordinary dramatists only in that he has a large mind and a scientific habit of using it. As a dramatist his theme is necessarily a conflict of some sort. As a dramatist of large mind he cannot be satisfied with the trumpery conflicts of the Divorce Court and the Criminal Court: of the husband with the seducer, of the policeman with the murderer. Having the scientific conscience in a higher degree than Zola (he has a better head), he could not be interested in imaginary conflicts which he himself would have had to invent like a child at play. The conflict which inspires his dramatic genius must be a big one and a real one. To ask an audience to spend three hours hanging on the question of which particular man some particular woman shall mate with does not strike him as a reasonable proceeding; and if the audience does not agree with him, why, it can go to some fashionable dramatist of the boulevard who does agree with it.

BRIEUX AND THE BOULEVARD

This involves Brieux in furious conflict with the boulevard. Up to quite recent times it was impossible for an Englishman to mention Brieux to a Parisian as the only French playwright who really counted in Europe without being met with astonished assurances that Brieux is not a playwright at all; that his plays are not plays; that he is not (in Sarcey's sense of the phrase) "du théâtre"; that he is a mere pamphleteer without even literary style. And when you expressed your natural gratification at learning that the general body of Parisian dramatists were so highly gifted that Brieux counted for nothing in Paris—when you respectfully asked for the names of a few of the most prominent of the geniuses who had eclipsed him, you were given three or four of which you had never heard, and one or two known to you as those of cynically commercial manipulators of the ménage à trois, the innocent wife discovered at the villain's rooms at midnight (to beg him to spare the virtue of a sister, the character of a son, or the life of a father), the compromising letter, the duel, and all the rest of the claptraps out of which dramatic playthings can be manu-

H 2

factured for the amusement of grown-up children. Not until the Academie Française elected Brieux did it occur to the boulevardiers that the enormous difference between him and their pet authors was a difference in which the superiority lay with Brieux.

THE PEDANTRY OF PARIS

Indeed it is difficult for the Englishman to understand how bigotedly the Parisians cling to the claptrap theatre. The English do not care enough about the theatre to cling to its traditions or persecute anyone for their sake; but the French do. Besides, in fine art, France is a nation of born pedants. The vulgar English painter paints vulgar pictures, and generally sells them. But the vulgar French painter paints classical ones, though whether he sells them or not I do not know: I hope not. The corresponding infatuation in the theatre is for dramas in alexandrines; and alexandrines are far worse than English blank verse, which is saying a good deal. Racine and Corneille, who established the alexandrine tradition, deliberately aimed at classicism, taking the Greek drama as their model. Even a foreigner can hear the music of their verse. Corneille wrote alexandrines as Dryden wrote heroic couplets, in a virile, stately, handsome and withal human way; and Racine had tenderness and beauty as well. This drama of Racine and Corneille, with the music of Gluck, gave the French in the XVII and XVIII centuries a body of art which was very beautiful, very refined, very delightful for cultivated people, and very tedious for the ignorant. When, through the spread of elementary education, the ignorant invaded the theatre in overwhelming numbers, this exquisite body of art became a dead body, and was practised by nobody except the amateurs—the people who love what has been already done in art and loathe the real life out of which living art must continually grow afresh. In their hands it passed from being a commercial failure to being an obsolete nuisance.

Commercially, the classic play was supplanted by a nuisance which was not a failure: to wit, the "well made play" of Scribe and his school. The manufacture of well made plays is not an art: it is an industry. It is not at all hard for a literary mechanic to acquire it: the only difficulty is to find a literary mechanic who is not by nature too much of an artist for the job; for nothing spoils a well made play more infallibly than the least alloy of high art or the least qualm of conscience on the part of the writer. "Art for art's sake" is the formula of the well made play, meaning in practice "Success for money's sake." Now great art is never produced for its own sake. It is too difficult to be worth the effort. All the great artists enter into a terrible struggle with the public, often involving bitter poverty and personal humiliation, and always involving calumny and persecution, because they believe they are apostles doing what used to be called the Will of God, and is now called by many prosaic names, of which "public work" is the least controversial. And when these artists have travailed and brought forth, and at last forced the public to associate keen pleasure and deep interest with their methods and morals, a crowd of smaller men—art confectioners, we may call them—hasten to make pretty entertainments out of scraps and crumbs from the masterpieces. Offenbach laid hands on Beethoven's Seventh Symphony and produced J'aime les militaires, to the disgust of Schumann, who was nevertheless doing precisely the same thing in a more pretentious way. And these confectioners are by no means mere plagiarists. They bring all sorts of engaging qualities to their work: love of beauty, desire to give pleasure, tenderness, humor, everything except the high republican conscience, the identification of the artist's purpose with the purpose of the universe, which alone makes an artist great.

But the well made play was not confectionery: it had not even the derived virtue of being borrowed from the great playwrights. Its formula grew up in the days when the spread of elementary schooling produced a huge mass of playgoers sufficiently educated to want plays instead of dog-fights, but not educated enough to enjoy or understand the masterpieces of dramatic art. Besides, education or no education, one cannot live on masterpieces alone, not only because there are not enough of them, but because new plays as well as great plays are needed, and there are not enough Molières and Shakespears in the world to keep the demand for novelty satisfied. Hence it has always been necessary to have some formula by which men of mediocre talent and no conscience can turn out plays for the theatrical market. Such men have written melodramas since the theatre existed. It was in the XIX century that the demand for manufactured plays was extended to drawing room plays in which the Forest of Bondy and the Auberge des Adrets, the Red Barn and the Cave at Midnight, had to be replaced by Lord Blank's flat in Whitehall Court and the Great Hall, Chevy Chace. Playgoers, being by that time mostly poor playgoers, wanted to see how the rich live; wanted to see them actually drinking champagne and wearing real fashionable dresses and trousers with a neatly ironed crease down the knee.

HOW TO WRITE A POPULAR PLAY

The formula for the well made play is so easy that I give it for the benefit of any reader who feels tempted to try his hand at making the fortune that awaits all successful manufacturers in this line. First, you "have an idea" for a dramatic situation. If it strikes you as a splendidly original idea whilst it is in fact as old as the hills, so much the better. For instance, the situation of an innocent person convicted by circumstances of a crime may always be depended on. If the person is a woman, she must be convicted of adultery. If a young officer, he must be convicted of selling information to the enemy, though it is really a fascinating female spy who has ensnared him and stolen the incriminating document. If the innocent wife, banished from her home, suffers agonies through her separation from her children, and, when one of them is dying (of any disease the dramatist chooses to inflict), disguises herself as a nurse and attends it through its dying convulsion until the doctor, who should be a serio-comic character, and if possible a faithful old admirer of the lady's, simultaneously announces the recovery of the child and the discovery of the wife's innocence, the success of the play may be regarded as assured if the writer has any sort of knack for his work. Comedy is more difficult, because it requires a sense of humor and a good deal of vivacity; but the process is essentially the same: it is the manufacture of a misunderstanding. Having manufactured it, you place its culmination at the end of the last act but one, which is the point at which the manufacture of the play begins. Then you make your first act out of the necessary introduction of the characters to the audience, after elaborate explanations, mostly conducted by servants, solicitors, and other low life personages (the principals must all be dukes and colonels and millionaires), of how the misunderstanding is going to come about. Your last act consists, of course, of clearing up the misunderstanding, and generally getting the audience out of the theatre as best you can.

Now please do not misunderstand me as pretending that this process is so mechanical that it offers no opportunity for the exercise of talent. On the contrary, it is so mechanical that without very conspicuous talent nobody can make much reputation by doing it, though they can and do make a living at it. And this often leads the cultivated classes to suppose that all plays are written by authors of talent. As a matter of fact the majority of those who in France and England make a living by writing plays are unknown and, as to education, all but illiterate. Their names are not worth putting on the playbill, because their audiences neither know nor care who the author is, and often believe that the actors improvise the whole piece, just as they in fact do sometimes improvise the dialogue. To rise out of this obscurity you must be a Scribe or a Sardou, doing essentially the same thing, it is true, but doing it wittily and ingeniously, at moments almost poetically, and giving the persons of the drama some touches of real observed character.

WHY THE CRITICS ARE ALWAYS WRONG

Now it is these strokes of talent that set the critics wrong. For the talent, being all expended on the formula, at last consecrates the formula in the eyes of the critics. Nay, they become so accustomed to the formula that at last they cannot relish or understand a play that has grown naturally, just as they cannot admire the Venus of Milo because she has neither a corset nor high heeled shoes. They are like the peasants who are so accustomed to food reeking with garlic that when food is served to them without it they declare that it has no taste and is not food at all.

This is the explanation of the refusal of the critics of all nations to accept great original dramatists like Ibsen and Brieux as real dramatists, or their plays as real plays. No writer of the first order needs the formula any more than a sound man needs a crutch. In his simplest mood, when he is only seeking to amuse, he does not manufacture a plot: he tells a story. He finds no difficulty in setting people on the stage to talk and act in an amusing, exciting, or touching way. His characters have adventures and ideas which are interesting in themselves, and need not be fitted into the Chinese puzzle of a plot.

THE INTERPRETER OF LIFE

But the great dramatist has something better to do than to amuse either himself or his audience. He has to interpret life. This sounds a mere pious phrase of literary criticism; but a moment's consideration will discover its meaning and its exactitude. Life as it appears to us in our daily experience is an unintelligible chaos of happenings. You pass Othello in the bazaar in Aleppo, Iago on the jetty in Cyprus, and Desdemona in the nave of St Mark's in Venice without the slightest clue to their relations to one another. The man you see stepping into a chemist's shop to buy the means of committing murder or suicide, may, for all you know, want nothing but a liver pill or a toothbrush. The statesman who has no other object than to make you vote for his party at the next election may be starting you on an incline at the foot of which lies war, or revolution, or a smallpox epidemic, or five years off your lifetime. The horrible murder of a whole family by the father who finishes by killing himself, or the driving of a young girl on to the streets, may be the result of your discharging an employee in a fit of temper a month before. To attempt to understand life from merely looking on at it as it happens in the streets is as hopeless as trying to understand public questions by studying snapshots of public demonstrations. If we possessed a series of cinematographs of all the executions during the Reign of Terror, they might be exhibited a thousand times without enlightening the audiences in the least as to the meaning of the Revolution: Robespierre would perish as "un monsieur" and Marie Antoinette as "une femme." Life as it occurs is senseless: a policeman may watch it and work in it for thirty years in the streets and courts of Paris without learning as much of it or from it as a child or a nun may learn from a single play by Brieux. For it is the business of Brieux to pick out the significant incidents from the chaos of daily happenings, and arrange them so that their relation to one another becomes significant, thus changing us from bewildered spectators of a monstrous confusion to men intelligently conscious of the world and its destinies. This is the highest function that man can perform—the greatest work he can set his hand to; and this is why the great dramatists of the world, from Euripides and Aristophanes to Shakespear and Molière, and from them to Ibsen and Brieux, take that majestic and pontifical rank which seems so strangely above all the reasonable pretensions of mere strolling actors and theatrical authors.

HOW THE GREAT DRAMATISTS TORTURE THE PUBLIC

Now if the critics are wrong in supposing that the formula of the well made play is not only indispensable in good playwrighting, but is actually the essence of the play itself—if their delusion is rebuked and confuted by the practice of every great dramatist even when he is only amusing himself by story telling, what must happen to their poor formula when it impertinently offers its services to a playwright who has taken on his supreme function as the Interpreter of Life? Not only has he no use for it; but he must attack and destroy it; for one of the very first lessons he has to teach to a play-ridden public is that the romantic conventions on which the formula proceeds are all false, and are doing incalculable harm in these days when everybody reads romances and goes to the theatre. Just as the historian can teach no real history until he has cured his readers of the romantic delusion that the greatness of a queen consists in her being a pretty woman and having her head cut off; so the playwright of the first order can do nothing with his audiences until he has cured them of looking at the stage through the keyhole and sniffing round the theatre as prurient people sniff round the divorce court. The cure is not a popular one. The public suffers from it exactly as a drunkard or a snuff taker suffers from an attempt to conquer the habit. The critics especially, who are forced by their profession to indulge immoderately in plays adulterated with falsehood and vice, suffer so acutely when forced to abstain for a whole evening, that they hurl disparagements and even abuse and insult at the merciless dramatist who is torturing them. To a bad play of the kind they are accustomed to they can be cruel through superciliousness, irony, impatience, contempt, or even a Rochefoucauldian pleasure in a friend's misfortune. But the hatred provoked by deliberately inflicted pain, the frantic denials as of a prisoner at the bar accused of a disgraceful crime, the clamor for vengeance thinly disguised as artistic justice, the suspicion that the dramatist is using private information and making a personal attack: all these are to be found only when the playwright is no mere *marchand de plaisir*, but, like Brieux, a ruthless revealer of hidden truth and a mighty destroyer of idols.

BRIEUX'S CONQUEST OF LONDON

So well does Brieux know this that he has written a play, La Foi, shewing how terrible truth is to men, and how false religions (theatrical romance, by the way, is the falsest and most fantastically held of all the false religions) are a necessity to them. With this play he achieved, for the first time on record, the feat of winning a success in a fashionable London theatre with a cold-blooded thesis play. Those who witnessed the performance of False Gods at His Majesty's Theatre this year were astonished to see that exceptionally large theatre filled with strangely attentive ordinary playgoers, to whose customary requirements and weaknesses no concession was made for a moment by the playwright. They were getting a lesson and nothing else. The same famous acting, the same sumptuous *mise en scène*, had not always saved other plays from failure. There was no enthusiasm: one might almost say there was no enjoyment. The audience for once had something better to do than to amuse themselves. The old playgoers and the critics, who, on the first night, had politely regretted an inevitable failure after waiting, like the maturer ladies at the sack of Ismail in Byron's poem, for the adultery to begin, asked one another incredulously whether there could really be money in this sort of thing. Such feats had been performed before at coterie theatres where the expenses were low and where the plays were seasoned with a good deal of ordinary amusing comedy; but in this play there was not a jest from beginning to end; and the size of the theatre and the expenses of production were on a princely scale. Yet La Foi held its own. The feat was quite unprecedented; and that it should have been achieved for the first time by a Frenchman is about a million times more remarkable than that the first man to fly across the channel (the two events were almost simultaneous) should also have been a Frenchman.

PARISIAN STUPIDITY

And here I must digress for a moment to remark that though Paris is easily the most prejudiced, old-fashioned, obsolete-minded city in the west of Europe, yet when she produces great men she certainly does not do it by halves. Unfortunately, there is nothing she hates more than a Frenchman of genius. When an Englishman says that you have to go back to Michael Angelo to find a sculptor who can be mentioned in the same breath as Rodin without manifest absurdity, the Parisians indignantly exclaim that only an ignorant foreigner could imagine that a man who was not a pupil at the Beaux Arts could possibly be a sculptor at all. And I have already described how they talk about Brieux, the only French dramatist whose fame crosses frontiers and channels, and fills the continent. To be quite frank, I cannot to this day understand why they made him an Academician instead of starving him to death and then giving him a statue. Can it be that in his early days, before he could gain his living by the theatre, he wrote a spelling book, or delivered a course of lectures on the use of pure line in Greek design? To suppose that they did it because he is a great man is to imply that they know a great Frenchman when they see him, which is contrary to all experience. They never know until the English tell them.

BRIEUX AND THE ENGLISH THEATRE

In England our knowledge of Brieux has been delayed by the childishness of our theatre. This childishness is by no means to be deplored: it means that the theatre is occupied with the elementary education of the masses instead of with the higher education of the classes. Those who desire dramatic performances of the higher sort have to provide for themselves by forming clubs, hiring theatres, engaging performers, and selecting plays for themselves. After 1889, when Ibsen first became known in London through A Doll's House, a succession of these clubs kept what may be called the serious adult drama fitfully alive until 1904, when Messrs Vedrenne and Barker took the field with a regular theatrical enterprise devoted to this class of work, and maintained it until the National Theatre project was set on foot, and provisional repertory schemes were announced by established commercial managements. It was through one of these clubs, the Stage Society, that Brieux reached the English stage with his Bienfaiteurs. Then the first two plays in this volume were performed, and, later on, Les Hannetons. The first of these performances settled for us the question of Brieux's rank among modern playwrights. After that his Robe Rouge introduced the ordinary playgoers to him; and he is now no longer one of the curiosities of the coterie theatre, as even Ibsen to some extent still is, but one of the conquerors of the general British public.

THE CENSORSHIP IN FRANCE AND ENGLAND

Unfortunately, he has not yet been able to conquer our detestable, discredited, but still all-powerful Censorship. In France he was attacked by the Censorship just as in England; but in France the Censorship broke itself against him and perished. The same thing would probably have occurred here but for the fact that our Censor, by a grotesque accident of history—to be precise, because Henry VIII began the Censorship of the theatre by appointing an officer of his own household to do the work—remains part of the King's retinue; and his abolition involves the curtailment of that retinue and therefore the reduction of the King's State, always a very difficult and delicate matter in a monarchical country. In France the Censorship was exercised by the Minister of Fine Arts (a portfolio that does not exist in our Cabinet) and was in the hands of two or three examiners of plays, who necessarily behaved exactly like our Mr Redford; for, as I have so often pointed out, the evils of censorship are made

compulsory by the nature of the office, and are not really the fault of the individual Censor. These gentlemen, then, prohibited the performance of Brieux's best and most useful plays just as Mr Redford did here. But as the French parliament, having nobody to consider but themselves and the interests of the nation, presently refused to vote the salaries of the Censors, the institution died a natural death. We have no such summary remedy here. Our Censor's salary is part of the King's civil list, and is therefore sacred. Years ago, our Playgoers' Club asked me how the Censorship could be abolished. I replied, to the great scandal of that loyal body: You must begin by abolishing the monarchy.

BRIEUX AND THE ENGLISH CENSORSHIP

Nevertheless, Brieux has left his mark even on the English Censorship. This year (1909) the prohibition of his plays was one of the strongest items in the long list of grievances by which the English playwrights compelled the Government to appoint a Select Committee of both houses of Parliament to inquire into the working of the Censorship. The report of that Committee admits the charge brought against the Censor of systematically suppressing plays dealing seriously with social problems whilst allowing frivolous and even pornographic plays to pass unchallenged. It advises that the submission of plays to the Censor shall in future be optional, though it does not dare to omit the customary sycophantic recommendation that the Lord Chamberlain shall still retain his privilege of licensing plays; and it proposes that the authors and managers of plays so licensed, though not exempt from prosecution, shall enjoy certain immunities denied in the case of unlicensed plays. There are many other conditions which need not be gone into here; but to a Frenchman the main fact that stands out is that the accident which has made the Censor an officer of the King's Household has prevented a parliamentary committee from recommending the abolition of his control over the theatre in a report which not only has not a word to say in his defence, but expressly declares that his license affords the public no guarantee that the plays he approves are decent, and that authors of serious plays need protection against his unenlightened despotism.

TABOO

We may therefore take it on the authority of the Select Committee that the prohibition by the English Censorship of the public performances of the three plays in this book does not afford the smallest reasonable ground for condemning them as improper—rather the contrary. As a matter of fact, most men, if asked to guess the passages to which the Censor took exception, would guess wrongly. Certainly a Frenchman would. The reason is that though in England as in France what is called decency is not a reasoned discrimination between what needs to be said and what ought not to be said, but simply the observance of a set of taboos, these taboos are not the same in England as in France. A Frenchman of scrupulously correct behavior will sometimes quite innocently make an English lady blush by mentioning something that is unmentionable in polite society in England though quite mentionable in France. To take a simple illustration, an Englishman, when he first visits France, is always embarrassed, and sometimes shocked, on finding that the person in charge of a public lavatory for men is a woman. I cannot give reciprocal instances of the ways in which Englishmen shock the French nation, because I am happily unconscious of all the *cochonneries* of which I am no doubt guilty when I am in France. But that I do occasionally shock the brave French bourgeois to the very marrow of his bones by my indelicacy, I have not the smallest doubt. There is only one epithet in universal use for foreigners. That epithet is "dirty."

THE ATTITUDE OF THE PEOPLE TO THE LITERARY ARTS

These differences between nation and nation also exist between class and class and between town and country. I will not here go into the vexed question of whether the peasant's way of blowing his nose or the squire's is the more cleanly and hygienic, though my experience as a municipal councillor of the way in which epidemics are spread by laundries make me incline to the side of the peasant. What is beyond all question is that each seems disgusting to the other. And when we come from physical facts to moral views and ethical opinions we find the same antagonism. To a great section—perhaps the largest section—of the people of England and France, all novels, plays, and songs are licentious; and the habit of enjoying them is a sign of a worthless character. To these people the distinctions made by the literary classes between books fit for young girls to read and improper books—between Paul and Virginia and Mademoiselle de Maupin or Une Vie, between Mrs Humphry Ward and Ouida—have no meaning: all writers of love stories and all readers of them are alike shameless. Cultivated Paris, cultivated London, are apt to overlook people who, as they seldom read and never write, have no means of making themselves heard. But such simple people heavily outnumber the cultivated; and if they could also outwit them, literature would perish. Yet their intolerance of fiction is as nothing to their intolerance of fact. I lately heard an English gentleman state a very simple fact in these terms: "I never could get on with my mother: she did not like me; and I did not like her: my brother was her pet." To an immense number of living English and French people this speech would suggest that its utterer ought to be burned alive, though the substitution of stepmother for mother and of half-brother for brother would suffice to make it seem quite probable and natural. And this, observe, not in the least because all these horrified people adore and are adored by their mothers, but simply because they have a fixed convention that the proper name of the relation between mother and son is love. However bitter and hostile it may in fact be in some cases, to call it by any other name is a breach of convention; and by the instinctive logic of timidity they infer that a man to whom convention is not sacred is a dangerous man. To them the ten commandments are nothing but arbitrary conventions; and the man who says today that he does not love his mother may, they conclude, tomorrow steal, rob, murder, commit adultery, and bear false witness against his neighbor.

THE DREAD OF THE ORIGINAL THINKER

This is the real secret of the terror inspired by an original thinker. In repudiating convention he is repudiating that on which his neighbors are relying for their sense of security. But he is usually also doing something even more unpopular. He is proposing new obligations to add to the already heavy burden of duty. When the boy Shelley elaborately and solemnly cursed his father for the entertainment of his friends, he only shocked us. But when the man Shelley told us that we should feed, clothe, and educate all the children in the country as carefully as if they were our immediate own, we lost our tempers with him and deprived him of the custody of his own children.

It is useless to complain that the conventional masses are unintelligent. To begin with, they are not unintelligent except in the sense in which all men are unintelligent in matters in which they are not experts. I object to be called unintelligent merely because I do not know enough about mechanical construction to be able to judge whether a motor car of new design is an improvement or not, and therefore prefer to buy one of the old type to which I am accustomed. The brave bourgeois whom Brieux scandalizes must not be dismissed with ridicule by the man of letters because, not being an expert in morals, he prefers the old ways and mistrusts the new. His position is a very reasonable one. He says, in effect, "If I am to enjoy any sense of security, I must be able to reckon on other people behaving in a certain ascertained way. Never mind whether it is the ideally right way or the ideally wrong way: it will suit me well enough if only it is convenient and, above all, unmistakeable. Lay it down if you like that people are not to pay debts and are to murder one another whenever they get a chance. In that case I can refuse to give credit and can carry weapons and learn to use them to defend myself. On the other hand, if you settle that debts are to be enforced and the peace kept by the police, I will give credit and renounce the practice of arms. But the one thing that I cannot stand is not knowing what the social contract is."

THE JUSTIFICATION OF CONVENTIONALITY

It is a cherished tradition in English politics that at a meeting of Lord Melbourne's Cabinet in the early days of Queen Victoria, the Prime Minister, when the meeting threatened to break up in confusion, put his back to the door and said, in the cynically profane manner then fashionable: "Gentlemen: we can tell the House the truth or we can tell it a lie: I do not care a damn which. All I insist on is that we shall all tell the same lie; and you shall not leave the room until you have settled what it is to be." Just so does the bourgeois perceive that the essential thing is not whether a convention is right or wrong, but that everybody shall know what it is and observe it. His cry is always: "I want to know where I stand." Tell him what he may do and what he may not do; and make him feel that he may depend on other people doing or not doing the same; and he feels secure, knowing where he stands and where other people stand. His dread and hatred of revolutions and heresies and men with original ideas is his dread of disorientation and insecurity. Those who have felt earthquakes assure us that there is no terror like the terror of the earth swaying under the feet that have always depended on it as the one immovable thing in the world. That is just how the ordinary respectable man feels when some man of genius rocks the moral ground beneath him by denying the validity of a convention. The popular phrases by which such innovators are described are always of the same kind. The early Christians were called men who wished to turn the world upside down. The modern critics of morals are reproached for "standing on their heads." There is no pretence of argument, or of any understanding of the proposals of the reformers: there is simply panic and a demand for suppression at all costs. The reformer is not forbidden to advance this or that definite opinion, because his assailants are too frightened to know or care what his opinions are: he is forbidden simply to speak in an unusual way about morals and religion, or to mention any subject that is not usually mentioned in public.

This is the terror which the English Censorship, like all other Censorships, gives effect to. It explains what puzzles most observers of the Censorship so much: namely, its scandalous laxity towards and positive encouragement of the familiar and customary pornographic side of theatrical art simultaneously with its intolerance of the higher drama, which is always unconventional and superbourgeois in its ethics. To illustrate, let me cite the point on which the English Censorship came into conflict with Brieux, when Les Hannetons was first performed by the Stage Society.

WHY LES HANNETONS WAS CENSORED

Les Hannetons is a very powerful and convincing demonstration of the delusiveness of that sort of freedom which men try to secure by refusing to marry, and living with a mistress instead. The play is a comedy: the audience laughs throughout; but the most dissolute man present leaves the theatre convinced that the unfortunate hero had better have been married ten times over than fallen into such bondage as his liaison has landed him in. To witness a performance might very wisely be made part of the curriculum of every university college and polytechnic in the country.

Now those who do not know the ways of the Censorship may jump to the conclusion that the objection of the Censor was to the exhibition on the stage of two persons living together in immoral relations. They would be greatly mistaken. The Censor made no difficulty whatever about that. Even the funny but ruthless scene where the woman cajoles the man by kissing him on a certain susceptible spot on his neck—a scene from which our shamed conscience shrinks as from a branding iron—was licensed without a word of remonstrance. But there is a searching passage in the play where the woman confesses to a girl friend that one of the lies by which she induced the man to enter into relations with her was that he was not her first lover. The friend is simple enough to express surprise, thinking that this, far from being an inducement, would have roused jealousy and disgust. The woman replies that, on the contrary, no man likes to face the responsibility of tempting a girl to her first step from the beaten path, and that girls take care accordingly not to let them know it.

This is one of those terrible stripping strokes by which a master of realism suddenly exposes a social sore which has been plastered over with sentimental nonsense about erring Magdalens, vicious nonsense about gaiety, or simply prudish silence. No young man or young woman hearing it, however anarchical their opinions may be as to sexual conduct, can possibly imagine afterwards that the relation between "les hannetons" is honest, charming, sentimentally interesting, or pardonable by the self-respect of either. It is felt instinctively to have something fundamentally dishonorable in it, in spite of the innocence of the natural affection of the pair for one another. Yet this is precisely the passage that the Censor refused to pass. All the rest was duly licensed. The exhibition of the pretty, scheming, lying, sensual girl fixing herself with triumphant success on the meanly prudent sensual man, and having what many women would consider rather a good time of it, was allowed and encouraged by the court certificate of propriety. But the deadly touch that made it impossible for even the most thoughtless pair in the audience to go and do likewise without loathing themselves, was forbidden.

MISADVENTURE OF A FRENCHMAN IN WESTMINSTER ABBEY

In short, the censorship did what it always does: it left the poison on the table and carefully locked up the antidote. And it did this, not from a fiendish design to destroy the souls of the people, but simply because the passage involved a reference by a girl to her virginity, which is unusual and therefore tabooed. The Censor never troubled himself as to the meaning or effect of the passage. It represented the woman as doing an unusual thing: therefore a dangerous, possibly subversive thing. In England, when we are scandalized and can give no direct reason why, we exclaim "What next?" That is the continual cry of the Censor's soul. If a girl may refer to her virginity on the stage, what may she not refer to? This instinctive regard to consequences was once impressed painfully on a pious Frenchman who, in Westminster Abbey, knelt down to pray. The verger, who had never seen such a thing happen before, promptly handed him over to the police and charged him with "brawling." Fortunately, the magistrate had compassion on the foreigner's ignorance; and even went the length of asking why he should not be allowed to pray in church. The reply of the verger was simple and obvious. "If we allowed that," he said, "we should have people praying all over the place." And to this day the rule in Westminster Abbey is that you may stroll about and look at the monuments; but you must not on any account pray. Similarly, on the stage you may represent murder, gluttony, sexual vice, and all the crimes in the calendar and out of it; but you must not say anything unusual about them.

MARRIAGE AND MALTHUS

If Brieux found himself blocked by the Censorship when he was exposing the vice of illicit unions, it will surprise no one to learn that his far more urgently needed exposures of the intemperance and corruption of marriage itself was fiercely banned. The vulgar, and consequently the official, view of marriage is that it hallows all the sexual relations of the parties to it. That it may mask all the vices of the coarsest libertinage with added elements of slavery and cruelty has always been true to some extent; but during the last forty years it has become so serious a matter that conscientious dramatists have to vivisect legal unions as ruthlessly as illegal ones. For it happens that just about forty years ago the propaganda of Neo-Malthusianism changed the bearing of children from an involuntary condition of marriage to a voluntary one. From the moment this momentous discovery was made, childless marriage became available to male voluptuaries as the cheapest way of keeping a mistress, and to female ones as the most convenient and respectable way of being kept in idle luxury by a man. The effects of this have already been startling, and will yet be revolutionary as far as marriage is concerned, both in law and custom. The work of keeping the populations of Europe replenished received a sudden check, amounting in France and England to a threat of actual retrogression. The appointment of a Royal Commission to inquire into the decline of the birthrate in the very sections of the population which most need to be maintained, is probably not very far off: the more far-seeing of those who know the facts have prophesied such a step for a long time past. The expectation of the Neo-Malthusians that the regulation of births in our families would give the fewer children born a better chance of survival in greater numbers and in fuller health and efficiency than the children of the old unrestricted families and of the mother exhausted by excessive childbearing has no doubt been fulfilled in some cases; but, on the whole, artificial sterility seems to be beating natural fertility; for as far as can be judged by certain sectional but typical private censuses, the average number of children produced is being dragged down to one and a half per family by the large proportion of intentionally childless marriages, and the heavy pressure of the cost of private childbearing on the scanty incomes of the masses.

That this will force us to a liberal State endowment of parentage, direct or indirect, is not now doubted by people who understand the problem: in fact, as I write, the first open step has already been taken by the Government's proposal to exempt parents from the full burden of taxation borne by the childless. There has also begun a change in public opinion as to the open abuse of marriage as a mere means by which any pair can procure a certificate of respectability by paying for it, which may quite possibly end in the disuse of the ceremony for all except fertile unions. From the point of view of the Church, it is a manifest profanation that couples whose only aim is a comfortable domesticity should obtain for it the sacrament of religious marriage on pretence of unselfish and publicly important purposes which they have not the smallest intention of carrying out. From the secular point of view there is no reason why couples who do not intend to have children should be allowed to enslave one another by all the complicated legal restrictions of their liberty and property which are attached to marriage solely to secure the responsibility of parents to the State for their children.

BRIEUX AND THE RESPECTABLE MARRIED MAN

All these by no means remote prospects, familiar though they are to the statesman and sociologist, are amazing to the bourgeois even when he is personally implicated in the change of practice that is creating the necessity for a change in law and in opinions. He has changed his practice privately, without talking about it except in secret, or in passages of unprintable Rabelaisian jocosity with his friends; and he is not only unable to see why anyone else should talk publicly about the change, but terrified lest what he is doing furtively and hypocritically should be suddenly dragged into the light, and his own case recorded, perhaps, in public statistics in support of innovations which vaguely suggest to him the destruction of morals and the break-up of the family. But both his pruderies and his terrors must give way before the absolute necessity for re-examining the foundations of our social structure after the shock they have received from the discovery of artificial sterilization, and their readjustment to the new strains they have to bear as a consequence of that discovery.

Tolstoy, with his Kreutzer Sonata, was the first to carry the war into the enemy's country by shewing that marriage intensified instead of eliminating every element of evil in sensual relations; but Brieux was the first dramatist to see not only the hard facts of the situation, but its political importance. He has seen in particular that a new issue has arisen in that eternal conflict of the sexes which is created by the huge difference between the transient pleasure of the man and the prolonged suffering of the woman in maintaining the population. Malthusianism, when it passed from being the speculation of an economist to being the ardent faith of a devoted band of propagandists, touched our feelings mainly as a protest against the burden of excessive childbearing imposed on married women. It was not then foreseen that the triumph of the propaganda might impose a still worse burden on them: the burden of enforced sterility. Before Malthus was born, cases were familiar enough in which wives who had borne two or three children as an inevitable consequence of their conjugal relations had thereupon rebelled against further travail and discontinued the relations by such a resolute assertion of selfishness as is not easy to an amiable woman and practically not possible to a loving or a jealous wife. But the case of a man refusing to fulfil his parental function and thereby denying the right of his wife to motherhood was unknown. Yet it immediately and inevitably arose the moment men became possessed of the means of doing this without self-denial. A wife could thus be put in a position intolerable to a woman of honor as distinguished from a frank voluptuary. She could be condemned to barren bodily slavery without remedy. To keep silence about so monstrous a wrong as this merely because the subject is a tabooed one was not possible to Brieux. Censorship or no Censorship, it had to be said, and indeed shouted from the housetops if nothing else would make people attend, that this infamy existed and must be remedied. And Brieux touched the evil at its worst spot in that section of the middle class in which the need for pecuniary prudence has almost swallowed up every more human feeling. In this most wretched of all classes there is no employment for women except the employment of wife and mother, and no provision for women without employment. The fathers are too poor to provide. The daughter must marry whom she can get: if the first chance, which she dares not refuse, is not that of a man whom she positively dislikes, she may consider herself fortunate. Her real hope of affection and self-respect lies in her children. And yet she above all women is subject to the danger that the dread of poverty which is the ruling factor in her husband's world may induce him to deny her right and frustrate her function of motherhood, using her simply as a housekeeper and a mistress without paying her the market price of such luxuries or forfeiting his respectability. To make us understand what this horror means, Brieux wrote Les Trois Filles de Monsieur Dupont, or, in equivalent English, The Three Daughters of Mr Smith. Mr Smith, in the person of the Censor, immediately shrieked "You must not mention such things." Mr Smith was wrong: they are just the things that must be mentioned, and mentioned again and yet again, until they are set right. Surely, of all the anomalies of our marriage law, there is nothing more mischievously absurd than that a woman can divorce a man for involuntary, but not for voluntary sterility. And a man cannot divorce a woman for sterility at all, although she now has the same power as he of frustrating the public purpose of all marriages.

BRIEUX SHEWS THE OTHER SIDE

But Brieux is not, as the ordinary man mostly is, a mere reactionist against the latest oversights and mistakes, becoming an atheist at every flaw discovered in popular theology, and recoiling into the grossest superstition when some Jesuit who happens by exception to be a clever and subtle man (about the last thing, by the way, that a real live Jesuit ever is) shews him that popular atheism is only theology without mind or purpose. The ordinary man, when Brieux makes him aware of the fact that Malthusianism has produced an unexpected and revolting situation, instantly conceives a violent prejudice against it, pointing to the declining population as evidence that it is bringing ruin on the human race, and clamoring for the return of the conjugal morality of his grandmother, as Theodore Roosevelt did when he was President of the United States of America. It therefore became necessary for Brieux to head him off in his frantic flight by writing another play, Maternity, to remind him of the case of Malthusianism, and to warn him—if he is capable of the warning—that progress is not achieved by panic-stricken rushes back and forward between one folly and another, but by sifting all movements and adding what survives the sifting to the fabric of our morality. For the fact that Malthusianism has made new crimes possible should not

discredit it, and cannot stop it, because every step gained by man in his continuous effort to control Nature necessarily does the same. Flying, for instance, which has become practical as a general human art for the first time this year, is capable of such alarming abuse that we are on the eve of a clamor for its restriction, and even for its prohibition, that will speedily make the present clamor against motor cars as completely forgotten as the clamor against bicycles was when motor cars appeared. But the motor car cannot be suppressed: it is improving our roads, improving the manners and screwing up the capacity and conduct of all who use them, improving our regulation of traffic, improving both locomotion and character as every victory over Nature finally improves the world and the race. Malthusianism is no exception to the rule: its obvious abuses, and the new need for protecting marriage from being made a mere charter of libertinage and slavery by its means, must be dealt with by improvements in conduct and law, and not by a hopeless attempt to turn the clock back to the time of Mrs Gamp. The tyranny which denies to the wife the right to become a mother has become possible through the discovery of the means of escape from the no less unbearable tyranny which compelled her to set another child at the table round which those she had already borne were starving because there was not enough food for them. When the French Government, like Colonel Roosevelt, could think of no better cure for the new tyranny than a revival of the old, Brieux added a play on the old tyranny to his play on the new tyranny.

This is the explanation of what stupid people call the inconsistencies of those modern dramatists who, like Ibsen and Brieux, are prophets as well as playwrights. Ibsen did not write The Wild Duck to ridicule the lesson he had already taught in Pillars of Society and An Enemy of the People: he did it to head off his disciples when, in their stampede from idealism, they forgot the need of ideals and illusions to men not strong enough to bear the truth. Brieux's La Foi has virtually the same theme. It is not an ultramontane tract to defend the Church against the sceptic. It is a solemn warning that you have not, as so many modern sceptics assume, disposed of the doctrine when you have proved that it is false. The miracle of St Januarius is worked, not by men who believe in it, but by men who know it to be a trick, but know also that men cannot be governed by the truth unless they are capable of the truth, and yet must be governed somehow, truth or no truth. Maternity and The Three Daughters of Mr Smith are not contradictory: they are complementary, like An Enemy of the People and The Wild Duck. I myself have had to introduce into one of my plays a scene in which a young man defends his vices on the ground that he is one of my disciples. I did so because the incident had actually occurred in a criminal court, where a young prisoner gave the same reason and was sentenced to six months imprisonment, less, I fear, for the offence than for the attempt to justify it.

THE MOST UNMENTIONABLE OF ALL SUBJECTS

Finally, Brieux attacked the most unmentionable subject of all: the subject of the diseases that dog profligacy in great cities and undermine high civilizations. The conspiracy of silence in this matter has long been intolerable to those who know the situation. It has not yet been generally realized that a startling change in the urgency of the question has been produced by recent advances in pathology. Briefly stated, the facts of the change are as follows. In the boyhood of those of us who are now of middle age,

the diseases in question were known as mainly of two kinds. One, admittedly very common, was considered transient, easily curable, harmless to future generations, and, to everyone but the sufferer, dismissible as a ludicrous incident. The other was admittedly one of the most formidable scourges of mankind, capable at its worst of hideous disfigurement and ruinous hereditary transmission, but not at all so common as the more trifling ailment, and fortunately shewing signs of dying out like typhus or plague. That is the belief still entertained by the elderly section of the community and those whom it has instructed.

This easy-going estimate of the situation was alarmingly upset in 1879 by Neisser's investigation of the supposedly lighter form of the disease, and the association with it of a newly discovered micro-organism called the gonococcus, a pathogenic germ of appalling malignity. It is said to be the commonest cause of blindness: it is transmitted from father to mother, from mother to child, from child to nurse, producing evils from which the individual attacked never gets securely free. A marriage contracted by a person actively affected in this way is perhaps the worst crime that can be committed in a civilized community with legal impunity. The danger of becoming the victim of such a crime is the worst danger that lurks in marriage for men and women, and in domestic service for nurses. And this affection, remember, is not the comparatively rare and receding scourge which used to be dreaded, but the frightfully common one of which all the men over forty now living were taught to make light.

Stupid people who are forced by these facts to admit that the simple taboo which forbids the subject to be mentioned at all is ruinous, still fall back on the plea that though the public ought to be warned, the theatre is not the proper place for the warning. When we ask them "What, then, *is* the proper place?" they plead that the proper place is out of hearing of the general public: that is, not in a school, not in a church, not in a newspaper, not in a public meeting, but in medical text-books which are read only by medical students. This, of course, is the taboo over again, only sufficiently ashamed of itself to resort to subterfuge. The common sense of the matter is that a public danger needs a public warning; and the more public the place the more effective the warning. But beyond this general consideration there is a special need for the warning in the theatre.

WHY THE UNMENTIONABLE MUST BE MENTIONED

The best friends of the theatre cannot deny, and need not seek to deny, that a considerable proportion of our theatrical entertainments stimulate the sexual instincts of the spectators. Indeed this is so commonly the case that the play which contains no sexual appeal is quite openly and commonly written of, even by professional critics of high standing, as being "undramatic," or "not a play at all." This is the basis of the prejudices against the theatre shewn by that section of English society in which sex is regarded as original sin, and the theatre, consequently, as the gate of hell. The prejudice is thoughtless: sex is a necessary and healthy instinct; and its nurture and education is one of the most important uses of all art, and, for the present at all events, the chief use of the theatre.

Now it may be an open question whether the theatre has proved itself worthy of being entrusted with so serious a function. I can conceive a community passing a law forbidding dramatic authors to deal with sex as a motive at all. Although such a law would consign the great bulk of existing dramatic literature to the waste paper basket, it would

neither destroy it wholly nor paralyze all future playwrights. The bowdlerization of Molière and Shakespear on the basis of such a law would leave a surprising quantity of their work intact. The novels of Dickens and his contemporaries are before us to prove how independent the imaginative writer is of the theme so often assumed to be indispensable in fiction. The works in which it is dragged in by the ears on this false assumption are far more numerous than the tales and plays—Manon Lescaut is an example—of which it forms the entire substance. Just as the European dramatist is able to write plays without introducing an accouchement, which is regarded as indispensable in all sympathetic Chinese plays, he can, if he is put to it, dispense with any theme that law or custom could conceivably forbid, and still find himself rich in dramatic material. Let us grant therefore that love might be ruled out by a written law as effectually as cholera is ruled out by an unwritten one without utterly ruining the theatre.

But what is none the less beyond all question by any reasonable and thoughtful person is that if we tolerate any subject on the stage we must not tolerate it by halves. It may be questioned whether we should allow war on the stage; but it cannot sanely be questioned that, if we do, we must allow its horrors to be represented as well as its glories. Destruction and murder, pestilence and famine, demoralization and cruelty, robbery and jobbery, must be allowed to contend with patriotism and military heroism on the boards as they do in actual war: otherwise the stage might inflame national hatreds and lead to their gratification with a recklessness that would make a cockpit of Europe. Again, if unscrupulous authors are to be allowed to make the stage a parade of champagne bottles, syphons, and tantaluses, scrupulous ones must be allowed to write such plays as L'Assommoir, which has, as a matter of simple fact, effectively deterred many young men from drunkenness. Nobody disputes the reasonableness of this freedom to present both sides. But when we come to sex, the taboo steps in, with the result that all the allurements of sex may be exhibited on the stage heightened by every artifice that the imagination of the voluptuary can devize, but not one of its dangers and penalties. You may exhibit seduction on the stage: but you must not even mention illegitimate conception and criminal abortion. We may, and do, parade prostitution to the point of intoxicating every young person in the theatre: yet no young person may hear a word as to the diseases that follow prostitution and avenge the prostitute to the third and fourth generation of them that buy her. Our shops and business offices are full of young men living in lonely lodgings, whose only artistic recreation is the theatre. In theatre we practise upon them every art that can make their loneliness intolerable and heighten the charm of the bait in the snares of the street as they go home. But when a dramatist is enlightened enough to understand the danger, and sympathetic enough to come to the rescue with a play to expose the snare and warn the victim, we forbid the manager to perform it on pain of ruin, and denounce the author as a corrupter of morals. One hardly knows whether to laugh or cry at such perverse stupidity.

BRIEUX AND VOLTAIRE

It is a noteworthy fact that when Brieux wrote Les Avariés (Damaged Goods) his experience with it recalled in one particular that of Voltaire.

It will be remembered that Voltaire, whose religious opinions were almost exactly those of most English Nonconformists today, took refuge from the Established Church of France near Geneva, the city of Calvin, where he established himself as the first and the greatest of modern Nonconformist philanthropists. The Genevese ministers found his theology so much to their taste that they were prevented from becoming open Voltaireans only by the scandal he gave by his ridicule of the current Genevese idolatry of the Bible, from which he was as free as any of our prominent Baptists and Congregationalists. In the same way, when Brieux, having had his Les Avariés condemned by the now extinct French Censorship, paid a visit to Switzerland, he was invited by a Swiss minister to read the play from the pulpit; and though the reading actually took place in a secular building, it was at the invitation and under the auspices of the minister. The minister knew what the Censor did not know: that what Brieux says in Les Avariés needs saying. The minister believed that when a thing needs saying, a man is in due course inspired to say it, and that such inspiration gives him a divine right to be heard. And this appears to be the simple truth of the matter in terms of the minister's divinity. For most certainly Brieux had every worldly inducement to refrain from writing this play, and no motive for disregarding these inducements except the motive that made Luther tear up the Pope's Bull, and Mahomet tell the idolatrous Arabs of Mecca that they were worshipping stones.

The reader will now understand why these three great plays have forced themselves upon us in England as they forced themselves upon Brieux's own countrymen. Just as Brieux had to write them, cost what it might, so we have had to translate them and perform them and finally publish them for those to read who are out of reach of the theatre. The evils they deal with are as rampant in England and America as they are in France. The gonococcus is not an exclusively French microbe: the possibility of sterilizing marriage is not bounded by the Channel, the Rhine, or the Alps. The furious revolt of poor women against bringing into the world more mouths to eat the bread that is already insufficient for their firstborn, rages with us exactly as it does in the final scene of Maternity. Therefore these three plays are given to the English-speaking peoples first. There are others to follow of like importance to us. And there are some like La Française, which we may read more light-heartedly when we have learnt the lesson of the rest. In La Française an American (who might just as well be an Englishman) has acquired his ideas of France and French life, not from the plays of Brieux, but from the conventional plays and romances which have only one theme: adultery. Visiting France, he is received as a friend in an ordinary respectable French household, where he conceives himself obliged, as a gallant man of the world, to invite his hostess to commit with him the adultery which he imagines to be a matter of course in every French *ménage*. The ignominious failure of his enterprise makes it much better comedy than his success would have made it in an ordinary fashionable play.

AS GOOD FISH IN THE SEA

The total number of plays produced by Brieux up to the date on which I write these lines is fifteen. The earliest dates as far back as 1890. It is therefore high time for us to begin to read him, as we have already begun to act him. The most pitiful sort of ignorance is ignorance of the few great men who are men of our own time. Most of us die without having heard of those contemporaries of ours for our opportunities of seeing and applauding whom posterity will envy us. Imagine meeting the ghost of an Elizabethan cockney in heaven, and, on asking him eagerly what Shakespear was like, being told either that the cockney had never heard of Shakespear, or knew of him vaguely as an objectionable writer of plays full of regrettable errors of taste. To save our own ghosts from disgracing themselves in this manner when they are asked about Brieux, is one of the secondary uses of this first instalment of his works in English.

POSTSCRIPT 1933. The war of 1914–18 broke down the obscurantism as to venereal disease which led to the disablement of so many soldiers; and since then the work of Marie Stopes in England and of Margaret Sanger in America has carried the propaganda of Birth Control into broader daylight and even established clinics to inculcate and teach its practice. Also the Church of England has for the first time flinched from condemning it. But as far as the law is concerned the situation is unchanged.

IX

MRS. WARREN'S PROFESSION

1894

Mrs Warren's Profession was written in 1894 to draw attention to the truth that prostitution is caused, not by female depravity and male licentiousness, but simply by underpaying, undervaluing, and overworking women so shamefully that the poorest of them are forced to resort to prostitution to keep body and soul together. Indeed all attractive unpropertied women lose money by being infallibly virtuous or contracting marriages that are not more or less venal. If on the large social scale we get what we call vice instead of what we call virtue it is simply because we are paying more for it. No normal woman would be a professional prostitute if she could better herself by being respectable, nor marry for money if she could afford to marry for love.

Also I desired to expose the fact that prostitution is not only carried on without organization by individual enterprise in the lodgings of solitary women, each her own mistress as well as every customer's mistress, but organized and exploited as a big international commerce for the profit of capitalists like any other commerce, and very lucrative to great city estates, including Church estates, through the rents of the houses in which it is practised.

I could not have done anything more injurious to my prospects at the outset of my career. My play was immediately stigmatized by the Lord Chamberlain, who by Act of Parliament has despotic and even supermonarchical power over our theatres, as "immoral and otherwise improper for the stage." Its performance was prohibited, I myself being branded by implication, to my great damage, as an unscrupulous and blackguardly author.

True, I have lived this defamation down, and am apparently none the worse. True too that the stage under the Censorship became so licentious after the war that the ban on a comparatively prudish play like mine became ridiculous and had to be lifted. Also I admit that my career as a revolutionary critic of our most respected social institutions kept me so continually in hot water that the addition of another jugful of boiling fluid by the Lord Chamberlain troubled me too little to entitle me to personal commiseration, especially as the play greatly strengthened my repute among serious readers. Besides, in 1894 the ordinary commercial theatres would have nothing to say to me, Lord Chamberlain or no Lord Chamberlain. None the less the injury done me, now admittedly indefensible, was real and considerable, and the injury to society much greater; for when the White Slave Traffic, as Mrs Warren's profession came to be called, was dealt with legislatively, all that Parliament did was to enact that prostitutes' male bullies and parasites should be flogged, leaving Mrs Warren in complete command of the situation, and its true nature more effectually masked than ever. It was the fault of the Censorship that our legislators and journalists were not better instructed.

In 1902 the Stage Society, technically a club giving private performances for the entertainment of its own members, and therefore exempt from the Lord Chamberlain's jurisdiction, resolved to perform the play. None of the public theatres dared brave his displeasure (he has absolute power to close them if they offend him) by harboring the performance; but another club which had a little stage, and which rather courted a pleasantly scandalous reputation, opened its doors for one night and one afternoon. Some idea of the resultant sensation may be gathered from the following polemic, which appeared as a preface to a special edition of the play, and was headed

THE AUTHOR'S APOLOGY

Mrs Warren's Profession has been performed at last, after a delay of only eight years; and I have once more shared with Ibsen the triumphant amusement of startling all but the strongest-headed of the London theatre critics clean out of the practice of their profession. No author who has ever known the exultation of sending the Press into an hysterical tumult of protest, of moral panic, of involuntary and frantic confession of sin, of a horror of conscience in which the power of distinguishing between the work of art on the stage and the real life of the spectator is confused and overwhelmed, will ever care for the stereotyped compliments which every successful farce or melodrama elicits from the newspapers. Give me that critic who rushed from my play to declare furiously that Sir George Crofts ought to be kicked. What a triumph for the actor, thus to reduce a jaded London journalist to the condition of the simple sailor in the Wapping gallery, who shouts execrations at Iago and warnings to Othello not to believe him! But dearer still than such simplicity is that sense of the sudden earthquake shock to the foundations of morality which sends a pallid crowd of critics into the street shrieking that the pillars of society are cracking and the ruin of the State at hand. Even the Ibsen champions of ten years ago remonstrate with me just as the veterans of those brave days remonstrated with them. Mr Grein, the hardy iconoclast who first launched my plays on the stage alongside Ghosts and The Wild Duck, exclaims that I have shattered his ideals. Actually his ideals! What would Dr Relling say? And Mr William Archer himself disowns me because I "cannot touch pitch without wallowing in it." Truly my play must be more needed than I knew; and yet I thought I knew how little the others know.

Do not suppose, however, that the consternation of the Press reflects any consternation among the general public. Anybody can upset the theatre critics, in a turn of the wrist, by substituting for the romantic commonplaces of the stage the moral commonplaces of the pulpit, the platform, or the library. Play Mrs Warren's Profession to an audience of clerical members of the Christian Social Union and of women well experienced in Rescue, Temperance, and Girls' Club work, and no moral panic will arise: every man and woman present will know that as long as poverty makes virtue hideous and the spare pocket-money of rich bachelordom makes vice dazzling, their daily hand-to-hand fight against prostitution with prayer and persuasion, shelters and scanty alms, will be a losing one. There was a time when they were able to urge that though "the white-lead factory where Anne Jane was poisoned" may be a far more terrible place than Mrs Warren's house, yet hell is still more dreadful. Nowadays they no longer believe in hell; and the girls among whom they are working know that they do not believe in it, and would laugh at them if they did. So well have the rescuers learnt that Mrs Warren's defence of herself and indictment of society is the thing that most needs saying, that those who know me personally reproach me, not for writing this play, but for wasting my energies on "pleasant plays" for the amusement of frivolous people, when I can build up such excellent stage sermons on their own work. Mrs Warren's Profession is the one play of mine which I could submit to a censorship without doubt of the result; only, it must not be the censorship of the minor theatre critic, nor of an innocent court official like the Lord Chamberlain's Examiner, much less of people who consciously profit by Mrs Warren's profession, or who personally make use of it, or who hold the widely whispered view that it is an indispensable safety-valve for the protection of domestic virtue, or, above all, who are smitten with a sentimental affection for our fallen sister, and would "take her up tenderly, lift her with care, fashioned so slenderly, young, and *so* fair." Nor am I prepared to accept the verdict of the medical gentlemen who would compulsorily examine and register Mrs Warren, whilst leaving Mrs Warren's patrons, especially her military patrons, free to destroy her health and anybody else's without fear of reprisals. But I should be quite content to have my play judged by, say, a joint committee of the Central Vigilance Society and the Salvation Army. And the sterner moralists the members of the committee were, the better.

Some of the journalists I have shocked reason so unripely that they will gather nothing from this but a confused notion that I am accusing the National Vigilance Association and the Salvation Army of complicity in my own scandalous immorality. It will seem to them that people who would stand this play would stand anything. They are quite mistaken. Such an audience as I have described would be revolted by many of our fashionable plays. They would leave the theatre convinced that the Plymouth Brother who still regards the playhouse as one of the gates of hell is perhaps the safest adviser on the subject of which he knows so little. If I do not draw the same conclusion, it is not because I am one of those who claim that art is exempt from moral obligations, and deny that the writing or performance of a play is a moral act, to be treated on exactly the same footing as theft or murder if it produces equally mischievous consequences. I am convinced that fine art is the subtlest, the most seductive, the most effective instrument of moral propaganda in the world, excepting only the example of personal conduct; and I waive even this exception in favor of the art of the stage, because it works by exhibiting examples of personal conduct made intelligible and moving to crowds of unobservant unreflecting people to whom real life means nothing. I have pointed out again and again that the influence of the theatre in England is growing so great that private conduct, religion, law, science, politics, and morals are becoming more and more theatrical, whilst the theatre itself remains impervious to common sense, religion, science, politics, and morals. That is why I fight the theatre, not with pamphlets and sermons and treatises, but with plays; and so effective do I find the dramatic method that I have no doubt I shall at last persuade even London to take its conscience and its brains with it when it goes to the theatre, instead of leaving them at home with its prayer-book as it does at present. Consequently, I am the last man to deny that if the net effect of performing Mrs Warren's Profession were an increase in the number of persons entering that profession or employing it, its performance might well be made an indictable offence.

Now let us consider how such recruiting can be encouraged by the theatre. Nothing is easier. Let the Lord Chamberlain's Examiner of Plays, backed by the Press, make an unwritten but perfectly well understood regulation that members of Mrs Warren's profession shall be tolerated on the stage only when they are beautiful, exquisitely dressed, and sumptuously lodged and fed; also that they shall, at the end of the play, die of consumption to the sympathetic tears of the whole audience, or step into the next room to commit suicide, or at least be turned out by their protectors and passed on to be "redeemed" by old and faithful lovers who have adored them in spite of all their levities. Naturally the poorer girls in the gallery will believe in the beauty, in the exquisite dresses, and the luxurious living, and will see that there is no real necessity for the consumption, the suicide, or the ejectment: mere pious forms, all of them, to save the Censor's face. Even if these purely official catastrophes carried any conviction, the majority of English girls remain so poor, so dependent, so well aware that the drudgeries of such honest work as is within their reach are likely enough to lead them eventually to lung disease, premature death, and domestic desertion or brutality, that they would still see reason to prefer the primrose path to the stony way of virtue, since both, vice at worst and virtue at best, lead to the same end in poverty and overwork. It is true that the Elementary School mistress will tell you that only girls of a certain kind will reason in this way. But alas! that certain kind turns out on inquiry to be simply the pretty, dainty kind: that is, the only kind that gets the chance of acting on such reasoning. Read the first report of the Commission on the Housing of the Working Classes [Bluebook C 4402, 1889]; read the Report on Home Industries (sacred word, Home!) issued by the Women's Industrial Council [Home Industries of Women in London, 1897, 1s.]; and ask yourself whether, if the lot in life therein described were your lot in life, you would not rather be a jewelled Vamp. If you can go deep enough into things to be able to say no, how many ignorant half-starved girls will believe you are speaking sincerely? To them the lot of the stage courtesan is heavenly in comparison with their own. Yet the Lord Chamberlain's Examiner, being an officer of the Royal Household, places the King in the position of saying to the dramatist "Thus, and thus only, shall you present Mrs Warren's profession on the stage, or you shall starve. Witness Shaw, who told the untempting truth about it, and whom We, by the Grace of God, accordingly disallow and suppress, and do what in Us lies to silence." Fortunately, Shaw cannot be silenced. "The harlot's cry from street to street" is louder than the voices of all the kings. I am not dependent on the theatre, and cannot be starved into making my play a standing advertisement of the attractive side of Mrs Warren's business.

Here I must guard myself against a misunderstanding. It is not the fault of their authors that the long string of wanton's tragedies, from Antony and Cleopatra to Iris, are snares to poor girls, and are objected to on that account by many earnest men and women who consider Mrs Warren's Profession an excellent sermon. Pinero is in no way bound to suppress the fact that his Iris is a person to be envied by millions of better women. If he made his play false to life by inventing fictitious disadvantages for her, he would be acting as unscrupulously as any tract-writer. If society chooses to provide for its Irises better than for its working women, it must not expect honest playwrights to manufacture spurious evidence to save its credit. The mischief lies in the deliberate suppression of the other side of the case: the refusal to allow Mrs Warren to expose the drudgery and repulsiveness of plying for hire among coarse tedious drunkards. All that, says the Examiner in effect, is horrifying, loathsome. Precisely: what does he expect it to be? would he have us represent it as beautiful and gratifying? His answer to this question amounts, I fear, to a blunt Yes; for it seems impossible to root out of an Englishman's mind the notion that vice is delightful, and that abstention from it is privation. At all events, as long as the tempting side of it is kept towards the public, and softened by plenty of sentiment and sympathy, it is welcomed by our Censor, whereas the slightest attempt to place it in the light of the policeman's lantern or the Salvation Army shelter is checkmated at once as not merely disgusting, but, if you please, unnecessary.

Everybody will, I hope, admit that this state of things is intolerable; that the subject of Mrs Warren's profession must be either tapu altogether, or else exhibited with the warning side as freely displayed as the tempting side. But many persons will vote for a complete tapu, and an impartial clean sweep from the boards of Mrs Warren and Gretchen and the rest: in short, for banishing the sexual instincts from the stage altogether. Those who think this impossible can hardly have considered the number and importance of the subjects which are actually banished from the stage. Many plays, among them Lear, Hamlet, Macbeth, Coriolanus, Julius Cæsar, have no sex complications: the thread of their action can be followed by children who could not understand a single scene of Mrs Warren's Profession or Iris. None of our plays rouse the sympathy of the audience by an exhibition of the pains of maternity, as Chinese plays constantly do. Each nation has its particular set of tapus in addition to the common human stock; and though each of these tapus limits the scope of the dramatist, it does not make drama impossible. If the Examiner were to refuse to license plays with female characters in them, he would only be doing to the stage what our tribal customs already do to the pulpit and the bar. I have myself written a rather entertaining play with only one woman in it, and she quite heartwhole; and I could just as easily write a play without a woman in it at all. I will even go as far as to promise the Examiner my support if he will introduce this limitation for part of the year, say during Lent, so as to make a close season for that dullest of stock dramatic subjects, adultery, and force our managers and authors to find out what all great dramatists find out spontaneously: to wit, that people who sacrifice every other consideration to love are as hopelessly unheroic on the stage as lunatics or dipsomaniacs. Hector and Hamlet are the world's heroes; not Paris and Antony.

But though I do not question the possibility of a drama in which love should be as effectively ignored as cholera is at present, there is not the slightest chance of that way out of the difficulty being taken by the Examiner. If he attempted it there would be a revolt in which he would be swept away, in spite of my singlehanded efforts to defend him. A complete tapu is politically impossible. A complete toleration is equally impossible to the Examiner, because his occupation would be gone if there were no tapu to enforce. He is therefore compelled to maintain the present compromise of a partial tapu, applied, to the best of his judgment, with a careful respect to persons and to public opinion. And a very sensible English solution of the difficulty, too, most readers will say. I should not dispute it if dramatic poets really were what English public opinion generally assumes them to be during their lifetime: that is, a licentiously irregular group to be kept in order in a rough and ready way by a magistrate who will stand no nonsense from them. But I cannot admit that the class represented by Eschylus, Sophocles, Aristophanes, Euripides, Shakespear, Goethe, Ibsen, and Tolstoy, not to mention our own contemporary playwrights, is as much in place in the Examiner's office as a pickpocket is in Bow Street. Further, it is not true that the Censorship, though it certainly suppresses Ibsen and Tolstoy, and would suppress Shakespear but for the absurd rule that a play once licensed is always licensed (so that Wycherley is permitted and Shelley prohibited), also suppresses unscrupulous playwrights. I challenge the Examiner to mention any extremity of sexual misconduct which any manager in his senses would risk presenting on the London stage that has not been presented under his license and that of his predecessor. The compromise, in fact, works out in practice in favor of loose plays as against earnest ones.

To carry conviction on this point, I will take the extreme course of narrating the plots of two plays witnessed within the last ten years by myself at London West End theatres, one licensed under Queen Victoria, the other under her successor. Both plots conform to the strictest rules of the period when La Dame aux Camellias was still a forbidden play, and when The Second Mrs Tanqueray would have been tolerated only on condition that she carefully explained to the audience that when she met Captain Ardale she sinned "but in intention."

Play number one. A prince is compelled by his parents to marry the daughter of a neighboring king, but loves another maiden. The scene represents a hall in the king's palace at night. The wedding has taken place that day; and the closed door of the nuptial chamber is in view of the audience. Inside, the princess awaits her bridegroom. A duenna is in attendance. The bridegroom enters. His sole desire is to escape from a marriage which is hateful to him. A means occurs to him. He will assault the duenna, and be ignominiously expelled from the palace by his indignant father-in-law. To his horror, when he proceeds to carry out this stratagem, the duenna, far from raising an alarm, is flattered, delighted, and compliant. The assaulter becomes the assaulted. He flings her angrily to the ground, where she remains placidly. He flies. The father enters; dismisses the duenna; and listens at the keyhole of his daughter's nuptial chamber, uttering various pleasantries, and declaring, with a shiver, that a sound of kissing, which he supposes to proceed from within, makes him feel young again.

Story number two. A German officer finds himself in an inn with a French lady who has wounded his national vanity. He resolves to humble her by committing a rape upon her. He announces his purpose. She remonstrates, implores, flies to the doors and finds them locked, calls for help and finds none at hand, runs screaming from side to side, and, after a harrowing scene, is overpowered and faints. Nothing further being possible on the stage without actual felony, the officer then relents and leaves her. When she recovers, she believes that he has carried out his threat; and during the rest of the play she is represented as vainly vowing vengeance upon him, whilst she is really falling in love with him under the influence of his imaginary crime against her. Finally she consents to marry him; and the curtain falls on their happiness.

This story was certified by the Examiner, acting for the Lord Chamberlain, as void in its general tendency of "anything immoral or otherwise improper for the stage." But let nobody conclude therefore that the Examiner is a monster, whose policy it is to deprave the theatre. As a matter of fact, both the above stories are strictly in order from the official point of view. The incidents of sex which they contain, though carried in both to the extreme point at which another step would be dealt with, not by the Examiner, but by the police, do not involve adultery, nor any allusion to Mrs Warren's profession, nor to the fact that the children of any polyandrous group will, when they grow up, inevitably be confronted, as those of Mrs Warren's group are in my play, with the insoluble problem of their own possible consanguinity. In short, by depending wholly on the coarse humors and the physical fascination of sex, they comply with all the formulable requirements of the Censorship, whereas plays in which these humors and fascinations are discarded, and the social problems created by sex seriously faced and dealt with, inevitably ignore the official formula and are suppressed. If the old rule against the exhibition of illicit sex relations on the stage were revived, and the subject absolutely barred, the only result would be that Antony and Cleopatra, Othello (because of the Bianca episode), Troilus and Cressida, Henry IV, Measure for Measure, Timon of Athens, La Dame aux Camellias, The Profligate, The Second Mrs Tanqueray, The Notorious Mrs Ebbsmith, The Gay Lord Quex, Mrs Dane's Defence, and Iris would be swept from the stage, and placed under the same ban as Tolstoy's Dominion of Darkness and Mrs Warren's Profession, whilst such plays as the two described above would have a monopoly of the theatre as far as sexual interest is concerned.

What is more, the repulsiveness of the worst of the certified plays would protect censorship against effective exposure and criticism. Not long ago an American Review of high standing asked me for an article on the Censorship of the English Stage. I replied that such an article would involve passages too disagreeable for publication in a magazine for general family reading. The editor persisted nevertheless; but not until he had declared his readiness to face this, and had pledged himself to insert the article unaltered (the particularity of the pledge extending even to a specification of the exact number of words in the article), did I consent to the proposal. What was the result? The editor, confronted with the two stories given above, threw his pledge to the winds, and, instead of returning the article, printed it with the illustrative examples omitted, and nothing left but the argument from political principle against the Censorship. In doing this he fired my broadside after withdrawing the cannon balls; for neither the Censor nor any other Englishman, except perhaps a few veterans of the dwindling old guard of Benthamism, cares a dump about political principle. The ordinary Briton thinks that if every other Briton is not under some form of tutelage, the more childish the better, he will abuse his freedom viciously. As far as its principle is concerned, the Censorship is the most popular institution in England; and the playwright who criticizes it is slighted as a blackguard agitating for impunity. Consequently nothing can really shake the confidence of the public in the Lord Chamberlain's department except a remorseless and unbowdlerized narration of the licentious fictions which slip through its net, and are hallmarked by it with the approval of the royal household. But as such stories cannot be made public without great difficulty, owing to the obligation an editor is under not to deal unexpectedly with matters that are not *virginibus puerisque*, the chances are heavily in favor of the Censor escaping all remonstrance. With the exception of such comments as I was able to make in my own critical articles in The World and The Saturday Review when the pieces I have described were first produced, and a few ignorant protests by churchmen against much better plays which they confessed they had not seen nor read, nothing has been said in the Press that could seriously disturb the easygoing notion that the stage would be much worse than it admittedly is but for the vigilance of the Examiner. The truth is, that no manager would dare produce on his own responsibility the pieces he can now get royal certificates for at two guineas per piece.

I hasten to add that I believe these evils

I

to be inherent in the nature of all censorship, and not merely a consequence of the form the institution takes in London. No doubt there is a staggering absurdity in appointing an ordinary clerk to see that the leaders of European literature do not corrupt the morals of the nation, and to restrain Sir Henry Irving from presuming to impersonate Samson or David on the stage, though any other sort of artist may daub these scriptural figures on a signboard or carve them on a tombstone without hindrance. If the General Medical Council, the Royal College of Physicians, the Royal Academy of Arts, the Incorporated Law Society, and Convocation were abolished, and their functions handed over to the Examiner, the Concert of Europe would presumably certify England as mad. Yet, though neither medicine nor painting nor law nor the Church moulds the character of the nation as potently as the theatre does, nothing can come on the stage unless its dimensions admit of its first passing through the Examiner's mind! Pray do not think that I question his honesty. I am quite sure that he sincerely thinks me a blackguard, and my play a grossly improper one, because, like Tolstoy's Dominion of Darkness, it produces, as they are both meant to produce, a very strong and very painful impression of evil. I do not doubt for a moment that the rapine play which I have described, and which he licensed, was quite incapable in manuscript of producing any particular effect on his mind at all, and that when he was once satisfied that the ill-conducted hero was a German and not an English officer, he passed the play without studying its moral tendencies. Even if he had undertaken that study, there is no more reason to suppose that he is a competent moralist than there is to suppose that I am a competent mathematician. But truly it does not matter whether he is a moralist or not. Let nobody dream for a moment that

what is wrong with the Censorship is the shortcoming of the gentleman who happens at any moment to be acting as Censor. Replace him tomorrow by an Academy of Letters and an Academy of Dramatic Poetry, and the new filter will still exclude original and epoch-making work, whilst passing conventional, old-fashioned, and vulgar work. The conclave which compiles the expurgatory index of the Roman Catholic Church is the most august, ancient, learned, famous, and authoritative censorship in Europe. Is it more enlightened, more liberal, more tolerant than the comparatively unqualified office of the Lord Chamberlain? On the contrary, it has reduced itself to a degree of absurdity which makes a Catholic university a contradiction in terms. All censorships exist to prevent anyone from challenging current conceptions and existing institutions. All progress is initiated by challenging current conceptions, and executed by supplanting existing institutions. Consequently the first condition of progress is the removal of censorships. There is the whole case against censorships in a nutshell.

It will be asked whether theatrical managers are to be allowed to produce what they like, without regard to the public interest. But that is not the alternative. The managers of our London music-halls are not subject to any censorship. They produce their entertainments on their own responsibility, and have no two-guinea certificates to plead if their houses are conducted viciously. They know that if they lose their character, the County Council will simply refuse to renew their license at the end of the year; and nothing in the history of popular art is more amazing than the improvement in music-halls that this simple arrangement has produced within a few years. Place the theatres on the same footing, and we shall promptly have a similar revolution: a whole class of frankly blackguardly plays, in which unscrupulous low comedians attract crowds to gaze at bevies of girls who have nothing to exhibit but their prettiness, will vanish like the obscene songs which were supposed to enliven the squalid dulness, incredible to the younger generation, of the music-halls fifteen years ago. On the other hand, plays which treat sex questions as problems for thought instead of as aphrodisiacs will be freely performed. Gentlemen of the Examiner's way of thinking will have plenty of opportunity of protesting against them in Council; but the result will be that the Examiner will find his natural level; Ibsen and Tolstoy theirs; so no harm will be done.

This question of the Censorship reminds me that I have to apologize to those who went to the recent performance of Mrs Warren's Profession expecting to find it what I have just called an aphrodisiac. That was not my fault: it was the Examiner's. After the specimens I have given of the tolerance of his department, it was natural enough for thoughtless people to infer that a play which overstepped his indulgence must be a very exciting play indeed. Accordingly, I find one critic so explicit as to the nature of his disappointment as to say candidly that "such airy talk as there is upon the matter is utterly unworthy of acceptance as being a representation of what people with blood in them think or do on such occasions." Thus am I crushed between the upper millstone of the Examiner, who thinks me a libertine, and the nether popular critic, who thinks me a prude. Critics of all grades and ages, middle-aged fathers of families no less than ardent young enthusiasts, are equally indignant with me. They revile me as lacking in passion, in feeling, in manhood. Some of them even sum the matter up by denying me any dramatic power: a melancholy betrayal of what dramatic power has come to mean on our stage under the

Censorship! Can I be expected to refrain from laughing at the spectacle of a number of respectable gentlemen lamenting because a playwright lures them to the theatre by a promise to excite their senses in a very special and sensational manner, and then, having successfully trapped them in exceptional numbers, proceeds to ignore their senses and ruthlessly improve their minds? But I protest again that the lure was not mine. The play had been in print for four years; and I have spared no pains to make known that my plays are built to induce, not voluptuous reverie but intellectual interest, not romantic rhapsody but humane concern. Accordingly, I do not find those critics who are gifted with intellectual appetite and political conscience complaining of want of dramatic power. Rather do they protest, not altogether unjustly, against a few relapses into staginess and caricature which betray the young playwright and the old playgoer in this early work of mine. As to the voluptuaries, I can assure them that the playwright, whether he be myself or another, will always disappoint them. The drama can do little to delight the senses: all the apparent instances to the contrary are instances of the personal fascination of the performers. The drama of pure feeling is no longer in the hands of the playwright: it has been conquered by the musician, after whose enchantments all the verbal arts seem cold and tame. Romeo and Juliet with the loveliest Juliet is dry, tedious, and rhetorical in comparison with Wagner's Tristan, even though Isolde be both fourteen stone and forty, as she often is in Germany. Indeed, it needed no Wagner to convince the public of this. The voluptuous sentimentality of Gounod's Faust and Bizet's Carmen has captured the common playgoer; and there is, flatly, no future now for any drama without music except the drama of thought. The attempt to produce a genus of opera without music (and this absurdity is what our fashionable theatres have been driving at for a long time past without knowing it) is far less hopeful than my own determination to accept problem as the normal material of the drama.

That this determination will throw me into a long conflict with our theatre critics, and with the few playgoers who go to the theatre as often as the critics, I well know; but I am too well equipped for the strife to be deterred by it, or to bear malice towards the losing side. In trying to produce the sensuous effects of opera, the fashionable drama has become so flaccid in its sentimentality, and the intellect of its frequenters so atrophied by disuse, that the reintroduction of problem, with its remorseless logic and iron framework of fact, inevitably produces at first an overwhelming impression of coldness and inhuman rationalism. But this will soon pass away. When the intellectual muscle and moral nerve of the critics has been developed in the struggle with modern problem plays, the pettish luxuriousness of the clever ones, and the sulky sense of disadvantaged weakness in the sentimental ones, will clear away; and it will be seen that only in the problem play is there any real drama, because drama is no mere setting up of the camera to nature: it is the presentation in parable of the conflict between Man's will and his environment: in a word, of problem. The vapidness of such drama as the pseudo-operatic plays contain lies in the fact that in them animal passion, sentimentally diluted, is shewn in conflict, not with real circumstances, but with a set of conventions and assumptions half of which do not exist off the stage, whilst the other half can either be evaded by a pretence of compliance or defied with complete impunity by any reasonably strong-minded person. Nobody can feel that such conventions are really compulsory; and consequently nobody can believe in the stage pathos that accepts them as an inexorable fate, or in the reality of the figures who indulge in such pathos. Sitting at such plays we do not believe: we make-believe. And the habit of make-believe becomes at last so rooted, that criticism of the theatre insensibly ceases to be criticism at all, and becomes more and more a chronicle of the fashionable enterprises of the only realities left on the stage: that is, the performers in their own persons. In this phase the playwright who attempts to revive genuine drama produces the disagreeable impression of the pedant who attempts to start a serious discussion at a fashionable at-home. Later on, when he has driven the tea services out and made the people who had come to use the theatre as a drawing room understand that it is they and not the dramatists who are the intruders, he has to face the accusation that his plays ignore human feeling, an illusion produced by that very resistance of fact and law to human feeling which creates drama. It is the *deus ex machina* who, by suspending that resistance, makes the fall of the curtain an immediate necessity, since drama ends exactly where resistance ends. Yet the introduction of this resistance produces so strong an impression of heartlessness nowadays that a distinguished critic has summed up the impression made on him by Mrs Warren's Profession, by declaring that "the difference between the spirit of Tolstoy and the spirit of Mr Shaw is the difference between the spirit of Christ and the spirit of Euclid." But the epigram would be as good if Tolstoy's name were put in place of mine and D'Annunzio's in place of Tolstoy's. At the same time I accept the enormous compliment to my reasoning powers with sincere complacency; and I promise my flatterer that when he is sufficiently accustomed to and therefore undazzled by problem on the stage to be able to attend to the familiar factor of humanity in it as well as to the unfamiliar one of a real environment, he will both see and feel that Mrs Warren's Profession is no mere theorem, but a play of instincts and temperaments in conflict with each other and with a flinty social problem that never yields an inch to mere sentiment.

I go further than this. I declare that the real secret of the cynicism and inhumanity of which shallower critics accuse me is the unexpectedness with which my characters behave like human beings, instead of conforming to the romantic logic of the stage. The axioms and postulates of that dreary mimanthropometry are so well known that it is almost impossible for its slaves to write tolerable last acts to their plays, so conventionally do their conclusions follow from their premises. Because I have thrown this logic ruthlessly overboard, I am accused of ignoring, not stage logic, but, of all things, human feeling. People with completely theatrified imaginations tell me that no girl would treat her mother as Vivie Warren does, meaning that no stage heroine would in a popular sentimental play. They say this just as they might say that no two straight lines would enclose a space. They do not see how completely inverted their vision has become even when I throw its preposterousness in their faces, as I repeatedly do in this very play. Praed, the sentimental artist (fool that I was not to make him a theatre critic instead of an architect!), burlesques them by expecting all through the piece that the feelings of the others will be logically deducible from their family relationships and from his "conventionally unconventional" social code. The sarcasm is lost on the critics: they, saturated with the same logic, only think him the sole sensible person on the stage. Thus it comes about that the more completely the dramatist is emancipated from

the illusion that men and women are primarily reasonable beings, and the more powerfully he insists on the ruthless indifference of their great dramatic antagonist, the external world, to their whims and emotions, the surer he is to be denounced as blind to the very distinction on which his whole work is built. Far from ignoring idiosyncrasy, will, passion, impulse, whim, as factors in human action, I have placed them so nakedly on the stage that the elderly citizen, accustomed to see them clothed with the veil of manufactured logic about duty, and to disguise even his own impulses from himself in this way, finds the picture as unnatural as Carlyle's suggested painting of parliament sitting without its clothes.

I now come to those critics who, intellectually baffled by the problem in Mrs Warren's Profession, have made a virtue of running away from it on the gentlemanly ground that the theatre is frequented by women as well as by men, and that such problems should not be discussed or even mentioned in the presence of women. With that sort of chivalry I cannot argue: I simply affirm that Mrs Warren's Profession is a play for women; that it was written for women; that it has been performed and produced mainly through the determination of women that it should be performed and produced; that the enthusiasm of women made its first performance excitingly successful; and that not one of these women had any inducement to support it except their belief in the timeliness and the power of the lesson the play teaches. Those who were "surprised to see ladies present" were men; and when they proceeded to explain that the journals they represented could not possibly demoralize the public by describing such a play, their editors cruelly devoted the space saved by their delicacy to reporting at unusual length an exceptionally abominable police case.

My old Independent Theatre manager, Mr Grein, besides that reproach to me for shattering his ideals, complains that Mrs Warren is not wicked enough, and names several romancers who would have clothed her black soul with all the terrors of tragedy. I have no doubt they would; but that is just what I did not want to do. Nothing would please our sanctimonious British public more than to throw the whole guilt of Mrs Warren's profession on Mrs Warren herself. Now the whole aim of my play is to throw that guilt on the British public itself. Mr Grein may remember that when he produced my first play, Widowers' Houses, exactly the same misunderstanding arose. When the virtuous young gentleman rose up in wrath against the slum landlord, the slum landlord very effectually shewed him that slums are the product, not of individual Harpagons, but of the indifference of virtuous young gentlemen to the condition of the city they live in, provided they live at the west end of it on money earned by somebody else's labor. The notion that prostitution is created by the wickedness of Mrs Warren is as silly as the notion—prevalent, nevertheless, to some extent in Temperance circles—that drunkenness is created by the wickedness of the publican. Mrs Warren is not a whit a worse woman than the reputable daughter who cannot endure her. Her indifference to the ultimate social consequences of her means of making money, and her discovery of that means by the ordinary method of taking the line of least resistance to getting it, are too common in English society to call for any special remark. Her vitality, her thrift, her energy, her outspokenness, her wise care of her daughter, and the managing capacity which has enabled her and her sister to climb from the fried fish shop down by the Mint to the establishments of which she boasts, are all high English social virtues. Her defence of herself is so overwhelming that it provokes the St James's Gazette to declare that "the tendency of the play is wholly evil" because "it contains one of the boldest and most specious defences of an immoral life for poor women that has ever been penned." Happily the St James's Gazette here speaks in its haste. Mrs Warren's defence of herself is not only bold and specious, but valid and unanswerable. But it is no defence at all of the vice which she organizes. It is no defence of an immoral life to say that the alternative offered by society collectively to poor women is a miserable life, starved, overworked, fetid, ailing, ugly. Though it is quite natural and *right* for Mrs Warren to choose what is, according to her lights, the least immoral alternative, it is none the less infamous of society to offer such alternatives. For the alternatives offered are not morality and immorality, but two sorts of immorality. The man who cannot see that starvation, overwork, dirt, and disease are as anti-social as prostitution—that they are the vices and crimes of a nation, and not merely its misfortunes—is (to put it as politely as possible) a hopelessly Private Person.

The notion that Mrs Warren must be a fiend is only an example of the violence and passion which the slightest reference to sex rouses in undisciplined minds, and which makes it seem natural to our lawgivers to punish silly and negligible indecencies with a ferocity unknown in dealing with, for example, ruinous financial swindling. Had my play been entitled Mr Warren's Profession, and Mr Warren been a bookmaker, nobody would have expected me to make him a villain as well. Yet gambling is a vice, and bookmaking an institution, for which there is absolutely nothing to be said. The moral and economic evil done by trying to get other people's money without working for it (and this is the essence of gambling) is not only enormous but uncompensated. There are no two sides to the question of gambling, no circumstances which force us to tolerate it lest its suppression lead to worse things, no consensus of opinion among responsible classes, such as magistrates and military commanders, that it is a necessity, no Athenian records of gambling made splendid by the talents of its professors, no contention that instead of violating morals it only violates a legal institution which is in many respects oppressive and unnatural, no possible plea that the instinct on which it is founded is a vital one. Prostitution can confuse the issue with all these excuses: gambling has none of them. Consequently, if Mrs Warren must needs be a demon, a bookmaker must be a cacodemon. Well, does anybody who knows the sporting world really believe that bookmakers are worse than their neighbors? On the contrary, they have to be a good deal better; for in that world nearly everybody whose social rank does not exclude such an occupation would be a bookmaker if he could; but the strength of character required for handling large sums of money and for strict settlements and unflinching payment of losses is so rare that successful bookmakers are rare too. It may seem that at least public spirit cannot be one of a bookmaker's virtues; but I can testify from personal experience that excellent public work is done with money subscribed by bookmakers. It is true that there are abysses in bookmaking: for example, welshing. Mr Grein hints that there are abysses in Mrs Warren's profession also. So there are in every profession: the error lies in supposing that every member of them sounds these depths. I sit on a public body which prosecutes Mrs Warren zealously; and I can assure Mr Grein that she is often leniently dealt with because she has conducted her business "respectably" and held herself above its vilest branches. The degrees in infamy are as numerous and as scrupulously observed as the degrees in the peerage: the moralist's notion that there are depths at which the moral atmosphere ceases is as delusive as the rich man's notion that there are no social jealousies or snobberies among the very poor. No: had I drawn Mrs Warren as a fiend in human form, the very people who now rebuke me for flattering her would probably be the first to deride me for deducing character logically from occupation instead of observing it accurately in society.

One critic is so enslaved by this sort of logic that he calls my portraiture of the Reverend Samuel Gardner an attack on religion. According to this view Subaltern Iago is an attack on the army, Sir John Falstaff an attack on knighthood, and King Claudius an attack on royalty. Here again the clamor for naturalness and human feeling, raised by so many critics when they are confronted by the real thing on the stage, is really a clamor for the most mechanical and superficial sort of logic. The dramatic reason for making the clergyman what Mrs Warren calls "an old stick-in-the-mud," whose son, in spite of much capacity and charm, is a cynically worthless member of society, is to set up a mordant contrast between him and the woman of infamous profession, with her well brought-up, straightforward, hardworking daughter. The critics who have missed the contrast have doubtless observed often enough that many clergymen are in the Church through no genuine calling, but simply because, in circles which can command preferment, it is the refuge of the fool of the family; and that clergymen's sons are often conspicuous reactionists against the restraints imposed on them in childhood by their father's profession. These critics must know, too, from history if not from experience, that women as unscrupulous as Mrs Warren have distinguished themselves as administrators and rulers, both commercially and politically. But both observation and knowledge are left behind when journalists go to the theatre. Once in their stalls, they assume that it is "natural" for clergymen to be saintly, for soldiers to be heroic, for lawyers to be hard-hearted, for sailors to be simple and generous, for doctors to perform miracles with little bottles, and for Mrs Warren to be a beast and a demon. All this is not only not natural, but not dramatic. A man's profession only enters into the drama of his life when it comes into conflict with his nature. The result of this conflict is tragic in Mrs Warren's case, and comic in the clergyman's case (at least we are savage enough to laugh at it); but in both cases it is illogical, and in both cases natural. I repeat, the critics who accuse me of sacrificing nature to logic are so sophisticated by their profession that to them logic is nature, and nature absurdity.

Many friendly critics are too little skilled in social questions and moral discussions to be able to conceive that respectable gentlemen like themselves, who would instantly call the police to remove Mrs Warren if she ventured to canvass them personally, could possibly be in any way responsible for her proceedings. They remonstrate sincerely, asking me what good such painful exposures can possibly do. They might as well ask what good Lord Shaftesbury did by devoting his life to the exposure of evils (by no means yet remedied) compared to which the worst things brought into view or even into surmise in this play are trifles. The good of mentioning them is that you make people so extremely uncomfortable about them that they finally stop blaming "human nature" for them, and begin to support measures for their reform. Can anything be more absurd than the copy of The Echo which contains a notice of the performance of my play? It is edited by a gentleman who, having devoted his life to work of the Shaftesbury type, exposes social evils and clamors for their reform in every column except one; and that one is occupied by the declaration of the paper's kindly theatre critic, that the performance left him "wondering what useful purpose the play was intended to serve." The balance has to be redressed by the more fashionable papers, which usually combine capable art criticism with West-End solecism on politics and sociology. It is very noteworthy, however, on comparing the Press explosion produced by Mrs Warren's Profession in 1902 with that produced by Widowers' Houses about ten years earlier, that whereas in 1892 the facts were frantically denied and the persons of the drama flouted as monsters of wickedness, in 1902 the facts are admitted, and the characters recognized, though it is suggested that this is exactly why no gentleman should mention them in public. Only one writer has ventured to imply this time that the poverty mentioned by Mrs Warren has since been quietly relieved, and need not have been dragged back to the footlights. I compliment him on his splendid mendacity, in which he is unsupported, save by a little plea in a theatrical paper which is innocent enough to think that ten guineas a year with board and lodging is an impossibly low wage for a barmaid. It goes on to cite Mr Charles Booth as having testified that there are many laborers' wives who are happy and contented on eighteen shillings a week. But I can go further than that myself. I have seen an Oxford agricultural laborer's wife looking cheerful on eight shillings a week; but that does not console me for the fact that agriculture in England is a ruined industry. If poverty does not matter as long as it is contented, then crime does not matter as long as it is unscrupulous. The truth is that it is only then that it does matter most desperately. Many persons are more comfortable when they are dirty than when they are clean; but that does not recommend dirt as a national policy.

In 1905 Arnold Daly produced Mrs Warren's Profession in New York. The Press of that city instantly raised a cry that such persons as Mrs Warren are "ordure" and should not be mentioned in the presence of decent people. This hideous repudiation of humanity and social conscience so took possession of the New York journalists that the few among them who kept their feet morally and intellectually could do nothing to check the epidemic of foul language, gross suggestion, and raving obscenity of word and thought that broke out. The writers abandoned all self-restraint under the impression that they were upholding virtue instead of outraging it. They infected each other with their hysteria until they were for all practical purposes indecently mad. They finally forced the police to arrest Daly and his company, and led the magistrate to express his loathing of the duty thus forced upon him of reading an unmentionable and abominable play. Of course the convulsion soon exhausted itself. The magistrate, naturally somewhat impatient when he found that what he had to read was a strenuously ethical play forming part of a book which had been in circulation unchallenged for eight years, and had been received without protest by the whole London and New York Press, gave the journalists a piece of his mind as to their moral taste in plays. By consent, he passed the case on to a higher court, which declared that the play was not immoral; acquitted Daly; and made an end of the attempt to use the law to declare living women to be "ordure," and thus enforce silence as to the far-reaching fact that you cannot cheapen women in the market for industrial purposes without cheapening them for other purposes as well. I hope Mrs Warren's Profession will be played everywhere, in season and out of season, until Mrs Warren has bitten that fact into the public conscience, and shamed the newspapers which support a tariff to keep up the price of every American commodity except American manhood and womanhood.

Unfortunately, Daly had already suffered the usual fate of those who direct public attention to the profits of the sweater or the pleasures of the voluptuary. He was morally lynched side by side with me. Months elapsed before the decision of the courts vindicated him; and even then, since his vindication implied the condemnation of the Press, which was by that time sober again, and ashamed of its orgy, his triumph received a rather sulky and grudging publicity. In the meantime he had hardly been able to approach an American city, including even those cities which had heaped applause on him as the defender of hearth and home when he produced Candida, without having to face articles discussing whether mothers could allow their daughters to attend such plays as You Never Can Tell, written by the infamous author of Mrs Warren's Profession, and acted by the monster who produced it. What made this harder to bear was that though no fact is better established in theatrical business than the financial disastrousness of moral discredit, the journalists who had done all the mischief kept paying vice the homage of assuming that it is enormously popular and lucrative, and that Daly and I, being exploiters of vice, must therefore be making colossal fortunes out of the abuse heaped on us, and had in fact provoked it and welcomed it with that express object. Ignorance of real life could hardly go further.

I was deeply disgusted by this unsavory mobbing. And I have certain sensitive places in my soul: I do not like that word "ordure." Apply it to my work, and I can afford to smile, since the world, on the whole, will smile with me. But to apply it to the woman in the street, whose spirit is of one substance with your own and her body no less holy: to look your women folk in the face afterwards and not go out and hang yourself: that is not on the list of pardonable sins.

Shortly after these events a leading New York newspaper, which was among the most abusively clamorous for the suppression of Mrs Warren's Profession, was fined heavily for deriving part of its revenue from advertisements of Mrs Warren's houses.

Many people have been puzzled by the fact that whilst stage entertainments which are frankly meant to act on the spectators as aphrodisiacs are everywhere tolerated, plays which have an almost horrifying contrary effect are fiercely attacked by persons and papers notoriously indifferent to public morals on all other occasions. The explanation is very simple. The profits of Mrs Warren's profession are shared not only by Mrs Warren and Sir George Crofts, but by the landlords of their houses, the newspapers which advertize them, the restaurants which cater for them, and, in short, all the trades to which they are good customers, not to mention the public officials and representatives whom they silence by complicity, corruption, or blackmail. Add to these the employers who profit by cheap female labor, and the shareholders whose dividends depend on it (you find such people everywhere, even on the judicial bench and in the highest places in Church and State), and you get a large and powerful class with a strong pecuniary incentive to protect Mrs Warren's profession, and a correspondingly strong incentive to conceal, from their own consciences no less than from

the world, the real sources of their gain. These are the people who declare that it is feminine vice and not poverty that drives women to the streets, as if vicious women with independent incomes ever went there. These are the people who, indulgent or indifferent to aphrodisiac plays, raise the moral hue and cry against performances of Mrs Warren's Profession, and drag actresses to the police court to be insulted, bullied, and threatened for fulfilling their engagements. For please observe that the judicial decision in New York State in favor of the play did not end the matter. In Kansas City, for instance, the municipality, finding itself restrained by the courts from preventing the performance, fell back on a local by-law against indecency. It summoned the actress who impersonated Mrs Warren to the police court, and offered her and her colleagues the alternative of leaving the city or being prosecuted under this by-law.

Now nothing is more possible than that the city councillors who suddenly displayed such concern for the morals of the theatre were either Mrs Warren's landlords, or employers of women at starvation wages, or restaurant keepers, or newspaper proprietors, or in some other more or less direct way sharers of the profits of her trade. No doubt it is equally possible that they were simply stupid men who thought that indecency consists, not in evil, but in mentioning it. I have, however, been myself a member of a municipal council, and have not found municipal councillors quite so simple and inexperienced as this. At all events I do not propose to give the Kansas councillors the benefit of the doubt. I therefore advise the public at large, which will finally decide the matter, to keep a vigilant eye on gentlemen who will stand anything at the theatre except a performance of Mrs Warren's Profession, and who assert in the same breath that (*a*) the play is too loathsome to be bearable by civilized people, and (*b*) that unless its performance is prohibited the whole town will throng to see it. They may be merely excited and foolish; but I am bound to warn the public that it is equally likely that they may be collected and knavish.

At all events, to prohibit the play is to protect the evil which the play exposes; and in view of that fact, I see no reason for assuming that the prohibitionists are disinterested moralists, and that the author, the managers, and the performers, who depend for their livelihood on their personal reputations and not on rents, advertisements, or dividends, are grossly inferior to them in moral sense and public responsibility.

It is true that in Mrs Warren's Profession, Society, and not any individual, is the villain of the piece; but it does not follow that the people who take offence at it are all champions of society. Their credentials cannot be too carefully examined.

PICCARD'S COTTAGE, *January* 1902.

P.S. (1930) On reading the above after a lapse of 28 years, with the ban on Mrs Warren withdrawn and forgotten, I should have discarded it as an overdone fuss about nothing that now matters were it not for a recent incident. Before describing this I must explain that with the invention of the cinematograph a new censorship has come into existence, created, not this time by Act of Parliament, but by the film manufacturers to provide themselves with the certificates of propriety which have proved so useful to the theatre managers. This private censorship has acquired public power through its acceptance by the local authorities, without whose license the films cannot be exhibited in place of public entertainment.

A lady who has devoted herself to the charitable work of relieving the homeless and penniless people who are to be found every night in London on the Thames Embankment had to deal largely with working men who had come to London from the country under the mistaken impression that there is always employment there for everybody, and with young women, also from the provinces, who had been lured to London by offers of situations which were really traps set for them by the agents of the White Slave traffic. The lady rightly concluded that much the best instrument for warning the men, and making known to the women the addresses of the organization for befriending unprotected girl travellers, is the cinema. She caused a film to be made for this purpose. The Film Censor immediately banned the part of the film which gave the addresses to the girls and shewed them the risks they ran. The lady appealed to me to help her to protest. After convincing myself by witnessing a private exhibition of the film that it was quite innocent I wrote to the Censor, begging him to examine the film personally, and remedy what seemed to be a rule-of-thumb mistake by his examiners. He not only confirmed their veto, but left uncontradicted a report in all the papers that he had given as his reason that the lady had paraded the allurements of vice, and that such parades could not be tolerated by him. The sole allurements were the smart motor car in which the heroine of the film was kidnapped, and the fashionable clothes of the two very repulsive agents who drugged her in it. In every other respect her experiences were as disagreeable as the sternest moralist could desire.

I then made a tour of the picture houses to see what the Film Censor considers allowable. Of the films duly licensed by him two were so nakedly pornographic that their exhibition could hardly have been risked without the

Censor's certificate of purity. One of them presented the allurements of a supposedly French brothel so shamelessly that I rose and fled in disgust long before the end, though I am as hardened to vulgar salacity in the theatre as a surgeon is to a dissecting room.

The only logical conclusion apparent is that the White Slave traffickers are in complete control of our picture theatres, and can close them to our Rescue workers as effectively as they can reserve them for advertisements of their own trade. I spare the Film Censor that conclusion. The conclusion I press upon him and on the public is my old one of twentyeight years ago: that all the evil effects of such corrupt control are inevitably produced gratuitously by Censors with the best intentions.

POSTSCRIPT 1933. In spite of the suppression of my play for so many years by the censorship the subject broke out into a campaign for the abolition of the White Slave Traffic which still occupies the League of Nations at Geneva. But my demonstration that the root of the evil is economic was ruthlessly ignored by the profiteering Press (that is, by the entire Press); and when at last parliament proceeded to legislate, its contribution to the question was to ordain that Mrs Warren's male competitors should be flogged instead of fined. This had the double effect of stimulating the perverted sexuality which delights in flogging, and driving the traffic into female hands, leaving Mrs Warren triumphant.

The ban on performances of the play has long since been withdrawn; and when it is performed the critics hasten to declare that the scandal of underpaid virtue and overpaid vice is a thing of the past. Yet when the war created an urgent demand for women's labor in 1914 the Government proceeded to employ women for twelve hours a day at a wage of five ha'pence an hour. It is amazing how the grossest abuses thrive on their reputation for being old unhappy far-off things in an age of imaginary progress.

X

THE DOCTOR'S DILEMMA

1906

ON DOCTORS

It is not the fault of our doctors that the medical service of the community, as at present provided for, is a murderous absurdity. That any sane nation, having observed that you could provide for the supply of bread by giving bakers a pecuniary interest in baking for you, should go on to give a surgeon a pecuniary interest in cutting off your leg, is enough to make one despair of political humanity. But that is precisely what we have done. And the more appalling the mutilation, the more the mutilator is paid. He who corrects the ingrowing toe-nail receives a few shillings: he who cuts your inside out receives hundreds of guineas, except when he does it to a poor person for practice.

Scandalized voices murmur that these operations are necessary. They may be. It may also be necessary to hang a man or pull down a house. But we take good care not to make the hangman and the housebreaker the judges of that. If we did, no man's neck would be safe and no man's house stable. But we do make the doctor the judge, and fine him anything from sixpence to several hundred guineas if he decides in our favor. I cannot knock my shins severely without forcing on some surgeon the difficult question, "Could I not make a better use of a pocketful of guineas than this man is making of his leg? Could he not write as well—or even better—on one leg than on two? And the guineas would make all the difference in the world to me just now. My wife—my pretty ones—the leg may mortify—it is always safer to operate—he will be well in a fortnight—artificial legs are now so well made that they are

really better than natural ones—evolution is towards motors and leglessness, etc. etc. etc."

Now there is no calculation that an engineer can make as to the behavior of a girder under a strain, or an astronomer as to the recurrence of a comet, more certain than the calculation that under such circumstances we shall be dismembered unnecessarily in all directions by surgeons who believe the operations to be necessary solely because they want to perform them. The process metaphorically called bleeding the rich man is performed not only metaphorically but literally every day by surgeons who are quite as honest as most of us. After all, what harm is there in it? The surgeon need not take off the rich man's (or woman's) leg or arm: he can remove the appendix or the uvula, and leave the patient none the worse after a fortnight or so in bed, whilst the nurse, the general practitioner, the apothecary, and the surgeon will be the better.

DOUBTFUL CHARACTER BORNE BY THE MEDICAL PROFESSION

Again I hear the voices indignantly muttering old phrases about the high character of a noble profession and the honor and conscience of its members. I must reply that the medical profession has not a high character; it has an infamous character. I do not know a single thoughtful and well-informed person who does not feel that the tragedy of illness at present is that it delivers you helplessly into the hands of a profession which you deeply mistrust, because it not only advocates and practises the most revolting cruelties in the pursuit of knowledge, and justifies them on grounds which would equally justify practising the same cruelties on yourself or your children, or burning down London to test a patent fire extinguisher, but, when it has shocked the public, tries to reassure it with lies of breath-bereaving brazenness. That is the character the medical profession has got just now. It may be deserved or it may not: there it is at all events: and the doctors who have not realized this are living in a fool's paradise. As to the honor and conscience of doctors, they have as much as any other class of men, no more and no less. And what other men dare pretend to be impartial where they have a strong pecuniary interest on one side? Nobody supposes that doctors are less virtuous than judges; but a judge whose salary and reputation depended on whether the verdict was for plaintiff or defendant, prosecutor or prisoner, would be as little trusted as a general in the pay of the enemy. To offer me a doctor as my judge, and then weight his decision with a bribe of a large sum of money and a virtual guarantee that if he makes a mistake it can never be proved against him, is to go wildly beyond the ascertained strain which human nature will bear. It is simply unscientific to allege or believe that doctors do not under existing circumstances perform unnecessary operations and manufacture and prolong lucrative illnesses. The only ones who can claim to be above suspicion are those who are so much sought after that their cured patients are immediately replaced by fresh ones. And there is this curious psychological fact to be remembered: a serious illness or a death advertizes the doctor exactly as a hanging advertizes the barrister who defended the person hanged. Suppose, for example, a royal personage gets something wrong with his throat, or has a pain in his inside. If a doctor effects some trumpery cure with a wet compress or a peppermint lozenge nobody takes the least notice of him. But if he operates on the throat and kills the patient, or extirpates an internal organ and keeps the whole nation palpitating for days whilst the patient hovers in pain and fever between life and death, his fortune is made: every rich man who omits to call him in when the same symptoms appear in his household is held not to have done his utmost duty to the patient. The wonder is that there is a king or queen left alive in Europe.

DOCTORS' CONSCIENCES

There is another difficulty in trusting to the honor and conscience of a doctor. Doctors are just like other Englishmen: most of them have no honor and no conscience: what they commonly mistake for these is sentimentality and an intense dread of doing anything that everybody else does not do, or omitting to do anything that everybody else does. This of course does amount to a sort of working or rule-of-thumb conscience; but it means that you will do anything, good or bad, provided you get enough people to keep you in countenance by doing it also. It is the sort of conscience that makes it possible to keep order on a pirate ship, or in a troop of brigands. It may be said that in the last analysis there is no other sort of honor or conscience in existence—that the assent of the majority is the only sanction known to ethics. No doubt this holds good in political practice. If mankind knew the facts, and agreed with the doctors, then the doctors would be in the right; and any person who thought otherwise would be a lunatic. But mankind does not agree, and does not know the facts. All that can be said for medical popularity is that until there is a practicable alternative to blind trust in the doctor, the truth about the doctor is so terrible that we dare not face it. Molière saw through the doctors; but he had to call them in just the same. Napoleon had no illusions about them; but he had to die under their treatment just as much as the most credulous ignoramus that ever paid sixpence for a bottle of strong medicine. In this predicament most people, to save themselves from unbearable mistrust and misery, or from being driven by their conscience into actual conflict with the law, fall back on the old rule that if you cannot have what you believe in you must believe in what you have. When your child is ill or your wife dying, and you happen to be very fond of them, or even when, if you are not fond of them, you are human enough to forget every personal grudge before the spectacle of a fellow creature in pain or peril, what you want is comfort, reassurance, something to clutch at, were it but a straw. This the doctor brings you. You have a wildly urgent feeling that something must be done; and the doctor does something. Sometimes what he does kills the patient; but you do not know that; and the doctor assures you that all that human skill could do has been done. And nobody has the brutality to say to the newly bereft father, mother, husband, wife, brother, or sister, "You have killed your lost darling by your credulity."

THE PECULIAR PEOPLE

Besides, the calling in of the doctor is now compulsory except in cases where the patient is an adult and not too ill to decide the steps to be taken. We are subject to prosecution for manslaughter or for criminal neglect if the patient dies without the consolations of the medical profession. This menace is kept before the public by the Peculiar People. The Peculiars, as they are called, have gained their name by believing that the Bible is infallible, and taking their belief quite seriously. The Bible is very clear as to the treatment of illness. The Epistle of James, chapter v., contains the following explicit directions:—

14. Is any sick among you? let him call for the elders of the Church; and let them pray over him, anointing him with oil in the name of the Lord:

15. And the prayer of faith shall save the sick, and the Lord shall raise him up; and if he have committed sins, they shall be forgiven him.

The Peculiars obey these instructions and dispense with doctors. They are therefore prosecuted for manslaughter when their children die.

When I was a young man, the Peculiars were usually acquitted. The prosecution broke down when the doctor in the witness box was asked whether, if the child had had medical attendance, it would have lived. It was, of course, impossible for any man of sense and honor to assume divine omniscience by answering this in the affirmative, or indeed pretending to be able to answer it at all. And on this the judge had to instruct the jury that they must acquit the prisoner. Thus a judge with a keen sense of law (a very rare phenomenon on the Bench, by the way) was spared the possibility of having to sentence one prisoner (under the Blasphemy Laws) for questioning the authority of Scripture, and another for ignorantly and superstitiously accepting it as a guide to conduct. Today all this is changed. The doctor never hesitates to claim divine omniscience, nor to clamor for laws to punish any scepticism on the part of laymen. A modern doctor thinks nothing of signing the death certificate of one of his own diphtheria patients, and then going into the witness box and swearing a Peculiar into prison for six months by assuring the jury, on oath, that if the prisoner's child, dead of diphtheria, had been placed under his treatment instead of that of St James, it would not have died. And he does so not only with impunity, but with public applause, though the logical course would be to prosecute him either for the murder of his own patient, or for perjury in the case of St James. Yet no barrister, apparently, dreams of asking for the statistics of the relative case-mortality in diphtheria among the Peculiars and among the believers in doctors, on which alone any valid opinion could be founded. The barrister is as superstitious as the doctor is infatuated; and the Peculiar goes un-pitied to his cell, though nothing what-ever has been proved except that his child died without the interference of a doctor as effectually as any of the hundreds of children who die every day of the same diseases in the doctor's care.

RECOIL OF THE DOGMA OF MEDICAL INFALLIBILITY ON THE DOCTOR

On the other hand, when the doctor is in the dock, or is the defendant in an action for malpractice, he has to struggle against the inevitable result of his former pretences to infinite knowledge and un-erring skill. He has taught the jury and the judge, and even his own counsel, to believe that every doctor can, with a glance at the tongue, a touch on the pulse, and a reading of the clinical thermo-meter, diagnose with absolute certainty a patient's complaint, also that on dissect-ing a dead body he can infallibly put his finger on the cause of death, and, in cases where poisoning is suspected, the nature of the poison used. Now all this sup-posed exactness and infallibility is imagin-ary; and to treat a doctor as if his mis-takes were necessarily malicious or cor-rupt malpractices (an inevitable deduction from the postulate that the doctor, being omniscient, cannot make mistakes) is as unjust as to blame the nearest apothecary for not being prepared to supply you with sixpenny-worth of the elixir of life, or the nearest motor garage for not having perpetual motion on sale in gallon tins.

But if apothecaries and motor car makers habitually advertized elixir of life and per-petual motion, and succeeded in creating a strong general belief that they could supply it, they would find themselves in an awkward position if they were indicted for allowing a customer to die, or for burning a chauffeur by putting petrol into his car. That is the predicament the doctor finds himself in when he has to defend himself against a charge of malpractice by a plea of ignorance and fallibility. His plea is received with flat incredulity; and he gets little sympathy, even from laymen who know, because he has brought the incredulity on himself. If he escapes, he can only do so by opening the eyes of the jury to the facts that medical science is as yet very imperfectly differentiated from common curemongering witchcraft; that diagnosis, though it means in many in-stances (including even the identification of pathogenic bacilli under the micro-scope) only a choice among terms so loose that they would not be accepted as definitions in any really exact science, is, even at that, an uncertain and difficult matter on which doctors often differ; and that the very best medical opinion and treatment varies widely from doctor to doctor, one practitioner prescribing six or seven scheduled poisons for so familiar a disease as enteric fever where another will not tolerate drugs at all; one starving a patient whom another would stuff; one urging an operation which another would regard as unnecessary and dangerous; one giving alcohol and meat which another would sternly forbid, etc. etc. etc.: all these discrepancies arising not between the opinion of good doctors and bad ones (the medical contention is, of course, that a bad doctor is an impossibility), but between practitioners of equal eminence and authority. Usually it is impossible to persuade the jury that these facts are facts. Juries seldom notice facts; and they have been taught to regard any doubts of the omniscience and omnipotence of doctors as blasphemy. Even the fact that doctors themselves die of the very diseases they profess to cure passes unnoticed. We do not shoot out our lips and shake our heads, saying, "They save others: themselves they cannot save": their reputation stands, like an African king's palace, on a foundation of dead bodies; and the result is that the verdict goes against the defendant when the defendant is a doctor accused of malpractice.

Fortunately for the doctors, they very seldom find themselves in this position, because it is so difficult to prove anything against them. The only evidence that can decide a case of malpractice is expert evidence: that is, the evidence of other doctors; and every doctor will allow a colleague to decimate a whole countryside sooner than violate the bond of professional etiquet by giving him away. It is the nurse who gives the doctor away in private, because every nurse has some particular doctor whom she likes; and she usually assures her patients that all the others are disastrous noodles, and soothes the tedium of the sick-bed by gossip about their blunders. She will even give a doctor away for the sake of making the patient believe that she knows more than the doctor. But she dare not, for her livelihood, give the doctor away in public. And the doctors stand by one another at all costs. Now and then some doctor in an unassailable position, like the late Sir William Gull, will go into the witness box and say what he really thinks about the way a patient has been treated; but such behavior is considered little short of infamous by his colleagues.

WHY DOCTORS DO NOT DIFFER

The truth is, there would never be any public agreement among doctors if they did not agree to agree on the main point of the doctor being always in the right. Yet the two guinea man never thinks that the five shilling man is right: if he did, he would be understood as confessing to an overcharge of £1:17s.; and on the same ground the five shilling man cannot encourage the notion that the owner of the sixpenny surgery round the corner is quite up to his mark. Thus even the layman has to be taught that infallibility is not quite infallible, because there are two qualities of it to be had at two prices.

But there is no agreement even in the same rank at the same price. During the first great epidemic of influenza towards the end of the nineteenth century a London evening paper sent round a journalist-patient to all the great consultants of that day, and published their advice and prescriptions: a proceeding passionately denounced by the medical papers as a breach of confidence of these eminent physicians. The case was the same; but the prescriptions were different, and so was the advice. Now a doctor cannot think his own treatment right and at the same time think his colleague right in prescribing a different treatment when the patient is the same. Anyone who has ever known doctors well enough to hear medical shop talked without reserve knows that they are full of stories about each other's blunders and errors, and that the theory of their omniscience and omnipotence no more holds good among themselves than it did with Molière and Napoleon. But for this very reason no doctor dare accuse another of malpractice. He is not sure enough of his own opinion to ruin another man by it. He knows that if such conduct were tolerated in his profession no doctor's livelihood or reputation would be worth a year's purchase. I do not blame him: I should do the same myself. But the effect of this state of things is to make the medical profession a conspiracy to hide its own shortcomings. No doubt the same may be said of all professions. They are all conspiracies against the laity; and I do not suggest that the medical conspiracy is either better or worse than the military conspiracy, the legal conspiracy, the sacerdotal conspiracy, the pedagogic conspiracy, the royal and aristocratic conspiracy, the literary and artistic conspiracy, and the innumerable industrial, commercial, and financial conspiracies, from the trade unions to the great exchanges, which make up the huge conflict which we call society. But it is less suspected. The Radicals who used to advocate, as an indispensable preliminary to social reform, the strangling of the last king with the entrails of the last priest, substituted compulsory vaccination for compulsory baptism without a murmur.

THE CRAZE FOR OPERATIONS

Thus everything is on the side of the doctor. When men die of disease they are said to die from natural causes. When they recover (and they mostly do) the doctor gets the credit of curing them. In surgery all operations are recorded as successful if the patient can be got out of the hospital or nursing home alive, though the subsequent history of the case may be such as would make an honest surgeon vow never to recommend or perform the operation again. The large range of operations which consist of amputating limbs and extirpating organs admits of no direct verification of their necessity. There is a fashion in operations as there is in sleeves and skirts: the triumph of some surgeon who has at last found out how to make a once desperate operation fairly safe is usually followed by a rage for that operation not only among the doctors, but actually among their patients. There are men and women whom the operating table seems to fascinate: half-alive people who through vanity, or hypochondria, or a craving to be the constant objects of anxious attention or what not, lose such feeble sense as they ever had of the value of their own organs and limbs. They seem to care as little for mutilation as lobsters or lizards, which at least have the excuse that they grow new claws and new tails if they lose the old ones. Whilst this book was being prepared for the press a case was tried in the Courts, of a man who sued a railway company for damages because a train had run over him and amputated both his legs. He lost his case because it was proved that he had deliberately contrived the occurrence himself for the sake of getting an idler's pension at the expense of the railway company, being too dull to realize how much more he had to lose than to gain by the bargain even if he had won his case and received damages above his utmost hopes.

This amazing case makes it possible to say, with some prospect of being believed, that there is in the classes who can afford to pay for fashionable operations a sprinkling of persons so incapable of appreciating the relative importance of preserving their bodily integrity (including the capacity for parentage) and the pleasure of talking about themselves and hearing themselves talked about as the heroes and heroines of sensational operations, that they tempt surgeons to operate on them not only with huge fees, but with personal solicitation. Now it cannot be too often repeated that when an operation is once performed, nobody can ever prove that it was unnecessary. If I refuse to allow my leg to be amputated, its mortification and my death may prove that I was wrong: but if I let the leg go, nobody can ever prove that it would not have mortified had I been obstinate. Operation is therefore the safe side for the surgeon as well as the lucrative side. The result is that we hear of "conservative surgeons" as a distinct class of practitioners who make it a rule not to operate if they can possibly help it, and who are sought after by the people who have vitality enough to regard an operation as a last resort. But no surgeon is bound to take the conservative view. If he believes that an organ is at best a useless survival, and that if he extirpates it the patient will be well and none the worse in a fortnight, whereas to await the natural cure would mean a month's illness, then he is clearly justified in recommending the operation even if the cure without operation is as certain as anything of the kind ever can be. Thus the conservative surgeon and the radical or extirpatory surgeon may both be right as far as the ultimate cure is concerned; so that their consciences do not help them out of their differences.

CREDULITY AND CHLOROFORM

There is no harder scientific fact in the world than the fact that belief can be produced in practically unlimited quantity and intensity, without observation or reasoning, and even in defiance of both, by the simple desire to believe founded on a strong interest in believing. Everybody recognizes this in the case of the amatory infatuations of the adolescents who see angels and heroes in obviously (to others) commonplace and even objectionable maidens and youths. But it holds good over the entire field of human activity. The hardest-headed materialist will become a consulter of table-rappers and slate-writers if he loses a child or a wife so beloved that the desire to revive and communicate with them becomes irresistible. The cobbler believes that there is nothing like leather. The Imperialist who regards the conquest of England by a foreign power as the worst of political misfortunes believes that the conquest of a foreign power by England would be a boon to the conquered. Doctors are no more proof against such illusions than other men. Can anyone then doubt that under existing conditions a great deal of unnecessary and mischievous operating is bound to go on, and that patients are encouraged to imagine that modern sur-

gery and anesthesia have made operations much less serious matters than they really are? When doctors write or speak to the public about operations, they imply, and often say in so many words, that chloroform has made surgery painless. People who have been operated on know better. The patient does not feel the knife, and the operation is therefore enormously facilitated for the surgeon; but the patient pays for the anesthesia with hours of wretched sickness; and when that is over there is the pain of the wound made by the surgeon, which has to heal like any other wound. This is why operating surgeons, who are usually out of the house with their fee in their pockets before the patient has recovered consciousness, and who therefore see nothing of the suffering witnessed by the general practitioner and the nurse, occasionally talk of operations very much as the hangman in Barnaby Rudge talked of executions, as if being operated on were a luxury in sensation as well as in price.

MEDICAL POVERTY

To make matters worse, doctors are hideously poor. The Irish gentleman doctor of my boyhood, who took nothing less than a guinea, though he might pay you four visits for it, seems to have no equivalent nowadays in English society. Better be a railway porter than an ordinary English general practitioner. A railway porter has from eighteen to twenty-three shillings a week from the Company merely as a retainer; and his additional fees from the public, if we leave the third-class twopenny tip out of account (and I am by no means sure that even this reservation need be made), are equivalent to doctor's fees in the case of second-class passengers, and double doctor's fees in the case of first. Any class of educated men thus treated tends to become a brigand class, and doctors are no exception to the rule. They are offered disgraceful prices for advice and medicine. Their patients are for the most part so poor and so ignorant that good advice would be resented as impracticable and wounding. When you are so poor that you cannot afford to refuse eighteen-pence from a man who is too poor to pay you any more, it is useless to tell him that what he or his sick child needs is not medicine, but more leisure, better clothes, better food, and a better drained and ventilated house. It is kinder to give him a bottle of something almost as cheap as water, and tell him to come again with another eighteenpence if it does not cure him. When you have done that over and over again every day for a week, how much scientific conscience have you left? If you are weak-minded enough to cling desperately to your eighteenpence as denoting a certain social superiority to the sixpenny doctor, you will be miser-ably poor all your life; whilst the sixpenny doctor, with his low prices and quick turnover of patients, visibly makes much more than you do and kills no more people.

A doctor's character can no more stand out against such conditions than the lungs of his patients can stand out against bad ventilation. The only way in which he can preserve his self-respect is by for-getting all he ever learnt of science, and clinging to such help as he can give without cost merely by being less ignor-ant and more accustomed to sick-beds than his patients. Finally, he acquires a certain skill at nursing cases under poverty-stricken domestic conditions, just as women who have been trained as domestic servants in some huge institu-tion with lifts, vacuum cleaners, electric lighting, steam heating, and machinery that turns the kitchen into a laboratory and engine house combined, manage, when they are sent out into the world to drudge as general servants, to pick up their business in a new way, learning the

slatternly habits and wretched make-shifts of homes where even bundles of kindling wood are luxuries to be anxiously economized.

THE SUCCESSFUL DOCTOR

The doctor whose success blinds public opinion to medical poverty is almost as completely demoralized. His promotion means that his practice becomes more and more confined to the idle rich. The proper advice for most of their ailments is typified in Abernethy's "Live on six-pence a day and earn it." But here, as at the other end of the scale, the right ad-vice is neither agreeable nor practicable. And every hypochondriacal rich lady or gentleman who can be persuaded that he or she is a lifelong invalid means anything from fifty to five hundred pounds a year for the doctor. Operations enable a sur-geon to earn similar sums in a couple of hours; and if the surgeon also keeps a nursing home, he may make considerable profits at the same time by running what is the most expensive kind of hotel. These gains are so great that they undo much of the moral advantage which the absence of grinding pecuniary anxiety gives the rich doctor over the poor one. It is true that the temptation to prescribe a sham treat-ment because the real treatment is too dear for either patient or doctor does not exist for the rich doctor. He always has plenty of genuine cases which can afford genuine treatment; and these provide him with enough sincere scientific professional work to save him from the ignorance, obsolescence, and atrophy of scientific conscience into which his poorer col-leagues sink. But on the other hand his expenses are enormous. Even as a bache-lor, he must, at London west end rates, make over a thousand a year before he can afford even to insure his life. His house, his servants, and his equipage (or autopage) must be on the scale to which his patients are accustomed, though a couple of rooms with a camp bed in one of them might satisfy his own requirements. Above all, the income which provides for these outgoings stops the moment he himself stops working. Unlike the man of business, whose managers, clerks, warehousemen, and laborers keep his business going whilst he is in bed or in his club, the doctor cannot earn a farthing by deputy. Though he is exceptionally exposed to infection, and has to face all weathers at all hours of the night and day, often not enjoying a complete night's rest for a week, the money stops coming in the moment he stops going out; and therefore illness has special terrors for him, and success no certain permanence. He dare not stop making hay while the sun shines; for it may set at any time. Men do not resist pressure of this intensity. When they come under it as doctors they pay unnecessary visits; they write prescriptions that are as absurd as the rub of chalk with which an Irish tailor once charmed away a wart from my father's finger; they conspire with surgeons to promote operations; they nurse the delusions of the *malade imaginaire* (who is always really ill because, as there is no such thing as perfect health, nobody is ever really well); they exploit human folly, vanity, and fear of death as ruthlessly as their own health, strength, and patience are exploited by selfish hypochondriacs. They must do all these things or else run pecuniary risks that no man can fairly be asked to run. And the healthier the world becomes, the more they are compelled to live by imposture and the less by that really helpful activity of which all doctors get enough to preserve them from utter corruption. For even the most hardened humbug who ever prescribed ether tonics to ladies whose need for tonics is of precisely the same character as the need of poorer women for a glass of gin, has to help a mother through childbearing often enough to feel that he is not living wholly in vain.

THE PSYCHOLOGY OF SELF-RESPECT IN SURGEONS

The surgeon, though often more unscrupulous than the general practitioner, retains his self-respect more easily. The human conscience can subsist on very questionable food. No man who is occupied in doing a very difficult thing, and doing it very well, ever loses his self-respect. The shirk, the duffer, the malingerer, the coward, the weakling, may be put out of countenance by his own failures and frauds; but the man who does evil skilfully, energetically, masterfully, grows prouder and bolder at every crime. The common man may have to found his self-respect on sobriety, honesty, and industry; but a Napoleon needs no such props for his sense of dignity. If Nelson's conscience whispered to him at all in the silent watches of the night, you may depend on it it whispered about the Baltic and the Nile and Cape St Vincent, and not about his unfaithfulness to his wife. A man who robs little children when no one is looking can hardly have much self-respect or even self-esteem; but an accomplished burglar must be proud of himself. In the play to which I am at present preluding I have represented an artist who is so entirely satisfied with his artistic conscience, even to the point of dying like a saint with its support, that he is utterly selfish and unscrupulous in every other relation without feeling at the smallest disadvantage. The same thing may be observed in women who have a genius for personal attractiveness: they expend more thought, labor, skill, inventiveness, taste, and endurance on making themselves lovely than would suffice to keep a dozen ugly women honest; and this enables them to maintain a high opinion of themselves, and an angry contempt for unattractive and personally careless women, whilst they lie and cheat and slander and sell themselves without a blush. The truth is, hardly any of us have ethical energy enough for more than one really inflexible point of honor. Andrea del Sarto, like Louis Dubedat in my play, must have expended on the attainment of his great mastery of design and his originality in fresco painting more conscientiousness and industry than go to the making of the reputations of a dozen ordinary mayors and churchwardens; but (if Vasari is to be believed) when the King of France entrusted him with money to buy pictures for him, he stole it to spend on his wife. Such cases are not confined to eminent artists. Unsuccessful, unskilful men are often much more scrupulous than successful ones. In the ranks of ordinary skilled labor many men are to be found who earn good wages and are never out of a job because they are strong, indefatigable, and skilful, and who therefore are bold in a high opinion of themselves; bu they are selfish and tyrannical, gluttonous and drunken, as their wives and children know to their cost.

Not only do these talented energetic people retain their self-respect through shameful misconduct: they do not even lose the respect of others, because their talents benefit and interest everybody, whilst their vices affect only a few. An actor, a painter, a composer, an author, may be as selfish as he likes without reproach from the public if only his art is superb; and he cannot fulfil this condition without sufficient effort and sacrifice to make him feel noble and martyred in spite of his selfishness. In may even happen that the selfishness of an artist may be a benefit to the public by enabling him to concentrate himself on their gratification with a recklessness of every other consideration that makes him highly dangerous to those about him. In sacrificing others to himself he is sacrificing them to the public he gratifies; and the public is quite content with that arrangement. The public actually has an interest in the artist's vices.

It has no such interest in the surgeon's vices. The surgeon's art is exercised at its expense, not for its gratification. We do not go to the operating table as we go to the theatre, to the picture gallery, to the concert room, to be entertained and delighted: we go to be tormented and maimed lest a worse thing should befall us. It is of the most extreme importance to us that the experts on whose assurance we face this horror and suffer this mutilation should have no interests but our own to think of; should judge our cases scientifically; and should feel about them kindly. Let us see what guarantees we have: first for the science, and then for the kindness.

ARE DOCTORS MEN OF SCIENCE?

I presume nobody will question the existence of a widely spread popular delusion that every doctor is a man of science. It is escaped only in the very small class which understands by science something more than conjuring with retorts and spirit lamps, magnets and microscopes, and discovering magical cures for disease. To a sufficiently ignorant man every captain of a trading schooner is a Galileo, every organ-grinder a Beethoven, every piano-tuner a Helmholtz, every Old Bailey barrister a Solon, every Seven Dials pigeon-dealer a Darwin, every scrivener a Shakespear, every locomotive engine a miracle, and its driver no less wonderful than George Stephenson. As a matter of fact, the rank and file of doctors are no more scientific than their tailors; or, if you prefer to put it the reverse way, their tailors are no less scientific than they. Doctoring is an art, not a science: any layman who is interested in science sufficiently to take in one of the scientific journals and follow the literature of the scientific movement, knows more about it than those doctors (probably a large majority) who are not interested in it, and practise only to earn their bread. Doctoring is not even the art of keeping people in health (no doctor seems able to advise you what to eat any better than his grandmother or the nearest quack): it is the art of curing illnesses. It does happen exceptionally that a practising doctor makes a contribution to science (my play describes a very notable one); but it happens much oftener that he draws disastrous conclusions from his clinical experience because he has no conception of scientific method, and believes, like any rustic, that the handling of evidence and statistics needs no expertness. The distinction between a quack doctor and a qualified one is mainly that only the qualified one is authorized to sign death certificates, for which both sorts seem to have about equal occasion. Unqualified practitioners now make large incomes as hygienists, and are resorted to as frequently by cultivated amateur scientists who understand quite well what they are doing as by ignorant people who are simply dupes. Bone-setters make fortunes under the very noses of our greatest surgeons from educated and wealthy patients; and some of the most successful doctors on the register use quite heretical methods of treating disease, and have qualified themselves solely for convenience. Leaving out of account the village witches who prescribe spells and sell charms, the humblest professional healers in this country are the herbalists. These men wander through the fields on Sunday seeking for herbs with magic properties of curing disease, preventing childbirth, and the like. Each of them believes that he is on the verge of a great discovery, in which Virginia Snake Root will be an ingredient, heaven knows why! Virginia Snake Root fascinates the imagination of the herbalist as mercury used to fascinate the alchemists. On week days he keeps a shop in which he sells packets of penny-

royal, dandelion, etc., labelled with little lists of the diseases they are supposed to cure, and apparently do cure to the satisfaction of the people who keep on buying them. I have never been able to perceive any distinction between the science of the herbalist and that of the duly registered doctor. A relative of mine recently consulted a doctor about some of the ordinary symptoms which indicate the need for a holiday and a change. The doctor satisfied himself that the patient's heart was a little depressed. Digitalis being a drug labelled as a heart specific by the profession, he promptly administered a stiff dose. Fortunately the patient was a hardy old lady who was not easily killed. She recovered with no worse result than her conversion to Christian Science, which owes its vogue quite as much to public despair of doctors as to superstition. I am not, observe, here concerned with the question as to whether the dose of digitalis was judicious or not: the point is, that a farm laborer consulting a herbalist would have been treated in exactly the same way.

BACTERIOLOGY AS A SUPERSTITION

The smattering of science that all— even doctors—pick up from the ordinary newspapers nowadays only makes the doctor more dangerous than he used to be. Wise men used to take care to consult doctors qualified before 1860, who were usually contemptuous of or indifferent to the germ theory and bacteriological therapeutics; but now that these veterans have mostly retired or died, we are left in the hands of the generations which, having heard of microbes much as St Thomas Aquinas heard of angels, suddenly concluded that the whole art of healing could be summed up in the formula: Find the microbe and kill it. And even that they did not know how to do. The simplest way to kill most microbes is to throw them into an open street or river and let the sun shine on them, which explains the fact that when great cities have recklessly thrown all their sewage into the open river the water has sometimes been cleaner twenty miles below the city than thirty miles above it. But doctors instinctively avoid all facts that are reassuring, and eagerly swallow those that make it a marvel that anyone could possibly survive three days in an atmosphere consisting mainly of countless pathogenic germs. They conceive microbes as immortal until slain by a germicide administered by a duly qualified medical man. All through Europe people are adjured, by public notices and even under legal penalties, not to throw their microbes into the sunshine, but to collect them carefully in a handkerchief; shield the handkerchief from the sun in the darkness and warmth of the pocket; and send it to a laundry to be mixed up with everybody else's handkerchiefs, with results only too familiar to local health authorities.

In the first frenzy of microbe killing, surgical instruments were dipped in carbolic oil, which was a great improvement on not dipping them in anything at all and simply using them dirty; but as microbes are so fond of carbolic oil that they swarm in it, it was not a success from the anti-microbe point of view. Formalin was squirted into the circulation of consumptives until it was discovered that formalin nourishes the tubercle bacillus handsomely and kills men. The popular theory of disease is the common medical theory: namely, that every disease had its microbe duly created in the garden of Eden, and has been steadily propagating itself and producing widening circles of malignant disease ever since. It was plain from the first that if this had been even approximately true, the whole human race would have been wiped out by the plague long ago, and that every epidemic, instead of fading out as mysteriously as it

rushed in, would spread over the whole world. It was also evident that the characteristic microbe of a disease might be a symptom instead of a cause. An unpunctual man is always in a hurry; but it does not follow that hurry is the cause of unpunctuality: on the contrary, what is the matter with the patient is sloth. When Florence Nightingale said bluntly that if you overcrowded your soldiers in dirty quarters there would be an outbreak of smallpox among them, she was snubbed as an ignorant female who did not know that smallpox can be produced only by the importation of its specific microbe.

If this was the line taken about smallpox, the microbe of which has never yet been run down and exposed under the microscope by the bacteriologist, what must have been the ardor of conviction as to tuberculosis, tetanus, enteric fever, Maltese fever, diphtheria, and the rest of the diseases in which the characteristic bacillus had been identified! When there was no bacillus it was assumed that, since no disease could exist without a bacillus, it was simply eluding observation. When the bacillus was found, as it frequently was, in persons who were not suffering from the disease, the theory was saved by simply calling the bacillus an impostor, or pseudo-bacillus. The same boundless credulity which the public exhibit as to a doctor's power of diagnosis was shewn by the doctors themselves as to the analytic microbe hunters. These witch finders would give you a certificate of the ultimate constitution of anything from a sample of the water from your well to a scrap of your lungs, for seven-and-six-pence. I do not suggest that the analysts were dishonest. No doubt they carried the analysis as far as they could afford to carry it for the money. No doubt also they could afford to carry it far enough to be of some use. But the fact remains that just as doctors perform for half-a-crown, without the least misgiving, operations which could not be thoroughly and safely performed with due scientific rigor and the requisite apparatus by an unaided private practitioner for less than some thousands of pounds, so did they proceed on the assumption that they could get the last word of science as to the constituents of their pathological samples for a two-hours cab fare.

ECONOMIC DIFFICULTIES OF IMMUNIZATION

I have heard doctors affirm and deny almost every possible proposition as to disease and treatment. I can remember the time when doctors no more dreamt of consumption and pneumonia being infectious than they now dream of sea-sickness being infectious, or than so great a clinical observer as Sydenham dreamt of smallpox being infectious. I have heard doctors deny that there is such a thing as infection. I have heard them deny the existence of hydrophobia as a specific disease differing from tetanus. I have heard them defend prophylactic measures and prophylactic legislation as the sole and certain salvation of mankind from zymotic disease; and I have heard them denounce both as malignant spreaders of cancer and lunacy. But the one objection I have never heard from a doctor is the objection that prophylaxis by the inoculatory methods most in vogue is an economic impossibility under our private practice system. They buy some stuff from somebody for a shilling, and inject a pennyworth of it under their patient's skin for half-a-crown, concluding that, since this primitive rite pays the somebody and pays them, the problem of prophylaxis has been satisfactorily solved. The results are sometimes no worse than the ordinary results of dirt getting into cuts; but neither the doctor nor the patient is quite satisfied unless the inoculation "takes": that is, unless it produces perceptible illness and disablement. Some-

times both doctor and patient get more value in this direction than they bargain for. The results of ordinary private-practice-inoculation at their worst are bad enough to be indistinguishable from those of the most discreditable and dreaded disease known; and doctors, to save the credit of the inoculation, have been driven to accuse their patient or their patient's parents of having contracted this disease independently of the inoculation, an excuse which naturally does not make the family any more resigned, and leads to public recriminations in which the doctors, forgetting everything but the immediate quarrel, naïvely excuse themselves by admitting, and even claiming as a point in their favor, that it is often impossible to distinguish the disease produced by their inoculation and the disease they have accused the patient of contracting. And both parties assume that what is at issue is the scientific soundness of the prophylaxis. It never occurs to them that the particular pathogenic germ which they intended to introduce into the patient's system may be quite innocent of the catastrophe, and that the casual dirt introduced with it may be at fault. When, as in the case of smallpox or cowpox, the germ has not yet been detected, what you inoculate is simply undefined matter that has been scraped off an anything but chemically clean calf suffering from the disease in question. You take your chance of the germ being in the scrapings, and, lest you should kill it, you take no precautions against other germs being in it as well. Anything may happen as the result of such an inoculation. Yet this is the only stuff of the kind which is prepared and supplied even in State establishments: that is, in the only establishments free from the commercial temptation to adulterate materials and scamp precautionary processes.

Even if the germ were identified, complete precautions would hardly pay. It is true that microbe farming is not expensive. The cost of breeding and housing two head of cattle would provide for the breeding and housing of enough microbes to inoculate the entire population of the globe since human life first appeared on it. But the precautions necessary to ensure that the inoculation shal consist of nothing else but the required germ in the proper state of attenuation are a very different matter from the precautions necessary in the distribution and consumption of beefsteaks. Yet people expect to find vaccines and anti-toxins and the like retailed at "popular prices" in private enterprise shops just as they expect to find ounces of tobacco and papers of pins.

THE PERILS OF INOCULATION

The trouble does not end with the matter to be inoculated. There is the question of the condition of the patient. The discoveries of Sir Almroth Wright have shewn that the appalling results which led to the hasty dropping in 1894 of Koch's tuberculin were not accidents, but perfectly orderly and inevitable phenomena following the injection of dangerously strong "vaccines" at the wrong moment, and reinforcing the disease instead of stimulating the resistance to it. To ascertain the right moment a laboratory and a staff of experts are needed. The general practitioner, having no such laboratory and no such experience, has always chanced it, and insisted, when he was unlucky, that the results were not due to the inoculation, but to some other cause: a favorite and not very tactful one being the drunkenness or licentiousness of the patient. But though a few doctors have now learnt the danger of inoculating without any reference to the patient's "opsonic index" at the moment of inoculation, and though those other doctors who are denouncing the danger as imaginary and opsonin as a craze or a

fad, obviously do so because it involves an operation which they have neither the means nor the knowledge to perform, there is still no grasp of the economic change in the situation. They have never been warned that the practicability of any method of extirpating disease depends not only on its efficacy, but on its cost. For example, just at present the world has run raving mad on the subject of radium, which has excited our credulity precisely as the apparitions at Lourdes excited the credulity of Roman Catholics. Suppose it were ascertained that every child in the world could be rendered absolutely immune from all disease during its entire life by taking half an ounce of radium to every pint of its milk. The world would be none the healthier, because not even a Crown Prince—no, not even the son of a Chicago Meat King, could afford the treatment. Yet it is doubtful whether doctors would refrain from prescribing it on that ground. The recklessness with which they now recommend wintering in Egypt or at Davos to people who cannot afford to go to Cornwall, and the orders given for champagne jelly and old port in households where such luxuries must obviously be acquired at the cost of stinting necessaries, often make one wonder whether it is possible for a man to go through a medical training and retain a spark of common sense.

This sort of inconsiderateness gets cured only in the classes where poverty, pretentious as it is even at its worst, cannot pitch its pretences high enough to make it possible for the doctor (himself often no better off than the patient) to assume that the average income of an English family is about £2000 a year, and that it is quite easy to break up a home, sell an old family seat at a sacrifice, and retire into a foreign sanatorium devoted to some "treatment" that did not exist two years ago and probably will not exist (except as a pretext for keeping an ordinary hotel) two years hence. In a poor practice the doctor must find cheap treatments for cheap people, or humiliate and lose his patients either by prescribing beyond their means or sending them to the public hospitals. When it comes to prophylactic inoculation, the alternative lies between the complete scientific process, which can only be brought down to a reasonable cost by being very highly organized as a public service in a public institution, and such cheap, nasty, dangerous and scientifically spurious imitations as ordinary vaccination, which will probably be ended, like its equally vaunted forerunner, eighteenth century inoculation, by a purely reactionary law making all sorts of vaccination, scientific or not, criminal offences. Naturally, the poor doctor (that is, the average doctor) defends ordinary vaccination frantically, as it means to him the bread of his children. To secure the vehement and practically unanimous support of the rank and file of the medical profession for any sort of treatment or operation, all that is necessary is that it can be easily practised by a rather shabbily dressed man in a surgically dirty room in a surgically dirty house without any assistance, and that the materials for it shall cost, say, a penny, and the charge for it to a patient with £100 a year be half-a-crown. And, on the other hand, a hygienic measure has only to be one of such refinement, difficulty, precision, and costliness as to be quite beyond the resources of private practice, to be ignored or angrily denounced as a fad.

TRADE UNIONISM AND SCIENCE

Here we have the explanation of the savage rancor that so amazes people who imagine that the controversy concerning vaccination is a scientific one. It has really nothing to do with science. The medical profession, consisting for the most part of very poor men struggling to keep up appearances beyond their means, find themselves threatened with the extinction of a considerable part of their incomes: a part, too, that is easily and regularly earned, since it is independent of disease, and brings every person born into the nation, healthy or not, to the doctors. To boot, there is the occasional windfall of an epidemic, with its panic and rush for revaccination. Under such circumstances, vaccination would be defended desperately were it twice as dirty, dangerous, and unscientific in method as it actually is. The note of fury in the defence, the feeling that the anti-vaccinator is doing a cruel, ruinous, inconsiderate thing in a mood of malignant folly: all this, so puzzling to the observer who knows nothing of the economic side of the question, and only sees that the anti-vaccinator, having nothing whatever to gain and a good deal to lose by placing himself in opposition to the law and to the outcry that adds private persecution to legal penalties, can have no interest in the matter except the interest of a reformer in abolishing a corrupt and mischievous superstition, becomes intelligible the moment the tragedy of medical poverty and the lucrativeness of cheap vaccination is taken into account.

In the face of such economic pressure as this, it is silly to expect that medical teaching, any more than medical practice, can possibly be scientific. The test to which all methods of treatment are finally brought is whether they are lucrative to doctors or not. It would be difficult to cite any proposition less obnoxious to science than that advanced by Hahnemann: to wit, that drugs which in large doses produce certain symptoms, counteract them in very small doses, just as in more modern practice it is found that a sufficiently small inoculation with typhoid rallies our powers to resist the disease instead of prostrating us with it. But Hahnemann and his followers were

frantically persecuted for a century by
generations of apothecary-doctors whose
incomes depended on the quantity of
drugs they could induce their patients to
swallow. These two cases of ordinary
vaccination and homeopathy are typical
of all the rest. Just as the object of a trade
union under existing conditions must
finally be, not to improve the technical
quality of the work done by its members,
but to secure a living wage for them, so
the object of the medical profession today
is to secure an income for the private
doctor; and to this consideration all concern for science and public health must
give way when the two come into conflict. Fortunately they are not always in
conflict. Up to a certain point doctors,
like carpenters and masons, must earn
their living by doing the work that the
public wants from them; and as it is not
in the nature of things possible that such
public want should be based on unmixed
disutility, it may be admitted that doctors
have their uses, real as well as imaginary.
But just as the best carpenter or mason
will resist the introduction of a machine
that is likely to throw him out of work,
or the public technical education of unskilled laborers' sons to compete with
him, so the doctor will resist with all his
powers of persecution every advance of
science that threatens his income. And as
the advance of scientific hygiene tends to
make the private doctor's visits rarer, and
the public inspector's frequenter, whilst
the advance of scientific therapeutics is in
the direction of treatments that involve
highly organized laboratories, hospitals,
and public institutions generally, it un-
luckily happens that the organization of
private practitioners which we call the
medical profession is coming more and
more to represent, not science, but desperate and embittered anti-science: a state
of things which is likely to get worse
until the average doctor either depends
upon or hopes for an appointment in
the public health service for his livelihood.

So much for our guarantees as to
medical science. Let us now deal with the
more painful subject of medical kindness.

DOCTORS AND VIVISECTION

The importance to our doctors of a
reputation for the tenderest humanity is
so obvious, and the quantity of benevolent work actually done by them for
nothing (a great deal of it from sheer
good nature) so large, that at first sight
it seems unaccountable that they should
not only throw all their credit away, but
deliberately choose to band themselves
publicly with outlaws and scoundrels by
claiming that in the pursuit of their professional knowledge they should be free
from the restraints of law, of honor, of
pity, of remorse, of everything that distinguishes an orderly citizen from a South
Sea buccaneer, or a philosopher from an
inquisitor. For here we look in vain for
either an economic or a sentimental motive. In every generation fools and blackguards have made this claim; and honest
and reasonable men, led by the strongest
contemporary minds, have repudiated it
and exposed its crude rascality. From
Shakespear and Dr Johnson to Ruskin
and Mark Twain, the natural abhorrence
of sane mankind for the vivisector's
cruelty, and the contempt of able thinkers
for his imbecile casuistry, have been expressed by the most popular spokesmen
of humanity. If the medical profession
were to outdo the Anti-Vivisection Societies in a general professional protest
against the practice and principles of the
vivisectors, every doctor in the kingdom
would gain substantially by the immense
relief and reconciliation which would
follow such a reassurance of the humanity
of the doctor. Not one doctor in a thousand is a vivisector, or has any interest
in vivisection, either pecuniary or intellectual, or would treat his dog cruelly or

allow anyone else to do it. It is true that the doctor complies with the professional fashion of defending vivisection, and assuring you that people like Shakespear and Dr Johnson and Ruskin and Mark Twain are ignorant sentimentalists, just as he complies with any other silly fashion: the mystery is, how it became the fashion in spite of its being so injurious to those who follow it. Making all possible allowance for the effect of the brazen lying of the few men who bring a rush of despairing patients to their doors by professing in letters to the newspapers to have learnt from vivisection how to cure certain diseases, and the assurances of the sayers of smooth things that the practice is quite painless under the law, it is still difficult to find any civilized motive for an attitude by which the medical profession has everything to lose and nothing to gain.

THE PRIMITIVE SAVAGE MOTIVE

I say civilized motive advisedly; for primitive tribal motives are easy enough to find. Every savage chief who is not a Mahomet learns that if he wishes to strike the imagination of his tribe—and without doing that he cannot rule them—he must terrify or revolt them from time to time by acts of hideous cruelty or disgusting unnaturalness. We are far from being as superior to such tribes as we imagine. It is very doubtful indeed whether Peter the Great could have effected the changes he made in Russia if he had not fascinated and intimidated his people by his monstrous cruelties and grotesque escapades. Had he been a nineteenth century king of England, he would have had to wait for some huge accidental calamity: a cholera epidemic, a war, or an insurrection, before waking us up sufficiently to get anything done. Vivisection helps the doctor to rule us as Peter ruled the Russians. The notion that the man who does dreadful things is superhuman, and that there-

fore he can also do wonderful things either as ruler, avenger, healer, or what not, is by no means confined to barbarians. Just as the manifold wickednesses and stupidities of our criminal code are supported, not by any general comprehension of law or study of jurisprudence, not even by simple vindictiveness, but by the superstition that a calamity of any sort must be expiated by a human sacrifice; so the wickednesses and stupidities of our medicine men are rooted in superstitions that have no more to do with science than the traditional ceremony of christening an ironclad has to do with the effectiveness of its armament. We have only to turn to Macaulay's description of the treatment of Charles II in his last illness to see how strongly his physicians felt that their only chance of cheating death was by outraging nature in tormenting and disgusting their unfortunate patient. True, this was more than two centuries ago; but I have heard my own nineteenth century grandfather describe the cupping and firing and nauseous medicines of his time with perfect credulity as to their beneficial effects; and some more modern treatments appear to me quite as barbarous. It is in this way that vivisection pays the doctor. It appeals to the fear and credulity of the savage in us; and without fear and credulity half the private doctor's occupation and seven-eighths of his influence would be gone.

THE HIGHER MOTIVE. THE TREE OF KNOWLEDGE

But the greatest force of all on the side of vivisection is the mighty and indeed divine force of curiosity. Here we have no decaying tribal instinct which men strive to root out of themselves as they strive to root out the tiger's lust for blood. On the contrary, the curiosity of the ape, or of the child who pulls out the legs and wings of a fly to see what it will do without them, or who, on being told that a cat dropped out of the window will always fall on its legs, immediately tries the experiment on the nearest cat from the highest window in the house (I protest I did it myself from the first floor only), is as nothing compared to the thirst for knowledge of the philosopher, the poet, the biologist, and the naturalist. I have always despised Adam because he had to be tempted by the woman, as she was by the serpent, before he could be induced to pluck the apple from the tree of knowledge. I should have swallowed every apple on the tree the moment the owner's back was turned. When Gray said "Where ignorance is bliss, 'tis folly to be wise," he forgot that it is godlike to be wise; and since nobody wants bliss particularly, or could stand more than a very brief taste of it if it were attainable, and since everybody, by the deepest law of the Life Force, desires to be godlike, it is stupid, and indeed blasphemous and despairing, to hope that the thirst for knowledge will either diminish or consent to be subordinated to any other end whatsoever. We shall see later on that the claim that has arisen in this way for the unconditioned pursuit of knowledge is as idle as all dreams of unconditioned activity; but none the less the right to knowledge must be regarded as a fundamental human right. The fact that men of science have had to fight so hard to secure its recognition, and are still so vigorously persecuted when they discover anything that is not quite palatable to vulgar people, makes them sorely jealous for that right; and when they hear a popular outcry for the suppression of a method of research which has an air of being scientific, their first instinct is to rally to the defence of that method without further consideration, with the result that they sometimes, as in the case of vivisection, presently find themselves fighting on a false issue.

THE FLAW IN THE ARGUMENT

I may as well pause here to explain their error. The right to know is like the right to live. It is fundamental and unconditional in its assumption that knowledge, like life, is a desirable thing, though any fool can prove that ignorance is bliss, and that "a little knowledge is a dangerous thing" (a little being the most that any of us can attain), as easily as that the pains of life are more numerous and constant than its pleasures, and that therefore we should all be better dead. The logic is unimpeachable; but its only effect is to make us say that if these are the conclusions logic leads to, so much the worse for logic, after which curt dismissal of Folly, we continue living and learning by instinct: that is, as of right. We legislate on the assumption that no man may be killed on the strength of a demonstration that he would be happier in his grave, not even if he is dying slowly of cancer and begs the doctor to despatch him quickly and mercifully. To get killed lawfully he must violate somebody's else's right to live by committing murder. But he is by no means free to live unconditionally. In society he can exercise his right to live only under very stiff conditions. In countries where there is compulsory military service he may even have to throw away his individual life to save the life of the community.

It is just so in the case of the right to knowledge. It is a right that is as yet very imperfectly recognized in practice. But in theory it is admitted that an adult person in pursuit of knowledge must not be refused it on the ground that he would be better or happier without it. Parents and priests may forbid knowledge to those who accept their authority; and social taboo may be made effective by acts of legal persecution under cover of repressing blasphemy, obscenity, and sedition; but no government now openly forbids its subjects to pursue knowledge on the ground that knowledge is in itself a bad thing, or that it is possible for any of us to have too much of it.

LIMITATIONS OF THE RIGHT TO KNOWLEDGE

But neither does any government exempt the pursuit of knowledge, any more than the pursuit of life, liberty, and happiness (as the American Constitution puts it), from all social conditions. No man is allowed to put his mother into the stove because he desires to know how long an adult woman will survive at a temperature of 500° Fahrenheit, no matter how important or interesting that particular addition to the store of human knowledge may be. A man who did so would have short work made not only of his right to knowledge, but of his right to live and all his other rights at the same time. The right to knowledge is not the only right; and its exercise must be limited by respect for other rights, and for its own exercise by others. When a man says to Society, "May I torture my mother in pursuit of knowledge?" Society replies "No." If he pleads, "What! Not even if I have a chance of finding out how to cure cancer by doing it?" Society still says, "Not even then." If the scientist, making the best of his disappointment, goes on to ask may he torture a dog, the stupid and callous people who do not realize that a dog is a fellow creature, and sometimes a good friend, may say Yes, though Shakespear, Dr Johnson, and their like may say No. But even those who say "You may torture *a* dog" never say "You may torture *my* dog." And nobody says, "Yes, because in the pursuit of knowledge you may do as you please." Just as even the stupidest people say, in effect, "If you cannot attain to knowledge without burning your mother you must do without knowledge," so the wisest people say, "If you cannot attain

to knowledge without torturing a dog, you must do without knowledge."

A FALSE ALTERNATIVE

But in practice you cannot persuade any wise man that this alternative can ever be forced on anyone but a fool, or that a fool can be trusted to learn anything from any experiment, cruel or humane. The Chinaman who burnt down his house to roast his pig was no doubt honestly unable to conceive any less disastrous way of cooking his dinner; and the roast must have been spoiled after all (a perfect type of the average vivisectionist experiment); but this did not prove that the Chinaman was right: it only proved that the Chinaman was an incapable cook and, fundamentally, a fool.

Take another celebrated experiment: one in sanitary reform. In the days of Nero Rome was in the same predicament as London today. If someone would burn down London, and it were rebuilt, as it would now have to be, subject to the sanitary by-laws and Building Act provisions enforced by the London County Council, it would be enormously improved; and the average lifetime of Londoners would be considerably prolonged. Nero argued in the same way about Rome. He employed incendiaries to set it on fire; and he played the harp in scientific raptures whilst it was burning. I am so far of Nero's way of thinking that I have often said, when consulted by despairing sanitary reformers, that what London needs to make her healthy is an earthquake. Why, then, it may be asked, do not I, as a public-spirited man, employ incendiaries to set it on fire, with a heroic disregard of the consequences to myself and others? Any vivisector would, if he had the courage of his opinions. The reasonable answer is that London can be made healthy without burning her down; and that as we have not enough civic virtue to make her healthy in a humane and economical way, we should not have enough to rebuild her in that way. In the old Hebrew legend, God lost patience with the world as Nero did with Rome, and drowned everybody except a single family. But the result was that the progeny of that family reproduced all the vices of their predecessors so exactly that the misery caused by the flood might just as well have been spared: things went on just as they did before. In the same way, the list of diseases which vivisection claims to have cured is long; but the returns of the Registrar-General shew that people still persist in dying of them as if vivisection had never been heard of. Any fool can burn down a city or cut an animal open; and an exceptionally foolish fool is quite likely to promise enormous benefits to the race as the result of such activities. But when the constructive, benevolent part of the business comes to be done, the same want of imagination, the same stupidity and cruelty, the same laziness and want of perseverance that prevented Nero or the vivisector from devizing or pushing through humane methods, prevents him from bringing order out of the chaos and happiness out of the misery he has made. At one time it seemed reasonable enough to declare that it was impossible to find whether or not there was a stone inside a man's body except by exploring it with a knife, or to find out what the sun is made of without visiting it in a balloon. Both these impossibilities have been achieved, but not by vivisectors. The Röntgen rays need not hurt the patient; and spectrum analysis involves no destruction. After such triumphs of humane experiment and reasoning, it is useless to assure us that there is no other key to knowledge except cruelty. When the vivisector offers us that assurance, we reply simply and contemptuously, "You mean that you are not clever or humane or energetic enough to find one."

CRUELTY FOR ITS OWN SAKE

It will now, I hope, be clear why the attack on vivisection is not an attack on the right to knowledge: why, indeed, those who have the deepest conviction of the sacredness of that right are the leaders of the attack. No knowledge is finally impossible of human attainment; for even though it may be beyond our present capacity, the needed capacity is not unattainable. Consequently no method of investigation is the only method; and no law forbidding any particular method can cut us off from the knowledge we hope to gain by it. The only knowledge we lose by forbidding cruelty is knowledge at first hand of cruelty itself, which is precisely the knowledge humane people wish to be spared.

But the question remains: Do we all really wish to be spared that knowledge? Are humane methods really to be preferred to cruel ones? Even if the experiments come to nothing, may not their cruelty be enjoyed for its own sake, as a sensational luxury? Let us face these questions boldly, not shrinking from the fact that cruelty is one of the primitive pleasures of mankind, and that the detection of its Protean disguises as law, education, medicine, discipline, sport and so forth, is one of the most difficult of the unending tasks of the legislator.

OUR OWN CRUELTIES

At first blush it may seem not only unnecessary, but even indecent, to discuss such a proposition as the elevation of cruelty to the rank of a human right. Unnecessary, because no vivisector confesses to a love of cruelty for its own sake or claims any general fundamental right to be cruel. Indecent, because there is an accepted convention to repudiate cruelty; and vivisection is only tolerated by the law on condition that, like judicial torture, it shall be done as mercifully as the nature of the practice allows. But the moment the controversy becomes embittered, the recriminations bandied between the opposed parties bring us face-to-face with some very ugly truths. On one occasion I was invited to speak at a large Anti-Vivisection meeting in the Queen's Hall in London. I found myself on the platform with fox hunters, tame stag hunters, men and women whose calendar was divided, not by pay days and quarter days, but by seasons for killing animals for sport: the fox, the hare, the otter, the partridge, and the rest having each its appointed date for slaughter. The ladies among us wore hats and cloaks and headdresses obtained by wholesale massacres, ruthless trappings, callous extermination of our fellow creatures. We insisted on our butchers supplying us with white veal, and were large and constant consumers of *pâté de foie gras*: both comestibles being obtained by revolting methods. We sent our sons to public schools where indecent flogging is a recognized method of taming the young human animal. Yet we were all in hysterics of indignation at the cruelties of the vivisectors. These, if any were present, must have smiled sardonically at such inhuman humanitarians, whose daily habits and fashionable amusements cause more suffering in England in a week than all the vivisectors of Europe do in a year. I made a very effective speech, not exclusively against vivisection, but against cruelty; and I have never been asked to speak since by that Society, nor do I expect to be, as I should probably give such offence to its most affluent subscribers that its attempts to suppress vivisection would be seriously hindered. But that does not prevent the vivisectors from freely using the "youre another" retort, and using it with justice.

We must therefore give ourselves no airs of superiority when denouncing the cruelties of vivisection. We all do just as

horrible things, with even less excuse. But in making that admission we are also making short work of the virtuous airs with which we are sometimes referred to the humanity of the medical profession as a guarantee that vivisection is not abused —much as if our burglars should assure us that they are too honest to abuse the practice of burgling. We are, as a matter of fact, a cruel nation; and our habit of disguising our vices by giving polite names to the offences we are determined to commit, does not, unfortunately for my own comfort, impose on me. Vivisectors can hardly pretend to be better than the classes from which they are drawn, or those above them; and if these classes are capable of sacrificing animals in various cruel ways under cover of sport, fashion, education, discipline, and even, when the cruel sacrifices are human sacrifices, of political economy, it is idle for the vivisector to pretend that he is incapable of practising cruelty for pleasure or profit or both under the cloak of science. We are all tarred with the same brush; and the vivisectors are not slow to remind us of it, and to protest vehemently against being branded as exceptionally cruel and as devizers of horrible instruments of torture by people whose main notion of enjoyment is cruel sport, and whose requirements in the way of villainously cruel traps occupy pages of the catalogue of the Army and Navy Stores.

THE SCIENTIFIC INVESTIGATION OF CRUELTY

There is in man a specific lust for cruelty which infects even his passion of pity and makes it savage. Simple disgust at cruelty is very rare. The people who turn sick and faint and those who gloat are often alike in the pains they take to witness executions, floggings, operations, or any other exhibitions of suffering, especially those involving bloodshed, blows, and laceration. A craze for cruelty

K

can be developed just as a craze for drink can; and nobody who attempts to ignore cruelty as a possible factor in the attraction of vivisection and even of anti-vivisection, or in the credulity with which we accept its excuses, can be regarded as a scientific investigator of it. Those who accuse vivisectors of indulging the well-known passion of cruelty under the cloak of research are therefore putting forward a strictly scientific psychological hypothesis, which is also simple, human, obvious, and probable. It may be as wounding to the personal vanity of the vivisector as Darwin's Origin of Species was to the people who could not bear to think that they were cousins to the monkeys (remember Goldsmith's anger when he was told that he could not move his upper jaw); but science has to consider only the truth of the hypothesis, and not whether conceited people will like it or not. In vain do the sentimental champions of vivisection declare themselves the most humane of men, inflicting suffering only to relieve it, scrupulous in the use of anesthetics, and void of all passion except the passion of pity for a disease-ridden world. The really scientific investigator answers that the question cannot be settled by hysterical protestations, and that if the vivisectionist rejects deductive reasoning, he had better clear his character by his own favorite method of experiment.

SUGGESTED LABORATORY TESTS OF THE VIVISECTOR'S EMOTIONS

Take the hackneyed case of the Italian who tortured mice, ostensibly to find out about the effects of pain rather less than the nearest dentist could have told him, and who boasted of the ecstatic sensations (he actually used the word love) with which he carried out his experiments. Or the gentleman who starved sixty dogs to death to establish the fact that a dog deprived of food gets progressively lighter and weaker, becoming remarkably emaciated, and finally dying: an undoubted truth, but ascertainable without laboratory experiments by a simple inquiry addressed to the nearest policeman, or, failing him, to any sane person in Europe. The Italian is diagnosed as a cruel voluptuary: the dog-starver is passed over as such a hopeless fool that it is impossible to take any interest in him. Why not test the diagnosis scientifically? Why not perform a careful series of experiments on persons under the influence of voluptuous ecstasy, so as to ascertain its physiological symptoms? Then perform a second series on persons engaged in mathematical work or machine designing, so as to ascertain the symptoms of cold scientific activity? Then note the symptoms of a vivisector performing a cruel experiment; and compare them with the voluptuary symptoms and the mathematical symptoms? Such experiments would be quite as interesting and important as any yet undertaken by the vivisectors. They might open a line of investigation which would finally make, for instance, the ascertainment of the guilt or innocence of an accused person a much exacter process than the very fallible methods of our criminal courts. But instead of proposing such an investigation, our vivisectors offer us all the pious protestations and all the huffy recriminations that any common unscientific mortal offers when he is accused of unworthy conduct.

ROUTINE

Yet most vivisectors would probably come triumphant out of such a series of experiments, because vivisection is now a routine, like butchering or hanging or flogging; and many of the men who practise it do so only because it has been established as part of the profession they have adopted. Far from enjoying it, they have simply overcome their natural repugnance and become indifferent to it, as men inevitably become indifferent to anything they do often enough. It is this dangerous power of custom that makes it so difficult to convince the common sense of mankind that any established commercial or professional practice has its root in passion. Let a routine once spring from passion, and you will presently find thousands of routineers following it passionlessly for a livelihood. Thus it always seems strained to speak of the religious convictions of a clergyman, because nine out of ten clergymen have no religious convictions: they are ordinary officials carrying on a routine of baptizing, marrying, and churching; praying, reciting, and preaching; and, like solicitors or doctors, getting away from their duties with relief to hunt, to garden, to keep bees, to go into society, and the like. In the same way many people do cruel and vile things without being in the least cruel or vile, because the routine to which they have been brought up is superstitiously cruel and vile. To say that every man who beats his children and every schoolmaster who flogs a pupil is a conscious debauchee is absurd: thousands of dull, conscientious people beat their children conscientiously, because they were beaten themselves and think children ought to be beaten. The ill-tempered vulgarity that instinctively strikes at and hurts a thing that annoys it (and all children are annoying), and the simple stupidity that requires from a child perfection beyond the reach of the wisest and best adults (perfect truthfulness coupled with perfect obedience is quite a common condition of leaving a child unwhipped), produce a good deal of flagellation among people who not only do not lust after it, but who hit the harder because they are angry at having to perform an uncomfortable duty. These people will beat merely to assert their authority, or to carry out what they conceive to be a divine order on the strength of the precept of Solomon recorded in the Bible, which carefully adds that Solomon completely spoilt his own son and turned away from the god of his fathers to the sensuous idolatry in which he ended his days.

In the same way we find men and women practising vivisection as senselessly as a humane butcher, who adores his fox terrier, will cut a calf's throat and hang it up by its heels to bleed slowly to death because it is the custom to eat veal and insist on its being white; or as a German purveyor nails a goose to a board and stuffs it with food because fashionable people eat *pâté de foie gras*; or as the crew of a whaler breaks in on a colony of seals and clubs them to death in wholesale massacre because ladies want sealskin jackets; or as fanciers blind singing birds with hot needles, and mutilate the ears and tails of dogs and horses. Let cruelty or kindness or anything else once become customary and it will be practised by people to whom it is not at all natural, but whose rule of life is simply to do only what everybody else does, and who would lose their employment and starve if they indulged in any peculiarity. A respectable man will lie daily, in speech and in print, about the qualities of the article he lives by selling, because it is customary to do so. He will flog his boy for telling a lie, because it is customary to do so. He will also flog him for not telling a lie if the boy tells inconvenient or disrespectful truths, because it is customary to do so. He will give the same boy a present on his birthday, and buy him a spade and bucket at the seaside, because it is customary to do so, being all the time neither particularly mendacious, nor particularly cruel, nor particularly generous, but simply incapable of ethical judgment or independent action.

Just so do we find a crowd of petty vivisectionists daily committing atrocities and stupidities, because it is the custom to do so. Vivisection is customary as part of the routine of preparing lectures in medical schools. For instance, there are two ways of making the action of the heart visible to students. One, a barbarous, ignorant, and thoughtless way, is to stick little flags into a rabbit's heart and let the students see the flags jump. The other, an elegant, ingenious, well-informed, and instructive way, is to put a sphygmograph on the student's wrist and let him see a record of his heart's action traced by a needle on a slip of smoked paper. But it has become the custom for lecturers to teach from the rabbit; and the lecturers are not original enough to get out of their groove. Then there are the demonstrations which are made by cutting up frogs with scissors. The most humane man, however repugnant the operation may be to him at first, cannot do it at lecture after lecture for months without finally—and that very soon—feeling no more for the frog than if he were cutting up pieces of paper. Such clumsy and lazy ways of teaching are based on the cheapness of frogs and rabbits. If machines were as cheap as frogs, engineers would not only be taught the anatomy of machines and the functions of their parts: they would also have machines misused and wrecked before them so that they might learn as much as possible by using their eyes, and as little as possible by using their brains and imaginations. Thus we have, as part of the routine of teaching, a routine of vivisection which soon produces complete indifference to it on the part even of those who are naturally humane. If they pass on from the routine of lecture preparation, not into general practice, but into research work, they carry this acquired indifference with them into the laboratory, where any atrocity is possible, because all atrocities satisfy curiosity. The routine man is in the majority in his profession always: consequently the moment his practice is tracked down to its source in human passion there is a great and quite sincere poohpoohing from himself, from the mass of the profession, and from the mass of the public, which sees that the average doctor is much too commonplace and decent a person to be capable of passionate wickedness of any kind.

Here, then, we have in vivisection, as in all the other tolerated and instituted cruelties, this anti-climax: that only a negligible percentage of those who practise and consequently defend it get any satisfaction out of it. As in Mr Galsworthy's play Justice the useless and detestable torture of solitary imprisonment is shewn at its worst without the introduction of a single cruel person into the drama, so it would be possible to represent all the torments of vivisection dramatically without introducing a single vivisector who had not felt sick at his first experience in the laboratory. Not that this can exonerate any vivisector from suspicion of enjoying his work (or *her* work: a good deal of the vivisection in medical schools is done by women). In every autobiography which records a real experience of school or prison life, we find that here and there among the routineers there is to be found the genuine amateur, the orgiastic flogging schoolmaster or the nagging warder, who has sought out a cruel profession for the sake of its cruelty. But it is the genuine routineer who is the bulwark of the practice, because, though you can excite public fury against a Sade, a Bluebeard, or a Nero, you cannot rouse any feeling against dull Mr Smith doing his duty; that is, doing the usual thing. He is so obviously no better and no worse than anyone else that it is difficult to conceive that the things he does are abominable. If you would see public dislike surging up in a moment against an individual, you must watch one who does something unusual, no matter how sensible it may be.

The name of Jonas Hanway lives as that of a brave man because he was the first who dared to appear in the streets of this rainy island with an umbrella.

THE OLD LINE BETWEEN MAN AND BEAST

But there is still a distinction to be clung to by those who dare not tell themselves the truth about the medical profession because they are so helplessly dependent on it when death threatens the household. That distinction is the line that separates the brute from the man in the old classification. Granted, they will plead, that we are all cruel; yet the tame stag hunter does not hunt men; and the sportsman who lets a leash of greyhounds loose on a hare would be horrified at the thought of letting them loose on a human child. The lady who gets her cloak by flaying a sable does not flay a negro; nor does it ever occur to her that her veal cutlet might be improved on by a slice of tender baby.

Now there was a time when some trust could be placed in this distinction. The Roman Catholic Church still maintains, with what it must permit me to call a stupid obstinacy, and in spite of St Francis and St Anthony, that animals have no souls and no rights; so that you cannot sin against an animal, or against God by anything you may choose to do to an animal. Resisting the temptation to enter on an argument as to whether you may not sin against your own soul if you are unjust or cruel to the least of those whom St Francis called his little brothers. I have only to point out here that nothing could be more despicably superstitious in the opinion of a vivisector than the notion that science recognizes any such step in evolution as the step from a physical organism to an immortal soul. That conceit has been taken out of all our men of science, and out of all our doctors, by the evolutionists; and when it is considered how completely obsessed biological science has become in our days, not by the full scope of evolution, but by that particular method of it which has neither sense nor purpose nor life nor anything human, much less godlike, in it: by the method that is, of so-called Natural Selection (meaning no selection at all, but mere dead accident and luck), the folly of trusting to vivisectors to hold the human animal any more sacred than the other animals becomes so clear that it would be waste of time to insist further on it. As a matter of fact the man who once concedes to the vivisector the right to put a dog outside the laws of honor and fellowship, concedes to him also the right to put himself outside them; for he is nothing to the vivisector but a more highly developed, and consequently more interesting-to-experiment-on vertebrate than the dog.

VIVISECTING THE HUMAN SUBJECT

I have in my hand a printed and published account by a doctor of how he tested his remedy for pulmonary tuberculosis, which was, to inject a powerful germicide directly into the circulation by stabbing a vein with a syringe. He was one of those doctors who are able to command public sympathy by saying, quite truly, that when they discovered that the proposed treatment was dangerous, they experimented thenceforth on themselves. In this case the doctor was devoted enough to carry his experiments to the point of running serious risks, and actually making himself very uncomfortable. But he did not begin with himself. His first experiment was on two hospital patients. On receiving a message from the hospital to the effect that these two martyrs to therapeutic science had all but expired in convulsions, he experimented on a rabbit, which instantly dropped dead. It was then, and not until then, that he began to experiment on himself, with the germicide modified in the direction indicated by the experiments made on the two patients and the rabbit. As a good many people countenance vivisection because they fear that if the experiments are not made on rabbits they will be made on themselves, it is worth noting that in this case, where both rabbits and men were equally available, the men, being of course enormously more instructive and costing nothing, were experimented on first. Once grant the ethics of the vivisectionists and you not only sanction the experiment on the human subject, but make it the first duty of the vivisector. If a guinea pig may be sacrificed for the sake of the very little that can be learnt from it, shall not a man be sacrificed for the sake of the great deal that can be learnt from him? At all events, he *is* sacrificed, as this typical case shows. I may add (not that it touches the argument) that the doctor, the patients, and the rabbit all suffered in vain, as far as the hoped-for rescue of the race from pulmonary consumption is concerned.

"THE LIE IS A EUROPEAN POWER"

Now at the very time when the lectures describing these experiments were being circulated in print and discussed eagerly by the medical profession, the customary denials that patients are experimented on were as loud, as indignant, as highminded as ever, in spite of the few intelligent doctors who point out rightly that all treatments are experiments on the patient. And this brings us to an obvious but mostly overlooked weakness in the vivisector's position: that is, his inevitable forfeiture of all claim to have his word believed. It is hardly to be expected that a man who does not hesitate to vivisect for the sake of science will hesitate to lie about it afterwards to protect it from what he deems the ignorant sentimentality of the laity. When the public conscience stirs uneasily and threatens suppression, there is never wanting some

doctor of eminent position and high character who will sacrifice himself devotedly to the cause of science by coming forward to assure the public on his honor that all experiments on animals are completely painless; although he must know that the very experiments which first provoked the anti-vivisection movement by their atrocity were experiments to ascertain the physiological effects of the sensation of extreme pain (the much more interesting physiology of pleasure remains uninvestigated) and that all experiments in which sensation is a factor are voided by its suppression. Besides, vivisection may be painless in cases where the experiments are very cruel. If a person scratches me with a poisoned dagger so gently that I do not feel the scratch, he has achieved a painless vivisection; but if I presently die in torment I am not likely to consider that his humanity is amply vindicated by his gentleness. A cobra's bite hurts so little that the creature is almost, legally speaking, a vivisector who inflicts no pain. By giving his victims chloroform before biting them he could comply with the law completely.

Here, then, is a pretty deadlock. Public support of vivisection is founded almost wholly on the assurances of the vivisectors that great public benefits may be expected from the practice. Not for a moment do I suggest that such a defence would be valid even if proved. But when the witnesses begin by alleging that in the cause of science all the customary ethical obligations (which include the obligation to tell the truth) are suspended, what weight can any reasonable person give to their testimony? I would rather swear fifty lies than take an animal which had licked my hand in good fellowship and torture it. If I did torture the dog, I should certainly not have the face to turn round and ask how any person dare suspect an honorable man like myself of telling lies. Most sensible and humane people would, I hope, reply flatly that honorable men do not behave dishonorably even to dogs. The murderer who, when asked by the chaplain whether he had any other crimes to confess, replied indignantly, "What do you take me for?" reminds us very strongly of the vivisectors who are so deeply hurt when their evidence is set aside as worthless.

AN ARGUMENT WHICH WOULD DEFEND ANY CRIME

The Achilles heel of vivisection, however, is not to be found in the pain it causes, but in the line of argument by which it is justified. The medical code regarding it is simply criminal anarchism at its very worst. Indeed, no criminal has yet had the impudence to argue as every vivisector argues. No burglar contends that as it is admittedly important to have money to spend, and as the object of burglary is to provide the burglar with money to spend, and as in many instances it has achieved this object, therefore the burglar is a public benefactor and the police are ignorant sentimentalists. No highway robber has yet harrowed us with denunciations of the puling moralist who allows his child to suffer all the evils of poverty because certain faddists think it dishonest to garotte an alderman. Thieves and assassins understand quite well that there are paths of acquisition, even of the best things, that are barred to all men of honor. Again, has the silliest burglar ever pretended that to put a stop to burglary is to put a stop to industry? All the vivisections that have been performed since the world began have produced nothing so important as the innocent and honorable discovery of radiography; and one of the reasons why radiography was not discovered sooner was that the men whose business it was to discover new clinical methods were coarsening and stupefying themselves with the sensual villainies and cutthroat's casuistries of vivisection. The law of the conservation of energy holds good in physiology as in other things: every vivisector is a deserter from the army of honorable investigators. But the vivisector does not see this. He not only calls his methods scientific: he contends that there are no other scientific methods. When you express your natural loathing for his cruelty and your natural contempt for his stupidity, he imagines that you are attacking science. Yet he has no inkling of the method and temper of science. The point at issue being plainly whether he is a rascal or not, he not only insists that the real point is whether some hotheaded anti-vivisectionist is a liar (which he proves by ridiculously unscientific assumptions as to the degree of accuracy attainable in human statement), but never dreams of offering any scientific evidence by his own methods.

There are many paths to knowledge already discovered; and no enlightened man doubts that there are many more waiting to be discovered. Indeed, all paths lead to knowledge; because even the vilest and stupidest action teaches us something about vileness and stupidity, and may accidentally teach us a good deal more: for instance, a cutthroat learns (and perhaps teaches) the anatomy of the carotid artery and jugular vein; and there can be no question that the burning of St Joan of Arc must have been a most instructive and interesting experiment to a good observer, and could have been made more so if it had been carried out by skilled physiologists under laboratory conditions. The earthquake in San Francisco proved invaluable as an experiment in the stability of giant steel buildings; and the ramming of the Victoria by the Camperdown settled doubtful points of the greatest importance in naval warfare. According to vivisectionist logic our builders would be justified in producing artificial earthquakes with dynamite, and our admirals in contriving catastrophes at naval manœuvres, in order to follow up the line of research thus accidentally discovered.

The truth is, if the acquisition of knowledge justifies every sort of conduct, it justifies any sort of conduct, from the illumination of Nero's feasts by burning human beings alive (another interesting experiment) to the simplest act of kindness. And in the light of that truth it is clear that the exemption of the pursuit of knowledge from the laws of honor is the most hideous conceivable enlargement of anarchy; worse, by far, than an exemption of the pursuit of money or political power, since these can hardly be attained without some regard for at least the appearances of human welfare, whereas a curious devil might destroy the whole race in torment, acquiring knowledge all the time from his highly interesting experiment. There is more danger in one respectable scientist countenancing such a monstrous claim than in fifty assassins or dynamitards. The man who makes it is ethically imbecile; and whoever imagines that it is a scientific claim has not the faintest conception of what science means. The paths to knowledge are countless. One of these paths is a path through darkness, secrecy, and cruelty. When a man deliberately turns from all other paths and goes down that one, it is scientific to infer that what attracts him is not knowledge, since there are other paths to that, but cruelty. With so strong and scientific a case against him, it is childish for him to stand on his honor and reputation and high character and the credit of a noble profession and so forth: he must clear himself either by reason or by experiment, unless he boldly contends that evolution has retained a passion of cruelty in man just because it is indispensable to the fulness of his knowledge.

THOU ART THE MAN

I shall not be at all surprised if what I have written above has induced in sym-pathetic readers a transport of virtuous indignation at the expense of the medical profession. I shall not damp so creditable and salutary a sentiment; but I must point out that the guilt is shared by all of us. It is not in his capacity of healer and man of science that the doctor vivisects or defends vivisection, but in his entirely vulgar lay capacity. He is made of the same clay as the ignorant, shallow, credulous, half-miseducated, pecuniarily anxious people who call him in when they have tried in vain every bottle and every pill the advertizing druggist can persuade them to buy. The real remedy for vivisection is the remedy for all the mischief that the medical profession and all the other professions are doing: namely, more knowledge. The juries which send the poor Peculiars to prison, and give vivisectionists heavy damages against humane persons who accuse them of cruelty; the editors and councillors and student-led mobs who are striving to make Vivisection one of the watchwords of our civilization, are not doctors; they are the British public, all so afraid to die that they will cling frantically to any idol which promises to cure all their diseases, and crucify anyone who tells them that they must not only die when their time comes, but die like gentlemen. In their paroxysms of cowardice and selfishness they force the doctors to humor their folly and ignorance. How complete and inconsiderate their ignorance is can only be realized by those who have some knowledge of vital statistics, and of the illusions which beset Public Health legislation.

WHAT THE PUBLIC WANTS AND WILL NOT GET

The demands of this poor public are not reasonable, but they are quite simple. It dreads disease and desires to be protected against it. But it is poor and wants to be protected cheaply. Scientific measures are too hard to understand, too costly, too clearly tending towards a rise in the rates and more public interference with the insanitary, because insufficiently financed, private house. What the public wants, therefore, is a cheap magic charm to prevent, and a cheap pill or potion to cure all disease. If forces all such charms on the doctors.

THE VACCINATION CRAZE

Thus it was really the public and not the medical profession that took up vaccination with irresistible faith, sweeping the invention out of Jenner's hands and establishing it in a form which he himself repudiated. Jenner was not a man of science; but he was not a fool; and when he found that people who had suffered from cowpox either by contagion in the milking shed or by vaccination, were not, as he had supposed, immune from smallpox, he ascribed the cases of immunity which had formerly misled him to a disease of the horse, which, perhaps because we do not drink its milk and eat its flesh, is kept at a greater distance in our imagination than our foster mother the cow. At all events, the public, which had been boundlessly credulous about the cow, would not have the horse on any terms; and to this day the law which prescribes Jennerian vaccination is carried out with an anti-Jennerian inoculation because the public would have it so in spite of Jenner. All the grossest lies and superstitions which have disgraced the vaccination craze were taught to the doctors by the public. It was not the doctors who first began to declare that all our old men remember the time when almost every face they saw in the street was horribly pitted with smallpox, and that all this disfigurement has vanished since the introduction of vaccination. Jenner himself alluded to this imaginary phenomenon before the introduction of vaccination, and attributed it to the older practice of smallpox inoculation, by which Voltaire, Catherine II, and Lady Mary Wortley Montagu so confidently expected to see the disease made harmless. It was not Jenner who set people declaring that smallpox, if not abolished by vaccination, had at least been made much milder: on the contrary, he recorded a pre-vaccination epidemic in which none of the persons attacked went to bed or considered themselves as seriously ill. Neither Jenner, nor any other doctor ever, as far as I know, inculcated the popular notion that everybody got smallpox as a matter of course before vaccination was invented. That doctors get infected with these delusions, and are in their unprofessional capacity as members of the public subject to them like other men, is true; but if we had to decide whether vaccination was first forced on the public by the doctors or on the doctors by the public, we should have to decide against the public.

STATISTICAL ILLUSIONS

Public ignorance of the laws of evidence and of statistics can hardly be exaggerated. There may be a doctor here and there who in dealing with the statistics of disease has taken at least the first step towards sanity by grasping the fact that as an attack of even the commonest disease is an exceptional event, apparently overwhelmingly statistical evidence in favor of any prophylactic can be produced by persuading the public that everybody caught the disease formerly. Thus if a disease is one which normally attacks fifteen per cent of the population, and if the effect of a prophylactic is actually to increase the proportion to twenty per cent, the publication of this figure of twenty per cent will convince the public that the prophylactic has reduced the percentage by eighty per cent instead of increasing it by five, because the public, left to itself and to the old gentlemen who are always ready to remember, on every possible subject, that things used to be much worse than they are now (such old gentlemen greatly outnumber the laudatores temporis acti), will assume that the former percentage was about 100. The vogue of the Pasteur treatment of hydrophobia, for instance, was due to the assumption by the public that every person bitten by a rabid dog necessarily got hydrophobia. I myself heard hydrophobia discussed in my youth by doctors in Dublin before a Pasteur Institute existed, the subject having been brought forward there by the scepticism of an eminent surgeon as to whether hydrophobia is really a specific disease or only ordinary tetanus induced (as tetanus was then supposed to be induced) by a lacerated wound. There were no statistics available as to the proportion of dog bites that ended in hydrophobia; but nobody ever guessed that the cases could be more than two or three per cent of the bites. On me, therefore, the results published by the Pasteur Institute produced no such effect as they did on the ordinary man who thinks that the bite of a mad dog means certain hydrophobia. It seemed to me that the proportion of deaths among the cases treated at the Institute was rather higher, if anything, than might have been expected had there been no Institute in existence. But to the public every Pasteur patient who did not die was miraculously saved from an agonizing death by the beneficent white magic of that most trusty of all wizards, the man of science.

Even trained statisticians often fail to appreciate the extent to which statistics are vitiated by the unrecorded assumptions of their interpreters. Their attention is too much occupied with the cruder tricks of those who make a corrupt use of statistics for advertizing purposes. There is, for example, the percentage dodge. In some hamlet, barely large enough to have a name, two people are attacked during a smallpox epidemic. One dies: the other recovers. One has vaccination marks: the other has none. Immediately the vaccinists or the anti-vaccinists publish the triumphant news that at such and such a place not a single vaccinated person died of smallpox whilst 100 per cent of the unvaccinated perished miserably; or, as the case may be, that 100 per cent of the unvaccinated recovered whilst the vaccinated succumbed to the last man. Or, to take another common instance, comparisons which are really comparisons between two social classes with different standards of nutrition and education are palmed off as comparisons between the results of a certain medical treatment and its neglect. Thus it is easy to prove that the wearing of tall hats and the carrying of umbrellas enlarges the chest, prolongs life, and confers comparative immunity from disease; for the statistics shew that the classes which use these articles are bigger, healthier, and live longer than the class which never dreams of possessing such things. It does not take much perspicacity to see that what really makes this difference is not the tall hat and the umbrella, but the wealth and nourishment of which they are evidence, and that a gold watch or membership of a club in Pall Mall might be proved in the same way to have the like sovereign virtues. A university degree, a daily bath, the owning of thirty pairs of trousers, a knowledge of Wagner's music, a pew in church, anything, in short, that implies more means and better nurture than the mass of laborers enjoy, can be statistically palmed off as a magic-spell conferring all sorts of privileges.

In the case of a prophylactic enforced by law, this illusion is intensified grotesquely, because only vagrants can evade it. Now vagrants have little power of resisting any disease: their death-rate and their case-mortality rate is always high relatively to that of respectable folk.

Nothing is easier, therefore, than to prove that compliance with any public regulation produces the most gratifying results. It would be equally easy even if the regulation actually raised the death-rate, provided it did not raise it sufficiently to make the average householder, who cannot evade regulations, die as early as the average vagrant who can.

THE SURPRISES OF ATTENTION AND NEGLECT

There is another statistical illusion which is independent of class differences. A common complaint of houseowners is that the Public Health Authorities frequently compel them to instal costly sanitary appliances which are condemned a few years later as dangerous to health, and forbidden under penalties. Yet these discarded mistakes are always made in the first instance on the strength of a demonstration that their introduction has reduced the death-rate. The explanation is simple. Suppose a law were made that every child in the nation should be compelled to drink a pint of brandy per month, but that the brandy must be administered only when the child was in good health, with its digestion and so forth working normally, and its teeth either naturally or artificially sound. Probably the result would be an immediate and startling reduction in child mortality, leading to further legislation increasing the quantity of brandy to a gallon. Not until the brandy craze had been carried to a point at which the direct harm done by it would outweigh the incidental good, would an anti-brandy party be listened to. That incidental good would be the substitution of attention to the general health of children for the neglect which is now the rule so long as the child is not actually too sick to run about and play as usual. Even if this attention were confined to the children's teeth, there would be an improvement which it would take a good deal of brandy to cancel.

This imaginary case explains the actual case of the sanitary appliances which our local sanitary authorities prescribe today and condemn tomorrow. No sanitary contrivance which the mind of even the very worst plumber can devize could be as disastrous as that total neglect for long periods which gets avenged by pestilences that sweep through whole continents, like the black death and the cholera. If it were proposed at this time of day to discharge all the sewage of London crude and untreated into the Thames, instead of carrying it, after elaborate treatment, far out into the North Sea, there would be a shriek of horror from all our experts. Yet if Cromwell had done that instead of doing nothing, there would probably have been no Great Plague of London. When the Local Health Authority forces every householder to have his sanitary arrangements thought about and attended to by somebody whose special business it is to attend to such things, then it matters not how erroneous or even directly mischievous may be the specific measures taken: the net result at first is sure to be an improvement. Not until attention has been effectually substituted for neglect as the general rule, will the statistics begin to shew the merits of the particular methods of attention adopted. And as we are far from having arrived at this stage, being as to health legislation only at the beginning of things, we have practically no evidence yet as to the value of methods. Simple and obvious as this is, nobody seems as yet to discount the effect of substituting attention for neglect in drawing conclusions from health statistics. Everything is put to the credit of the particular method employed, although it may quite possibly be raising the death-rate by five per thousand whilst the attention incidental to it is reducing the death-rate fifteen per thousand. The net gain of ten per thousand is credited to the method, and made the excuse for enforcing more of it.

STEALING CREDIT FROM CIVILIZATION

There is yet another way in which specifics which have no merits at all, either direct or incidental, may be brought into high repute by statistics. For a century past civilization has been cleaning away the conditions which favor bacterial fevers. Typhus, once rife, has vanished: plague and cholera have been stopped at our frontiers by a sanitary blockade. We still have epidemics of smallpox and typhoid; and diphtheria and scarlet fever are endemic in the slums. Measles, which in my childhood was not regarded as a dangerous disease, has now become so mortal that notices are posted publicly urging parents to take it seriously. But even in these cases the contrast between the death and recovery rates in the rich districts and in the poor ones has led to the general conviction among experts that bacterial diseases are preventible; and they already are to a large extent prevented. The dangers of infection and the way to avoid it are better understood than they used to be. It is barely twenty years since people exposed themselves recklessly to the infection of consumption and pneumonia in the belief that these diseases were not "catching." Nowadays the troubles of consumptive patients are greatly increased by the growing disposition to treat them as lepers. No doubt there is a good deal of ignorant exaggeration and cowardly refusal to face a human and necessary share of the risk. That has always been the case. We now know that the medieval horror of leprosy was out of all proportion to the danger of infection, and was accompanied by apparent blindness to the infectiousness of smallpox, which has since been worked up by our disease terrorists into the position formerly held by leprosy. But the scare of infection, though it sets even doctors talking as if the only really scientific thing to do with a fever patient is to throw him into the nearest ditch and pump carbolic acid on him from a safe distance until he is ready to be cremated on the spot, has led to much greater care and cleanliness. And the net result has been a series of victories over disease.

Now let us suppose that in the early nineteenth century somebody had come forward with a theory that typhus fever always begins at the top joint of the little finger; and that if this joint be amputated immediately after birth, typhus fever will disappear. Had such a suggestion been adopted, the theory would have been triumphantly confirmed; for as a matter of fact, typhus fever *has* disappeared. On the other hand cancer and madness have increased (statistically) to an appalling extent. The opponents of the little finger theory would therefore be pretty sure to allege that the amputations were spreading cancer and lunacy. The vaccination controversy is full of such contentions. So is the controversy as to the docking of horses' tails and the cropping of dogs' ears. So is the less widely known controversy as to circumcision and the declaring certain kinds of flesh unclean by the Jews. To advertize any remedy or operation, you have only to pick out all the most reassuring advances made by civilization, and boldly present the two in the relation of cause and effect: the public will swallow the fallacy without a wry face. It has no idea of the need for what is called a control experiment. In Shakespear's time and for long after it, mummy was a favorite medicament. You took a pinch of the dust of a dead Egyptian in a pint of the hottest water you could bear to drink; and it did you a great deal of good. This, you thought, proved what a sovereign healer mummy was. But if you had tried the control experiment of taking the hot water without the mummy, you might have found the effect exactly the same, and that any hot drink would have done as well.

BIOMETRIKA

Another difficulty about statistics is the technical difficulty of calculation. Before you can even make a mistake in drawing your conclusion from the correlations established by your statistics you must ascertain the correlations. When I turn over the pages of Biometrika, a quarterly journal in which is recorded the work done in the field of biological statistics by Professor Karl Pearson and his colleagues, I am out of my depth at the first line, because mathematics are to me only a concept: I never used a logarithm in my life, and could not undertake to extract the square root of four without misgiving. I am therefore unable to deny that the statistical ascertainment of the correlations between one thing and another must be a very complicated and difficult technical business, not to be tackled successfully except by high mathematicians; and I cannot resist Professor Karl Pearson's immense contempt for, and indignant sense of grave social danger in, the unskilled guesses of the ordinary sociologist.

Now the man in the street knows nothing of Biometrika: all he knows is that "you can prove anything by figures," though he forgets this the moment figures are used to prove anything he wants to believe. If he did take in Biometrika he would probably become abjectly credulous as to all the conclusions drawn in it from the correlations so learnedly worked out; though the mathematician whose correlations would fill a Newton with admiration, may, in collecting and accepting data and drawing conclusions from them, fall into quite crude errors by just such popular oversights as I have been describing.

PATIENT-MADE THERAPEUTICS

To all these blunders and ignorances doctors are no less subject than the rest of us. They are not trained in the use of evidence, nor in biometrics, nor in the psychology of human credulity, nor in the incidence of economic pressure. Further, they must believe, on the whole, what their patients believe, just as they must wear the sort of hat their patients wear. The doctor may lay down the law despotically enough to the patient at points where the patient's mind is simply blank; but when the patient has a prejudice the doctor must either keep it in countenance or lose his patient. If people are persuaded that night air is dangerous to health and that fresh air makes them catch cold, it will not be possible for a doctor to make his living in private practice if he prescribes ventilation. We have to go back no further than the days of The Pickwick Papers to find ourselves in a world where people slept in four-post beds with curtains drawn closely round to exclude as much air as possible. Had Mr Pickwick's doctor told him that he would be much healthier if he slept on a camp bed by an open window, Mr Pickwick would have regarded him as a crank and called in another doctor. Had he gone on to forbid Mr Pickwick to drink brandy and water whenever he felt chilly, and assured him that if he were deprived of meat or salt for a whole year, he would not only not die, but would be none the worse, Mr Pickwick would have fled from his presence as from that of a dangerous madman. And in these matters the doctor cannot cheat his patient. If he has no faith in drugs or vaccination, and the patient has, he can cheat him with colored water and pass his lancet through the flame of a spirit lamp before scratching his arm. But he cannot make him change his daily habits without knowing it.

THE REFORMS ALSO COME FROM THE LAITY

In the main, then, the doctor learns that if he gets ahead of the superstitions of his patients he is a ruined man; and the result is that he instinctively takes care not to get ahead of them. That is why all the changes come from the laity. It was not until an agitation had been conducted for many years by laymen, including quacks and faddists of all kinds, that the public was sufficiently impressed to make it possible for the doctors to open their minds and their mouths on the subject of fresh air, cold water, temperance, and the rest of the new fashions in hygiene. At present the tables have been turned on many old prejudices. Plenty of our most popular elderly doctors believe that cold tubs in the morning are unnatural, exhausting, and rheumatic; that fresh air is a fad, and that everybody is the better for a glass or two of port wine every day; but they no longer dare say as much until they know exactly where they are; for many very desirable patients in country houses have lately been persuaded that their first duty is to get up at six in the morning and begin the day by taking a walk barefoot through the dewy grass. He who shews the least scepticism as to this practice is at once suspected of being "an old-fashioned doctor," and dismissed to make room for a younger man.

In short, private medical practice is governed not by science but by supply and demand; and however scientific a treatment may be, it cannot hold its place in the market if there is no demand for it; nor can the grossest quackery be kept off the market if there is a demand for it.

FASHIONS AND EPIDEMICS

A demand, however, can be inculcated. This is thoroughly understood by fashionable tradesmen, who find no difficulty in persuading their customers to renew articles that are not worn out and to buy things they do not want. By making doctors tradesmen, we compel them to learn the tricks of trade; consequently we find that the fashions of the year include treatments, operations, and particular drugs, as well as hats, sleeves, ballads, and games. Tonsils, vermiform appendices, uvulas, even ovaries are sacrificed because it is the fashion to get them cut out, and because the operations are highly profitable. The psychology of fashion becomes a pathology; for the cases have every air of being genuine: fashions, after all, are only induced epidemics, proving that epidemics can be induced by tradesmen, and therefore by doctors.

THE DOCTOR'S VIRTUES

It will be admitted that this is a pretty bad state of things. And the melodramatic instinct of the public, always demanding that every wrong shall have, not its remedy, but its villain to be hissed, will blame, not its own apathy, superstition, and ignorance, but the depravity of the doctors. Nothing could be more unjust or mischievous. Doctors, if no better than other men, are certainly no worse. I was reproached during the performances of The Doctor's Dilemma at the Court Theatre in 1907 because I made the artist a rascal, the journalist an illiterate incapable, and all the doctors "angels." But I did not go beyond the warrant of my own experience. It has been my luck to have doctors among my friends for nearly forty years past (all perfectly aware of my freedom from the usual credulity as to the miraculous powers and knowledge attributed to them); and though I know that there are medical blackguards as well as military, legal, and clerical blackguards (one soon finds that out when one is privileged to hear doctors talking shop among themselves), the fact that I was no more at a loss for private medical advice and attendance when I had not a penny in my pocket than I was later on when I could afford fees on the highest scale, has made it impossible for me to share that hostility to the doctor as a man which exists and is growing as an inevitable result of the present condition of medical practice. Not that the interest in disease and aberrations which turns some men and women to medicine and surgery is not sometimes as morbid as the interest in misery and vice which turns some others to philanthropy and "rescue work." But the true doctor is inspired by a hatred of ill-health, and a divine impatience of any waste of vital forces. Unless a man is led to medicine or surgery through a very exceptional technical aptitude, or because doctoring is a family tradition, or because he regards it unintelligently as a lucrative and gentlemanly profession, his motives in choosing the career of a healer are clearly generous. However actual practice may disillusion and corrupt him, his selection in the first instance is not a selection of a base character.

THE DOCTOR'S HARDSHIPS

A review of the counts in the indictment I have brought against private medical practice will shew that they arise out of the doctor's position as a competitive private tradesman: that is, out of his poverty and dependence. And it should be borne in mind that doctors are expected to treat other people specially well whilst themselves submitting to specially inconsiderate treatment. The butcher and baker are not expected to feed the hungry unless the hungry can pay; but a doctor who allows a fellow creature to suffer or perish without aid is regarded as a monster. Even if we must dismiss hospital service as really venal, the fact remains that most doctors do a good deal of gratuitous work in private practice all through their careers. And in his paid work the doctor is on a different footing to the tradesman. Although the articles he sells, advice and treatment, are the same for all classes, his fees have to be graduated like the income tax. The successful fashionable doctor may weed his poorer patients out from time to time, and finally use the College of Physicians to place it out of his own power to accept low fees; but the ordinary general practitioner never makes out his bills without considering the taxable capacity of his patients.

Then there is the disregard of his own health and comfort which results from the fact that he is, by the nature of his work, an emergency man. We are polite and considerate to the doctor when there is nothing the matter, and we meet him as a friend or entertain him as a guest; but when the baby is suffering from croup, or its mother has a temperature of 104°, or its grandfather has broken his leg, nobody thinks of the doctor except as a healer and savior. He may be hungry, weary, sleepy, run down by several successive nights disturbed by that instrument of torture, the night bell; but who ever thinks of this in the face of sudden sickness or accident? We think no more of the condition of a doctor attending a case than of the condition of a fireman at a fire. In other occupations night-work is specially recognized and provided for. The worker sleeps all day; has his breakfast in the evening; his lunch or dinner at midnight; his dinner or supper before going to bed in the morning; and he changes to day-work if he cannot stand night-work. But a doctor is expected to work day and night. In practices which consist largely of workmen's clubs, and in which the patients are therefore taken on wholesale terms and very numerous, the unfortunate assistant, or the principal if he has no assistant, often does not undress, knowing that he will be called up before he has snatched an hour's sleep. To the strain of such inhuman conditions must be added the constant risk of infection. One wonders why the impatient doctors do not become savage and unmanageable, and the patient ones imbecile. Perhaps they do, to some extent. And the pay is wretched, and so uncertain that refusal to attend without payment in advance becomes often a necessary measure of self-defence, whilst the County Court has long ago put an end to the tradition that the doctor's fee is an honorarium. Even the most eminent physicians, as such biographies as those of Paget shew, are sometimes miserably, inhumanly poor until they are past their prime.

In short, the doctor needs our help for the moment much more than we often need his. The ridicule of Molière, the death of a well-informed and clever writer like the late Harold Frederic in the hands of Christian Scientists (a sort of sealing with his blood of the contemptuous disbelief in and dislike of doctors he had bitterly expressed in his books), the scathing and quite justifiable exposure of medical practice in the novel by Mr Maarten Maartens entitled The New Religion: all these trouble the doctor very little, and are in any case well set off by the popularity of Sir Luke Fildes' famous picture, and by the verdicts in which juries from time to time express their conviction that the doctor can do no wrong. The real woes of the doctor are the shabby coat, the wolf at the door, the tyranny of ignorant patients, the work-day of 24 hours, and the uselessness of honestly prescribing what most of the patients really need: that is, not medicine, but money.

THE PUBLIC DOCTOR

What then is to be done?

Fortunately we have not to begin absolutely from the beginning: we already have, in the Medical Officer of Health, a sort of doctor who is free from the worst hardships, and consequently from the worst vices, of the private practitioner. His position depends, not on the number of people who are ill, and whom he can keep ill, but on the number of people who are well. He is judged, as all doctors and treatments should be judged, by the vital statistics of his district. When the death-rate goes up his credit goes down. As every increase in his salary depends on the issue of a public debate as to the health of the constituency under his charge, he has every inducement to strive towards the ideal of a clean bill of health. He has a safe, dignified, responsible, independent position based wholly on the public health; whereas the private practitioner has a precarious, shabby-genteel, irresponsible, servile position, based wholly on the prevalence of illness.

It is true, there are grave scandals in the public medical service. The public doctor may be also a private practitioner eking out his earnings by giving a little time to public work for a mean payment. There are cases in which the position is one which no successful practitioner will accept, and where, therefore, incapables or drunkards get automatically selected for the post, faute de mieux; but even in these cases the doctor is less disastrous in his public capacity than in his private one: besides, the conditions which produce these bad cases are doomed, as the evil is now recognized and understood. A popular but unstable remedy is to enable local authorities, when they are too small to require the undivided time of such men as the Medical Officers of our great municipalities, to combine for public health purposes so that each may share the services of a highly paid official of the best class; but the right remedy is a larger area as the sanitary unit.

MEDICAL ORGANIZATION

Another advantage of public medical work is that it admits of organization, and consequently of the distribution of the work in such a manner as to avoid wasting the time of highly qualified experts on trivial jobs. The individualism of private practice leads to an appalling waste of time on trifles. Men whose dexterity as operators or almost divinatory skill in diagnosis are constantly needed for difficult cases, are poulticing whitlows, vaccinating, changing unimportant dressings, prescribing ether drams for ladies with timid leanings towards dipsomania, and generally wasting their time in the pursuit of private fees. In no other profession is the practitioner expected to do all the work involved in it from the first day of his professional career to the last as the doctor is. The judge passes sentence of death; but he is not expected to hang the criminal with his own hands, as he would be if the legal profession were as unorganized as the medical. The bishop is not expected to blow the organ or wash the baby he baptizes. The general is not asked to plan a campaign or conduct a battle at half-past twelve and to play the drum at half-past two. Even if they were, things would still not be as bad as in the medical profession; for in it not only is the first-class man set to do third-class work, but, what is much more terrifying, the third-class man is expected to do first-class work. Every general practitioner is supposed to be capable of the whole range of medical and surgical work at a moment's notice; and the country doctor, who has not a specialist nor a crack consultant at the end of his telephone, often has to tackle without hesitation cases which no sane practitioner in a town would take in hand without assistance. No doubt this develops the resourcefulness of the country doctor, and makes him a more capable man than his suburban colleague; but it cannot develop the second-class man into a first-class one. If the practice of law not only led to a judge having to hang, but the hangman to judge, or if in the army

matters were so arranged that it would be possible for the drummer boy to be in command at Waterloo whilst the Duke of Wellington was playing the drum in Brussels, we should not be consoled by the reflection that our hangmen were thereby made a little more judicial-minded, and our drummers more responsible, than in foreign countries where the legal and military professions recognized the advantages of division of labor.

Under such conditions no statistics as to the graduation of professional ability among doctors are available. Assuming that doctors are normal men and not magicians (and it is unfortunately very hard to persuade people to admit so much and thereby destroy the romance of doctoring) we may guess that the medical profession, like the other professions, consists of a small percentage of highly gifted persons at one end, and a small percentage of altogether disastrous duffers at the other. Between these extremes comes the main body of doctors (also, of course, with a weak and a strong end) who can be trusted to work under regulations with more or less aid from above according to the gravity of the case. Or, to put it in terms of the cases, there are cases that present no difficulties, and can be dealt with by a nurse or student at one end of the scale, and cases that require watching and handling by the very highest existing skill at the other; whilst between come the great mass of cases which need visits from the doctor of ordinary ability and from the chiefs of the profession in the proportion of, say, seven to none, seven to one, three to one, one to one, or, for a day or two, none to one. Such a service is organized at present only in hospitals; though in large towns the practice of calling in the consultant acts, to some extent, as a substitute for it. But in the latter case it is quite unregulated except by professional etiquet, which, as we have seen, has for its object, not the health of the patient or of the community at large, but the protection of the doctor's livelihood and the concealment of his errors. And as the consultant is an expensive luxury, he is a last resource rather than, as he should be, a matter of course in all cases where the general practitioner is not equal to the occasion: a predicament in which a very capable man may find himself at any time through the cropping up of a case of which he has had no clinical experience.

THE SOCIAL SOLUTION OF THE MEDICAL PROBLEM

The social solution of the medical problem, then, depends on that large, slowly advancing, pettishly resisted integration of society called generally Socialism. Until the medical profession becomes a body of men trained and paid by the country to keep the country in health it will remain what it is at present: a conspiracy to exploit popular credulity and human suffering. Already our M.O.H.s (Medical Officers of Health) are in the new position: what is lacking is appreciation of the change, not only by the public but by the private doctors. For, as we have seen, when one of the first-rate posts becomes vacant in one of the great cities, and all the leading M.O.H.s compete for it, they must appeal to the good health of the cities of which they have been in charge, and not to the size of the incomes the local private doctors are making out of the ill-health of their patients. If a competitor can prove that he has utterly ruined every sort of medical private practice in a large city except obstetric practice and the surgery of accidents, his claims are irresistible; and this is the ideal at which every M.O.H. should aim. But the profession at large should none the less welcome him and set its house in order for the social change which will finally be its own salvation. For the M.O.H. as we know him is only

the beginning of that army of Public Hygiene which will presently take the place in general interest and honor now occupied by our military and naval forces. It is silly that an Englishman should be more afraid of a German soldier than of a British disease germ, and should clamor for more barracks in the same newspapers that protest against more school clinics, and cry out that if the State fights disease for us it makes us paupers, though they never say that if the State fights the Germans for us it makes us cowards. Fortunately, when a habit of thought is silly it only needs steady treatment by ridicule from sensible and witty people to be put out of countenance and perish. Every year sees an increase in the number of persons employed in the Public Health Service, who would formerly have been mere adventurers in the Private Illness Service. To put it another way, a host of men and women who have now a strong incentive to be mischievous and even murderous rogues will have a much stronger, because a much honester, incentive to be not only good citizens but active benefactors to the community. And they will have no anxiety whatever about their incomes.

THE FUTURE OF PRIVATE PRACTICE

It must not be hastily concluded that this involves the extinction of the private practitioner. What it will really mean for him is release from his present degrading and scientifically corrupting slavery to his patients. As I have already shewn, the doctor who has to live by pleasing his patients in competition with everybody who has walked the hospitals, scraped through the examinations, and bought a brass plate, soon finds himself prescribing water to teetotallers and brandy or champagne jelly to drunkards; beefsteaks and stout in one house, and "uric acid free" vegetarian diet over the way; shut windows, big fires, and heavy overcoats to old Colonels, and open air and as much nakedness as is compatible with decency to young faddists, never once daring to say either "I dont know," or "I dont agree." For the strength of the doctor's, as of every other man's position when the evolution of social organization at last reaches his profession, will be that he will always have open to him the alternative of public employment when the private employer becomes too tyrannous. And let no one suppose that the words doctor and patient can disguise from the parties the fact that they are employer and employee. No doubt doctors who are in great demand can be as high-handed and independent as employees are in all classes when a dearth in their labor market makes them indispensable; but the average doctor is not in this position: he is struggling for life in an overcrowded profession, and knows well that "a good bedside manner" will carry him to solvency through a morass of illness, whilst the least attempt at plain dealing with people who are eating too much or drinking too much, or frowsting too much (to go no further in the list of intemperances that make up so much of family life) would soon land him in the Bankruptcy Court.

Private practice, thus protected, would itself protect individuals, as far as such protection is possible, against the errors and superstitions of State medicine, which are at worst no worse than the errors and superstitions of private practice, being, indeed, all derived from it. Such monstrosities as vaccination are, as we have seen, founded, not on science, but on half-crowns. If the Vaccination Acts, instead of being wholly repealed as they are already half repealed, were strengthened by compelling every parent to have his child vaccinated by a public officer whose salary was completely independent of the number of vaccinations performed by him, and for whom there was plenty of alternative public health work waiting, vaccination would be dead in two years, as the vaccinator would not only not gain by it, but would lose credit through the depressing effects on the vital statistics of his district of the illness and deaths it causes, whilst it would take from him all the credit of that freedom from smallpox which is the result of good sanitary administration and vigilant prevention of infection. Such absurd panic scandals as that of the last London epidemic, where a fee of half-a-crown per revaccination produced raids on houses during the absence of parents, and the forcible seizure and revaccination of children left to answer the door, can be prevented simply by abolishing the half-crown and all similar follies, paying, not for this or that ceremony of witchcraft, but for immunity from disease, and paying, too, in a rational way. The officer with a fixed salary saves himself trouble by doing his business with the least possible interference with the private citizen. The man paid by the job loses money by not forcing his job on the public as often as possible without reference to its results.

THE TECHNICAL PROBLEM

As to any technical medical problem specially involved, there is none. If there were, I should not be competent to deal with it, as I am not a technical expert in medicine: I deal with the subject as an economist, a politician, and a citizen exercising my common sense. Everything that I have said applies equally to all the medical techniques, and will hold good whether public hygiene be based on the poetic fancies of Christian Science, the tribal superstitions of the druggist and the vivisector, or the best we can make of our real knowledge. But I may remind those who confusedly imagine that the medical problem is also the scientific problem, that all problems are finally scientific problems. The notion that therapeutics or hygiene or surgery is any more or less scientific than making or cleaning boots is entertained only by people to whom a man of science is still a magician who can cure diseases, transmute metals, and enable us to live for ever. It may still be necessary for some time to come to practise on popular credulity, popular love and dread of the marvellous, and popular idolatry, to induce the poor to comply with the sanitary regulations they are too ignorant to understand. As I have elsewhere confessed, I have myself been responsible for ridiculous incantations with burning sulphur, experimentally proved to be quite useless, because poor people are convinced, by the mystical air of the burning and the horrible smell, that it exorcizes the demons of smallpox and scarlet fever and makes it safe for them to return to their houses. To assure them that the real secret is sunshine and soap is only to convince them that you do not care whether they live or die, and wish to save money at their expense. So you perform the incantation; and back they go to their houses, satisfied. A religious ceremony—a poetic blessing of the threshold, for instance—would be much better; but unfortunately our religion is weak on the sanitary side. One of the worst misfortunes of Christendom was that reaction against the voluptuous bathing of the imperial Romans which made dirty habits a part of Christian piety, and in some unlucky places (the Sandwich Islands, for example) made the introduction of Christianity also the introduction of disease, because the formulators of the superseded native religion, like Mahomet, had been enlightened enough to introduce as religious duties such sanitary measures as ablution and the most careful and reverent treatment of everything cast off by the human body, even to nail clippings and hairs; and our missionaries thoughtlessly discredited this godly doctrine without supplying its place, which was promptly taken by laziness and neglect. If the priests of Ireland could only be persuaded to teach their flocks that it is a deadly insult to the Blessed Virgin to place her image in a cottage that is not kept up to that high standard of Sunday cleanliness to which all her worshippers must believe she is accustomed, and to represent her as being especially particular about stables because her son was born in one, they might do more in one year than all the Sanitary Inspectors in Ireland could do in twenty; and they could hardly doubt that Our Lady would be delighted. Perhaps they do nowadays; for Ireland is certainly a transfigured country since my youth as far as clean faces and pinafores can transfigure it. In England, where so many of the inhabitants are too gross to believe in poetic faiths, too respectable to tolerate the notion that the stable at Bethany was a common peasant farmer's stable instead of a first-rate racing one, and too savage to believe that anything can really cast out the devil of disease unless it be some terrifying hoodoo of tortures and stinks, the M.O.H. will no doubt for a long time to come have to preach to fools according to their folly, promising miracles, and threatening hideous personal consequences of neglect of by-laws and the like; therefore it will be important that every M.O.H. shall have, with his (or her) other qualifications, a sense of humor, lest he (or she) should come at last to believe all the nonsense that must needs be talked. But he must, in his capacity of an expert advising the authorities, keep the government itself free of superstition. If Italian peasants are so ignorant that the Church can get no hold of them except by miracles, why, miracles there must be. The blood of St Januarius must liquefy whether the Saint is in the humor or not. To trick a heathen into being a dutiful Christian is no worse than to trick a whitewasher into trusting himself in a room where a smallpox patient has lain, by pretending to exorcize the disease with burning sulphur. But woe to the Church if in deceiving the peasant it also deceives itself; for then the Church is lost, and the peasant too, unless he revolt against it. Unless the Church works the pretended miracle painfully against the grain, and is continually urged by its dislike of the imposture to strive to make the peasant susceptible to the true reasons for behaving well, the Church will become an instrument of his corruption and an exploiter of his ignorance, and will find itself launched upon that persecution of scientific truth of which all priesthoods are accused—and none with more justice than the scientific priesthood.

And here we come to the danger that terrifies so many of us: the danger of having a hygienic orthodoxy imposed on us. But we must face that: in such crowded and poverty ridden civilizations as ours any orthodoxy is better than laisser-faire. If our population ever comes to consist exclusively of well-to-do, highly cultivated, and thoroughly instructed free persons in a position to take care of themselves, no doubt they will make short work of a good deal of official regulation that is now of life-and-death necessity to us; but under existing circumstances, I repeat, almost any sort of attention that democracy will stand is better than neglect. Attention and activity lead to mistakes as well as to successes; but a life spent in making mistakes is not only more honorable but more useful than a life spent doing nothing. The one lesson that comes out of all our theorizing and experimenting is that there is only one really scientific progressive method; and that is the method of trial and error. If you come to that, what is laisser-faire but an orthodoxy? the most tyrannous and disastrous of all the orthodoxies, since it forbids you even to learn.

THE LATEST THEORIES

Medical theories are so much a matter of fashion, and the most fertile of them are modified so rapidly by medical practice and biological research, which are international activities, that the play which furnishes the pretext for this preface is already slightly outmoded, though I believe it may be taken as a faithful record for the year (1906) in which it was begun. I must not expose any professional man to ruin by connecting his name with the entire freedom of criticism which I, as a layman, enjoy; but it will be evident to all experts that my play could not have been written but for the work done by Sir Almroth Wright in the theory and practice of securing immunization from bacterial diseases by the inoculation of "vaccines" made of their own bacteria: a practice incorrectly called vaccinetherapy (there is nothing vaccine about it) apparently because it is what vaccination ought to be and is not. Until Sir Almroth Wright, following up one of Metchnikoff's most suggestive biological romances, discovered that the white corpuscles or phagocytes which attack and devour disease germs for us do their work only when we butter the disease germs appetizingly for them with a natural sauce which Sir Almroth named opsonin, and that our production of this condiment continually rises and falls rhythmically from negligibility to the highest efficiency, nobody had been able even to conjecture why the various serums that were from time to time introduced as having effected marvellous cures, presently made such direful havoc of some unfortunate patient that they had to be dropped hastily. The quantity of sturdy lying that was necessary to save the credit of inoculation in those days was prodigious; and had it not been for the devotion shewn by the military authorities throughout Europe, who would order the entire disappearance of some disease from their armies, and bring it about by the simple plan of changing the name under which the cases were reported, or for our own Metropolitan Asylums Board, which carefully suppressed all the medical reports that revealed the sometimes quite appalling effects of epidemics of revaccination, there is no saying what popular reaction might not have taken place against the whole immunization movement in therapeutics.

The situation was saved when Sir Almroth Wright pointed out that if you inoculated a patient with pathogenic germs at a moment when his powers of cooking them for consumption by the phagocytes was receding to its lowest point, you would certainly make him a good deal worse and perhaps kill him, whereas if you made precisely the same inoculation when the cooking power was rising to one of its periodical climaxes, you would stimulate it to still further exertions and produce just the opposite result. And he invented a technique for ascertaining in which phase the patient happened to be at any given moment. The dramatic possibilities of this discovery and invention will be found in my play. But it is one thing to invent a technique: it is quite another to persuade the medical profession to acquire it. Our general practitioners, I gather, simply declined to acquire it, being mostly unable to afford either the acquisition or the practice of it when acquired. Something simple, cheap, and ready at all times for all comers, is, as I have shewn, the only thing that is economically possible in general practice, whatever may be the case in Sir Almroth's famous laboratory in St Mary's Hospital. It would have become necessary to denounce opsonin in the trade papers as a fad and Sir Almroth as a dangerous man if his practice in the laboratory had not led him to the conclusion that the customary inoculations were very

much too powerful, and that a comparatively infinitesimal dose would not precipitate a negative phase of cooking activity, and might induce a positive one. And thus it happens that the refusal of our general practitioners to acquire the new technique is no longer quite so dangerous in practice as it was when The Doctor's Dilemma was written: nay, that Sir Ralph Bloomfield Bonington's way of administering inoculations as if they were spoonfuls of squills may sometimes work fairly well. For all that, I find Sir Almroth Wright, on the 23rd May 1910, warning the Royal Society of Medicine that "the clinician has not yet been prevailed upon to reconsider his position," which means that the general practitioner ("the doctor," as he is called in our homes) is going on just as he did before, and could not afford to learn or practise a new technique even if he had ever heard of it. To the patient who does not know about it he will say nothing. To the patient who does, he will ridicule it, and disparage Sir Almroth. What else can he do, except confess his ignorance and starve?

But now please observe how "the whirligig of time brings its revenges." This latest discovery of the remedial virtue of a very very tiny hair of the dog that bit you reminds us, not only of Arndt's law of protoplasmic reaction to stimuli, according to which weak and strong stimuli provoke opposite reactions, but of Hahnemann's homeopathy, which was founded on the fact alleged by Hahnemann that drugs which produce certain symptoms when taken in ordinary perceptible quantities, will, when taken in infinitesimally small quantities, provoke just the opposite symptoms; so that the drug that gives you a headache will also cure a headache if you take little enough of it. I have already explained that the savage opposition which homeopathy encountered from the medical profession was not a scientific opposition;

for nobody seems to deny that some drugs act in the alleged manner. It was opposed simply because doctors and apothecaries lived by selling bottles and boxes of doctor's stuff to be taken in spoonfuls or in pellets as large as peas; and people would not pay as much for drops and globules no bigger than pins' heads. Nowadays, however, the more cultivated folk are beginning to be so suspicious of drugs, and the incorrigibly superstitious people so profusely supplied with patent medicines (the medical advice to take them being wrapped round the bottle and thrown in for nothing) that homeopathy has become a way of rehabilitating the trade of prescription compounding, and is consequently coming into professional credit. At which point the theory of opsonins comes very opportunely to shake hands with it.

Add to the newly triumphant homeopathist and the opsonist that other remarkable innovator, the Swedish masseur, who does not theorize about you, but probes you all over with his powerful thumbs until he finds out your sore spots and rubs them away, besides cheating you into a little wholesome exercise; and you have nearly everything in medical practice today that is not flat witchcraft or pure commercial exploitation of human credulity and fear of death. Add to them a good deal of vegetarian and teetotal controversy raging round a clamor for scientific eating and drinking, and resulting in little so far except calling digestion Metabolism and dividing the public between the eminent doctor who tells us that we do not eat enough fish, and his equally eminent colleague who warns us that a fish diet must end in leprosy, and you have all that opposes with any sort of countenance the rise of Christian Science with its cathedrals and congregations and zealots and miracles and cures: all very silly, no doubt, but sane and sensible, poetic and hopeful, compared to the pseudo science of the commercial general practitioner, who foolishly clamors for the prosecution and even the execution of the Christian Scientists when their patients die, forgetting the long deathroll of his own patients.

By the time this preface is in print the kaleidoscope may have had another shake; and opsonin may have gone the way of phlogiston at the hands of its own restless discoverer. I will not say that Hahnemann may have gone the way of Diafoirus; for Diafoirus we have always with us. But we shall still pick up all our knowledge in pursuit of some Will o' the Wisp or other. What is called science has always pursued the Elixir of Life and the Philosopher's Stone, and is just as busy after them today as ever it was in the days of Paracelsus. We call them by different names: Immunization or radiotherapy or what not; but the dreams which lure us into the adventures from which we learn are always at bottom the same. Science becomes dangerous only when it imagines that it has reached its goal. What is wrong with priests and popes is that instead of being apostles and saints, they are nothing but empirics who say "I know" instead of "I am learning," and pray for credulity and inertia as wise men pray for scepticism and activity. Such abominations as the Inquisition and the Vaccination Acts are possible only in the famine years of the soul, when the great vital dogmas of honor, liberty, courage, the kinship of all life, faith that the unknown is greater than the known and is only the As Yet Unknown, and resolution to find a manly highway to it, have been forgotten in a paroxysm of littleness and terror in which nothing is active except concupiscence and the fear of death, playing on which any trader can filch a fortune, any blackguard gratify his cruelty, and any tyrant make us his slaves.

Lest this should seem too rhetorical a conclusion for our professional men of science, who are mostly trained not to believe anything unless it is worded in the jargon of those writers who, because they never really understand what they are trying to say, cannot find familiar words for it, and are therefore compelled to invent a new language of nonsense for every book they write, let me sum up my conclusions as dryly as is consistent with accurate thought and live conviction.

1. Nothing is more dangerous than a poor doctor: not even a poor employer or a poor landlord.

2. Of all the anti-social vested interests the worst is the vested interest in ill-health.

3. Remember that an illness is a misdemeanor; and treat the doctor as an accessory unless he notifies every case to the Public Health Authority.

4. Treat every death as a possible and, under our present system, a probable murder, by making it the subject of a reasonably conducted inquest; and execute the doctor, if necessary, *as* a doctor, by striking him off the register.

5. Make up your mind how many doctors the community needs to keep it well. Do not register more or less than this number; and let registration constitute the doctor a civil servant with a dignified living wage paid out of public funds.

6. Municipalize Harley Street.

7. Treat the private operator exactly as you would treat a private executioner.

8. Treat persons who profess to be able to cure disease as you treat fortune tellers.

9. Keep the public carefully informed, by special statistics and announcements of individual cases, of all illnesses of doctors or in their families.

10. Make it compulsory for a doctor using a brass plate to have inscribed on it, in addition to the letters indicating his qualifications, the words "Remember that I too am mortal."

11. In legislation and social organization, proceed on the principle that invalids, meaning persons who cannot keep themselves alive by their own activities, cannot, beyond reason, expect to be kept alive by the activity of others. There is a point at which the most energetic policeman or doctor, when called upon to deal with an apparently drowned person, gives up artificial respiration, although it is never possible to declare with certainty, at any point short of decomposition, that another five minutes of the exercise would not effect resuscitation. The theory that every individual alive is of infinite value is legislatively impracticable. No doubt the higher the life we secure to the individual by wise social organization, the greater his value is to the community, and the more pains we shall take to pull him through any temporary danger or disablement. But the man who costs more than he is worth is doomed by sound hygiene as inexorably as by sound economics.

12. Do not try to live for ever. You will not succeed.

13. Use your health, even to the point of wearing it out. That is what it is for. Spend all you have before you die; and do not outlive yourself.

14. Take the utmost care to get well born and well brought up. This means that your mother must have a good doctor. Be careful to go to a school where there is what they call a school clinic, where your nutrition and teeth and eyesight and other matters of importance to you will be attended to. Be particularly careful to have all this done at the expense of the nation, as otherwise it will not be done at all, the chances being about forty to one against your being able to pay for it directly yourself, even if you know how to set about it. Otherwise you will be what most people are at present: an unsound citizen of an unsound nation, with-

out sense enough to be ashamed or unhappy about it.

1911.

POSTSCRIPT 1930. During the year which have elapsed since the foregoing preface was penned, the need for bringing the medical profession under responsible and effective public control has become constantly more pressing as the inevitable collisions between the march of discovery in therapeutic science and the reactionary obsolescence of the General Medical Council have become more frequent and sensational. A later volume in the present edition of my works deals with this development.

POSTSCRIPT 1933. The condition of the medical profession is now so scandalous that unregistered practitioners obtain higher fees and are more popular with educated patients than registered ones. I have dealt with this fully in my volume entitled Doctors' Delusions; but I may mention here that my demand for lay representation on the General Medical Council at last moved the Government to impose one of their best men, Sir Edward Hilton Young, on that body. But as it immediately imposed on him several other whole-time jobs, culminating in the overwhelming business of Slum Clearance, it was evident that no serious importance was attached to his appointment. Until the General Medical Council is composed of hardworking representatives of the suffering public, with doctors who live by private practice rigidly excluded except as assessors, we shall still be decimated by the vested interest of the private side of the profession in disease.

XI

IMPRISONMENT (ENGLISH LOCAL GOVERNMENT, BY SIDNEY AND BEATRICE WEBB)

Dec.–Jan. 1921–22

FOREWORD

When I was a boy in my teens in Dublin I was asked by an acquaintance of mine who was clerk to a Crown Solicitor, and had business in prisons, whether I would like to go through Mountjoy Prison, much as he might have asked me whether I would like to go through the Mint, or the cellars at the docks. I accepted the invitation with my head full of dungeons and chains and straw pallets and stage gaolers: in short, of the last acts of Il Trovatore and Gounod's Faust, and of the Tower of London in Richard III. I expected the warders to look like murderers, and the murderers like heroes. At least I suppose I did, because what struck me most was that the place was as bright and clean as whitewash and scrubbing and polish could make it, with all the warders looking thoroughly respectable, and all the prisoners ruffianly and degenerate, except one tall delicate figure tramping round in the exercise ring, a Lifer by the color of his cap, who had chopped up his family with a hatchet, and been recommended to mercy on account of his youth. I thought, and still think, imprisonment for life a curious sort of mercy. My main impression of the others, and the one that has stuck longest and hardest, was that as it was evidently impossible to reform such men, it was useless to torture them, and dangerous to release them.

I have never been imprisoned myself; but in my first years as a public speaker I had to volunteer for prison martyrdom in two Free Speech conflicts with the police. As my luck would have it, on the first occasion the police capitulated on the eve of the day on which I had undertaken to address a prohibited meeting and refuse to pay a fine; and on the second a rival political organization put up a rival martyr, and, on a division, carried his election over my head, to my great relief. These incidents are not very impressive now; but the fact that my acquaintance with the subject of the following essay began with the sight of an actual prison, and that twice afterwards I was for a week or so firmly convinced that I was about to spend at least a fortnight and possibly a month in the cells, gave me an interest in the subject less perfunctory than that of the ordinary citizen to whom prison is only a reference in the police news, denoting simply a place where dishonest and violent people are very properly locked up.

This comfortable ignorance, by the way, is quite commonly shared by judges. A Lord Chief Justice of England, grieved at hearing from a lady of social importance that her son had been sent to prison as a Conscientious Objector, told her that he hoped she would get to see him often, and keep up his spirits with frequent letters, and send him in nice things to eat. He was amazed to learn from her that he might just as well have suggested a motor ride every afternoon and a visit to the opera in the evening. He had been sentencing people all through his judicial career to terms of imprisonment, some of them for life, without knowing that it meant anything more than being confined to the house and wearing a dress with broad arrows all over it. No doubt he thought, quite rightly, that such confinement was bad enough for anybody, however wicked.

I had no such illusions about prison life. My political activities often brought me into contact with men of high character and ability who had been victims of modern forms of persecution under the very elastic headings of treason, sedition, obstruction, blasphemy, offences against press laws, and so forth. I knew that Karl Marx had declared that British prisons were the cruellest in the world; and I thought it quite probable that he was right. I knew Prince Peter Kropotkin, who, after personal experience of the most villainous convict prisons in Siberia and the best model prison in France, said that they were both so bad that the difference was not worth talking about. What with European "politicals" and amnestied Irish Fenians, those who, like myself, were in the way of meeting such people could hardly feel easy in their consciences about the established methods of handling criminals.

Also I was in occasional touch with certain efforts made by the now extinct Humanitarian League, and by a little Society called the Police and Public Vigilance Society, to call attention to the grievances of prisoners. The League dealt with punishments: the Society, which was really an agitation conducted by one devoted man with very slender means, the late James Timewell, tried to obtain redress for people who alleged that they had been the victims of petty frame-ups by the police. But the witnesses on whose testimony these two bodies had to proceed were mostly either helpless creatures who could not tell the truth or scoundrels who would not tell it. The helpless creatures told you what they wanted to believe themselves: the scoundrels told you what they wanted you to believe.

Anyone who has tried to find out what war is like from our demobilized soldiers will understand. Their consciousness is limited and utterly uncritical; their memory is inaccurate and confused; their judgment is perverted by personal dislikes and vanities; and as to reflection, reason, self-criticism, and the rest of the intellectual counterchecks, they have no more of them than a mouse has of mathematics. If this is the case with normal men like soldiers, even less is to be expected from subnormal men like criminals. Neither the Humanitarian League nor Mr Timewell could rouse general public compunction with such testimony, or attract special subscriptions enough to enable them to conduct a serious investigation. And John Galsworthy had not then arisen to smite our consciences with such plays as The Silver Box and Justice.

This situation was changed by the agitation for Votes for Women and the subsequent war of 1914–18, both of which threw into prison an unprecedented number of educated, critical, public-spirited, conscientious men and women who under ordinary circumstances would have learnt no more about prisons than larks learn about coal mines. They came out of prison unembittered by their personal sufferings: their grievance was the public grievance of the whole prison system and its intense irreligiousness. In prison they had been capable of observing critically what they saw; and out of prison they were able to describe it. The official whitewash of the Prison Commissioners could not impose on them. They and their friends had money enough to take an office and engage a secretarial staff, besides supplying some voluntary educated labor. They formed a committee with Lord Olivier as chairman, which investigated the condition of English prisons and incidentally read some interesting reports of American ones. Eventually they issued their report as a volume entitled English Prisons Today, edited by Stephen Hobhouse and Fenner Brockway, who had both been in prison during the war.

I was a member of that committee; and the essay which follows was written as a preface to the report. But I did not find it possible to keep a thorough sifting of the subject within the limits of the sixth commandment, on which Mr Hobhouse took an uncompromising stand. Fortunately my friends Sidney and Beatrice Webb were just then reinforcing the work of the committee by issuing the volume of their monumental history of English Local Government which deals with prisons. By transferring my preface to their book I was able to secure the intended publicity for it, and to please everybody concerned, myself included.

I give this history of the essay lest it should be taken as a fanciful exercise by a literary man making up the subject out of his own head. I have not made a parade of facts and figures because my business is to change the vindictive attitude towards criminals which has made the facts possible; but I know the facts better, apparently, than the Prison Commissioners, and relevant figures quite as well.

However, the matter did not stop with the issue of Mr and Mrs Webb's Prisons Under Local Government. That work, though read throughout the civilized world by serious students of political science, has a specialized circulation. Fortunately, my preface to it attracted the attention of the Department of Christian Social Service of the National Council of the Protestant Episcopal Church in the United States. That body put it into general circulation in America.

[It now appears among my own works for the first time in the British Isles, 1931.]

G. B. S.

Madeira, January 1925.

THE SPIRIT IN WHICH TO READ THIS ESSAY

Imprisonment as it exists today is a worse crime than any of those committed by its victims; for no single criminal can be as powerful for evil, or as unrestrained in its exercise, as an organized nation. Therefore, if any person is addressing himself to the perusal of this dreadful subject in the spirit of a philanthropist bent on reforming a necessary and beneficent public institution, I beg him to put it down and go about some other business. It is just such reformers who have in the past made the neglect, oppression, corruption, and physical torture of the old common gaol the pretext for transforming it into that diabolical den of torment, mischief, and damnation, the modern model prison.

If, on the contrary, the reader comes as a repentant sinner, let him read on.

THE OBSTACLE OF VINDICTIVENESS

The difficulty in finding repentant sinners when this crime is in question has two roots. The first is that we are all brought up to believe that we may inflict injuries on anyone against whom we can make out a case of moral inferiority. We have this thrashed into us in our childhood by the infliction on ourselves of such injuries by our parents and teachers, or indeed by any elder who happens to be in charge of us. The second is that we are all now brought up to believe, not that the king can do no wrong, because kings have been unable to keep up that pretence, but that Society can do no wrong. Now not only does Society commit more frightful crimes than any individual, king or commoner: it legalizes its crimes, and forges certificates of righteousness for them, besides torturing anyone who dares expose their true character. A society like ours, which will, without remorse, ruin a boy body and soul for life for trying to sell newspapers in a railway station, is not likely to be very tender to people who venture to tell it that its laws would shock the Prince of Darkness himself if he had not been taught from his earliest childhood to respect as well as fear them.

Consequently we have a desperately sophisticated public, as well as a quite frankly vindictive one. Judges spend their lives consigning their fellow-creatures to prison; and when some whisper reaches them that prisons are horribly cruel and destructive places, and that no creature fit to live should be sent there, they only remark calmly that prisons are not meant to be comfortable, which is no doubt the consideration that reconciled Pontius Pilate to the practice of crucifixion.

THE OBSTACLE OF STUPIDITY

Another difficulty is the sort of stupidity that comes from lack of imagination. When I tell people that I have seen with these eyes a man (no less a man than Richard Wagner, by the way) who once met a crowd going to see a soldier broken on the wheel by the crueller of the two legalized methods of carrying out that hideous sentence, they shudder, and are amazed to hear that what they call medieval torture was used in civilized Europe so recently. They forget that the punishment of half-hanging, unmentionably mutilating, beheading, and quartering, was on the British statute book within my own memory. The same people will read of a burglar being sentenced to ten years' penal servitude without turning a hair. They are like Ibsen's Peer Gynt, who was greatly reassured when he was told that the pains of hell are mental: he thought they cannot be so very bad if there is no actual burning brimstone. When such people are terrified by an outburst of robbery with violence, or Sadistically excited by reports of the White Slave traffic, they clamor to have sentences of two years' hard labor supplemented by a flogging, which is a joke by comparison. They will try to lynch a criminal who illtreats a child in some sensationally cruel manner; but on the most trifling provocation they will inflict on the child the prison demoralization and the prison stigma which condemn it for the rest of its life to crime as the only employment open to a prison child. The public conscience would be far more active if the punishment of imprisonment were abolished, and we went back to the rack, the stake, the pillory, and the lash at the cart's tail.

BLOOD SPORTS DISGUISED AS PUNISHMENT ARE LESS CRUEL THAN IMPRISONMENT BUT MORE DEMORALIZING TO THE PUBLIC

The objection to retrogression is not that such punishments are more cruel than imprisonment. They are less cruel, and far less permanently injurious. The decisive objection to them is that they are sports in disguise. The pleasure to the spectators, and not the pain to the criminal, condemns them. People will go to see Titus Oates flogged or Joan of Arc burnt with equal zest as an entertainment. They will pay high prices for a good view. They will reluctantly admit that they must not torture one another as long as certain rules are observed; but they will hail a breach of the rules with delight as an excuse for a bout of cruelty. Yet they can be shamed at last into recognizing that such exhibitions are degrading and demoralizing; that the executioner is a wretch whose hand no decent person cares to take; and that the enjoyment of the spectators is fiendish. We have then to find some form of torment which can give no sensual satisfaction to the tormentor, and which is hidden from public view. That is how imprisonment, being just such a torment, became the normal penalty. The fact that it may be worse for the criminal is not taken into account. The public is seeking its own salvation, not that of the lawbreaker. For him it would be far better to suffer in the public eye; for among the crowd of sightseers there might be a Victor Hugo or a Dickens, able and willing to make the sightseers think of what they are doing and ashamed of it. The prisoner has no such chance. He envies the unfortunate animals in the Zoo, watched daily by thousands of disinterested observers who never try to convert a tiger into a Quaker by solitary confinement, and would set up a resounding agitation in the papers if even the most ferocious maneater were made to suffer what the most docile convict suffers. Not only has the convict no such protection: the secrecy of his prison makes it hard to convince the public that he is suffering at all.

HOW WE ALL BECOME INURED TO IMPRISONMENT

There is another reason for this incredulity. The vast majority of our city populations are inured to imprisonment from their childhood. The school is a prison. The office and the factory are prisons. The home is a prison. To the young who have the misfortune to be what is called well brought up it is sometimes a prison of inhuman severity. The children of John Howard, as far as their liberty was concerned, were treated very much as he insisted criminals should be treated, with the result that his children were morally disabled, like criminals. This imprisonment in the home, the school, the office, and the factory is kept up by browbeating, scolding, bullying, punishing, disbelief of the prisoner's statements and acceptance of those of the official, essentially as in a criminal prison. The freedom given by the adult's right to walk out of his prison is only a freedom to go into another or starve: he can choose the prison where he is best treated: that is all. On the other hand, the imprisoned criminal is free from care as to his board, lodging, and clothing: he pays no taxes, and has no responsibilities. Nobody expects him to work as an unconvicted man

must work if he is to keep his job: nobody expects him to do his work well, or cares twopence whether it is well done or not.

Under such circumstances it is very hard to convince the ordinary citizen that the criminal is not better off than he deserves to be, and indeed on the verge of being positively pampered. Judges, magistrates, and Home Secretaries are so commonly under the same delusion that people who have ascertained the truth about prisons have been driven to declare that the most urgent necessity of the situation is that every judge, magistrate, and Home Secretary should serve a six months' sentence incognito; so that when he is dealing out and enforcing sentences he should at least know what he is doing.

COMPETITION IN EVIL BETWEEN PRISON AND SLUM

When we get down to the poorest and most oppressed of our population we find the conditions of their life so wretched that it would be impossible to conduct a prison humanely without making the lot of the criminal more eligible than that of many free citizens. If the prison does not underbid the slum in human misery, the slum will empty and the prison will fill. This does in fact take place to a small extent at present, because slum life at its worst is so atrocious that its victims, when they are intelligent enough to study alternatives instead of taking their lot blindly, conclude that prison is the most comfortable place to spend the winter in, and qualify themselves accordingly by committing an offence for which they will get six months. But this consideration affects only those people whose condition is not defended by any responsible publicist: the remedy is admittedly not to make the prison worse but the slum better. Unfortunately the admitted claims of the poor on life are pitifully modest. The moment the treatment of the criminal is decent and merciful enough to give him a chance of moral recovery, or, in incorrigible cases, to avoid making bad worse, the official descriptions of his lot become so rosy that a clamor arises against thieves and murderers being better off than honest and kindly men; for the official reports tell us only of the care that is taken of the prisoner and the advantages he enjoys, or can earn by good conduct, never of his sufferings; and the public is not imaginative or thoughtful enough to supply the deficiency.

What sane man, I ask the clamorers, would accept an offer of free board, lodging, clothing, waiters in attendance at a touch of the bell, medical treatment, spiritual advice, scientific ventilation and sanitation, technical instruction, liberal education, and the use of a carefully selected library, with regular exercise daily and sacred music at frequent intervals, even at the very best of the Ritz Hotels, if the conditions were that he should never leave the hotel, never speak, never sing, never laugh, never see a newspaper, and write only one sternly censored letter and have one miserable interview at long intervals through the bars of a cage under the eye of a warder? And when the prison is not the Ritz Hotel, when the lodging, the food, the bed, are all deliberately made so uncomfortable as to be instruments of torture, when the clothes are rags promiscuously worn by all your fellow-prisoners in turn with yourself, when the exercise is that of a turnspit, when the ventilation and sanitation are noisome, when the instruction is a sham, the education a fraud, when the doctor is a bully to whom your ailments are all malingerings, and the chaplain a moral snob with no time for anything but the distribution of unreadable books, when the waiters are bound by penalties not to speak to you except to give you an order or a rebuke, and then to address you as you would not dream of addressing your dog, when the manager holds over your head a continual threat of starvation and confinement in a punishment cell (as if your own cell were not punishment enough), then what man in his senses would voluntarily exchange even the most harassed freedom for such a life, much less wallow luxuriously in it, as the Punch burglar always does on paper the moment anyone suggests the slightest alleviation of the pains of imprisonment?

GIVING THEM HELL

Yet people cannot be brought to see this. They ask, first, what right the convict has to complain when he has brought it on himself by his own misconduct, and second, what he has to complain of. You reply that his grievances are silence, solitude, idleness, waste of time, and irresponsibility. The retort is, "Why call that torture, as if it were boiling oil or red hot irons or something like that? Why, I have taken a cottage in the country for the sake of silence and solitude; and I should be only too glad to get rid of my responsibilities and waste my time in idleness like a real gentleman. A jolly sight too well off, the fellows are. I should give them hell."

Thus imprisonment is at once the most cruel of punishments and the one that those who inflict it without having ever experienced it cannot believe to be cruel. A country gentleman with a big hunting stable will indignantly discharge a groom and refuse him a reference for cruelly thrashing a horse. But it never occurs to him that his stables are horse prisons, and the stall a cell in which it is quite unnatural for the horse to be immured. In my youth I saw the great Italian actress Ristori play Mary Stuart; and nothing in her performance remains more vividly with me than her representation of the relief of Mary at finding herself in the open air after months of imprisonment. When I first saw a stud of hunters turned out to grass, they reminded me so strongly of Ristori that I at once understood that they had been prisoners in their stables, a fact which, obvious as it was, I had not thought of before. And this sort of thoughtlessness, being continuous and unconscious, inflicts more suffering than all the malice and passion in the world. In prison you get one piled on the other: to the cruelty that is intended and contrived, that grudges you even the inevitable relief of sleep, and makes your nights miserable by plank beds and the like, is added the worse cruelty that is not intended as cruelty, and, when its perpetrators can be made conscious of it at all, deludes them by a ghastly semblance of pampered indulgence.

THE THREE OFFICIAL AIMS OF IMPRISONMENT

And now comes a further complication. When people are at last compelled to think about what they are doing to our unfortunate convicts, they think so unsuccessfully and confusedly that they only make matters worse. Take for example the official list of the results aimed at by the Prison Commissioners. First, imprisonment must be "retributory" (the word vindictive is not in official use). Second, it must be deterrent. Third, it must be reformative.

THE RETRIBUTION MUDDLE

Now, if you are to punish a man retributively, you must injure him. If you are to reform him, you must improve him. And men are not improved by injuries. To propose to punish and reform people by the same operation is exactly as if you were to take a man suffering from pneumonia, and attempt to combine punitive and curative treatment. Arguing that a man with pneumonia is a danger to the community, and that he need not catch it if he takes proper care of his health, you resolve that he shall have a severe lesson, both to punish him for his negligence and

pulmonary weakness and to deter others from following his example. You therefore strip him naked, and in that condition stand him all night in the snow. But as you admit the duty of restoring him to health if possible, and discharging him with sound lungs, you engage a doctor to superintend the punishment and administer cough lozenges, made as unpleasant to the taste as possible so as not to pamper the culprit. A Board of Commissioners ordering such treatment would prove thereby that either they were imbeciles or else they were hotly in earnest about punishing the patient and not in the least in earnest about curing him.

When our Prison Commissioners pretend to combine punishment with moral reformation they are in the same dilemma. We are told that the reformation of the criminal is kept constantly in view; yet the destruction of the prisoner's self-respect by systematic humiliation is deliberately ordered and practised; and we learn from a chaplain that he "does not think it is good to give opportunity for the exercise of Christian and social virtues one towards another" among prisoners. The only consolation for such contradictions is their demonstration that, as the tormentors instinctively feel that they must be liars and hypocrites on the subject, their consciences cannot be very easy about the torment. But the contradictions are obvious here only because I put them on the same page. The Prison Commissioners keep them a few pages apart; and the average reader's memory, it seems, is not long enough to span the gap when his personal interests are not at stake.

PLAUSIBILITY OF THE DETERRENCE DELUSION

Deterrence, which is the real object of the courts, has much more to be said for it, because it is neither simply and directly wicked like retribution, nor a false excuse for wickedness like reformation. It is an unquestionable fact that, by making rules and forcing those who break them to suffer so severely that others like them become afraid to break them, discipline can be maintained to a certain extent among creatures without sense enough to understand its necessity, or, if they do understand it, without conscience enough to refrain from violating it. This is the crude basis of all our disciplines: home discipline, school discipline, factory discipline, army and navy discipline, as well as of prison discipline, and of the whole fabric of criminal law. It is imposed not only by cruel rulers, but by unquestionably humane ones: the only difference being that the cruel rulers impose it with alacrity and gloat over its execution, and the humane rulers are driven to it reluctantly by the failure of their appeals to the consciences of people who have no conscience. Thus we find Mahomet, a conspicuously humane and conscientious Arab, keeping his fierce staff in order, not by unusual punishments, but by threats of a hell after death which he invented for the purpose in revolting detail of a kind which suggests that Mahomet had perhaps too much of the woman and the artist in him to know what would frighten a Bedouin most. Wellington, a general so humane that he sacrificed the exercise of a military genius of the first order to his moral horror of war and his freedom from its illusions, nevertheless hanged and flogged his soldiers mercilessly because he had learnt from experience that, as he put it, nothing is worse than impunity. All revolutions have been the work of men who, like Robespierre, were sentimental humanitarians and conscientious objectors to capital punishment and to the severities of military and prison discipline; yet all the revolutions have after a very brief practical experience been driven to Terrorism (the proper name of Deterrence) as ruthless as the Counter-Revolutionary Terror of Sulla, a late

example being that of the Russian revolution of 1917. Whether it is Sulla, Robespierre, Trotsky, or the fighting mate of a sailing ship with a crew of loafers and wastrels, the result is the same: there are people to be dealt with who will not obey the law unless they are afraid to disobey it, and whose disobedience would mean disaster.

CRIME CANNOT BE KILLED BY KINDNESS

It is useless for humanitarians to shirk this hard fact, and proclaim their conviction that all lawbreakers can be reformed by kindness. That may be true in many cases, provided you can find a very gifted practitioner to take the worst ones in hand, with unlimited time and means to treat them. But if these conditions are not available, and a policeman and an executioner who will disable the wrongdoer instantaneously are available, the police remedy is the only practicable one, even for rulers filled with the spirit of the Sermon on the Mount. The late G. V. Foote, President of the English National Secular Society, a strenuous humanitarian, once had to persuade a very intimate friend of his, a much smaller and weaker man, to allow himself to be taken to an asylum for lunatics. It took four hours of humanitarian persuasion to get the patient from the first floor of his house to the cab door. Foote told me that he had not only recognized at once that no asylum attendant, with several patients to attend to, could possibly spend four hours in getting each of them downstairs, but found his temper so intolerably strained by the unnatural tax on his patience that if the breaking point had been reached, as it certainly would have been in the case of a warder or asylum attendant, he would have been far more violent, not to say savage, than if he had resorted to force at once, and finished the job in five minutes.

From resorting to this rational and

L

practically compulsory use of kindly physical coercion to making it so painful that the victim will be afraid to give any trouble next time is a pretty certain step. In prisons the warders have to protect themselves against violence from prisoners, of which there is a constant risk and very well founded dread, as there are always ungovernably savage criminals who have little more power of refraining from furious assaults than some animals, including quite carefully bred dogs and horses, have of refraining from biting and savaging. The official punishment is flogging and putting in irons for months. But the immediate rescue of the assaulted warder has to be effected by the whole body of warders within reach; and whoever supposes that the prisoner suffers nothing more at their hands than the minimum of force necessary to restrain him knows nothing of prison life and less of human nature.

Any criticism of the deterrent theory of our prison system which ignores the existence of ungovernable savages will be discredited by the citation of actual cases. I should be passed over as a sentimentalist if I lost sight of them for a moment. On any other subject I could dispose of the matter by reminding my critics that hard cases make bad law. On this subject I recognize that the hard cases are of such a nature that provision must be made for them. Indeed hard cases may be said to be the whole subject matter of criminal law; for the normal human case is not that of the criminal, but of the law-abiding person on whose collar the grip of the policeman never closes. Only, it does not follow that the hardest cases should dictate the treatment of the relatively soft ones.

THE SEAMY SIDE OF DETERRENCE

Let us now see what are the objections to the Deterrent or Terrorist system.

It necessarily leaves the interests of the victim wholly out of account. It injures and degrades him; destroys the reputation without which he cannot get employment; and when the punishment is imprisonment under our system, atrophies his powers of fending for himself in the world. Now this would not materially hurt anyone but himself if, when he had been duly made an example of, he were killed like a vivisected dog. But he is not killed. He is, at the expiration of his sentence, flung out of the prison into the streets to earn his living in a labor market where nobody will employ an ex-prisoner, betraying himself at every turn by his ignorance of the common news of the months or years he has passed without newspapers, lamed in speech, and terrified at the unaccustomed task of providing food and lodging for himself. There is only one lucrative occupation available for him; and that is crime. He has no compunction as to Society: why should he have any? Society having for its own selfish protection done its worst to him, he has no feeling about it except a desire to get a bit of his own back. He seeks the only company in which he is welcome: the society of criminals; and sooner or later, according to his luck, he finds himself in prison again. The figures of recidivism shew that the exceptions to this routine are so few as to be negligible for the purposes of our argument. The criminal, far from being deterred from crime, is forced into it; and the citizen whom his punishment was meant to protect suffers from his depredations.

OUR PLAGUE OF UNRESTRAINED CRIME

It is, in fact, admitted that the deterrent system does not deter the convicted criminal. Its real efficacy is sought in its deterrent effect on the free citizens who would commit crimes but for their fear of punishment. The Terrorist can point to the wide range of evil-doing which, not being punished by law, is rampant among us;

for though a man can get himself hanged for a momentary lapse of self-control under intolerable provocation by a nagging woman, or into prison for putting the precepts of Christ above the orders of a Competent Military Authority, he can be a quite infernal scoundrel without breaking any penal law. If it be true, as it certainly is, that it is conscience and not the fear of punishment that makes civilized life possible, and that Dr. Johnson's

How small, of all that human hearts endure,
That part that laws or kings can cause or
    cure!

is as applicable to crime as to human activity in general, it is none the less true that commercial civilization presents an appalling spectacle of pillage and parasitism, of corruption in the press and in the pulpit, of lying advertisements which make people buy rank poisons in the belief that they are health restorers, of traps to catch the provision made for the widow and the fatherless and divert it to the pockets of company promoting rogues, of villainous oppression of the poor and cruelty to the defenceless; and it is arguable that most of this could, like burglary and forgery, be kept within bearable bounds if its perpetrators were dealt with as burglars and forgers are dealt with today. It is, let us not forget, equally arguable that if we can afford to leave so much villainy unpunished we can afford to leave all villainy unpunished. Unfortunately, we cannot afford it: our toleration is threatening our civilization. The prosperity that consists in the wicked flourishing like a green bay tree, and the humble and contrite hearts being thoroughly despised, is a commercial delusion. Facts must be looked in the face, rascals told what they are, and all men called on to justify their ways to God and Man up to the point at which the full discharge of their social duties leaves them free to exercise their individual fancies.

Restraint from evil-doing is within the rights as well as within the powers of organized society over its members; and it cannot be denied that the exercise of these powers, as far as it could be made inevitable, would incidentally deter from crime a certain number of people with only marginal consciences or none at all, and that an extension of the penal code would create fresh social conscience by enlarging the list of things which law-abiding people make it a point of honor not to do, besides calling the attention of the community to grave matters in which they have hitherto erred through thoughtlessness.

DETERRENCE A FUNCTION OF CERTAINTY, NOT OF SEVERITY

But there is all the difference in the world between deterrence as an incident of the operation of criminal law, and deterrence as its sole object and justification. In a purely deterrent system, for instance, it matters not a jot who is punished provided somebody is punished and the public persuaded that he is guilty. The effect of hanging or imprisoning the wrong man is as deterrent as hanging or imprisoning the right one. This is the fundamental explanation of the extreme and apparently fiendish reluctance of the Home Office to release a prisoner when, as in the Beck case, the evidence on which he was convicted has become discredited to a point at which no jury would maintain its verdict of guilty. The reluctance is not to confess that an innocent man is being punished, but to proclaim that a guilty man has escaped. For if escape is possible deterrence shrinks almost to nothing. There is no better established rule of criminology than that it is not the severity of punishment that deters, but its certainty. And the flaw in the case of Terrorism is that it is impossible to obtain enough certainty to deter. The police are compelled to confess every year, when they publish their statistics, that against the list of crimes reported to them they can set only a percentage of detections and convictions. And the list of reported crimes can form only a percentage, how large or small it is impossible to say, but probably small, of the crimes actually committed; for it is the greatest mistake to suppose that everyone who is robbed runs to the police: on the contrary, only foolish and ignorant or very angry people do so without very serious consideration and great reluctance. In most cases it costs nothing to let the thief off, and a good deal to prosecute him. The burglar in Heartbreak House, who makes his living by breaking into people's houses, and then blackmailing them by threatening to give himself up to the police and put them to the expense and discomfort of attending his trial and giving evidence after enduring all the worry of the police enquiries, is not a joke; he is a comic dramatization of a process that is going on every day. As to the black sheep of respectable families who blackmail them by offering them the alternative of making good their thefts and frauds, even to the extent of honoring their forged cheques, or having the family name disgraced, ask any experienced family solicitor.

Besides the chances of not being prosecuted, there are the chances of acquittal; but I doubt whether they count for much except with very attractive women. Still, it is worth mentioning that juries will snatch at the flimsiest pretexts for refusing to send people who engage their sympathy to the gallows or to penal servitude, even on evidence of murder or theft which would make short work of a repulsive person.

SOME PERSONAL EXPERIENCES

Take my own experience as probably common enough. Fifty years ago a friend of mine, hearing that a legacy had been left him, lent himself the expected sum out of his employers' cash; concealed the defalcation by falsifying his accounts; and was detected before he could repay. His employers angrily resented the fraud, and had certainly no desire to spare him. But a public exposure of the affair would have involved shock to their clients' sense of security, loss of time and consequently of money, an end to all hope of his ever making good the loss, and the unpleasantness of attendance in court at the trial. All this put any recourse to the police out of the question; and my friend obtained another post after a very brief interval during which he supported himself as a church organist. This, by the way, was a quite desirable conclusion, as he was for all ordinary practical purposes a sufficiently honest man. It would have been pure mischief to make him a criminal; but that is not the present point. He serves here as an illustration of the fact that our criminal law, far from inviting prosecution, attaches serious losses and inconveniences to it.

It may be said that whatever the losses and inconveniences may be, it is a public duty to prosecute. But is it? Is it not a Christian duty not to prosecute? A man stole £500 from me by a trick. He speculated in my character with subtlety and success; and yet he ran risks of detection which no quite sensible man would have ventured on. It was assumed that I would resort to the police. I asked why. The answer was that he should be punished to deter others from similar crimes. I naturally said, "You have been punishing people cruelly for more than a century for this kind of fraud; and the result is that I am robbed of £500. Evidently your deterrence does not deter. What it does do is to torment the swindler for years, and then throw him back upon society, a worse man in every respect, with no other employment open to him except that of fresh swindling. Besides, your elaborate arrangements to deter me from prosecuting are convincing and effective. I could earn £500 by useful work in the time it would take to prosecute this man vindictively and worse than uselessly. So I wish him joy of his booty, and invite him to swindle me again if he can." Now this was not sentimentality. I am not a bit fonder of being swindled than other people; and if society would treat swindlers properly I should denounce them without the slightest remorse, and not grudge a reasonable expenditure of time and energy in the business. But to throw good money after bad in setting to work a wicked and mischievous routine of evil would be to stamp myself as a worse man than the swindler, who earned the money more energetically, and appropriated it no more unjustly, if less legally, than I earn and appropriate my dividends.

I must however warn our thieves that I can promise them no immunity from police pursuit if they rob me. Some time after the operation just recorded, an uninvited guest came to a luncheon party in my house. He (or she) got away with an overcoat and a pocketful of my wife's best table silver. But instead of selecting my overcoat, he took the best overcoat, which was that of one of my guests. My guest was insured against theft; the insurance company had to buy him a new overcoat; and the matter thus passed out of my hands into those of the police. But the result, as far as the thief was concerned, was the same. He was not captured; and he had the social satisfaction of providing employment for others in converting into a strongly fortified obstacle the flimsy gate through which he had effected an entrance, thereby giving my flat the appearance of a private madhouse.

On another occasion a drunken woman obtained admission by presenting an authentic letter from a soft-hearted member of the House of Lords. I had no guests at the moment; and as she, too, wanted an overcoat, she took mine, and actually interviewed me with it most perfunctorily concealed under her jacket. When I called her attention to it she handed it back to me effusively; begged me to shake hands with her; and went her way.

Now these things occur by the dozen every day, in spite of the severity with which they are punished when the thief is dealt with by the police. I daresay all my readers, if not too young to have completed a representative experience, could add two or three similar stories. What do they go to prove? Just that detection is so uncertain that its consequences have no really effective deterrence for the potential offender, whilst the unpleasant and expensive consequences of prosecution, being absolutely certain, have a very strong deterrent effect indeed on the prosecutor. In short, all the hideous cruelty practised by us for the sake of deterrence is wasted: we are damning our souls at great expense and trouble for nothing.

JUDICIAL VENGEANCE AS AN ALTERNATIVE TO LYNCH LAW

Thus we see that of the three official objects of our prison system: vengeance, deterrence, and reformation of the criminal, only one is achieved; and that is the one which is nakedly abominable. But there is a plea for it which must be taken into account, and which brings us to the root of the matter in our own characters. It is said, and it is in a certain degree true, that if the Government does not lawfully organize and regulate popular vengeance, the populace will rise up and execute this vengeance lawlessly for itself. The standard defence of the Inquisition is that without it no heretic's life would have been safe. In Texas today the people are not satisfied with the prospect of knowing that a murderer or ravisher will be electrocuted inside a gaol if a jury can resist the defence put up by his lawyer. They tear him from the hands of the sheriff; pour lamp oil over him; and burn him alive. Now the burning of human beings is not only an expression of outraged public morality: it is also a sport for which a taste can be acquired much more easily and rapidly than a taste for coursing hares, just as a taste for drink can be acquired from brandy and cocktails more easily and rapidly than from beer or sauterne. Lynching mobs begin with negro ravishers and murderers; but they presently go on to any sort of delinquent, provided he is black. Later on, as a white man will burn as amusingly as a black one, and a white woman react to tarring and feathering as thrillingly as a negress, the color line is effaced by what professes to be a rising wave of virtuous indignation, but is in fact an epidemic of Sadism. The defenders of our penal systems take advantage of it to assure us that if they did not torment and ruin a boy guilty of sleeping in the open air, an indignant public would rise and tear that boy limb from limb.

Now the reply to such a plea, from the point of view of civilized law, cannot be too sweeping. The government which cannot restrain a mob from taking the law into its own hands is no government at all. If Landru could go to the guillotine unmolested in France, and his British prototype who drowned all his wives in their baths could be peaceably hanged in England, Texas can protect its criminals by simply bringing its civilization up to the French and British level. But indeed the besetting sin of the mob is a morbid hero worship of great criminals rather than a ferocious abhorrence of them. In any case nobody will have the effrontery to pretend that the number of criminals who excite popular feeling enough to provoke lynching is more than a negligible percentage of the whole. The theory that the problem of crime is only

one of organizing, regulating, and executing the vengeance of the mob will not bear plain statement, much less discussion. It is only the retributive theory over again in its most impudent form.

THE HARD CASES THAT MAKE BAD LAW

Having now disposed of all the official theories as the trash they are, let us return to the facts, and deal with the hard ones first. Everyone who has any extensive experience of domesticated animals, human or other, knows that there are negatively bad specimens who have no consciences, and positively bad ones who are incurably ferocious. The negative ones are often very agreeable and even charming companions; but they beg, borrow, steal, defraud, and seduce almost by reflex action: they cannot resist the most trifling temptation. They are indulged and spared to the extreme limit of endurance; but in the end they have to be deprived of their liberty in some way. The positive ones enjoy no such tolerance. Unless they are physically restrained they break people's bones, knock out their eyes, rupture their organs, or kill them.

Then there are the cruel people, not necessarily unable to control their tempers, nor fraudulent, nor in any other way disqualified for ordinary social activity or liberty, possibly even with conspicuous virtues. But, by a horrible involution, they lust after the spectacle of suffering, mental and physical, as normal men lust after love. Torture is to them a pleasure except when it is inflicted on themselves. In scores of ways, from the habitual utterance of wounding speeches, and the contriving of sly injuries and humiliations for which they cannot be brought to book legally, to thrashing their wives and children or, as bachelors, paying prostitutes of the hardier sort to submit to floggings, they seek the satisfaction of their desire wherever and however they can.

POSSIBILITIES OF THERAPEUTIC TREATMENT

Now in the present state of our knowledge it is folly to talk of reforming these people. By this I do not mean that even now they are all quite incurable. The cases of no conscience are sometimes, like Parsifal's when he shot the swan, cases of unawakened conscience. Violent and quarrelsome people are often only energetic people who are underworked: I have known a man cured of wife-beating by setting him to beat the drum in a village band; and the quarrels that make country life so very unarcadian are picked mostly because the quarrelers have not enough friction in their lives to keep them goodhumored.

Psycho-analysis, too, which is not all quackery and pornography, might conceivably cure a case of Sadism as it might cure any of the phobias. And psychoanalysis is a mere fancy compared to the knowledge we now pretend to concerning the function of our glands and their effect on our character and conduct. In the nineteenth century this knowledge was pursued barbarously by crude vivisectors whose notion of finding out what a gland was for was to cut it violently out and see what would happen to the victim, meanwhile trying to bribe the public to tolerate such horrors by promising to make old debauchees young again. This was rightly felt to be a villainous business; besides, who could suppose that the men who did these things would hesitate to lie about the results when there was plenty of money to be made by representing them as cures for dreaded diseases? But today we are not asked to infer that because something has happened to a violently mutilated dog it must happen also to an unmutilated human being. We can now make authentic pictures of internal organs by means of rays to which flesh is transparent. This makes it possible to take a criminal and say authoritatively that he is a case, not of original sin, but of an inefficient, or excessively efficient, thyroid gland, or pituitary gland, or adrenal gland, as the case may be. This of course does not help the police in dealing with a criminal: they must apprehend and bring him to trial all the same. But if the prison doctor were able to say "Put some iodine in this man's skilly, and his character will change," then the notion of punishing instead of curing him would become ridiculous. Of course the matter is not so simple as that; and all this endocrinism, as it is called, may turn out to be only the latest addition to our already very extensive collection of pseudo-scientific mares' nests; still, we cannot ignore the fact that a considerable case is being made out by eminent physiologists for at least a conjecture that many cases which are now incurable may be disposed of in the not very remote future by inducing the patient to produce more thyroxin or pituitrin or adrenalin or what not, or even administering them to him as thyroxin is at present administered in cases of myxœdema. Yet the reports of the work of our prison medical officers suggest that hardly any of them has ever heard of these discoveries, or regards a convict as anything more interesting scientifically than a malingering rascal.

THE INCORRIGIBLE VILLAINS

It will be seen that I am prepared to go to lengths which still seem fantastic as to the possibility of changing a criminal into an honest man. And I have more faith than most prison chaplains seem to have in the possibilities of religious conversion. But I cannot add too emphatically that the people who imagine that all criminals can be reformed by setting chaplains to preach at them, by giving them pious books and tracts to read, by separating them from their companions in crime and locking them up in solitude to reflect on their sins and repent, are far worse enemies both to the criminal and to Society than those who face the fact that these are merely additional cruelties which make their victims worse, or even than those who frankly use them as a means of "giving them hell." But when this is recognized, and the bigoted reformers with their sermons, their tracts, their horrors of separation, silence, and solitude to avoid contamination, are bundled out of our prisons as nuisances, the problem remains, how are you to deal with your incorrigibles? Here you have a man who supports himself by gaining the confidence and affection of lonely women; seducing them; spending all their money; and then burning them in a stove or drowning them in a bath. He is quite an attractive fellow, with a genuine taste for women and no taste at all for murder, which is only his way of getting rid of them when their money is spent and they are in the way of the next woman. There is no more malice or Sadism about the final operation than there is about tearing up a letter when it is done with, and throwing it into the waste paper basket. You electrocute him or hang him or chop his head off. But presently you have to deal with a man who lives in exactly the same way, but has not executive force or courage enough to commit murder. He only abandons his victims and turns up in a fresh place with a fresh name. He generally marries them, as it is easier to seduce them so.

Alongside him you have a married couple united by a passion for cruelty. They amuse themselves by tying their children to the bedstead; thrashing them with straps; and branding them with red-hot pokers. You also have to deal with a man who on the slightest irritation flings his wife under a dray, or smashes a lighted kerosene lamp into her face. He has been in prison again and again for outbursts of this kind; and always, within a week of his release, or within a few hours of it, he has done it again.

Now you cannot get rid of these nuisances and monsters by simply cataloguing them as subthyroidics and superadrenals or the like. At present you torment them for a fixed period, at the end of which they are set free to resume their operations with a savage grudge against the community which has tormented them. That is stupid. Nothing is gained by punishing people who cannot help themselves, and on whom deterrence is thrown away. Releasing them is like releasing the tigers from the Zoo to find their next meal in the nearest children's playing ground.

THE LETHAL CHAMBER

The most obvious course is to kill them. Some of the popular objections to this may be considered for a moment. Death, it is said, is irrevocable; and after all, they may turn out to be innocent. But really you cannot handle criminals on the assumption that they may be innocent. You are not supposed to handle them at all until you have convinced yourself by an elaborate trial that they are guilty. Besides, imprisonment is as irrevocable as hanging. Each is a method of taking a criminal's life; and when he prefers hanging or suicide to imprisonment for life, as he sometimes does, he says, in effect, that he had rather you took his life all at once, painlessly, than minute by minute in long-drawn-out torture. You can give a prisoner a pardon; but you cannot give him back a moment of his imprisonment. He may accept a reprieve willingly in the hope of a pardon or an escape or a revolution or an earthquake or what not; but as you do not mean him to evade his sentence in any way whatever, it is not for you to take such clutchings at straws into account.

Another argument against the death penalty for anything short of murder is the practical one of the policeman and the householder, who plead that if you hang burglars they will shoot to avoid capture on the ground that they may as well be hanged for a sheep as for a lamb. But this can be disposed of by pointing out, first, that even under existing circumstances the burglar occasionally shoots, and, second, that acquittals, recommendations to mercy, verdicts of manslaughter, successful pleas of insanity and so forth, already make the death penalty so uncertain that even red-handed murderers shoot no oftener than burglars—less often, in fact. This uncertainty would be actually increased if the death sentence were, as it should be, made applicable to other criminals than those convicted of wilful murder, and no longer made compulsory in any case.

THE SACREDNESS OF HUMAN LIFE
FROM THE WARDER'S SIDE

Then comes the plea for the sacredness of human life. The State should not set the example of killing, or of clubbing a rioter with a policeman's baton, or of dropping bombs on a sleeping city, or of doing many things that States nevertheless have to do. But let us take the plea on its own ground, which is, fundamentally, that life is the most precious of all things, and its waste the worst of crimes. We have already seen that imprisonment does not spare the life of the criminal: it takes it and wastes it in the most cruel way. But there are others to be considered beside the criminal and the citizens who fear him so much that they cannot sleep in peace unless he is locked up. There are the people who have to lock him up, and fetch him his food, and watch him. Why are their lives to be wasted? Warders, and especially wardresses, are almost as much tied to the prison by their occupation, and by their pensions, which they dare not

forfeit by seeking other employment, as the criminals are. If I had to choose between a spell under preventive detention among hardened criminals in Camp Hill and one as warder in an ordinary prison, I think I should vote for Camp Hill. Warders suffer in body and mind from their employment; and if it be true, as our examination seems to prove, that they are doing no good to society, but very active harm, their lives are wasted more completely than those of the criminals; for most criminals are discharged after a few weeks or months; but the warder never escapes until he is superannuated, by which time he is an older gaolbird than any Lifer in the cells.

THE PRICE OF LIFE IN COMMUNITIES

How then does the case stand with your incurable pathological case of crime? If you treat the life of the criminal as sacred, you find yourself not only taking his life but sacrificing the lives of innocent men and women to keep him locked up. There is no sort of sense or humanity in such a course. The moment we face it frankly we are driven to the conclusion that the community has a right to put a price on the right to live in it. That price must be sufficient self-control to live without wasting and destroying the lives of others, whether by direct attack like a tiger, parasitic exploitation like a leech, or having to be held in a leash with another person at the end of it. Persons lacking such self-control have been thrust out into the sage-brush to wander there until they die of thirst, a cruel and cowardly way of killing them. The dread of clean and wilful killing often leads to evasions of the commandment "Thou shalt not kill" which are far more cruel than its frank violation. It has never been possible to obey it unreservedly, either with men or with animals; and the attempts to keep the letter of it have led to burying vestal virgins and nuns alive,

L 2

crushing men to death in the press-yard, handing heretics over to the secular arm, and the like, instead of killing them humanely and without any evasion of the heavy responsibility involved. It was a horrible thing to build a vestal virgin into a wall with food and water enough for a day; but to build her into a prison for years as we do, with just enough loathsome food to prevent her from dying, is more than horrible: it is diabolical. If no better alternatives to death can be found than these, then who will not vote for death? If people are fit to live, let them live under decent human conditions. If they are not fit to live, kill them in a decent human way. Is it any wonder that some of us are driven to prescribe the lethal chamber as the solution for the hard cases which are at present made the excuse for dragging all the other cases down to their level, and the only solution that will create a sense of full social responsibility in modern populations?

THE SIXTH COMMANDMENT

The slaughtering of incorrigibly dangerous persons, as distinguished from the punitive execution of murderers who have violated the commandment not to kill, cannot be established summarily by these practical considerations. In spite of their cogency we have not only individuals who are resolutely and uncompromisingly opposed to slaying under any provocation whatever, we have nations who have abolished the death penalty, and regard our grim retention of it as barbarous. Wider than any nation we have the Roman Catholic Church, which insists literally on absolute obedience to the commandment, and condemns as murder even the killing of an unborn child to save the mother's life. In practice this obligation has been evaded so grossly—by the Inquisition, for example, which refused to slay the heretic, but handed him over to the secular arm

with a formal recommendation to mercy, knowing that the secular arm would immediately burn him—that the case of the Church might be cited to illustrate the uselessness of barring the death penalty. But it also illustrates the persistence and antiquity of a point of conscience which still defies the argument from expediency. That point of conscience may be called a superstition because it is as old as the story of Cain and Abel, and because it is difficult to find any rational basis for it. But there is something to be said for it all the same.

Killing is a dangerously cheap way out of a difficulty. "Stone dead hath no fellow" was a handy formula for Cromwell's troops in dealing with the Irish; still, that precedent is not very reassuring. All the social problems of all the countries can be got rid of by extirpating the inhabitants; but to get rid of a problem is not to solve it. Even perfectly rational solutions of our problems must be humane as well if they are to be accepted by good men: otherwise the logic of the inquisitor, the dynamiter, and the vivisectionist would rule the world for ever as it unfortunately does to far too great an extent already. It may also be argued that if society were to forgo its power of slaying, and also its practice of punishment, it would have a stronger incentive to find out how to correct the apparently incorrigible. Although whenever it has renounced its power to slay sane criminals it has substituted a horribly rigorous and indeed virtually lethal imprisonment, this does not apply to homicidal lunatics, the comparatively lenient treatment of whom could obviously be extended to sane murderers. The Oxford Dictionary owes several of its pages to a homicide who was detained at Broadmoor (the English Asylum for Criminal Lunatics) during the pleasure of the Crown. As to the cases which, when not disposed of by the lethal method, involve caging men as tigers are caged, can they not be dealt with by the padded room? Granted that it is questionable whether the public conscience which tolerates such caging is really more sensitive or thoughtful than that which demands the lethal solution, and that at the present time executions, and even floggings, do not harden the authorities and lower the standard of humanity all through our penal system as much as continuing penalties do, yet the reluctance to kill persists. The moment it is pointed out that if we kill incurable criminals we may as well also kill incurable troublesome invalids, people realize with a shock that the urge of horror, hatred, and vengeance is needed to nerve them—or unnerve them—to slay. When I force humane people to face their political powers of life and death apart from punishment as I am doing now, I produce a terrified impression that I want to hang everybody. In vain I protest that I am dealing with a very small class of human monsters, and that as far as crime is concerned our indiscriminate hanging of wilful murderers and traitors slays more in one year than dispassionate lethal treatment would be likely to slay in ten. I am asked at once who is to be trusted with the appalling responsibility of deciding whether a man is to live or die, and what government could be trusted not to kill its enemies under the pretence that they are enemies of society.

GOVERNMENTS MUST PRESUME OR ABDICATE

The reply is obvious. Such responsibilities must be taken, whether we are fit for them or not, if civilized society is to be organized. No unofficial person denies that they are abused: the whole effect of this essay is to shew that they are horribly abused. I can say for my own part as a vehement critic and opponent of all the governments of which I have had any experience that I am the last person to forget that governments use the criminal law to suppress and exterminate their opponents whenever the opposition becomes really acute, and that the more virtuous the revolutionist and the more vicious the government, the more likely it is to kill him, and to do so under pretence of his being one of the dangerous persons for whom the lethal treatment would be reserved. It has been pointed out again and again that it is in the very nature of power to corrupt those to whom it is entrusted, and that to God alone belongs the awful prerogative of dismissing the soul from the body. Tolstoy has exhausted the persuasions of literary art in exhorting us that we resist not evil; and men have suffered abominable persecutions sooner than accept military service with its chief commandment, Thou shalt kill.

All this leaves the problem just where it was. The irresponsible humanitarian citizen may indulge his pity and sympathy to his heart's content, knowing that whenever a criminal passes to his doom there, but for the grace of God, goes he; but those who have to govern find that they must either abdicate, and that promptly, or else take on themselves as best they can many of the attributes of God. They must decide what is good and what evil; they must force men to do certain things and refrain from doing certain other things whether individual consciences approve or not; they must resist evil resolutely and continually, possibly and preferably without malice or revenge, but certainly with the effect of disarming it, preventing it, stamping it out, and creating public opinion against it. In short, they must do all sorts of things which they are manifestly not ideally fit to do, and, let us hope, do with becoming misgiving, but which must be done, all the same, well or ill, somehow and by somebody. If I were to ignore this, everyone who has had any experience of government would throw these pages aside as those of an inexperienced sentimentalist or an Impossibilist Anarchist.

Nevertheless, certain lines have to be drawn limiting the activities of governments, and allowing the individual to be a law unto himself. For instance, we are obliged (if we are wise) to tolerate sedition and blasphemy to a considerable extent because sedition and blasphemy are nothing more than the advocacy of changes in the established forms of government, morals, and religion; and without such changes there can be no social evolution. But as governments are not always wise, it is difficult enough to secure this intellectual anarchy, or as we call it, freedom of speech and conscience; and anyone who proposed to extend it to such actions as are contemplated by the advocates of lethal treatment would be dismissed as insane. No country at peace will tolerate murder, whether it is done on principle or in sin. What is more, no country at war will tolerate a refusal to murder the enemy. Thus, whether the powers of the country are being exercised for good or evil, they never remain in abeyance, and whoever proposes to set to those powers the limit of an absolute obedience to the commandment "Thou shalt not kill," must do so quite arbitrarily. He cannot give any reason that I can discover for saying that it is wickeder to break a man's neck than to cage him for life: he can only say that his instinct places an overwhelming ban on the one and not on the other; and he must depend on the existence of a similar instinct in the community for his success in having legal slaying ruled out.

THE RUTHLESSNESS OF THE PURE HEART

In this he will have little difficulty as long as the slaying is an act of revenge and expiation, as it is at present: that is why capital punishment has been abolished in some countries, and why its abolition is agitated for in the countries which still practise it. But if these sinful elements be discarded, and the slaying is made a matter of pure expediency, the criminal being pitied as sincerely as a mad dog is pitied, the most ardent present advocate of the abolition of capital punishment may not only consent to the slaying as he does in the case of the mad dog, but even demand it to put an end to an unendurable danger and horror. Malice and fear are narrow things, and carry with them a thousand inhibitions and terrors and scruples. A heart and brain purified of them gain an enormous freedom; and this freedom is shewn not only in the many civilized activities that are tabooed in the savage tribe, but also in the ruthlessness with which the civilized man destroys things that the savage prays to and propitiates. The attempt to reform an incurably dangerous criminal may come to be classed with the attempt to propitiate a sacred rattlesnake. The higher civilization does not make still greater sacrifices to the snake: it kills it.

I am driven to conclude, that though, if voluntary custodians can be found for dangerous incorrigibles, as they doubtless can by attaching compensating advantages to their employment, it is quite possible to proceed with slaying absolutely barred, there is not enough likelihood of this renunciation by the State of the powers of life and death to justify me in leaving lethal treatment out of the question. In any case it would be impossible to obtain any clear thinking on the question unless its possibilities were frankly faced and to some extent explored. I have faced them frankly and explored them as far as seems necessary; and at that I must leave it. Nothing that I have to say about the other sorts of criminals will be in the least invalidated if it should be decided that killing is to be ruled out. I think it quite likely that it may be ruled out on sentimental grounds. By the time we have reached solid ground the shock of reintroducing it (though this has been effected and even clamored for in some countries) may be too great to be faced under normal conditions. Also, as far as what we call crime is concerned, the matter is not one of the first importance. I should be surprised if, even in so large a population as ours, it would ever be thought necessary to extirpate one criminal as utterly unmanageable every year; and this means, of course, that if we decide to cage such people, the cage need not be a very large one.

I am not myself writing as an advocate one way or the other. I have to deal with European and American civilization, which, having no longer than a century ago executed people for offences now punished by a few months or even weeks of imprisonment, has advanced to a point at which less than half a dozen crimes are punishable by death: murder, piracy, rape, arson, and (in Scotland) vitriol throwing. The opponents of capital punishment usually believe, naturally enough, that the effect of abandoning the notion of punishment altogether as sinful (which it is) will sweep away the scaffold from these crimes also, and thus make an end of the death penalty. No doubt it will; but I foresee that it will reintroduce the idea of killing dangerous people simply because they are dangerous, without the least desire to punish them, and without specific reference to the actions which have called attention to their dangerousness. That extremity may be met with an absolute veto, or it may not. I cannot foresee which side I should take: a wise man does not ford a stream till he gets to it. But I am so sure that the situation will arise, that I have to deal with it here as impersonally as may be, without committing myself or anyone else one way or the other.

THE SOFT CASES THAT WE TURN INTO HARD ONES

Now let us look at the other end of the scale, where the soft cases are. Here we are confronted with the staggering fact that many of our prisoners have not been convicted of any offence at all. They are awaiting their trial, and are too poor and friendless to find bail; whilst others have been convicted of mere breaches of by-laws of which they were ignorant, and which they could not have guessed by their sense of right and wrong; for many by-laws have no ethical character whatever. For example, a boy sells a newspaper on the premises of a railway company, and thereby infringes a by-law the object of which is to protect the commercial monopoly of the newsagents who have paid the company for the right to have a bookstall on the platform. The boy's brother jostles a passenger who is burdened with hand luggage, and says "Carry your bag, sir?" These perfectly innocent lads are sent to prison, though the warders themselves admit that a sentence of imprisonment is so ruinous to a boy's morals that they would rather see their own sons dead than in prison.

But let us take the guilty. The great majority of them have been convicted of petty frauds compared to which the common practices of the commercial world are serious crimes. Herbert Spencer's essays on the laxity of the morals of trade have called no trader successfully to repentance. It is not too much to say that any contractor in Europe or America who does not secure business by tenders and estimates and specifications for work and materials which he has not the smallest intention of doing or putting in, and who does not resort to bribery to have the work and materials he actually does do and put in passed by anybody whose duty it is to check them, is an exceptional man. The usage is so much a matter of course, and competition has made it so compulsory, that conscience is awakened only when the fraud is carried to some unusual length. I can remember two cases which illustrate what I mean very well. A builder of high commercial standing contracted to put up a public building. When the work began he found that the clerk of the works, whose business it was to check the work on behalf of the purchaser, lived opposite the building site. The contractor immediately protested that this was not part of the bargain, and that his estimate had been obtained on false pretences. The other is the case of the omnibus conductors of London when the alarum punch was invented and introduced. They immediately struck for higher wages, and got them, frankly on the ground that the punch had cut off the percentage they had been accustomed to add to their wages by peculation, and that it should be made up to them.

Both these cases prove that dishonesty does not pay when it becomes general. The contractor might just as well estimate for the work he really does and the material he actually uses; for, after all, since his object is to tempt the purchaser by keeping prices down, he has to give him the benefit of the fraud. If the purchaser finds him out and says, for example, "You estimated for galvanized pipes; and you have put in plain ones," the contractor can reply, "If I had put in galvanized pipes I should have had to charge you more." In the same way, the bus conductors might just as well have struck for an increase of wage as stolen it: the event proved they could have got it. But they thought they could secure employment more easily by asking for a low wage and making it up to their needs surreptitiously. It is one of the grievances of clerks in many businesses that they have to connive at dishonest practices as part of the regular routine of the office; but neither they nor their employers are any the richer, because business always finally settles down to the facts, and is conducted in terms not of the pretence but of the reality.

MOST PRISONERS NO WORSE THAN OURSELVES

We may take it, then, that the thief who is in prison is not necessarily more dishonest than his fellows at large, but mostly only one who, through ignorance or stupidity, steals in a way that is not customary. He snatches a loaf from the baker's counter and is promptly run into gaol. Another man snatches bread from the tables of hundreds of widows and orphans and simple credulous souls who do not know the ways of company promoters; and, as likely as not, he is run into Parliament. You may say that the remedy for this is not to spare the lesser offender but to punish the greater; but there you miss my present point, which is, that as the great majority of prisoners are not a bit more dishonest naturally than thousands of people who are not only at liberty, but highly pampered, it is no use telling me that society will fall into anarchic dissolution if these unlucky prisoners are treated with common humanity. On the contrary, when we see the outrageous extent to which the most shamelessly selfish rogues and rascals can be granted not only impunity but encouragement and magnificent remuneration, we are tempted to ask ourselves have we any right to restrain anyone at all from doing his worst to us. The first prison I ever saw had inscribed on it CEASE TO DO EVIL: LEARN TO DO WELL; but as the inscription was on the outside, the prisoners could not read it. It should have been addressed to the self-righteous free spectator in the street, and should have run ALL HAVE SINNED, AND FALLEN SHORT OF THE GLORY OF GOD.

We must get out of the habit of painting human character in soot and whitewash. It is not true that men can be divided into absolutely honest persons and absolutely dishonest ones. Our honesty varies with the strain put on it: this is proved by the fact that every additional penny of income tax brings in less than the penny preceding. The purchaser of a horse or motor-car has to beware much more carefully than the purchaser of an article worth five shillings. If you take Landru at one extreme, and at the other the prisoner whose crime is sleeping out: that is to say, whose crime is no crime at all, you can place every sane human being, from the monarch to the tramp, somewhere on the scale between them. Not one of them has a blank page in the books of the Recording Angel. From the people who tell white lies about their ages, social positions, and incomes, to those who grind the faces of the poor, or marry whilst suffering from contagious disease, or buy valuable properties from inexperienced owners for a tenth of their value, or sell worthless shares for the whole of a widow's savings, or obtain vast sums on false pretences held forth by lying advertisements, to say nothing of bullying and beating in their homes, and drinking and debauching in their bachelorhood, you could at any moment find dozens of people who have never been imprisoned and never will be, and are yet worse citizens than any but the very worst of our convicts. Much of the difference between the bond and the free is a difference in circumstances only: if a man is not hungry, and his children are ailing only because they are too well fed, nobody can tell whether he would steal a loaf if his children were crying for bread and he himself had not tasted a mouthful for twenty-four hours. Therefore, if you are in an attitude of moral superiority to our convicts: if you are one of the Serve Them Right and Give Them Hell brigade, you may justly be invited, in your own vernacular, either to Come Off It, or else Go Inside and take the measure you are meting out to others no worse than yourself.

GOOD SOLDIERS OFTEN BAD CITIZENS, AND BAD CITIZENS GOOD PRISONERS

The distinction between the people the criminal law need deal with and those it may safely leave at large is not a distinction between depravity and good nature: it is a distinction between people who cannot, as they themselves put it, go straight except in leading strings, and those who can. Incurable criminals make well-behaved soldiers and prisoners. The war of 1914–18 almost emptied our prisons of able-bodied men; and in the leading strings of military discipline these men ceased to be criminals. Some soldiers who were discharged with not only first-rate certificates of their good conduct as soldiers, but with a Victoria Cross "For Valor," were no sooner cast adrift into ordinary civil life than they were presently found in the dock pleading their military services and good character as soldiers in mitigation of sentences of imprisonment for frauds and thefts of the meanest sort. When we consider how completely a soldier is enslaved by military discipline, and how abhorrent military service consequently is to civically capable people, we cannot doubt, even if there were no first-hand testimony on the subject, that many men enlist voluntarily, not because they want to lead a drunken and dissolute life (the reason given by the Iron Duke), or because they are under any of the romantic illusions on which the recruiting sergeant is supposed to practise, but because they know themselves to be unfit for full moral responsibility, and conclude that they had better have their lives ordered for them than face the effort (intolerably difficult for them) of ordering it themselves.

This effort is not made easier by our civilization. A man who treated his children as every laborer treated them as a matter of course a hundred years ago would now be imprisoned for neglecting them and keeping them away from school. The statute book is crammed with offences unknown to our grandfathers and unintelligible to uneducated men; and the list needs startling extension; for, as Mr H. G. Wells has pointed out, its fundamental items date from the Mosaic period, when modern Capitalism, which involves a new morality, was unknown. In more obvious matters we notice how the standard of dress, manners, and lodging which qualifies a man socially for employment as a factory hand or mechanic has risen since the days when no person of any refinement could travel, as everybody now travels, third-class.

REMEDIES IN THE ROUGH

We may now begin to arrange our problem comprehensively. The people who have to be dealt with specially by the Government because for one reason or another they cannot deal satisfactorily with themselves may be roughly divided into three sections. First, the small number of dangerous or incorrigibly mischievous human animals. With them should be associated all hopeless defectives, from the idiot children who lie like stranded jellyfish on asylum floors, and have to be artificially fed, to the worst homicidal maniacs. Second, a body of people who cannot provide for or order their lives for themselves, but who, under discipline and tutelage, with their board and lodging and clothing provided for them, as in the case of soldiers, are normally happy, well-behaved, useful citizens. (There would be several degrees of tutelage through which they might be promoted if they are fit and willing.) Third, all normal persons who have trespassed in some way during one of those lapses of self-discipline which are as common as colds, and who have been unlucky enough to fall into the hands of the police in consequence. These last should never be imprisoned. They should be required to compensate the State for the injury done to the body politic by their misdeeds, and, when possible, to compensate the victims, as well as pay the costs of bringing them to justice. Until they have done this they cannot complain if they find themselves distrained upon; harassed by frequent compulsory appearances in court to excuse themselves; and threatened with consignment to the second class as defectives. It is quite easy to make carelessness and selfishness or petty violence and dishonesty unremunerative and disagreeable, without resorting to imprisonment. In the cases where the offender has fallen into bad habits and bad company, the stupidest course to take is to force him into the worst of all habits and the worst of all company: that is, prison habits and prison company. The proper remedies are good habits and good company. If these are not available, then the offender must be put into the second class, and kept straight under tutelage until he is fit for freedom.

DIFFICULTY OF THE UNDISCIPLINED

The difficulty lies, it will be seen, in devizing a means of dealing with the second class. The first is easy: too easy, in fact. You kill or you cage: that is all. In the third class, summoning and fining and admonishing are easy and not mischievous: you may worry a man considerably by badgering him about his conduct and dunning him for money in a police court occasionally; but you do not permanently disable him morally and physically thereby. It is the offender of the second class, too good to be killed or caged, and not good enough for normal liberty, whose treatment bothers us.

THE INDETERMINATE SENTENCE

Any proposal to place men under compulsory tutelage immediately raises the vexed question of what is called "the indeterminate sentence." The British parliament has never been prevailed on to create a possibility of a criminal being "detained preventively" for life: it has set a limit of ten years to that condition. This is inevitable as long as the tutelage is primarily not a tutelage but a punishment. In England there is a law under which a drunkard, politely called an inebriate, can voluntarily sentence himself to a term of detention for the sake of being restrained from yielding to a temptation which he is unable to resist when left to himself. Under existing circumstances nobody is likely to do that twice, or even once if he has any knowledge of how the unfortunate inebriates are treated. The only system of detention available is the prison system; and the only sort of prisoner the officials have any practice in dealing with is the criminal. Every detained person is therefore put through the dismal routine of punishment in the first place, deterrence in the second place, and reform in the very remote third place. The inebriate volunteer prisoner very soon finds that he is being treated as a criminal, and tries in vain to revoke his renunciation of his liberty.

Otherwise, say the authorities very truly, they would be overwhelmed with volunteers. This reminds us of the Westminster Abbey verger who charged a French gentleman with brawling in church. The magistrate, inquiring what, exactly, the foreigner had done, was told that he had knelt in prayer. "But," said the magistrate, "is not that what a church is for?" The verger was scandalized. "If we allowed that," he said, "we should have people praying all over the place." The Prison Commissioners know that if prisons were made reasonably happy places, and thrown open to volunteers like the army, they might speedily be overcrowded. And this, with its implied threat of an enormous increase of taxa-tion, seems a conclusive objection.

THE ECONOMY ASPECT

But if its effect would be to convert a large mass of more or less dishonest, unproductive or half productive, unsatisfactory, feckless, nervous, anxious, wretched people into good citizens, it is absurd to object to it as costly. It would be unbearably costly, of course, if the life and labor of its subjects were as stupidly wasted as they are in our prisons; but any scheme into which the conditions of our present system are read will stand condemned at once. Whether the labor of the subject be organized by the State, as in Government dockyards, post offices, municipal industries and services and so forth, or by private employers obtaining labor service from the authorities, organized and used productively it must be; and anyone who maintains that such organization and production costs the nation more than wasting the labor power of able-bodied men and women either by imprisonment or by throwing criminals on the streets to prey on society and on themselves, is maintaining a monstrous capitalistic paradox. Obviously it will not cost the nation anything at all: it will enrich it and protect it. The real commercial objection to it is that it would reduce the supply of sweatable labor available for unscrupulous private employers. But so much the better if it does. Sweating may make profits for private persons here and there; but their neighbors have to pay through the nose for these profits in poor rates, police rates, public health rates (mostly disease rates), and all the rest of the gigantic expenditure, all pure waste and mischief, which falls on the rate-payer and taxpayer in his constant struggle with the fruits of the poverty which he is nevertheless invited to maintain for the sake of making two or three of his neighbors unwholesomely and unjustly rich.

It is not altogether desirable that State tutelage should be available without limit for all who may volunteer for it. We can imagine a magistrate's court as a place in which men clamoring to be literally "taken in charge" are opposed by Crown lawyers and court officials determined to prove, if possible, that these importunate volunteers are quite well able to take care of themselves if they choose. Evidence of defective character would be sternly demanded; and if these were manufactured (as in the not uncommon case of a poor woman charging her son with theft to get him taken off her hands and sent to a reformatory) the offender would be ruthlessly consigned to my third division, consisting of offenders who are not to be taken in charge at all, but simply harried and bothered and attached and sold up until they pay the damages of their offences.

But as a matter of experience men do not seek the avowed tutelage of conditions which imply deficiency of character. Most of them resent any sort of tutelage unless they are brought up to it and therefore do not feel it as an infringement of their individuality. The army and navy are not overcrowded, though the army has always been the refuge of the sort of imbecile called a ne'er-do-well. Indeed the great obstacle to the realization of the Socialist dream of a perfectly organized and highly prosperous community, without poverty or overwork or idleness, is the intense repugnance of the average man to the degree of public regulation of his life which it would involve. This repugnance is certainly not weaker in England and America than elsewhere. Both Americans and Englishmen are born Anarchists; and, as complete Anarchism is practically impossible, they seek the minimum of public interference with their personal initiative, and overshoot the mark so excessively that it is no exaggeration to say that civilization is perishing of Anarchism. If civilization is to be saved for the first time in history it will have to be by a much greater extension of public regulation and organization than any community has hitherto been willing to submit to. When this extension takes place it will provide the discipline of public service for large masses of the population who now look after themselves very indifferently, and are only nominally free to control their own destinies; and in this way many people of the sort that now finds itself in prison will be kept straight automatically. But in any case there is no danger of a tutelary system being swamped by a rush of volunteers qualifying themselves for it by hurling stones through shop windows or the like.

All this does not mean that we must have indeterminate sentences of tutelage. The mischief of the present system is not that the criminal under preventive detention must be released at the end of ten years, but that if he relapses he is sent to penal servitude instead of being simply and sensibly returned to Camp Hill. What it does mean is that if the tutelage be made humane and profitable, the criminal, far from demanding his discharge, will rather threaten the authorities with a repetition of his crime if they turn him out of doors. The change that is needed is to add to the present power of the detaining authorities to release the prisoner at any time if they consider him fit for self-responsibility, the power of the prisoner to remain if he finds himself more comfortable and safe under tutelage, as voluntary soldiers feel themselves more comfortable in the army, or enclosed nuns in a convent, than cast on the world on his own resources.

WHITHER THE FACTS ARE DRIVING US

So much for the difficulty of the indeterminate sentence, which is quite manageable. Its discussion has led us to the discovery that in spite of the unchristian spirit of our criminal law, and the cruelty of its administration, the mere logic of facts is driving us to humane solutions. Already in England no judge or magistrate is obliged to pass any sentence whatever for a first offence except when dealing with a few extraordinary crimes which have affected our imagination so strongly that we feel bound to mark our abhorrence of them by special rigor not only to those convicted of them, but to those accused of them: for example, persons accused of high treason were formerly not allowed the help of counsel in defending themselves. And when the account of the English system of preventive detention at Camp Hill is studied in connection with the remarkable series of experiments now being made in America, it will be seen that nothing stands between us and humanity and decency but our cruelty, vindictiveness, terror, and thoughtless indifference.

CRIME AS DISEASE

It must not be imagined that any system will reach every anti-social deed that is committed. I have already shewn that most crime goes undetected, unreported, and even unforbidden; and I have suggested that if our system of dealing with crime were one with which any humane and thoughtful person could conscientiously co-operate, if we compensated injured persons for bringing criminals to justice instead of, as at present, making the process expensive and extremely disagreeable and even terrifying to them, and if we revised our penal laws by striking out of their list of criminal acts a few which ought not to be there and adding a good many which ought to be there, we might have a good many more delinquents to deal with than at present unless we concurrently improved the education and condition of the masses sufficiently to do away with the large part of law-breaking which is merely one of the symptoms

of poverty, and would disappear with it. But in any case we should diligently read Samuel Butler's Erewhon, and accustom ourselves to regard crime as pathological, and the criminal as an invalid, curable or incurable. There is, in fact, hardly an argument that can be advanced for the stern suppression of crime by penal methods that does not apply equally to the suppression of disease; and we have already an elaborate sanitary code under which persons neglecting certain precautions against disease are not only prosecuted but in some instances (sometimes quite mistaken ones, as the history of vaccination has proved) persecuted very cruelly. We actually force parents to subject their children to surgical operations, some of which are both dangerous and highly questionable. But we have so far stopped short of making it a punishable offence to be attacked by smallpox or typhus fever, though no legal assumption is more certain than that both diseases can be extinguished by sanitation more completely than crime by education. Yet there would be no greater injustice in such punishment than there is in the imprisonment of any thief; and the sanctimonious speech in which the judge in Erewhon, sentencing a man for phthisis, recapitulated the career of crime which began with an accident in childhood, and ended with pulmonary tuberculosis, was not a whit more ridiculous than the similar speeches made at every session by our own judges. Why a man who is punished for having an inefficient conscience should be privileged to have an inefficient lung is a debatable question. If one is sent to prison and the other to hospital, why make the prison so different from the hospital?

But I make the parallel here because it brings out the significance of the fact that we admit without protest that we have to put up with a good deal of illness in the world, and to treat the sufferers with special indulgence and consideration, instead of turning on them like a herd of buffaloes and goring them to death, as we do in the case of our moral invalids. We even punish people very severely for neglecting their invalids or treating them in such a way as to make them worse instead of better: that is, for doing to them exactly what we should do ourselves if instead of doing wrong in body and losing health they had gone wrong in mind and stolen a handkerchief. There are people in the world so incredibly foolish that they expect their children to be always perfectly truthful and perfectly obedient; but even these idiots do not expect their children to be perfectly well always, nor thrash them if they catch cold. In short, if crime were not punished at all, the world would not come to an end any more than it does now that disease is not punished at all. The real gist of the distinction we make is that the consequences of crime, if unpunished, are pleasant, whereas the consequences of catching a chill are its own punishment; but this will not bear examination. A bad conscience is quite as uncomfortable as a bad cold; and though there are people so hardily constituted in this respect that they can behave very selfishly without turning a hair, so are there people of such hardy physical constitution that they can abuse their bodies with impunity to an extent that would be fatal to ordinary persons. Anyhow, it is not proposed that abnormal subjects should be unrestrained.

On the other hand avoidable illnesses are just like avoidable crimes in respect of being the result of some form of indulgence, positive or negative. For all practical purposes the parallel between the physical and moral invalid holds good; only, we may have to consider the absolute sacredness of the physical invalid's life. I shall not here attempt to prejudge the result of that consideration; but it is clear that if we decide that this sacredness must be maintained at all costs, and that the idiot in Darenth, who lies there having food poured into it so that its heart may continue to beat and its lungs to breathe automatically (for it can do nothing voluntarily), must be preserved from death much more laboriously than Einstein, then we must hold the criminal equally fetish unless we are to keep the whole subject in its present disastrous confusion.

REFORMING OUR CONSCIENCES

The change in the public conscience which is necessary before these considerations can take effect in abolishing our villainous system of dealing with crime will never be induced by sympathy with the criminal or even disgust at the prison. The proportion of the population directly concerned is so small that to the great majority imprisonment is something so unlikely to occur—indeed, so certain statistically never to occur—that they cannot be persuaded to take any interest in the matter. As long as the question is only one of the comfort of the prisoner, nothing will be done, because as long as the principle of punishment is admitted, and the Sermon on the Mount ridiculed as an unpractical outburst of anarchism and sentimentality, the public will always be reassured by learning from the judges (none of whom, by the way, seems to know what really happens to a prisoner after he leaves the dock) that our prisons are admirable institutions, and by the romances of Prison Commissioners like Du Cane and Sir Evelyn Ruggles-Brise, who arrange prisons as children build houses with toy bricks, and finally become so pleased with their arrangements that they describe them in terms which make us wonder that they do not commit serious crimes to qualify themselves for prolonged residence in their pet paradises. I must therefore attack the punitive position at another angle by dealing with its psychological effect on the criminal.

EXPIATION AND MORAL ACCOUNTANCY

No ordinary criminal will agree with me for a moment that punishment is a mistake and a sin. His opinions on that point are precisely those of the policeman who arrests him; and if I were to preach this gospel of mine to the convicts in a prison I should be dismissed as a hopeless crank far more summarily than if I were to interview the Chief Commissioner at Scotland Yard about it.

Punishment is not a simple idea: it is a very complex one. It is not merely some injury that an innocent person inflicts on a guilty one, and that the guilty one evades by every means in his power. It is also a balancing of accounts with the soul. People who feel guilty are apt to inflict it on themselves if nobody will take the job off their hands. Confessions, though less common than they would be if the penalties were not so soul-destroying, are received without surprise. From the criminals' point of view punishment is expiation; and their bitterest complaints of injustice refer, not to their sentences, but to the dishonesty with which society, having exacted the price of the crime, still treats the criminal as a defaulter. Even so sophisticated a man of the world as Oscar Wilde claimed that by his two years' imprisonment he had settled accounts with the world and was entitled to begin again with a clean slate. But the world persisted in ostracizing him as if it had not punished him at all.

This was inevitable; but it was dishonest. If we are absurd enough to engage in a retributive trade in crime, we should at least trade fairly and give clean receipts when we are paid. If we did, we should soon find that the trade is impracticable and ridiculous; for neither party can deliver the goods. No discharge that the authorities can give can procure the ex-prisoner an eligible situation; and no atonement that a thief or murderer can make in suffering can make him any the less a thief or murderer. And nobody shirks this demonstration as much as the thief himself. Human self-respect wants so desperately to have its sins washed away, however purgatorially, that we are willing to go through the most fantastic ceremonies, conjurations, and ordeals to have our scarlet souls made whiter than snow. We naturally prefer to lay our sins on scapegoats or on the Cross, if our neighbors will let us off so easily; but when they will not, then we will cleanse ourselves by suffering a penalty sooner than be worried by our consciences. This is the real foundation of the criminal law in human superstition. This is why, when we refuse to employ a discharged prisoner, he invariably pleads that what he did is paid for, and that we have no right to bring it against him after he has suffered the appointed penalty.

As we cannot admit the plea, we should consider whether we should exact the penalty. I am not arguing that the plea should be admitted: I am arguing that the bargain should never have been made. I am more merciless than the criminal law, because I would destroy the evil-doer's delusion that there can be any forgiveness of sin. What is done cannot be undone; and the man who steals must remain a thief until he becomes another man, no matter what reparation or expiation he may make or suffer. A punishment system means a pardon system: the two go together inseparably. Once admit that if I do something wicked to you we are quits when you do something equally wicked to me and you are bound to admit also that the two blacks make a white. Our criminal system is an organized attempt to produce white by two blacks. Common sense should doggedly refuse to believe that evil can be abolished by duplicating it. But common sense is not so logical; and thus we get the present grotesque spectacle of a judge committing thousands of horrible crimes in order that thousands of criminals may feel that they have balanced their moral accounts.

FAMILIAR FRAUDS OF THE TRADE IN SIN

It is a game at which there is plenty of cheating. The prisoner pleads Not Guilty, and tries his best to get off, or to have as light a sentence as possible. The commercial brigand, fining himself for his plunderings by subscribing to charities, never subscribes as much as he stole. But through all the folly and absurdity of the business, and the dense mental confusion caused by the fact that it is never frankly faced and clearly stated, there shines the fact that conscience is part of the equipment of the normal man, and that it never fails in its work. It is retributive because it makes him uncomfortable; it is deterrent because detection and retribution are absolutely certain; and it is reformative because reformation is the only way of escape. That is to say, it does to perfection by divine methods what the Prison Commissioners are trying to do by diabolical methods without hope or even possibility of success.

REVENGE THE DESTROYER OF CONSCIENCE

The effect of revenge, or retribution from without, is to destroy the conscience of the aggressor instantly. If I stand on the corn of a man in the street, and he winces or cries out, I am all remorse, and overwhelm him with heartfelt apologies. But if he sets about me with his fists, the first blow he lands changes my mind completely; and I bend all my energies on doing intentionally to his eyes and nose and jaw what I did unintentionally to his toes. Vengeance is mine, saith the Lord; and that means that it is not the Lord Chief Justice's. A violent punishing, such as a flogging, carries no sense of expia-

tion with it: whilst its effect lasts, which is fortunately not very long, its victim is in a savage fury in which he would burn down the gaol and roast the warders and the governor and the justices alive in it with intense satisfaction if he could.

Imprisonment, on the other hand, gives the conscience a false satisfaction. The criminal feels that he is working off his crime, though he is doing it involuntarily, and would escape at any moment if he could. He preserves his sense of solvency without ceasing to be a thief, as a gambler preserves it by paying his losses without ceasing to be a gambler.

THE SENTIMENTALITY OF REVENGE

There is a mysterious psychological limit to punishment. We somehow dare not kill a hopelessly diseased or dangerous man by way of punishment for any offence short of murder, though we chloroform a hopelessly diseased or dangerous dog by way of kindness without the least misgiving. Until we have purged our souls of malice, which is pure sentiment, we cannot get rid of sentimentality; and the sentimentality which makes us abominably cruel in one direction makes us foolishly and superstitiously afraid to act sternly in others. Homicidal lunatics say in their asylums "They cannot hang *us*." I could give here, but refrain for obvious reasons, simple instructions by carrying out which any person can commit a murder with the certainty, if detected, of being sent to an asylum instead of to the gallows. They ought to have just the contrary effect; for the case of the homicidal lunatic is the clearest case for judicial killing that exists. It is the killing of the sane murderer that requires consideration: it should never be a matter of course, because there are murders which raise no convincing presumption that those who commit them are exceptionally likely to commit another. But about a chronically homicidal lunatic there should be no hesitation whatever as long as we practise judicial killing at all; and there would not be if we simply considered without malice the question of his fitness to live in society. We spare him because the gallows is a punishment, and we feel that we have no right to punish a lunatic. When we realize that we have no right to punish anybody, the problem of disposing of impossible people will put itself on its proper footing. We shall drop our moral airs; but unless we rule killing out absolutely, persons who give more trouble than they are worth will run the risk of being apologetically, sympathetically, painlessly, but effectually returned to the dust from which they sprung.

MAN IN SOCIETY MUST JUSTIFY HIS EXISTENCE

This would at least create a sense of moral responsibility in our citizens. We are all too apt to take our lives as a matter of course, In a civilized community life is not a matter of course: it can be maintained only on complicated artificial conditions; and whoever enlarges his life by violating these conditions enlarges it at the expense of the lives of others. The extent to which we tolerate such vital embezzlement at present is quite outrageous: we have whole classes of persons who waste, squander, and luxuriate in the hard-earned income of the nation without even a pretence of social service or contribution of any kind; and instead of sternly calling on them to justify their existence or go to the scrap heap, we encourage and honor them, and indeed conduct the whole business of the country as if its object were to produce and pamper them. How can a prison chaplain appeal with any effect to the conscience of a professional criminal who knows quite well that his illegal and impecunious modes of preying on society are no worse morally, and enormously less mischievous materially, than the self-legalized plutocratic modes practised by the chaplain's most honored friends with the chaplain's full approval? The moment we cease asking whether men are good or bad, and ascertain simply whether they are pulling their weight in the social boat, our persistent evildoers may have a very unpleasant surprise. Far from having an easy time under a Government of soft-hearted and soft-headed sentimentalists, cooing that "to understand everything is to pardon everything," they may find themselves disciplined to an extent at present undreamed of by the average man-about-town.

CIVILIZED MAN IS NOT BORN FREE

And here it will occur to some of my readers that a book about imprisonment should be also a book about freedom. Rousseau said that Man is born free. Rousseau was wrong. No government of a civilized State can possibly regard its citizens as born free. On the contrary, it must regard them as born in debt, and as necessarily incurring fresh debt every day they live; and its most pressing duty is to hold them to that debt and see that they pay it. Not until it is paid can any freedom begin for the individual. When he cannot walk a hundred yards without using such a very expensive manufactured article as a street, care must be taken that he produces his share of its cost. When he has paid scot and lot his leisure begins, and with it his liberty. He can then say boldly, "Having given unto Cæsar the things that are Cæsar's I shall now, under no tutelage or compulsion except that of my conscience, give to God the things that are God's." That is the only possible basis for civil liberty; and we are unable to attain it because our governments corruptly shirk the duties of Cæsar; usurp the attributes of God; and make an unholy mess of which this horrible prison system of ours is only one symptom.

OUR NATURE NOT SO BAD AS OUR PRISON SYSTEM

We must, however, be on our guard against ascribing all the villainy of that system to our cruelty and selfish terrors. I have pointed out how the operation of the criminal law is made very uncertain, and therefore loses the deterrence it aims at, by the reluctance of sympathetic people to hand over offenders to the police. Vindictive and frivolous as we are, we are not downright fiends, as we should be if our modern prison system had been deliberately invented and constructed by us all in one piece. It has grown upon us, and grown evilly, having evil roots; but its worst developments have been well meant; for the road to hell is paved with good intentions, not with bad ones. The history of it is too long to be told here in detail; but a word or two of it is needed to save the reader from closing the volume in despair of human nature.

THE HISTORY OF OUR PRISONS

Imprisonment was not originally a punishment any more than chaining up a dog, cruel as that practice is, is a punishment. It was simply a method of detention. The officer responsible for the custody of an offender had to lock or chain him up somewhere to prevent him from running away, and to be able to lay his hand on him on the day of trial or execution. This was regarded as the officer's own affair: the law looked to him for the delivery of the offender, and did not concern itself as to how it was effected. This seems strange nowadays; but I can remember a case of a lunatic on a battleship, who had one man told off to act as his keeper. The lunatic was violent and troublesome, and gave his keeper plenty of severe exercise; but the rest of the crew looked on with the keenest enjoyment of the spectacle, and gave the lunatic the strictest fair play by letting his keeper fight it out with him unaided. And that is what the law did mostly in England until well into the nineteenth century. To this day there is no prison in some of the Virgin Islands. The prisoner is tied by the leg to a tree, and plays cards with the constable who guards him.

The result was that the provision of lock-ups became a private commercial speculation, undertaken and conducted for the sake of what could be made out of it by the speculator. There was no need for these places to be lock-ups: the accused could be chained up or gyved or manacled if no safe prison was available; and when lock-ups came to be provided as a matter of business, the practice of chaining was continued as a matter of tradition, and formed a very simple method of extorting money from prisoners by torture. No food was provided by the State: what the prisoner ate was charged against him as if he were in a hotel; and it often happened that when he was acquitted he was taken back to prison as security for his bill and kept there until he had paid it.

Under these circumstances the prison was only a building into which all classes and sorts of detained persons were thrown indiscriminately. The rich could buy a private room, like Mr Pickwick in the Fleet; but the general herd of poor criminals, old and young, innocent and hardened, virgin and prostitute, mad and sane, clean and verminous, diseased and whole, pigged together in indescribable promiscuity. I repeat: nobody invented this. Nobody intended it. Nobody defended it except the people who made money by it. Nobody else except the prisoners knew about it: they were as innocent as Mr Pickwick of what went on inside the prison walls. And, as usual in England, nobody bothered about it, because people with money could avoid its grossest discomforts on the negligibly rare occasions when they fell into the hands of the officers of the law. It was by the mere accident of being pricked for sheriff that John Howard learned what the inside of a gaol was like.

HOWARD'S GOOD INTENTIONS

As a result of Howard's agitation prisons are now State prisons: the State accepts full responsibility for the prisoner from the moment of his arrest. So far, so good. But in the meantime imprisonment, instead of being a means of detention, has become not only a punishment, but, for the reasons given at the outset of this essay, *the* punishment. And official shallowness, prevailing against the poet Crabbe's depth, has made it an infernal punishment. Howard saw that the prisoners in the old gaol contaminated one another; and his remedy was to give them separate cells in which they could meditate on their crimes and repent. When prisons with separate cells were built accordingly, the prison officials soon found that it saved trouble to keep the prisoners locked up in them; and the philanthropists out-Howarded Howard in their efforts to reform criminals by silence, separation, and the wearing of masks, lest they should contaminate one another by the expression of their faces. Until 1920 the convicts in Belgian prisons wore iron masks. Our own convicts wore cloth masks for some time, and would probably be wearing them still had not our solicitude for their salvation killed and driven them mad in such numbers that we were forced to admit that thorough segregation, though no doubt correct in principle (which is just where it is fatally incorrect) does not work. Frightful things in the way of solitude, separation, and silence, not for months, but for many years at a time, were done in American prisons.

The reader will find as much as he can stand in English Prisons Under Local Government, by Sidney and Beatrice Webb, and a good deal more in English Prisons Today, edited by Stephen Hobhouse and Fenner Brockway, in which the system is described from the prison cells, not by common criminals, but by educated and thoughtful men and women who, as agitators for Votes for Women or as Conscientious Objectors to military service, have been condemned to imprisonment of late years. Our horror at their disclosures must not blind us to my immediate point, which is that our prison system is a horrible accidental growth and not a deliberate human invention, and that its worst features have been produced with the intention, not of making it worse, but of making it better. Howard is not responsible: he warned us that "absolute solitude is more than human nature can bear without the hazard of distraction and despair." Elizabeth Fry saw nothing but mischief in prison silence and prison solitude. Their followers were fools: that is all.

THE SO-CALLED CRIMINAL TYPE

Perhaps the most far-reaching service done by the Brockway-Hobhouse report is the light it throws on the alleged phenomenon of a Criminal Type. The belief in this has gone through several vicissitudes. At first a criminal was supposed to be a beetle-browed, bulldog-jawed person for whom no treatment could be too bad. This suited the prison authorities, as nothing is so troublesome to them as waves of public sympathy with criminals, founded on imaginative idealizations of them. But the authorities changed their note when a scientific account of the type was put forward by Lombroso and a body of investigators calling themselves psychiatrists. These gentlemen found that criminals had asymmetrical features and other stigmata (an effective word). They contended that the criminals were the victims of these congenital peculiarities, and could not help themselves. As the obvious conclusion was that they were not morally responsible for their actions, and therefore should not be punished for them, the prison authorities saw their occupation threatened, and denied that there was any criminal type, always excepting the beetle-brows and bulldog-jaws which the criminal was assumed to have imposed on his naturally Grecian features by a life of villainy. They were able to point out that everybody has asymmetrical features, and that the alleged stigmata of the Lombrosic criminal are as characteristic of the Church, the Stock Exchange, the Bench, and the Legislature as of Portland and Dartmoor. That settled the matter for the moment. The criminal type was off.

But nobody who has ever visited a prison has any doubt that there is a prison type, and a very marked one at that. And if he is saturated with the teachings of the Natural Selectionists, according to which changes of type are the result of the slow accumulation of minute variations, and therefore cannot be visibly produced in less than, say, a million years, he will conclude, like Lombroso, that the criminal is a natural species, and therefore incorrigible.

HOW TYPES ARE MANUFACTURED

But twentieth century observation has lately been knocking nineteenth century science into a cocked hat by shewing that the types that were said to take a million years to produce can be produced in five. I have in my hand number seventy-four of the privately printed opuscula issued by the Society which calls itself the Set of Odd Volumes. It is entitled The Influence Which Our Surroundings Exert On Us, and is the work of Sir William Arbuthnot Lane, one of our most distinguished surgeons. In it he shews that by keeping a man at work as a deal porter, a coal trimmer, a shoemaker or what not, you can, within a period no longer than that spent in prison by typical criminals, produce a typical deal porter, coal trimmer, and so on, the changes involved being visible grotesque skeletal changes for which Huxley or Owen would have demanded a whole evolutionary epoch. No Bolshevik has yet written so revolutionary a pamphlet as this little record of a recent after-dinner speech.

What it means is that the criminal type is an artificial type, manufactured in prison by the prison system. It means that the type is not one of the accidents of the system, but must be produced by imprisonment no matter how normal the victim is at the beginning, or how anxious the authorities are to keep him so. The simple truth is that the typical criminal is a normal man when he first enters a prison, and develops the type during his imprisonment.

PSYCHIATRISTS AND ENDOCRINISTS

This does not mean that no other types are to be noted in prison. By all means let the endocrinists go on dividing abnormal people, in prison and out, into hyper and sub pituitaries and thyroidics and adrenals. They need not, as the habit of the scientific world is, quarrel furiously with me for remarking that another type can be externally imposed on their pituitaries and thyroidics and adrenals impartially. The fact that a man has an excessive adrenal secretion may be a reason for trying to check it instead of punishing him. It does not alter the fact that if you keep one adrenal in penal servitude and another in the House of Lords for ten years, the one will shew the stigmata of a typical convict, and the other of a typical peer, in addition to the stigmata of adrenalism.

To realize the importance of this, we must recall the discredit into which Lombroso fell when it was pointed out that by his diagnosis everybody was more or less a criminal. I suggest that this was not quite so complete a reductio ad absurdum as it seemed. I have already accounted for the curious insensibility of the public to the misery they are inflicting on their prisoners by the fact that some of the most mischievous and unhappy conditions of prison life are imposed on all respectably brought-up children as a matter of course. It is arguable that what Lombroso took to be criminal stigmata were genuine prison stigmata, and that their prevalence among respectable people who have never been in gaol is due to the prison conditions to which such people are conventionally subjected for the first twenty years of their life.

THE CASE OF QUEEN VICTORIA

I take up another much discussed and most readable modern book: Queen Victoria, by Lytton Strachey. It contains some shocking pages, made bearable by the comedic power of the author, but still ghastly reading. Queen Victoria was very carefully brought up. When she was eighteen they came to her and told her that she was Queen of England. She asked whether she could really do what she liked; and when this was reluctantly admitted by her careful mother, Victoria considered what wonderful and hitherto impossible happiness she could confer on herself by her new powers. And she could think of nothing more delightful than an hour of separate solitary confinement. She had never been alone before, never been unwatched by people whose business it was to see that she behaved herself, and to rebuke her and punish her if she did anything they disapproved of. In short, she had been treated as a dangerous criminal, unfit to be trusted with any initiative or moral responsibility.

It would carry me too far to trace the effects of this monstrous bringing-up on the course of history. The book should be given to every prisoner who finds his solitary confinement every day from half-past four in the afternoon to next morning more than he can bear. He will find that there are worse things than solitude when the only company available is that of the warders and governor. And he will understand why the next thing the queen did was to turn her mother practically out of the house. She was, as he would put it, getting a bit of her own back. Let him then, if he is an intellectually curious prisoner, and has not been long enough in prison to have his intellect atrophied, make a list of the miseries that are common to the lot of our little Queen Victorias out of prison and our thieves and murderers in prison. Confinement, obedience, silence at associated work, continual supervision by hostile guardians reporting every infraction of rule for punishment, regulation of every moment of one's life from outside, compulsory exercise instead of play, systematic extirpation of initiative and responsibility, uncongenial and sometimes impossible tasks, and a normal assumption that every original and undictated action will be a wrong action. This is the lot of the well-brought-up child, whether heiress to a throne or heir to a country rector, like Samuel Butler, who was beaten by his father until he acquired and retained until his death some of the stigmata of a chained dog. The British statesman Mr Winston Churchill, a duke's grandson, tells us in his reminiscences that when he was a child of seven he was sent to an expensive school where the discipline was more ferocious than would be permitted in a Reformatory for young criminals of twice that age.

PREVALENCE OF CRIMINAL CHARACTERISTICS IN POLITE SOCIETY

Butler, a man of exceptionally strong character which reacted violently against his training, would have been what the Prison Commissioners call a bad prisoner, and therefore does not illustrate the normal social effect of the system. Even

Queen Victoria, with all her characteristic prison transitions from tutelage to tyranny, and her inability to understand or tolerate any other conditions, was too energetic, uneducated, and original, not to react vigorously against her circumstances. It is when we look at modern civilization in bulk that we are forced to admit that child training (or rather taming), as we practise it, produces moral imbecility. About a dozen millions of persons, on whose education enormous sums had been spent publicly and privately, went like sheep to the slaughter in 1914–1918; and the survivors are making elaborate arrangements to go again. A glance at the newspapers which cater specially for the classes which go through the respectable routine of preparatory school, public school, and university, will shew that the ideals of those classes, their points of honor, their sense of humor, their boasts, their anticipations of future exploits, are precisely those of criminals. They always are ready (Steady, boys, steady) to fight and to conquer again and again. Ned Kelly, Charles Peace, Dick Turpin and Claude Duval, the Black Prince, Harry the Fifth, Robin Hood, Paul Jones, Clive, Nelson and Captain Kidd, Cortez and Lord Roberts, were not all on the side of the law; but their morality was the same: they all held that pugnacity, the will to conquer, and the sort of courage that makes pugnacity and the will to conquer effective, are virtues so splendid that they sanctify plunder, devastation, and murder in direct proportion to the magnitude of these operations. The relaxations of the operators are love affairs and luxurious banquets. Now pray what else is the romance of the thieves' kitchen and of the surreptitious conversations of the prison exercise ring and associated labor shop? The difference is no more essential than that between whiskey and champagne, between an ounce of shag and a box of Havanas, between a burglary and a bombardment, between a jemmy and a bayonet, between a chloroformed pad and a gas shell, between a Browning pistol bought at a pawnbroker's and a service revolver. Gild the reputable end of it as thickly as we like with the cant of courage, patriotism, national prestige, security, duty, and all the rest of it: smudge the disreputable end with all the vituperation that the utmost transports of virtuous indignation can inspire: such tricks will not induce the divine judgment, by which all mankind must finally stand or fall, to distinguish between the victims of these two bragging predatory insects the criminal and the gentleman.

The gentleman beats the criminal hollow in the magnitude of his operations and the number of people employed in them. For the depredations of the criminal are negligibly small compared to the military holocausts and ravaged areas, the civic slums, the hospitals, the cemeteries crowded with the prematurely dead, and the labor markets in which men and women are exposed for sale for all purposes, honorable and dishonorable. These are the products of criminal ideas imposed on the entire population. The common thief and burglar, miserably sweated by the receiver to whom he has to sell his plunder, steals a few spoons or diamonds at a monstrous risk, and gets less than a tenth of their value from a rascal who runs no risk worth considering; and the poor wretch is content with the trumpery debauch his hard-earned percentage brings him. The gentleman steals a whole country, or a perpetual income for himself and his descendants, and is never satisfied until he has more conquests and more riches to boast of. What is more, the illicit thief does not defend his conduct ethically. He may cry "To hell with the parsons and with honesty and white-livered respectability!" and so forth; but he does so as a defier of God, a public enemy, a Satanic hero. The gentleman really believes that he is a creator of national prestige, a defender of the faith, a pillar of society; and with this conviction to strengthen him he is utterly unscrupulous in his misplaced pride and honor, and plays the wholesaler in evil to the criminal's petty retail enterprises.

THE ROOT OF THE EVIL

And what is at the bottom of it all? Just the belief that virtue is something to be imposed on us from without, like the tricks taught to a performing animal, by the whip. Such manufactured virtue has no ethical value whatever, as appears promptly enough when the whip is removed. All communities must live finally by their ethical values: that is, by their genuine virtues. Living virtuously is an art that can be learnt only by living in full responsibility for our own actions; and as the process is one of trial and error even when seeking the guidance of others' experience, society must, whether it likes it or not, put up with a certain burden of individual error. The man who has never made a mistake will never make anything; and the man who has never done any harm will never do any good. The disastrous people are the indelicate and conceited busybodies who want to reform criminals and mould children's characters by external pressure and abortion. The cowards who refuse to accept the inevitable risks of human society, and would have everybody handcuffed if they could lest they should have their pockets picked or their heads punched, are bad enough; and the flagellomaniacs who are for ever shrieking the exploded falsehood that garotting was put down by flogging, and that all crimes, especially the sexually exciting ones, can be put down by more flogging, are worse; but such obvious cases of phobia and libido soon make themselves ridiculous if they are given a free platform. It is the busybody, the quack, the pseudo God Almighty, the Dr Moreau of Mr H. G. Wells's ghastliest romance, continually lusting to lay hands on living creatures and by reckless violation of their souls and bodies abort them into some monster representing their ideal of a Good Man, or a Model Citizen, or a Perfect Wife and Mother: he is the irreconcilable enemy, the ubiquitous and iniquitous nuisance, and the most difficult to get rid of because he has imposed his moral pretensions on public opinion, and is accepted as just the sort of philanthropist our prisons and criminals should be left to, whereas he (or she) is really the only sort of person who should never be admitted to any part of a prison except the gallows on which so many less mischievous egotists have expired. No one who has not a profound instinctive respect for the right of all living creatures to moral and religious liberty: that is, to liberty of moral and religious experiment on themselves, limited only by their obligations not to become unduly burdensome to others, should be let come within ten miles of a child, a criminal, or any other person in a condition of tutelage. Indelicacy on this point is the most conclusive of social disqualifications. When it is ignorant and short-sighted it produces criminals. When it is worldly-wise and pompous it produces Prison Commissioners.

RECAPITULATION

For the reader's mental convenience, I recapitulate the contentions presented above.

1. Modern imprisonment: that is, imprisonment practised as a punishment as well as a means of detention, is extremely cruel and mischievous, and therefore extremely wicked. The word extremely is used advisedly because the system has been pushed to a degree at which prison mortality and prison insanity forced it back to the point at which it is barely endurable, which point may therefore be

regarded as the practicable extreme.

2. Although public vindictiveness and public dread are largely responsible for this wickedness, some of the most cruel features of the prison system are not understood by the public, and have not been deliberately invented and contrived for the purpose of increasing the prisoner's torment. The worst of these are (a) unsuccessful attempts at reform, (b) successful attempts to make the working of the prison cheaper for the State and easier for the officials, and (c) accidents of the evolution of the old privately owned detention prison into the new punitive State prison.

3. The prison authorities profess three objects: (a) Retribution (a euphemism for vengeance), (b) Deterrence (a euphemism for Terrorism), and (c) Reform of the prisoner. They achieve the first by simple atrocity. They fail in the second through lack of the necessary certainty of detection, prosecution, and conviction; partly because their methods are too cruel and mischievous to secure the co-operation of the public; partly because the prosecutor is put to serious inconvenience and loss of time; partly because most people desire to avoid an unquestionable family disgrace much more than to secure a very questionable justice; and partly because the proportion of avowedly undetected crimes is high enough to hold out reasonable hopes to the criminal that he will never be called to account. The third (Reform) is irreconcilable with the first (Retribution); for the figures of recidivism, and the discovery that the so-called Criminal Type is really a prison type, prove that the retributive process is one of uncompensated deterioration.

4. The cardinal vice of the system is the anti-Christian vice of vengeance, or the intentional duplication of malicious injuries partly in pure spite, partly in compliance with the expiatory superstition that two blacks make a white. The criminal accepts this, but claims that punishment absolves him if the injuries are equivalent, and still more if he has the worse of the bargain, as he almost always has. Consequently, when absolution on his release is necessarily denied him, and he is forced back into crime by the refusal to employ him, he feels that he is entitled to revenge this injustice by becoming an enemy of society. No beneficial reform of our treatment of criminals is possible unless and until this superstition of expiation and this essentially sentimental vice of vengeance are unconditionally eradicated.

5. Society has a right of self-defence, extending to the destruction or restraint of lawbreakers. This right is separable from the right to revenge or punish: it need have no more to do with punishment or revenge than the caging or shooting of a man-eating tiger. It arises from the existence of (A) intolerably mischievous human beings, and (B) persons defective in the self-control needed for free life in modern society, but well behaved and at their ease under tutelage and discipline. Class A can be painlessly killed or permanently restrained. The requisite tutelage and discipline can be provided for Class B without rancor or insult. The rest can be treated not as criminals but as civil defendants, and made to pay for their depredations in the same manner. At present many persons guilty of conduct much viler than that for which poor men are sent to prison suffer nothing worse than civil actions for damages when they do not (unhappily) enjoy complete impunity.

6. The principle to be kept before the minds of all citizens is that as civilized society is a very costly arrangement necessary to their subsistence and security they must justify their enjoyment of it by contributing their share to its cost, and giving no more than their share of trouble, subject to every possible provision by insurance against innocent disability. This is a condition precedent to freedom, and

justifies us in removing cases of incurable noxious disability by simply putting an end to their existence.

7. An unconquerable repugnance to judicial killing having led to the abolition of capital punishment in several countries, and to its reservation for specially dangerous or abhorrent crimes in all the others, it is possible that the right to kill may be renounced by all civilized States. This repugnance may be intensified as we cease to distinguish between sin and infirmity, or, in prison language, between crime and disease, because of our fear of being led to the extirpation of the incurable invalid who is excessively troublesome as well as to that of the incurable criminal.

On the other hand, the opposite temperament, which is not squeamish about making short work of hard cases, and which is revolted by the daily sacrifice of the lives of prison officials, and of relatives and nurses, to incurable criminals and invalids, may be reinforced by the abandonment of ethical pretentiousness, vengeance, malice, and all uncharitableness in the matter, and may become less scrupulous than at present in advocating euthanasia for all incurables.

Whichever party may prevail, punishment as such is likely to disappear, and with it the ear-marking of certain offences as calling for specially deterrent severities. But it does not follow that lethal treatment of extreme cases will be barred. On the contrary, it may be extended from murder to social incompatibility of all sorts. If it be absolutely barred, sufficient restraint must be effected, not as a punishment but as a necessity for public safety. But there will be no excuse for making it more unpleasant than it need be.

8. When detention and restraint are necessary, the criminal's right to contact with all the spiritual influences of his day should be respected, and its exercise encouraged and facilitated. Conversation, access to books and pictures and music, unfettered scientific, philosophic, and religious activity, change of scene and occupation, the free formation of friendships and acquaintances, marriage and parentage: in short, all the normal methods of creation and recreation, must be available for criminals as for other persons, partly because deprivation of these things is severely punitive, and partly because it is destructive to the victim, and produces what we call the criminal type, making a cure impossible. Any specific liberty which the criminal's specific defects lead him to abuse will, no doubt, be taken from him; but if his life is spared his right to live must be accepted in the fullest sense, and not, as at present, merely as a right to breathe and circulate his blood. In short, a criminal should be treated, not as a man who has forfeited all normal rights and liberties by the breaking of a single law, but as one who, through some specific weakness or weaknesses, is incapable of exercising some specific liberty or liberties.

9. The main difficulty in applying this concept of individual freedom to the criminal arises from the fact that the concept itself is as yet unformed. We do not apply it to children, at home or at school, nor to employees, nor to persons of any class or age who are in the power of other persons. Like Queen Victoria, we conceive Man as being either in authority or subject to authority, each person doing only what he is expressly permitted to do, or what the example of the rest of his class encourages him to consider as tacitly permitted. The concept of the evolving free man in an evolving society, making all sorts of experiments in conduct, and therefore doing everything he likes as far as he can unless there are express prohibitions to which he is politically a consenting party, is still unusual, and consequently terrifying, in spite of all the individualist pamphlets of the eighteenth

and nineteenth centuries. It will be found that those who are most scandalized by the liberties I am claiming for the convict would be equally scandalized if I claimed them for their own sons, or even for themselves.

The conclusion is that imprisonment cannot be fully understood by those who do not understand freedom. But it can be understood quite well enough to have it made a much less horrible, wicked, and wasteful thing than it is at present.

POLITICAL

M

XII

THE APPLE CART

1930

The first performances of this play at home and abroad provoked several confident anticipations that it would be published with an elaborate prefatory treatise on Democracy to explain why I, formerly a notorious democrat, have apparently veered round to the opposite quarter and become a devoted Royalist. In Dresden the performance was actually prohibited as a blasphemy against Democracy.

What was all this pother about? I had written a comedy in which a King defeats an attempt by his popularly elected Prime Minister to deprive him of the right to influence public opinion through the Press and the platform: in short, to reduce him to a cipher. The King's reply is that rather than be a cipher he will abandon his throne and take his obviously very rosy chance of becoming a popularly elected Prime Minister himself. To those who believe that our system of votes for everybody produces parliaments which represent the people it should seem that this solution of the difficulty is completely democratic, and that the Prime Minister must at once accept it joyfully as such. He knows better. The change would rally the anti-democratic royalist vote against him, and impose on him a rival in the person of the only public man whose ability he has to fear. The comedic paradox of the situation is that the King wins, not by exercising his royal authority, but by threatening to resign it and go to the democratic poll.

That so many critics who believe themselves to be ardent democrats should take the entirely personal triumph of the hereditary king over the elected minister to be a triumph of autocracy over democracy, and its dramatization an act of political apostasy on the part of the author, convinces me that our professed devotion to political principles is only a mask for our idolatry of eminent persons. The Apple Cart exposes the unreality of both democracy and royalty as our idealists conceive them. Our Liberal democrats believe in a figment called a constitutional monarch, a sort of Punch puppet who cannot move until his Prime Minister's fingers are in his sleeves. They believe in another figment called a responsible minister, who moves only when similarly actuated by the million fingers of the electorate. But the most superficial inspection of any two such figures shews that they are not puppets but living men, and that the supposed control of one by the other and of both by the electorate amounts to no more than a not very deterrent fear of uncertain and under ordinary circumstances quite remote consequences. The nearest thing to a puppet in our political system is a Cabinet minister at the head of a great public office. Unless he possesses a very exceptional share of dominating ability and relevant knowledge he is helpless in the hands of his officials. He must sign whatever documents they present to him, and repeat whatever words they put into his mouth when answering questions in parliament, with a docility which cannot be imposed on a king who works at his job; for the king works continuously whilst his ministers are in office for spells only, the spells being few and brief, and often occurring for the first time to men of advanced age with little or no training for an experience of supreme responsibility. George the Third and Queen Victoria were not, like Queen Elizabeth, the natural superiors of their ministers in political genius and general capacity; but they were for many purposes of State necessarily superior to them in experience, in cunning, in exact knowledge of the limits of their responsibility and consequently of the limits of their irresponsibility: in short, in the authority and practical power that these superiorities produce. Very clever men who have come into contact with monarchs have been so impressed that they have attributed to them extraordinary natural qualifications which they, as now visible to us in historical perspective, clearly did not possess. In conflicts between monarchs and popularly elected ministers the monarchs win every time when personal ability and good sense are at all equally divided.

In The Apple Cart this equality is assumed. It is masked by a strong contrast of character and methods which has led my less considerate critics to complain that I have packed the cards by making the King a wise man and the minister a fool. But that is not at all the relation between the two. Both play with equal skill; and the King wins, not by greater astuteness, but because he has the ace of trumps in his hand and knows when to play it. As the prettier player of the two he has the sympathy of the audience. Not being as pampered and powerful as an operatic prima donna, and depending as he does not on some commercially valuable talent but on his conformity to the popular ideal of dignity and perfect breeding, he has to be trained, and to train himself, to accept good manners as an indispensable condition of his intercourse with his subjects, and to leave to the less highly placed such indulgences as tempers, tantrums, bullyings, sneerings, swearings, kickings: in short, the commoner violences and intemperances of authority.

His ministers have much laxer standards. It is open to them, if it will save their time, to get their own way by making scenes, flying into calculated rages, and substituting vulgar abuse for argument. A clever minister, not having had a royal training, will, if he finds himself involved in a duel with his king, be careful not to choose the weapons at which the king can beat him. Rather will he in cold blood oppose to the king's perfect behavior an intentional misbehavior and apparently childish petulance which he can always drop at the right moment for a demeanor as urbane as that of the king himself, thus employing two sets of weapons to the king's one. This gives him the advantages of his own training as a successful ambitious man who has pushed his way from obscurity to celebrity: a process involving a considerable use of the shorter and more selfish methods of dominating the feebly recalcitrant, the unreasonable, the timid, and the stupid, as well as a sharp sense of the danger of these methods when dealing with persons of strong character in strong positions.

In this light the style of fighting adopted by the antagonists in the scrap between King Magnus and Mr Joseph Proteus is seen to be a plain deduction from their relative positions and antecedents, and not a manufactured contrast between democracy and royalty to the disadvantage of the former. Those who so mistook it are out of date. They still regard democracy as the under dog in the conflict. But to me it is the king who is doomed to be tragically in that position in the future into which the play is projected: in fact, he is visibly at least half in it already; and the theory of constitutional monarchy assumes that he is wholly in it, and has been so since the end of the seventeenth century.

Besides, the conflict is not really between royalty and democracy. It is between both and plutocracy, which, having destroyed the royal power by frank force under democratic pretexts, has bought and swallowed democracy. Money talks: money prints: money broadcasts: money reigns; and kings and labor leaders alike have to register its decrees, and even, by a staggering paradox, to finance its enterprises and guarantee its profits. Democracy is no longer bought: it is bilked. Ministers who are Socialists to the backbone are as helpless in the grip of Breakages Limited as its acknowledged henchmen: from the moment when they attain to what is with unintentional irony called power (meaning the drudgery of carrying on for the plutocrats) they no longer dare even to talk of nationalizing any industry, however socially vital, that has a farthing of profit for plutocracy still left in it, or that can be made to yield a farthing for it by subsidies.

King Magnus's little tactical victory, which bulks so largely in the playhouse, leaves him in a worse plight than his defeated opponent, who can always plead that he is only the instrument of the people's will, whereas the unfortunate monarch, making a desperate bid for dictatorship on the perfectly true plea that democracy has destroyed all other responsibility (has not Mussolini said that there is a vacant throne in every country in Europe waiting for a capable man to fill it?), is compelled to assume full responsibility himself, and face all the reproaches that Mr Proteus can shirk. In his Cabinet there is only one friendly man who has courage, principle, and genuine good manners when he is courteously treated; and that man is an uncompromising republican, his rival for the dictatorship. The splendidly honest and devoted Die-hard lady is too scornfully tactless to help much; but with a little more experience in the art of handling effective men and women as distinguished from the art of handling mass meetings Mr Bill Boanerges might surprise those who, because he makes them laugh, see nothing in him but a caricature.

In short, those critics of mine who have taken The Apple Cart for a story of a struggle between a hero and a roomful of guys have been grossly taken in. It is never safe to take my plays at their suburban face value: it ends in your finding in them only what you bring to them, and so getting nothing for your money.

On the subject of Democracy generally I have nothing to say that can take the problem farther than I have already carried it in my Intelligent Woman's Guide to Socialism and Capitalism. We have to solve two inseparable main problems: the economic problem of how to produce and distribute our subsistence, and the political problem of how to select our rulers and prevent them from abusing their authority in their own interests or those of their class or religion. Our solution of the economic problem is the Capitalist system, which achieves miracles in production, but fails so ludicrously and disastrously to distribute its products rationally, or to produce in the order of social need, that it is always complaining of being paralyzed by its "overproduction" of things of which millions of us stand in desperate want. Our solution of the political problem is Votes for Everybody and Every Authority Elected by Vote, an expedient originally devized to prevent rulers from tyrannizing by the very effectual method of preventing them from doing anything, and thus leaving everything to irresponsible private enterprise. But as private enterprise will do nothing that is not profitable to its little self, and the very existence of civilization now depends on the swift and unhampered public execution of enterprises that supersede private enterprise and are not merely profitable but vitally necessary to the whole community, this purely inhibitive check on tyranny has become a stranglehold on genuine democracy. Its painfully evolved machinery of parliament and Party System and Cabinet is so effective in obstruction that we take thirty years by constitutional methods to do thirty minutes work, and shall presently be forced to clear up thirty years arrears in thirty minutes by unconstitutional ones unless we pass a Reform Bill that will make a complete revolution in our political machinery and procedure. When we see parliaments like ours kicked into the gutter by dictators, both in kingdoms and republics, it is foolish to wait until the dictator dies or collapses, and then do nothing but pick the poor old things up and try to scrape the mud off them: the only sane course is to take the step by which the dictatorship could have been anticipated and averted, and construct a political system for rapid positive work instead of slow nugatory work, made to fit into the twentieth century instead of into the sixteenth.

Until we face this task and accomplish it we shall not be able to produce electorates capable of doing anything by their votes except pave the way to their own destruction. An election at present, considered as a means of selecting the best qualified rulers, is so absurd that if the last dozen parliaments had consisted of the candidates who were at the foot of the poll instead of those who were at the head of it there is no reason to suppose that we should have been a step more or less advanced than we are today. In neither case would the electorate have had any real choice of representatives. If it had, we might have had to struggle with parliaments of Titus Oateses and Lord George Gordons dominating a few generals and artists, with Cabinets made up of the sort of orator who is said to carry away his hearers by his eloquence because, having first ascertained by a few cautious feelers what they are ready to applaud, he gives it to them a dozen times over in an overwhelming crescendo, and is in effect carried away by them. As it is, the voters have no real choice of candidates: they have to take what they can get and make the best of it according to their lights, which is often the worst of it by the light of heaven. By chance rather than by judgment they find themselves represented in parliament by a fortunate proportion of reasonably honest and public spirited persons who happen to be also successful public speakers. The rest are in parliament because they can afford it and have a fancy for it or an interest in it.

Last October (1929) I was asked to address the enormous audience created by the new invention of Wireless Broadcast on a range of political and cultural topics introduced by a previous speaker under the general heading of Points of View. Among the topics was Democracy, presented, as usual, in a completely abstract guise as an infinitely beneficent principle in which we must trust though it slay us. I was determined that this time Votes for Everybody and Every Authority Elected by Vote should not escape by wearing its imposing mask. I delivered myself as follows:

Your Majesties, your Royal Highnesses, your Excellencies, your Graces and Reverences, my Lords, Ladies and Gentlemen, fellow citizens of all degrees: I am going to talk to you about Democracy objectively: that is, as it exists and as we must all reckon with it equally, no matter what our points of view may be. Suppose I were to talk to you not about Democracy, but about the sea, which is in some respects rather like Democracy! We all have our own views of the sea. Some of us hate it and are never well when we are at it or on it. Others love it, and are never so happy as when they are in it or on it or looking at it. Some of us regard it as Britain's natural realm and surest bulwark: others want a Channel Tunnel. But certain facts about the sea are quite independent of our feelings towards it. If I take it for granted that the sea exists, none of you will contradict me. If I say that the sea is sometimes furiously violent and always uncertain, and that those who are most familiar with it trust it least, you will not immediately shriek out that I do not believe in the sea; that I am an enemy of the sea; that I want to abolish the sea; that I am going to make bathing illegal; that I am out to ruin our carrying trade and lay waste all our seaside resorts and scrap the British Navy. If I tell you that you cannot breathe in the sea, you will not take that as a personal insult and ask me indignantly if I consider you inferior to a fish. Well, you must please be equally sensible when I tell you some hard facts about Democracy. When I tell you that it is sometimes furiously violent and always dangerous and treacherous, and that those who are familiar with it as practical statesmen trust it least, you must not at once denounce me as a paid agent of Benito Mussolini, or declare that I have become a Tory Die-hard in my old age, and accuse me of wanting to take away your votes and make an end of parliament, and the franchise, and free speech, and public meeting, and trial by jury. Still less must you rise in your places and give me three rousing cheers as a champion of medieval monarchy and feudalism. I am quite innocent of any such extravagances. All I mean is that whether we are Democrats or Tories, Catholics or Protestants, Communists or Fascists, we are all face to face with a certain force in the world called Democracy; and we must understand the nature of that force whether we want to fight it or to forward it. Our business is not to deny the perils of Democracy, but to provide against them as far as we can, and then consider whether the risks we cannot provide against are worth taking.

Democracy, as you know it, is seldom more than a long word beginning with a capital letter, which we accept reverently or disparage contemptuously without asking any questions. Now we should never accept anything reverently until we have asked it a great many very searching questions, the first two being What are you? and Where do you live? When I put these questions to Democracy the answer I get is "My name is Demos; and I live in the British Empire, the United States of America, and wherever the love of liberty burns in the heart of man. You, my friend Shaw, are a unit of Democracy: your name is also Demos: you are a citizen of a great democratic community: you are a potential constituent of the Parliament of Man, the Federation of the World." At this I usually burst into loud cheers, which do credit to my enthusiastic nature. Tonight, however, I shall do nothing of the sort: I shall say "Dont talk nonsense. My name is not Demos: it is Bernard Shaw. My address is not the British Empire, nor the United States of America, nor wherever the love of liberty burns in the heart of man: it is at such and such a number in such and such a street in London; and it will be time enough to discuss my seat in the Parliament of Man when that celebrated institution comes into existence. I dont believe your name is Demos: nobody's name is Demos; and all I can make of your address is that you have no address, and are just a tramp—if indeed you exist at all."

You will notice that I am too polite to call Demos a windbag or a hot air merchant; but I am going to ask you to begin our study of Democracy by considering it first as a big balloon, filled with gas or hot air, and sent up so that you shall be kept looking up at the sky whilst other people are picking your pockets. When the balloon comes down to earth every five years or so you are invited to get into the basket if you can throw out one of the people who are sitting tightly in it; but as you can afford neither the time nor the money, and there are forty millions of you and hardly room for six hundred in the basket, the balloon goes up again with much the same lot in it and leaves you where you were before. I think you will admit that the balloon as an image of Democracy corresponds to the parliamentary facts.

Now let us examine a more poetic conception of Democracy. Abraham Lincoln is represented as standing amid the carnage of the battlefield of Gettysburg, and declaring that all that slaughter of Americans by Americans occurred in order that Democracy, defined as government *of* the people *for* the people *by* the people, should not perish from the earth. Let us pick this famous peroration to pieces and see what there really is inside it. (By the way, Lincoln did not really declaim it on the field of Gettysburg; and the American Civil War was not fought in defence of any such principle, but, on the contrary, to enable one half of the United States to force the other half to be governed as they did not wish to be governed. But never mind that. I mentioned it only to remind you that it seems impossible for statesmen to make speeches about Democracy, or journalists to report them, without obscuring it in a cloud of humbug).

Now for the three articles of the definition. Number One: Government *of* the people: that, evidently, is necessary: a human community can no more exist without a government than a human being can exist without a co-ordinated control of its breathing and blood circulation. Number Two: Government *for* the people, is most important. Dean Inge put it perfectly for us when he called Democracy a form of society which means equal consideration for all. He added that it is a Christian principle, and that, as a Christian, he believes in it. So do I. That is why I insist on equality of income. Equal consideration for a person with a

hundred a year and one with a hundred thousand is impossible. But Number Three: Government *by* the people, is quite a different matter. All the monarchs, all the tyrants, all the dictators, all the Die-hard Tories are agreed that we must be governed. Democrats like the Dean and myself are agreed that we must be governed with equal consideration for everybody. But we repudiate Number Three on the ground that the people cannot govern. The thing is a physical impossibility. Every citizen cannot be a ruler any more than every boy can be an engine driver or a pirate king. A nation of prime ministers or dictators is as absurd as an army of field marshals. Government by the people is not and never can be a reality: it is only a cry by which demagogues humbug us into voting for them. If you doubt this—if you ask me "Why should not the people make their own laws?" I need only ask you "Why should not the people write their own plays?" They cannot. It is much easier to write a good play than to make a good law. And there are not a hundred men in the world who can write a play good enough to stand daily wear and tear as long as a law must.

Now comes the question, If we cannot govern ourselves, what can we do to save ourselves from being at the mercy of those who *can* govern, and who may quite possibly be thoroughpaced grafters and scoundrels? The primitive answer is that as we are always in a huge majority we can, if rulers oppress us intolerably, burn their houses and tear them to pieces. This is not satisfactory. Decent people never do it until they have quite lost their heads; and when they have lost their heads they are as likely as not to burn the wrong house and tear the wrong man to pieces. When we have what is called a popular movement very few people who take part in it know what it is all about. I once saw a real popular movement in

London. People were running excitedly through the streets. Everyone who saw them doing it immediately joined in the rush. They ran simply because everyone else was doing it. It was most impressive to see thousands of people sweeping along at full speed like that. There could be no doubt that it was literally a popular movement. I ascertained afterwards that it was started by a runaway cow. That cow had an important share in my education as a political philosopher; and I can assure you that if you will study crowds, and lost and terrified animals, and things like that, instead of reading books and newspaper articles, you will learn a great deal about politics from them. Most general elections, for instance, are nothing but stampedes. Our last but one was a conspicuous example of this. The cow was a Russian one.

I think we may take it that neither mob violence nor popular movements can be depended on as checks upon the abuse of power by governments. One might suppose that at least they would act as a last resort when an autocrat goes mad and commits outrageous excesses of tyranny and cruelty. But it is a curious fact that they never do. Take two famous cases: those of Nero and Tsar Paul the First of Russia. If Nero had been an ordinary professional fiddler he would probably have been no worse a man than any member of the wireless orchestra. If Paul had been a lieutenant in a line regiment we should never have heard of him. But when these two poor fellows were invested with absolute powers over their fellow creatures they went mad, and did such appalling things that they had to be killed like mad dogs. Only, it was not the people that rose up and killed them. They were dispatched quite privately by a very select circle of their own bodyguards. For a genuinely democratic execution of unpopular statesmen we must turn to the brothers De Witt, who were torn to pieces by a Dutch mob in the seventeenth century. They were neither tyrants nor autocrats. On the contrary, one of them had been imprisoned and tortured for his resistance to the despotism of William of Orange; and the other had come to meet him as he came out of prison. The mob was on the side of the autocrat. We may take it that the shortest way for a tyrant to get rid of a troublesome champion of liberty is to raise a hue and cry against him as an unpatriotic person, and leave the mob to do the rest after supplying them with a well tipped ringleader. Nowadays this is called direct action by the revolutionary proletariat. Those who put their faith in it soon find that proletariats are never revolutionary, and that their direct action, when it is controlled at all, is usually controlled by police agents.

Democracy, then, cannot be government by the people: it can only be government by consent of the governed. Unfortunately, when democratic statesmen propose to govern us by our own consent, they find that we dont want to be governed at all, and that we regard rates and taxes and rents and death duties as intolerable burdens. What we want to know is how little government we can get along with without being murdered in our beds. That question cannot be answered until we have explained what we mean by getting along. Savages manage to get along. Unruly Arabs and Tartars get along. The only rule in the matter is that the civilized way of getting along is the way of corporate action, not individual action; and corporate action involves more government than individual action.

Thus government, which used to be a comparatively simple affair, today has to manage an enormous development of Socialism and Communism. Our industrial and social life is set in a huge communistic framework of public roadways, streets, bridges, water supplies, power supplies, lighting, tramways, schools,

M 2

dockyards, and public aids and conveniences, employing a prodigious army of police, inspectors, teachers, and officials of all grades in hundreds of departments. We have found by bitter experience that it is impossible to trust factories, workshops, and mines to private management. Only by stern laws enforced by constant inspection have we stopped the monstrous waste of human life and welfare it cost when it was left uncontrolled by the Government. During the war our attempt to leave the munitioning of the army to private enterprise led us to the verge of defeat and caused an appalling slaughter of our soldiers. When the Government took the work out of private hands and had it done in national factories it was at once successful. The private firms were still allowed to do what little they could; but they had to be taught to do it economically, and to keep their accounts properly, by Government officials. Our big capitalist enterprises now run to the Government for help as a lamb runs to its mother. They cannot even make an extension of the Tube railway in London without Government aid. Unassisted private capitalism is breaking down or getting left behind in all directions. If all our Socialism and Communism and the drastic taxation of unearned incomes which finances it were to stop, our private enterprises would drop like shot stags, and we should all be dead in a month. When Mr Baldwin tried to win the last election by declaring that Socialism had been a failure whenever and wherever it had been tried, Socialism went over him like a steam roller and handed his office to a Socialist Prime Minister. Nothing could save us in the war but a great extension of Socialism; and now it is clear enough that only still greater extensions of it can repair the ravages of the war and keep pace with the growing requirements of civilization.

What we have to ask ourselves, then, is not whether we will have Socialism and Communism or not, but whether Democracy can keep pace with the developments of both that are being forced on us by the growth of national and international corporate action.

Now corporate action is impossible without a governing body. It may be the central Government: it may be a municipal corporation, a county council, a district council, or a parish council. It may be the board of directors of a joint stock company, or of a trust made by combining several joint stock companies. Such boards, elected by the votes of the shareholders, are little States within the State, and very powerful ones, too, some of them. If they have not laws and kings, they have by-laws and chairmen. And you and I, the consumers of their services, are more at the mercy of the boards that organize them than we are at the mercy of parliament. Several active politicians who began as Liberals and are now Socialists have said to me that they were converted by seeing that the nation had to choose, not between governmental control of industry and control by separate private individuals kept in order by their competition for our custom, but between governmental control and control by gigantic trusts wielding great power without responsibility, and having no object but to make as much money out of us as possible. Our Government is at this moment having much more trouble with the private corporations on whom we are dependent for our coals and cotton goods than with France or the United States of America. We are in the hands of our corporate bodies, public or private, for the satisfaction of our everyday needs. Their powers are life and death powers. I need not labor this point: we all know it.

But what we do not all realize is that we are equally dependent on corporate action for the satisfaction of our religious needs. Dean Inge tells us that our general elections have become public auctions at which the contending parties bid against one another for our votes by each promising us a larger share than the other of the plunder of the minority. Now that is perfectly true. The contending parties do not as yet venture to put it exactly in those words; but that is what it comes to. And the Dean's profession obliges him to urge his congregation, which is much wider than that of St Paul's (it extends across the Atlantic), always to vote for the party which pledges itself to go farthest in enabling those of us who have great possessions to sell them and give the price to the poor. But we cannot do this as private persons. It must be done by the Government or not at all. Take my own case. I am not a young man with great possessions; but I am an old man paying enough in income tax and surtax to provide doles for some hundreds of unemployed and old age pensioners. I have not the smallest objection to this: on the contrary, I advocated it strongly for years before I had any income worth taxing. But I could not do it if the Government did not arrange it for me. If the Government ceased taxing my superfluous money and redistributing it among people who have no incomes at all, I could do nothing by myself. What could I do? Can you suggest anything? I could send my war bonds to the Chancellor of the Exchequer and invite him to cancel the part of the National Debt that they represent; and he would undoubtedly thank me in the most courteous official terms for my patriotism. But the poor would not get any of it. The other payers of surtax and income tax and death duties would save the interest they now have to pay on it: that is all. I should only have made the rich richer and myself poorer. I could burn all my share certificates and inform the secretaries of the companies that they might write off that much of their capital indebtedness. The result

would be a bigger dividend for the rest of the shareholders, with the poor out in the cold as before. I might sell my war bonds and share certificates for cash, and throw the money into the street to be scrambled for; but it would be snatched up, not by the poorest, but by the best fed and most able-bodied of the scramblers. Besides, if we all tried to sell our bonds and shares— and this is what you have to consider; for Christ's advice was not addressed to me alone but to all who have great possessions —the result would be that their value would fall to nothing, as the Stock Exchange would immediately become a market in which there were all sellers and no buyers. Accordingly, any spare money that the Government leaves me is invested where I can get the highest interest and the best security, as thereby I can make sure that it goes where it is most wanted and gives immediate employment. This is the best I can do without Government interference: indeed any other way of dealing with my spare money would be foolish and demoralizing, but the result is that I become richer and richer, and the poor become relatively poorer and poorer. So you see I cannot even be a Christian except through Government action; and neither can the Dean.

Now let us get down to our problem. We cannot govern ourselves; yet if we entrust the immense powers and revenues which are necessary in an effective modern Government to an absolute monarch or dictator, he goes more or less mad unless he is a quite extraordinary and therefore very seldom obtainable person. Besides, modern government is not a one-man job: it is too big for that. If we resort to a committee or parliament of superior persons, they will set up an oligarchy and abuse their power for their own benefit. Our dilemma is that men in the lump cannot govern themselves; and yet, as William Morris put it, no man is good enough to be another man's master. We need to be governed, and yet to control our governors. But the best governors will not accept any control except that of their own consciences; and, as we who are governed are also apt to abuse any power of control we have, our ignorance, our passions, our private and immediate interests are constantly in conflict with the knowledge, the wisdom, and the public spirit and regard for the future of our best qualified governors.

Still, if we cannot control our governors, can we not at least choose them and change them if they do not suit?

Let me invent a primitive example of democratic choice. It is always best to take imaginary examples: they offend nobody. Imagine then that we are the inhabitants of a village. We have to elect somebody for the office of postman. There are several candidates; but one stands out conspicuously, because he has frequently treated us at the public-house, has subscribed a shilling to our little flower show, has a kind word for the children when he passes, and is a victim of oppression by the squire because his late father was one of our most successful poachers. We elect him triumphantly, and he is duly installed, uniformed, provided with a red bicycle, and given a batch of letters to deliver. As his motive in seeking the post has been pure ambition, he has not thought much beforehand about his duties; and it now occurs to him for the first time that he cannot read. So he hires a boy to come round with him and read the addresses. The boy conceals himself in the lane whilst the postman delivers the letters at the house, takes the Christmas boxes, and gets the whole credit of the transaction. In course of time he dies with a high reputation for efficiency in the discharge of his duties; and we elect another equally illiterate successor on similar grounds. But by this time the boy has grown up and become an institution.

He presents himself to the new postman as an established and indispensable feature of the postal system and finally becomes recognized and paid by the village as such.

Here you have the perfect image of a popularly elected Cabinet Minister and the Civil Service department over which he presides. It may work very well; for our postman, though illiterate, may be a very capable fellow; and the boy who reads the addresses for him may be quite incapable of doing anything more. But this does not always happen. Whether it happens or not, the system is not a democratic reality: it is a democratic illusion. The boy, when he has ability enough to take advantage of the situation, is the master of the man. The person elected to do the work is not really doing it: he is a popular humbug who is merely doing what a permanent official tells him to do. That is how it comes about that we are now governed by a Civil Service which has such enormous power that its regulations are taking the place of the laws of England, though some of them are made for the convenience of the officials without the slightest regard to the convenience or even the rights of the public. And how are our Civil Servants selected? Mostly by an educational test which nobody but an expensively schooled youth can pass, thus making the most powerful and effective part of our government an irresponsible class government.

Now, what control have you or I over the Services? We have votes. I have used mine a few times to see what it is like. Well, it is like this. When the election approaches, two or three persons of whom I know nothing write to me soliciting my vote and enclosing a list of meetings, an election address, and a polling card. One of the addresses reads like an article in The Morning Post, and has a Union Jack on it. Another is like The Daily News or Manchester Guardian. Both might have been compiled from the editorial waste paper baskets of a hundred years ago. A third address, more up-to-date and much better phrased, convinces me that the sender has had it written for him at the headquarters of the Labor Party. A fourth, the most hopelessly out of date of them all, contains scraps of the early English translations of the Communist Manifesto of 1848. I have no guarantee that any of these documents were written by the candidates. They convey nothing whatever to me as to their character or political capacity. The half-tone photographic portraits which adorn the front pages do not even tell me their ages, having been taken twenty years ago. If I go to one of the meetings I find a schoolroom packed with people who find an election meeting cheaper and funnier than a theatre. On the platform sit one or two poor men who have worked hard to keep party politics alive in the constituency. They ought to be the candidates; but they have no more chance of such eminence than they have of possessing a Rolls-Royce car. They move votes of confidence in the candidate, though as the candidate is a stranger to them and to everybody else present nobody can possibly feel any such confidence. They lead the applause for him; they prompt him when questions are asked; and when he is completely floored they jump up and cry "Let me answer that, Mr Chairman!" and then pretend that he has answered it. The old shibboleths are droned over; and nothing has any sense or reality in it except the vituperation of the opposition party, which is received with shouts of relief by the audience. Yet it is nothing but an exhibition of bad manners. If I vote for one of these candidates, and he or she is elected, I am supposed to be enjoying a democratic control of the government—to be exercising government *of* myself, *for* myself, *by* myself. Do you wonder that the Dean cannot believe such nonsense? If I believed it I should not be fit to vote at all. If this is Democracy, who can blame Signor Mussolini for describing it as a putrefying corpse?

The candidates may ask me what more they can do for me but present themselves and answer any questions I may put to them. I quite admit that they can do nothing; but that does not mend matters. What I should like is a real test of their capacity. Shortly before the war a doctor in San Francisco discovered that if a drop of a candidate's blood can be obtained on a piece of blotting paper it is possible to discover within half an hour what is wrong with him physically. What I am waiting for is the discovery of a process by which on delivery of a drop of his blood or a lock of his hair we can ascertain what is right with him mentally. We could then have a graded series of panels of capable persons for all employments, public or private, and not allow any person, however popular, to undertake the employment of governing us unless he or she were on the appropriate panel. At the lower end of the scale there would be a panel of persons qualified to take part in a parish meeting; at the higher end a panel of persons qualified to act as Secretaries of State for Foreign Affairs or Finance Ministers. At present not more than two per thousand of the population would be available for the highest panel. I should then be in no danger of electing a postman and finding that he could neither read nor write. My choice of candidates would be perhaps more restricted than at present; but I do not desire liberty to choose windbags and nincompoops to represent me in parliament; and my power to choose between one qualified candidate and another would give me as much control as is either possible or desirable. The voting and counting would be done by machinery: I should connect my telephone with the proper office; touch a button; and the machinery would do the rest.

Pending such a completion of the American doctor's discovery, how are we to go on? Well, as best we can, with the sort of government that our present system produces. Several reforms are possible without any new discovery. Our present parliament is obsolete: it can no more do the work of a modern State than Julius Cæsar's galley could do the work of an Atlantic liner. We need in these islands two or three additional federal legislatures, working on our municipal committee system instead of our parliamentary party system. We need a central authority to co-ordinate the federal work. Our obsolete little internal frontiers must be obliterated, and our units of local government enlarged to dimensions compatible with the recent prodigious advances in facility of communication and co-operation. Commonwealth affairs and supernational activities through the League of Nations or otherwise will have to be provided for, and Cabinet function to be transformed. All the pseudo-democratic obstructive functions of our political machinery must be ruthlessly scrapped, and the general problem of government approached from a positive viewpoint at which mere anarchic national sovereignty as distinguished from self-government will have no meaning.

I must conclude by warning you that when everything has been done that can be done, civilization will still be dependent on the consciences of the governors and the governed. Our natural dispositions may be good; but we have been badly brought up, and are full of antisocial personal ambitions and prejudices and snobberies. Had we not better teach our children to be better citizens than ourselves? We are not doing that at present. The Russians *are*. That is my last word. Think over it.

So much for my broadcast on Democracy! And now a word about Breakages, Limited. Like all Socialists who know their business I have an exasperated sense of the mischief done by our system of private Capitalism in setting up huge vested interests in destruction, waste, and disease. The armament firms thrive on war; the glaziers gain by broken windows; the operating surgeons depend on cancer for their children's bread; the distillers and brewers build cathedrals to sanctify the profits of drunkenness; and the prosperity of Dives costs the privation of a hundred Lazaruses.

The title Breakages, Limited, was suggested to me by the fate of that remarkable genius, the late Alfred Warwick Gattie, with whom I was personally acquainted. I knew him first as the author of a play. He was a disturbing man, afflicted—or, as it turned out, gifted—with chronic hyperæsthesia, feeling everything violently and expressing his feelings vehemently and on occasion volcanically. I concluded that he was not sufficiently cold-blooded to do much as a playwright; so that when, having lost sight of him for some years, I was told that he had made an invention of first-rate importance, I was incredulous, and concluded that the invention was only a Utopian project. Our friend Henry Murray was so provoked by my attitude that to appease him I consented to investigate the alleged great invention in person on Gattie's promising to behave like a reasonable being during the process, a promise which he redeemed with the greatest dignity, remaining silent whilst an engineer explained his miracles to me, and contenting himself with the reading of a brief statement shewing that the adoption of his plan would release from industry enough men to utterly overwhelm the Central Empires with whom we were then at war.

I approached the investigation very sceptically. Our friend spoke of "the works." I could not believe that Gattie had any works, except in his fervid imagination. He mentioned "the company." That was more credible: anyone may form a company; but that it had any resources seemed to me doubtful. However, I suffered myself to be taken to Battersea; and there, sure enough, I found a workshop, duly labelled as the premises of The New Transport Company, Limited, and spacious enough to accommodate a double railway line with a platform. The affair was unquestionably real, so far. The platform was not provided with a station: its sole equipment was a table with a row of buttons on it for making electrical contacts. Each line of railway had on it a truck with a steel lid. The practical part of the proceedings began by placing an armchair on the lid of one of the trucks and seating me in it. A brimming glass of water was then set at my feet. I could not imagine what I was expected to do with the water or what was going to happen; and there was a suggestion of electrocution about the chair which made me nervous. Gattie then sat down majestically at the table on the platform with his hand hovering over the buttons. Intimating that the miracle would take place when my truck passed the other truck, he asked me to choose whether it should occur at the first passage or later, and to dictate the order in which it should be repeated. I was by that time incapable of choosing; so I said the sooner the better, and the two trucks started. When the other truck had passed mine I found myself magically sitting on it, chair and all, with the glass of water unspilled at my feet.

The rest of the story is a tragi-comedy. When I said to Gattie apologetically (I felt deeply guilty of having underrated him) that I had never known that he was an engineer, and had taken him to be the usual amateur inventor with no professional training, he told me that this was exactly what he was: just like Sir Christo-

pher Wren. He had been concerned in an electric lighting business, and had been revolted by the prodigious number of breakages of glass bulbs involved by the handling of the crates in which they were packed for transport by rail and road. What was needed was a method of transferring the crates from truck to truck, and from truck to road lorry, and from road lorry to warehouse lift without shock, friction, or handling, Gattie, being I suppose, by natural genius an inventor though by mistaken vocation a playwright, solved the mechanical problem without apparent difficulty, and offered his nation the means of effecting an enormous saving of labor and smash. But instead of being received with open arms as a social benefactor he found himself up against Breakages, Limited. The glass blowers whose employment was threatened, the exploiters of the great industry of repairing our railway trucks (every time a goods train is stopped a series of 150 violent collisions is propagated from end to end of the train, as those who live within earshot know to their cost), and the railway porters who dump the crates from truck to platform and then hurl them into other trucks, shattering bulbs, battering cans, and too often rupturing themselves in the process, saw in Gattie an enemy of the human race, a wrecker of homes and a starver of innocent babes. He fought them undauntedly; but they were too strong for him; and in due time his patents expired and he died almost unrecognized, whilst Unknown Soldiers were being canonized throughout the world. So far, The Apple Cart is his only shrine; and as it does not even bear his name, I have written it here pending its tardy appearance in the roll of fame.

I must not leave my readers to assume that Gattie was an easy man to deal with, or that he handled the opposition in a conciliatory manner with due allowance for the inertia of a somewhat unimaginative officialdom which had not, like myself, sat on his trucks, and probably set him down as a Utopian (a species much dreaded in Government departments) and thus missed the real point, which was that he was an inventor. Like many men of genius he could not understand why things obvious to him should not be so at once to other people, and found it easier to believe that they were corrupt than that they could be so stupid. Once, after I had urged him to be more diplomatic, he brought me, with some pride, a letter to the Board of Trade which he considered a masterpiece of tact and good temper. It contained not a word descriptive of his invention; and it began somewhat in this fashion: "Sir, If you are an honest man you cannot deny that among the worst abuses of this corrupt age is the acceptance of city directorships by retired members of the Board of Trade." Clearly it was not easy for the Board of Trade to deal with an inventor who wished to interest them, not in his new machines, but in the desirability of its abolishing itself as infamous.

The last time I saw him he called on me to unfold a new scheme of much greater importance, as he declared, than his trucks. He was very interesting on that occasion. He began by giving me a vivid account of the pirates who used to infest the Thames below London Bridge before the docks were built. He described how the docks had come into existence not as wharves for loading and unloading but as strongholds in which ships and their cargoes could be secure from piracy. They are now, he declared, a waste of fabulously valuable ground; and their work should be done in quite another way. He then produced plans of a pier to be built in the middle of the river, communicating directly by rail and road with the shore and the great main lines. The ships would come alongside the pier; and by a simple system of hoists the contents of their holds would be lifted out and transferred (like myself in the armchair) to railway trucks or motor lorries without being touched by a human hand and therefore without risk of breakage. It was all so masterly, so simple in its complexity, so convincing as to its practicability, and so prodigiously valuable socially, that I, taking it very seriously, proceeded to discuss what could be done to interest the proper people in it.

To my amazement Gattie began to shew unmistakeable signs of disappointment and indignation, "You do not seem to understand me," he said. "I have shewn you all this mechanical stuff merely by way of illustration. What I have come to consult you about is a great melodrama I am going to write, the scene of which will be the Pool of London in the seventeenth century among the pirates!"

What could I or anyone do with a man like that? He was naïvely surprised when I laughed; and he went away only half persuaded that his scheme for turning the docks into building land; expediting the Thames traffic; saving much dangerous and demoralizing casual labor; and transfiguring the underpaid stevedore into a fullfed electrician, was stupendously more important than any ridiculous melodrama. He admitted that there was of course all that in it; but I could see that his heart was in the melodrama.

As it was evident that officialdom, writhing under his insults and shocked by his utter lack of veneration for bigwigs, besides being hampered as all our Government departments are by the vested interests of Breakages, Limited, would do nothing for him, I induced some less embarrassed public persons to take a ride in the trucks and be convinced that they really existed and worked. But here again the parallel between Gattie and his fellow-amateur Sir Chrisopher Wren came in. Wren was not content to redesign and rebuild St Paul's: he wanted to redesign London as well. He was quite right: what we have lost by not letting him do it is incalculable. Similarly, Gattie was not content to improve the luggage arrangements of our railways: he would not listen to you if your mind was not large enough to grasp the immediate necessity for a new central clearing house in Farringdon Market, connected with the existing railways by a system of new tubes. He was of course right; and we have already lost by sticking to our old ways more than the gigantic sum his scheme would have cost. But neither the money nor the enterprise was available just then, with the war on our hands. The Clearing House, like the Thames pier, remains on paper; and Gattie is in his grave. But I still hold that there must have been something great in a man who, having not only imagined them but invented their machinery, could, far from being crushed by their rejection, exclaim "Perish all my mechanical trash if only it provides material for one bad play!"

This little history will explain how it actually did provide material for Breakages, Limited, and for the bitter cry of the Powermistress General. Not until Breakages is itself broken will it cease to have a message for us.

XIII

TOO TRUE TO BE GOOD

1931

MONEY AND HAPPINESS

Somehow my play, Too True To Be Good, has in performance excited an animosity and an enthusiasm which will hardly be accounted for by the printed text. Some of the spectators felt that they had had a divine revelation, and overlooked the fact that the eloquent gentleman through whose extremely active mouth they had received it was the most hopeless sort of scoundrel: that is, one whose scoundrelism consists in the absence of conscience rather than in any positive vices, and is masked by good looks and agreeable manners. The less intellectual journalist critics sulked as they always do when their poverty but not their will consents to their witnessing a play of mine; but over and above the resultant querulousness to which I have long been accustomed I thought I detected an unusual intensity of resentment, as if I had hit them in some new and unbearably sore spot.

Where, then, was the offence that so exceedingly disgruntled these unhappy persons? I think it must have been the main gist and moral of the play, which is not, as usual, that our social system is unjust to the poor, but that it is cruel to the rich. Our revolutionary writers have dwelt on the horrors of poverty. Our conventional and romantic writers have ignored those horrors, dwelling pleasantly on the elegances of an existence free from pecuniary care. The poor have been pitied for miseries which do not, unfortunately, make them unbearably miserable. But who has pitied the idle rich or really believed that they have a worse time of it than those who have to live on ten shillings a day or less, and earn it? My play is a story of three reckless young people who come into possession of, for the moment, unlimited riches, and set out to have a thoroughly good time with all the modern machinery of pleasure to aid them. The result is that they get nothing for their money but a multitude of worries and a maddening dissatisfaction.

THE VAMPIRE AND THE CALF

I doubt whether this state of things is ever intentionally produced. We see a man apparently slaving to place his children in the position of my three adventurers; but on closer investigation we generally find that he does not care twopence for his children, and is wholly wrapped up in the fascinating game of making money. Like other games it is enjoyable only by people with an irresistible and virtually exclusive fancy for it, and enough arithmetical ability and flair for market values to play it well; but with these qualifications the poorest men can make the most astounding fortunes. They accumulate nothing but powers of extracting money every six months from their less acquisitive neighbors; and their children accumulate nothing but obligations to spend it. As between these two processes of bleeding and being bled, bleeding is the better fun. The vampire has a better time than the calf hung up by the heels with its throat cut. The money-getter spends less on his food, clothes, and amusements than his clerks do, and is happy. His wife and sons and daughters, spending fabulous sums on themselves, are no happier than their housemaids, if so happy; for the routine of fashion is virtually as compulsory as the routine of a housemaid, its dressing is as much dictated as her uniform, its snubbings are as humiliating, and its monotony is more tedious because more senseless and useless, not to mention that it must be pleasanter to be tipped than to tip. And, as I surmise, the housemaid's day off or evening off is really off: in those hard earned hours she ceases to be a housemaid and can be herself; but the lady of fashion never has a moment off: she has to be fashionable even in her little leisure, and dies without ever having had any self at all. Here and there you find rich ladies taking up occupations and interests which keep them so busy doing professional or public work that they might as well have five hundred a year as fifty thousand "for all the good it does them" as the poor say in their amazement when they see people who could afford to be fashionable and extravagant working hard and dressing rather plainly. But that requires a personal endowment of tastes and talents quite out of the common run.

I remember a soldier of the old never-do-well type drifting into a little Socialist Society which I happened to be addressing more than fifty years ago. As he had evidently blundered into the wrong shop and was half drunk, some of the comrades began to chaff him, and finally held me up to him as an example of the advantages of teetotalism. With the most complete conviction he denounced me as a hypocrite and a liar, affirming it to be a well-known and inexorable law of nature that no man with money in his pocket could pass a public house without going in for a drink.

THE OLD SOLDIER AND THE PUBLIC HOUSE

I have never forgotten that soldier, because his delusion, in less crude forms, and his conception of happiness, seem to afflict everybody in England more or less. When I say less crude forms I do not mean truer forms; for the soldier, being half drunk, was probably happier than he would have been if quite sober, whereas the plutocrat who has spent a hundred pounds in a day in the search for pleasure is not happier than if he had spent only five shillings. For it must be admitted that a private soldier, outside that surprising centre of culture, the Red Army of Russia, has so little to be happy about when sober that his case is hardly a fair one. But it serves to illustrate the moral of my play, which is, that our capitalistic system, with its golden exceptions of idle richery and its leaden rule of anxious poverty, is as desperate a failure from the point of view of the rich as of the poor. We are all amazed and incredulous, like the soldier, when we hear of the multimillionaire passing the public house without going in and drinking himself silly; and we envy his sons and daughters who do go in and drink themselves silly. The vulgar pub may be in fact a Palace Hotel, and the pints of beer or glasses of whisky an elaborate dinner with many courses and wines culminating in cigars and liqueurs; but the illusion and the results are cognate.

I therefore plead for a science of happiness to cure us of the miserable delusion that we can achieve it by becoming richer than our neighbors. Modern colossal fortunes have demonstrated its vanity. When country parsons were "passing rich with forty pounds a year" there was some excuse for believing that to be rich was to be happy, as the conception of riches did not venture beyond enough to pay for the necessities of a cultivated life. A hundred years ago Samuel Warren wrote a famous novel about a man who became enormously rich. The title of the novel was Ten Thousand a Year; and this, to any resident Irish family in my boyhood, represented an opulence beyond which only Lords Lieutenant and their like could aspire. The scale has changed since then. I have just seen in the papers a picture of the funeral of a shipping magnate whose income, if the capital value of the property left by him be correctly stated, must have been over four thousand pounds a day or a million and a half a year. If happiness is to be measured by riches he must have been fourteen thousand times as happy as the laborer lucky enough to be earning two pounds a week. Those who believe that riches are the reward of virtue are bound to conclude that he was also fourteen thousand times as sober, honest, and industrious, which would lead to the quaint conclusion that if he drank a bottle of wine a day the laborer must have drunk fourteen thousand.

THE UNLOADING MILLIONAIRES

This is so obviously monstrous that it may now be dismissed as an illusion of the poor who know nothing of the lives of the rich. Poverty, when it involves continual privation and anxiety, is, like toothache, so painful that the victim can desire nothing happier than the cessation of the pain. But it takes no very extraordinary supply of money to enable a humble person to say "I want for nothing"; and when that modest point is reached the power of money to produce happiness vanishes, and the trouble which an excess of it brings begins to assert itself, and finally reaches a point at which the multimillionaires are seen frantically unloading on charitable, educational, scientific, religious, and even (though rarely) artistic and political "causes" of all kinds, mostly without stopping to examine whether the causes produce any effects, and if so what effects. And far from suffering a loss of happiness every time they give away a thousand pounds, they find themselves rather in the enviable state of mind of the reveller in The Pilgrim's Progress with his riddle "There was a man, though some did think him mad, the more he gave away the more he had."

DELUSIONS OF POVERTY

The notion that the rich must be happy is complemented by the delusion that the poor must be miserable. Our society is so constituted that most people remain all their lives in the condition in which they were born, and have to depend on their imagination for their notions of what it is like to be in the opposite condition. The upstarts and the downstarts, though we hear a great deal about them either as popular celebrities or criminals, are exceptional. The rich, it is said, do not know how the poor live; but nobody insists on the more mischievous fact that the poor do not know how the rich live. The rich are a minority; and they are not consumed with envy of the poor. But the poor are a huge majority and they are so demoralized by the notion that they would be happy if only they were rich, that they make themselves poorer, if hopefuller, by backing horses and buying sweepstake tickets on the chance of realizing their daydreams of unearned fortunes. Our penny newspapers now depend for their circulation, and consequently for their existence, on the sale of what are virtually lottery coupons. The real opposition to Socialism comes from the fear (well founded) that it would cut off the possibilities of becoming rich beyond those dreams of avarice which our capitalist system encourages. The odds against a poor person becoming a millionaire are of astronomical magnitude; but they are sufficient to establish and maintain the Totalisator as a national institution, and to produce unlimited daydreams of bequests from imaginary long lost uncles in Australia or a lucky ticket in the Calcutta or Irish Sweeps.

TRYING IT FOR AN HOUR

Besides, even quite poor people save up for holidays during which they can be idle and rich, if not for life, at least for an hour, an afternoon, or even a week. And for the poor these moments derive such a charm from the change from the monotony of daily toil and servitude, that the most intolerable hardships and discomforts and fatigues in excursion trains and overcrowded lodgings seem delightful, and leave the reveller with a completely false notion of what a lifetime of such revelry would be.

I maintain that nobody with a sane sense of values can feel that the sole prize which our villainous capitalist system has to offer, the prize of admission to the ranks of the idle rich, can possibly confer either happiness or health or freedom on its winner. No one can convict me of crying sour grapes; for during the last thirty-five years I have been under no compulsion to work, nor had any material privation or social ostracism to fear as a consequence of not working. But, like all the intelligent rich people of my acquaintance, I have worked as hard, ate and drunk no more, and dressed no better than when I had to work or starve. When my pockets were empty I did not buy any of the luxuries in the London shops because I had no money to buy them with. When, later on, I had enough to buy anything that London could tempt me with, the result was the same: I returned home day after day without having made a single purchase. And I am no ascetic: no man alive is freer than I from the fancy that selfmortification will propitiate a spiteful deity or increase my balance in a salvation bank in a world beyond the grave. I would and could live the life of the idle rich if I liked it; and my sole reason for not living it is that I dont like it. I have every opportunity of observing it both in its daily practice and its remoter results; and I know that a year of it would make me more unhappy than anything else of an accepted kind that I can imagine. For, just as the beanfeaster can live like a lord for an afternoon, and the Lancashire factory operative have a gorgeous week at Blackpool when the wakes are on, so I have had my afternoons as an idle rich man, and know only too well what it is like. It makes me feel suicidal.

You may say that I am an exceptional man. So I am, in respect of being able to write plays and books; but as everybody is exceptional in respect of being able to do something that most other people cannot do, there is nothing in that. Where I am really a little exceptional is in respect of my having experienced both poverty and riches, servitude and selfgovernment, and also having for some reason or other (possibly when I was assured in my infancy that some nasty medicine was delicious) made up my mind early in life never to let myself be persuaded that I am enjoying myself gloriously when I am, as a matter of fact, being bored and pestered and plundered and worried and tired. You cannot humbug me on this point: I understand perfectly why Florence Nightingale fled from fashionable society in London to the horrors of the Crimean hospitals rather than behave like a lady, and why my neighbor Mr Apsley Cherry-Garrard, the sole survivor of what he calls with good reason "the worst journey in the world" through the Antarctic winter, was no poor sailorman driven by his need for daily bread to make a hard living before the mast, but a country gentleman opulent enough to choose the best that London society could offer him if he chose. Better the wards of the most terrible of field hospitals than a drawingroom in Mayfair: better the South Pole at its blackest six months winter night and its most murderous extremities of cold than Sunday by the Serpentine in the height of the season.

CONSOLATIONS OF THE LANDED GENTRY

To some extent this misery of riches is a new thing. Anyone who has the run of our country houses, with their great parks and gardens, their staffs of retainers, indoor and outdoor, and the local public work that is always available for the resident landed gentry, will at once challenge the unqualified assertion that the rich, in a lump, are miserable. Clearly they are nothing of the sort, any more than the poor in a lump. But then they are neither idle nor free. A lady with a big house to manage, and the rearing of a family to supervise, has a reasonably busy time of it even without counting her share in the routine of sport and entertainment and occasional travel which to people brought up to it is a necessary and important part of a well ordered life. The landed gentry have enough exercise and occupation and sense of social importance and utility to keep them on very good terms with themselves and their neighbors. If you suddenly asked them whether they really enjoyed their routine and whether they would not rather be Communists in Russia they would be more sincerely scandalized than if you had turned to them in church and asked them whether they really believed every clause in the Apostles' Creed. When one of their ugly ducklings becomes a revolutionist it is not because countryhouse life is idle, but because its activities are uncongenial and because the duckling has tastes or talents which it thwarts, or a faculty for social criticism which discovers that the great country house is not built on the eternal rock but on the sandy shore of an ocean of poverty which may at any moment pass from calm to tempest. On the whole, there is no reason why a territorial lady should not be as happy as her dairymaid, or her husband be as happy as his gamekeeper. The riches of the county families are attached to property; and the only miserable county people are those who will not work at their job.

MISERIES OF THE VAGRANT ROOT-LESS RICH

But the new thing is riches detached from real property: that is, detached from work, from responsibility, from tradition, and from every sort of prescribed routine, even from the routine of going to the village church every Sunday, paying and receiving calls, and having every month set apart for the killing of some particular bird or animal. It means being a tramp without the daily recurrent obligation to beg or steal your dinner and the price of your bed. Instead, you have the daily question " What shall I do? Where shall I go?" and the daily answer "Do what you please: go where you like: it doesnt matter what you do or where you go." In short, the perfect liberty of which slaves dream because they have no experience of its horrors. Of course the answer of outraged Nature is drowned for a time by the luxury merchants shouting "Come and shop, whether you need anything or not. Come to our palace hotels. Come round the world in our liners. Come and wallow in our swimming pools. Come and see our latest model automobile: we have changed the inventor's design for-better-for-worse solely to give you an excuse for buying a new one and selling your old one at scrap iron prices. Come and buy our latest fashions in dress: you cannot possibly be seen in last season's garments." And so on and so forth. But the old questions come home to the rich tourists in the palace hotels and luxury liners just as they do to the tramps on the highroad. They come up when you have the latest car and the latest wardrobe and all the rest of it. The only want that money can satisfy without satiating for more than a few hours is the need for food and drink and sleep. So from one serious meal a day and two very minor ones you go on to three serious meals a day and two minor ones. Then you work another minor one between breakfast and lunch "to sustain you"; and you soon find that you cannot tackle any meal without a cocktail, and that you cannot sleep. That obliges you to resort to the latest soporific drug, guaranteed in the advertisements to have none of the ruinous effects of its equally guaranteed forerunner. Then comes the doctor, with his tonics, which are simply additional cocktails, and his sure knowledge that if he tells you the truth about yourself and refuses to prescribe the tonics and the drugs, his children will starve. If you indulge in such a luxury as a clerical spiritual adviser it is his duty to tell you that what is the matter with you is that you are an idle useless glutton and drunkard and that you are going to hell; but alas! he, like the doctor, cannot afford this, as he may have to ask you for a subscription tomorrow to keep his church going. And that is "Liberty: thou choicest treasure."

This sort of life has been made possible, and indeed inevitable, by what William Cobbett, who had a sturdy sense of vital values, denounced as The Funding System. It was a product of war, which obliged belligerent governments to obtain enormous sums from all and sundry by giving them in exchange the right to live for nothing on the future income of the country until their money was returned: a system now so popular among people with any money to spare that they can be induced to part with it only on condition that the Government promises not to repay it before a certain more or less remote day. When joint stock companies were formed to run big industrial concerns with money raised on the still more tempting terms that the money is never to be repaid, the system became so extensive that the idle upstart rich became a definitely mischievous and miserable class quite different in character from the old feudal rich.

THE REDEMPTION FROM PROPERTY

When I propose the abolition of our capitalistic system to redeem mankind from the double curse of poverty and riches, loud wailings arise. The most articulate sounds in the hubbub are to the effect that the wretched slaves of the curse will lose their liberty if they are forced to earn their living honorably. The retort that they have nothing to lose but their chains, with the addition that the gold chains are as bad as the iron ones, cannot silence them, because they think they are free, and have been brought up to believe that unless the country remains the private property of irresponsible owners maintaining a parliament to make any change impossible, with churches schools and universities to inculcate the sacredness of private property and party government disguised as religion education and democracy, civilization must perish. I am accused of every sort of reactionary extravagance by the people who think themselves advanced, and of every sort of destructive madness by people who thank God they are no wiser than their fathers.

Now I cannot profitably discuss politics religion and economics with terrified ignoramuses who understand neither what they are defending nor what they are attacking. But it happens that Mr Gilbert Chesterton, who is not an ignoramus and not in the least terrified, and whose very interesting conversion to Roman Catholicism has obliged him to face the problem of social organization fundamentally, discarding the Protestant impostures on English history which inspired the vigorous Liberalism of his salad days, has lately taken me to task for the entirely imaginary offence of advocating government by a committee of celebrities. To clear up the matter I have replied to Mr Chesterton very fully and in Catholic terms. Those who have read my reply in the magazines in which it appeared need read no further, unless they wish, as I should advise, to read it twice. For the benefit of the rest, and to put it on permanent record, here it is.

FUNDAMENTAL NATURAL CONDITIONS OF HUMAN SOCIETY

1. Government is necessary wherever two or three are gathered together—or

two or three billions—for keeps.

2. Government is neither automatic nor abstract: it must be performed by human rulers and agents as best they can.

3. The business of the rulers is to check disastrously selfish or unexpected behavior on the part of individuals in social affairs.

4. This business can be done only by devizing and enforcing rules of social conduct codifying the greatest common measure of agreement as to the necessary sacrifice of individual liberty to the good of the community.

5. The paradox of government is that as the good of the community involves a maximum of individual liberty for all its members the rulers have at the same time to enslave everyone ruthlessly and to secure for everyone the utmost possible freedom.

6. In primitive communities people feed and lodge themselves without bothering the Government. In big civilizations this is impossible; so the first business of the Government is to provide for the production and distribution of wealth from day to day and the just sharing of the labor and leisure involved. Thus the individual citizen has to be compelled not only to behave himself properly, but to work productively.

7. The moral slavery of the compulsion to behave properly is a whole-time compulsion admitting of no liberty; but the personal slavery of the compulsion to work lasts only as many hours daily as suffice to discharge the economic duties of the citizen, the remaining hours (over and above those needed for feeding, sleeping, locomotion, etc.) being his leisure.

8. Leisure is the sphere of individual liberty: labor is the sphere of slavery.

9. People who think they can be honestly free all the time are idiots: people who seek whole-time freedom by putting their share of productive work on others are thieves.

10. The use of the word slavery to denote subjection to public government has grown up among the idiots and thieves, and is resorted to here only because it is expedient to explain things to fools according to their folly.

So much for the fundamental natural conditions of social organization. They are as completely beyond argument as the precession of the equinoxes; but they present different problems to different people. To the thief, for instance, the problem is how to evade his share in the labor of production, to increase his share in the distribution of the product, and to corrupt the Government so that it may protect and glorify his chicaneries instead of liquidating him. To Mr Chesterton the Distributist (or Extreme Left Communist) and Catholic (or Equalitarian Internationalist) it is how to select rulers who will govern righteously and impartially in accordance with the fundamental natural conditions.

The history of civilization is the history of the conflict between these rival views of the situation. The Pirate King, the Robber Baron, and the Manchester Man produced between them a government which they called the Empire, the State, the Realm, the Republic, or any other imposing name that did not give away its central purpose. The Chestertonians produced a government which they called The Church; and in due time the Last of the Chestertons joined this Catholic Church, like a very large ship entering a very small harbor, to the great peril of its many rickety old piers and wharves, and the swamping of all the small craft in its neighborhood. So let us see what the Catholic Church made of its governmental problem.

THE CATHOLIC SOLUTION

To begin with, the Church, being catholic, was necessarily democratic to the extent that its aim was to save the souls of all persons without regard to their age, sex, nationality, class, or color. The nobleman who felt that God would not lightly damn a man of his quality received no countenance from the Church in that conviction. Within its fold all souls were equal before God.

But the Church did not draw the ridiculous conclusion that all men and women are equally qualified or equally desirous to legislate, to govern, to administer, to make decisions, to manage public affairs or even their own private affairs. It faced the fact that only about five per cent. of the population are capable of exercising these powers, and are certain to be corrupted by them unless they have an irresistible religious vocation for public work and a faith in its beneficence which will induce them to take vows to abstain from any profit that is not shared by all the rest, and from all indulgences which might blunt their consciences or subject them to the family influences so bitterly deprecated by Jesus.

This natural "called" minority was never elected in the scandalous way we call democratic. Its members were in the first instance self-elected: that is, they voluntarily lived holy lives and devoted themselves to the public welfare in obedience to the impulse of the Holy Ghost within them. This impulse was their vocation. They were called from above, not chosen by the uncalled. To protect themselves and obtain the necessary power, they organized themselves, and called their organization The Church. After that, the genuineness and sufficiency of the vocation of the new recruits were judged by The Church. If the judgment was favorable, and the candidates took certain vows, they were admitted to the official priesthood and set to govern as priests in the parish and spiritual directors in the family, all of them being eligible, if they had the requisite ability, for promotion to the work of governing the Church itself as bishops or cardinals, or to the supreme rank of Pope or Vicar of Christ on earth. And all this without the smallest reference to the opinions of the uncalled and unordained.

NEED FOR A COMMON FAITH

Now comes the question, why should persons of genuine vocation be asked to take vows before being placed in authority? Is not the vocation a sufficient guarantee of their wisdom?

No. Before priests can govern they must have a common faith as to the fundamental conditions of a stable human society. Otherwise the result might be an assembly of random men of genius unable to agree on a single legislative measure or point of policy. An ecumenical council consisting of Einstein and Colonel Lynch, Aquinas and Francis Bacon, Dante and Galileo, Lenin and Lloyd George, could seldom come to a unanimous decision, if indeed to any decision except in the negative against a minority of one, on any point beyond the capacity of a coroner's jury. The Pope must not be an eccentric genius presiding over a conclave of variously disposed cardinals: he must have an absolutely closed mind on what Herbert Spencer called Social Statics; and in this the cardinals must resemble and agree with him. What is more, they must to some extent represent the conscience of the common people; for it is evident that if they made laws and gave personal directions which would produce general horror or be taken as proofs of insanity their authority would collapse. Hence the need for vows committing all who take them to definite articles of faith on social statics, and to their logical consequences in law and custom. Such vows automatically exclude revolutionary geniuses, who, being uncommon, are not representative, more especially scientific geniuses, with whom it is a point of honor to have unconditionally open minds even on the most apparently sacred subjects.

RUSSIA REDISCOVERS THE CHURCH SYSTEM

A tremendous importance is given to a clear understanding of the Catholic system at this moment by the staggering fact that the biggest State in the modern world, having made a clean sweep of its Church by denouncing its religion as dope, depriving its priests and bishops of any greater authority than a quack can pick up at a fair, encouraging its most seriously minded children to form a League of the Godless, shooting its pious Tsar, turning its cathedrals into historical museums illustrating the infamies of ecclesiastical history and expressly entitling them anti-religious: in short, addressing itself solemnly and implacably to a root-and-branch extermination of everything that we associate with priesthood, has, under pressure of circumstances, unconsciously and spontaneously established as its system of government an as-close-as-possible reproduction of the hierarchy of the Catholic Church. The nomenclature is changed, of course: the Church is called the Communist Party; and the Holy Office and its familiars are known as the Komintern and the Gay Pay Oo. There is the popular safeguard of having the symptoms of the priestly vocation verified in the first instance by the group of peasants or industrial workers with whom the postulant's daily life has been passed, thus giving a genuine democratic basis to the system; and the hierarchy elected on this basis is not only up to date for the moment, but amenable to the daily lessons of trial and error in its practical operations and in no way pledged against change and innovation as such. But essentially the system is that of the old Christian Catholic Church, even to its fundamental vow of Communism and the death penalty on Ananias and Sapphira for violating it.

If our newspapers knew what is really happening in the world, or could discriminate between the news value of a bicycle accident in Clapham and that of a capsize of civilization, their columns would be full of this literally epoch-making event. And the first question they would address to Russia would be "Why, seeing that the Christian system has been such a hopeless failure, do you go back to it, and invite us to go back to it?"

WHY THE CHRISTIAN SYSTEM FAILED

The answer is that the Christian system failed, not because it was wrong in its psychology, its fundamental postulate of equality, or its anticipation of Lenin's principle that the rulers must be as poor as the ruled so that they can raise themselves only by raising their people, but because the old priests' ignorance of economics and political science blinded them to the mischief latent in the selfishness of private property in the physical earth. Before the Church knew where it was (it has not quite located itself yet) it found itself so prodigiously rich that the Pope was a secular Italian prince with armies and frontiers, enjoying not only the rent of Church lands, but selling salvation on such a scale that when Torquemada began burning Jews instead of allowing them to ransom their bodies by payments to the Roman treasury, and leaving their souls to God, a first-rate quarrel between the Church and the Spanish Inquisition was the result.

But the riches of the Church were nothing compared to the riches of the Church's great rival, the Empire. And the poverty of the priest was opulence compared to the poverty of the proletarian. Whilst the Church was being so corrupted by its own property, and by the influence on it of the lay proprietors, that it lost all its moral prestige, the warriors and robbers of the Empire had been learning from experience that a pirate ship needs a hierarchy of officers and an iron discipline even more than police boats, and that the work of robbing the poor all the time involves a very elaborate system of government to ensure that the poor shall, like bees, continue to produce not only their own subsistence but the surplus that can be robbed from them without bringing on them the doom of the goose that lays the golden eggs. Naked coercion is so expensive that it became necessary to practise on the imaginations of the poor to the extent of making them believe that it is a pious duty to be robbed, and that their moment of life in this world is only a prelude to an eternity in which the poor will be blest and happy, and the rich horribly tortured.

Matters at last reached a point at which there was more law and order in the Empire than in The Church. Emperor Philip of Spain was enormously more respectable and pious, if less amiable, than Pope Alexander Borgia. The Empire gained moral prestige as The Church lost it until the Empire, virtuously indignant, took it on itself to reform The Church, all the more readily as the restoration of priestly poverty was a first-rate excuse for plundering it.

Now The Church could not with any decency allow itself to be reformed by a plutocracy of pirate kings, robber barons, commercial adventurers, moneylenders, and deserters from its own ranks. It reformed itself from within by its own saints and the Orders they founded, and thus "dished" the Reformation; whilst the Reformers set up national Churches and free Churches of their own under the general definition of Protestants, and thereby found themselves committed to a curious adulteration of their doctrine of Individualism, or the right of private judgment, with most of the ecclesiastical corruptions against which they had protested. And as neither Church nor Empire would share the government of mankind with the other nor allow the common people any say in the matter, the Catholics and Protestants set to work to exterminate one another with rack and stake, fire, sword, and gunpowder, aided by the poison gas of scurrilous calumny, until the very name of religion began to stink in the nostrils of all really charitable and faithful people.

GOVERNMENT BY EVERYBODY

The moral drawn from all this was that as nobody could be trusted to govern the people the people must govern themselves, which was nonsense. Nevertheless it was assumed that by inscribing every man's name on a register of voters we could realize the ideal of every man his own Solon and his own Plato, as to which one could only ask why not every man his own Shakespear and his own Einstein? But this assumption suited the plutocrats very well, as they had only to master the easy art of stampeding elections by their newspapers to do anything they liked in the name of the people. Votes for everybody (called for short, Democracy) ended in government neither of the best nor of the worst, but in an official government which could do nothing but talk, and an actual government of landlords, employers, and financiers at war with an Opposition of trade unionists, strikers, pickets, and—occasionally—rioters. The resultant disorder, indiscipline, and breakdown of distribution, produced a reaction of pure disappointment and distress in which the people looked wildly round for a Savior, and were ready to give a hopeful trial to anyone bold enough to assume dictatorship and kick aside the impotent official government until he had completely muzzled and subjugated it.

FAILURE ALL ROUND

That is the history of Catholicism and Protestantism, Church and Empire, Liberalism and Democracy, up to date.

Clearly a ghastly failure, both positively as an attempt to solve the problem of government and negatively as an attempt to secure freedom of thought and facility of change to keep pace with thought.

Now this does not mean in the least that the original Catholic plan was wrong. On the contrary, all the disasters to which it has led have been demonstrations of the eternal need for it. The alternative to vocational government is a mixture of a haporth of very incompetent official government with an intolerable deal of very competent private tyranny. Providence, or Nature if you prefer that expression, has not ordained that all men shall have a vocation for being "servants of all the rest" as saints or rulers. Providence knows better than to provide armies consisting exclusively of commanders-in-chief or factories staffed exclusively with managing directors; and to that inexorable natural fact we shall always have to come back, just as the Russian revolutionists, who were reeking with Protestant Liberal superstitions at the beginning, have had to come back to it. But we have now thought out much more carefully than St Peter the basic articles of faith, without which the vocation of the priest is inevitably pushed out by the vocation of the robbers and the racketeers, self-elected as gentlemen and ladies. We know that private property distributes wealth, work, and leisure so unevenly that a wretchedly poor and miserably overworked majority are forced to maintain a minority inordinately rich and passionately convinced that labor is so disgraceful to them that they dare not be seen carrying a parcel down Bond Street. We know that the strains set up by such a division of interests also destroy peace, justice, religion, good breeding, honor, reasonable freedom, and everything that government exists to secure, and that all this iniquity arises automatically when we thoughtlessly allow a person to own a thousand acres of land in the middle of London much more completely than he owns the pair of boots in which he walks over it; for he may not kick me out of my house into the street with his boots; but he may do so with his writ of ejectment. And so we are driven to the conclusion that the modern priesthood must utterly renounce, abjure, abhor, abominate, and annihilate private property as the very worst of all the devil's inventions for the demoralization and damnation of mankind. Civilized men and women must live by their ordered and equal share in the work needed to support the community, and must find their freedom in their ordered and equal share of the leisure produced by scientific economy in producing that support. It still takes some conviction to repudiate an institution so well spoken of as private property; but the facts must be faced: our clandestine methods of violating it by income tax and surtax, which mean only "What a thief stole steal thou from the thief," will no longer serve; for a modern government, as the Russians soon found out, must not take money, even from thieves, until it is ready to employ it productively. To throw it away in doles as our governing duffers do, is to burn the candle at both ends and precipitate the catastrophe they are trying to avert.

OBSOLETE VOWS

As to the vows, some of the old ones must go. The Catholic Church and our Board of Education insist on celibacy, the one for priests and the other for schoolmistresses. That is a remnant of the cynical superstition of original sin. Married people have a right to married rulers; mothers have a right to have their children taught and handled by mothers; and priests and pastors who meddle with family affairs should know what they are talking about.

Another important modern discovery

is that government is not a whole-time job for all its agents. A council of peasants derives its ancient wisdom from its normal day's work on the land, without which it would be a council of tramps and village idiots. It is not desirable that an ordinary parish priest should have no other occupation, nor an abnormal occupation, even that of a scholar. Nor is it desirable that his uniform should be too sacerdotal; for that is the method of idolatry, which substitutes for rational authority the superstitious awe produced by a contrived singularity. St Vincent de Paul knew thoroughly well what he was about when he constituted his Sisterhood of Charity on the rule that the sister should not be distinguishable from an ordinary respectable woman. Unfortunately, the costume prescribed under this rule has in the course of the centuries become as extraordinary as that of the Bluecoat boy; and St Vincent's idea is consequently lost; but modern industrial experience confirms it; for the latest rediscovery of the Vincentian principle has been made by Mr Ford, who has testified that if you want a staff of helpful persons who will turn their hands to anything at need you must not give them either title, rank, or uniform, as the immediate result will be their partial disablement by the exclusion from their activities of many of the most necessary jobs as beneath their dignity.

Another stipulation made by St Vincent, who already in the sixteenth century was far ahead of us, was that no sister may pledge herself for longer than a year at a time, however often she may renew her vows. Thus the sisters can never lose their freedom nor suffer from cold feet. If he were alive today St Vincent would probably propose a clean sweep of all our difficulties about marriage and divorce by forbidding people to marry for longer than a year, and make them renew their vows every twelve months. In Russia the members of the Communist Party cannot dedicate themselves eternally: they can drop out into the laity when they please, and if they do not please and nevertheless have become slack in their ministry, they are pushed out.

SUPERNATURAL PRETENSIONS

Furthermore, modern priests must not make supernatural pretensions. They must not be impostors. A vocation for politics, though essentially a religious vocation, must be on the same footing as a vocation for music or mathematics or cooking or nursing or acting or architecture or farming or billiards or any other born aptitude. The authority which must attach to all public officials and councils must rest on their ability and efficiency. In the Royal Navy every mishap to a ship involves a court martial on the responsible officer: if the officer makes a mistake he forfeits his command unless he can convince the court that he is still worthy it. In no other way can our hackneyed phrase "responsible government" acquire any real meaning. When a Catholic priest goes wrong (or too right) he is silenced: when a Russian Commissar goes wrong, he is expelled from the Party. Such responsibility necessarily makes official authority very authoritative and frightens off the unduly nervous. Stalin and Mussolini are the most responsible statesmen in Europe because they have no hold on their places except their efficiency; and their authority is consequently greater than that of any of the monarchs, presidents, and prime ministers who have to deal with them. Stalin is one of the higher functionaries with whom governing is necessarily a whole-time job. But he is no richer than his neighbors, and can "better himself" only by bettering them, not by buttering them like a British demagogue.

ECLECTIC DEMOCRACY

I think my views on intellectual aristocracy and democracy and all the rest of it are now plain enough. As between the intentions of The Church and the intentions of The Empire (unrealized ideals both) I am on the side of The Church. As to the evil done by The Church with the best intentions and the good done by The Empire with the worst, I am an Eclectic: there is much to be learnt from each. I harp on Russia because the Moscow experiment is the only really new departure from Tweedledum and Tweedledee: Fascism is still wavering between Empire and Church, between private property and Communism. Years ago, I said that what democracy needed was a trustworthy anthropometric machine for the selection of qualified rulers. Since then I have elaborated this by demanding the formation of panels of tested persons eligible for the different grades in the governmental hierarchy. Panel A would be for diplomacy and international finance, Panel B for national affairs, Panel C for municipal and county affairs, Panel D for the village councils and so forth. Under such a panel system the voters would lose their present liberty to return such candidates as the late Horatio Bottomley to parliament by enormous majorities; but they would gain the advantage of at least knowing that their rulers know how to read and write, which they do not enjoy at present.

Nobody ventured to disagree with me when I urged the need for such panels; but when I was challenged to produce my anthropometric machine or my endocrine or phrenological tests, I was obliged to confess that they had not yet been invented, and that such existing attempts at them as competitive examinations are so irrelevant and misleading as to be worse than useless as tests of vocation. But the Soviet system, hammered out under the sternest pressure of circumstances, supplies an excellent provisional solution, which turns out to be the solution of the old Catholic Church purged of supernatural pretension, assumption of final perfection, and the poison of private property with its fatal consequences. Mr Stalin is not in the least like an Emperor, nor an Archbishop, nor a Prime Minister, nor a Chancellor; but he would be strikingly like a Pope, claiming for form's sake an apostolic succession from Marx, were it not for his frank method of Trial and Error, his entirely human footing, and his liability to removal at a moment's notice if his eminence should upset his mental balance. At the other end of the scale are the rank and file of the Communist Party, doing an ordinary day's work with the common folk, and giving only their leisure to the Party. For their election as representatives of the commons they must depend on the votes of their intimate and equal neighbors and workmates. They have no incentive to seek election except the vocational incentive; for success, in the first instance, means, not release from the day's ordinary work, but the sacrifice of all one's leisure to politics, and, if promotion to the whole-time grades be achieved, a comparatively ascetic discipline and virtually no pecuniary gain.

If anyone can suggest a better practically tested plan, now is the time to do it; for it is all up with the old Anarchist-Liberal parliamentary systems in the face of thirty millions of unemployed, and World Idiotic Conferences at which each nation implores all the others to absorb its unemployed by a revival of international trade. Mr Chesterton says truly that a government, if it is to govern, "cannot select one ruler to do something and another to undo it, one intellectual to restore the nation and another to ruin the nation." But that is precisely what our parliamentary party system does. Mr Chesterton has put it in a nutshell; and I hope he will appreciate the sound Catholicism with which I have cracked it.

XIV

ON THE ROCKS

1933

EXTERMINATION

In this play a reference is made by a Chief of Police to the political necessity for killing people: a necessity so distressing to the statesmen and so terrifying to the common citizen that nobody except myself (as far as I know) has ventured to examine it directly on its own merits, although every Government is obliged to practise it on a scale varying from the execution of a single murderer to the slaughter of millions of quite innocent persons. Whilst assenting to these proceedings, and even acclaiming and celebrating them, we dare not tell ourselves what we are doing or why we are doing it; and so we call it justice or capital punishment or our duty to king and country or any other convenient verbal whitewash for what we instinctively recoil from as from a dirty job. These childish evasions are revolting. We must strip off the whitewash and find out what is really beneath it. Extermination must be put on a scientific basis if it is ever to be carried out humanely and apologetically as well as thoroughly.

KILLING AS A POLITICAL FUNCTION

That killing is a necessity is beyond question by any thoughtful person. Unless rabbits and deer and rats and foxes are killed, or "kept down" as we put it, mankind must perish; and that section of mankind which lives in the country and is directly and personally engaged in the struggle with Nature for a living has no sentimental doubts that they must be killed. As to tigers and poisonous snakes, their incompatibility with human civilization is unquestioned. This does not excuse the use of cruel steel traps, agonizing poisons, or packs of hounds as methods of extermination. Killing can be cruelly or kindly done; and the deliberate choice of cruel ways, and their organization as popular pleasures, is sinful; but the sin is in the cruelty and the enjoyment of it, not in the killing.

THE SACREDNESS OF HUMAN LIFE

In law we draw a line between the killing of human animals and non-human ones, setting the latter apart as brutes. This was founded on a general belief that humans have immortal souls and brutes none. Nowadays more and more people are refusing to make this distinction. They may believe in The Life Everlasting and The Life to Come; but they make no distinction between Man and Brute, because some of them believe that brutes have souls, whilst others refuse to believe that the physical materializations and personifications of The Life Everlasting are themselves everlasting. In either case the mystic distinction between Man and Brute vanishes; and the murderer pleading that though a rabbit should be killed for being mischievous he himself should be spared because he has an immortal soul and a rabbit has none is as hopelessly out of date as a gentleman duellist pleading his clergy. When the necessity for killing a dangerous human being arises, as it still does daily, the only distinction we make between a man and a snared rabbit is that we very quaintly provide the man with a minister of religion to explain to him that we are not killing him at all, but only expediting his transfer to an eternity of bliss.

The political necessity for killing him is precisely like that for killing the cobra or the tiger: he is so ferocious or unscrupulous that if his neighbors do not kill him he will kill or ruin his neighbors; so that there is nothing for it but to disable him once for all by making an end of him, or else waste the lives of useful and harmless people in seeing that he does no mischief, and caging him cruelly like a lion in a show.

Here somebody is sure to interject that there is the alternative of teaching him better manners; but I am not here dealing with such cases: the real necessity arises only in dealing with untameable persons who are constitutionally unable to restrain their violent or acquisitive impulses, and have no compunction about sacrificing others to their own immediate convenience. To punish such persons is ridiculous: we might as reasonably punish a tile for flying off a roof in a storm and knocking a clergyman on the head. But to kill them is quite reasonable and very necessary.

PRESENT EXTERMINATIONS

All this so far is mere elementary criminology, already dealt with very fully by me in my Essay on Prisons, which I recommend to those readers who may feel impelled to ramble away at this point into the prosings about Deterrence beloved by our Prison Commissioners and judges. It disposes of the dogma of the unconditional sacredness of human life, or any other incarnation of life; but it covers only a corner of the field opened up by modern powers of extermination. In Germany it is suggested that the Nordic race should exterminate the Latin race. As both these lingual stocks are hopelessly interbred by this time, such a sacrifice to ethnological sciolism is not practicable; but its discussion familiarizes the idea and clears the way for practicable suggestions. The extermination of whole races and classes has been not only advocated but actually attempted. The extirpation of the Jew as such figured for a few

mad moments in the program of the Nazi party in Germany. The extermination of the peasant is in active progress in Russia, where the extermination of the class of ladies and gentlemen of so-called independent means has already been accomplished; and an attempt to exterminate the old Conservative professional class and the kulak or prosperous farmer class has been checked only by the discovery that they cannot as yet be done without. Outside Russia the extermination of Communists is widely advocated; and there is a movement in the British Empire and the United States for the extermination of Fascists. In India the impulse of Moslems and Hindus to exterminate one another is complicated by the impulse of the British Empire to exterminate both when they happen to be militant Nationalists.

PREVIOUS ATTEMPTS MISS THE POINT

The novelty and significance of these instances consists in the equal status of the parties. The extermination of what the exterminators call inferior races is as old as history. "Stone dead hath no fellow" said Cromwell when he tried to exterminate the Irish. "The only good nigger is a dead nigger" say the Americans of the Ku-Klux temperament. "Hates any man the thing he would not kill?" said Shylock naïvely. But we white men, as we absurdly call ourselves in spite of the testimony of our looking glasses, regard all differently colored folk as inferior species. Ladies and gentlemen class rebellious laborers with vermin. The Dominicans, the watchdogs of God, regarded the Albigenses as the enemies of God, just as Torquemada regarded the Jews as the murderers of God. All that is an old story: what we are confronted with now is a growing perception that if we desire a certain type of civilization and culture we must exterminate the sort of people who do not fit into it. There is a difference between the shooting at sight of aboriginal natives in the back blocks of Australia and the massacres of aristocrats in the terror which followed the foreign attacks on the French Revolution. The Australian gunman pots the aboriginal natives to satisfy his personal antipathy to a black man with uncut hair. But nobody in the French Republic had this feeling about Lavoisier, nor can any German Nazi have felt that way about Einstein. Yet Lavoisier was guillotined; and Einstein has had to fly for his life from Germany. It was silly to say that the Republic had no use for chemists; and no Nazi has stultified his party to the extent of saying that the new National Socialist Fascist State in Germany has no use for mathematician-physicists. The proposition is that aristocrats (Lavoisier's class) and Jews (Einstein's race) are unfit to enjoy the privilege of living in a modern society founded on definite principles of social welfare as distinguished from the old promiscuous aggregations crudely policed by chiefs who had no notion of social criticism and no time to invent it.

KING CHARLES'S HEAD

It was, by the way, the English Revolution which introduced the category of Malignant or Man of Blood, and killed the King as an affirmation that even kings must not survive if they are malignant. This was much more advanced than the execution in the following century of Louis XV as an ordinary traitor, or of the Tsar in our own time to prevent his being captured by the Tchekoslovakian contingent and used as a standard to rally the royalist reaction. Charles affirmed a divine personal right to govern as against the parliament and would keep no bargain with it. Parliament denied his right, and set up against it a divine right of election winners to govern. They fought it out; and the victorious election winners exterminated the king, very logically. Finding

that their authority still needed a royal disguise they drove a hard bargain for a crown with his son, and, after ejecting the next king who broke it, a still harder one with his Dutch grandson before they allowed the title of king, with nine tenths of the meaning knocked out of it, to be used as a matter of convenience again in England. Nobody had a word to say against Charles's private character. It was solely for incompatibility of politics that he was eliminated, or "liquidated" as we say now. There was a real novelty in the transaction. The Church had for centuries before compelled the secular State to liquidate heretics; and the slaughter of rebels who tried to substitute one dynasty for another, or to seize the throne for themselves, was common routine. But Charles was neither a heretic nor a rebel. He was the assertor of a divine right to govern without winning elections; and because that right could not co-exist with the supremacy of a much richer and more powerful plutocracy off went his head.

Charles was only the first victim. After Culloden the defeated Highland chiefs and their clansmen were butchered like sheep on the field. Had they been merely prisoners of war, this would have been murder. But as they were also Incompatibles with British civilization, it was only liquidation.

RIGHT TO EXTERMINATE CONFERRED BY PRIVATE PROPERTY

Having disposed of the divine right of kings the political liquidators turned their attention slowly to its derivatory the divine right of landlords, which had gradually disguised itself as private property in land. For when a tract of land becomes the private property of an individual who has to depend on it for his subsistence, the relation between him and the inhabitants of that tract becomes an economic one; and if they become economically superfluous or wasteful, he must

N

exterminate them. This is continually happening wherever private property in land exists. If I possess land and find it profitable to grow wheat on it, I need many agricultural laborers to enable me to do it; and I tolerate their existence accordingly. If I presently find that it is more profitable to cover my land with sheep and sell their wool, I have to tolerate the existence of the sheep; but I no longer need tolerate the existence of the laborers; so I drive them off my land, which is my legal method of extermination, retaining only a few to act as shepherds. Later on I find that it is more profitable to cover my land with wild deer, and collect money from gentlemen and ladies who enjoy shooting them. I then exterminate my shepherds and keep only a few gamekeepers. But I may do much better by letting my land to industrialists for the erection of factories. They exterminate the sheep and the deer; but they need far more men than I needed even when I grew wheat. The driven-offs crowd into the factories and multiply like rabbits; and for the moment population grows instead of diminishing. But soon machines come along and make millions of proletarians economically superfluous. The factory owner accordingly sacks them, which is his legal method of extermination. During these developments the exterminated, or, as we call them, the evicted and sacked, try to avoid starvation partly by emigration, but mostly by offering themselves for all sorts of employment as soldiers, servants, prostitutes, police officers, scavengers, and operators of the immense machinery of amusement and protection for the idle rich classes created by the private property system. By organization in trade unions, municipal and parliamentary Labor Parties, and the like, and maintaining a sort of continual civil war consisting of strikes and riots, they extort from the proprietors enough to reduce the rate of extermination (shewn by the actuarial expectation of life of the unpropertied) for periods described as progressive, until the proprietors, by engaging in suicidal wars, are forced to intensify their economies, and the rate of extermination rises again.

DISGUISES UNDER WHICH PRIVATE EXTERMINATION OPERATES

Note that during all this the Registrar General's returns do not give us the deaths of the exterminated as such, because the exterminated do not starve as lost travellers starve in the desert. Their starvation is more or less protracted; and when the final catastrophe arrives, it is disguised under an imposing array of doctors' names for moribundity. The victims die mostly in their first year, and subsequently at all ages short of the age at which properly nourished people die. Sometimes they are starved into attaining an age at which people with well filled pockets eat themselves to death. Either way and all ways the extermination is a real and permanent feature of private property civilization, though it is never mentioned as such, and ladies and gentlemen are carefully educated to be unconscious of its existence and to talk nonsense about its facts when they are too obvious or become too scandalous to be ignored, when they often advocate emigration or Birth Control or war as remedies. And against the facts there is a chronic humanitarian revolt expressing itself either underground or overground in revolutionary movements; making our political constitutions very unstable; and imposing an habitual disingenuousness on conservative statesmen.

PRIVATE POWERS OF LIFE AND DEATH

Now the central fact of all these facts is that the private proprietors have irresponsible powers of life and death in the State. Such powers may be tolerated as long as the Government is in effect a committee of private proprietors; yet if such a committee be widened into or superseded by a Government acting in the interest of the whole people, that Government will not suffer any private class to hold the lives of the citizens at its mercy and thereby become their real masters. A popular Government, before it fully grasps the situation, usually begins by attempting to redistribute property in such a manner as to make everyone a petty proprietor, as in the French Revolution. But when the impossibility of doing this (except in the special case of agricultural land) becomes apparent, and the question is probed to the bottom by unpropertied political philosophers like Proudhon and Marx, private property is sooner or later excommunicated and abolished; and what was formerly called "real property" is replaced by ordinary personal property and common property administered by the State.

All modern progressive and revolutionary movements are at bottom attacks on private property. A Chancellor of the Exchequer apologizing for an increase in the surtax, a Fascist dictator organizing a Corporate State, a Soviet Commissar ejecting a kulak and adding his acres to a collective farm, are all running the same race, though all of them except the Commissar may be extremely reluctant to win it. For in the long run the power to exterminate is too grave to be left in any hands but those of a thoroughly Communist Government responsible to the whole community. The landlord with his writ of ejectment and the employer with his sack, must finally go the way of the nobleman with his sword and his benefit of clergy, and of Hannibal Chollop with his bowie knife and pistol.

Let us then assume that private property, already maimed by factory legislation, surtax, and a good deal of petty persecution in England, and in Russia

tolerated only provisionally as a disgraceful necessity pending its complete extirpation, is finally discarded by civilized communities, and the duty of maintaining it at all costs replaced by the duty of giving effect to the dogma that every ablebodied and ablebodied and ablesouled person has an absolute right to an equal share in the national dividend. Would the practice of extermination thereupon disappear? I suggest that, on the contrary, it might continue much more openly and intelligently and scientifically than at present, because the humanitarian revolt against it would probably become a humanitarian support of it; and there would be an end of the hypocrisy, the venal special pleading, and the concealment or ignoring of facts which are imposed on us at present because extermination for the benefit of a handful of private persons against the interests of the race is permitted and practised. The old doctrine of the sacredness of human life, which in our idiot asylums at Darenth and elsewhere still terrifies us into wasting the lives of capable people in preserving the lives of monsters, was a crude expedient for beginning civilization. At present we discard it in dealing with murderers, heretics, traitors, and (in Scotland) vitriol throwers, who can be legally killed. A runaway convict can also be summarily shot by a warder to save the trouble of pursuing and recapturing him; and although the convict is not under capital sentence and the case is therefore clearly one of wilful murder, coroners' juries persist in treating it as a harmless and necessary incident in prison routine.

Unfortunately the whole question is bedevilled by our anti-Christian vice of punishment, expiation, sacrifice, and all the cognate tribal superstitions which are hammered into us in our childhood by barbarous scripturists, irascible or sadist parents, and a hideous criminal code. When the horrors of anarchy force us to set up laws that forbid us to fight and torture one another for sport, we still snatch at every excuse for declaring individuals outside the protection of law and torturing them to our hearts' content.

CRUELTY'S EXCUSES

There have been summits of civilization at which heretics like Socrates, who was killed because he was wiser than his neighbors, have not been tortured, but ordered to kill themselves in the most painless manner known to their judges. But from that summit there was a speedy relapse into our present savagery. For Wallace, whom the Scots adored as a patriot and the English executed as a traitor, the most cruel and obscene method of killing that the human imagination could conceive at its vilest was specially invented to punish him for being a traitor (or "larn him to be a toad"); and this sentence has been passed, though not carried out, within the memory of persons now living. John of Leyden, for being a Communist, was tortured so frightfully before being hung up in a cage on the church tower to starve to death in sight of all the citizens and their little children, that the bishop who was officially obliged to witness it died of horror. Joan of Arc, for wearing men's clothes and being a Protestant and a witch, was burnt alive, after a proposal to torture her had been barely defeated. The people who saw her burnt were quite accustomed to such spectacles, and regarded them as holiday attractions. A woman's sex was made an excuse for burning her instead of more mercifully hanging her. Male criminals were broken on the wheel: that is, battered to death with iron bars, until well into the nineteenth century. This was a public spectacle; and the prolongation of the victim's suffering was so elaborately studied and arranged that Cartouche, one of the kings of scoundrelism, was bribed to betray his accomplices by the promise that he should be killed by the sixth blow of the bar. The wheel and the stake have lately gone out of use; but the Sadist mania for flogging seems ineradicable; for after a partially successful attempt to discard it in Victorian times it has revived again with redoubled ferocity: quite recently a criminal was sentenced to a flogging and ten years penal servitude; and although the victim escaped his punishment and gave a sensational advertisement to its savagery by committing suicide, nobody protested, though thirty years ago there would have been a strenuous outcry against it, raised by the old Humanitarian League, and voiced in Parliament by the Irish Nationalists. Alas! the first thing the Irish did when they at last enjoyed self-government was to get rid of these sentimental Nationalists and put flogging on their statute book in a series of Coercion Acts that would have horrified Dublin Castle. In a really civilized state flogging would cease because it would be impossible to induce any decent citizen to flog another. Among us a perfectly respectable official will do it for half a crown, and probably enjoy the job.

LEADING CASE OF JESUS CHRIST

I dislike cruelty, even cruelty to other people, and should therefore like to see all cruel people exterminated. But I should recoil with horror from a proposal to punish them. Let me illustrate my attitude by a very famous, indeed far too famous, example of the popular conception of criminal law as a means of delivering up victims to the normal popular lust for cruelty which has been mortified by the restraint imposed on it by civilization. Take the case of the extermination of Jesus Christ. No doubt there was a strong case for it. Jesus was from the point of view of the High Priest a heretic and an impostor. From the point of view of the merchants he was a rioter and a Communist. From the Roman Imperialist point of view he was a traitor. From the commonsense point of view he was a dangerous madman. From the snobbish point of view, always a very influential one, he was a penniless vagrant. From the police point of view he was an obstructor of thoroughfares, a beggar, an associate of prostitutes, an apologist of sinners, and a disparager of judges; and his daily companions were tramps whom he had seduced into vagabondage from their regular trades. From the point of view of the pious he was a Sabbath breaker, a denier of the efficacy of circumcision and the advocate of a strange rite of baptism, a gluttonous man and a winebibber. He was abhorrent to the medical profession as an unqualified practitioner who healed people by quackery and charged nothing for the treatment. He was not anti-Christ: nobody had heard of such a power of darkness then; but he was startlingly anti-Moses. He was against the priests, against the judiciary, against the military, against the city (he declared that it was impossible for a rich man to enter the kingdom of heaven), against all the interests, classes, principalities and powers, inviting everybody to abandon all these and follow him. By every argument, legal, political, religious, customary, and polite, he was the most complete enemy of the society of his time ever brought to the bar. He was guilty on every count of the indictment, and on many more that his accusers had not the wit to frame. If he was innocent then the whole world was guilty. To acquit him was to throw over civilization and all its institutions. History has borne out the case against him; for no State has ever constituted itself on his principles or made it possible to live according to his commandments: those States who have taken his name have taken it as an alias to enable them to persecute his followers more plausibly.

It is not surprising that under these circumstances, and in the absence of any defence, the Jerusalem community and the Roman government decided to exterminate Jesus. They had just as much right to do so as to exterminate the two thieves who perished with him. But there was neither right nor reason in torturing him. He was entitled to the painless death of Socrates. We may charitably suppose that if the death could have been arranged privately between Pilate and Caiaphas Jesus would have been dispatched as quickly and suddenly as John the Baptist. But the mob wanted the horrible fun of seeing somebody crucified: an abominably cruel method of execution. Pilate only made matters worse by trying to appease them by having Jesus flogged. The soldiers, too, had to have their bit of sport, to crown him with thorns and, when they buffeted him, challenge him ironically to guess which of them had struck the blow.

"CROSSTIANITY"

All this was cruelty for its own sake, for the pleasure of it. And the fun did not stop there. Such was and is the attraction of these atrocities that the spectacle of them has been reproduced in pictures and waxworks and exhibited in churches ever since as an aid to piety. The chief instrument of torture is the subject of a special Adoration. Little models of it in gold and ivory are worn as personal ornaments; and big reproductions in wood and marble are set up in sacred places and on graves. Contrasting the case with that of Socrates, one is forced to the conclusion that if Jesus had been humanely exterminated his memory would have lost ninetynine per cent of its attraction for posterity. Those who were specially susceptible to his morbid attraction were not satisfied with symbolic crosses which hurt nobody. They soon got busy with "acts of faith" which consisted of great public shows at which Jews and Protestants or

Catholics, and anyone else who could be caught out on a point of doctrine, were burnt alive. Cruelty is so infectious that the very compassion it rouses is infuriated to take revenge by still viler cruelties.

The tragedy of this—or, if you will, the comedy—is that it was his clearness of vision on this very point that set Jesus so high above his persecutors. He taught that two blacks do not make a white; that evil should not be countered by worse evil but by good; that revenge and punishment only duplicate wrong; that we should conceive God not as an irascible and vindictive tyrant but as an affectionate father. No doubt many private amiabilities have been inspired by this teaching; but politically it has received no more quarter than Pilate gave it. To all Governments it has remained paradoxical and impracticable. A typical acknowledgment of it was the hanging of a crucifix above the seat of the judge who was sentencing evildoers to be broken on the wheel.

CHRISTIANITY AND THE SEVENTH COMMANDMENT

Now it is not enough to satirize this. We must examine why it occurred. It is not enough to protest that evildoers must not be paid in their own coin by treating them as cruelly as they have treated others. We still have to stop the mischief they do. What is to be done with them? It is easy to suggest that they should be reformed by gentleness and shamed by non-resistance. By all means, if they respond to that treatment. But if gentleness fails to reform them and non-resistance encourages them to further aggression, what then? A month spent in a Tolstoyan community will convince anybody of the soundness of the nearest police inspector's belief that every normal human group contains not only a percentage of saints but also a percentage of irreclaimable scoundrels and good-for-noughts who will wreck any community unless they are expensively restrained or cheaply exterminated. Our Mosaic system of vindictive punishment, politely called "retributory" by Prison Commissioners, disposes of them temporarily; but it wastes the lives of honest citizens in guarding them; sets a horrible example of cruelty and malicious injury; costs a good deal of money that might be better spent; and, after all, sooner or later lets the scoundrel loose again to recommence his depredations. It would be much more sensible and less cruel to treat him as we treat mad dogs or adders, without malice or cruelty, and without reference to catalogues of particular crimes. The notion that persons should be safe from extermination as long as they do not commit wilful murder, or levy war against the Crown, or kidnap, or throw vitriol, is not only to limit social responsibility unnecessarily, and to privilege the large range of intolerable misconduct that lies outside them, but to divert attention from the essential justification for extermination, which is always incorrigible social incompatibility and nothing else.

THE RUSSIAN EXPERIMENT

The only country which has yet awakened to this extension of social responsibility is Russia. When the Soviet Government undertook to change over from Capitalism to Communism it found itself without any instruments for the maintenance of order except a list of crimes and punishments administered through a ritual of criminal law. And in the list of crimes the very worst offences against Communist society had no place: on the contrary they were highly honored and rewarded. As our English doggerel runs, the courts could punish a man for stealing the goose from off the common, but not the man who stole the common from the goose. The idler, that common enemy of mankind who robs everybody all the time, though he is so carefully protected from having his own pocket picked, incurred no penalty, and had actually passed the most severe laws against any interference with his idling. It was the business of the Soviet to make all business public business and all persons public servants; but the view of the ordinary Russian citizen was that a post in a public service was an exceptional stroke of good luck for the holder because it was a sinecure carrying with it the privilege of treating the public insolently and extorting bribes from it. For example, when the Russian railways were communized, some of the local stationmasters interpreted the change as meaning that they might now be as lazy and careless as they pleased, whereas in fact it was of life-or-death importance that they should redouble their activity and strain every nerve to make the service efficient. The unfortunate Commissar who was Minister of Transport found himself obliged to put a pistol in his pocket and with his own hand shoot stationmasters who had thrown his telegrams into the dustbin instead of attending to them, so that he might the more impressively ask the rest of the staff whether they yet grasped the fact that orders are meant to be executed.

INADEQUACY OF PENAL CODES

Now being Minister of Transport, or Minister of any other public service, is a whole-time job: it cannot be permanently combined with that of amateur executioner, carrying with it the reputation in all the capitalist papers of the west of being a ferocious and coldblooded murderer. And no conceivable extension of the criminal code nor of the service disciplines, with their lists of specific offences and specific penalties, could have provided for instant exemplary exterminations of this kind, any more than for the growing urgency of how to dispose of people who would not or could not fit themselves into the new order of things by conforming to its new morality. It would have been easy to specify certain offences and certain penalties in the old fashion: as, for instance, if you hoard money you will be shot; if you speculate in the difference in purchasing power of the rouble in Moscow and Berlin you will be shot; if you buy at the Co-operative to sell at the private trader's shop you will be shot; if you take bribes you will be shot; if you falsify farm or factory balance sheets you will be shot; if you exploit labor you will be shot; and it will be useless to plead that you have been brought up to regard these as normal business activities, and that the whole of respectable society outside Russia agrees with you. But the most elaborate code of this sort would still have left unspecified a hundred ways in which wreckers of Communism could have side-tracked it without ever having to face the essential questions: are you pulling your weight in the social boat? are you giving more trouble than you are worth? have you earned the privilege of living in a civilized community? That is why the Russians were forced to set up an Inquisition or Star Chamber, called at first the Cheka and now the Gay Pay Oo (Ogpu), to go into these questions and "liquidate" persons who could not answer them satisfactorily. The security against the abuse of this power of life and death was that the Cheka had no interest in liquidating anybody who could be made publicly useful, all its interests being in the opposite direction.

LIMITED LIABILITY IN MORALS

Such a novelty is extremely terrifying to us, who are still working on a system of limited liability in morals. Our "free" British citizens can ascertain exactly what they may do and what they may not do if they are to keep out of the hands of the police. Our financiers know that they must not forge share certificates nor overstate their assets in the balance sheets they send to their shareholders. But provided they observe a few conditions of this kind they are free to enter upon a series of quite legitimate but not the less nefarious operations. For example, making a corner in wheat or copper or any other cornerable commodity and forcing up prices so as to make enormous private fortunes for themselves, or making mischief between nations through the Press to stimulate the private trade in armaments. Such limited liability no longer exists in Russia, and is not likely to exist in the future in any highly civilized state. It may be quite impossible to convict a forestaller or regrator under a criminal code of having taken a single illegal step, but quite easy to convince any reasonable body of judges that he is what the people call "a wrong one." In Russia such a conviction would lead to his disappearance and the receipt by his family of a letter to say that they need not wait up for him, as he would not return home any more.[1] In our country he would enjoy his gains in high honor and personal security, and thank his stars that he lived in a free country and not in Communist Russia.

But as the new tribunal has been forced on Russia by pressure of circumstances and not planned and thought out at leisure, the two institutions, the Ogpu and the ordinary police administering the criminal code, work side by side, with the odd result that the surest way to escape the Ogpu is to commit an ordinary crime and take refuge in the arms of the police and the magistrate, who cannot exterminate you because capital punishment has been abolished in Russia (liquidation by the Ogpu is not punishment: it

is only "weeding the garden"); and the sentence of imprisonment, though it may seem severe to us in view of the cruelty of our treatment of criminals, will be carried out with comparative leniency, and probably, if the culprit behaves well, be remitted after a while. As four years imprisonment is considered enough for any reasonable sort of murder, a cornerer who finds himself in imminent danger of detection and liquidation by the Ogpu would be well advised to lose his temper and murder his mother-in-law, thereby securing a lease of life for at least four years.

Sooner or later this situation will have to be thoroughly studied and thought out to its logical conclusion in all civilized countries. The lists of crimes and penalties will obsolesce like the doctors' lists of diseases and medicines; and it will become possible to be a judge without ceasing to be a Christian. And extermination, my present subject, will become a humane science instead of the miserable mixture of piracy, cruelty, vengeance, race conceit, and superstition it now is.

NATURAL LIMIT TO EXTERMINATION

Fortunately the more frankly and realistically it is faced the more it detaches itself from the associations with crude slaughter which now make it terrible. When Charlemagne founded the Holy Roman Empire (as far as anyone can be said to have founded it) he postulated that all its subjects must be Catholic Christians, and made an amateurish attempt to secure this condition of social stability by killing everyone who fell into his power and refused to be baptized. But he cannot ever have got very far with it, because there is one sort of bird you must not kill on any pretext whatever: namely, the goose that lays the golden eggs. In Russia the Soviet Government began by a Charlemagnesque attempt to exterminate the bourgeoisie by classing them as

---

[1] Note, however, that a sentence of extermination should never be so certain as to make it worth the delinquent's while to avoid arrest by murdering his or her pursuers.

intelligentsia, restricting their rations, and putting their children at the foot of the overcrowded educational list. They also proscribed the kulak, the able, hard-headed, hardfisted farmer who was richer than his neighbors and liked to see them poorer than himself. Him they rudely took by the shoulders and threw destitute into the lane. There were plausible reasons for this beginning of selection in population; for the moral outlook of the bourgeoisie and the kulaks was danger-ously anti-social. But the results were disastrous. The bourgeoisie contained the professional class and the organizing business class. Without professional men and business organizers nothing could be done in the industries; and the hope that picked members of the proletariat could take up professional and organizing work on the strength of their native talent in sufficient numbers was crushingly dis-appointed. When the kulak was thrown out of his farm, and his farming ability paralyzed, food ran short. Very soon the kulak had to be thrown back into his farm and told to carry on until his hour had come; and a pleasant convention was established whereby all educated persons, however obviously ladies or gentlemen, who were willing to assure the authorities that their fathers had "worked on the land with their hands" were accepted as genuine proletarians, and transferred from the infamous category of intelli-gentsia to the honorable one of "the in-tellectual proletariat." Even Lenin and his colleagues, all ultra-bourgeois (otherwise they would never have so absurdly over-estimated the intellectual resources of the proletariat and been so contemptuous of the pretension of their own class to be indispensable), allowed their parents to be described as hornyhanded cultivators of the soil. The pretence has now become a standing joke; but you will still come up against it if you accuse any Russian of being a lady or gentleman.

INCOMPATIBILITY OF PEASANTRY WITH MODERN CIVILIZATION

These, however, are merely expedients of transition. The Russian proletariat is now growing its own professional and organizing class; and the ex-bourgeois is dying out, after seeing his children receive a sound Communist education and being lectured by them on his old-fashioned prejudices. And the planners of the Soviet State have no time to bother about moribund questions; for they are confronted with the new and over-whelming necessity for exterminating the peasants, who still exist in formidable numbers. The notion that a civilized State can be made out of any sort of human material is one of our old Radical delusions. As to building Communism with such trash as the Capitalist system produces it is out of the question. For a Communist Utopia we need a population of Utopians; and Utopians do not grow wild on the bushes nor are they to be picked up in the slums: they have to be cultivated very carefully and expensively. Peasants will not do; yet without the peasants the Communists could never have captured the Russian Revolution. Nominally it was the Soviets of peasants and soldiers who backed Lenin and saved Communism when all Western Europe set on him like a pack of hounds on a fox. But as all the soldiers were peasants, and all the peasants hungry for property, the military element only added to the peas-ants' cry of Give us land, the soldiers' cry of Give us peace. Lenin said, in effect, Take the land; and if feudally minded persons obstruct you, exterminate them; but do not burn their houses, as you will need them to live in. And it was the re-sultant legions of petty landed proprietors that made Lenin's position impregnable, and provided Trotsky and Stalin with the Red soldiers who defeated the counter-revolutionists of 1918. For the counter-revolution, in which we, to our eternal shame, took part (England sets the example of revolution and then attacks all other countries which presume to follow it), meant bringing the old landlords back; and the peasant fought against that as the mercenaries and conscripts of the Capitalist armies would not fight in favor of it.

A PEASANT VICTORY IS A VICTORY FOR PRIVATE PROPERTY

So far so good for Lenin; but the war against the counter-revolutionists, when it ended in victory for the peasant proprietor, was really a victory for private property, and was therefore succeeded by a fiercer struggle between the fanatically Communist Government and the fiercely individualist peasant proprietor, who wanted the produce of his plot for himself, and had no notion of pooling it with anybody, least of all with the urban proletarians who seemed like another species to him. Left to themselves the moujiks would have reproduced Capitalist civilization at its American worst in ten years. Thus the most urgent task before the victorious Communist Government was the extermination of the moujik; and yet the moujik, being still the goose that laid the golden eggs, could not be exterminated summarily without incidentally exterminating the whole Russian nation.

The way out of this deadlock was obvious enough, though very expensive and tedious. You can exterminate any human class not only by summary violence but by bringing up its children to be different. In the case of the Russian peasantry the father lives in a lousy kennel, at no man's call but his own, and extracts a subsistence by primitive methods from a strip of land on which a tractor could hardly turn even if he could afford such a luxury, but which is his very own. His book is a book of Nature, from which all wisdom can be gathered by those who have been taught to read it by due practice on printed books; but he has not been so practised, and for cultural purposes has to be classed as ignorant, though he knows things that university professors do not know. He is brutalized by excessive muscular labor; he is dirty; his freedom from civilized control leaves him so unprotected from the tyranny of Nature that it becomes evident to his children that the highly regulated people in the nearest collectivist farm, where thousands of acres are cultivated by dozens of tractors, and nobody can put his foot on one of the acres or his hand on one of the tractors and say "This is my own to do what I like with," are better fed and housed, nicer, and much more leisured, and consequently free, than he ever is.

PREVENTIVE EXTERMINATION: ITS DIFFICULTIES

In short, you exterminate the peasant by bringing up his children to be scientifically mechanized farmers and to live a collegiate life in cultivated society. It sounds simple; but the process requires better planning than is always forthcoming (with local famines and revolts as the penalty); for while the grass grows the steed starves; and when education means not only schools and teachers, but giant collective farms equipped with the most advanced agricultural machinery, which means also gigantic engineering works for the production of the machinery, you may easily find that you have spent too much on these forms of capitalization and are running short of immediately consumable goods, presenting the spectacle of the nation with the highest level of general culture running short of boots and tightening its belt for lack of sufficient food.

I must not suggest that this has occurred all over Russia; for I saw no underfed people there; and the children were remarkably plump. And I cannot trust the reports; for I have no sooner read in The Times a letter from Mr Kerensky assuring me that in the Ukraine the starving people are eating one another, than M. Herriot, the eminent French statesman, goes to Russia and insists on visiting the Ukraine so that he may have ocular proof of the alleged cannibalism, but can find no trace of it. Still, between satiety and starvation mitigated by cannibalism there are many degrees of shortage; and it is no secret that the struggle of the Russian Government to provide more collective farms and more giant factories to provide agricultural machinery for them has to be carried on against a constant clamor from the workers for new boots and clothes, and more varied food and more of it: in short, less sacrifice of the present to the future. As Stalin said quaintly "They will be demanding silver watches next." The constant correction of the inevitable swerves towards one extreme or the other, analogous to the control of the Bank rate by the Bank of England (only enormously more laborious), strains all the wit and industry of the Russian rulers; and occasional sideslips must be inevitable during these years when the ablest and oldest Communists are still learners.

TEMPERAMENTAL DIFFICULTIES

Even when the extinction of the bourgeoisie and the kulaks and the old aristocracy is complete, and the Russian population consists of citizens educated as Communists, there will still be questions to settle which are at bottom questions as to the sort of civilization that is desirable; and this involves a decision as to the sort of people that are desirable and undesirable. Some of us, believing that a more primitive life than ours would be happier and better, advocate "a return to nature." Others dream of a much more mechanized, specialized, and complicated life. Some of us value machinery because it makes a shorter working day possible for us: others value it because it enriches us by increasing the product per hour. Some of us would like to take things easy and retire at 60: others would like to work their utmost and retire at 40. Some of us will say Let us be content with £200 a year: others No: let us live at the rate of £20,000 a year and strain every faculty to earn it. Some of us want a minimum of necessary work and a maximum of liberty to think and discover and experiment in the extension of science and art, philosophy and religion, sport and exploration: others, caring for none of these things, and desiring nothing more than to be saved the trouble of thinking and to be told what to do at every turn, would prefer thoughtless and comfortable tutelage and routine, not knowing what to do with themselves when at liberty. A life filled with scientific curiosity would be hell for the people who would not cross the street to find out whether the earth is flat or round; and a person with no ear for music would strenuously object to work for the support of municipal bands, whilst people of Shakespear's tastes would agitate for the extermination of the unmusical.

IMPORTANCE OF LAZINESS FOR FALLOWING

Some of these differences could be settled on give-and-take lines. The division of society into classes with different tastes and capacities—different natures, as folks call it—would not shake social stability provided everyone had an equal share of the national dividend. It is not true that it takes all sorts to make a world; for there are some sorts that would destroy any world very soon if they were suffered to live and have their way; but it is true that in the generations of men continuous high cultivation is not expedient: there must be fallows, or at least light croppings, between the intense cultivations; for we cannot expect the very energetic and vital Napoleon to be the son of an equally energetic father or the father of an equally vital son. Nobody has yet calculated how many lazy ancestors it takes to produce an indefatigable prodigy; but it is certain that dynasties of geniuses do not occur, and that this is the decisive objection to hereditary rulers (though not, let me hasten to add, to hereditary figure heads). There is a large field for toleration here: the clever people must suffer fools gladly, and the easygoing ones find out how to keep the energetic ones busy. There may be as good biological reasons for the existence of the workshy as of the workmad. Even one and the same person may have spells of intense activity and slackness varying from weeks to years.

STANDARD RELIGION INDISPENSABLE

Nevertheless there will be conflicts to the death in the creation of artificial humanity. There is nothing that can be changed more completely than human nature when the job is taken in hand early enough. Such artificial products as our agricultural laborers and urban mechanics, our country gentlemen and city plutocrats, though they are from the same human stock, are so different that they cannot live together without great discomfort, and are practically not intermarriageable. It is possible to get rid of their social incompatibility by giving them all the same education and income, and ranking them all in the same class. For example, Lord Lonsdale is not in the least socially incompatible with Dean Inge, though a really critical naturalist would as soon class Shetland ponies with zebras as lump these two gentlemen under the same heading. But the question remains, what is this same education to be? The training of the scholar and the sportsman may split and diverge as they adolesce; but they must start from a common training

and a common morality as children. And when the state has to prescribe a uniform moral curriculum the variety of our temperaments makes it impossible to please everybody. The Quaker and the Ritualist, the Fundamentalist and the Freethinker, the Vegetarian and the flesh eater, the missionary and the cannibal, the humanitarian and the sportsman-hunter, the military terrorist and the Christian, will not agree as to the faiths and habits to be inculcated upon the children of the community in order that they may be good citizens. Each temperament will demand the extermination of the other through the schools and nurseries, and the establishment of its temperamental faith and habits as standard in these factories of future citizens. All will agree to exterminate illiteracy by compulsory reading, writing, and arithmetic: indeed they have already done so. But all will not agree on a standard religion. Yet a standard religion is indispensable, however completely it may shed the old theologies. Every attempt to banish religion from the schools proves that in this respect Nature abhors a vacuum, and that the community must make up its mind, or have its mind made up for it by its official thinkers, as to what its children are to be taught to believe and how they should be trained to behave. Compromise is ruled out by the nature of the case. What compromise is possible between myself, for instance, who believe in the religion of Creative Evolution, the economics of Socialism, and a diet from which the dead bodies of men, fish, fowls, and animals are rigidly excluded, and my Fundamentalist neighbors who believe that all Evolutionists go to hell; that children languish and die without beefsteaks; and that without private property civilization must perish? We cannot exterminate oneanother at present; but the time cannot be very far off when the education authorities will have to consider which set of beliefs is the better qualification for citizenship in Utopia.

ECLECTIC RELIGIONS

They will probably pigeon-hole both, and proceed eclectically to compile several creeds suitable to the several capacities and ages of the children. For there is clearly no sense in offering the religion of a mature and scholarly philosopher to a child of five, nor attempting to bring the cosmogonies of Dante and Aquinas, Hegel and Marx, within the comprehension of a village dunce. Nurses rule their little charges by threatening them with bogies in whose existence no nurse believes, exactly as Mahomet ruled his Arabs by promises of a paradise and threats of a hell the details of which he must have known to be his own invention even if he did believe generally in a post mortem life of rewards and punishments for conduct in this world. Therefore I do not suggest that the education authorities in Utopia will seek for absolute truth in order to inculcate it though the heavens fall. Nor do I advise a return to Queen Elizabeth's plan of 39 Articles to please everybody by alternately affirming and denying all the disputed beliefs. The likeliest outcome is an elaborate creed of useful illusions, to be discarded bit by bit as the child is promoted from standard to standard or form to form, except such of them as adults may be allowed to comfort themselves with for the sake of the docility they produce.

There would be nothing new in this: it is what our authorities do at present, except that they do it unsystematically and unconsciously, being mostly more or less duped themselves by the illusions. Unfortunately they allow the illusions to fall behind the times and become incredible, at which point they become exceedingly dangerous; for when people are brought up on creeds which they cannot believe, they are left with no creeds at all, and are apt to buy pistols and take to banditry bag snatching and racketeering when employment fails and they find themselves short of money. It is the importance of keeping our inculcated illusions up to date that throws our higher professional classes into wild alarm when the individual liberty of thought, speech, and conscience which they think they possess (this is one of their inculcated illusions) is threatened by the dictatorships which are springing up all over the world as our pseudo-democratic parliamentary institutions reduce themselves more and more disastrously to absurdity.

IMPORTANCE OF FREE THOUGHT

Let me try to straighten this out for them. It was very generally believed as lately as in Victorian times that religious education consisted in imparting to children certain eternal, final, and absolute truths. I, for instance, being the son of an Irish Protestant gentleman, found myself, at the dawn of my infant conscience, absolutely convinced that all Roman Catholics go to hell when they die, a conviction which involved not only a belief in the existence of hell but a whole series of implications as to the nature and character of God. Now that I am older I cannot regard this as anything more than a provisional hypothesis which, on consideration, I must definitely reject. As the more pious of my uncles would have put it, I have lost my religious faith and am in peril of damnation as an Apostate. But I do not present my creed of Creative Evolution as anything more than another provisional hypothesis. It differs from the old Dublin brimstone creed solely in its greater credibility: that is, its more exact conformity to the facts alleged by our scientific workers, who have somehow won that faith in their infallibility formerly enjoyed by our priests. No future education authority, unless it is as badly educated as our present ones, will imagine that it has any final and eternal truths to inculcate: it can only select the most useful working hypotheses and inculcate them very much as it inculcates standard behavior throughout that vast field of civilized conduct in which it does not matter in the least how people act in particular situations provided they all act in the same way, as in the rule of the road. All the provisional hypotheses may be illusions; but if they conduce to beneficial conduct they must be inculcated and acted on by Governments until better ones arrive.

TOLERATION MOSTLY ILLUSORY

But, cry the professors, are the hypotheses never to be questioned? Is disillusion to be punished as a crime? That will always depend a good deal on circumstances. One of the best religious brains in England has said that the war of 1914–18 was foolish and unnecessary; and nobody now dreams of prosecuting him; but he would not have been allowed to go through the trenches from platoon to platoon saying so just before zero hour, with or without the addition "Sirs, ye are brethren: why do ye wrong one to another?" I have no illusion of being free to say and write what I please. I went round the world lately preaching that if Russia were thrust back from Communism into competitive Capitalism, and China developed into a predatory Capitalist State, either independently or as part of a Japanese Asiatic hegemony, all the western States would have to quintuple their armies and lie awake at nights in continual dread of hostile aeroplanes, the obvious moral being that whether we choose Communism for ourselves or not, it is our clear interest, even from the point of view of our crudest and oldest militarist diplomacy, to do everything in our power to sustain Communism in Russia and extend it in China, where at present provinces containing at the least of many

conflicting estimates eighteen millions of people, have adopted it. Now I was not physically prevented from saying this, nor from writing and printing it. But in a western world suffering badly from Marxphobia, and frantically making itself worse like a shrew in a bad temper, I could not get a single newspaper to take up my point or report my utterance. When I say anything silly, or am reported as saying anything reactionary, it runs like wildfire through the Press of the whole world. When I say anything that could break the carefully inculcated popular faith in Capitalism the silence is so profound as to be almost audible. I do not complain, because I do not share the professorial illusion that there is any more freedom for disillusionists in the British Empire and the United States of North America than in Italy, Germany, and Russia. I have seen too many newspapers suppressed and editors swept away, not only in Ireland and India but in London in my time, to be taken in by Tennyson's notion that we live in a land where a man can say the thing he will. There is no such country. But this is no excuse for the extravagances of censorship indulged in by jejune governments of revolutionists, and by Churches who imagine they possess the eternal truth about everything, to say nothing of hereditary autocrats who conceive that they are so by divine right. Our papers are silent about the suppression of liberty in Imperialist Japan, though in Japan it is a crime to have "dangerous thoughts." In my native Ireland, now nominally a Free State, one of my books is on the index; and I have no doubt all the rest will follow as soon as the clerical censorship discovers their existence. In Austria my chronicle play St Joan had to be altered to please Catholic authorities who know much less about Catholicism than I do. In America books which can be bought anywhere in Europe are forbidden. The concentration of British and

American attention on the intolerances of Fascism and Communism creates an illusion that they do not exist elsewhere; but they exist everywhere, and must be met, not with ridiculous hotheaded attacks on Germany, Italy, and Russia, but by a restatement of the case for Toleration in general.

LEADING CASES: SOCRATES AND JESUS

It is a historical misfortune that the most world-famous victims of persecution made no valid defence. Socrates and Jesus are the most talked of in Christian countries. Socrates at his trial was in full possession of his faculties, and was allowed to say everything he had to say in his defence; but instead of defending his right to criticize he infuriated his accusers by launching at them a damning contrast between their infamous corruption and mendacity and his own upright disinterestedness and blameless record as citizen and soldier. Jesus made no defence at all. He did not regard himself as a prisoner being tried for a vulgar offence and using all his wit to escape condemnation. He believed that he was going through a sacrificial rite in which he should be slain, after which he should rise from the dead and come again in glory to establish his kingdom on earth for ever. It does not matter to our present purpose whether this was the delusion of a madman or a hard and holy fact: in either case the question of toleration was not at issue for him; therefore he did not raise it.

THE CASE OF GALILEO

In the epoch which Jesus inaugurated, or at least in which his name was habitually taken in vain, we have Joan of Arc and John of Leyden, Giordano Bruno and Galileo, Servetus and John Hus and the heroes of Foxe's Book of Martyrs standing out in our imagination from thousands of forgotten martyrdoms. Galileo is a favored subject with our scientists;

but they miss the point because they think that the question at issue at his trial was whether the earth went round the sun or was the stationary centre round which the sun circled. Now that was not the issue. Taken by itself it was a mere question of physical fact without any moral significance, and therefore no concern of the Church. As Galileo was not burnt and certainly not abhorred, it is quite credible that both his immediate judges and the Pope believed with at least half their minds that he was right about the earth and the sun. But what they had to consider was whether the Christian religion, on which to the best of their belief not only the civilization of the world but its salvation depended, and which had accepted the Hebrew scriptures and the Greek testament as inspired revelations, could stand the shock of the discovery that many of its tales, from the tactics of Joshua in the battle of Gibeon to the Ascension, must have been written by somebody who did not know what the physical universe was really like. I am quite familiar with the pre-Galileo universe of the Bible and St Augustine. As a child I thought of the earth as being an immense ground floor with a star studded ceiling which was the floor of heaven, and a basement which was hell. That Jesus should be taken up into the clouds as the shortest way to heaven seemed as natural to me as that, at the Opera, Mephistopheles should come up from hell through a trap in the floor. But if instead of telling me that Jesus was taken up into the clouds and that the disciples saw him no more, which still makes me feel quite holy, you tell me that he went up like a balloon into the stratosphere, I do not feel holy: I laugh obstreperously. The exalting vision has suddenly become a ribald joke. That is what the Church feared; and that is what has actually happened. Is it any wonder that the Pope told Galileo that he really must keep his discoveries to himself, and that Galileo consented to deny them? Possibly it was the Pope who, to console him, whispered "E pur se muove."

FIGMENT OF THE SELFREGARDING ACTION

St Joan did not claim toleration: she was so far from believing in it that she wanted to lead a crusade of extermination against the Husites, though she was burnt for sharing their heresy. That is how all the martyrs have missed the point of their defence. They all claimed to possess absolute truth as against the error of their persecutors, and would have considered it their duty to persecute for its sake if they had had the power. Real toleration: the toleration of error and falsehood, never occurred to them as a principle possible for any sane government. And so they have left us no model defence. And there is no modern treatise known to me which quite supplies this need. Stuart Mill's Essay on Liberty satisfied the nineteenth century, and was my own first textbook on the subject; but its conclusion that selfregarding actions should not be interfered with by the authorities carries very little weight for Socialists who perceive that in a complex modern civilization there are no purely selfregarding actions in the controversial sphere. The color of a man's braces or a woman's garters may concern the wearers alone; but people have never been burnt for wearing black underclothes instead of white; and the notion that preaching a sermon or publishing a pamphlet can be classed as a selfregarding action is manifestly absurd. All great Art and Literature is propaganda. Most certainly the heresies of Galileo were not selfregarding actions: his feat of setting the earth rolling was as startling as Joshua's feat of making the sun stand still. The Church's mistake was not in interfering with his liberty, but in imagining that the secret of the earth's

motion could be kept, and fearing that religion could not stand the shock of its disclosure, or a thousand such. It was idiotic to try to adapt Nature to the Church instead of continually adapting the Church to Nature by changing its teaching on physical matters with every advance made in our knowledge of Nature. In treating the legend of Joshua's victory as a religious truth instead of insisting that it did not make the smallest difference to religion whether Joshua was any more real than Jack the Giant Killer, and that Galileo might play skittles with the whole solar system without moving the Eternal Throne and the Papal Chair which was its visible tangible symbol on earth a single inch, it lost a great opportunity, as it has since lost many others, leaving itself open to the reproach of stupidity in not understanding Galileo's argument, of pride in not having humility enough to admit that it had been wrong in its astronomy, and of feebleness of faith and confusion of the temporal with the spiritual as aforesaid, laying itself open to much damaging Protestant and scientific disparagement, both mostly open to precisely the same reproaches.

INCOMPLETENESS OF THE GREAT TRIALS

No doubt Galileo missed the real point at issue as completely as Socrates or Jesus. For this we need not blame him: he was a physicist and not a politician; and to him the only questions at issue were whether the earth moved or not, and whether a ten pound cannon ball would fall twice as fast as a five pound one or only just as fast and no faster. But Socrates was by vocation and habit a solver of problems of conduct, both personal and political; and Jesus, who had spent his life in propounding the most staggering paradoxes on the same subject, not by any means always in the abstract, but as personal directions to his followers, must, if he had any sense of moral responsibility, have been challenged by his own conscience again and again as to whether he had any right to set men on a path which was likely to lead the best of them to the cross and the worst of them to the moral destruction described by St Augustine. No man could expressly admit that his word would bring not peace but a sword without having satisfied himself that he was justified in doing so. He must have been told as frequently as I have been told that he was giving pain to many worthy people; and even with the fullest allowance for the strain of impishness with which the Life Force endows those of us who are destined by it to *épater le bourgeois*, he cannot have believed that the mere satisfaction of this Punchesque *Schadenfreude* could justify him in hurting anyone's feelings. What, then, would have been his defence if, at his trial, he had been his old self, defending himself as an accused man threatened with a horrible penalty, instead of a god going through an inevitable ordeal as a prelude to the establishment of his kingdom on earth?

A MODERN PASSION PLAY IMPOSSIBLE

The question is of such importance at the present crisis, when the kingdoms are breaking up, and upstart rulers are sowing their wild oats by such grotesque persecutions that Galileo's great successor Einstein is a plundered fugitive from officially threatened extermination, that I must endeavor to dramatize the trial of Jesus as it might have proceeded had it taken place before Peter uttered his momentous exclamation "Thou art the Christ." I have been asked repeatedly to dramatize the Gospel story, mostly by admirers of my dramatization of the trial of St Joan. But the trial of a dumb prisoner, at which the judge who puts the crucial question to him remains unanswered, cannot be dramatized unless the judge is to be the hero of the play.

Now Pilate, though perhaps a trifle above the average of colonial governors, is not a heroic figure. Joan tackled her judges valiantly and wittily: her trial was a drama ready made, only needing to be brought within theatrical limits of time and space to be a thrilling play. But Jesus would not defend himself. It was not that he had not a word to say for himself, nor that he was denied the opportunity of saying it. He was not only allowed but challenged to defend himself. He was an experienced public speaker, able to hold multitudes with his oratory, happy and ready in debate and repartee, full of the illustrative hypothetical cases beloved of lawyers (called parables in the Gospels), and never at a loss when plied with questions. If ever there was a full dress debate for the forensic championship to be looked forward to with excited confidence by the disciples of the challenged expert it was this trial of Christ. Yet their champion put up no fight: he went like a lamb to the slaughter, dumb. Such a spectacle is disappointing on the stage, which is the one thing that a drama must not be; and when the disappointment is followed by scourging and crucifixion it is unbearable: not even the genius of our Poet Laureate, with all the magic of Canterbury Cathedral for scenery, can redeem it except for people who enjoy horror and catastrophe for their own sake and have no intellectual expectations to be disappointed.

DIFFERENCE BETWEEN READER AND SPECTATOR

It may be asked why the incident of the trial and execution must fail on the stage, seeing that the Gospel narrative is so pathetic, and so many of us have read it without disappointment. The answer is very simple: we have read it in childhood; and children go on from horror to horror breathlessly, knowing nothing of the constitutional questions at issue. Some of them remain in this condition of intellectual innocence to the end of their lives, whilst the cleverer ones seldom reconsider the impressions they have received as little children. Most Christians, I suspect, are afraid to think about it critically at all, having been taught to consider criticism blasphemous when applied to Bible stories. Besides, there are a thousand things that will pass in a well told story that will not bear being brought to actuality on the stage. The evangelists can switch off our attention from Jesus to Peter hearing the cock crow (or the bugle blow) or to Pilate chaffering with the crowd about Barabbas; but on the stage the dumb figure cannot be got rid of: it is to him that we look for a speech that will take us up to heaven, and not to the weeping of Peter and the bawling of the mob, which become unbearable interruptions instead of skilful diversions.

For my part, when I read the story over again as an adult and as a professional critic to boot, I felt the disappointment so keenly that I have been ever since in the condition of the musician who, when he had gone to bed, heard somebody play an unresolved discord, and could not go to sleep until he had risen to play the resolution on his piano. What follows is my attempt to resolve Pilate's discord. I begin with the narrative of St John, the only one of the four which represents Jesus as saying anything more than any crazy person might in the same circumstances.

PILATE. Are you the king of the Jews?

JESUS. Do you really want to know? or have those people outside put it into your head to ask me?

PILATE. Am I a Jew, that I should trouble myself about you? Your own people and their priests have brought you to me for judgment. What have you done?

JESUS. My kingdom is not of this world: if it were, my followers would have fought the police and rescued me. But that sort of thing does not happen in my kingdom.

PILATE. Then you are a king?

JESUS. You say so. I came into this world and was born a common man for no other purpose than to reveal the truth. And everyone capable of receiving the truth recognizes it in my voice.

PILATE. What is truth?

JESUS. You are the first person I have met intelligent enough to ask me that question.

PILATE. Come on! no flattery. I am a Roman, and no doubt seem exceptionally intelligent to a Jew. You Jews are always talking about truth and righteousness and justice: you feed on words when you are tired of making money, or too poor to have anything else to feed on. They want me to nail you up on a cross; but as I do not yet see what particular harm you have done I prefer to nail you down to an argument. Fine words butter no parsnips in Rome. You say your vocation is to reveal the truth. I take your word for it; but I ask you what is truth?

JESUS. It is that which a man must tell even if he be stoned or crucified for telling it. I am not offering you the truth at a price for my own profit: I am offering it freely to you for your salvation at the peril of my own life. Would I do that if I were not driven by God to do it against all the protests of my shrinking flesh?

PILATE. You Jews are a simple folk. You have found only one god. We Romans have found many; and one of them is a God of Lies. Even you Jews have to admit a Father of Lies whom you call the devil, deceiving yourselves with words as usual. But he is a very potent god, is he not? And as he delights not only in lies but in all other mischief such as stonings and crucifixions of innocent men, how am I to judge whether it is he who is driving you to sacrifice yourself for a lie, or Minerva driving you to be sacrificed for the truth? I ask you again, what is truth?

JESUS. It is what you know by your experience to be true or feel in your soul must be true.

PILATE. You mean that truth is a correspondence between word and fact. It is true that I am sitting in this chair; but I am not the truth and the chair is not the truth: we are only the facts. My perception that I am sitting here may be only a dream; therefore my perception is not the truth.

JESUS. You say well. The truth is the truth and nothing else. That is your answer.

PILATE. Aye; but how far is it discoverable? We agree that it is true that I am sitting in this chair because our senses tell us so; and two men are not likely to be dreaming the same dream at the same moment. But when I rise from my chair this truth is no longer true. Truth is of the present, not of the future. Your hopes for the future are not the truth. Even in the present your opinions are not the truth. It is true that I sit in this chair. But is it true that it is better for your people that I should sit in this chair and impose on them the peace of Rome than that they should be left to slaughter oneanother in their own native savagery, as they are now clamoring to me to slaughter you?

JESUS. There is the peace of God that is beyond our understanding; and that peace shall prevail over the peace of Rome when God's hour strikes.

PILATE. Very pretty, my friend; but the hour of the gods is now and always; and all the world knows what the peace of your Jewish God means. Have I not read it in the campaigns of Joshua? We Romans have purchased the *pax Romana* with our blood; and we prefer it as a plain understandable thing which keeps men's knives off oneanother's throats to your peace which is beyond understand-

ing because it slaughters man woman and child in the name of your God. But that is only our opinion. It is not yours. Therefore it is not necessarily the truth. I must act on it, because a governor must act on something: he cannot loaf round the roads and talk beautifully as you do. If you were a responsible governor instead of a poetic vagrant, you would soon discover that my choice must lie, not between truth and falsehood, neither of which I can ever ascertain, but between reasonable and well informed opinion and sentimental and ill informed impulse.

JESUS. Nevertheless, opinion is a dead thing and impulse a live thing. You cannot impose on me with your reasonable and well informed opinion. If it is your will to crucify me, I can find you a dozen reasons for doing so; and your police can supply you with a hundred facts to support the reasons. If it is your will to spare me I can find you just as many reasons for that; and my disciples will supply you with more facts than you will have time or patience to listen to. That is why your lawyers can plead as well for one side as another, and can therefore plead without dishonor for the side that pays them, like the hackney charioteer who will drive you north as readily as south for the same fare.

PILATE. You are cleverer than I thought; and you are right. There is my will; and there is the will of Cæsar to which my will must give way; and there is above Cæsar the will of the gods. But these wills are in continual conflict with oneanother; therefore they are not truth; for truth is one, and cannot conflict with itself. There are conflicting opinions and conflicting wills; but there is no truth except the momentary truth that I am sitting in this chair. Yet you tell me that you are here to bear witness to the truth! You, a vagrant, a talker, who have never had to pass a sentence nor levy a tax nor issue an edict! What have you to say that I should not have the presumption scourged out of you by my executioners?

JESUS. Scourging is not a cure for presumption, nor is it justice, though you will perhaps call it so in your report to Cæsar: it is cruelty; and that cruelty is wicked and horrible because it is the weapon with which the sons of Satan slay the sons of God is part of the eternal truth you seek.

PILATE. Leave out cruelty: all government is cruel; for nothing is so cruel as impunity. A salutary severity—

JESUS. Oh please! You must excuse me, noble Governor; but I am so made by God that official phrases make me violently sick. Salutary severity is ipecacuanha to me. I have spoken to you as one man to another, in living words. Do not be so ungrateful as to answer me in dead ones.

PILATE. In the mouth of a Roman words mean something: in the mouth of a Jew they are a cheap substitute for strong drink. If we allowed you you would fill the whole world with your scriptures and psalms and talmuds; and the history of mankind would become a tale of fine words and villainous deeds.

JESUS. Yet the word came first, before it was made flesh. The word was the beginning. The word was with God before he made us. Nay, the word was God.

PILATE. And what may all that mean, pray?

JESUS. The difference between man and Roman is but a word; but it makes all the difference. The difference between Roman and Jew is only a word.

PILATE. It is a fact.

JESUS. A fact that was first a thought; for a thought is the substance of a word. I am no mere chance pile of flesh and bone: if I were only that, I should fall into corruption and dust before your eyes. I am the embodiment of a thought of God: I am the Word made flesh: that is what holds me together standing before

you in the image of God.

PILATE. That is well argued; but what is sauce for the goose is sauce for the gander; and it seems to me that if you are the Word made flesh so also am I.

JESUS. Have I not said so again and again? Have they not stoned me in the streets for saying it? Have I not sent my apostles to proclaim this great news to the Gentiles and to the very ends of the world? The Word is God. And God is within you. It was when I said this that the Jews—my own people—began picking up stones. But why should you, the Gentile, reproach me for it?

PILATE. I have not reproached you for it. I pointed it out to you.

JESUS. Forgive me. I am so accustomed to be contradicted—

PILATE. Just so. There are many sorts of words; and they are all made flesh sooner or later. Go among my soldiers and you will hear many filthy words and witness many cruel and hateful deeds that began as thoughts. I do not allow those words to be spoken in my presence. I punish those deeds as crimes. Your truth, as you call it, can be nothing but the thoughts for which you have found words which will take effect in deeds if I set you loose to scatter your words broadcast among the people. Your own people who bring you to me tell me that your thoughts are abominable and your words blasphemous. How am I to refute them? How am I to distinguish between the blasphemies of my soldiers reported to me by my centurions and your blasphemies reported to me by your High Priest?

JESUS. Woe betide you and the world if you do not distinguish!

PILATE. So you think. I am not frightened. Why do you think so?

JESUS. I do not think: I know. I have it from God.

PILATE. I have the same sort of knowledge from several gods.

JESUS. In so far as you know the truth you have it from my God, who is your heavenly father and mine. He has many names and his nature is manifold. Call him what you will: he is still Our Father. Does a father tell his children lies?

PILATE. Yes: many lies. You have an earthly father and an earthly mother. Did they tell you what you are preaching?

JESUS. Alas! no.

PILATE. Then you are defying your father and mother. You are defying your Church. You are breaking your God's commandments, and claiming a right to do so. You are pleading for the poor, and declaring that it is easier for a camel to pass through the eye of a needle than for a rich man to enter your God's paradise. Yet you have feasted at the tables of the rich, and encouraged harlots to spend on perfume for your feet money that might have been given to the poor, thereby so disgusting your treasurer that he has betrayed you to the High Priest for a handful of silver. Well, feast as much as you please: I do not blame you for refusing to play the fakir and make yourself a walking exhibition of silly austerities; but I must draw the line at your making a riot in the temple and throwing the gold of the moneychangers to be scrambled for by your partizans. I have a law to administer. The law forbids obscenity, sedition, and blasphemy. You are accused of sedition and blasphemy. You do not deny them: you only talk about the truth, which turns out to be nothing but what you like to believe. Your blasphemy is nothing to me: the whole Jewish religion is blasphemy from beginning to end from my Roman point of view; but it means a great deal to the High Priest; and I cannot keep order in Jewry except by dealing with Jewish fools according to Jewish folly. But sedition concerns me and my office very closely; and when you undertook to supersede the Roman Empire by a kingdom in which you and not Cæsar are to occupy the throne, you were guilty of the uttermost sedition. I am loth to have you crucified; for though you are only a Jew, and a half baked young one at that, yet I perceive that you are in your Jewish way a man of quality; and it makes me uneasy to throw a man of quality to the mob, even if his quality be only a Jewish quality. For I am a patrician and therefore myself a man of quality; and hawks should not pick out hawks' eyes. I am actually condescending to parley with you at this length in the merciful hope of finding an excuse for tolerating your blasphemy and sedition. In defence you offer me nothing but an empty phrase about the truth. I am sincere in wishing to spare you; for if I do not release you I shall have to release that blackguard Barabbas, who has gone further than you and killed somebody, whereas I understand that you have only raised a Jew from the dead. So for the last time set your wits to work, and find me a sound reason for letting a seditious blasphemer go free.

JESUS. I do not ask you to set me free; nor would I accept my life at the price of Barabbas's death even if I believed that you could countermand the ordeal to which I am predestined. Yet for the satisfaction of your longing for the truth I will tell you that the answer to your demand is your own argument that neither you nor the prisoner whom you judge can prove that he is in the right; therefore you must not judge me lest you be yourself judged. Without sedition and blasphemy the world would stand still and the kingdom of God never be a stage nearer. The Roman Empire began with a wolf suckling two human infants. If these infants had not been wiser than their fostermother your empire would be a pack of wolves. It is by children who are wiser than their fathers, subjects who are wiser than their emperors, beggars and vagrants who are wiser than their priests, that men rise from being beasts of prey to believing in me and being saved.

PILATE. What do you mean by believing in you?

JESUS. Seeing the world as I do. What else could it mean?

PILATE. And you are the Christ, the Messiah, eh?

JESUS. Were I Satan, my argument would still hold.

PILATE. And I am to spare and encourage every heretic, every rebel, every lawbreaker, every rapscallion lest he should turn out to be wiser than all the generations who made the Roman law and built up the Roman Empire on it?

JESUS. By their fruits ye shall know them. Beware how you kill a thought that is new to you. For that thought may be the foundation of the kingdom of God on earth.

PILATE. It may also be the ruin of all kingdoms, all law, and all human society. It may be the thought of the beast of prey striving to return.

JESUS. The beast of prey is not striving to return: the kingdom of God is striving to come. The empire that looks back in terror shall give way to the kingdom that looks forward with hope. Terror drives men mad: hope and faith give them divine wisdom. The men whom you fill with fear will stick at no evil and perish in their sin: the men whom I fill with faith shall inherit the earth. I say to you Cast out fear. Speak no more vain things to me about the greatness of Rome. The greatness of Rome, as you call it, is nothing but fear: fear of the past and fear of the future, fear of the poor, fear of the rich, fear of the High Priests, fear of the Jews and Greeks who are learned, fear of the Gauls and Goths and Huns who are barbarians, fear of the Carthage you destroyed to save you from your fear of it and now fear worse than ever, fear of imperial Cæsar, the idol you have yourself created, and fear of me, the penniless vagrant, buffeted and mocked, fear of everything except the rule of God: faith in nothing but blood and iron and gold. You, standing for Rome, are the universal coward: I, standing for the kingdom of God, have braved everything, lost everything, and won an eternal crown.

PILATE. You have won a crown of thorns; and you shall wear it on the cross. You are a more dangerous fellow than I thought. For your blasphemy against the god of the high priests I care nothing: you may trample their religion into hell for all I care; but you have blasphemed against Cæsar and against the Empire; and you mean it, and have the power to turn men's hearts against it as you have half turned mine. Therefore I must make an end of you whilst there is still some law left in the world.

JESUS. Law is blind without counsel. The counsel men agree with is vain: it is only the echo of their own voices. A million echoes will not help you to rule righteously. But he who does not fear you and shews you the other side is a pearl of the greatest price. Slay me and you go blind to your damnation. The greatest of God's names is Counsellor; and when your Empire is dust and your name a byword among the nations the temples of the living God shall still ring with his praise as Wonderful! Counsellor! the Everlasting Father, the Prince of Peace.

THE SACREDNESS OF CRITICISM

And so the last word remains with Christ and Handel; and this must stand as the best defence of Tolerance until a better man than I makes a better job of it.

Put shortly and undramatically the case is that a civilization cannot progress without criticism, and must therefore, to save itself from stagnation and putrefaction, declare impunity for criticism. This means impunity not only for propositions which, however novel, seem interesting, statesmanlike, and respectable, but for propositions that shock the uncritical as obscene, seditious, blasphemous, heretical, and revolutionary. That sound Catholic institution, the Devil's Advocate, must be privileged as possibly the Herald of the World to Come. The difficulty is to distinguish between the critic and the criminal or lunatic, between liberty of precept and liberty of example. It may be vitally necessary to allow a person to advocate Nudism; but it may not be expedient to allow that person to walk along Piccadilly stark naked. Karl Marx writing the death warrant of private property in the reading room of the British Museum was sacred; but if Karl Marx had sent the rent of his villa in Maitland Park to the Chancellor of the Exchequer, and shot the landlord's agents when they came to distrain on his furniture or execute a writ of ejectment, he could hardly have escaped hanging by pleading his right to criticize. Not until the criticism changes the law can the magistrate allow the critic to give effect to it. We are so dangerously uneducated in citizenship that most of us assume that we have an unlimited right to change our conduct the moment we have changed our minds. People who have a vague notion that Socialism is a state of society in which everyone gives away everything he possesses to everybody else occasionally reproach me because I, being a Socialist, do not immediately beggar myself in this fashion. People who imagined, more specifically, that a Socialist could not consistently keep a motor car, almost succeeded in making a public question of the possession of such a vehicle by a Prime Minister who at that time professed Socialism. But even if these idiots had really understood what they were talking about, they would have been wrong in supposing that a hostile critic of the existing social order either could or should behave as if he were living in his own particular Utopia. He may, at most, be a little eccentric at the cost of being indulged as slightly cracked.

On the other hand the Government, too, has not only a right but a duty of criticism. If it is to abandon once for all its savage superstition that whoever breaks the law is fair game for the torturers, and that the wrong wrought by the evildoer can be expiated and undone by a worse wrong done to him by judges and priests: if it is to substitute the doctrine of Jesus that punishment is only a senseless attempt to make a white out of two blacks, and to abolish the monstrous list of crimes and punishments by which these superstitions have been reduced to practice for routine officials, then there must be a stupendous extension of governmental criticism; for every crime will raise the essential critical question whether the criminal is fit to live at all, and if so whether he is fit to live under more or less tutelage and discipline like a soldier, or at normal liberty under an obligation to make good the damage he has cost.

For such functions as these we shall need critics educated otherwise than our judges of today; but the same may be said of all whose public functions transcend the application of a routine.

I have no doubt that the eradication of malice, vindictiveness, and Sadist libido on these terms from the personal contacts of citizens with their rulers, far from having a reassuring effect, is likely to be rather terrifying at first, as all people with any tenderness of conscience will feel the deepest misgivings as to whether they are really worth keeping alive in a highly civilized community; but that will wear off as standards of worth get established and known by practice. In the meantime the terror will act as a sort of social conscience which is dangerously lacking at present, and which none of our model educational establishments ever dreams of inculcating.

XV

HEARTBREAK HOUSE

1919

WHERE HEARTBREAK HOUSE STANDS

Heartbreak House is not merely the name of the play which follows this preface. It is cultured, leisured Europe before the war. When the play was begun not a shot had been fired; and only the professional diplomatists and the very few amateurs whose hobby is foreign policy even knew that the guns were loaded. A Russian playwright, Tchekov, had produced four fascinating dramatic studies of Heartbreak House, of which three, The Cherry Orchard, Uncle Vanya, and The Seagull, had been performed in England. Tolstoy, in his Fruits of Enlightenment, had shewn us through it in his most ferociously contemptuous manner. Tolstoy did not waste any sympathy on it: it was to him the house in which Europe was stifling its soul; and he knew that our utter enervation and futilization in that overheated drawing-room atmosphere was delivering the world over to the control of ignorant and soulless cunning and energy, with the frightful consequences which have now overtaken it. Tolstoy was no pessimist: he was not disposed to leave the house standing if he could bring it down about the ears of its pretty and amiable voluptuaries; and he wielded the pickaxe with a will. He treated the case of the inmates as one of opium poisoning, to be dealt with by seizing the patients roughly and exercising them violently until they were broad awake. Tchekov, more of a fatalist, had no faith in these charming people extricating themselves. They would, he thought, be sold up and sent adrift by the bailiffs; therefore he had no scruple in exploiting and even flattering their charm.

THE INHABITANTS

Tchekov's plays, being less lucrative than swings and roundabouts, got no further in England, where theatres are only ordinary commercial affairs, than a couple of performances by the Stage Society. We stared and said, "How Russian!" They did not strike me in that way. Just as Ibsen's intensely Norwegian plays exactly fitted every middle and professional class suburb in Europe, these intensely Russian plays fitted all the country houses in Europe in which the pleasures of music, art, literature, and the theatre had supplanted hunting, shooting, fishing, flirting, eating, and drinking. The same nice people, the same utter futility. The nice people could read; some of them could write; and they were the only repositories of culture who had social opportunities of contact with our politicians, administrators, and newspaper proprietors, or any chance of sharing or influencing their activities. But they shrank from that contact. They hated politics. They did not wish to realize Utopia for the common people: they wished to realize their favorite fictions and poems in their own lives; and, when they could, they lived without scruple on incomes which they did nothing to earn. The women in their girlhood made themselves look like variety theatre stars, and settled down later into the types of beauty imagined by the previous generation of painters. They took the only part of our society in which there was leisure for high culture, and made it an economic, political, and, as far as practicable, a moral vacuum; and as Nature, abhorring the vacuum, immediately filled it up with sex and with all sorts of refined pleasures, it was a very delightful place at its best for moments of relaxation. In other moments it was disastrous. For prime ministers and their like, it was a veritable Capua.

HORSEBACK HALL

But where were our front benchers to nest if not here? The alternative to Heartbreak House was Horseback Hall, consisting of a prison for horses with an annex for the ladies and gentlemen who rode them, hunted them, talked about them, bought them and sold them, and gave nine-tenths of their lives to them, dividing the other tenth between charity, churchgoing (as a substitute for religion), and conservative electioneering (as a substitute for politics). It is true that the two establishments got mixed at the edges. Exiles from the library, the music room, and the picture gallery would be found languishing among the stables, miserably discontented; and hardy horsewomen who slept at the first chord of Schumann were born, horribly misplaced, into the garden of Klingsor; but sometimes one came upon horsebreakers and heartbreakers who could make the best of both worlds. As a rule, however, the two were apart and knew little of one another; so the prime minister folk had to choose between barbarism and Capua. And of the two atmospheres it is hard to say which was the more fatal to statesmanship.

REVOLUTION ON THE SHELF

Heartbreak House was quite familiar with revolutionary ideas on paper. It aimed at being advanced and freethinking, and hardly ever went to church or kept the Sabbath except by a little extra fun at week-ends. When you spent a Friday to Tuesday in it you found on the shelf in your bedroom not only the books of poets and novelists, but of revolutionary biologists and even economists. Without at least a few plays by myself and Mr Granville Barker, and a few stories by Mr H. G. Wells, Mr Arnold Bennett, and Mr John Galsworthy, the house would have been out of the movement. You would find Blake among the poets, and beside him Bergson, Butler, Scott Haldane, the poems of Meredith and Thomas Hardy, and, generally speaking, all the literary implements for forming the mind of the perfect modern Socialist and Creative Evolutionist. It was a curious experience to spend Sunday in dipping into these books, and on Monday morning to read in the daily paper that the country had just been brought to the verge of anarchy because a new Home Secretary or chief of police, without an idea in his head that his great-grandmother might not have had to apologize for, had refused to "recognize" some powerful Trade Union, just as a gondola might refuse to recognize a 20,000-ton liner.

In short, power and culture were in separate compartments. The barbarians were not only literally in the saddle, but on the front bench in the House of Commons, with nobody to correct their incredible ignorance of modern thought and political science but upstarts from the counting-house, who had spent their lives furnishing their pockets instead of their minds. Both, however, were practised in dealing with money and with men, as far as acquiring the one and exploiting the other went; and although this is as undesirable an expertness as that of the medieval robber baron, it qualifies men to keep an estate or a business going in its old routine without necessarily understanding it, just as Bond Street tradesmen and domestic servants keep fashionable society going without any instruction in sociology.

THE CHERRY ORCHARD

The Heartbreak people neither could nor would do anything of the sort. With their heads as full of the Anticipations of

Mr H. G. Wells as the heads of our actual rulers were empty even of the anticipations of Erasmus or Sir Thomas More, they refused the drudgery of politics, and would have made a very poor job of it if they had changed their minds. Not that they would have been allowed to meddle anyhow, as only through the accident of being a hereditary peer can anyone in these days of Votes for Everybody get into parliament if handicapped by a serious modern cultural equipment; but if they had, their habit of living in a vacuum would have left them helpless and ineffective in public affairs. Even in private life they were often helpless wasters of their inheritance, like the people in Tchekov's Cherry Orchard. Even those who lived within their incomes were really kept going by their solicitors and agents, being unable to manage an estate or run a business without continual prompting from those who have to learn how to do such things or starve.

From what is called Democracy no corrective to this state of things could be hoped. It is said that every people has the Government it deserves. It is more to the point that every Government has the electorate it deserves; for the orators of the front bench can edify or debauch an ignorant electorate at will. Thus our democracy moves in a vicious circle of reciprocal worthiness and unworthiness.

NATURE'S LONG CREDITS

Nature's way of dealing with unhealthy conditions is unfortunately not one that compels us to conduct a solvent hygiene on a cash basis. She demoralizes us with long credits and reckless overdrafts, and then pulls us up cruelly with catastrophic bankruptcies. Take, for example, common domestic sanitation. A whole city generation may neglect it utterly and scandalously, if not with absolute impunity, yet without any evil consequences that anyone thinks of tracing to it. In a hospital two generations of medical students may tolerate dirt and carelessness, and then go out into general practice to spread the doctrine that fresh air is a fad, and sanitation an imposture set up to make profits for plumbers. Then suddenly Nature takes her revenge. She strikes at the city with a pestilence and at the hospital with an epidemic of hospital gangrene, slaughtering right and left until the innocent young have paid for the guilty old, and the account is balanced. And then she goes to sleep again and gives another period of credit, with the same result.

This is what has just happened in our political hygiene. Political science has been as recklessly neglected by Governments and electorates during my lifetime as sanitary science was in the days of Charles the Second. In international relations diplomacy has been a boyishly lawless affair of family intrigues, commercial and territorial brigandage, torpors of pseudo-goodnature produced by laziness, and spasms of ferocious activity produced by terror. But in these islands we muddled through. Nature gave us a longer credit than she gave to France or Germany or Russia. To British centenarians who died in their beds in 1914, any dread of having to hide underground in London from the shells of an enemy seemed more remote and fantastic than a dread of the appearance of a colony of cobras and rattlesnakes in Kensington Gardens. In the prophetic works of Charles Dickens we were warned against many evils which have since come to pass; but of the evil of being slaughtered by a foreign foe on our own doorsteps there was no shadow. Nature gave us a very long credit; and we abused it to the utmost. But when she struck at last she struck with a vengeance. For four years she smote our firstborn and heaped on us plagues of which Egypt never dreamed. They were all as preventible as the great Plague of London, and came solely because they had not been prevented. They were not undone by winning the war. The earth is still bursting with the dead bodies of the victors.

THE WICKED HALF CENTURY

It is difficult to say whether indifference and neglect are worse than false doctrine; but Heartbreak House and Horseback Hall unfortunately suffered from both. For half a century before the war civilization had been going to the devil very precipitately under the influence of a pseudo-science as disastrous as the blackest Calvinism. Calvinism taught that as we are predestinately saved or damned, nothing that we do can alter our destiny. Still, as Calvinism gave the individual no clue as to whether he had drawn a lucky number or an unlucky one, it left him a fairly strong interest in encouraging his hopes of salvation and allaying his fear of damnation by behaving as one of the elect might be expected to behave rather than as one of the reprobate. But in the middle of the XIX century naturalists and physicists assured the world, in the name of Science, that salvation and damnation are all nonsense, and that predestination is the central truth of religion, inasmuch as human beings are produced by their environment, their sins and good deeds being only a series of chemical and mechanical reactions over which they have no control. Such figments as mind, choice, purpose, conscience, will, and so forth, are, they taught, mere illusions, produced because they are useful in the continual struggle of the human machine to maintain its environment in a favorable condition, a process incidentally involving the ruthless destruction or subjection of its competitors for the supply (assumed to be limited) of subsistence available. We taught Prussia this religion; and Prussia bettered our instruction so effectively

that we presently found ourselves confronted with the necessity of destroying Prussia to prevent Prussia destroying us. And that has just ended in each destroying the other to an extent doubtfully reparable in our time.

It may be asked how so imbecile and dangerous a creed ever came to be accepted by intelligent beings. I will answer that question more fully in my next volume of plays, which will be entirely devoted to the subject. For the present I will only say that there were better reasons than the obvious one that such sham science as this opened a scientific career to very stupid men, and all the other careers to shameless rascals, provided they were industrious enough. It is true that this motive operated very powerfully; but when the new departure in scientific doctrine which is associated with the name of the great naturalist Charles Darwin began, it was not only a reaction against a barbarous pseudo-evangelical teleology intolerably obstructive to all scientific progress, but was accompanied, as it happened, by discoveries of extraordinary interest in physics, chemistry, and that lifeless method of evolution which its investigators called Natural Selection. Howbeit, there was only one result possible in the ethical sphere, and that was the banishment of conscience from human affairs, or, as Samuel Butler vehemently put it, "of mind from the universe."

HYPOCHONDRIA

Now Heartbreak House, with Butler and Bergson and Scott Haldane alongside Blake and the other major poets on its shelves (to say nothing of Wagner and the tone poets), was not so completely blinded by the doltish materialism of the laboratories as the uncultured world outside. But being an idle house it was a hypochrondriacal house, always running after cures. It would stop eating meat, not on valid Shelleyan grounds, but in order to get rid of a bogey called Uric Acid; and it would actually let you pull all its teeth out to exorcize another demon named Pyorrhea. It was superstitious, and addicted to table-rapping, materialization séances, clairvoyance, palmistry, crystal-gazing and the like to such an extent that it may be doubted whether ever before in the history of the world did soothsayers, astrologers, and unregistered therapeutic specialists of all sorts flourish as they did during this half century of the drift to the abyss. The registered doctors and surgeons were hard put to it to compete with the unregistered. They were not clever enough to appeal to the imagination and sociability of the Heartbreakers by the arts of the actor, the orator, the poet, the winning conversationalist. They had to fall back coarsely on the terror of infection and death. They prescribed inoculations and operations. Whatever part of a human being could be cut out without necessarily killing him they cut out; and he often died (unnecessarily of course) in consequence. From such trifles as uvulas and tonsils they went on to ovaries and appendices until at last no one's inside was safe. They explained that the human intestine was too long, and that nothing could make a child of Adam healthy except short circuiting the pylorus by cutting a length out of the lower intestine and fastening it directly to the stomach. As their mechanist theory taught them that medicine was the business of the chemist's laboratory, and surgery of the carpenter's shop, and also that Science (by which they meant their practices) was so important that no consideration for the interests of any individual creature, whether frog or philosopher, much less the vulgar commonplaces of sentimental ethics, could weigh for a moment against the remotest offchance of an addition to the body of scientific knowledge, they operated and

vivisected and inoculated and lied on a stupendous scale, clamoring for and actually acquiring such legal powers over the bodies of their fellow citizens as neither king, pope, nor parliament dare ever have claimed. The Inquisition itself was a Liberal institution compared to the General Medical Council.

THOSE WHO DO NOT KNOW HOW TO LIVE MUST MAKE A MERIT OF DYING

Heartbreak House was far too lazy and shallow to extricate itself from this palace of evil enchantment. It rhapsodized about love; but it believed in cruelty. It was afraid of the cruel people; and it saw that cruelty was at least effective. Cruelty did things that made money, whereas Love did nothing but prove the soundness of Larochefoucauld's saying that very few people would fall in love if they had never read about it. Heartbreak House, in short, did not know how to live, at which point all that was left to it was the boast that at least it knew how to die: a melancholy accomplishment which the outbreak of war presently gave it practically unlimited opportunities of displaying. Thus were the firstborn of Heartbreak House smitten; and the young, the innocent, the hopeful expiated the folly and worthlessness of their elders.

WAR DELIRIUM

Only those who have lived through a first-rate war, not in the field, but at home, and kept their heads, can possibly understand the bitterness of Shakespear and Swift, who both went through this experience. The horror of Peer Gynt in the madhouse, when the lunatics, exalted by illusions of splendid talent and visions of a dawning millennium, crowned him as their emperor, was tame in comparison. I do not know whether anyone really kept his head completely except those who had to keep it because they had to conduct the war at first hand. I should not have kept my own (as far as I did keep it) if I had not at once understood that as a scribe and speaker I too was under the most serious public obligation to keep my grip on realities; but this did not save me from a considerable degree of hyperæsthesia. There were of course some happy people to whom the war meant nothing: all political and general matters lying outside their little circle of interest. But the ordinary war-conscious civilian went mad, the main symptom being a conviction that the whole order of nature had been reversed. All foods, he felt, must now be adulterated. All schools must be closed. No advertisements must be sent to the newspapers, of which new editions must appear and be bought up every ten minutes. Travelling must be stopped, or, that being impossible, greatly hindered. All pretences about fine art and culture and the like must be flung off as an intolerable affectation; and the picture galleries and museums and schools at once occupied by war workers. The British Museum itself was saved only by a hairsbreadth. The sincerity of all this, and of much more which would not be believed if I chronicled it, may be established by one conclusive instance of the general craziness. Men were seized with the illusion that they could win the war by giving away money. And they not only subscribed millions to Funds of all sorts with no discoverable object, and to ridiculous voluntary organizations for doing what was plainly the business of the civil and military authorities, but actually handed out money to any thief in the street who had the presence of mind to pretend that he (or she) was "collecting" it for the annihilation of the enemy. Swindlers were emboldened to take offices; label themselves Anti-Enemy Leagues; and simply pocket the money that was heaped on them. Attractively dressed young women found that they had nothing to do but parade the streets, collecting-box in hand, and live gloriously on the profits. Many months elapsed before, as a first sign of returning sanity, the police swept an Anti-Enemy secretary into prison *pour encourager les autres*, and the passionate penny collecting of the Flag Days was brought under some sort of regulation.

MADNESS IN COURT

The demoralization did not spare the Law Courts. Soldiers were acquitted, even on fully proved indictments for wilful murder, until at last the judges and magistrates had to announce that what was called the Unwritten Law, which meant simply that a soldier could do what he liked with impunity in civil life, was not the law of the land, and that a Victoria Cross did not carry with it a perpetual plenary indulgence. Unfortunately the insanity of the juries and magistrates did not always manifest itself in indulgence. No person unlucky enough to be charged with any sort of conduct, however reasonable and salutary, that did not smack of war delirium had the slightest chance of acquittal. There were in the country, too, a certain number of people who had conscientious objections to war as criminal or unchristian. The Act of Parliament introducing Compulsory Military Service thoughtlessly exempted these persons, merely requiring them to prove the genuineness of their convictions. Those who did so were very ill-advised from the point of view of their own personal interest; for they were persecuted with savage logicality in spite of the law; whilst those who made no pretence of having any objection to war at all, and had not only had military training in Officers' Training Corps, but had proclaimed on public occasions that they were perfectly ready to engage in civil war on behalf of their political opinions, were allowed the benefit of the

Act on the ground that they did not approve of this particular war. For the Christians there was no mercy. In cases where the evidence as to their being killed by ill treatment was so unequivocal that the verdict would certainly have been one of wilful murder had the prejudice of the coroner's jury been on the other side, their tormentors were gratuitously declared to be blameless. There was only one virtue, pugnacity: only one vice, pacifism. That is an essential condition of war; but the Government had not the courage to legislate accordingly; and its law was set aside for Lynch law.

The climax of legal lawlessness was reached in France. The greatest Socialist statesman in Europe, Jaurès, was shot and killed by a gentleman who resented his efforts to avert the war. M. Clemenceau was shot by another gentleman of less popular opinions, and happily came off no worse than having to spend a precautionary couple of days in bed. The slayer of Jaurès was recklessly acquitted: the would-be slayer of M. Clemenceau was carefully found guilty. There is no reason to doubt that the same thing would have happened in England if the war had begun with a successful attempt to assassinate Keir Hardie, and ended with an unsuccessful one to assassinate Mr Lloyd George.

THE LONG ARM OF WAR

The pestilence which is the usual accompaniment of war was called influenza. Whether it was really a war pestilence or not was made doubtful by the fact that it did its worst in places remote from the battle-fields, notably on the west coast of North America and in India. But the moral pestilence, which was unquestionably a war pestilence, reproduced this phenomenon. One would have supposed that the war fever would have raged most furiously in the countries actually under fire, and that the others would be more reasonable. Belgium and Flanders, where over large districts literally not one stone was left upon another as the opposed armies drove each other back and forward over it after terrific preliminary bombardments, might have been pardoned for relieving their feelings more emphatically than by shrugging their shoulders and saying "C'est la guerre." England, inviolate for so many centuries that the swoop of war on her homesteads had long ceased to be more credible than a return of the Flood, could hardly be expected to keep her temper sweet when she knew at last what it was to hide in cellars and underground railway stations, or lie quaking in bed, whilst bombs crashed, houses crumbled, and aircraft guns distributed shrapnel on friend and foe alike until certain shop windows in London, formerly full of fashionable hats, were filled with steel helmets. Slain and mutilated women and children, and burnt and wrecked dwellings, excuse a good deal of violent language, and produce a wrath on which many suns go down before it is appeased. Yet it was in the United States of America, where nobody slept the worse for the war, that the war fever went beyond all sense and reason. In European Courts there was vindictive illegality: in American Courts there was raving lunacy. It is not for me to chronicle the extravagances of an Ally: let some candid American do that. I can only say that to us sitting in our gardens in England, with the guns in France making themselves felt by a throb in the air as unmistakeable as an audible sound, or with tightening hearts studying the phases of the moon in London in their bearing on the chances whether our houses would be standing or ourselves alive next morning, the newspaper accounts of the sentences American Courts were passing on young girls and old men alike for the expression of opinions which were being uttered amid thundering applause before huge audiences in England, and the more private records of the methods by which the American War Loans were raised, were so amazing that they would put the guns and the possibilities of a raid clean out of our heads for the moment.

THE RABID WATCHDOGS OF LIBERTY

Not content with these rancorous abuses of the existing law, the war maniacs made a frantic rush to abolish all constitutional guarantees of liberty and well-being. The ordinary law was superseded by Acts under which newspapers were seized and their printing machinery destroyed by simple police raids *à la Russe*, and persons arrested and shot without any pretence of trial by jury or publicity of procedure or evidence. Though it was urgently necessary that production should be increased by the most scientific organization and economy of labor, and though no fact was better established than that excessive duration and intensity of toil reduces production heavily instead of increasing it, the factory laws were suspended, and men and women recklessly overworked until the loss of their efficiency became too glaring to be ignored. Remonstrances and warnings were met either with an accusation of pro-Germanism or the formula, "Remember that we are at war now." I have said that men assumed that war had reversed the order of nature, and that all was lost unless we did the exact opposite of everything we had found necessary and beneficial in peace. But the truth was worse than that. The war did not change men's minds in any such impossible way. What really happened was that the impact of physical death and destruction, the one reality that every fool can understand, tore off the masks of education, art, science, and religion from our ignorance and barbarism, and left us glorying grotesquely in the licence suddenly accorded to our vilest passions and most abject terrors. Ever since Thucydides wrote his history, it has been on record that when the angel of death sounds his trumpet the pretences of civilization are blown from men's heads into the mud like hats in a gust of wind. But when this scripture was fulfilled among us, the shock was not the less appalling because a few students of Greek history were not surprised by it. Indeed these students threw themselves into the orgy as shamelessly as the illiterate. The Christian priest joining in the war dance without even throwing off his cassock first, and the respectable school governor expelling the German professor with insult and bodily violence, and declaring that no English child should ever again be taught the language of Luther and Goethe, were kept in countenance by the most impudent repudiations of every decency of civilization and every lesson of political experience on the part of the very persons who, as university professors, historians, philosophers, and men of science, were the accredited custodians of culture. It was crudely natural, and perhaps necessary for recruiting purposes, that German militarism and German dynastic ambition should be painted by journalists and recruiters in black and red as European dangers (as in fact they are), leaving it to be inferred that our own militarism and our own political constitution are millennially democratic (which they certainly are not); but when it came to frantic denunciations of German chemistry, German biology, German poetry, German music, German literature, German philosophy, and even German engineering, as malignant abominations standing towards British and French chemistry and so forth in the relation of heaven to hell, it was clear that the utterers of such barbarous ravings had never really understood or cared for the arts and sciences they professed and were profaning, and were only the appallingly degenerate descendants of the men of the seventeenth and eighteenth centuries who, recognizing no national frontiers in the great realm of the human mind, kept the European comity of that realm loftily and even ostentatiously above the rancors of the battle-field. Tearing the Garter from the Kaiser's leg, striking the German dukes from the roll of our peerage, changing the King's illustrious and historically appropriate surname for that of a traditionless locality, was not a very dignified business; but the erasure of German names from the British rolls of science and learning was a confession that in England the little respect paid to science and learning is only an affectation which hides a savage contempt for both. One felt that the figure of St George and the Dragon on our coinage should be replaced by that of the soldier driving his spear through Archimedes. But by that time there was no coinage: only paper money in which ten shillings called itself a pound as confidently as the people who were disgracing their country called themselves patriots.

THE SUFFERINGS OF THE SANE

The mental distress of living amid the obscene din of all these carmagnoles and corobberies was not the only burden that lay on sane people during the war. There was also the emotional strain, complicated by the offended economic sense, produced by the casualty lists. The stupid, the selfish, the narrow-minded, the callous and unimaginative were spared a great deal. "Blood and destruction shall be so in use that mothers shall but smile when they behold their infants quartered by the hands of war," was a Shakespearean prophecy that very nearly came true; for when nearly every house had a slaughtered son to mourn, we should all have gone quite out of our senses if we had taken our own and

our friends' bereavements at their peace value. It became necessary to give them a false value; to proclaim the young life worthily and gloriously sacrificed to redeem the liberty of mankind, instead of to expiate the heedlessness and folly of their fathers, and expiate it in vain. We had even to assume that the parents and not the children had made the sacrifice, until at last the comic papers were driven to satirize fat old men, sitting comfortably in club chairs, and boasting of the sons they had "given" to their country.

No one grudged these anodynes to acute personal grief; but they only embittered those who knew that the young men were having their teeth set on edge because their parents had eaten sour political grapes. Then think of the young men themselves! Many of them had no illusions about the policy that led to the war: they went clear-sighted to a horribly repugnant duty. Men essentially gentle and essentially wise, with really valuable work in hand, laid it down voluntarily and spent months forming fours in the barrack yard, and stabbing sacks of straw in the public eye, so that they might go out to kill and maim men as gentle as themselves. These men, who were perhaps, as a class, our most efficient soldiers (Frederick Keeling, for example), were not duped for a moment by the hypocritical melodrama that consoled and stimulated the others. They left their creative work to drudge at destruction, exactly as they would have left it to take their turn at the pumps in a sinking ship. They did not, like some of the conscientious objectors, hold back because the ship had been neglected by its officers and scuttled by its wreckers. The ship had to be saved, even if Newton had to leave his fluxions and Michael Angelo his marbles to save it; so they threw away the tools of their beneficent and ennobling trades, and took up the bloodstained bayonet and the murderous bomb, forcing themselves to pervert their divine instinct for perfect artistic execution to the effective handling of these diabolical things, and their economic faculty for organization to the contriving of ruin and slaughter. For it gave an ironic edge to their tragedy that the very talents they were forced to prostitute made the prostitution not only effective, but even interesting; so that some of them were rapidly promoted, and found themselves actually becoming artists in war, with a growing relish for it, like Napoleon and all the other scourges of mankind, in spite of themselves. For many of them there was not even this consolation. They "stuck it," and hated it, to the end.

EVIL IN THE THRONE OF GOOD

This distress of the gentle was so acute that those who shared it in civil life, without having to shed blood with their own hands, or witness destruction with their own eyes, hardly care to obtrude their own woes. Nevertheless, even when sitting at home in safety, it was not easy for those who had to write and speak about the war to throw away their highest conscience, and deliberately work to a standard of inevitable evil instead of to the ideal of life more abundant. I can answer for at least one person who found the change from the wisdom of Jesus and St Francis to the morals of Richard III and the madness of Don Quixote extremely irksome. But that change had to be made; and we are all the worse for it, except those for whom it was not really a change at all, but only a relief from hypocrisy.

Think, too, of those who, though they had neither to write nor to fight, and had no children of their own to lose, yet knew the inestimable loss to the world of four years of the life of a generation wasted on destruction. Hardly one of the epoch-making works of the human mind might not have been aborted or destroyed by taking their authors away from their natural work for four critical years. Not only were Shakespears and Platos being killed outright; but many of the best harvests of the survivors had to be sown in the barren soil of the trenches. And this was no mere British consideration. To the truly civilized man, to the good European, the slaughter of the German youth was as disastrous as the slaughter of the English. Fools exulted in "German losses." They were our losses as well. Imagine exulting in the death of Beethoven because Bill Sikes dealt him his death blow!

STRAINING AT THE GNAT AND SWALLOWING THE CAMEL

But most people could not comprehend these sorrows. There was a frivolous exultation in death for its own sake, which was at bottom an inability to realize that the deaths were real deaths and not stage ones. Again and again, when an air raider dropped a bomb which tore a child and its mother limb from limb, the people who saw it, though they had been reading with great cheerfulness of thousands of such happenings day after day in their newspapers, suddenly burst into furious imprecations on "the Huns" as murderers, and shrieked for savage and satisfying vengeance. At such moments it became clear that the deaths they had not seen meant no more to them than the mimic deaths of the cinema screen. Sometimes it was not necessary that death should be actually witnessed: it had only to take place under circumstances of sufficient novelty and proximity to bring it home almost as sensationally and effectively as if it had been actually visible.

For example, in the spring of 1915 there was an appalling slaughter of our young soldiers at Neuve Chapelle and at the Gallipoli landing. I will not go so far as to say that our civilians were delighted to have such exciting news to read at breakfast. But I cannot pretend that I noticed either in the papers, or in general intercourse, any feeling beyond the usual one that the cinema show at the front was going splendidly, and that our boys were the bravest of the brave. Suddenly there came the news that an Atlantic liner, the Lusitania, had been torpedoed, and that several well-known first-class passengers, including a famous theatrical manager and the author of a popular farce, had been drowned, among others. The others included Sir Hugh Lane; but as he had only laid the country under great obligations in the sphere of the fine arts, no great stress was laid on that loss.

Immediately an amazing frenzy swept through the country. Men who up to that time had kept their heads now lost them utterly. "Killing saloon passengers! What next?" was the essence of the whole agitation; but it is far too trivial a phrase to convey the faintest notion of the rage which possessed us. To me, with my mind full of the hideous cost of Neuve Chapelle, Ypres, and the Gallipoli landing, the fuss about the Lusitania seemed almost a heartless impertinence, though I was well acquainted personally with the three best-known victims, and understood, better perhaps than most people, the misfortune of the death of Lane. I even found a grim satisfaction, very intelligible to all soldiers, in the fact that the civilians who found the war such splendid British sport should get a sharp taste of what it was to the actual combatants. I expressed my impatience very freely, and found that my very straightforward and natural feeling in the matter was received as a monstrous and heartless paradox. When I asked those who gaped at me whether they had anything to say about the holocaust of Festubert, they gaped wider than before, having totally forgotten it, or rather, having never realized it. They were not heartless any more than I was; but the big catastrophe was too big for them to grasp, and the little one had been just the right size for them. I was not surprised. Have I not seen a public body for just the same reason pass a vote for £30,000 without a word, and then spend three special meetings, prolonged into the night, over an item of seven shillings for refreshments?

LITTLE MINDS AND BIG BATTLES

Nobody will be able to understand the vagaries of public feeling during the war unless they bear constantly in mind that the war in its entire magnitude did not exist for the average civilian. He could not conceive even a battle, much less a campaign. To the suburbs the war was nothing but a suburban squabble. To the miner and navvy it was only a series of bayonet fights between German champions and English ones. The enormity of it was quite beyond most of us. Its episodes had to be reduced to the dimensions of a railway accident or a shipwreck before it could produce any effect on our minds at all. To us the ridiculous bombardments of Scarborough and Ramsgate were colossal tragedies, and the battle of Jutland a mere ballad. The words "after thorough artillery preparation" in the news from the front meant nothing to us; but when our seaside trippers learned that an elderly gentleman at breakfast in a week-end marine hotel had been interrupted by a bomb dropping into his egg-cup, their wrath and horror knew no bounds. They declared that this would put a new spirit into the army, and had no suspicion that the soldiers in the trenches roared with laughter over it for days, and told each other that it would do the blighters at home good to have a taste of what the army was up against. Sometimes the smallness of view was pathetic. A man would work at home regardless of the call "to make the world safe for democracy." His brother would be killed at the front. Immediately he would throw up his work and take up the war as a family blood feud against the Germans. Sometimes it was comic. A wounded man, entitled to his discharge, would return to the trenches with a grim determination to find the Hun who had wounded him and pay him out for it.

It is impossible to estimate what proportion of us, in khaki or out of it, grasped the war and its political antecedents as a whole in the light of any philosophy of history or knowledge of what war is. I doubt whether it was as high as our proportion of higher mathematicians. But there can be no doubt that it was prodigiously outnumbered by the comparatively ignorant and childish. Remember that these people had to be stimulated to make the sacrifices demanded by the war, and that this could not be done by appeals to a knowledge which they did not possess, and a comprehension of which they were incapable. When the armistice at last set me free to tell the truth about the war at the following general election, a soldier said to a candidate whom I was supporting "If I had known all that in 1914, they would never have got me into khaki." And that, of course, was precisely why it had been necessary to stuff him with a romance that any diplomatist would have laughed at. Thus the natural confusion of ignorance was increased by a deliberately propagated confusion of nursery bogey stories and melodramatic nonsense, which at last overreached itself and made it impossible to stop the war before we had not only achieved the triumph of vanquishing the German army and thereby overthrowing its militarist monarchy, but made the very serious mistake of ruining the centre of Europe, a thing that no sane European State could afford to do.

THE DUMB CAPABLES AND THE NOISY INCAPABLES

Confronted with this picture of insensate delusion and folly, the critical reader will immediately counterplead that England all this time was conducting a war which involved the organization of several millions of fighting men and of the workers who were supplying them with provisions, munitions, and transport, and that this could not have been done by a mob of hysterical ranters. This is fortunately true. To pass from the newspaper offices and political platforms and club fenders and suburban drawing rooms to the Army and the munition factories was to pass from Bedlam to the busiest and sanest of workaday worlds. It was to rediscover England, and find solid ground for the faith of those who still believed in her. But a necessary condition of this efficiency was that those who were efficient should give all their time to their business and leave the rabble raving to its hearts' content. Indeed the raving was useful to the efficient, because, as it was always wide of the mark, it often distracted attention very conveniently from operations that would have been defeated or hindered by publicity. A precept which I endeavored vainly to popularize early in the war, "If you have anything to do go and do it: if not, for heaven's sake get out of the way," was only half carried out. Certainly the capable people went and did it; but the incapables would by no means get out of the way: they fussed and bawled and were only prevented from getting very seriously into the way by the blessed fact that they never knew where the way was. Thus whilst all the efficiency of England was silent and invisible, all its imbecility was deafening the heavens with its clamor and blotting out the sun with its dust. It was also unfortunately intimidating the Government by its blusterings into using the irresistible powers of the State to intimidate the sensible people, thus enabling a despicable minority of would-be lynchers to set up a reign of terror which could at any time have been broken by a single stern word from a responsible minister. But our ministers had not that sort of courage: neither Heartbreak House nor Horseback Hall had bred it, much less the suburbs. When matters at last came to the looting of shops by criminals under patriotic pretexts, it was the police force and not the Government that put its foot down. There was even one deplorable moment, during the submarine scare, in which the Government yielded to a childish cry for the maltreatment of naval prisoners of war, and, to our great disgrace, was forced by the enemy to behave itself. And yet behind all this public blundering and misconduct and futile mischief, the effective England was carrying on with the most formidable capacity and activity. The ostensible England was making the empire sick with its incontinences, its ignorances, its ferocities, its panics, and its endless and intolerable blarings of Allied national anthems in season and out. The esoteric England was proceeding irresistibly to the conquest of Europe.

THE PRACTICAL BUSINESS MEN

From the beginning the useless people set up a shriek for "practical business men." By this they meant men who had become rich by placing their personal interests before those of the country, and measuring the success of every activity by the pecuniary profit it brought to them and to those on whom they depended for their supplies of capital. The pitiable failure of some conspicuous samples from the first batch we tried of these poor devils helped to give the whole public side of the war an air of monstrous and hopeless farce. They proved not only

that they were useless for public work, but that in a well-ordered nation they would never have been allowed to control private enterprise.

HOW THE FOOLS SHOUTED THE WISE MEN DOWN

Thus, like a fertile country flooded with mud, England shewed no sign of her greatness in the days when she was putting forth all her strength to save herself from the worst consequences of her littleness. Most of the men of action, occupied to the last hour of their time with urgent practical work, had to leave to idler people, or to professional rhetoricians, the presentation of the war to the reason and imagination of the country and the world in speeches, poems, manifestos, picture posters, and newspaper articles. I have had the privilege of hearing some of our ablest commanders talking about their work; and I have shared the common lot of reading the accounts of that work given to the world by the newspapers. No two experiences could be more different. But in the end the talkers obtained a dangerous ascendancy over the rank and file of the men of action; for though the great men of action are always inveterate talkers and often very clever writers, and therefore cannot have their minds formed for them by others, the average man of action, like the average fighter with the bayonet, can give no account of himself in words even to himself, and is apt to pick up and accept what he reads about himself and other people in the papers, except when the writer is rash enough to commit himself on technical points. It was not uncommon during the war to hear a soldier, or a civilian engaged on war work, describing events within his own experience that reduced to utter absurdity the ravings and maunderings of his daily paper, and yet echo the opinions of that paper like a parrot. Thus, to escape from the prevailing confusion and folly, it was not enough to seek the company of the ordinary man of action: one had to get into contact with the master spirits. This was a privilege which only a handful of people could enjoy. For the unprivileged citizen there was no escape. To him the whole country seemed mad, futile, silly, incompetent, with no hope of victory except the hope that the enemy might be just as mad. Only by very resolute reflection and reasoning could he reassure himself that if there was nothing more solid beneath these appalling appearances the war could not possibly have gone on for a single day without a total breakdown of its organization.

THE MAD ELECTION

Happy were the fools and the thoughtless men of action in those days. The worst of it was that the fools were very strongly represented in parliament, as fools not only elect fools, but can persuade men of action to elect them too. The election that immediately followed the armistice was perhaps the maddest that has ever taken place. Soldiers who had done voluntary and heroic service in the field were defeated by persons who had apparently never run a risk or spent a farthing that they could avoid, and who even had in the course of the election to apologize publicly for bawling Pacifist or Pro-German at their opponent. Party leaders seek such followers, who can always be depended on to walk tamely into the lobby at the party whip's orders, provided the leader will make their seats safe for them by the process which was called, in derisive reference to the war rationing system, "giving them the coupon." Other incidents were so grotesque that I cannot mention them without enabling the reader to identify the parties, which would not be fair, as they were no more to blame than thousands of others who must necessarily be nameless. The general result was patently absurd; and the electorate, disgusted at its own work, instantly recoiled to the opposite extreme, and cast out all the coupon candidates at the earliest bye-elections by equally silly majorities. But the mischief of the general election could not be undone; and the Government had not only to pretend to abuse its European victory as it had promised, but actually to do it by starving the enemies who had thrown down their arms. It had, in short, won the election by pledging itself to be thriftlessly wicked, cruel, and vindictive; and it did not find it as easy to escape from this pledge as it had from nobler ones. The end, as I write, is not yet; but it is clear that this thoughtless savagery will recoil on the heads of the Allies so severely that we shall be forced by the sternest necessity to take up our share of healing the Europe we have wounded almost to death instead of attempting to complete her destruction.

THE YAHOO AND THE ANGRY APE

Contemplating this picture of a state of mankind so recent that no denial of its truth is possible, one understands Shakespear comparing Man to an angry ape, Swift describing him as a Yahoo rebuked by the superior virtue of the horse, and Wellington declaring that the British can behave themselves neither in victory nor defeat. Yet none of the three had seen war as we have seen it. Shakespear blamed great men, saying that "Could great men thunder as Jove himself does Jove would ne'er be quiet; for every pelting petty officer would use his heaven for thunder: nothing but thunder." What would Shakespear have said if he had seen something far more destructive than thunder in the hand of every village laborer, and found on the Messines Ridge the craters of the nineteen volcanoes that were let loose there at the touch of a finger that might have been a child's finger without the result being a whit less ruinous? Shakespear may have seen a Stratford cottage struck by one of Jove's thunderbolts, and have helped to extinguish the lighted thatch and clear away the bits of the broken chimney. What would he have said if he had seen Ypres as it is now, or returned to Stratford, as French peasants are returning to their homes today, to find the old familiar signpost inscribed "To Stratford, 1 mile," and at the end of the mile nothing but some holes in the ground and a fragment of a broken churn here and there? Would not the spectacle of the angry ape endowed with powers of destruction that Jove never pretended to, have beggared even his command of words?

And yet, what is there to say except that war puts a strain on human nature that breaks down the better half of it, and makes the worse half a diabolical virtue? Better for us if it broke it down altogether; for then the warlike way out of our difficulties would be barred to us, and we should take greater care not to get into them. In truth, it is, as Byron said, "not difficult to die," and enormously difficult to live: that explains why, at bottom, peace is not only better than war, but infinitely more arduous. Did any hero of the war face the glorious risk of death more bravely than the traitor Bolo faced the ignominious certainty of it? Bolo taught us all how to die: can we say that he taught us all how to live? Hardly a week passes now without some soldier who braved death in the field so recklessly that he was decorated or specially commended for it, being haled before our magistrates for having failed to resist the paltriest temptations of peace, with no better excuse than the old one that "a man must live." Strange that one who, sooner than do honest work, will sell his honor for a bottle of wine, a visit to the theatre, and an hour with a strange woman, all obtained by passing a worthless cheque, could yet stake his life on the most desperate chances of the battlefield! Does it not seem as if, after all, the glory of death were cheaper than the glory of life? If it is not easier to attain, why do so many more men attain it? At all events it is clear that the kingdom of the Prince of Peace has not yet become the kingdom of this world. His attempts at invasion have been resisted far more fiercely than the Kaiser's. Successful as that resistance has been, it has piled up a sort of National Debt that is not the less oppressive because we have no figures for it and do not intend to pay it. A blockade that cuts off "the grace of our Lord" is in the long run less bearable than the blockades which merely cut off raw materials; and against that blockade our Armada is impotent. In the blockader's house, he has assured us, there are many mansions; but I am afraid they do not include either Heartbreak House or Horseback Hall.

PLAGUE ON BOTH YOUR HOUSES!

Meanwhile the Bolshevist picks and petards are at work on the foundations of both buildings; and though the Bolshevists may be buried in the ruins, their deaths will not save the edifices. Unfortunately they can be built again. Like Doubting Castle, they have been demolished many times by successive Greathearts, and rebuilt by Simple, Sloth, and Presumption, by Feeble Mind and Much Afraid, and by all the jurymen of Vanity Fair. Another generation of "secondary education" at our ancient public schools and the cheaper institutions that ape them will be quite sufficient to keep the two going until the next war.

For the instruction of that generation I leave these pages as a record of what civilian life was during the war: a matter on which history is usually silent. Fortunately it was a very short war. It is true that the people who thought it could not last more than six months were very signally refuted by the event. As Sir Douglas Haig has pointed out, its Waterloos lasted months instead of hours. But there would have been nothing surprising in its lasting thirty years. If it had not been for the fact that the blockade achieved the amazing feat of starving out Europe, which it could not possibly have done had Europe been properly organized for war, or even for peace, the war would have lasted until the belligerents were so tired of it that they could no longer be compelled to compel themselves to go on with it. Considering its magnitude, the war of 1914–18 will certainly be classed as the shortest in history. The end came so suddenly that the combatants literally stumbled over it; and yet it came a full year later than it should have come if the belligerents had not been far too afraid of one another to face the situation sensibly. Germany, having failed to provide for the war she began, failed again to surrender before she was dangerously exhausted. Her opponents, equally improvident, went as much too close to bankruptcy as Germany to starvation. It was a bluff at which both were bluffed. And, with the usual irony of war, it remains doubtful whether Germany and Russia, the defeated, will not be the gainers; for the victors are already busy fastening on themselves the chains they have struck from the limbs of the vanquished.

HOW THE THEATRE FARED

Let us now contract our view rather violently from the European theatre of war to the theatre in which the fights are sham fights, and the slain, rising the moment the curtain has fallen, go comfortably home to supper after washing off their rosepink wounds. It is nearly twenty years since I was last obliged to introduce a play in the form of a book for lack of an opportunity of presenting it in its proper mode by a performance in a theatre. The war has thrown me back on this expedient. Heartbreak House has not yet reached the stage. I have withheld it because the war has completely upset the economic conditions which formerly enabled serious drama to pay its way in London. The change is not in the theatres nor in the management of them, nor in the authors and actors, but in the audiences. For four years the London theatres were crowded every night with thousands of soldiers on leave from the front. These soldiers were not seasoned London playgoers. A childish experience of my own gave me a clue to their condition. When I was a small boy I was taken to the opera. I did not then know what an opera was, though I could whistle a good deal of opera music. I had seen in my mother's album photographs of all the great opera singers, mostly in evening dress. In the theatre I found myself before a gilded balcony filled with persons in evening dress whom I took to be the opera singers. I picked out one massive dark lady as Alboni, and wondered how soon she would stand up and sing. I was puzzled by the fact that I was made to sit with my back to the singers instead of facing them. When the curtain went up, my astonishment and delight were unbounded.

THE SOLDIER AT THE THEATRE FRONT

In 1915 I saw in the theatres men in khaki in just the same predicament. To everyone who had my clue to their state of mind it was evident that they had never been in a theatre before and did not know what it was. At one of our great variety theatres I sat beside a young officer, not at all a rough specimen, who, even when the curtain rose and enlightened him as to the place where he had to look for his entertainment, found the dramatic part of it utterly incomprehensible. He did not know how to play his part of the game. He could understand the people on the stage singing and dancing and performing gymnastic feats. He not only understood but intensely enjoyed an artist who imitated cocks crowing and pigs squeaking. But the people who pretended that they were somebody else, and that the painted picture behind them was real, bewildered him. In his presence I realized how very sophisticated the natural man has to become before the conventions of the theatre can be easily acceptable, or the purpose of the drama obvious to him.

Well, from the moment when the routine of leave for our soldiers was established, such novices, accompanied by damsels (called flappers) often as innocent as themselves, crowded the theatres to the doors. It was hardly possible at first to find stuff crude enough to nurse them on. The best music-hall comedians ransacked their memories for the oldest quips and the most childish antics to avoid carrying the military spectators out of their depth. I believe that this was a mistake as far as the novices were concerned. Shakespear, or the dramatized histories of George Barnwell, Maria Martin, or the Demon Barber of Fleet Street, would probably have been quite popular with them. But the novices were only a minority after all. The cultivated soldier, who in time of peace would look at nothing theatrical except the most advanced post-Ibsen plays in the most artistic settings, found himself, to his own astonishment, thirsting for silly jokes, dances, and brainlessly sensuous exhibitions of pretty girls. The author of some of the most grimly serious plays of our time told me that after enduring the trenches for months without a glimpse of the female of his species, it gave him an entirely innocent but delightful pleasure merely to see a flapper. The reaction from the battle-field produced a condition of hyperæsthesia in which all the theatrical values were altered. Trivial things gained intensity and stale things novelty. The actor, instead of having to coax his audiences out of the boredom which had driven them to the theatre in an ill humor to seek some sort of distraction, had only to exploit the bliss of smiling men who were no longer under fire and under military discipline, but actually clean and comfortable and in a mood to be pleased with anything and everything that a bevy of pretty girls and a funny man, or even a bevy of girls pretending to be pretty and a man pretending to be funny, could do for them.

Then could be seen every night in the theatres old-fashioned farcical comedies, in which a bedroom, with four doors on each side and a practicable window in the middle, was understood to resemble exactly the bedroom in the flats beneath and above, all three inhabited by couples consumed with jealousy. When these people came home drunk at night; mistook their neighbor's flats for their own; and in due course got into the wrong beds, it was not only the novices who found the resulting complications and scandals exquisitely ingenious and amusing, nor their equally verdant flappers who could not help squealing in a manner that astonished the oldest performers when the gentleman who had just come in drunk through the window pretended to undress, and allowed glimpses of his naked person to be descried from time to time. Men who had just read the news that Charles Wyndham was dying, and were thereby sadly reminded of Pink Dominos and the torrent of farcical comedies that followed it in his heyday until every trick of that trade had become so stale that the laughter they provoked turned to loathing: these veterans also, when they returned from the field, were as much pleased by what they knew to be stale and foolish as the novices by what they thought fresh and clever.

COMMERCE IN THE THEATRE

Wellington said that an army moves on its belly. So does a London theatre. Before a man acts he must eat. Before he performs plays he must pay rent. In London we have no theatres for the welfare of the people: they are all for the sole purpose of producing the utmost obtainable rent for the proprietor. If the twin flats and twin beds produce a guinea more than Shakespear, out goes Shakespear, and in come the twin flats and the twin beds. If the brainless bevy of pretty girls and the funny man outbid Mozart, out goes Mozart.

UNSER SHAKESPEAR

Before the war an effort was made to remedy this by establishing a national theatre in celebration of the tercentenary of the death of Shakespear. A committee was formed; and all sorts of illustrious and influential persons lent their names to a grand appeal to our national culture. My play, The Dark Lady of The Sonnets, was one of the incidents of that appeal. After some years of effort the result was a single handsome subscription from a German gentleman. Like the celebrated swearer in the anecdote when the cart containing all his household goods lost its tailboard at the top of the hill and let its contents roll in ruin to the bottom, I can only say, "I cannot do justice to this situation," and let it pass without another word.

THE HIGHER DRAMA PUT OUT OF ACTION

The effect of the war on the London theatres may now be imagined. The beds and the bevies drove every higher form of art out of it. Rents went up to an unprecedented figure. At the same time prices doubled everywhere except at the theatre pay-boxes, and raised the expenses of management to such a degree that unless the houses were quite full every night, profit was impossible. Even bare solvency could not be attained without a very wide popularity. Now what had made serious drama possible to a limited extent before the war was that a play could pay its way even if the theatre were only half full until Saturday and three-quarters full then. A manager who was an enthusiast and a desperately hard worker, with an occasional grant-in-aid from an artistically disposed millionaire, and a due proportion of those rare and happy accidents by which plays of the higher sort turn out to be potboilers as well, could hold out for some years, by which time a relay might arrive in the person of another enthusiast. Thus and not otherwise occurred that remarkable revival of the British drama at the beginning of the century which made my own career as a playwright possible in England. In America I had already established myself, not as part of the ordinary theatre system, but in association with the exceptional genius of Richard Mansfield. In Germany and Austria I had no difficulty: the system of publicly aided theatres there, Court and Municipal, kept drama of the kind I dealt in alive; so that I was indebted to the Emperor of Austria for magnificent productions of my works at a time when the sole official attention paid me by the British Court was the announcement to the English-speaking world that certain plays of mine were unfit for public performance, a substantial set-off against this being that the British Court, in the course of its private playgoing, paid no regard to the bad character given me by the chief officer of its household.

Howbeit, the fact that my plays effected a lodgment on the London stage, and were presently followed by the plays of Granville Barker, Gilbert Murray, John Masefield, St John Hankin, Laurence Housman, Arnold Bennett, John Galsworthy, John Drinkwater, and others which would in the XIX century have stood rather less chance of production at a London theatre than the Dialogues of Plato, not to mention revivals of the ancient Athenian drama, and a restoration to the stage of Shakespear's plays as he wrote them, was made economically possible solely by a supply of theatres which could hold nearly twice as much money as it cost to rent and maintain them. In such theatres work appealing to a relatively small class of cultivated persons, and therefore attracting only from half to three-quarters as many spectators as the more popular pastimes, could nevertheless keep going in the hands of young adventurers who were doing it for its own sake, and had not yet been forced by advancing age and responsibilities to consider the commercial value of their time and energy too closely. The war struck this foundation away in the manner I have just described. The expenses of running the cheapest west-end theatres rose to a sum which exceeded by twenty-five per cent the utmost that the higher drama can, as an ascertained matter of fact, be depended on to draw. Thus the higher drama, which has never really been a commercially sound speculation, now became an impossible one. Accordingly, attempts are being made to provide a refuge for it in suburban theatres in London and repertory theatres in the provinces. But at the moment when the army has at last disgorged the survivors of the gallant band of dramatic pioneers whom it swallowed, they find that the economic conditions which formerly made their work no worse than precarious now put it out of the question altogether, as far as the west end of London is concerned.

CHURCH AND THEATRE

I do not suppose many people care particularly. We are not brought up to care; and a sense of the national importance of the theatre is not born in mankind; the natural man, like so many of the soldiers at the beginning of the war, does not know what a theatre is. But please note that all these soldiers who did not know what a theatre was, knew what a church was. And they had been taught to respect churches. Nobody had ever warned them against a church as a place where frivolous women paraded in their best clothes; where stories of improper females like Potiphar's wife, and erotic poetry like the Song of Songs, were read aloud; where the sensuous and sentimental music of Schubert, Mendelssohn, Gounod, and Brahms was more popular than severe music by greater composers; where the prettiest sort of pretty pictures of pretty saints assailed the imagination and senses through stained-glass windows; and where sculpture and architecture came to the help of painting. Nobody ever reminded them that these things had sometimes produced such developments of erotic idolatry that men who were not only enthusiastic amateurs of literature, painting, and music, but famous practitioners of them, had actually exulted when mobs and even regular troops under express command had mutilated church statues, smashed church windows, wrecked church organs, and torn up the sheets from which the church music was read and sung. When they saw broken statues in churches, they were told that this was the work of wicked godless rioters, instead of, as it was, the work partly of zealots bent on driving the world, the flesh, and the devil out of the temple, and partly of insurgent men who had become intolerably poor because the temple had become a den of thieves. But all the sins and perversions that were so carefully hidden from them in the history of the Church were laid on the shoulders of the Theatre: that stuffy, uncomfortable place of penance in which we suffer so much inconvenience on the slenderest chance of gaining a scrap of food for our starving souls. When the Germans bombed the Cathedral of Rheims the world rang with the horror of the sacrilege. When they bombed the Little Theatre in the Adelphi, and narrowly missed bombing two writers of plays who lived within a few yards of it, the fact was not even mentioned in the papers. In point of appeal to the senses no theatre ever built could touch the fane at Rheims: no actress could rival its Virgin in beauty, nor any operatic tenor look otherwise than a fool beside its David. Its picture glass was glorious even to those who had seen the glass of Chartres. It was wonderful in its very grotesques: who would look at the Blondin Donkey after seeing its leviathans? In spite of the Adam-Adelphian decoration on which Miss Kingston had lavished so much taste and care, the Little Theatre was in comparison with Rheims the gloomiest of little conventicles: indeed the cathedral must, from the Puritan point of view, have debauched a million voluptuaries for every one whom the Little Theatre had sent home thoughtful to a chaste bed after Mr Chesterton's Magic or Brieux's Les Avariés. Perhaps that is the real reason why the Church is lauded and the Theatre reviled. Whether or no, the fact remains that the lady to whose public spirit and sense of the national value of the theatre I owed the first regular public performance of a play of mine had to conceal her action as if it had been a crime, whereas if she had given the money to the Church she would have worn a halo for it. And I admit, as I have always done, that this state of things may have been a very sensible one. I have asked Londoners again and again why they pay half a guinea to go to a theatre when they can go to St Paul's or Westminster Abbey for nothing. Their only possible reply is that they want to see something new and possibly something wicked; but the theatres mostly disappoint both hopes. If ever a revolution makes me Dictator, I shall establish a heavy charge for admission to our churches. But everyone who pays at the church door shall receive a ticket entitling him or her to free admission to one performance at any theatre he or she prefers. Thus shall the sensuous charms of the church service be made to subsidize the sterner virtue of the drama.

THE NEXT PHASE

The present situation will not last. Although the newspaper I read at breakfast this morning before writing these words contains a calculation that no less than twenty-three wars are at present being waged to confirm the peace, England is no longer in khaki; and a violent reaction is setting in against the crude theatrical fare of the four terrible years. Soon the rents of theatres will once more be fixed on the assumption that they cannot always be full, nor even on the average half full week in and week out. Prices will change. The higher drama will be at no greater disadvantage than it was before the war; and it may benefit, first, by the fact that many of us have been torn from the fools' paradise in which the theatre formerly traded, and thrust upon the sternest realities and necessities until we have lost both faith in and patience with the theatrical pretences that had no root either in reality or necessity; second, by the startling change made by the war in the distribution of income. It seems only the other day that a millionaire was a man with £50,000 a year. Today, when he has paid his income tax and super tax, and insured his life for the amount of his death duties, he is lucky if his net income is £10,000, though his nominal property remains the same. And this is the result of a Budget which is called "a respite for the rich." At the other end of the scale millions of persons have had regular incomes for the first time in their lives; and their men have been regularly clothed, fed, lodged, and taught to make up their minds that certain things have to be done, also for the first time in their lives. Hundreds of thousands of women have been taken out of their domestic cages and tasted both discipline and independence. The thoughtless and snobbish middle classes have been pulled up short by the very unpleasant experience of being ruined to an unprecedented extent. We have all had a tremendous jolt; and although the widespread notion that the shock of the war would automatically make a new heaven and a new earth, and that the dog would never go back to his vomit nor the sow to her wallowing in the mire, is already seen to be a delusion, yet we are far more conscious of our condition than we were, and far less disposed to submit to it. Revolution, lately only a sensational chapter in history or a demagogic claptrap, is now a possibility so imminent that hardly by trying to suppress it in other countries by arms and defamation, and calling the process anti-Bolshevism, can our Government stave it off at home.

Perhaps the most tragic figure of the day is the American President who was once a historian. In those days it became his task to tell us how, after that great war in America which was more clearly than any other war of our time a war for an idea, the conquerors, confronted with a heroic task of reconstruction, turned recreant, and spent fifteen years in abusing their victory under cover of pretending to accomplish the task they were doing what they could to make impossible. Alas! Hegel was right when he said that we learn from history that men never learn anything from history. With what anguish of mind the President sees that we, the new conquerors, forgetting everything we professed to fight for, are sitting down with watering mouths to a good square meal of ten years revenge upon

and humiliation of our prostrate foe, can only be guessed by those who know, as he does, how hopeless is remonstrance, and how happy Lincoln was in perishing from the earth before his inspired messages became scraps of paper. He knows well that from the Peace Conference will come, in spite of his utmost, no edict on which he will be able, like Lincoln, to invoke "the considerate judgment of mankind, and the gracious favor of Almighty God." He led his people to destroy the militarism of Zabern; and the army they rescued is busy in Cologne imprisoning every German who does not salute a British officer; whilst the Government at home, asked whether it approves, replies that it does not propose even to discontinue this Zabernism when the Peace is concluded, but in effect looks forward to making Germans salute British officers until the end of the world. That is what war makes of men and women. It will wear off; and the worst it threatens is already proving impracticable; but before the humble and contrite heart ceases to be despised, the President and I, being of the same age, will be dotards. In the meantime there is, for him, another history to write; for me, another comedy to stage. Perhaps, after all, that is what wars are for, and what historians and playwrights are for. If men will not learn until their lessons are written in blood, why, blood they must have, their own for preference.

THE EPHEMERAL THRONES AND THE ETERNAL THEATRE

To the theatre it will not matter. Whatever Bastilles fall, the theatre will stand. Apostolic Hapsburg has collapsed; All Highest Hohenzollern languishes in Holland, threatened with trial on a capital charge of fighting for his country against England; Imperial Romanoff, said to have perished miserably by a more summary method of murder, is perhaps alive or perhaps dead: nobody cares more than if he had been a peasant; the lord of Hellas is level with his lackeys in republican Switzerland; Prime Ministers and Commanders-in-Chief have passed from a brief glory as Solons and Cæsars into failure and obscurity as closely on one another's heels as the descendants of Banquo; but Euripides and Aristophanes, Shakespear and Molière, Goethe and Ibsen remain fixed in their everlasting seats.

HOW WAR MUZZLES THE DRAMATIC POET

As for myself, why, it may be asked, did I not write two plays about the war instead of two pamphlets on it? The answer is significant. You cannot make war on war and on your neighbor at the same time. War cannot bear the terrible castigation of comedy, the ruthless light of laughter that glares on the stage. When men are heroically dying for their country, it is not the time to shew their lovers and wives and fathers and mothers how they are being sacrificed to the blunders of boobies, the cupidity of capitalists, the ambition of conquerors, the electioneering of demagogues, the Pharisaism of patriots, the lusts and lies and rancors and bloodthirsts that love war because it opens their prison doors, and sets them in the thrones of power and popularity. For unless these things are mercilessly exposed they will hide under the mantle of the ideals on the stage just as they do in real life.

And though there may be better things to reveal, it may not, and indeed cannot, be militarily expedient to reveal them whilst the issue is still in the balance.

Truth telling is not compatible with the defence of the realm. We are just now reading the revelations of our generals and admirals, unmuzzled at last by the armistice. During the war, General A, in his moving despatches from the field, told how General B had covered himself with deathless glory in such and such a battle. He now tells us that General B came within an ace of losing us the war by disobeying his orders on that occasion, and fighting instead of running away as he ought to have done. An excellent subject for comedy now that the war is over, no doubt; but if General A had let this out at the time, what would have been the effect on General B's soldiers? And had the stage made known what the Prime Minister and the Secretary of State for War who overruled General A thought of him, and what he thought of them, as now revealed in raging controversy, what would have been the effect on the nation? That is why comedy, though sorely tempted, had to be loyally silent; for the art of the dramatic poet knows no patriotism; recognizes no obligation but truth to natural history; cares not whether Germany or England perish; is ready to cry with Brynhild, "Lass' uns verderben, lachend zu grunde geh'n" sooner than deceive or be deceived; and thus becomes in time of war a greater military danger than poison, steel, or trinitrotoluene. That is why I had to withhold Heartbreak House from the footlights during the war; for the Germans might on any night have turned the last act from play into earnest, and even then might not have waited for their cues.

XVI

THE SHEWING-UP OF BLANCO POSNET

1909

THE CENSORSHIP

This little play is really a religious tract in dramatic form. If our silly censorship would permit its performance, it might possibly help to set right-side-up the perverted conscience and re-invigorate the starved self-respect of our considerable class of loose-lived playgoers whose point of honor is to deride all official and conventional sermons. As it is, it only gives me an opportunity of telling the story of the Select Committee of both Houses of Parliament which sat last year to inquire into the working of the censorship, against which it was alleged by myself and others that as its imbecility and mischievousness could not be fully illustrated within the limits of decorum imposed on the press, it could only be dealt with by a parliamentary body subject to no such limits.

A READABLE BLUEBOOK

Few books of the year 1909 can have been cheaper and more entertaining than the report of this Committee. Its full title is REPORT FROM THE JOINT SELECT COMMITTEE OF THE HOUSE OF LORDS AND THE HOUSE OF COMMONS ON THE STAGE PLAYS (CENSORSHIP) TOGETHER WITH THE PROCEEDINGS OF THE COMMITTEE, MINUTES OF EVIDENCE, AND APPENDICES. What the phrase "the Stage Plays" means in this title I do not know; nor does anyone else. The number of the Bluebook is 214. How interesting it is may be judged from the fact that it contains verbatim reports of long and animated interviews between the Committee and such witnesses as Mr William Archer, Mr Granville Barker, Mr J. M. Barrie, Mr Forbes Robertson, Mr Cecil Raleigh, Mr John

Galsworthy, Mr Laurence Housman, Sir Herbert Beerbohm Tree, Mr W. L. Courtney, Sir William Gilbert, Mr A. B. Walkley, Miss Lena Ashwell, Professor Gilbert Murray, Mr George Alexander, Mr George Edwardes, Mr Comyns Carr, the Speaker of the House of Commons, the Bishop of Southwark, Mr Hall Caine, Mr Israel Zangwill, Sir Squire Bancroft, Sir Arthur Pinero, and Mr Gilbert Chesterton, not to mention myself and a number of gentlemen less well known to the general public, but important in the world of the theatre. The publication of a book by so many famous contributors would be beyond the means of any commercial publishing firm. His Majesty's Stationery Office sells it to all comers by weight at the very reasonable price of three-and-threepence a copy.

HOW NOT TO DO IT

It was pointed out by Charles Dickens in Little Dorrit, which remains the most accurate and penetrating study of the genteel littleness of our class governments in the English language, that whenever an abuse becomes oppressive enough to persuade our party parliamentarians that something must be done, they immediately set to work to face the situation and discover How Not To Do It. Since Dickens's day the exposures effected by the Socialists have so shattered the self-satisfaction of modern commercial civilization that it is no longer difficult to convince our governments that something must be done, even to the extent of attempts at a reconstruction of civilization on a thoroughly uncommercial basis. Consequently, the first part of the process described by Dickens: that in which the reformers were snubbed by front bench demonstrations that the administrative departments were consuming miles of red tape in the correctest forms of activity, and that everything was for the best in the best of all possible worlds, is out of fashion; and we are in that other phase, familiarized by the history of the French Revolution, in which the primary assumption is that the country is in danger, and that the first duty of all parties, politicians, and governments is to save it. But as the effect of this is to give governments a great many more things to do, it also gives a powerful stimulus to the art of How Not To Do Them: that is to say, the art of contriving methods of reform which will leave matters exactly as they are.

The report of the Joint Select Committee is a capital illustration of this tendency. The case against the censorship was overwhelming; and the defence was more damaging to it than no defence at all could have been. Even had this not been so, the mere caprice of opinion had turned against the institution; and a reform was expected, evidence or no evidence. Therefore the Committee was unanimous as to the necessity of reforming the censorship; only, unfortunately, the majority attached to this unanimity the usual condition that nothing should be done to disturb the existing state of things. How this was effected may be gathered from the recommendations finally agreed on, which are as follows.

1. The drama is to be set entirely free by the abolition of the existing obligation to procure a licence from the Censor before performing a play; but every theatre lease is in future to be construed as if it contained a clause giving the landlord power to break it and evict the lessee if he produces a play without first obtaining the usual licence from the Lord Chamberlain.

2. Some of the plays licensed by the Lord Chamberlain are so vicious that their present practical immunity from prosecution must be put an end to; but no manager who procures the Lord Chamberlain's licence for a play can be punished in any way for producing it, though a special tribunal may order him to discontinue the performance; and even this order must not be recorded to his disadvantage on the licence of his theatre, nor may it be given as a judicial reason for cancelling that licence.

3. Authors and managers producing plays without first obtaining the usual licence from the Lord Chamberlain shall be perfectly free to do so, and shall be at no disadvantage compared to those who follow the existing practice, except that they may be punished, have the licences of their theatres endorsed and cancelled, and have the performance stopped pending the proceedings without compensation in the event of the proceedings ending in their acquittal.

4. Authors are to be rescued from their present subjection to an irresponsible secret tribunal which can condemn their plays without giving reasons, by the substitution for that tribunal of a Committee of the Privy Council, which is to be the final authority on the fitness of a play for representation; and this Committee is to sit *in camera* if and when it pleases.

5. The power to impose a veto on the production of plays is to be abolished because it may hinder the growth of a great national drama; but the Office of Examiner of Plays shall be continued; and the Lord Chamberlain shall retain his present powers to license plays, but shall be made responsible to Parliament to the extent of making it possible to ask questions there concerning his proceedings, especially now that members have discovered a method of doing this indirectly.

And so on, and so forth. The thing is to be done; and it is not to be done. Everything is to be changed and nothing is to be changed. The problem is to be faced and the solution to be shirked. And the word of Dickens is to be justified.

THE STORY OF THE JOINT SELECT COMMITTEE

Let me now tell the story of the Committee in greater detail, partly as a contribution to history; partly because, like most true stories, it is more amusing than the official story.

All commissions of public enquiry are more or less intimidated both by the interests on which they have to sit in judgment and, when their members are party politicians, by the votes at the back of those interests; but this unfortunate Committee sat under a quite exceptional cross fire. First, there was the king. The Censor is a member of his household retinue; and as a king's retinue has to be jealously guarded to avoid curtailment of the royal state no matter what may be the function of the particular retainer threatened, nothing but an express royal intimation to the contrary, which is a constitutional impossibility, could have relieved the Committee from the fear of displeasing the king by any proposal to abolish the censorship of the Lord Chamberlain. Now all the lords on the Committee and some of the commoners could have been wiped out of society (in their sense of the word) by the slightest intimation that the king would prefer not to meet them; and this was a heavy risk to run on the chance of "a great and serious national drama" ensuing on the removal of the Lord Chamberlain's veto on Mrs Warren's Profession. Second, there was the Nonconformist conscience, holding the Liberal Government responsible for the Committee it had appointed, and holding also, to the extent of votes enough to turn the scale in some constituencies, that the theatre is the gate of hell, to be tolerated, as vice is tolerated, only because the power to suppress it

could not be given to any public body without too serious an interference with certain Liberal traditions of liberty which are still useful to Nonconformists in other directions. Third, there was the commercial interest of the theatrical managers and their syndicates of backers in the City, to whom, as I shall shew later on, the censorship affords a cheap insurance of enormous value. Fourth, there was the powerful interest of the trade in intoxicating liquors, fiercely determined to resist any extension of the authority of teetotaller-led local governing bodies over theatres. Fifth, there were the playwrights, without political power, but with a very close natural monopoly of a talent not only for play-writing but for satirical polemics. And since every interest has its opposition, all these influences had created hostile bodies by the operation of the mere impulse to contradict them, always strong in English human nature.

WHY THE MANAGERS LOVE THE CENSORSHIP

The only one of these influences which seems to be generally misunderstood is that of the managers. It has been assumed repeatedly that managers and authors are affected in the same way by the censorship. When a prominent author protests against the censorship, his opinion is supposed to be balanced by that of some prominent manager who declares that the censorship is the mainstay of the theatre, and his relations with the Lord Chamberlain and the Examiner of Plays a cherished privilege and an inexhaustible joy. This error was not removed by the evidence given before the Joint Select Committee. The managers did not make their case clear there, partly because they did not understand it, and partly because their most eminent witnesses were not personally affected by it, and would not condescend to plead it, feeling themselves, on the contrary, compelled by their self-respect to admit and even emphasize the fact that the Lord Chamberlain in the exercise of his duties as licenser had done those things which he ought not to have done, and left undone those things which he ought to have done. Mr Forbes Robertson and Sir Herbert Tree, for instance, had never felt the real disadvantage of which managers have to complain. This disadvantage was not put directly to the Committee; and though the managers are against me on the question of the censorship, I will now put their case for them as they should have put it themselves, and as it can be read between the lines of their evidence when once the reader has the clue.

The manager of a theatre is a man of business. He is not an expert in politics, religion, art, literature, philosophy, or law. He calls in a playwright just as he calls in a doctor, or consults a lawyer, or engages an architect, depending on the playwright's reputation and past achievements for a satisfactory result. A play by an unknown man may attract him sufficiently to induce him to give that unknown man a trial; but this does not occur often enough to be taken into account: his normal course is to resort to a well-known author and take (mostly with misgiving) what he gets from him. Now this does not cause any anxiety to Mr Forbes Robertson and Sir Herbert Tree, because they are only incidentally managers and men of business: primarily they are highly cultivated artists, quite capable of judging for themselves anything that the most abstruse playwright is likely to put before them. But the plain-sailing tradesman who must be taken as the typical manager (for the west end of London is not the whole theatrical world) is by no means equally qualified to judge whether a play is safe from prosecution or not. He may not understand it, may not like it, may not know what the author

is driving at, may have no knowledge of the ethical, political, and sectarian controversies which may form the intellectual fabric of the play, and may honestly see nothing but an ordinary "character part" in a stage figure which may be a libellous and unmistakeable caricature of some eminent living person of whom he has never heard. Yet if he produces the play he is legally responsible just as if he had written it himself. Without protection he may find himself in the dock answering a charge of blasphemous libel, seditious libel, obscene libel, or all three together, not to mention the possibility of a private action for defamatory libel. His sole refuge is the opinion of the Examiner of Plays, his sole protection the licence of the Lord Chamberlain. A refusal to license does not hurt him, because he can produce another play: it is the author who suffers. The granting of the licence practically places him above the law; for though it may be legally possible to prosecute a licensed play, nobody ever dreams of doing it. The really responsible person, the Lord Chamberlain, could not be put into the dock; and the manager could not decently be convicted when he could produce in his defence a certificate from the chief officer of the King's Household that the play was a proper one.

A TWO GUINEA INSURANCE POLICY

The censorship, then, provides the manager, at the negligible premium of two guineas per play, with an effective insurance against the author getting him into trouble, and a complete relief from all conscientious responsibility for the character of the entertainment at his theatre. Under such circumstances, managers would be more than human if they did not regard the censorship as their most valuable privilege. This is the simple explanation of the rally of the managers and their Associations to the defence of the censorship, of their reiterated resolutions of confidence in the Lord Chamberlain, of their presentations of plate, and, generally, of their enthusiastic contentment with the present system, all in such startling contrast to the denunciations of the censorship by the authors. It also explains why the managerial witnesses who had least to fear from the Censor were the most reluctant in his defence, whilst those whose practice it is to strain his indulgence to the utmost were almost rapturous in his praise. There would be absolute unanimity among the managers in favor of the censorship if they were all simply tradesmen. Even those actor-managers who made no secret before the Committee of their contempt for the present operation of the censorship, and their indignation at being handed over to a domestic official as casual servants of a specially disorderly kind, demanded, not the abolition of the institution, but such a reform as might make it consistent with their dignity and unobstructive to their higher artistic aims. Feeling no personal need for protection against the author, they perhaps forgot the plight of many a manager to whom the modern advanced drama is so much Greek; but they did feel very strongly the need of being protected against Vigilance Societies and Municipalities and common informers in a country where a large section of the community still believes that art of all kinds is inherently sinful.

WHY THE GOVERNMENT INTERFERED

It may now be asked how a Liberal government had been persuaded to meddle at all with a question in which so many conflicting interests were involved, and which had probably no electoral value whatever. Many simple souls believed that it was because certain severely virtuous plays by Ibsen, by M. Brieux, by Mr Granville Barker, and by me, were suppressed by the censorship, whilst plays of a scandalous character were licensed without demur. No doubt this influenced public opinion; but those who imagine that it could influence British governments little know how remote from public opinion and how full of their own little family and party affairs British governments, both Liberal and Unionist, still are. The censorship scandal had existed for years without any parliamentary action being taken in the matter, and might have existed for as many more had it not happened in 1906 that Mr Robert Vernon Harcourt entered parliament as a member of the Liberal Party, of which his father had been one of the leaders during the Gladstone era. Mr Harcourt was thus a young man marked out for office both by his parentage and his unquestionable social position as one of the governing class. Also, and this was much less usual, he was brilliantly clever, and was the author of a couple of plays of remarkable promise. Mr Harcourt informed his leaders that he was going to take up the subject of the censorship. The leaders, recognizing his hereditary right to a parliamentary canter of some sort as a prelude to his public career, and finding that all the clever people seemed to be agreed that the censorship was an anti-Liberal institution and an abominable nuisance to boot, indulged him by appointing a Select Committee of both Houses to investigate the subject. The then Chancellor of the Duchy of Lancaster, Mr Herbert Samuel (now Postmaster-General), who had made his way into the Cabinet twenty years ahead of the usual age, was made Chairman. Mr Robert Harcourt himself was of course a member. With him, representing the Commons, were Mr Alfred Mason, a man of letters who had won a seat in parliament as offhandedly as he has since discarded it, or as he once appeared on the stage to help me out of a difficulty in casting Arms and the Man when that piece was the newest thing in the advanced drama. There was Mr Hugh Law, an Irish member, son of an Irish Chancellor, presenting a keen and joyous front to English intellectual sloth. Above all, there was Colonel Lockwood to represent at one stroke the Opposition and the average popular man. This he did by standing up gallantly for the Censor, to whose support the Opposition was in no way committed, and by visibly defying the most cherished conventions of the average man with a bunch of carnations in his buttonhole as large as a dinnerplate, which would have made a Bunthorne blench, and which very nearly did make Mr Granville Barker (who has an antipathy to the scent of carnations) faint.

THE PEERS ON THE JOINT SELECT COMMITTEE

The House of Lords then proceeded to its selection. As fashionable drama in Paris and London concerns itself almost exclusively with adultery, the first choice fell on Lord Gorell, who had for many years presided over the Divorce Court. Lord Plymouth, who had been Chairman to the Shakespear Memorial project (now merged in the Shakespear Memorial National Theatre), was obviously marked out for selection; and it was generally expected that the Lords Lytton and Esher, who had taken a prominent part in the same movement, would have been added. This expectation was not fulfilled. Instead, Lord Willoughby de Broke, who had distinguished himself as an amateur actor, was selected along with Lord Newton, whose special qualifications for the Committee, if he had any, were unknown to the public. Finally Lord Ribblesdale, the argute son of a Scotch mother, was thrown in to make up for any shortcoming in intellectual subtlety that might arise in the case of his younger colleagues; and this completed the two teams.

THE COMMITTEE'S ATTITUDE TOWARDS THE THEATRE

In England, thanks chiefly to the censorship, the theatre is not respected. It is indulged and despised as a department of what is politely called gaiety. It is therefore not surprising that the majority of the Committee began by taking its work uppishly and carelessly. When it discovered that the contemporary drama, licensed by the Lord Chamberlain, included plays which could be described only behind closed doors, and in the discomfort which attends discussions of very nasty subjects between men of widely different ages, it calmly put its own convenience before its public duty by ruling that there should be no discussion of particular plays, much as if a committee on temperance were to rule that drunkenness was not a proper subject of conversation among gentlemen.

A BAD BEGINNING

This was a bad beginning. Everybody knew that in England the censorship would not be crushed by the weight of the constitutional argument against it, heavy as that was, unless it were also brought home to the Committee and to the public that it had sanctioned and protected the very worst practicable examples of the kind of play it professed to extirpate. For it must be remembered that the other half of the practical side of the case, dealing with the merits of the plays it had suppressed, could never secure a unanimous assent. If the Censor had suppressed Hamlet, as he most certainly would have done had it been submitted to him as a new play, he would have been supported by a large body of people to whom incest is a tabooed subject which must not be mentioned on the stage or anywhere else outside a criminal court. Hamlet, Œdipus, and The Cenci, Mrs Warren's Profession, Brieux's Maternité, and Les Avariés, Maeterlinck's Monna Vanna and Mr Granville Barker's Waste may or may not be great poems, or edifying sermons, or important documents, or charming romances: our tribal citizens know nothing about that and do not want to know anything: all that they do know is that incest, prostitution, abortion, contagious diseases, and nudity are improper, and that all conversations, or books, or plays in which they are discussed are improper conversations, improper books, improper plays, and should not be allowed. The Censor may prohibit all such plays with complete certainty that there will be a chorus of "Quite right too" sufficient to drown the protests of the few who know better. The Achilles heel of the censorship is therefore not the fine plays it has suppressed, but the abominable plays it has licensed: plays which the Committee itself had to turn the public out of the room and close the doors before it could discuss, and which I myself have found it impossible to expose in the press because no editor of a paper or magazine intended for general family reading could admit into his columns the baldest narration of the stories which the Censor has not only tolerated but expressly certified as fitting for presentation on the stage. When the Committee ruled out this part of the case it shook the confidence of the authors in its impartiality and its seriousness. Of course it was not able to enforce its ruling thoroughly. Plays which were merely lightminded and irresponsible in their viciousness were repeatedly mentioned by Mr Harcourt and others. But the really detestable plays, which would have damned the censorship beyond all apology or salvation, were never referred to; and the moment Mr Harcourt or anyone else made the Committee uncomfortable by a move in their direction, the ruling was appealed to at once, and the censorship saved.

A COMIC INTERLUDE

It was part of this nervous dislike of the unpleasant part of its business that led to the comic incident of the Committee's sudden discovery that I had insulted it, and its suspension of its investigation for the purpose of elaborately insulting me back again. Comic to the lookers-on, that is; for the majority of the Committee made no attempt to conceal the fact that they were wildly angry with me; and I, though my public experience and skill in acting enabled me to maintain an appearance of imperturbable good-humor, was equally furious. The friction began as follows.

The precedents for the conduct of the Committee were to be found in the proceedings of the Committee of 1892. That Committee, no doubt recognizing the absurdity of calling on distinguished artists to give their views before it, and then refusing to allow them to state their views except in nervous replies to such questions as it might suit members to put to them, allowed Sir Henry Irving and Sir John Hare to prepare and read written statements, and formally invited them to read them to the Committee before being questioned. I accordingly prepared such a statement. For the greater convenience of the Committee, I offered to have this statement printed at my own expense, and to supply the members with copies. The offer was accepted; and the copies supplied. I also offered to provide the Committee with copies of those plays of mine which had been refused a licence by the Lord Chamberlain. That offer also was accepted; and the books duly supplied.

AN ANTI-SHAVIAN PANIC

As far as I can guess, the next thing that happened was that some timid or unawakened member of the Committee read my statement and was frightened or scandalized out of his wits by it. At all events it is certain that the majority of the Committee allowed themselves to be persuaded to refuse to allow any statement to be read; but to avoid the appearance of pointing this expressly at me, the form adopted was a resolution to adhere strictly to precedent, the Committee being then unaware that the precedents were on my side. Accordingly, when I appeared before the Committee, and proposed to read my statement "according to precedent," the Committee was visibly taken aback. The Chairman was bound by the letter of the decision arrived at to allow me to read my statement, since that course was according to precedent; but as this was exactly what the decision was meant to prevent, the majority of the Committee would have regarded this hoisting of them with their own petard as a breach of faith on the part of the Chairman, who, I infer, was not in agreement with the suppressive majority. There was nothing for it, after a somewhat awkward pause, but to clear me and the public out of the room and reconsider the situation *in camera*. When the doors were opened again I was informed simply that the Committee would not hear my statement. But as the Committee could not very decently refuse my evidence altogether, the Chairman, with a printed copy of my statement in his hand as "proof," was able to come to the rescue to some extent by putting to me a series of questions to which no doubt I might have replied by taking another copy out of my pocket, and quoting my statement paragraph by paragraph, as some of the later witnesses did. But as in offering the Committee my statement for burial in their bluebook I had made a considerable sacrifice, being able to secure greater publicity for it by independent publication on my own account; and as, further, the circumstances of the refusal made it offensive enough to take all heart out of the scrupulous consideration with which I had so far treated the Committee, I was not disposed to give its majority a second chance, or to lose the opportunity offered me by the questions to fire an additional broadside into the censorship. I pocketed my statement, and answered the questions *viva voce*. At the conclusion of this, my examination-in-chief, the Committee adjourned, asking me to present myself again for (virtually) cross-examination. But this cross-examination never came off, as the sequel will shew.

A RARE AND CURIOUS FIRST EDITION

The refusal of the Committee to admit my statement had not unnaturally created the impression that it must be a scandalous document; and a lively demand for copies at once set in. And among the very first applicants were members of the majority which had carried the decision to exclude the document. They had given so little attention to the business that they did not know, or had forgotten, that they had already been supplied with copies at their own request. At all events, they came to me publicly and cleaned me out of the handful of copies I had provided for distribution to the press. And after the sitting it was intimated to me that yet more copies were desired for the use of the Committee: a demand, under the circumstances, of breath-bereaving coolness. At the same time, a brisk demand arose outside the Committee, not only among people who were anxious to read what I had to say on the subject, but among victims of the craze for collecting first editions, copies of privately circulated pamphlets, and other real or imaginary rarities. Such maniacs will cheerfully pay five guineas for any piece of discarded old rubbish of mine when they will not pay as many shillings for a clean new copy of it, because everyone else can get it for the same price too.

THE TIMES TO THE RESCUE

The day after the refusal of the Committee to face my statement, I transferred the scene of action to the columns of The Times, which did yeoman's service to the public on this, as on many other occasions, by treating the question as a public one without the least regard to the supposed susceptibilities of the Court on the one side, or the avowed prejudices of the Free Churches or the interests of the managers or theatrical speculators on the other. The Times published the summarized conclusions of my statement, and gave me an opportunity of saying as much as it was then advisable to say of what had occurred. For it must be remembered that, however impatient and contemptuous I might feel of the intellectual cowardice shewn by the majority of the Committee face to face with myself, it was none the less necessary to keep up its prestige in every possible way, not only for the sake of the dignity and importance of the matter with which it had to deal, and in the hope that the treatment of subsequent witnesses and the final report might make amends for a feeble beginning, but also out of respect and consideration for the minority. For it is fair to say that the majority was never more than a bare majority, and that the worst thing the Committee did—the exclusion of references to particular plays —was perpetrated in the absence of the Chairman.

I, therefore, had to treat the Committee in The Times very much better than its majority deserved, an injustice for which I now apologize. I did not, however, resist the temptation to hint, quite good-humoredly, that my politeness to the Committee had cost me quite enough already, and that I was not prepared to supply the members of the Committee, or anyone else, with extra copies merely as collectors' curiosities.

THE COUNCIL OF TEN

Then the fat was in the fire. The majority, chaffed for its eagerness to obtain copies of scarce pamphlets retailable at five guineas, went dancing mad. When I presented myself, as requested, for cross-examination, I found the doors of the Committee room shut, and the corridors of the House of Lords filled by a wondering crowd, to whom it had somehow leaked out that something terrible was happening inside. It could not be another licensed play too scandalous to be discussed in public, because the Committee had decided to discuss no more of these examples of the Censor's notions of purifying the stage; and what else the Committee might have to discuss that might not be heard by all the world was not easily guessable.

Without suggesting that the confidence of the Committee was in any way violated by any of its members further than was absolutely necessary to clear them from suspicion of complicity in the scene which followed, I think I may venture to conjecture what was happening. It was felt by the majority, first, that it must be cleared at all costs of the imputation of having procured more than one copy each of my statement, and that one not from any interest in an undesirable document by an irreverent author, but in the reluctant discharge of its solemn public duty; second, that a terrible example must be made of me by the most crushing public snub in the power of the Committee to administer. To throw my wretched little pamphlet at my head and to kick me out of the room was the passionate impulse which prevailed in spite of all the remonstrances of the Commoners, seasoned to the give-and-take of public life, and of the single peer who kept his head. The others, for the moment, had no heads to keep. And the fashion in which they proposed to wreak their vengeance was as follows.

THE SENTENCE

I was to be admitted, as a lamb to the slaughter, and allowed to take my place as if for further examination. The Chairman was then to inform me coldly that the Committee did not desire to have anything more to say to me. The members were thereupon solemnly to hand me back the copies of my statement as so much waste paper, and I was to be suffered to slink away with what countenance I could maintain in such disgrace.

But this plan required the active co-operation of every member of the Committee; and whilst the majority regarded it as an august and impressive vindication of the majesty of parliament, the minority regarded it with equal conviction as a puerile tomfoolery, and declined altogether to act their allotted parts in it. Besides, they did not all want to part with the books. For instance, Mr Hugh Law, being an Irishman, with an Irishman's sense of how to behave like a gallant gentleman on occasion, was determined to be able to assure me that nothing should induce him to give up my statement or prevent him from obtaining and cherishing as many copies as possible. (I quote this as an example to the House of Lords of the right thing to say in such emergencies.) So the program had to be modified. The minority could not prevent the enraged majority from refusing to examine me further; nor could the Chairman refuse to communicate that decision to me. Neither could the minority object to the secretary handing me back such copies as he could collect from the majority. And at that the matter was left. The doors were opened; the audience trooped in; I was called to my place in the dock (so to speak); and all was ready for the sacrifice.

THE EXECUTION

Alas! the majority reckoned without Colonel Lockwood. That hardy and undaunted veteran refused to shirk his share in the scene merely because the minority was recalcitrant and the majority perhaps subject to stage fright. When Mr Samuel had informed me that the Committee had no further questions to ask me with an urbanity which gave the public no clue as to the temper of the majority; when I had jumped up with the proper air of relief and gratitude; when the secretary had handed me his little packet of books with an affability which effectually concealed his dramatic function as executioner; when the audience was simply disappointed at being baulked of the entertainment of hearing Mr Robert Harcourt cross-examine me; in short, when the situation was all but saved by the tact of the Chairman and secretary, Colonel Lockwood rose, with all his carnations blazing, and gave away the whole case by handing me, with impressive simplicity and courtesy, his *two* copies of the precious statement. And I believe that if he had succeeded in securing ten, he would have handed them all back to me with the most sincere conviction that every one of the ten must prove a crushing addition to the weight of my discomfiture. I still cherish that second copy, a little blue-bound pamphlet, methodically autographed "Lockwood B" among my most valued literary trophies.

An innocent lady told me afterwards that she never knew that I could smile so beautifully, and that she thought it shewed very good taste on my part. I was not conscious of smiling; but I should have embraced the Colonel had I dared. As it was, I turned expectantly to his colleagues, mutely inviting them to follow his example. But there was only one Colonel Lockwood on that Committee. No eye met mine except minority eyes, dancing with mischief. There was nothing more to be said. I went home to my morning's work, and returned in the afternoon to receive the apologies of the minority for the conduct of the majority, and to see Mr Granville Barker, overwhelmed by the conscience-stricken politeness of the now almost abject Committee, and by a powerful smell of carnations, heading the long list of playwrights who came there to testify against the censorship, and whose treatment, I am happy to say, was everything they could have desired.

After all, ridiculous as the scene was, Colonel Lockwood's simplicity and courage were much more serviceable to his colleagues than their own inept *coup de théâtre* would have been if he had not spoiled it. It was plain to everyone that he had acted in entire good faith, without a thought as to these apparently insignificant little books being of any importance or having caused me or anybody else any trouble, and that he was wounded in his most sensitive spot by the construction my Times letter had put on his action. And in Colonel Lockwood's case one saw the case of his party on the Committee. They had simply been thoughtless in the matter.

I hope nobody will suppose that this in any way exonerates them. When people accept public service for one of the most vital duties that can arise in our society, they have no right to be thoughtless. In spite of the fun of the scene on the surface, my public sense was, and still is, very deeply offended by it. It made an end for me of the claim of the majority to be taken seriously. When the Government comes to deal with the question, as it presumably will before long, I invite it to be guided by the Chairman, the minority, and by the witnesses according to their weight, and to pay no attention whatever to those recommendations which were obviously inserted solely to conciliate the majority and get the report through and the Committee done with.

My evidence will be found in the Blue-book, pp. 46-53. And here is the terrible statement which the Committee went through so much to suppress.

THE REJECTED STATEMENT— PART I

THE WITNESS'S QUALIFICATIONS

I am by profession a playwright. I have been in practice since 1892. I am a member of the Managing Committee of the Society of Authors and of the Dramatic Sub-Committee of that body. I have written nineteen plays, some of which have been translated and performed in all European countries except Turkey, Greece, and Portugal. They have been performed extensively in America. Three of them have been refused licences by the Lord Chamberlain. In one case a licence has since been granted. The other two are still unlicensed. I have suffered both in pocket and reputation by the action of the Lord Chamberlain. In other countries I have not come into conflict with the censorship except in Austria, where the production of a comedy of mine was postponed for a year because it alluded to the part taken by Austria in the Servo-Bulgarian war. This comedy was not one of the plays suppressed in England by the Lord Chamberlain. One of the plays so suppressed was prosecuted in America by the police in consequence of an immense crowd of disorderly persons having been attracted to the first performance by the Lord Chamberlain's condemnation of it; but on appeal to a higher court it was decided that the representation was lawful and the intention innocent, since when it has been repeatedly performed.

I am not an ordinary playwright in general practice. I am a specialist in immoral and heretical plays. My reputation has been gained by my persistent struggle to force the public to reconsider its morals. In particular, I regard much current morality as to economic and sexual relations as disastrously wrong; and I regard certain doctrines of the Christian religion as understood in England today with abhorrence. I write plays with the deliberate object of converting the nation to my opinions in these matters. I have no other effectual incentive to write plays, as I am not dependent on the theatre for my livelihood. If I were prevented from producing immoral and heretical plays, I should cease to write for the theatre, and propagate my views from the platform and through books. I mention these facts to shew that I have a special interest in the achievement by my profession of those rights of liberty of speech and conscience which are matters of course in other professions. I object to censorship not merely because the existing form of it grievously injures and hinders me individually, but on public grounds.

THE DEFINITION OF IMMORALITY

In dealing with the question of the censorship, everything depends on the correct use of the word immorality, and a careful discrimination between the powers of a magistrate or judge to administer a code, and those of a censor to please himself.

Whatever is contrary to established manners and customs is immoral. An immoral act or doctrine is not necessarily a sinful one: on the contrary, every advance in thought and conduct is by definition immoral until it has converted the majority. For this reason it is of the most enormous importance that immorality should be protected jealously against the attacks of those who have no standard except the standard of custom, and who regard any attack on custom—that is, on morals—as an attack on society, on religion, and on virtue.

A censor is never intentionally a protector of immorality. He always aims at the protection of morality. Now morality is extremely valuable to society. It imposes conventional conduct on the great mass of persons who are incapable of original ethical judgment, and who would be quite lost if they were not in leading-strings devized by lawgivers, philosophers, prophets, and poets for their guidance. But morality is not dependent on censorship for protection. It is already powerfully fortified by the magistracy and the whole body of law. Blasphemy, indecency, libel, treason, sedition, obscenity, profanity, and all the other evils which a censorship is supposed to avert, are punishable by the civil magistrate with all the severity of vehement prejudice. Morality has not only every engine that lawgivers can devize in full operation for its protection, but also that enormous weight of public opinion enforced by social ostracism which is stronger than all the statutes. A censor pretending to protect morality is like a child pushing the cushions of a railway carriage to give itself the sensation of making the train travel at sixty miles an hour. It is immorality, not morality, that needs protection: it is morality, not immorality, that needs restraint; for morality, with all the dead weight of human inertia and superstition to hang on the back of the pioneer, and all the malice of vulgarity and prejudice to threaten him, is responsible for many persecutions and many martyrdoms.

Persecutions and martyrdoms, however, are trifles compared to the mischief done by censorships in delaying the general march of enlightenment. This can be brought home to us by imagining what would have been the effect of applying to all literature the censorship we still apply to the stage. The works of Linnæus and the evolutionists of 1790–1830, of Darwin, Wallace, Huxley, Helmholtz, Tyndall, Spencer, Carlyle, Ruskin, and Samuel Butler, would not have been published, as they were all immoral and heretical in the very highest degree, and gave pain to many worthy and pious people. They are at present condemned by the Greek and Roman Catholic censorships as unfit for general reading. A censorship of conduct would have been equally disastrous. The disloyalty of Hampden and of Washington; the revolting immorality of Luther in not only marrying when he was a priest, but actually marrying a nun; the heterodoxy of Galileo; the shocking blasphemies and sacrileges of Mahomet against the idols whom he dethroned to make way for his conception of one god; the still more startling blasphemy of Jesus when He declared God to be the son of man and Himself to be the son of God, are all examples of shocking immoralities (every immorality shocks somebody), the suppression and extinction of which would have been more disastrous than the utmost mischief that can be conceived as ensuing from the toleration of vice.

These facts, glaring as they are, are disguised by the promotion of immoralities into moralities which is constantly going on. Christianity and Mahometanism, once thought of and dealt with exactly as Anarchism is thought of and dealt with today, have become established religions; and fresh immoralities are persecuted in their name. The truth is that the vast majority of persons professing these religions have never been anything but simple moralists. The respectable Englishman who is a Christian because he was born in Clapham would be a Mahometan for the cognate reason if he had been born in Constantinople. He has never willingly tolerated immorality. He did not adopt any innovation until it had become moral; and then he adopted it, not on its merits, but solely because it had become moral. In doing so he never realized that it had ever been immoral: consequently its early struggles taught him no lesson; and he has opposed the next step in human progress as indignantly as if neither manners, customs, nor thought had ever changed since the beginning of the world. Toleration must be imposed on him as a mystic and painful duty by his spiritual and political leaders, or he will condemn the world to stagnation, which is the penalty of an inflexible morality.

WHAT TOLERATION MEANS

This must be done all the more arbitrarily because it is not possible to make the ordinary moral man understand what toleration and liberty really mean. He will accept them verbally with alacrity, even with enthusiasm, because the word toleration has been moralized by eminent Whigs; but what he means by toleration is toleration of doctrines that he considers enlightened, and, by liberty, liberty to do what he considers right: that is, he does not mean toleration or liberty at all; for there is no need to tolerate what appears enlightened or to claim liberty to do what most people consider right. Toleration and liberty have no sense or use except as toleration of opinions that are considered damnable, and liberty to do what seems wrong. Setting Englishmen free to marry their deceased wife's sisters is not tolerated by the people who approve of it, but by the people who regard it as incestuous. Catholic Emancipation and the admission of Jews to parliament needed no toleration from Catholics and Jews: the toleration they needed was that of the people who regarded the one measure as a facilitation of idolatry, and the other as a condonation of the crucifixion. Clearly such toleration is not clamored for by the multitude or by the press which reflects its prejudices. It is essentially one of those abnegations of passion and prejudice which the common man submits to because uncommon men whom he respects as wiser than himself assure him that it must be so, or the higher affairs of human destiny will suffer.

Such submission is the more difficult because the arguments against tolerating immorality are the same as the arguments against tolerating murder and theft; and this is why the Censor seems to the inconsiderate as obviously desirable a functionary as the police magistrate. But there is this simple and tremendous difference between the cases: that whereas no evil can conceivably result from the total suppression of murder and theft, and all communities prosper in direct proportion to such suppression, the total suppression of immorality, especially in matters of religion and sex, would stop enlightenment, and produce what used to be called a Chinese civilization until the Chinese lately took to immoral courses by permitting railway contractors to desecrate the graves of their ancestors, and their soldiers to wear clothes which indecently revealed the fact that they had legs and waists and even posteriors. At about the same moment a few bold Englishwomen ventured on the immorality of riding astride their horses, a practice that has since established itself so successfully that before another generation has passed away there may not be a new side-saddle in England, or a woman who could use it if there was.

THE CASE FOR TOLERATION

Accordingly, there has risen among wise and far-sighted men a perception of the need for setting certain departments of human activity entirely free from legal interference. This has nothing to do with any sympathy these liberators may themselves have with immoral views. A man with the strongest conviction of the Divine ordering of the universe and of the superiority of monarchy to all forms of government may nevertheless quite consistently and conscientiously be ready to lay down his life for the right of every man to advocate Atheism or Republicanism if he believes in them. An attack on morals may turn out to be the salvation of the race. A hundred years ago nobody foresaw that Tom Paine's centenary would be the subject of a laudatory special article in The Times; and only a few understood that the persecution of his works and the transportation of men for the felony of reading them was a mischievous mistake. Even less, perhaps, could they have guessed that Proudhon, who became notorious by his essay entitled "What is Property? It is Theft," would have received, on the like occasion and in the same paper, a respectful consideration which nobody would now dream of according to Lord Liverpool or Lord Brougham. Nevertheless there was a mass of evidence to shew that such a development was not only possible but fairly probable, and that the risks of suppressing liberty of propaganda were far graver than the risk of Paine's or Proudhon's writings wrecking civilization. Now there was no such evidence in favor of tolerating the cutting of throats and the robbing of tills. No case whatever can be made out for the statement that a nation cannot do without common thieves and homicidal ruffians. But an overwhelming case can be made out for the statement that no nation can prosper or even continue to exist without heretics and advocates of shockingly immoral doctrines. The Inquisition and the Star Chamber, which were nothing but censorships, made ruthless war on impiety and immorality. The result was once familiar to Englishmen, though of late years it seems to have been forgotten. It cost England a revolution to get rid of the Star Chamber. Spain did not get rid of the Inquisition, and paid for that omission by becoming a barely third-rate power politically, and intellectually no power at all, in the Europe she had once dominated as the mightiest of the Christian empires.

THE LIMITS TO TOLERATION

But the large toleration these considerations dictate has limits. For example, though we tolerate, and rightly tolerate, the propaganda of Anarchism as a political theory which embraces all that is valuable in the doctrine of Laisser-Faire and the method of Free Trade as well as all that is shocking in the views of Bakounine, we clearly cannot, or at all events will not, tolerate assassination of rulers on the ground that it is "propaganda by deed" or sociological experiment. A play inciting to such an assassination cannot claim the privileges of heresy or immorality, because no case can be made out in support of assassination as an indispensable instrument of progress. Now it happens that we have in the Julius Cæsar of Shakespear a play which the Tsar of Russia or the Governor-General of India would hardly care to see performed in their capitals just now. It is an artistic treasure; but it glorifies a murder which Goethe described as the silliest crime ever committed. It may quite possibly have helped the regicides of 1649 to see themselves, as it certainly helped generations of Whig statesmen to see them, in a heroic light; and it unquestionably vindicates and ennobles a conspirator who assassinated the head of the Roman State not because he abused his position but solely because he occupied it, thus affirming the extreme republican principle that all kings, good or bad, should be killed because kingship and freedom cannot live together. Under certain circumstances this vindication and ennoblement might act as an incitement to an actual assassination as well as to Plutarchian republicanism; for it is one thing to advocate republicanism or royalism: it is quite another to make a hero of Brutus or Ravaillac, or a heroine of Charlotte Corday. Assassination is the extreme form of censorship; and it seems hard to justify an incitement to it on anti-censorial principles. The very people who would have scouted the notion of prohibiting the performances of Julius Cæsar at His Majesty's Theatre in London last year, might now entertain very seriously a proposal to exclude Indians from them, and to suppress the play completely in Calcutta and Dublin; for if the assassin of Cæsar was a hero, why not the assassins of Lord Frederick Cavendish, Presidents Lincoln and McKinley, and Sir Curzon Wyllie? Here is a strong case for some constitutional means of preventing the performance of a play. True, it is an equally strong case for preventing the circulation of the Bible, which was always in the hands of our regicides; but as the Roman Catholic Church does not hesitate to accept that consequence of the censorial principle, it does not invalidate the argument.

Take another actual case. A modern comedy, Arms and The Man, though not a comedy of politics, is nevertheless so far historical that it reveals the unacknowledged fact that as the Servo-Bulgarian War of 1885 was much more than a struggle between the Servians and Bulgarians, the troops engaged were officered by two European Powers of the first magnitude. In consequence, the performance of the play was for some time forbidden in Vienna, and more recently it gave offence in Rome at a moment when popular feeling was excited as to the relations of Austria with the Balkan States. Now if a comedy so remote from political passion as Arms and The Man can, merely because it refers to political facts, become so inconvenient and inopportune that Foreign Offices take the trouble to have its production postponed, what may not be the effect of what is called a patriotic drama produced at a moment when the balance is quivering between peace and war? Is there not something to be said for a political censorship, if not for a moral one? May not those continental governments who leave the stage practically free in every other respect, but muzzle it politically, be justified by the practical exigencies of the situation?

THE DIFFERENCE BETWEEN LAW AND CENSORSHIP

The answer is that a pamphlet, a newspaper article, or a resolution moved at a political meeting can do all the mischief that a play can, and often more; yet we do not set up a permanent censorship of the press or of political meetings. Any journalist may publish an article, any demagogue may deliver a speech without giving notice to the government or obtaining its licence. The risk of such freedom is great; but as it is the price of our political liberty, we think it worth paying. We may abrogate it in emergencies by a Coercion Act, a suspension of the Habeas Corpus Act, or a proclamation of martial law, just as we stop the traffic in a street during a fire, or shoot thieves at sight if they loot after an earthquake. But when the emergency is past, liberty is restored everywhere except in the theatre. The Act of 1843 is a permanent Coercion Act for the theatre, a permanent suspension of the Habeas Corpus Act as far as plays are concerned, a permanent proclamation of martial law with a single official substituted for a court martial. It is, in fact, assumed that actors, playwrights, and theatre managers are dangerous and dissolute characters whose existence creates a chronic state of emergency, and who must be treated as earthquake looters are treated. It is not necessary now to discredit this assumption. It was broken down by the late Sir Henry Irving when he finally shamed the Government into extending to his profession the official recognition enjoyed by the other branches of fine art. Today we have on the roll of knighthood actors, authors, and managers. The rogue and

vagabond theory of the depravity of the theatre is as dead officially as it is in general society; and with it has perished the sole excuse for the Act of 1843 and for the denial to the theatre of the liberties secured, at far greater social risk, to the press and the platform.

There is no question here of giving the theatre any larger liberties than the press and the platform, or of claiming larger powers for Shakespear to eulogize Brutus than Lord Rosebery has to eulogize Cromwell. The abolition of the censorship does not involve the abolition of the magistrate and of the whole civil and criminal code. On the contrary, it would make the theatre more effectually subject to them than it is at present; for once a play now runs the gauntlet of the censorship, it is practically placed above the law. It is almost humiliating to have to demonstrate the essential difference between a censor and a magistrate or a sanitary inspector; but it is impossible to ignore the carelessness with which even distinguished critics of the theatre assume that all the arguments proper to the support of a magistracy and body of jurisprudence apply equally to a censorship.

A magistrate has laws to administer: a censor has nothing but his own opinion. A judge leaves the question of guilt to the jury: the Censor is jury and judge as well as lawgiver. A magistrate may be strongly prejudiced against an atheist or an anti-vaccinator, just as a sanitary inspector may have formed a careful opinion that drains are less healthy than cesspools; but the magistrate must allow the atheist to affirm instead of to swear, and must grant the anti-vaccinator an exemption certificate, when their demands are lawfully made; and in cities the inspector must compel the builder to make drains and must prosecute him if he makes cesspools. The law may be only the intolerance of the community; but it is a defined and limited intolerance. The limitation is sometimes carried so far that a judge cannot inflict the penalty for housebreaking on a burglar who can prove that he found the door open and therefore made only an unlawful entry. On the other hand, it is sometimes so vague, as for example in the case of the American law against obscenity, that it makes the magistrate virtually a censor. But in the main a citizen can ascertain what he may do and what he may not do; and, though no one knows better than a magistrate that a single ill-conducted family may demoralize a whole street, no magistrate can imprison or otherwise restrain its members on the ground that their immorality may corrupt their neighbors. He can prevent any citizen from carrying certain specified weapons, but not from handling pokers, table-knives, bricks, or bottles of corrosive fluid, on the ground that he might use them to commit murder or inflict malicious injury. He has no general power to prevent citizens from selling unhealthy or poisonous substances, or judging for themselves what substances are unhealthy and what wholesome, what poisonous and what innocuous: what he *can* do is to prevent anybody who has not a specific qualification from selling certain specified poisons of which a schedule is kept. Nobody is forbidden to sell minerals without a licence; but everybody is forbidden to sell silver without a licence. When the law has forgotten some atrocious sin— for instance, contracting marriage whilst suffering from contagious disease—the magistrate cannot arrest or punish the wrongdoer, however he may abhor his wickedness. In short, no man is lawfully at the mercy of the magistrate's personal caprice, prejudice, ignorance, superstition, temper, stupidity, resentment, timidity, ambition, or private conviction. But a playwright's livelihood, his reputation, and his inspiration and mission are at the personal mercy of the Censor. The two

do not stand, as the criminal and the judge stand, in the presence of a law that binds them both equally, and was made by neither of them, but by the deliberate collective wisdom of the community. The only law that affects them is the Act of 1843, which empowers one of them to do absolutely and finally what he likes with the other's work. And when it is remembered that the slave in this case is the man whose profession is that of Eschylus and Euripides, of Shakespear and Goethe, of Tolstoy and Ibsen, and the master the holder of a party appointment which by the nature of its duties practically excludes the possibility of its acceptance by a serious statesman or great lawyer, it will be seen that the playwrights are justified in reproaching the framers of that Act for having failed not only to appreciate the immense importance of the theatre as a most powerful instrument for teaching the nation how and what to think and feel, but even to conceive that those who make their living by the theatre are normal human beings with the common rights of English citizens. In this extremity of inconsiderateness it is not surprising that they also did not trouble themselves to study the difference between a censor and a magistrate. And it will be found that almost all the people who disinterestedly defend the censorship today are defending him on the assumption that there is no constitutional difference between him and any other functionary whose duty it is to restrain crime and disorder.

One further difference remains to be noted. As a magistrate grows old his mind may change or decay; but the law remains the same. The censorship of the theatre fluctuates with every change in the views and character of the man who exercises it. And what this implies can only be appreciated by those who can imagine what the effect on the mind must be of the duty of reading through every play that is produced in the kingdom year in, year out.

WHY THE LORD CHAMBERLAIN?

What may be called the high political case against censorship as a principle is now complete. The pleadings are those which have already freed books and pulpits and political platforms in England from censorship, if not from occasional legal persecution. The stage alone remains under a censorship of a grotesquely unsuitable kind. No play can be performed if the Lord Chamberlain happens to disapprove of it. And the Lord Chamberlain's functions have no sort of relationship to dramatic literature. A great judge of literature, a far-seeing statesman, a born champion of liberty of conscience and intellectual integrity—say a Milton, a Chesterfield, a Bentham—would be a very bad Lord Chamberlain: so bad, in fact, that his exclusion from such a post may be regarded as decreed by natural law. On the other hand, a good Lord Chamberlain would be a stickler for morals in the narrowest sense, a busybody, a man to whom a matter of two inches in the length of a gentleman's sword or the absence of a feather from a lady's head-dress would be a graver matter than the Habeas Corpus Act. The Lord Chamberlain, as Censor of the theatre, is a direct descendant of the King's Master of the Revels, appointed in 1544 by Henry VIII to keep order among the players and musicians of that day when they performed at Court. This first appearance of the theatrical censor in politics as the whipper-in of the player, with its conception of the player as a rich man's servant hired to amuse him, and, outside his professional duties, as a gay, disorderly, anarchic spoilt child, half privileged, half outlawed, probably as much vagabond as actor, is the real foundation of the subjection of the whole profession, actors, managers, authors and all, to the despotic authority of an officer whose business it is to preserve decorum among menials. It must be remembered that it was not until a hundred years later, in the reaction against the Puritans, that a woman could appear on the English stage without being pelted off as the Italian actresses were. The theatrical profession was regarded as a shameless one; and it is only of late years that actresses have at last succeeded in living down the assumption that actress and prostitute are synonymous terms, and made good their position in respectable society. This makes the survival of the old ostracism in the Act of 1843 intolerably galling; and though it explains the apparently unaccountable absurdity of choosing as Censor of dramatic literature an official whose functions and qualifications have nothing whatever to do with literature, it also explains why the present arrangement is not only criticized as an institution, but resented as an insult.

THE DIPLOMATIC OBJECTION TO THE LORD CHAMBERLAIN

There is another reason, quite unconnected with the susceptibilities of authors, which makes it undesirable that a member of the King's Household should be responsible for the character and tendency of plays. The drama, dealing with all departments of human life, is necessarily political. Recent events have shewn—what indeed needed no demonstration—that it is impossible to prevent inferences being made, both at home and abroad, from the action of the Lord Chamberlain. The most talked-about play of the present year (1909), An Englishman's Home, has for its main interest an invasion of England by a fictitious power which is understood, as it is meant to be understood, to represent Germany. The lesson taught by the play is the danger of invasion and the need for every English citizen to be a soldier. The Lord Chamberlain licensed this play, but refused to license a parody of it. Shortly afterwards he refused to license another play in which the fear of a German invasion was ridiculed. The German press drew the inevitable inference that the Lord Chamberlain was an anti-German alarmist, and that his opinions were a reflection of those prevailing in St James's Palace. Immediately after this, the Lord Chamberlain licensed the play. Whether the inference, as far as the Lord Chamberlain was concerned, was justified, is of no consequence. What is important is that it was sure to be made, justly or unjustly, and extended from the Lord Chamberlain to the Throne.

THE OBJECTION OF COURT ETIQUET

There is another objection to the Lord Chamberlain's censorship which affects the author's choice of subject. Formerly very little heed was given in England to the susceptibilities of foreign courts. For instance, the notion that the Mikado of Japan should be as sacred to the English playwright as he is to the Japanese Lord Chamberlain would have seemed grotesque a generation ago. Now that the maintenance of *entente cordiale* between nations is one of the most prominent and most useful functions of the Crown, the freedom of authors to deal with political subjects, even historically, is seriously threatened by the way in which the censorship makes the King responsible for the contents of every play. One author— the writer of these lines, in fact—has long desired to dramatize the life of Mahomet. But the possibility of a protest from the Turkish Ambassador—or the fear of it— causing the Lord Chamberlain to refuse to license such a play has prevented the play from being written. Now, if the censorship were abolished, nobody but the author could be held responsible for the play. The Turkish Ambassador does not now protest against the publication of Carlyle's essay on the prophet, or of

the English translations of the Koran in the prefaces to which Mahomet is criticized as an impostor, or of the older books in which he is reviled as Mahound and classed with the devil himself. But if these publications had to be licensed by the Lord Chamberlain it would be impossible for the King to allow the licence to be issued, as he would thereby be made responsible for the opinions expressed. This restriction of the historical drama is an unmixed evil. Great religious leaders are more interesting and more important subjects for the dramatist than great conquerors. It is a misfortune that public opinion would not tolerate a dramatization of Mahomet in Constantinople. But to prohibit it here, where public opinion would tolerate it, is an absurdity which, if applied in all directions, would make it impossible for the Queen to receive a Turkish ambassador without veiling herself, or the Dean and Chapter of St Paul's to display a cross on the summit of their Cathedral in a city occupied largely and influentially by Jews. Court etiquet is no doubt an excellent thing for court ceremonies; but to attempt to impose it on the drama is about as sensible as an attempt to make everybody in London wear court dress.

WHY NOT AN ENLIGHTENED CENSORSHIP?

In the above cases the general question of censorship is separable from the question of the present form of it. Everyone who condemns the principle of censorship must also condemn the Lord Chamberlain's control of the drama; but those who approve of the principle do not necessarily approve of the Lord Chamberlain being the Censor *ex officio*. They may, however, be entirely opposed to popular liberties, and may conclude from what has been said, not that the stage should be made as free as the church, press, or platform, but that these institutions should be censored as strictly as the stage. It will seem obvious to them that nothing is needed to remove all objections to a censorship except the placing of its powers in better hands.

Now though the transfer of the censorship to, say, the Lord Chancellor, or the Primate, or a Cabinet Minister, would be much less humiliating to the persons immediately concerned, the inherent vices of the institution would not be appreciably less disastrous. They would even be aggravated, for reasons which do not appear on the surface, and therefore need to be followed with some attention.

It is often said that the public is the real censor. That this is to some extent true is proved by the fact that plays which are licensed and produced in London have to be expurgated for the provinces. This does not mean that the provinces are more strait-laced, but simply that in many provincial towns there is only one theatre for all classes and all tastes, whereas in London there are separate theatres for separate sections of playgoers: so that, for example, Sir Herbert Beerbohm Tree can conduct His Majesty's Theatre without the slightest regard to the tastes of the frequenters of the Gaiety Theatre; and Mr George Edwardes can conduct the Gaiety Theatre without catering in any way for lovers of Shakespear. Thus the farcical comedy which has scandalized the critics in London by the libertinage of its jests is played to the respectable dress circle of Northampton with these same jests slurred over so as to be imperceptible by even the most prurient spectator. The public, in short, takes care that nobody shall outrage it.

But the public also takes care that nobody shall starve it, or regulate its dramatic diet as a schoolmistress regulates the reading of her pupils. Even when it wishes to be debauched, no censor can—or at least no censor does—stand out against it. If a play is irresistibly amusing, it gets licensed no matter what its moral aspect may be. A brilliant instance is the Divorçons of the late Victorien Sardou, which may not have been the naughtiest play of the 19th century, but was certainly the very naughtiest that any English manager in his senses would have ventured to produce. Nevertheless, being a very amusing play, it passed the licenser with the exception of a reference to impotence as a ground for divorce which no English actress would have ventured on in any case. Within the last few months a very amusing comedy with a strongly polygamous moral was found irresistible by the Lord Chamberlain. Plenty of fun and a happy ending will get anything licensed, because the public will have it so, and the Examiner of Plays, as the holder of the office testified before the Commission of 1892 (Report, page 330), feels with the public, and knows that his office could not survive a widespread unpopularity. In short, the support of the mob—that is, of the unreasoning, unorganized, uninstructed mass of popular sentiment—is indispensable to the censorship as it exists today in England. This is the explanation of the toleration by the Lord Chamberlain of coarse and vicious plays. It is not long since a judge before whom a licensed play came in the course of a lawsuit expressed his scandalized astonishment at the licensing of such a work. Eminent churchmen have made similar protests. In some plays the simulation of criminal assaults on the stage has been carried to a point at which a step further would have involved the interference of the police. Provided the treatment of the theme is gaily or hypocritically popular, and the ending happy, the indulgence of the Lord Chamberlain can be counted on. On the other hand, anything unpleasing and unpopular is rigorously censored. Adultery and prostitution are tolerated and even encouraged to such an extent that plays which do not deal with them are commonly said not to be

P

plays at all. But if any of the unpleasing consequences of adultery and prostitution—for instance, an *unsuccessful* illegal operation (successful ones are tolerated) or venereal disease—are mentioned, the play is prohibited. This principle of shielding the playgoer from unpleasant reflections is carried so far that when a play was submitted for licence in which the relations of a prostitute with all the male characters in the piece was described as "immoral," the Examiner of Plays objected to that passage, though he made no objection to the relations themselves. The Lord Chamberlain dare not, in short, attempt to exclude from the stage the tragedies of murder and lust, or the farces of mendacity, adultery, and dissolute gaiety in which vulgar people delight. But when these same vulgar people are threatened with an unpopular play in which dissoluteness is shewn to be no laughing matter, it is prohibited at once amid the vulgar applause, the net result being that vice is made delightful and virtue banned by the very institution which is supported on the understanding that it produces exactly the opposite result.

THE WEAKNESS OF THE LORD CHAMBERLAIN'S DEPARTMENT

Now comes the question, Why is our censorship, armed as it is with apparently autocratic powers, so scandalously timid in the face of the mob? Why is it not as autocratic in dealing with playwrights below the average as with those above it? The answer is that its position is really a very weak one. It has no direct coercive forces, no funds to institute prosecutions and recover the legal penalties of defying it, no powers of arrest or imprisonment, in short, none of the guarantees of autocracy. What it can do is to refuse to renew the licence of a theatre at which its orders are disobeyed. When it happens that a theatre is about to be demolished, as was the case recently with the Imperial

Theatre after it had passed into the hands of the Wesleyan Methodists, unlicensed plays can be performed, technically in private, but really in full publicity, without risk. The prohibited plays of Brieux and Ibsen have been performed in London in this way with complete impunity. But the impunity is not confined to condemned theatres. Not long ago a West End manager allowed a prohibited play to be performed at his theatre, taking his chance of losing his licence in consequence. The event proved that the manager was justified in regarding the risk as negligible; for the Lord Chamberlain's remedy—the closing of a popular and well-conducted theatre—was far too extreme to be practicable. Unless the play had so outraged public opinion as to make the manager odious and provoke a clamor for his exemplary punishment, the Lord Chamberlain could only have had his revenge at the risk of having his powers abolished as unsupportably tyrannical.

The Lord Chamberlain then has his powers so adjusted that he is tyrannical just where it is important that he should be tolerant, and tolerant just where he could screw up the standard a little by being tyrannical. His plea that there are unmentionable depths to which managers and authors would descend if he did not prevent them is disproved by the plain fact that his indulgence goes as far as the police, and sometimes further than the public, will let it. If our judges had so little power there would be no law in England. If our churches had so much, there would be no theatre, no literature, no science, no art, possibly no England. The institution is at once absurdly despotic and abjectly weak.

AN ENLIGHTENED CENSORSHIP STILL WORSE THAN THE LORD CHAMBERLAIN'S

Clearly a censorship of judges, bishops, or statesmen would not be in this abject condition. It would no doubt make short work of the coarse and vicious pieces which now enjoy the protection of the Lord Chamberlain, or at least of those of them in which the vulgarity and vice are discoverable by merely reading the prompt copy. But it would certainly disappoint the main hope of its advocates: the hope that it would protect and foster the higher drama. It would do nothing of the sort. On the contrary, it would inevitably suppress it more completely than the Lord Chamberlain does, because it would understand it better. The one play of Ibsen's which is prohibited on the English stage, Ghosts, is far less subversive than A Doll's House. But the Lord Chamberlain does not meddle with such far-reaching matters as the tendency of a play. He refuses to license Ghosts exactly as he would refuse to license Hamlet if it were submitted to him as a new play. He would license even Hamlet if certain alterations were made in it. He would disallow the incestuous relationship between the King and Queen. He would probably insist on the substitution of some fictitious country for Denmark in deference to the near relations of our reigning house with that realm. He would certainly make it an absolute condition that the closet scene, in which a son, in an agony of shame and revulsion, reproaches his mother for her relations with his uncle, should be struck out as unbearably horrifying and improper. But compliance with these conditions would satisfy him. He would raise no speculative objections to the tendency of the play.

This indifference to the larger issues of a theatrical performance could not be safely predicated of an enlightened censorship. Such a censorship might be more liberal in its toleration of matters which are only objected to on the ground that they are not usually discussed in general social conversation or in the presence of children; but it would presumably have a far deeper insight to and concern for the real ethical tendency of the play. For instance, had it been in existence during the last quarter of a century, it would have perceived that those plays of Ibsen's which have been licensed without question are fundamentally immoral to an altogether extraordinary degree. Every one of them is a deliberate act of war on society as at present constituted. Religion, marriage, ordinary respectability, are subjected to a destructive exposure and criticism which seems to mere moralists —that is, to persons of no more than average depth of mind—to be diabolical. It is no exaggeration to say that Ibsen gained his overwhelming reputation by undertaking a task of no less magnitude than changing the mind of Europe with the view of changing its morals. Now you cannot license work of that sort without making yourself responsible for it. The Lord Chamberlain accepted the responsibility because he did not understand it or concern himself about it. But what really enlightened and conscientious official dare take such a responsibility? The strength of character and range of vision which made Ibsen capable of it are not to be expected from any official, however eminent. It is true that an enlightened censor might, whilst shrinking even with horror from Ibsen's views, perceive that any nation which suppressed Ibsen would presently find itself falling behind the nations which tolerated him just as Spain fell behind England; but the proper action to take on such a conviction is the abdication of censorship, not the practice of it. As long as a censor is a censor, he cannot endorse by his licence opinions which seem to him dangerously heretical.

We may, therefore, conclude that the more enlightened a censorship is, the worse it would serve us. The Lord Chamberlain, an obviously unenlightened Censor, prohibits Ghosts and licenses all the rest of Ibsen's plays. An enlightened censorship would possibly license Ghosts; but it would certainly suppress many of the other plays. It would suppress subversiveness as well as what is called bad taste. The Lord Chamberlain prohibits one play by Sophocles because, like Hamlet, it mentions the subject of incest; but an enlightened censorship might suppress all the plays of Euripides because Euripides, like Ibsen, was a revolutionary Freethinker. Under the Lord Chamberlain, we can smuggle a good deal of immoral drama and almost as much coarsely vulgar and furtively lascivious drama as we like. Under a college of cardinals, or bishops, or judges, or any other conceivable form of experts in morals, philosophy, religion, or politics, we should get little except stagnant mediocrity.

THE PRACTICAL IMPOSSIBILITIES
OF CENSORSHIP

There is, besides, a crushing material difficulty in the way of an enlightened censorship. It is not too much to say that the work involved would drive a man of any intellectual rank mad. Consider, for example, the Christmas pantomimes. Imagine a judge of the High Court, or an archbishop, or a Cabinet Minister, or an eminent man of letters, earning his living by reading through the mass of trivial doggerel represented by all the pantomimes which are put into rehearsal simultaneously at the end of every year. The proposal to put such mind-destroying drudgery upon an official of the class implied by the demand for an enlightened censorship falls through the moment we realize what it implies in practice.

Another material difficulty is that no play can be judged by merely reading the dialogue. To be fully effective a censor should witness the performance. The *mise-en-scène* of a play is as much a part of it as the words spoken on the stage. No censor could possibly object to such a speech as "Might I speak to you for a moment, miss?" yet that apparently innocent phrase has often been made offensively improper on the stage by popular low comedians, with the effect of changing the whole character and meaning of the play as understood by the official Examiner. In one of the plays of the present season, the dialogue was that of a crude melodrama dealing in the most conventionally correct manner with the fortunes of a good-hearted and virtuous girl. Its morality was that of the Sunday school. But the principal actress, between two speeches which contained no reference to her action, changed her underclothing on the stage! It is true that in this case the actress was so much better than her part that she succeeded in turning what was meant as an impropriety into an inoffensive stroke of realism; yet it is none the less clear that stage business of this character, on which there can be no check except the actual presence of a censor in the theatre, might convert any dialogue, however innocent, into just the sort of entertainment against which the Censor is supposed to protect the public.

It was this practical impossibility that prevented the London County Council from attempting to apply a censorship of the Lord Chamberlain's pattern to the London music halls. A proposal to examine all entertainments before permitting their performance was actually made; and it was abandoned, not in the least as contrary to the liberty of the stage, but because the executive problem of how to do it at once reduced the proposal to absurdity. Even if the Council devoted all its time to witnessing rehearsals of variety performances, and putting each item to the vote, possibly after a prolonged discussion followed by a division, the work would still fall into arrear. No committee could be induced to undertake such a task. The attachment of an inspector of morals to each music hall would have meant an appreciable addition to the rate-payers' burden. In the face of such difficulties the proposal melted away. Had it been pushed through, and the inspectors appointed, each of them would have become a censor, and the whole body of inspectors would have become a *police des mœurs*. Those who know the history of such police forces on the Continent will understand how impossible it would be to procure inspectors whose characters would stand the strain of their opportunities of corruption, both pecuniary and personal, at such salaries as a local authority could be persuaded to offer.

It has been suggested that the present censorship should be supplemented by a board of experts, who should deal, not with the whole mass of plays sent up for licence, but only those which the Examiner of Plays refuses to pass. As the number of plays which the Examiner refuses to pass is never great enough to occupy a Board in permanent session with regular salaries, and as casual employment is not compatible with public responsibility, this proposal would work out in practice as an addition to the duties of some existing functionary. A Secretary of State would be objectionable as likely to be biased politically. An ecclesiastical referee might be biased against the theatre altogether. A judge in chambers would be the proper authority. This plan would combine the inevitable intolerance of an enlightened censorship with the popular laxity of the Lord Chamberlain. The judge would suppress the pioneers, whilst the Examiner of Plays issued two guinea certificates for the vulgar and vicious plays. For this reason the plan would no doubt be popular; but it would be very much as a relaxation of the administration of the Public Health Acts accompanied by the cheapening of gin would be popular.

THE ARBITRATION PROPOSAL

On the occasion of a recent deputation of playwrights to the Prime Minister it was suggested that if a censorship be inevitable, provision should be made for an appeal from the Lord Chamberlain in cases of refusal of licence. The authors of this suggestion propose that the Lord Chamberlain shall choose one umpire and the author another. The two umpires shall then elect a referee, whose decision shall be final.

This proposal is not likely to be entertained by constitutional lawyers. It is a naïve offer to accept the method of arbitration in what is essentially a matter, not between one private individual or body and another, but between a public offender and the State. It will presumably be ruled out as a proposal to refer a case of manslaughter to arbitration would be ruled out. But even if it were constitutionally sound, it bears all the marks of that practical inexperience which leads men to believe that arbitration either costs nothing or is at least cheaper than law. Who is to pay for the time of the three arbitrators, presumably men of high professional standing? The author may not be able: the manager may not be willing: neither of them should be called upon to pay for a public service otherwise than by their contributions to the revenue. Clearly the State should pay. But even so, the difficulties are only beginning. A licence is seldom refused except on grounds which are controversial. The two arbitrators selected by the opposed parties to the controversy are to agree to leave the decision to a third party unanimously chosen by themselves. That is very far from being a simple solution. An attempt to shorten and simplify the passing of the Finance Bill by referring it to an arbitrator chosen unanimously by Mr Asquith and Mr Balfour might not improbably cost more and last longer than a civil war. And why should the chosen referee—if he ever succeeded in getting chosen—be assumed to be a safer authority than the Examiner of Plays? He would certainly be a less responsible one: in fact, being (however eminent) a casual person called in to settle a single case, he would be virtually irresponsible. Worse still, he would take all responsibility away from the Lord Chamberlain, who is at least an official of the King's Household and a nominee of the Government. The Lord Chamberlain, with all his shortcomings, thinks twice before he refuses a licence, knowing that his refusal is final and may promptly be made public. But if he could transfer his responsibility to an arbitrator, he would naturally do so whenever he felt the slightest misgiving, or whenever, for diplomatic reasons, the licence would come more gracefully from an authority unconnected with the court. These considerations, added to the general objection to the principle of censorship, seem sufficient to put the arbitration expedient quite out of the question.

END OF THE FIRST PART OF THE
REJECTED STATEMENT

THE REJECTED STATEMENT—
PART II

THE LICENSING OF THEATRES

THE DISTINCTION BETWEEN LICENSING AND CENSORSHIP

It must not be concluded that the uncompromising abolition of all censorship involves the abandonment of all control and regulation of theatres. Factories are regulated in the public interest; but there is no censorship of factories. For example, many persons are sincerely convinced that cotton clothing is unhealthy; that alcoholic drinks are demoralizing; and that playing-cards are the devil's picture-books. But though the factories

in which cotton, whiskey, and cards are manufactured are stringently regulated under the factory code and the Public Health and Building Acts, the inspectors appointed to carry out these Acts never go to a manufacturer and inform him that unless he manufactures woollens instead of cottons, ginger-beer instead of whiskey, Bibles instead of playing-cards, he will be forbidden to place his products on the market. In the case of premises licensed for the sale of spirits the authorities go a step further. A public-house differs from a factory in the essential particular that whereas disorder in a factory is promptly and voluntarily suppressed, because every moment of its duration involves a measurable pecuniary loss to the proprietor, disorder in a public-house may be a source of profit to the proprietor by its attraction for disorderly customers. Consequently a publican is compelled to obtain a licence to pursue his trade; and this licence lasts only a year, and need not be renewed if his house has been conducted in a disorderly manner in the meantime.

PROSTITUTION AND DRINK IN THEATRES

The theatre presents the same problem as the public-house in respect to disorder. To begin with, a theatre is actually a place licensed for the sale of spirits. The bars at a London theatre can be let without difficulty for £30 a week and upwards. And though it is clear that nobody will pay from a shilling to half a guinea for access to a theatre bar when he can obtain access to an ordinary public-house for nothing, there is no law to prevent the theatre proprietor from issuing free passes broadcast and recouping himself by the profit on the sale of drink. Besides, there may be some other attraction than the sale of drink. When this attraction is that of the play no objection need be made. But it happens that the auditorium of a theatre, with its brilliant lighting and luxurious decorations, makes a very effective shelter and background for the display of fine dresses and pretty faces. Consequently theatres have been used for centuries in England as markets by prostitutes. From the Restoration to the days of Macready all theatres were made use of in this way as a matter of course; and to this, far more than to any prejudice against dramatic art, we owe the Puritan formula that the theatre door is the gate of hell. Macready had a hard struggle to drive the prostitutes from his theatre; and since his time the London theatres controlled by the Lord Chamberlain have become respectable and even socially pretentious. But some of the variety theatres still derive a revenue by selling admissions to women who do not look at the performance, and men who go to purchase or admire the women. And in the provinces this state of things is by no means confined to the variety theatres. The real attraction is sometimes not the performance at all. The theatre is not really a theatre: it is a drink shop and a prostitution market; and the last shred of its disguise is stripped by the virtually indiscriminate issue of free tickets to the men. Access to the stage is also easily obtained; and the plays preferred by the management are those in which the stage is filled with young women who are not in any serious technical sense of the word actresses at all. Considering that all this is now possible at any theatre, and actually occurs at some theatres, the fact that our best theatres are as respectable as they are is much to their credit; but it is still an intolerable evil that respectable managers should have to fight against the free tickets and disorderly housekeeping of unscrupulous competitors. The dramatic author is equally injured. He finds that unless he writes plays which make suitable side-shows for drinking-bars and brothels, he may be excluded from towns where there is not room for two theatres,

and where the one existing theatre is exploiting drunkenness and prostitution instead of carrying on a legitimate dramatic business. Indeed everybody connected with the theatrical profession suffers in reputation from the detestable tradition of such places, against which the censorship has proved quite useless.

Here we have a strong case for applying either the licensing system or whatever better means may be devized for securing the orderly conduct of houses of public entertainment, dramatic or other. Liberty must, no doubt, be respected in so far that no manager should have the right to refuse admission to decently dressed, sober, and well-conducted persons, whether they are prostitutes, soldiers in uniform, gentlemen not in evening dress, Indians, or what not; but when disorder is stopped, disorderly persons will either cease to come or else reform their manners. It is, however, quite arguable that the indiscriminate issue of free admissions, though an apparently innocent and good-natured, and certainly a highly popular proceeding, should expose the proprietor of the theatre to the risk of a refusal to renew his licence.

WHY THE MANAGERS DREAD LOCAL CONTROL

All this points to the transfer of the control of theatres from the Lord Chamberlain to the municipality. And this step is opposed by the long-run managers, partly because they take it for granted that municipal control must involve municipal censorship of plays, so that plays might be licensed in one town and prohibited in the next, and partly because, as they have no desire to produce plays which are in advance of public opinion, and as the Lord Chamberlain in every other respect gives more scandal by his laxity than trouble by his severity, they find in the present system a cheap and easy means of procuring a certificate which relieves them of all social responsibility, and provides them with so strong a weapon of defence in case of a prosecution that it acts in practice as a bar to any such proceedings. Above all, they know that the Examiner of Plays is free from the pressure of that large body of English public opinion already alluded to, which regards the theatre as the Prohibitionist Teetotaller regards the public-house: that is, as an abomination to be stamped out unconditionally. The managers rightly dread this pressure more than anything else; and they believe that it is so strong in local governments as to be a characteristic bias of municipal authority. In this they are no doubt mistaken. There is not a municipal authority of any importance in the country in which a proposal to stamp out the theatre, or even to treat it illiberally, would have a chance of adoption. Municipal control of the variety theatres (formerly called music halls) has been very far from illiberal, except in the one particular in which the Lord Chamberlain is equally illiberal. That particular is the assumption that a draped figure is decent and an undraped one indecent. It is useless to point to actual experience, which proves abundantly that naked or apparently naked figures, whether exhibited as living pictures, animated statuary, or in a dance, are at their best not only innocent, but refining in their effect, whereas those actresses and skirt dancers who have brought the peculiar aphrodisiac effect which is objected to to the highest pitch of efficiency wear twice as many petticoats as an ordinary lady does, and seldom exhibit more than their ankles. Unfortunately, municipal councillors persist in confusing decency with drapery; and both in London and the provinces certain positively edifying performances have been forbidden or withdrawn under pressure, and replaced by coarse and vicious ones. There is not the slightest reason to suppose that the Lord Chamberlain would have been any more tolerant; but this does not alter the fact that the municipal licensing authorities have actually used their powers to set up a censorship which is open to all the objections to censorship in general, and which, in addition, sets up the objection from which central control is free: namely, the impossibility of planning theatrical tours without the serious commercial risk of having the performance forbidden in some of the towns booked. How can this be prevented?

DESIRABLE LIMITATIONS OF LOCAL CONTROL

The problem is not a difficult one. The municipality can be limited just as the monarchy is limited. The Act transferring theatres to local control can be a charter of the liberties of the stage as well as an Act to reform administration. The power to refuse to grant or renew a licence to a theatre need not be an arbitrary one. The municipality may be required to state the ground of refusal; and certain grounds can be expressly declared as unlawful; so that it shall be possible for the manager to resort to the courts for a mandamus to compel the authority to grant a licence. It can be declared unlawful for a licensing authority to demand from the manager any disclosure of the nature of any entertainment he proposes to give, or to prevent its performance, or to refuse to renew his licence on the ground that the tendency of his entertainments is contrary to religion and morals, or that the theatre is an undesirable institution, or that there are already as many theatres as are needed, or that the theatre draws people away from the churches, chapels, mission halls, and the like in its neighborhood. The assumption should be that every citizen has a right to open and conduct a theatre, and therefore has a right to a licence unless he has forfeited that right by allowing his theatre to become a disorderly house, or failing to provide a building which complies with the regulations concerning sanitation and egress in case of fire, or being convicted of an offence against public decency. Also, the licensing powers of the authority should not be delegated to any official or committee; and the manager or lessee of the theatre should have a right to appear in person or by counsel to plead against any motion to refuse to grant or renew his licence. With these safeguards the licensing power could not be stretched to censorship. The manager would enjoy liberty of conscience as far as the local authority is concerned; but on the least attempt on his part to keep a disorderly house under cover of opening a theatre he would risk his licence.

But the managers will not and should not be satisfied with these limits to the municipal power. If they are deprived of the protection of the Lord Chamberlain's licence, and at the same time efficiently protected against every attempt at censorship by the licensing authority, the enemies of the theatre will resort to the ordinary law, and try to get from the prejudices of a jury what they are debarred from getting from the prejudices of a County Council or City Corporation. Moral Reform Societies, "Purity" Societies, Vigilance Societies, exist in England and America for the purpose of enforcing the existing laws against obscenity, blasphemy, Sabbath-breaking, the debauchery of children, prostitution, and so forth. The paid officials of these societies, in their anxiety to produce plenty of evidence of their activity in the annual reports which go out to the subscribers, do not always discriminate between an obscene postcard and an artistic one, or to put it more exactly, between a naked figure and an indecent one. They often combine a narrow but terribly sincere sectarian bigotry with a complete ignorance of art and history. Even when they have some culture, their livelihood is at the mercy of subscribers and committee men who have none. If these officials had any power of distinguishing between art and blackguardism, between morality and virtue, between immorality and vice, between conscientious heresy and mere baseness of mind and foulness of mouth, they might be trusted by theatrical managers not to abuse the powers of the common informer. As it is, it has been found necessary, in order to enable good music to be performed on Sunday, to take away these powers in that particular, and vest them solely in the Attorney-General. This disqualification of the common informer should be extended to the initiation of all proceedings of a censorial character against theatres. Few people are aware of the monstrous laws against blasphemy which still disgrace our statute book. If any serious attempt were made to carry them out, prison accommodation would have to be provided for almost every educated person in the country, beginning with the Archbishop of Canterbury. Until some government with courage and character enough to repeal them comes into power, it is not too much to ask that such infamous powers of oppression should be kept in responsible hands and not left at the disposal of every bigot ignorant enough to be unaware of the social dangers of persecution. Besides, the common informer is not always a sincere bigot who believes he is performing an action of signal merit in silencing and ruining a heretic. He is unfortunately just as often a blackmailer, who has studied his powers as a common informer in order that he may extort money for refraining from exercising them. If the manager is to be responsible he should be made responsible to a responsible functionary. To be responsible to every fanatical ignoramus who chooses to prosecute him for exhibiting a cast of the Hermes of Praxiteles in his vestibule, or giving a performance of Measure for Measure, is mere slavery. It is made bearable at present by the protection of the Lord Chamberlain's certificate. But when that is no longer available, the common informer must be disarmed if the manager is to enjoy security.

SUMMARY

The general case against censorship as a principle, and the particular case against the existing English censorship and against its replacement by a more enlightened one, is now complete. The following is a recapitulation of the propositions and conclusions contended for.

1. The question of censorship or no censorship is a question of high political principle and not of petty policy.

2. The toleration of heresy and shocks to morality on the stage, and even their protection against the prejudices and superstitions which necessarily enter largely into morality and public opinion, are essential to the welfare of the nation.

3. The existing censorship of the Lord Chamberlain does not only intentionally suppress heresy and challenges to morality in their serious and avowed forms, but unintentionally gives the special protection of its official licence to the most extreme impropriety that the lowest section of London playgoers will tolerate in theatres especially devoted to their entertainment, licensing everything that is popular and forbidding any attempt to change public opinion or morals.

4. The Lord Chamberlain's censorship is open to the special objection that its application to political plays is taken to indicate the attitude of the Crown on questions of domestic and foreign policy, and that it imposes the limits of etiquet on the historical drama.

5. A censorship of a more enlightened and independent kind, exercised by the most eminent available authorities, would prove in practice more disastrous than the censorship of the Lord Chamberlain, because the more eminent its members were the less possible would it be for them to accept the responsibility for heresy or immorality by licensing them, and because the many heretical and immoral plays which now pass the Lord Chamberlain because he does not understand them, would be understood and suppressed by a more highly enlightened censorship.

6. A reconstructed and enlightened censorship would be armed with summary and effective powers which would stop the evasions by which heretical and immoral plays are now performed in spite of the Lord Chamberlain; and such powers would constitute a tyranny which would ruin the theatre spiritually by driving all independent thinkers from the drama into the uncensored forms of art.

7. The work of critically examining all stage plays in their written form, and of witnessing their performance in order to see that the sense is not altered by the stage business, would, even if it were divided among so many officials as to be physically possible, be mentally impossible to persons of taste and enlightenment.

8. Regulation of theatres is an entirely different matter from censorship, inasmuch as a theatre, being not only a stage, but a place licensed for the sale of spirits, and a public resort capable of being put to disorderly use, and needing special provision for the safety of audiences in cases of fire, etc., cannot be abandoned wholly to private control, and may therefore reasonably be made subject to an annual licence like those now required before allowing premises to be used publicly for music and dancing.

9. In order to prevent the powers of the licensing authority being abused so as to constitute a virtual censorship, any Act transferring the theatres to the control of a licensing authority should be made also a charter of the rights of dramatic authors and managers by the following provisions:

A. The public prosecutor (the Attorney-General) alone should have the right to set the law in operation against the manager of a theatre or the author of a play in respect of the character of the play or entertainment.

B. No disclosure of the particulars of a theatrical entertainment shall be required before performance.

C. Licences shall not be withheld on the ground that the existence of theatres is dangerous to religion and morals, or on the ground that any entertainment given or contemplated is heretical or immoral.

D. The licensing area shall be no less than that of a County Council or City Corporation, which shall not delegate its licensing powers to any minor local authority or to any official or committee; it shall decide all questions affecting the existence of a theatrical licence by vote of the entire body; managers, lessees, and proprietors of theatres shall have the right to plead, in person or by counsel, against a proposal to withhold a licence; and the licence shall not be withheld except for stated reasons, the validity of which shall be subject to the judgment of the high courts.

E. The annual licence, once granted, shall not be cancelled or suspended unless the manager has been convicted by public prosecution of an offence against the ordinary laws against disorderly housekeeping, indecency, blasphemy, etc., except in cases where some structural or sanitary defect in the building necessitates immediate action for the protection of the public against physical injury.

F. No licence shall be refused on the ground that the proximity of the theatre to a church, mission hall, school, or other place of worship, edification, instruction, or entertainment (including another theatre) would draw the public away from such places into its own doors.

PREFACE RESUMED

MR GEORGE ALEXANDER'S PROTEST

On the facts mentioned in the foregoing statement, and in my evidence before the Joint Select Committee, no controversy arose except on one point. Mr George Alexander protested vigorously and indignantly against my admission that theatres, like public-houses, need special control on the ground that they can profit by disorder, and are sometimes conducted with that end in view. Now, Mr Alexander is a famous actor-manager; and it is very difficult to persuade the public that the more famous an actor-manager is the less he is likely to know about any theatre except his own. When the Committee of 1892 reported, I was considered guilty of a perverse paradox when I said that the witness who knew least about the theatre was Henry Irving. Yet a moment's consideration would have shewn that the paradox was a platitude. For about quarter of a century Irving was confined night after night to his own theatre and his own dressing-room, never seeing a play even there because he was himself part of the play; producing the works of long departed authors; and, to the extent to which his talent was extraordinary, necessarily making his theatre unlike any other theatre. When he went to the provinces or to America, the theatres to which he went were swept and garnished for him, and their staffs replaced—as far as he came in contact with them—by his own lieutenants. In the end, there was hardly a first-nighter in his gallery who did not know more about the London theatres and the progress of dramatic art than he; and as to the provinces, if any chief constable had told him the real history and character of many provincial theatres, he would have denounced that chief constable as an ignorant libeller of a noble profession. But the constable would have been right for all that. Now if this was true of Sir Henry Irving, who did not become a London manager until he had roughed it for years in the provinces, how much more true must it be of, say, Mr George Alexander, whose successful march through his profession has passed as far from the purlieus of our theatrical world as the king's naval career from the Isle of Dogs? The moment we come to that necessary part of the censorship question which deals with the control of theatres from the point of view of those who know how much money can be made out of them by managers who seek to make the auditorium attractive rather than the stage, you find the managers divided into two sections. The first section consists of honorable and successful managers like Mr Alexander, who know nothing of such abuses, and deny, with perfect sincerity and indignant vehemence, that they exist except, perhaps, in certain notorious variety theatres. The other is the silent section which knows better, but is very well content to be publicly defended and privately amused by Mr Alexander's innocence. To accept a West End manager as an expert in theatres because he is an actor is much as if we were to accept the organist of St Paul's Cathedral as an expert on music halls because he is a musician. The real experts are all in the conspiracy to keep the police out of the theatre. And they are so successful that even the police do not know as much as they should.

The police should have been examined by the Committee, and the whole question of the extent to which theatres are disorderly houses in disguise sifted to the bottom. For it is on this point that we discover behind the phantoms of the corrupt dramatists who are restrained by the censorship from debauching the stage, the reality of the corrupt managers and theatre proprietors who actually do debauch it without let or hindrance from the censorship. The whole case for giving control over theatres to local authorities rests on this reality.

ELIZA AND HER BATH

The persistent notion that a theatre is an Alsatia where the king's writ does not run, and where any wickedness is possible in the absence of a special tribunal and a special police, was brought out by an innocent remark made by Sir William Gilbert, who, when giving evidence before the Committee, was asked by Colonel Lockwood whether a law sufficient to restrain impropriety in books would also restrain impropriety in plays. Sir William replied: "I should say there is a very wide distinction between what is read and what is seen. In a novel one may read that 'Eliza stripped off her dressing-gown and stepped into her bath' without any harm; but I think if that were presented on the stage it would be shocking." All the stupid and inconsiderate people seized eagerly on this illustration as if it were a successful attempt to prove that without a censorship we should be unable to prevent actresses from appearing naked on the stage. As a matter of fact, if an actress could be persuaded to do such a thing (and it would be about as easy to persuade a bishop's wife to appear in church in the same condition) the police would simply arrest her on a charge of indecent exposure. The extent to which this obvious safeguard was overlooked may be taken as a measure of the thoughtlessness and frivolity of the excuses made for the censorship. It should be added that the artistic representation of a bath, with every suggestion of nakedness that the law as to decency allows, is one of the most familiar subjects of scenic art. From the Rhine maidens in Wagner's Trilogy, and the bathers in the second act of Les Huguenots, to the ballets of water nymphs in our Christmas pantomimes and at our variety theatres, the sound hygienic propaganda of the bath, and the charm of the undraped human figure, are exploited without offence on the stage to an extent never dreamt of by any novelist.

A KING'S PROCTOR

Another hare was started by Professor Gilbert Murray and Mr Laurence Housman, who, in pure kindness to the managers, asked whether it would not be possible to establish for their assistance a sort of King's Proctor to whom plays might be referred for an official legal opinion as to their compliance with the law before production. There are several objections to this proposal; and they may as well be stated in case the proposal should be revived. In the first place, no lawyer with the most elementary knowledge of the law of libel in its various applications to sedition, obscenity, and blasphemy, could answer for the consequences of producing any play whatsoever as to which the smallest question could arise in the mind of any sane person. I have been a critic and an author in active service for thirty years; and though nothing I have written has ever been prosecuted in England or made the subject of legal proceedings, yet I have never published in my life an article, a play, or a book, as to which, if I had taken legal advice, an expert could have assured me that I was proof against prosecution or against an action for damages by the persons criticized. No doubt a sensible solicitor might have advised me that the risk was no greater than all men have to take in dangerous trades; but such an opinion, though it may encourage a client, does not protect him. For example, if a publisher asks his solicitor whether he may venture on an edition of Sterne's Sentimental Journey, or a manager whether he may produce King Lear without risk of prosecution, the solicitor will advise him to go ahead. But if the solicitor or counsel consulted by him were asked for a guarantee that neither of these works was a libel, he would have to reply that he could give no such guarantee; that, on the contrary, it was his duty to warn his client that both of them are obscene libels; that King Lear, containing as it does perhaps the most appalling blasphemy that despair ever uttered, is a blasphemous libel, and that it is doubtful whether it could not be construed as a seditious libel as well. As to Ibsen's Brand (the play which made him popular with the most earnestly religious people) no sane solicitor would advise his client even to chance it except in a broadly cultivated and tolerant (or indifferent) modern city. The lighter plays would be no better off. What lawyer could accept any responsibility for the production of Sardou's Divorçons or Clyde Fitch's The Woman in the Case? Put the proposed King's Proctor in operation tomorrow; and what will be the result? The managers will find that instead of insuring them as the Lord Chamberlain does, he will warn them that every play they submit to him is vulnerable to the law, and that they must produce it not only on the ordinary risk of acting on their own responsibility, but at the very grave additional risk of doing so in the teeth of an official warning. Under such circumstances, what manager would resort a second time to the Proctor; and how would the Proctor live without fees, unless indeed the Government gave him a salary for doing nothing? The institution would not last a year, except as a job for somebody.

COUNSEL'S OPINION

The proposal is still less plausible when it is considered that at present, without any new legislation at all, any manager who is doubtful about a play can obtain the advice of his solicitor, or Counsel's opinion, if he thinks it will be of any service to him. The verdict of the proposed King's Proctor would be nothing but Counsel's opinion without the liberty of choice of Counsel, possibly cheapened, but sure to be adverse; for an official cannot give practical advice as a friend and a man of the world; he must stick to the letter of the law and take no chances. And as far as the law is concerned, journalism, literature, and the drama exist only by custom or sufferance.

WANTED: A NEW MAGNA CHARTA

This leads us to a very vital question. Is it not possible to amend the law so as to make it possible for a lawyer to advise his client that he may publish the works of Blake, Zola, and Swinburne, or produce the plays of Ibsen and Mr Granville Barker, or print an ordinary criticism in his newspaper, without the possibility of finding himself in prison, or mulcted in damages and costs in consequence? No doubt it is; but only by a declaration of constitutional right to blaspheme, rebel, and deal with tabooed subjects. Such a declaration is not just now within the scope of practical politics, although we are compelled to act to a great extent as if it was actually part of the constitution. All that can be done is to take my advice and limit the necessary public control of the theatres in such a manner as to prevent its being abused as a censorship. We have ready to our hand the machinery of licensing as applied to public-houses. A licensed victualler can now be assured confidently by his lawyer that a magistrate cannot refuse to renew his licence on the ground that he (the magistrate) is a teetotaller and has seen too much of the evil of drink to sanction its sale. The magistrate must give a judicial reason for his refusal, meaning really a constitutional reason; and his teetotalism is not such a reason. In the same way you can protect a theatrical manager by ruling out certain reasons as unconstitutional, as suggested in my statement. Combine this with the abolition of the common informer's power to initiate proceedings; and you will have gone as far as seems possible at present. You will have local control of the theatres for police purposes and sanitary purposes without censorship; and I do not see what more is possible until we get a formal Magna Charta declaring all the categories of libel and the blasphemy laws contrary to public liberty, and repealing and defining accordingly.

PROPOSED: A NEW STAR CHAMBER

Yet we cannot mention Magna Charta without recalling how useless such documents are to a nation which has no more political comprehension nor political virtue than King John. When Henry VII calmly proceeded to tear up Magna Charta by establishing the Star Chamber (a criminal court consisting of a committee of the Privy Council without a jury) nobody objected until, about a century and a half later, the Star Chamber began cutting off the ears of eminent Nonconformist divines and standing them in the pillory; and then the Nonconformists, and nobody else, abolished the Star Chamber. And if anyone doubts that we are quite ready to establish the Star Chamber again, let him read the Report of the Joint Select Committee, on which I now venture to offer a few criticisms.

The report of the Committee, which will be found in the bluebook, should be read with attention and respect as far as page x, up to which point it is an able and well-written statement of the case. From page x onward, when it goes on from diagnosing the disease to prescribing the treatment, it should be read with even greater attention but with no respect whatever, as the main object of the treatment is to conciliate the How Not To Do It majority. It contains, however, one very notable proposal, the same being nothing more nor less than to revive the Star Chamber for the purpose of dealing with heretical or seditious plays and their authors, and indeed with all charges against theatrical entertainments except common police cases of indecency. The reason given is that for which the Star Chamber was created by Henry VII: that is, the inadequacy of the ordinary law. "We consider," says the report, "that the law which prevents or punishes indecency, blasphemy and libel in printed publications [it does not, by the way, except in the crudest police cases] would not be adequate for the control of the drama." Therefor a committee of the Privy Council is to be empowered to suppress plays and punish managers and authors at its pleasure, on the motion of the Attorney-General, without a jury. The members of the Committee will, of course, be men of high standing and character: otherwise they would not be on the Privy Council. That is to say, they will have all the qualifications of Archbishop Laud.

Now I have no guarantee that any member of the majority of the Joint Select Committee ever heard of the Star Chamber or of Archbishop Laud. One of them did not know that politics meant anything more than party electioneering. Nothing is more alarming than the ignorance of our public men of the commonplaces of our history, and their consequent readiness to repeat experiments which have in the past produced national catastrophes. At all events, whether they knew what they were doing or not, there can be no question as to what they did. They proposed virtually that the Act of the Long Parliament in 1641 shall be repealed, and the Star Chamber re-established, in order that playwrights and managers may be punished for unspecified offences unknown to the law. When I say unspecified, I should say specified as follows (see page xi of the report) in the case of a play:—

(a) To be indecent.

(b) To contain offensive personalities.

(c) To represent on the stage in an invidious manner a living person, or any person recently dead.

(d) To do violence to the sentiment of religious reverence.

(e) To be calculated to conduce to vice or crime.

(f) To be calculated to impair friendly relations with any foreign power.

(g) To be calculated to cause a breach of the peace.

Now it is clear that there is no play yet written, or possible to be written, in this world, that might not be condemned under one or other of these heads. How any sane man, not being a professed enemy of public liberty, could put his hand to so monstrous a catalogue passes my understanding. Had a comparatively definite and innocent clause been added forbidding the affirmation or denial of the doctrine of Transubstantiation, the country would have been up in arms at once. Lord Ribblesdale made an effort to reduce the seven categories to the old formula "not to be fitting for the preservation of good manners, decorum, or the public peace"; but this proposal was not carried; whilst on Lord Gorell's motion a final widening of the net was achieved by adding the phrase "to be calculated to"; so that even if a play does not produce any of the results feared, the author can still be punished on the ground that his play is "calculated" to produce them. I have no hesitation in saying that a committee capable of such an outrageous display of thoughtlessness and historical ignorance as this paragraph of its report implies deserves to be haled before the tribunal it has itself proposed, and dealt with under a general clause levelled at conduct "calculated to" overthrow the liberties of England.

POSSIBILITIES OF THE PROPOSAL

Still, though I am certainly not willing to give Lord Gorell the chance of seeing me in the pillory with my ears cut off if I can help it, I daresay many authors would rather take their chance with a Star Chamber than with a jury, just as some soldiers would rather take their chance with a court-martial than at Quarter Sessions. For that matter, some of them would rather take their chance with the Lord Chamberlain than with either. And though this is no reason for depriving the whole body of authors of the benefit of Magna Charta, still, if the right of the proprietor of a play to refuse the good offices of the Privy Council and to perform the play until his accusers had indicted him at law, and obtained the verdict of a jury against him, were sufficiently guarded, the proposed Committee might be set up and used for certain purposes. For instance, it might be made a condition of the intervention of the Attorney-General or the Director of Public Prosecutions that he should refer an accused play to the Committee, and obtain their sanction before taking action, offering the proprietor of the play, if the Committee thought fit, an opportunity of voluntarily accepting trial by the Committee as an alternative to prosecution in the ordinary course of law. But the Committee should have no powers of punishment beyond the power (formidable enough) of suspending performances of the play. If it thought that additional punishment was called for, it could order a prosecution without allowing the pro-

prietor or author of the play the alternative of a trial by itself. The author of the play should be made a party to all proceedings of the Committee, and have the right to defend himself in person or by counsel. This would provide a check on the Attorney-General (who might be as bigoted as any of the municipal aldermen who are so much dreaded by the actor-managers) without enabling the Committee to abuse its powers for party, class, or sectarian ends beyond that irreducible minimum of abuse which a popular jury would endorse, for which minimum there is no remedy.

But when everything is said for the Star Chamber that can be said, and every precaution taken to secure to those whom it pursues the alternative of trial by jury, the expedient still remains a very questionable one, to be endured for the sake of its protective rather than its repressive powers. It should abolish the present quaint toleration of rioting in theatres. For example, if it is to be an offence to perform a play which the proposed new Committee shall condemn, it should also be made an offence to disturb a performance which the Committee has not condemned. "Brawling" at a theatre should be dealt with as severely as brawling in church if the censorship is to be taken out of the hands of the public. At present Jenny Geddes may throw her stool at the head of a playwright who preaches unpalatable doctrine to her, or rather, since her stool is a fixture, she may hiss and hoot and make it impossible to proceed with the performance, even although nobody has compelled her to come to the theatre or suspended her liberty to stay away, and although she has no claim on an unendowed theatre for her spiritual necessities, as she has on her parish church. If mob censorship cannot be trusted to keep naughty playwrights in order, still less can it be trusted to keep the pioneers of thought in countenance;

and I submit that anyone hissing a play permitted by the new censorship should be guilty of contempt of court.

STAR CHAMBER SENTIMENTALITY

But what is most to be dreaded in a Star Chamber is not its sternness but its sentimentality. There is no worse censorship than one which considers only the feelings of the spectators, except perhaps one which considers the feelings of people who do not even witness the performance. Take the case of the Passion Play at Oberammergau. The offence given by a representation of the Crucifixion on the stage is not bounded by frontiers: further, it is an offence of which the voluntary spectators are guilty no less than the actors. If it is to be tolerated at all: if we are not to make war on the German Empire for permitting it, nor punish the English people who go to Bavaria to see it and thereby endow it with English money, we may as well tolerate it in London, where nobody need go to see it except those who are not offended by it. When Wagner's Parsifal becomes available for representation in London, many people will be sincerely horrified when the miracle of the Mass is simulated on the stage of Covent Garden, and the Holy Ghost descends in the form of a dove. But if the Committee of the Privy Council, or the Lord Chamberlain, or anyone else, were to attempt to keep Parsifal from us to spare the feelings of these people, it would not be long before even the most thoughtless champions of the censorship would see that the principle of doing nothing that could shock anybody had reduced itself to absurdity. No quarter whatever should be given to the bigotry of people so unfit for social life as to insist not only that their own prejudices and superstitions should have the fullest toleration but that everybody else should be compelled to think and act as they do. Every service in St Paul's Cathedral is an outrage to the opinions of the congregation of the Roman Catholic Cathedral of Westminster. Every Liberal meeting is a defiance and a challenge to the most cherished opinions of the Unionists. A law to compel the Roman Catholics to attend service at St. Paul's, or the Liberals to attend the meetings of the Primrose League would be resented as an insufferable tyranny. But a law to shut up both St Paul's and the Westminster Cathedral, and to put down political meetings and associations because of the offence given by them to many worthy and excellent people, would be a far worse tyranny, because it would kill the religious and political life of the country outright, whereas to compel people to attend the services and meetings of their opponents would greatly enlarge their minds, and would actually be a good thing if it were enforced all round. I should not object to a law to compel everybody to read two newspapers, each violently opposed to the other in politics; but to forbid us to read newspapers at all would be to maim us mentally and cashier our country in the ranks of civilization. I deny that anybody has the right to demand more from me, over and above lawful conduct in a general sense, than liberty to stay away from the theatre in which my plays are represented. If he is unfortunate enough to have a religion so petty that it can be insulted (any man is as welcome to insult my religion, if he can, as he is to insult the universe) I claim the right to insult it to my heart's content, if I choose, provided I do not compel him to come and hear me. If I think this country ought to make war on any other country, then, so long as war remains lawful, I claim full liberty to write and perform a play inciting the country to that war without interference from the ambassadors of the menaced country. I may "give pain to many worthy people, and pleasure to none," as the Censor's pet phrase puts it: I may even make

Europe a cockpit and Asia a shambles: no matter: if preachers and politicians, statesmen and soldiers, may do these things—if it is right that such things should be done, then I claim my share in the right to do them. If the proposed Committee is meant to prevent me from doing these things whilst men of other professions are permitted to do them, then I protest with all my might against the formation of such a Committee. If it is to protect me, on the contrary, against the attacks that bigots and corrupt pornographers may make on me by appealing to the ignorance and prejudices of common jurors, then I welcome it; but is that really the object of its proposers? And if it is, what guarantee have I that the new tribunal will not presently resolve into a mere committee to avoid unpleasantness and keep the stage "in good taste"? It is no more possible for me to do my work honestly as a playwright without giving pain than it is for a dentist. The nation's morals are like its teeth: the more decayed they are the more it hurts to touch them. Prevent dentists and dramatists from giving pain, and not only will our morals become as carious as our teeth, but toothache and the plagues that follow neglected morality will presently cause more agony than all the dentists and dramatists at their worst have caused since the world began.

ANYTHING FOR A QUIET LIFE

Another doubt: would a Committee of the Privy Council really face the risks that must be taken by all communities as the price of our freedom to evolve? Would it not rather take the popular English view that freedom and virtue generally are sweet and desirable only when they cost nothing? Nothing worth having is to be had without risk. A mother risks her child's life every time she lets it ramble through the countryside, or cross the street, or clamber over the rocks on the shore by itself. A father risks his son's morals when he gives him a latchkey. The members of the Joint Select Committee risked my producing a revolver and shooting them when they admitted me to the room without having me handcuffed. And these risks are no unreal ones. Every day some child is maimed or drowned and some young man infected with disease; and political assassinations have been appallingly frequent of late years. Railway travelling has its risks; motoring has its risks; aeroplaning has its risks; every advance we make costs us a risk of some sort. And though these are only risks to the individual, to the community they are certainties. It is not certain that I will be killed this year in a railway accident; but it is certain that somebody will. The invention of printing and the freedom of the press have brought upon us, not merely risks of their abuse, but the establishment as part of our social routine of some of the worst evils a community can suffer from. People who realize these evils shriek for the suppression of motor cars, the virtual imprisonment and enslavement of the young, the passing of Press Laws (especially in Egypt, India, and Ireland), exactly as they shriek for a censorship of the stage. The freedom of the stage will be abused just as certainly as the complaisance and innocence of the censorship is abused at present. It will also be used by writers like myself for raising very difficult and disturbing questions, social, political, and religious, at moments which may be extremely inconvenient to the government. Is it certain that a Committee of the Privy Council would stand up to all this as the price of liberty? I doubt it. If I am to be at the mercy of a nice amiable Committee of elderly gentlemen (I know all about elderly gentlemen, being one myself) whose motto is the highly popular one, "Anything for a quiet life," and who will make the inevitable abuses of freedom by our blackguards an excuse for interfering with any disquieting use of it by myself, then I shall be worse off than I am with the Lord Chamberlain, whose mind is not broad enough to obstruct the whole range of thought. If it were, he would be given a more difficult post.

SHALL THE EXAMINER OF PLAYS STARVE?

And here I may be reminded that if I prefer the Lord Chamberlain I can go to the Lord Chamberlain, who is to retain all his present functions for the benefit of those who prefer to be judged by him. But I am not so sure that the Lord Chamberlain will be able to exercise those functions for long if resort to him is to be optional. Let me be kinder to him than he has been to me, and uncover for him the pitfalls which the Joint Select Committee have dug (and concealed) in his path. Consider how the voluntary system must inevitably work. The Joint Select Committee expressly urges that the Lord Chamberlain's licence must not be a bar to a prosecution. Granted that in spite of this reservation the licence would prove in future as powerful a defence as it has been in the past, yet the voluntary clause nevertheless places the manager at the mercy of any author who makes it a condition of his contract that his play shall not be submitted for licence. I should probably take that course without opposition from the manager. For the manager, knowing that three of my plays have been refused a licence, and that it would be far safer to produce a play for which no licence had been asked than one for which it had been asked and refused, would agree that it was more prudent, in my case, to avail himself of the power of dispensing with the Lord Chamberlain's licence. But now mark the consequences. The manager, having thus discovered that his best policy was to dispense with the licence in the few doubtful cases, would presently ask himself why he should spend two guineas each on licences for the many plays as to which no question could conceivably arise. What risk does any manager run in producing such works as Sweet Lavender, Peter Pan, The Silver King, or any of the 99 per cent of plays that are equally neutral on controversial questions. Does anyone seriously believe that the managers would continue to pay the Lord Chamberlain two guineas a play out of mere love and loyalty, only to create an additional risk in the case of controversial plays, and to guard against risks that do not exist in the case of the great bulk of other productions? Only those would remain faithful to him who produce such plays as the Select Committee began by discussing *in camera*, and ended by refusing to discuss at all because they were too nasty. These people would still try to get a licence, and would still no doubt succeed as they do today. But could the King's Reader of Plays live on his fees from these plays alone; and if he could how long would his post survive the discredit of licensing only pornographic plays? It is clear to me that the Examiner would be starved out of existence, and the censorship perish of desuetude. Perhaps that is exactly what the Select Committee contemplated. If so, I have nothing more to say, except that I think sudden death would be more merciful.

LORD GORELL'S AWAKENING

In the meantime, conceive the situation which would arise if a licensed play were prosecuted. To make it clearer, let us imagine any other offender—say a company promoter with a fraudulent prospectus—pleading in Court that he had induced the Lord Chamberlain to issue a certificate that the prospectus contained nothing objectionable, and that on the strength of that certificate he issued it; also, that by law the Court could do nothing to him except order him to wind up his company. Some such vision as this must have come to Lord Gorell when he at last grappled seriously with the problem. Mr Harcourt seized the opportunity to make a last rally. He seconded Lord Gorell's proposal that the Committee should admit that its scheme of an optional censorship was an elaborate absurdity, and report that all censorship before production was out of the question. But it was too late: the *volte face* was too sudden and complete. It was Lord Gorell whose vote had turned the close division which took place on the question of receiving my statement. It was Lord Gorell without whose countenance and authority the farce of the books could never have been performed. Yet here was Lord Gorell, after assenting to all the provisions for the optional censorship paragraph by paragraph, suddenly informing his colleagues that they had been wrong all through and that I had been right all through, and inviting them to scrap half their work and adopt my conclusion. No wonder Lord Gorell got only one vote: that of Mr Harcourt. But the incident is not the less significant. Lord Gorell carried more weight than any other member of the Committee on the legal and constitutional aspect of the question. Had he begun where he left off—had he at the outset put down his foot on the notion that an optional penal law could ever be anything but a gross contradiction in terms, that part of the Committee's proposals would never have come into existence.

JUDGES: THEIR PROFESSIONAL LIMITATIONS

I do not, however, appeal to Lord Gorell's judgment on all points. It is inevitable that a judge should be deeply impressed by his professional experience with a sense of the impotence of judges and laws and courts to deal satisfactorily with evils which are so Protean and elusive as to defy definition, and which yet seem to present quite simple problems to the common sense of men of the world. You have only to imagine the Privy Council as consisting of men of the world highly endowed with common sense, to persuade yourself that the supplementing of the law by the common sense of the Privy Council would settle the whole difficulty. But no man knows what he means by common sense, though every man can tell you that it is very uncommon, even in Privy Councils. And since every ploughman is a man of the world, it is evident that even the phrase itself does not mean what it says. As a matter of fact, it means in ordinary use simply a man who will not make himself disagreeable for the sake of a principle: just the sort of man who should never be allowed to meddle with political rights. Now to a judge a political right, that is, a dogma which is above our laws and conditions our laws, instead of being subject to them, is anarchic and abhorrent. That is why I trust Lord Gorell when he is defending the integrity of the law against the proposal to make it in any sense optional, whilst I very strongly mistrust him, as I mistrust all professional judges, when political rights are in danger.

CONCLUSION

I must conclude by recommending the Government to take my advice wherever it conflicts with that of the Joint Select Committee. It is, I think, obviously more deeply considered and better informed, though I say it that should not. At all events, I have given my reasons; and at that I must leave it. As the tradition which makes Malvolio not only Master of the Revels but Master of the Mind of England, and which has come down to us from Henry VIII, is manifestly doomed to the dustbin, the sooner it goes there the better; for the democratic control which naturally succeeds it can easily be limited so as to prevent it becoming either a censorship or a tyranny. The Examiner of Plays should receive a generous pension, and be set free to practise privately as an expert adviser of theatrical managers. There is no reason why they should be deprived of the counsel they so highly value.

It only remains to say that public performances of The Shewing-up of Blanco Posnet are still prohibited in Great Britain by the Lord Chamberlain. An attempt was made to prevent even its performance in Ireland by some indiscreet Castle officials in the absence of the Lord Lieutenant. This attempt gave extraordinary publicity to the production of the play; and every possible effort was made to persuade the Irish public that the performance would be an outrage to their religion, and to provoke a repetition of the rioting that attended the first performances of Synge's Playboy of the Western World before the most sensitive and, on provocation, the most turbulent audience in the kingdom. The directors of the Irish National Theatre, Lady Gregory and Mr William Butler Yeats, rose to the occasion with inspiriting courage. I am a conciliatory person, and was willing, as I always am, to make every concession in return for having my own way. But Lady Gregory and Mr Yeats not only would not yield an inch, but insisted, within the due limits of gallant warfare, on taking the field with every circumstance of defiance, and winning the battle with every trophy of victory. Their triumph was as complete as they could have desired. The performance exhausted the possibilities of success, and provoked no murmur, though it inspired several approving sermons. Later on, Lady Gregory and Mr Yeats brought the play to London and performed it under the Lord Chamberlain's nose, through the instrumentality of the Stage Society. After this, the play was again sub-mitted to the Lord Chamberlain. But, though beaten, he, too, understands the art of How Not To Do It. He licensed the play, but endorsed on his licence the condition that all the passages which implicated God in the history of Blanco Posnet must be omitted in representation. All the coarseness, the profligacy, the prostitution, the violence, the drinking-bar humor into which the light shines in the play are licensed, but the light itself is extinguished. I need hardly say that I have not availed myself of this licence, and do not intend to. There is enough licensed darkness in our theatres today without my adding to it.

AYOT ST LAWRENCE,
 14th July 1910.

POSTSCRIPT.—Since the above was written the Lord Chamberlain has made an attempt to evade his responsibility and perhaps to postpone his doom by appointing an advisory committee, unknown to the law, on which he will presumably throw any odium that may attach to refusals of licences in the future. This strange and lawless body will hardly reassure our moralists, who object much more to the plays he licenses than to those he suppresses, and are therefore unmoved by his plea that his refusals are few and far between. It consists of two eminent actors (one retired), an Oxford professor of literature, and two eminent barristers. As their assembly is neither created by statute nor sanctioned by custom, it is difficult to know what to call it until it advises the Lord Chamberlain to deprive some author of his means of livelihood, when it will, I presume, become a conspiracy, and be indictable accordingly; unless, indeed, it can persuade the Courts to recognize it as a new Estate of the Realm, created by the Lord Chamberlain. This constitutional position is so questionable that I strongly advise the members to resign promptly before the Lord Chamberlain gets them into trouble.

POSTSCRIPT 1933.—The censorship of plays remains unaltered, though of late years it has been much more liberally and intelligently exercised. None of my plays is now on the index.

But an unofficial censorship of films has been set up to safeguard their unprecedented licence in pornographic art. As an example of its operation I may cite the case of a lady who, when doing charitable work among the outcasts on the Thames Embankment, was appalled by the extent to which men were lured to London by visions of unlimited employment there, and girls coming on the same errand found themselves helpless in the hands of White Slave traffickers because they did not know of the existence of the bodies which exist for the protection of unescorted young women travellers. She accordingly at great expense had a film made to warn the men, and not only to make known to young women the existence of the protective and rescue agencies but to make their addresses known by exhibition on the screen.

This film was immediately banned as immoral by the unofficial trade censorship. The lady, bewildered by this attack on her personal character, appealed to me. I saw the film at a private exhibition, and satisfied myself that it was useful and quite irreproachable. In the same week I visited two leading picture houses in London. In one of them the dressing quarters of a company of ballet dancers were shewn; and the attraction of this scene, which did not further the story, and was introduced solely for its own sake, consisted in the row of dancers suddenly and simultaneously turning their backs to the audience, bending down, and changing their underclothing. The other film shewed a French seaport brothel in which two sailors began by watching an undressing woman through a skylight, and then entered the brothel and did everything that could be done without incurring a police prosecution.

Without mentioning these films, and in the friendliest fashion, I begged the Censor to have a look at the lady's film, as I thought its prohibition must have been a mistake. My attempt at being conciliatory was thrown away: I was informed in the stiffest and loftiest manner that the prohibition was quite deliberate and fully justified. It was then stated in the Press without contradiction that the film was banned as an incitement to vice, at which breath-bereaving lie I had to drop the matter and assure the unfortunate benefactress that she had no remedy. The effect of the censorship was to leave pornography triumphant and to suppress the address of the Rescue Society. I cannot believe that this result was intended by the gentleman who took so high a tone with me; but, if not, the incident proves my contention that even the best intentioned and most highminded censors are often more disastrous than the Laodicean or corrupt ones.

As to my licensing proposal, I have never succeeded in making any of my critics understand it or any statesman notice it. Theatre critics assume that every member of a local authority is a Holy Willy fanatically biased against the theatre, and that I propose to set up a censorship of such persons, each reading all the plays and having a veto on its performances. Meanwhile, thanks to their hysterical ignorance, the drama remains at the mercy not only of the Lord Chamberlain, but of that most dangerous of Holy Willies, the common informer.

XVII

JOHN BULL'S OTHER ISLAND

1904

PREFACE FOR POLITICIANS
(TO THE FIRST EDITION IN 1906)

John Bull's Other Island was written in 1904 at the request of Mr William Butler Yeats, as a patriotic contribution to the repertory of the Irish Literary Theatre. Like most people who have asked me to write plays, Mr Yeats got rather more than he bargained for. The play was at that time beyond the resources of the new Abbey Theatre, which the Irish enterprise owed to the public spirit of Miss A. E. F. Horniman (an Englishwoman, of course), who, twelve years ago, played an important part in the history of the modern English stage as well as in my own personal destiny by providing the necessary capital for that memorable season at the Avenue Theatre which forced my Arms and The Man and Mr Yeats's Land of Heart's Desire on the recalcitrant London playgoer, and gave a third Irish playwright, Dr John Todhunter, an opportunity which the commercial theatres could not have afforded him.

There was another reason for changing the destination of John Bull's Other Island. It was uncongenial to the whole spirit of the neo-Gaelic movement, which is bent on creating a new Ireland after its own ideal, whereas my play is a very uncompromising presentment of the real old Ireland. The next thing that happened was the production of the play in London at the Court Theatre by Messrs Vedrenne and Barker, and its immediate and enormous popularity with delighted and flattered English audiences. This constituted it a successful commercial play, and made it unnecessary to resort to the special machinery or tax the special resources of the Irish Literary Theatre for its production.

HOW TOM BROADBENT TOOK IT

Now I have a good deal more to say about the relations between the Irish and the English than will be found in my play. Writing the play for an Irish audience, I thought it would be good for them to be shewn very clearly that the loudest laugh they could raise at the expense of the absurdest Englishman was not really a laugh on their side; that he would succeed where they would fail; that he could inspire strong affection and loyalty in an Irishman who knew the world and was moved only to dislike, mistrust, impatience and even exasperation by his own countrymen; that his power of taking himself seriously, and his insensibility to anything funny in danger and destruction, was the first condition of economy and concentration of force, sustained purpose, and rational conduct. But the need for this lesson in Ireland is the measure of its demoralizing superfluousness in England. English audiences very naturally swallowed it eagerly and smacked their lips over it, laughing all the more heartily because they felt that they were taking a caricature of themselves with the most tolerant and large-minded goodhumor. They were perfectly willing to allow me to represent Tom Broadbent as infatuated in politics, hypnotized by his newspaper leader-writers and parliamentary orators into an utter paralysis of his common sense, without moral delicacy or social tact, provided I made him cheerful, robust, goodnatured, free from envy, and above all, a successful muddler-through in business and love. Not only did no English critic allow that the success in business of Messrs English Broadbent and Irish Doyle might possibly have been due to some extent to Doyle, but one writer actually dwelt with much feeling on the pathos of Doyle's failure as an engineer (a circumstance not mentioned nor suggested in my play) in contrast with Broadbent's solid success. No doubt, when the play is performed in Ireland, the Dublin critics will regard it as self-evident that without Doyle Broadbent would have become bankrupt in six months. I should say, myself, that the combination was probably much more effective than either of the partners would have been alone. I am persuaded further—without pretending to know more about it than anyone else—that Broadbent's special contribution was simply the strength, self-satisfaction, social confidence and cheerful bumptiousness that money, comfort, and good feeding bring to all healthy people; and that Doyle's special contribution was the freedom from illusion, the power of facing facts, the nervous industry, the sharpened wits, the sensitive pride of the imaginative man who has fought his way up through social persecution and poverty. I do not say that the confidence of the Englishman in Broadbent is not for the moment justified. The virtues of the English soil are not less real because they consist of coal and iron, not of metaphysical sources of character. The virtues of Broadbent are not less real because they are the virtues of the money that coal and iron have produced. But as the mineral virtues are being discovered and developed in other soils, their derivative virtues are appearing so rapidly in other nations that Broadbent's relative advantage is vanishing. In truth I am afraid (the misgiving is natural to a by-this-time slightly elderly playwright) that Broadbent is out of date. The successful Englishman of today, when he is not a transplanted Scotchman or Irishman, often turns out on investigation to be, if not an American, an Italian, or a Jew, at least to be depending on the brains, the nervous energy, and the freedom from romantic illusions (often called cynicism) of such foreigners for the management of his sources of income. At all events I am persuaded that a modern nation that is satisfied with Broadbent is in a dream. Much as I like him, I object to be governed by him, or entangled in his political destiny. I therefore propose to give him a piece of my mind here, as an Irishman, full of an instinctive pity for those of my fellow-creatures who are only English.

WHAT IS AN IRISHMAN?

When I say that I am an Irishman I mean that I was born in Ireland, and that my native language is the English of Swift and not the unspeakable jargon of the mid-XIX century London newspapers. My extraction is the extraction of most Englishmen: that is, I have no trace in me of the commercially imported North Spanish strain which passes for aboriginal Irish: I am a genuine typical Irishman of the Danish, Norman, Cromwellian, and (of course) Scotch invasions. I am violently and arrogantly Protestant by family tradition; but let no English Government therefore count on my allegiance: I am English enough to be an inveterate Republican and Home Ruler. It is true that one of my grandfathers was an Orangeman; but then his sister was an abbess; and his uncle, I am proud to say, was hanged as a rebel. When I look round me on the hybrid cosmopolitans, slum poisoned or square pampered, who call themselves Englishmen today, and see them bullied by the Irish Protestant garrison as no Bengalee now lets himself be bullied by an Englishman; when I see the Irishman everywhere standing clearheaded, sane, hardily callous to the boyish sentimentalities, susceptibilities, and credulities that make the Englishman the dupe of every charlatan and the idolater of every numskull, I perceive that Ireland is the only spot on earth which still produces the ideal Englishman of history. Blackguard, bully, drunkard, liar, foulmouth, flatterer, beggar, backbiter, venal functionary, corrupt judge, envious friend, vindictive opponent, unparalleled political traitor: all these your Irishman may easily be, just as he may be a gentleman (a species extinct in England, and nobody a penny the worse); but he is never quite the hysterical, nonsense-crammed, fact-proof, truth-terrified, unballasted sport of all the bogey panics and all the silly enthusiasms that now calls itself "God's Englishman." England cannot do without its Irish and its Scots today, because it cannot do without at least a little sanity.

THE PROTESTANT GARRISON

The more Protestant an Irishman is— the more English he is, if it flatters you to have it put that way, the more intolerable he finds it to be ruled by English instead of Irish folly. A "loyal" Irishman is an abhorrent phenomenon, because it is an unnatural one. No doubt English rule is vigorously exploited in the interests of the property, power, and promotion of the Irish classes as against the Irish masses. Our delicacy is part of a keen sense of reality which makes us a very practical, and even, on occasion, a very coarse people. The Irish soldier takes the King's shilling and drinks the King's health; and the Irish squire takes the title deeds of the English settlement and rises uncovered to the strains of the English national anthem. But do not mistake this cupboard loyalty for anything deeper. It gains a broad base from the normal attachment of every reasonable man to the established government as long as it is bearable; for we all, after a certain age, prefer peace to revolution and order to chaos, other things being equal. Such considerations produce loyal Irishmen as they produce loyal Poles and Fins, loyal Hindoos, loyal Filipinos, and faithful slaves. But there is nothing more in it than that. If there is an entire lack of gall in the feeling of the Irish gentry towards the English, it is because the Englishman is always gaping admiringly at the Irishman as at some clever child prodigy. He overrates him with a generosity born of a traditional conviction of his own superiority in the deeper aspects of human character. As the Irish gentleman, tracing his pedigree to the conquest or one of the invasions, is equally convinced that if this superiority really exists, he is the genuine true blue heir to it, and as he is easily able to hold his own in all the superficial social accomplishments, he finds English society agreeable, and English houses very comfortable, Irish establishments being generally straitened by an attempt to keep a park and a stable on an income which would not justify an Englishman in venturing upon a wholly detached villa.

OUR TEMPERAMENTS CONTRASTED

But however pleasant the relations between the Protestant garrison and the English gentry may be, they are always essentially of the nature of an *entente cordiale* between foreigners. Personally I like Englishmen much better than Irishmen (no doubt because they make more of me) just as many Englishmen like Frenchmen better than Englishmen, and never go on board a Peninsular and Oriental steamer when one of the ships of the Messageries Maritimes is available. But I never think of an Englishman as my countryman. I should as soon think of applying that term to a German. And the Englishman has the same feeling. When a Frenchman fails to make the distinction, we both feel a certain disparagement involved in the misapprehension. Macaulay, seeing that the Irish had in Swift an author worth stealing, tried to annex him by contending that he must be classed as an Englishman because he was not an aboriginal Celt. He might as well have refused the name of Briton to Addison because he did not stain himself blue and attach scythes to the poles of his sedan chair. In spite of all such trifling with facts, the actual distinction between the idolatrous Englishman and the fact-facing Irishman, of the same extraction though they be, remains to explode those two hollowest of fictions, the Irish and English "races." There is no Irish race any more than there is an English race or a Yankee race. There *is* an Irish climate, which will stamp an immigrant more deeply and durably in two years, apparently, than the English climate will in two hundred. It is reinforced by an artificial economic climate which does some of the work attributed to the natural geographic one; but the geographic climate is eternal and irresistible, making a mankind and a womankind that Kent, Middlesex, and East Anglia cannot produce and do not want to imitate.

How can I sketch the broad lines of the contrast as they strike me? Roughly I should say that the Englishman is wholly at the mercy of his imagination, having no sense of reality to check it. The Irishman, with a far subtler and more fastidious imagination, has one eye always on things as they are. If you compare Moore's visionary Minstrel Boy with Mr Rudyard Kipling's quasi-realistic Soldiers Three, you may yawn over Moore or gush over him, but you will not suspect him of having had any illusions about the contemporary British private; whilst as to Mr Kipling, you will see that he has not, and unless he settles in Ireland for a few years will always remain constitutionally and congenitally incapable of having, the faintest inkling of the reality which he idolizes as Tommy Atkins. Perhaps you have never thought of illus-

trating the contrast between English and Irish by Moore and Mr Kipling, or even by Parnell and Gladstone. Sir Boyle Roche and Shakespear may seem more to your point. Let me find you a more dramatic instance. Think of the famous meeting between the Duke of Wellington, that intensely Irish Irishman, and Nelson, that intensely English Englishman. Wellington's contemptuous disgust at Nelson's theatricality as a professed hero, patriot, and rhapsode, a theatricality which in an Irishman would have been an insufferably vulgar affectation, was quite natural and inevitable. Wellington's formula for that kind of thing was a well-known Irish one: "Sir: dont be a damned fool." It is the formula of all Irishmen for all Englishmen to this day. It is the formula of Larry Doyle for Tom Broadbent in my play, in spite of Doyle's affection for Tom. Nelson's genius, instead of producing intellectual keenness and scrupulousness, produced mere delirium. He was drunk with glory, exalted by his fervent faith in the sound British patriotism of the Almighty, nerved by the vulgarest anti-foreign prejudice, and apparently unchastened by any reflections on the fact that he had never had to fight a technically capable and properly equipped enemy except on land, where he had never been successful. Compare Wellington, who had to fight Napoleon's armies, Napoleon's marshals, and finally Napoleon himself, without one moment of illusion as to the human material he had to command, without one gush of the "Kiss me, Hardy" emotion which enabled Nelson to idolize his crews and his staff, without forgetting even in his dreams that the normal British officer of that time was an incapable amateur (as he still is) and the normal British soldier a never-do-well (he is now a depressed and respectable young man). No wonder Wellington became an accomplished comedian in the art of anti-climax, scandalizing the unfortunate Croker, responding to the demand for glorious sentiments by the most disenchanting touches of realism, and, generally, pricking the English windbag at its most explosive crises of distention. Nelson, intensely nervous and theatrical, made an enormous fuss about victories so cheap that he would have deserved shooting if he had lost them, and, not content with lavishing splendid fighting on helpless adversaries like the heroic De Brueys or Villeneuve (who had not even the illusion of heroism when he went like a lamb to the slaughter), got himself killed by his passion for exposing himself to death in that sublime defiance of it which was perhaps the supreme tribute of the exquisite coward to the King of Terrors (for, believe me, you cannot be a hero without being a coward: supersense cuts both ways), the result being a tremendous effect on the gallery. Wellington, most capable of captains, was neither a hero nor a patriot: perhaps not even a coward; and had it not been for the Nelsonic anecdotes invented for him—"Up guards, and at em" and so forth—and the fact that the antagonist with whom he finally closed was such a master of theatrical effect that Wellington could not fight him without getting into his limelight, nor overthrow him (most unfortunately for us all) without drawing the eyes of the whole world to the catastrophe, the Iron Duke would have been almost forgotten by this time. Now that contrast is English against Irish all over, and is the more delicious because the real Irishman in it is the Englishman of tradition, whilst the real Englishman is the traditional theatrical foreigner.

The value of the illustration lies in the fact that Nelson and Wellington were both in the highest degree efficient, and both in the highest degree incompatible with one another on any other footing than one of independence. The govern-ment of Nelson by Wellington or of Wellington by Nelson is felt at once to be a dishonorable outrage to the governed and a finally impossible task for the governor.

I daresay some Englishman will now try to steal Wellington as Macaulay tried to steal Swift. And he may plead with some truth that though it seems impossible that any other country than England could produce a hero so utterly devoid of common sense, intellectual delicacy, and international chivalry as Nelson, it may be contended that Wellington was rather an eighteenth century aristocratic type, than a specifically Irish type. George IV and Byron, contrasted with Gladstone, seem Irish in respect of a certain humorous blackguardism, and a power of appreciating art and sentiment without being duped by them into mistaking romantic figments for realities. But faithlessness and the need for carrying off the worthlessness and impotence that accompany it, produce in all nations a gay, sceptical, amusing, blaspheming, witty fashion which suits the flexibility of the Irish mind very well; and the contrast between this fashion and the energetic infatuations that have enabled intellectually ridiculous men, without wit or humor, to go on crusades and make successful revolutions, must not be confused with the contrast between the English and Irish idiosyncrasies. The Irishman makes a distinction which the Englishman is too lazy intellectually (the intellectual laziness and slovenliness of the English is almost beyond belief) to make. The Englishman, impressed with the dissoluteness of the faithless wits of the Restoration and the Regency, and with the victories of the wilful zealots of the patriotic, religious, and revolutionary wars, jumps to the conclusion that wilfulness is the main thing. In this he is right. But he overdoes his jump so far as to conclude also that stupidity and wrongheadedness are better guarantees of efficiency and trustworthiness than intellectual vivacity, which he mistrusts as a common symptom of worthlessness, vice, and instability. Now in this he is most dangerously wrong. Whether the Irishman grasps the truth as firmly as the Englishman may be open to question; but he is certainly comparatively free from the error. That affectionate and admiring love of sentimental stupidity for its own sake, both in men and women, which shines so steadily through the novels of Thackeray would hardly be possible in the works of an Irish novelist. Even Dickens, though too vital a genius and too severely educated in the school of shabby-genteel poverty to have any doubt of the national danger of fatheadedness in high places, evidently assumes rather too hastily the superiority of Mr Meagles to Sir John Chester and Harold Skimpole. On the other hand, it takes an Irishman years of residence in England to learn to respect and like a blockhead. An Englishman will not respect nor like anyone else. Every English statesman has to maintain his popularity by pretending to be ruder, more ignorant, more sentimental, more superstitious, more stupid than any man who has lived behind the scenes of public life for ten minutes can possibly be. Nobody dares to publish really intimate memoirs of him or really private letters of his until his whole generation has passed away, and his party can no longer be compromised by the discovery that the platitudinizing twaddler and hypocritical opportunist was really a man of some perception as well as of strong constitution, peg-away industry, personal ambition, and party keenness.

ENGLISH STUPIDITY EXCUSED

I do not claim it as a natural superiority in the Irish nation that it dislikes and mistrusts fools, and expects its political leaders to be clever and humbug-proof.

It may be that if our resources included the armed force and virtually unlimited money which push the political and military figureheads of England through bungled enterprises to a muddled success, and create an illusion of some miraculous and divine innate English quality that enables a general to become a conqueror with abilities that would not suffice to save a cabman from having his licence marked, and a member of parliament to become Prime Minister with the outlook on life of a sporting country solicitor educated by a private governess, we should lapse into gross intellectual sottishness, and prefer leaders who encouraged our vulgarities by sharing them, and flattered us by associating them with purchased successes, to our betters. But as it is, we cannot afford that sort of encouragement and flattery in Ireland. The odds against which our leaders have to fight would be too heavy for the fourth-rate Englishmen whose leadership consists for the most part in marking time ostentatiously until they are violently shoved, and then stumbling blindly forward (or backward) wherever the shove sends them. We cannot crush England as a Pickford's van might crush a perambulator. We are the perambulator and England the Pickford. We must study her and our real weaknesses and real strength; we must practise upon her slow conscience and her quick terrors; we must deal in ideas and political principles since we cannot deal in bayonets; we must outwit, outwork, outstay her; we must embarrass, bully, even conspire and assassinate when nothing else will move her, if we are not all to be driven deeper and deeper into the shame and misery of our servitude. Our leaders must be not only determined enough, but clever enough to do this. We have no illusions as to the existence of any mysterious Irish pluck, Irish honesty, Irish bias on the part of Providence, or sterling Irish solidity of character, that will enable an Irish block-head to hold his own against England. Blockheads are of no use to us: we were compelled to follow a supercilious, un-popular, tongue-tied, aristocratic Pro-testant Parnell, although there was no lack among us of fluent imbeciles, with majestic presences and oceans of dignity and sentiment, to promote into his place could they have done his work for us. It is obviously convenient that Mr Red-mond should be a better speaker and rhetorician than Parnell; but if he began to use his powers to make himself agree-able instead of making himself reckoned with by the enemy; if he set to work to manufacture and support English shams and hypocrisies instead of exposing and denouncing them; if he constituted him-self the permanent apologist of doing nothing, and, when the people insisted on his doing something, only roused himself to discover how to pretend to do it without really changing anything, he would lose his leadership as certainly as an English politician would, by the same course, attain a permanent place on the front bench. In short, our circumstances place a premium on political ability whilst the circumstances of England discount it; and the quality of the supply naturally follows the demand. If you miss in my writings that hero-worship of dotards and duffers which is planting England with statues of disastrous statesmen and absurd generals, the explanation is simply that I am an Irishman and you an Englishman.

IRISH PROTESTANTISM REALLY PROTESTANT

When I repeat that I am an Irish Pro-testant, I come to a part of the relation between England and Ireland that you will never understand unless I insist on explaining it to you with that Irish insist-ence on intellectual clarity to which my English critics are so intensely recal-citrant.

First, let me tell you that in Ireland Protestantism is really Protestant. It is true that there is an Irish Protestant Church (disestablished some 35 years ago) in spite of the fact that a Protestant Church is, fundamentally, a contradic-tion in terms. But this means only that the Protestants use the word Church to denote their secular organization, with-out troubling themselves about the meta-physical sense of Christ's famous pun, "Upon this rock I will build my church." The Church of England, which is a re-formed Anglican Catholic Anti-Protest-ant Church, is quite another affair. An Anglican is acutely conscious that he is not a Wesleyan; and many Anglican clergymen do not hesitate to teach that all Methodists incur damnation. In Ire-land all that the member of the Irish Protestant Church knows is that he is not a Roman Catholic. The decorations of even the "lowest" English Church seem to him to be extravagantly Ritualistic and Popish. I myself entered the Irish Church by baptism, a ceremony performed by my uncle in "his own church." But I was sent, with many boys of my own de-nomination, to a Wesleyan school where the Wesleyan catechism was taught with-out the least protest on the part of the parents, although there was so little pre-sumption in favor of any boy there being a Wesleyan that if all the Church boys had been withdrawn at any moment, the school would have become bankrupt. And this was by no means analogous to the case of those working class members of the Church of England in London, who send their daughters to Roman Catholic schools rather than to the public elementary schools. They do so for the definite reason that the nuns teach girls good manners and sweetness of speech, which have no place in the County Coun-cil curriculum. But in Ireland the Church parent sends his son to a Wesleyan school (if it is convenient and socially eligible) because he is indifferent to the form of Protestantism, provided it is Protestantism. There is also in Ireland a characteristically Protestant refusal to take ceremonies and even sacraments very seriously except by way of strenuous objection to them when they are conducted with candles or incense. For example, I was never confirmed, although the ceremony was specially needed in my case as the failure of my appointed godfather to appear at my baptism had led to his responsibilities being assumed on the spot, at my uncle's order, by the sexton. And my case was a very common one, even among people quite untouched by modern scepticisms. Apart from the weekly churchgoing, which holds its own as a respectable habit, the initiations are perfunctory, the omissions regarded as negligible. The distinction between churchman and dissenter, which in England is a class distinction, a political distinction, and even occasionally a religious distinction, does not exist. Nobody is surprised in Ireland to find that the squire who is the local pillar of the formerly established Church is also a Plymouth Brother, and, except on certain special or fashionable occasions, attends the Methodist meeting-house. The parson has no priestly character and no priestly influence: the High Church curate of course exists and has his vogue among religious epicures of the other sex; but the general attitude of his congregation towards him is that of Dr Clifford. The clause in the Apostles' Creed professing belief in a Catholic Church is a standing puzzle to Protestant children; and when they grow up they dismiss it from their minds more often than they solve it, because they really are not Catholics but Protestants to the extremest practicable degree of individualism. It is true that they talk of church and chapel with all the Anglican contempt for chapel; but in Ireland the chapel means the Roman Catholic church,

for which the Irish Protestant reserves all the class rancor, the political hostility, the religious bigotry, and the bad blood generally that in England separates the Establishment from the non-conforming Protestant organizations. When a vulgar Irish Protestant speaks of a "Papist" he feels exactly as a vulgar Anglican vicar does when he speaks of a Dissenter. And when the vicar is Anglican enough to call himself a Catholic priest, wear a cassock, and bless his flock with two fingers, he becomes horrifically incomprehensible to the Irish Protestant Churchman, who, on his part, puzzles the Anglican by regarding a Methodist as tolerantly as an Irishman who likes grog regards an Irishman who prefers punch.

A FUNDAMENTAL ANOMALY

Now nothing can be more anomalous, and at bottom impossible, than a Conservative Protestant party standing for the established order against a revolutionary Catholic party. The Protestant is theoretically an anarchist as far as anarchism is practicable in human society: that is, he is an individualist, a free-thinker, a self-helper, a Whig, a Liberal, a mistruster and vilifier of the State, a rebel. The Catholic is theoretically a Collectivist, a self-abnegator, a Tory, a Conservative, a supporter of Church and State one and undivisible, an obeyer. This would be a statement of fact as well as of theory if men were Protestants and Catholics by temperament and adult choice instead of by family tradition. The peasant who supposed that Wordsworth's son would carry on the business now the old gentleman was gone was not a whit more foolish than we who laugh at his ignorance of the nature of poetry whilst we take it as a matter of course that a son should "carry on" his father's religion. Hence, owing to our family system, the Catholic Churches are recruited daily at the font by temperamental Protestants, and the Protestant organizations by temperamental Catholics, with consequences most disconcerting to those who expect history to be deducible from the religious professions of the men who make it.

Still, though the Roman Catholic Church may occasionally catch such Tartars as Luther and Voltaire, or the Protestant organizations as Newman and Manning, the general run of mankind takes its impress from the atmosphere in which it is brought up. In Ireland the Roman Catholic peasant cannot escape the religious atmosphere of his Church. Except when he breaks out like a naughty child he is docile; he is reverent; he is content to regard knowledge as something not his business; he is a child before his Church, and accepts it as the highest authority in science and philosophy. He speaks of himself as a son of the Church, calling his priest father instead of brother or Mister. To rebel politically, he must break away from parish tutelage and follow a Protestant leader on national questions. His Church naturally fosters his submissiveness. The British Government and the Vatican may differ very vehemently as to whose subject the Irishman is to be; but they are quite agreed as to the propriety of his being a subject. Of the two, the British Government allows him more liberty, giving him as complete a democratic control of local government as his means will enable him to use, and a voice in the election of a formidable minority in the House of Commons, besides allowing him to read and learn what he likes—except when it makes a tufthunting onslaught on a seditious newspaper. But if he dared to claim a voice in the selection of his parish priest, or a representative at the Vatican, he would be denounced from the altar as an almost inconceivable blasphemer; and his educational opportunities are so restricted by his Church that he is heavily handicapped in every walk of life that requires any literacy. It is the aim of his priest to make him and keep him a submissive Conservative; and nothing but gross economic oppression and religious persecution could have produced the strange phenomenon of a revolutionary movement not only tolerated by the Clericals, but, up to a certain point, even encouraged by them. If there is such a thing as political science, with natural laws like any other science, it is certain that only the most violent external force could effect and maintain this unnatural combination of political revolution with Papal reaction, and of hardy individualism and independence with despotism and subjugation.

That violent external force is the clumsy thumb of English rule. If you would be good enough, ladies and gentlemen of England, to take your thumb away and leave us free to do something else than bite it, the unnaturally combined elements in Irish politics would fly asunder and recombine according to their proper nature with results entirely satisfactory to real Protestantism.

THE NATURE OF POLITICAL HATRED

Just reconsider the Home Rule question in the light of that very English characteristic of the Irish people, their political hatred of priests. Do not be distracted by the shriek of indignant denial from the Catholic papers and from those who have witnessed the charming relations between the Irish peasantry and their spiritual fathers. I am perfectly aware that the Irish love their priests as devotedly as the French loved them before the Revolution or as the Italians loved them before they imprisoned the Pope in the Vatican. They love their landlords too: many an Irish gentleman has found in his nurse a foster-mother more interested in him than his actual mother. They love the English, as every Englishman who travels in Ireland can testify. Please do not suppose that I speak satirically: the world is full of authentic examples of the concurrence of human kindliness with political rancor. Slaves and schoolboys often love their masters; Napoleon and his soldiers made desperate efforts to save from drowning the Russian soldiers under whom they had broken the ice with their cannon; even the relations between nonconformist peasants and country parsons in England are not invariably unkindly; in the southern States of America planters are often traditionally fond of negroes and kind to them, with substantial returns in humble affection; soldiers and sailors often admire and cheer their officers sincerely and heartily; nowhere is actual personal intercourse found compatible for long with the intolerable friction of hatred and malice. But people who persist in pleading these amiabilities as political factors must be summarily bundled out of the room when questions of State are to be discussed. Just as an Irishman may have English friends whom he may prefer to any Irishman of his acquaintance, and be kind, hospitable, and serviceable in his intercourse with Englishmen, whilst being perfectly prepared to make the Shannon run red with English blood if Irish freedom could be obtained at that price; so an Irish Catholic may like his priest as a man and revere him as a confessor and spiritual pastor whilst being implacably determined to seize the first opportunity of throwing off his yoke. This is political hatred: the only hatred that civilization allows to be mortal hatred.

THE REVOLT AGAINST THE PRIEST

Realize, then, that the popular party in Ireland is seething with rebellion against the tyranny of the Church. Imagine the feelings of an English farmer if the parson refused to marry him for less than £20, and if he had virtually no other way of getting married! Imagine the Church Rates revived in the form of an unofficial Income Tax scientifically adjusted to your taxable capacity by an intimate knowledge of your affairs verified in the confessional! Imagine being one of a peasantry reputed the poorest in the world, under the thumb of a priesthood reputed the richest in the world! Imagine a Catholic middle class continually defeated in the struggle of professional, official, and fashionable life by the superior education of its Protestant competitors, and yet forbidden by its priests to resort to the only efficient universities in the country! Imagine trying to get a modern education in a seminary of priests, where every modern book worth reading is on the index, and the earth is still regarded, not perhaps as absolutely flat, yet as being far from so spherical as Protestants allege! Imagine being forbidden to read this preface because it proclaims your own grievance! And imagine being bound to submit to all this because the popular side must hold together at all costs in the face of the Protestant enemy! That is, roughly, the predicament of Roman Catholic Ireland.

PROTESTANT LOYALTY: A FORECAST

Now let us have a look at Protestant Ireland. I have already said that a "loyal" Irishman is an abhorrent phenomenon, because he is an unnatural one. In Ireland it is not "loyalty" to drink the English king's health and stand uncovered to the English national anthem: it is simply exploitation of English rule in the interests of the property, power, and promotion of the Irish classes as against the Irish masses. From any other point of view it is cowardice and dishonor. I have known a Protestant go to Dublin Castle to be sworn in as a special constable, quite resolved to take the baton and break the heads of a patriotic faction just then upsetting the peace of the town, yet back out at the last moment because he could not bring himself to swallow the oath of allegiance tendered with the baton. There is no such thing as genuine loyalty in Ireland. There is a separation of the Irish people into two hostile camps: one Protestant, gentlemanly, and oligarchical; the other Roman Catholic, popular, and democratic. The oligarchy governs Ireland as a bureaucracy deriving authority from the king of England. It cannot cast him off without casting off its own ascendancy. Therefore it naturally exploits him sedulously, drinking his health, waving his flag, playing his anthem, and using the foolish word "traitor" freely in its cups. But let the English Government make a step towards the democratic party, and the Protestant garrison revolts at once, not with tears and prayers and anguish of soul and years of trembling reluctance, as the parliamentarians of the XVII century revolted against Charles I, but with acrid promptitude and strident threatenings. When England finally abandons the garrison by yielding to the demand for Home Rule, the Protestants will not go under, nor will they waste much time in sulking over their betrayal, and comparing their fate with that of Gordon left by Gladstone to perish on the spears of heathen fanatics. They cannot afford to retire into an Irish Faubourg St Germain. They will take an energetic part in the national government, which will be sorely in need of parliamentary and official forces independent of Rome. They will get not only the Protestant votes, but the votes of Catholics in that spirit of toleration which is everywhere extended to heresies that happen to be politically serviceable to the orthodox. They will not relax their determination to hold every inch of the government of Ireland that they can grasp; but as that government will then be a national Irish government instead of as now an English government, their determination will make them the vanguard of Irish Nationalism and Democracy as against Roman-

ism and Sacerdotalism, leaving English Unionists grieved and shocked at their discovery of the true value of an Irish Protestant's loyalty.

But there will be no open break in the tradition of the party. The Protestants will still be the party of Union, which will then mean, not the Repeal of Home Rule, but the maintenance of the Federal Union of English-speaking commonwealths, now theatrically called the Empire. They will pull down the Union Jack without the smallest scruple; but they know the value of the Channel Fleet, and will cling closer than brothers to that and any other Imperial asset that can be exploited for the protection of Ireland against foreign aggression or the sharing of expenses with the British taxpayer. They know that the Irish coast is for the English invasion-scaremonger the heel of Achilles, and that they can use this to make him pay for the boot.

PROTESTANT PUGNACITY

If any Englishman feels incredulous as to this view of Protestantism as an essentially Nationalist force in Ireland, let him ask himself which leader he, if he were an Irishman, would rather have back from the grave to fight England: the Catholic Daniel O'Connell or the Protestant Parnell. O'Connell organized the Nationalist movement only to draw its teeth, to break its determination, and to declare that Repeal of the Union was not worth the shedding of a drop of blood. He died in the bosom of his Church, not in the bosom of his country. The Protestant leaders, from Lord Edward Fitzgerald to Parnell, have never divided their devotion. If any Englishman thinks that they would have been more sparing of blood than the English themselves are, if only so cheap a fluid could have purchased the honor of Ireland, he greatly mistakes the Irish Protestant temper. The notion that Ireland is the only country in the world

Q

not worth shedding a drop of blood for is not a Protestant one, and certainly not countenanced by English practice. It was hardly reasonable to ask Parnell to shed blood *quant. suff.* in Egypt to put an end to the misgovernment of the Khedive and replace him by Lord Cromer for the sake of the English bondholders, and then to expect him to become a Tolstoyan or an O'Connellite in regard to his own country. With a wholly Protestant Ireland at his back he might have bullied England into conceding Home Rule; for the insensibility of the English governing classes to philosophical, moral, social considerations—in short, to any considerations which require a little intellectual exertion and sympathetic alertness—is tempered, as we Irish well know, by an absurd susceptibility to intimidation.

For let me halt a moment here to impress on you, O English reader, that no fact has been more deeply stamped into us than that we can do nothing with an English Government unless we frighten it, any more than you can yourself. When power and riches are thrown haphazard into children's cradles as they are in England, you get a governing class without industry, character, courage, or real experience; and under such circumstances reforms are produced only by catastrophes followed by panics in which "something must be done." Thus it costs a cholera epidemic to achieve a Public Health Act, a Crimean War to reform the Civil Service, and a gunpowder plot to disestablish the Irish Church. It was by the light, not of reason, but of the moon, that the need for paying serious attention to the Irish land question was seen in England. It cost the American War of Independence and the Irish Volunteer movement to obtain the Irish parliament of 1782, the constitution of which far overshot the nationalist mark of today in the matter of independence.

It is vain to plead that this is human nature and not class weakness. The Japanese have proved that it is possible to conduct social and political changes intelligently and providentially instead of drifting along helplessly until public disasters compel a terrified and inconsiderate rearrangement. Innumerable experiments in local government have shewn that when men are neither too poor to be honest nor too rich to understand and share the needs of the people—as in New Zealand, for example—they can govern much more providently than our little circle of aristocrats and plutocrats.

THE JUST ENGLISHMAN

English Unionists, when asked what they have to say in defence of their rule of subject peoples, often reply that the Englishman is just, leaving us divided between our derision of so monstrously inhuman a pretension, and our impatience with so gross a confusion of the mutually exclusive functions of judge and legislator. For there is only one condition on which a man can do justice between two litigants, and that is that he shall have no interest in common with either of them, whereas it is only by having every interest in common with both of them that he can govern them tolerably. The indispensable preliminary to Democracy is the representation of every interest: the indispensable preliminary to justice is the elimination of every interest. When we want an arbitrator or an umpire, we turn to a stranger: when we want a government, a stranger is the one person we will not endure. The Englishman in India, for example, stands, a very statue of justice, between two natives. He says, in effect, "I am impartial in your religious disputes because I believe in neither of your religions. I am impartial in your conflicts of custom and sentiment because your customs and sentiments are different from, and abysmally inferior to, my own. Finally, I am impartial as to your interests, because they are both equally opposed to mine, which is to keep you both equally powerless against me in order that I may extract money from you to pay salaries and pensions to myself and my fellow Englishmen as judges and rulers over you. In return for which you get the inestimable benefit of a government that does absolute justice as between Indian and Indian, being wholly preoccupied with the maintenance of absolute injustice as between India and England."

It will be observed that no Englishman, without making himself ridiculous, could pretend to be perfectly just or disinterested in English affairs, or would tolerate a proposal to establish the Indian or Irish system in Great Britain. Yet if the justice of the Englishman is sufficient to ensure the welfare of India or Ireland, it ought to suffice equally for England. But the English are wise enough to refuse to trust to English justice themselves, preferring democracy. They can hardly blame the Irish for taking the same view.

In short, dear English reader, the Irish Protestant stands outside that English Mutual Admiration Society which you call the Union or the Empire. You may buy a common and not ineffective variety of Irish Protestant by delegating your powers to him, and in effect making him the oppressor and you his sorely bullied and bothered catspaw and military maintainer; but if you offer him nothing for his loyalty except the natural superiority of the English character, you will—well, try the experiment, and see what will happen! You would have a ten-times better chance with the Roman Catholic; for he has been saturated from his youth up with the Imperial idea of foreign rule by a spiritually superior international power, and is trained to submission and abnegation of his private judgment. A Roman Catholic garrison would take its orders from England and let her rule Ireland if England were Roman Catholic.

The Protestant garrison simply seizes on the English power; uses it for its own purposes; and occasionally orders the English Government to remove an Irish secretary who has dared to apply English ideas to the affairs of the garrison. Whereupon the English Government abjectly removes him, and implores him, as a gentleman and a loyal Englishman, not to reproach it in the face of the Nationalist enemy.

Such incidents naturally do not shake the sturdy conviction of the Irish Protestant that he is more than a match for any English Government in determination and intelligence. Here, no doubt, he flatters himself; for his advantage is not really an advantage of character, but of comparative directness of interest, concentration of force on one narrow issue, simplicity of aim, with freedom from the scruples and responsibilities of world-politics. The business is Irish business, not English; and he is Irish. And his object, which is simply to secure the dominance of his own caste and creed behind the power of England, is simpler and clearer than the confused aims of English Cabinets struggling ineptly with the burdens of empire, and biassed by the pressure of capital anywhere rather than in Ireland. He has no responsibility, no interest, no status outside his own country and his own movement, which means that he has no conscience in dealing with England; whereas England, having a very uneasy conscience, and many hindering and hampering responsibilities and interests in dealing with him, gets bullied and driven by him, and finally learns sympathy with Nationalist aims by her experience of the tyranny of the Orange party.

IRISH CATHOLICISM FORECAST

Let us suppose that the establishment of a national government were to annihilate the oligarchic party by absorbing the Protestant garrison and making it a Protestant National Guard. The Roman Catholic laity, now a cipher, would organize itself; and a revolt against Rome and against the priesthood would ensue. The Roman Catholic Church would become the official Irish Church. The Irish parliament would insist on a voice in the promotion of churchmen; fees and contributions would be regulated; blackmail would be resisted; sweating in conventual factories and workshops would be stopped; and the ban would be taken off the universities. In a word, the Roman Catholic Church, against which Dublin Castle is powerless, would meet the one force on earth that can cope with it victoriously. That force is Democracy, a thing far more Catholic than itself. Until that force is let loose against it, the Protestant garrison can do nothing to the priesthood except consolidate it and drive the people to rally round it in defence of their altars against the foreigner and the heretic. When it *is* let loose, the Catholic laity will make as short work of sacerdotal tyranny in Ireland as it has done in France and Italy. And in doing so it will be forced to face the old problem of the relations of Church and State. A Roman Catholic party must submit to Rome: an anti-clerical Catholic party must of necessity become an Irish Catholic party. The Holy Roman Empire, like the other Empires, has no future except as a Federation of national Catholic Churches; for Christianity can no more escape Democracy than Democracy can escape Socialism. It is noteworthy in this connection that the Anglican Catholics have played and are playing a notable part in the Socialist movement in England in opposition to the individualist Secularists of the urban proletariat; but they are quit of the preliminary dead lift that awaits the Irish Catholic. Their Church has thrown off the yoke of Rome, and is safely and permanently Anglicized. But the Catholic Church in Ireland is still Roman. Home Rule will herald the day when the Vatican will go the way of Dublin Castle, and the island of the saints assume the headship of her own Church. It may seem incredible that long after the last Orangeman shall lay down his chalk for ever, the familiar scrawl on every blank wall in the north of Ireland "To hell with the Pope!" may reappear in the south, traced by the hands of Catholics who shall have forgotten the traditional counter legend, "To hell with King William!" (of glorious, pious, and immortal memory); but it may happen so. "The island of the saints" is no idle phrase. Religious genius is one of our national products; and Ireland is no bad rock to build a Church on. Holy and beautiful is the soul of Catholic Ireland: her prayers are lovelier than the teeth and claws of Protestantism, but not so effective in dealing with the English.

ENGLISH VOLTAIREANISM

Let me familiarize the situation by shewing how closely it reproduces the English situation in its essentials. In England, as in France, the struggle between the priesthood and the laity has produced a vast body of Voltaireans. But the essential identity of the French and English movements has been obscured by the ignorance of the ordinary Englishman, who, instead of knowing the distinctive tenets of his church or sect, vaguely believes them to be the eternal truth as opposed to the damnable error of all the other denominations. He thinks of Voltaire as a French "infidel," instead of as the champion of the laity against the official theocracy of the State Church. The Nonconformist leaders of our Free Churches are all Voltaireans. The warcry of the Passive Resisters is Voltaire's warcry, "Écrasez l'infâme." No account need be taken of the technical difference between Voltaire's "infâme" and Dr Clifford's. One was the unreformed Roman Church of France; the other is the reformed Anglican Church; but in both cases the attack has been on a priestly tyranny and a professional monopoly. Voltaire convinced the Genevan ministers that he was the philosophic champion of their Protestant, Individualistic, Democratic Deism against the State Church of Roman Catholic France; and his heroic energy and beneficence as a philanthropist, which now only makes the list of achievements on his monument at Ferney the most impressive epitaph in Europe, then made the most earnest of the Lutheran ministers glad to claim a common inspiration with him. Unfortunately Voltaire had an irrepressible sense of humor. He joked about Habakkuk; and jokes about Habakkuk smelt too strongly of brimstone to be tolerated by Protestants to whom the Bible was not a literature but a fetish and a talisman. And so Voltaire, in spite of the church he "erected to God," became in England the bogey-atheist of three generations of English ignoramuses, instead of the legitimate successor of Martin Luther and John Knox.

Nowadays, however, Voltaire's jokes are either forgotten or else fall flat on a world which no longer venerates Habakkuk; and his true position is becoming apparent. The fact that Voltaire was a Roman Catholic layman, educated at a Jesuit college, is the conclusive reply to the shallow people who imagine that Ireland delivered up to the Irish democracy—that is, to the Catholic laity—would be delivered up to the tyranny of the priesthood.

SUPPOSE!

Suppose, now, that the conquest of France by Henry V of England had endured, and that France in the XVIII century had been governed by an English viceroy through a Huguenot bureaucracy and a judicial bench appointed on the understanding that loyalty for them meant loyalty to England, and patriotism a willingness to die in defence of the English conquest and of the English Church, would not Voltaire in that case have been the meanest of traitors and self-seekers if he had played the game of England by joining in its campaign against his own and his country's Church? The energy he threw into the defence of Calas and Sirven would have been thrown into the defence of the Frenchmen whom the English would have called "rebels"; and he would have been forced to identify the cause of freedom and democracy with the cause of "l'infâme." The French revolution would have been a revolution against England and English rule instead of against aristocracy and ecclesiasticism; and all the intellectual and spiritual forces in France, from Turgot to De Tocqueville, would have been burnt up in mere anti-Anglicism and nationalist dithyrambs instead of contributing to political science and broadening the thought of the world.

What would have happened in France is what has happened in Ireland; and that is why it is only the small-minded Irish, incapable of conceiving what religious freedom means to a country, who do not loathe English rule. For in Ireland England is nothing but the Pope's policeman. She imagines she is holding the Vatican cardinals at bay when she is really strangling the Voltaires, the Foxes and Penns, the Cliffords, Hortons, Campbells, Walters, and Silvester Hornes, who are to be found among the Roman Catholic laity as plentifully as among the Anglican Catholic laity in England. She gets nothing out of Ireland but infinite trouble, infinite confusion and hindrance in her own legislation, a hatred that circulates through the whole world and poisons it against her, a reproach that makes her professions of sympathy with Finland

and Macedonia ridiculous and hypocritical, whilst the priest takes all the
spoils, in money, in power, in pride, and
in popularity.

IRELAND'S REAL GRIEVANCE

But it is not the spoils that matter. It is
the waste, the sterilization, the perversion
of fruitful brain power into flatulent protest against unnecessary evil, the use of
our very entrails to tie our own hands
and seal our own lips in the name of our
honor and patriotism. As far as money or
comfort is concerned, the average Irishman has a more tolerable life—especially
now that the population is so scanty—
than the average Englishman. It is true
that in Ireland the poor man is robbed
and starved and oppressed under judicial
forms which confer the imposing title of
justice on a crude system of bludgeoning
and perjury. But so is the Englishman.
The Englishman, more docile, less dangerous, too lazy intellectually to use such
political and legal power as lies within his
reach, suffers more and makes less fuss
about it than the Irishman. But at least he
has nobody to blame but himself and his
fellow countrymen. He does not doubt
that if an effective majority of the English
people made up their minds to alter the
Constitution, as the majority of the Irish
people have made up their minds to obtain Home Rule, they could alter it without having to fight an overwhelmingly
powerful and rich neighboring nation,
and fight, too, with ropes round their
necks. He can attack any institution in
his country without betraying it to foreign
vengeance and foreign oppression. True,
his landlord may turn him out of his
cottage if he goes to a Methodist chapel
instead of to the parish church. His customers may stop their orders if he votes
Liberal instead of Conservative. English
ladies and gentlemen who would perish
sooner than shoot a fox do these things
without the smallest sense of indecency

and dishonor. But they cannot muzzle his
intellectual leaders. The English philosopher, the English author, the English
orator can attack every abuse and expose
every superstition without strengthening
the hands of any common enemy. In Ireland every such attack, every such exposure, is a service to England and a stab
to Ireland. If you expose the tyranny and
rapacity of the Church, it is an argument
in favor of Protestant ascendancy. If you
denounce the nepotism and jobbery of
the new local authorities, you are demonstrating the unfitness of the Irish to
govern themselves, and the superiority of
the old oligarchical grand juries.

And there is the same pressure on the
other side. The Protestant must stand by
the garrison at all costs: the Unionist
must wink at every bureaucratic abuse,
connive at every tyranny, magnify every
official blockhead, because their exposure
would be a victory for the Nationalist
enemy. Every Irishman is in Lancelot's
position: his honor rooted in dishonor
stands; and faith unfaithful keeps him
falsely true.

THE CURSE OF NATIONALISM

It is hardly possible for an Englishman
to understand all that this implies. A conquered nation is like a man with cancer:
he can think of nothing else, and is forced
to place himself, to the exclusion of all
better company, in the hands of quacks
who profess to treat or cure cancer. The
windbags of the two rival platforms are
the most insufferable of all windbags. It
requires neither knowledge, character,
conscience, diligence in public affairs,
nor any virtue, private or communal, to
thump the Nationalist or Orange tub:
nay, it puts a premium on the rancor or
callousness that has given rise to the proverb that if you put an Irishman on a spit
you can always get another Irishman to
baste him. Jingo oratory in England is
sickening enough to serious people: in-

deed one evening's mafficking in London produced a determined call for the police. Well, in Ireland all political oratory is Jingo oratory; and all political demonstrations are maffickings. English rule is such an intolerable abomination that no other subject can reach the people. Nationalism stands between Ireland and the light of the world. Nobody in Ireland of any intelligence likes Nationalism any more than a man with a broken arm likes having it set. A healthy nation is as unconscious of its nationality as a healthy man of his bones. But if you break a nation's nationality it will think of nothing else but getting it set again. It will listen to no reformer, to no philosopher, to no preacher, until the demand of the Nationalist is granted. It will attend to no business, however vital, except the business of unification and liberation.

That is why everything is in abeyance in Ireland pending the achievement of Home Rule. The great movements of the human spirit which sweep in waves over Europe are stopped on the Irish coast by the English guns of the Pigeon House Fort. Only a quaint little offshoot of English pre-Raphaelitism called the Gaelic movement has got a footing by using Nationalism as a stalking-horse, and popularizing itself as an attack on the native language of the Irish people, which is most fortunately also the native language of half the world, including England. Every election is fought on nationalist grounds; every appointment is made on nationalist grounds; every judge is a partisan in the nationalist conflict; every speech is a dreary recapitulation of nationalist twaddle; every lecture is a corruption of history to flatter nationalism or defame it; every school is a recruiting station; every church is a barrack; and every Irishman is unspeakably tired of the whole miserable business, which nevertheless is and perforce must remain his first business until Home Rule makes an end of it, and sweeps the nationalist and the garrison hack together into the dustbin.

There is indeed no greater curse to a nation than a nationalist movement, which is only the agonizing symptom of a suppressed natural function. Conquered nations lose their place in the world's march because they can do nothing but strive to get rid of their nationalist movements by recovering their national liberty. All demonstrations of the virtues of a foreign government, though often conclusive, are as useless as demonstrations of the superiority of artificial teeth, glass eyes, silver windpipes, and patent wooden legs to the natural products. Like Democracy, national self-government is not for the good of the people: it is for the satisfaction of the people. One Antonine emperor, one St Louis, one Richelieu, may be worth ten democracies in point of what is called good government; but there is no satisfaction for the people in them. To deprive a dyspeptic of his dinner and hand it over to a man who can digest it better is a highly logical proceeding; but it is not a sensible one. To take the government of Ireland away from the Irish and hand it over to the English on the ground that they can govern better would be a precisely parallel case if the English had managed their own affairs so well as to place their superior faculty for governing beyond question. But as the English are avowed muddlers —rather proud of it, in fact—even the logic of that case against Home Rule is not complete. Read Mr Charles Booth's account of London, Mr Rowntree's account of York, and the latest official report on Dundee; and then pretend, if you can, that Englishmen and Scotchmen have not more cause to hand over their affairs to an Irish parliament than to clamor for another nation's cities to devastate and another people's business to mismanage.

A NATURAL RIGHT

The question is not one of logic at all, but of natural right. English universities have for some time past encouraged an extremely foolish academic exercise which consists in disproving the existence of natural rights on the ground that they cannot be deduced from the principles of any known political system. If they could, they would not be natural rights but acquired ones. Acquired rights are deduced from political constitutions; but political constitutions are deduced from natural rights. When a man insists on certain liberties without the slightest regard to demonstrations that they are not for his own good, nor for the public good, nor moral, nor reasonable, nor decent, nor compatible with the existing constitution of society, then he is said to claim a natural right to that liberty. When, for instance, he insists on living, in spite of the irrefutable demonstrations of many able pessimists, from the author of the book of Ecclesiastes to Schopenhauer, that life is an evil, he is asserting a natural right to live. When he insists on a vote in order that his country may be governed according to his ignorance instead of the wisdom of the Privy Council, he is asserting a natural right to self-government. When he insists on guiding himself at 21 by his own inexperience and folly and immaturity instead of by the experience and sagacity of his father, or the well-stored mind of his grandmother, he is asserting a natural right to independence. Even if Home Rule were as unhealthy as an Englishman's eating, as intemperate as his drinking, as filthy as his smoking, as licentious as his domesticity, as corrupt as his elections, as murderously greedy as his commerce, as cruel as his prisons, and as merciless as his streets, Ireland's claim to self-government would still be as good as England's. King James the First proved so cleverly and conclusively that the satis-faction of natural rights was incompatible with good government that his courtiers called him Solomon. We, more enlightened, call him Fool, solely because we have learnt that nations insist on being governed by their own consent—or, as they put it, by themselves and for themselves—and that they will finally upset a good government which denies them this even if the alternative be a bad government which at least creates and maintains an illusion of democracy. America, as far as one can ascertain, is much worse governed, and has a much more disgraceful political history than England under Charles I; but the American Republic is the stabler government because it starts from a formal concession of natural rights, and keeps up an illusion of safeguarding them by an elaborate machinery of democratic election. And the final reason why Ireland must have Home Rule is that she has a natural right to it.

A WARNING

Finally, some words of warning to both nations. Ireland has been deliberately ruined again and again by England. Unable to compete with us industrially, she has destroyed our industries by the brute force of prohibitive taxation. She was perfectly right. That brute force was a more honorable weapon than the poverty which we used to undersell her. We lived with and as our pigs, and let loose our wares in the Englishman's market at prices which he could compete with only by living like a pig himself. Having the alternative of stopping our industry altogether, he very naturally and properly availed himself of it. We should have done the same in his place. To bear malice against him on that score is to poison our blood and weaken our constitutions with unintelligent rancor. In wrecking all the industries that were based on the poverty of our people England did us an enormous service. In omitting to do the same on her own soil, she did herself a wrong that has rotted her almost to the marrow. I hope that when Home Rule is at last achieved, one of our first legislative acts will be to fortify the subsistence of our people behind the bulwark of a standard wage, and to impose crushing import duties on every English trade that flourishes in the slum and fattens on the starvation of our unfortunate English neighbors.

DOWN WITH THE SOLDIER!

Now for England's share of warning. Let her look to her Empire; for unless she makes it such a Federation for civil strength and defence that all free peoples will cling to it voluntarily, it will inevitably become a military tyranny to prevent them from abandoning it; and such a tyranny will drain the English taxpayer of his money more effectually than its worst cruelties can ever drain its victims of their liberty. A political scheme that cannot be carried out except by soldiers will not be a permanent one. The soldier is an anachronism of which we must get rid. Among people who are proof against the suggestions of romantic fiction there can no longer be any question of the fact that military service produces moral imbecility, ferocity, and cowardice, and that the defence of nations must be undertaken by the civil enterprise of men enjoying all the rights and liberties of citizenship, and trained by the exacting discipline of democratic freedom and responsibility. For permanent work the soldier is worse than useless: such efficiency as he has is the result of dehumanization and disablement. His whole training tends to make him a weakling. He has the easiest of lives: he has no freedom and no responsibility. He is politically and socially a child, with rations instead of rights, treated like a child, punished like a child, dressed prettily and washed and combed like a child, excused

for outbreaks of naughtiness like a child, forbidden to marry like a child, and called Tommy like a child. He has no real work to keep him from going mad except housemaid's work: all the rest is forced exercise, in the form of endless rehearsals for a destructive and terrifying performance which may never come off, and which, when it does come off, is not like the rehearsals. His officer has not even housekeeper's work to keep him sane. The work of organizing and commanding bodies of men, which builds up the character and resource of the large class of civilians who live by it, only demoralizes the military officer, because his orders, however disastrous or offensive, must be obeyed without regard to consequences: for instance, if he calls his men dogs, and perverts a musketry drill order to make them kneel to him as an act of personal humiliation, and thereby provokes a mutiny among men not yet thoroughly broken in to the abjectness of the military condition, he is not, as might be expected, shot, but, at worst, reprimanded, whilst the leader of the mutiny, instead of getting the Victoria Cross and a public testimonial, is condemned to five years' penal servitude by Lynch Law (technically called martial law) administered by a trade union of officers. Compare with this the position of, for instance, our railway managers or our heads of explosive factories. They have to handle large bodies of men whose carelessness or insubordination may cause wholesale destruction of life and property; yet any of these men may insult them, defy them, or assault them without special penalties of any sort. The military commander dares not face these conditions: he lives in perpetual terror of his men, and will undertake their command only when they are stripped of all their civil rights, gagged, and bound hand and foot by a barbarous slave code. Thus the officer learns to punish, but never to rule; and when an emergency like the Indian Mutiny comes, he breaks down; and the situation has to be saved by a few untypical officers with character enough to have retained their civilian qualities in spite of the messroom. This, unfortunately, is learnt by the public, not on the spot, but from Lord Roberts fifty years later.

Besides the Mutiny we have had the Crimean and South African wars, the Dreyfus affair in France, the incidents of the anti-militarist campaign by the Social-Democrats in Germany, and now the Denshawai affair in the Nile delta, all heaping on us sensational demonstrations of the fact that soldiers pay the penalty of their slavery and outlawry by becoming, relatively to free civilians, destructive, cruel, dishonest, tyrannical, hysterical, mendacious, alarmists at home and terrorists abroad, politically reactionary, and professionally incapable. If it were humanly possible to militarize all the humanity out of a man, there would be absolutely no defence to this indictment. But the military system is so idiotically academic and impossible, and renders its victims so incapable of carrying it out with any thoroughness except when, in an occasional hysterical outburst of terror and violence, that hackneyed comedy of civil life, the weak man putting his foot down, becomes the military tragedy of the armed man burning, flogging, and murdering in a panic, that a body of soldiers and officers is in the main, and under normal circumstances, much like any other body of laborers and gentlemen. Many of us count among our personal friends and relatives officers whose amiable and honorable character seems to contradict everything I have just said about the military character. You have only to describe Lynch courts and acts of terrorism to them as the work of Ribbonmen, Dacoits, Moonlighters, Boxers, or —to use the general term most familiar to them—"natives," and their honest and generous indignation knows no bounds: they feel about them like men, not like soldiers. But the moment you bring the professional side of them uppermost by describing precisely the same proceedings to them as the work of regular armies, they defend them, applaud them, and are ready to take part in them as if their humanity had been blown out like a candle. You find that there is a blind spot on their moral retina, and that this blind spot is the military spot.

The excuse, when any excuse is made, is that discipline is supremely important in war. Now most soldiers have no experience of war; and to assume that those who have are therefore qualified to legislate for it, is as absurd as to assume that a man who has been run over by an omnibus is thereby qualified to draw up wise regulations for the traffic of London. Neither our military novices nor our veterans are clever enough to see that in the field, discipline either keeps itself or goes to pieces; for humanity under fire is a quite different thing from humanity in barracks: when there is danger the difficulty is never to find men who will obey, but men who can command. It is in time of peace, when an army is either a police force (in which case its work can be better done by a civilian constabulary) or an absurdity, that discipline is difficult, because the wasted life of the soldier is unnatural, except to a lazy man, and his servitude galling and senseless, except to a docile one. Still, the soldier is a man, and the officer sometimes a gentleman in the literal sense of the word; and so, what with humanity, laziness, and docility combined, they manage to rub along with only occasional outbursts of mutiny on the one side and class rancor and class cowardice on the other.

They are not even discontented; for the military and naval codes simplify life for them just as it is simplified for children. No soldier is asked to think for himself, to judge for himself, to consult his own honor and manhood, to dread any consequence except the consequence of punishment to his own person. The rules are plain and simple; the ceremonies of respect and submission are as easy and mechanical as a prayer wheel; the orders are always to be obeyed thoughtlessly, however inept or dishonorable they may be. As the late Laureate said in the two stinging lines in which he branded the British soldier with the dishonor of Esau, "theirs not to reason why, theirs but to do and die." To the moral imbecile and political sluggard these conditions are as congenial and attractive as they are abhorrent and intolerable to the William Tell temperament. Just as the most incorrigible criminal is always, we are told, the best behaved convict, so the man with least conscience and initiative makes the best behaved soldier, and that not wholly through mere fear of punishment, but through a genuine fitness for and consequent happiness in the childlike military life. Such men dread freedom and responsibility as a weak man dreads a risk or a heavy burden; and the objection to the military system is that it tends to produce such men by a weakening disuse of the moral muscles. No doubt this weakness is just what the military system aims at, its ideal soldier being, not a complete man, but a docile unit of cannon-fodder which can be trusted to respond promptly and certainly to the external stimulus of a shouted order, and is intimidated to the pitch of being afraid to run away from a battle. It may be doubted whether even in the Prussian heyday of the system, when floggings of hundreds and even thousands of lashes were matters of ordinary routine, this detestable ideal was ever realized; but your courts-martial are not practical enough to take that into account: it is characteristic of the military mind continually to ignore human nature and cry for the moon instead of facing modern social facts and accepting modern democratic conditions. And when I say the military mind, I repeat that I am not forgetting the patent fact that the military mind and the humane mind can exist in the same person; so that an officer who will take all the civilian risks, from city traffic to fox-hunting, without uneasiness, and who will manage all the civil employees on his estate and in his house and stables without the aid of a Mutiny Act, will also, in his military capacity, frantically declare that he dare not walk about in a foreign country unless every crime of violence against an Englishman in uniform is punished by the bombardment and destruction of a whole village, or the wholesale flogging and execution of every native in the neighborhood, and also that unless he and his fellow officers have power, without the intervention of a jury, to punish the slightest self-assertion or hesitation to obey orders, however grossly insulting or disastrous those orders may be, with sentences which are reserved in civil life for the worst crimes, he cannot secure the obedience and respect of his men, and the country will accordingly lose all its colonies and dependencies, and be helplessly conquered in the German invasion which he confidently expects to occur in the course of a fortnight or so. That is to say, in so far as he is an ordinary gentleman he behaves sensibly and courageously; and in so far as he is a military man he gives way without shame to the grossest folly, cruelty, and poltroonery. If any other profession in the world had been stained by these vices, and by false witness, forgery, swindling, torture, compulsion of men's families to attend their executions, digging up and mutilation of dead enemies, all wantonly added to the devastation proper to its own business, as the military profession has been within recent memory in England, France, and the United States of America (to mention no other countries), it would be very difficult to induce men of capacity and character to enter it. And in England it is, in fact, largely dependent for its recruits on the refuse of industrial life, and for its officers on the aristocratic and plutocratic refuse of political and diplomatic life, who join the army and pay for their positions in the more or less fashionable clubs which the regimental messes provide them with—clubs which, by the way, occasionally figure in ragging scandals as circles of extremely coarse moral character.

Now in countries which are denied Home Rule: that is, in which the government does not rest on the consent of the people, it must rest on military coercion; and the bureaucracy, however civil and legal it may be in form and even in the character of its best officials, must connive at all the atrocities of military rule, and become infected in the end with the chronic panic characteristic of militarism. In recent witness whereof, let me shift the scene from Ireland to Egypt, and tell the story of the Denshawai affair of June 1906 by way of object-lesson.

THE DENSHAWAI HORROR

Denshawai is a little Egyptian village in the Nile delta. Besides the dilapidated huts among the reeds by the roadside, and the palm trees, there are towers of unbaked brick, as unaccountable to an English villager as a Kentish oast-house to an Egyptian. These towers are pigeon-houses; for the villagers keep pigeons just as an English farmer keeps poultry.

Try to imagine the feelings of an English village if a party of Chinese officers suddenly appeared and began shooting the ducks, the geese, the hens, and the turkeys, and carried them off, asserting that they were wild birds, as everybody in China knew, and that the pretended indignation of the farmers was a cloak for hatred of the Chinese, and perhaps for a plot to overthrow the religion of Con-

fucius and establish the Church of England in its place! Well, that is the British equivalent of what happened at Denshawai when a party of English officers went pigeon-shooting there the year before last. The inhabitants complained and memorialized; but they obtained no redress: the law failed them in their hour of need. So one leading family of pigeon farmers, Mahfouz by name, despaired of the law; and its head, Hassan Mahfouz, aged 60, made up his mind not to submit tamely to a repetition of the outrage. Also, British officers were ordered not to shoot pigeons in the villages without the consent of the Omdeh, or headman, though nothing was settled as to what might happen to the Omdeh if he ventured to refuse.

Fancy the feelings of Denshawai when on the 13th of June last there drove to the village four khaki-clad British officers with guns, one of them being a shooter of the year before, accompanied by one other officer on horseback, and also by a dragoman and an Ombashi, or police official! The oriental blood of Hassan Mahfouz boiled; and he warned them that they would not be allowed to shoot pigeons; but as they did not understand his language, the warning had no effect. They sent their dragoman to ask the Omdeh's permission to shoot; but the Omdeh was away; and all the interpreter could get from the Omdeh's deputy, who knew better than to dare an absolute refusal, was the pretty obvious reply that they might shoot if they went far enough away from the village. On the strength of this welcome, they went from 100 to 300 yards away from the houses (these distances were afterwards officially averaged at 500 yards), and began shooting the villagers' pigeons. The villagers remonstrated and finally seized the gun of the youngest officer. It went off in the struggle, and wounded three men and the wife of one Abd-el-Nebi, a young man of 25. Now the lady, though, as it turned out, only temporarily disabled by a charge of pigeon shot in the softest part of her person, gave herself up for dead; and the feeling in the village was much as if our imaginary Chinese officers, on being interfered with in their slaughter of turkeys, had killed an English farmer's wife. Abd-el-Nebi, her husband, took the matter to heart, not altogether without reason, we may admit. His threshing-floor also caught fire somehow (the official English theory is that he set it on fire as a signal for revolt to the entire Moslem world); and all the lads and loafers in the place were presently on the spot. The other officers, seeing their friend in trouble, joined him. Abd-el-Nebi hit the supposed murderer of his wife with a stick; Hassan Mahfouz used a stick also; and the lads and loafers began to throw stones and bricks. Five London policemen would have seen that there was nothing to be done but fight their way out, as there is no use arguing with an irritated mob, especially if you do not know its language. Had the shooting party been in the charge of a capable non-commissioned officer, he would perhaps have got it safely off. As it was, the officers tried propitiation, making their overtures in pantomime. They gave up their guns; they offered watches and money to the crowd, crying Baksheesh; and the senior officer actually collared the junior and pretended to arrest him for the murder of the woman. Naturally they were mobbed worse than before; and what they did not give to the crowd was taken from them, whether as payment for the pigeons, blood money, or simple plunder was not gone into. The officers, two Irishmen and three Englishmen, having made a hopeless mess of it, and being now in serious danger, made for their carriages, but were dragged out of them again, one of the coachmen being knocked senseless. They then "agreed to run," the arrangement being that the Englishmen, being the juniors, should run away to camp and bring help to the Irishmen. They bolted accordingly; but the third, the youngest, seeing the two Irishmen hard put to it, went back and stood by them. Of the two fugitives, one, after a long race in the Egyptian afternoon sun, got to the next village and there dropped, smitten by sunstroke, of which he died. The other ran on and met a patrol, which started to the rescue.

Meanwhile, the other three officers had been taken out of the hands of the lads and the loafers, of Abd-el-Nebi and Hassan Mahfouz, by the elders and watchmen, and saved from further injury, but not before they had been severely knocked about, one of them having one of the bones of his left arm broken near the wrist—simple fracture of the thin end of the ulna. They were also brought to the threshing-floor; shewn the wounded woman; informed by gestures that they deserved to have their throats cut for murdering her; and kicked (with naked feet, fortunately); but at this point the elders and constables stopped the mobbing. Finally the three were sent off to camp in their carriages; and the incident ended for that day.

No English mob, under similar provocation, would have behaved any better; and few would have done as little mischief. It is not many months since an old man—not a foreigner and not an unbeliever—was kicked to death in the streets of London because the action of a park constable in turning him out of a public park exposed him to suspicion of misconduct. At Denshawai, the officers were not on duty. In their private capacity as sportsmen, they committed a serious depredation on a very poor village by slaughtering its stock. In an English village they would have been tolerated because the farmers would have expected compensation for damage, and the villagers coals and blankets and employment in country house, garden, and stable, or as beaters, huntsmen, and the like, from them. But Denshawai had no such inducements to submit to their thoughtless and selfish aggression. One of them had apparently killed a woman and wounded three men with his gun: in fact his own comrade virtually convicted him of it before the crowd by collaring him as a prisoner. In short, the officers had given outrageous provocation; and they had shewn an amiable but disastrous want of determination and judgment in dealing with the riot they provoked. They should have been severely reprimanded and informed that they had themselves to thank for what happened to them; and the villagers who assaulted them should have been treated with leniency, and assured that pigeon-shooting would not be allowed in future.

That is what should have ensued. Now for what actually did ensue.

Abd-el-Nebi, in consideration of the injury to his wife, was only sentenced to penal servitude for life. And our clemency did not stop there. His wife was not punished at all—not even charged with stealing the shot which was found in her person. And lest Abd-el-Nebi should feel lonely at 25 in beginning penal servitude for the rest of his days, another young man, of 20, was sent to penal servitude for life with him.

No such sentimentality was shewn to Hassan Mahfouz. An Egyptian pigeon farmer who objects to British sport; threatens British officers and gentlemen when they shoot his pigeons; and actually hits those officers with a substantial stick, is clearly a ruffian to be made an example of. Penal servitude was not enough for a man of 60 who looked 70, and might not have lived to suffer five years of it. So Hassan was hanged; but as a special mark of consideration for his family, he was hanged in full view of his own house,

with his wives and children and grandchildren enjoying the spectacle from the roof. And lest this privilege should excite jealousy in other households, three other Denshavians were hanged with him. They went through the ceremony with dignity, professing their faith ("Mahometan, I regret to say," Mr Pecksniff would have said). Hassan, however, "in a loud voice invoked ruin upon the houses of those who had given evidence against him"; and Darweesh was impatient and presumed to tell the hangman to be quick. But then Darweesh was a bit of a brigand: he had been imprisoned for bearing false witness; and his resistance to the British invasion is the only officially recorded incident of his life which is entirely to his credit. He and Abd-el-Nebi (who had been imprisoned for theft) were the only disreputable characters among the punished. Ages of the four hanged men respectively, 60, 50, 22, and 20.

Hanging, however, is the least sensational form of public execution: it lacks those elements of blood and torture for which the military and bureaucratic imagination lusts. So, as they had room for only one man on the gallows, and had to leave him hanging half an hour to make sure work and give his family plenty of time to watch him swinging ("slowly turning round and round on himself," as the local papers described it), thus having two hours to kill as well as four men, they kept the entertainment going by flogging eight men with fifty lashes each: eleven more than the utmost permitted by the law of Moses in times which our Army of Occupation no doubt considers barbarous. But then Moses conceived his law as being what he called the law of God, and not simply an instrument for the gratification of his own cruelty and terror. It is unspeakably reassuring to learn from the British official reports laid before parliament that "due dignity was observed in carrying out the executions," that "all possible humanity was shewn in carrying them out," and that "the arrangements were admirable, and reflect great credit on all concerned." As this last testimonial apparently does not refer to the victims, they are evidently officially considered not to have been concerned in the proceedings at all. Finally, Lord Cromer certifies that the Englishman in charge of the proceedings is "a singularly humane man, and is very popular amongst the natives of Egypt by reason of the great sympathy he has always shewn for them." It will be seen that Parliamentary Papers, Nos. 3 and 4, Egypt, 1906, are not lacking in unconscious humor. The official walrus pledges himself in every case for the kindliness of the official carpenter.

One man was actually let off, to the great danger of the British Empire perhaps. Still, as he was an epileptic, and had already had several fits in the court of Judge Lynch, the doctor said Better not; and he escaped. This was very inconvenient; for the number of floggees had been made up solely to fill the time occupied by the hangings at the rate of two floggings per hanging; and the breakdown of the arrangement through Said Suleiman Kheirallah's inconsiderate indisposition made the execution of Darweesh tedious, as he was hanging for fully quarter of an hour without any flogging to amuse his fellow villagers and the officers and men of the Inniskilling Dragoons, the military mounted police, and the mounted infantry. A few spare sentences of flogging should have been kept in hand to provide against accidents.

In any case there was not time to flog everybody, nor to flog three of the floggees enough; so these three had a year's hard labor apiece in addition to their floggings. Six others were not flogged at all, but were sent to penal servitude for seven years each. One man got fifteen years. Total for the morning's work: four hanged, two to penal servitude for life,

one to fifteen years penal servitude, six to seven years penal servitude, three to imprisonment for a year with hard labor and fifty lashes, and five to fifty lashes.

Lord Cromer certifies that these proceedings were "just and necessary." He also gives his reasons. It appears that the boasted justice introduced into Egypt by the English in 1882 was imaginary, and that the real work of coping with Egyptian disorder was done by Brigandage Commissions, composed of Egyptians. These Commissions, when an offence was reported, descended on the inculpated village; seized everybody concerned; and plied them with tortures, mentionable and unmentionable, until they accused everybody they were expected to accuse. The accused were in turn tortured until they confessed anything and everything they were accused of. They were then killed, flogged, or sent to penal servitude. This was the reality behind the illusion that soothed us after bombarding Alexandria. The bloodless, white-gloved native courts set up to flatter our sense of imperial justice had, apparently, about as much to do with the actual government of the fellaheen as the annual court which awards the Dunmow flitch of bacon has to do with our divorce court. Eventually a Belgian judge, who was appointed Procureur-Général, exposed the true state of affairs.

Then the situation had to be faced. Order had to be maintained somehow; but the regular native courts which saved the face of the British Occupation were useless for the purpose; and the Brigandage Commissions were so abominable and demoralizing that they made more mischief than they prevented. Besides, there was Mr Wilfrid Scawen Blunt on the warpath against tyranny and torture, threatening to get questions asked in parliament. A new sort of tribunal in the nature of a court-martial had therefore to be invented to replace the Brigandage

Commissions; but simple British military courts-martial, though probably the best available form of official Lynch Law, were made impossible by the jealousy of the "loyal" (to England) Egyptians, who, it seems, rule the Occupation and bully England exactly as the "loyal" Irish rule the Garrison and bully the Unionists nearer home. That kind of loyalty, not being a natural product, has to be purchased; and the price is an official job of some sort with a position and a salary attached. Hence we got, in 1895, a tribunal constituted in which three English officials sat with two Egyptian officials, exercising practically unlimited powers of punishment without a jury and without appeal. They represent the best of our judicial and military officialism. And what that best is may be judged by the sentences on the Denshawai villagers.

Lord Cromer's justification of the tribunal is practically that, bad as it is, the Brigandage Commissions were worse. Also (lest we should propose to carry our moral superiority any further) that the Egyptians are so accustomed to associate law and order with floggings, executions, torture, and Lynch Law, that they will not respect any tribunal which does not continue these practices. This is a far-reaching argument: for instance, it suggests that Church of England missionaries might do well to adopt the rite of human sacrifice when evangelizing tribes in whose imagination that practice is inseparably bound up with religion. It suggests that the sole reason why the Denshawai tribunal did not resort to torture for the purpose of extorting confessions and evidence was that parliament might not stand it—though really a parliament which stood the executions would, one would think, stand anything. The tribunal had certainly no intention of allowing witnesses to testify against British officers; for, as it happened, the Ombashi who accompanied them on the two shoot-

ing expeditions, one Ahmed Hassan Zakzouk, aged 26, was rash enough to insist that after the shot that struck the woman, the officers fired on the mob twice. This appears in the parliamentary paper; but the French newspaper *L'Égypte* is quoted by Mr Wilfrid Scawen Blunt as reporting that Zakzouk, on being asked by one of the English judges whether he was not afraid to say such a thing, replied "Nobody in the world is able to frighten me: the truth is the truth," and was promptly told to stand down. Mr Blunt adds that Zakzouk was then tried for his conduct in connection with the affair before a Court of Discipline, which awarded him two years imprisonment and fifty lashes. Without rudely calling this a use of torture to intimidate anti-British witnesses, I may count on the assent of most reasonable people when I say that Zakzouk probably regards himself as having received a rather strong hint to make his evidence agreeable to the Occupation in future.

Not only was there of course no jury at the trial, but considerably less than no defence. Barristers of sufficient standing to make it very undesirable for them to offend the Occupation were instructed to "defend" the prisoners. Far from defending them, they paid high compliments to the Occupation as one of the choicest benefits rained by Heaven on their country, and appealed for mercy for their miserable clients, whose conduct had "caused the unanimous indignation of all Egyptians." "Clemency," they said, "was above equity." The tribunal in delivering judgment remarked that "the counsel for the defence had a full hearing: nevertheless the defence broke down completely, and all that their counsel could say on behalf of the prisoners practically amounted to an appeal to the mercy of the Court."

Now the proper defence, if put forward, would probably have convinced

Lord Cromer that nothing but the burning of the village and the crucifixion of all its inhabitants could preserve the British Empire. That defence was obvious enough: the village was invaded by five armed foreigners who attempted for the second time to slaughter the villagers' farming stock and carry it off; in resisting an attempt to disarm them four villagers had been wounded; the villagers had lost their tempers and knocked the invaders about; and the older men and watchmen had finally rescued the aggressors and sent them back with no worse handling than they would have got anywhere for the like misconduct.

One can imagine what would have happened to the man, prisoner or advocate, who should have dared to tell the truth in this fashion. The prisoners knew better than to attempt it. On the scaffold, Darweesh turned to his house as he stood on the trap, and exclaimed "May God compensate us well for this world of meanness, for this world of injustice, for this world of cruelty." If he had dared in court thus to compare God with the tribunal to the disadvantage of the latter, he would no doubt have had fifty lashes before his hanging, to teach him the greatness of the Empire. As it was, he kept his views to himself until it was too late to do anything worse to him than hang him. In court, he did as all the rest did. They lied; they denied; they set up desperate alibis; they protested they had been in the next village, or tending cattle a mile off, or threshing, or what not. One of them, when identified, said "All men are alike." He had only one eye. Darweesh, who had secured one of the officers' guns, declared that his enemies had come in the night and buried it in his house, where his mother sat on it, like Rachel on Laban's stolen teraphim, until she was dragged off. A pitiable business, yet not so pitiable as the virtuous indignation with which Judge Lynch, himself provable by his own judgment to be a prevaricator, hypocrite, tyrant, and coward of the first water, preened himself at its expense. When Lord Cromer, in his official apology for Judge Lynch, says that "the prisoners had a perfectly fair trial"—not, observe, a trial as little unfair as human frailty could make it, which is the most that can be said for any trial on earth, but "a *perfectly* fair trial"—he no doubt believes what he says; but his opinion is interesting mainly as an example of the state of his mind, and of the extent to which, after thirty years of official life in Egypt, one loses the plain sense of English words.

Lord Cromer recalls how, in the eighties, a man threatened with the courbash by a Moudir in the presence of Sir Claude MacDonald, said "You dare not flog me now that the British are here." "So bold an answer," says Lord Cromer, "was probably due to the presence of a British officer." What would that man say now? What does Lord Cromer say now? He deprecates "premature endeavors to thrust Western ideas on an Eastern people," by which he means that when you are in Egypt you must do as the Egyptians do: terrorize by the lash and the scaffold. Thus does the East conquer its conquerors. In 1883 Lord Dufferin was abolishing the bastinado as "a horrible and infamous punishment." In 1906 Lord Cromer guarantees ferocious sentences of flogging as "just and necessary," and can see "nothing reprehensible in the manner in which they were carried out." "I have," he adds, "passed nearly thirty years of my life in an earnest endeavor to raise the moral and material condition of the people of Egypt. I have been assisted by a number of very capable officials, all of whom, I may say, have been animated by the same spirit as myself." Egypt may well shudder as she reads those words. If the first thirty years have been crowned by the Denshawai incident, what will

Egypt be like at the end of another thirty years of moral elevation "animated by the same spirit"?

It is pleasanter to return to Lord Cromer's first letter on Denshawai, written to Sir Edward Grey the day after the shooting party. It says that "orders will shortly be issued by the General prohibiting officers in the army from shooting pigeons in the future under any circumstances whatever." But pray why this prohibition, if, as the tribunal declared, the officers were "guests [actually *guests!*] who had done nothing to deserve blame"?

Mr Findlay is another interesting official correspondent of Sir Edward. Even after the trial, at which it had been impossible to push the medical evidence further than to say that the officer who died of sunstroke had been predisposed to it by the knocking about he had suffered and by his flight under the Egyptian sun, whilst the officers who had remained defenceless in the hands of the villagers were in court, alive and well, Mr Findlay writes that the four hanged men were "convicted of a brutal and premeditated murder," and complains that "the native press disregards the fact" and "is being conducted with such an absolute disregard for truth as to make it evident that large sums of money have been expended." Mr Findlay is also a bit of a philosopher. "The Egyptian, being a fatalist," he says, "does not greatly fear death, and there is therefore much to be said for flogging as a judicial punishment in Egypt." Logically, then, the four hanged men ought to have been flogged instead. But Mr Findlay does not draw that conclusion. Logic is not his strong point: he is a man of feeling, and a very nervous one at that. "I do not believe that this brutal attack on British officers had anything directly to do with political animosity. It is, however, due to the insubordinate spirit which has been sedulously fostered during the last year by

unscrupulous and interested agitators." Again, "it is my duty to warn you of the deplorable effect which is being produced in Egypt by the fact that Members of Parliament have seriously called in question the unanimous sentence passed by a legally constituted Court, of which the best English and the best native Judge were members. This fact will, moreover, supply the lever which has, up to the present, been lacking to the venal agitators who are at the head of the so-called patriotic party." I find Mr Findlay irresistible, so exquisitely does he give us the measure and flavor of officialism. "A few days after the Denshawai affray some natives stoned and severely injured an irrigation inspector. Two days ago three natives knocked a soldier off his donkey and kicked him in the stomach: his injuries are serious. In the latter case theft appears to have been the motive. My object in mentioning these instances is to shew the results to be expected if once respect for the law is shaken. Should the present state of things continue, and, still more, should the agitation in this country find support at home, the date is not far distant when the necessity will arise for bringing in a press law and for considerably increasing the army of occupation." Just think of it! In a population of nearly ten millions, one irrigation inspector is stoned. The Denshawai executions are then carried out to make the law respected. The result is that three natives knock a soldier off his donkey and rob him. Thereupon Mr Findlay, appalled at the bankruptcy of civilization, sees nothing for it now but suppression of the native newspapers and a considerable increase in the army of occupation! And Lord Cromer writes "All I need say is that I concur generally in Mr Findlay's remarks, and that, had I remained in Egypt, I should in every respect have adopted the same course as that which he pursued."

But I must resolutely shut this rich parliamentary paper. I have extracted enough to paint the picture, and enforce my warning to England that if her Empire means ruling the world as Denshawai has been ruled in 1906—and that, I am afraid, is what the Empire does mean to the main body of our aristocratic-military caste and to our Jingo plutocrats—then there can be no more sacred and urgent political duty on earth than the disruption, defeat, and suppression of the Empire, and, incidentally, the humanization of its supporters by the sternest lessons of that adversity which comes finally to institutions which make themselves abhorred by the aspiring will of humanity towards divinity. As for the Egyptians, any man cradled by the Nile who, after the Denshawai incident, will ever voluntarily submit to British rule, or accept any bond with us except the bond of a Federation of free and equal states, will deserve the worst that Lord Cromer can consider "just and necessary" for him. That is what you get by attempting to prove your supremacy by the excesses of frightened soldiers and denaturalized officials instead of by courageous helpfulness and moral superiority.

In any case let no Englishman who is content to leave Abd-el-Nebi and his twenty-year-old neighbor in penal servitude for life, and to plume himself on the power to do it, pretend to be fit to govern either my country or his own. The responsibility cannot be confined to the tribunal and to the demoralized officials of the Occupation. The House of Commons had twenty-four hours clear notice, with the telegraph under the hand of Sir Edward Grey, to enable it to declare that England was a civilized Power and would not stand these barbarous lashings and vindictive hangings. Yet Mr Dillon, representing the Irish party, which well knows what British Occupations and Findlay "loyalism" mean, protested in vain. Sir Edward, on behalf of the new Liberal Government (still simmering with virtuous indignation at the flogging of Chinamen and the military executions in South Africa in the forced presence of the victims' families under the late Imperialist Government), not only permitted and defended the Denshawai executions, but appealed to the House almost passionately not to criticize or repudiate them, on the ground—how incredible it now appears!—that Abd-el-Nebi and Hassan Mahfouz and Darweesh and the rest were the fuglemen of a gigantic Moslem plot to rise against Christendom in the name of the Prophet and sweep Christendom out of Africa and Asia by a colossal second edition of the Indian Mutiny. That this idiotic romance, gross and ridiculous as the lies of Falstaff, should have imposed on any intelligent and politically experienced human being, is strange enough—though the secret shame of revolted humanity will make cabinet ministers snatch at fantastic excuses—but what humanity will not forgive our foreign secretary for is his failure to see that even if such a conspiracy really existed, England should have faced it and fought it bravely by honorable means, instead of wildly lashing and strangling a handful of poor peasants to scare Islam into terrified submission. Were I abject enough to grant to Sir Edward Grey as valid that main asset of "thinking Imperially," the conviction that we are all going to be murdered, I should still suggest to him that we can at least die like gentlemen? Might I even be so personal as to say that the reason for giving him a social position and political opportunities that are denied to his tradesmen is that he is supposed to understand better than they that honor is worth its danger and its cost, and that life is worthless without honor? It is true that Sir John Falstaff did not think so; but Sir John is hardly a model for Sir Edward.

Yet even Sir John would have had enough gumption to see that the Denshawai panic was more dangerous to the Empire than the loss of ten pitched battles.

As cowardice is highly infectious, would it not be desirable to supersede officials who, after years of oriental service, have lost the familiar art of concealing their terrors? I am myself a sedentary literary civilian, constitutionally timid; but I find it possible to keep up appearances, and can even face the risk of being run over, or garotted, or burnt out in London without shrieking for martial law, suppression of the newspapers, exemplary flogging and hanging of motorbus drivers, and compulsory police service. Why are soldiers and officials on foreign service so much more cowardly than citizens? Is it not clearly because the whole Imperial military system of coercion and terrorism is unnatural, and that the truth formulated by William Morris that "no man is good enough to be another man's master" is true also of nations, and very specially true of those plutocrat-ridden Powers which have of late stumbled into an enormous increase of material wealth without having made any intelligent provision for its proper distribution and administration?

However, the economic reform of the Empire is a long business, whereas the release of Abd-el-Nebi and his neighbors is a matter of the stroke of a pen, once public opinion is shamed into activity. I fear I have stated their case very unfairly and inadequately, because I am hampered, as an Irishman, by my implacable hostility to English domination. Mistrusting my own prejudices, I have taken the story from the two parliamentary papers in which our officials have done their utmost to whitewash the tribunals and the pigeon-shooting party, and to blackwash the villagers. Those who wish to have it told to them by an Englishman of unquestionable personal and social credentials, and an intimate knowledge of Egypt and the Egyptians, can find it in Mr Wilfrid Scawen Blunt's pamphlet entitled "Atrocities of British Rule in Egypt." When they have read it they will appreciate my forbearance; and when I add that English rule in Ireland has been "animated by the same spirit" (I thank Lord Cromer for the phrase) as English rule in Egypt, and that this is the inevitable spirit of all coercive military rule, they will perhaps begin to understand why Home Rule is a necessity not only for Ireland, but for all constituents of those Federations of Commonwealths which are now the only permanently practicable form of Empire.

POSTSCRIPT. These sheets had passed through the press when the news came of Lord Cromer's resignation. As he accuses himself of failing health, he will perhaps forgive me for accusing him of failing judgment, and for suggesting that his retirement from office might well be celebrated in Egypt by the retirement, at his intercession, of Abd-el-Nebi and the rest from penal servitude.

A YEAR LATER. It may be a relief to some of my readers to learn that very shortly after the publication of the above account of the Denshawai atrocity, I received a private assurance that Abd-el-Nebi and his fellow-prisoners would be released on the following New Year's Day, which is the customary occasion in Egypt for such acts of grace and clemency as the Occupation may allow the Khedive to perform, and that in the meantime their detention would not be rigorous. As the hanged men could not be unhanged nor the flogged men unflogged, this was all that could be done. I am bound to add, in justice to the Government, that this was, as far as I could ascertain, an act of pure conscience on the part of the Cabinet: for there was no sign of any serious pressure of public opinion. One or two newspapers seemed to be amused at my calling the Denshawai villagers Denshavians; but they shewed no other interest in the matter: another illustration of how hopeless it is to induce one modern nation, preoccupied as it necessarily is with its own affairs, to take any real interest in the welfare of another, even when it professes to govern that other in a superior manner for its good. Sir Edward Grey's reputation as a great Minister for Foreign Affairs was not shaken in the least: the eulogies which were heaped on him by both parties increased in volume; and an attempt which I made to call attention to the real character of the Anglo-Russian agreement as to Persia, which was held up as a masterpiece of his diplomacy (I was apparently the only person who had taken the trouble to read it) had no effect. Not until Sir Edward ventured to threaten a really formidable European Power in 1911, and threatened it successfully from his point of view, did a sudden and violent agitation against him spring up. Until then, men of both parties idolized him without knowing why, just as they had formerly idolized Lord Cromer and Lord Milner without knowing why. They will now very possibly turn on him and rend him, also without knowing why. The one thing they will not do is to blame themselves, which is the only blaming that can be of any profit to them.

TWENTYFOUR YEARS LATER. The sequel to these events confirmed my unheeded warning with a sanguinary completeness of which I had no prevision. At Easter 1916 a handful of Irishmen seized the Dublin Post Office and proclaimed an Irish Republic, with one of their number, a schoolmaster named Pearse, as President. If all Ireland had risen at this gesture it would have been a serious matter for England, then up to her neck in the war against the Central Empires. But there was no response: the gesture was a complete failure. All that was necessary was to blockade the Post Office until its microcosmic republic was starved out and made ridiculous. What actually happened would be incredible if there were not so many living witnesses of it. From a battery planted at Trinity College (the Irish equivalent of Oxford University), and from a warship in the river Liffey, a bombardment was poured on the centre of the city which reduced more than a square mile of it to such a condition that when, in the following year, I was taken through Arras and Ypres to shew me what the German artillery had done to these cities in two and a half years, I laughed and said, "You should see what the British artillery did to my native city in a week." It would not be true to say that not one stone was left upon another; for the marksmanship was so bad that the Post Office itself was left standing amid a waste of rubbish heaps; and enough scraps of wall were left for the British Army, which needed recruits, to cover with appeals to the Irish to remember Belgium lest the fate of Louvain should befall their own hearths and homes.

Having thus worked up a harebrained romantic adventure into a heroic episode in the struggle for Irish freedom, the victorious artillerists proceeded to kill their prisoners of war in a drawn-out string of executions. Those who were executed accordingly became not only national heroes, but the martyrs whose blood was the seed of the present Irish Free State. Among those who escaped was its first President. Nothing more blindly savage, stupid, and terror-mad could have been devised by England's worst enemies. It was a very characteristic example of the mentality produced by the conventional gentleman-militarist education at Marlborough and Sandhurst and the conventional gentleman-diplomatist education at Eton and Oxford, Harrow and Cambridge. Is it surprising that the Russian Soviet Government, though fanatically credulous as to the need for popular education, absolutely refused to employ as teachers anyone who had been touched by the equivalent public school and university routine in Russia, and stuck to its resolution even at the cost of carrying on for some years with teachers who were hardly a day ahead of their pupils?

But the Post Office episode was eclipsed by an event which was much more than an episode, as it shattered the whole case for parliamentary government throughout the world. The Irish Nationalists, after thirty years of constitutional procedure in the British Parliament, had carried an Act to establish Irish Home Rule, as it was then called, which duly received the royal assent and became a statute of the realm. Immediately the British officers on service in Ireland mutinied, refusing to enforce the Act or operate against the northern Orangemen who were openly arming themselves to resist it. They were assured of support by their fellow-officers at home. The Act was suspended after prominent English statesmen had taken part in the military manœuvres of the Orangemen. The Prime Minister publicly pledged himself that Belfast, the Orange capital, would not in any case be coerced. In short, the Act was shelved under a threat of civil war; and the Clan na Gael, which in America had steadfastly maintained that the constitutional movement was useless, as England would in the last resort repudiate the constitution and hold Ireland against the Irish by physical force, and had been rebuked, lectured, and repudiated by the parliamentary Home Rulers for a whole generation for saying so, was justified. The Catholic Irish accordingly armed themselves and drilled as Volunteers in spite of the hostility of the Government, which meanwhile gave every possible

assistance to the parallel preparations of the Orangemen. An Irish parliament (or Dail) sat in Dublin and claimed to be the national government. Irish courts were set up for the administration of Irish justice; Irish order was kept by Irish police; Irish taxes were collected by Irish officials; and British courts were boycotted. Upon this interesting but hopeless attempt to ignore British rule the Government let loose a specially recruited force (known to history as the Black and Tans) with *carte blanche* to kill, burn, and destroy, save only that they must stop short of rapine. They wrecked the Irish courts and produced a state of anarchy. They struck at the Irish through the popular co-operative stores and creameries, which they burnt. The people found a civil leader in Arthur Griffiths and a military one in Michael Collins. The Black and Tans had the British Government at their back: Collins had the people at his back. He threatened that for every creamery or co-operative store or cabin or cottage burnt by the Black and Tans he would burn two country houses of the Protestant gentry. The country houses that were not burnt were raided at night and laid under contribution for needed supplies. If the occupants reported the raid, the house was burnt. The Black and Tans and the ordinary constabulary were treated as enemies in uniform: that is, they were shot at sight and their stations burnt; or they were ambushed and killed in petty battles. Those who gave warnings or information of any helpful kind to them were mercilessly executed without privilege of sex or benefit of clergy. Collins, with allies in every street and hamlet, proved able to carry out his threat. He won the crown of the Reign of Terror; and the position of the Protestant gentry became unbearable.

Thus by fire and bullet, murder and torture and devastation, a situation was produced in which the British Government had either to capitulate at the cost of a far more complete concession of self-government to Ireland than that decreed by the repudiated Home Rule Act, or to let loose the military strength of England in a Cromwellian reconquest, massacre, and replantation which it knew that public opinion in England and America would not tolerate; for some of the most conspicuous English champions of Ulster warned the Government that they could stand no more of the Black and Tan terrorism. And so we settled the Irish Question, not as civilized and reasonable men should have settled it, but as dogs settle a dispute over a bone.

Future historians will probably see in these catastrophes a ritual of human sacrifice without which the savages of the twentieth century could not effect any redistribution of political power or wealth. Nothing was learnt from Denshawai or the Black and Tan terror. In India, which is still struggling for self-government, and obviously must finally have it, a military panic led to the cannonading of a forbidden public meeting at Amritsar, the crowd being dealt with precisely as if it were a body of German shocktroops rushing the British trenches in Flanders. In London the police would have broken a score or two of heads and dragged a handful of ringleaders to the police courts. And there was the usual combination of mean spite with hyperbolical violence. Indians were forced to crawl past official buildings on their hands and knees. The effect was to make British imperial rule ridiculous in Europe, and implacably resented in India.

In Egypt the British domination died of Denshawai; but at its deathbed the British Sirdar was assassinated, whereupon the British Government, just then rather drunk after a sweeping election victory secured by an anti-Russian scare, announced to an amazed world that it was going to cut off the Nile at its source

and destroy Egypt by stopping its water supply. Of course nothing happened but an ignominious climb down; but the incident illustrates my contention that our authority, when it is too far flung (as our patriotic rhapsodists put it), goes stark mad at the periphery if a pin drops. As to what further panics and atrocities will ensue before India is left to govern itself as much as Ireland and Egypt now are I am in the dark until the event enlightens me. But on the folly of allowing military counsels to prevail in political settlements I may point to the frontiers established by the victors after the war of 1914–18. Almost every one of these frontiers has a new war implicit in it, because the soldier recognizes no ethnographical, linguistic, or moral boundaries: he demands a line that he can defend, or rather that Napoleon or Wellington could have defended; for he has not yet learnt to think of offence and defence in terms of airplanes which ignore his Waterloo ridges. And the inevitable nationalist rebellions against these military frontiers, and the atrocities by which they are countered, are in full swing as I write.

Meanwhile, John Bull's Other Island, though its freedom has destroyed all the romantic interest that used to attach to it, has become at last highly interesting to the student of political science as an experiment in political structure. Protestant Ulster, which armed against the rest of Ireland and defied the British Parliament to the cry of "We wont have it," meaning that they would die in the last ditch singing "O God, our help in ages past" rather than suffer or tolerate Home Rule, is now suffering and indeed hugging Home Rule on a much more homely scale than the Home Rulers ever demanded or dreamt of; for it has a Belfast Home Rule Parliament instead of an Irish one. And it has allowed Catholic Ireland to secure the Irish parliament. Thus, of the two regional parliaments which have been established on a sectarian basis, Protestant Ulster has been left with the smaller. Now it happens that Protestant Ulster is industrial Ireland and Catholic Ireland agricultural Ireland. And throughout the world for a century past the farmer, the peasant, and the Catholic have been the bulwark of the industrial capitalists against the growing political power of the industrial proletariat organized in trade unions, Labor parties, and the ubiquitous sodalities of that new ultra-Catholic Church called Socialism.

From this defensive alliance the Ulster employers, blinded by an obsolete bigotry and snobbery, have deliberately cut themselves off. In my preface of 1906, and again in my 1912 preface to a sixpenny edition of this play called the Home Rule edition, I exhorted the Protestants to take their chance, trust their grit, and play their part in a single parliament ruling an undivided Ireland. They did not take my advice. Probably they did not even read it, being too deeply absorbed in the History of Maria Monk, or the latest demonstration that all the evil in the world is the work of an underground conspiracy entitled by them "the Jesuits." It is a pity they did not begin their political education, as I began mine, by reading Karl Marx. It is true that I had occasion to point out that Marx was not infallible; but he left me with a very strong disposition to back the economic situation to control all the other situations, religious, nationalist, or romantic, in the long run. And so I do not despair of seeing Protestant Ulster seeking the alliance it repudiated. The Northern Parliament will not merge into the Oireachtas; for until both of them are superseded by a completely modernized central government, made for action and not for obstruction, they will remain more effective as regional parliaments than they would be as national ones; but they will soon have to take counsel together through conferences which will recur until they become a permanent institution and finally develop into what the Americans call Congress, or Federal Government of the whole island. No doubt this will be received in Belfast (if noticed at all) with shouts of "We wont have it." But I have heard that cry before, and regard it as a very hopeful sign that they will have it gladly enough when they have the luck to get it.

AYOT ST LAWRENCE,
November 1929.

XVIII

FAMILY LIFE IN GERMANY UNDER THE BLOCKADE
1919

We are at present [1919] at a climax of national exultation over the most magnificent military triumph in our long record of victory. We are the happiest and proudest of empires. Such pageantry of peace, such panoply of war, has never before been seen by living men. The defeat of the Armada, the overthrow of Louis XIV, the conquest of India and Canada, the chaining of Napoleon, were child's play to this last and most tremendous of our exploits. We have stretched out a mighty hand upon the most dreaded power in the world (except ourselves) and choked it until it lies half dead at our feet, buying its bare life from us by concessions so abject that the more generous souls among us are ashamed of having exacted so much. We have been taken into the high mountain as of old; and we have not turned our backs on the power and the glory offered to us.

But the splendor of the end, which is the work of our imagination, had better not blind us to the grimness of the means, which were the work of our hands. Triumphs of this kind cannot be had for nothing. It is now too late to ask whether this one was worth what it cost: the question is not merely could we afford another (our military authorities are already urging us to prepare for it), but whether we can afford to push this one any further, or even to refrain from undoing, as far as possible, a good deal of what we have done, and saving as many lives as we can from the wreck we have made. When Napoleon caught the Russians on a frozen lake, he turned his guns on the ice and broke it. He then took extraordinary pains to rescue the drowning soldiers. Once they were defeated he had no quarrel with them. To win this war, we did a far more horrible thing than the ice-breaking. We starved the children of Germany, and of many other lands as well. Having defeated our enemies by that means, are we going to feed the starving children as Napoleon rescued the drowning soldiers, or are we out, not merely for defeat, but for extermination?

Superficially, extermination seems a logical procedure both during the war and after the victory. But it never works smoothly. When soldiers are asked to do it they refuse, because the fortune of the vanquished may be that of the victor tomorrow; and just as prize-fighting would be impossible if pugilists were not protected by a very strict limitation of the extent to which the winner may abuse his victory, so war would be impossible if there were not precisely analogous limits to the abuse of military victories in the field. Everyone must have noticed during the war the contrast between the ferocity of our civilians and the reasonableness and compunction of our soldiers from the front, even of the wounded soldiers who had suffered personally and acutely from the operations of the enemy. The civilian called the German the Hun, and, in the comparative safety of home, clamored for his extermination with a full mouth. The soldier called him Jerry, meaning "companion in misfortune," and spoke no evil of him except when he was specifically ordered to. When the civilian mercilessly went on starving the German children after the armistice, the British soldier fed them out of his rations; and it was from the army that the first protest came against the infernal cruelty of the continued blockade.

This does not mean that the British civilian is one sort of person and the

British soldier another. It means that the civilian neither sees nor knows what he is doing, and that the soldier sees it and has to do it. In Coventry it is easy to forget all about the German children, and work yourself up into a drunken frenzy of determination that the Kaiser shall be hanged to avenge the victims of the submarine campaign. In Cologne, with famine-wasted children begging for the refuse of your meals, or mutely watching every morsel you eat with a hungry eye, it is impossible. In the early days of voluntary recruiting, we were exhorted from every hoarding to remember that some day our children would ask us what we did in the great war. That question was dropped when compulsory military service was instituted. It might very well be revived in the form, "Daddy: what did you do when the war was over?" The man who can say "I shared my ration with the poor starving children in Germany," will have a considerable moral advantage over the ardent patriot who has nothing better to say than "I voted for hanging the Kaiser; and he was not hanged after all."

But even men who are naturally cruel, or so desperately afraid of the Germans that no victory can reassure them, are sooner or later forced to behave themselves by economic considerations. If we and the Germans were two Red Indian tribes, each sufficient to itself for all its needs, then one could exterminate the other and feel all the safer for it without being a penny the worse, except for the incidental casualties. Many of our journalists, like the citizens who accept them as their political instructors, have such primitive notions of society that they are unable to conceive European relations as anything more complicated. But if this were so, we could never have starved Germany, and the war would still be going on with a prospect of lasting until human nature could no longer bear it. Germany was beaten because she was de-

pendent for her very existence on trade with her enemies. But trade means exchange of goods. If Germany lived by selling her products to us, we lived equally by selling our products to Germany. Our blockade cut Germany off from all alternative sources, and so starved her out; but there were moments during the war when Germany, by her submarine campaign, came so near to cutting us off that for some months we read the lists of sunken ships with our hearts in our mouths. It was a frightful starving match, and for nearly a year we were racing neck and neck, or at least seemed to be; for we did not then know how impossible it was for Germany to keep up her submarine fleet.

However, from our point of view all's well that ends well. We won the race. But how is our trade with Germany to be restored? Our primitives say that they do not want it to be restored. They will never shake hands with a Hun as long as they live. They will never buy from him or sell to him. In other words, they have not sense enough to understand modern civilization. In the very same breath with which they gasp out these follies, they declare that Germany must be made to pay for the war; and the Peace Treaty has already imposed on the vanquished a colossal tribute. How is that tribute to be paid if German industry is ruined and German labor is starving? Granted that the Germans are to be our slaves for the next fifty years, must not slaves be fed as well as beaten? There is nothing to be got out of beating them except labor; and how can they labor if they are not fed? Stick is not a very productive diet, is it?

The tribute can be paid only if Germany buys things from us at more than cost price, and sells things to us at less than cost price until her ransom is paid. There is no other way in which it can be done under existing European conditions. That means that German production must continue side-by-side with British production. If we are to have the spoils of victory, German industry must be restored. And if German industry is to be restored, German labor must be fed. That is why, in starving the Germans, we are biting our noses to spite our faces. If our vengeance-mongers cannot divine by spiritual intuition that we are members one of another, they will have it rubbed into them most unsympathetically and uncomfortably by the hard fact that there will be no business doing in many of their own trades until German demand revives: that is, until Germany is producing enough to pay *more than enough* for British goods.

The pages which follow do not go into this economic consideration. They appeal, not to an elementary knowledge of international trade and finance, which most of their readers unfortunately do not possess, but simply, like Athenian tragedy, to pity and horror. There is no literary art about them: they just say crudely to the British conqueror, "Thus didst thou." If he replies that he could not help it, he must be told that he can help it now. The military necessity for starvation has passed: it is now not only a vile revenge on the innocent, but a suicidal blunder.

Also, it is a dangerous precedent. We were able to form an irresistible combination against the late German Empire solely because it had made itself feared throughout the world, and because its military traditions had boasted overmuch of their pseudo-realism and real ruthlessness. Now that we have cast it down from that perilous eminence, we have left ourselves in the position of the most dreaded nation militarily. If we, too, now set up a tradition of the same spurious realism and genuine ruthlessness, the Germany we have emancipated will find it quite easy to form a combination against us which may one day leave us at the mercy of those who are now at our mercy. The old rule, "Treat your friend as one who may some day be your enemy, and your enemy as one who may some day be your friend," is hardly the golden rule; but it is a sound one for those who scorn golden rules.

Let us look to it accordingly.

RELIGIOUS

XIX

BACK TO METHUSELAH

1921

THE INFIDEL HALF CENTURY

THE DAWN OF DARWINISM

One day early in the eighteen hundred and sixties, I, being then a small boy, was with my nurse, buying something in the shop of a petty newsagent, bookseller, and stationer in Camden Street, Dublin, when there entered an elderly man, weighty and solemn, who advanced to the counter, and said pompously, "Have you the works of the celebrated Buffoon?"

My own works were at that time unwritten, or it is possible that the shop assistant might have misunderstood me so far as to produce a copy of Man and Superman. As it was, she knew quite well what he wanted; for this was before the Education Act of 1870 had produced shop assistants who know how to read and know nothing else. The celebrated Buffoon was not a humorist, but the famous naturalist Buffon. Every literate child at that time knew Buffon's Natural History as well as Esop's Fables. And no living child had heard the name that has since obliterated Buffon's in the popular consciousness: the name of Darwin.

Ten years elapsed. The celebrated Buffoon was forgotten; I had doubled my years and my length; and I had discarded the religion of my forefathers. One day the richest and consequently most dogmatic of my uncles came into a restaurant where I was dining, and found himself, much against his will, in conversation with the most questionable of his nephews. By way of making myself agreeable, I spoke of modern thought and Darwin. He said, "Oh, thats the fellow who wants to make out that we all have tails like monkeys." I tried to explain that what Darwin had

insisted on in this connection was that some monkeys have no tails. But my uncle was as impervious to what Darwin really said as any Neo-Darwinian nowadays. He died impenitent, and did not mention me in his will.

Twenty years elapsed, If my uncle had been alive, he would have known all about Darwin, and known it all wrong. In spite of the efforts of Grant Allen to set him right, he would have accepted Darwin as the discoverer of Evolution, of Heredity, and of modification of species by Selection. For the pre-Darwinian age had come to be regarded as a Dark Age in which men still believed that the book of Genesis was a standard scientific treatise, and that the only additions to it were Galileo's demonstration of Leonardo da Vinci's simple remark that the earth is a moon of the sun, Newton's theory of gravitation, Sir Humphry Davy's invention of the safety-lamp, the discovery of electricity, the application of steam to industrial purposes, and the penny post. It was just the same in other subjects. Thus Nietzsche, by the two or three who had come across his writings, was supposed to have been the first man to whom it occurred that mere morality and legality and urbanity lead nowhere, as if Bunyan had never written Badman. Schopenhauer was credited with inventing the distinction between the Covenant of Grace and the Covenant of Works which troubled Cromwell on his deathbed. People talked as if there had been no dramatic or descriptive music before Wagner; no impressionist painting before Whistler; whilst as to myself, I was finding that the surest way to produce an effect of daring innovation and originality was to revive the ancient attraction of long rhetorical speeches; to stick closely to the methods of Molière; and to lift characters bodily out of the pages of Charles Dickens.

THE ADVENT OF THE NEO-DARWINIANS

This particular sort of ignorance does not always or often matter. But in Darwin's case it did matter. If Darwin had really led the world at one bound from the book of Genesis to Heredity, to Modification of Species by Selection, and to Evolution, he would have been a philosopher and a prophet as well as an eminent professional naturalist, with geology as a hobby. The delusion that he had actually achieved this feat did no harm at first, because if people's views are sound, about evolution or anything else, it does not make two straws difference whether they call the revealer of their views Tom or Dick. But later on such apparently negligible errors have awkward consequences. Darwin was given an imposing reputation as not only an Evolutionist, but as *the* Evolutionist, with the immense majority who never read his books. The few who never read any others were led by them to concentrate exclusively on Circumstantial Selection as the explanation of all the transformations and adaptations which were the evidence for Evolution. And they presently found themselves so cut off by this specialization from the majority who knew Darwin only by his spurious reputation, that they were obliged to distinguish themselves, not as Darwinians, but as Neo-Darwinians.

Before ten more years had elapsed, the Neo-Darwinians were practically running current Science. It was 1906; I was fifty; I had published my own view of evolution in a play called Man and Superman; and I found that most people were unable to understand how I could be an Evolutionist and not a Neo-Darwinian, or why I habitually derided Neo-Darwinism as a ghastly idiocy, and would fall on its professors slaughterously in public discussions. It was in the hope of making me clear the matter up that the Fabian Society, which was then organizing a series of lectures on Prophets of the Nineteenth Century, asked me to deliver a lecture on the prophet Darwin. I did so; and scraps of that lecture, which was never published, variegate these pages.

POLITICAL INADEQUACY OF THE HUMAN ANIMAL

Ten more years elapsed. Neo-Darwinism in politics had produced a European catastrophe of a magnitude so appalling, and a scope so unpredictable, that as I write these lines in 1920, it is still far from certain whether our civilization will survive it. The circumstances of this catastrophe, the boyish cinema-fed romanticism which made it possible to impose it on the people as a crusade, and especially the ignorance and errors of the victors of Western Europe when its violent phase had passed and the time for reconstruction arrived, confirmed a doubt which had grown steadily in my mind during my forty years public work as a Socialist: namely, whether the human animal, as he exists at present, is capable of solving the social problems raised by his own aggregation, or, as he calls it, his civilization.

COWARDICE OF THE IRRELIGIOUS

Another observation I had made was that goodnatured unambitious men are cowards when they have no religion. They are dominated and exploited not only by greedy and often half-witted and half-alive weaklings who will do anything for cigars, champagne, motor cars, and the more childish and selfish uses of money, but by able and sound administrators who can do nothing else with them than dominate and exploit them. Government and exploitation become synonymous under such circumstances; and the world is finally ruled by the childish, the brigands, and the blackguards. Those who refuse to stand in with them are persecuted and occasionally executed when they give any trouble to the exploiters. They fall into poverty when they lack lucrative specific talents. At the present moment one half of Europe, having knocked the other half down, is trying to kick it to death, and may succeed: a procedure which is, logically, sound Neo-Darwinism. And the goodnatured majority are looking on in helpless horror, or allowing themselves to be persuaded by the newspapers of their exploiters that the kicking is not only a sound commercial investment, but an act of divine justice of which they are the ardent instruments.

But if Man is really incapable of organizing a big civilization, and cannot organize even a village or a tribe any too well, what is the use of giving him a religion? A religion may make him hunger and thirst for righteousness: but will it endow him with the practical capacity to satisfy that appetite? Good intentions do not carry with them a grain of political science, which is a very complicated one. The most devoted and indefatigable, the most able and disinterested students of this science in England, as far as I know, are my friends Sidney and Beatrice Webb. It has taken them forty years of preliminary work, in the course of which they have published several treatises comparable to Adam Smith's Wealth of Nations, to formulate a political constitution adequate to existing needs. If this is the measure of what can be done in a lifetime by extraordinary ability, keen natural aptitude, exceptional opportunities, and freedom from the preoccupations of breadwinning, what are we to expect from the parliament man to whom political science is as remote and distasteful as the differential calculus, and to whom such an elementary but vital point as the law of economic rent is a *pons asinorum* never to be approached, much less crossed? Or from the common voter who is mostly so hard at work all day earning a living that he cannot keep awake for five minutes over a book?

IS THERE ANY HOPE IN EDUCATION?

The usual answer is that we must educate our masters: that is, ourselves. We must teach citizenship and political science at school. But must we? There is no must about it, the hard fact being that we must *not* teach political science or citizenship at school. The schoolmaster who attempted it would soon find himself penniless in the streets without pupils, if not in the dock pleading to a pompously worded indictment for sedition against the exploiters. Our schools teach the morality of feudalism corrupted by commercialism, and hold up the military conqueror, the robber baron, and the profiteer, as models of the illustrious and the successful. In vain do the prophets who see through this imposture preach and teach a better gospel: the individuals whom they convert are doomed to pass away in a few years; and the new generations are dragged back in the schools to the morality of the fifteenth century, and think themselves Liberal when they are defending the ideas of Henry VII, and gentlemanly when they are opposing to them the ideas of Richard III. Thus the educated man is a greater nuisance than the uneducated one: indeed it is the inefficiency and sham of the educational side of our schools (to which, except under compulsion, children would not be sent by their parents at all if they did not act as prisons in which the immature are kept from worrying the mature) that save us from being dashed on the rocks of false doctrine instead of drifting down the midstream of mere ignorance. There is no way out through the schoolmaster.

R

HOMEOPATHIC EDUCATION

In truth, mankind cannot be saved from without, by schoolmasters or any other sort of masters: it can only be lamed and enslaved by them. It is said that if you wash a cat it will never again wash itself. This may or may not be true: what is certain is that if you teach a man anything he will never learn it; and if you cure him of a disease he will be unable to cure himself the next time it attacks him. Therefore, if you want to see a cat clean, you throw a bucket of mud over it, when it will immediately take extraordinary pains to lick the mud off, and finally be cleaner than it was before. In the same way doctors who are up-to-date (say ·00005 per cent of all the registered practitioners, and 20 per cent of the unregistered ones), when they want to rid you of a disease or a symptom, inoculate you with that disease or give you a drug that produces that symptom, in order to provoke you to resist it as the mud provokes the cat to wash itself.

Now an acute person will ask me why, if this be so, our false education does not provoke our scholars to find out the truth. My answer is that it sometimes does. Voltaire was a pupil of the Jesuits; Samuel Butler was the pupil of a hopelessly conventional and erroneous country parson. But then Voltaire was Voltaire, and Butler was Butler: that is, their minds were so abnormally strong that they could throw off the doses of poison that paralyze ordinary minds. When the doctors inoculate you and the homeopathists dose you, they give you an infinitesimally attenuated dose. If they gave you the virus at full strength it would overcome your resistance and produce its direct effect. The doses of false doctrine given at public schools and universities are so big that they overwhelm the resistance that a tiny dose would provoke. The normal student is corrupted beyond redemption, and will drive the genius who resists out of the country if he can. Byron and Shelley had to fly to Italy, whilst Castlereagh and Eldon ruled the roost at home. Rousseau was hunted from frontier to frontier; Karl Marx starved in exile in a Soho lodging; Ruskin's articles were refused by the magazines (he was too rich to be otherwise persecuted), whilst mindless forgotten nonentities governed the land; sent men to the prison or the gallows for blasphemy and sedition (meaning the truth about Church and State); and sedulously stored up the social disease and corruption which explode from time to time in gigantic boils that have to be lanced by a million bayonets. This is the result of allopathic education. Homeopathic education has not yet been officially tried, and would obviously be a delicate matter if it were. A body of schoolmasters inciting their pupils to infinitesimal peccadilloes with the object of provoking them to exclaim, "Get thee behind me, Satan," or telling them white lies about history for the sake of being contradicted, insulted, and refuted, would certainly do less harm than our present educational allopaths do; but then nobody will advocate homeopathic education. Allopathy has produced the poisonous illusion that it enlightens instead of darkening. The suggestion may, however, explain why, whilst most people's minds succumb to inculcation and environment, a few react vigorously: honest and decent people coming from thievish slums, and sceptics and realists from country parsonages.

THE DIABOLICAL EFFICIENCY OF TECHNICAL EDUCATION

But meanwhile—and here comes the horror of it—our technical instruction is honest and efficient. The public schoolboy who is carefully blinded, duped, and corrupted as to the nature of a society based on profiteering, and is taught to honor parasitic idleness and luxury, learns to shoot and ride and keep fit with all the assistance and guidance that can be procured for him by the most anxiously sincere desire that he may do these things well, and if possible superlatively well. In the army he learns to fly; to drop bombs; to use machine - guns to the utmost of his capacity. The discovery of high explosives is rewarded and dignified: instruction in the manufacture of the weapons, battleships, submarines, and land batteries by which they are applied destructively, is quite genuine: the instructors know their business, and really mean the learners to succeed. The result is that powers of destruction that could hardly without uneasiness be entrusted to infinite wisdom and infinite benevolence are placed in the hands of romantic schoolboy patriots who, however generous by nature, are by education ignoramuses, dupes, snobs, and sportsmen to whom fighting is a religion and killing an accomplishment; whilst political power, useless under such circumstances except to militarist imperialists in chronic terror of invasion and subjugation, pompous tufthunting fools, commercial adventurers to whom the organization by the nation of its own industrial services would mean checkmate, financial parasites on the money market, and stupid people who cling to the *status quo* merely because they are used to it, is obtained by heredity, by simple purchase, by keeping newspapers and pretending that they are organs of public opinion, by the wiles of seductive women, and by prostituting ambitious talent to the service of the profiteers, who call the tune because, having secured all the spare plunder, they alone can afford to pay the piper. Neither the rulers nor the ruled understand high politics. They do not even know that there is such a branch of knowledge as political science; but between them they can coerce and enslave with the deadliest efficiency, even to the wiping out of civilization, because their education as slayers has been honestly and thoroughly carried out. Essentially the rulers are all defectives; and there is nothing worse than government by defectives who wield irresistible powers of physical coercion. The commonplace sound people submit, and compel the rest to submit, because they have been taught to do so as an article of religion and a point of honor. Those in whom natural enlightenment has reacted against artificial education submit because they are compelled; but they would resist, and finally resist effectively, if they were not cowards. And they are cowards because they have neither an officially accredited and established religion nor a generally recognized point of honor, and are all at sixes and sevens with their various private speculations, sending their children perforce to the schools where they will be corrupted for want of any other schools. The rulers are equally intimidated by the immense extension and cheapening of the means of slaughter and destruction. The British Government is more afraid of Ireland now that submarines, bombs, and poison gas are cheap and easily made than it was of the German Empire before the war; consequently the old British caution which maintained a balance of power through command of the sea is intensified into a terror that sees security in nothing short of absolute military mastery of the entire globe: that is, in an impossibility that will yet seem possible in detail to soldiers and to parochial and insular patriotic civilians.

FLIMSINESS OF CIVILIZATION

This situation has occurred so often before, always with the same result of a collapse of civilization (Professor Flinders Petrie has let out the secret of previous collapses), that the rich are instinctively crying "Let us eat and drink; for tomorrow we die," and the poor, "How long, O Lord, how long?" But the pitiless reply still is that God helps those who help themselves. This does not mean that if Man cannot find the remedy no remedy will be found. The power that produced Man when the monkey was not up to the mark, can produce a higher creature than Man if Man does not come up to the mark. What it means is that if Man is to be saved, Man must save himself. There seems no compelling reason why he should be saved. He is by no means an ideal creature. At his present best many of his ways are so unpleasant that they are unmentionable in polite society, and so painful that he is compelled to pretend that pain is often a good. Nature holds no brief for the human experiment: it must stand or fall by its results. If Man will not serve, Nature will try another experiment.

What hope is there then of human improvement? According to the Neo-Darwinists, to the Mechanists, no hope whatever, because improvement can come only through some senseless accident which must, on the statistical average of accidents, be presently wiped out by some other equally senseless accident.

CREATIVE EVOLUTION

But this dismal creed does not discourage those who believe that the impulse that produces evolution is creative. They have observed the simple fact that the will to do anything can and does, at a certain pitch of intensity set up by conviction of its necessity, create and organize new tissue to do it with. To them therefore mankind is by no means played out yet. If the weight lifter, under the trivial stimulus of an athletic competition, can "put up a muscle," it seems reasonable to believe that an equally earnest and convinced philosopher could "put up a brain." Both are directions of vitality to a certain end. Evolution shews us this direction of

vitality doing all sorts of things: providing the centipede with a hundred legs, and ridding the fish of any legs at all; building lungs and arms for the land and gills and fins for the sea; enabling the mammal to gestate its young inside its body, and the fowl to incubate hers outside it; offering us, we may say, our choice of any sort of bodily contrivance to maintain our activity and increase our resources.

VOLUNTARY LONGEVITY

Among other matters apparently changeable at will is the duration of individual life. Weismann, a very clever and suggestive biologist who was unhappily reduced to idiocy by Neo-Darwinism pointed out that death is not an eternal condition of life, but an expedient introduced to provide for continual renewal without overcrowding. Now Circumstantial Selection does not account for natural death: it accounts only for the survival of species in which the individuals have sense enough to decay and die on purpose. But the individuals do not seem to have calculated very reasonably: nobody can explain why a parrot should live ten times as long as a dog, and a turtle be almost immortal. In the case of man, the operation has overshot its mark: men do not live long enough: they are, for all the purposes of high civilization, mere children when they die; and our Prime Ministers though rated as mature, divide their time between the golf course and the Treasury Bench in parliament. Presumably, however, the same power that made this mistake can remedy it. If on opportunist grounds Man now fixes the term of his life at three score and ten years, he can equally fix it at three hundred, or three thousand, or even at the genuine Circumstantial Selection limit, which would be until a sooner-or-later-inevitable fatal accident makes an end of the individual. All that is necessary to make him extend his present span is that tremendous catatrophes such as the late war shall convince him of the necessity of at least outliving his taste for golf and cigars if the race is to be saved. This is not fantastic speculation: it is deductive biology, if there is such a science as biology. Here, then, is a stone that we have left unturned, and that may be worth turning. To make the suggestion more entertaining than it would be to most people in the form of a biological treatise, I have written Back to Methuselah as a contribution to the modern Bible.

Many people, however, can read treatises and cannot read Bibles. Darwin could not read Shakespear. Some who can read both, like to learn the history of their ideas. Some are so entangled in the current confusion of Creative Evolution with Circumstantial Selection by their historical ignorance that they are puzzled by any distinction between the two. For all their sakes I must give here a little history of the conflict between the view of Evolution taken by the Darwinians (though not altogether by Darwin himself) and called Natural Selection, and that which is emerging, under the title of Creative Evolution, as the genuinely scientific religion for which all wise men are now anxiously looking.

THE EARLY EVOLUTIONISTS

The idea of Evolution, or Transformation as it is now sometimes called, was not first conceived by Charles Darwin, nor by Alfred Russel Wallace, who observed the operation of Circumstantial Selection simultaneously with Charles. The celebrated Buffoon was a better Evolutionist than either of them; and two thousand years before Buffon was born, the Greek philosopher Empedocles opined that all forms of life are transformations of four elements, Fire, Air, Earth, and Water, effected by the two innate forces of attraction and repulsion, or love and hate. As lately as 1860 I myself was taught

as a child that everything was made out of these four elements. Both the Empedocleans and the Evolutionists were opposed to those who believed in the separate creation of all forms of life as described in the book of Genesis. This "conflict between religion and science," as the phrase went then, did not perplex my infant mind in the least: I knew perfectly well, without knowing that I knew it, that the validity of a story is not the same as the occurrence of a fact. But as I grew up I found that I had to choose between Evolution and Genesis. If you believed that dogs and cats and snakes and birds and beetles and oysters and whales and men and women were all separately designed and made and named in Eden garden at the beginning of things, and have since survived simply by reproducing their kind, then you were not an Evolutionist. If you believed, on the contrary, that all the different species are modifications, variations, and elaborations of one primal stock, or even of a few primal stocks, then you were an Evolutionist. But you were not necessarily a Darwinian; for you might have been a modern Evolutionist twenty years before Charles Darwin was born, and a whole lifetime before he published his Origin of Species. For that matter, when Aristotle grouped animals with backbones as blood relations, he began the sort of classification which, when extended by Darwin to monkeys and men, so shocked my uncle.

Genesis had held the field until the time (1707–1778) of Linnæus the famous botanist. In the meantime the microscope had been invented. It revealed a new world of hitherto invisible creatures called Infusorians, as common water was found to be an infusion of them. In the eighteenth century naturalists were very keen on the Infusorian Amœbas, and were much struck by the way in which the members of this old family behaved and developed. But it was still possible for

Linnæus to begin a treatise by saying "There are just so many species as there were forms created in the beginning," though there were hundreds of commonplace Scotch gardeners, pigeon fanciers, and stock breeders then living who knew better. Linnæus himself knew better before he died. In the last edition of his System of Nature, he began to wonder whether the transmutation of species by variation might not be possible. Then came the great poet who jumped over the facts to the conclusion. Goethe said that all the shapes of creation were cousins; that there must be some common stock from which all the species had sprung; that it was the environment of air that had produced the eagle, of water the seal, and of earth the mole. He could not say how this happened; but he divined that it did happen. Erasmus Darwin, the grandfather of Charles, carried the environment theory much further, pointing out instance after instance of modifications made in species apparently to adapt it to circumstances and environment: for instance, that the brilliant colors of the leopard, which make it so conspicuous in Regent's Park, conceal it in a tropical jungle. Finally he wrote, as his declaration of faith, "The world has been evolved, not created: it has arisen little by little from a small beginning, and has increased through the activity of the elemental forces embodied in itself, and so has rather grown than come into being at an almighty word. What a sublime idea of the infinite might of the great Architect, the Cause of all causes, the Father of all fathers, the Ens Entium! For if we would compare the Infinite, it would surely require a greater Infinite to cause the causes of effects than to produce the effects themselves." In this, published in the year 1794, you have nineteenth century Evolution precisely defined. And Erasmus Darwin was by no means its only apostle. It was in the air then. A German biologist named Treviranus, whose book was published in 1802, wrote, "In every living being there exists a capacity for endless diversity of form. Each possesses the power of adapting its organization to the variations of the external world; and it is this power, called into activity by cosmic changes, which has enabled the simple zoophytes of the primitive world to climb to higher and higher stages of organization, and has brought endless variety into nature." There you have your evolution of Man from the amœba all complete whilst Nelson was still alive on the seas. And in 1809, before the battle of Waterloo, a French soldier named Lamarck, who had beaten his musket into a microscope and turned zoologist, declared that species were an illusion produced by the shortness of our individual lives, and that they were constantly changing and melting into one another and into new forms as surely as the hand of a clock is continually moving, though it moves so slowly that it looks stationary to us. We have since come to think that its industry is less continuous: that the clock stops for a long time, and then is suddenly "put on" by a mysterious finger. But never mind that just at present.

THE ADVENT OF THE NEO-LAMARCKIANS

I call your special attention to Lamarck, because later on there were Neo-Lamarckians as well as Neo-Darwinians. I was a Neo-Lamarckian. Lamarck passed on from the conception of Evolution as a general law to Charles Darwin's department of it, which was the method of Evolution. Lamarck, whilst making many ingenious suggestions as to the reactions of external causes on life and habit, such as changes of climate, food supply, geological upheavals and so forth, really held as his fundamental proposition that living organisms changed because they wanted to. As he stated it, the great factor in

Evolution is use and disuse. If you have no eyes, and want to see, and keep trying to see, you will finally get eyes. If, like a mole or a subterranean fish, you have eyes and dont want to see, you will lose your eyes. If you like eating the tender tops of trees enough to make you concentrate all your energies on the stretching of your neck, you will finally get a long neck, like the giraffe. This seems absurd to inconsiderate people at the first blush; but it is within the personal experience of all of us that it is just by this process that a child tumbling about the floor becomes a boy walking erect; and that a man sprawling on the road with a bruised chin, or supine on the ice with a bashed occiput, becomes a bicyclist and a skater. The process is not continuous, as it would be if mere practice had anything to do with it; for though you may improve at each bicycling lesson *during* the lesson, when you begin your next lesson you do not begin at the point at which you left off: you relapse apparently to the beginning. Finally, you succeed quite suddenly, and do not relapse again. More miraculous still, you at once exercise the new power unconsciously. Although you are adapting your front wheel to your balance so elaborately and actively that the accidental locking of your handle bars for a second will throw you off; though five minutes before you could not do it at all, yet now you do it as unconsciously as you grow your finger nails. You have a new faculty, and must have created some new bodily tissue as its organ. And you have done it solely by willing. For here there can be no question of Circumstantial Selection, or the survival of the fittest. The man who is learning how to ride a bicycle has no advantage over the non-cyclist in the struggle for existence: quite the contrary. He has acquired a new habit, an automatic unconscious habit, solely because he wanted to, and kept trying until it was added unto him.

HOW ACQUIREMENTS ARE INHERITED

But when your son tries to skate or bicycle in his turn, he does not pick up the accomplishment where you left it, any more than he is born six feet high with a beard and a tall hat. The set-back that occurred between your lessons occurs again. The race learns exactly as the individual learns. Your son relapses, not to the very beginning, but to a point which no mortal method of measurement can distinguish from the beginning. Now this is odd; for certain other habits of yours, equally acquired (to the Evolutionist, of course, all habits are acquired), equally unconscious, equally automatic, are transmitted without any perceptible relapse. For instance, the very first act of your son when he enters the world as a separate individual is to yell with indignation: that yell which Shakespear thought the most tragic and piteous of all sounds. In the act of yelling he begins to breathe: another habit, and not even a necessary one, as the object of breathing can be achieved in other ways, as by deep sea fishes. He circulates his blood by pumping it with his heart. He demands a meal, and proceeds at once to perform the most elaborate chemical operations on the food he swallows. He manufactures teeth; discards them; and replaces them with fresh ones. Compared to these habitual feats, walking, standing upright, and bicycling are the merest trifles; yet it is only by going through the wanting, trying process that he can stand, walk, or cycle, whereas in the other and far more difficult and complex habits he not only does not consciously want nor consciously try, but actually consciously objects very strongly. Take that early habit of cutting the teeth: would he do that if he could help it? Take that later habit of decaying and eliminating himself by death—equally an acquired habit, remember—how he abhors it! Yet the habit has become so rooted, so automatic, that he must do it in spite of himself, even to his own destruction.

We have here a routine which, given time enough for it to operate, will finally produce the most elaborate forms of organized life on Lamarckian lines without the intervention of Circumstantial Selection at all. If you can turn a pedestrian into a cyclist, and a cyclist into a pianist or violinist, without the intervention of Circumstantial Selection, you can turn an amœba into a man, or a man into a superman, without it. All of which is rank heresy to the Neo-Darwinian, who imagines that if you stop Circumstantial Selection, you not only stop development but inaugurate a rapid and disastrous degeneration.

Let us fix the Lamarckian evolutionary process well in our minds. You are alive; and you want to be more alive. You want an extension of consciousness and of power. You want, consequently, additional organs, or additional uses of your existing organs: that is, additional habits. You get them because you want them badly enough to keep trying for them until they come. Nobody knows how: nobody knows why: all we know is that the thing actually takes place. We relapse miserably from effort to effort until the old organ is modified or the new one created, when suddenly the impossible becomes possible and the habit is formed. The moment we form it we want to get rid of the consciousness of it so as to economize our consciousness for fresh conquests of life; as all consciousness means preoccupation and obstruction. If we had to think about breathing or digesting or circulating our blood we should have no attention to spare for anything else, as we find to our cost when anything goes wrong with these operations. We want to be unconscious of them just as we wanted to acquire them; and we finally win what we want. But we win unconsciousness of our habits at the cost

of losing our control of them; and we also build one habit and its corresponding functional modification of our organs on another, and so become dependent on our old habits. Consequently we have to persist in them even when they hurt us. We cannot stop breathing to avoid an attack of asthma, or to escape drowning. We can lose a habit and discard an organ when we no longer need them, just as we acquired them; but this process is slow and broken by relapses; and relics of the organ and the habit long survive its utility. And if other and still indispensable habits and modifications have been built on the ones we wish to discard, we must provide a new foundation for them before we demolish the old one. This is also a slow process and a very curious one.

THE MIRACLE OF CONDENSED RECAPITULATION

The relapses between the efforts to acquire a habit are important because, as we have seen, they recur not only from effort to effort in the case of the individual, but from generation to generation in the case of the race. This relapsing from generation to generation is an invariable characteristic of the evolutionary process. For instance, Raphael, though descended from eight uninterrupted generations of painters, had to learn to paint apparently as if no Sanzio had ever handled a brush before. But he had also to learn to breathe, and digest, and circulate his blood. Although his father and mother were fully grown adults when he was conceived, he was not conceived or even born fully grown: he had to go back and begin as a speck of protoplasm, and to struggle through an embryonic lifetime, during part of which he was indistinguishable from an embryonic dog, and had neither a skull nor a backbone. When he at last acquired these articles, he was for some time doubtful whether he was a bird or a fish. He had to compress untold centuries of development into nine months before he was human enough to break loose as an independent being. And even then he was still so incomplete that his parents might well have exclaimed "Good Heavens! have you learnt nothing from our experience that you come into the world in this ridiculously elementary state? Why cant you talk and walk and paint and behave decently?" To that question Baby Raphael had no answer. All he could have said was that this is how evolution or transformation happens. The time may come when the same force that compressed the development of millions of years into nine months may pack many more millions into even a shorter space; so that Raphaels may be born painters as they are now born breathers and blood circulators. But they will still begin as specks of protoplasm, and acquire the faculty of painting in their mother's womb at quite a late stage of their embryonic life. They must recapitulate the history of mankind in their own persons, however briefly they may condense it.

Nothing was so astonishing and significant in the discoveries of the embryologists, nor anything so absurdly little appreciated, as this recapitulation, as it is now called: this power of hurrying up into months a process which was once so long and tedious that the mere contemplation of it is unendurable by men whose span of life is three-score-and-ten. It widened human possibilities to the extent of enabling us to hope that the most prolonged and difficult operations of our minds may yet become instantaneous, or, as we call it, instinctive. It also directed our attention to examples of this packing up of centuries into seconds which were staring us in the face in all directions. As I write these lines the newspapers are occupied by the exploits of a child of eight, who has just defeated twenty adult chess players in twenty games played simultaneously, and has been able afterwards to reconstruct all the twenty games without any apparent effort of memory. Most people, including myself, play chess (when they play it at all) from hand to mouth, and can hardly recall the last move but one, or foresee the next but two. Also, when I have to make an arithmetical calculation, I have to do it step by step with pencil and paper, slowly, reluctantly, and with so little confidence in the result that I dare not act on it without "proving" the sum by a further calculation involving more ciphering. But there are men who can neither read, write, nor cipher, to whom the answer to such sums as I can do is instantly obvious without any conscious calculation at all; and the result is infallible. Yet some of these natural arithmeticians have but a small vocabulary; are at a loss when they have to find words for any but the simplest everyday occasions; and cannot for the life of them describe mechanical operations which they perform daily in the course of their trade; whereas to me the whole vocabulary of English literature, from Shakespear to the latest edition of the Encyclopædia Britannica, is so completely and instantaneously at my call that I have never had to consult even a thesaurus except once or twice when for some reason I wanted a third or fourth synonym. Again, though I have tried and failed to draw recognizable portraits of persons I have seen every day for years, Mr Bernard Partridge, having seen a man once, will, without more strain than is involved in eating a sandwich, draw him to the life. The keyboard of a piano is a device I have never been able to master; yet Mr Cyril Scott uses it exactly as I use my own fingers; and to Sir Edward Elgar an orchestral score is as instantaneously intelligible at sight as a page of Shakespear is to me. One man cannot, after trying for years, finger the flute fluently.

Another will take up a flute with a newly invented arrangement of keys on it, and play it at once with hardly a mistake. We find people to whom writing is so difficult that they prefer to sign their name with a mark, and beside them men who master systems of shorthand and improvise new systems of their own as easily as they learnt the alphabet. These contrasts are to be seen on all hands, and have nothing to do with variations in general intelligence, nor even in the specialized intelligence proper to the faculty in question: for example, no composer or dramatic poet has ever pretended to be able to perform all the parts he writes for the singers, actors, and players who are his executants. One might as well expect Napoleon to be a fencer, or the Astronomer Royal to know how many beans make five any better than his bookkeeper. Even exceptional command of language does not imply the possession of ideas to express: Mezzofanti, the master of fifty-eight languages, had less to say in them than Shakespear with his little Latin and less Greek; and public life is the paradise of voluble windbags.

All these examples, which might be multiplied by millions, are cases in which a long, laborious, conscious, detailed process of acquirement has been condensed into an instinctive and unconscious inborn one. Factors which formerly had to be considered one by one in succession are integrated into what seems a single simple factor. Chains of hardly soluble problems have coalesced in one problem which solves itself the moment it is raised. What is more, they have been pushed back (or forward, if you like) from post-natal to pre-natal ones. The child in the womb may take some time over them; but it is a miraculously shortened time.

The time phenomena involved are curious, and suggest that we are either wrong about our history or else that we enormously exaggerate the periods required for the pre-natal acquirement of habits. In the nineteenth century we talked very glibly about geological periods, and flung millions of eons about in the most lordly manner in our reaction against Archbishop Ussher's chronology. We had a craze for big figures, and positively liked to believe that the progress made by the child in the womb in a month was represented in prehistoric time by ages and ages. We insisted that Evolution advanced more slowly than any snail ever crawled, and that Nature does not proceed by leaps and bounds. This was all very well as long as we were dealing with such acquired habits as breathing or digestion. It was possible to believe that dozens of epochs had gone to the slow building up of these habits. But when we have to consider the case of a man born not only as an accomplished metabolist, but with such an aptitude for shorthand and keyboard manipulation that he is a stenographer or pianist at least five sixths ready-made as soon as he can control his hands intelligently, we are forced to suspect either that keyboards and shorthand are older inventions than we suppose, or else that acquirements can be assimilated and stored as congenital qualifications in a shorter time than we think; so that, as between Lyell and Archbishop Ussher, the laugh may not be with Lyell quite so uproariously as it seemed fifty years ago.

HEREDITY AN OLD STORY

It is evident that the evolutionary process is a hereditary one, or, to put it less drily, that human life is continuous and immortal. The Evolutionists took heredity for granted. So did everybody. The human mind has been soaked in heredity as long back as we can trace its thought. Hereditary peers, hereditary monarchs, hereditary castes and trades and classes were the best known of social institutions, and in some cases of public nuisances. Pedigree men counted pedigree dogs and pedigree horses among their most cherished possessions. Far from being unconscious of heredity, or sceptical, men were insanely credulous about it: they not only believed in the transmission of qualities and habits from generation to generation, but expected the son to begin mentally where the father left off.

This belief in heredity led naturally to the practice of Intentional Selection. Good blood and breeding were eagerly sought after in human marriage. In dealing with plants and animals, selection with a view to the production of new varieties and the improvement and modification of species had been practised ever since men began to cultivate them. My pre-Darwinian uncle knew as well as Darwin that the race-horse and the dray-horse are not separate creations from the Garden of Eden, but adaptations by deliberate human selection of the medieval war-horse to modern racing and industrial haulage. He knew that there are nearly two hundred different sorts of dogs, all capable of breeding with one another and of producing cross varieties unknown to Adam. He knew that the same thing is true of pigeons. He knew that gardeners had spent their lives trying to breed black tulips and green carnations and unheard-of orchids, and had actually produced flowers just as strange to Eve. His quarrel with the Evolutionists was not a quarrel with the evidence for Evolution: he had accepted enough of it to prove Evolution ten times over before he ever heard of it. What he repudiated was cousinship with the ape, and the implied suspicion of a rudimentary tail, because it was offensive to his sense of his own dignity, and because he thought that apes were ridiculous, and tails diabolical when associated with the erect posture. Also he believed that Evolution was a heresy

which involved the destruction of Christianity, of which, as a member of the Irish Church (the pseudo-Protestant one), he conceived himself a pillar. But this was only his ignorance; for a man may deny his descent from an ape and be eligible as a churchwarden without being any the less a convinced Evolutionist.

DISCOVERY ANTICIPATED BY DIVINATION

What is more, the religious folk can claim to be among the pioneers of Evolutionism. Weismann, Neo-Darwinist though he was, devoted a long passage in his History of Evolution to the Nature Philosophy of Lorenz Oken, published in 1809. Oken defined natural science as "the science of the everlasting transmutations of the Holy Ghost in the world." His religion had started him on the right track, and not only led him to think out a whole scheme of Evolution in abstract terms, but guided his aim in a significantly good scientific shot which brought him within the scope of Weismann. He not only defined the original substance from which all forms of life have developed as protoplasm, or, as he called it, primitive slime (*Urschleim*), but actually declared that this slime took the form of vesicles out of which the universe was built. Here was the modern cell morphology guessed by a religious thinker long before the microscope and the scalpel forced it on the vision of mere laboratory workers who could not think and had no religion. They worked hard to discover the vital secrets of the glands by opening up dogs and cutting out the glands, or tying up their ducts, or severing their nerves, thereby learning, negatively, that the governors of our vital forces do not hold their incessant conversations through the nerves, and, positively, how miserably a horribly injured dog can die, leaving us to infer that we shall probably perish likewise if we grudge our guineas to Harley Street.

Lorenz Oken *thought* very hard to find out what was happening to the Holy Ghost, and thereby made a contribution of extraordinary importance to our understanding of uninjured creatures. The man who was scientific enough to see that the Holy Ghost is a scientific fact got easily in front of the blockheads who could only sin against it. Hence my uncle was turning his back on very respectable company when he derided Evolution, and would probably have recanted and apologized at once had anybody pointed out to him what a solecism he was committing.

The metaphysical side of Evolution was thus no novelty when Darwin arrived. Had Oken never lived, there would still have been millions of persons trained from their childhood to believe that we are continually urged upwards by a force called the Will of God. In 1819 Schopenhauer published his treatise on The World as Will, which is the metaphysical complement to Lamarck's natural history, as it demonstrates that the driving force behind Evolution is a will-to-live, and to live, as Christ said long before, more abundantly. And the earlier philosophers, from Plato to Leibnitz, had kept the human mind open for the thought of the universe as one idea behind all its physically apprehensible transformations.

CORRECTED DATES FOR THE DISCOVERY OF EVOLUTION

All this, remember, is the state of things in the pre-Darwin period, which so many of us still think of as a pre-evolutionary period. Evolutionism was the rage before Queen Victoria came to the throne. To fix this chronology, let me repeat the story told by Weismann of the July revolution in Paris in 1830, when the French got rid of Charles the Tenth. Goethe was then still living; and a French friend of his called on him and found him wildly excited. "What do you think of the great event?" said Goethe. "The volcano is in eruption; and all is in flames. There can no longer be discussion with closed doors." The Frenchman replied that no doubt it was a terrible business; but what could they expect with such a ministry and such a king? "Stuff!" said Goethe: "I am not thinking of these people at all, but of the open rupture in the French Academy between Cuvier and St Hilaire. It is of the utmost importance to science." The rupture Goethe meant was about Evolution, Cuvier contending that there were four species, and St Hilaire that there was only one.

From 1830, when Darwin was an apparently unpromising lad of twentyone, until 1859, when he turned the world upside down by his Origin of Species, there was a slump in Evolutionism. The first generation of its enthusiasts was ageing and dying out; and their successors were being taught from the Book of Genesis, just as Edward VI was (and Edward VII too, for that matter). Nobody who knew the theory was adding anything to it. This slump not only heightened the impression of entire novelty when Darwin brought the subject to the front again: it probably prevented him from realizing how much had been done before, even by his own grandfather, to whom he was accused of being unjust. Besides, he was not really carrying on the family business. He was an entirely original worker; and he was on a new tack, as we shall see presently. And he would not in any case have thought much, as a practical naturalist, of the more or less mystical intellectual speculations of the Deists of 1790–1830. Scientific workers were very tired of Deism just then. They had given up the riddle of the Great First Cause as insoluble, and were calling themselves, accordingly, Agnostics. They had turned from the inscrutable question of Why things existed, to the spade work of discovering What was really occurring in the world and How it really occurred.

With all his attention bent in this new direction, Darwin soon noticed that a good deal was occurring in an entirely unmystical and even unmeaning way of which the older speculative Deist-Evolutionists had taken little or no account. Nowadays, when we are turning in weary disgust and disillusion from Neo-Darwinism and Mechanism to Vitalism and Creative Evolution, it is difficult to imagine how this new departure of Darwin's could possibly have appealed to his contemporaries as exciting, agreeable, above all as hopeful. Let me therefore try to bring back something of the atmosphere of that time by describing a scene, very characteristic of its superstitions, in which I took what was then considered an unspeakably shocking part.

DEFYING THE LIGHTNING: A FRUSTRATED EXPERIMENT

One evening in 1878 or thereabouts, I, being then in my earliest twenties, was at a bachelor party of young men of the professional class in the house of a doctor in the Kensingtonian quarter of London. They fell to talking about religious revivals; and an anecdote was related of a man who, having incautiously scoffed at the mission of Messrs Moody and Sankey, a then famous firm of American evangelists, was subsequently carried home on a shutter, slain by divine vengeance as a blasphemer. A timid minority, without quite venturing to question the truth of the incident—for they naturally did not care to run the risk of going home on shutters themselves—nevertheless shewed a certain disposition to cavil at those who exulted in it; and something approaching to an argument began. At last it was alleged by the most evangelical of the disputants that Charles Bradlaugh, the most formidable atheist on the Secularist platform, had taken out his watch publicly and challenged the Almighty to strike him dead in five minutes if he really existed and disapproved of atheism. The leader of the cavillers, with great heat, repudiated this as a gross calumny, declaring that Bradlaugh had repeatedly and indignantly contradicted it, and implying that the atheist champion was far too pious a man to commit such a blasphemy. This exquisite confusion of ideas roused my sense of comedy. It was clear to me that the challenge attributed to Charles Bradlaugh was a scientific experiment of a quite simple, straightforward, and proper kind to ascertain whether the expression of atheistic opinions really did involve any personal risk. It was certainly the method taught in the Bible, Elijah having confuted the prophets of Baal in precisely that way, with every circumstance of bitter mockery of their god when he failed to send down fire from heaven. Accordingly I said that if the question at issue were whether the penalty of questioning the theology of Messrs Moody and Sankey was to be struck dead on the spot by an incensed deity, nothing could effect a more convincing settlement of it than the very obvious experiment attributed to Mr Bradlaugh, and that consequently if he had not tried it, he ought to have tried it. The omission, I added, was one which could easily be remedied there and then, as I happened to share Mr Bradlaugh's views as to the absurdity of the belief in these violent interferences with the order of nature by a short-tempered and thin-skinned supernatural deity. Therefore—and at that point I took out my watch.

The effect was electrical. Neither sceptics nor devotees were prepared to abide the result of the experiment. In vain did I urge the pious to trust in the accuracy of their deity's aim with a thunderbolt, and the justice of his discrimination between the innocent and the guilty. In vain did I appeal to the sceptics to accept the logical outcome of their scepticism: it soon appeared that when thunderbolts were in question there were no sceptics. Our host, seeing that his guests would vanish precipitately if the impious challenge were uttered, leaving him alone with a solitary infidel under sentence of extermination in five minutes, interposed and forbade the experiment, pleading at the same time for a change of subject. I of course complied, but could not refrain from remarking that though the dreadful words had not been uttered, yet, as the thought had been formulated in my mind, it was very doubtful whether the consequences could be averted by sealing my lips. However, the rest appeared to feel that the game would be played according to the rules, and that it mattered very little what I thought so long as I said nothing. Only the leader of the evangelical party, I thought, was a little preoccupied until five minutes had elapsed and the weather was still calm.

IN QUEST OF THE FIRST CAUSE

Another reminiscence. In those days we thought in terms of time and space, of cause and effect, as we still do; but we do not now demand from a religion that it shall explain the universe completely in terms of cause and effect, and present the world to us as a manufactured article and as the private property of its Manufacturer. We did then. We were invited to pity the delusion of certain heathens who held that the world is supported by an elephant who is supported by a tortoise. Mahomet decided that the mountains are great weights to keep the world from being blown away into space. But we refuted these orientals by asking triumphantly what the tortoise stands on? Freethinkers asked which came first: the owl or the egg. Nobody thought of saying that the ultimate problem of existence, being clearly insoluble and even unthinkable on causation lines, could not

be a causation problem. To pious people this would have been flat atheism, because they assumed that God must be a Cause, and sometimes called him The Great First Cause, or, in still choicer language, The Primal Cause. To the Rationalists it would have been a renunciation of reason. Here and there a man would confess that he stood as with a dim lantern in a dense fog, and could see but a little way in any direction into infinity. But he did not really believe that infinity was infinite or that the eternal was also sempiternal: he assumed that all things, known and unknown, were caused.

Hence it was that I found myself one day towards the end of the eighteen-seventies in a cell in the old Brompton Oratory arguing with Father Addis, who had been called by one of his flock to attempt my conversion to Roman Catholicism. The universe exists, said the father: somebody must have made it. If that somebody exists, said I, somebody must have made him. I grant that for the sake of argument, said the Oratorian. I grant you a maker of God. I grant you a maker of the maker of God. I grant you as long a line of makers as you please; but an infinity of makers is unthinkable and extravagant: it is no harder to believe in number one than in number fifty thousand or fifty million; so why not accept number one and stop there, since no attempt to get behind him will remove your logical difficulty? By your leave, said I, it is as easy for me to believe that the universe made itself as that a maker of the universe made himself: in fact much easier; for the universe visibly exists and makes itself as it goes along, whereas a maker for it is a hypothesis. Of course we could get no further on these lines. He rose and said that we were like two men working a saw, he pushing it forward and I pushing it back, and cutting nothing; but when we had dropped the subject and were walking through the refectory, he returned to it for a moment to say that he should go mad if he lost his belief. I, glorying in the robust callousness of youth and the comedic spirit, felt quite comfortable and said so; though I was touched, too, by his evident sincerity.

These two anecdotes are superficially trivial and even comic; but there is an abyss of horror beneath them. They reveal a condition so utterly irreligious that religion means nothing but belief in a nursery bogey, and its inadequacy is demonstrated by a toy logical dilemma, neither the bogey nor the dilemma having anything to do with religion, or being serious enough to impose on or confuse any properly educated child over the age of six. One hardly knows which is the more appalling: the abjectness of the credulity or the flippancy of the scepticism. The result was inevitable. All who were strongminded enough not to be terrified by the bogey were left stranded in empty contemptuous negation, and argued, when they argued at all, as I argued with Father Addis. But their position was not intellectually comfortable. A member of parliament expressed their discomfort when, objecting to the admission of Charles Bradlaugh into parliament, he said "Hang it all, a man should believe in something or somebody." It was easy to throw the bogey into the dustbin; but none the less the world, our corner of the universe, did not look like a pure accident: it presented evidences of design in every direction. There was mind and purpose behind it. As the anti-Bradlaugh member would have put it, there must be somebody behind the something: no atheist could get over that.

PALEY'S WATCH

Paley had put the argument in an apparently unanswerable form. If you found a watch, full of mechanism exquisitely adapted to produce a series of operations all leading to the fulfilment of one central purpose of measuring for mankind the march of the day and night, could you believe that it was not the work of a cunning artificer who had designed and contrived it all to that end? And here was a far more wonderful thing than a watch, a man with all his organs ingeniously contrived, cords and levers, girders and kingposts, circulating systems of pipes and valves, dialysing membranes, chemical retorts, carburettors, ventilators, inlets and outlets, telephone transmitters in his ears, light recorders and lenses in his eyes: was it conceivable that this was the work of chance? that no artificer had wrought here? that there was no purpose in this, no design, no guiding intelligence? The thing was incredible. In vain did Helmholtz declare that "the eye has every possible defect that can be found in an optical instrument, and even some peculiar to itself," and that "if an optician tried to sell me an instrument which had all these defects I should think myself quite justified in blaming his carelessness in the strongest terms, and sending him back his instrument." To discredit the optician's skill was not to get rid of the optician. The eye might not be so cleverly made as Paley thought, but it was made somehow, by somebody.

And then my argument with Father Addis began all over again. It was easy enough to say that every man makes his own eyes: indeed the embryologists had actually caught him doing it. But what about the very evident purpose that prompted him to do it? Why did he want to see, if not to extend his consciousness and his knowledge and his power? That purpose was at work everywhere, and must be something bigger than the individual eye-making man. Only the stupidest muckrakers could fail to see this, and even to know it as part of their own consciousness. Yet to admit it seemed to involve letting the bogey come back, so inextricably had we managed to mix up belief in the bogey's existence with belief in the existence of design in the universe.

THE IRRESISTIBLE CRY OF ORDER, ORDER!

Our scornful young scientific and philosophic lions of today must not blame the Church of England for this confusion of thought. In 1562 the Church, in convocation in London "for the avoiding of diversities of opinions and for the establishment of consent touching true religion," proclaimed in their first utterance, and as an Article of Religion, that God is "without body, parts, or passions," or, as we say, an *Élan Vital* or Life Force. Unfortunately neither parents, parsons, nor pedagogues could be induced to adopt that article. St John might say that "God is spirit" as pointedly as he pleased; our Sovereign Lady Elizabeth might ratify the Article again and again; serious divines might feel as deeply as they could that a God with body, parts, and passions could be nothing but an anthropomorphic idol: no matter: people at large could not conceive a God who was not anthropomorphic: they stood by the Old Testament legends of a God whose parts had been seen by one of the patriarchs, and finally set up as against the Church a God who, far from being without body, parts, or passions, was composed of nothing else, and of very evil passions too. They imposed this idol in practice on the Church itself, in spite of the First Article, and thereby homeopathically produced the atheist, whose denial of God was simply a denial of the idol and a demonstration against an unbearable and most unchristian idolatry. The idol was, as Shelley had been expelled from Oxford for pointing out, an almighty fiend, with a petty character and unlimited power, spiteful, cruel, jealous, vindictive, and physically violent. The most villainous schoolmasters, the most tyrannical parents, fell far short in their attempts to imitate it. But it was not its social vices that brought it low. What made it scientifically intolerable was that it was ready at a moment's notice to upset the whole order of the universe on the most trumpery provocation, whether by stopping the sun in the valley of Ajalon or sending an atheist home dead on a shutter (the shutter was indispensable because it marked the utter unpreparedness of the atheist, who, unable to save himself by a deathbed repentance, was subsequently roasted through all eternity in blazing brimstone). It was this disorderliness, this refusal to obey its own laws of nature, that created a scientific need for its destruction. Science could stand a cruel and unjust god; for nature was full of suffering and injustice. But a disorderly god was impossible. In the Middle Ages a compromise had been made by which two different orders of truth, religious and scientific, had been recognized, in order that a schoolman might say that two and two make four without being burnt for heresy. But the nineteenth century, steeped in a meddling, presumptuous, reading-and-writing, socially and politically powerful ignorance inconceivable by Thomas Aquinas or even Roger Bacon, was incapable of so convenient an arrangement; and science was strangled by bigoted ignoramuses claiming infallibility for their interpretation of the Bible, which was regarded, not as a literature nor even as a book, but partly as an oracle which answered and settled all questions, and partly as a talisman to be carried by soldiers in their breast pockets or placed under the pillows of persons who were afraid of ghosts. The tract shops exhibited in their windows bullet-dinted testaments, mothers' gifts to their soldier sons whose lives had been saved by it; for the muzzle-loaders of those days could not drive a projectile through so many pages.

THE MOMENT AND THE MAN

This superstition of a continual capricious disorder in nature, of a lawgiver who was also a lawbreaker, made atheists in all directions among clever and lightminded people. But atheism did not account for Paley's watch. Atheism accounted for nothing; and it was the business of science to account for everything that was plainly accountable. Science had no use for mere negation: what was desired by it above all things just then was a demonstration that the evidences of design could be explained without resort to the hypothesis of a personal designer. If only some genius, whilst admitting Paley's facts, could knock the brains out of Paley by the discovery of a method whereby watches could happen without watchmakers, that genius was assured of such a welcome from the thought of his day as no natural philosopher had ever enjoyed before.

The time being thus ripe, the genius appeared; and his name was Charles Darwin. And now, what did Darwin really discover?

Here, I am afraid, I shall require once more the assistance of the giraffe, or, as he was called in the days of the celebrated Buffoon, the camelopard (by children, cammyleopard). I do not remember how this animal imposed himself illustratively on the Evolution controversy; but there was no getting away from him then; and I am old-fashioned enough to be unable to get away from him now. How did he come by his long neck? Lamarck would have said, by wanting to get at the tender leaves high up on the tree, and trying until he succeeded in wishing the necessary length of neck into existence. Another answer was also possible: namely, that some prehistoric stock-breeder, wishing to produce a natural curiosity, selected the longest-necked animals he could find, and bred from them until at last an animal with an abnormally long neck was evolved by intentional selection, just as the racehorse or the fantail pigeon has been evolved. Both these explanations, you will observe, involve consciousness, will, design, purpose, either on the part of the animal itself or on the part of a superior intelligence controlling its destiny. Darwin pointed out—and this and no more was Darwin's famous discovery—that a third explanation, involving neither will nor purpose nor design either in the animal or anyone else, was on the cards. If your neck is too short to reach your food, you die. That may be the simple explanation of the fact that all the surviving animals that feed on foliage have necks or trunks long enough to reach it. So bang goes your belief that the necks must have been designed to reach the food. But Lamarck did not believe that the necks were so designed in the beginning: he believed that the long necks were evolved by wanting and trying. Not necessarily, said Darwin. Consider the effect on the giraffes of the natural multiplication of their numbers, as insisted on by Malthus. Suppose the average height of the foliage-eating animals is four feet, and that they increase in numbers until a time comes when all the trees are eaten away to within four feet of the ground. Then the animals who happen to be an inch or two short of the average will die of starvation. All the animals who happen to be an inch or so above the average will be better fed and stronger than the others. They will secure the strongest and tallest mates; and their progeny will survive whilst the average ones and the sub-average ones will die out. This process, by which the species gains, say, an inch in reach, will repeat itself until the giraffe's neck is so long that he can always find food enough within his reach, at which point, of course, the selective process stops and the length of the giraffe's neck stops with it. Otherwise, he would grow until he could browse off the trees in the moon. And this, mark you, without the intervention of any stock-breeder, human or divine, and without will, purpose, design, or even consciousness beyond the blind will to satisfy hunger. It is true that this blind will, being in effect a will to live, gives away the whole case; but still, as compared to the open-eyed intelligent wanting and trying of Lamarck, the Darwinian process may be described as a chapter of accidents. As such, it seems simple, because you do not at first realize all that it involves. But when its whole significance dawns on you, your heart sinks into a heap of sand within you. There is a hideous fatalism about it, a ghastly and damnable reduction of beauty and intelligence, of strength and purpose, of honor and aspiration, to such casually picturesque changes as an avalanche may make in a mountain landscape, or a railway accident in a human figure. To call this Natural Selection is a blasphemy, possible to many for whom Nature is nothing but a casual aggregation of inert and dead matter, but eternally impossible to the spirits and souls of the righteous. If it be no blasphemy, but a truth of science, then the stars of heaven, the showers and dew, the winter and summer, the fire and heat, the mountains and hills, may no longer be called to exalt the Lord with us by praise: their work is to modify all things by blindly starving and murdering everything that is not lucky enough to survive in the universal struggle for hogwash.

THE BRINK OF THE BOTTOMLESS PIT

Thus did the neck of the giraffe reach out across the whole heavens and make men believe that what they saw there was a gloaming of the gods. For if this sort of selection could turn an antelope into a giraffe, it could conceivably turn a pond full of amœbas into the French Academy. Though Lamarck's way, the way of life, will, aspiration, and achievement, re-mained still possible, this newly shewn way of hunger, death, stupidity, delusion, chance, and bare survival was also possible: was indeed most certainly the way in which many apparently intelligently designed transformations had actually come to pass. Had I not preluded with the apparently idle story of my revival of the controversial methods of Elijah, I should be asked how it was that the explorer who opened up this gulf of despair, far from being stoned or crucified as the destroyer of the honor of the race and the purpose of the world, was hailed as Deliverer, Savior, Prophet, Redeemer, Enlightener, Rescuer, Hope Giver, and Epoch Maker; whilst poor Lamarck was swept aside as a crude and exploded guesser hardly worthy to be named as his erroneous forerunner. In the light of my anecdote, the explanation is obvious. The first thing the gulf did was to swallow up Paley, and the Disorderly Designer, and Shelley's Almighty Fiend, and all the rest of the pseudo-religious rubbish that had blocked every upward and onward path since the hopes of men had turned to Science as their true Savior. It seemed such a convenient grave that nobody at first noticed that it was nothing less than the bottomless pit, now become a very real terror. For though Darwin left a path round it for his soul, his followers presently dug it right across the whole width of the way. Yet for the moment, there was nothing but wild rejoicing: a sort of scientific mafficking. We had been so oppressed by the notion that everything that happened in the world was the arbitrary personal act of an arbitrary personal god of dangerously jealous and cruel personal character, so that even the relief of the pains of childbed and the operating table by chloroform was objected to as an interference with his arrangements which he would probably resent, that we just jumped at Darwin. When Napoleon was asked what would happen when he died, he said that Europe would express its intense relief with a great "Ouf!" Well, when Darwin killed the god who objected to chloroform, everybody who had ever thought about it said "Ouf!" Paley was buried fathoms deep with his watch, now fully accounted for without any divine artificer at all. We were so glad to be rid of both that we never gave a thought to the consequences. When a prisoner sees the door of his dungeon open, he dashes for it without stopping to think where he shall get his dinner outside. The moment we found that we could do without Shelley's almighty fiend intellectually, he went into the gulf that seemed only a dustbin with a suddenness that made our own lives one of the most astonishing periods in history. If I had told that uncle of mine that within thirty years from the date of our conversation I should be exposing myself to suspicions of the grossest superstition by questioning the sufficiency of Darwin; maintaining the reality of the Holy Ghost; and declaring that the phenomenon of the Word becoming Flesh was occurring daily, he would have regarded me as the most extravagant madman our family had ever produced. Yet it was so. In 1906 I might have vituperated Jehovah more heartily than ever Shelley did without eliciting a protest in any circle of thinkers, or shocking any public audience accustomed to modern discussion; but when I described Darwin as "an intelligent and industrious pigeon fancier," that blasphemous levity, as it seemed, was received with horror and indignation. The tide has now turned; and every puny whipster may say what he likes about Darwin; but anyone who wants to know what it was to be a Lamarckian during the last quarter of the nineteenth century has only to read Mr Festing Jones's memoir of Samuel Butler to learn how completely even a man of genius could isolate himself by antagonizing Darwin on the one hand and the Church on the other.

WHY DARWIN CONVERTED THE CROWD

I am well aware that in describing the effect of Darwin's discovery on naturalists and on persons capable of serious reflection on the nature and attributes of God, I am leaving the vast mass of the British public out of account. I have pointed out elsewhere that the British nation does not consist of atheists and Plymouth Brothers; and I am not now going to pretend that it ever consisted of Darwinians and Lamarckians. The average citizen is irreligious and unscientific: you talk to him about cricket and golf, market prices and party politics, not about evolution and relativity, transubstantiation and predestination. Nothing will knock into his head the fateful distinction between Evolution as promulgated by Erasmus Darwin, and Circumstantial (so-called Natural) Selection as revealed by his grandson. Yet the doctrine of Charles reached him, though the doctrine of Erasmus had passed over his head. Why did not Erasmus Darwin popularize the word Evolution as effectively as Charles?

The reason was, I think, that Circumstantial Selection is easier to understand, more visible and concrete, than Lamarckian evolution. Evolution as a philosophy and physiology of the will is a mystical process, which can be apprehended only by a trained, apt, and comprehensive thinker. Though the phenomena of use and disuse, of wanting and trying, of the manufacture of weight lifters and wrestlers from men of ordinary strength, are familiar enough as facts, they are extremely puzzling as subjects of thought, and lead you into metaphysics the moment you try to account for them. But pigeon fanciers, dog fanciers, gardeners, stockbreeders, or stud grooms, can understand Circumstantial Selection, because it is their business to produce transformation by imposing on flowers and animals a Selection From Without. All that Darwin had to say to them was that the mere chapter of accidents is always doing on a huge scale what they themselves are doing on a very small scale. There is hardly a laborer attached to an English country house who has not taken a litter of kittens or puppies to the bucket, and drowned all of them except the one he thinks the most promising. Such a man has nothing to learn about the survival of the fittest except that it acts in more ways than he has yet noticed; for he knows quite well, as you will find if you are not too proud to talk to him, that this sort of selection occurs naturally (in Darwin's sense) too: that, for instance, a hard winter will kill off a weakly child as the bucket kills off a weakly puppy. Then there is the farm laborer. Shakespear's Touchstone, a court-bred fool, was shocked to find in the shepherd a natural philosopher, and opined that he would be damned for the part he took in the sexual selection of sheep. As to the production of new species by the selection of variations, that is no news to your gardener. Now if you are familiar with these three processes: the survival of the fittest, sexual selection, and variation leading to new kinds, there is nothing to puzzle you in Darwinism.

That was the secret of Darwin's popularity. He never puzzled anybody. If very few of us have read The Origin of Species from end to end, it is not because it overtaxes our mind, but because we take in the whole case and are prepared to accept it long before we have come to the end of the innumerable instances and illustrations of which the book mainly consists. Darwin becomes tedious in the manner of a man who insists on continuing to prove his innocence after he has been acquitted. You assure him that there is not a stain on his character, and beg him to leave the court; but he will not be content with enough evidence: he will have

you listen to all the evidence that exists in the world. Darwin's industry was enormous. His patience, his perseverance, his conscientiousness reached the human limit. But he never got deeper beneath or higher above his facts than an ordinary man could follow him. He was not conscious of having raised a stupendous issue, because, though it arose instantly, it was not his business. He was conscious of having discovered a process of transformation and modification which accounted for a great deal of natural history. But he did not put it forward as accounting for the whole of natural history. He included it under the heading of Evolution, though it was only pseudo-evolution at best; but he revealed it as *a* method of evolution, not as *the* method of evolution. He did not pretend that it excluded other methods, or that it was the chief method. Though he demonstrated that many transformations which had been taken as functional adaptations (the current phrase for Lamarckian evolution) either certainly were or conceivably might be due to Circumstantial Selection, he was careful not to claim that he had superseded Lamarck or disproved Functional Adaptation. In short, he was not a Darwinian, but an honest naturalist working away at his job with so little preoccupation with theological speculation that he never quarrelled with the theistic Unitarianism into which he was born, and remained to the end the engagingly simple and socially easy-going soul he had been in his boyhood, when his elders doubted whether he would ever be of much use in the world.

HOW WE RUSHED DOWN A STEEP PLACE

Not so the rest of us intellectuals. We all began going to the devil with the utmost cheerfulness. Everyone who had a mind to change, changed it. Only Samuel Butler, on whom Darwin had acted homeopathically, reacted against him furiously; ran up the Lamarckian flag to the top-gallant peak; declared with penetrating accuracy that Darwin had "banished mind from the universe"; and even attacked Darwin's personal character, unable to bear the fact that the author of so abhorrent a doctrine was an amiable and upright man. Nobody would listen to him. He was so completely submerged by the flowing tide of Darwinism that when Darwin wanted to clear up the misunderstanding on which Butler was basing his personal attacks, Darwin's friends, very foolishly and snobbishly, persuaded him that Butler was too ill-conditioned and negligible to be answered. That they could not recognize in Butler a man of genius mattered little: what did matter was that they could not understand the provocation under which he was raging. They actually regarded the banishment of mind from the universe as a glorious enlightenment and emancipation for which he was ignorantly ungrateful. Even now, when Butler's eminence is unchallenged, and his biographer, Mr Festing Jones, is enjoying a vogue like that of Boswell or Lockhart, his memoirs shew him rather as a shocking example of the bad controversial manners of our country parsonages than as a prophet who tried to head us back when we were gaily dancing to our damnation across the rainbow bridge which Darwinism had thrown over the gulf which separates life and hope from death and despair. We were intellectually intoxicated with the idea that the world could make itself without design, purpose, skill, or intelligence: in short, without life. We completely overlooked the difference between the modification of species by adaptation to their environment and the appearance of new species: we just threw in the word "variations" or the word "sports" (fancy a man of science talking of an unknown factor as a sport instead of as x!) and left them

to "accumulate" and account for the difference between a cockatoo and a hippopotamus. Such phrases set us free to revel in demonstrating to the Vitalists and Bible worshippers that if we once admit the existence of any kind of force, however unintelligent, and stretch out the past to unlimited time for such force to operate accidentally in, that force may conceivably, by the action of Circumstantial Selection, produce a world in which every function has an organ perfectly adapted to perform it, and therefore presents every appearance of having been designed, like Paley's watch, by a conscious and intelligent artificer for the purpose. We took a perverse pleasure in arguing, without the least suspicion that we were reducing ourselves to absurdity, that all the books in the British Museum library might have been written word for word as they stand on the shelves if no human being had ever been conscious, just as the trees stand in the forest doing wonderful things without consciousness.

And the Darwinians went far beyond denying consciousness to trees. Weismann insisted that the chick breaks out of its eggshell automatically; that the butterfly, springing into the air to avoid the pounce of the lizard, "does not wish to avoid death; knows nothing about death," what has happened being simply that a flight instinct evolved by Circumstantial Selection reacts promptly to a visual impression produced by the lizard's movement. His proof is that the butterfly immediately settles again on the flower, and repeats the performance every time the lizard springs, thus shewing that it learns nothing from experience, and—Weismann concludes—is not conscious of what it does.

It should hardly have escaped so curious an observer that when the cat jumps up on the dinner table, and you put it down, it instantly jumps up again, and finally establishes its right to a place on the cloth by convincing you that if you put it down a hundred times it will jump up a hundred and one times; so that if you desire its company at dinner you can have it only on its own terms. If Weismann really thought that cats act thus without any consciousness or any purpose, immediate or ulterior, he must have known very little about cats. But a thorough-going Weismannite, if any such still survive from those mad days, would contend that I am not at present necessarily conscious of what I am doing; that my writing of these lines, and your reading of them, are effects of Circumstantial Selection; that I need know no more about Darwinism than a butterfly knows of a lizard's appetite; and that the proof that I actually am doing it unconsciously is that as I have spent forty years in writing in this fashion without, as far as I can see, producing any visible effect on public opinion, I must be incapable of learning from experience, and am therefore a mere automaton. And the Weismannite demonstration of this would of course be an equally unconscious effect of Circumstantial Selection.

DARWINISM NOT FINALLY REFUTABLE

Do not too hastily say that this is inconceivable. To Circumstantial Selection all mechanical and chemical reactions are possible, provided you accept the geologists' estimates of the great age of the earth, and therefore allow time enough for the circumstances to operate. It is true that mere survival of the fittest in the struggle for existence plus sexual selection fail as hopelessly to account for Darwin's own life work as for my conquest of the bicycle; but who can prove that there are not other soulless factors, unnoticed or undiscovered, which only require imagination enough to fit them to the evolution of an automatic Jesus or Shakespear? When a man tells you that you are a product of Circumstantial Selection solely, you cannot finally disprove it. You can only tell him out of the depths of your inner conviction that he is a fool and a liar. But as this, though British, is uncivil, it is wiser to offer him the counter-assurance that you are the product of Lamarckian evolution, formerly called Functional Adaptation and now Creative Evolution, and challenge him to disprove *that*, which he can no more do than you can disprove Circumstantial Selection, both forces being conceivably able to produce anything if you only give them rope enough. You may also defy him to act for a single hour on the assumption that he may safely cross Oxford Street in a state of unconsciousness, trusting to his dodging reflexes to react automatically and promptly enough to the visual impression produced by a motor bus, and the audible impression produced by its hooter. But if you allow yourself to defy him to explain any particular action of yours by Circumstantial Selection, he should always be able to find some explanation that will fit the case if only he is ingenious enough and goes far enough to find it. Darwin found several such explanations in his controversies. Anybody who really wants to believe that the universe has been produced by Circumstantial Selection co-operating with a force as inhuman as we conceive magnetism to be can find a logical excuse for his belief if he tries hard enough.

THREE BLIND MICE

The stultification and damnation which ensued are illustrated by a comparison of the ease and certainty with which Butler's mind moved to humane and inspiring conclusions with the grotesque stupidities and cruelties of the idle and silly controversy which arose among the Darwinians as to whether acquired habits can be transmitted from parents to offspring. Consider, for example, how Weismann set to work on that subject. An Evolutionist with a live mind would first have dropped the popular expression "acquired habits," because to an Evolutionist there are no other habits and can be no others, a man being only an amœba with acquirements. He would then have considered carefully the process by which he himself had acquired his habits. He would have assumed that the habits with which he was born must have been acquired by a similar process. He would have known what a habit is: that is, an action voluntarily attempted until it has become more or less automatic and involuntary; and it would never have occurred to him that injuries or accidents coming from external sources against the will of the victim could possibly establish a habit; that, for instance, a family could acquire a habit of being killed in railway accidents.

And yet Weismann began to investigate the point by behaving like the butcher's wife in the old catch. He got a colony of mice, and cut off their tails. Then he waited to see whether their children would be born without tails. They were not, as Butler could have told him beforehand. He then cut off the children's tails, and waited to see whether the grandchildren would be born with at least rather short tails. They were not, as I could have told him beforehand. So with the patience and industry on which men of science pride themselves, he cut off the grandchildren's tails too, and waited, full of hope, for the birth of curtailed greatgrandchildren. But their tails were quite up to the mark, as any fool could have told him beforehand. Weismann then gravely drew the inference that acquired habits cannot be transmitted. And yet Weismann was not a born imbecile. He was an exceptionally clever and studious man, not without roots of imagination and philosophy in him which Darwinism killed as weeds. How was it that he did not see that he was not experimenting with habits or characteristics at all? How had he overlooked the glaring fact that

his experiment had been tried for many generations in China on the feet of Chinese women without producing the smallest tendency on their part to be born with abnormally small feet? He must have known about the bound feet even if he knew nothing of the mutilations, the clipped ears and docked tails, practised by dog fanciers and horse breeders on many generations of the unfortunate animals they deal in. Such amazing blindness and stupidity on the part of a man who was naturally neither blind nor stupid is a telling illustration of what Darwin unintentionally did to the minds of his disciples by turning their attention so exclusively towards the part played in Evolution by accident and violence operating with entire callousness to suffering and sentiment.

A vital conception of Evolution would have taught Weismann that biological problems are not to be solved by assaults on mice. The scientific form of his experiment would have been something like this. First, he should have procured a colony of mice highly susceptible to hypnotic suggestion. He should then have hypnotized them into an urgent conviction that the fate of the musque world depended on the disappearance of its tail, just as some ancient and forgotten experimenter seems to have convinced the cats of the Isle of Man. Having thus made the mice desire to lose their tails with a life-or-death intensity, he would very soon have seen a few mice born with little or no tail. These would be recognized by the other mice as superior beings, and privileged in the division of food and in sexual selection. Ultimately the tailed mice would be put to death as monsters by their fellows, and the miracle of the tailless mouse completely achieved.

The objection to this experiment is not that it seems too funny to be taken seriously, and is not cruel enough to overawe the mob, but simply that it is impossible because the human experimenter cannot get at the mouse's mind. And that is what is wrong with all the barren cruelties of the laboratories. Darwin's followers did not think of this. Their only idea of investigation was to imitate "Nature" by perpetrating violent and senseless cruelties, and watch the effect of them with a paralyzing fatalism which forbade the smallest effort to use their minds instead of their knives and eyes, and established an abominable tradition that the man who hesitates to be as cruel as Circumstantial Selection itself is a traitor to science. For Weismann's experiment upon the mice was a mere joke compared to the atrocities committed by other Darwinians in their attempts to prove that mutilations could not be transmitted. No doubt the worst of these experiments were not really experiments at all, but cruelties committed by cruel men who were attracted to the laboratory by the fact that it was a secret refuge left by law and public superstition for the amateur of passionate torture. But there is no reason to suspect Weismann of Sadism. Cutting off the tails of several generations of mice is not voluptuous enough to tempt a scientific Nero. It was a mere piece of one-eyedness; and it was Darwin who put out Weismann's humane and sensible eye. He blinded many another eye and paralyzed many another will also. Ever since he set up Circumstantial Selection as the creator and ruler of the universe, the scientific world has been the very citadel of stupidity and cruelty. Fearful as the tribal god of the Hebrews was, nobody ever shuddered as they passed even his meanest and narrowest Little Bethel or his proudest war-consecrating cathedral as we shudder now when we pass a physiological laboratory. If we dreaded and mistrusted the priest, we could at least keep him out of the house; but what of the modern Darwinist surgeon whom we dread and mistrust ten times more, but into whose hands

we must all give ourselves from time to time? Miserably as religion had been debased, it did at least still proclaim that our relation to one another was that of a fellowship in which we were all equal and members one of another before the judgment-seat of our common father. Darwinism proclaimed that our true relation is that of competitors and combatants in a struggle for mere survival, and that every act of pity or loyalty to the old fellowship is a vain and mischievous attempt to lessen the severity of the struggle and preserve inferior varieties from the efforts of Nature to weed them out. Even in Socialist Societies which existed solely to substitute the law of fellowship for the law of competition, and the method of providence and wisdom for the method of rushing violently down a steep place into the sea, I found myself regarded as a blasphemer and an ignorant sentimentalist because whenever the Neo-Darwinian doctrine was preached there I made no attempt to conceal my intellectual contempt for its blind coarseness and shallow logic, or my natural abhorrence of its sickening inhumanity.

THE GREATEST OF THESE IS SELF-CONTROL

As there is no place in Darwinism for free will, or any other sort of will, the Neo-Darwinists held that there is no such thing as self-control. Yet self-control is just the one quality of survival value which Circumstantial Selection must invariably and inevitably develop in the long run. Uncontrolled qualities may be selected for survival and development for certain periods and under certain circumstances. For instance, since it is the ungovernable gluttons who strive the hardest to get food and drink, their efforts would develop their strength and cunning in a period of such scarcity that the utmost they could do would not enable them to over-eat themselves. But a change of circumstances involving a plentiful supply of food would destroy them. We see this very thing happening often enough in the case of the healthy and vigorous poor man who becomes a millionaire by one of the accidents of our competitive commerce, and immediately proceeds to dig his grave with his teeth. But the self-controlled man survives all such changes of circumstance, because he adapts himself to them, and eats neither as much as he can hold nor as little as he can scrape along on, but as much as is good for him. What *is* self-control? It is nothing but a highly developed vital sense, dominating and regulating the mere appetites. To overlook the very existence of this supreme sense; to miss the obvious inference that it is the quality that distinguishes the fittest to survive; to omit, in short, the highest moral claim of Evolutionary Selection: all this, which the Neo-Darwinians did in the name of Natural Selection, shewed the most pitiable want of mastery of their own subject, the dullest lack of observation of the forces upon which Natural Selection works.

A SAMPLE OF LAMARCKO-SHAVIAN INVECTIVE

The Vitalist philosophers made no such mistakes. Nietzsche, for example, thinking out the great central truth of the Will to Power instead of cutting off mouse-tails, had no difficulty in concluding that the final objective of this Will was power over self, and that the seekers after power over others and material possessions were on a false scent.

The stultification naturally became much worse as the first Darwinians died out. The prestige of these pioneers, who had the older evolutionary culture to build on, and were in fact no more Darwinian in the modern sense than Darwin himself, ceased to dazzle us when Huxley and Tyndall and Spencer and Darwin passed away, and we were left with the smaller people who began with Darwin and took in nothing else. Accordingly, I find that in the year 1906 I indulged my temper by hurling invectives at the Neo-Darwinians in the following terms.

"I really do not wish to be abusive; but when I think of these poor little dullards, with their precarious hold of just that corner of evolution that a blackbeetle can understand—with their retinue of twopenny-halfpenny Torquemadas wallowing in the infamies of the vivisector's laboratory, and solemnly offering us as epoch-making discoveries their demonstrations that dogs get weaker and die if you give them no food; that intense pain makes mice sweat; and that if you cut off a dog's leg the three-legged dog will have a four-legged puppy, I ask myself what spell has fallen on intelligent and humane men that they allow themselves to be imposed on by this rabble of dolts, blackguards, impostors, quacks, liars, and, worst of all, credulous conscientious fools. Better a thousand times Moses and Spurgeon [a then famous preacher] back again. After all, you cannot understand Moses without imagination nor Spurgeon without metaphysics; but you can be a thorough-going Neo-Darwinian without imagination, metaphysics, poetry, conscience, or decency. For 'Natural Selection' has no moral significance: it deals with that part of evolution which has no purpose, no intelligence, and might more appropriately be called accidental selection, or better still, Unnatural Selection, since nothing is more unnatural than an accident. If it could be proved that the whole universe had been produced by such Selection, only fools and rascals could bear to live."

THE HUMANITARIANS AND THE PROBLEM OF EVIL

Yet the humanitarians were as delighted as anybody with Darwinism at first. They had been perplexed by the Problem of Evil and the Cruelty of Nature. They were Shelleyists, but not atheists. Those who believed in God were at a terrible disadvantage with the atheist. They could not deny the existence of natural facts so cruel that to attribute them to the will of God is to make God a demon. Belief in God was impossible to any thoughtful person without belief in the Devil as well. The painted Devil, with his horns, his barbed tail, and his abode of burning brimstone, was an incredible bogey; but the evil attributed to him was real enough; and the atheists argued that the author of evil, if he exists, must be strong enough to overcome God, else God is morally responsible for everything he permits the Devil to do. Neither conclusion delivered us from the horror of attributing the cruelty of nature to the workings of an evil will, or could reconcile it with our impulses towards justice, mercy, and a higher life.

A complete deliverance was offered by the discovery of Circumstantial Selection: that is to say, of a method by which horrors having every appearance of being elaborately planned by some intelligent contriver are only accidents without any moral significance at all. Suppose a watcher from the stars saw a frightful accident produced by two crowded trains at full speed crashing into one another! How could he conceive that a catastrophe brought about by such elaborate machinery, such ingenious preparation, such skilled direction, such vigilant industry, was quite unintentional? Would he not conclude that the signal-men were devils?

Well, Circumstantial Selection is largely a theory of collisions: that is, a theory of the innocence of much apparently designed devilry. In this way Darwin brought intense relief as well as an enlarged knowledge of facts to the humanitarians. He destroyed the omnipotence

of God for them; but he also exonerated God from a hideous charge of cruelty. Granted that the comfort was shallow, and that deeper reflection was bound to shew that worse than all conceivable devil-deities is a blind, deaf, dumb, heartless, senseless mob of forces that strike as a tree does when it is blown down by the wind, or as the tree itself is struck by lightning. That did not occur to the humanitarians at the moment: people do not reflect deeply when they are in the first happiness of escape from an intolerably oppressive situation. Like Bunyan's pilgrim they could not see the wicket gate, nor the Slough of Despond, nor the castle of Giant Despair; but they saw the shining light at the end of the path, and so started gaily towards it as Evolutionists.

And they were right; for the problem of evil yields very easily to Creative Evolution. If the driving power behind Evolution is omnipotent only in the sense that there seems no limit to its final achievement; and if it must meanwhile struggle with matter and circumstance by the method of trial and error, then the world must be full of its unsuccessful experiments. Christ may meet a tiger, or a High Priest arm-in-arm with a Roman Governor, and be the unfittest to survive under the circumstances. Mozart may have a genius that prevails against Emperors and Archbishops, and a lung that succumbs to some obscure and noxious property of foul air. If all our calamities are either accidents or sincerely repented mistakes, there is no malice in the Cruelty of Nature and no Problem of Evil in the Victorian sense at all. The theology of the women who told us that they became atheists when they sat by the cradles of their children and saw them strangled by the hand of God is succeeded by the theology of Blanco Posnet, with his "It was early days when He made the croup, I guess. It was the best He could think of then; but when it turned out wrong on His hands He made you and me to fight the croup for Him."

HOW ONE TOUCH OF DARWIN MAKES THE WHOLE WORLD KIN

Another humanitarian interest in Darwinism was that Darwin popularized Evolution generally, as well as making his own special contribution to it. Now the general conception of Evolution provides the humanitarian with a scientific basis, because it establishes the fundamental equality of all living things. It makes the killing of an animal murder in exactly the same sense as the killing of a man is murder. It is sometimes necessary to kill men as it is always necessary to kill tigers; but the old theoretic distinction between the two acts has been obliterated by Evolution. When I was a child and was told that our dog and our parrot, with whom I was on intimate terms, were not creatures like myself, but were brutal whilst I was reasonable, I not only did not believe it, but quite consciously and intellectually formed the opinion that the distinction was false; so that afterwards, when Darwin's views were first unfolded to me, I promptly said that I had found out all that for myself before I was ten years old; and I am far from sure that my youthful arrogance was not justified; for this sense of the kinship of all forms of life is all that is needed to make Evolution not only a conceivable theory, but an inspiring one. St Anthony was ripe for the Evolution theory when he preached to the fishes, and St Francis when he called the birds his little brothers. Our vanity, and our snobbish conception of Godhead as being, like earthly kingship, a supreme class distinction instead of the rock on which Equality is built, had led us to insist on God offering us special terms by placing us apart from and above all the rest of his creatures. Evolution took that conceit out of us; and now, though we may kill a flea without the smallest remorse, we at all events know that we are killing our cousin. No doubt it shocks the flea when the creature that an almighty Celestial Flea created expressly for the food of fleas, destroys the jumping lord of creation with his sharp and enormous thumbnail; but no flea will ever be so foolish as to preach that in slaying fleas Man is applying a method of Natural Selection which will finally evolve a flea so swift that no man can catch him, and so hardy of constitution that Insect Powder will have no more effect on him than strychnine on an elephant.

WHY DARWIN PLEASED THE SOCIALISTS

The Humanitarians were not alone among the agitators in their welcome to Darwin. He had the luck to please everybody who had an axe to grind. The Militarists were as enthusiastic as the Humanitarians, the Socialists as the Capitalists. The Socialists were specially encouraged by Darwin's insistence on the influence of environment. Perhaps the strongest moral bulwark of Capitalism is the belief in the efficacy of individual righteousness. Robert Owen made desperate efforts to convince England that her criminals, her drunkards, her ignorant and stupid masses, were the victims of circumstance: that if we would only establish his new moral world we should find that the masses born into an educated and moralized community would be themselves educated and moralized. The stock reply to this is to be found in Lewes's Life of Goethe. Lewes scorned the notion that circumstances govern character. He pointed to the variety of character in the governing rich class to prove the contrary. Similarity of circumstance can hardly be carried to a more desolating dead level than in the case of the individuals who are born and bred in English country houses, and sent first to Eton or

Harrow, and then to Oxford or Cambridge, to have their minds and habits formed. Such a routine would destroy individuality if anything could. Yet individuals come out from it as different as Pitt from Fox, as Lord Russell from Lord Curzon, as Mr Winston Churchill from Lord Robert Cecil. This acceptance of the congenital character of the individual as the determining factor in his destiny had been reinforced by the Lamarckian view of Evolution. If the giraffe can develop his neck by wanting and trying, a man can develop his character in the same way. The old saying, "Where there is a will, there is a way," condenses Lamarck's theory of functional adaptation into a proverb. This felt bracingly moral to strong minds, and reassuringly pious to feeble ones. There was no more effective retort to the Socialist than to tell him to reform himself before he pretends to reform society. If you were rich, how pleasant it was to feel that you owed your riches to the superiority of your own character! The industrial revolution had turned numbers of greedy dullards into monstrously rich men. Nothing could be more humiliating and threatening to them than the view that the falling of a shower of gold into their pockets was as pure an accident as the falling of a shower of hail on their umbrellas, and happened alike to the just and unjust. Nothing could be more flattering and fortifying to them than the assumption that they were rich because they were virtuous.

Now Darwinism made a clean sweep of all such self-righteousness. It more than justified Robert Owen by discovering in the environment of an organism an influence on it more potent than Owen had ever claimed. It implied that street arabs are produced by slums and not by original sin: that prostitutes are produced by starvation wages and not by feminine concupiscence. It threw the authority of science on the side of the Socialist who said that he who would reform himself must first reform society. It suggested that if we want healthy and wealthy citizens we must have healthy and wealthy towns; and that these can exist only in healthy and wealthy countries. It could be led to the conclusion that the type of character which remains indifferent to the welfare of its neighbors as long as its own personal appetite is satisfied is the disastrous type, and the type which is deeply concerned about its environment the only possible type for a permanently prosperous community. It shewed that the surprising changes which Robert Owen had produced in factory children by a change in their circumstances which does not seem any too generous to us nowadays were as nothing to the changes—changes not only of habits but of species, not only of species but of orders—which might conceivably be the work of environment acting on individuals without any character or intellectual consciousness whatever. No wonder the Socialists received Darwin with open arms.

DARWIN AND KARL MARX

Besides, the Socialists had an evolutionary prophet of their own, who had discredited Manchester as Darwin discredited the Garden of Eden. Karl Marx had proclaimed in his Communist Manifesto of 1848 (now enjoying Scriptural authority in Russia) that civilization is an organism evolving irresistibly by circumstantial selection; and he published the first volume of his Das Kapital in 1867. The revolt against anthropomorphic idolatry, which was, as we have seen, the secret of Darwin's success, had been accompanied by a revolt against the conventional respectability which covered not only the brigandage and piracy of the feudal barons, but the hypocrisy, inhumanity, snobbery, and greed of the bourgeoisie, who were utterly corrupted by an essentially diabolical identification of success in life with big profits. The moment Marx shewed that the relation of the bourgeoisie to society was grossly immoral and disastrous, and that the whited wall of starched shirt fronts concealed and defended the most infamous of all tyrannies and the basest of all robberies, he became an inspired prophet in the mind of every generous soul whom his book reached. He had said and proved what they wanted to have proved; and they would hear nothing against him. Now Marx was by no means infallible: his economics, half borrowed, and half home-made by a literary amateur, were not, when strictly followed up, even favorable to Socialism. His theory of civilization had been promulgated already in Buckle's History of Civilization, a book as epoch-making in the minds of its readers as Das Kapital. There was nothing about Socialism in the widely read first volume of Das Kapital: every reference it made to workers and capitalists shewed that Marx had never breathed industrial air, and had dug his case out of bluebooks in the British Museum. Compared to Darwin, he seemed to have no power of observation: there was not a fact in Das Kapital that had not been taken out of a book, nor a discussion that had not been opened by somebody else's pamphlet. No matter: he exposed the bourgeoisie and made an end of its moral prestige. That was enough: like Darwin he had for the moment the World Will by the ear. Marx had, too, what Darwin had not: implacability and a fine Jewish literary gift, with terrible powers of hatred, invective, irony, and all the bitter qualities bred, first in the oppression of a rather pampered young genius (Marx was the spoilt child of a well-to-do family) by a social system utterly uncongenial to him, and later on by exile and poverty. Thus Marx and Darwin between them toppled over two closely related idols, and became the prophets of two new creeds.

WHY DARWIN PLEASED THE PROFITEERS ALSO

But how, at this rate, did Darwin succeed with the capitalists too? It is not easy to make the best of both worlds when one of the worlds is preaching a Class War, and the other vigorously practising it. The explanation is that Darwinism was so closely related to Capitalism that Marx regarded it as an economic product rather than as a biological theory. Darwin got his main postulate, the pressure of population on the available means of subsistence, from the treatise of Malthus on Population, just as he got his other postulate of a practically unlimited time for that pressure to operate from the geologist Lyell, who made an end of Archbishop Ussher's Biblical estimate of the age of the earth as 4004 B.C. plus A.D. The treatises of the Ricardian economists on the Law of Diminishing Return, which was only the Manchester School's version of the giraffe and the trees, were all very fiercely discussed when Darwin was a young man. In fact the discovery in the eighteenth century by the French Physiocrats of the economic effects of Commercial Selection in soils and sites, and by Malthus of a competition for subsistence which he attributed to pressure of population on available subsistence, had already brought political science into that unbreathable atmosphere of fatalism which is the characteristic blight of Darwinism. Long before Darwin published a line, the Ricardo - Malthusian economists were preaching the fatalistic Wages Fund doctrine, and assuring the workers that Trade Unionism is a vain defiance of the inexorable laws of political economy, just as the Neo-Darwinians were presently assuring us that Temperance Legislation is a vain defiance of Natural Selection, and that the true way to deal with drunkenness is to flood the country with cheap gin and let the fittest survive. Cobdenism is, after all, nothing but the abandonment of trade to Circumstantial Selection.

It is hardly possible to exaggerate the importance of this preparation for Darwinism by a vast political and clerical propaganda of its moral atmosphere. Never in history, as far as we know, had there been such a determined, richly subsidized, politically organized attempt to persuade the human race that all progress, all prosperity, all salvation, individual and social, depend on an unrestrained conflict for food and money, on the suppression and elimination of the weak by the strong, on Free Trade, Free Contract, Free Competition, Natural Liberty, Laisser-faire: in short, on "doing the other fellow down" with impunity, all interference by a guiding government, all organization except police organization to protect legalized fraud against fisticuffs, all attempt to introduce human purpose and design and forethought into the industrial welter, being "contrary to the laws of political economy." Even the proletariat sympathized, though to them Capitalist liberty meant only wage slavery without the legal safeguards of chattel slavery. People were tired of governments and kings and priests and providences, and wanted to find out how Nature would arrange matters if she were let alone. And they found it out to their cost in the days when Lancashire used up nine generations of wage slaves in one generation of their masters. But their masters, becoming richer and richer, were very well satisfied, and Bastiat proved convincingly that Nature had arranged Economic Harmonies which would settle social questions far better than theocracies or aristocracies or mobocracies, the real *deus ex machina* being unrestrained plutocracy.

THE POETRY AND PURITY OF MATERIALISM

Thus the stars in their courses fought for Darwin. Every faction drew a moral from him; every catholic hater of faction founded a hope on him; every blackguard felt justified by him; and every saint felt encouraged by him. The notion that any harm could come of so splendid an enlightenment seemed as silly as the notion that the atheists would steal all our spoons. The physicists went further than the Darwinians. Tyndall declared that he saw in Matter the promise and potency of all forms of life, and with his Irish graphic lucidity made a picture of a world of magnetic atoms, each atom with a positive and a negative pole, arranging itself by attraction and repulsion in orderly crystalline structure. Such a picture is dangerously fascinating to thinkers oppressed by the bloody disorders of the living world. Craving for purer subjects of thought, they find in the contemplation of crystals and magnets a happiness more dramatic and less childish than the happiness found by the mathematicians in abstract numbers, because they see in the crystals beauty and movement without the corrupting appetites of fleshly vitality. In such Materialism as that of Lucretius and Tyndall there is a nobility which produces poetry: John Davidson found his highest inspiration in it. Even its pessimism as it faces the cooling of the sun and the return of the ice-caps does not degrade the pessimist: for example, the Quincy Adamses, with their insistence on modern democratic degradation as an inevitable result of solar shrinkage, are not dehumanized as the vivisectionists are. Perhaps nobody is at heart fool enough to believe that life is at the mercy of temperature: Dante was not troubled by the objection that Brunetto could not have lived in the fire nor Ugolino in the ice.

But the physicists found their intellectual vision of the world incommunicable to those who were not born with it. It came to the public simply as Materialism; and Materialism lost its peculiar purity and dignity when it entered into the Darwinian reaction against Bible fetichism. Between the two of them religion was knocked to pieces; and where there had been a god, a cause, a faith that the universe was ordered however inexplicable by us its order might be, and therefore a sense of moral responsibility as part of that order, there was now an utter void. Chaos had come again. The first effect was exhilarating: we had the runaway child's sense of freedom before it gets hungry and lonely and frightened. In this phase we did not desire our God back again. We printed the verses in which William Blake, the most religious of our great poets, called the anthropomorphic idol Old Nobodaddy, and gibed at him in terms which the printer had to leave us to guess from his blank spaces. We had heard the parson droning that God is not mocked; and it was great fun to mock Him to our hearts' content and not be a penny the worse. It did not occur to us that Old Nobodaddy, instead of being a ridiculous fiction, might be only an impostor, and that the exposure of this Koepenik Captain of the heavens, far from proving that there was no real captain, rather proved the contrary: that, in short, Nobodaddy could not have impersonated anybody if there had not been Somebodaddy to impersonate. We did not see the significance of the fact that on the last occasion on which God had been "expelled with a pitchfork," men so different as Voltaire and Robespierre had said, the one that if God did not exist it would be necessary to invent him, and the other that after an honest attempt to dispense with a Supreme Being in practical politics, some such hypothesis had been found quite indispensable, and could not be replaced by a mere Goddess of Reason. If these two opinions were quoted at all, they were quoted as jokes at the expense of Nobodaddy. We were quite sure for the moment that whatever lingering superstition might have daunted these men of the eighteenth century, we Darwinians could do without God, and had made a good riddance of Him.

THE VICEROYS OF THE KING OF KINGS

Now in politics it is much easier to do without God than to do without his viceroys and vicars and lieutenants; and we begin to miss the lieutenants long before we begin to miss their principal. Roman Catholics do what their confessors advise without troubling God; and Royalists are content to worship the King and ask the policeman. But God's trustiest lieutenants often lack official credentials. They may be professed atheists who are also men of honor and high public spirit. The old belief that it matters dreadfully to God whether a man thinks himself an atheist or not, and that the extent to which it matters can be stated with exactness as one single damn, was an error: for the divinity is in the honor and public spirit, not in the mouthed *credo* or *non credo*. The consequences of this error became grave when the fitness of a man for public trust was tested, not by his honor and public spirit, but by asking him whether he believed in Nobodaddy or not. If he said yes, he was held fit to be a Prime Minister, though, as our ablest Churchman has said, the real implication was that he was either a fool, a bigot, or a liar. Darwin destroyed this test; but when it was only thoughtlessly dropped, there was no test at all; and the door to public trust was open to the man who had no sense of God because he had no sense of anything beyond his own business interests and personal appetites and ambitions. As a result, the people who did not feel in the least inconvenienced by being no longer governed by Nobodaddy soon found themselves very acutely inconvenienced by being governed by fools and commercial adventurers. They had forgotten not only

God but Goldsmith, who had warned them that "honor sinks where commerce long prevails."

The lieutenants of God are not always persons: some of them are legal and parliamentary fictions. One of them is Public Opinion. The pre-Darwinian statesmen and publicists were not restrained directly by God; but they restrained themselves by setting up an image of a Public Opinion which would not tolerate any attempt to tamper with British liberties. Their favorite way of putting it was that any Government which proposed such and such an infringement of such and such a British liberty would be hurled from office in a week. This was not true: there was no such public opinion, no limit to what the British people would put up with in the abstract, and no hardship short of immediate and sudden starvation that it would not and did not put up with in the concrete. But this very helplessness of the people had forced their rulers to pretend that they were not helpless, and that the certainty of a sturdy and unconquerable popular resistance forbade any trifling with Magna Carta or the Petition of Rights or the authority of parliament. Now the reality behind this fiction was the divine sense that liberty is a need vital to human growth. Accordingly, though it was difficult enough to effect a political reform, yet, once parliament had passed it, its wildest opponent had no hope that the Government would cancel it, or shelve it, or be bought off from executing it. From Walpole to Campbell-Bannerman there was no Prime Minister to whom such renagueing or trafficking would ever have occurred, though there were plenty who employed corruption unsparingly to procure the votes of members of parliament for their policy.

POLITICAL OPPORTUNISM IN EXCELSIS

The moment Nobodaddy was slain by Darwin, Public Opinion, as divine deputy, lost its sanctity. Politicians no longer told themselves that the British public would never suffer this or that: they allowed themselves to know that for their own personal purposes, which are limited to their ten or twenty years on the front benches in parliament, the British Public can be humbugged and coerced into believing and suffering everything that it pays to impose on them, and that any false excuse for an unpopular step will serve if it can be kept in countenance for a fortnight: that is, until the terms of the excuse are forgotten. The people, untaught or mistaught, are so ignorant and incapable politically that this in itself would not greatly matter; for a statesman who told them the truth would not be understood, and would in effect mislead them more completely than if he dealt with them according to their blindness instead of to his own wisdom. But though there is no difference in this respect between the best demagogue and the worst, both of them having to present their cases equally in terms of melodrama, there is all the difference in the world between the statesman who is humbugging the people into allowing him to do the will of God, in whatever disguise it may come to him, and one who is humbugging them into furthering his personal ambition and the commercial interests of the plutocrats who own the newspapers and support him on reciprocal terms. And there is almost as great a difference between the statesman who does this naïvely and automatically, or even does it telling himself that he is ambitious and selfish and unscrupulous, and the one who does it on principle, believing that if everyone takes the line of least material resistance the result will be the survival of the fittest in a perfectly harmonious universe. Once produce an atmosphere of fatalism on principle, and it matters little what the opinions or superstitions of the individual statesmen concerned may be. A Kaiser who is a devout reader of sermons, a Prime Minister who is an emotional singer of hymns, and a General who is a bigoted Roman Catholic may be the executants of the policy; but the policy itself will be one of unprincipled opportunism; and all the Governments will be like the tramp who walks always with the wind and ends as a pauper, or the stone that rolls down the hill and ends as an avalanche: their way is the way to destruction.

THE BETRAYAL OF WESTERN CIVILIZATION

Within sixty years from the publication of Darwin's Origin of Species political opportunism had brought parliaments into contempt; created a popular demand for direct action by the organized industries ("Syndicalism"); and wrecked the centre of Europe in a paroxysm of that chronic terror of one another, that cowardice of the irreligious, which, masked in the bravado of militarist patriotism, had ridden the Powers like a nightmare since the Franco-Prussian war of 1870–1871. The sturdy old cosmopolitan Liberalism vanished almost unnoticed. At the present moment all the new ordinances for the government of our Crown Colonies contain, as a matter of course, prohibitions of all criticism, spoken or written, of their ruling officials, which would have scandalized George III and elicited Liberal pamphlets from Catherine II. Statesmen are afraid of the suburbs, of the newspapers, of the profiteers, of the diplomatists, of the militarists, of the country houses, of the trade unions, of everything ephemeral on earth except the revolutions they are provoking; and they would be afraid of these if they were not too ignorant of society and history to appreciate the risk, and to know that a revolution always seems hopeless and impossible the day before it breaks out, and indeed never does break out until it seems hopeless and

impossible; for rulers who think it possible take care to insure the risk by ruling reasonably. This brings about a condition fatal to all political stability: namely, that you never know where to have the politicians. If the fear of God was in them it might be possible to come to some general understanding as to what God disapproves of; and Europe might pull together on that basis. But the present panic, in which Prime Ministers drift from election to election, either fighting or running away from everybody who shakes a fist at them, makes a European civilization impossible. Such peace and prosperity as we enjoyed before the war depended on the loyalty of the Western States to their own civilization. That loyalty could find practical expression only in an alliance of the highly civilized Western Powers against the primitive tyrannies of the East. Britain, Germany, France, and the United States of America could have imposed peace on the world, and nursed modern civilization in Russia, Turkey, and the Balkans. Every meaner consideration should have given way to this need for the solidarity of the higher civilization. What actually happened was that France and England, through their clerks the diplomatists, made an alliance with Russia to defend themselves against Germany; Germany made an alliance with Turkey to defend herself against the three; and the two unnatural and suicidal combinations fell on one another in a war that came nearer to being a war of extermination than any wars since those of Timur the Tartar; whilst the United States held aloof as long as they could, and the other States either did the same or joined in the fray through compulsion, bribery, or their judgment as to which side their bread was buttered. And at the present moment, though the main fighting has ceased through the surrender of Germany on terms which the victors have never dreamt of observing, the extermination

s

by blockade and famine, which was what forced Germany to surrender, still continues, although it is certain that if the vanquished starve the victors will starve too, and Europe will liquidate its affairs by going, not into bankruptcy, but into chaos.

Now all this, it will be noticed, was fundamentally nothing but an idiotic attempt on the part of each belligerent State to secure for itself the advantage of the survival of the fittest through Circumstantial Selection. If the Western Powers had selected their allies in the Lamarckian manner intelligently, purposely, and vitally, *ad majorem Dei gloriam*, as what Nietzsche called good Europeans, there would have been a League of Nations and no war. But because the selection relied on was purely circumstantial opportunist selection, so that the alliances were mere marriages of convenience, they have turned out, not merely as badly as might have been expected, but far worse than the blackest pessimist had ever imagined possible.

CIRCUMSTANTIAL SELECTION IN FINANCE

How it will all end we do not yet know. When wolves combine to kill a horse, the death of the horse only sets them fighting one another for the choicest morsels. Men are no better than wolves if they have no better principles: accordingly, we find that the Armistice and the Treaty have not extricated us from the war. A handful of Serbian regicides flung us into it as a sporting navvy throws a bull pup at a cat; but the Supreme Council, with all its victorious legions and all its prestige, cannot get us out of it, though we are heartily sick and tired of the whole business, and know now very well that it should never have been allowed to happen. But we are helpless before a slate scrawled with figures of National Debts. As there is no money to pay them because it was all

spent on the war (wars have to be paid for on the nail) the sensible thing to do is to wipe the slate and let the wrangling States distribute what they can spare, on the sound communist principle of from each according to his ability, to each according to his need. But no: we have no principles left, not even commercial ones; for what sane commercialist would decree that France must not pay for her failure to defend her own soil; that Germany must pay for her success in carrying the war into the enemy's country; and that as Germany has not the money to pay, and under our commercial system can make it only by becoming once more a commercial competitor of England and France, which neither of them will allow, she must borrow the money from England, or America, or even from France: an arrangement by which the victorious creditors will pay one another, and wait to get their money back until Germany is either strong enough to refuse to pay or ruined beyond the possibility of paying? Meanwhile Russia, reduced to a scrap of fish and a pint of cabbage soup a day, has fallen into the hands of rulers who perceive that Materialist Communism is at all events more effective than Materialist Nihilism, and are attempting to move in an intelligent and ordered manner, practising a very strenuous Intentional Selection of workers as fitter to survive than idlers; whilst the Western Powers are drifting and colliding and running on the rocks, in the hope that if they continue to do their worst they will get Naturally Selected for survival without the trouble of thinking about it.

THE HOMEOPATHIC REACTION AGAINST DARWINISM

When, like the Russians, our Nihilists have it urgently borne in on them, by the brute force of rising wages that never overtake rising prices, that they are being Naturally Selected for destruction, they will perhaps remember that "Dont Care came to a bad end," and begin to look round for a religion. And the whole purpose of this book is to shew them where to look. For, throughout all the godless welter of the infidel half-century, Darwinism has been acting not only directly but homeopathically, its poison rallying our vital forces not only to resist it and cast it out, but to achieve a new Reformation and put a credible and healthy religion in its place. Samuel Butler was the pioneer of the reaction as far as the casting out was concerned; but the issue was confused by the physiologists, who were divided on the question into Mechanists and Vitalists. The Mechanists said that life is nothing but physical and chemical action; that they have demonstrated this in many cases of so-called vital phenomena; and that there is no reason to doubt that with improved methods they will presently be able to demonstrate it in all of them. The Vitalists said that a dead body and a live one are physically and chemically identical, and that the difference can be accounted for only by the existence of a Vital Force. This seems simple; but the Anti-Mechanists objected to be called Vitalists (obviously the right name for them) on two contradictory grounds. First, that vitality is scientifically inadmissible, because it cannot be isolated and experimented with in the laboratory. Second, that force, being by definition anything that can alter the speed or direction of matter in motion (briefly, that can overcome inertia) is essentially a mechanistic conception. Here we had the New Vitalist only half extricated from the Old Mechanist, objecting to be called either, and unable to give a clear lead in the new direction. And there was a deeper antagonism. The Old Vitalists, in postulating a Vital Force, were setting up a comparatively mechanical conception as against the divine idea of the life breathed into the clay nostrils of Adam, whereby he became a living soul. The New Vitalists, filled by their laboratory researches with a sense of the miraculousness of life that went far beyond the comparatively uninformed imaginations of the authors of the Book of Genesis, regarded the Old Vitalists as Mechanists who had tried to fill up the gulf between life and death with an empty phrase denoting an imaginary physical force.

These professional faction fights are ephemeral, and need not trouble us here. The Old Vitalist, who was essentially a Materialist, has evolved into the New Vitalist, who is, as every genuine scientist must be, finally a metaphysician. And as the New Vitalist turns from the disputes of his youth to the future of his science, he will cease to boggle at the name Vitalist, or at the inevitable, ancient, popular, and quite correct use of the term Force to denote metaphysical as well as physical overcomers of inertia.

Since the discovery of Evolution as the method of the Life Force, the religion of metaphysical Vitalism has been gaining the definiteness and concreteness needed to make it assimilable by the educated critical man. But it has always been with us. The popular religions, disgraced by their Opportunist cardinals and bishops, have been kept in credit by canonized saints whose secret was their conception of themselves as the instruments and vehicles of divine power and aspiration: a conception which at moments becomes an actual experience of ecstatic possession by that power. And above and below all have been millions of humble and obscure persons, sometimes totally illiterate, sometimes unconscious of having any religion at all, sometimes believing in their simplicity that the gods and temples and priests of their district stood for their instinctive righteousness, who have kept sweet the tradition that good people follow a light that shines within and above and ahead of them, that bad people care only for themselves, and that the good are saved and blessed and the bad damned and miserable. Protestantism was a movement towards the pursuit of a light called an inner light because every man must see it with his own eyes and not take any priest's word for it or any Church's account of it. In short, there is no question of a new religion, but rather of redistilling the eternal spirit of religion and thus extricating it from the sludgy residue of temporalities and legends that are making belief impossible, though they are the stock-in-trade of all the Churches and all the Schools.

RELIGION AND ROMANCE

It is the adulteration of religion by the romance of miracles and paradises and torture chambers that makes it reel at the impact of every advance in science, instead of being clarified by it. If you take an English village lad, and teach him that religion means believing that the stories of Noah's Ark and the Garden of Eden are literally true on the authority of God himself, and if that boy becomes an artisan and goes into the town among the sceptical city proletariat, then, when the jibes of his mates set him thinking, and he sees that these stories cannot be literally true, and learns that no candid prelate now pretends to believe them, he does not make any fine distinctions: he declares at once that religion is a fraud, and parsons and teachers hypocrites and liars. He becomes indifferent to religion if he has little conscience, and indignantly hostile to it if he has a good deal.

The same revolt against wantonly false teaching is happening daily in the professional classes whose recreation is reading and whose intellectual sport is controversy. They banish the Bible from their houses, and sometimes put into the hands of their unfortunate children Ethical and Rationalist tracts of the deadliest dullness, compelling these wretched infants to sit

out the discourses of Secularist lecturers (I have delivered some of them myself), who bore them at a length now forbidden by custom in the established pulpit. Our minds have reacted so violently towards provable logical theorems and demonstrable mechanical or chemical facts that we have become incapable of metaphysical truth, and try to cast out incredible and silly lies by credible and clever ones, calling in Satan to cast out Satan, and getting more into his clutches than ever in the process. Thus the world is kept sane less by the saints than by the vast mass of the indifferent, who neither act nor react in the matter. Butler's preaching of the gospel of Laodicea was a piece of common sense founded on his observation of this.

But indifference will not guide nations through civilization to the establishment of the perfect city of God. An indifferent statesman is a contradiction in terms; and a statesman who is indifferent on principle, a Laisser-faire or Muddle-Through doctrinaire, plays the deuce with us in the long run. Our statesmen must get a religion by hook or crook; and as we are committed to Adult Suffrage it must be a religion capable of vulgarization. The thought first put into words by the Mills when they said "There is no God; but this is a family secret," and long held unspoken by aristocratic statesmen and diplomatists, will not serve now; for the revival of civilization after the war cannot be effected by artificial breathing: the driving force of an undeluded popular consent is indispensable, and will be impossible until the statesman can appeal to the vital instincts of the people in terms of a common religion. The success of the Hang the Kaiser cry at the last General Election shews us very terrifyingly how a common irreligion can be used by myopic demagogy; and common irreligion will destroy civilization unless it is countered by common religion.

THE DANGER OF REACTION

And here arises the danger that when we realize this we shall do just what we did half a century ago, and what Pliable did in The Pilgrim's Progress when Christian landed him in the Slough of Despond: that is, run back in terror to our old superstitions. We jumped out of the frying-pan into the fire; and we are just as likely to jump back again, now that we feel hotter than ever. History records very little in the way of mental activity on the part of the mass of mankind except a series of stampedes from affirmative errors into negative ones and back again. It must therefore be said very precisely and clearly that the bankruptcy of Darwinism does not mean that Nobodaddy was Somebodaddy *with* "body, parts, and passions" after all; that the world was made in the year 4004 B.C.; that damnation means an eternity of blazing brimstone; that the Immaculate Conception means that sex is sinful and that Christ was parthenogenetically brought forth by a virgin descended in like manner from a line of virgins right back to Eve; that the Trinity is an anthropomorphic monster with three heads which are yet only one head; that in Rome the bread and wine on the altar become flesh and blood, and in England, in a still more mystical manner, they do and they do not; that the Bible is an infallible scientific manual, an accurate historical chronicle, and a complete guide to conduct; that we may lie and cheat and murder and then wash ourselves innocent in the blood of the lamb on Sunday at the cost of a *credo* and a penny in the plate, and so on and so forth. Civilization cannot be saved by people not only crude enough to believe these things, but irreligious enough to believe that such belief constitutes a religion. The education of children cannot safely be left in their hands. If dwindling sects like the Church of England, the Church of Rome, the Greek Church, and the rest, persist in trying to cramp the human mind within the limits of these grotesque perversions of natural truths and poetic metaphors, then they must be ruthlessly banished from the schools until they either perish in general contempt or discover the soul that is hidden in every dogma. The real Class War will be a war of intellectual classes; and its conquest will be the souls of the children.

A TOUCHSTONE FOR DOGMA

The test of a dogma is its universality. As long as the Church of England preaches a single doctrine that the Brahman, the Buddhist, the Mussulman, the Parsee, and all the other sectarians who are British subjects cannot accept, it has no legitimate place in the counsels of the British Commonwealth, and will remain what it is at present, a corrupter of youth, a danger to the State, and an obstruction to the fellowship of the Holy Ghost. This has never been more strongly felt than at present, after a war in which the Church failed grossly in the courage of its profession, and sold its lilies for the laurels of the soldiers of the Victoria Cross. All the cocks in Christendom have been crowing shame on it ever since; and it will not be spared for the sake of the two or three faithful who were found even among the bishops. Let the Church take it on authority, even my authority (as a professional legend maker) if it cannot see the truth by its own light: no dogma can be a legend. A legend can pass an ethnical frontier as a legend, but not as a truth; whilst the only frontier to the currency of a sound dogma as such is the frontier of capacity for understanding it.

This does not mean that we should throw away legend and parable and drama: they are the natural vehicles of dogma; but woe to the Churches and rulers who substitute the legend for the dogma, the parable for the history, the drama for the religion! Better by far declare the throne of God empty than set a liar and a fool on it. What are called wars of religion are always wars to destroy religion by affirming the historical truth or material substantiality of some legend, and killing those who refuse to accept it as historical or substantial. But who has ever refused to accept a good legend with delight *as* a legend? The legends, the parables, the dramas, are among the choicest treasures of mankind. No one is ever tired of stories of miracles. In vain did Mahomet repudiate the miracles ascribed to him: in vain did Christ furiously scold those who asked him to give them an exhibition as a conjuror: in vain did the saints declare that God chose them not for their powers but for their weaknesses; that the humble might be exalted, and the proud rebuked. People will have their miracles, their stories, their heroes and heroines and saints and martyrs and divinities to exercise their gifts of affection, admiration, wonder, and worship, and their Judases and devils to enable them to be angry and yet feel that they do well to be angry. Every one of these legends is the common heritage of the human race; and there is only one inexorable condition attached to their healthy enjoyment, which is that no one shall believe them literally. The reading of stories and delighting in them made Don Quixote a gentleman: the believing them literally made him a madman who slew lambs instead of feeding them. In England today good books of Eastern religious legends are read eagerly; and Protestants and Atheists read Roman Catholic legends of the Saints with pleasure. But such fare is shirked by Indians and Roman Catholics. Freethinkers read the Bible: indeed they seem to be its only readers now except the reluctant parsons at the church lecterns, who communicate their discomfort to the congregation by gargling the words in their throats in an unnatural manner that is as repulsive as it is unintelligible. And this is because the imposition of the legends as literal truths at once changes them from parables into falsehoods. The feeling against the Bible has become so strong at last that educated people not only refuse to outrage their intellectual consciences by reading the legend of Noah's Ark, with its funny beginning about the animals and its exquisite end about the birds: they will not read even the chronicles of King David, which may very well be true, and are certainly more candid than the official biographies of our contemporary monarchs.

WHAT TO DO WITH THE LEGENDS

What we should do, then, is to pool our legends and make a delightful stock of religious folk-lore on an honest basis for all mankind. With our minds freed from pretence and falsehood we could enter into the heritage of all the faiths. China would share her sages with Spain, and Spain her saints with China. The Ulster man who now gives his son an unmerciful thrashing if the boy is so tactless as to ask how the evening and the morning could be the first day before the sun was created, or to betray an innocent calf-love for the Virgin Mary, would buy him a bookful of legends of the creation and of mothers of God from all parts of the world, and be very glad to find his laddie as interested in such things as in marbles or Police and Robbers. That would be better than beating all good feeling towards religion out of the child, and blackening his mind by teaching him that the worshippers of the holy virgins, whether of the Parthenon or St Peter's, are fire-doomed heathens and idolaters. All the sweetness of religion is conveyed to the world by the hands of story-tellers and image-makers. Without their fictions the truths of religion would for the multitude be neither intelligible nor even apprehensible; and the prophets would prophesy and the teachers teach in vain. And nothing stands between the people and the fictions except the silly falsehood that the fictions are literal truths, and that there is nothing in religion but fiction.

A LESSON FROM SCIENCE TO THE CHURCHES

Let the Churches ask themselves why there is no revolt against the dogmas of mathematics though there is one against the dogmas of religion. It is not that the mathematical dogmas are more comprehensible. The law of inverse squares is as incomprehensible to the common man as the Athanasian creed. It is not that science is free from legends, witchcraft, miracles, biographic boostings of quacks as heroes and saints, and of barren scoundrels as explorers and discoverers. On the contrary, the iconography and hagiology of Scientism are as copious as they are mostly squalid. But no student of science has yet been taught that specific gravity consists in the belief that Archimedes jumped out of his bath and ran naked through the streets of Syracuse shouting Eureka, Eureka, or that the law of inverse squares must be discarded if anyone can prove that Newton was never in an orchard in his life. When some unusually conscientious or enterprising bacteriologist reads the pamphlets of Jenner, and discovers that they might have been written by an ignorant but curious and observant nurserymaid, and could not possibly have been written by any person with a scientifically trained mind, he does not feel that the whole edifice of science has collapsed and crumbled, and that there is no such thing as smallpox. It may come to that yet; for hygiene, as it forces its way into our schools, is being taught as falsely as religion is taught there; but in mathematics and physics the faith is still kept pure, and you may take the law and leave the legends without suspicion of heresy. Accordingly, the tower of the mathematician stands unshaken whilst the temple of the priest rocks to its foundation.

THE RELIGIOUS ART OF THE TWENTIETH CENTURY

Creative Evolution is already a religion, and is indeed now unmistakeably the religion of the twentieth century, newly arisen from the ashes of pseudo-Christianity, of mere scepticism, and of the soulless affirmations and blind negations of the Mechanists and Neo-Darwinians. But it cannot become a popular religion until it has its legends, its parables, its miracles. And when I say popular I do not mean apprehensible by villagers only. I mean apprehensible by Cabinet Ministers as well. It is unreasonable to look to the professional politician and administrator for light and leading in religion. He is neither a philosopher nor a prophet: if he were, he would be philosophizing and prophesying, and not neglecting both for the drudgery of practical government. Socrates and Coleridge did not remain soldiers, nor could John Stuart Mill remain the representative of Westminster in the House of Commons even when he was willing. The Westminster electors admired Mill for telling them that much of the difficulty of dealing with them arose from their being inveterate liars. But they would not vote a second time for the man who was not afraid to break the crust of mendacity on which they were all dancing; for it seemed to them that there was a volcanic abyss beneath, not having his philosophic conviction that the truth is the solidest standing ground in the end. Your front bench man will always be an exploiter of the popular religion or irreligion. Not being an expert, he must take it as he finds it; and before he can take it, he must have been told stories about it in his childhood and had before him all his life an elaborate iconography of it produced by writers, painters, sculptors, temple architects, and artists of all the higher sorts. Even if, as sometimes happens, he is a bit of an amateur in metaphysics as well as a professional politician, he must still govern according to the popular iconography, and not according to his own personal interpretations if these happen to be heterodox.

It will be seen then that the revival of religion on a scientific basis does not mean the death of art, but a glorious rebirth of it. Indeed art has never been great when it was not providing an iconography for a live religion. And it has never been quite contemptible except when imitating the iconography after the religion had become a superstition. Italian painting from Giotto to Carpaccio is all religious painting; and it moves us deeply and has real greatness. Compare with it the attempts of our painters a century ago to achieve the effects of the old masters by imitation when they should have been illustrating a faith of their own. Contemplate, if you can bear it, the dull daubs of Hilton and Haydon, who knew so much more about drawing and scumbling and glazing and perspective and anatomy and "marvellous foreshortening" than Giotto, the latchet of whose shoe they were nevertheless not worthy to unloose. Compare Mozart's Magic Flute, Beethoven's Ninth Symphony, Wagner's Ring, all of them reachings-forward to the new Vitalist art, with the dreary pseudo-sacred oratorios and cantatas which were produced for no better reason than that Handel had formerly made splendid thunder in that way, and with the stale confectionery, mostly too would-be pious to be even cheerfully toothsome, of Spohr and Mendelssohn, Stainer and Parry, which spread indigestion at our musical festivals until I publicly told Parry the bludgeoning truth about his Job and woke him to conviction of sin. Compare Flaxman and Thorwaldsen and Gibson with Phidias and Praxiteles, Stevens with Michael Angelo, Bouguereau's Virgin with Cimabue's, or the best operatic Christs of Scheffer and Müller with the worst Christs that the worst painters could paint before the end of the fifteenth century, and you must feel that until we have a great religious movement we cannot hope for a great artistic one. The disillusioned Raphael could paint a mother and child, but not a queen of Heaven as much less skilful men had done in the days of his great-grandfather; yet he could reach forward to the twentieth century and paint a Transfiguration of the Son of Man as they could not. Also, please note, he could decorate a house of pleasure for a cardinal very beautifully with voluptuous pictures of Cupid and Psyche; for this simple sort of Vitalism is always with us, and, like portrait painting, keeps the artist supplied with subject matter in the intervals between the ages of faith; so that your sceptical Rembrandts and Velasquezs are at least not compelled to paint shop fronts for want of anything else to paint in which they can really believe.

THE ARTIST-PROPHETS

And there are always certain rare but intensely interesting anticipations. Michael Angelo could not very well believe in Julius II or Leo X, or in much that they believed in; but he could paint the Superman three hundred years before Nietzsche wrote Also Sprach Zarathustra and Strauss set it to music. Michael Angelo won the primacy among all modern painters and sculptors solely by his power of shewing us superhuman persons. On the strength of his decoration and color alone he would hardly have survived his own death twenty years; and even his design would have had only an academic interest; but as a painter of prophets and sibyls he is greatest among the very greatest in his craft, because we aspire to a world of prophets and sibyls. Beethoven never heard of radio-activity nor of electrons dancing in vortices of inconceivable energy; but pray can anyone explain the last movement of his Hammerklavier Sonata, Opus

106, otherwise than as a musical picture of these whirling electrons? His contemporaries said he was mad, partly perhaps because the movement was so hard to play; but we, who can make a pianola play it to us over and over until it is as familiar as Pop Goes the Weasel, know that it is sane and methodical. As such, it must represent something; and as all Beethoven's serious compositions represent some process within himself, some nerve storm or soul storm, and the storm here is clearly one of physical movement, I should much like to know what other storm than the atomic storm could have driven him to this oddest of all those many expressions of cyclonic energy which have given him the same distinction among musicians that Michael Angelo has among draughtsmen.

In Beethoven's day the business of art was held to be "the sublime and beautiful." In our day it has fallen to be the imitative and voluptuous. In both periods the word passionate has been freely employed; but in the eighteenth century passion meant irresistible impulse of the loftiest kind: for example, a passion for astronomy or for truth. For us it has come to mean concupiscence and nothing else. One might say to the art of Europe what Antony said to the corpse of Cæsar: "Are all thy conquests, glories, triumphs, spoils, shrunk to this little measure?" But in fact it is the mind of Europe that has shrunk, being, as we have seen, wholly preoccupied with a busy spring-cleaning to get rid of its superstitions before readjusting itself to the new conception of Evolution.

EVOLUTION IN THE THEATRE

On the stage (and here I come at last to my own particular function in the matter), Comedy, as a destructive, derisory, critical, negative art, kept the theatre open when sublime tragedy perished. From Molière to Oscar Wilde we had a line of comedic playwrights who, if they had nothing fundamentally positive to say, were at least in revolt against falsehood and imposture, and were not only, as they claimed, "chastening morals by ridicule," but, in Johnson's phrase, clearing our minds of cant, and thereby shewing an uneasiness in the presence of error which is the surest symptom of intellectual vitality. Meanwhile the name of Tragedy was assumed by plays in which everyone was killed in the last act, just as, in spite of Molière, plays in which everyone was married in the last act called themselves comedies. Now neither tragedies nor comedies can be produced according to a prescription which gives only the last moments of the last act. Shakespear did not make Hamlet out of its final butchery, nor Twelfth Night out of its final matrimony. And he could not become the conscious iconographer of a religion because he had no conscious religion. He had therefore to exercise his extraordinary natural gifts in the very entertaining art of mimicry, giving us the famous "delineation of character" which makes his plays, like the novels of Scott, Dumas, and Dickens, so delightful. Also, he developed that curious and questionable art of building us a refuge from despair by disguising the cruelties of Nature as jokes. But with all his gifts, the fact remains that he never found the inspiration to write an original play. He furbished up old plays, and adapted popular stories, and chapters of history from Holinshed's Chronicle and Plutarch's biographies, to the stage. All this he did (or did not; for there are minus quantities in the algebra of art) with a recklessness which shewed that his trade lay far from his conscience. It is true that he never takes his characters from the borrowed story, because it was less trouble and more fun to him to create them afresh; but none the less he heaps the murders and villainies of the borrowed story on his own essentially gentle creations without scruple, no matter how incongruous they may be. And all the time his vital need for a philosophy drives him to seek one by the quaint professional method of introducing philosophers as characters into his plays, and even of making his heroes philosophers; but when they come on the stage they have no philosophy to expound: they are only pessimists and railers; and their occasional would-be philosophic speeches, such as The Seven Ages of Man and The Soliloquy on Suicide, shew how deeply in the dark Shakespear was as to what philosophy means. He forced himself in among the greatest of playwrights without having once entered that region in which Michael Angelo, Beethoven, Goethe, and the antique Athenian stage poets are great. He would really not be great at all if it were not that he had religion enough to be aware that his religionless condition was one of despair. His towering King Lear would be only a melodrama were it not for its express admission that if there is nothing more to be said of the universe than Hamlet has to say, then "as flies to wanton boys are we to the gods: they kill us for their sport."

Ever since Shakespear, playwrights have been struggling with the same lack of religion; and many of them were forced to become mere panders and sensation-mongers because, though they had higher ambitions, they could find no better subject matter. From Congreve to Sheridan they were so sterile in spite of their wit that they did not achieve between them the output of Molière's single lifetime; and they were all (not without reason) ashamed of their profession, and preferred to be regarded as mere men of fashion with a rakish hobby. Goldsmith's was the only saved soul in that pandemonium.

The leaders among my own contemporaries (now veterans) snatched at minor social problems rather than write entirely without any wider purpose than to win money and fame. One of them expressed to me his envy of the ancient Greek playwrights because the Athenians asked them, not for some "new and original" disguise of the half-dozen threadbare plots of the modern theatre, but for the deepest lesson they could draw from the familiar and sacred legends of their country. "Let us all," he said, "write an Electra, an Antigone, an Agamemnon, and shew what we can do with it." But he did not write any of them, because these legends are no longer religious: Aphrodite and Artemis and Poseidon are deader than their statues. Another, with a commanding position and every trick of British farce and Parisian drama at his fingers' ends, finally could not write without a sermon to preach, and yet could not find texts more fundamental than the hypocrisies of sham Puritanism, or the matrimonial speculation which makes our young actresses as careful of their reputations as of their complexions. A third, too tender-hearted to break our spirits with the realities of a bitter experience, coaxed a wistful pathos and a dainty fun out of the fairy cloudland that lay between him and the empty heavens. The giants of the theatre of our time, Ibsen and Strindberg, had no greater comfort for the world than we: indeed much less; for they refused us even the Shakespearian-Dickensian consolation of laughter at mischief, accurately called comic relief. Our emancipated young successors scorn us, very properly. But they will be able to do no better whilst the drama remains pre-Evolutionist. Let them consider the great exception of Goethe. He, no richer than Shakespear, Ibsen, or Strindberg in specific talent as a playwright, is in the empyrean whilst they are gnashing their teeth in impotent fury in the mud, or at best finding an acid enjoyment in the irony of their predicament. Goethe is Olympian: the other giants are infernal in everything but their veracity and their repudiation of the irreligion of their time: that is, they are bitter and hopeless. It is not a question of mere dates. Goethe was an Evolutionist in 1830: many playwrights, even young ones, are still untouched by Creative Evolution in 1920. Ibsen was Darwinized to the extent of exploiting heredity on the stage much as the ancient Athenian playwrights exploited the Eumenides; but there is no trace in his plays of any faith in or knowledge of Creative Evolution as a modern scientific fact. True, the poetic aspiration is plain enough in his Emperor or Galilean; but it is one of Ibsen's distinctions that nothing was valid for him but science; and he left that vision of the future which his Roman seer calls "the third Empire" behind him as a Utopian dream when he settled down to his serious grapple with realities in those plays of modern life with which he overcame Europe, and broke the dusty windows of every dry-rotten theatre in it from Moscow to Manchester.

MY OWN PART IN THE MATTER

In my own activities as a playwright I found this state of things intolerable. The fashionable theatre prescribed one serious subject: clandestine adultery: the dullest of all subjects for a serious author, whatever it may be for audiences who read the police intelligence and skip the reviews and leading articles. I tried slum-landlordism, doctrinaire Free Love (pseudo-Ibsenism), prostitution, militarism, marriage, history, current politics, natural Christianity, national and individual character, paradoxes of conventional society, husband - hunting, questions of conscience, professional delusions and impostures, all worked into a series of comedies of manners in the classic fashion, which was then very much out of fashion, the mechanical tricks of Parisian "construction" being *de rigueur* in the theatre. But this, though it occupied me and established me professionally, did not constitute me an iconographer of the religion of my time, and thus fulfil my natural function as an artist. I was quite conscious of this; for I had always known that civilization needs a religion as a matter of life or death; and as the conception of Creative Evolution developed I saw that we were at last within reach of a faith which complied with the first condition of all the religions that have ever taken hold of humanity: namely, that it must be, first and fundamentally, a science of metabiology. This was a crucial point with me; for I had seen Bible fetishism, after standing up to all the rationalistic batteries of Hume, Voltaire, and the rest, collapse before the onslaught of much less gifted Evolutionists, solely because they discredited it as a biological document; so that from that moment it lost its hold, and left literate Christendom faithless. My own Irish eighteenth-centuryism made it impossible for me to believe anything until I could conceive it as a scientific hypothesis, even though the abominations, quackeries, impostures, venalities, credulities, and delusions of the camp followers of science, and the brazen lies and priestly pretensions of the pseudo-scientific curemongers, all sedulously inculcated by modern "secondary education," were so monstrous that I was sometimes forced to make a verbal distinction between science and knowledge lest I should mislead my readers. But I never forgot that without knowledge even wisdom is more dangerous than mere opportunist ignorance, and that somebody must take the Garden of Eden in hand and weed it properly.

Accordingly, in 1901, I took the legend of Don Juan in its Mozartian form and made it a dramatic parable of Creative Evolution. But being then at the height of my invention and comedic talent, I decorated it too brilliantly and lavishly. I surrounded it with a comedy of which it formed only one act, and that act was so completely episodical (it was a dream which did not affect the action of the piece) that the comedy could be detached and played by itself: indeed it could hardly be played at full length owing to the enormous length of the entire work, though that feat has been performed a few times in Scotland by Mr Esmé Percy, who led one of the forlorn hopes of the advanced drama at that time. Also I supplied the published work with an imposing framework consisting of a preface, an appendix called The Revolutionist's Handbook, and a final display of aphoristic fireworks. The effect was so vertiginous, apparently, that nobody noticed the new religion in the centre of the intellectual whirlpool. Now I protest I did not cut these cerebral capers in mere inconsiderate exuberance. I did it because the worst convention of the criticism of the theatre current at that time was that intellectual seriousness is out of place on the stage; that the theatre is a place of shallow amusement; that people go there to be soothed after the enormous intellectual strain of a day in the city: in short, that a playwright is a person whose business it is to make unwholesome confectionery out of cheap emotions. My answer to this was to put all my intellectual goods in the shop window under the sign of Man and Superman. That part of my design succeeded. By good luck and acting, the comedy triumphed on the stage; and the book was a good deal discussed. Since then the sweet-shop view of the theatre has been out of countenance; and its critical exponents have been driven to take an intel-

lectual pose which, though often more trying than their old intellectually nihilistic vulgarity, at least concedes the dignity of the theatre, not to mention the usefulness of those who live by criticizing it. And the younger playwrights are not only taking their art seriously, but being taken seriously themselves. The critic who ought to be a newsboy is now comparatively rare.

I now find myself inspired to make a second legend of Creative Evolution without distractions and embellishments. My sands are running out; the exuberance of 1901 has aged into the garrulity of 1920; and the war has been a stern intimation that the matter is not one to be trifled with. I abandon the legend of Don Juan with its erotic associations, and go back to the legend of the Garden of Eden. I exploit the eternal interest of the philosopher's stone which enables men to live for ever. I am not, I hope, under more illusion than is humanly inevitable as to the crudity of this my beginning of a Bible for Creative Evolution. I am doing the best I can at my age. My powers are waning; but so much the better for those who found me unbearably brilliant when I was in my prime. It is my hope that a hundred apter and more elegant parables by younger hands will soon leave mine as far behind as the religious pictures of the fifteenth century left behind the first attempts of the early Christians at iconography. In that hope I withdraw and ring up the curtain.

XX

ANDROCLES AND THE LION
1916

ON THE PROSPECTS OF CHRISTIANITY

WHY NOT GIVE CHRISTIANITY A TRIAL?

The question seems a hopeless one after 2000 years of resolute adherence to the old cry of "Not this man, but Barabbas." Yet it is beginning to look as if Barabbas was a failure, in spite of his strong right hand, his victories, his empires, his millions of money, and his moralities and churches and political constitutions. "This man" has not been a failure yet; for nobody has ever been sane enough to try his way. But he has had one quaint triumph. Barabbas has stolen his name and taken his cross as a standard. There is a sort of compliment in that. There is even a sort of loyalty in it, like that of the brigand who breaks every law and yet claims to be a patriotic subject of the king who makes them. We have always had a curious feeling that though we crucified Christ on a stick, he somehow managed to get hold of the right end of it, and that if we were better men we might try his plan. There have been one or two grotesque attempts at it by inadequate people, such as the Kingdom of God in Munster, which was ended by a crucifixion so much more atrocious than the one on Calvary that the bishop who took the part of Annas went home and died of horror. But responsible people have never made such attempts. The moneyed, respectable, capable world has been steadily anti-Christian and Barabbasque since the crucifixion; and the specific doctrine of Jesus has not in all that time been put into political or general social practice. I am no more a Christian than Pilate was,

or you, gentle reader; and yet, like Pilate, I greatly prefer Jesus to Annas and Caiaphas; and I am ready to admit that after contemplating the world and human nature for nearly sixty years, I see no way out of the world's misery but the way which would have been found by Christ's will if he had undertaken the work of a modern practical statesman.

Pray do not at this early point lose patience with me and shut the book. I assure you I am as sceptical and scientific and modern a thinker as you will find anywhere. I grant you I know a great deal more about economics and politics than Jesus did, and can do things he could not do. I am by all Barabbasque standards a person of much better character and standing, and greater practical sense. I have no sympathy with vagabonds and talkers who try to reform society by taking men away from their regular productive work and making vagabonds and talkers of them too; and if I had been Pilate I should have recognized as plainly as he the necessity for suppressing attacks on the existing social order, however corrupt that order might be, by people with no knowledge of government and no power to construct political machinery to carry out their views, acting on the very dangerous delusion that the end of the world was at hand. I make no defence of such Christians as Savonarola and John of Leyden: they were scuttling the ship before they had learned how to build a raft; and it became necessary to throw them overboard to save the crew. I say this to set myself right with respectable society; but I must still insist that if Jesus could have worked out the practical problems of a Communist constitution, an admitted obligation to deal with crime without revenge or punishment, and a full assumption by humanity of divine responsibilities, he would have conferred an incalculable benefit on mankind, because these distinctive demands of his are now turning out to be good sense and sound economics.

I say distinctive, because his common humanity and his subjection to time and space (that is, to the Syrian life of his period) involved his belief in many things, true and false, that in no way distinguish him from other Syrians of that time. But such common beliefs do not constitute specific Christianity any more than wearing a beard, working in a carpenter's shop, or believing that the earth is flat and that the stars could drop on it from heaven like hailstones. Christianity interests practical statesmen now because of the doctrines that distinguished Christ from the Jews and the Barabbasques generally, including ourselves.

WHY JESUS MORE THAN ANOTHER?

I do not imply, however, that these doctrines were peculiar to Christ. A doctrine peculiar to one man would be only a craze, unless its comprehension depended on a development of human faculty so rare that only one exceptionally gifted man possessed it. But even in this case it would be useless, because incapable of spreading. Christianity is a step in moral evolution which is independent of any individual preacher. If Jesus had never existed (and that he ever existed in any other sense than that in which Shakespear's Hamlet existed has been vigorously questioned) Tolstoy would have thought and taught and quarrelled with the Greek Church all the same. Their creed has been fragmentarily practised to a considerable extent in spite of the fact that the laws of all countries treat it, in effect, as criminal. Many of its advocates have been militant atheists. But for some reason the imagination of white mankind has picked out Jesus of Nazareth as *the* Christ, and attributed all the Christian doctrines to him; and as it is the doctrine and not the man that matters, and as, besides, one symbol is as good as another provided everyone attaches the same meaning to it, I raise, for the moment, no question as to how far the gospels are original, and how far they consist of Greek and Chinese interpolations. The record that Jesus said certain things is not invalidated by a demonstration that Confucius said them before him. Those who claim a literal divine paternity for him cannot be silenced by the discovery that the same claim was made for Alexander and Augustus. And I am not just now concerned with the credibility of the gospels as records of fact; for I am not acting as a detective, but turning our modern lights on to certain ideas and doctrines in them which disentangle themselves from the rest because they are flatly contrary to common practice, common sense, and common belief, and yet have, in the teeth of dogged incredulity and recalcitrance, produced an irresistible impression that Christ, though rejected by his posterity as an unpractical dreamer, and executed by his contemporaries as a dangerous anarchist and blasphemous madman, was greater than his judges.

WAS JESUS A COWARD?

I know quite well that this impression of superiority is not produced on everyone, even of those who profess extreme susceptibility to it. Setting aside the huge mass of inculcated Christ-worship which has no real significance because it has no intelligence, there is, among people who are really free to think for themselves on the subject, a great deal of hearty dislike of Jesus and of contempt for his failure to save himself and overcome his enemies by personal bravery and cunning as Mahomet did. I have heard this feeling expressed far more impatiently by persons brought up in England as Christians than by Mahometans, who are, like their prophet, very civil to Jesus, and allow him a place in their esteem and veneration at least as high as we accord to John the Baptist. But this British bulldog contempt is founded on a complete misconception of his reasons for submitting voluntarily to an ordeal of torment and death. The modern Secularist is often so determined to regard Jesus as a man like himself and nothing more, that he slips unconsciously into the error of assuming that Jesus shared that view. But it is quite clear from the New Testament writers (the chief authorities for believing that Jesus ever existed) that Jesus at the time of his death believed himself to be the Christ, a divine personage. It is therefore absurd to criticize his conduct before Pilate as if he were Colonel Roosevelt or Admiral von Tirpitz or even Mahomet. Whether you accept his belief in his divinity as fully as Simon Peter did, or reject it as a delusion which led him to submit to torture and sacrifice his life without resistance in the conviction that he would presently rise again in glory, you are equally bound to admit that, far from behaving like a coward or a sheep, he shewed considerable physical fortitude in going through a cruel ordeal against which he could have defended himself as effectually as he cleared the money-changers out of the temple. "Gentle Jesus, meek and mild" is a snivelling modern invention, with no warrant in the gospels. St Matthew would as soon have thought of applying such adjectives to Judas Maccabeus as to Jesus; and even St Luke, who makes Jesus polite and gracious, does not make him meek. The picture of him as an English curate of the farcical comedy type, too meek to fight a policeman, and everybody's butt, may be useful in the nursery to soften children; but that such a figure could ever have become a centre of the world's attention is too absurd for discussion: grown men and women may speak kindly of a harmless creature who utters amiable sentiments and is a helpless nincompoop when he is called on to defend them; but they will not follow him, nor do what he tells them, because they do not wish to share his defeat and disgrace.

WAS JESUS A MARTYR?

It is important therefore that we should clear our minds of the notion that Jesus died, as some of us are in the habit of declaring, for his social and political opinions. There have been many martyrs to those opinions; but he was not one of them, nor, as his words shew, did he see any more sense in martyrdom than Galileo did. He was executed by the Jews for the blasphemy of claiming to be a God; and Pilate, to whom this was a mere piece of superstitious nonsense, let them execute him as the cheapest way of keeping them quiet, on the formal plea that he had committed treason against Rome by saying that he was the King of the Jews. He was not falsely accused, nor denied full opportunities of defending himself. The proceedings were quite straightforward and regular; and Pilate, to whom the appeal lay, favored him and despised his judges, and was evidently willing enough to be conciliated. But instead of denying the charge, Jesus repeated the offence. He knew what he was doing: he had alienated numbers of his own disciples and been stoned in the streets for doing it before. He was not lying: he believed literally what he said. The horror of the High Priest was perfectly natural: he was a Primate confronted with a heterodox street preacher uttering what seemed to him an appalling and impudent blasphemy. The fact that the blasphemy was to Jesus a simple statement of fact, and that it has since been accepted as such by all western nations, does not invalidate the proceedings, nor give us the right to regard Annas and Caiaphas as worse men than the Archbishop of Canterbury and the Head Master of Eton. If Jesus had been indicted in a modern court, he would have been examined by two doctors; found to be obsessed by a delusion; declared incapable of pleading; and sent to an asylum: that is the whole difference. But please note that when a man is charged before a modern tribunal (to take a case that happened the other day) of having asserted and maintained that he was an officer returned from the front to receive the Victoria Cross at the hands of the King, although he was in fact a mechanic, nobody thinks of treating him as afflicted with a delusion. He is punished for false pretences, because his assertion is credible and therefore misleading. Just so, the claim to divinity made by Jesus was to the High Priest, who looked forward to the coming of a Messiah, one that might conceivably have been true, and might therefore have misled the people in a very dangerous way. That was why he treated Jesus as an impostor and a blasphemer where we should have treated him as a madman.

THE GOSPELS WITHOUT PREJUDICE

All this will become clear if we read the gospels without prejudice. When I was young it was impossible to read them without fantastic confusion of thought. The confusion was so utterly confounded that it was called the proper spirit to read the Bible in. Jesus was a baby; and he was older than creation. He was a man who could be persecuted, stoned, scourged, and killed; and he was a god, immortal and all-powerful, able to raise the dead and call millions of angels to his aid. It was a sin to doubt either view of him: that is, it was a sin to reason about him; and the end was that you did not reason about him, and read about him only when you were compelled. When you heard the gospel stories read in church, or learnt them from painters and poets, you came out with an impression of their contents that would have astonished a Chinaman who had read the story without prepossession. Even sceptics who were specially on their guard, put the Bible in the dock, and read the gospels with the object of detecting discrepancies in the four narratives to shew that the writers were as subject to error as the writers of yesterday's newspaper.

All this has changed greatly within two generations. Today the Bible is so little read that the language of the Authorized Version is rapidly becoming obsolete; so that even in the United States, where the old tradition of the verbal infallibility of "the book of books" lingers more strongly than anywhere else except perhaps in Ulster, retranslations into modern English have been introduced perforce to save its bare intelligibility. It is quite easy today to find cultivated persons who have never read the New Testament, and on whom therefore it is possible to try the experiment of asking them to read the gospels and state what they have gathered as to the history and views and character of Christ.

THE GOSPELS NOW UNINTELLIGIBLE TO NOVICES

But it will not do to read the gospels with a mind furnished only for the reception of, say, a biography of Goethe. You will not make sense of them, nor even be able without impatient weariness to persevere in the task of going steadily through them, unless you know something of the history of the human imagination as applied to religion. Not long ago I asked a writer of distinguished intellectual competence whether he had made a study of the gospels since his childhood. His reply was that he had lately tried, but "found it all such nonsense that I could not stick it." As I do not want to send anyone to the gospels with this result, I had better here give a brief exposition of how much of the history of religion is needed to make the gospels and the conduct and ultimate fate of Jesus intelligible and interesting.

WORLDLINESS OF THE MAJORITY

The first common mistake to get rid of is that mankind consists of a great mass of religious people and a few eccentric atheists. It consists of a huge mass of worldly people, and a small percentage of persons deeply interested in religion and concerned about their own souls and other people's; and this section consists mostly of those who are passionately affirming the established religion and those who are passionately attacking it, the genuine philosophers being very few. Thus you never have a nation of millions of Wesleys and one Tom Paine. You have a million Mr Worldly Wisemans, one Wesley, with his small congregation, and one Tom Paine, with *his* smaller congregation. The passionately religious are a people apart; and if they were not hopelessly outnumbered by the worldly, they would turn the world upside down, as St Paul was reproached, quite justly, for wanting to do. Few people can number among their personal acquaintances a single atheist or a single Plymouth Brother. Unless a religious turn in ourselves has led us to seek the little Societies to which these rare birds belong, we pass our lives among people who, whatever creeds they may repeat, and in whatever temples they may avouch their respectability and wear their Sunday clothes, have robust consciences, and hunger and thirst, not for righteousness, but for rich feeding and comfort and social position and attractive mates and ease and pleasure and respect and consideration: in short, for love and money. To these people one morality is as good as another provided they are used to it and can put up with its restrictions without unhappiness; and in the maintenance of this morality they will fight and punish and coerce without scruple. They may not be the salt of the earth, these Philistines; but they are the substance of civilization; and they save society from ruin by criminals and conquerors as well as by Savonarolas and Knipperdollings. And as they know, very sensibly, that a little religion is good for children and serves morality, keeping the poor in goodhumor or in awe by promising rewards in heaven or threatening torments in hell, they encourage the religious people up to a certain point: for instance, if Savonarola only tells the ladies of Florence that they ought to tear off their jewels and finery and sacrifice them to God, they offer him a cardinal's hat, and praise him as a saint; but if he induces them to actually do it, they burn him as a public nuisance.

RELIGION OF THE MINORITY.
SALVATIONISM

The religion of the tolerated religious minority has always been essentially the same religion: that is why its changes of name and form have made so little difference. That is why, also, a nation so civilized as the English can convert negroes to their faith with great ease, but cannot convert Mahometans or Jews. The negro finds in civilized Salvationism an unspeakably more comforting version of his crude creed; but neither Saracen nor Jew sees any advantage in it over his own version. The Crusader was surprised to find the Saracen quite as religious and moral as himself, and rather more than less civilized. The Latin Christian has nothing to offer the Greek Christian that Greek Christianity has not already provided. They are all, at root, Salvationists.

Let us trace this religion of Salvation from its beginnings. So many things that man does not himself contrive or desire are always happening: death, plagues, tempests, blights, floods, sunrise and sunset, growths and harvests and decay, and Kant's two wonders of the starry heavens above us and the moral law within us, that we conclude that somebody must be doing it all, or that somebody is doing the good and somebody else doing the evil, or that armies of invisible persons, beneficent and malevolent, are doing it; hence you postulate gods and devils, angels and demons. You propitiate these powers with presents, called sacrifices, and flatteries, called praises. Then the Kantian moral law within you makes you conceive your god as a judge; and straightway you try to corrupt him, also with presents and flatteries. This seems shocking to us; but our objection to it is quite a recent development: no longer ago than Shakespear's time it was thought quite natural that litigants should give presents to human judges; and the buying off of divine wrath by actual money payments to priests, or, in the reformed churches which discountenance this, by subscriptions to charities and church building and the like, is still in full swing. Its practical disadvantage is that though it makes matters very easy for the rich, it cuts off the poor from all hope of divine favor. And this quickens the moral criticism of the poor to such an extent, that they soon find the moral law within them revolting against the idea of buying off the deity with gold and gifts, though they are still quite ready to buy him off with the paper money of praise and professions of repentance. Accordingly, you will find that though a religion may last unchanged for many centuries in primitive communities where the conditions of life leave no room for poverty and riches, and the process of propitiating the supernatural powers is as well within the means of the least of the members as within those of the headman, yet when commercial civilization arrives, and capi-talism divides the people into a few rich and a great many so poor that they can barely live, a movement for religious reform will arise among the poor, and will be essentially a movement for cheap or entirely gratuitous salvation.

To understand what the poor mean by propitiation, we must examine for a moment what they mean by justice.

THE DIFFERENCE BETWEEN ATONEMENT AND PUNISHMENT

The primitive idea of justice is partly legalized revenge and partly expiation by sacrifice. It works out from both sides in the notion that two blacks make a white, and that when a wrong has been done, it should be paid for by an equivalent suffering. It seems to the Philistine majority a matter of course that this compensating suffering should be inflicted on the wrongdoer for the sake of its deterrent effect on other would-be wrongdoers; but a moment's reflection will shew that this utilitarian application corrupts the whole transaction. For example, the shedding of innocent blood cannot be balanced by the shedding of guilty blood. Sacrificing a criminal to propitiate God for the murder of one of his righteous servants is like sacrificing a mangy sheep or an ox with the rinderpest: it calls down divine wrath instead of appeasing it. In doing it we offer God as a sacrifice the gratification of our own revenge and the protection of our own lives without cost to ourselves; and cost to ourselves is the essence of sacrifice and expiation. However much the Philistines have succeeded in confusing these things in practice, they are to the Salvationist sense distinct and even contrary. The Baronet's cousin in Dickens's novel, who, perplexed by the failure of the police to discover the murderer of the baronet's solicitor, said "Far better hang wrong fellow than no fellow," was not only expressing a very common sentiment, but trembling on the brink of the rarer Salvationist opinion that it is much better to hang the wrong fellow: that, in fact, the wrong fellow is the right fellow to hang.

The point is a cardinal one, because until we grasp it not only does historical Christianity remain unintelligible to us, but those who do not care a rap about historical Christianity may be led into the mistake of supposing that if we discard revenge, and treat murderers exactly as God treated Cain: that is, exempt them from punishment by putting a brand on them as unworthy to be sacrificed, and let them face the world as best they can with that brand on them, we should get rid both of punishment and sacrifice. It would not at all follow: on the contrary, the feeling that there must be an expiation of the murder might quite possibly lead to our putting some innocent person—the more innocent the better—to a cruel death to balance the account with divine justice.

SALVATION AT FIRST A CLASS PRIVILEGE; AND THE REMEDY

Thus, even when the poor decide that the method of purchasing salvation by offering rams and goats or bringing gold to the altar must be wrong because they cannot afford it, we still do not feel "saved" without a sacrifice and a victim. In vain do we try to substitute mystical rites that cost nothing, such as circumcision, or, as a substitute for that, baptism. Our sense of justice still demands an expiation, a sacrifice, a sufferer for our sins. And this leaves the poor man still in his old difficulty; for if it was impossible for him to procure rams and goats and shekels, how much more impossible is it for him to find a neighbor who will voluntarily suffer for his sins: one who will say cheerfully "You have committed a murder. Well, never mind: I am willing to be hanged for it in your stead"?

Our imagination must come to our rescue. Why not, instead of driving our-

selves to despair by insisting on a separate atonement by a separate redeemer for every sin, have one great atonement and one great redeemer to compound for the sins of the world once for all? Nothing easier, nothing cheaper. The yoke is easy, the burden light. All you have to do when the redeemer is once found (or invented by the imagination) is to believe in the efficacy of the transaction, and you are saved. The rams and goats cease to bleed; the altars which ask for expensive gifts and continually renewed sacrifices are torn down; and the Church of the single redeemer and the single atonement rises on the ruins of the old temples, and becomes a single Church of the Christ.

RETROSPECTIVE ATONEMENT; AND THE EXPECTATION OF THE REDEEMER

But this does not happen at once. Between the old costly religion of the rich and the new gratuitous religion of the poor there comes an interregnum in which the redeemer, though conceived by the human imagination, is not yet found. He is awaited and expected under the names of the Christ, the Messiah, Baldur the Beautiful, or what not; but he has not yet come. Yet the sinners are not therefore in despair. It is true that they cannot say, as we say, "The Christ has come, and has redeemed us"; but they can say "The Christ will come, and will redeem us," which, as the atonement is conceived as retrospective, is equally consoling. There are periods when nations are seething with this expectation and crying aloud with prophecy of the Redeemer through their poets. To feel that atmosphere we have only to take up the Bible and read Isaiah at one end of such a period and Luke and John at the other.

COMPLETION OF THE SCHEME BY LUTHER AND CALVIN

We now see our religion as a quaint but quite intelligible evolution from crude attempts to propitiate the destructive forces of Nature among savages to a subtle theology with a costly ritual of sacrifice possible only to the rich as a luxury, and finally to the religion of Luther and Calvin. And it must be said for the earlier forms that they involved very real sacrifices. The sacrifice was not always vicarious, and is not yet universally so. In India men pay with their own skins, torturing themselves hideously to attain holiness. In the west, saints amazed the world with their austerities and self-scourgings and confessions and vigils. But Luther delivered us from all that. His reformation was a triumph of imagination and a triumph of cheapness. It brought you complete salvation and asked you for nothing but faith. Luther did not know what he was doing in the scientific sociological way in which we know it; but his instinct served him better than knowledge could have done; for it was instinct rather than theological casuistry that made him hold so resolutely to Justification by Faith as the trump card by which he should beat the Pope, or, as he would have put it, the sign in which he should conquer. He may be said to have abolished the charge for admission to heaven. Paul had advocated this; but Luther and Calvin did it.

JOHN BARLEYCORN

There is yet another page in the history of religion which must be conned and digested before the career of Jesus can be fully understood. People who can read long books will find it in Frazer's Golden Bough. Simpler folk will find it in the peasant's song of John Barleycorn, now made accessible to our drawing room amateurs in the admirable collections of Somersetshire Folk Songs by Mr Cecil Sharp. From Frazer's *magnum opus* you will learn how the same primitive logic which makes the Englishman believe today that by eating a beefsteak he can acquire the strength and courage of the bull, and to hold that belief in the face of the most ignominious defeats by vegetarian wrestlers and racers and bicyclists, led the first men who conceived God as capable of incarnation to believe that they could acquire a spark of his divinity by eating his flesh and drinking his blood. And from the song of John Barleycorn you may learn how the miracle of the seed, the growth, and the harvest, still the most wonderful of all the miracles and as inexplicable as ever, taught the primitive husbandman, and, as we must now affirm, taught him quite rightly, that God is in the seed, and that God is immortal. And thus it became the test of Godhead that nothing that you could do to it could kill it, and that when you buried it, it would rise again in renewed life and beauty and give mankind eternal life on condition that it was eaten and drunk, and again slain and buried, to rise again for ever and ever. You may, and indeed must, use John Barleycorn "right barbarouslee," cutting him "off at knee" with your scythes, scourging him with your flails, burying him in the earth; and he will not resist you nor reproach you, but will rise again in golden beauty amidst a great burst of sunshine and bird music, and save you and renew your life. And from the interweaving of these two traditions with the craving for the Redeemer, you at last get the conviction that when the Redeemer comes he will be immortal; he will give us his body to eat and his blood to drink; and he will prove his divinity by suffering a barbarous death without resistance or reproach, and rise from the dead and return to the earth in glory as the giver of life eternal.

LOOKING FOR THE END OF THE WORLD

Yet another persistent belief has beset the imagination of the religious ever since religion spread among the poor, or, rather, ever since commercial civilization produced a hopelessly poor class cut off from enjoyment in this world. That belief is that the end of this world is at hand, and that it will presently pass away and be replaced by a kingdom of happiness, justice, and bliss in which the rich and the oppressors and the unjust shall have no share. We are all familiar with this expectation: many of us cherish some pious relative who sees in every great calamity a sign of the approaching end. Warning pamphlets are in constant circulation: advertisements are put in the papers and paid for by those who are convinced, and who are horrified at the indifference of the irreligious to the approaching doom. And revivalist preachers, now as in the days of John the Baptist, seldom fail to warn their flocks to watch and pray, as the great day will steal upon them like a thief in the night, and cannot be long deferred in a world so wicked. This belief also associates itself with Barleycorn's second coming; so that the two events become identified at last.

There is the other and more artificial side of this belief, on which it is an inculcated dread. The ruler who appeals to the prospect of heaven to console the poor and keep them from insurrection also curbs the vicious by threatening them with hell. In the Koran we find Mahomet driven more and more to this expedient of government; and experience confirms his evident belief that it is impossible to govern without it in certain phases of civilization. We shall see later on that it gives a powerful attraction to the belief in a Redeemer, since it adds to remorse of conscience, which hardened men bear very lightly, a definite dread of hideous and eternal torture.

THE HONOR OF DIVINE PARENTAGE

One more tradition must be noted. The consummation of praise for a king is to declare that he is the son of no earthly father, but of a god. His mother goes into the temple of Apollo, and Apollo comes to her in the shape of a serpent, or the like. The Roman emperors, following the example of Augustus, claimed the title of God. Illogically, such divine kings insist a good deal on their royal human ancestors. Alexander, claiming to be the son of Apollo, is equally determined to be the son of Philip. As the gospels stand, St Matthew and St Luke give genealogies (the two are different) establishing the descent of Jesus through Joseph from the royal house of David, and yet declare that not Joseph but the Holy Ghost was the father of Jesus. It is therefore now held that the story of the Holy Ghost is a later interpolation borrowed from the Greek and Roman imperial tradition. But experience shews that simultaneous faith in the descent from David and the conception by the Holy Ghost is possible. Such double beliefs are entertained by the human mind without uneasiness or consciousness of the contradiction involved. Many instances might be given: a familiar one to my generation being that of the Tichborne claimant, whose attempt to pass himself off as a baronet was supported by an association of laborers on the ground that the Tichborne family, in resisting it, were trying to do a laborer out of his rights. It is quite possible that Matthew and Luke may have been unconscious of the contradiction: indeed the interpolation theory does not remove the difficulty, as the interpolators themselves must have been unconscious of it. A better ground for suspecting interpolation is that St Paul knew nothing of the divine birth, and taught that Jesus came into the world at his birth as the son of Joseph, but rose from the dead after three days as the son of God. Here again, few notice the discrepancy: the three views are accepted simultaneously without intellectual discomfort. We can provisionally entertain half a dozen contradictory versions of an event if we feel either that it does not greatly matter, or that there is a category attainable in which the contradictions are reconciled.

But that is not the present point. All that need be noted here is that the legend of divine birth was sure to be attached sooner or later to very eminent persons in Roman imperial times, and that modern theologians, far from discrediting it, have very logically affirmed the miraculous conception not only of Jesus but of his mother.

With no more scholarly equipment than a knowledge of these habits of the human imagination, anyone may now read the four gospels without bewilderment, and without the contemptuous incredulity which spoils the temper of many modern atheists, or the senseless credulity which sometimes makes pious people force us to shove them aside in emergencies as impracticable lunatics when they ask us to meet violence and injustice with dumb submission in the belief that the strange demeanor of Jesus before Pilate was meant as an example of normal human conduct. Let us admit that without the proper clues the gospels are, to a modern educated person, nonsensical and incredible, whilst the apostles are unreadable. But with the clues, they are fairly plain sailing. Jesus becomes an intelligible and consistent person. His reasons for going "like a lamb to the slaughter" instead of saving himself as Mahomet did, become quite clear. The narrative becomes as credible as any other historical narrative of its period.

MATTHEW

THE ANNUNCIATION: THE MASSACRE: THE FLIGHT

Let us begin with the gospel of Matthew, bearing in mind that it does not profess to be the evidence of an eye-witness. It is a chronicle, founded, like other chronicles, on such evidence and records as the chronicler could get hold of. The only one of the evangelists who professes to give first-hand evidence as an eye-witness naturally takes care to say so; and the fact that Matthew makes no such pretension, and writes throughout as a chronicler, makes it clear that he is telling the story of Jesus as Holinshed told the story of Macbeth, except that, for a reason to be given later on, he must have collected his material and completed his book within the lifetime of persons contemporary with Jesus. Allowance must also be made for the fact that the gospel is written in the Greek language, whilst the first-hand traditions and the actual utterances of Jesus must have been in Aramaic, the dialect of Palestine. These distinctions are important, as you will find if you read Holinshed or Froissart and then read Benvenuto Cellini. You do not blame Holinshed or Froissart for believing and repeating the things they had read or been told, though you cannot always believe these things yourself. But when Cellini tells you that he saw this or did that, and you find it impossible to believe him, you lose patience with him, and are disposed to doubt everything in his autobiography. Do not forget, then, that Matthew is Holinshed and not Benvenuto. The very first pages of his narrative will put your attitude to the test.

Matthew tells us that the mother of Jesus was betrothed to a man of royal pedigree named Joseph, who was rich enough to live in a house in Bethlehem to which kings could bring gifts of gold without provoking any comment. An angel announces to Joseph that Jesus is the son of the Holy Ghost, and that he must not accuse her of infidelity because of her bearing a son of which he is not the father; but this episode disappears from the subsequent narrative: there is no record of its having been told to Jesus, nor any indication of his having any knowledge of it. The narrative, in fact, proceeds in all respects as if the annunciation formed no part of it.

Herod the Tetrarch, believing that a child has been born who will destroy him, orders all the male children to be slaughtered; and Jesus escapes by the flight of his parents into Egypt, whence they return to Nazareth when the danger is over. Here it is necessary to anticipate a little by saying that none of the other evangelists accepts this story, as none of them except John, who throws over Matthew altogether, shares his craze for treating history and biography as mere records of the fulfilment of ancient Jewish prophecies. This craze no doubt led him to seek for some legend bearing out Hosea's "Out of Egypt have I called my son," and Jeremiah's Rachel weeping for her children: in fact, he says so. Nothing that interests us nowadays turns on the credibility of the massacre of the innocents and the flight into Egypt. We may forget them, and proceed to the important part of the narrative, which skips at once to the manhood of Jesus.

JOHN THE BAPTIST

At this moment, a Salvationist prophet named John is stirring the people very strongly. John has declared that the rite of circumcision is insufficient as a dedication of the individual to God, and has substituted the rite of baptism. To us, who are accustomed to baptism as a matter of course, and to whom circumcision is a rather ridiculous foreign practice of no consequence, the sensational effect of such a heresy as this on the Jews is not apparent: it seems to us as natural that John should have baptized people as that the rector of our village should do so. But, as St Paul found to his cost later on, the discarding of circumcision for baptism was to the Jews as startling a heresy as the discarding of

transubstantiation in the Mass was to the Catholics of the XVI century.

JESUS JOINS THE BAPTISTS

Jesus entered as a man of thirty (Luke says) into the religious life of his time by going to John the Baptist and demanding baptism from him, much as certain well-to-do young gentlemen forty years ago "joined the Socialists." As far as established Jewry was concerned, he burnt his boats by this action, and cut himself off from the routine of wealth, respectability, and orthodoxy. He then began preaching John's gospel, which, apart from the heresy of baptism, the value of which lay in its bringing the Gentiles (that is, the uncircumcized) within the pale of salvation, was a call to the people to repent of their sins, as the kingdom of heaven was at hand. Luke adds that he also preached the communism of charity; told the surveyors of taxes not to over-assess the taxpayers; and advised soldiers to be content with their wages and not to be violent or lay false accusations. There is no record of John going beyond this.

THE SAVAGE JOHN AND THE CIVILIZED JESUS

Jesus went beyond it very rapidly, according to Matthew. Though, like John, he became an itinerant preacher, he departed widely from John's manner of life. John went into the wilderness, not into the synagogues; and his baptismal font was the river Jordan. He was an ascetic, clothed in skins and living on locusts and wild honey, practising a savage austerity. He courted martyrdom, and met it at the hands of Herod. Jesus saw no merit either in asceticism or martyrdom. In contrast to John he was essentially a highly-civilized, cultivated person. According to Luke, he pointed out the contrast himself, chaffing the Jews for complaining that John must be possessed by the devil because he was a teetotaller and vegetarian, whilst, because Jesus was neither one nor the other, they reviled him as a gluttonous man and a winebibber, the friend of the officials and their mistresses. He told straitlaced disciples that they would have trouble enough from other people without making any for themselves, and that they should avoid martyrdom and enjoy themselves whilst they had the chance. "When they persecute you in this city," he says, "flee into the next." He preaches in the synagogues and in the open air indifferently, just as they come. He repeatedly says, "I desire mercy and not sacrifice," meaning evidently to clear himself of the inveterate superstition that suffering is gratifying to God. "Be not, as the Pharisees, of a sad countenance," he says. He is convivial, feasting with Roman officials and sinners. He is careless of his person, and is remonstrated with for not washing his hands before sitting down to table. The followers of John the Baptist, who fast, and who expect to find the Christians greater ascetics than themselves, are disappointed at finding that Jesus and his twelve friends do not fast; and Jesus tells them that they should rejoice in him instead of being melancholy. He is jocular, and tells them they will all have as much fasting as they want soon enough, whether they like it or not. He is not afraid of disease, and dines with a leper. A woman, apparently to protect him against infection, pours a costly unguent on his head, and is rebuked because what it cost might have been given to the poor. He poohpoohs that lowspirited view, and says, as he said when he was reproached for not fasting, that the poor are always there to be helped, but that he is not there to be anointed always, implying that you should never lose a chance of being happy when there is so much misery in the world. He breaks the Sabbath; is impatient of conventionality when it is uncomfortable or obstructive; and outrages the feelings of the Jews by breaches of it. He is apt to accuse people who feel that way of hypocrisy. Like the late Samuel Butler, he regards disease as a department of sin, and on curing a lame man, says "Thy sins are forgiven" instead of "Arise and walk," subsequently maintaining, when the Scribes reproach him for assuming power to forgive sin as well as to cure disease, that the two come to the same thing. He has no modest affectations, and claims to be greater than Solomon or Jonah. When reproached, as Bunyan was, for resorting to the art of fiction when teaching in parables, he justifies himself on the ground that art is the only way in which the people can be taught. He is, in short, what we should call an artist and a Bohemian in his manner of life.

JESUS NOT A PROSELYTIST

A point of considerable practical importance today is that he expressly repudiates the idea that forms of religion, once rooted, can be weeded out and replanted with the flowers of a foreign faith. "If you try to root up the tares you will root up the wheat as well." Our proselytizing missionary enterprises are thus flatly contrary to his advice; and their results appear to bear him out in his view that if you convert a man brought up in another creed, you inevitably demoralize him. He acts on this view himself, and does not convert his disciples from Judaism to Christianity. To this day a Christian would be in religion a Jew initiated by baptism instead of circumcision, and accepting Jesus as the Messiah, and his teachings as of higher authority than those of Moses, but for the action of the Jewish priests, who, to save Jewry from being submerged in the rising flood of Christianity after the capture of Jerusalem and the destruction of the Temple, set up what was practically a new religious order, with new Scriptures and elaborate new observances, and to heir list of the accursed added one Ieschu, a bastard magician, whose comic rogueries brought him to a bad end like Punch or Til Eulenspiegel: an invention which cost them dear when the Christians got the upper hand of them politically. The Jew as Jesus, himself a Jew, knew him, never dreamt of such things, and could follow Jesus without ceasing to be a Jew.

THE TEACHINGS OF JESUS

So much for his personal life and temperament. His public career as a popular preacher carries him equally far beyond John the Baptist. He lays no stress on baptism or vows, and preaches conduct incessantly. He advocates communism, the widening of the private family with its cramping ties into the great family of mankind under the fatherhood of God, the abandonment of revenge and punishment, the counteracting of evil by good instead of by a hostile evil, and an organic conception of society in which you are not an independent individual but a member of society, your neighbor being another member, and each of you members one of another, as two fingers on a hand, the obvious conclusion being that unless you love your neighbor as yourself and he reciprocates you will both be the worse for it. He conveys all this with extraordinary charm, and entertains his hearers with fables (parables) to illustrate them. He has no synagogue or regular congregation, but travels from place to place with twelve men whom he has called from their work as he passed, and who have abandoned it to follow him.

THE MIRACLES

He has certain abnormal powers by which he can perform miracles. He is ashamed of these powers, but, being extremely compassionate, cannot refuse to exercise them when afflicted people beg him to cure them, when multitudes of people are hungry, and when his disciples are terrified by storms on the lakes. He asks for no reward, but begs the people not to mention these powers of his. There are two obvious reasons for his dislike of being known as a worker of miracles. One is the natural objection of all men who possess such powers, but have far more important business in the world than to exhibit them, to be regarded primarily as charlatans, besides being pestered to give exhibitions to satisfy curiosity. The other is that his view of the effect of miracles upon his mission is exactly that taken later on by Rousseau. He perceives that they will discredit him and divert attention from his doctrine by raising an entirely irrelevant issue between his disciples and his opponents.

Possibly my readers may not have studied Rousseau's Letters Written From The Mountain, which may be regarded as the classic work on miracles as credentials of divine mission. Rousseau shews, as Jesus foresaw, that the miracles are the main obstacle to the acceptance of Christianity, because their incredibility (if they were not incredible they would not be miracles) makes people sceptical as to the whole narrative, credible enough in the main, in which they occur, and suspicious of the doctrine with which they are thus associated. "Get rid of the miracles," said Rousseau, "and the whole world will fall at the feet of Jesus Christ." He points out that miracles offered as evidence of divinity, and failing to convince, make divinity ridiculous. He says, in effect, there is nothing in making a lame man walk: thousands of lame men have been cured and have walked without any miracle. Bring me a man with only one leg and make another grow instantaneously on him before my eyes, and I will be really impressed; but mere cures of ailments that have often been cured before are quite useless as evidence of anything else than desire to help and power to cure.

Jesus, according to Matthew, agreed so entirely with Rousseau, and felt the danger so strongly, that when people who were not ill or in trouble came to him and asked him to exercise his powers as a sign of his mission, he was irritated beyond measure, and refused with an indignation which they, not seeing Rousseau's point, must have thought very unreasonable. To be called "an evil and adulterous generation" merely for asking a miracle worker to give an exhibition of his powers, is rather a startling experience. Mahomet, by the way, also lost his temper when people asked him to perform miracles. But Mahomet expressly disclaimed any unusual powers; whereas it is clear from Matthew's story that Jesus (unfortunately for himself, as he thought) had some powers of healing. It is also obvious that the exercise of such powers would give rise to wild tales of magical feats which would expose their hero to condemnation as an impostor among people whose good opinion was of great consequence to the movement started by his mission.

But the deepest annoyance arising from the miracles would be the irrelevance of the issue raised by them. Jesus's teaching has nothing to do with miracles. If his mission had been simply to demonstrate a new method of restoring lost eyesight, the miracle of curing the blind would have been entirely relevant. But to say "You should love your enemies; and to convince you of this I will now proceed to cure this gentleman of cataract" would have been, to a man of Jesus's intelligence, the proposition of an idiot. If it could be proved today that not one of the miracles of Jesus actually occurred, that proof would not invalidate a single one of his didactic utterances; and conversely, if it could be proved that not only did the miracles actually occur, but that he had wrought a thousand other miracles a thousand times more wonderful, not a jot of weight would be added

to his doctrine. And yet the intellectual energy of sceptics and divines has been wasted for generations in arguing about the miracles on the assumption that Christianity is at stake in the controversy as to whether the stories of Matthew are false or true. According to Matthew himself, Jesus must have known this only too well; for wherever he went he was assailed with a clamor for miracles, though his doctrine created bewilderment.

So much for the miracles! Matthew tells us further, that Jesus declared that his doctrines would be attacked by Church and State, and that the common multitude were the salt of the earth and the light of the world. His disciples, in their relations with the political and ecclesiastical organizations, would be as sheep among wolves.

MATTHEW IMPUTES BIGOTRY TO JESUS

Matthew, like most biographers, strives to identify the opinions and prejudices of his hero with his own. Although he describes Jesus as tolerant even to carelessness, he draws the line at the Gentile, and represents Jesus as a bigoted Jew who regards his mission as addressed exclusively to "the lost sheep of the house of Israel." When a woman of Canaan begged Jesus to cure her daughter, he first refused to speak to her, and then told her brutally that "It is not meet to take the children's bread and cast it to the dogs." But when the woman said, "Truth, Lord; yet the dogs eat of the crumbs which fall from their master's table," she melted the Jew out of him and made Christ a Christian. To the woman whom he had just called a dog he said, "O woman, great is thy faith: be it unto thee even as thou wilt." This is somehow one of the most touching stories in the gospel; perhaps because the woman rebukes the prophet by a touch of his own finest quality. It is certainly out of character; but as the sins of good men are always out of character, t is not safe to reject the story as invented in the interest of Matthew's determination that Jesus shall have nothing to do with the Gentiles. At all events, there the story is; and it is by no means the only instance in which Matthew reports Jesus, in spite of the charm of his preaching, as extremely uncivil in private intercourse.

THE GREAT CHANGE

So far the history is that of a man sane and interesting apart from his special gifts as orator, healer, and prophet. But a startling change occurs. One day, after the disciples have discouraged him for a long time by their misunderstandings of his mission, and their speculations as to whether he is one of the old prophets come again, and if so, which, his disciple Peter suddenly solves the problem by exclaiming, "Thou art the Christ, the son of the living God." At this Jesus is extraordinarily pleased and excited. He declares that Peter has had a revelation straight from God. He makes a pun on Peter's name, and declares him the founder of his Church. And he accepts his destiny as a god by announcing that he will be killed when he goes to Jerusalem; for if he is really the Christ, it is a necessary part of his legendary destiny that he shall be slain. Peter, not understanding this, rebukes him for what seems mere craven melancholy; and Jesus turns fiercely on him and cries, "Get thee behind me, Satan."

Jesus now becomes obsessed with a conviction of his divinity, and talks about it continually to his disciples, though he forbids them to mention it to others. They begin to dispute among themselves as to the position they shall occupy in heaven when his kingdom is established. He rebukes them strenuously for this, and repeats his teaching that greatness means service and not domination; but he himself, always instinctively somewhat haughty, now becomes arrogant, dicta-

torial, and even abusive, never replying to his critics without an insulting epithet, and even cursing a fig-tree which disappoints him when he goes to it for fruit. He assumes all the traditions of the folklore gods, and announces that, like John Barleycorn, he will be barbarously slain and buried, but will rise from the earth and return to life. He attaches to himself the immemorial tribal ceremony of eating the god, by blessing bread and wine and handing them to his disciples with the words "This is my body: this is my blood." He forgets his own teaching and threatens eternal fire and eternal punishment. He announces, in addition to his Barleycorn resurrection, that he will come to the world a second time in glory and establish his kingdom on earth. He fears that this may lead to the appearance of impostors claiming to be himself, and declares explicitly and repeatedly that no matter what wonders these impostors may perform, his own coming will be unmistakeable, as the stars will fall from heaven, and trumpets be blown by angels. Further he declares that this will take place during the lifetime of persons then present.

JERUSALEM AND THE MYSTICAL SACRIFICE

In this new frame of mind he at last enters Jerusalem amid great popular curiosity; drives the moneychangers and sacrifice sellers out of the temple in a riot; refuses to interest himself in the beauties and wonders of the temple building on the ground that presently not a stone of it shall be left on another; reviles the high priests and elders in intolerable terms; and is arrested by night in a garden to avoid a popular disturbance. He makes no resistance, being persuaded that it is part of his destiny as a god to be murdered and to rise again. One of his followers shews fight, and cuts off the ear of one of his captors. Jesus rebukes him, but does not attempt to heal the wound, though he declares that if he wished to resist he could easily summon twelve million angels to his aid. He is taken before the high priest and by him handed over to the Roman governor, who is puzzled by his silent refusal to defend himself in any way, or to contradict his accusers or their witnesses, Pilate having naturally no idea that the prisoner conceives himself as going through an inevitable process of torment, death, and burial as a prelude to resurrection. Before the high priest he has also been silent except that when the priest asks him is he the Christ, the Son of God, he replies that they shall all see the Son of Man sitting at the right hand of power, and coming on the clouds of heaven. He maintains this attitude with frightful fortitude whilst they scourge him, mock him, torment him, and finally crucify him between two thieves. His prolonged agony of thirst and pain on the cross at last breaks his spirit, and he dies with a cry of "My God: why hast Thou forsaken me?"

NOT THIS MAN BUT BARABBAS

Meanwhile he has been definitely rejected by the people as well as by the priests. Pilate, pitying him, and unable to make out exactly what he has done (the blasphemy that has horrified the high priest does not move the Roman), tries to get him off by reminding the people that they have, by custom, the right to have a prisoner released at that time, and suggests that he should release Jesus. But they insist on his releasing a prisoner named Barabbas instead, and on having Jesus crucified. Matthew gives no clue to the popularity of Barabbas, describing him simply as "a notable prisoner." The later gospels make it clear, very significantly, that his offence was sedition and insurrection; that he was an advocate of physical force; and that he had killed his man. The choice of Barabbas thus appears as a popular choice of the militant advocate of physical force as against the unresisting advocate of mercy.

THE RESURRECTION

Matthew then tells how after three days an angel opened the family vault of one Joseph, a rich man of Arimathea, who had buried Jesus in it, whereupon Jesus rose and returned from Jerusalem to Galilee and resumed his preaching with his disciples, assuring them that he would now be with them to the end of the world.

At that point the narrative abruptly stops. The story has no ending.

DATE OF MATTHEW'S NARRATIVE

One effect of the promise of Jesus to come again in glory during the lifetime of some of his hearers is to date the gospel without the aid of any scholarship. It must have been written during the lifetime of Jesus's contemporaries: that is, whilst it was still possible for the promise of his Second Coming to be fulfilled. The death of the last person who had been alive when Jesus said "There be some of them that stand here that shall in no wise taste death til they see the Son of Man coming in his kingdom" destroyed the last possibility of the promised Second Coming, and bore out the incredulity of Pilate and the Jews. And as Matthew writes as one believing in that Second Coming, and in fact left his story unfinished to be ended by it, he must have produced his gospel within a lifetime of the crucifixion. Also, he must have believed that reading books would be one of the pleasures of the kingdom of heaven on earth.

CLASS TYPE OF MATTHEW'S JESUS

One more circumstance must be noted as gathered from Matthew. Though he begins his story in such a way as to suggest that Jesus belonged to the privileged classes, he mentions later on that when Jesus attempted to preach in his own country, and had no success there, the people said, "Is not this the carpenter's son?" But Jesus's manner throughout is that of an aristocrat, or at the very least the son of a rich bourgeois, and by no means a lowly-minded one at that. We must be careful therefore to conceive Joseph, not as a modern proletarian carpenter working for weekly wages, but as a master craftsman of royal descent. John the Baptist may have been a Keir Hardie; but the Jesus of Matthew is of the Ruskin-Morris class.

This haughty characterization is so marked that if we had no other documents concerning Jesus than the gospel of Matthew, we should not feel as we do about him. We should have been much less loth to say, "There is a man here who was sane until Peter hailed him as the Christ, and who then became a monomaniac." We should have pointed out that his delusion is a very common delusion among the insane, and that such insanity is quite consistent with the retention of the argumentative cunning and penetration which Jesus displayed in Jerusalem after his delusion had taken complete hold of him. We should feel horrified at the scourging and mocking and crucifixion just as we should if Ruskin had been treated in that way when he also went mad, instead of being cared for as an invalid. And we should have had no clear perception of any special significance in his way of calling the Son of God the Son of Man. We should have noticed that he was a Communist; that he regarded much of what we call law and order as machinery for robbing the poor under legal forms; that he thought domestic ties a snare for the soul; that he agreed with the proverb "The nearer the Church, the farther from God"; that he saw very plainly that the masters of the community should be its servants and not its oppressors and parasites; and that though he did not tell us not to fight our enemies, he did tell us to love them, and warned us that they who draw the sword shall perish by the sword. All this shews a great power of seeing through vulgar illusions, and a capacity for a higher morality than has yet been established in any civilized community; but it does not place Jesus above Confucius or Plato, not to mention more modern philosophers and moralists.

MARK

THE WOMEN DISCIPLES AND THE ASCENSION

Let us see whether we can get anything more out of Mark, whose gospel, by the way, is supposed to be older than Matthew's. Mark is brief; and it does not take long to discover that he adds nothing to Matthew except the ending of the story by Christ's ascension into heaven, and the news that many women had come with Jesus to Jerusalem, including Mary Magdalene, out of whom he had cast seven devils. On the other hand Mark says nothing about the birth of Jesus, and does not touch his career until his adult baptism by John. He apparently regards Jesus as a native of Nazareth, as John does, and not of Bethlehem, as Matthew and Luke do, Bethlehem being the city of David, from whom Jesus is said by Matthew and Luke to be descended. He describes John's doctrine as "Baptism of repentance unto remission of sins": that is, a form of Salvationism. He tells us that Jesus went into the synagogues and taught, not as the Scribes but as one having authority: that is, we infer, he preaches his own doctrine as an original moralist instead of repeating what the books say. He describes the miracle of Jesus reaching the boat by walking across the sea, but says nothing about Peter trying to do the same. Mark sees what he relates more vividly than Matthew, and gives touches of detail that bring the event more clearly before the reader. He says, for instance, that when Jesus walked on the waves to the boat, he was passing it by when the disciples called out to him. He seems to feel that Jesus's treatment of the woman of Canaan requires some apology, and therefore says that she was a Greek of Syrophenician race, which probably excused any incivility to her in Mark's eyes. He represents the father of the boy whom Jesus cured of epilepsy after the transfiguration as a sceptic who says "Lord, I believe: help thou mine unbelief." He tells the story of the widow's mite, omitted by Matthew. He explains that Barabbas was "lying bound with them that made insurrection, men who in the insurrection had committed murder." Joseph of Arimathea, who buried Jesus in his own tomb, and who is described by Matthew as a disciple, is described by Mark as "one who also himself was looking for the kingdom of God," which suggests that he was an independent seeker. Mark earns our gratitude by making no mention of the old prophecies, and thereby not only saves time, but avoids the absurd implication that Christ was merely going through a predetermined ritual, like the works of a clock, instead of living. Finally Mark reports Christ as saying, after his resurrection, that those who believe in him will be saved and those who do not, damned; but it is impossible to discover whether he means anything by a state of damnation beyond a state of error. The paleographers regard this passage as tacked on by a later scribe.

On the whole Mark leaves the modern reader where Matthew left him.

LUKE

LUKE THE LITERARY ARTIST

When we come to Luke, we come to a later story-teller, and one with a stronger natural gift for his art. Before you have read twenty lines of Luke's gospel you are aware that you have passed from the chronicler writing for the sake of recording important facts, to the artist, telling the story for the sake of telling it. At the very outset he achieves the most charming idyll in the Bible: the story of Mary crowded out of the inn into the stable and laying her newly-born son in the manger, and of the shepherds abiding in the field keeping watch over their flocks by night, and how the angel of the Lord came upon them, and the glory of the Lord shone around them, and suddenly there was with the angel a multitude of the heavenly host. These shepherds go to the stable and take the place of the kings in Matthew's chronicle. So completely has this story conquered and fascinated our imagination that most of us suppose all the gospels to contain it; but it is Luke's story and his alone: none of the others have the smallest hint of it.

THE CHARM OF LUKE'S NARRATIVE

Luke gives the charm of sentimental romance to every incident. The Annunciation, as described by Matthew, is made to Joseph, and is simply a warning to him not to divorce his wife for misconduct. In Luke's gospel it is made to Mary herself, at much greater length, with a sense of the ecstasy of the bride of the Holy Ghost. Jesus is refined and softened almost out of recognition: the stern peremptory disciple of John the Baptist, who never addresses a Pharisee or a Scribe without an insulting epithet, becomes a considerate, gentle, sociable, almost urbane person; and the Chauvinist Jew becomes a pro-Gentile who is thrown out of the synagogue in his own town for reminding the congregation that the prophets had sometimes preferred Gentiles to Jews. In fact they try to throw him down from a sort of Tarpeian rock which they use for executions; but he makes his way through them and escapes:

the only suggestion of a feat of arms on his part in the gospels. There is not a word of the Syrophenician woman. At the end he is calmly superior to his sufferings; delivers an address on his way to execution with unruffled composure; does not despair on the cross; and dies with perfect dignity, commending his spirit to God, after praying for the forgiveness of his persecutors on the ground that "They know not what they do." According to Matthew, it is part of the bitterness of his death that even the thieves who are crucified with him revile him. According to Luke, only one of them does this; and he is rebuked by the other, who begs Jesus to remember him when he comes into his kingdom. To which Jesus replies, "This day shalt thou be with me in Paradise," implying that he will spend the three days of his death here. In short, every device is used to get rid of the ruthless horror of the Matthew chronicle, and to relieve the strain of the Passion by touching episodes, and by representing Christ as superior to human suffering. It is Luke's Jesus who has won our hearts.

THE TOUCH OF PARISIAN ROMANCE

Luke's romantic shrinking from unpleasantness, and his sentimentality, are illustrated by his version of the woman with the ointment. Matthew and Mark describe it as taking place in the house of Simon the Leper, where it is objected to as a waste of money. In Luke's version the leper becomes a rich Pharisee; the woman becomes a Dame aux Camellias; and nothing is said about money and the poor. The woman washes the feet of Jesus with her tears and dries them with her hair; and he is reproached for suffering a sinful woman to touch him. It is almost an adaptation of the unromantic Matthew to the Parisian stage. There is a distinct attempt to increase the feminine interest all through. The slight lead given by Mark is taken up and developed. More is said about Jesus's mother and her feelings. Christ's following of women, just mentioned by Mark to account for their presence at his tomb, is introduced earlier; and some of the women are named; so that we are introduced to Joanna the wife of Chuza, Herod's steward, and Susanna. There is the quaint little domestic episode between Mary and Martha. There is the parable of the Prodigal Son, appealing to the indulgence romance has always shewn to Charles Surface and Des Grieux. Women follow Jesus to the cross; and he makes them a speech beginning "Daughters of Jerusalem." Slight as these changes may seem, they make a great change in the atmosphere. The Christ of Matthew could never have become what is vulgarly called a woman's hero (though the truth is that the popular demand for sentiment, as far as it is not simply human, is more manly than womanly); but the Christ of Luke has made possible those pictures which now hang in many ladies' chambers, in which Jesus is represented exactly as he is represented in the Lourdes cinematograph, by a handsome actor. The only touch of realism which Luke does not instinctively suppress for the sake of producing this kind of amenity is the reproach addressed to Jesus for sitting down to table without washing his hands; and that is retained because an interesting discourse hangs on it.

WAITING FOR THE MESSIAH

Another new feature in Luke's story is that it begins in a world in which everyone is expecting the advent of the Christ. In Matthew and Mark, Jesus comes into a normal Philistine world like our own of today. Not until the Baptist foretells that one greater than himself shall come after him does the old Jewish hope of a Messiah begin to stir again; and as Jesus begins as a disciple of John, and is baptized by him, nobody connects him with that hope until Peter has the sudden inspiration which produces so startling an effect on Jesus. But in Luke's gospel men's minds, and especially women's minds, are full of eager expectation of a Christ not only before the birth of Jesus, but before the birth of John the Baptist, the event with which Luke begins his story. Whilst Jesus and John are still in their mothers' wombs, John leaps at the approach of Jesus when the two mothers visit one another. At the circumcision of Jesus pious men and women hail the infant as the Christ.

The Baptist himself is not convinced; for at quite a late period in his former disciple's career he sends two young men to ask Jesus is he really the Christ. This is noteworthy because Jesus immediately gives them a deliberate exhibition of miracles, and bids them tell John what they have seen, and ask him what he thinks *now*. This is in complete contradiction to what I have called the Rousseau view of miracles as inferred from Matthew. Luke shews all a romancer's thoughtlessness about miracles: he regards them as "signs": that is, as proofs of the divinity of the person performing them, and not merely of thaumaturgic powers. He revels in miracles just as he revels in parables: they make such capital stories. He cannot allow the calling of Peter, James, and John from their boats to pass without a comic miraculous overdraft of fishes, with the net sinking the boats and provoking Peter to exclaim, "Depart from me; for I am a sinful man, O Lord," which should probably be translated, "I want no more of your miracles: natural fishing is good enough for my boats."

There are some other novelties in Luke's version. Pilate sends Jesus to Herod, who happens to be in Jerusalem just then, because Herod had expressed some curiosity about him; but nothing comes of it: the prisoner will not speak to him. When Jesus is ill received in a Samaritan village James and John propose to call down fire from heaven and destroy it; and Jesus replies that he is come not to destroy lives but to save them. The bias of Jesus against lawyers is emphasized and also his resolution not to admit that he is more bound to his relatives than to strangers. He snubs a woman who blesses his mother. As this is contrary to the traditions of sentimental romance, Luke would presumably have avoided it had he not become persuaded that the brotherhood of Man and the Fatherhood of God are superior even to sentimental considerations. The story of the lawyer asking what are the two chief commandments is changed by making Jesus put the question to the lawyer instead of answering it.

As to doctrine, Luke is only clear when his feelings are touched. His logic is weak; for some of the sayings of Jesus are pieced together wrongly, as anyone who has read them in the right order and context in Matthew will discover at once. He does not make anything new out of Christ's mission, and, like the other evangelists, thinks that the whole point of it is that Jesus was the long expected Christ, and that he will presently come back to earth and establish his kingdom, having duly died and risen again after three days. Yet Luke not only records the teaching as to communism and the discarding of hate, which have, of course, nothing to do with the Second Coming, but quotes one very remarkable saying which is not compatible with it, which is that people must not go about asking where the kingdom of heaven is, and saying "Lo, here!" and "Lo, there!" because the kingdom of heaven is within them. But Luke has no sense that this belongs to a quite different order of thought to his Christianity, and retains undisturbed his view of the kingdom as a locality as definite as Jerusalem or Madagascar.

JOHN

A NEW STORY AND A NEW CHARACTER

The gospel of John is a surprise after the others. Matthew, Mark, and Luke describe the same events in the same order (the variations in Luke are negligible), and their gospels are therefore called the synoptic gospels. They tell substantially the same story of a wandering preacher who at the end of his life came to Jerusalem. John describes a preacher who spent practically his whole adult life in the capital, with occasional visits to the provinces. His circumstantial account of the calling of Peter and the sons of Zebedee is quite different from the others; and he says nothing about their being fishermen. He says expressly that Jesus, though baptized by John, did not himself practise baptism, and that his disciples did. Christ's agonized appeal against his doom in the garden of Gethsemane becomes a cold-blooded suggestion made in the temple at a much earlier period. Jesus argues much more; complains a good deal of the unreasonableness and dislike with which he is met; is by no means silent before Caiaphas and Pilate; lays much greater stress on his resurrection and on the eating of his body (losing all his disciples except the twelve in consequence); says many apparently contradictory and nonsensical things to which no ordinary reader can now find any clue; and gives the impression of an educated, not to say sophisticated mystic, different both in character and schooling from the simple and downright preacher of Matthew and Mark, and the urbane easy-minded charmer of Luke. Indeed, the Jews say of him "How knoweth this man letters, having never learnt?"

JOHN THE IMMORTAL EYE-WITNESS

John, moreover, claims to be not only a chronicler but a witness. He declares that he is "the disciple whom Jesus loved," and that he actually leaned on the bosom of Jesus at the last supper and asked in a whisper which of them it was that should betray him. Jesus whispered that he would give a sop to the traitor, and thereupon handed one to Judas, who ate it and immediately became possessed by the devil. This is more natural than the other accounts, in which Jesus openly indicates Judas without eliciting any protest or exciting any comment. It also implies that Jesus deliberately bewitched Judas in order to bring about his own betrayal. Later on John claims that Jesus said to Peter "If I will that John tarry til I come, what is that to thee?"; and John, with a rather obvious mock modesty, adds that he must not claim to be immortal, as the disciples concluded; for Christ did not use that expression, but merely remarked "If I will that he tarry til I come." No other evangelist claims personal intimacy with Christ, or even pretends to be his contemporary (there is no ground for identifying Matthew the publican with Matthew the Evangelist); and John is the only evangelist whose account of Christ's career and character is hopelessly irreconcilable with Matthew's. He is almost as bad as Matthew, by the way, in his repeated explanations of Christ's actions as having no other purpose than to fulfil the old prophecies. The impression is more unpleasant, because, as John, unlike Matthew, is educated, subtle, and obsessed with artificial intellectual mystifications, the discovery that he is stupid or superficial in so simple a matter strikes one with distrust and dislike, in spite of his great literary charm, a good example of which is his transfiguration of the harsh episode of the Syrophenician woman into the pleasant story of the woman of Samaria. This perhaps is why his claim to be John the disciple, or to be a contemporary of Christ or even of any survivor of Christ's generation, has been

T

disputed, and finally, it seems, disallowed. But I repeat, I take no note here of the disputes of experts as to the date of the gospels, not because I am not acquainted with them, but because, as the earliest codices are Greek manuscripts of the fourth century A.D., and the Syrian ones are translations from the Greek, the paleographic expert has no difficulty in arriving at whatever conclusion happens to suit his beliefs or disbeliefs; and he never succeeds in convincing the other experts except when they believe or disbelieve exactly as he does. Hence I conclude that the dates of the original narratives cannot be ascertained, and that we must make the best of the evangelists' own accounts of themselves. There is, as we have seen, a very marked difference between them, leaving no doubt that we are dealing with four authors of well-marked diversity; but they all end in an attitude of expectancy of the Second Coming which they agree in declaring Jesus to have positively and unequivocally promised within the lifetime of his contemporaries. Any believer compiling a gospel after the last of these contemporaries had passed away would either reject and omit the tradition of that promise on the ground that since it was not fulfilled, and could never now be fulfilled, it could not have been made, or else have had to confess to the Jews, who were the keenest critics of the Christians, that Jesus was either an impostor or the victim of a delusion. Now all the evangelists except Matthew expressly declare themselves to be believers; and Matthew's narrative is obviously not that of a sceptic. I therefore assume as a matter of common sense that, interpolations apart, the gospels are derived from narratives written in the first century A.D. I include John, because though it may be claimed that he hedged his position by claiming that Christ, who specially loved him, endowed him with a miraculous life until the Second Coming, the conclusion being that John is alive at this moment, I cannot believe that a literary forger could hope to save the situation by so outrageous a pretension. Also, John's narrative is in many passages nearer to the realities of public life than the simple chronicle of Matthew or the sentimental romance of Luke. This may be because John was obviously more a man of the world than the others, and knew, as mere chroniclers and romancers never know, what actually happens away from books and desks. But it may also be because he saw and heard what happened instead of collecting traditions about it. The paleographers and daters of first quotations may say what they please: John's claim to give evidence as an eye-witness whilst the others are only compiling history is supported by a certain verisimilitude which appeals to me as one who has preached a new doctrine and argued about it, as well as written stories. This verisimilitude may be dramatic art backed by knowledge of public life; but even at that we must not forget that the best dramatic art is the operation of a divinatory instinct for truth. Be that as it may, John was certainly not the man to believe in the Second Coming and yet give a date for it after that date had passed. There is really no escape from the conclusion that the originals of all the gospels date from the period within which there was still a possibility of the Second Coming occurring at the promised time.

THE PECULIAR THEOLOGY OF JESUS

In spite of the suspicions roused by John's idiosyncrasies, his narrative is of enormous importance to those who go to the gospels for a credible modern religion. For it is John who adds to the other records such sayings as that "I and my father are one"; that "God is a spirit"; that the aim of Jesus is not only that the people should have life, but that they should have it "more abundantly" (a distinction much needed by people who think a man is either alive or dead, and never consider the important question how much alive he is); and that men should bear in mind what they were told in the 82nd Psalm: that they are gods, and are responsible for the doing of the mercy and justice of God. The Jews stoned him for saying these things, and, when he remonstrated with them for stupidly stoning one who had done nothing to them but good works, replied "For a good work we stone thee not; but for blasphemy, because that thou, being a man, makest thyself God." He insists (referring to the 82nd Psalm) that if it is part of their own religion that they are gods on the assurance of God himself, it cannot be blasphemy for him, whom the Father sanctified and sent into the world, to say "I am the son of God." But they will not have this at any price; and he has to escape from their fury. Here the point is obscured by the distinction made by Jesus between himself and other men. He says, in effect, "If you are gods, then, *à fortiori*, I am a god." John makes him say this, just as he makes him say "I am the light of the world." But Matthew makes him say to the people "Ye are the light of the world." John has no grip of the significance of these scraps which he has picked up: he is far more interested in a notion of his own that men can escape death and do even more extraordinary things than Christ himself: in fact, he actually represents Jesus as promising this explicitly, and is finally led into the audacious hint that he, John, is himself immortal in the flesh. Still, he does not miss the significant sayings altogether. However inconsistent they may be with the doctrine he is consciously driving at, they appeal to some sub-intellectual instinct in him that makes him stick them in, like a child sticking tinsel stars on the robe of a toy angel.

John does not mention the ascension; and the end of his narrative leaves Christ restored to life, and appearing from time to time among his disciples. It is on one of these occasions that John describes the miraculous draught of fishes which Luke places at the other end of Christ's career, at the call of the sons of Zebedee.

JOHN AGREED AS TO THE TRIAL AND CRUCIFIXION

Although John, following his practice of shewing Jesus's skill as a debater, makes him play a less passive part at his trial, he still gives substantially the same account of it as all the rest. And the question that would occur to any modern reader never occurs to him, any more than it occurred to Matthew, Mark, or Luke. That question is, Why on earth did not Jesus defend himself, and make the people rescue him from the High Priest? He was so popular that they were unable to prevent him driving the moneychangers out of the temple, or to arrest him for it. When they did arrest him afterwards, they had to do it at night in a garden. He could have argued with them as he had often done in the temple, and justified himself both to the Jewish law and to Caesar. And he had physical force at his command to back up his arguments: all that was needed was a speech to rally his followers; and he was not gagged. The reply of the evangelists would have been that all these inquiries are idle, because if Jesus had wished to escape, he could have saved himself all that trouble by doing what John describes him as doing: that is, casting his captors to the earth by an exertion of his miraculous power. If you asked John why he let them get up again and torment and execute him, John would have replied that it was part of the destiny of God to be slain and buried and to rise again, and that to have avoided this destiny would have been to repudiate his Godhead. And that is the only apparent explanation. Whether you believe with the evangelists that Christ could have rescued himself by a miracle, or, as a modern Secularist, point out that he could have defended himself effectually, the fact remains that according to all the narratives he did not do so. He had to die like a god, not to save himself "like one of the princes." [1] The consensus on this point is important, because it proves the absolute sincerity of Jesus's declaration that he was a god. No impostor would have accepted such dreadful consequences without an effort to save himself. No impostor would have been nerved to endure them by the conviction that he would rise from the grave and live again after three days. If we accept the story at all, we must believe this, and believe also that his promise to return in glory and establish his kingdom on earth within the lifetime of men then living, was one which he believed that he could, and indeed must fulfil. Two evangelists declare that in his last agony he despaired, and reproached God for forsaking him. The other two represent him as dying in unshaken conviction and charity with the simple remark that the ordeal was finished. But all four testify that his faith was not deceived, and that he actually rose again after three days. And I think it unreasonable to doubt that all four wrote their narratives in full faith that the other promise would be fulfilled too, and that they themselves might live to witness the Second Coming.

CREDIBILITY OF THE GOSPELS

It will be noted by the older among my readers, who are sure to be obsessed more or less by elderly wrangles as to whether the gospels are credible as matter-of-fact narratives, that I have hardly raised this question, and have accepted the credible and incredible with equal complacency. I have done this because credibility is a subjective condition, as the evolution of religious belief clearly shews. Belief is not dependent on evidence and reason. There is as much evidence that the miracles occurred as that the battle of Waterloo occurred, or that a large body of Russian troops passed through England in 1914 to take part in the war on the western front. The reasons for believing in the murder of Pompey are the same as the reasons for believing in the raising of Lazarus. Both have been believed and doubted by men of equal intelligence. Miracles, in the sense of phenomena we cannot explain, surround us on every hand: life itself is the miracle of miracles. Miracles in the sense of events that violate the normal course of our experience are vouched for every day: the flourishing Church of Christ Scientist is founded on a multitude of such miracles. Nobody believes all the miracles: everybody believes some of them. I cannot tell why men who will not believe that Jesus ever existed yet believe firmly that Shakespear was Bacon. I cannot tell why people who believe that angels appeared and fought on our side at the battle of Mons, and who believe that miracles occur quite frequently at Lourdes, nevertheless boggle at the miracle of the liquefaction of the blood of St Januarius, and reject it as a trick of priestcraft. I cannot tell why people who will not believe Matthew's story of three kings bringing costly gifts to the cradle of Jesus, believe Luke's story of the shepherds and the stable. I cannot tell why people, brought up to believe the Bible in the old literal way as an infallible record and revelation, and rejecting that view later on, begin by rejecting the Old

[1] Jesus himself had referred to that psalm (LXXXII) in which men who have judged unjustly and accepted the persons of the wicked (including by anticipation practically all the white inhabitants of the British Isles and the North American continent, to mention no other places) are condemned in the words, "I have said, ye are gods; and all of ye are children of the Most High; but ye shall die like men, and fall like one of the princes."

Testament, and give up the belief in a brimstone hell before they give up (if they ever do) the belief in a heaven of harps, crowns, and thrones. I cannot tell why people who will not believe in baptism on any terms believe in vaccination with the cruel fanaticism of inquisitors. I am convinced that if a dozen sceptics were to draw up in parallel columns a list of the events narrated in the gospels which they consider credible and incredible respectively, their lists would be different in several particulars. Belief is literally a matter of taste.

FASHIONS IN BELIEF

Now matters of taste are mostly also matters of fashion. We are conscious of a difference between medieval fashions in belief and modern fashions. For instance, though we are more credulous than men were in the Middle Ages, and entertain such crowds of fortune-tellers, magicians, miracle workers, agents of communication with the dead, discoverers of the elixir of life, transmuters of metals, and healers of all sorts, as the Middle Ages never dreamed of as possible, yet we will not take our miracles in the form that convinced the Middle Ages. Arithmetical numbers appealed to the Middle Ages just as they do to us, because they are difficult to deal with, and because the greatest masters of numbers, the Newtons and Leibnitzes, rank among the greatest men. But there are fashions in numbers too. The Middle Ages took a fancy to some familiar number like seven; and because it was an odd number, and the world was made in seven days, and there are seven stars in Charles's Wain, and for a dozen other reasons, they were ready to believe anything that had a seven or a seven times seven in it. Seven deadly sins, seven swords of sorrow in the heart of the Virgin, seven champions of Christendom, seemed obvious and reasonable things to believe in simply because they were seven. To us, on the contrary, the number seven is the stamp of superstition. We will believe in nothing less than millions. A medieval doctor gained his patient's confidence by telling him that his vitals were being devoured by seven worms. Such a diagnosis would ruin a modern physician. The modern physician tells his patient that he is ill because every drop of his blood is swarming with a million microbes and the patient believes him abjectly and instantly. Had a bishop told William the Conqueror that the sun was seventy-seven miles distant from the earth, William would have believed him not only out of respect for the Church, but because he would have felt that seventy-seven miles was the proper distance. The Kaiser, knowing just as little about it as the Conqueror, would send that bishop to an asylum. Yet he (I presume) unhesitatingly accepts the estimate of ninety-two and nine-tenths millions of miles, or whatever the latest big figure may be.

CREDIBILITY AND TRUTH

And here I must remind you that our credulity is not to be measured by the truth of the things we believe. When men believed that the earth was flat, they were not credulous: they were using their common sense, and, if asked to prove that the earth was flat, would have said simply, "Look at it." Those who refuse to believe that it is round are exercising a wholesome scepticism. The modern man who believes that the earth is round is grossly credulous. Flat Earth men drive him to fury by confuting him with the greatest ease when he tries to argue about it. Confront him with a theory that the earth is cylindrical, or annular, or hour-glass shaped, and he is lost. The thing he believes may be true, but that is not why he believes it: he believes it because in some mysterious way it appeals to his imagination. If you ask him why he believes that the sun is ninety-odd million miles off, either he will have to confess that he doesnt know, or he will say that Newton proved it. But he has not read the treatise in which Newton proved it, and does not even know that it was written in Latin. If you press an Ulster Protestant as to why he regards Newton as an infallible authority, and St Thomas Aquinas or the Pope as superstitious liars whom, after his death, he will have the pleasure of watching from his place in heaven whilst they roast in eternal flame, or if you ask me why I take into serious consideration Colonel Sir Almroth Wright's estimates of the number of streptococci contained in a given volume of serum whilst I can only laugh at the earlier estimates of the number of angels that can be accommodated on the point of a needle, no reasonable reply is possible except that somehow sevens and angels are out of fashion, and billions and streptococci are all the rage. I simply cannot tell you why Bacon, Montaigne, and Cervantes had a quite different fashion of credulity and incredulity from the Venerable Bede and Piers Plowman and the divine doctors of the Aquinas-Aristotle school, who were certainly no stupider, and had the same facts before them. Still less can I explain why, if we assume that these leaders of thought had all reasoned out their beliefs, their authority seemed conclusive to one generation and blasphemous to another, neither generation having followed the reasoning or gone into the facts of the matter for itself at all.

It is therefore idle to begin disputing with the reader as to what he should believe in the gospels and what he should disbelieve. He will believe what he can, and disbelieve what he must. If he draws any lines at all, they will be quite arbitrary ones. St John tells us that when Jesus explicitly claimed divine honors by the sacrament of his body and blood, so many of his disciples left him that their number was reduced to twelve. Many modern readers will not hold out so long: they will give in at the first miracle. Others will discriminate. They will accept the healing miracles, and reject the feeding of the multitude. To some the walking on the water will be a legendary exaggeration of a swim, ending in an ordinary rescue of Peter; and the raising of Lazarus will be only a similar glorification of a commonplace feat of artificial respiration, whilst others will scoff at it as a planned imposture in which Lazarus acted as a confederate. Between the rejection of the stories as wholly fabulous and the acceptance of them as the evangelists themselves mean them to be accepted, there will be many shades of belief and disbelief, of sympathy and derision. It is not a question of being a Christian or not. A Mahometan Arab will accept literally and without question parts of the narrative which an English Archbishop has to reject or explain away; and many Theosophists and lovers of the wisdom of India, who never enter a Christian Church except as sightseers, will revel in parts of John's gospel which mean nothing to a pious matter-of-fact Bradford manufacturer. Every reader takes from the Bible what he can get. In submitting a précis of the gospel narratives I have not implied any estimate either of their credibility or of their truth. I have simply informed him or reminded him, as the case may be, of what those narratives tell us about their hero.

CHRISTIAN ICONOLATRY AND THE PERIL OF THE ICONOCLAST

I must now abandon this attitude, and make a serious draft on the reader's attention by facing the question whether, if and when the medieval and Methodist will-to-believe the Salvationist and miraculous side of the gospel narratives fails us, as it plainly has failed the leaders of modern thought, there will be anything left of the mission of Jesus: whether, in short, we may not throw the gospels into the waste-paper basket, or put them away on the fiction shelf of our libraries. I venture to reply that we shall be, on the contrary, in the position of the man in Bunyan's riddle who found that "the more he threw away, the more he had." We get rid, to begin with, of the idolatrous or iconographic worship of Christ. By this I mean literally that worship which is given to pictures and statues of him, and to finished and unalterable stories about him. The test of the prevalence of this is that if you speak or write of Jesus as a real live person, or even as a still active God, such worshippers are more horrified than Don Juan was when the statue stepped from its pedestal and came to supper with him. You may deny the divinity of Jesus; you may doubt whether he ever existed; you may reject Christianity for Judaism, Mahometanism, Shintoism, or Fire Worship; and the iconolaters, placidly contemptuous, will only classify you as a freethinker or a heathen. But if you venture to wonder how Christ would have looked if he had shaved and had his hair cut, or what size in shoes he took, or whether he swore when he stood on a nail in the carpenter's shop, or could not button his robe when he was in a hurry, or whether he laughed over the repartees by which he baffled the priests when they tried to trap him into sedition and blasphemy, or even if you tell any part of his story in the vivid terms of modern colloquial slang, you will produce an extraordinary dismay and horror among the iconolaters. You will have made the picture come out of its frame, the statue descend from its pedestal, the story become real, with all the incalculable consequences that may flow from this terrifying miracle. It is at such moments that you realize that the iconolaters have never for a moment conceived Christ as a real person who meant what he said, as a fact, as a force like electricity, only needing the invention of suitable political machinery to be applied to the affairs of mankind with revolutionary effect.

Thus it is not disbelief that is dangerous in our society: it is belief. The moment it strikes you (as it may any day) that Christ is not the lifeless harmless image he has hitherto been to you, but a rallying centre for revolutionary influences which all established States and Churches fight, you must look to yourselves; for you have brought the image to life; and the mob may not be able to bear that horror.

THE ALTERNATIVE TO BARABBAS

But mobs must be faced if civilization is to be saved. It did not need the present war to shew that neither the iconographic Christ nor the Christ of St Paul has succeeded in effecting the salvation of human society. Whilst I write, the Turks are said to be massacring the Armenian Christians on an unprecedented scale; but Europe is not in a position to remonstrate; for her Christians are slaying one another by every device which civilization has put within their reach as busily as they are slaying the Turks. Barabbas is triumphant everywhere; and the final use he makes of his triumph is to lead us all to suicide with heroic gestures and resounding lies. Now those who, like myself, see the Barabbasque social organization as a failure, and are convinced that the Life Force (or whatever you choose to call it) cannot be finally beaten by any failure, and will even supersede humanity by evolving a higher species if we cannot master the problems raised by the multiplication of our own numbers, have always known that Jesus had a real message, and have felt the fascination of his character and doctrine. Not that we should nowadays dream of claiming any supernatural authority for him, much less the technical authority which attaches to an educated modern philosopher and jurist. But when, having entirely got rid of Salvationist Christianity, and even contracted a prejudice against Jesus on the score of his involuntary connection with it, we engage on a purely scientific study of economics, criminology, and biology, and find that our practical conclusions are virtually those of Jesus, we are distinctly pleased and encouraged to find that we were doing him an injustice, and that the nimbus that surrounds his head in the pictures may be interpreted some day as a light of science rather than a declaration of sentiment or a label of idolatry.

The doctrines in which Jesus is thus confirmed are, roughly, the following:

1. The kingdom of heaven is within you. You are the son of God; and God is the son of man. God is a spirit, to be worshipped in spirit and in truth, and not an elderly gentleman to be bribed and begged from. We are members one of another; so that you cannot injure or help your neighbor without injuring or helping yourself. God is your father: you are here to do God's work; and you and your father are one.

2. Get rid of property by throwing it into the common stock. Dissociate your work entirely from money payments. If you let a child starve you are letting God starve. Get rid of all anxiety about tomorrow's dinner and clothes, because you cannot serve two masters: God and Mammon.

3. Get rid of judges and punishment and revenge. Love your neighbor as yourself, he being a part of yourself. And love your enemies: they are your neighbors.

4. Get rid of your family entanglements. Every mother you meet is as much your mother as the woman who bore you. Every man you meet is as much your brother as the man she bore after you. Dont waste your time at family funerals grieving for your relatives: attend to life, not to death: there are as good fish in the sea as ever came out of it, and better. In the kingdom of heaven, which, as aforesaid, is within you, there is no marriage nor giving in marriage, because you cannot devote your life to two divinities: God and the person you are married to.

Now these are very interesting propositions; and they become more interesting every day, as experience and science drive us more and more to consider them favorably. In considering them, we shall waste our time unless we give them a reasonable construction. We must assume that the man who saw his way through such a mass of popular passion and illusion as stands between us and a sense of the value of such teaching was quite aware of all the objections that occur to an average stockbroker in the first five minutes. It is true that the world is governed to a considerable extent by the considerations that occur to stockbrokers in the first five minutes; but as the result is that the world is so badly governed that those who know the truth can hardly bear to live in it, an objection from an average stockbroker constitutes in itself a *prima facie* case for any social reform.

THE REDUCTION TO MODERN PRACTICE OF CHRISTIANITY

All the same, we must reduce the ethical counsels and proposals of Jesus to modern practice if they are to be of any use to us. If we ask our stockbroker to act simply as Jesus advised his disciples to act, he will reply, very justly, "You are advising me to become a tramp." If we urge a rich man to sell all that he has and give it to the poor, he will inform us that such an operation is impossible. If he sells his shares and his lands, their purchaser will continue all those activities which oppress the poor. If all the rich men take the advice simultaneously the shares will fall to zero and the lands be unsaleable. If one man sells out and throws the money into the slums, the only result will be to add himself and his dependents to the list of the poor, and to do no good to the poor beyond giving a chance few of them a drunken spree. We must therefore bear in mind that whereas, in the time of Jesus, and in the ages which grew darker and darker after his death until the darkness, after a brief false dawn in the Reformation and the Renascence, culminated in the commercial night of the nineteenth century, it was believed that you could not make men good by Act of Parliament, we now know that you cannot make them good in any other way, and that a man who is better than his fellows is a nuisance. The rich man must sell up not only himself but his whole class; and that can be done only through the Chancellor of the Exchequer. The disciple cannot have his bread without money until there is bread for everybody without money; and that requires an elaborate municipal organization of the food supply, rate supported. Being members one of another means One Man One Vote, and One Woman One Vote, and universal suffrage and equal incomes and all sorts of modern political measures. Even in Syria in the time of Jesus his teachings could not possibly have been realized by a series of independent explosions of personal righteousness on the part of the separate units of the population. Jerusalem could not have done what even a village community cannot do, and what Robinson Crusoe himself could not have done if his conscience, and the stern compulsion of Nature, had not imposed a common rule on the half dozen Robinson Crusoes who struggled within him for not wholly compatible satisfactions. And what cannot be done in Jerusalem or Juan Fernandez cannot be done in London, New York, Paris, and Berlin.

In short, Christianity, good or bad, right or wrong, must perforce be left out of the question in human affairs until it is made practically applicable to them by complicated political devices; and to pretend that a field preacher under the governorship of Pontius Pilate, or even Pontius Pilate himself in council with all the wisdom of Rome, could have worked out applications of Christianity or any other system of morals for the twentieth century, is to shelve the subject much more effectually than Nero and all its other persecutors ever succeeded in doing. Personal righteousness, and the view that you cannot make people moral by Act of Parliament, is, in fact, the favorite defensive resort of the people who, consciously or subconsciously, are quite determined not to have their property meddled with by Jesus or any other reformer.

MODERN COMMUNISM

Now let us see what modern experience and sociology have to say to the suggestion of Jesus that you should get rid of your property by throwing it into the common stock. One can hear the Pharisees of Jerusalem and Chorazin and Bethsaida saying, "My good fellow, if you were to divide up the wealth of Judea equally today, before the end of the year you would have rich and poor, poverty and affluence, just as you have today; for there will always be the idle and the industrious, the thrifty and the wasteful, the drunken and the sober; and, as you yourself have very justly observed, the poor we shall have always with us." And we can hear the reply, "Woe unto you, liars and hypocrites; for ye have this very day divided up the wealth of the country yourselves, as must be done every day (for man liveth not otherwise than from hand to mouth, nor can fish and eggs endure for ever); and ye have divided it unjustly; also ye have said that my reproach to you for having the poor always with you was a law unto you that this evil should persist and stink in the nostrils of God to all eternity; wherefore I think that Lazarus will yet see you beside Dives in hell." Modern Capitalism has made short work of the primitive pleas for inequality. The Pharisees themselves have organized communism in capital. Joint stock is the order of the day. An attempt to return to individual properties as the basis of our production would smash civilization more completely than ten revolutions. You cannot get the fields tilled today until the farmer becomes a co-operator. Take the shareholder to his railway, and ask him to point out to you the particular length of rail, the particular seat in the railway carriage, the particular lever in the engine that is his very own and nobody else's; and he will shun you as a madman, very wisely. And if, like Ananias and Sapphira, you try to hold back your little shop or what not from the common stock, represented by the Trust, or Combine, or Kartel, the Trust will presently freeze you out and rope you in and finally strike you dead industrially as thoroughly as St Peter himself. There is no longer any practical question open as to Communism in production: the struggle today is over the distribution of the product: that is, over the daily dividing-up which is the first necessity of organized society.

REDISTRIBUTION

Now it needs no Christ to convince anybody today that our system of distribution is wildly and monstrously wrong. We have million-dollar babies side by side with paupers worn out by a long life of unremitted drudgery. One person in every five dies in a workhouse, a public hospital, or a madhouse. In cities like London the proportion is very nearly one in two. Naturally so outrageous a distribution has to be effected by violence pure and simple. If you demur, you are sold up. If you resist the selling up you are bludgeoned and imprisoned, the process being euphemistically called the maintenance of law and order. Iniquity can go no further. By this time nobody who knows the figures of the distribution defends them. The most bigoted British Conservative hesitates to say that his king should be much poorer than Mr Rockefeller, or to proclaim the moral superiority of prostitution to needlework on the ground that it pays better. The need for a drastic redistribution of income in all civilized countries is now as obvious and as generally admitted as the need for sanitation.

SHALL HE WHO MAKES, OWN?

It is when we come to the question of the proportions in which we are to redistribute that controversy begins. We are bewildered by an absurdly unpractical notion that in some way a man's income should be given to him, not to enable him to live, but as a sort of Sunday School Prize for good behavior. And this folly is complicated by a less ridiculous but quite as unpractical belief that it is possible to assign to each person the exact portion of the national income that he or she has produced. To a child it seems that the blacksmith has made a horse-shoe, and that therefore the horse-shoe is his. But the blacksmith knows that the horse-shoe does not belong solely to him, but to his landlord, to the rate collector and taxgatherer, to the men from whom he bought the iron and anvil and the coals, leaving only a scrap of its value for himself; and this scrap he has to exchange with the butcher and baker and the clothier for the things that he really appropriates as living tissue or its wrappings, paying for all of them more than their cost; for these fellow traders of his have also their landlords and moneylenders to satisfy. If, then, such simple and direct village examples of apparent individual production turn out on a moment's examination to be the products of an elaborate social organization, what is to be said of such products as dreadnoughts, factory-made pins and needles, and steel pens? If God takes the dreadnought in one hand and a steel pen in the other, and asks Job who made them, and to whom they should belong by maker's right, Job must scratch his puzzled head with a potsherd and be dumb, unless indeed it strikes him that God is the ultimate maker, and that all we have a right to do with the product is to feed his lambs.

LABOR TIME

So maker's right as an alternative to taking the advice of Jesus would not work. In practice nothing was possible in that direction but to pay a worker by labor time: so much an hour or day or week or year. But how much? When that question came up, the only answer was "as little as he can be starved into accepting," with the ridiculous results already mentioned, and the additional anomaly that the largest share went to the people who did not work at all, and the least to those who worked hardest. In England nine-tenths of the wealth goes into the pockets of one-tenth of the population.

THE DREAM OF DISTRIBUTION ACCORDING TO MERIT

Against this comes the protest of the Sunday School theorists "Why not distribute according to merit?" Here one imagines Jesus, whose smile has been broadening down the ages as attempt after attempt to escape from his teaching has led to deeper and deeper disaster, laughing outright. Was ever so idiotic a project mooted as the estimation of virtue in money? The London School of Economics is, we must suppose, to set examination papers with such questions as "Taking the money value of the virtues of Jesus as 100, and of Judas Iscariot as zero, give the correct figures for, respectively, Pontius Pilate, the proprietor of the Gadarene swine, the widow who put her mite in the poor-box, Mr Horatio Bottomley, Shakespear, Mr Jack Johnson, Sir Isaac Newton, Palestrina, Offenbach, Sir Thomas Lipton, Mr Paul Cinquevalli, your family doctor, Florence Nightingale, Mrs Siddons, your charwoman, the Archbishop of Canterbury, and the common hangman." Or "The late Mr Barney Barnato received as his lawful income three thousand times as much money as an English agricultural laborer of good general character. Name the principal virtues in which Mr Barnato exceeded the laborer three thousandfold; and give in figures the loss sustained by civilization when Mr Barnato was driven to despair and suicide by the reduction of his multiple to one thousand." The Sunday School idea, with its principle "to each the income he deserves," is really too silly for discussion. Hamlet disposed of it three hundred years ago. "Use every man after his deserts, and who shall 'scape whipping?" Jesus remains unshaken as the practical man; and we stand exposed as the fools, the blunderers, the unpractical visionaries. The moment you try to reduce the Sunday School idea to figures you find that it brings you back to the hopeless plan of paying for a man's time; and your examination paper will read "The time of Jesus was worth nothing (he complained that the foxes had holes and the birds of the air nests whilst he had not a place to lay his head). Dr Crippen's time was worth, say, three hundred and fifty pounds a year. Criticize this arrangement; and, if you dispute its justice, state in pounds, dollars, francs and marks, what their relative time wages ought to have been." Your answer may be that the question is in extremely bad taste and that you decline to answer it. But you cannot object to being asked how many minutes of a bookmaker's time are worth two hours of an astronomer's?

VITAL DISTRIBUTION

In the end you are forced to ask the question you should have asked at the beginning. What do you give a man an income for? Obviously to keep him alive. Since it is evident that the first condition on which he can be kept alive without enslaving somebody else is that he shall produce an equivalent for what it costs to keep him alive, we may quite rationally compel him to abstain from idling by whatever means we employ to compel him to abstain from murder, arson, forgery, or any other crime. The one supremely foolish thing to do with him is to do nothing: that is to be as idle, lazy, and heartless in dealing with him as he is in dealing with us. Even if we provided work for him instead of basing, as we do, our whole industrial system on successive competitive waves of overwork with their ensuing troughs of unemployment, we should still sternly deny him the alternative of not doing it; for the result must be that he will become poor and make his children poor if he has any; and poor people are cancers in the commonwealth, costing far more than if they were handsomely pensioned off as incurables. Jesus had more sense than to propose anything of the sort. He said to his disciples, in effect, "Do your work for love; and let the other people lodge and feed and clothe you for love." Or, as we should put it nowadays, "for nothing." All human experience and all natural uncommercialized human aspiration point to this as the right path. The Greeks said, "First secure an independent income; and then practise virtue." We all strive towards an independent income. We all know as well as Jesus did that if we have to take thought for the morrow as to whether there shall be anything to eat or drink it will be impossible for us to think of nobler things, or live a higher life than that of a mole, whose life is from beginning to end a frenzied pursuit of food. Until the community is organized in such a way that the fear of bodily want is forgotten as completely as the fear of wolves already is in civilized capitals, we shall never have a decent social life. Indeed the whole attraction of our present arrangement lies in the fact that it does relieve a handful of us from this fear; but as the relief is effected stupidly and wickedly by making the favored handful parasitic on the rest, they are smitten with the degeneracy which seems to be the inevitable biological penalty of complete parasitism. They corrupt culture and statecraft instead of contributing to them, their excessive leisure being as mischievous as the excessive toil of the laborers. Anyhow, the moral is clear. The two main problems of organized society: how to produce subsistence enough for all its members, and how to prevent the theft of that subsistence by idlers, should be carefully dissociated; for the triumphant solution of the first by our inventors and chemists has been offset by the disastrous failure of our rulers to solve the other. Optimism on this point is only wilful blindness: we all have the hard fact of the failure before us. The only people who cling to the lazy delusion that it is possible to find a just distribution that will work automatically are those who postulate some revolutionary change like land nationalization, which by itself would obviously only force into greater urgency the problem of how to distribute the product of the land among all the individuals in the community.

EQUAL DISTRIBUTION

When that problem is at last faced, the question of the proportion in which the national income shall be distributed can have only one answer. All our shares must be equal. It has always been so: it always will be so. It is true that the incomes of robbers vary considerably from individual to individual; and the variation is reflected in the incomes of their parasites. The commercialization of certain exceptional talents has also produced exceptional incomes, direct and derivative. Persons who live on rent of land and capital are economically, though not legally, in the category of robbers, and have grotesquely different incomes. But in the huge mass of mankind variation of income from individual to individual is unknown, because it is ridiculously impracticable. As a device for persuading a carpenter that a judge is a creature of superior nature to himself, to be deferred and submitted to even to the death, we may give a carpenter a hundred pounds a year and a judge five thousand; but the wage for one carpenter is the wage for all the carpenters: the salary for one judge is the salary for all the judges.

THE CAPTAIN AND THE CABIN BOY

Nothing, therefore, is really in question, or ever has been, but the differences between class incomes. Already there is economic equality between captains, and economic equality between cabin boys. What is at issue still is whether there shall be economic equality between captains and cabin boys. What would Jesus have said? Presumably he would have said that if your only object is to produce a captain and a cabin boy for the purpose of transferring you from Liverpool to New York, or to manœuvre a fleet and carry powder from the magazine to the gun, then you need give no more than a shilling to the cabin boy for every pound you give to the more expensively trained captain. But if in addition to this you desire to allow the two human souls which are inseparable from the captain and the cabin boy, and which alone

differentiate them from the donkey-engine, to develop all their possibilities, then you may find the cabin boy costing rather more than the captain, because cabin boy's work does not do so much for the soul as captain's work. Consequently you will have to give him at least as much as the captain unless you definitely wish him to be a lower creature, in which case the sooner you are hanged as an abortionist the better. That is the fundamental argument.

THE POLITICAL AND BIOLOGICAL OBJECTIONS TO INEQUALITY

But there are other reasons for objecting to class stratification of income which have heaped themselves up since the time of Jesus. In politics it defeats every form of government except that of a necessarily corrupt oligarchy. Democracy in the most democratic modern republics: France and the United States for example, is an imposture and a delusion. It reduces justice and law to a farce: law becomes merely an instrument for keeping the poor in subjection; and accused workmen are tried, not by a jury of their peers, but by conspiracies of their exploiters. The press is the press of the rich and the curse of the poor: it becomes dangerous to teach men to read. The priest becomes the mere complement of the policeman in the machinery by which the country-house oppresses the village. Worst of all, marriage becomes a class affair: the infinite variety of choice which nature offers to the young in search of a mate is narrowed to a handful of persons of similar income; and beauty and health become the dreams of artists and the advertisements of quacks instead of the normal conditions of life. Society is not only divided but actually destroyed in all directions by inequality of income between classes: such stability as it has is due to the huge blocks of people between whom there is equality of income.

JESUS AS ECONOMIST

It seems therefore that we must begin by holding the right to an income as sacred and equal, just as we now begin by holding the right to life as sacred and equal. Indeed the one right is only a restatement of the other. To hang me for cutting a dock laborer's throat after making much of me for leaving him to starve when I do not happen to have a ship for him to unload is idiotic; for as he does far less mischief with his throat cut than when he is starving, a rational society would esteem the cutthroat more highly than the capitalist. The thing has become so obvious, and the evil so unendurable, that if our attempt at civilization is not to perish like all the previous ones, we shall have to organize our society in such a way as to be able to say to every person in the land, "Take no thought, saying What shall we eat? or What shall we drink? or Wherewithal shall we be clothed?" We shall then no longer have a race of men whose hearts are in their pockets and safes and at their bankers. As Jesus said, where your treasure is, there will your heart be also. That was why he recommended that money should cease to be a treasure, and that we should take steps to make ourselves utterly reckless of it, setting our minds free for higher uses. In other words, that we should all be gentlemen and take care of our country because our country takes care of us, instead of the commercialized cads we are, doing everything and anything for money, and selling our souls and bodies by the pound and the inch after wasting half the day haggling over the price. Decidedly, whether you think Jesus was God or not, you must admit that he was a first-rate political economist.

JESUS AS BIOLOGIST

He was also, as we now see, a first-rate biologist. It took a century and a half of evolutionary preachers, from Buffon and Goethe to Butler and Bergson, to convince us that we and our father are one; that as the kingdom of heaven is within us we need not go about looking for it and crying Lo here! and Lo there!; that God is not a picture of a pompous person in white robes in the family Bible, but a spirit; that it is through this spirit that we evolve towards greater abundance of life; that we are the lamps in which the light of the world burns: that, in short, we are gods though we die like men. All that is today sound biology and psychology; and the efforts of Natural Selectionists like Weismann to reduce evolution to mere automatism have not touched the doctrine of Jesus, though they have made short work of the theologians who conceived God as a magnate keeping men and angels as Lord Rothschild keeps buffaloes and emus at Tring.

MONEY THE MIDWIFE OF SCIENTIFIC COMMUNISM

It may be asked here by some simple-minded reader why we should not resort to crude Communism as the disciples were told to do. This would be quite practicable in a village where production was limited to the supply of the primitive wants which nature imposes on all human beings alike. We know that people need bread and boots without waiting for them to come and ask for these things and offer to pay for them. But when civilization advances to the point at which articles are produced that no man absolutely needs and that only some men fancy or can use, it is necessary that individuals should be able to have things made to their order and at their own cost. It is safe to provide bread for everybody because everybody wants and eats bread; but it would be absurd to provide microscopes and trombones, pet snakes and polo mallets, alembics and test tubes for everybody, as nine-tenths of them would be wasted;

and the nine-tenths of the population who do not use such things would object to their being provided at all. We have in the invaluable instrument called money a means of enabling every individual to order and pay for the particular things he desires over and above the things he must consume in order to remain alive, plus the things the State insists on his having and using whether he wants to or not: for example, clothes, sanitary arrangements, armies and navies. In large communities, where even the most eccentric demands for manufactured articles average themselves out until they can be foreseen within a negligible margin of error, direct communism (Take what you want without payment, as the people do in Morris's News From Nowhere) will, after a little experience, be found not only practicable but highly economical to an extent that now seems impossible. The sportsmen, the musicians, the physicists, the biologists will get their apparatus for the asking as easily as their bread, or, as at present, their paving, street lighting, and bridges; and the deaf man will not object to contribute to communal flutes when the musician has to contribute to communal ear trumpets. There are cases (for example, radium) in which the demand may be limited to the merest handful of laboratory workers, and in which nevertheless the whole community must pay because the price is beyond the means of any individual worker. But even when the utmost allowance is made for extensions of communism that now seem fabulous, there will still remain for a long time to come regions of supply and demand in which men will need and use money or individual credit, and for which, therefore, they must have individual incomes. Foreign travel is an obvious instance. We are so far from even national communism still, that we shall probably have considerable developments of local communism before it becomes possible for a Manchester man to go up to London for a day without taking any money with him. The modern practical form of the communism of Jesus is therefore, for the present, equal distribution of the surplus of the national income that is not absorbed by simple communism.

JUDGE NOT

In dealing with crime and the family, modern thought and experience have thrown no fresh light on the views of Jesus. When Swift had occasion to illustrate the corruption of our civilization by making a catalogue of the types of scoundrels it produces, he always gave judges a conspicuous place alongside of them they judged. And he seems to have done this not as a restatement of the doctrine of Jesus, but as the outcome of his own observation and judgment. One of Mr Gilbert Chesterton's stories has for its hero a judge who, whilst trying a criminal case, is so overwhelmed by the absurdity of his position and the wickedness of the things it forces him to do, that he throws off the ermine there and then, and goes out into the world to live the life of an honest man instead of that of a cruel idol. There has also been a propaganda of a soulless stupidity called Determinism, representing man as a dead object driven hither and thither by his environment, antecedents, circumstances, and so forth, which nevertheless does remind us that there are limits to the number of cubits an individual can add to his stature morally or physically, and that it is silly as well as cruel to torment a man five feet high for not being able to pluck fruit that is within the reach of men of average height. I have known a case of an unfortunate child being beaten for not being able to tell the time after receiving an elaborate explanation of the figures on a clock dial, the fact being that she was short-sighted and could not see them. This is a typical illustration of the absurdities and cruelties into which we are led by the counter-stupidity to Determinism: the doctrine of Free Will. The notion that people can be good if they like, and that you should give them a powerful additional motive for goodness by tormenting them when they do evil, would soon reduce itself to absurdity if its application were not kept within the limits which nature sets to the self-control of most of us. Nobody supposes that a man with no ear for music or no mathematical faculty could be compelled on pain of death, however cruelly inflicted, to hum all the themes of Beethoven's symphonies or to complete Newton's work on fluxions.

LIMITS TO FREE WILL

Consequently such of our laws as are not merely the intimidations by which tyrannies are maintained under pretext of law, can be obeyed through the exercise of a quite common degree of reasoning power and self-control. Most men and women can endure the ordinary annoyances and disappointments of life without committing murderous assaults. They conclude therefore that any person can refrain from such assaults if he or she chooses to, and proceed to reinforce self-control by threats of severe punishment. But in this they are mistaken. There are people, some of them possessing considerable powers of mind and body, who can no more restrain the fury into which a trifling mishap throws them than a dog can restrain himself from snapping if he is suddenly and painfully pinched. People fling knives and lighted paraffin lamps at one another in a dispute over a dinner-table. Men who have suffered several long sentences of penal servitude for murderous assaults will, the very day after they are released, seize their wives and cast them under drays at an irritating word. We have not only people who cannot resist an opportunity of stealing for the sake of satisfying their wants, but even people who have a specific mania for stealing, and do it when they are in no need of the things they steal. Burglary fascinates some men as sailoring fascinates some boys. Among respectable people how many are there who can be restrained by the warnings of their doctors and the lessons of experience from eating and drinking more than is good for them? It is true that between self-controlled people and ungovernable people there is a narrow margin of moral malingerers who can be made to behave themselves by the fear of consequences; but it is not worth while maintaining an abominable system of malicious, deliberate, costly and degrading ill-treatment of criminals for the sake of these marginal cases. For practical dealing with crime, Determinism or Predestination is quite a good working rule. People without self-control enough for social purposes may be killed, or may be kept in asylums with a view to studying their condition and ascertaining whether it is curable. To torture them and give ourselves virtuous airs at their expense is ridiculous and barbarous; and the desire to do it is vindictive and cruel. And though vindictiveness and cruelty are at least human qualities when they are frankly proclaimed and indulged, they are loathsome when they assume the robes of Justice. Which, I take it, is why Shakespear's Isabella gave such a dressing-down to Judge Angelo, and why Swift reserved the hottest corner of his hell for judges. Also, of course, why Jesus said "Judge not that ye be not judged" and "If any man hear my words and believe not, I judge him not" because "he hath one that judgeth him": namely, the Father who is one with him.

When we are robbed we generally appeal to the criminal law, not considering that if the criminal law were effective we should not have been robbed. That convicts us of vengeance.

I need not elaborate the argument further. I have dealt with it sufficiently elsewhere. I have only to point out that we have been judging and punishing ever since Jesus told us not to; and I defy anyone to make out a convincing case for believing that the world has been any better than it would have been if there had never been a judge, a prison, or a gallows in it all that time. We have simply added the misery of punishment to the misery of crime, and the cruelty of the judge to the cruelty of the criminal. We have taken the bad man, and made him worse by torture and degradation, incidentally making ourselves worse in the process. It does not seem very sensible, does it? It would have been far easier to kill him as kindly as possible, or to label him and leave him to his conscience, or to treat him as an invalid or a lunatic is now treated (it is only of late years, by the way, that madmen have been delivered from the whip, the chain, and the cage); and this, I presume, is the form in which the teaching of Jesus could have been put into practice.

JESUS ON MARRIAGE AND THE FAMILY

When we come to marriage and the family, we find Jesus making the same objection to that individual appropriation of human beings which is the essence of matrimony as to the individual appropriation of wealth. A married man, he said, will try to please his wife, and a married woman to please her husband, instead of doing the work of God. This is another version of "Where your treasure is, there will your heart be also." Eighteen hundred years later we find a very different person from Jesus, Talleyrand to wit, saying the same thing. A married man with a family, said Talleyrand, will do anything for money. Now this, though not a scientifically precise statement, is true enough to be a moral objection to marriage. As long

as a man has a right to risk his life or his livelihood for his ideas he needs only courage and conviction to make his integrity unassailable. But he forfeits that right when he marries. It took a revolution to rescue Wagner from his Court appointment at Dresden; and his wife never forgave him for being glad and feeling free when he lost it and threw her back into poverty. Millet might have gone on painting potboiling nudes to the end of his life if his wife had not been of a heroic turn herself. Women, for the sake of their children and parents, submit to slaveries and prostitutions that no unattached woman would endure.

This was the beginning and the end of the objection of Jesus to marriage and family ties, and the explanation of his conception of heaven as a place where there should be neither marrying nor giving in marriage. Now there is no reason to suppose that when he said this he did not mean it. He did not, as St Paul did afterwards in his name, propose celibacy as a rule of life; for he was not a fool, nor, when he denounced marriage, had he yet come to believe, as St Paul did, that the end of the world was at hand and there was therefore no more need to replenish the earth. He must have meant that the race should be continued without dividing with women and men the allegiance the individual owes to God within him. This raises the practical problem of how we are to secure the spiritual freedom and integrity of the priest and the nun without their barrenness and uncompleted experience. Luther the priest did not solve the problem by marrying a nun: he only testified in the most convincing and practical way to the fact that celibacy was a worse failure than marriage.

WHY JESUS DID NOT MARRY

To all appearance the problem oppresses only a few exceptional people.

Thoroughly conventional women married to thoroughly conventional men should not be conscious of any restriction: the chain not only leaves them free to do whatever they want to do, but greatly facilitates their doing it. To them an attack on marriage is not a blow struck in defence of their freedom but at their rights and privileges. One would expect that they would not only demur vehemently to the teachings of Jesus in this matter, but object strongly to his not having been a married man himself. Even those who regard him as a god descended from his throne in heaven to take on humanity for a time might reasonably declare that the assumption of humanity must have been incomplete at its most vital point if he were a celibate. But the facts are flatly contrary. The mere thought of Jesus as a married man is felt to be blasphemous by the most conventional believers; and even those of us to whom Jesus is no supernatural personage, but a prophet only as Mahomet was a prophet, feel that there was something more dignified in the bachelordom of Jesus than in the spectacle of Mahomet lying distracted on the floor of his harem whilst his wives stormed and squabbled and henpecked round him. We are not surprised that when Jesus called the sons of Zebedee to follow him, he did not call their father, and that the disciples, like Jesus himself, were all men without family entanglements. It is evident from his impatience when people excused themselves from following him because of their family funerals, or when they assumed that his first duty was to his mother, that he had found family ties and domestic affections in his way at every turn, and had become persuaded at last that no man could follow his inner light until he was free from their compulsion. The absence of any protest against this tempts us to declare that on this question of marriage there are no conventional people; and that every one of us is at heart a good Christian sexually.

INCONSISTENCY OF THE SEX INSTINCT

But the question is not so simple as that. Sex is an exceedingly subtle and complicated instinct; and the mass of mankind neither know nor care much about freedom of conscience, which is what Jesus was thinking about, and are concerned almost to obsession with sex, as to which Jesus said nothing. In our sexual natures we are torn by an irresistible attraction and an overwhelming repugnance and disgust. We have two tyrannous physical passions: concupiscence and chastity. We become mad in pursuit of sex: we become equally mad in the persecution of that pursuit. Unless we gratify our desire the race is lost: unless we restrain it we destroy ourselves. We are thus led to devize marriage institutions which will at the same time secure opportunities for the gratification of sex and raise up innumerable obstacles to it; which will sanctify it and brand it as infamous; which will identify it with virtue and with sin simultaneously. Obviously it is useless to look for any consistency in such institutions; and it is only by continual reform and readjustment, and by a considerable elasticity in their enforcement, that a tolerable result can be arrived at. I need not repeat here the long and elaborate examination of them that I prefixed to my play entitled Getting Married. Here I am concerned only with the views of Jesus on the question; and it is necessary, in order to understand the attitude of the world towards them, that we should not attribute the general approval of the decision of Jesus to remain unmarried as an endorsement of his views. We are simply in a state of confusion on the subject; but it is part of the confusion that we should conclude that Jesus was a celibate, and shrink even from the idea that his birth was a natural one, yet cling with ferocity to the sacredness of the institution which provides a refuge from celibacy.

FOR BETTER FOR WORSE

Jesus, however, did not express a complicated view of marriage. His objection to it was quite simple, as we have seen. He perceived that nobody could live the higher life unless money and sexual love were obtainable without sacrificing it; and he saw that the effect of marriage as it existed among the Jews (and as it still exists among ourselves) was to make the couples sacrifice every higher consideration until they had fed and pleased one another. The worst of it is that this dangerous preposterousness in marriage, instead of improving as the general conduct of married couples improves, becomes much worse. The selfish man to whom his wife is nothing but a slave, the selfish woman to whom her husband is nothing but a scapegoat and a breadwinner, are not held back from spiritual or any other adventures by fear of their effect on the welfare of their mates. Their wives do not make recreants and cowards of them: their husbands do not chain them to the cradle and the cooking range when their feet should be beautiful on the mountains. It is precisely as people become more kindly, more conscientious, more ready to shoulder the heavier part of the burden (which means that the strong shall give way to the weak and the slow hold back the swift), that marriage becomes an intolerable obstacle to individual evolution. And that is why the revolt against marriage of which Jesus was an exponent always recurs when civilization raises the standard of marital duty and affection, and at the same time produces a greater need for individual freedom in pursuit of a higher evolution.

THE REMEDY

This, fortunately, is only one side of marriage; and the question arises, can it not be eliminated? The reply is reassuring: of course it can. There is no mortal reason in the nature of things why a married couple should be economically dependent on one another. The Communism advocated by Jesus, which we have seen to be entirely practicable, and indeed inevitable if our civilization is to be saved from collapse, gets rid of that difficulty completely. And with the economic dependence will go the force of the outrageous claims that derive their real sanction from the economic pressure behind them. When a man allows his wife to turn him from the best work he is capable of doing, and to sell his soul at the highest commercial prices obtainable; when he allows her to entangle him in a social routine that is wearisome and debilitating to him, or tie him to her apron strings when he needs that occasional solitude which is one of the most sacred of human rights, he does so because he has no right to impose eccentric standards of expenditure and unsocial habits on her, and because these conditions have produced by their pressure so general a custom of chaining wedded couples to one another that married people are coarsely derided when their partners break the chain. And when a woman is condemned by her parents to wait in genteel idleness and uselessness for a husband when all her healthy social instincts call her to acquire a profession and work, it is again her economic dependence on them that makes their tyranny effective.

THE CASE FOR MARRIAGE

Thus, though it would be too much to say that everything that is obnoxious in marriage and family life will be cured by Communism, yet it can be said that it will cure what Jesus objected to in these institutions. He made no comprehensive study of them: he only expressed his own grievance with an overwhelming sense that it is a grievance so deep that all the considerations on the other side are as dust in the balance. Obviously there are such considerations, and very weighty ones too. When Talleyrand said that a married man with a family is capable of anything, he meant anything evil; but an optimist may declare, with equal half truth, that a married man is capable of anything good; that marriage turns vagabonds into steady citizens; and that men and women will, for love of their mates and children, practise virtues that unattached individuals are incapable of. It is true that too much of this domestic virtue is self-denial, which is not a virtue at all; but then the following of the inner light at all costs is largely self-indulgence, which is just as suicidal, just as weak, just as cowardly as self-denial. Ibsen, who takes us into the matter far more resolutely than Jesus, is unable to find any golden rule: both Brand and Peer Gynt come to a bad end; and though Brand does not do as much mischief as Peer, the mischief he does do is of extraordinary intensity.

CELIBACY NO REMEDY

We must, I think, regard the protest of Jesus against marriage and family ties as the claim of a particular kind of individual to be free from them because they hamper his own work intolerably. When he said that if we are to follow him in the sense of taking up his work we must give up our family ties, he was simply stating a fact; and to this day the Roman Catholic priest, the Buddhist lama, and the fakirs of all the eastern denominations accept the saying. It is also accepted by the physically enterprising, the explorers, the restlessly energetic of all kinds: in short, by the adventurous. The greatest sacrifice in marriage is the sacrifice of the adventurous attitude towards life: the being settled. Those who are born tired may crave for settlement; but to fresher and stronger spirits it is a form of suicide.

Now to say of any institution that it is incompatible with both the contemplative and adventurous life is to disgrace it so vitally that all the moralizings of all the Deans and Chapters cannot reconcile our souls to its slavery. The unmarried Jesus and the unmarried Beethoven, the unmarried Joan of Arc, Clare, Teresa, Florence Nightingale seem as they should be; and the saying that there is always something ridiculous about a married philosopher becomes inevitable. And yet the celibate is still more ridiculous than the married man: the priest, in accepting the alternative of celibacy, disables himself; and the best priests are those who have been men of this world before they became men of the world to come. But as the taking of vows does not annul an existing marriage, and a married man cannot become a priest, we are again confronted with the absurdity that the best priest is a reformed rake. Thus does marriage, itself intolerable, thrust us upon intolerable alternatives. The practical solution is to make the individual economically independent of marriage and the family, and to make marriage as easily dissoluble as any other partnership: in other words, to accept the conclusions to which experience is slowly driving both our sociologists and our legislators. This will not instantly cure all the evils of marriage, nor root up at one stroke its detestable tradition of property in human bodies. But it will leave Nature free to effect a cure; and in free soil the root may wither and perish.

This disposes of all the opinions and teachings of Jesus which are still matters of controversy. They are all in line with the best modern thought. He told us what we have to do; and we have had to find the way to do it. Most of us are still, as most were in his own time, extremely recalcitrant, and are being forced along that way by painful pressure of circumstances, protesting at every step that nothing will induce us to go; that is a ridiculous way, a disgraceful way, a socialistic way, an atheistic way, an immoral way, and that the vanguard ought to be ashamed of themselves and must be made to turn back at once. But they find that they have to follow the vanguard all the same if their lives are to be worth living.

AFTER THE CRUCIFIXION

Let us now return to the New Testament narrative; for what happened after the disappearance of Jesus is instructive. Unfortunately, the crucifixion was a complete political success. I remember that when I described it in these terms once before, I greatly shocked a most respectable newspaper in my native town, the Dublin Daily Express, because my journalistic phrase shewed that I was treating it as an ordinary event like Home Rule or the Insurance Act: that is (though this did not occur to the editor), as a real event which had really happened, instead of a portion of the Church service. I can only repeat, assuming as I am that it *was* a real event and did actually happen, that it was as complete a success as any in history. Christianity as a specific doctrine was slain with Jesus, suddenly and utterly. He was hardly cold in his grave, or high in his heaven (as you please), before the apostles dragged the tradition of him down to the level of the thing it has remained ever since. And that thing the intelligent heathen may study, if they would be instructed in it by modern books, in Samuel Butler's novel, The Way of All Flesh.

THE VINDICTIVE MIRACLES AND THE STONING OF STEPHEN

Take, for example, the miracles. Of Jesus alone of all the Christian miracle workers there is no record, except in certain gospels that all men reject, of a malicious or destructive miracle. A barren fig-tree was the only victim of his anger. Every one of his miracles on sentient subjects was an act of kindness. John declares that he healed the wound of the man whose ear was cut off (by Peter, John says) at the arrest in the garden. One of the first things the apostles did with their miraculous power was to strike dead a wretched man and his wife who had defrauded them by holding back some money from the common stock. They struck people blind or dead without remorse, judging because they had been judged. They healed the sick and raised the dead apparently in a spirit of pure display and advertisement. Their doctrine did not contain a ray of that light which reveals Jesus as one of the redeemers of men from folly and error. They cancelled him, and went back straight to John the Baptist and his formula of securing remission of sins by repentance and the rite of baptism (being born again of water and the spirit). Peter's first harangue softens us by the human touch of its exordium, which was a quaint assurance to his hearers that they must believe him to be sober because it was too early in the day to get drunk; but of Jesus he had nothing to say except that he was the Christ foretold by the prophets as coming from the seed of David, and that they must believe this and be baptized. To this the other apostles added incessant denunciations of the Jews for having crucified him, and threats of the destruction that would overtake them if they did not repent: that is, if they did not join the sect which the apostles were now forming. A quite intolerable young speaker named Stephen delivered an oration to the council, in which he first inflicted on them a tedious sketch of the history of Israel, with which they were presumably as well acquainted as he, and then reviled them in the most insulting terms as "stiff-necked and uncircumcized." Finally, after boring and annoying them to the utmost bearable extremity, he looked up and declared that he saw the heavens open, and Christ standing on the right hand of God. This was too much: they threw him out of the city and stoned him to death. It was a severe way of suppressing a tactless and conceited bore; but it was pardonable and human in comparison to the slaughter of poor Ananias and Sapphira.

PAUL

Suddenly a man of genius, Paul, violently anti-Christian, enters on the scene, holding the clothes of the men who are stoning Stephen. He persecutes the Christians with great vigor, a sport which he combines with the business of a tentmaker. This temperamental hatred of Jesus, whom he has never seen, is a pathological symptom of that particular sort of conscience and nervous constitution which brings its victims under the tyranny of two delirious terrors: the terror of sin and the terror of death, which may be called also the terror of sex and the terror of life. Now Jesus, with his healthy conscience on his higher plane, was free from these terrors. He consorted freely with sinners, and was never concerned for a moment, as far as we know, about whether his conduct was sinful or not; so that he has forced us to accept him as the man without sin. Even if we reckon his last days as the days of his delusion, he none the less gave a fairly convincing exhibition of superiority to the fear of death. This must have both fascinated and horrified Paul, or Saul, as he was first called. The horror accounts for his fierce persecution of the Christians. The fascination accounts for the strangest of his fancies: the fancy for attaching the name of Jesus Christ to the great idea which flashed upon him on the road to Damascus, the idea that he could not only make a religion of his two terrors, but that the movement started by Jesus offered him the nucleus for his new Church. It was a monstrous idea; and the shock of it, as he afterwards declared, struck him blind for days. He heard Jesus calling to him from the clouds, "Why persecute me?" His natural hatred of the teacher for whom Sin and Death had no terrors turned into a wild personal worship of him which has the ghastliness of a beautiful thing seen in a false light.

The chronicler of the Acts of the Apostles sees nothing of the significance of this. The great danger of conversion in all ages has been that when the religion of the high mind is offered to the lower mind, the lower mind, feeling its fascination without understanding it, and being incapable of rising to it, drags it down to its level by degrading it. Years ago I said that the conversion of a savage to Christianity is the conversion of Christianity to savagery. The conversion of Paul was no conversion at all: it was Paul who converted the religion that has raised one man above sin and death into a religion that delivered millions of men so completely into their dominion that their own common nature became a horror to them, and the religious life became a denial of life. Paul had no intention of surrendering either his Judaism or his Roman citizenship to the new moral world (as Robert Owen called it) of Communism and Jesuism. Just as in our own time Karl Marx, not content to take political economy as he found it, insisted on rebuilding it from the bottom upwards in his own way, and thereby gave a new lease of life to the errors it was just outgrowing, so Paul reconstructed the old Salvationism from which Jesus had vainly tried to redeem him, and produced a fantastic theology which is still the most amazing thing of the kind known to us. Being intellectually an inveterate Roman Rationalist, always discarding the irrational real thing for the unreal but ratiocinable postulate, he began by discarding Man as he is, and substituted a postulate which he called Adam. And when he was asked, as he surely must have been in a world not wholly mad, what had become of the natural man, he replied "Adam *is* the natural man." This was confusing to simpletons, because according to tradition Adam was certainly the name of the natural man as created in the garden of Eden. It was as if a preacher of our own time had described as typically British Frankenstein's monster, and called him Smith, and somebody, on demanding what about the man in the street, had been told "Smith *is* the man in the street." The thing happens often enough; for indeed the world is full of these Adams and Smiths and men in the street and average sensual men and economic men and womanly women and what not, all of them imaginary Atlases carrying imaginary worlds on their unsubstantial shoulders.

The Eden story provided Adam with a sin: the "original sin" for which we are all damned. Baldly stated, this seems ridiculous; nevertheless it corresponds to something actually existent not only in Paul's consciousness but in our own. The original sin was not the eating of the forbidden fruit, but the consciousness of sin which the fruit produced. The moment Adam and Eve tasted the apple they found themselves ashamed of their sexual relation, which until then had seemed quite innocent to them; and there is no getting over the hard fact that this shame, or state of sin, has persisted to this day, and is one of the strongest of our instincts. Thus Paul's postulate of Adam as the natural man was pragmatically true: it worked. But the weakness of Pragmatism is that most theories will work if you put your back into making them work, provided they have some point of contact with human nature. Hedonism will pass the pragmatic test as well as

Stoicism. Up to a certain point every social principle that is not absolutely idiotic works: Autocracy works in Russia and Democracy in America; Atheism works in France, Polytheism in India, Monotheism throughout Islam, and Pragmatism, or No-ism, in England. Paul's fantastic conception of the damned Adam, represented by Bunyan as a pilgrim with a great burden of sins on his back, corresponded to the fundamental condition of evolution, which is, that life, including human life, is continually evolving, and must therefore be continually ashamed of itself and its present and past. Bunyan's pilgrim wants to get rid of his bundle of sins; but he also wants to reach "yonder shining light"; and when at last his bundle falls off him into the sepulchre of Christ, his pilgrimage is still unfinished and his hardest trials still ahead of him. His conscience remains uneasy; "original sin" still torments him; and his adventure with Giant Despair, who throws him into the dungeon of Doubting Castle, from which he escapes by the use of a skeleton key, is more terrible than any he met whilst the bundle was still on his back. Thus Bunyan's allegory of human nature breaks through the Pauline theology at a hundred points. His theological allegory, The Holy War, with its troops of Election Doubters, and its cavalry of "those that rode Reformadoes," is, as a whole, absurd, impossible, and, except in passages where the artistic old Adam momentarily got the better of the Salvationist theologian, hardly readable.

Paul's theory of original sin was to some extent idiosyncratic. He tells us definitely that he finds himself quite well able to avoid the sinfulness of sex by practising celibacy; but he recognizes, rather contemptuously, that in this respect he is not as other men are, and says that they had better marry than burn, thus admitting that though marriage may lead to placing the desire to please wife or husband before the desire to please God, yet preoccupation with unsatisfied desire may be even more ungodly than preoccupation with domestic affection. This view of the case inevitably led him to insist that a wife should be rather a slave than a partner, her real function being, not to engage a man's love and loyalty, but on the contrary to release them for God by relieving the man of all preoccupation with sex just as in her capacity of housekeeper and cook she relieves his preoccupation with hunger by the simple expedient of satisfying his appetite. This slavery also justifies itself pragmatically by working effectively; but it has made Paul the eternal enemy of Woman. Incidentally it has led to many foolish surmises about Paul's personal character and circumstances, by people so enslaved by sex that a celibate appears to them a sort of monster. They forget that not only whole priesthoods, official and unofficial, from Paul to Carlyle and Ruskin, have defied the tyranny of sex, but immense numbers of ordinary citizens of both sexes have, either voluntarily or under pressure of circumstances easily surmountable, saved their energies for less primitive activities.

Howbeit, Paul succeeded in stealing the image of Christ crucified for the figure‑head of his Salvationist vessel, with its Adam posing as the natural man, its doctrine of original sin, and its damnation avoidable only by faith in the sacrifice of the cross. In fact, no sooner had Jesus knocked over the dragon of superstition than Paul boldly set it on its legs again in the name of Jesus.

THE CONFUSION OF CHRISTENDOM

Now it is evident that two religions having such contrary effects on mankind should not be confused as they are under a common name. There is not one word of Pauline Christianity in the characteristic utterances of Jesus. When Saul watched the clothes of the men who stoned Stephen, he was not acting upon beliefs which Paul renounced. There is no record of Christ's having ever said to any man: "Go and sin as much as you like: you can put it all on me." He said "Sin no more," and insisted that he was putting up the standard of conduct, not debasing it, and that the righteousness of the Christian must exceed that of the Scribe and Pharisee. The notion that he was shedding his blood in order that every petty cheat and adulterator and libertine might wallow in it and come out whiter than snow, cannot be imputed to him on his own authority. "I come as an infallible patent medicine for bad consciences" is not one of the sayings in the gospels. If Jesus could have been consulted on Bunyan's allegory as to that business of the burden of sin dropping from the pilgrim's back when he caught sight of the cross, we must infer from his teaching that he would have told Bunyan in forcible terms that he had never made a greater mistake in his life, and that the business of a Christ was to make self-satisfied sinners feel the burden of their sins and stop committing them instead of assuring them that they could not help it, as it was all Adam's fault, but that it did not matter as long as they were credulous and friendly about himself. Even when he believed himself to be a god, he did not regard himself as a scapegoat. He was to take away the sins of the world by good government, by justice and mercy, by setting the welfare of little children above the pride of princes, by casting all the quackeries and idolatries which now usurp and malversate the power of God into what our local authorities quaintly call the dust destructor, and by riding on the clouds of heaven in glory instead of in a thousand-guinea motor car. That was delirious, if you like; but it was the delirium of a free soul, not of a shame-bound one like Paul's. There has really never been a more monstrous imposition perpetrated than the imposition of the limitations of Paul's soul upon the soul of Jesus.

THE SECRET OF PAUL'S SUCCESS

Paul must soon have found that his followers had gained peace of mind and victory over death and sin at the cost of all moral responsibility; for he did his best to reintroduce it by making good conduct the test of sincere belief, and insisting that sincere belief was necessary to salvation. But as his system was rooted in the plain fact that as what he called sin includes sex and is therefore an ineradicable part of human nature (why else should Christ have had to atone for the sin of all future generations?) it was impossible for him to declare that sin, even in its wickedest extremity, could forfeit the sinner's salvation if he repented and believed. And to this day Pauline Christianity is, and owes its enormous vogue to being, a premium on sin. Its consequences have had to be held in check by the worldlywise majority through a violently anti-Christian system of criminal law and stern morality. But of course the main restraint is human nature, which has good impulses as well as bad ones, and refrains from theft and murder and cruelty, even when it is taught that it can commit them all at the expense of Christ and go happily to heaven afterwards, simply because it does not always want to murder or rob or torture.

It is now easy to understand why the Christianity of Jesus failed completely to establish itself politically and socially, and was easily suppressed by the police and the Church, whilst Paulinism overran the whole western civilized world, which was at that time the Roman Empire, and was adopted by it as its official faith, the old avenging gods falling helplessly before the new Redeemer. It still retains, as we may see in Africa, its power of bringing to simple people a message of hope and consolation that no other religion offers.

But this enchantment is produced by its spurious association with the personal charm of Jesus, and exists only for untrained minds. In the hands of a logical Frenchman like Calvin, pushing it to its utmost conclusions, and devizing "institutes" for hardheaded adult Scots and literal Swiss, it becomes the most infernal of fatalisms; and the lives of civilized children are blighted by its logic whilst negro piccaninnies are rejoicing in its legends.

PAUL'S QUALITIES

Paul, however, did not get his great reputation by mere imposition and reaction. It is only in comparison with Jesus (to whom many prefer him) that he appears common and conceited. Though in The Acts he is only a vulgar revivalist, he comes out in his own epistles as a genuine poet, though by flashes only. He is no more a Christian than Jesus was a Baptist: he is a disciple of Jesus only as Jesus was a disciple of John. He does nothing that Jesus would have done, and says nothing that Jesus would have said, though much, like the famous ode to charity, that he would have admired. He is more Jewish than the Jews, more Roman than the Romans, proud both ways, full of startling confessions and self-revelations that would not surprise us if they were slipped into the pages of Nietzsche, tormented by an intellectual conscience that demanded an argued case even at the cost of sophistry, with all sorts of fine qualities and occasional illuminations, but always hopelessly in the toils of Sin, Death, and Logic, which had no power over Jesus. As we have seen, it was by introducing this bondage and terror of his into the Christian doctrine that he adapted it to the Church and State systems which Jesus transcended, and made it practicable by destroying the specifically Jesuist side of it. He would have been quite in his place in any modern Protestant State; and he, not Jesus, is the true head and founder of our Reformed Church, as Peter is of the Roman Church. The followers of Paul and Peter made Christendom, whilst the Nazarenes were wiped out.

THE ACTS OF THE APOSTLES

Here we may return to the narrative called The Acts of the Apostles, which we left at the point where the stoning of Stephen was followed by the introduction of Paul. The author of The Acts, though a good story-teller, like Luke, was (herein also like Luke) much weaker in power of thought than in imaginative literary art. Hence we find Luke credited with the authorship of The Acts by people who like stories and have no aptitude for theology, whilst the book itself is denounced as spurious by Pauline theologians because Paul, and indeed all the apostles, are represented in it as very commonplace revivalists, interesting us by their adventures more than by any qualities of mind or character. Indeed, but for the epistles, we should have a very poor opinion of the apostles. Paul in particular is described as setting a fashion which has remained in continual use to this day. Whenever he addresses an audience, he dwells with great zest on his misdeeds before his pseudo conversion, with the effect of throwing into stronger relief his present state of blessedness; and he tells the story of that conversion over and over again, ending with exhortations to the hearers to come and be saved, and threats of the wrath that will overtake them if they refuse. At any revival meeting today the same thing may be heard, followed by the same conversions. This is natural enough; but it is totally unlike the preaching of Jesus, who never talked about his personal history, and never "worked up" an audience to hysteria. It aims at a purely nervous effect; it brings no enlightenment; the most ignorant man has only to become intoxicated with his own vanity, and mistake his self-satisfaction for the Holy Ghost, to become qualified as an apostle; and it has absolutely nothing to do with the characteristic doctrines of Jesus. The Holy Ghost may be at work all round producing wonders of art and science, and strengthening men to endure all sorts of martyrdoms for the enlargement of knowledge, and the enrichment and intensification of life ("that ye may have life more abundantly"); but the apostles, as described in The Acts, take no part in the struggle except as persecutors and revilers. To this day, when their successors get the upper hand, as in Geneva (Knox's "perfect city of Christ") and in Scotland and Ulster, every spiritual activity but moneymaking and churchgoing is stamped out; heretics are ruthlessly persecuted; and such pleasures as money can purchase are suppressed so that its possessors are compelled to go on making money because there is nothing else to do. And the compensation for all this privation is partly an insane conceit of being the elect of God, with a reserved seat in heaven, and partly, since even the most infatuated idiot cannot spend his life admiring himself, the less innocent excitement of punishing other people for not admiring him, and the nosing out of the sins of the people who, being intelligent enough to be incapable of mere dull self-righteousness, and highly susceptible to the beauty and interest of the real workings of the Holy Ghost, try to live more rational and abundant lives. The abominable amusement of terrifying children with threats of hell is another of these diversions, and perhaps the vilest and most mischievous of them. The net result is that the imitators of the apostles, whether they are called Holy Willies or Stigginses in derision, or, in admiration, Puritans or saints, are, outside their own congregations, and to a considerable extent inside them, heartily detested. Now nobody detests Jesus, though many who have been tormented in their childhood in his name include him in their general loathing of everything connected with the word religion; whilst others, who know him only by misrepresentation as a sentimental pacifist and an ascetic, include him in their general dislike of that type of character. In the same way a student who has had to "get up" Shakespear as a college subject may hate Shakespear; and people who dislike the theatre may include Molière in that dislike without ever having read a line of his or witnessed one of his plays; but nobody with any knowledge of Shakespear or Molière could possibly detest them, or read without pity and horror a description of their being insulted, tortured, and killed. And the same is true of Jesus. But it requires the most strenuous effort of conscience to refrain from crying "Serve him right" when we read of the stoning of Stephen; and nobody has ever cared twopence about the martyrdom of Peter: many better men have died worse deaths: for example, honest Hugh Latimer, who was burned by us, was worth fifty Stephens and a dozen Peters. One feels at last that when Jesus called Peter from his boat, he spoiled an honest fisherman, and made nothing better out of the wreck than a salvation monger.

THE CONTROVERSIES ON BAPTISM AND TRANSUBSTANTIATION

Meanwhile the inevitable effect of dropping the peculiar doctrines of Jesus and going back to John the Baptist, was to make it much easier to convert Gentiles than Jews; and it was by following the line of least resistance that Paul became the apostle to the Gentiles. The Jews had their own rite of initiation: the rite of circumcision; and they were fiercely jealous for it, because it marked them as the chosen people of God, and set them apart from the Gentiles, who were simply the uncircumcised. When Paul, finding that baptism made way faster among the Gentiles than among the Jews, as it enabled them to plead that they too were sanctified by a rite of later and higher authority than the Mosaic rite, he was compelled to admit that circumcision did not matter; and this, to the Jews, was an intolerable blasphemy. To Gentiles like ourselves, a good deal of the Epistle to the Romans is now tedious to unreadableness because it consists of a hopeless attempt by Paul to evade the conclusion that if a man were baptized it did not matter a rap whether he was circumcized or not. Paul claims circumcision as an excellent thing in its way for a Jew; but if it has no efficacy towards salvation, and if salvation is the one thing needful—and Paul was committed to both propositions —his pleas in mitigation only made the Jews more determined to stone him.

Thus from the very beginning of apostolic Christianity, it was hampered by a dispute as to whether salvation was to be attained by a surgical operation or by a sprinkling of water: mere rites on which Jesus would not have wasted twenty words. Later on, when the new sect conquered the Gentile west, where the dispute had no practical application, the other ceremony—that of eating the god —produced a still more disastrous dispute, in which a difference of belief, not as to the obligation to perform the ceremony, but as to whether it was a symbolic or a real ingestion of divine substance, produced persecution, slaughter, hatred, and everything that Jesus loathed, on a monstrous scale.

But long before that, the superstitions which had fastened on the new faith made trouble. The parthenogenetic birth of Christ, simple enough at first as a popular miracle, was not left so simple by the theologians. They began to ask of what substance Christ was made in the womb of the virgin. When the Trinity was added to the faith the question arose, was the virgin the mother of God or only the mother of Jesus? Arian schisms and Nestorian schisms arose on these questions; and the leaders of the resultant agitations rancorously deposed one another and excommunicated one another according to their luck in enlisting the emperors on their side. In the IV century they began to burn one another for differences of opinion in such matters. In the VIII century Charlemagne made Christianity compulsory by killing those who refused to embrace it; and though this made an end of the voluntary character of conversion, Charlemagne may claim to be the first Christian who put men to death for any point of doctrine that really mattered. From his time onward the history of Christian controversy reeks with blood and fire, torture and warfare. The Crusades, the persecutions in Albi and elsewhere, the Inquisition, the "wars of religion" which followed the Reformation, all presented themselves as Christian phenomena; but who can doubt that they would have been repudiated with horror by Jesus? Our own notion that the massacre of St Bartholomew's was an outrage on Christianity, whilst the campaigns of Gustavus Adolphus, and even of Frederick the Great, were a defence of it, is as absurd as the opposite notion that Frederick was Antichrist, and Torquemada and Ignatius Loyola men after the very heart of Jesus. Neither they nor their exploits had anything to do with him. It is probable that Archbishop Laud and John Wesley died equally persuaded that he in whose name they had made themselves famous on earth would receive them in Heaven with open arms. George Fox the Quaker would have had ten times their chance; and yet Fox made rather a miserable business of life.

Nevertheless all these perversions of the doctrine of Jesus derived their moral force from his credit, and so had to keep his gospel alive. When the Protestants translated the Bible into the vernacular and let it loose among the people, they did an extremely dangerous thing, as the mischief which followed proves; but they incidentally let loose the sayings of Jesus in open competition with the sayings of Paul and Koheleth and David and Solomon and the authors of Job and the Pentateuch; and, as we have seen, Jesus seems to be the winning name. The glaring contradiction between his teaching and the practice of all the States and all the Churches is no longer hidden. And it may be that though nineteen centuries have passed since Jesus was born (the date of his birth is now quaintly given as 7 B.C., though some contend for 100 B.C.), and though his Church has not yet been founded nor his political system tried, the bankruptcy of all the other systems when audited by our vital statistics, which give us a final test for all political systems, is driving us hard into accepting him, not as a scapegoat, but as one who was much less of a fool in practical matters than we have hitherto all thought him.

THE ALTERNATIVE CHRISTS

Let us now clear up the situation a little. The New Testament tells two stories for two different sorts of readers. One is the old story of the achievement of our salvation by the sacrifice and atonement of a divine personage who was barbarously slain and rose again on the third day: the story as it was accepted by the apostles. And in this story the political, economic, and moral views of the Christ have no importance: the atonement is everything; and we are saved by our faith in it, and not by works or opinions (other than that particular opinion) bearing on practical affairs.

The other is the story of a prophet who, after expressing several very interesting opinions as to practical conduct, both personal and political, which are now of pressing importance, and instructing his disciples to carry them out in their daily life, lost his head; believed himself to be a crude legendary form of god; and under that delusion courted and suffered a cruel execution in the belief that he would rise from the dead and come in glory to reign over a regenerated world. In this form, the political, economic, and moral opinions of Jesus, as guides to conduct, are interesting and important: the rest is mere psychopathy and superstition. The accounts of the resurrection, the parthenogenetic birth, and the more incredible miracles are rejected as inventions; and such episodes as the conversation with the devil are classed with similar conversations recorded of St Dunstan, Luther, Bunyan, Swedenborg, and Blake.

CREDULITY NO CRITERION

This arbitrary acceptance and rejection of parts of the gospel is not peculiar to the Secularist view. We have seen Luke and John reject Matthew's story of the massacre of the innocents and the flight into Egypt without ceremony. The notion that Matthew's manuscript is a literal and infallible record of facts, not subject to the errors that beset all earthly chroniclers, would have made John stare, being as it is a comparatively modern fancy of intellectually untrained people who keep the Bible on the same shelf with Napoleon's Book of Fate, Old Moore's Almanack, and handbooks of therapeutic herbalism. You may be a fanatical Salvationist and reject more miracle stories than Huxley did; and you may utterly repudiate Jesus as the Savior and yet cite him as a historical witness to the possession by men of the most marvellous thaumaturgical powers. "Christ Scientist" and Jesus the Mahatma are preached by people whom Peter would have struck dead as worse infidels than Simon Magus; and the Atonement is preached by Baptist and Congregationalist ministers whose views of the miracles are those of Inger-

soll and Bradlaugh. Luther, who made a clean sweep of all the saints with their million miracles, and reduced the Blessed Virgin herself to the status of an idol, concentrated Salvationism to a point at which the most execrable murderer who believes in it when the rope is round his neck, flies straight to the arms of Jesus, whilst Tom Paine and Shelley fall into the bottomless pit to burn there to all eternity. And sceptical physicists like Sir William Crookes demonstrate by laboratory experiments that "mediums" like Dunglas Home can make the pointer of a spring-balance go round without touching the weight suspended from it.

BELIEF IN PERSONAL IMMORTALITY NO CRITERION

Nor is belief in individual immortality any criterion. Theosophists, rejecting vicarious atonement so sternly that they insist that the smallest of our sins brings its Karma, also insist on individual immortality and metempsychosis in order to provide an unlimited field for Karma to be worked out by the unredeemed sinner. The belief in the prolongation of individual life beyond the grave is far more real and vivid among table-rapping Spiritualists than among conventional Christians. The notion that those who reject the Christian (or any other) scheme of salvation by atonement must reject also belief in personal immortality and in miracles is as baseless as the notion that if a man is an atheist he will steal your watch.

I could multiply these instances to weariness. The main difference that set Gladstone and Huxley by the ears is not one between belief in supernatural persons or miraculous events and the sternest view of such belief as a breach of intellectual integrity: it is the difference between belief in the efficacy of the crucifixion as an infallible cure for guilt, and a congenital incapacity for believing this, or (the same thing) desiring to believe it.

THE SECULAR VIEW NATURAL, NOT RATIONAL, THEREFORE INEVITABLE

It must therefore be taken as a flat fundamental modern fact, whether we like it or not, that whilst many of us cannot believe that Jesus got his curious grip of our souls by mere sentimentality, neither can we believe that he was John Barleycorn. The more our reason and study lead us to believe that Jesus was talking the most penetrating good sense when he preached Communism; when he declared that the reality behind the popular belief in God was a creative spirit in ourselves called by him the Heavenly Father and by us Evolution, Élan Vital, Life Force and other names; when he protested against the claims of marriage and the family to appropriate that high part of our energy that was meant for the service of his Father, the more impossible it becomes for us to believe that he was talking equally good sense when he so suddenly announced that he was himself a visible concrete God; that his flesh and blood were miraculous food for us; that he must be tortured and slain in the traditional manner and would rise from the dead after three days; and that at his Second Coming the stars would fall from heaven and he become king of an earthly paradise. But it is easy and reasonable to believe that an overwrought preacher at last went mad as Swift and Ruskin and Nietzsche went mad. Every asylum has in it a patient suffering from the delusion that he is a god, yet otherwise sane enough. These patients do not nowadays declare that they will be barbarously slain and will rise from the dead, because they have lost that tradition of the destiny of godhead; but they claim everything appertaining to divinity that is within their knowledge.

Thus the gospels as memoirs and sug-gestive statements of sociological and biological doctrine, highly relevant to modern civilization, though ending in the history of a psychopathic delusion, are quite credible, intelligible, and interesting to modern thinkers. In any other light they are neither credible, intelligible, nor interesting except to people upon whom the delusion imposes.

"THE HIGHER CRITICISM"

Historical research and paleographic criticism will no doubt continue their demonstrations that the New Testament, like the Old, seldom tells a single story or expounds a single doctrine, and gives us often an accretion and conglomeration of widely discrete and even unrelated traditions and doctrines. But these disintegrations, though technically interesting to scholars, and gratifying or exasperating, as the case may be, to people who are merely defending or attacking the paper fortifications of the infallibility of the Bible, have hardly anything to do with the purpose of these pages. I have mentioned the fact that most of the authorities are now agreed (for the moment) that the date of the birth of Jesus may be placed at about 7 B.C.; but they do not therefore date their letters 1923, nor, I presume, do they expect me to do so. What I am engaged in is a criticism (in the Kantian sense) of an established body of belief which has become an actual part of the mental fabric of my readers; and I should be the most exasperating of triflers and pedants if I were to digress into a criticism of some other belief or no-belief which my readers might conceivably profess if they were erudite Scriptural paleographers and historians, in which case, by the way, they would have to change their views so frequently that the gospel they received in their childhood would dominate them after all by its superior persistency. The chaos of mere facts in which the Sermon on the Mount and the Ode to Charity suggest nothing but disputes as to whether they are interpolations or not, in which Jesus becomes nothing but a name suspected of belonging to ten different prophets or executed persons, in which Paul is only the man who could not possibly have written the epistles attributed to him, in which Chinese sages, Greek philosophers, Latin authors, and writers of ancient anonymous inscriptions are thrown at our heads as the sources of this or that scrap of the Bible, is neither a religion nor a criticism of religion: one does not offer the fact that a good deal of the medieval building in Peterborough Cathedral was found to be flagrant jerry-building as a criticism of the Dean's sermons. For good or evil, we have made a synthesis out of the literature we call the Bible; and though the discovery that there is a good deal of jerry-building in the Bible is interesting in its way, because everything about the Bible is interesting, it does not alter the synthesis very materially even for the paleographers, and does not alter it at all for those who know no more about modern paleography than Archbishop Ussher did. I have therefore indicated little more of the discoveries than Archbishop Ussher might have guessed for himself if he had read the Bible without prepossessions.

For the rest, I have taken the synthesis as it really lives and works in men. After all, a synthesis is what you want: it is the case you have to judge brought to an apprehensible issue for you. Even if you have little more respect for synthetic biography than for synthetic rubber, synthetic milk, and the still unachieved synthetic protoplasm which is to enable us to make different sorts of men as a pastry-cook makes different sorts of tarts, the practical issue still lies as plainly before you as before the most credulous votaries of what pontificates as the Higher Criticism.

THE PERILS OF SALVATIONISM

The secular view of Jesus is powerfully reinforced by the increase in our day of the number of people who have had the means of educating and training themselves to the point at which they are not afraid to look facts in the face, even such terrifying facts as sin and death. The result is greater sternness in modern thought. The conviction is spreading that to encourage a man to believe that though his sins be as scarlet he can be made whiter than snow by an easy exercise of self-conceit, is to encourage him to be a rascal. It did not work so badly when you could also conscientiously assure him that if he let himself be caught napping in the matter of faith by death, a red-hot hell would roast him alive to all eternity. In those days a sudden death—the most enviable of all deaths—was regarded as the most frightful calamity. It was classed with plague, pestilence, and famine, battle and murder, in our prayers. But belief in that hell is fast vanishing. All the leaders of thought have lost it; and even for the rank and file it has fled to those parts of Ireland and Scotland which are still in the seventeenth century. Even there, it is tacitly reserved for the other fellow.

THE IMPORTANCE OF HELL IN THE SALVATION SCHEME

The seriousness of throwing over hell whilst still clinging to the Atonement is obvious. If there is no punishment for sin there can be no self-forgiveness for it. If Christ paid our score, and if there is no hell and therefore no chance of our getting into trouble by forgetting the obligation, then we can be as wicked as we like with impunity inside the secular law, even from self-reproach, which becomes mere ingratitude to the Savior. On the other hand, if Christ did not pay our score, it still stands against us; and such debts make us extremely uncomfortable. The drive of evolution, which we call conscience and honor, seizes on such slips, and shames us to the dust for being so low in the scale as to be capable of them. The "saved" thief experiences an ecstatic happiness which can never come to the honest atheist: he is tempted to steal again to repeat the glorious sensation. But if the atheist steals he has no such happiness. He is a thief and knows that he is a thief. Nothing can rub that off him. He may try to soothe his shame by some sort of restitution or equivalent act of benevolence; but that does not alter the fact that he did steal; and his conscience will not be easy until he has conquered his will to steal and changed himself into an honest man by developing that divine spark within him which Jesus insisted on as the everyday reality of what the atheist denies.

Now though the state of the believers in the Atonement may thus be the happier, it is most certainly not more desirable from the point of view of the community. The fact that a believer is happier than a sceptic is no more to the point than the fact that a drunken man is happier than a sober one. The happiness of credulity is a cheap and dangerous quality of happiness, and by no means a necessity of life. Whether Socrates got as much happiness out of life as Wesley is an unanswerable question; but a nation of Socrateses would be much safer and happier than a nation of Wesleys; and its individuals would be higher in the evolutionary scale. At all events it is in the Socratic man and not in the Wesleyan that our hope lies now.

THE RIGHT TO REFUSE ATONEMENT

Consequently, even if it were mentally possible for all of us to believe in the Atonement, we should have to cry off it, as we evidently have a right to do. Every man to whom salvation is offered has an inalienable natural right to say "No,

thank you: I prefer to retain my full moral responsibility: it is not good for me to be able to load a scapegoat with my sins: I should be less careful how I committed them if I knew they would cost me nothing." Then, too, there is the attitude of Ibsen: that iron moralist to whom the whole scheme of salvation was only an ignoble attempt to cheat God; to get into heaven without paying the price. To be let off, to beg for and accept eternal life as a present instead of earning it, would be mean enough even if we accepted the contempt of the Power on whose pity we were trading; but to bargain for a crown of glory as well! that was too much for Ibsen: it provoked him to exclaim, "Your God is an old man whom you cheat," and to lash the deadened conscience of the nineteenth century back to life with a whip of scorpions.

THE TEACHING OF CHRISTIANITY

And there I must leave the matter to such choice as your nature allows you. The honest teacher who has to make known to a novice the facts about Christianity cannot in any essential regard, I think, put the facts otherwise than as I have put them. If children are to be delivered from the proselytizing atheist on the one hand, and the proselytizing nun in the convent school on the other, with all the other proselytizers that lie between them, they must not be burdened with idle controversies as to whether there was ever such a person as Jesus or not. When Hume said that Joshua's campaigns were impossible, Whately did not wrangle about it: he proved, on the same lines, that the campaigns of Napoleon were impossible. Only fictitious characters will stand Hume's sort of examination: nothing will ever make Edward the Confessor and St Louis as real to us as Don Quixote and Mr Pickwick. We must cut the controversy short by declaring that there is the same evidence for the existence of Jesus as for that of any other person of his time; and the fact that you may not believe everything Matthew tells you no more disproves the existence of Jesus than the fact that you do not believe everything Macaulay tells you disproves the existence of William III. The gospel narratives in the main give you a biography which is quite credible and accountable on purely secular grounds when you have trimmed off everything that Hume or Grimm or Rousseau or Huxley or any modern bishop could reject as fanciful. Without going further than this, you can become a follower of Jesus just as you can become a follower of Confucius or Lao Tse, and may therefore call yourself a Jesuist, or even a Christian, if you hold, as the strictest Secularist quite legitimately may, that all prophets are inspired, and all men with a mission, Christs.

The teacher of Christianity has then to make known to the child, first the song of John Barleycorn, with the fields and seasons as witness to its eternal truth. Then, as the child's mind matures, it can learn, as historical and psychological phenomena, the tradition of the scapegoat, the Redeemer, the Atonement, the Resurrection, the Second Coming, and how, in a world saturated with this tradition, Jesus has been largely accepted as the long expected and often prophesied Redeemer, the Messiah, *the* Christ. It is open to the child also to accept him. If the child is built like Gladstone, he will accept Jesus as his Savior, and Peter and John the Baptist as the Savior's revealer and forerunner respectively. If he is built like Huxley, he will take the secular view, in spite of all that a pious family can do to prevent him. The important thing now is that the Gladstones and Huxleys should no longer waste their time irrelevantly and ridiculously wrangling about the Gadarene swine, and that they should make up their minds as to the soundness of the secular doctrines of Jesus; for it is about these that they may come to blows in our own time.

CHRISTIANITY AND THE EMPIRE

Finally, let us ask why it is that the old superstitions have so suddenly lost countenance that although, to the utter disgrace of the nation's leaders and rulers, the laws by which persecutors can destroy or gag all freedom of thought and speech in these matters are still unrepealed and ready to the hand of our bigots and fanatics (quite recently a respectable shopkeeper was convicted of "blasphemy" for saying that if a modern girl accounted for an illicit pregnancy by saying she had conceived of the Holy Ghost, we should know what to think: a remark which would never have occurred to him had he been properly taught how the story was grafted on the gospel), yet somehow they are used only against poor men, and that only in a half-hearted way. When we consider that from the time when the first scholar ventured to whisper as a professional secret that the Pentateuch could not possibly have been written by Moses to the time within my own recollection when Bishop Colenso, for saying the same thing openly, was inhibited from preaching and actually excommunicated, eight centuries elapsed (the point at issue, though technically interesting to paleographers and historians, having no more bearing on human welfare than the controversy as to whether uncial or cursive is the older form of writing); yet now, within fifty years of Colenso's heresy, there is not a Churchman of any authority living, or an educated layman, who could without ridicule declare that Moses wrote the Pentateuch as Pascal wrote his Thoughts or D'Aubigny his History of the Reformation, or that St Jerome wrote the passage about the three witnesses in the Vulgate, or that there are less than three different

U

accounts of the creation jumbled together in the book of Genesis. Now the maddest Progressive will hardly contend that our growth in wisdom and liberality has been greater in the last half century than in the sixteen half centuries preceding: indeed it would be easier to sustain the thesis that the last fifty years have witnessed a distinct reaction from Victorian Liberalism to Collectivism which has perceptibly strengthened the State Churches. Yet the fact remains that whereas Byron's Cain, published a century ago, is a leading case on the point that there is no copyright in a blasphemous book, the Salvation Army might now include it among its publications without shocking anyone.

I suggest that the causes which have produced this sudden clearing of the air include the transformation of many modern States, notably the old self-contained French Republic and the tight little Island of Britain, into empires which overflow the frontiers of all the Churches. In India, for example, there are less than four million Christians out of a population of three hundred and sixteen and a half millions. The King of England is the defender of the faith; but what faith is now *the* faith? The inhabitants of this island would, within the memory of persons still living, have claimed that their faith is surely *the* faith of God, and that all others are heathen. But we islanders are only forty-five millions; and if we count ourselves all as Christians, there are still seventy-seven and a quarter million Mahometans in the Empire. Add to these the Hindoos and Buddhists, Sikhs and Jains, whom I was taught in my childhood, by way of religious instruction, to regard as gross idolaters consigned to eternal perdition, but whose faith I can now be punished for disparaging by a provocative word, and you have a total of over three hundred and forty-two and a quarter million heretics to swamp

our forty-five million Britons, of whom, by the way, only six thousand call themselves distinctively "disciples of Christ," the rest being members of the Church of England and other denominations whose discipleship is less emphatically affirmed. In short, the Englishman of today, instead of being, like the forefathers whose ideas he clings to, a subject of a State practically wholly Christian, is now crowded, and indeed considerably overcrowded, into a corner of an Empire in which the Christians are a mere eleven per cent of the population; so that the Nonconformist who allows his umbrella stand to be sold up rather than pay rates towards the support of a Church of England school, finds himself paying taxes not only to endow the Church of Rome in Malta, but to send Christians to prison for the blasphemy of offering Bibles for sale in the streets of Khartoum.

Turn to France, a country ten times more insular in its preoccupation with its own language, its own history, its own character, than we, who have always been explorers and colonizers and grumblers. This once self-centred nation is forty millions strong. The total population of the French Republic is about one hundred and fourteen millions. The French are not in our hopeless Christian minority of eleven per cent; but they are in a minority of thirty-five per cent, which is fairly conclusive. And, being a more logical people than we, they have officially abandoned Christianity and declared that the French State has no specific religion.

Neither has the British State, though it does not say so. No doubt there are many innocent people in England who take Charlemagne's view, and would, as a matter of course, offer our eighty-nine per cent of "pagans, I regret to say" the alternative of death or Christianity but for a vague impression that these lost ones are all being converted gradually by the missionaries. But no statesman can entertain such ludicrously parochial delusions. No English king or French president can possibly govern on the assumption that the theology of Peter and Paul, Luther and Calvin, has any objective validity, or that the Christ is more than the Buddha, or Jehovah more than Krishna, or Jesus more or less human than Mahomet or Zoroaster or Confucius. He is actually compelled, in so far as he makes laws against blasphemy at all, to treat all the religions, including Christianity, as blasphemous when paraded before people who are not accustomed to them and do not want them. And even that is a concession to a mischievous intolerance which an empire should use its control of education to eradicate.

On the other hand, Governments cannot really divest themselves of religion, or even of dogma. When Jesus said that people should not only live but live more abundantly, he was dogmatizing; and many Pessimist sages, including Shakespear, whose hero begged his friend to refrain from suicide in the words "Absent thee from felicity awhile," would say dogmatizing very perniciously. Indeed many preachers and saints declare, some of them in the name of Jesus himself, that this world is a vale of tears, and that our lives had better be passed in sorrow and even in torment, as a preparation for a better life to come. Make these sad people comfortable; and they baffle you by putting on hair shirts.

None the less, Governments must proceed on dogmatic assumptions, whether they call them dogmas or not; and they must clearly be assumptions common enough to stamp those who reject them as eccentrics or lunatics. And the greater and more heterogeneous the population the commoner the assumptions must be. A Trappist monastery can be conducted on assumptions which would in twenty-four hours provoke the village at its gates to insurrection. That is because the monastery selects its people; and if a Trappist does not like it he can leave it. But a subject of the British Empire or the French Republic is not selected; and if he does not like it he must lump it; for emigration is practicable only within narrow limits, and seldom provides an effective remedy, all civilizations being now much alike.

To anyone capable of comprehending government at all it must be evident without argument that the set of fundamental assumptions drawn up in the thirty-nine articles or in the Westminster Confession are wildly impossible as political constitutions for modern empires. A personal profession of them by any person disposed to take such professions seriously would practically disqualify him for high imperial office. A Calvinist Viceroy of India and a Particular Baptist Secretary of State for Foreign Affairs would wreck the empire. The Stuarts wrecked even the tight little island which was the nucleus of the empire by their Scottish logic and theological dogma; and it may be sustained very plausibly that the alleged aptitude of the English for self-government, which is contradicted by every chapter of their history, is really only an incurable inaptitude for theology, and indeed for co-ordinated thought in any direction, which makes them equally impatient of systematic despotism and systematic good government: their history being that of a badly governed and accidentally free people (comparatively). Thus our success in colonizing, as far as it has not been produced by exterminating the natives, has been due to our indifference to the salvation of our subjects. Ireland is the exception which proves the rule; for Ireland, the standing instance of the inability of the English to colonize without extermination of natives, is also the one country under British rule in which the conquerors and colonizers proceeded on the assumption that their business was to establish Protestantism as well as to make money and thereby secure at least the lives of the unfortunate inhabitants out of whose labor it could be made. At this moment Ulster is refusing to accept fellow-citizenship with the other Irish provinces because the south believes in St Peter and Bossuet, and the north in St Paul and Calvin. Imagine the effect of trying to govern India or Egypt from Belfast or from the Vatican!

The position is perhaps graver for France than for England, because the sixty-five per cent of French subjects who are neither French nor Christian nor Modernist includes some thirty millions of negroes who are susceptible, and indeed highly susceptible, of conversion to those salvationist forms of pseudo-Christianity which have produced all the persecutions and religious wars of the last fifteen hundred years. When the late explorer Sir Henry Stanley told me of the emotional grip which Christianity had over the Baganda tribes, and read me their letters, which were exactly like medieval letters in their literal faith and ever-present piety, I said "Can these men handle a rifle?" To which Stanley replied with some scorn "Of course they can, as well as any white man." Now at this moment (1915) a vast European war is being waged, in which the French are using Senegalese soldiers. I ask the French Government, which, like our own Government, is deliberately leaving the religious instruction of these negroes in the hands of missions of Petrine Catholics and Pauline Calvinists, whether they have considered the possibility of a new series of crusades, by ardent African Salvationists, to rescue Paris from the grip of the modern scientific "infidel," and to raise the cry of "Back to the Apostles: back to Charlemagne!"

We are more fortunate in that an overwhelming majority of our subjects are Hindoos, Mahometans, and Buddhists: that is, they have, as a prophylactic against salvationist Christianity, highly civilized religions of their own. Mahometanism, which Napoleon at the end of his career classed as perhaps the best popular religion for modern political use, might in some respects have arisen as a reformed Christianity if Mahomet had had to deal with a population of seventeenth century Christians instead of Arabs who worshipped stones. As it is, men do not reject Mahomet for Calvin; and to offer a Hindoo so crude a theology as ours in exchange for his own, or our Jewish canonical literature as an improvement on Hindoo scripture, is to offer old lamps for older ones in a market where the oldest lamps, like old furniture in England, are the most highly valued.

Yet, I repeat, government is impossible without a religion: that is, without a body of common assumptions. The open mind never acts: when we have done our utmost to arrive at a reasonable conclusion, we still, when we can reason and investigate no more, must close our minds for the moment with a snap, and act dogmatically on our conclusions. The man who waits to make an entirely reasonable will dies intestate. A man so reasonable as to have an open mind about theft and murder, or about the need for food and reproduction, might just as well be a fool and a scoundrel for any use he could be as a legislator or a State official. The modern pseudo-democratic statesman, who says that he is only in power to carry out the will of the people, and moves only as the cat jumps, is clearly a political and intellectual brigand. The rule of the negative man who has no convictions means in practice the rule of the positive mob. Freedom of conscience as Cromwell used the phrase is an excellent thing; nevertheless if any man had proposed to give effect to freedom of conscience as to cannibalism in England,

Cromwell would have laid him by the heels almost as promptly as he would have laid a Roman Catholic, though in Fiji at the same moment he would have supported heartily the freedom of conscience of a vegetarian who disparaged the sacred diet of Long Pig.

Here then comes in the importance of the repudiation by Jesus of proselytism. His rule "Dont pull up the tares: sow the wheat: if you try to pull up the tares you will pull up the wheat with it" is the only possible rule for a statesman governing a modern empire, or a voter supporting such a statesman. There is nothing in the teaching of Jesus that cannot be assented to by a Brahman, a Mahometan, a Buddhist, or a Jew, without any question of their conversion to Christianity. In some ways it is easier to reconcile a Mahometan to Jesus than a British parson, because the idea of a professional priest is unfamiliar and even monstrous to a Mahometan (the tourist who persists in asking who is the dean of St Sophia puzzles beyond words the sacristan who lends him a huge pair of slippers); and Jesus never suggested that his disciples should separate themselves from the laity: he picked them up by the wayside, where any man or woman might follow him. For priests he had not a civil word; and they shewed their sense of his hostility by getting him killed as soon as possible. He was, in short, a thoroughgoing anti-Clerical. And though, as we have seen, it is only by political means that his doctrine can be put into practice, he not only never suggested a sectarian theocracy as a form of government, and would certainly have prophesied the downfall of the late President Kruger if he had survived to his time, but, when challenged, he refused to teach his disciples not to pay tribute to Cæsar, admitting that Cæsar, who presumably had the kingdom of heaven within him as much as any disciple, had his place in the scheme of things. Indeed the apostles made this an excuse for carrying subservience to the State to a pitch of idolatry that ended in the theory of the divine right of kings, and provoked men to cut kings' heads off to restore some sense of proportion in the matter. Jesus certainly did not consider the overthrow of the Roman empire or the substitution of a new ecclesiastical organization for the Jewish Church or for the priesthood of the Roman gods as part of his program. He said that God was better than Mammon; but he never said that Tweedledum was better than Tweedledee; and that is why it is now possible for British citizens and statesmen to follow Jesus, though they cannot possibly follow either Tweedledum or Tweedledee without bringing the empire down with a crash on their heads. And at that I must leave it.

XXI

SAINT JOAN

1924

JOAN THE ORIGINAL AND PRESUMPTUOUS

Joan of Arc, a village girl from the Vosges, was born about 1412; burnt for heresy, witchcraft, and sorcery in 1431; rehabilitated after a fashion in 1456; designated Venerable in 1904; declared Blessed in 1908; and finally canonized in 1920. She is the most notable Warrior Saint in the Christian calendar, and the queerest fish among the eccentric worthies of the Middle Ages. Though a professed and most pious Catholic, and the projector of a Crusade against the Husites, she was in fact one of the first Protestant martyrs. She was also one of the first apostles of Nationalism, and the first French practitioner of Napoleonic realism in warfare as distinguished from the sporting ransom-gambling chivalry of her time. She was the pioneer of rational dressing for women, and, like Queen Christina of Sweden two centuries later, to say nothing of Catalina de Erauso and innumerable obscure heroines who have disguised themselves as men to serve as soldiers and sailors, she refused to accept the specific woman's lot, and dressed and fought and lived as men did.

As she contrived to assert herself in all these ways with such force that she was famous throughout western Europe before she was out of her teens (indeed she never got out of them), it is hardly surprising that she was judicially burnt, ostensibly for a number of capital crimes which we no longer punish as such, but essentially for what we call unwomanly and insufferable presumption. At eighteen Joan's pretensions were beyond those of the proudest Pope or the haughtiest emperor. She claimed to be the ambassador and plenipotentiary of God, and to be, in effect, a member of the Church Triumphant whilst still in the flesh on earth. She patronized her own king, and summoned the English king to repentance and obedience to her commands. She lectured, talked down, and overruled statesmen and prelates. She pooh-poohed the plans of generals, leading their troops to victory on plans of her own. She had an unbounded and quite unconcealed contempt for official opinion, judgment, and authority, and for War Office tactics and strategy. Had she been a sage and monarch in whom the most venerable hierarchy and the most illustrious dynasty converged, her pretensions and proceedings would have been as trying to the official mind as the pretensions of Cæsar were to Cassius. As her actual condition was pure upstart, there were only two opinions about her. One was that she was miraculous: the other that she was unbearable.

JOAN AND SOCRATES

If Joan had been malicious, selfish, cowardly or stupid, she would have been one of the most odious persons known to history instead of one of the most attractive. If she had been old enough to know the effect she was producing on the men whom she humiliated by being right when they were wrong, and had learned to flatter and manage them, she might have lived as long as Queen Elizabeth. But she was too young and rustical and inexperienced to have any such arts. When she was thwarted by men whom she thought fools, she made no secret of her opinion of them or her impatience with their folly; and she was naïve enough to expect them to be obliged to her for setting them right and keeping them out of mischief. Now it is always hard for superior wits to understand the fury roused by their exposures of the stupidities of comparative dullards. Even Socrates, for all his age and experience, did not defend himself at his trial like a man who understood the long accumulated fury that had burst on him, and was clamoring for his death. His accuser, if born 2300 years later, might have been picked out of any first class carriage on a suburban railway during the evening or morning rush from or to the City; for he had really nothing to say except that he and his like could not endure being shewn up as idiots every time Socrates opened his mouth. Socrates, unconscious of this, was paralyzed by his sense that somehow he was missing the point of the attack. He petered out after he had established the fact that he was an old soldier and a man of honorable life, and that his accuser was a silly snob. He had no suspicion of the extent to which his mental superiority had roused fear and hatred against him in the hearts of men towards whom he was conscious of nothing but good will and good service.

CONTRAST WITH NAPOLEON

If Socrates was as innocent as this at the age of seventy, it may be imagined how innocent Joan was at the age of seventeen. Now Socrates was a man of argument, operating slowly and peacefully on men's minds, whereas Joan was a woman of action, operating with impetuous violence on their bodies. That, no doubt, is why the contemporaries of Socrates endured him so long, and why Joan was destroyed before she was fully grown. But both of them combined terrifying ability with a frankness, personal modesty, and benevolence which made the furious dislike to which they fell victims absolutely unreasonable, and therefore inapprehensible by themselves. Napoleon, also possessed of terrifying ability, but neither frank nor disinterested, had no illusions as to the nature of his popularity. When he was asked how the world would take his death, he said it would give a gasp of relief. But it is not so easy for mental giants who neither hate nor intend to injure their fellows to realize that nevertheless their fellows hate mental giants and would like to destroy them, not only enviously because the juxtaposition of a superior wounds their vanity, but quite humbly and honestly because it frightens them. Fear will drive men to any extreme; and the fear inspired by a superior being is a mystery which cannot be reasoned away. Being immeasurable it is unbearable when there is no presumption or guarantee of its benevolence and moral responsibility: in other words, when it has no official status. The legal and conventional superiority of Herod and Pilate, and of Annas and Caiaphas, inspires fear; but the fear, being a reasonable fear of measurable and avoidable consequences which seem salutary and protective, is bearable; whilst the strange superiority of Christ and the fear it inspires elicit a shriek of Crucify Him from all who cannot divine its benevolence. Socrates has to drink the hemlock, Christ to hang on the cross, and Joan to burn at the stake, whilst Napoleon, though he ends in St Helena, at least dies in his bed there; and many terrifying but quite comprehensible official scoundrels die natural deaths in all the glory of the kingdoms of this world, proving that it is far more dangerous to be a saint than to be a conqueror. Those who have been both, like Mahomet and Joan, have found that it is the conqueror who must save the saint, and that defeat and capture mean martyrdom. Joan was burnt without a hand lifted on her own side to save her. The comrades she had led to victory and the enemies she had disgraced and defeated, the French king she had crowned and the English king whose crown she had kicked into the Loire, were equally glad to be rid of her.

WAS JOAN INNOCENT OR GUILTY?

As this result could have been produced by a crapulous inferiority as well as by a sublime superiority, the question which of the two was operative in Joan's case has to be faced. It was decided against her by her contemporaries after a very careful and conscientious trial; and the reversal of the verdict twentyfive years later, in form a rehabilitation of Joan, was really only a confirmation of the validity of the coronation of Charles VII. It is the more impressive reversal by a unanimous Posterity, culminating in her canonization, that has quashed the original proceedings, and put her judges on their trial, which, so far, has been much more unfair than their trial of her. Nevertheless the rehabilitation of 1456, corrupt job as it was, really did produce evidence enough to satisfy all reasonable critics that Joan was not a common termagant, not a harlot, not a witch, not a blasphemer, no more an idolater than the Pope himself, and not ill conducted in any sense apart from her soldiering, her wearing of men's clothes, and her audacity, but on the contrary good-humored, an intact virgin, very pious, very temperate (we should call her meal of bread soaked in the common wine which is the drinking water of France ascetic), very kindly, and, though a brave and hardy soldier, unable to endure loose language or licentious conduct. She went to the stake without a stain on her character except the overweening presumption, the superbity as they called it, that led her thither. It would therefore be waste of time now to prove that the Joan of the first part of the Elizabethan chronicle play of Henry VI (supposed to have been tinkered by Shakespear) grossly libels her in its concluding scenes in deference to Jingo patriotism. The

mud that was thrown at her has dropped off by this time so completely that there is no need for any modern writer to wash up after it. What is far more difficult to get rid of is the mud that is being thrown at her judges, and the whitewash which disfigures her beyond recognition. When Jingo scurrility had done its worst to her, sectarian scurrility (in this case Protestant scurrility) used her stake to beat the Roman Catholic Church and the Inquisition. The easiest way to make these institutions the villains of a melodrama was to make The Maid its heroine. That melodrama may be dismissed as rubbish. Joan got a far fairer trial from the Church and the Inquisition than any prisoner of her type and in her situation gets nowadays in any official secular court; and the decision was strictly according to law. And she was not a melodramatic heroine: that is, a physically beautiful lovelorn parasite on an equally beautiful hero, but a genius and a saint, about as completely the opposite of a melodramatic heroine as it is possible for a human being to be.

Let us be clear about the meaning of the terms. A genius is a person who, seeing farther and probing deeper than other people, has a different set of ethical valuations from theirs, and has energy enough to give effect to this extra vision and its valuations in whatever manner best suits his or her specific talents. A saint is one who having practised heroic virtues, and enjoyed revelations or powers of the order which The Church classes technically as supernatural, is eligible for canonization. If a historian is an Anti-Feminist, and does not believe women to be capable of genius in the traditional masculine departments, he will never make anything of Joan, whose genius was turned to practical account mainly in soldiering and politics. If he is Rationalist enough to deny that saints exist, and to hold that new ideas cannot come otherwise than by conscious ratiocination, he will never catch Joan's likeness. Her ideal biographer must be free from nineteenth century prejudices and biases; must understand the Middle Ages, the Roman Catholic Church, and the Holy Roman Empire much more intimately than our Whig historians have ever understood them; and must be capable of throwing off sex partialities and their romance, and regarding woman as the female of the human species, and not as a different kind of animal with specific charms and specific imbecilities.

JOAN'S GOOD LOOKS

To put the last point roughly, any book about Joan which begins by describing her as a beauty may be at once classed as a romance. Not one of Joan's comrades, in village, court, or camp, even when they were straining themselves to please the king by praising her, ever claimed that she was pretty. All the men who alluded to the matter declared most emphatically that she was unattractive sexually to a degree that seemed to them miraculous, considering that she was in the bloom of youth, and neither ugly, awkward, deformed, nor unpleasant in her person. The evident truth is that like most women of her hardy managing type she seemed neutral in the conflict of sex because men were too much afraid of her to fall in love with her. She herself was not sexless: in spite of the virginity she had vowed up to a point, and preserved to her death, she never excluded the possibility of marriage for herself. But marriage, with its preliminary of the attraction, pursuit, and capture of a husband, was not her business: she had something else to do. Byron's formula, "Man's love is of man's life a thing apart: 'tis woman's whole existence," did not apply to her any more than to George Washington or any other masculine worker on the heroic scale. Had she lived in our

time, picture postcards might have been sold of her as a general: they would not have been sold of her as a sultana. Nevertheless there is one reason for crediting her with a very remarkable face. A sculptor of her time in Orleans made a statue of a helmeted young woman with a face that is unique in art in point of being evidently not an ideal face but a portrait, and yet so uncommon as to be unlike any real woman one has ever seen. It is surmised that Joan served unconsciously as the sculptor's model. There is no proof of this; but those extraordinarily spaced eyes raise so powerfully the question "If this woman be not Joan, who is she?" that I dispense with further evidence, and challenge those who disagree with me to prove a negative. It is a wonderful face, but quite neutral from the point of view of the operatic beauty fancier.

Such a fancier may perhaps be finally chilled by the prosaic fact that Joan was the defendant in a suit for breach of promise of marriage, and that she conducted her own case and won it.

JOAN'S SOCIAL POSITION

By class Joan was the daughter of a working farmer who was one of the headmen of his village, and transacted its feudal business for it with the neighboring squires and their lawyers. When the castle in which the villagers were entitled to take refuge from raids became derelict, he organized a combination of half a dozen farmers to obtain possession of it so as to occupy it when there was any danger of invasion. As a child, Joan could please herself at times with being the young lady of this castle. Her mother and brothers were able to follow and share her fortune at court without making themselves notably ridiculous. These facts leave us no excuse for the popular romance that turns every heroine into either a princess or a beggarmaid. In the somewhat similar case of Shakespear a

U 2

whole inverted pyramid of wasted research has been based on the assumption
that he was an illiterate laborer, in the
face of the plainest evidence that his
father was a man of business, and at one
time a very prosperous one, married to
a woman of some social pretensions.
There is the same tendency to drive Joan
into the position of a hired shepherd girl,
though a hired shepherd girl in Domrémy would have deferred to her as the
young lady of the farm.

The difference between Joan's case and
Shakespear's is that Shakespear was not
illiterate. He had been to school, and
knew as much Latin and Greek as most
university passmen retain: that is, for
practical purposes, none at all. Joan was
absolutely illiterate. "I do not know A
from B" she said. But many princesses at
that time and for long after might have
said the same. Marie Antoinette, for instance, at Joan's age could not spell her
own name correctly. But this does not
mean that Joan was an ignorant person,
or that she suffered from the diffidence
and sense of social disadvantage now felt
by people who cannot read or write. If
she could not write letters, she could and
did dictate them and attach full and indeed excessive importance to them. When
she was called a shepherd lass to her face
she very warmly resented it, and challenged any woman to compete with her
in the household arts of the mistresses of
well furnished houses. She understood
the political and military situation in
France much better than most of our
newspaper fed university women-gradu-
ates understand the corresponding situation of their own country today. Her first
convert was the neighboring commandant at Vaucouleurs; and she converted
him by telling him about the defeat of the
Dauphin's troops at the Battle of Her-
rings so long before he had official news
of it that he concluded she must have had
a divine revelation. This knowledge of

and interest in public affairs was nothing
extraordinary among farmers in a war-
swept countryside. Politicians came to
the door too often sword in hand to be
disregarded: Joan's people could not
afford to be ignorant of what was going
on in the feudal world. They were not
rich; and Joan worked on the farm as her
father did, driving the sheep to pasture
and so forth; but there is no evidence or
suggestion of sordid poverty, and no
reason to believe that Joan had to work
as a hired servant works, or indeed to
work at all when she preferred to go to
confession, or dawdle about waiting for
visions and listening to the church bells
to hear voices in them. In short, much
more of a young lady, and even of an intellectual, than most of the daughters of
our petty bourgeoisie.

JOAN'S VOICES AND VISIONS

Joan's voices and visions have played
many tricks with her reputation. They
have been held to prove that she was mad,
that she was a liar and impostor, that she
was a sorceress (she was burned for this),
and finally that she was a saint. They do
not prove any of these things; but the
variety of the conclusions reached shew
how little our matter-of-fact historians
know about other people's minds, or even
about their own. There are people in the
world whose imagination is so vivid that
when they have an idea it comes to them
as an audible voice, sometimes uttered by
a visible figure. Criminal lunatic asylums
are occupied largely by murderers who
have obeyed voices. Thus a woman may
hear voices telling her that she must cut
her husband's throat and strangle her
child as they lie asleep; and she may feel
obliged to do what she is told. By a
medico-legal superstition it is held in our
courts that criminals whose temptations
present themselves under these illusions
are not responsible for their actions, and
must be treated as insane. But the seers

of visions and the hearers of revelations are not always criminals. The inspirations and intuitions and unconsciously reasoned conclusions of genius sometimes assume similar illusions. Socrates, Luther, Swedenborg, Blake saw visions and heard voices just as Saint Francis and Saint Joan did. If Newton's imagination had been of the same vividly dramatic kind he might have seen the ghost of Pythagoras walk into the orchard and explain why the apples were falling. Such an illusion would have invalidated neither the theory of gravitation nor Newton's general sanity. What is more, the visionary method of making the discovery would not be a whit more miraculous than the normal method. The test of sanity is not the normality of the method but the reasonableness of the discovery. If Newton had been informed by Pythagoras that the moon was made of green cheese, then Newton would have been locked up. Gravitation, being a reasoned hypothesis which fitted remarkably well into the Copernican version of the observed physical facts of the universe, established Newton's reputation for extraordinary intelligence, and would have done so no matter how fantastically he had arrived at it. Yet his theory of gravitation is not so impressive a mental feat as his astounding chronology, which establishes him as the king of mental conjurors, but a Bedlamite king whose authority no one now accepts. On the subject of the eleventh horn of the beast seen by the prophet Daniel he was more fantastic than Joan, because his imagination was not dramatic but mathematical and therefore extraordinarily susceptible to numbers: indeed if all his works were lost except his chronology we should say that he was as mad as a hatter. As it is, who dares diagnose Newton as a madman?

In the same way Joan must be judged a sane woman in spite of her voices because they never gave her any advice that might not have come to her from her mother wit exactly as gravitation came to Newton. We can all see now, especially since the late war threw so many of our women into military life, that Joan's campaigning could not have been carried on in petticoats. This was not only because she did a man's work, but because it was morally necessary that sex should be left out of the question as between her and her comrades-in-arms. She gave this reason herself when she was pressed on the subject; and the fact that this entirely reasonable necessity came to her imagination first as an order from God delivered through the mouth of Saint Catherine does not prove that she was mad. The soundness of the order proves that she was unusually sane; but its form proves that her dramatic imagination played tricks with her senses. Her policy was also quite sound: nobody disputes that the relief of Orleans, followed up by the coronation at Rheims of the Dauphin as a counterblow to the suspicions then current of his legitimacy and consequently of his title, were military and political masterstrokes that saved France. They might have been planned by Napoleon or any other illusionproof genius. They came to Joan as an instruction from her Counsel, as she called her visionary saints; but she was none the less an able leader of men for imagining her ideas in this way.

THE EVOLUTIONARY APPETITE

What then is the modern view of Joan's voices and visions and messages from God? The nineteenth century said that they were delusions, but that as she was a pretty girl, and had been abominably ill-treated and finally done to death by a superstitious rabble of medieval priests hounded on by a corrupt political bishop, it must be assumed that she was the innocent dupe of these delusions. The twentieth century finds this explanation too vapidly commonplace, and demands something more mystic. I think the twentieth century is right, because an explanation which amounts to Joan being mentally defective instead of, as she obviously was, mentally excessive, will not wash. I cannot believe, nor, if I could, could I expect all my readers to believe, as Joan did, that three ocularly visible well dressed persons, named respectively Saint Catherine, Saint Margaret, and Saint Michael, came down from heaven and gave her certain instructions with which they were charged by God for her. Not that such a belief would be more improbable or fantastic than some modern beliefs which we all swallow; but there are fashions and family habits in belief, and it happens that, my fashion being Victorian and my family habit Protestant, I find myself unable to attach any such objective validity to the form of Joan's visions.

But that there are forces at work which use individuals for purposes far transcending the purpose of keeping these individuals alive and prosperous and respectable and safe and happy in the middle station in life, which is all any good bourgeois can reasonably require, is established by the fact that men will, in the pursuit of knowledge and of social readjustments for which they will not be a penny the better, and are indeed often many pence the worse, face poverty, infamy, exile, imprisonment, dreadful hardship, and death. Even the selfish pursuit of personal power does not nerve men to the efforts and sacrifices which are eagerly made in pursuit of extensions of our power over nature, though these extensions may not touch the personal life of the seeker at any point. There is no more mystery about this appetite for knowledge and power than about the appetite for food: both are known as facts and as facts only, the difference between them

being that the appetite for food is necessary to the life of the hungry man and is therefore a personal appetite, whereas the other is an appetite for evolution, and therefore a superpersonal need.

The diverse manners in which our imaginations dramatize the approach of the superpersonal forces is a problem for the psychologist, not for the historian. Only, the historian must understand that visionaries are neither impostors nor lunatics. It is one thing to say that the figure Joan recognized as St Catherine was not really St Catherine, but the dramatization by Joan's imagination of that pressure upon her of the driving force that is behind evolution which I have just called the evolutionary appetite. It is quite another to class her visions with the vision of two moons seen by a drunken person, or with Brocken spectres, echoes and the like. Saint Catherine's instructions were far too cogent for that; and the simplest French peasant who believes in apparitions of celestial personages to favored mortals is nearer to the scientific truth about Joan than the Rationalist and Materialist historians and essayists who feel obliged to set down a girl who saw saints and heard them talking to her as either crazy or mendacious. If Joan was mad, all Christendom was mad too; for people who believe devoutly in the existence of celestial personages are every whit as mad in that sense as the people who think they see them. Luther, when he threw his inkhorn at the devil, was no more mad than any other Augustinian monk: he had a more vivid imagination, and had perhaps eaten and slept less: that was all.

THE MERE ICONOGRAPHY DOES NOT MATTER

All the popular religions in the world are made apprehensible by an array of legendary personages, with an Almighty Father, and sometimes a mother and divine child, as the central figures. These are presented to the mind's eye in childhood; and the result is a hallucination which persists strongly throughout life when it has been well impressed. Thus all the thinking of the hallucinated adult about the fountain of inspiration which is continually flowing in the universe, or about the promptings of virtue and the revulsions of shame: in short, about aspiration and conscience, both of which forces are matters of fact more obvious than electro-magnetism, is thinking in terms of the celestial vision. And when in the case of exceptionally imaginative persons, especially those practising certain appropriate austerities, the hallucination extends from the mind's eye to the body's, the visionary sees Krishna or the Buddha or the Blessed Virgin or St Catherine as the case may be.

THE MODERN EDUCATION WHICH JOAN ESCAPED

It is important to everyone nowadays to understand this, because modern science is making short work of the hallucinations without regard to the vital importance of the things they symbolize. If Joan were reborn today she would be sent, first to a convent school in which she would be mildly taught to connect inspiration and conscience with St Catherine and St Michael exactly as she was in the fifteenth century, and then finished up with a very energetic training in the gospel of Saints Louis Pasteur and Paul Bert, who would tell her (possibly in visions but more probably in pamphlets) not to be a superstitious little fool, and to empty out St Catherine and the rest of the Catholic hagiology as an obsolete iconography of exploded myths. It would be rubbed into her that Galileo was a martyr, and his persecutors incorrigible ignoramuses, and that St Teresa's hormones had gone astray and left her incurably hyperpituitary or hyperadrenal or hysteroid or epileptoid or anything but asteroid. She would have been convinced by precept and experiment that baptism and receiving the body of her Lord were contemptible superstitions, and that vaccination and vivisection were enlightened practices. Behind her new Saints Louis and Paul there would be not only Science purifying Religion and being purified by it, but hypochondria, melancholia, cowardice, stupidity, cruelty, muckraking curiosity, knowledge without wisdom, and everything that the eternal soul in Nature loathes, instead of the virtues of which St Catherine was the figure head. As to the new rites, which would be the saner Joan? the one who carried little children to be baptized of water and the spirit, or the one who sent the police to force their parents to have the most villainous racial poison we know thrust into their veins? the one who told them the story of the angel and Mary, or the one who questioned them as to their experiences of the Edipus complex? the one to whom the consecrated wafer was the very body of the virtue that was her salvation, or the one who looked forward to a precise and convenient regulation of her health and her desires by a nicely calculated diet of thyroid extract, adrenalin, thymin, pituitrin, and insulin, with pick-me-ups of hormone stimulants, the blood being first carefully fortified with antibodies against all possible infections by inoculations of infected bacteria and serum from infected animals, and against old age by surgical extirpation of the reproductive ducts or weekly doses of monkey gland?

It is true that behind all these quackeries there is a certain body of genuine scientific physiology. But was there any the less a certain body of genuine psychology behind St Catherine and the Holy Ghost? And which is the healthier mind? the saintly mind or the monkey gland mind? Does not the present cry of Back to the Middle Ages, which has been incubating ever since the pre-Raphaelite movement began, mean that it is no longer our Academy pictures that are intolerable, but our credulities that have not the excuse of being superstitions, our cruelties that have not the excuse of barbarism, our persecutions that have not the excuse of religious faith, our shameless substitution of successful swindlers and scoundrels and quacks for saints as objects of worship, and our deafness and blindness to the calls and visions of the inexorable power that made us, and will destroy us if we disregard it? To Joan and her contemporaries we should appear as a drove of Gadarene swine, possessed by all the unclean spirits cast out by the faith and civilization of the Middle Ages, running violently down a steep place into a hell of high explosives. For us to set up our condition as a standard of sanity, and declare Joan mad because she never condescended to it, is to prove that we are not only lost but irredeemable. Let us then once for all drop all nonsense about Joan being cracked, and accept her as at least as sane as Florence Nightingale, who also combined a very simple iconography of religious belief with a mind so exceptionally powerful that it kept her in continual trouble with the medical and military panjandrums of her time.

FAILURES OF THE VOICES

That the voices and visions were illusory, and their wisdom all Joan's own, is shewn by the occasions on which they failed her, notably during her trial, when they assured her that she would be rescued. Here her hopes flattered her; but they were not unreasonable: her military colleague La Hire was in command of a considerable force not so very far off; and if the Armagnacs, as her party was called, had really wanted to rescue her, and had put anything like her own vigor into the enterprise, they could have attempted it with very fair chances of suc-cess. She did not understand that they were glad to be rid of her, nor that the rescue of a prisoner from the hands of the Church was a much more serious business for a medieval captain, or even a medieval king, than its mere physical difficulty as a military exploit suggested. According to her lights her expectation of a rescue was reasonable; therefore she heard Madame Saint Catherine assuring her it would happen, that being her way of finding out and making up her own mind. When it became evident that she had miscalculated: when she was led to the stake, and La Hire was not thundering at the gates of Rouen nor charging Warwick's men at arms, she threw over Saint Catherine at once, and recanted. Nothing could be more sane or practical. It was not until she discovered that she had gained nothing by her recantation but close imprisonment for life that she withdrew it, and deliberately and explicitly chose burning instead: a decision which shewed not only the extraordinary decision of her character, but also a Rationalism carried to its ultimate human test of suicide. Yet even in this the illusion persisted; and she announced her relapse as dictated to her by her voices.

JOAN A GALTONIC VISUALIZER

The most sceptical scientific reader may therefore accept as a flat fact, carrying no implication of unsoundness of mind, that Joan was what Francis Galton and other modern investigators of human faculty call a visualizer. She saw imaginary saints just as some other people see imaginary diagrams and landscapes with numbers dotted about them, and are thereby able to perform feats of memory and arithmetic impossible to non-visualizers. Visualizers will understand this at once. Non-visualizers who have never read Galton will be puzzled and incredulous. But a very little inquiry among their acquaintances will reveal to them that the mind's eye is more or less a magic lantern, and that the street is full of normally sane people who have hallucinations of all sorts which they believe to be part of the normal permanent equipment of all human beings.

JOAN'S MANLINESS AND MILITARISM

Joan's other abnormality, too common among uncommon things to be properly called a peculiarity, was her craze for soldiering and the masculine life. Her father tried to frighten her out of it by threatening to drown her if she ran away with the soldiers, and ordering her brothers to drown her if he were not on the spot. This extravagance was clearly not serious: it must have been addressed to a child young enough to imagine that he was in earnest. Joan must therefore as a child have wanted to run away and be a soldier. The awful prospect of being thrown into the Meuse and drowned by a terrible father and her big brothers kept her quiet until the father had lost his terrors and the brothers yielded to her natural leadership; and by that time she had sense enough to know that the masculine and military life was not a mere matter of running away from home. But the taste for it never left her, and was fundamental in determining her career.

If anyone doubts this, let him ask himself why a maid charged with a special mission from heaven to the Dauphin (this was how Joan saw her very able plan for retrieving the desperate situation of the uncrowned king) should not have simply gone to the court as a maid, in woman's dress, and urged her counsel upon him in a woman's way, as other women with similar missions had come to his mad father and his wise grandfather. Why did she insist on having a soldier's dress and arms and sword and horse and equipment, and on treating her escort of soldiers as comrades, sleeping side by side with them on the floor at night as if there were no difference of sex between them? It may be answered that this was the safest way of travelling through a country infested with hostile troops and bands of marauding deserters from both sides. Such an answer has no weight because it applies to all the women who travelled in France at that time, and who never dreamt of travelling otherwise than as women. But even if we accept it, how does it account for the fact that when the danger was over, and she could present herself at court in feminine attire with perfect safety and obviously with greater propriety, she presented herself in her man's dress, and instead of urging Charles, like Queen Victoria urging the War Office to send Roberts to the Transvaal, to send D'Alençon, De Rais, La Hire and the rest to the relief of Dunois at Orleans, insisted that she must go herself and lead the assault in person? Why did she give exhibitions of her dexterity in handling a lance, and of her seat as a rider? Why did she accept presents of armor and chargers and masculine surcoats, and in every action repudiate the conventional character of a woman? The simple answer to all these questions is that she was the sort of woman that wants to lead a man's life. They are to be found wherever there are armies on foot or navies on the seas, serving in male disguise, eluding detection for astonishingly long periods, and sometimes, no doubt, escaping it entirely. When they are in a position to defy public opinion they throw off all concealment. You have your Rosa Bonheur painting in male blouse and trousers, and George Sand living a man's life and almost compelling her Chopins and De Mussets to live women's lives to amuse her. Had Joan not been one of those "unwomanly women," she might have been canonized much sooner.

But it is not necessary to wear trousers and smoke big cigars to live a man's life any more than it is necessary to wear petticoats to live a woman's. There are plenty of gowned and bodiced women in ordinary civil life who manage their own affairs and other people's, including those of their menfolk, and are entirely masculine in their tastes and pursuits. There always were such women, even in the Victorian days when women had fewer legal rights than men, and our modern women magistrates, mayors, and members of Parliament were unknown. In reactionary Russia in our own century a woman soldier organized an effective regiment of amazons, which disappeared only because it was Aldershottian enough to be against the Revolution. The exemption of women from military service is founded, not on any natural inaptitude that men do not share, but on the fact that communities cannot reproduce themselves without plenty of women. Men are more largely dispensable, and are sacrificed accordingly.

WAS JOAN SUICIDAL?

These two abnormalities were the only ones that were irresistibly prepotent in Joan; and they brought her to the stake. Neither of them was peculiar to her. There was nothing peculiar about her except the vigor and scope of her mind and character, and the intensity of her vital energy. She was accused of a suicidal tendency; and it is a fact that when she attempted to escape from Beaurevoir Castle by jumping from a tower said to be sixty feet high, she took a risk beyond reason, though she recovered from the crash after a few days fasting. Her death was deliberately chosen as an alternative to life without liberty. In battle she challenged death as Wellington did at Waterloo, and as Nelson habitually did when he walked his quarter deck during his battles with all his decorations in full blaze. As neither Nelson nor Wellington nor any of those who have performed desperate feats, and preferred death to captivity, has been accused of suicidal mania, Joan need not be suspected of it. In the Beaurevoir affair there was more at stake than her freedom. She was distracted by the news that Compiègne was about to fall; and she was convinced that she could save it if only she could get free. Still, the leap was so perilous that her conscience was not quite easy about it; and she expressed this, as usual, by saying that Saint Catherine had forbidden her to do it, but forgave her afterwards for her disobedience.

JOAN SUMMED UP

We may accept and admire Joan, then, as a sane and shrewd country girl of extraordinary strength of mind and hardihood of body. Everything she did was thoroughly calculated; and though the process was so rapid that she was hardly conscious of it, and ascribed it all to her voices, she was a woman of policy and not of blind impulse. In war she was as much a realist as Napoleon: she had his eye for artillery and his knowledge of what it could do. She did not expect besieged cities to fall Jerichowise at the sound of her trumpet, but, like Wellington, adapted her methods of attack to the peculiarities of the defence; and she anticipated the Napoleonic calculation that if you only hold on long enough the other fellow will give in: for example, her final triumph at Orleans was achieved after her commander Dunois had sounded the retreat at the end of a day's fighting without a decision. She was never for a moment what so many romancers and playwrights have pretended: a romantic young lady. She was a thorough daughter of the soil in her peasantlike matter-of-factness and doggedness, and her acceptance of great lords and kings and prelates as such without idolatry or snobbery, seeing at a glance how much they were individually good for. She had the respectable countrywoman's sense of the value of public decency, and would not tolerate foul language and neglect of religious observances, nor allow disreputable women to hang about her soldiers. She had one pious ejaculation "En nom Dé!" and one meaningless oath "Par mon martin"; and this much swearing she allowed to the incorrigibly blasphemous La Hire equally with herself. The value of this prudery was so great in restoring the self-respect of the badly demoralized army that, like most of her policy, it justified itself as soundly calculated. She talked to and dealt with people of all classes, from laborers to kings, without embarrassment or affectation, and got them to do what she wanted when they were not afraid or corrupt. She could coax and she could hustle, her tongue having a soft side and a sharp edge. She was very capable: a born boss.

JOAN'S IMMATURITY AND IGNORANCE

All this, however, must be taken with one heavy qualification. She was only a girl in her teens. If we could think of her as a managing woman of fifty we should seize her type at once; for we have plenty of managing women among us of that age who illustrate perfectly the sort of person she would have become had she lived. But she, being only a lass when all is said, lacked their knowledge of men's vanities and of the weight and proportion of social forces. She knew nothing of iron hands in velvet gloves: she just used her fists. She thought political changes much easier than they are, and, like Mahomet in his innocence of any world but the tribal world, wrote letters to kings calling on them to make millennial rearrangements. Consequently it was only in the enterprises that were really simple and compassable by swift physical force, like the coronation and the Orleans campaign, that she was successful.

Her want of academic education dis-

abled her when she had to deal with such elaborately artificial structures as the great ecclesiastical and social institutions of the Middle Ages. She had a horror of heretics without suspecting that she was herself a heresiarch, one of the precursors of a schism that rent Europe in two, and cost centuries of bloodshed that is not yet staunched. She objected to foreigners on the sensible ground that they were not in their proper place in France; but she had no notion of how this brought her into conflict with Catholicism and Feudalism, both essentially international. She worked by commonsense; and where scholarship was the only clue to institutions she was in the dark, and broke her shins against them, all the more rudely because of her enormous self-confidence, which made her the least cautious of human beings in civil affairs.

This combination of inept youth and academic ignorance with great natural capacity, push, courage, devotion, originality and oddity, fully accounts for all the facts in Joan's career, and makes her a credible historical and human phenomenon; but it clashes most discordantly both with the idolatrous romance that has grown up round her, and the belittling scepticism that reacts against that romance.

THE MAID IN LITERATURE

English readers would probably like to know how these idolizations and reactions have affected the books they are most familiar with about Joan. There is the first part of the Shakespearean, or pseudo-Shakespearean trilogy of Henry VI, in which Joan is one of the leading characters. This portrait of Joan is not more authentic than the descriptions in the London papers of George Washington in 1780, of Napoleon in 1803, of the German Crown Prince in 1915, or of Lenin in 1917. It ends in mere scurrility. The impression left by it is that the playwright, having begun by an attempt to make Joan a beautiful and romantic figure, was told by his scandalized company that English patriotism would never stand a sympathetic representation of a French conqueror of English troops, and that unless he at once introduced all the old charges against Joan of being a sorceress and a harlot, and assumed her to be guilty of all of them, his play could not be produced. As likely as not, this is what actually happened: indeed there is only one other apparent way of accounting for the sympathetic representation of Joan as a heroine culminating in her eloquent appeal to the Duke of Burgundy, followed by the blackguardly scurrility of the concluding scenes. That other way is to assume that the original play was wholly scurrilous, and that Shakespear touched up the earlier scenes. As the work belongs to a period at which he was only beginning his practice as a tinker of old works, before his own style was fully formed and hardened, it is impossible to verify this guess. His finger is not unmistakeably evident in the play, which is poor and base in its moral tone; but he may have tried to redeem it from downright infamy by shedding a momentary glamor on the figure of The Maid.

When we jump over two centuries to Schiller, we find Die Jungfrau von Orleans drowned in a witch's caldron of raging romance. Schiller's Joan has not a single point of contact with the real Joan, nor indeed with any mortal woman that ever walked this earth. There is really nothing to be said of his play but that it is not about Joan at all, and can hardly be said to pretend to be; for he makes her die on the battlefield, finding her burning unbearable. Before Schiller came Voltaire, who burlesqued Homer in a mock epic called La Pucelle. It is the fashion to dismiss this with virtuous indignation as an obscene libel; and I certainly cannot defend it against the charge of extravagant indecorum. But its purpose was not to depict Joan, but to kill with ridicule everything that Voltaire righteously hated in the institutions and fashions of his own day. He made Joan ridiculous, but not contemptible nor (comparatively) unchaste; and as he also made Homer and St Peter and St Denis and the brave Dunois ridiculous, and the other heroines of the poem very unchaste indeed, he may be said to have let Joan off very easily. But indeed the personal adventures of the characters are so outrageous, and so Homerically free from any pretence at or even possibility of historical veracity, that those who affect to take them seriously only make themselves Pecksniffian. Samuel Butler believed The Iliad to be a burlesque of Greek Jingoism and Greek religion, written by a hostage or a slave; and La Pucelle makes Butler's theory almost convincing. Voltaire represents Agnes Sorel, the Dauphin's mistress, whom Joan never met, as a woman with a consuming passion for the chastest concubinal fidelity, whose fate it was to be continually falling into the hands of licentious foes and suffering the worst extremities of rapine. The combats in which Joan rides a flying donkey, or in which, taken unaware with no clothes on, she defends Agnes with her sword, and inflicts appropriate mutilations on her assailants, can be laughed at as they are intended to be without scruple; for no sane person could mistake them for sober history; and it may be that their ribald irreverence is more wholesome than the beglamored sentimentality of Schiller. Certainly Voltaire should not have asserted that Joan's father was a priest; but when he was out to écraser l'infâme (the French Church) he stuck at nothing.

So far, the literary representations of The Maid were legendary. But the publication by Quicherat in 1841 of the reports of her trial and rehabilitation placed the subject on a new footing. These entirely realistic documents created a living interest in Joan which Voltaire's mock Homerics and Schiller's romantic nonsense missed. Typical products of that interest in America and England are the histories of Joan by Mark Twain and Andrew Lang. Mark Twain was converted to downright worship of Joan directly by Quicherat. Later on, another man of genius, Anatole France, reacted against the Quicheratic wave of enthusiasm, and wrote a Life of Joan in which he attributed Joan's ideas to clerical prompting and her military success to an adroit use of her by Dunois as a *mascotte*: in short, he denied that she had any serious military or political ability. At this Andrew saw red, and went for Anatole's scalp in a rival Life of her which should be read as a corrective to the other. Lang had no difficulty in shewing that Joan's ability was not an unnatural fiction to be explained away as an illusion manufactured by priests and soldiers, but a straightforward fact.

It has been lightly pleaded in explanation that Anatole France is a Parisian of the art world, into whose scheme of things the able, hardheaded, hardhanded female, though she dominates provincial France and business Paris, does not enter; whereas Lang was a Scot, and every Scot knows that the grey mare is as likely as not to be the better horse. But this explanation does not convince me. I cannot believe that Anatole France does not know what everybody knows. I wish everybody knew all that he knows. One feels antipathies at work in his book. He is not anti-Joan; but he is anti-clerical, anti-mystic, and fundamentally unable to believe that there ever was any such person as the real Joan.

Mark Twain's Joan, skirted to the ground, and with as many petticoats as Noah's wife in a toy ark, is an attempt to combine Bayard with Esther Summerson from Bleak House into an unimpeachable American school teacher in armor. Like Esther Summerson she makes her creator ridiculous, and yet, being the work of a man of genius, remains a credible human goodygoody in spite of her creator's infatuation. It is the description rather than the valuation that is wrong. Andrew Lang and Mark Twain are equally determined to make Joan a beautiful and most ladylike Victorian; but both of them recognize and insist on her capacity for leadership, though the Scots scholar is less romantic about it than the Mississippi pilot. But then Lang was, by lifelong professional habit, a critic of biographies rather than a biographer, whereas Mark Twain writes his biography frankly in the form of a romance.

PROTESTANT MISUNDERSTANDINGS OF THE MIDDLE AGES

They had, however, one disability in common. To understand Joan's history it is not enough to understand her character: you must understand her environment as well. Joan in a nineteenth-twentieth century environment is as incongruous a figure as she would appear were she to walk down Piccadilly today in her fifteenth century armor. To see her in her proper perspective you must understand Christendom and the Catholic Church, the Holy Roman Empire and the Feudal System, as they existed and were understood in the Middle Ages. If you confuse the Middle Ages with the Dark Ages, and are in the habit of ridiculing your aunt for wearing "medieval clothes," meaning those in vogue in the eighteen-nineties, and are quite convinced that the world has progressed enormously, both morally and mechanically, since Joan's time, then you will never understand why Joan was burnt, much less feel that you might have voted for burning her yourself if you had been a member of the court that tried her; and until you feel that you know nothing essential about her.

That the Mississippi pilot should have broken down on this misunderstanding is natural enough. Mark Twain, the Innocent Abroad, who saw the lovely churches of the Middle Ages without a throb of emotion, author of A Yankee at the Court of King Arthur, in which the heroes and heroines of medieval chivalry are guys seen through the eyes of a street arab, was clearly out of court from the beginning. Andrew Lang was better read; but, like Walter Scott, he enjoyed medieval history as a string of Border romances rather than as the record of a high European civilization based on a catholic faith. Both of them were baptized as Protestants, and impressed by all their schooling and most of their reading with the belief that Catholic bishops who burnt heretics were persecutors capable of any villainy; that all heretics were Albigensians or Husites or Jews or Protestants of the highest character; and that the Inquisition was a Chamber of Horrors invented expressly and exclusively for such burnings. Accordingly we find them representing Peter Cauchon, Bishop of Beauvais, the judge who sent Joan to the stake, as an unconscionable scoundrel, and all the questions put to her as "traps" to ensnare and destroy her. And they assume unhesitatingly that the two or three score of canons and doctors of law and divinity who sat with Cauchon as assessors, were exact reproductions of him on slightly less elevated chairs and with a different headdress.

COMPARATIVE FAIRNESS OF JOAN'S TRIAL

The truth is that Cauchon was threatened and insulted by the English for being too considerate to Joan. A recent French writer denies that Joan was burnt, and holds that Cauchon spirited her away and burnt somebody or something else in her place, and that the pretender who subsequently personated her at Orleans and elsewhere was not a pretender but the real authentic Joan. He is able to cite Cauchon's pro-Joan partiality in support of his view. As to the assessors, the objection to them is not that they were a row of uniform rascals, but that they were political partisans of Joan's enemies. This is a valid objection to all such trials; but in the absence of neutral tribunals they are unavoidable. A trial by Joan's French partisans would have been as unfair as the trial by her French opponents; and an equally mixed tribunal would have produced a deadlock. Such recent trials as those of Edith Cavell by a German tribunal and Roger Casement by an English one were open to the same objection; but they went forward to the death nevertheless, because neutral tribunals were not available. Edith, like Joan, was an arch heretic: in the middle of the war she declared before the world that "Patriotism is not enough." She nursed enemies back to health, and assisted their prisoners to escape, making it abundantly clear that she would help any fugitive or distressed person without asking whose side he was on, and acknowledging no distinction before Christ between Tommy and Jerry and Pitou the *poilu*. Well might Edith have wished that she could bring the Middle Ages back, and have fifty civilians, learned in the law or vowed to the service of God, to support two skilled judges in trying her case according to the Catholic law of Christendom, and to argue it out with her at sitting after sitting for many weeks. The modern military Inquisition was not so squeamish. It shot her out of hand; and her countrymen, seeing in this a good opportunity for lecturing the enemy on his intolerance, put up a statue to her, but took particular care not to inscribe on the pedestal "Patriotism is not enough," for which omission, and the lie it implies, they will need Edith's intercession when they are themselves brought to judgment, if any heavenly power thinks such moral cowards capable of pleading to an intelligible indictment.

The point need be no further labored. Joan was persecuted essentially as she would be persecuted today. The change from burning to hanging or shooting may strike us as a change for the better. The change from careful trial under ordinary law to recklessly summary military terrorism may strike us a change for the worse. But as far as toleration is concerned the trial and execution in Rouen in 1431 might have been an event of today; and we may charge our consciences accordingly. If Joan had to be dealt with by us in London she would be treated with no more toleration than Miss Sylvia Pankhurst, or the Peculiar People, or the parents who keep their children from the elementary school, or any of the others who cross the line we have to draw, rightly or wrongly, between the tolerable and the intolerable.

JOAN NOT TRIED AS A POLITICAL OFFENDER

Besides, Joan's trial was not, like Casement's, a national political trial. Ecclesiastical courts and the courts of the Inquisition (Joan was tried by a combination of the two) were Courts Christian: that is, international courts; and she was tried, not as a traitress, but as a heretic, blasphemer, sorceress and idolater. Her alleged offences were not political offences against England, nor against the Burgundian faction in France, but against God and against the common morality of Christendom. And although the idea we call Nationalism was so foreign to the medieval conception of Christian society that it might almost have been directly charged against Joan as an additional heresy, yet it was not so charged; and it is unreasonable to suppose that the political bias of a body of Frenchmen like the assessors would on this point have run strongly in favor of the English foreigners (even if they had been making themselves particularly agreeable in France instead of just the contrary) against a Frenchwoman who had vanquished them.

The tragic part of the trial was that Joan, like most prisoners tried for anything but the simplest breaches of the ten commandments, did not understand what they were accusing her of. She was much more like Mark Twain than like Peter Cauchon. Her attachment to the Church was very different from the Bishop's, and does not, in fact, bear close examination from his point of view. She delighted in the solaces the Church offers to sensitive souls: to her, confession and communion were luxuries beside which the vulgar pleasures of the senses were trash. Her prayers were wonderful conversations with her three saints. Her piety seemed superhuman to the formally dutiful people whose religion was only a task to them. But when the Church was not offering her her favorite luxuries, but calling on her to accept its interpretation of God's will, and to sacrifice her own, she flatly refused, and made it clear that her notion of a Catholic Church was one in which the Pope was Pope Joan. How could the Church tolerate that, when it had just destroyed Hus, and had watched the career of Wycliffe with a growing anger that would have brought him, too, to the stake, had he not died a natural death before the wrath fell on him in his grave? Neither Hus nor Wycliffe was as bluntly defiant as Joan: both were reformers of the Church like Luther; whilst Joan, like Mrs Eddy, was quite prepared to supersede St Peter as the rock on which the Church was built, and, like Mahomet, was always ready with a private revelation from God to settle every question and fit every occasion.

The enormity of Joan's pretension was proved by her own unconsciousness of it, which we call her innocence, and her friends called her simplicity. Her solutions of the problems presented to her seemed, and indeed mostly were, the plainest commonsense, and their revelation to her by her Voices was to her a simple matter of fact. How could plain commonsense and simple fact seem to her to be that hideous thing, heresy? When rival prophetesses came into the field, she was down on them at once for liars and humbugs; but she never thought of them as heretics. She was in a state of invincible ignorance as to the Church's view; and the Church could not tolerate her pretensions without either waiving its authority or giving her a place beside the Trinity during her lifetime and in her teens, which was unthinkable. Thus an irresistible force met an immovable obstacle, and developed the heat that consumed poor Joan.

Mark and Andrew would have shared her innocence and her fate had they been dealt with by the Inquisition: that is why their accounts of the trial are as absurd as hers might have been could she have written one. All that can be said for their assumption that Cauchon was a vulgar villain, and that the questions put to Joan were traps, is that it has the support of the inquiry which rehabilitated her twentyfive years later. But this rehabilitation was as corrupt as the contrary proceeding applied to Cromwell by our Restoration reactionaries. Cauchon had been dug up, and his body thrown into the common sewer. Nothing was easier than to accuse him of cozenage, and declare the whole trial void on that account. That was what everybody wanted, from Charles the Victorious, whose credit was bound up with The Maid's, to the patriotic Nationalist populace, who idolized Joan's memory. The English were gone; and a verdict in their favor would have been an outrage on the throne and on the patriotism which Joan had set on foot. We have none of these overwhelming

motives of political convenience and popularity to bias us. For us the first trial stands valid; and the rehabilitation would be negligible but for the mass of sincere testimony it produced as to Joan's engaging personal character. The question then arises: how did The Church get over the verdict at the first trial when it canonized Joan five hundred years later?

THE CHURCH UNCOMPROMISED BY ITS AMENDS

Easily enough. In the Catholic Church, far more than in law, there is no wrong without a remedy. It does not defer to Joanesque private judgment as such, the supremacy of private judgment for the individual being the quintessence of Protestantism; nevertheless it finds a place for private judgment *in excelsis* by admitting that the highest wisdom may come as a divine revelation to an individual. On sufficient evidence it will declare that individual a saint. Thus, as revelation may come by way of an enlightenment of the private judgment no less than by the words of a celestial personage appearing in a vision, a saint may be defined as a person of heroic virtue whose private judgment is privileged. Many innovating saints, notably Francis and Clare, have been in conflict with the Church during their lives, and have thus raised the question whether they were heretics or saints. Francis might have gone to the stake had he lived longer. It is therefore by no means impossible for a person to be excommunicated as a heretic, and on further consideration canonized as a saint. Excommunication by a provincial ecclesiastical court is not one of the acts for which the Church claims infallibility. Perhaps I had better inform my Protestant readers that the famous Dogma of Papal Infallibility is by far the most modest pretension of the kind in existence. Compared with our infallible democracies, our infallible medical councils, our infallible astronomers, our infallible judges, and our infallible parliaments, the Pope is on his knees in the dust confessing his ignorance before the throne of God, asking only that as to certain historical matters on which he has clearly more sources of information open to him than anyone else his decision shall be taken as final. The Church may, and perhaps some day will, canonize Galileo without compromising such infallibility as it claims for the Pope, if not without compromising the infallibility claimed for the Book of Joshua by simple souls whose rational faith in more important things has become bound up with a quite irrational faith in the chronicle of Joshua's campaigns as a treatise on physics. Therefore the Church will probably not canonize Galileo yet awhile, though it might do worse. But it has been able to canonize Joan without any compromise at all. She never doubted that the sun went round the earth: she had seen it do so too often.

Still, there was a great wrong done to Joan and to the conscience of the world by her burning. *Tout comprendre, c'est tout pardonner*, which is the Devil's sentimentality, cannot excuse it. When we have admitted that the tribunal was not only honest and legal, but exceptionally merciful in respect of sparing Joan the torture which was customary when she was obdurate as to taking the oath, and that Cauchon was far more self-disciplined and conscientious both as priest and lawyer than any English judge ever dreams of being in a political case in which his party and class prejudices are involved, the human fact remains that the burning of Joan of Arc was a horror, and that a historian who would defend it would defend anything. The final criticism of its physical side is implied in the refusal of the Marquesas islanders to be persuaded that the English did not eat Joan. Why, they ask, should anyone take the trouble to roast a human being except

with that object? They cannot conceive its being a pleasure. As we have no answer for them that is not shameful to us, let us blush for our more complicated and pretentious savagery before we proceed to unravel the business further, and see what other lessons it contains for us.

CRUELTY, MODERN AND MEDIEVAL

First, let us get rid of the notion that the mere physical cruelty of the burning has any special significance. Joan was burnt just as dozens of less interesting heretics were burnt in her time. Christ, in being crucified, only shared the fate of thousands of forgotten malefactors. They have no pre-eminence in mere physical pain: much more horrible executions than theirs are on record, to say nothing of the agonies of so-called natural death at its worst.

Joan was burnt more than five hundred years ago. More than three hundred years later: that is, only about a hundred years before I was born, a woman was burnt on Stephen's Green in my native city of Dublin for coining, which was held to be treason. In my preface to the recent volume on English Prisons under Local Government, by Sidney and Beatrice Webb, I have mentioned that when I was already a grown man I saw Richard Wagner conduct two concerts, and that when Richard Wagner was a young man he saw and avoided a crowd of people hastening to see a soldier broken on the wheel by the more cruel of the two ways of carrying out that hideous method of execution. Also that the penalty of hanging, drawing, and quartering, unmentionable in its details, was abolished so recently that there are men living who have been sentenced to it. We are still flogging criminals, and clamoring for more flogging. Not even the most sensationally frightful of these atrocities inflicted on its victim the misery, degradation, and conscious waste and loss of life suffered in our modern prisons, especially the model ones, without, as far as I can see, rousing any more compunction than the burning of heretics did in the Middle Ages. We have not even the excuse of getting some fun out of our prisons as the Middle Ages did out of their stakes and wheels and gibbets. Joan herself judged this matter when she had to choose between imprisonment and the stake, and chose the stake. And thereby she deprived The Church of the plea that it was guiltless of her death, which was the work of the secular arm. The Church should have confined itself to excommunicating her. There it was within its rights: she had refused to accept its authority or comply with its conditions; and it could say with truth "You are not one of us: go forth and find the religion that suits you, or found one for yourself." It had no right to say "You may return to us now that you have recanted; but you shall stay in a dungeon all the rest of your life." Unfortunately, The Church did not believe that there was any genuine soul saving religion outside itself; and it was deeply corrupted, as all the Churches were and still are, by primitive Calibanism (in Browning's sense), or the propitiation of a dreaded deity by suffering and sacrifice. Its method was not cruelty for cruelty's sake, but cruelty for the salvation of Joan's soul. Joan, however, believed that the saving of her soul was her own business, and not that of *les gens d'église*. By using that term as she did, mistrustfully and contemptuously, she announced herself as, in germ, an anti-Clerical as thoroughgoing as Voltaire or Anatole France. Had she said in so many words "To the dustbin with the Church Militant and its blackcoated officials: I recognize only the Church Triumphant in heaven," she would hardly have put her view more plainly.

CATHOLIC ANTI-CLERICALISM

I must not leave it to be inferred here that one cannot be an anti-Clerical and a good Catholic too. All the reforming Popes have been vehement anti-Clericals, veritable scourges of the clergy. All the great Orders arose from dissatisfaction with the priests: that of the Franciscans with priestly snobbery, that of the Dominicans with priestly laziness and Laodiceanism, that of the Jesuits with priestly apathy and ignorance and indiscipline. The most bigoted Ulster Orangeman or Leicester Low Church bourgeois (as described by Mr Henry Nevinson) is a mere Gallio compared to Machiavelli, who, though no Protestant, was a fierce anti-Clerical. Any Catholic may, and many Catholics do, denounce any priest or body of priests, as lazy, drunken, idle, dissolute, and unworthy of their great Church and their function as the pastors of their flocks of human souls. But to say that the souls of the people are no business of the Churchmen is to go a step further, a step across the Rubicon. Joan virtually took that step.

CATHOLICISM NOT YET CATHOLIC ENOUGH

And so, if we admit, as we must, that the burning of Joan was a mistake, we must broaden Catholicism sufficiently to include her in its charter. Our Churches must admit that no official organization of mortal men whose vocation does not carry with it extraordinary mental powers (and this is all that any Church Militant can in the face of fact and history pretend to be), can keep pace with the private judgment of persons of genius except when, by a very rare accident, the genius happens to be Pope, and not even then unless he is an exceedingly overbearing Pope. The Churches must learn humility as well as teach it. The Apostolic Succession cannot be secured or confined by the laying on of hands: the tongues of fire have descended on heathens and outcasts too often for that, leaving anointed Churchmen to scandalize History as worldly rascals. When the Church Militant behaves as if it were already the Church Triumphant, it makes these appalling blunders about Joan and Bruno and Galileo and the rest which make it so difficult for a Freethinker to join it; and a Church which has no place for Freethinkers: nay, which does not inculcate and encourage freethinking with a complete belief that thought, when really free, must by its own law take the path that leads to The Church's bosom, not only has no future in modern culture, but obviously has no faith in the valid science of its own tenets, and is guilty of the heresy that theology and science are two different and opposite impulses, rivals for human allegiance.

I have before me the letter of a Catholic priest. "In your play," he writes, "I see the dramatic presentation of the conflict of the Regal, sacerdotal, and Prophetical powers, in which Joan was crushed. To me it is not the victory of any one of them over the others that will bring peace and the Reign of the Saints in the Kingdom of God, but their fruitful interaction in a costly but noble state of tension." The Pope himself could not put it better; nor can I. We must accept the tension, and maintain it nobly without letting ourselves be tempted to relieve it by burning the thread. This is Joan's lesson to The Church; and its formulation by the hand of a priest emboldens me to claim that her canonization was a magnificently Catholic gesture as the canonization of a Protestant saint by the Church of Rome. But its special value and virtue cannot be apparent until it is known and understood as such. If any simple priest for whom this is too hard a saying tells me that it was not so intended, I shall remind him that the Church is in the hands of God, and not, as simple priests imagine, God in the hands of the Church; so if he answers too confidently for God's intentions he may be asked "Hast thou entered into the springs of the sea? or hast thou walked in the recesses of the deep?" And Joan's own answer is also the answer of old: "Though He slay me, yet will I trust in Him; *but I will maintain my own ways before Him.*"

THE LAW OF CHANGE IS THE LAW OF GOD

When Joan maintained her own ways she claimed, like Job, that there was not only God and the Church to be considered, but the Word made Flesh: that is, the unaveraged individual, representing life possibly at its highest actual human evolution and possibly at its lowest, but never at its merely mathematical average. Now there is no deification of the democratic average in the theory of the Church: it is an avowed hierarchy in which the members are sifted until at the end of the process an individual stands supreme as the Vicar of Christ. But when the process is examined it appears that its successive steps of selection and election are of the superior by the inferior (the cardinal vice of democracy), with the result that great popes are as rare and accidental as great kings, and that it has sometimes been safer for an aspirant to the Chair and the Keys to pass as a moribund dotard than as an energetic saint. At best very few popes have been canonized, or could be without letting down the standard of sanctity set by the self-elected saints.

No other result could have been reasonably expected; for it is not possible that an official organization of the spiritual needs of millions of men and women, mostly poor and ignorant, should compete successfully in the selection of its principals with the direct choice of the Holy Ghost as it flashes with unerring aim upon the individual. Nor can any College of Cardinals pray effectively that its choice may be inspired. The conscious prayer of the inferior may be that his choice may light on a greater than himself; but the sub-conscious intention of his self-preserving individuality must be to find a trustworthy servant for his own purposes. The saints and prophets, though they may be accidentally in this or that official position or rank, are always really self-selected, like Joan. And since neither Church nor State, by the secular necessities of its constitution, can guarantee even the recognition of such self-chosen missions, there is nothing for us but to make it a point of honor to privilege heresy to the last bearable degree on the simple ground that all evolution in thought and conduct must at first appear as heresy and misconduct. In short, though all society is founded on intolerance, all improvement is founded on tolerance, or the recognition of the fact that the law of evolution is Ibsen's law of change. And as the law of God in any sense of the word which can now command a faith proof against science is a law of evolution, it follows that the law of God is a law of change, and that when the Churches set themselves against change as such, they are setting themselves against the law of God.

CREDULITY, MODERN AND MEDIEVAL

When Abernethy, the famous doctor, was asked why he indulged himself with all the habits he warned his patients against as unhealthy, he replied that his business was that of a direction post, which points out the way to a place, but does not go thither itself. He might have added that neither does it compel the traveller to go thither, nor prevent him from seeking some other way. Unfortunately our clerical direction posts always do coerce the traveller when they have the political power to do so. When the Church was a temporal as well as a spiritual power, and for long after to the full extent to which it could control or influence the temporal power, it enforced conformity by persecutions that were all the more ruthless because their intention was so excellent. Today, when the doctor has succeeded to the priest, and can do practically what he likes with parliament and the press through the blind faith in him which has succeeded to the far more critical faith in the parson, legal compulsion to take the doctor's prescription, however poisonous, is carried to an extent that would have horrified the Inquisition and staggered Archbishop Laud. Our credulity is grosser than that of the Middle Ages, because the priest had no such direct pecuniary interest in our sins as the doctor has in our diseases: he did not starve when all was well with his flock, nor prosper when they were perishing, as our private commercial doctors must. Also the medieval cleric believed that something extremely unpleasant would happen to him after death if he was unscrupulous, a belief now practically extinct among persons receiving a dogmatically materialist education. Our professional corporations are Trade Unions without souls to be damned; and they will soon drive us to remind them that they have bodies to be kicked. The Vatican was never soulless: at worst it was a political conspiracy to make the Church supreme temporally as well as spiritually. Therefore the question raised by Joan's burning is a burning question still, though the penalties involved are not so sensational. That is why I am probing it. If it were only an historical curiosity I would not waste my readers' time and my own on it for five minutes.

TOLERATION, MODERN AND MEDIEVAL

The more closely we grapple with it the more difficult it becomes. At first sight we are disposed to repeat that Joan should have been excommunicated and then left to go her own way, though she would have protested vehemently against so cruel a deprivation of her spiritual food; for confession, absolution, and the body of her Lord were first necessaries of life to her. Such a spirit as Joan's might have got over that difficulty as the Church of England got over the Bulls of Pope Leo, by making a Church of her own, and affirming it to be the temple of the true and original faith from which her persecutors had strayed. But as such a proceeding was, in the eyes of both Church and State at that time, a spreading of damnation and anarchy, its toleration involved a greater strain on faith in freedom than political and ecclesiastical human nature could bear. It is easy to say that the Church should have waited for the alleged evil results instead of assuming that they would occur, and what they would be. That sounds simple enough; but if a modern Public Health Authority were to leave people entirely to their own devices in the matter of sanitation, saying, "We have nothing to do with drainage or your views about drainage; but if you catch smallpox or typhus we will prosecute you and have you punished very severely like the authorities in Butler's Erewhon," it would either be removed to the County Asylum or reminded that A's neglect of sanitation may kill the child of B two miles off, or start an epidemic in which the most conscientious sanitarians may perish.

We must face the fact that society is founded on intolerance. There are glaring cases of the abuse of intolerance; but they are quite as characteristic of our own age as of the Middle Ages. The typical modern example and contrast is compulsory inoculation replacing what was virtually compulsory baptism. But compulsion to inoculate is objected to as a crudely unscientific and mischievous anti-sanitary quackery, not in the least because we think it wrong to compel people to protect their children from disease. Its opponents would make it a crime, and will probably succeed in doing so; and that will be just as intolerant as making it compulsory.

Neither the Pasteurians nor their opponents the Sanitarians would leave parents free to bring up their children naked, though that course also has some plausible advocates. We may prate of toleration as we will; but society must always draw a line somewhere between allowable conduct and insanity or crime, in spite of the risk of mistaking sages for lunatics and saviors for blasphemers. We must persecute, even to the death; and all we can do to mitigate the danger of persecution is, first, to be very careful what we persecute, and second, to bear in mind that unless there is a large liberty to shock conventional people, and a well informed sense of the value of originality, individuality, and eccentricity, the result will be apparent stagnation covering a repression of evolutionary forces which will eventually explode with extravagant and probably destructive violence.

VARIABILITY OF TOLERATION

The degree of tolerance attainable at any moment depends on the strain under which society is maintaining its cohesion. In war, for instance, we suppress the gospels and put Quakers in prison, muzzle the newspapers, and make it a serious offence to shew a light at night. Under the strain of invasion the French Government in 1792 struck off 4000 heads, mostly on grounds that would not in time of settled peace have provoked any Government to chloroform a dog; and in 1920 the British Government slaughtered and burnt in Ireland to persecute the advocates of a constitutional change which it had presently to effect itself. Later on the Fascisti in Italy did everything that the Black and Tans did in Ireland, with some grotesquely ferocious variations, under the strain of an unskilled attempt at industrial revolution by Socialists who understood Socialism even less than Capitalists understand Capitalism. In the United States an incredibly savage persecution of Russians took place during the scare spread by the Russian Bolshevik revolution after 1917. These instances could easily be multiplied; but they are enough to shew that between a maximum of indulgent toleration and a ruthlessly intolerant Terrorism there is a scale through which toleration is continually rising or falling, and that there was not the smallest ground for the self-complacent conviction of the nineteenth century that it was more tolerant than the fifteenth, or that such an event as the execution of Joan could not possibly occur in what we call our own more enlightened times. Thousands of women, each of them a thousand times less dangerous and terrifying to our Governments than Joan was to the Government of her day, have within the last ten years been slaughtered, starved to death, burnt out of house and home, and what not that Persecution and Terror could do to them, in the course of Crusades far more tyrannically pretentious than the medieval Crusades which proposed nothing more hyperbolical than the rescue of the Holy Sepulchre from the Saracens. The Inquisition, with its English equivalent the Star Chamber, are gone in the sense that their names are now disused; but can any of the modern substitutes for the Inquisition, the Special Tribunals and Commissions, the punitive expeditions, the suspensions of the Habeas Corpus Act, the proclamations of martial law and of minor states of siege, and the rest of them, claim that their victims have as fair a trial, as well considered a body of law to govern their cases, or as conscientious a judge to insist on strict legality of procedure as Joan had from the Inquisition and from the spirit of the Middle Ages even when her country was under the heaviest strain of civil and foreign war? From us she would have had no trial and no law except a Defence of The Realm Act suspending all law; and for judge she would have had, at best, a bothered major, and at worst a promoted advocate in ermine and scarlet to whom the scruples of a trained ecclesiastic like Cauchon would seem ridiculous and ungentlemanly.

THE CONFLICT BETWEEN GENIUS AND DISCIPLINE

Having thus brought the matter home to ourselves, we may now consider the special feature of Joan's mental constitution which made her so unmanageable. What is to be done on the one hand with rulers who will not give any reason for their orders, and on the other with people who cannot understand the reasons when they are given? The government of the world, political, industrial, and domestic, has to be carried on mostly by the giving and obeying of orders under just these conditions. "Dont argue: do as you are told" has to be said not only to children and soldiers, but practically to everybody. Fortunately most people do not want to argue: they are only too glad to be saved the trouble of thinking for themselves. And the ablest and most independent thinkers are content to understand their own special department. In other departments they will unhesitatingly ask for and accept the instructions of a policeman or the advice of a tailor without demanding or desiring explanations.

Nevertheless, there must be some ground for attaching authority to an order. A child will obey its parents, a soldier his officer, a philosopher a railway porter, and a workman a foreman, all without question, because it is generally accepted that those who give the orders understand what they are about, and are duly authorized and even obliged to give them, and because, in the practical emergencies of daily life, there is no time for lessons and explanations, or for arguments as to their validity. Such obediences are as necessary to the continuous operation of our social system as the revolutions of the earth are to the succession of night and day. But they are not so spontaneous as they seem: they have to be very carefully arranged and maintained. A bishop will defer to and obey a king; but let a curate venture to give him an order, however necessary and sensible, and the bishop will forget his cloth and damn the curate's impudence. The more obedient a man is to accredited authority the more jealous he is of allowing any unauthorized person to order him about.

With all this in mind, consider the career of Joan. She was a village girl, in authority over sheep and pigs, dogs and chickens, and to some extent over her father's hired laborers when he hired any, but over no one else on earth. Outside the farm she had no authority, no prestige, no claim to the smallest deference. Yet she ordered everybody about, from her uncle to the king, the archbishop, and the military General Staff. Her uncle obeyed her like a sheep, and took her to the castle of the local commander, who, on being ordered about, tried to assert himself, but soon collapsed and obeyed. And so on up to the king, as we have seen. This would have been unbearably irritating even if her orders had been offered as rational solutions of the desperate difficulties in which her social superiors found themselves just then. But they were not so offered. Nor were they offered as the expression of Joan's arbitrary will. It was never "I say so," but always "God says so."

JOAN AS THEOCRAT

Leaders who take that line have no trouble with some people, and no end of trouble with others. They need never fear a lukewarm reception. Either they are messengers of God, or they are blasphemous impostors. In the Middle Ages the general belief in witchcraft greatly intensified this contrast, because when an apparent miracle happened (as in the case of the wind changing at Orleans) it proved the divine mission to the credulous, and proved a contract with the devil to the sceptical. All through, Joan had to depend on those who accepted her as an incarnate angel against those who added to an intense resentment of her presumption a bigoted abhorrence of her as a witch. To this abhorrence we must add the extreme irritation of those who did not believe in the voices, and regarded her as a liar and impostor. It is hard to conceive anything more infuriating to a statesman or a military commander, or to a court favorite, than to be overruled at every turn, or to be robbed of the ear of the reigning sovereign, by an impudent young upstart practising on the credulity of the populace and the vanity and silliness of an immature prince by exploiting a few of those lucky coincidences which pass as miracles with uncritical people. Not only were the envy, snobbery, and competitive ambition of the baser natures exacerbated by Joan's success, but among the friendly ones that were clever enough to be critical a quite reasonable scepticism and mistrust of her ability, founded on a fair observation of her obvious ignorance and temerity, were at work against her. And as she met all remonstrances and all criticisms, not with arguments or persuasion, but with a flat appeal to the authority of God and a claim to be in God's special confidence, she must have seemed, to all who were not infatuated by her, so insufferable that nothing but an unbroken chain of overwhelming successes in the military and political field could have saved her from the wrath that finally destroyed her.

UNBROKEN SUCCESS ESSENTIAL IN THEOCRACY

To forge such a chain she needed to be the King, the Archbishop of Rheims, the

Bastard of Orleans, and herself into the bargain; and that was impossible. From the moment when she failed to stimulate Charles to follow up his coronation with a swoop on Paris she was lost. The fact that she insisted on this whilst the king and the rest timidly and foolishly thought they could square the Duke of Burgundy, and effect a combination with him against the English, made her a terrifying nuisance to them; and from that time onward she could do nothing but prowl about the battlefields waiting for some lucky chance to sweep the captains into a big move. But it was to the enemy that the chance came: she was taken prisoner by the Burgundians fighting before Compiègne, and at once discovered that she had not a friend in the political world. Had she escaped she would probably have fought on until the English were gone, and then had to shake the dust of the court off her feet, and retire to Domrémy as Garibaldi had to retire to Caprera.

MODERN DISTORTIONS OF JOAN'S HISTORY

This, I think, is all that we can now pretend to say about the prose of Joan's career. The romance of her rise, the tragedy of her execution, and the comedy of the attempts of posterity to make amends for that execution, belong to my play and not to my preface, which must be confined to a sober essay on the facts. That such an essay is badly needed can be ascertained by examining any of our standard works of reference. They give accurately enough the facts about the visit to Vaucouleurs, the annunciation to Charles at Chinon, the raising of the siege of Orleans and the subsequent battles, the coronation at Rheims, the capture at Compiègne, and the trial and execution at Rouen, with their dates and the names of the people concerned; but they all break down on the melodramatic legend of the wicked bishop and the en-trapped maiden and the rest of it. It would be far less misleading if they were wrong as to the facts, and right in their view of the facts. As it is, they illustrate the too little considered truth that the fashion in which we think changes like the fashion of our clothes, and that it is difficult, if not impossible, for most people to think otherwise than in the fashion of their own period.

HISTORY ALWAYS OUT OF DATE

This, by the way, is why children are never taught contemporary history. Their history books deal with periods of which the thinking has passed out of fashion, and the circumstances no longer apply to active life. For example, they are taught history about Washington, and told lies about Lenin. In Washington's time they were told lies (the same lies) about Washington, and taught history about Cromwell. In the fifteenth and sixteenth centuries they were told lies about Joan, and by this time might very well be told the truth about her. Unfortunately the lies did not cease when the political circumstances became obsolete. The Reformation, which Joan had unconsciously anticipated, kept the questions which arose in her case burning up to our own day (you can see plenty of the burnt houses still in Ireland), with the result that Joan has remained the subject of anti-Clerical lies, of specifically Protestant lies, and of Roman Catholic evasions of her unconscious Protestantism. The truth sticks in our throats with all the sauces it is served with: it will never go down until we take it without any sauce at all.

THE REAL JOAN NOT MARVELLOUS ENOUGH FOR US

But even in its simplicity, the faith demanded by Joan is one which the anti-metaphysical temper of nineteenth century civilization, which remains powerful in England and America, and is tyrannical in France, contemptuously refuses her. We do not, like her contemporaries, rush to the opposite extreme in a recoil from her as from a witch self-sold to the devil, because we do not believe in the devil nor in the possibility of commercial contracts with him. Our credulity, though enormous, is not boundless; and our stock of it is quite used up by our mediums, clairvoyants, hand readers, slate writers, Christian Scientists, psycho-analysts, electronic vibration diviners, therapeutists of all schools registered and unregistered, astrologers, astronomers who tell us that the sun is nearly a hundred million miles away and that Betelgeuse is ten times as big as the whole universe, physicists who balance Betelgeuse by describing the incredible smallness of the atom, and a host of other marvel mongers whose credulity would have dissolved the Middle Ages in a roar of sceptical merriment. In the Middle Ages people believed that the earth was flat, for which they had at least the evidence of their senses: we believe it to be round, not because as many as one per cent of us could give the physical reasons for so quaint a belief, but because modern science has convinced us that nothing that is obvious is true, and that everything that is magical, improbable, extraordinary, gigantic, microscopic, heartless, or outrageous is scientific.

I must not, by the way, be taken as implying that the earth is flat, or that all or any of our amazing credulities are delusions or impostures. I am only defending my own age against the charge of being less imaginative than the Middle Ages. I affirm that the nineteenth century, and still more the twentieth, can knock the fifteenth into a cocked hat in point of susceptibility to marvels and miracles and saints and prophets and magicians and monsters and fairy tales of all kinds. The proportion of marvel to immediately credible statement in the latest edition of the Encyclopædia Britannica is enormously greater than in the Bible. The medieval doctors of divinity who did not pretend to settle how many angels could dance on the point of a needle cut a very poor figure as far as romantic credulity is concerned beside the modern physicists who have settled to the billionth of a millimetre every movement and position in the dance of the electrons. Not for worlds would I question the precise accuracy of these calculations or the existence of electrons (whatever they may be). The fate of Joan is a warning to me against such heresy. But why the men who believe in electrons should regard themselves as less credulous than the men who believed in angels is not apparent to me. If they refuse to believe, with the Rouen assessors of 1431, that Joan was a witch, it is not because that explanation is too marvellous, but because it is not marvellous enough.

THE STAGE LIMITS OF HISTORICAL REPRESENTATION

For the story of Joan I refer the reader to the play which follows. It contains all that need be known about her; but as it is for stage use I have had to condense into three and a half hours a series of events which in their historical happening were spread over four times as many months; for the theatre imposes unities of time and place from which Nature in her boundless wastefulness is free. Therefore the reader must not suppose that Joan really put Robert de Baudricourt in her pocket in fifteen minutes, nor that her excommunication, recantation, relapse, and death at the stake were a matter of half an hour or so. Neither do I claim more for my dramatizations of Joan's contemporaries than that some of them are probably slightly more like the originals than those imaginary portraits of all the Popes from Saint Peter onward through the Dark Ages which are still gravely exhibited in the Uffizi in Florence (or were when I was there last). My Dunois would do equally well for the Duc d'Alençon. Both left descriptions of Joan so similar that, as a man always describes himself unconsciously whenever he describes anyone else, I have inferred that these goodnatured young men were very like one another in mind; so I have lumped the twain into a single figure, thereby saving the theatre manager a salary and a suit of armor. Dunois' face, still on record at Châteaudun, is a suggestive help. But I really know no more about these men and their circle than Shakespear knew about Falconbridge and the Duke of Austria, or about Macbeth and Macduff. In view of the things they did in history, and have to do again in the play, I can only invent appropriate characters for them in Shakespear's manner.

A VOID IN THE ELIZABETHAN DRAMA

I have, however, one advantage over the Elizabethans. I write in full view of the Middle Ages, which may be said to have been rediscovered in the middle of the nineteenth century after an eclipse of about four hundred and fifty years. The Renascence of antique literature and art in the sixteenth century, and the lusty growth of Capitalism, between them buried the Middle Ages; and their resurrection is a second Renascence. Now there is not a breath of medieval atmosphere in Shakespear's histories. His John of Gaunt is like a study of the old age of Drake. Although he was a Catholic by family tradition, his figures are all intensely Protestant, individualist, sceptical, self-centred in everything but their love affairs, and completely personal and selfish even in them. His kings are not statesmen: his cardinals have no religion: a novice can read his plays from one end to the other without learning that the world is finally governed by forces ex-pressing themselves in religions and laws which make epochs rather than by vulgarly ambitious individuals who make rows. The divinity which shapes our ends, rough hew them how we will, is mentioned fatalistically only to be forgotten immediately like a passing vague apprehension. To Shakespear as to Mark Twain, Cauchon would have been a tyrant and a bully instead of a Catholic, and the inquisitor Lemaître would have been a Sadist instead of a lawyer. Warwick would have had no more feudal quality than his successor the King Maker has in the play of Henry VI. We should have seen them all completely satisfied that if they would only to their own selves be true they could not then be false to any man (a precept which represents the reaction against medievalism at its intensest) as if they were beings in the air, without public responsibilities of any kind. All Shakespear's characters are so: that is why they seem natural to our middle classes, who are comfortable and irresponsible at other people's expense, and are neither ashamed of that condition nor even conscious of it. Nature abhors this vacuum in Shakespear; and I have taken care to let the medieval atmosphere blow through my play freely. Those who see it performed will not mistake the startling event it records for a mere personal accident. They will have before them not only the visible and human puppets, but the Church, the Inquisition, the Feudal System, with divine inspiration always beating against their too inelastic limits: all more terrible in their dramatic force than any of the little mortal figures clanking about in plate armor or moving silently in the frocks and hoods of the order of St Dominic.

TRAGEDY, NOT MELODRAMA

There are no villains in the piece. Crime, like disease, is not interesting: it is something to be done away with by general consent, and that is all about it. It is what men do at their best, with good intentions, and what normal men and women find that they must and will do in spite of their intentions, that really concern us. The rascally bishop and the cruel inquisitor of Mark Twain and Andrew Lang are as dull as pickpockets; and they reduce Joan to the level of the even less interesting person whose pocket is picked. I have represented both of them as capable and eloquent exponents of The Church Militant and The Church Litigant, because only by doing so can I maintain my drama on the level of high tragedy and save it from becoming a mere police court sensation. A villain in a play can never be anything more than a *diabolus ex machina*, possibly a more exciting expedient than a *deus ex machina*, but both equally mechanical, and therefore interesting only as mechanism. It is, I repeat, what normally innocent people do that concerns us; and if Joan had not been burnt by normally innocent people in the energy of their righteousness her death at their hands would have no more significance than the Tokyo earthquake, which burnt a great many maidens. The tragedy of such murders is that they are not committed by murderers. They are judicial murders, pious murders; and this contradiction at once brings an element of comedy into the tragedy: the angels may weep at the murder, but the gods laugh at the murderers.

THE INEVITABLE FLATTERIES OF TRAGEDY

Here then we have a reason why my drama of Saint Joan's career, though it may give the essential truth of it, gives an inexact picture of some accidental facts. It goes almost without saying that the old Jeanne d'Arc melodramas, reducing everything to a conflict of villain and hero, or in Joan's case villain and heroine, not only miss the point entirely, but falsify the characters, making Cauchon a scoundrel, Joan a prima donna, and Dunois a lover. But the writer of high tragedy and comedy, aiming at the innermost attainable truth, must needs flatter Cauchon nearly as much as the melodramatist vilifies him. Although there is, as far as I have been able to discover, nothing against Cauchon that convicts him of bad faith or exceptional severity in his judicial relations with Joan, or of as much anti-prisoner, pro-police, class and sectarian bias as we now take for granted in our own courts, yet there is hardly more warrant for classing him as a great Catholic churchman, completely proof against the passions roused by the temporal situation. Neither does the inquisitor Lemaître, in such scanty accounts of him as are now recoverable, appear quite so able a master of his duties and of the case before him as I have given him credit for being. But it is the business of the stage to make its figures more intelligible to themselves than they would be in real life; for by no other means can they be made intelligible to the audience. And in this case Cauchon and Lemaître have to make intelligible not only themselves but the Church and the Inquisition, just as Warwick has to make the feudal system intelligible, the three between them having thus to make a twentieth-century audience conscious of an epoch fundamentally different from its own. Obviously the real Cauchon, Lemaître, and Warwick could not have done this: they were part of the Middle Ages themselves, and therefore as unconscious of its peculiarities as of the atomic formula of the air they breathed. But the play would be unintelligible if I had not endowed them with enough of this consciousness to enable them to explain their attitude to the twentieth century. All I claim is that by this inevitable sacrifice of verisimilitude I have secured in the only possible way sufficient veracity to justify me in claiming that as far as I can gather from the available documentation, and from such powers of divination as I possess, the things I represent these three exponents of the drama as saying are the things they actually would have said if they had known what they were really doing. And beyond this neither drama nor history can go in my hands.

SOME WELL-MEANT PROPOSALS FOR THE IMPROVEMENT OF THE PLAY

I have to thank several critics on both sides of the Atlantic, including some whose admiration for my play is most generously enthusiastic, for their heartfelt instructions as to how it can be improved. They point out that by the excision of the epilogue and all the references to such undramatic and tedious matters as the Church, the feudal system, the Inquisition, the theory of heresy and so forth, all of which, they point out, would be ruthlessly blue pencilled by any experienced manager, the play could be considerably shortened. I think they are mistaken. The experienced knights of the blue pencil, having saved an hour and a half by disembowelling the play, would at once proceed to waste two hours in building elaborate scenery, having real water in the river Loire and a real bridge across it, and staging an obviously sham fight for possession of it, with the victorious French led by Joan on a real horse. The coronation would eclipse all previous theatrical displays, shewing, first, the procession through the streets of Rheims, and then the service in the cathedral, with special music written for both. Joan would be burnt on the stage, as Mr Matheson Lang always is in The Wandering Jew, on the principle that it does not matter in the least why a woman is burnt provided she is burnt, and people can pay to see it done. The intervals between the acts whilst these splendors were being built up and then demolished by the stage carpenters would seem eternal, to the great profit of the refreshment bars. And the weary and demoralized audience would lose their last trains and curse me for writing such inordinately long and intolerably dreary and meaningless plays. But the applause of the press would be unanimous. Nobody who knows the stage history of Shakespear will doubt that this is what would happen if I knew my business so little as to listen to these well intentioned but disastrous counsellors: indeed it probably will happen when I am no longer in control of the performing rights. So perhaps it will be as well for the public to see the play while I am still alive.

THE EPILOGUE

As to the epilogue, I could hardly be expected to stultify myself by implying that Joan's history in the world ended unhappily with her execution, instead of beginning there. It was necessary by hook or crook to shew the canonized Joan as well as the incinerated one; for many a woman has got herself burnt by carelessly whisking a muslin skirt into the drawing room fireplace, but getting canonized is a different matter, and a more important one. So I am afraid the epilogue must stand.

TO THE CRITICS, LEST THEY SHOULD FEEL IGNORED

To a professional critic (I have been one myself) theatre-going is the curse of Adam. The play is the evil he is paid to endure in the sweat of his brow; and the sooner it is over, the better. This would seem to place him in irreconcilable opposition to the paying playgoer, from whose point of view the longer the play, the more entertainment he gets for his money. It does in fact so place him, especially in the provinces, where the playgoer goes to the theatre for the sake of the play solely, and insists so effectively on a certain number of hours' entertainment that touring managers are sometimes seriously embarrassed by the brevity of the London plays they have to deal in.

For in London the critics are reinforced by a considerable body of persons who go to the theatre as many others go to church, to display their best clothes and compare them with other people's; to be in the fashion, and have something to talk about at dinner parties; to adore a pet performer; to pass the evening anywhere rather than at home: in short, for any or every reason except interest in dramatic art as such. In fashionable centres the number of irreligious people who go to church, of unmusical people who go to concerts and operas, and of undramatic people who go to the theatre, is so prodigious that sermons have been cut down to ten minutes and plays to two hours; and, even at that, congregations sit longing for the benediction and audiences for the final curtain, so that they may get away to the lunch or supper they really crave for, after arriving as late as (or later than) the hour of beginning can possibly be made for them.

Thus from the stalls and in the Press an atmosphere of hypocrisy spreads. Nobody says straight out that genuine drama is a tedious nuisance, and that to ask people to endure more than two hours of it (with two long intervals of relief) is an intolerable imposition. Nobody says "I hate classical tragedy and comedy as I hate sermons and symphonies; but I like police news and divorce news and any kind of dancing or decoration that has an aphrodisiac effect on me or on my wife or husband. And whatever superior people may pretend, I cannot associate pleasure with any sort of intellectual activity; and I dont believe anyone else can either." Such things are not said; yet nine-tenths of what is offered as criticism of the drama in the metropolitan Press of Europe and America is nothing but a muddled paraphrase of it. If it does not mean that, it means nothing.

I do not complain of this, though it complains very unreasonably of me. But I can take no more notice of it than Einstein of the people who are incapable of mathematics. I write in the classical manner for those who pay for admission to a theatre because they like classical comedy or tragedy for its own sake, and like it so much when it is good of its kind and well done that they tear themselves away from it with reluctance to catch the very latest train or omnibus that will take them home. Far from arriving late from an eight or half-past eight o'clock dinner so as to escape at least the first half-hour of the performance, they stand in queues outside the theatre doors for hours beforehand in bitingly cold weather to secure a seat. In countries where a play lasts a week, they bring baskets of provisions and sit it out. These are the patrons on whom I depend for my bread. I do not give them performances twelve hours long, because circumstances do not at present make such entertainments feasible; though a performance beginning after breakfast and ending at sunset is as possible physically and artistically in Surrey or Middlesex as in Ober-Ammergau; and an all-night sitting in a theatre would be at least as enjoyable as an all-night sitting in the House of Commons, and much more useful. But in St Joan I have done my best by going to the well-established classical limit of three and a half hours practically continuous playing, barring the one interval imposed by considerations which have nothing to do with art. I know that this is hard on the pseudo-critics and on the fashionable people whose playgoing is a hypocrisy. I cannot help feeling some compassion for them when they assure me that my play, though a great play, must fail hopelessly, because it does not begin at a quarter to nine and end at eleven. The facts are overwhelmingly against them. They forget that all men are not as they are. Still, I am sorry for them; and though I cannot for their sakes undo my work and help the people who hate the theatre to drive out the people who love it, yet I may point out to them that they have several remedies in their own hands. They can escape the first part of the play by their usual practice of arriving late. They can escape the epilogue by not waiting for it. And if the irreducible minimum thus attained is still too painful, they can stay away altogether. But I deprecate this extreme course, because it is good neither for my pocket nor for their own souls. Already a few of them, noticing that what matters is not the absolute length of time occupied by a play, but the speed with which that time passes, are discovering that the theatre, though purgatorial in its Aristotelian moments, is not necessarily always the dull place they have so often found it. What do its discomforts matter when the play makes us forget them?

XXII

THE ADVENTURES OF THE BLACK GIRL IN HER SEARCH FOR GOD

1932

I was inspired to write this tale when I was held up in Knysna for five weeks in the African summer and English winter of 1932. My intention was to write a play in the ordinary course of my business as a playwright; but I found myself writing the story of the black girl instead. And now, the story being written, I proceed to speculate on what it means, though I cannot too often repeat that I am as liable as anyone else to err in my interpretation, and that pioneer writers, like other pioneers, often mistake their destination as Columbus did. That is how they sometimes run away in pious horror from the conclusions to which their revelations manifestly lead. I hold, as firmly as St Thomas Aquinas, that all truths, ancient or modern, are divinely inspired; but I know by observation and introspection that the instrument on which the inspiring force plays may be a very faulty one, and may even end, like Bunyan in The Holy War, by making the most ridiculous nonsense of his message.

However, here is my own account of the matter for what it is worth.

It is often said, by the heedless, that we are a conservative species, impervious to new ideas. I have not found it so. I am often appalled at the avidity and credulity with which new ideas are snatched at and adopted without a scrap of sound evidence. People will believe anything that amuses them, gratifies them, or promises them some sort of profit. I console myself, as Stuart Mill did, with the notion that in time the silly ideas will lose their charm and drop out of fashion and out of existence, that the false promises, when broken, will pass through cynical derision into oblivion; and that after this sifting process the sound ideas, being indestructible (for even if suppressed or forgotten they are rediscovered again and again) will survive and be added to the body of ascertained knowledge we call Science. In this way we acquire a well tested stock of ideas to furnish our minds, such furnishing being education proper as distinguished from the pseudo-education of the schools and universities.

Unfortunately there is a snag in this simple scheme. It forgets the prudent old precept, "Dont throw out your dirty water until you get in your clean" which is the very devil unless completed by "This also I say unto you, that when you get your fresh water you must throw out the dirty, and be particularly careful not to let the two get mixed."

Now this is just what we never do. We persist in pouring the clean water into the dirty; and our minds are always muddled in consequence. The educated human of today has a mind which can be compared only to a store in which the very latest and most precious acquisitions are flung on top of a noisome heap of rag-and-bottle refuse and worthless antiquities from the museum lumber room. The store is always bankrupt; and the men in possession include William the Conqueror and Henry the Seventh, Moses and Jesus, St Augustine and Sir Isaac Newton, Calvin and Wesley, Queen Victoria and Mr H. G. Wells; whilst among the distraining creditors are Karl Marx, Einstein, and dozens of people more or less like Stuart Mill and myself. No mind can operate reasonably in such a mess. And as our current schooling and colleging and graduating consists in reproducing this mess in the minds of every fresh generation of children, we are provoking revolutionary emergencies in which persons muddled by university degrees will have to be politically disfranchised and disqualified as, in effect, certified lunatics, and the direction of affairs given over to the self-educated and the simpletons.

The most conspicuous example of this insane practice of continually taking in new ideas without ever clearing out the ideas they supersede, is the standing of the Bible in those countries in which the extraordinary artistic value of the English translation has given it a magical power over its readers. That power is now waning because, as sixteenth century English is a dying tongue, new translations are being forced on us by the plain fact that the old one is no longer intelligible to the masses. These new versions have—the good ones by their admirable homeliness and the ordinary ones by their newspapery everydayness—suddenly placed the Bible narratives in a light of familiar realism which obliges their readers to apply common sense tests to them.

But the influence of these modern versions is not yet very wide. It seems to me that those who find the old version unintelligible and boresome do not resort to modern versions: they simply give up reading the Bible. The few who are caught and interested by the new versions stumble on them by accidents which, being accidents, are necessarily rare. But they still hear Lessons read in church in the old version in a specially reverent tone; children at Sunday School are made to learn its verses by heart, and are rewarded by little cards inscribed with its texts; and bedrooms and nurseries are still decorated with its precepts, warnings, and consolations. The British and Foreign Bible Society has distributed more than three million copies annually for a century past; and though many of these copies may be mere churchgoers' luggage, never opened on weekdays, or gifts in discharge of the duties of godparents; yet they count. There is still on the statute book a law which no statesman dare repeal, which makes it felony for a professed Christian to question the scientific truth and supernatural authority of any word of Holy Scripture, the penalties extending to ruinous outlawry; and the same acceptance of the Bible as an infallible encyclopedia is one of the Articles of the Church of England, though another Article, and that the very first, flatly denies the corporeal and voracious nature of God insisted on in the Pentateuch.

In all these instances the Bible means the translation authorized by King James the First of the best examples in ancient Jewish literature of natural and political history, of poetry, morality, theology, and rhapsody. The translation was extraordinarily well done because to the translators what they were translating was not merely a curious collection of ancient books written by different authors in different stages of culture, but the Word of God divinely revealed through his chosen and expressly inspired scribes. In this conviction they carried out their work with boundless reverence and care and achieved a beautifully artistic result. It did not seem possible to them that they could flatter the original texts; for who could improve on God's own style? And as they could not conceive that divine revelation could conflict with what they believed to be the truths of their religion, they did not hesitate to translate a negative by a positive where such a conflict seemed to arise, as they could hardly trust their own fallible knowledge of ancient Hebrew when it contradicted the very foundations of their faith, nor doubt that God would, as they prayed Him to do, take care that his message should not suffer corruption in their hands. In this state of exaltation they made a translation so magnificent that to this day the common human Britisher or citizen of the United States of North America accepts and worships it as a single book by a single author, the book being the Book of Books and the author being God. Its charm, its promise of salvation, its pathos, and its majesty have been raised to transcendence by Handel, who can still make atheists cry and give materialists the thrill of the sublime with his Messiah. Even the ignorant, to whom religion is crude fetichism and magic, prize it as a paper talisman that will exorcise ghosts, prevent witnesses from lying, and, if carried devoutly in a soldier's pocket, stop bullets.

Now it is clear that this supernatural view of the Bible, though at its best it may achieve sublimity by keeping its head in the skies, may also make itself both ridiculous and dangerous by having its feet off the ground. It is a matter of daily experience that a book taken as an infallible revelation, whether the author be Moses, Ezekiel, Paul, Swedenborg, Joseph Smith, Mary Baker Eddy, or Karl Marx, may bring such hope, consolation, interest, and happiness into our individual lives that we may well cherish it as the key of Paradise. But if the paradise be a fool's paradise, as it must be when its materials are imaginary, then it must not be made the foundation of a State, and must be classed with anodynes, opiates, and anæsthetics. It is not for nothing that the fanatically religious leaders of the new Russia dismissed the religion of the Greek Church as "dope." That is precisely what a religion becomes when it is divorced from reality. It is useful to ambitious rulers in corrupt political systems as a sedative to popular turbulence (that is why the tyrant always makes much of the priest); but in the long run civilization must get back to honest reality or perish.

At present we are at a crisis in which one party is keeping the Bible in the clouds in the name of religion, and another is trying to get rid of it altogether in the name of Science. Both names are so recklessly taken in vain that the Bishop of Birmingham has just warned his flock that the scientific party is drawing nearer to Christ than the Church congregations. I, who am a sort of unofficial Bishop of Everywhere, have repeatedly warned the scientists that the Quakers are fundamentally far more scientific than the official biologists. In this confusion I venture to suggest that we neither leave the Bible in the clouds nor attempt the impossible task of suppressing it. Why not simply bring it down to the ground, and take it for what it really is?

To maintain good humor I am quite willing to concede to my Protestant friends that the Bible in the clouds was sometimes turned to good account in the struggles to maintain Protestant Freethought (such as it was) against the Churches and Empires. The soldier who had his Bible in one hand and his weapon in the other fought with the strength of ten under Cromwell, William of Orange, and Gustavus Adolphus. The very old-fashioned may still permit themselves a little romance about the Huguenots at La Rochelle, the psalm of the Ironsides at Dunbar, the ships that broke the boom and relieved the siege of Londonderry, and even about Dugald Dalgetty. But the struggle between Guelph and Ghibelline is so completely over that in its last and bloodiest war the ministers of the Guelph king did not even know what his name meant, and made him discard it in the face of the Ghibelline Kaiser and the Holy Roman Empire. And the soldier fought with the trigger of a machine gun in one hand and a popular newspaper in the other. Thanks to the machine gun he fought with the strength of a thousand; but the idolized Bible was still at the back of the popular newspaper, full of the spirit of the campaigns of Joshua, holding up our sword as the sword of the Lord and Gideon, and hounding us on to the slaughter of those modern Amalekites and Canaanites, the Germans, as idolators and children of the devil. Though the formula (King and Country) was different, the spirit was the same: it was the old imaginary conflict of Jehovah against Baal; only, as the Germans were also fighting for King and Country, and were quite as convinced as we that Jehovah, the Lord strong and mighty, the Lord mighty in battle, the Lord of Hosts (now called big battalions), was their God, and that ours was his enemy, the fighting, though fearfully slaughterous, was so completely neutralized that the victory had to be won by blockade. But the wounds to civilization were so serious that we do not as yet know whether they are not going to prove mortal, because they are being kept open by the Old Testament spirit and methods and superstitions. And here again it is important to notice that the only country which seems to be vigorously recovering is Russia, which has thrown the Old Testament violently and contemptuously into the waste paper basket, and even, in the intensity of its reaction against it, organized its children into a League of the Godless, thereby unexpectedly suffering them to obey the invitation of Jesus to come unto him, whilst we are organizing our children in Officers' Training Corps: a very notable confirmation of the Bishop of Birmingham's observation that scientific atheism moves towards Christ whilst official Christianity pulls savagely in the opposite direction.

The situation is past trifling. The ancient worshippers of Jehovah, armed with sword and spear, and demoralized by a clever boy with a sling, could not murder and destroy wholesale. But with machine gun and amphibious tank, aeroplane and gas bomb, operating on cities where millions of inhabitants are depending for light and heat, water and food, on central-ized mechanical organs like great steel hearts and arteries, that can be smashed in half an hour by a boy in a bomber, we really must take care that the boy is better educated than Noah and Joshua. In plain words, as we cannot get rid of the Bible, it will get rid of us unless we learn to read it "in the proper spirit," which I take to be the spirit of intellectual integrity that obliges honest thinkers to read every line which pretends to divine authority with all their wits about them, and to judge it exactly as they judge the Koran, the Upanishads, the Arabian Nights, this morning's leading article in The Times, or last week's cartoon in Punch, knowing that all written words are equally open to inspiration from the eternal fount and equally subject to error from the mortal imperfection of their authors.

Then say, of what use is the Bible nowadays to anyone but the antiquary and the literary connoisseur? Why not boot it into the dustbin as the Soviet has done? Well, there is a *prima facie* case to be made out for that. Let us first do justice to it.

What about the tables of the law? the ten commandments? They did not suffice even for the wandering desert tribe upon whom they were imposed by Moses, who, like Mahomet later on, could get them respected only by pretending that they were supernaturally revealed to him. They had to be supplemented by the elaborate codes of Leviticus and Deuteronomy, which the most fanatically observant Jew could not now obey without outraging our modern morality and violating our criminal law. They are mere lumber nowadays; for their simpler validities are the necessary commonplaces of human society and need no Bible to reveal them or give them authority. The second commandment, taken to heart by Islam, is broken and ignored throughout Christendom, though its warning against the enchantments of fine art is worthy the deepest consideration, and, had its author known the magic of word-music as he knew that of the graven image, might stand as a warning against our idolatry of the Bible. The whole ten are unsuited and inadequate to modern needs, as they say not a word against those forms of robbery, legalized by the robbers, which have uprooted the moral foundation of our society and will condemn us to slow social decay if we are not wakened up, as Russia has been, by a crashing collapse.

In addition to these negative drawbacks there is the positive one that the religion inculcated in the earlier books is a crudely atrocious ritual of human sacrifice to propitiate a murderous tribal deity who was, for example, induced to spare the human race from destruction in a second deluge by the pleasure given him by the smell of burning flesh when Noah "took of every clean beast and of every clean fowl, and offered burnt offerings on the altar." And though this ritual is in the later books fiercely repudiated, and its god denied in express terms, by the prophet Micah, shewing how it was outgrown as the Jews progressed in culture, yet the tradition of a blood sacrifice whereby the vengeance of a terribly angry god can be bought off by a vicarious and hideously cruel blood sacrifice persists even through the New Testament, where it attaches itself to the torture and execution of Jesus by the Roman governor of Jerusalem, idolizing that horror in Noah's fashion as a means by which we can all cheat our consciences, evade our moral responsibilities, and turn our shame into self-congratulation by loading all our infamies on to the scourged shoulders of Christ. It would be hard to imagine a more demoralizing and unchristian doctrine: indeed it would not be at all unreasonable for the Intellectual Co-operation Committee of the League of Nations to follow the example of the Roman Catholic Church by objecting to the promiscuous circulation of the Bible (except under conditions amounting to careful spiritual direction) until the supernatural claims made for its authority are finally and unequivocally dropped.

As to Bible science, it has over the nineteenth-century materialistic fashion in biology the advantage of being a science of life and not an attempt to substitute physics and chemistry for it; but it is hopelessly pre-evolutionary; its descriptions of the origin of life and morals are obviously fairy tales; its astronomy is terracentric; its notions of the starry universe are childish; its history is epical and legendary: in short, people whose education in these departments is derived from the Bible are so absurdly misinformed as to be unfit for public employment, parental responsibility, or the franchise. As an encyclopedia, therefore, the Bible must be shelved with the first edition of the Encyclopædia Britannica as a record of what men once believed, and a measure of how far they have left their obsolete beliefs behind.

Granted all this to Russia, it does not by any means dispose of the Bible. A great deal of the Bible is much more alive than this morning's paper and last night's parliamentary debate. Its chronicles are better reading than most of our fashionable histories, and less intentionally mendacious. In revolutionary invective and Utopian aspiration it cuts the ground from under the feet of Ruskin, Carlyle, and Karl Marx; and in epics of great leaders and great rascals it makes Homer seem superficial and Shakespear unbalanced. And its one great love poem is the only one that can satisfy a man who is really in love. Shelley's Epipsychidion is, in comparison, literary gas and gaiters.

In sum, it is an epitome, illustrated with the most stirring examples, of the history of a tribe of mentally vigorous, imaginative, aggressively acquisitive humans who developed into a nation through ruthless conquest, encouraged by the delusion that they were "the chosen people of God" and, as such, the natural inheritors of all the earth, with a reversion to a blissful eternity hereafter in the kingdom of heaven. And the epitome in no way suppresses the fact that this delusion led at last to their dispersion, denationalization, and bigoted persecution by better disciplined states which, though equally confident of a monopoly of divine favor earned by their own merits, paid the Jews the compliment of adopting the Hebrew gods and prophets, as, on the whole, more useful to imperialist rulers than the available alternatives.

Now the difference between an illiterate savage and a person who has read such an epitome (with due skipping of its genealogical rubbish and the occasional nonsenses produced by attempts to translate from imperfectly understood tongues) is enormous. A community on which such a historical curriculum is imposed in family and school may be more dangerous to its neighbors, and in greater peril of collapse from intolerance and megalomania, than a community that reads either nothing or silly novels, football results, and city articles; but it is beyond all question a more highly educated one. It is therefore not in the least surprising nor unreasonable that when the only generally available alternative to Bible education is no liberal education at all, many who have no illusions about the Bible, and fully comprehend its drawbacks, vote for Bible education *faute de mieux*. This is why mere criticism of Bible education cuts so little ice. Ancient Hebrew history and literature, half fabulous as it is, is better than no history and no literature; and I neither regret nor resent my own Bible education, especially as my mind soon grew strong enough to take it at its real value. At worst the Bible gives a child a better start in life than the gutter.

This testimonial will please our Bible idolators; but it must not for a moment soothe them into believing that their fetichism can now be defended by the plea that it was better to be Noah or Abraham or Sir Isaac Newton than a London street arab. Street arabs are not very common in these days of compulsory attendance at the public elementary school. The alternative to the book of Genesis at present is not mere ignorant nescience, but Mr H. G. Wells's Outline of History, and the host of imitations and supplements which its huge success has called into existence. Within the last two hundred years a body of history, literature, poetry, science, and art has been inspired and created by precisely the same mysterious impulse that inspired and created the Bible. In all these departments it leaves the Bible just nowhere. It is the Bible-educated human who is now the ignoramus. If you doubt it, try to pass an examination for any practical employment by giving Bible answers to the examiners' questions. You will be fortunate if you are merely plucked and not certified as a lunatic. Throughout the whole range of Science which the Bible was formerly supposed to cover with an infallible authority, it is now hopelessly superseded, with one exception. That exception is the science of theology, which is still so completely off the ground—so metaphysical, as the learned say, that our materialist scientists contemptuously deny it the right to call itself science at all.

But there is no surer symptom of a sordid and fundamentally stupid mind, however powerful it may be in many practical activities, than a contempt for metaphysics. A person may be supremely able as a mathematician, engineer, parliamentary tactician, or racing bookmaker; but if that person has contemplated the universe all through life without ever asking "What the devil does it all mean?" he (or she) is one of those people for whom Calvin accounted by placing them in his category of the predestinately damned.

Hence the Bible, scientifically obsolete in all other respects, remains interesting as a record of how the idea of God, which is the first effort of civilized mankind to account for the existence and origin and purpose of as much of the universe as we are conscious of, develops from a childish idolatry of a thundering, earthquaking, famine striking, pestilence launching, blinding, deafening, killing, destructively omnipotent Bogey Man, maker of night and day and sun and moon, of the four seasons and their miracles of seed and harvest, to a braver idealization of a benevolent sage, a just judge, an affectionate father, evolving finally into the incorporeal word that never becomes flesh, at which point modern science and philosophy takes up the problem with its *Vis Naturae*, its *Élan Vital*, its Life Force, its Evolutionary Appetite, its still more abstract Categorical Imperative, and what not?

Now the study of this history of the development of a hypothesis from savage idolatry to a highly cultivated metaphysic is as interesting, instructive, and reassuring as any study can be to an open mind and an honest intellect. But we spoil it all by that lazy and sluttish practice of not throwing out the dirty water when we get in the clean. The Bible presents us with a succession of gods, each being a striking improvement on the previous one, marking an Ascent of Man to a nobler and deeper conception of Nature, every step involving a purification of the water of life and calling for a thorough emptying and cleansing of the vessel before its replenishment by a fresh and cleaner supply. But we baffle the blessing by just sloshing the water from the new fountain into the contents of the dirty old bucket, and repeat this folly until our minds are in such a filthy mess that we are objects of pity to the superficial but clearheaded atheists who are content without metaphysics and can see nothing in the whole business but its confusions and absurdities. Practical men of business refuse to be bothered with such crazy matters at all.

Take the situation in detail as it develops through the Bible. The God of Noah is not the God of Job. Contemplate first the angry deity who drowned every living thing on earth, except one family of each species, in a fit of raging disgust at their wickedness, and then allowed the head of the one human family to appease him by "the sweet savour" of a heap of burning flesh! Is he identical with the tolerant, argumentative, academic, urbane philosophic speculator who entertained the devil familiarly and made a wager with him that he could not drive Job to despair of divine benevolence? People who cannot see the difference between these two Gods cannot pass the most elementary test of intelligence: they cannot distinguish between similars and dissimilars.

But though Job's god is a great advance on Noah's god, he is a very bad debater, unless indeed we give him credit for deliberately saving himself from defeat by the old expedient: "No case: abuse the plaintiff's attorney." Job having raised the problem of the existence of evil and its incompatibility with omnipotent benevolence, it is no valid reply to jeer at him for being unable to create a whale or to play with it as with a bird. And there is a very suspicious touch of Noah's God in the offer to overlook the complicity of Job's friends in his doubts in consideration of a sacrifice of seven bullocks and seven rams. God's attempt at an argument is only a repetition and elaboration of the sneers of Elihu, and is so abruptly tacked on to them that one concludes that it must be a pious forgery to conceal the fact that the original poem left the problem of evil unsolved and Job's criticism unanswered, as indeed it remained until Creative Evolution solved it.

When we come to Micah we find him throwing out the dirty water fearlessly. He will not have Noah's God, nor even Job's God with his seven bullocks and seven rams. He raises the conception of God to the highest point it has ever attained by his fiercely contemptuous denunciation of the blood sacrifices, and his inspired and inspiring demand "What doth the Lord require of thee but to do justly, and to love mercy, and to walk humbly with thy God?" Before this victory of the human spirit over crude superstition Noah's God and Job's God go down like skittles: there is an end of them. And yet our children are taught, not to exult in this great triumph of spiritual insight over mere animal terror of the Bogey Man, but to believe that Micah's God and Job's God and Noah's God are one and the same, and that every good child must revere the spirit of justice and mercy and humility equally with the appetite for burnt flesh and human sacrifice, such indiscriminate and nonsensical reverence being inculcated as religion.

Later on comes Jesus, who dares a further flight. He suggests that godhead is something which incorporates itself in man: in himself, for instance. He is immediately stoned by his horrified hearers, who can see nothing in the suggestion but a monstrous attempt on his part to impersonate Jehovah. This misunderstanding, typical of dirty water theology, was made an article of religion eighteen hundred years later by Emanuel Swedenborg. But the unadulterated suggestion of Jesus is an advance on the theology of Micah; for Man walking humbly before an external God is an ineffective creature compared to Man exploring as the instrument and embodiment of God with no other guide than the spark of divinity within him. It is certainly the greatest break in the Bible between the old and the new testament. Yet the dirty water still spoils it; for we find Paul holding up Christ to the Ephesians as "an offering and a sacrifice to God for a sweet smelling savour," thereby dragging Christianity back and down to the level of Noah. None of the apostles rose above that level; and the result was that the great advances made by Micah and Jesus were cancelled; and historical Christianity was built up on the sacrificial altars of Jehovah, with Jesus as the sacrifice. What he and Micah would say if they could return and see their names and credit attached to the idolatries they abhorred can be imagined only by those who understand and sympathize with them.

Jesus could be reproached for having chosen his disciples very unwisely if we could believe that he had any real choice. There are moments when one is tempted to say that there was not one Christian among them, and that Judas was the only one who shewed any gleams of common sense. Because Jesus had mental powers and insight quite beyond their comprehension they worshipped him as a superhuman and indeed supernatural phenomenon, and made his memory the nucleus of their crude belief in magic, their Noahism, their sentimentality, their masochist Puritanism, and their simple morality with its punitive sanctions, decent and honest and amiable enough, some of it, but never for a moment on the intellectual level of Jesus, and at worst pregnant with all the horrors of the later wars of religion, the Jew burnings of Torquemada, and the atrocities of which all the pseudo-Christian Churches were guilty the moment they became powerful enough to persecute.

Most unfortunately the death of Jesus helped to vulgarize his reputation and obscure his doctrine. The Romans, though they executed their own political criminals by throwing them from the Tarpeian rock, punished slave revolts by crucifixion. They crucified six thousand of the followers of the revolutionary gladiator, Spartacus, a century before Jesus was denounced to them by the Jewish high priest as an agitator of the same kidney. He was accordingly tortured and killed in this hideous manner, with the infinitely more hideous result that the cross and the other instruments of his torture were made the symbols of the faith legally established in his name three hundred years later. They are still accepted as such throughout Christendom. The crucifixion thus became to the Churches what the Chamber of Horrors is to a waxwork: the irresistible attraction for children and for the crudest adult worshippers. Christ's clean water of life is befouled by the dirtiest of dirty water from the idolatries of his savage forefathers; and our prelates and proconsuls take Caiaphas and Pontius Pilate for their models in the name of their despised and rejected victim.

The case was further complicated by the pitiable fact that Jesus himself, shaken by the despair which unsettled the reason of Swift and Ruskin and many others at the spectacle of human cruelty, injustice, misery, folly, and apparently hopeless political incapacity, and perhaps also by the worship of his disciples and of the multitude, had allowed Peter to persuade him that he was the Messiah, and that death could not prevail against him nor prevent his returning to judge the world and establish his reign on earth for ever and ever. As this delusion came as easily within the mental range of his disciples as his social doctrine had been far over their heads, "Crosstianity" became established on the authority of Jesus himself. Later on, in a curious record of the visions of a drug addict which was absurdly admitted to the canon under the title of Revelation, a thousand years were specified as the period that was to elapse before Jesus was to return as he had promised. In 1000 A.D. the last possibility of the promised advent expired; but by that time people were so used to the delay that they readily substituted for the Second Advent a Second Postponement. Pseudo-Christianity was, and always will be, fact proof.

The whole business is an amazing muddle, which has held out not only because the views of Jesus were above the heads of all but the best minds, but because his appearance was followed by the relapse in civilization which we call the Dark Ages, from which we are only just emerging sufficiently to begin to pick up the thread of Christ's most advanced thought and rescue it from the mess the apostles and their successors made of it.

Six hundred years after Jesus, Mahomet founded Islam and made a colossal stride ahead from mere stock-and-stone idolatry to a very enlightened Unitarianism; but though he died a conqueror, and therefore escaped being made the chief attraction in an Arabian Chamber of Horrors, he found it impossible to control his Arabs without enticing and intimidating them by promises of a delightful life for the faithful, and threats of an eternity of disgusting torment for the wicked, after their bodily death, and also, after some honest protests, by accepting the supernatural character thrust on him by the childish superstition of his followers; so that he, too, now needs to be rediscovered in his true nature before Islam can come back to earth as a living faith.

And now I think the adventures of the black girl as revealed to me need no longer puzzle anyone. They could hardly have happened to a white girl steeped from her birth in the pseudo-Christianity of the Churches. I take it that the missionary lifted her straight out of her native tribal fetichism into an unbiassed contemplation of the Bible with its series of gods marking stages in the development of the conception of God from the monster Bogey Man to the Father; then to the spirit without body, parts, nor passions; and finally to the definition of that spirit in the words God is Love. For the primitive two her knobkerry suffices; but when she reaches the end she has to point out that Love is not enough (like Edith Cavell making the same discovery about Patriotism) and that it is wiser to take Voltaire's advice by cultivating her garden and bringing up her piccaninnies than to spend her life imagining that she can find a complete explanation of the universe by laying about her with a knobkerry.

Still, the knobkerry has to be used as far as the way is clear. Mere agnosticism leads nowhere. When the question of the existence of Noah's idol is raised on the point, vital to high civilization, whether our children shall continue to be brought up to worship it and compound for their sins by sacrificing to it, or, more cheaply, by sheltering themselves behind another's sacrifice to it, then whoever hesitates to bring down the knobkerry with might and main is ludicrously unfit to have any part in the government of a modern State. The importance of a message to that effect at the present world crisis is probably at the bottom of my curious and sudden inspiration to write this tale instead of cumbering theatrical literature with another stage comedy.

AUTOBIOGRAPHICAL AND PROFESSIONAL

XXIII

IMMATURITY

1930

The scene of one of Mr Arnold Bennett's novels is laid in a certain *cul de sac* off the Brompton Road, nearly opposite the West Brompton District Post Office. He calls it Alexandra Grove; but its actual name is Victoria Grove. As he describes it, the houses now contrive a double rent to pay, as the gardens have been fitted up with studios, thus quietly modernizing London by the back-to-back housing so vehemently denounced as a relic of barbarism in Leeds. When I arrived there as an Irish emigrant of 20, this intensification of population had not occurred. The houses were semi-detached villas with plenty of air space round them (you could call it garden). On the other side of the back wall were orchards; for the huge Poor Law Infirmary which now occupies this space, with its tower on the Fulham Road, was not yet built. The land between West Brompton and Fulham and Putney, now closely packed with streets and suburban roads, had still plenty of orchard and market garden to give it a countrified air and to make it possible to live there, as I did for years, without feeling that one must flee to the country or wither in the smoke. All the parallel Groves connected the Fulham Road with King's Road, Chelsea, where Cremorne Gardens, an unlaid ghost from the eighteenth century, was desperately fighting off its final exorcism as a rendezvous of the half world. Hence these now blameless thoroughfares were then reputed Bohemian, whilst Victoria Grove, as a blind alley, remained as respectable as Clapham.

I came to London from Dublin in the spring of 1876, and found my mother and my one surviving sister (I had no brothers) established in No. 13 Victoria Grove, trying to turn their musical accomplishments to account: my mother by teaching, my sister by singing. My father, left in Dublin, spared us a pound a week from his slender resources; and by getting into debt and occasionally extracting ourselves by drawing on a maternal inheritance of £4000 over which my mother had a power of appointment, and which therefore could be realized bit by bit as her three children came of age, we managed to keep going somehow.

Impecuniosity was necessarily chronic in the household. And here let me distinguish between this sort of poverty and that which furnishes an element of romance in the early lives of many famous men. I am almost tempted to say that it is the only sort of poverty that counts, short of the privations that make success impossible. We all know the man whose mother brought him up with nineteen brothers and sisters on an income of eighteen shillings a week earned by her own labor. The road from the log cabin to the White House, from the bench in the factory to the Treasury Bench, from the hovel to the mansion in Park Lane, if not exactly a crowded road, always has a few well fed figures at the end of it to tell us all about it. I always assure these gentlemen that they do not know what poverty and failure is. Beginning with as much as they expected or were accustomed to, they have known nothing but promotion. At each step they have had the income of the society in which they moved, and been able to afford its clothes, its food, its habits, its rents and rates. What more has any prince? If you would know what real poverty is, ask the younger son of a younger son of a younger son. To understand his plight you must start at the top without the income of the top, and curse your stars that you were not lucky enough to start at the bottom.

Our institution of primogeniture may have been a feudal necessity. It kept the baronies together; and the barons and their retainers kept the king and the country supplied with an army, a magistracy, and a network of local governments. But it took no account of the younger sons. These unhappy ones were brought up in the baronial castle. Let us represent the income of the barony by the figure 1000. Both sons and daughters were brought up to know no other mode of life than life at this figure. When the eldest took all, what was there left for the girls' dowries and the boys' allowances? Only the scrapings and leavings of the mother's dowry, and such charity as the new baron might choose (if he could afford it) to bestow on his poor relations. A younger son's figure, especially if he had many brothers, might easily be 20 or less, even to zero. What was the poor wretch to do, knowing no other way of living but the way that cost 1000? Easy to tell him that he must cut his coat according to his cloth. Impossible to do it without being trained to that measure from childhood. Impossible anyhow without dropping every relative and friend in the world, and stepping down, a mistrusted, ridiculous, incongruous stranger, into the social circle of his mother's maid and his brother's butler. Impossible often even to go into the army, where an officer cannot live on his pay unless he is a promoted ranker in a line regiment, and not even then with any ease. There is nothing for it but to live beyond one's income, to spunge, to beg, to take credit at the shops without means, to borrow without the prospect of being able to repay, and to blackmail the baron by presenting him with a choice between paying up and having his brother haled before the criminal courts for swindling. The alternative (to marry the daughter of a rich *parvenu*,

American or British) is not always available. Who would be an Honorable on such terms if he could help it?

But think of his son, and of his son's son: the undisguised commoner, for whom, because it costs too much, there is not even the public school and university education of the baron's cadet, and who cannot avail himself of the public elementary and secondary schools because such a step would disclass the man of family! Think of the attempt to go into business with some pitiful little capital! think of the struggle to make the loathed occupation yield a living! think of the son for whom there is nothing but a clerkship in the office of some good-natured business acquaintance! and bear in mind that the descent implies that every generation is, like the original younger son, brought up to a mode of life more expensive than its income can compass; so that it is condemned to pull the devil by the tail from its adolescence to its grave! My able and flourishing friend A tells me that he knows what poverty is and what drink is: was he not brought up in the Borough by a drunken mother? B, rolling in wealth, tells me that when he was a boy he had meat only twice a year. C, wallowing in fame, calls me a snob, after gleefully narrating his experiences in the kitchen of his father's small shop, and how he was enabled to study country house society by a childish privilege of visiting the servants' hall. How easily I cap these zests to success by the simple statement that my father was second cousin to a baronet, and my mother the daughter of a country gentleman whose rule was, when in difficulties, mortgage. That was my sort of poverty. The Shaws were younger sons from the beginning, as I shall shew when I reveal my full pedigree. Even the baronetcy was founded on the fortunes of a fifth son who came to Dublin and made that city his oyster. Let who will preen himself on his Mother

Hubbard's bare cupboard, and play for sympathy as an upstart: I was a downstart and the son of a downstart. But for the accident of a lucrative talent I should today be poorer than Spinoza; for he at least knew how to grind lenses, whereas I could not afford to learn any art. Luckily Nature taught me one.

This social *degringolade* never stops in these islands. It produces a class which deserves a history all to itself. Do not talk of the middle class: the expression is meaningless except when it is used by an economist to denote the man of business who stands in the middle between land and capital on the one hand, and labor on the other, and organizes business for both. I sing my own class: the Shabby Genteel, the Poor Relations, the Gentlemen who are No Gentlemen. If you want to know exactly where I came in, you will get at such facts as that of my many uncles only one, the eldest, contrived to snatch a university education. The rest shifted as best they could without it (rather better than he, mostly). One distinguished himself as a civil servant. He had a gun, and went shooting. One made a fortune in business, and attained to carriage horses; but he lost the fortune in a premature attempt to develop the mineral resources of Ireland without waiting for the new railways produced by the late war. Two emigrated to Tasmania, and, like Mr Micawber, made history there. One was blind and dependent on his brothers: another became blind later, but remained independent and capable. One aunt married the rector of St Bride's (now demolished) in Dublin. The others married quite prosperously, except the eldest, whose conception of the family dignity was so prodigious (the family snobbery being unmitigated in her case by the family sense of humor) that she would have refused an earl because he was not a duke, and so died a very ancient virgin. Dead or alive, there were fourteen of

them; and they all, except perhaps the eldest, must have had a very straitened time of it in their childhood after their father died, leaving my grandmother to bring up an unconscionable lot of children on very inadequate means. The baronet came to the rescue by giving her a quaint cottage, with Gothically pointed windows, to live in at Terenure (we called the place Roundtown). It stands in, or rather creeps picturesquely along, its little walled garden near the tram terminus to this day, though my grandfather's brass helmet and sword (he was in the Yeomanry or Militia as a gentleman amateur soldier) no longer hang in the hall. Professionally, he was some sort of combination of solicitor, notary public, and stockbroker that prevailed at that time. I suspect that his orphans did not always get enough to eat; for the younger ones, though invincibly healthy and long lived, were not athletic, and exhibited such a remarkable collection of squints (my father had a stupendous squint) that to this day a squint is so familiar to me that I notice it no more than a pair of spectacles or even a pair of boots.

On the whole, they held their cherished respectability in the world in spite of their lack of opportunity. They owed something perhaps, to the confidence given them by their sense of family. In Irish fashion they talked of themselves as the Shaws, as who should say the Valois, the Bourbons, the Hohenzollerns, the Hapsburgs, or the Romanoffs; and their world conceded the point to them. I had an enormous contempt for this family snobbery, as I called it, until I was completely reconciled to it by a certain Mr Alexander Mackintosh Shaw, a clansman who, instead of taking his pedigree for granted in the usual Shaw manner, hunted it up, and published 100 copies privately in 1877. Somebody sent me a copy; and my gratification was unbounded when I read the first sentence of the first chapter, which ran: "It is the general tradition, says the Rev. Lachlan Shaw [bless him!], that the Shaws are descended of McDuff, Earl of Fife." I hastily skipped to the chapter about the Irish Shaws to make sure that they were my people; and there they were, baronet and all, duly traced to the third son of that immortalized yet un-born Thane of Fife who, invulnerable to normally accouched swordsmen, laid on and slew Macbeth. It was as good as being descended from Shakespear, whom I had been unconsciously resolved to reincar-nate from my cradle.

Years after this discovery I was staying on the shores of Loch Fyne, and being cooked for and housekept by a lady named McFarlane, who treated me with a con-sideration which I at first supposed to be due to my eminence as an author. But she undeceived me one day by telling me that the McFarlanes and the Shaws were de-scended from the Thanes of Fife, and that I must not make myself too cheap. She added that the McFarlanes were the elder branch.

My uncles did not trouble about Mac-duff: it was enough for them that they were Shaws. They had an impression that the Government should give them employment, preferably sinecure, if no-thing else could be found; and I suppose this was why my father, after essaying a clerkship or two (one of them in an iron-works), at last had his position recog-nized by a post in the Four Courts, per-haps because his sister had married the brother of a law baron. Anyhow the office he held was so undeniably superfluous that it actually got abolished before I was born; and my father naturally demanded a pension as compensation for the out-rage. Having got it, he promptly sold it, and set up in business as a merchant deal-ing wholesale (the family dignity made retail business impossible) in flour and its cereal concomitants. He had an office and warehouse in Jervis Street in the city; and

he had a mill in Dolphin's Barn on the country side of the canal, at the end of a rather pretty little village street called Rutland Avenue. The mill has now fallen to pieces; but some relics of it are still to be seen from the field with the millpond behind Rutland House at the end of the avenue, with its two stone eagles on the gateposts. My father used to take me sometimes to this mill before breakfast (a long walk for a child); and I used to like playing about it. I do not think it had any other real use; for it never paid its way; and the bulk of my father's business was commissioned: he was a middleman. I should mention that as he knew nothing about the flour business, and as his part-ner, a Mr Clibborn, having been appren-ticed to the cloth trade, knew if possible less, the business, purchased readymade, must have proceeded by its own momen-tum, and produced its results, such as they were, automatically in spite of its proprietors. They did not work the in-dustry: it worked them. It kept alive, but did not flourish. Early in its history the bankruptcy of one of its customers dealt it such a blow that my father's partner broke down in tears, though he was forti-fied by a marriage with a woman of pro-perty, and could afford to regard his busi-ness as only a second string to his bow. My father, albeit ruined, found the magni-tude of the catastrophe so irresistibly amusing that he had to retreat hastily from the office to an empty corner of the warehouse, and laugh until he was ex-hausted. The business struggled on and even supported my father until he died, enabling him to help his family a little after they had solved a desperate financial situation by emigrating to London: or, to put it in another way, by deserting him. His last years were soothed and dis-embarrassed by this step. He never, as far as I know, made the slightest movement towards a reunion; and none of us ever dreamt of there being any unkindness in the arrangement. In our family we did not bother about conventionalities or sentimentalities.

Our ridiculous poverty was too common in our class, and not conspicuous enough in a poor country, to account wholly for our social detachment from my father's family, a large and (for Ireland) not unprosperous one. In early days the baronet, being a bachelor, was clannishly accessible: he entertained even his second cousins at Bushy Park, and was specially attentive to my mother. I was never at Bushy Park myself except once, on the occasion of his funeral (the Shaw funerals were prodigies of black pomp); but if my father had been able to turn his social opportunities to account, I might have had a quite respectable and normal social training. My mother, socially very eligible, was made welcome in all directions. She sang very well; and the Shaws were naturally a musical family. All the women could "pick out tunes" on the piano, and support them with the chords of the tonic, subdominant, dominant, and tonic again. Even a Neapolitan sixth was not beyond them. My father played the trombone, and could vamp a bass on it to any tune that did not modulate too distractingly. My eldest uncle (Barney: I suppose I was called Bernard after him; but he himself was Uncle William) played the ophicleide, a giant keyed brass bugle, now superseded by the tuba. Berlioz has described it as a chromatic bullock; but my uncle could make it moo and bellow very melodiously. My aunt Emily played the violoncello. Aunt Shah (Charlotte), having beautiful hands, and refinements of person and character to match them, used the harp and tambourine to display them. Modern readers will laugh at the picture of an evening at Bushy Park, with the bachelor Sir Robert and his clan seated round an ottoman on which my uncle Barney stood, solemnly playing Annie Laurie on the ophicleide. The present

distinguished inheritor of the title may well find it incredible. But in those days it was the fashion for guests to provide their own music and gentlemen to play wind instruments as a social accomplishment: indeed that age of brass is still remembered and regretted by the few makers of musical instruments whose traditions go back far enough.

And now you will ask why, with such unexceptional antecedents and social openings, was I not respectably brought up? Unfortunately or fortunately (it all depends on how you look at it) my father had a habit which eventually closed all doors to him, and consequently to my mother, who could not very well be invited without him. If you asked him to dinner or to a party, he was not always quite sober when he arrived; and he was invariably scandalously drunk when he left. Now a convivial drunkard may be exhilarating in convivial company. Even a quarrelsome or boastful drunkard may be found entertaining by people who are not particular. But a miserable drunkard —and my father, in theory a teetotaller, was racked with shame and remorse even in his cups—is unbearable. We were finally dropped socially. After my early childhood I cannot remember ever paying a visit at a relative's house. If my mother and father had dined out, or gone to a party, their children would have been much more astonished than if the house had caught fire.

How my mother rescued herself from this predicament by her musical talent I will tell elsewhere. My father reduced his teetotalism from theory to practice when a mild fit, which felled him on our doorstep one Sunday afternoon, convinced him that he must stop drinking or perish. It had no worse effect; but his reform, though complete and permanent, came too late to save the social situation; and I, cut off from the social drill which puts one at one's ease in private society, grew up frightfully shy and utterly ignorant of social routine. My mother, who had been as carefully brought up as Queen Victoria, was too humane to inflict what she had suffered on any child; besides, I think she imagined that correct behavior is inborn, and that much of what she had been taught was natural to her. Anyhow, she never taught it to us, leaving us wholly to the promptings of our blood's blueness, with results which may be imagined.

In England, if people are reasonably goodnatured and amiable, they are forgiven any sort of eccentricity of behavior if only they are unaffected and all of one piece. If when I came to London I had been merely shy provincially, with incorrect table manners and wrong clothes; if I had eaten peas with a knife and worn a red tie with an evening suit, kind people would have taken me in hand and drilled me in spite of the infernal and very silly Irish pride which will never admit the need of such tuition. But my difficulties were not of that easily remediable kind. I was sensible enough to inform myself so exactly as to what I should do with a finger bowl when it was placed before me on a dessert plate, that I could give a lead in such matters to other novices who were hopelessly floored by that staggering problem. Clever sympathetic women might divine at a glance that I was mortally shy; but people who could not see through my skin, and who were accustomed to respect, and even veneration, from the young, may well have found me insufferable, aggressive, and impudent. When a young man has achieved nothing and is doing nothing, and when he is obviously so poor that he ought to be doing something very energetically, it is rather trying to find him assuming an authority in conversation, and an equality in terms, which only conspicuous success and distinguished ability could make becoming. Yet this is what is done, quite unconsciously, by young persons who have in

them the potentiality of such success and ability. Napoleon could hardly have felt much reverence for his average French generals before the French Revolution, when he was apparently only a by-no-means irreproachable subaltern from Corsica. No such general could possibly have liked him or his manners at that time, though after Austerlitz even first rate generals blushed with gratification at the most condescending word of praise from him. It must have been intolerable in Stratford-on-Avon in 1584 for a local magnate of mature age, knight of the shire and justice of the peace, to be contemplated *de haut en bas* by a dissolute young poacher, and even to amuse him by intellectual inadequacy. I am sure Shakespear was too civil by nature to make any such demonstration consciously; but it is inconceivable that the future author of Lear, who was to die a landowning magnate, and be described in the parish register as a Gent., could have treated Sir Thomas Lucy quite as an ordinary country gentleman of mature age expects to be treated by an ordinary poacher in his teens.

The truth is that all men are in a false position in society until they have realized their possibilities, and imposed them on their neighbors. They are tormented by a continual shortcoming in themselves; yet they irritate others by a continual overweening. This discord can be resolved by acknowledged success or failure only: everyone is ill at ease until he has found his natural place, whether it be above or below his birthplace. The overrated inheritor of a position for which he has no capacity, and the underrated nobody who is a born genius, are alike shy because they are alike out of place. Besides, this finding of one's place may be made very puzzling by the fact that there is no place in ordinary society for extraordinary individuals. For the worldly wiseman, with common ambitions, the matter is simple enough: money, title, precedence, a seat in parliament, a portfolio in the cabinet, will mean success both to him and his circle. But what about people like St Francis and St Clare? Of what use to them are the means to live the life of the country house and the west end mansion? They have literally no business in them, and must necessarily cut an unhappy and ridiculous figure there. They have to make a society of Franciscans and Poor Clares for themselves before they can work or live socially. It is true that those who are called saints are not saintly all the time and in everything. In eating and drinking, lodging and sleeping, chatting and playing: in short, in everything but working out their destiny as saints, what is good enough for a ploughman is good enough for a poet, a philosopher, a saint, or a higher mathematician. But Hodge's work is not good enough for Newton, nor Falstaff's conversation holy enough for Shelley. Christ adapted himself so amiably to the fashionable life of his time in his leisure that he was reproached for being a gluttonous man and a winebibber, and for frequenting frivolous and worthless sets. But he did not work where he feasted, nor flatter the Pharisees, nor ask the Romans to buy him with a sinecure. He knew when he was being entertained, well treated, lionized: not an unpleasant adventure for once in a way; and he did not quarrel with the people who were so nice to him. Besides, to sample society is part of a prophet's business: he must sample the governing class above all, because his inborn knowledge of human nature will not explain the anomalies produced in it by Capitalism and Sacerdotalism. But he can never feel at home in it. The born Communist, before he knows what he is, and understands why, is always awkward and unhappy in plutocratic society and in the poorer societies which ape it to the extent of their little means: in short, wherever spiritual values are assessed like Income Tax. In his nonage he is imposed on by the prestige which the propertied classes have conferred on themselves and inculcated in the schools, and by the comfort and refinement and splendor of their equipment in contrast to the squalor of the proletariat. If he has been brought up to regard himself as one of the propertied classes, and has its whole equipment of false standards of worth, lacking nothing but the indispensable pecuniary equipment without which his education is utterly meaningless, his embarrassment and bewilderment are pitiable, and his isolation often complete; for he is left alone between the poor whom he regards as beneath him and the rich whose standards of expenditure are beyond his means. He is ashamed of his poverty, in continual dread of doing the wrong thing, resentfully insubordinate and seditious in a social order which he not only accepts but in which he actually claims a privileged part.

As I write, there is a craze for what is called psycho-analysis, or the cure of diseases by explaining to the patient what is the matter with him: an excellent plan if you happen to know what is the matter with him, especially when the explanation is that there is nothing the matter with him. Thus a bee, desperately trying to reach a flower bed through a window pane, concludes that he is the victim of evil spirits or that he is mad, his end being exhaustion, despair, and death. Yet, if he only knew, there is nothing wrong with him: all he has to do is go out as he came in, through open window or door. Your born Communist begins like the bee on the pane. He worries himself and everybody else until he dies of peevishness, or else is led by some propagandist pamphlet, or by his own intellectual impulses (if he has any), to investigate the economic structure of our society.

Immediately everything becomes clear to him. Property is theft: respectability founded on poverty is blasphemy: marriage founded on property is prostitution: it is easier for a camel to go through the eye of a needle than for a rich man to enter the kingdom of heaven. He now knows where he is, and where this society which has so intimidated him is. He is cured of his *mauvaise honte*, and may now be as much at his ease with the princes of this world as Caesar was with the pirates whom he intended to crucify when, as presently happened, the fortune of war made their captive their conqueror.

If he be not a born Communist, but a predatory combative man, eager to do the other fellow down, and happy in a contrast between his prosperity and the indigence of others, happy also in a robust contempt for cowards and weaklings, the very same discovery of the nature of our Capitalism will nerve him to play the Capitalist game for all it and he are worth. But for the most part men drift with the society into which they are born, and make the best of its accidents without changing its morals or understanding its principles.

As it happens, I was a born Communist and Iconoclast (or Quaker) without knowing it; and I never got on easy terms with plutocracy and snobbery until I took to the study of economics, beginning with Henry George and Karl Marx. In my twentieth year, at Victoria Grove, not being on Caesarian easy terms with the pirates or their retainers, I felt much as Caesar might have done if he had imagined the pirate ship to be the Mayflower, and was still more inclined to mistrust himself than to mistrust the crew, however little respect they might pay him. Not that my opinions were conventional. Read my preface to Back to Methuselah, and you will see me as the complete infidel of that day. I had read much poetry; but only one poet was sacred to me: Shelley. I had read his works piously from end to end, and was in my nega-tions atheist and republican to the backbone. I say in my negations; for I had not reached any affirmative position. When, at a public meeting of the Shelley Society, I scandalized many of the members by saying that I had joined because, like Shelley, I was a Socialist, an atheist, and a vegetarian, I did not know that I could have expressed my position more accurately by simply saying that my conception of God was that insisted on in the first Article of the Church of England, then as now vehemently repudiated by all pious persons, who will have it that God is a substantial gentleman of uncertain and occasionally savage temper, and a spirit only in the sense in which an archbishop is a spirit. I had never thought of reading the Articles of the Church of England; and if I had I should still have used the word atheist as a declaration that I was on the side of Bradlaugh and Foote and others who, as avowed Secularists and Atheists, were being persecuted and imprisoned for my opinions. From my childhood I had been accustomed to regard myself as a sceptic outside institutional religion, and therefore one to whom the conventional religious observances were fair game for scoffing. In this my manners were no better and no worse than those of my class generally. It never occurred to pious ladies and gentlemen to respect a sceptic; and it never occurred to a sceptic to respect a believer: reprobation and ostracism were considered natural and even obligatory on the one side, like derision, even to blasphemy, on the other. In Ireland Protestants and Catholics despised, insulted, and ostracized one another as a matter of course. In England Church people persecuted Dissenters; and Dissenters hated the Church with a bitterness incredible to anyone who has never known what it is to be a little village Dissenter in a Church school. I am not sure that controversial manners are any better now; but they certainly were odious then: you thought it your right and your duty to sneer at the man who was a heretic to your faith if you could not positively injure him in some way. As my manners in this respect were no better than other people's, and my satirical powers much more formidable, I can only hope that my natural civility, which led me to draw back when I found I was hurting people's feelings, may have mitigated my offensiveness in those early days when I still regarded controversy as admitting of no quarter. I lacked both cruelty and will-to-victory.

It may be asked here how I came by my heterodox opinions, seeing that my father's alcoholic neurosis, though it accounts for my not going into society, does not account for my not going to church. My reply, if put in the conventional terms of that day, would be that I was badly brought up because my mother was so well brought up. Her character reacted so strongly against her strict and loveless training that churchgoing was completely dropped in our family before I was ten years old. In my childhood I exercised my literary genius by composing my own prayers. I cannot recall the words of the final form I adopted; but I remember that it was in three movements, like a sonata, and in the best Church of Ireland style. It ended with the Lord's Prayer; and I repeated it every night in bed. I had been warned by my nurse that warm prayers were no use, and that only by kneeling by my bedside in the cold could I hope for a hearing; but I criticised this admonition unfavorably on various grounds, the real one being my preference for warmth and comfort. I did not disparage my nurse's authority in these matters because she was a Roman Catholic: I even tolerated her practice of sprinkling me with holy water occasionally. But her asceticism did not fit the essentially artistic and luxurious character of my devotional exploits. Besides, the penalty did not apply to my prayer; for it was not a petition. I had too much sense to risk my faith by begging for things I knew very well I should not get; so I did not care whether my prayers were answered or not: they were a literary performance for the entertainment and propitiation of the Almighty; and though I should not have dreamt of daring to say that if He did not like them He might lump them (perhaps I was too confident of their quality to apprehend such a rebuff), I certainly behaved as if my comfort were an indispensable condition of the performance taking place at all.

The Lord's Prayer I used once or twice as a protective spell. Thunderstorms are much less common in Ireland than in England; and the first two I remember frightened me horribly. During the second I bethought me of the Lord's Prayer, and steadied myself by repeating it.

I continued these pious habits long after the conventional compulsion to attend church and Sunday School had ceased, and I no longer regarded such customs as having anything to do with an emancipated spirit like mine. But one evening, as I was wandering through the furze bushes on Torca Hill in the dusk, I suddenly asked myself why I went on repeating my prayer every night when, as I put it, I did not believe in it. Being thus brought to book by my intellectual conscience I felt obliged in common honesty to refrain from superstitious practices; and that night, for the first time since I could speak, I did not say my prayers. I missed them so much that I asked myself another question. Why am I so uncomfortable about it? Can this be conscience? But next night the discomfort wore off so much that I hardly noticed it; and the night after I had forgotten all about my prayers as completely as if I had been born a heathen. It is worth adding that this sacrifice of the grace of God, as I had been taught it, to intellectual integrity synchronized with that dawning of moral passion in me which I have described in the first act of Man and Superman. Up to that time I had not experienced the slightest remorse in telling lies whenever they seemed likely to help me out of a difficulty: rather did I revel in the exercise of dramatic invention involved. Even when I was a good boy I was so only theatrically, because, as actors say, I saw myself in the character; and this occurred very seldom, my taste running so strongly on stage villains and stage demons (I painted the whitewashed wall in my bedroom in Dalkey with watercolor frescoes of Mephistopheles) that I must have actually bewitched myself; for, when Nature completed my countenance in 1880 or thereabouts (I had only the tenderest sprouting of hair on my face until I was 24), I found myself equipped with the upgrowing moustaches and eyebrows, and the sarcastic nostrils of the operatic fiend whose airs (by Gounod) I had sung as a child, and whose attitudes I had affected in my boyhood. Later on, as the generations moved past me, I saw the fantasies of actors and painters come to life as living men and women, and began to perceive that imaginative fiction is to life what the sketch is to the picture or the conception to the statue. The world is full of ugly little men who were taken to the theatre to see the Yellow Dwarf or Rumpelstiltskin when they were children; and we shall soon have women in all directions with the features of Movie Vamps because in childhood they were taken to the picture palaces and inspired with an ambition to be serpents of Old Nile.

My father disapproved of the detachment of his family from the conventional observances that were associated with the standing of the Shaw family. But he was in the grip of a humorous sense of anticlimax which I inherited from him and used with much effect when I became a writer of comedy. The more sacred an idea or a situation was by convention, the more irresistible was it to him as the jumping-off place for a plunge into laughter. Thus, when I scoffed at the Bible he would instantly and quite sincerely rebuke me, telling me, with what little sternness was in his nature, that I should not speak so; that no educated man would make such a display of ignorance; that the Bible was universally recognized as a literary and historical masterpiece; and as much more to the same effect as he could muster. But when he had reached the point of feeling really impressive, a convulsion of internal chuckling would wrinkle up his eyes; and (I knowing all the time quite well what was coming) would cap his eulogy by assuring me, with an air of perfect fairness, that even the worst enemy of religion could say no worse of the Bible than that it was the damndest parcel of lies ever written. He would then rub his eyes and chuckle for quite a long time. It became an unacknowledged game between us that I should provoke him to exhibitions of this kind.

With such a father my condition was clearly hopeless as far as the conventions of religion were concerned. In essential matters his influence was as good as his culture permitted. One of my very earliest recollections is reading the Pilgrim's Progress to him, and being corrected by him for saying grievious instead of grievous. I never saw him, as far as I can remember, reading anything but the newspaper; but he had read Sir Walter Scott and other popular classics; and he always encouraged me to do the same, and to frequent the National Gallery, and to go to the theatre and the opera when I could afford it. His anticlimaxes depended for their effect on our sense of the sacredness he was reacting against: there would have been no fun whatever in saying that the Adventures of Munchausen (known to us as Baron Mun Chawzon) were a parcel of lies. If my mother's pastors and masters had had a little of his humor, she would not simply have dropped the subject of religion with her children in silent but implacable dislike of what had helped to make her childhood miserable, and resolved that it should not do the same to them. The vacuum she left by this policy had, I think, serious disadvantages for my two sisters (the younger of whom died just before I came to London); but in my case it only made a clear space for positive beliefs later on.

My mother, I may say here, had no comedic impulses, and never uttered an epigram in her life: all my comedy is a Shavian inheritance. She had plenty of imagination, and really lived in it and on it. Her brother, my uncle Walter, who stayed with us from time to time in the intervals of his trips across the Atlantic as a surgeon on the Inman Liners, had an extraordinary command of picturesque language, partly derived by memory from the Bible and Prayer Book, and partly natural. The conversation of the navigating staffs and pursers of our ocean services was at that time (whatever it may be today) extremely Rabelaisian and profane. Falstaff himself could not have held his own with my uncle in obscene anecdotes, unprintable limericks, and fantastic profanity; and it mattered nothing to him whether his audience consisted of his messmates on board ship or his schoolboy nephew: he performed before each with equal gusto. To do him justice, he was always an artist in his obscenity and blasphemy, and therefore never sank to the level of incontinent blackguardism. His efforts were controlled, deliberate, fastidiously chosen and worded. But they were all the more effective in destroying all my inculcated childish reverence for the verbiage of religion, for its legends and personifications and parables. In view of my subsequent work in the world it seems providential that I was driven to the essentials of religion by the reduction of every factitious or fictitious element in it to the most irreverent absurdity.

It would be the greatest mistake to conclude that this shocking state of affairs was bad for my soul. In so far as the process of destroying reverence for the inessential trappings of religion was indecent, it was deplorable; and I wish my first steps to grace had been lighted by my uncle's wit and style without his obscenity. My father's comedy was entirely decent. But that the process was necessary to my salvation I have no doubt whatever. A popular book in my youth was Mark Twain's New Pilgrim's Progress, which horrified the thoughtlessly pious by making fun of what they called sacred things. Yet Mark Twain was really a religious force in the world: his Yankee at the Court of King Arthur was his nearest approach to genuine blasphemy; and that came from want of culture, not from perversity of soul. His training as a Mississippi pilot must have been, as to religion, very like my training as the nephew of a Transatlantic surgeon.

Later on, I discovered that in the Ages of Faith the sport of making fun of the accessories and legends of religion was organized and practised by the Church to such an extent that it was almost part of its ritual. The people were instructed in spiritual history and hagiology by stage plays full of comic passages which might have been written by my uncle. For instance, my uncle taught me an elaborate conversation supposed to have passed between Daniel in the lion's den and King Darius, in which each strove to outdo the other in Rabelaisian repartee. The medieval playwright, more daring than my uncle, put on the stage comical conversations between Cain and his Creator, in which Cain's language was no more respectful than that of Fielding's Squire Western, and similarly indecent. In all Catholic countries there is a hagiology that is fit for publication and a hagiology that is not. In the Middle Ages they may have condemned a story as lewd or blasphemous; but it did not occur to them that God or His Church could be shaken by it. No man with any faith worth respecting in any religion worth holding ever dreams that it can be shaken by a joke, least of all by an obscene joke. It is Messieurs Formalist and Hypocrisy who feel that religion is crumbling when the forms are not observed. The truth is, humor is one of the great purifiers of religion, even when it is itself anything but pure.

The institution of the family, which is the centre of reverence for carefully brought-up children, was just the opposite for me. In a large family there are always a few skeletons in the cupboard; and in my father's clan there were many uncles and aunts and cousins, consequently many cupboards, consequently some skeletons. Our own particular skeleton was my father's drunkenness. It was combined with a harmlessness and humaneness which made him the least formidable of men; so that it was impossible for him to impress his children in the manner that makes awe and dread almost an instinct with some children. It is much to his credit that he was incapable of deliberately practising any such impressiveness, drunk or sober; but unfortunately the drunkenness was so humiliating that it would have been unendurable if we had not taken refuge in laughter. It had to be either a family tragedy or a family joke; and it was on the whole a healthy instinct that decided us to get what ribald fun was possible out of it, which, however, was very little indeed. If Noah had made a habit of drinking, his sons would soon have worn out the pious solicitude which they displayed on the occasion of his single lapse from sobriety. A boy who has seen "the governor," with an imperfectly wrapped-up goose under one arm and a ham in the same condition under the other (both purchased under heaven knows what delusion of festivity), butting at the garden wall in the belief that he was pushing open the gate, and transforming his tall hat to a concertina in the process, and who, instead of being overwhelmed with shame and anxiety at the spectacle, has been so disabled by merriment (uproariously shared by the maternal uncle) that he has hardly been able to rush to the rescue of the hat and pilot its wearer to safety, is clearly not a boy who will make tragedies of trifles instead of making trifles of tragedies. If you cannot get rid of the family skeleton, you may as well make it dance.

Then there was my Uncle William, a most amiable man, with great natural dignity. In early manhood he was not only an inveterate smoker, but so insistent a toper that a man who made a bet that he would produce Barney Shaw sober, and knocked him up at six in the morning with that object, lost his bet. But this might have happened to any common drunkard. What gave the peculiar Shaw finish and humor to the case was that my uncle suddenly and instantly gave up smoking and drinking at one blow, and devoted himself to his accomplishment of playing the ophicleide. In this harmless and gentle pursuit he continued, a blameless old bachelor, for many years, and then, to the amazement of Dublin, renounced the ophicleide and all its works, and married a lady of distinguished social position and great piety. She declined, naturally, to have anything to do with us; and, as far as I know, treated the rest of the family in the same way. Anyhow, I never saw her, and only saw my uncle furtively by the roadside after his marriage, when he would make hopeless attempts to save me, in the pious sense of the word, not perhaps without some secret Shavian enjoyment of the irreverent pleasantries with which I scattered my path to perdition. He was reputed to sit with a Bible on his knees, and an opera glass to his eyes, watching the ladies' bathing place in Dalkey; and my sister, who was a swimmer, confirmed this gossip as far as the opera glass was concerned.

But this was only the prelude to a very singular conclusion, or rather catastrophe. The fantastic imagery of the Bible so gained on my uncle that he took off his boots, explaining that he expected to be taken up to heaven at any moment like Elijah, and that he felt that his boots would impede his celestial flight. He then went a step further, and hung his room with all the white fabrics he could lay hands on, alleging that he was the Holy Ghost. At last he became silent, and remained so to the end. His wife, warned that his harmless fancies might change into dangerous ones, had him removed to an asylum in the north of Dublin. My father thought that a musical appeal might prevail with him, and went in search of the ophicleide. But it was nowhere to be found. He took a flute to the asylum instead; for every Shaw of that generation seemed able to play any wind instrument at sight. My uncle, still obstinately mute, contemplated the flute for a while, and then played Home Sweet Home on it. My father had to be content with this small success, as nothing more could be got out of his brother. A day or two later my uncle, impatient for heaven, resolved to expedite his arrival there. Every possible weapon had been carefully removed from his reach; but his custodians reckoned without the Shavian originality. They had left him somehow within reach of a carpet bag. He put his head into it, and in a strenuous effort to decapitate or strangle himself by closing it on his neck, perished of heart failure. I should be glad to believe that, like Elijah, he got the heavenly reward he sought; for he was a fine upstanding man and a gentle creature, nobody's enemy but his own, as the saying is.

Still, what sort of gravity could a boy maintain with a family history of this kind? However, I must not imply that all my uncles were like that. They were mostly respectable normal people. I can recall only two other exceptions to this rule. One of my uncles married an elegant and brilliant lady, from whom he separated after scandalizing the family by beating her; but as Job himself would have beaten her when she lost her very unstable temper, nobody who knew her intimately ever blamed him. Though the neurosis which produced my father's joyless craving for alcohol had the same effect, with the same curious recalcitrance and final impermanence, in one or two other cases, and was perhaps connected with occasional family paroxysms of Evangelical piety, and some share of my father's comedic love of anticlimax, yet on the whole our collection of skeletons was not exceptionally large. But as, compared with similar English families, we had a power of derisive dramatization that made the bones of the Shavian skeletons rattle more loudly; and as I possessed this power in an abnormal degree, and frequently entertained my friends with stories of my uncles (so effectively, by the way, that nobody ever believed them), the family, far from being a school of reverence for me, was rather a mine from which I could dig highly amusing material without the trouble of inventing a single incident. What idle fancy of mine could have improved on the hard facts of the Life and Death of Uncle William?

Thus the immediate result of my family training in my Victoria Grove days was that I presented myself to the unprepared stranger as a most irreverent young man. My Mephistophelean moustache and eyebrows had not yet grown; and there was nothing in my aspect to break the shock of my diabolical opinions.

Later on, when I had made a public reputation as an iconoclast, people who met me in private were surprised at my mildness and sociability. But I had no public reputation then: consequently expectation in my regard was normal. And I was not at all reticent of the diabolical opinions. I felt them to be advantageous, just as I felt that I was in a superior position as an Irishman, without a shadow of any justification for that patriotic arrogance. As it never occurred to me to conceal my opinions any more than my nationality, and as I had, besides, an unpleasant trick of contradicting everyone from whom I thought I could learn anything in order to draw him out and enable me to pick his brains, I think I must have impressed many amiable persons as an extremely disagreeable and undesirable young man.

And yet I was painfully shy, and was simply afraid to accept invitations, with the result that I very soon ceased to get any. I was told that if I wanted to get on, I must not flatly refuse invitations— actually dinner invitations—which were meant to help me, and the refusal of which was nothing short of a social outrage. But I knew very well that introductions could be of no use to one who had no profession and could do nothing except what any clerk could do. I knew I was useless, worthless, penniless, and that until I had qualified myself to do something, and proved it by doing it, all this business of calling on people who might perhaps do something for me, and dining out without money to pay for a cab, was silly. Fortunately for me, the realism that made me face my own position so ruthlessly also kept before me the fact that if I borrowed money I could not pay it back, and therefore might more candidly beg or steal it. I knew quite well that if I borrowed £5 from a friend and could not pay it back, I was selling a friend for £5, and that this was a foolish bargain. So

I did not borrow, and therefore did not lose my friends; though some of them, who could have had no illusions about my financial capacity, hinted that they were quite willing, and indeed anxious, to call a gift a loan.

I feel bound to confess here, in reference to my neglect of the few invitations and offers of introductions that reached me, that behind the conviction that they could lead to nothing that I wanted lay the unspoken fear that they might lead to something I did not want: that is, commercial employment. I had had enough of that. No doubt it would have been a great relief to my mother if I could have earned something. No doubt I could have earned something if I had really meant to. No doubt if my father had died, and my mother been struck dumb and blind, I should have had to go back to the office desk (the doom of shabby gentility) and give up all hope of acquiring a profession; for even the literary profession, though its exacts no academic course and costly equipment, does exact all one's time and the best of one's brains. As it was, I dodged every opening instinctively. With an excellent testimonial and an unexceptionable character, I was an incorrigible Unemployable. I kept up pretences (to myself as much as to others) for some time. I answered advertisements, not too offensively. I actually took a berth in a telephone Company (then a sensational novelty) and had some difficulty in extricating myself from the Company which bought it up. I can remember an interview with a bank manager in Onslow Gardens (procured for me, to my dismay, by an officious friend with whom I *had* dined) with a view to employment in the bank. I entertained him so brilliantly (if I may use an adverb with which in later years I was much plagued by friendly critics) that we parted on the best of terms, he declaring that, though I certainly ought to get something to do without the least difficulty, he did not feel that a bank clerkship was the right job for me.

I have said that I had an excellent testimonial as an employee in a business office. I had, as a matter of fact, spent four and a half years at a desk in Dublin before I emigrated. I have already given the economic reasons why boys of my class have to do without university education, just as they have to do without horses and guns. And yet I cannot deny that clergymen no better off than my father do manage somehow to start their sons in life with a university degree. They regard it as an absolute necessity, and therefore do not consider whether they can afford it or not. They must afford it. The need for it may be an illusion; but we are subject to such illusions: one man cannot live without a grand piano, another without a boat, another without a butler, another without a horse, and so on through a whole range of psychological imperatives. I have known women set up orphanages because they could not do without children to beat. Place their necessities in any rational order, and you will find that many of them cannot afford these things. They get out of the difficulty by simply rearranging your rational order as a psychological order, and putting their fancies at the top and their needs at the bottom. It is no use telling a woman that she needs good food and plenty of it much more vitally than she needs a seven guinea hat, a bottle of hair dye, a supply of face powder and rouge, a puff and a haresfoot. She will live on tea and rashers for months rather than forego them. And men are just as unreasonable. To say that my father could not afford to give me a university education is like saying that he could not afford to drink, or that I could not afford to become an author. Both statements are true; but he drank and I became an author all the same. I must therefore explain, just as seriously as if my father had had fifty thousand a year, why I did not graduate at Trinity College, Dublin.

I cannot learn anything that does not interest me. My memory is not indiscriminate: it rejects and selects; and its selections are not academic. I have no competitive instinct; nor do I crave for prizes and distinctions: consequently I have no interest in competitive examinations: if I won, the disappointment of my competitors would distress me instead of gratifying me: if I lost, my self-esteem would suffer. Besides, I have far too great a sense of my own importance to feel that it could be influenced by a degree or a gold medal or what not. There is only one sort of school that could have qualified me for academic success; and that is the sort in which the teachers take care that the pupils shall be either memorizing their lessons continuously, with all the desperate strenuousness that terror can inspire, or else crying with severe physical pain. I was never in a school where the teachers cared enough about me, or about their ostensible profession, or had enough conviction and cruelty, to take any such trouble; so I learnt nothing at school, not even what I could and would have learned if any attempt had been made to interest me. I congratulate myself on this; for I am firmly persuaded that every unnatural activity of the brain is as mischievous as any unnatural activity of the body, and that pressing people to learn things they do not want to know is as unwholesome and disastrous as feeding them on sawdust. Civilization is always wrecked by giving the governing classes what is called secondary education, which produces invincible ignorance and intellectual and moral imbecility as a result of unnatural abuse of the apprehensive faculty. No child would ever learn to walk or dress itself if its hands and feet were kept in irons and allowed to move only when and as its guardians pulled and pushed them.

I somehow knew this when I began,

as a boy entering on my teens, to think about such things. I remember saying, in some discussion that arose on the subject of my education, that T.C.D. men were all alike (by which I meant all wrong), and that I did not want to go through college. I was entirely untouched by university idealism. When it reached me later on, I recognized how ignorantly I had spoken in my boyhood; but when I went still further and learnt that this idealism is never realized in our schools and universities, and operates only as a mask and a decoy for our system of impressing and enslaving children and stultifying adults, I concluded that my ignorance had been inspired, and had served me very well. I have not since changed my mind.

However that may be, I decided, at thirteen or thereabouts, that for the moment I must go into business and earn some money and begin to be a grown-up man. There was at that time, on one of the quays in Dublin, a firm of cloth merchants, by name Scott, Spain, and Rooney. A friend of ours knew Scott, and asked him to give me a start in life with some employment. I called on this gentleman by appointment. I had the vaguest notion of what would happen: all I knew was that I was "going into an office." I thought I should have preferred to interview Spain, as the name was more romantic. Scott turned out to be a smart handsome man, with moustachios; and I suppose a boy more or less in his warehouse did not matter to him when there was a friend to be obliged: at all events, he said only a few perfunctory things and was settling my employment, when, as my stars would have it, Rooney appeared. Mr Rooney was much older, not at all smart, but long, lean, grave, and respectable.

The last time I saw the late Sir George Alexander (the actor) he described to me his own boyhood, spent in a cloth warehouse in Cheapside, where they loaded him with bales, and praised him highly for his excellent conduct, even rewarding him after some years to the extent of sixteen shillings a week. Rooney saved me from the bales. He talked to me a little, and then said quite decisively that I was too young, and that the work was not suitable to me. He evidently considered that my introducer, my parents, and his young partner, had been inconsiderate; and I presently descended the stairs, reprieved and unemployed. As Mr Rooney was certainly fifty then at least, he must be a centenarian if, as I hope, he still lives. If he does, I offer him the assurance that I have not forgotten his sympathy.

A year later, or thereabouts, my uncle Frederick, an important official in the Valuation Office, whom no land agent or family solicitor in Dublin could afford to disoblige, asked a leading and terribly respectable firm of land agents, carrying on business at 15 Molesworth Street, to find a berth for me. They did so; and I became their office boy (junior clerk I called myself) at eighteen shillings a month. It was a very good opening for anyone with a future as a land agent, which in Ireland at that time was a business of professional rank. It was utterly thrown away on me. However, as the office was overstaffed with gentlemen apprentices, who had paid large fees for the privilege of singing operatic selections with me when the principals were out, there was nothing to complain of socially, even for a Shaw; and the atmosphere was as uncommercial as that of an office can be. Thus I learnt business habits without being infected with the business spirit. By the time I had attained to thirty shillings a month, the most active and responsible official in the office, the cashier, vanished; and as we were private bankers to some extent, our clients drawing cheques on us, and so forth, someone had to take his place without an hour's delay. An elder substitute grumbled at the strange job, and, though an able man in his way, could not make his cash balance. It became necessary, after a day or two of confusion, to try the office boy as a stopgap whilst the advertisements for a new cashier of appropriate age and responsibility were going forward. Immediately the machine worked again quite smoothly. I, who never knew how much money I had of my own (except when the figure was zero), proved a model of accuracy as to the money of others. I acquired my predecessor's very neat handwriting, my own being too sloped and straggly for the cash book. The efforts to fill my important place more worthily slackened. I bought a tailed coat, and was chaffed about it by the apprentices. My salary was raised to £48 a year, which was as much as I expected at sixteen and much less than the firm would have had to pay to a competent adult: in short, I made good in spite of myself, and found, to my dismay, that Business, instead of expelling me as the worthless impostor I was, was fastening upon me with no intention of letting me go.

Behold me therefore in my twentieth year, with a business training, in an occupation which I detested as cordially as any sane person lets himself detest anything he cannot escape from. In March 1876 I broke loose. I gave a month's notice. My employers naturally thought I was discontented with my salary (£84, I think, by that time), and explained to me quietly that they hoped to make my position more eligible. My only fear was that they should make it so eligible that all excuse for throwing it up would be taken from me. I thanked them and said I was resolved to go; and I had, of course, no reason in the world to give them for my resolution. They were a little hurt, and explained to my uncle that they had done their best, but that I seemed to have made up my mind. I had. After enjoying for a few days the luxury of not having

to go to the office, and being, if not my own master, at least not anyone else's slave, I packed a carpet bag; boarded the North Wall boat; and left the train next morning at Euston, where, on hearing a porter cry, in an accent quite strange to me (I had hardly ever heard an h dropped before), "Ensm' faw weel?" which I rightly interpreted as "Hansom or four wheel?" I was afraid to say hansom, because I had never been in one and was not sure that I should know how to get in. So I solemnly drove in a growler through streets whose names Dickens had made familiar to me, London being at its spring best, which is its very best, to Victoria Grove, where the driver accepted four shillings as a reasonable fare for the journey.

I did not set foot in Ireland again until 1905, and not then on my own initiative. I went back to please my wife; and a curious reluctance to retrace my steps made me land in the south and enter Dublin through the backdoor from Meath rather than return as I came, through the front door on the sea. In 1876 I had had enough of Dublin. James Joyce in his Ulysses has described, with a fidelity so ruthless that the book is hardly bearable, the life that Dublin offers to its young men, or, if you prefer to put it the other way, that its young men offer to Dublin. No doubt it is much like the life of young men everywhere in modern urban civilization. A certain flippant futile derision and belittlement that confuses the noble and serious with the base and ludicrous seems to me peculiar to Dublin; but I suppose that is because my only personal experience of that phase of youth was a Dublin experience; for when I left my native city I left that phase behind me, and associated no more with men of my age until, after about eight years of solitude in this respect, I was drawn into the Socialist revival of the early eighties, among Englishmen intensely serious and burning

Y

with indignation at very real and very fundamental evils that affected all the world; so that the reaction against them bound the finer spirits of all the nations together instead of making them cherish hatred of one another as a national virtue. Thus, when I left Dublin I left (a few private friendships apart) no society that did not disgust me. To this day my sentimental regard for Ireland does not include the capital. I am not enamored of failure, of poverty, of obscurity, and of the ostracism and contempt which these imply; and these were all that Dublin offered to the enormity of my unconscious ambition. The cities a man likes are the cities he has conquered. Napoleon did not turn from Paris to sentimentalize over Ajaccio, nor Catherine from St Petersburg to Stettin as the centre of her universe.

On this question of ambition let me say a word. In the ordinary connotation of the word I am the least ambitious of men. I have said, and I confirm it here, that I am so poor a hand at pushing and struggling, and so little interested in their rewards, that I have risen by sheer gravitation, too industrious by acquired habit to stop working (I work as my father drank), and too lazy and timid by nature to lay hold of half the opportunities or a tenth of the money that a conventionally ambitious man would have grasped strenuously. I never thought of myself as destined to become what is called a great man: indeed I was diffident to the most distressing degree; and I was ridiculously credulous as to the claims of others to superior knowledge and authority. But one day in the office I had a shock. One of the apprentices, by name C. J. Smyth, older than I and more a man of the world, remarked that every young chap thought he was going to be a great man. On a really modest youth this commonplace would have had no effect. It gave me so perceptible a jar that I suddenly became aware that I had never thought I was to

be a great man simply because I had always taken it as a matter of course. The incident passed without leaving any preoccupation with it to hamper me; and I remained as diffident as ever because I was still as incompetent as ever. But I doubt whether I ever recovered my former complete innocence of subconscious intention to devote myself to the class of work that only a few men excel in, and to accept the responsibilities that attach to its dignity.

Now this bore directly on my abandonment of Dublin, for which many young Irishmen of today find it impossible to forgive me. My business in life could not be transacted in Dublin out of an experience confined to Ireland. I had to go to London just as my father had to go to the Corn Exchange. London was the literary centre for the English language, and for such artistic culture as the realm of the English language (in which I proposed to be king) could afford. There was no Gaelic League in those days, nor any sense that Ireland had in herself the seed of culture. Every Irishman who felt that his business in life was on the higher planes of the cultural professions felt that he must have a metropolitan domicile and an international culture: that is, he felt that his first business was to get out of Ireland. I had the same feeling. For London as London, or England as England, I cared nothing. If my subject had been science or music I should have made for Berlin or Leipsic. If painting, I should have made for Paris: indeed many of the Irish writers who have made a name in literature escaped to Paris with the intention of becoming painters. For theology I should have gone to Rome, and for Protestant philosophy to Weimar. But as the English language was my weapon, there was nothing for it but London. In 1914 the Germans, resenting my description of their Imperial political situation as Potsdamnation, denounced me as a father-landless fellow. They were quite right. I was no more offended than if they had called me unparochial. They had never reproached me for making pilgrimages to Bayreuth when I could as easily have made them to the Hill of Tara. If you want to make me homesick, remind me of the Thuringian Fichtelgebirge, of the broad fields and delicate airs of France, of the Gorges of the Tarn, of the Passes of the Tyrol, of the North African desert, of the Golden Horn, of the Swedish lakes, or even of the Norwegian fiords where I have never been except in imagination, and you may stir that craving in me as easily—probably more easily—as in any exiled native of these places. It was not until I went back to Ireland as a tourist that I perceived that the charm of my country was quite independent of the accident of my having been born in it, and that it could fascinate a Spaniard or an Englishman more powerfully than an Irishman, in whose feeling for it there must always be a strange anguish, because it is the country where he has been unhappy and where vulgarity is vulgar to him. And so I am a tolerably good European in the Nietzschean sense, but a very bad Irishman in the Sinn Fein or Chosen People sense.

For the first couple of years of my life in London I did nothing decisive. I acted as ghost for a musician who had accepted a berth as musical critic; and as such ghosts must not appear, and I was therefore cut off from the paper and could not correct proofs, my criticisms, mostly very ruthless ones, appeared with such misprints, such mutilations and venal interpolations by other hands, so inextricably mixed up with other criticisms most offensive to my artistic sense, that I have ever since hidden this activity of mine as a guilty secret, lest someone should dig out these old notices and imagine that I was responsible for everything in them and with them. Even now I can hardly bring myself to reveal that the name of the paper was The Hornet, and that it had passed then into the hands of a certain Captain Donald Shaw, who was not related to me, and whom I never met. It died on his hands, and partly, perhaps, at mine.

Then my cousin, Mrs Cashel Hoey, a woman of letters, daughter of the aunt who played the tambourine with her beautiful hands, gave me an introduction to Arnold White, then secretary to the Edison Telephone Company. He found a berth for me in the Way Leave Department of that shortlived company; and I presently found myself studying the topography of the east end of London, and trying to persuade all sorts of people to allow the Company to put insulators and poles and derricks and the like on their roofs to carry the telephone lines. I liked the exploration involved; but my shyness made the business of calling on strangers frightfully uncongenial; and my sensitiveness, which was extreme, in spite of the brazen fortitude which I simulated, made the impatient rebuffs I had to endure occasionally, especially from much worried women who mistook me for an advertisement canvasser, ridiculously painful to me. But I escaped these trials presently; for I soon had to take charge of the department, and organize the work of more thick-skinned adventurers instead of doing it myself. Further particulars will be found in the preface to my second novel, The Irrational Knot. The Edison Telephone Company was presently swallowed up by the Bell Telephone Company; and I seized the opportunity to recover my destitute freedom by refusing to apply for the employment promised by the amalgamation to the disbanded staff. This was the end of my career as a commercial employee. I soon dropped even the pretence of seeking any renewal of it. Except for a day or two in 1881, when I earned a few pounds by counting the votes at an election in Leyton, I was an Unemployable, an ablebodied pauper in fact if not in law, until the year 1885, when for the first time I earned enough money directly by my pen to pay my way. My income for that year amounted to £112; and from that time until the war of 1914–18 momentarily threatened us all with bankruptcy, I had no pecuniary anxieties except those produced by the possession of money, not by the lack of it. My penury phase was over.

The telephone episode occurred in 1879; and in that year I had done what every literary adventurer did in those days, and many do still. I had written a novel. My office training had left me with a habit of doing something regularly every day as a fundamental condition of industry as distinguished from idleness. I knew I was making no headway unless I was doing this, and that I should never produce a book in any other fashion. I bought supplies of white paper, demy size, by sixpennorths at a time; folded it in quarto; and condemned myself to fill five pages of it a day, rain or shine, dull or inspired. I had so much of the schoolboy and the clerk still in me that if my five pages ended in the middle of a sentence I did not finish it until next day. On the other hand, if I missed a day, I made up for it by doing a double task on the morrow. On this plan I produced five novels in five years. It was my professional apprenticeship, doggedly suffered with all the diffidence and dissatisfaction of a learner with a very critical master, myself to wit, whom there was no pleasing and no evading, and persevered in to save my self-respect in a condition of impecuniosity which, for two acute moments (I still recall them with a wry face), added broken boots and carefully hidden raggedness to cuffs whose edges were trimmed by the scissors, and a tall hat so limp with age that I had to wear it back-to-front to enable me to take it off without doubling up the brim.

I had no success as a novelist. I sent the five novels to all the publishers in London and some in America. None would venture on them. Fifty or sixty refusals without a single acceptance forced me into a fierce self-sufficiency. I became undiscourageable, acquiring a superhuman insensitiveness to praise or blame which has been useful to me at times since, though at other times it has retarded my business affairs by making me indifferent to the publication and performances of my works, and even impatient of them as an unwelcome interruption to the labor of writing their successors. Instead of seizing every opportunity of bringing them before the public, I have often, on plausible but really trivial pretexts, put off proposals which I should have embraced with all the normal author's keenness for publicity.

Thus, after five years of novel writing, I was a complete professional failure. The more I wrote and the better I wrote the less I pleased the publishers. This first novel of mine, though rejected, at least elicited some expressions of willingness to read any future attempts. Blackwood actually accepted and then revoked. Sir George Macmillan, then a junior, not only sent me a longish and evidently considered report by the firm's reader, John (afterwards Lord) Morley, but suggested to him that I might be of some use to him in his capacity as editor of the Pall Mall Gazette.

All such responses ceased with my second novel; and I had no means of knowing, and was too young and inexperienced to guess, that what was the matter was not any lack of literary competence on my part, but the antagonism raised by my hostility to respectable Victorian thought and society. I was left without a ray of hope; yet I did not stop writing novels until, having planned my fifth effort on a colossal scale, I found at the end of what were to me only the first two sections of it, that I had no more to say and had better wait until I had educated myself much farther. And when, after an interval of critical journalism, I resumed the writing of fiction, I did so as a playwright and not as a novelist.

Four of the five novels of my nonage, as I call them, at last got into print as described in the preface already cited. But the first of them never got published at all. Opening the old parcel, as I do now (it is like opening a grave that has been closed for forty-two years), I find a pile of cahiers of twenty pages each, and realize with some dismay that I am face-to-face with a novel containing nearly 200,000 words. The title is Immaturity. The handwriting, which slopes slightly backwards, has all the regularity and legibility of my old cash book. Unfortunately, the mice have eaten so much of two of the cahiers that the ends of the lines are missing. This is awkward; for I have just told myself that I must make no attempt to correct the work of the apprentice with the hand of the master; that such as it is it must remain; that I am too old now to touch it without producing new incongruities more disagreeable than any that are possible between the style of 1879 and the taste of 1921. Yet, if the mice have eaten much, I must play the sedulous ape, like Stevenson, and imitate my own youthful manner like any literary forger.

It may be asked why I should print the thing at all: why not let ill alone? I am quite disposed to do so; but somehow one must not do such things. If Beethoven had destroyed his septet for wind instruments when he had advanced to the ninth symphony and the Mass in D, many people who delight in the septet and cannot make head or tail of symphony or Mass would suffer a wanton deprivation; and though my early style now makes me laugh at its pedantry, yet I have a great respect for the priggish conscientiousness of my first efforts. They prove too that, like Goethe, I knew all along, and have added more to my power of handling, illustrating, and addressing my material than to the material itself.

Anyhow, I have little doubt that Immaturity will be at least readable by the easygoing bookbuyers who will devour anything in the shape of a novel, however ridiculously out of fashion it may be. I know that some readers will like it much better than my later works. There must be a certain quality of youth in it which I could not now recapture, and which may even have charm as well as weakness and absurdity. Having re-read the other four novels for publication and republication at one time or another, I can guarantee the propriety of my early style. It was the last thing in correctness. I have never aimed at style in my life: style is a sort of melody that comes into my sentences by itself. If a writer says what he has to say as accurately and effectively as he can, his style will take care of itself, if he has a style. But I did set up one condition in my early days. I resolved that I would write nothing that should not be intelligible to a foreigner with a dictionary, like the French of Voltaire; and I therefore avoided idiom. (Later on I came to seek idiom as being the most highly vitalized form of language.) Consequently I do not expect to find the English of Immaturity idiomatic. Also, there will be nothing of the voice of the public speaker in it: the voice that rings through so much of my later work. Not until Immaturity was finished, late in 1879, did I for the first time rise to my feet in a little debating club called The Zetetical Society, to make, in a condition of heartbreaking nervousness, my first assault on an audience.

Perhaps I had better add a word as to the characters in the book. I do so with some reluctance, because it is misleading to mention even the smallest circumstance connecting a fictitious person with a living one. If Shakespear had happened to mention that he made the Prince of Denmark carry a set of tablets and make notes in them because he had seen Sir Walter Raleigh doing so, it would by this time be an invincible tradition in English literature that Raleigh was the original of Hamlet. We should have writers following up the clue, as they would call it, to the conclusion that Raleigh was the real author of the play. One day, as I was sitting in the reading room of the British Museum, beginning my fifth and last novel, An Unsocial Socialist, I saw a young lady with an attractive and arresting expression, bold, vivid, and very clever, working at one of the desks. On that glimpse of a face I instantly conceived the character and wrote the description of Agatha Wylie. I have never exchanged a word with that lady; never made her acquaintance; saw her again under the same circumstances but very few times; yet if I mention her name, which became well known in literature (she too was writing a novel then, probably, and perhaps had the hero suggested to her by my profile), she will be set down as Agatha Wylie to her dying day, with heaven knows how much more scandalous invention added to account for my supposed intimate knowledge of her character. Before and since, I have used living models as freely as a painter does, and in much the same way: that is, I have sometimes made a fairly faithful portrait founded on intimate personal intercourse, and sometimes, as in Agatha's case, developed what a passing glance suggested to my imagination. In the latter case it has happened sometimes that the incidents I have invented on the spur of such a glance have hit the facts so nearly that I have found myself accused of unpardonable violations of personal privacy. I hardly expect to be believed when I say that I once invented a servant for one of my models and found afterwards that he actually had just such a servant. Between the two extremes of actual portraiture and pure fancy work suggested by a glance or an anecdote, I have copied nature with many degrees of fidelity, combining studies from life in the same book or play with those types and composites and traditional figures of the novel and the stage which are called pure fictions. Many of the characters in this first novel of mine owed something to persons I had met, including members of my family (not to mention myself); but none of them are portraits; and with one exception the models are unknown to the public. That exception was Cecil Lawson, whose early death lost us the only landscape painter who ever reminded me of the spacious and fascinating experiments of Rubens in that branch of painting. When I lived at Victoria Grove the Lawsons: father, mother, Malcolm, and two sisters, lived in one of the handsome old houses in Cheyne Walk, Chelsea. Cecil and another brother, being married, boarded out. Malcolm was a musician; and the sisters sang. One, a soprano, dark, quick, plump and bright, sang joyously. The other, a contralto, sang with heartbreaking intensity of expression, which she deepened by dressing esthetically, as it was called then, meaning in the Rossettian taste. Miss Lawson produced this effect, not by the ugly extravagances which made the fashionable milliners' version of the esthetic mode ridiculous, but by very simple grey and brown gowns which somehow harmonized with her habitual expression of sadness and even suffering; so that when she sang "Oh, dont deceive me: oh, never leave me," she produced a picture as well as a tone poem. Cecil, who had just acquired a position by the few masterpieces which remain to us, was very much "in the movement" at the old Grosvenor Gallery (now the Aeolian Hall), then new, and passing through the sensational vogue achieved by its revelations of Burne Jones and Whistler.

Malcolm was conducting a Gluck Society, at which I had discovered Gluck through a recital of Alceste, in which Theo Marzials, who had a charming baritone voice, sang the part of Hercules. My mother had met Marzials in the course of her musical activities: he introduced her to Malcolm Lawson: she lent him a hand in the chorus of the Gluck Society; and the result was that I found myself invited to visit the Lawsons, who were at home in Cheyne Walk every Sunday evening. I suffered such agonies of shyness that I sometimes walked up and down the Embankment for twenty minutes or more before venturing to knock at the door: indeed I should have funked it altogether, and hurried home asking myself what was the use of torturing myself when it was so easy to run away, if I had not been instinctively aware that I must never let myself off in this manner if I meant ever to do anything in the world. Few men can have suffered more than I did in my youth from simple cowardice or been more horribly ashamed of it. I shirked and hid when the peril, real or imaginary, was of the sort that I had no vital interest in facing; but when such an interest was at stake, I went ahead and suffered accordingly. The worst of it was that when I appeared in the Lawsons' drawingroom I did not appeal to the goodnature of the company as a pardonably and even becomingly bashful novice. I had not then tuned the Shavian note to any sort of harmony; and I have no doubt the Lawsons found me discordant, crudely self-assertive, and insufferable. I hope they, and all the others on whom I jarred at this time, forgave me in later years, when it turned out that I really had something to assert after all. The house and its artistic atmosphere were most congenial to me; and I liked all the Lawsons; but I had not mastered the art of society at that time, and could not bear making an inartistic exhibition of myself; so I soon ceased to plague them, and, except for an occasional chance meeting with Malcolm, passed out of their lives after touching them very lightly in passing.

Cecil Lawson was the spoilt child of that household. He pontificated on art in a wayward grumbling incoherent musing fashion of his own. When, following my youthful and very irritating system of contradicting everyone from whom I thought I could learn anything, I suggested that Whistler was something short of the greatest artist of all time, he could not form a sentence to crush me with, but groaned inarticulately for a moment, like a clock about to strike, and then uttered the words Titian Turner Rembrandt Velasquez Whistler. He was goodlooking, not a big man, but trimly built, with just enough crisply curled hair to proclaim the artist without compromising the man. I had seen his work in the public exhibitions (never in private); and, thanks to my boyish prowlings in the Dublin National Gallery (as a boy I wanted to be a painter, never a writer), I knew its value. His untimely death, which occurred soon after my visits, must have broken up the Sunday evenings at Cheyne Walk very badly. I did not venture to intrude after it.

I used him in Immaturity as a model for the artist Cyril Scott, an invented name which has since been made famous by a British composer. I chose it because Cyril resembled Cecil metrically, and because I thought Lawson was a Scot (he was, I learn, born in Shropshire). But I must again warn the reader against taking the man in the book as an authentic portrait of the great painter, or inferring that his courtship and marriage or any of the circumstances I have invented for him, represent facts in Lawson's life. I knew nothing whatever about him except what I saw of him during my few visits to

Cheyne Walk; and I have learnt nothing since. He set my imagination to work: that was all.

I have now told as much as seems to me necessary of the circumstances and relevant antecedents of my first book. It is the book of a raw youth, still quite out of touch with the country to which he had transported himself; and if I am to be entirely communicative on this subject, I must add that the mere rawness which so soon rubs off was complicated by a deeper strangeness which has made me all my life a sojourner on this planet rather than a native of it. Whether it be that I was born mad or a little too sane, my kingdom was not of this world: I was at home only in the realm of my imagination, and at my ease only with the mighty dead. Therefore I had to become an actor, and create for myself a fantastic personality fit and apt for dealing with men, and adaptable to the various parts I had to play as author, journalist, orator, politician, committee man, man of the world, and so forth. In this I succeeded later on only too well. In my boyhood I saw Charles Mathews act in a farce called Cool as a Cucumber. The hero was a young man just returned from a tour of the world, upon which he had been sent to cure him of an apparently hopeless bashfulness; and the fun lay in the cure having overshot the mark and transformed him into a monster of outrageous impudence. I am not sure that something of the kind did not happen to me; for when my imposture was at last accomplished, and I daily pulled the threads of the puppet who re-

presented me in the public press, the applause that greeted it was not unlike that which Mathews drew in Cool as a Cucumber. Certainly the growls of resentful disgust with which my advances were resisted closely resembled those of the unfortunate old gentleman in the farce whose pictures and furniture the young man so coolly rearranged to his own taste. At the time of which I am writing, however, I had not yet learnt to act, nor come to understand that my natural character was impossible on the great stage of London. When I had to come out of the realm of imagination into that of actuality I was still uncomfortable. I was outside society, outside politics, outside sport, outside the Church. If the term had been invented then I should have been called The Complete Outsider. But the epithet would have been appropriate only within the limits of British barbarism. The moment music, painting, literature, or science came into question the positions were reversed: it was I who was the Insider. I had the intellectual habit; and my natural combination of critical faculty with literary resource needed only a clear comprehension of life in the light of an intelligible theory: in short, a religion, to set it in triumphant operation. It was the lack of this last qualification that lamed me in those early days in Victoria Grove, and that set limits to this ungainly first novel of mine, which you will not lose very much by skipping.

Ayot St Lawrence
Summer 1921

XXIV

THE IRRATIONAL KNOT

1905

This novel was written in the year 1880; but this preface was not written until 25 years later for an American edition. In 1880 I was twentyfour; and four years had elapsed since I had exported myself from Dublin to London in a condition of extreme rawness and inexperience concerning the specifically English side of the life with which the book pretends to deal. Everybody wrote novels then. It was my second attempt; and it shared the fate of my first. Nobody would publish it, though I tried all the London publishers and some American ones. And I should not greatly blame them if I could feel sure that it was the book's faults and not its qualities that repelled them.

I have narrated elsewhere how in the course of time the rejected MS. became Mrs Annie Besant's excuse for lending me her ever-helping hand by publishing it as a serial in a little propagandist magazine of hers. That was how it got loose beyond all possibility of recapture. It is out of my power now to stand between it and the American public.

At present, of course, I am not the author of The Irrational Knot. Physiologists inform us that the substance of our bodies (and consequently of our souls) is shed and renewed at such a rate that no part of us lasts longer than eight years: I am therefore not now in any atom of me the person who wrote The Irrational Knot in 1880. The last of that author perished in 1888; and two of his successors have since joined the majority. Fourth of his line, I cannot be expected to take any very lively interest in the novels of my literary great-grandfather. Even my personal recollections of him are becoming vague and overlaid with those most misleading of all traditions, the traditions founded on the lies a man tells, and at last comes to believe, about himself *to* himself. Certain things, however, I remember very well. For instance, I am significantly clear as to the price of the paper on which I wrote The Irrational Knot. It was cheap—a white demy of unpretentious quality—so that sixpennorth lasted a long time. My daily allowance of composition was five pages of this demy in quarto; and I held my natural laziness sternly to that task day in, day out, to the end. I remember also that Bizet's Carmen being then new in London, I used it as a safety-valve for my romantic impulses. When I was tired of the sordid realism of Edward Conolly (whose name does not rhyme to Polly, as the Irish stress is on the first syllable) I threw down my pen and went to the piano to forget him in the glamorous society of Carmen and her crimson toreador and yellow dragoon. Not that Bizet's music could infatuate me as it infatuated Nietzsche. Nursed on greater masters, I thought less of him than he deserved; but the Carmen music was—in places—exquisite of its kind, and could enchant a young man romantic enough to have come to the end of romance before I began to create in art for myself. I still could enjoy other people's romances.

When I say that *I* did and felt these things, I mean, of course, that the predecessor whose name I bear did and felt them. The I of today is (? am) cool towards Carmen; and Carmen, I regret to say, does not take the slightest interest in him (? me). And now enough of this juggling with past and present Shaws. The grammatical complications of being a first person and several extinct third persons at the same moment are so frightful that I must return to the ordinary misusage, and ask the reader to make the necessary corrections in his or her own mind.

This book is not wholly a compound of intuition and ignorance. Take for example the profession of my hero, an Irish-American electrical engineer. That was by no means a flight of fancy. For you must not suppose, because I am a man of letters, that I never tried to earn an honest living. I began trying to commit that sin against my nature when I was fifteen, and persevered, from youthful timidity and diffidence, until I was twentythree. My last attempt was in 1879, when a company was formed in London to exploit an ingenious invention by Mr Thomas Alva Edison: a much too ingenious invention as it proved, being nothing less than a telephone of such stentorian efficiency that it bellowed your most private communications all over the house instead of whispering them with some sort of discretion. This was not what the British stockbroker wanted; so the company was soon merged in the National Telephone Company after making a place for itself in the history of literature, quite unintentionally, by providing me with a job. Whilst the Edison Telephone Company lasted, it crowded the basement of a huge pile of offices in Queen Victoria Street with American artificers. These deluded and romantic men gave me a glimpse of the skilled proletariat of the United States. They sang obsolete sentimental songs with genuine emotion; and their language was frightful even to an Irishman. They worked with a ferocious energy which was out of all proportion to the actual result achieved. Indomitably resolved to assert their republican manhood by taking no orders from a tall-hatted Englishman whose stiff politeness covered his conviction that they were, relatively to himself, inferior and common persons, they insisted on being slave-driven with genuine American oaths by a genuine free and equal American foreman. They utterly despised the artfully slow British workman who did as little for his wages as he possibly could; never hurried himself; and had a deep reverence for anyone whose pocket could be tapped by respectful behavior. Need I add that they were contemptuously wondered at by this same British workman as a parcel of outlandish adult boys, who sweated themselves for their employer's benefit instead of looking after their own interests? They adored Mr Edison as the greatest man of all time in every possible department of science, art, and philosophy, and execrated Mr Graham Bell, the inventor of the rival telephone, as his Satanic adversary; but each of them had (or pretended to have) on the brink of completion, an improvement on the telephone, usually a new transmitter. They were free-souled creatures, excellent company: sensitive, cheerful, and profane; liars, braggarts, and hustlers; with an air of making slow old England hum which never left them even when, as often happened, they were wrestling with difficulties of their own making, or struggling in no-thoroughfares from which they had to be retrieved like strayed sheep by Englishmen without imagination enough to go wrong.

In this environment I remained for some months. As I was interested in physics and had read Tyndall and Helmholtz, besides having learnt something in Ireland through a friendship with one of Mr Graham Bell's cousins who was also a chemist and physicist, I was, I believe, the only person in the entire establishment who knew the current scientific explanation of telephony; and as I soon struck up a friendship with our official lecturer, a Colchester man whose strong point was pre-scientific agriculture, I often discharged his duties for him in a manner which, I am persuaded, laid the foundation of Mr Edison's London reputation: my sole reward being my boyish delight in the half-concealed incredulity of our visitors (who were convinced by the hoarsely startling utterances of the telephone that the speaker, alleged by me to be twenty miles away, was really using a speaking-trumpet in the next room), and their obvious uncertainty, when the demonstration was over, as to whether they ought to tip me or not: a question they either decided in the negative or never decided at all; for I never got anything.

So much for my electrical engineer! To get him into contact with fashionable society before he became famous was also a problem easily solved. I knew of three English peers who actually preferred physical laboratories to stables, and scientific experts to gamekeepers: in fact, one of the experts was a friend of mine. And I knew from personal experience that if science brings men of all ranks into contact, art, especially music, does the same for men and women. An electrician who can play an accompaniment can go anywhere and know anybody. As far as mere access and acquaintance go there are no class barriers for him. My difficulty was not to get my hero into society, but to give any sort of plausibility to my picture of society when I got him into it. I lacked the touch of the literary diner-out; and I had, as the reader will probably find to his cost, the classical tradition which makes all the persons in a novel, except the comically vernacular ones, or the speakers of phonetically spelt dialect, utter themselves in the formal phrases and studied syntax of eighteenth century rhetoric. In short, I wrote in the style of Scott and Dickens; and as fashionable society then spoke and behaved, as it still does, in no style at all, my transcriptions of Oxford and Mayfair may nowadays suggest an unaccountable and ludicrous ignorance of a very superficial and access-ible code of manners. I was not, however, so ignorant as might have been inferred at that time from my unpresentable and almost desperate financial condition.

I had, to begin with, a sort of back-stairs knowledge; for in my teens I struggled for life in the office of an Irish gentleman who acted as land agent and private banker for many persons of distinction. Now it is possible for a London author to dine out in the highest circles for twenty years without learning as much about the human frailties of his hosts as the family solicitor or (in Ireland) the family land agent learns in twenty days; and some of this knowledge inevitably reaches his clerks, especially the clerk who keeps the cash, which was my particular department. He learns, if capable of the lesson, that the aristocratic profession has as few geniuses as any other profession; so that if you want a peerage of more than, say, half a dozen members, you must fill it up with many common persons, and even with some deplorably mean ones. For "service is no inheritance" either in the kitchen or the House of Lords; and the case presented by Mr Barrie in his play of The Admirable Crichton, where the butler is the man of quality, and his master, the Earl, the man of rank, is no fantasy but a quite common occurrence, and indeed to some extent an inevitable one, because the English are extremely particular in selecting their butlers, whilst they do not select their barons at all, taking them as the accident of birth sends them. The consequences include much ironic comedy. For instance, we have in England a curious belief in first rate people, meaning all the people we do not know; and this consoles us for the undeniable second-rateness of the people we do know, besides saving the credit of aristocracy as an institution. The unmet aristocrat is devoutly believed in; but he is always round the corner, never at hand. That *the* smart set exists; that there is above and beyond that smart set a class so blue of blood and exquisite in nature that it looks down even on the King with haughty condescension; that scepticism on this nice point is a stigma of plebeian baseness: all these imaginings are so common here that they constitute the real popular sociology of England as much as an unlimited credulity as to vaccination constitutes the real popular science of England. It is, of course, a timid superstition. A British peer or peeress who happens by chance to be genuinely noble is just as isolated at court as Goethe would have been among all the other grandsons of publicans, if they had formed a distinct class in Frankfurt or Weimar. This I knew very well when I wrote my novels; and if, as I suspect, I failed to create a convincingly verisimilar atmosphere of aristocracy, it was not because I had any illusions or ignorances as to the common humanity of the peerage, and not because I gave literary style to its conversation, but because, as I had no money, I had to blind myself to its enormous importance, with the result that I missed the point of view, and with it the whole moral basis, of the class which rightly values money, and plenty of it, as the first condition of a bearable life.

Money is indeed the most important thing in the world; and all sound and successful personal and national morality should have this fact for its basis. Every teacher or twaddler who denies it or suppresses it, is an enemy of life. Money controls morality; and what makes the United States of America look so foolish even in foolish Europe is that they are always in a state of flurried concern and violent interference with morality, whereas they throw their money into the street to be scrambled for, and presently find that their cash reserves are not in their own hands, but in the pockets of a few millionaires who, bewildered by their luck, and unspeakably incapable of making any truly economic use of it, endeavor to "do good" with it by letting themselves be fleeced by philanthropic committee men, building contractors, librarians and professors, in the name of education, science, art, and what not; so that sensible people exhale relievedly when the pious millionaire dies, and his heirs, demoralized by being brought up on his outrageous income, begin the socially beneficent work of scattering his fortune through the channels of the trades that flourish by riotous living.

This, as I have said, I did not then understand; for I knew money only by the want of it. Ireland is a poor country; and my father was a poor man in a poor country. By this I do not mean that he was hungry and homeless, a hewer of wood and a drawer of water. My friend Mr James Huneker, a man of gorgeous imagination and incorrigible romanticism, has described me to the American public as a peasant lad who has raised himself, as all American presidents are assumed to have raised themselves, from the humblest departments of manual labor to the loftiest eminence. James flatters me. Had I been born a peasant, I should now be a tramp. My notion of my father's income is even vaguer than his own was —and that is saying a good deal—but he always had an income of at least three figures (four, if you count in dollars instead of pounds); and what made him poor was that he conceived himself as born to a social position which even in Ireland could have been maintained in dignified comfort only on twice or thrice what he had. And he married on that assumption. Fortunately for me, social opportunity is not always to be measured by income. There is an important economic factor, first analysed by an American economist (General Walker), and called rent of ability. Now this rent, when the ability is of the artistic or political sort, is often paid in kind. For example, a

London possessor of such ability may, with barely enough money to maintain a furnished bedroom and a single presentable suit of clothes, see everything worth seeing that a millionaire can see, and know everybody worth knowing that he can know. Long before I reached this point myself, a very trifling accomplishment gave me glimpses of the sort of fashionable life a peasant never sees. Thus I remember one evening during the novel-writing period when nobody would pay a farthing for a stroke of my pen, walking along Sloane Street in that blessed shield of literary shabbiness, evening dress. A man accosted me with an eloquent appeal for help, ending with the assurance that he had not a penny in the world. I replied, with exact truth, "Neither have I." He thanked me civilly, and went away, apparently not in the least surprised, leaving me to ask myself why I did not turn beggar too, since I felt sure that a man who did it as well as he must be in comfortable circumstances.

Another reminiscence. A little past midnight, in the same costume, I was turning from Piccadilly into Bond Street, when a lady of the pavement, out of luck that evening so far, confided to me that the last bus for Brompton had passed, and that she should be grateful to any gentleman who would give her a lift in a hansom. My old-fashioned Irish gallantry had not then been worn off by age and England: besides, as a novelist who could find no publisher, I was touched by the similarity of our trades and predicaments. I excused myself very politely on the ground that my wife (invented for the occasion) was waiting for me at home, and that I felt sure so attractive a lady would have no difficulty in finding another escort. Unfortunately this speech made so favorable an impression on her that she immediately took my arm and declared her willingness to go anywhere with me, on the flattering ground that I was a perfect gentleman. In vain did I try to persuade her that in coming up Bond Street and deserting Piccadilly she was throwing away her last chance of a hansom: she attached herself so devotedly to me that I could not without actual violence shake her off. At last I made a stand at the end of Old Bond Street. I took out my purse; opened it; and held it upside down. Her countenance fell, poor girl! She turned on her heel with a melancholy flirt of her skirt, and vanished.

Now on both these occasions I had been in the company of people who spent at least as much in a week as I did in a year. Why was I, a penniless and unknown young man, admitted there? Simply because, though I was an execrable pianist, and never improved until the happy invention of the pianola made a Paderewski of me, I could play a simple accompaniment at sight more congenially to a singer than most amateurs. It is true that the musical side of London society, with its streak of Bohemianism, and its necessary toleration of foreign ways and professional manners, is far less typically English than the sporting side or the political side or the Philistine side; so much so, indeed, that people may and do pass their lives in it without ever discovering what English plutocracy in the mass is really like: still, if you wander in it nocturnally for a fitful year or so as I did, with empty pockets and an utter impossibility of approaching it by daylight (owing to the too obvious decay of the morning wardrobe), you have something more actual to go on than the hallucinations of a peasant lad setting his foot manfully on the lowest rung of the social ladder. I never climbed any ladder: I have achieved eminence by sheer gravitation; and I hereby warn all peasant lads not to be duped by my pretended example into regarding their present servitude as a practicable first step to a celebrity so dazzling that its subject cannot even suppress his own bad novels.

Conceive me then at the writing of The Irrational Knot as a person neither belonging to the world I describe nor wholly ignorant of it, and on certain points quite incapable of conceiving it intuitively. A whole world of art which did not exist for it lay open to me. I was familiar with the greatest in that world: mighty poets, painters, and musicians were my intimates. I found the world of artificial greatness founded on convention and money so repugnant and contemptible by comparison that I had no sympathetic understanding of it. People are fond of blaming valets because no man is a hero to his valet. But it is equally true that no man is a valet to his hero; and the hero, consequently, is apt to blunder very ludicrously about valets, through judging them from an irrelevant standard of heroism: heroism, remember, having its faults as well as its qualities. I, always on the heroic plane imaginatively, had two disgusting faults which I did not recognize as faults because I could not help them. I was poor and (by day) shabby. I therefore tolerated the gross error that poverty, though an inconvenience and a trial, is not a sin and a disgrace; and I stood for my self-respect on the things I had: probity, ability, knowledge of art, laboriousness, and whatever else came cheaply to me. Because I could walk into Hampton Court Palace and the National Gallery (on free days) and enjoy Mantegna and Michael Angelo whilst millionaires were yawning miserably over inept gluttonies; because I could suffer more by hearing a movement of Beethoven's Ninth Symphony taken at a wrong tempo than a duchess by losing a diamond necklace, I was indifferent to the repulsive fact that if I had fallen in love with the duchess I did not possess a morning suit in which I could reasonably have expected her to touch me with the furthest protended pair of tongs; and I did not see that to remedy this I should have been prepared to wade through seas of other people's blood. Indeed it is this perception which constitutes an aristocracy nowadays. It is the secret of all our governing classes, which consist finally of people who, though perfectly prepared to be generous, humane, cultured, philanthropic, public spirited and personally charming in the second instance, are unalterably resolved, in the first, to have money enough for a handsome and delicate life, and will, in pursuit of that money, batter in the doors of their fellow-men, sell them up, sweat them in fetid dens, shoot, stab, hang, imprison, sink, burn, and destroy them in the name of law and order. And this shows their fundamental sanity and rightmindedness; for a sufficient income is indispensable to the practice of virtue; and the man who will let any unselfish consideration stand between him and its attainment is a weakling, a dupe, and a predestined slave. If I could convince our impecunious mobs of this, the world would be reformed before the end of the week; for the sluggards who are content to be wealthy without working and the dastards who are content to work without being wealthy, together with all the pseudo-moralists and ethicists and cowardice mongers generally, would be exterminated without shrift, to the unutterable enlargement of life and ennoblement of humanity. We might even make some beginnings of civilization under such happy circumstances.

In the days of The Irrational Knot I had not learnt this lesson; consequently I did not understand the British peerage, just as I did not understand that glorious and beautiful phenomenon, the "heartless" rich American woman, who so thoroughly and admirably understands that conscience is a luxury, and should be indulged in only when the vital needs of life have been abundantly satisfied. The instinct which has led the British peerage to fortify itself by American alliances is healthy and well inspired. Thanks to it, we shall still have a few people to maintain the tradition of a handsome, free, proud, costly life, whilst the craven mass of us are keeping up our starveling pretence that it is more important to be good than to be rich, and piously cheating, robbing, and murdering one another by doing our duty as policemen, soldiers, bailiffs, jurymen, turnkeys, hangmen, tradesmen, and curates, at the command of those who know that the golden grapes are *not* sour. Why, good heavens! we shall all pretend that this straightforward truth of mine is mere Swiftian satire, because it would require a little courage to take it seriously and either act on it or make me drink the hemlock for uttering it.

There was the less excuse for my blindness because I was at that very moment laying the foundations of my high fortune by the most ruthless disregard of all the quack duties which lead the peasant lad of fiction to the White House, and harness the real peasant boy to the plough until he is finally swept, as rubbish, into the workhouse. I was an ablebodied and ableminded young man in the strength of my youth; and my family, then heavily embarrassed, needed my help urgently. That I should have chosen to be a burden to them instead was, according to all the conventions of peasant lad fiction, monstrous. Well, without a blush I embraced the monstrosity. I did not throw myself into the struggle for life: I threw my mother into it. I was not a staff to my father's old age: I hung on to his coat tails. His reward was to live just long enough to read a review of one of these silly novels written in an obscure journal by a personal friend of my own (now eminent in literature as Mr John Mackinnon Robertson) prefiguring me to some extent as a considerable author. I

think, myself, that this was a handsome reward, far better worth having than a nice pension from a dutiful son struggling slavishly for his parent's bread in some sordid trade. Handsome or not, it was the only return he ever had for the little pension he contrived to export from Ireland for his family. My mother reinforced it by drudging in her elder years at the art of music which she had followed in her prime freely for love. I only helped to spend it. People wondered at my heartlessness: one young and romantic lady had the courage to remonstrate openly and indignantly with me, "for the which," as Pepys said of the shipwright's wife who refused his advances, "I did respect her." Callous as Comus to moral babble, I steadily wrote my five pages a day and made a man of myself (at my mother's expense) instead of a slave. And I protest that I will not suffer James Huneker or any romanticist to pass me off as a peasant boy qualifying for a chapter in Smiles's Self Help, or a good son supporting a helpless mother, instead of a stupendously selfish artist leaning with the full weight of his hungry body on an energetic and capable woman. No, James: such lies are not only unnecessary, but fearfully depressing and fundamentally immoral, besides being hardly fair to the supposed peasant lad's parents. My mother worked for my living instead of preaching that it was my duty to work for hers: therefore take off your hat to her, and blush.

It is now open to any one who pleases to read The Irrational Knot. I do not recommend him to; but it is possible that the same mysterious force which drove me through the labor of writing it may have had some purpose which will sustain others through the labor of reading it, and even reward them with some ghastly enjoyment of it. For my own part I cannot stand it. It is to me only one of the heaps of spoiled material that all apprenticeship involves. I consent to its publication because I remember that British colonel who called on Beethoven when the elderly composer was working at his posthumous quartets, and offered him a commission for a work in the style of his jejune septet. Beethoven drove the Colonel out of the house with objurgation. I think that was uncivil. There is a time for the septet, and a time for the posthumous quartets. It is true that if a man called on me now and asked me to write something like The Irrational Knot I should have to exercise great self-control. But there are people who read Man and Superman, and then tell me (actually to my face) that I have never done anything so good as Cashel Byron's Profession. After this, there may be a public for even The Irrational Knot; so let it go.

LONDON, *May* 26, 1905.

P.S.—Since writing the above I have looked through the proof-sheets of this book, and found, with some access of respect for my youth, that it is a fiction of the first order. By this I do not mean that it is a masterpiece in that order, or even a pleasant example of it, but simply that, such as it is, it is one of those fictions in which the morality is original and not ready-made. Now this quality is the true diagnostic of the first order in literature, and indeed in all the arts, including the art of life. It is, for example, the distinction that sets Shakespear's Hamlet above his other plays, and that sets Ibsen's work as a whole above Shakespear's work as a whole. Shakespear's morality is a mere reach-me-down; and because Hamlet does not feel comfortable in it and struggles against the misfit, he suggests something better, futile as his struggle is, and incompetent as Shakespear shews himself in his effort to think out the revolt of his feeling against ready-made morality.

Ibsen's morality is original all through: he knows well that the men in the street have no use for principles, because they can neither understand nor apply them; and that what they can understand and apply are arbitrary rules of conduct, often frightfully destructive and inhuman, but at least definite rules enabling the common stupid man to know where he stands and what he may do and not do without getting into trouble. Now to all writers of the first order, these rules, and the need for them produced by the moral and intellectual incompetence of the ordinary human animal, are no more invariably beneficial and respectable than the sunlight which ripens the wheat in Sussex and leaves the desert deadly in Sahara, making the cheeks of the ploughman's child rosy in the morning and striking the ploughman brain-sick or dead in the afternoon; no more inspired (and no less) than the religion of the Andaman islanders; as much in need of frequent throwing away and replacement as the community's boots. By writers of the second order the readymade morality is accepted as the basis of all moral judgment and criticism of the characters they portray, even when their genius forces them to represent their most attractive heroes and heroines as violating the readymade code in all directions. Far be it from me to pretend that the first order is more readable than the second! Shakespear, Scott, Dickens, Dumas *père* are not, to say the least, less readable than Euripides and Ibsen. Nor is the first order always more constructive; for Byron, Oscar Wilde, and Larochefoucauld did not get further in positive philosophy than Ruskin and Carlyle, though they could snuff Ruskin's Seven Lamps with their fingers without flinching. Still, the first order remains the first order and the second the second for all that: no man who shuts his eyes and opens his mouth when religion and morality are offered to him on a long spoon can share the same Parnassian bench with those who make an original contribution to religion and morality, were it only a criticism.

Therefore on coming back to this Irrational Knot as a stranger after twenty-five years, I am proud to find that its morality is not ready-made. The drunken prima donna of a bygone type of musical burlesque is not depicted as an immoral person, but as a person with a morality of her own, no worse in its way than the morality of her highly respectable wine merchant in *its* way. The sociology of the successful inventor is his own sociology too; and it is by his originality in this respect that he passes irresistibly through all the readymade prejudices that are set up to bar his promotion. And the heroine, nice, amiable, benevolent, and anxious to please and behave well, but hopelessly secondhand in her morals and nicenesses, and consequently without any real moral force now that the threat of hell has lost its terrors for her, is left destitute among the failures which are so puzzling to thoughtless people. "I cannot understand why she is so unlucky: she is such a nice woman!": that is the formula. As if people with any force in them ever were altogether nice!

And so I claim the first order for this jejune exploit of mine, and invite you to note that the final chapter, so remote from Scott and Dickens and so close to Ibsen, was written years before Ibsen came to my knowledge, thus proving that the revolt of the Life Force against ready-made morality in the nineteenth century was not the work of a Norwegian microbe, but would have worked itself into expression in English literature had Norway never existed. In fact, when Miss Lord's translation of A Doll's House ap-

peared in the eighteen-eighties, and so excited some of my Socialist friends that they got up a private reading of it in which I was cast for the part of Krogstad, its novelty as a morally original study of a marriage did not stagger me as it staggered Europe. I had made a morally original study of a marriage myself, and made it, too, without any melodramatic forgeries, spinal diseases, and suicides, though I had to confess to a study of dipsomania. At all events, I chattered and ate caramels in the back drawing-room (our green-room) whilst Eleanor Marx, as Nora, brought Helmer to book at the other side of the folding doors. Indeed I concerned myself very little about Ibsen until, later on, William Archer translated Peer Gynt to me *viva voce*, when the magic of the great poet opened my eyes in a flash to the importance of the social philosopher.

I seriously suggest that The Irrational Knot may be regarded as an early attempt on the part of the Life Force to write A Doll's House in English by the instrumentality of a very immature writer aged 24. And though I say it that should not, the choice was not such a bad shot for a stupid instinctive force that has to work and become conscious of itself by means of human brains. If we could only realize that though the Life Force supplies us with its own purpose it has no other brains to work with than those it has painfully and imperfectly evolved in our heads, the peoples of the earth would learn some pity for their gods; and we should have a religion that would not be contradicted at every turn by the Thing-That-Is giving the lie to the Thing-That-Ought-To-Be.

WELYWN, *Sunday, June 25, 1905.*

XXV

CASHEL BYRON'S PROFESSION

NOVELS OF MY NONAGE

I never think of Cashel Byron's Profession without a shudder at the narrowness of my escape from becoming a successful novelist at the age of twenty-six. At that moment an adventurous publisher might have ruined me. Fortunately for me, there were no adventurous publishers at that time; and I was forced to fight my way, instead of being ingloriously bought off at the first brush. Not that Cashel Byron's Profession was my very first novel. It was my fourth, and was followed by yet another. I recall these five remote products of my nonage as five heavy brown paper parcels which were always coming back to me from some publisher, and raising the very serious financial question of the sixpence to be paid to Messrs Carter, Paterson, and Co., the carriers, for passing them on to the next publisher. Eventually, Carter, Paterson, and Co. were the only gainers; for the publishers had to pay their readers' fees for nothing but a warning not to publish me; and I had to pay the sixpences for sending my parcels on a bootless errand. At last I grew out of novel-writing, and set to work to find out what the world was really like. The result of my investigations, so far, entirely confirms the observation of Goethe as to the amazement, the incredulity, the moral shock with which the poet discovers that what he supposed to be the real world does not exist, and that men and women are made by their own fancies in the image of the imaginary creatures in his youthful fictions, only much stupider.

Unfortunately for the immature poet, he has not in his nonage the satisfaction of knowing that his guesses at life are true. Bring a peasant into a drawing-room, and though his good sense may lead him to behave very properly, yet he will suffer torments of misgiving that everything he does must be a solecism. In my earlier excursions into literature I confess I felt like the peasant in the drawing room. I was, on the whole, glad to get out of it. Looking back now with the eyes of experience, I find that I certainly did make blunders in matters outside the scope of poetic divination. To take a very mild example, I endowed the opulent heroine of this very book with a park of thirty acres in extent, being then fully persuaded that this was a reasonable estimate of the size of the Isle of Wight or thereabouts. But it is not by the solecisms of ignorance that the young man makes himself most ridiculous. Far more unnatural than these were my proprieties and accuracies and intelligences. I did not know my England then. I was young, raw from eighteenth century Ireland, modest, and anxious lest my poverty and provinciality should prevent me from correctly representing the intelligence, refinement, conscience, and good breeding which I supposed to be as natural and common in English society as in Scott's novels. I actually thought that educated people conscientiously learnt their manners and studied their opinions—were really educated, in short —instead of merely picking up the habits and prejudices of their set, and confidently presenting the resultant absurd equipment of class solecisms to the world as a perfect gentility. Consequently the only characters which were natural in my novels were the comic characters, because the island was (and is) populated exclusively by comic characters. Take them seriously in fiction, and the result is the

Dickens heroine or the Sarah Grand hero: pathetically unattractive figments both of them. Thus my imaginary persons of quality became quite unlike any actual persons at large in England, being superior to them in a priggish manner which would nowadays rouse the humor of our younger publishers' readers very inopportunely. In 1882, however, the literary fashion which distinguished the virtuous and serious characters in a novel by a decorous stylishness and scrupulousness of composition, as if all their speeches had been corrected by their governesses and schoolmasters, had not yet been exploded by the "New Journalism" of 1888 and the advent of a host of authors who had apparently never read anything, catering for a proletariat newly made literate by the Education Act. The distinction between the naturalness of Caleb Balderstone and the artificiality of Edgar and Lucy was still regarded as one of the social decencies by the seniors of literature; and this probably explains the fact that the only intimations I received that my work had made some impression, and had even been hesitatingly condemned, were from the older and more august houses whose readers were all grave elderly lovers of literature. And the more I progressed towards my own individual style and ventured upon the freer expression of my own ideas, the more I disappointed them. As to the regular novel-publishing houses, whose readers were merely on the scent of popularity, they gave me no quarter at all. And so between the old stool of my literary conscientiousness and the new stool of a view of life that did not reach publishing-point in England until about ten years later, when Ibsen drove it in, my novels fell to the ground.

I was to find later on that a book is like a child: it is easier to bring it into the world than to control it when it is launched there. As long as I kept sending my novels to the publishers, they were as safe from publicity as they would have been in the fire, where I had better, perhaps, have put them. But when I flung them aside as failures they almost instantly began to shew signs of life.

The Socialist revival of the eighties, into which I had plunged, produced the usual crop of propagandist magazines, in the conduct of which payment of the printer was the main problem, payment of contributors being quite out of the question. The editor of such a magazine can never count on a full supply of live matter to make up his tale of pages. But if he can collect a stock of unreadable novels, the refuse of the publishing trade, and a stock of minor poems (the world is full of such trash), an instalment of serial novel and a few verses will always make up the magazine to any required size. And this was how I found a use at last for my brown paper parcels. It seemed a matter of no more consequence than stuffing so many broken window-panes with them; but it had momentous consequences; for in this way four of the five got printed and published in London, and thus incidentally became the common property of the citizens of the United States of America. These pioneers did not at first appreciate their new acquisition; and nothing particular happened except that the first novel (No. 5; for I ladled them out to the Socialist magazine editors in inverse order of composition) made me acquainted with William Morris, who, to my surprise, had been reading the monthly instalments with a certain relish. But that only proved how much easier it is to please a great man than a little one, especially when you share his politics. No. 5, called An Unsocial Socialist, was followed by No. 4, Cashel Byron's Profession; and Cashel Byron would not lie quiet in his serial grave, but presently rose and walked as a book.

It happened in this way. The name of the magazine was To-Day, not the present paper of that name, but one of the many To-days which are now Yester-days. It had several editors, among them Mr Belfort Bax and the late James Leigh Joynes; but all the editors were in part-nership with Mr Henry Hyde Champion, who printed the magazine, and conse-quently went on for ever, whilst the others came and went. It was a fantastic busi-ness, Joynes having thrown up an Eton mastership, and Champion a commission in the army, at the call of Socialism. But Champion's pugnacity survived his abdi-cated adjutancy: he had an unregenerate taste for pugilism, and liked Cashel Byron so much that he stereotyped the pages of To-Day which it occupied, and in spite of my friendly remonstrances, hurled on the market a misshapen shilling edition. My friend Mr William Archer reviewed it prominently; the Saturday Review, al-ways susceptible in those days to the arts of self-defence, unexpectedly declared it the novel of the age; Mr W. E. Henley wanted to have it dramatized; Stevenson wrote a letter about it, of which more presently; the other papers hastily searched their waste-paper baskets for it and re-viewed it, mostly rather disappointedly; and the public preserved its composure and did not seem to care.

That shilling edition began with a thou-sand copies; but it proved immortal. I never got anything out of it; and Mr Champion never got anything out of it; for he presently settled in Australia, and his printing presses and stereo plates were dispersed. But from that time forth the book was never really out of print; and though Messrs Walter Scott soon placed a revised shilling edition on the market, I suspect that still, in some obscure print-ing office, those old plates of Mr Cham-pion's from time to time produce a "re-mainder" of the original Modern Press edition, which is to the present what the Quarto Hamlet is to the Folio.

On the passing of To-Day, I became novelist in ordinary to a magazine called Our Corner, edited by Mrs Annie Besant. It had the singular habit of paying for its contributions, and was, I am afraid, to some extent a device of Mrs Besant's for relieving necessitous young propagand-ists without wounding their pride by open almsgiving. She was an incorrigible benefactress, and probably revenged her-self for my freely expressed scorn for this weakness by drawing on her private ac-count to pay me for my jejune novels. At last Our Corner went the way of all propagandist magazines, completing a second nonage novel and its own career at the same moment. This left me with only one unprinted masterpiece, my Opus 1, which had cost me an unconscionable quantity of paper, and was called, with merciless fitness, Immaturity. Part of it had by this time been devoured by mice, though even they had not been able to finish it. To this day it has never escaped from its old brown paper travelling suit; and I only mention it because some of its characters appear, Trollope fashion, in the later novels. I do not think any of them got so far as Cashel Byron's Pro-fession; but the Mrs Hoskyn and her guests who appear in that absurd Chapter VI are all borrowed from previous works.

The unimportance of these particulars must be my apology for detailing them to a world that finds something romantic in what are called literary struggles. How-ever, I must most indignantly deny that I ever struggled. I wrote the books: it was the publishers who struggled with them, and struggled in vain. The public now takes up the struggle, impelled, not by any fresh operations of mine, but by Literary Destiny. For there is a third act to my tragedy.

Not long ago, when the memory of the brown paper parcels of 1879–1883 had been buried under twenty years of work, I learnt from the American papers that the list of book sales in one of the

United States was headed by a certain novel called An Unsocial Socialist, by Bernard Shaw. This was unmistakeably Opus 5 of the Novels of My Nonage. Columbia was beginning to look after her hitherto neglected acquisition. Apparently the result was encouraging; for presently the same publisher produced a new edition of Cashel Byron's Profession (Opus 4), in criticizing which the more thoughtful reviewers, unaware that the publisher was working backwards through the list, pointed out the marked advance in my style, the surer grip, the clearer form, the finer art, the maturer view of the world, and so forth. As it was clearly unfair that my own American publishers should be debarred by delicacy towards me from exploiting the new field of derelict fiction, I begged them to make the most of their national inheritance; and with my full approval, Opus 3, called Love Among the Artists (a paraphrase of the forgotten line Love Among the Roses) followed. No doubt it will pay its way: people who will read An Unsocial Socialist will read anything. But the new enthusiasm for Cashel Byron did not stop here. American ladies were seized with a desire to go on the stage and be Lydia Carew for two thrilling hours. American actors "saw themselves" as Cashel. Mr James Corbett has actually appeared on the New York stage in the part. There can be no doubt now that my novels, so long left for dead in the forlorn-hope magazines of the eighties, have arisen and begun to propagate themselves vigorously throughout the new world at the rate of a dollar and a half per copy, free of all royalty to the flattered author.

Blame not me, then, reader, if these exercises of a raw apprentice break loose again and insist on their right to live. The world never did know chalk from cheese in matters of art; and, after all, since it is only the young and the old who have time to read, the rest being too busy living, my exercises may be fitter for the market than my masterpieces.

Cashel Byron's Profession is not a very venturesome republication, because, as I have said, the story has never been really out of print. But for some years after the expiration of my agreement with Messrs Walter Scott I did my best to suppress it, though by that time it had become the subject of proposals from a new generation of publishers. The truth is, the preference for this particular novel annoyed me. In novel-writing there are two trustworthy dodges for capturing the public. One is to slaughter a child and pathosticate over its deathbed for a whole chapter. The other is to describe either a fight or a murder. There is a fight in Cashel Byron's Profession: that profession itself is fighting; and here lay the whole schoolboy secret of the book's little vogue. I had the old grievance of the author: people will admire him for the feats that any fool can achieve, and bear malice against him for boring them with better work. Besides, my conscience was not quite easy in the matter. In spite of all my pains to present the prizefighter and his pursuits without any romantic glamor (for indeed the true artistic material of the story is the comedy of the contrast between the realities of the ring and the common romantic glorification or sentimental abhorrence of it), yet our noncombatant citizens are so fond of setting other people to fight that the only effect of such descriptions as I have incidentally given of Cashel's professional performances is to make people want to see something of the sort and take steps accordingly. This tendency of the book was repugnant to me; and if prizefighting were a sleeping dog, I should certainly let it lie, in spite of the American editions.

Unfortunately the dog is awake, barking and biting vigorously. Twenty years ago prizefighting was supposed to be dead. Few living men remembered the palmy days when Tom and Jerry went to Jackson's rooms (where Byron—not Cashel, but the poet—studied "the noble art") to complete their education as Corinthians; when Cribb fought Molyneux and was to Tom Spring what Skene was to Cashel Byron; when Kemble engaged Dutch Sam to carry on the war with the O.P. rioters; when Sharples' portraits of leading bruisers were engraved on steel; when Bell's Life was a fashionable paper, and Pierce Egan's Boxiana a more expensive publishing enterprise than any modern Badminton volume. The sport was supposed to have died of its own blackguardism by the second quarter of the century; but the connoisseur who approaches the subject without moral bias will, I think, agree with me that it must have lived by its blackguardism and died of its intolerable tediousness; for all prizefighters are not Cashel Byrons, and in barren dreariness and futility no spectacle on earth can contend with that of two exhausted men trying for hours to tire one another out at fisticuffs for the sake of their backers. The Sayers revival in the sixties only left the ring more discredited than ever, since the injuries formerly reserved for the combatants began, after their culmination in the poisoning of Heenan, to be showered on the referee; and as the referee was usually the representative of the Bell's Life type of paper, which naturally organized the prizefights it lived by reporting, the ring went under again, this time undoubtedly through its blackguardism and violence driving away its only capable organizers.

In the eighties many apparently lost causes and dead enthusiasms unexpectedly revived: Imperialism, Patriotism, Religion, Socialism, and many other things, including prizefighting in an aggravated form, and on a scale of commercial profit and publicity which soon made its palmy days insignificant and ridiculous by contrast. A modern American pugilist makes more by a single defeat than Cribb made by all his victories. It is this fact that has decided me to give up my attempt to suppress Cashel Byron's Profession. Silence may be the right policy on a dropped subject; but on a burning one every word that can cool the fervor of idolatry with a dash of cold fact has its value.

I need not postpone a comment on the vast propaganda of pugnacity in modern fiction: a propaganda that must be met, not by shocked silence, but by counter-propaganda. And this counter-propaganda must not take the usual form of "painting the horrors." Horror is fascinating: the great criminal is always a popular hero. People are seduced by romance because they are ignorant of reality; and this is as true of the prize ring as of the battlefield. The intelligent prizefighter is not a knight-errant: he is a disillusioned man of business trying to make money at a certain weight and at certain risks, not of bodily injury (for a bruise is soon cured), but of pecuniary loss. When he is a Jew, a negro, a gypsy, or a recruit from that gypsified, nomadic, poaching, tinkering, tramping class which exists in all countries, he differs from the phlegmatic John Bull pugilist (an almost extinct species) exactly as he would differ from him in any other occupation: that is, he is a more imaginative liar, a more obvious poser, a more plausible talker, a vainer actor, a more reckless gambler, and more easily persuaded that he is beaten or even killed when he has only received an unusually hard punch. The unintelligent prizefighter is often the helpless tool of a gang of gamblers, backers, and showmen, who set him on to fight as they might set on a dog. And the spectacle of a poor human animal fighting faithfully for his backers, like a terrier killing rats, or a racehorse doing its best to win a race for its owner, is one which ought to persuade any sensible person of the folly of treating the actual combatants as "the principals" in a prizefight. Cockfighting was not suppressed by imprisoning the cocks; and prizefighting will not be suppressed by imprisoning the pugilists. But, intelligent or unintelligent, first rate like Cashel Byron, second rate like Skene, or third rate like William Paradise in this story, the prizefighter is no more what the spectators imagine him to be than the lady with the wand and star in the pantomime is really a fairy queen. And since Cashel Byron's Profession, on its prizefighting side, is an attempt to take the reader behind the scenes without unfairly confusing professional pugilism with the blackguardly environment which is no more essential to it than to professional cricket, and which is now losing its hold on the pugilist through the substitution of gate-money at boxing exhibitions for stakes at prizefights as his means of living, I think I may let it go its way with a reasonable prospect of seeing it do more good than harm.

It may even help in the Herculean task of eliminating romantic fisticuffs from English novels, and so clear them from the reproach of childishness and crudity which they certainly deserve in this respect. Even in the best nineteenth century novels the heroes knock the villains down. Bulwer Lytton's Kenelm Chillingly was a "scientific" pugilist, though his technique will hardly be recognized by experts. Thackeray, who, when defeated in a parliamentary election, publicly compared himself to Gregson beaten by Gully, loved a fight almost as much as he loved a fool. Even the great Dickens himself never quite got away from this sort of schoolboyishness; for though Jo Gargery knocking down Orlick is much more plausible than Oliver Twist punching the head of Noah Claypole, still the principle is the same: virtue still insists on victory, domination, and triumphant assault and battery. It is true that Dombey and Son contains a pious attempt to caricature a

prizefighter; but no qualified authority will pretend that Dickens caught The Chicken's point of view, or did justice to the social accomplishments of the ring. Mr Toots's silly admiration of the poor boxer, and the manner in which the Chicken and other professors of the art of self-defence used to sponge on him, is perfectly true to life; but in the real pugilistic world so profitable a gull would soon have been taken out of the hands of the Chicken and preyed upon by much better company. It is true that if the Chicken had been an unconquerable fighter, he might have maintained a gloomy eminence in spite of his dulness and disagreeable manners; but Dickens gave away this one possible excuse by allowing The Larky Boy to defeat the Chicken with ignominy. That is what is called poetic justice. It is really poetic criminal law; and it is almost as dishonest and vindictive as real criminal law. In plain fact the pugilistic profession is like any other profession: common sense, good manners, and a social turn count for as much in it as they do elsewhere: and as the pugilist makes a good deal of money by teaching gentlemen to box, he has to learn to behave himself, and often succeeds very much better than the average middle-class professional man. Shakespear was much nearer the mark when he made Autolycus better company, and Charles the Wrestler a better-mannered man, than Ajax or Cloten. If Dickens had really known the ring, he would have made the Chicken either a Sayers in professional ability or a Sam Weller in sociability. A successful combination of personal repulsiveness with professional incompetence is as impossible there as at the bar or in the faculty. The episode of the Chicken, then, must be dismissed, in spite of its hero's tempting suggested remedy for Mr Dombey's stiffness, as a futile atonement for the heroic fisticuffs of Oliver Twist and Co.

There is an abominable vein of retaliatory violence all through the literature of the nineteenth century. Whether it is Macaulay describing the flogging of Titus Oates, or Dickens inventing the scene in which old Martin Chuzzlewit bludgeons Pecksniff, the curious childishness of the English character, its naughty relish for primitive brutalities and tolerance of physical indignities, its unreasoning destructiveness when incommoded, crop up in all directions. The childishness has its advantages: its want of foresight prevents the individual from carrying weapons, as it prevents the nation from being prepared for war; its forgetfulness prevents vendettas and prolonged malice-bearing; its simplicity and transparency save it from the more ingenious and complicated forms of political corruption. In short, it has those innocences of childhood which are a necessary result of its impotences. But it has no true sense of human dignity. The son of a Russian noble is not flogged at school, because he commits suicide sooner than survive the outrage to his self-respect. The son of an English noble has no more sense of dignity than the master who flogs him: flogging may be troublesome to the flogger and painful to the floggee; but the notion that the transaction is disgusting to the public and dishonorable and disgraceful to the parties is as unintelligible and fantastic in England as it is in a nursery anywhere. The moment the Englishman gets away from Eton, he begins to enjoy and boast of flogging as an institution. A school where boys are flogged and where they settle their quarrels by fighting with their fists he calls, not, as one might expect, a school of childishness, but a school of manliness. And he gradually persuades himself that all Englishmen can use their fists, which is about as true as the parallel theory that every Frenchman can handle a foil and that every Italian carries a stiletto. And so, though he himself has never fought a pitched battle at school, and does not, pugilistically speaking, know his right hand from his left; though his neighbors are as peaceful and as nervous as he; though if he knocked a man down or saw one of his friends do it, the event would stand out in his history like a fire or a murder; yet he not only tolerates unstinted knockings-down in fiction, but actually founds his conception of his nation and its destiny on these imaginary outrages, and at last comes to regard a plain statement of the plain fact that the average respectable Englishman knows rather less about fighting than he does about flying, as a paradoxical extravagance.

And so every popular English novel becomes a gospel of pugilism. Cashel Byron's Profession, then, is like any other novel in respect of its hero punching people's heads. Its novelty consists in the fact that an attempt is made to treat the art of punching seriously, and to detach it from the general elevation of moral character with which the ordinary novelist persists in associating it.

Here, therefore, the prizefighter is not idolized. I have given Cashel Byron every advantage a prizefighter can have: health and strength and pugilistic genius. But by pugilistic genius I mean nothing vague, imaginary, or glamorous. In all walks of life men are to be found who seem to have powers of divination. For example, you propound a complicated arithmetical problem: say the cubing of a number containing four digits. Give me a slate and half an hour's time, and I can produce a wrong answer. But there are men to whom the right answer is instantly obvious without any consciousness of calculation on their part. Ask such a man to write a description or put a somewhat complicated thought into words; and he will take my slate and blunder over it in search of words for half an hour, finally putting down the wrong ones; whilst for a Shakespear the words are there in due style and measure as soon as the consciousness of the thing to be described or the formation of the thought. Now there are pugilists to whom the process of aiming and estimating distance in hitting, of considering the evidence as to what their opponent is going to do, arriving at a conclusion, and devizing and carrying out effective counter-measures, is as instantaneous and unconscious as the calculation of the born arithmetician or the verbal expression of the born writer. This is not more wonderful than the very complicated and deeply considered feats of breathing and circulating the blood, which everybody does continually without thinking; but it is much rarer, and so has a miraculous appearance. A man with this gift, and with no physical infirmities to disable him, is a born prizefighter. He need have no other exceptional qualities, courage least of all: indeed there are instances on record of prizefighters who have only consented to persevere with a winning fight when a mirror has been brought to convince them that their faces were undamaged and their injuries and terrors imaginary. "Stage fright" is as common in the ring as elsewhere: I have myself seen a painful exhibition of it from a very rough customer who presently knocked out his opponent without effort, by instinct. The risks of the ring are limited by rules and conditions to such an extent that the experienced prizefighter is much more afraid of the blackguardism of the spectators than of his opponent: he takes care to have a strong body of supporters in his corner, and to keep carefully away from the opposite corner. Courage is if anything rather scarcer, because less needed, in the ring than out of it; and there are civil occupations which many successful prizefighters would fail in, or fear to enter, for want of nerve. For the ring, like all romantic institutions, has a natural attraction for hysterical people.

When a pugilistic genius of the Cashel Byron type appeared in the ring of his day, it soon became evident to the betting men on whom the institution depended, that it was useless to back clever boxers against him; for, as the second Lytton (Owen Meredith) wrote—

Talk not of genius baffled: genius is master of man.
Genius does what it must; and Talent does what it can.

But there is a well-known way of defeating the pugilistic genius. There are hard-fisted, hard-hitting men in the world, who will, with the callousness of a ship's figurehead, and almost with its helplessness in defence, take all the hammering that genius can give them, and, when genius can hammer no more from mere exhaustion, give it back its blows with interest and vanquish it. All pugilism lies between these two extremes typified by Cashel Byron and William Paradise; and it is because the Paradises are as likely to win as the Byrons, and are by no means so scarce, that the case for fist fighting, with gloves or without, as a discipline in the higher athletic qualities, moral and physical, imposes only on people who have no practical knowledge of the subject.

On a previous page I have alluded to a letter from Robert Louis Stevenson to Mr William Archer about Cashel Byron's Profession. Part of that letter has been given to the public in the second volume of Mr Sidney Colvin's edition of Stevenson's letters (Methuen, 1900). But no document concerning a living person of any consequence (by which I mean a person with money enough to take an action for libel) is ever published in England unless its contents are wholly complimentary. Stevenson's letters were probably all unfit for publication in this respect. Certainly the one about Cashel Byron's Profession was; and Mr Sidney Colvin, out of consideration for me and for his publishers and printers, politely abbreviated it. Fortunately the original letter is still in the hands of Mr Archer. I need not quote the handsome things which Mr Colvin selected, as they have been extensively reprinted in America to help the sale of the reprints there. But here is the suppressed portion, to which I leave the last word, having no more to say than that the book is now reprinted, not from the old Modern Press edition which Stevenson read, but from the revised text issued afterwards by Messrs Walter Scott, from which certain "little bits of Socialism daubed in" for the edification of the readers of To-Day were either painted out or better harmonized with the rest. I had intended to make no further revision; and I have in fact made none of any importance; but in reading the proofs my pen positively jumped to humanize a few passages in which the literary professionalism with which my heroine expresses herself (this professionalism is usually called "style" in England) went past all bearing. I have also indulged myself by varying a few sentences, and inserting one or two new ones, so as to enable the American publisher to secure copyright in this edition. But I have made no attempt to turn an 1882 novel into a twentieth century one; and the few alterations are, except for legal purposes, quite negligible.

And now for the suppressed part of Stevenson's verdict, which is in the form of an analysis of the book's composition.

"Charles Reade . . 1 part
Henry James or some kindred author, badly assimilated . . 1 part
Disraeli (perhaps unconscious) . . . $\frac{1}{2}$ part
Struggling, overlaid original talent . . $1\frac{1}{2}$ part
Blooming gaseous folly . 1 part

"That is the equation as it stands. What it may become, I dont know, nor any other man. *Vixere fortes*—O, let him remember that—let him beware of his damned century: his gifts of insane chivalry and animated narration are just those that might be slain and thrown out like an untimely birth by the Dæmon of the Epoch.

"And if he only knew how I had enjoyed the chivalry! Bashville — O Bashville! *j'en chortle!* (which is finely polygot)."

1901.

POSTSCRIPT TWENTYNINE YEARS LATER. Pages viii and ix[1] of this preface must be read with some reservations. Belfort Bax, Henry Hyde Champion, William Archer, and W. E. Henley are no longer Misters: they are all dead. And the novel that "never escaped from its brown travelling suit" has at last escaped, to be published for the first time in the Collected Edition of my works fifty years after I wrote Finis on its last page.

1930.

[1] Page 660 of this volume.

XXVI

WIDOWERS' HOUSES

1893

THE AUTHOR'S PREFACE

The early history of the play which forms this first volume of the "Independent Theatre Series" has been given by Mr William Archer in The World of the 14th December 1892, in the following terms:—

"Partly to facilitate the labours of Mr George Bernard Shaw's biographers, and partly by way of relieving my own conscience, I think I ought to give a short history of the genesis of Widowers' Houses. Far away back in the olden days [1885], while as yet the Independent Theatre slumbered in the womb of Time, together with the New Drama, the New Criticism, the New Humour, and all the other glories of our renovated world, I used to be a daily frequenter of the British Museum Reading Room. Even more assiduous in his attendance was a young man of tawny complexion and attire, beside whom I used frequently to find myself seated. My curiosity was piqued by the odd conjunction of his subjects of research. Day after day for weeks he had before him two books, which he studied alternately, if not simultaneously—Karl Marx's Das Kapital (in French), and an orchestral score of Tristan und Isolde. I did not know then how exactly this quaint juxtaposition symbolised the main interests of his life. Presently I met him at the house of a common acquaintance, and we conversed for the first time. I learned from himself that he was the author of several unpublished masterpieces of fiction. Construction, he owned with engaging modesty, was not his strong point, but his dialogue was incomparable. Now, in those days,

I had still a certain hankering after the rewards, if not the glories, of the playwright. With a modesty in no way inferior to Mr Shaw's, I had realised that I could not write dialogue a bit; but I still considered myself a born constructor. So I proposed, and Mr Shaw agreed to, a collaboration. I was to provide him with one of the numerous plots I kept in stock, and he was to write the dialogue. So said, so done. I drew out, scene by scene, the scheme of a twaddling cup-and-saucer comedy vaguely suggested by Augier's Ceinture Dorée. The details I forget, but I know it was to be called Rhinegold, was to open, as Widowers' Houses actually does, in a hotel-garden on the Rhine, and was to have two heroines, a sentimental and a comic one, according to the accepted Robertson-Byron-Carton formula. I fancy the hero was to propose to the sentimental heroine, believing her to be the poor niece instead of the rich daughter of the sweater, or slum-landlord, or whatever he may have been; and I know he was to carry on in the most heroic fashion, and was ultimately to succeed in throwing the tainted treasure of his father-in-law, metaphorically speaking, into the Rhine. All this I gravely propounded to Mr Shaw, who listened with no less admirable gravity. Then I thought the matter had dropped, for I heard no more of it for many weeks. I used to see Mr Shaw at the Museum, laboriously writing page after page of the most exquisitely neat shorthand at the rate of about three words a minute; but it did not occur to me that this was our play. After about six weeks he said to me, 'Look here, I've written half the first act of that comedy, and I've used up all your plot. Now I want some more to go on with.' I told him that my plot was a rounded and perfect organic whole, and that I could no more eke it out in this fashion than I could provide him or myself with a set of supplementary arms and legs. I begged him to extend his shorthand and let me see what he had done; but this would have taken him far too long. He tried to decipher some of it orally, but the process was too lingering and painful for endurance. So he simply gave me an outline in narrative of what he had done; and I saw that, so far from having used up my plot, he had not even touched it. There the matter rested for months and years. Mr Shaw would now and then hold out vague threats of finishing 'our play,' but I felt no serious alarm. I thought (judging from my own experience in other cases) that when he came to read over in cold blood what he had written, he would see what impossible stuff it was. Perhaps my free utterance of this view piqued him; perhaps he felt impelled to remove from the Independent Theatre the reproach of dealing solely in foreign products. The fire of his genius, at all events, was not to be quenched by my persistent applications of the wet-blanket. He finished his play; Mr Grein, as in duty bound, accepted it; and the result was the performance of Friday last [9th Dec. 1892] at the Independent Theatre."

To this history I have little to add. The circumstances occurred, in the main, as Mr Archer states them. But I most strenuously deny that there is any such great difference between his Rhinegold and Widowers' Houses as he supposes. I appeal to the impartial public, which has now both my play and Mr Archer's story before it, to judge whether I did not deal faithfully with him. The Rhine hotel garden, the hero proposing to the heroine in ignorance of the source of her father's wealth, the "tainted treasure of the father-in-law," the renunciation of it by the lover: all these will be found as promi-

nently in the pages of the play as in Mr Archer's description of the fable which he persists in saying I did "not even touch." As a matter of fact the dissolution of partnership between us came when I told him that I had finished up the renunciation and wanted some more story to go on with, as I was only in the middle of the second act. He said that according to his calculation the renunciation ought to have landed me at the end of the play. I could only reply that his calculation did not work out, and that he must supply further material. This he most unreasonably refused to do; and I had eventually to fish up the tainted treasure out of the Rhine, so to speak, and make it last out another act and a half, which I had to invent all by myself. Clearly, then, he was the defaulter; and I am the victim.

It will have been noted by the attentive reader that what I have called a story, Mr Archer calls a plot; and that he mentions two heroines, introduced for the sole purpose of being mistaken for one another. Now, I confess to discarding the second daughter. She was admittedly a mere joist in the plot; and I had then, have now, and have always had, an utter contempt for "constructed" works of art. How any man in his senses can deliberately take as his model the sterile artifice of Wilkie Collins or Scribe, and repudiate the natural artistic activity of Fielding, Goldsmith, Defoe and Dickens, not to mention Æschylus and Shakespear, is beyond argument with me: those who entertain such preferences are obviously incapable people, who prefer a "well made play" to King Lear exactly as they prefer acrostics to sonnets. As a fictionist, my natural way is to imagine characters and spin out a story about them, whether I am writing a novel or a play; and I please myself by reflecting that this has been the way of all great masters of fiction. At the same time I am quite aware that a writer with the necessary constructive ingenuity, and the itch for exercising it for its own sake, can entertain audiences or readers very agreeably by carefully constructing and unravelling mysteries and misunderstandings; and that this ingenuity may be associated with sufficient creative imagination to give a considerable show of humanity and some interest of character to the puppets contrived for the purpose of furthering the plot. The line between the authors who place their imagination at the service of their ingenuity and those who place their ingenuity at the service of their imagination may be hard to draw with precise justice (to Edgar Allan Poe, for instance!); but it is clear that if we draw it as an equator, Scribe and the plot constructors will be at the south pole, and Æschylus and the dramatic poets at the north. Now, Archer's Rhinegold, in the absence of any convincing evidence that I was an Æschylus, was designed for the southern hemisphere; and Widowers' Houses was built for the north. I told the story, but discarded the plot; and Archer at once perceived that this step made the enterprise entirely my own, since the resultant play, whether good or bad, must on my method be a *growth* out of the stimulated imagination of the actual writer, and not a manufactured article constructed by an artisan according to plans and specifications supplied by an inventor. The collaboration was therefore dropped; and after finishing the second act, so as to avoid leaving a loose end, and noting such beginnings of the third as had already sprouted, I left the work aside for seven years and thought no more of it. Last August, having been rather overworked by the occurrence of a General Election at the busiest part of the journalistic season in London, I could do nothing for a while but potter aimlessly over my old papers, among which I came across the manuscript of the play; and it so tickled me that I there and then sat down and finished it. But for Mr Grein

and the Independent Theatre Society it would probably have gone back to its drawer and lain there for another seven years, if not for ever.

Some idea of the discussion which followed the performance may be gathered from the appendices which will be found at the end of this preface. The entire novelty on the stage of the standpoint taken, which is impartially Socialistic, greatly confused the critics, especially those who are in the habit of accepting as Socialism that spirit of sympathy with the poor and indignant protest against suffering and injustice which, in modern literature, culminated in Victor Hugo's Les Miserables, and has lately been forced into the theatre by the pressure of the Socialist propaganda outside. This "stage Socialism" is represented in my play by the good-natured compunction of my hero, who conceives the horrors of the slums as merely the result of atrocious individual delinquency on the part of the slum landlord. In spite of the unanswerable way in which the shallowness and impracticability of this view are exposed at once by a single speech from a practical business man, many of my critics were unable to rid themselves of it. They dismissed the man of business as a sophistical villain, and so got hopelessly astray as to the characterization in the piece. My portraiture of Lickcheese, the slum rent collector, an effective but quite common piece of work, pleased better than any of the rest. My technical skill as a playwright sustained many attacks, all based on the assumption that the only admissible stage technique is the technique of plot construction, an assumption which excludes Shakespear and Goethe from the ranks of competent stage workmen, and which therefore appears to me to reduce itself to absurdity, although I am well aware that many of our critics look on Shakespear and Goethe as literary men who were unfortunately disabled from producing good acting plays by their deficiency in the stagecraft of the ordinary farcical comedy writer and melodramatist. It was further objected that my play, being didactic, was therefore not a work of art—a proposition which, if examined, will be found to mean either that the world's acknowledged masterpieces are not works of art, or else exactly nothing at all. Now, I submit that I could not reasonably be expected to defer to the authority of canons of art which no artist acknowledges, and in subjection to which no art would be possible, even if I had not, by my practice in the profession of music critic during the remarkable development effected both in that art and in its criticism by Richard Wagner, been sufficiently trained in critical processes to recognize the objections I have cited as nothing more than the common fallacies and ineptitudes into which all critics fall when first confronted with a progressive movement. I have also practised picture criticism, and have had to make up my mind as to the pre-Raphaelite movement and the Impressionist movement, with the result that I have come to suspect dramatic critics of never having had to make up their minds about anything, owing to the fact that until the advent of Ibsen the other day there had not for many years been anything worth calling a movement in dramatic art. I by no means undervalued their like or dislike of my work, which was written as much to please them as anyone else; but, as an expert, I found their critical analysis anything but skilful, and their power of imposing on themselves by phrase-making, boundless. Even the best of the younger school will occasionally be satisfied that he has quite accounted for an unexpected speech by dismissing it as a wanton paradox (without any consciousness of having insulted the author); or he will dispose of an incident by pointing out that it is "inconsistent"; or, if he wishes to be specially ingenious, he will say of a character

—a red-haired one, for instance—that it is not a human being at all, but a type of the red-haired variety of mankind. I make free to criticize my critics thus because some of them are my personal friends; others have dealt so handsomely by me that I cannot very well except them without a ridiculous appearance of returning the compliment; and the rest will be all the better for being brought to book. Besides, I may offer my Quintessence of Ibsenism, written and published before there was any question of finishing or producing Widowers' Houses, as a substantial proof that my interest in the art of criticism is not at bottom merely the protest of my own sensitiveness against the very disrespectful way in which my work has been handled in various quarters. There must, however, be no mistake as to the ground upon which I challenge criticism for the play, now that I submit it in print to the public. It is a propagandist play— a didactic play—a play with a purpose; but I do not therefore claim any special indulgence for it from people who go to the theatre to be entertained. I offer it as a technically good practicable stage play, one which will, if adequately acted, hold its proper audience and drive its story home to the last word.

But in claiming place for my play among works of art, I must make a melancholy reservation. One or two friendly readers may find it interesting, amusing, even admirable, as far as a mere topical farce can excite admiration; but nobody will find it a beautiful or lovable work. It is saturated with the vulgarity of the life it represents: the people do not speak nobly, live gracefully, or sincerely face their own position: the author is not giving expression in pleasant fancies to the underlying beauty and romance of happy life, but dragging up to the smooth surface of "respectability" a handful of the slime and foulness of its polluted bed, and playing off your laughter at the scandal of the exposure against your shudder at its blackness. I offer it as my own criticism of the author of Widowers' Houses that the disillusion which makes all great dramatic poets tragic has here made him only derisive; and derision is by common consent a baser atmosphere than that of tragedy. I had better have written a beautiful play, like Twelfth Night, or a grand play, like the tragic masterpieces; but, frankly, I was not able to: modern commercialism is a bad art school, and cannot, with all its robberies, murders and prostitutions, move us in the grand manner to pity and terror: it is squalid, futile, blundering, mean, ridiculous, for ever uneasily pretending to be the wide-minded, humane, enterprising thing it is not. It is not my fault, reader, that my art is the expression of my sense of moral and intellectual perversity rather than of my sense of beauty. My life has been passed mostly in big modern towns, where my sense of beauty has been starved whilst my intellect has been gorged with problems like that of the slums in this play, until at last I have come, in a horrible sort of way, to relish them enough to make them the subjects of my essays as an artist. Such art as can come out of these conditions for a man of my endowment I claim to have put into my work; and therefore you will please judge it, not as a pamphlet in dialogue, but as in intention a work of art as much as any comedy of Molière's is a work of art, and as pretending to be a better made play for actual use and long wear on the boards than anything that has yet been turned out by the patent constructive machinery. And I claim that its value in both respects is enhanced by the fact that it deals with a burning social question, and is deliberately intended to induce people to vote on the Progressive side at the next County Council election in London. So, as the clown says in All's Well, "Spare not me." I am no novice in the current critical theories of dramatic art; and what I have done I have done on purpose.

LONDON, *March* 1893.

APPENDIX I

THE AUTHOR TO THE DRAMATIC CRITICS

FELLOW-CRITICS

It is one of my advantages that I can discuss criticism, not merely as an author, but as a critic. I have no illusions about critics being authors who have failed. I know, as one who has practised both crafts, that authorship is child's play compared to criticism; and I have, you may depend upon it, my full share of the professional instinct which regards the romancer as a mere adventurer in literature, and the critic as a highly skilled workman. Ask any novelist or dramatist whether he can write a better novel or play than I; and he will blithely say Yes. Ask him to take my place as critic for one week; and he will blench from the test. The truth is that the critic stands between popular authorship, for which he is not silly enough, and great authorship, for which he has not genius enough. It is certainly true that the status of popular author is much coveted by critics; but that is because the popular author is much better paid for much easier work. Thackeray, like many other eminent authors, coveted a government sinecure; but nobody therefore supposes that authors are merely unsuccessful sinecurists, or that a well paid post in the civil service would have been intellectually a promotion for Thackeray. He who publishes a critical essay well knows how few care to read such things; whereas some donkey of an author, with the imagination of a schoolboy, or some sentimental young lady perhaps, will turn out a story too absurd to be thinkable by an ordinarily competent critic, and yet have it bought by scores and hundreds of thousands of readers of fiction. It is the natural desire to wallow in the profits of romantic make-believe instead of toiling for the scanty wages of "the intolerable fatigue of thought" that drives the critic to envy the author.

You will now feel, fellow-critics, that in turning dramatist I have not turned traitor. It is for the honor of our guild that I venture to suggest that even in the intellectual department the authors are getting ahead of us. I do not wish to rake up the case of Ibsen and his Ghosts again: I think it will be admitted now that the most old - fashioned school for young ladies in the country would have made almost as good a job of that discussion as we did. It was not a question of our liking Ibsen or not liking him, agreeing with him or not agreeing with him. Whichever way our bias lay it was our business to analyse his position skilfully and pronounce on it coolly. Under no circumstances should we have forgotten ourselves so far as to scold at him and cry Fie! like a bevy of illiterate prudes. This, however, is what too many of us did; and now, since what is done cannot be undone, we had better put up a few posts to warn future critics off the dangerous places where we come to grief oftenest.

The first warning I propose is: Do not let us raise the cry of "Ibsen" whenever we find a modern idea in a play. See what it has led to in the following passages culled from criticisms—some of them friendly and able ones—of Widowers' Houses.

"As an ardent admirer of Ibsen's methods, he has not scrupled to follow the method of that writer to extremes."— Daily Telegraph. "The lesson is trite in the case of creeds that the disciple not seldom distances the master. Ibsen has justly been charged, etc., etc."—Athenæum. "The London Ibsen [ironical]. One can see that all this is meant to be ex-

ceedingly Ibsenesque."—Sunday Sun. "I really think it is time the Independent Theatre Society made an effort to secure a play that is not moulded on the lines laid down by the great and only Ibsen." —Pelican. "Mr Shaw is a zealous Ibsenite."—Weekly Dispatch. "A rather silly play by a rather clever man, which may be either worship or satire of Ibsenius the Great."—Saturday Review. "Mr Shaw is the high priest, one may say, of Ibsenism."—Piccadilly. "Like all the Ibsenians he ruins his argument", etc.—Modern Society. "Mr Shaw is an Ibsenite and is consequently quite up to date."—Freeman's Journal. "A promising young tigress of a daughter, who is drawn on the severest principles of Ibsenite heredity." —Western Mercury.

Now the first two acts of Widowers' Houses were written in 1885, when I knew nothing about Ibsen; and I must add that the authors of the lines quoted above should have guessed this, because there is not one idea in the play that cannot be more easily referred to half a dozen English writers than to Ibsen; whilst of his peculiar retrospective method, by which his plays are made to turn upon events supposed to have happened before the rise of the curtain, there is not a trace in my work. The subjects which seem most strongly to suggest Ibsen to modern critics are (1) Heredity, (2) the Emancipation of Woman, (3) any adverse criticism whatever of our marriage laws and customs, and (4) any mixture of wickedness and goodness in the same character. It is therefore necessary to remind ourselves that modern English culture was saturated with the conception of heredity by Herbert Spencer, Darwin, Huxley, Tyndall, and Galton before Ibsen's name was known here; that the Married Women's Property Act, the result of a long and strenuous crusade against what I may call the anti-Ibsenite ideal of marriage, was passed in England before A Doll's House was written; that the two most famous works on the subject of Women's Rights are Mary Wollstonecraft's Vindication and John Stuart Mill's Subjection of Women, dated respectively 1792, and 1869; and that those who may never have studied the complex characters in the fiction of Balzac, George Eliot, George Meredith, and other well-known modern writers, may at least be presumed to have read the history of King David in the Bible, and to have learnt from it that Nature does not keep heroism exclusively for one set of men and villainy exclusively for another, merely to enable us all to become dramatists and "paint character" with a bucket of whitewash and a jar of lampblack. These things are the more important for a critic to observe, because matters have taken such a course in England for the last fifty years that the man who has neither the culture of the Bible nor that of the Evolutionist school is in ninety-nine cases out of a hundred a man with no culture at all—a suspicion not to be lightly incurred by anyone whose calling it is to bring culture to bear on dramatic literature. Be warned therefore; for it is hard to see how a critic who has dipped into modern English literature even to the modest extent of reading one of Mr Grant Allen's novels, could write as if every idea in physics and morals that is not to be found in Chambers' Vestiges of Creation and Dr Watts' poems must necessarily be a recent Norwegian importation.

The second warning is: Let us not try to encourage the hypocrisy of the theatre, already greater than that of the conventicle, by being more austere in our judgment of *dramatis personæ* than of real men and women. Imitate that excellent critic of mine (known to me only through his very agreeable notice of my play) the London correspondent of the Glasgow Herald, who says:—

"The characters are depicted naturally, and not in the glorified form so common upon the conventional stage. . . . It was a treat for once to see a hero (like one of Thackeray's) no better than one of his fellow-men; to listen to the worldliness of the slum landlord and his clerk; and particularly to welcome a heroine who shows her temper to her betrothed, and still more to her father, and who, like other estimable womankind whom we frequently meet in real life, though rarely on the stage, is always ready to quarrel on a point of feminine dignity, but when 'cornered' is always anxious to forgive and to make friends again."

That is what I call a reasonable criticism. Now listen to some of the others:—

"There can hardly be said to be a single estimable personage in the whole play." —Times. "All his *dramatis personæ* are entirely selfish and despicable."—Daily Telegraph. "Revolting picture of middle-class life. . . . Remorselessly the eccentric one [the author] laid bare his idealized essence of snobbishness compressed from all the worst specimens of his fellow-men, and bade us believe that he was painting from life. . . . The abominable Blanche appears in a worse light than ever; and the eccentricity ends with the smothering of what small spark of decency remained in the heart of the only person of the whole bunch who ever had any."—Morning Leader. "It is already impossible, we should hope, to find a set of people so peculiar and unsympathetic as those introduced in this play."—Morning Advertiser. "In such a world what is to be done but to show hands all round and caper to the tune of 'rogues all'?"—Globe. "Mr Gilbert possesses an uncanny habit of turning up the seamy side of life's robe; but Mr Shaw's world has not rags enough to cover its nudity. He aims to show with Zolaesque exactitude that middle-class life is foul and leprous. The play means that

z

the middle class, even to its womanhood, is brutal at heart, or it means nothing."— Athenæum. "A set of blood-suckers. Every one is ill-conditioned, quarrelsome, fractious, apt to behave, at a moment's notice, like a badly-brought-up child."— World. "The mere word 'mortgage' suffices to turn hero into rascal. Mr Shaw will say that is his point—scratch a middle-class hero and you find a rascal." —Speaker. "Revelation of a distorted and myopic outlook on society."—Sunday Sun. "Very disagreeable heroine . . . all the other characters in the play—the poor parlormaid alone excepted—are as hateful as that heroine."—Era. "Mr Shaw devotes all his energies to making his characters unsympathetic, sordid, soulless— ending even worse than they began."— Stage. "Heartless young lady . . . cads of diverse temperaments."—Weekly Dispatch. "He goes further than Ibsen, whose characters are a mixture of knaves and fools; whereas in Widowers' Houses they are all knaves."—Modern Society. "Mr Shaw starts with a total disbelief in human nature."—Freeman's Journal. "All the characters were villains except a pretty parlormaid."—Western Mercury. "The moral seems to be the utter selfishness of human nature outside a progressive County Council."—Umpire. "I could not help noticing that the only thoroughly decent character in the play was a sort of Mrs Harris in the shape of the parson, who was only allowed to be talked about, but who did not appear."—Mr Ben. Greet, addressing the Church and Stage Guild.

I remember once hearing Mr Moody the Evangelist preach on the text, "All have sinned and fallen short of the glory of God." He declared strenuously that in morals a miss is as good as a mile, and that the most venial sin damns as effectually as the most atrocious crime. To have fallen short of the glory of God is enough, whether by an inch or a league does not matter. I must say that from any other point of view than Mr Moody's, the passages set forth above appear to me to be ludicrous exaggerations. Even after making all allowance for the effect on the writers of the way in which, for the first time on the stage (as far as I know) they saw the citizen with his share in the guilt of our industrial system brought home to him, I still think that they might have paused to ask themselves in what respect Trench, Sartorius, Blanche, Cokane and Lickcheese are any worse, I will not say than themselves, but than the characters in any of the comedies, ancient or modern, to which they have taken no exception on this score. I certainly had no intention of spoiling the moral of my play by making the characters at all singular; and I suggest that the following considerations will explain my apparent cynicism.

Formerly, a man was responsible only for his private conduct and for the maintenance of his own household. Today, as an inevitable consequence of Democracy, he is responsible for the state of the whole community which he helps to govern as a citizen and a voter. Now a man may discharge his private responsibility very well, and yet not even realize that his public responsibility exists. Just as Charles I was an excellent private gentleman and an intolerable king, so most men today are reasonably good friends and fathers, but execrable citizens. Sartorius is the ordinary man of business, voting for the candidate who promises to keep down the rates, and getting on the vestry solely to prevent the vestry from interfering with his property. And he does so in a hypocritical way only because that is the custom—not in the least because he is a Pecksniff. I have drawn him as a man of strong and masterful character, unscrupulous but not a law-breaker, a kind and unselfish father, and much more reasonable and even magnanimous with Trench than the typical villa owner, who is a comparatively spiteful and huffy person. He is, in short, distinctly an exceptional and superior specimen of the middle-class man whose business it is to deal *directly* with the poor. His rascality—for from the social point of view he certainly is a callous rascal—does not lie in his refusing to spend money on his rookeries, since his plea that his tenants would burn his improvements is perfectly well founded. It lies altogether in his indifference to defects in our social system which produce a class of persons so poor that they are driven by constant physical privation to turn everything they can lay hands on into more fuel and more food. When we find a castaway at sea chewing his boots to appease his hunger, we do not stigmatize him as a creature too degraded to appreciate the right use of boots: we take him aboard and relieve his hunger, after which he wears his boots as appreciatively as a West End gentleman. But Sartorius is not ashamed to explain the disappearance of his banisters and cistern lids on the absurd ground that "these people do not know how to live in handsome houses." He has found out that there is no use in treating them goodnaturedly; and he has not enough social conscience to proceed to ask why there is no use, and to find out how, as a citizen and an elector, to remedy the abject poverty which makes a woman willing, for the sake of having a good warm, to burn the handrail that is put up to save her and her neighbors from falling downstairs. The point may not be obvious at once to a critic who has only to ring the bell for another scuttle of Wallsend when his fire runs low, any more than it was obvious to Sartorius. Consequently, in every denunciation of Sartorius as a monster, we may see the hand of Sartorius himself.[1]

[1] On this subject of current middle-class morality, see also the letters I have addressed to the Press in answer to my critics, extracts from which will be found in the second appendix.

I now come to a string of remonstrances partly brought on me by a passage in an interview published in the Star newspaper (November 29th, 1892), in which I declared that I wished to appeal to the audience "on the solid ground of political economy," and to have a blackboard on the stage with diagrams to illustrate my points, with much more chaff of the same kind. Here is the result:—

"A kind of leading article of the slashing type."—Morning. "An exposition in dialogue of the New Economics. . . . What has this farrago of newspaper leaders and Fabian essays to do with the play?" —Star. "Undramatic attempt to cut up a Parliamentary Report into uneven stage lengths. . . . Published as one of the dialogues sometimes given in the Fortnightly Review it would be effective."—Echo. "A discussion, with open doors, of the pros and cons of slum landlordism . . . a good sermon."—Black and White. "A new form of didactic Socialistic demonstration, like the practicable laundries with the poor washerwomen at work which figured in a recent procession in Hyde Park."—Sunday Sun. "It would be readable and might be useful as a Fabian pamphlet."—Weekly Dispatch. "In no sense a drama, but a succession of dialogues in which the author sets forth his views concerning Socialist questions."— Lloyds. "Not a play—a pamphlet."— Encore. "The exposure of certain social sins connected with the letting of tenement houses afforded the sole *raison d'être* of Mr Shaw's feeble little play."—Observer. "His propaganda—I beg pardon, his new play."—Penny Illustrated Paper. "Merely a lecture."—Financial Observer. "Mr Shaw wishes to utter a tirade against certain abuses; and he thinks the theatre a suitable pulpit for his utterances."— Colonies and India. "The play is a pamphlet in dramatic form."—Western Mercury. "The whole of the three acts is occupied with a dreary discussion of the ethics of slum property."—Birmingham Post. "Three acts of dreary dissertation on the familiar text that 'rent is robbery.'"—Yorkshire Post. "Mr Bernard Shaw is an amiable Fabian who believes that 'rent is robbery.'"—Yorkshire Evening Post.

Now I think it must be evident at this rate to all who have read the play, that if I had written The Merchant of Venice it would have been denounced as a dissertation on the Jewish question, complicated by a crude exposition of the peculiar views of the Fabian Society on the law of contract. All I need say on the Fabian point is that any person who would like to see the difference between an essay on rent and Widowers' Houses can buy Fabian Essays, containing just such an essay by me, for ninepence. Fabian pamphlets, in which I have had a hand, can be obtained for a penny; and a comparison of them with this play will shew how little the critics quoted above know how merciful I have been to them. Let me say, however, that it is impossible for any fictionist, dramatic or other, to make true pictures of modern society without some knowledge of the economic anatomy of it. And since what the dramatist ought to know the critic ought to know, a course of Fabian literature would most unquestionably do incalculable good to both dramatists and critics, if they could be persuaded to go through it. For all that, I see that it would be useless to blame a critic today for not being an economist, or even an ordinarily competent politician and man of business. Nobody expects it from him; and he himself benightedly ridicules the idea. But what I do expect him to know is that "bluebook plays" hold the stage far better than conventionally idealist dramas. I need only mention the irrepressible Never too Late to Mend to prove that Widowers' Houses, far from

being a play of so new a sort that its very title to the name of drama is questionable, is, on its bluebook side, a sample (whether good or bad is not here in question) of one of the most familiar, popular, and firmly established genres in English dramatic literature. It is a matter of experience that the dramatized or novelized bluebook or Fabian Essay (so to speak) has ten times as much chance of success as the mere romance, though it is also, of course, a much more difficult job for the writer. My warning therefore is against the folly of assuming that the reverse is the case, and that a play is handicapped by a basis of bluebook. A wary critic, if he wished to "slate" Widowers' Houses, would begin somewhat in this fashion: "Not even with all the advantages of his profound economic knowledge and his complete acquaintance with the wealth of dramatic material stored in our national bluebook literature was Mr Shaw able to produce a tolerable play." It is mere perversity to assume that the less a dramatist knows and cares about real life, the better his plays are likely to be.

There are a dozen other warnings that I could formulate for the sake of our younger and weaker brethren, who are being severely tested by the dramatic revival now beginning. But as I very much doubt whether they have read thus far into what must be to them a piece of heavy literature, I will indulge myself by laying down a just now rather weary pen, confident that the really able brothers of the craft will forgive my preaching, seeing that they best know how much the rest stand in need of a sermon. My sole object is to knock on the head a few empty formulas which take up the space in dramatic criticism which should be occupied by real live ideas, and which have been trotted out in the last few years whenever a play has been produced with any pretension to represent modern life as it is really lived.

APPENDIX II

The following extracts from letters addressed by the author to the press after the performance of Widowers' Houses are reprinted here to give the reading public some idea of the commotion which can be made in a theatre by a work which, if published as a novel, would surprise no one. First, as to the extent of the commotion, hear The Era of the 24th December, 1892:—

"Hardly any recent play has provoked so much newspaper and other controversy as Mr Bernard Shaw's Widowers' Houses. At least two of the daily papers, on the day after its production, devoted leading articles to its consideration, besides special criticisms of almost unprecedented length. We should be afraid to say how many journals gave two long columns to it. Then all last week a controversy on its merits and demerits raged in a morning paper; and it was held up as an example of the kind of play the Lord Chamberlain did *not* object to by Mrs Aveling in her lecture to the Playgoers; and, finally, it was one of the subjects of an interesting lecture delivered last Sunday night to the Socialists of Hammersmith. The last fact, however, becomes less surprising when we find that the lecturer was Mr Bernard Shaw."

This account is not exaggerated. The play occupied the press for weeks after its production to an extent which, in a really healthy and active phase of dramatic art, would have been absurd. The discussion raged chiefly round matters of fact, most of the writers seeming to have no definite idea of the sources of the revenues enjoyed by the propertied classes under our industrial system. In replying to these criticisms the author carefully abstained from confusing issues of fact with the artistic issues alluded to in the preface to the present volume; and it should be noted that whereas in that preface the play is defended as a work of art, here it is justified mainly as a document. To the editor of The Star the author is indebted for the publication, on the 19th December, 1892, of a letter of which the following is an abridgment:—

"Sir,—The critics of my play Widowers' Houses have now had their say. Will you be so good as to let the author have a turn? I have gone through every criticism I could get hold of; and I think it is now clear that 'the new drama' has no malice to fear from the serious critics. The care with which every possible admission in my favor has been made, even in the notices of those who found the play intolerably disagreeable and the author intolerably undramatic, shews that the loss of critical balance produced by the first shock of Ibsen's Ghosts was only momentary, and that the most unconventional and obnoxious agitator-dramatist, even when he has gone out of his way to attack his critics, need not fear a Press vendetta.

"However, the fairness of criticism is one thing, its adequacy quite another. I do not hesitate to say that many of my critics have been completely beaten by the play simply because they are ignorant of society. Do not let me be misunderstood: I do not mean that they eat with their knives, drink the contents of their finger-bowls, or sit down to dinner in ulsters and green neckties. What I mean is that they do not know life well enough to recognize it in the glare of the footlights. They denounce Sartorius, my house-knacking widower, as a monstrous libel on the middle and upper class, because he grinds his money remorselessly out of the poor. But they do not (and cannot) answer his argument as to the impossibility of his acting otherwise under our social system; nor do they notice the fact that though he is a bad landlord he is not in the least a bad man as men go. Even in his economic capacity I have made him a rather favorable specimen of his class. I might have made him a shareholder in a match factory where avoidable 'phossy jaw' is not avoided, or in a tram company working its men seventeen and a half hours a day, or in a railway company with a terrible death-roll of mangled shunters, or in a whitelead factory or chemical works—in short, I might have piled on the agony beyond the endurance of my audience, and yet not made him one whit worse than thousands of personally amiable and respected men who have invested in the most lucrative way the savings they have earned or inherited. I will not ask those critics who are so indignant with my 'distorted and myopic outlook on society' what they will do with the little money their profession may enable them to save. I will simply tell them what they *must* do with it, and that is follow the advice of their stockbroker as to the safest and most remunerative investment, reserving their moral scruples for the expenditure of the interest, and their sympathies for the treatment of the members of their own families. Even in spending the interest they will have no alternative but to get the best value they can for their money without regard to the conditions under which the articles they buy are produced. They will take a domestic pride in their comfortable homes, full of furniture made by 'slaughtered' (*i.e.* extra-sweated) cabinet makers, and go to church on Sunday in shirts sewn by women who can only bring their wages up to subsistence point by prostitution. What will they say to Sartorius then? What, indeed, can they say to him now? —these 'guilty creatures sitting at a play,' who, instead of being struck to the soul and presently proclaiming their malefactions, are naïvely astonished and revolted at the spectacle of a man on the stage act-

ing as we are all acting perforce every day. The notion that the people in Widowers' Houses are abnormally vicious or odious could only prevail in a community in which Sartorius is absolutely typical in his unconscious villainy. Like my critics, he lacks conviction of sin. Now, the didactic object of my play is to bring conviction of sin—to make the Pharisee who repudiates Sartorius as either a Harpagon or a diseased dream of mine, and thanks God that such persons do not represent his class, recognize that Sartorius is his own photograph. In vain will the virtuous critic tell me that he does not own slum property: all I want to see is the label on his matchbox, or his last week's washing-bill, to judge for myself whether he really ever gives a second thought to Sartorius's tenants, who make his matchboxes and wash his stockings so cheaply.

"As to the highly connected young gentleman, naturally straightforward and easygoing, who bursts into genuine indignation at the sufferings of the poor, and, on being shewn that he cannot help them, becomes honestly cynical and throws off all responsibility whatever, that is nothing but the reality of the everyday process known as disillusion. His allowing the two business men to get his legs under their mahogany, and to persuade him to 'stand in' with a speculation of which he understands nothing except that he is promised some money out of it, will surprise no one who knows the City, and has seen the exploitation of aristocratic names by City promoters spread from needy guinea-pig colonels, and lords with courtesy titles, to eldest sons of the noblest families. If I had even represented Harry Trench as letting himself in for eighteen months' hard labor for no greater crime than that of being gambler enough to be the too willing dupe of a swindler, the incident would be perfectly true to life. As to the compensation speculation in the third act being a fraud which no gentleman would have countenanced, that opinion is too innocent to be discussed. I can only say that as the object of the scheme is to make a haul at the expense of the ratepayers collectively, it is much less cruel and treacherous in its incidence than the sort of speculation which made the late Mr Jay Gould universally respected during his lifetime. I shall be told next that Panama is a dream of mine.

"There is a curious idea in the minds of some of my critics that I have given away my case by representing the poor man, Lickcheese, as behaving, when he gets the chance, exactly as the rich man does. These gentlemen believe that, according to me, what is wrong with society is that the rich, who are all wicked, oppress the poor, who are all virtuous. I will not waste the space of The Star by dealing with such a misconception further than to curtly but good-humoredly inform those who entertain it that they are fools. I administer the remark, not as an insult, but as a tonic.

"Now comes the question, How far does all this touch the merits of the play as a work of art? Obviously not at all; but it has most decidedly touched the value of the opinions of my critics on that point. The evidence of the notices (I have sheaves of them before me) is irresistible. With hardly an exception the men who find my sociology wrong are also the men who find my dramatic workmanship bad; and *vice versa*. Even the criticism of the acting is biassed in the same way. The effect on me, of course, is to reassure me completely as to my own competence as a playwright. The very success with which I have brought all the Philistines and sentimental idealists down on me proves the velocity and penetration with which my realism got across the footlights. I am well accustomed to judge of the execution I have done by the cries of the wounded.

"On one point, however, I heartily thank my critics for their unanimous forbearance. Not one of them has betrayed the licenses I have taken in the political and commercial details of the play. Considering that I have made a resident in Surbiton eligible as a St Giles' vestryman; that I have made the London County Council contemporary with the 1885 Royal Commission on the Housing of the Working Classes; that I have represented an experienced man of business as paying 7 per cent on a first mortgage—considering, in short, that I have recklessly sacrificed realism to dramatic effect in the machinery of the play, I feel, as may be well imagined, deeply moved by the compliments which have been paid me on my perfect knowledge of economics and business."

Before giving the rest of the letter, it is convenient to refer here to a very funny discussion which arose over the scene in the second act in which Blanche assaults the servant. Although nothing is commoner on the stage than bodily violence threatened or executed by indignant heroes, heroines have hitherto been excluded by convention from this method of displaying their prowess. The author resolved to redress this injustice to Woman by making his heroine attack her servant much as Othello attacks his ancient. The resultant sensation testified to the hardihood of the experiment. The critics were highly scandalized; and their view of the incident was expressed in the following passage from a notice which appeared the day after the performance:—

"What a ludicrous incident! How we all shrieked with laughter! What has such a scene to do with the play? Why did Mr Shaw introduce it? I will tell you why. Because Mr Shaw wishes to present Blanche as a *type*, a type of the modern middle-class Englishwoman (as he sees her), the woman who will not hear about the poor wretches in their tenement houses because it is so unpleasant, and who, in her own drawing-room, can, in a fit of temper, use brutal violence to her own dependants."

It was not possible for the author to seriously discuss the notion that he regarded temper and violence as class characteristics. He was only able to say, in a letter to The Speaker, "Some people think that ladies with tempers are never personally violent. I happen to know that they are; and so I leave the matter." It is true that the ideal lady—the "typical" lady if that term be preferred—never strikes, never swears, never smokes, never gambles, never drinks, never nags, never makes advances to inept wooers, never, in short, does anything "unladylike," whether "in her own drawing-room" or elsewhere. Just so the ideal clergyman never hunts, never goes to the theatre, and regards the poorest laborer as his equal and his brother by their common Father, God. The author confesses to having jilted *the* ideal lady for *a* real one. He did it intentionally; and he will probably do it again, and yet again, even at the risk of having the real ones mistaken for counter-ideals. Why Blanche should be held to indicate any belief on his part that all ladies are hot-tempered, any more than Hamlet is held to indicate a belief on Shakespear's part that all princes are philosophers, is not apparent to him.

Here is a final extract from the letter to The Star on the subject of Blanche:—

"On another point in her conduct one critic makes an objection which, I confess, amazed me. Sartorius, as the son of a very poor woman, knows that the poor are human beings exactly like himself. But his daughter, brought up as a lady, conceives them as a different and inferior species. 'I hate the poor,' she says—'at least, I hate those dirty, drunken, disreputable people who live like pigs.' The critic in question, whose bias towards myself is altogether friendly, cannot conceive that a young lady would avow such inhuman sentiments: hypocrisy, he contends, would prevent her if her heart did not. I can only refer him, if he has really never heard such sentiments boasted of by ladies, to the comments of The Times and the St James's Gazette (to name no other papers written by gentlemen for gentlemen) on the unemployed, on the starving Irish peasants whose rents have since been reduced wholesale in the Irish land courts, or on the most heavily sweated classes of workers whose miserable plight has been exposed before Parliamentary Committees and Royal Commissions, to prove that the thinkers and writers of Blanche Sartorius's party vie with each other in unconscious—nay, conscientious—brutality, callousness, and class prejudice when they speak of the proletariat. Hypocrisy with them takes the shape of dissembling sympathy with the working class when they really feel it, not of affecting it when they do not feel it. My friend and critic must remember the savage caricatures of William Morris, John Burns, Miss Helen Taylor, Mrs Besant, etc., in which Punch once indulged, as well as the outrageous calumnies which were heaped on the late Charles Bradlaugh during his struggle to enter Parliament, not to mention the cases of unsocial conduct by county gentlemen and magistrates exposed every week in the 'Pillory' columns of Truth. Am I to be told that the young ladies who read these papers in our suburban villas are less narrow and better able to see across the frontiers of their own class than the writers whom their fathers support? The fact is that Blanche's class prejudices, like those of the other characters in the play, are watered down instead of exaggerated. The whole truth is too monstrous to be told otherwise than by degrees."

To this a writer in The Lady's Pictorial (24th December, 1892) retorts:—

"So it comes to this, that Mr Shaw's defence for drawing a middle-class English girl as a virago who batters her maid and vilifies the starving poor, is that in professedly political papers (written by men for men—women not entering into the question at all), the other side is held up to ridicule by mud being flung upon their humble allies! as though the political game played by political journals has anything whatever to do with the attributes of humanity common to the average woman and the average man!"

It only remains for the author to meet this defence by citing the journalism written by women for women, and by denying most strenuously that the indifference of women to political journalism can be interpreted in any other way than as a selfish and narrow insensibility to the social questions which form the real substance of politics.

The only other utterance of the author's which need be quoted is from a letter to The Speaker (31st December, 1892). It is not a defence of the artistic value of the play, which cannot be established or disestablished by argument, but a renewal of the author's insistence on the impossibility of appreciating a work of art without adequate knowledge of its subject-matter:—

"I now approach the question which is really the most interesting from the critical point of view. Is it possible to treat the artistic quality of a play altogether independently of its scientific quality? For example, is it possible for a critic to be perfectly appreciative and perfectly incredulous and half insensible at the same time? I do not believe it for a moment. No point in a drama can produce any effect at all unless the spectator perceives it and accepts it as a real point; and this primary condition being satisfied, the force of the effect will depend on the extent to which the point interests the spectator—that is, seems momentous to him. The spectacle of Hamlet fencing with an opponent whose foil is 'unbated' produces its effect because the audience knows the danger; but there are risks just as thrilling to those who understand them, risks of cutting arteries in surgical operations, risks of losing large sums by a momentary loss of nerve in the money market, risks of destroying one's whole character by an apparently trifling step, perils of all sorts which may give the most terrible intensity to a scene in the eyes of those who have the requisite technical knowledge or experience of life to fathom the full significance of what they are witnessing, but which would produce as little effect on others as the wheeling forward of a machine gun would on a hostile tribe of savages unacquainted with the 'resources of civilization.'

"It has long been clear to me that nothing will be done for the theatre until the most able dramatists refuse to write down to the level of that imaginary monster the British Public. We want a theatre for people who have lived, thought, and felt, and who have some real sense that women are human beings just like men, only worse brought up, and consequently worse behaved. In such a theatre the merely literary man who has read and written instead of living until he has come to feel fiction as experience and to resent experience as fiction, would be as much out of place as the ideal British Public itself. Well, let him sit out his first mistaken visit quietly and not come again; for it is clear that only by holding the mirror up to literature can the dramatist please him, whereas it is by holding it up to nature that good work is produced. In such a theatre Widowers' Houses would rank as a trumpery farcical comedy; whereas today it is excitedly discussed as a daringly original sermon, political essay,

Z 2

satire, Drapier letter or what not, even by those who will not accept it as a play on any terms because its hero did not, when he learnt that his income came from slum property, at once relinquish it (*i.e.* make it a present to Sartorius without benefiting the tenants) and go to the goldfields to dig out nuggets with his strong right arm, so that he might return to wed his Blanche after a shipwreck (witnessed by her in a vision), just in time to rescue her from beggary, brought upon her by the discovery that Lickcheese was the rightful heir to the property of Sartorius, who had dispossessed and enslaved him by a series of forgeries unmasked by the faithful Cokane. Was it really lack of capacity that led me to forego all this 'drama' by making my hero do exactly what he would have done in real life—that is, apologize like a gentleman (in the favorable sense) for accusing another man of his own unconscious rascality, and admit his inability to change a world that will not take the trouble to change itself?"

The reader will now be in a position to understand the sort of controversy which has so magnified the importance of Widowers' Houses.

APPENDIX III

The following is an item of news from The Star newspaper of the 2nd January, 1893:—

"A dangerous staircase has proved fatal to Elizabeth H——, aged 40, a charwoman, of X Buildings. The evidence at St Giles's Coroner's Court on Saturday showed that the deceased was found lying at the bottom of the stairs at her lodgings on Tuesday morning, at half-past twelve, in an insensible condition. She was carried upstairs and put to bed, but died the same day.

"The Coroner's officer: 'The stairs are very dangerous at night. They are insufficiently lighted.'

"Dr Brennan deposed that death was due to extensive fracture of the skull. He said he found the stairs dark and slippery. A handrail was needed.

"The Coroner: 'There is, I understand, no resident landlord on the premises.' Over a hundred families live at these buildings. The jury, in returning a verdict of 'Accidental death,' added the subjoined rider: 'The jurors, having heard in evidence that the staircases leading to X Buildings are insufficiently lighted, and that there are no handrails, would call the attention of the landlord to this condition of things, with a view to their immediate improvement.'"

The report of the Royal Commission of 1885 on the Housing of the Working Classes, alluded to in the third act of the play, may also be consulted as to the ordinary rent and condition of a single-room tenement in London.

Finally, it may not be amiss to observe that the author has himself made collections of weekly rents from very poor tenants, and is conversant with the attitude of the middle-class proprietor towards the laborer tenant.

PostScript 1933. On the question of the slums this earliest play of mine is still up to date more than forty years after its first performance. Not only are the overcrowded tenements and cellar dwellings as bad as ever, but highly respectable looking houses, covering whole residential districts formerly inhabited by single families, are now partitioned to accommodate two families, whilst gardens and backyards are filled up with quaintly called "villages" or "studios," the result being back-to-back dwellings much worse than the back-to-backs of Leeds so vehemently denounced there by housing reformers, but left unnoticed in London because the change is invisible from the street.

The population question is still treated as if it were concerned solely with the food supply and not with the supply of space. Plans for crowding up the over-populated quarters still more by covering in the railways and building on the squares are still current although there are streets and streets of little old two-storey houselets which could be replaced by commodious and sanitary piles of flats. It seems as if nothing adequate can be done until the poor are taught to burn their own dwellings instead of other people's when their housing conditions become unbearable.

XXVII

PLAYS UNPLEASANT
1898

MAINLY ABOUT MYSELF

There is an old saying that if a man has not fallen in love before forty, he had better not fall in love after. I long ago perceived that this rule applied to many other matters as well: for example, to the writing of plays; and I made a rough memorandum for my own guidance that unless I could produce at least half a dozen plays before I was forty, I had better let playwriting alone. It was not so easy to comply with this provision as might be supposed. Not that I lacked the dramatist's gift. As far as that is concerned, I have encountered no limit but my own laziness to my power of conjuring up imaginary people in imaginary places, and finding pretexts for theatrical scenes between them. But to obtain a livelihood by this insane gift, I must have conjured so as to interest not only my own imagination, but that of at least some seventy or a hundred thousand contemporary London playgoers. To fulfil this condition was hopelessly out of my power. I had no taste for what is called popular art, no respect for popular morality, no belief in popular religion, no admiration for popular heroics. As an Irishman I could pretend to patriotism neither for the country I had abandoned nor the country that had ruined it. As a humane person I detested violence and slaughter, whether in war, sport, or the butcher's yard. I was a Socialist, detesting our anarchical scramble for money, and believing in equality as the only possible permanent basis of social organization, discipline, subordination, good manners, and selection of fit persons for high functions. Fashionable life, open on indulgent terms to unencumbered "brill-iant" persons, I could not endure, even if I had not feared its demoralizing effect on a character which required looking after as much as my own. I was neither a sceptic nor a cynic in these matters: I simply understood life differently from the average respectable man; and as I certainly enjoyed myself more—mostly in ways which would have made him unbearably miserable—I was not splenetic over our variance.

Judge then, how impossible it was for me to write fiction that should delight the public. In my nonage I had tried to obtain a foothold in literature by writing novels, and had actually produced five long works in that form without getting further than an encouraging compliment or two from the most dignified of the London and American publishers, who unanimously declined to venture their capital upon me. Now it is clear that a novel cannot be too bad to be worth publishing, provided it is a novel at all, and not merely an ineptitude. I was not convinced that the publishers' view was commercially sound until I got a clue to my real condition from a friend of mine, a physician who had devoted himself specially to ophthalmic surgery. He tested my eyesight one evening, and informed me that it was quite uninteresting to him because it was normal. I naturally took this to mean that it was like everybody else's; but he rejected this construction as paradoxical, and hastened to explain to me that I was an exceptional and highly fortunate person optically, normal sight conferring the power of seeing things accurately, and being enjoyed by only about ten per cent of the population, the remaining ninety per cent being abnormal. I immediately perceived the explanation of my want of success in fiction. My mind's eye, like my body's, was "normal": it saw things differently from other people's eyes, and saw them better.

This revelation produced a considerable effect on me. At first it struck me that I might live by selling my works to the ten per cent who were like myself; but a moment's reflection shewed me that these must all be as penniless as I, and that we could not live by taking in oneanother's literary washing. How to earn daily bread by my pen was then the problem. Had I been a practical commonsense moneyloving Englishman, the matter would have been easy enough: I should have put on a pair of abnormal spectacles and aberred my vision to the liking of the ninety per cent of potential bookbuyers. But I was so prodigiously self-satisfied with my superiority, so flattered by my abnormal normality, that the resource of hypocrisy never occurred to me. Better see rightly on a pound a week than squint on a million. The question was, how to get the pound a week. The matter, once I gave up writing novels, was not so very difficult. Every despot must have one disloyal subject to keep him sane. Even Louis the Eleventh had to tolerate his confessor, standing for the eternal against the temporal throne. Democracy has now handed the sceptre of the despot to the sovereign people; but they, too, must have their confessor, whom they call Critic. Criticism is not only medicinally salutary: it has positive popular attractions in its cruelty, its gladiatorship, and the gratification given to envy by its attacks on the great, and to enthusiasm by its praises. It may say things which many would like to say, but dare not, and indeed for want of skill could not even if they durst. Its iconoclasms, seditions, and blasphemies, if well turned, tickle those whom they shock; so that the critic adds the privileges of the court jester to those of the confessor. Garrick,

had he called Dr Johnson Punch, would have spoken profoundly and wittily; whereas Dr Johnson, in hurling that epithet at him, was but picking up the cheapest sneer an actor is subject to.

It was as Punch, then, that I emerged from obscurity. All I had to do was to open my normal eyes, and with my utmost literary skill put the case exactly as it struck me, or describe the thing exactly as I saw it, to be applauded as the most humorously extravagant paradoxer in London. The only reproach with which I became familiar was the everlasting "Why can you not be serious?" Soon my privileges were enormous and my wealth immense. I had a prominent place reserved for me on a prominent journal every week to say my say as if I were the most important person in the kingdom. My pleasing toil was to report upon all the works of fine art the capital of the world can attract to its exhibitions, its opera house, its concerts and its theatres. The classes eagerly read my essays: the masses patiently listened to my harangues. I enjoyed the immunities of impecuniosity with the opportunities of a millionaire. If ever there was a man without a grievance, I was that man.

But alas! the world grew younger as I grew older: its vision cleared as mine dimmed: it began to read with the naked eye the writing on the wall which now began to remind me that the age of spectacles was at hand. My opportunities were still there: nay, they multiplied tenfold; but the strength and youth to cope with them began to fail, and to need eking out with the shifty cunning of experience. I had to shirk the platform; to economize my health; even to take holidays. In my weekly columns, which I once filled full from a magic well that never ran dry or lost its sparkle provided I pumped hard enough, I began to repeat myself; to fall into a style which, to my great peril, was recognized as at least partly serious; to find the pump tiring me and the water lower in the well; and, worst symptom of all, to reflect with little tremors on the fact that my mystic wealth could not, like the money for which other men threw it away, be stored up against my second childhood. The younger generation, reared in an enlightenment unknown to my schooldays, came knocking at the door too: I glanced back at my old columns and realized that I had timidly botched at thirty what newer men do now with gay confidence in their cradles. I listened to their vigorous knocks with exultation for the race, with penurious alarm for my own old age. When I talked to this generation, it called me Mister, and, with its frank, charming humanity, respected me as one who had done good work in my time. A famous playwright wrote a long play to shew that people of my age were on the shelf; and I laughed at him with the wrong side of my mouth.

It was at this bitter moment that my fellow citizens, who had previously repudiated all my offers of political service, contemptuously allowed me to become a vestryman: *me*, the author of Widowers' Houses! Then, like any other harmless useful creature, I took the first step rearward. Up to that fateful day I had never penuriously spooned up the spilt drops of my well into bottles. Time enough for that when the well was empty. But now I listened to the voice of the publisher for the first time since he had refused to listen to mine. I turned over my articles again; but to serve up the weekly paper of five years ago as a novelty! no: I had not yet fallen so low, though I see that degradation looming before me as an agricultural laborer sees the workhouse. So I said "I will begin with small sins: I will publish my plays."

How! you will cry: plays! What plays?

Let me explain. One of the worst privations of life in London for persons of serious intellectual and artistic interests is the want of a suitable playhouse. I am fond of the play, and am, as intelligent readers of this preface will have observed, myself a bit of an actor. Consequently, when I found myself coming across projects of all sorts for the foundation of a theatre which should be to the newly gathered intellectual harvest of the nineteenth century what Shakespear's theatre was to the harvest of the Renascence, I was warmly interested. But it soon appeared that the languid demand of a small and uppish group for a form of entertainment which it had become thoroughly accustomed to do without, could never provide the intense energy necessary for the establishment of the New Theatre (we of course called everything advanced "the New" at that time: see The Philanderer, the second play in "Plays Unpleasant"). That energy could be set free only by the genius of the actor and manager finding in the masterpieces of the New Drama its characteristic and necessary mode of expression, and revealing their fascination to the public. Clearly the way to begin was to pick up a masterpiece or two. Masterpieces, however, do not grow on the bushes. The New Theatre would never have come into existence but for the plays of Ibsen, just as the Bayreuth Festival Playhouse would never have come into existence but for Wagner's Nibelungen tetralogy. Every attempt to extend the repertory proved that it is the drama that makes the theatre and not the theatre the drama. Not that this needed fresh proof, since the whole difficulty had arisen through the drama of the day being written for the theatres instead of from its own inner necessity. Still, a thing that nobody believes cannot be proved too often.

Ibsen, then, was the hero of the new departure. It was in 1889 that the first really effective blow was struck by the production of A Doll's House by Charles

Charrington and Janet Achurch. Whilst they were taking that epoch-making play round the world, Mr Grein followed up the campaign in London with his Independent Theatre. It got on its feet by producing Ibsen's Ghosts; but its search for unacted native dramatic masterpieces was so complete a failure that in the autumn of 1892 it had not yet produced a single original piece of any magnitude by an English author. In this humiliating national emergency, I proposed to Mr Grein that he should boldly announce a play by me. Being an extraordinarily sanguine and enterprising man, he took this step without hesitation. I then raked out, from my dustiest pile of discarded and rejected manuscripts, two acts of a play I had begun in 1885, shortly after the close of my novel writing period, in collaboration with my friend William Archer.

Archer has himself described how I proved the most impossible of collaborators. Laying violent hands on his thoroughly planned scheme for a sympathetically romantic "well made play" of the Parisian type then in vogue, I perversely distorted it into a grotesquely realistic exposure of slum landlordism, municipal jobbery, and the pecuniary and matrimonial ties between them and the pleasant people with "independent" incomes who imagine that such sordid matters do not touch their own lives. The result was revoltingly incongruous; for though I took my theme seriously enough, I did not then take the theatre quite seriously, even in taking it more seriously than it took itself. The farcical trivialities in which I followed the fashion of the times became silly and irritating beyond all endurance when intruded upon a subject of such depth, reality, and force as that into which I had plunged my drama. Archer, perceiving that I had played the fool both with his plan and my own theme, promptly disowned me; and the project, which neither of us had

much at heart, was dropped, leaving me with two abortive acts of an unfinished and condemned play. Exhuming this as aforesaid seven years later, I saw that the very qualities which had made it impossible for ordinary commercial purposes in 1885 might be exactly those needed by the Independent Theatre in 1892. So I completed it by a third act; gave it the farfetched Scriptural title of Widowers' Houses; and handed it over to Mr Grein, who launched it at the public in the Royalty Theatre with all its original tomfooleries on its head. It made a sensation out of all proportion to its merits or even its demerits; and I at once became infamous as a playwright. The first performance was sufficiently exciting: the Socialists and Independents applauded me furiously on principle; the ordinary playgoing first-nighters hooted me frantically on the same ground; I, being at that time in some practice as what is impolitely called a mob orator, made a speech before the curtain; the newspapers discussed the play for a whole fortnight not only in the ordinary theatrical notices and criticisms, but in leading articles and letters; and finally the text of the play was published with an introduction by Mr Grein, an amusing account by Archer of the original collaboration, and a long preface and several elaborate controversial appendices in my most energetically egotistic fighting style. The volume, forming number one of the Independent Theatre series of plays, now extinct, is a curious relic of that nine days wonder; and as it contains the original text of the play with all its silly pleasantries, I can recommend it to collectors of quarto Hamlets, and of all those scarce and superseded early editions which the unfortunate author would so gladly annihilate if he could.

I had not achieved a success; but I had provoked an uproar; and the sensation was so agreeable that I resolved to try again. In the following year, 1893, when the discussion about Ibsenism, "the New Woman," and the like, was at its height, I wrote for the Independent Theatre the topical comedy called The Philanderer. But even before I finished it, it was apparent that its demands on the most expert and delicate sort of high comedy acting went beyond the resources then at the disposal of Mr Grein. I had written a part which nobody but Charles Wyndham could act, in a play which was impossible at his theatre: a feat comparable to the building of Robinson Crusoe's first boat. I immediately threw it aside, and, returning to the vein I had worked in Widowers' Houses, wrote a third play, Mrs Warren's Profession, on a social subject of tremendous force. That force justified itself in spite of the inexperience of the playwright. The play was everything that the Independent Theatre could desire: rather more, if anything, than it bargained for. But at this point I came upon the obstacle that makes dramatic authorship intolerable in England to writers accustomed to the freedom of the Press. I mean, of course, the Censorship.

In 1737, Henry Fielding, the greatest practising dramatist, with the single exception of Shakespear, produced by England between the Middle Ages and the nineteenth century, devoted his genius to the task of exposing and destroying parliamentary corruption, then at its height. Walpole, unable to govern without corruption, promptly gagged the stage by a censorship which is in full force at the present moment. Fielding, driven out of the trade of Molière and Aristophanes, took to that of Cervantes; and since then the English novel has been one of the glories of literature, whilst the English drama has been its disgrace. The extinguisher which Walpole dropped on Fielding descends on me in the form of the Lord Chamberlain's Examiner of Plays, a gentleman who robs, insults, and suppresses me as irresistibly as if he were the Tsar of Russia and I the meanest of his subjects. The robbery takes the form of making me pay him two guineas for reading every play of mine that exceeds one act in length. I do not want him to read it (at least officially: personally he is welcome): on the contrary, I strenuously resent that impertinence on his part. But I must submit in order to obtain from him an insolent and insufferable document, which I cannot read without boiling of the blood, certifying that in his opinion—*his* opinion!—my play "does not in its general tendency contain anything immoral or otherwise improper for the stage," and that the Lord Chamberlain therefore "allows" its performance (confound his impudence!). In spite of this certificate he still retains his right, as an ordinary citizen, to prosecute me, or instigate some other citizen to prosecute me, for an outrage on public morals if he should change his mind later on. Besides, if he really protects the public against my immorality, why does not the public pay him for the service? The policeman does not look to the thief for his wages, but to the honest man whom he protects against the thief. And yet, if I refuse to pay, this tyrant can practically ruin any manager who produces my play in defiance of him. If, having been paid, he is afraid to license the play: that is, if he is more afraid of the clamor of the opponents of my opinions than of their supporters, then he can suppress it, and impose a mulct of £50 on everybody who takes part in a representation of it, from the callboy to the principal tragedian. And there is no getting rid of him. Since he lives, not at the expense of the taxpayer, but by blackmailing the author, no political party would gain ten votes by abolishing him. Private political influence cannot touch him; for such private influence, moving only at the promptings of individual benevolence to individuals, makes nice little places to job nice little people into instead of doing away with them. Nay, I myself, though I know that the Examiner is necessarily an odious and mischievous official, and that if I were appointed to his post (which I shall probably apply for at the next vacancy) I could no more help being odious and mischievous than a ramrod could if it were stuck into the wheels of a steam engine, am loth to stir up the question lest the Press, having now lost all tradition of liberty, and being able to conceive no alternative to the Lord Chamberlain's Examiner than a Home Secretary's Examiner or some other seven-headed devil to replace the oneheaded one, should make the remedy worse than the disease. Thus I cling to the Censorship as many Radicals cling to the House of Lords or the Throne, or as domineering women shun masterful men, and marry weak and amiable ones. Until the nation is prepared for Freedom of The Stage on the same terms as it now enjoys Freedom of The Press, by allowing the playwright and manager to perform anything they please and take the consequences before the ordinary law as authors and editors do, I shall cherish the Lord Chamberlain's Examiner as the apple of my eye. I once thought of organizing a Petition of Right from all the managers and authors to the Prime Minister; but as it was obvious that nine out of ten of these victims of oppression, far from daring to offend their despot, would promptly extol him as the most salutary of English institutions, and spread themselves with unctuous flattery on the perfectly irrelevant question of his estimable personal character, I abandoned the notion. What is more, many of them, in taking this safe course, would be pursuing a sound business policy, since the managers and authors to whom the existing system has brought success not only have no incentive to change it for another which would expose them to wider competition, but have for the most part the

greatest dread of the "New" ideas which the abolition of the Censorship would let loose on the stage. And so long live the Lord Chamberlain's Examiner!

In 1893 this post was occupied by a gentleman, now deceased, whose ideas had in the course of nature become quite obsolete. He was openly hostile to the New movement; and his evidence before the Select Committee of the House of Commons on Theatres and Places of Entertainment in 1892 (Blue Book No. 240, pp. 328-335) is probably the best compendium in existence of every fallacy that can make a Censor obnoxious. In dealing with him Mr Grein was at a heavy disadvantage. Without a license, Mrs Warren's Profession could only be performed in some building not a theatre, and therefore not subject to reprisals from the Lord Chamberlain. The audience would have to be invited as guests only; so that the support of the public paying money at the doors, a support with which the Independent Theatre could not afford to dispense, was out of the question. To apply for a license was to court a practically certain refusal, entailing the £50 penalty on all concerned in any subsequent performance whatever. The deadlock was complete. The play was ready; the Independent Theatre was ready; and the cast was ready; but the mere existence of the Censorship, without any action or knowledge of the play on its part, was sufficient to paralyze all these forces. So I threw Mrs Warren's Profession aside too, and, like another Fielding, closed my career as playwright in ordinary to the Independent Theatre.

Fortunately, though the Stage is bond, the Press is free. And even if the Stage were freed, none the less would it be necessary to publish plays as well as perform them. Had the two performances of Widowers' Houses achieved by Mr Grein been multiplied by fifty, it would still have remained unknown to those who either dwell out of reach of a theatre, or, as a matter of habit, prejudice, comfort, health, or age, abstain altogether from playgoing. Many people who read with delight all the classic dramatists, from Eschylus to Ibsen, only go to the theatre on the rare occasions when they are offered a play by an author whose work they have already learnt to value as literature, or a performance by an actor of the first rank. Even our habitual playgoers have no true habit of playgoing. If on any night at the busiest part of the theatrical season in London, the audiences were cordoned by the police and examined individually as to their views on the subject, there would probably not be a single house-owning native among them who would not conceive a visit to the theatre, or indeed to any public assembly, artistic or political, as an exceptional way of spending an evening, the normal English way being to sit in separate families in separate houses, each person silently occupied with a book, a paper, or a game of halma, cut off equally from the blessings of society and solitude. You may make the acquaintance of a thousand streets of middle-class English families without coming on a trace of any consciousness of citizenship, or any artistic cultivation of the senses. The condition of the men is bad enough, in spite of their daily escape into the city, because they carry the exclusive and unsocial habits of "the home" with them into the wider world of their business. Amiable and companionable enough by nature, they are, by home training, so incredibly ill-mannered, that not even their interest as men of business in welcoming a possible customer in every inquirer can correct their habit of treating everybody who has not been "introduced" as a stranger and intruder. The women, who have not even the city to educate them, are much worse: they are positively unfit for civilized intercourse: graceless, ignorant, narrow-minded to a quite appalling degree. In public places these homebred people cannot be taught to understand that the right they are themselves exercising is a common right. Whether they are in a second-class railway carriage or in a church, they receive every additional fellow passenger or worshipper as a Chinaman receives the "foreign devil" who has forced him to open his ports.

In proportion as this horrible domestic institution is broken up by the active social circulation of the upper classes in their own orbit, or its stagnant isolation made impossible by the conditions of working class life, manners improve enormously. In the middle classes themselves the revolt of a single clever daughter (nobody has yet done justice to the modern clever Englishwoman's loathing of the very word Home), and her insistence on qualifying herself for an independent working life, humanizes her whole family in an astonishingly short time; and such communal enjoyments as a visit to the suburban theatre once a week, or to the Monday Popular Concerts, or both, softens the worst symptoms of its unsociableness. But none of these breaches in the English survival of the hareem can be made without a cannonade of books and pianoforte music. The books and music cannot be kept out, because they alone can make the hideous boredom of the hearth bearable. If its victims may not live real lives, they may at least read about imaginary ones, and perhaps learn from them to doubt whether a class that not only submits to home life, but actually boasts about it, is really a class worth belonging to. For the sake of the unhappy prisoners of the home, then, let my plays be printed as well as acted.

But the dramatic author has reasons for publishing his plays which would hold good even if English families went to the theatre as regularly as they take in the newspaper. A perfectly adequate and successful stage representation of a play requires a combination of circumstances so extraordinarily fortunate that I doubt whether it has ever occurred in the history of the world. Take the case of the most successful English dramatist of the first rank: Shakespear. Although he wrote three centuries ago, he still holds his own so well that it is not impossible to meet old playgoers who have witnessed public performances of more than thirty out of his thirty-seven reputed plays, a dozen of them fairly often, and half a dozen over and over again. I myself, though I have by no means availed myself of all my opportunities, have seen twenty-three of his plays publicly acted. But if I had not read them as well, my impression of them would be not merely incomplete, but violently distorted and falsified. It is only within the last few years that some of our younger actor-managers have been struck with the idea, quite novel in their profession, of performing Shakespear's plays as he wrote them, instead of using them as a cuckoo uses a sparrow's nest. In spite of the success of these experiments, the stage is still dominated by Garrick's conviction that the manager and actor must adapt Shakespear's plays to the modern stage by a process which no doubt presents itself to the adapter's mind as one of masterly amelioration, but which must necessarily be mainly one of debasement and mutilation whenever, as occasionally happens, the adapter is inferior to the author. The living author can protect himself against this extremity of misrepresentation; but the more unquestioned his authority is on the stage, and the more friendly and willing the co-operation of the manager and the company, the more completely does he get convinced of the impossibility of achieving an authentic representation of his piece as well as an effective and successful one. It is quite possible for a piece to enjoy the most sensational success on the basis of a complete misunderstanding of its philosophy: indeed, it is not too much to say that it is only by a capacity for succeeding in spite of its philosophy that a dramatic work of serious poetic import can become popular. In the case of the first part of Goethe's Faust we have this frankly avowed by the extraction from the great original of popular entertainments like Gounod's opera or the Lyceum version, in which poetry and philosophy are replaced by romance, which is the recognized spurious substitute for both and is destructive of them. Not even when a drama is performed without omission or alteration by actors who are enthusiastic disciples of the author does it escape transfiguration. We have lately seen some remarkably sympathetic stage interpretations of poetic drama, from the experiments of Charles Charrington with Ibsen, and of Lugné Poë with Maeterlinck, under comparatively inexpensive conditions, to those of the Wagner Festival Playhouse at Bayreuth on the costliest scale; and readers of Ibsen and Maeterlinck, and pianoforte students of Wagner, are rightly warned that they cannot fully appreciate the force of a dramatic masterpiece without the aid of the theatre. But I have never found an acquaintance with a dramatist founded on the theatre alone, or with a composer founded on the concert room alone, a really intimate and accurate one. The very originality and genius of the performers conflicts with the originality and genius of the author. Imagine Shakespear confronted with Sir Henry Irving at a rehearsal of The Merchant of Venice, or Sheridan with Miss Ada Rehan at one of The School for Scandal. It is easy to imagine the speeches that might pass on such occasions. For example "As I look at your playing, Sir Henry, I seem to see Israel mourning the Captivity and crying, 'How long, O Lord, how long?' It is a little startling to see Shylock's strong feelings operating through a romantic intellect instead of through an entirely commercial one; but pray dont alter your conception, which will be abundantly profitable to us both." Or "My dear Miss Rehan: let me congratulate you on a piece of tragic acting which has made me ashamed of the triviality of my play, and obliterated Sir Peter Teazle from my consciousness, though I meant him to be the hero of the scene. I foresee an enormous success for both of us in this fortunate misrepresentation of my intention." Even if the author had nothing to gain pecuniarily by conniving at the glorification of his play by the performer, the actor's excess of power would still carry its own authority and win the sympathy of the author's histrionic instinct, unless he were a Realist of fanatical integrity. And that would not save him either; for his attempts to make powerful actors do less than their utmost would be as futile as his attempts to make feeble ones do more.

In short, the fact that a skilfully written play is infinitely more adaptable to all sorts of acting than available acting is to all sorts of plays (the actual conditions thus exactly reversing the desirable ones) finally drives the author to the conclusion that his own view of his work can only be conveyed by himself. And since he could not act the play singlehanded even if he were a trained actor, he must fall back on his powers of literary expression, as other poets and fictionists do. So far, this has hardly been seriously attempted by dramatists. Of Shakespear's plays we have not even complete prompt copies: the folio gives us hardly anything but the bare lines. What would we not give for the copy of Hamlet used by Shakespear at rehearsal, with the original stage business scrawled by the prompter's pencil? And if we had in addition the descriptive directions which the author gave on the stage: above all, the character sketches, however brief, by which he tried to con-

vey to the actor the sort of person he meant him to incarnate, what a light they would shed, not only on the play, but on the history of the sixteenth century! Well, we should have had all this and much more if Shakespear, instead of merely writing out his lines, had prepared the plays for publication in competition with fiction as elaborate as that of Meredith. It is for want of this elaboration that Shakespear, unsurpassed as poet, storyteller, character draughtsman, humorist, and rhetorician, has left us no intellectually coherent drama, and could not afford to pursue a genuinely scientific method in his studies of character and society, though in such unpopular plays as All's Well, Measure for Measure, and Troilus and Cressida, we find him ready and willing to start at the twentieth century if the seventeenth would only let him.

Such literary treatment is much more needed by modern plays than by Shakespear's, because in his time the acting of plays was very imperfectly differentiated from the declamation of verses; and descriptive or narrative recitation did what is now done by scenery, furniture, and stage business. Anyone reading the mere dialogue of an Elizabethan play understands all but half a dozen unimportant lines of it without difficulty; whilst many modern plays, highly successful on the stage, are not merely unreadable but positively unintelligible without visible stage business. Recitation on a platform, with the spectators seated round the reciter in the Elizabethan fashion, would reduce them to absurdity. The extreme instance is a pure pantomime, like L'Enfant Prodigue, in which the dialogue, though it exists, is not spoken. If a dramatic author were to publish a pantomime, it is clear that he could make it intelligible to a reader only by giving him the words which the pantomimist is supposed to be uttering. Now it is not a whit less impossible to make a modern practical stage play intelligible to an audience by dialogue alone, than to make a pantomime intelligible to a reader without it.

Obvious as this is, the presentation of plays through the literary medium has not yet become an art; and the result is that it is very difficult to induce the English public to buy and read plays. Indeed, why should they, when they find nothing in them except the bare words, with a few carpenter's and costumier's directions as to the heroine's father having a grey beard, and the drawing room having three doors on the right, two doors and an entrance through the conservatory on the left, and a French window in the middle? It is astonishing to me that Ibsen, devoting two years to the production of a three-act play, the extraordinary quality of which depends on a mastery of character and situation which can only be achieved by working out a good deal of the family and personal history of the individuals represented, should nevertheless give the reading public very little more than the technical memorandum required by the carpenter, the electrician, and the prompter. Who will deny that the resultant occasional mysteriousness of effect, enchanting though it may be, is produced at the cost of intellectual obscurity? Ibsen, interrogated as to his meaning, replied "What I have said, I have said." Precisely; but the point is that what he hasnt said, he hasnt said. There are perhaps people (though I doubt it, not being one of them myself) to whom Ibsen's plays, as they stand, speak sufficiently for themselves. There are certainly others who could not understand them on any terms. Granting that on both these classes further explanations would be thrown away, is nothing to be done for the vast majority to whom a word of explanation makes all the difference?

Finally, may I put in a plea for the actors themselves? Born actors have a susceptibility to dramatic emotion which enables them to seize the moods of their parts intuitively. But to expect them to be intuitive as to intellectual meaning and circumstantial conditions as well, is to demand powers of divination from them: one might as well expect the Astronomer Royal to tell the time in a catacomb. And yet the actor generally finds his part full of emotional directions which he could supply as well or better than the author, whilst he is left quite in the dark as to the political or religious conditions under which the character he impersonates is supposed to be acting. Definite conceptions of these are always implicit in the best plays, and are often the key to their appropriate rendering; but most actors are so accustomed to do without them that they would object to being troubled with them, although it is only by such educative trouble that an actor's profession can place him on the level of the lawyer, the physician, the churchman, and the statesman. Even as it is, Shylock as a Jew and usurer, Othello as a Moor and a soldier, Cæsar, Cleopatra, and Antony as figures in defined political circumstances, are enormously more real to the actor than the countless heroes as to whom nothing is ever known except that they wear nice clothes, love the heroine, baffle the villain, and live happily ever after.

The case, then, is overwhelming not only for printing and publishing the dialogue of plays, but for a serious effort to convey their full content to the reader. This means the institution of a new art; and I daresay that before these two volumes are ten years old, the bald attempt they make at it will be left far behind, and that the customary brief and unreadable scene specification at the head of an act will have expanded into a chapter, or even a series of chapters. No doubt one result of this will be the production, under cover of the above arguments, of works of a mixture of kinds, part narrative, part homily, part description, part dialogue, and (possibly) part drama: works that could be read, but not acted. I have no objection to such works; but my own aim has been that of the practical dramatist: if anything my eye has been too much on the stage. At all events, I have tried to put down nothing that is irrelevant to the actor's performance, and, through it, to the audience's comprehension of the play. I have of course been compelled to omit many things that a stage representation could convey, simply because the art of letters, though highly developed grammatically, is still in its infancy as a technical speech notation: for example, there are fifty ways of saying Yes, and five hundred of saying No, but only one way of writing them down. Even the use of spaced letters instead of italics for underlining, though familiar to foreign readers, will have to be learned by the English public before it becomes effective. But if my readers do their fair share of the work, I daresay they will understand nearly as much of the plays as I do myself.

Finally, a word as to why I have labelled the three plays in this first volume Unpleasant. The reason is pretty obvious: their dramatic power is used to force the spectator to face unpleasant facts. No doubt all plays which deal sincerely with humanity must wound the monstrous conceit which it is the business of romance to flatter. But here we are confronted, not only with the comedy and tragedy of individual character and destiny, but with those social horrors which arise from the fact that the average homebred Englishman, however honorable and goodnatured he may be in his private capacity, is, as a citizen, a wretched creature who, whilst clamoring for a gratuitous millennium, will shut his eyes to the most villainous abuses if the remedy threatens to add another penny in the pound to the rates and taxes which he has

to be half cheated, half coerced into paying. In Widowers' Houses I have shewn middle-class respectability and younger son gentility fattening on the poverty of the slum as flies fatten on filth. That is not a pleasant theme.

In The Philanderer I have shewn the grotesque sexual compacts made between men and women under marriage laws which represent to some of us a political necessity (especially for other people), to some a divine ordinance, to some a romantic ideal, to some a domestic profession for women, and to some that worst of blundering abominations, an institution which society has outgrown but not modified, and which "advanced" individuals are therefore forced to evade. The scene with which The Philanderer opens, the atmosphere in which it proceeds, and the marriage with which it ends, are, for the intellectually and artistically conscious classes in modern society, typical; and it will hardly be denied, I think, that they are unpleasant.

In Mrs Warren's Profession I have gone straight at the fact that, as Mrs Warren puts it, "the only way for a woman to provide for herself decently is for her to be good to some man that can afford to be good to her." There are certain questions on which I am, like most Socialists, an extreme Individualist. I believe that any society which desires to found itself on a high standard of integrity of character in its units should organize itself in such a fashion as to make it possible for all men and all women to maintain themselves in reasonable comfort by their industry without selling their affections and their convictions. At present we not only condemn women as a sex to attach themselves to breadwinners, licitly or illicitly, on pain of heavy privation and disadvantage; but we have great prostitute classes of men: for instance, the playwrights and journalists, to whom I myself belong, not to mention the legions of lawyers, doctors, clergymen, and platform politicians who are daily using their highest faculties to belie their real sentiments: a sin compared to which that of a woman who sells the use of her person for a few hours is too venial to be worth mentioning; for rich men without conviction are more dangerous in modern society than poor women without chastity. Hardly a pleasant subject, this!

I must, however, warn my readers that my attacks are directed against themselves, not against my stage figures. They cannot too thoroughly understand that the guilt of defective social organization does not lie alone on the people who actually work the commercial makeshifts which the defects make inevitable, and who often, like Sartorius and Mrs Warren, display valuable executive capacities and even high moral virtues in their administration, but with the whole body of citizens whose public opinion, public action, and public contribution as ratepayers, alone can replace Sartorius's slums with decent dwellings, Charteris's intrigues with reasonable marriage contracts, and Mrs Warren's profession with honorable industries guarded by a humane industrial code and a "moral minimum" wage.

How I came, later on, to write plays which, dealing less with the crimes of society, and more with its romantic follies and with the struggles of individuals against those follies, may be called, by contrast, Pleasant, is a story which I shall tell on resuming this discourse for the edification of the readers of the second volume.

XXVIII

PLAYS PLEASANT

1898

Readers of the discourse with which the "Unpleasant" volume commences will remember that I turned my hand to play-writing when a great deal of talk about "the New Drama," followed by the actual establishment of a "New Theatre" (the Independent), threatened to end in the humiliating discovery that the New Drama, in England at least, was a figment of the revolutionary imagination. This was not to be endured. I had rashly taken up the case; and rather than let it collapse I manufactured the evidence.

Man is a creature of habit. You cannot write three plays and then stop. Besides, the New movement did not stop. In 1894, Florence Farr, who had already produced Ibsen's Rosmersholm, was placed in command of the Avenue Theatre in London for a season on the new lines by Miss A. E. F. Horniman, who had family reasons for not yet appearing openly as a pioneer-manageress. There were, as available New Dramatists, myself, discovered by the Independent Theatre (at my own suggestion); Dr John Todhunter, who had been discovered before (his play The Black Cat had been one of the Independent's successes); and Mr W. B. Yeats, a genuine discovery. Dr Todhunter supplied A Comedy of Sighs: Mr Yeats, The Land of Heart's Desire. I, having nothing but unpleasant plays in my desk, hastily completed a first attempt at a pleasant one, and called it Arms and The Man, taking the title from the first line of Dryden's Virgil. It passed for a success, the applause on the first night being as promising as could be wished; and it ran from the 21st of April to the 7th of July. To witness it the public paid £1777:5:6, an average of £23:2:5 per representation (including nine mat-inées). A publisher receiving £1700 for a book would have made a satisfactory profit: experts in West End theatrical management will contemplate that figure with a grim smile.

In the autumn of 1894 I spent a few weeks in Florence, where I occupied myself with the religious art of the Middle Ages and its destruction by the Renascence. From a former visit to Italy on the same business I had hurried back to Birmingham to discharge my duties as musical critic at the Festival there. On that occasion a very remarkable collection of the works of our British "pre-Raphaelite" painters was on view. I looked at these, and then went into the Birmingham churches to see the windows of William Morris and Burne-Jones. On the whole, Birmingham was more hopeful than the Italian cities; for the art it had to shew me was the work of living men, whereas modern Italy had, as far as I could see, no more connection with Giotto than Port Said has with Ptolemy. Now I am no believer in the worth of any mere taste for art that cannot produce what it professes to appreciate. When my subsequent visit to Italy found me practising the playwright's craft, the time was ripe for a modern pre-Raphaelite play. Religion was alive again, coming back upon men, even upon clergymen, with such power that not the Church of England itself could keep it out. Here my activity as a Socialist had placed me on sure and familiar ground. To me the members of the Guild of St Matthew were no more "High Church clergymen," Dr Clifford no more "an eminent Nonconformist divine," than I was to them "an infidel." There is only one religion, though there are a hundred versions of it. We all had the same thing to say; and though some of us cleared our throats to say it by singing revolutionary lyrics and republican hymns, we thought nothing of singing them to the music of Sullivan's Onward Christian Soldiers or Haydn's God Preserve the Emperor.

Now unity, however desirable in political agitations, is fatal to drama; for every drama must present a conflict. The end may be reconciliation or destruction; or, as in life itself, there may be no end; but the conflict is indispensable: no conflict, no drama. Certainly it is easy to dramatize the prosaic conflict of Christian Socialism with vulgar Unsocialism: for instance, in Widowers' Houses, the clergyman, who does not appear on the stage at all, is the real antagonist of the slum landlord. But the obvious conflicts of unmistakeable good with unmistakeable evil can only supply the crude drama of villain and hero, in which some absolute point of view is taken, and the dissentients are treated by the dramatist as enemies to be piously glorified or indignantly vilified. In such cheap wares I do not deal. Even in my unpleasant propagandist plays I have allowed every person his or her own point of view, and have, I hope, to the full extent of my understanding of him, been as sympathetic with Sir George Crofts as with any of the more genial and popular characters in the present volume. To distil the quintessential drama from pre-Raphaelitism, medieval or modern, it must be shewn at its best in conflict with the first broken, nervous, stumbling attempts to formulate its own revolt against itself as it develops into something higher. A coherent explanation of any such revolt, addressed intelligibly and prosaically to the intellect, can only come when the work is done, and indeed *done with*: that is to say, when the development, accomplished, admitted, and assimilated, is a story of yesterday. Long before any such understanding can be reached, the eyes of men begin to turn towards the distant light of the new age. Discernible at first only by the eyes of the man of genius, it must be focussed by him on the speculum of a work of art, and flashed back from that into the eyes of the common man. Nay, the artist himself has no other way of making himself conscious of the ray: it is by a blind instinct that he keeps on building up his masterpieces until their pinnacles catch the glint of the unrisen sun. Ask him to explain himself prosaically, and you find that he "writes like an angel and talks like poor Poll," and is himself the first to make that epigram at his own expense. John Ruskin has told us clearly enough what is in the pictures of Carpaccio and Bellini: let him explain, if he can, where we shall be when the sun that is caught by the summits of the work of his favorite Tintoretto, of his aversion Rembrandt, of Mozart, of Beethoven and Wagner, of Blake and of Shelley, shall have reached the valleys. Let Ibsen explain, if he can, why the building of churches and happy homes is not the ultimate destiny of Man, and why, to thrill the unsatisfied younger generations, he must mount beyond it to heights that now seem unspeakably giddy and dreadful to him, and from which the first climbers must fall and dash themselves to pieces. He cannot explain it: he can only shew it to you as a vision in the magic glass of his artwork; so that you may catch his presentiment and make what you can of it. And this is the function that raises dramatic art above imposture and pleasure hunting, and enables the playwright to be something more than a skilled liar and pandar.

Here, then, was the higher but vaguer and timider vision, the incoherent, mischievous, and even ridiculous unpracticalness, which offered me a dramatic antagonist for the clear, bold, sure, sensible, benevolent, salutarily shortsighted Christian Socialist idealism. I availed myself of it in Candida, the drunken scene in which has been much appreciated, I am told, in Aberdeen. I purposely contrived the play in such a way as to make the expenses of representation insignificant; so that, without pretending that I could appeal to a very wide circle of playgoers, I could reasonably sound a few of our more enlightened managers as to an experiment with half a dozen afternoon performances. They admired the play generously: indeed I think that if any of them had been young enough to play the poet, my proposal might have been acceded to, in spite of many incidental difficulties. Nay, if only I had made the poet a cripple, or at least blind, so as to combine an easier disguise with a larger claim for sympathy, something might have been done. Richard Mansfield, who had, with apparent ease, made me quite famous in America by his productions of my plays, went so far as to put the play actually into rehearsal before he would confess himself beaten by the physical difficulties of the part. But they did beat him; and Candida did not see the footlights until my old ally the Independent Theatre, making a propagandist tour through the provinces with A Doll's House, added Candida to its repertory, to the great astonishment of its audiences.

In an idle moment in 1895 I began the little scene called The Man of Destiny, which is hardly more than a bravura piece to display the virtuosity of the two principal performers.

In the meantime I had devoted the spare moments of 1896 to the composition of two more plays, only the first of which appears in this volume.[1] You Never Can Tell was an attempt to comply with many requests for a play in which the much paragraphed "brilliancy" of Arms and The Man should be tempered by some consideration for the requirements of managers in search of fashionable

[1] Plays Pleasant.

comedies for West End theatres. I had no difficulty in complying, as I have always cast my plays in the ordinary practical comedy form in use at all the theatres; and far from taking an unsympathetic view of the popular preference for fun, fashionable dresses, a little music, and even an exhibition of eating and drinking by people with an expensive air, attended by an if-possible-comic waiter, I was more than willing to shew that the drama can humanize these things as easily as they, in the wrong hands, can dehumanize the drama. But as often happens it was easier to do this than to persuade those who had asked for it that they had indeed got it. A chapter in Cyril Maude's history of the Haymarket Theatre records how the play was rehearsed there, and why I withdrew it. And so I reached the point at which, as narrated in the preface to the "Unpleasant" volume, I resolved to avail myself of my literary expertness to put my plays before the public in my own way.

It will be noticed that I have not been driven to this expedient by any hostility on the part of our managers. I will not pretend that the modern actor-manager's talent as player can in the nature of things be often associated with exceptional critical insight. As a rule, by the time a manager has experience enough to make him as safe a judge of plays as a Bond Street dealer is of pictures, he begins to be thrown out in his calculations by the slow but constant change of public taste, and by his own growing conservatism. But his need for new plays is so great, and the few accredited authors are so little able to keep pace with their commissions, that he is always apt to overrate rather than to underrate his discoveries in the way of new pieces by new authors. An original work by a man of genius like Ibsen may, of course, baffle him as it baffles many professed critics; but in the beaten path of drama no unacted works of merit, suitable to his purposes, have been discovered; whereas the production, at great expense, of very faulty plays written by novices (not "backers") is by no means an unknown event. Indeed, to anyone who can estimate, even vaguely, the complicated trouble, the risk of heavy loss, and the initial expense and thought, involved by the production of a play, the ease with which dramatic authors, known and unknown, get their works performed must needs seem a wonder.

Only, authors must not expect managers to invest many thousands of pounds in plays, however fine (or the reverse), which will clearly not attract perfectly commonplace people. Playwriting and theatrical management, on the present commercial basis, are businesses like other businesses, depending on the patronage of great numbers of very ordinary customers. When the managers and authors study the wants of these customers, they succeed: when they do not, they fail. A public-spirited manager, or an author with a keen artistic conscience, may choose to pursue his business with the minimum of profit and the maximum of social usefulness by keeping as close as he can to the highest marketable limit of quality, and constantly feeling for an extension of that limit through the advance of popular culture. An unscrupulous manager or author may aim simply at the maximum of profit with the minimum of risk. These are the opposite poles of our system, represented in practice by our first rate managements at the one end, and the syndicates which exploit pornographic farces at the other. Between them there is plenty of room for most talents to breathe freely: at all events there is a career, no harder of access than any cognate career, for all qualified playwrights who bring the manager what his customers want and understand, or even enough of it to induce them to swallow at the same time a great deal that they neither want nor understand; for the public is touchingly humble in such matters.

For all that, the commercial limits are too narrow for our social welfare. The theatre is growing in importance as a social organ. Bad theatres are as mischievous as bad schools or bad churches; for modern civilization is rapidly multiplying the class to which the theatre is both school and church. Public and private life become daily more theatrical: the modern Kaiser, Dictator, President, or Prime Minister is nothing if not an effective actor; all newspapers are now edited histrionically; and the records of our law courts shew that the stage is affecting personal conduct to an unprecedented extent, and affecting it by no means for the worse, except in so far as the theatrical education of the persons concerned has been romantic: that is, spurious, cheap, and vulgar. The truth is that dramatic invention is the first effort of man to become intellectually conscious. No frontier can be marked between drama and history or religion, or between acting and conduct, nor any distinction made between them that is not also the distinction between the masterpieces of the great dramatic poets and the commonplaces of our theatrical seasons. When this chapter of science is convincingly written, the national importance of the theatre will be as unquestioned as that of the army, the fleet, the Church, the law, and the schools.

For my part, I have no doubt that the commercial limits should be overstepped, and that the highest prestige, with a financial position of reasonable security and comfort, should be attainable in theatrical management by keeping the public in constant touch with the highest achievements of dramatic art. Our managers will not dissent to this: the best of them are so willing to get as near that position as they can without ruining themselves, that they can all point to honorable losses incurred through aiming "over the heads of the public," and will no doubt risk such loss again, for the sake of their reputation as artists, as soon as a few popular successes enable them to afford it. But even if it were possible for them to educate the nation at their own private cost, why should they be expected to do it? There are much stronger objections to the pauperization of the public by private doles than were ever entertained, even by the Poor Law Commissioners of 1834, to the pauperization of private individuals by public doles. If we want a theatre which shall be to the drama what the National Gallery and British Museum are to painting and literature, we can get it by endowing it in the same way. In the meantime there are many possibilities of local activity. Groups of amateurs can form permanent societies and persevere until they develop into professional companies in established repertory theatres. In big cities it should be feasible to form influential committees, preferably without any actors, critics, or playwrights on them, and with as many persons of title as possible, for the purpose of approaching one of the leading local managers with a proposal that they shall, under a guarantee against loss, undertake a certain number of afternoon performances of the class required by the committee, in addition to their ordinary business. If the committee is influential enough, the offer will be accepted. In that case, the first performance will be the beginning of a classic repertory for the manager and his company which every subsequent performance will extend. The formation of the repertory will go hand in hand with the discovery and habituation of a regular audience for it; and it will eventually become profitable for the manager to multiply the number of performances at his own risk. It might even become worth his while to take a second

theatre and establish the repertory permanently in it. In the event of any of his classic productions proving a fashionable success, he could transfer it to his fashionable house and make the most of it there. Such managership would carry a knighthood with it; and such a theatre would be the needed nucleus for municipal or national endowment. I make the suggestion quite disinterestedly; for as I am not an academic person, I should not be welcomed as an unacted classic by such a committee; and cases like mine would still leave forlorn hopes like The Independent Theatre its reason for existing. The committee plan, I may remind its critics, has been in operation in London for two hundred years in support of Italian opera.

Returning now to the actual state of things, it is clear that I have no grievance against our theatres. Knowing quite well what I was doing, I have heaped difficulties in the way of the performance of my plays by ignoring the majority of the manager's customers: nay, by positively making war on them. To the actor I have been more considerate, using all my cunning to enable him to make the most of his technical methods; but I have not hesitated on occasion to tax his intelligence very severely, making the stage effect depend not only on *nuances* of execution quite beyond the average skill produced by the routine of the English stage in its present condition, but on a perfectly sincere and straightforward conception of states of mind which still seem cynically perverse to most people, and on a goodhumoredly contemptuous or profoundly pitiful attitude towards ethical conventions which seem to them validly heroic or venerable. It is inevitable that actors should suffer more than most of us from the sophistication of their consciousness by romance; and my view of romance as the great heresy to be swept off from art and life—as the food of modern pessimism and the bane of modern self-respect, is far more puzzling to the performers than it is to the pit. It is hard for an actor whose point of honor it is to be a perfect gentleman, to sympathize with an author who regards gentility as a dishonest folly, and gallantry and chivalry as treasonable to women and stultifying to men.

The misunderstanding is complicated by the fact that actors, in their demonstrations of emotion, have made a second nature of stage custom, which is often very much out of date as a representation of contemporary life. Sometimes the stage custom is not only obsolete, but fundamentally wrong: for instance, in the simple case of laughter and tears, in which it deals too liberally, it is certainly not based on the fact, easily enough discoverable in real life, that we only cry now in the effort to bear happiness, whilst we laugh and exult in destruction, confusion, and ruin. When a comedy is performed, it is nothing to me that the spectators laugh: any fool can make an audience laugh. I want to see how many of them, laughing or grave, are in the melting mood. And this result cannot be achieved, even by actors who thoroughly understand my purpose, except through an artistic beauty of execution unattainable without long and arduous practice, and an intellectual effort which my plays probably do not seem serious enough to call forth.

Beyond the difficulties thus raised by the nature and quality of my work, I have none to complain of. I have come upon no ill will, no inaccessibility, on the part of the very few managers with whom I have discussed it. As a rule I find that the actor-manager is over-sanguine, because he has the artist's habit of underrating the force of circumstances and exaggerating the power of the talented individual to prevail against them; whilst I have acquired the politician's habit of regarding the individual, however talented, as having no choice but to make the most of his circumstances. I half suspect that those managers who have had most to do with me, if asked to name the main obstacle to the performance of my plays, would unhesitatingly and unanimously reply "The author." And I confess that though as a matter of business I wish my plays to be performed, as a matter of instinct I fight against the inevitable misrepresentation of them with all the subtlety needed to conceal my ill will from myself as well as from the manager.

The main difficulty, of course, is the incapacity for serious drama of thousands of playgoers of all classes whose shillings and half guineas will buy as much in the market as if they delighted in the highest art. But with them I must frankly take the superior position. I know that many managers are wholly dependent on them, and that no manager is wholly independent of them; but I can no more write what they want than Joachim can put aside his fiddle and oblige a happy company of beanfeasters with a marching tune on the German concertina. They must keep away from my plays: that is all.

There is no reason, however, why I should take this haughty attitude towards those representative critics whose complaint is that my talent, though not unentertaining, lacks elevation of sentiment and seriousness of purpose. They can find, under the surface-brilliancy for which they give me credit, no coherent thought or sympathy, and accuse me, in various terms and degrees, of an inhuman and freakish wantonness; of preoccupation with "the seamy side of life"; of paradox, cynicism, and eccentricity, reducible, as some contend, to a trite formula of treating bad as good and good as bad, important as trivial and trivial as important, serious as laughable and laughable as serious, and so forth. As to this formula I can only say that if any gentleman is simple enough to think that even a good comic opera can be produced by it, I invite him to try his hand, and see whether anything resembling one of my plays will reward him.

I could explain the matter easily enough if I chose; but the result would be that the people who misunderstand the plays would misunderstand the explanation ten times more. The particular exceptions taken are seldom more than symptoms of the underlying fundamental disagreement between the romantic morality of the critics and the natural morality of the plays. For example, I am quite aware that the much criticized Swiss officer in Arms and The Man is not a conventional stage soldier. He suffers from want of food and sleep; his nerves go to pieces after three days under fire, ending in the horrors of a rout and pursuit; he has found by experience that it is more important to have a few bits of chocolate to eat in the field than cartridges for his revolver. When many of my critics rejected these circumstances as fantastically improbable and cynically unnatural, it was not necessary to argue them into common sense: all I had to do was to brain them, so to speak, with the first half dozen military authorities at hand, beginning with the present Commander in Chief. But when it proved that such unromantic (but all the more dramatic) facts implied to them a denial of the existence of courage, patriotism, faith, hope, and charity, I saw that it was not really mere matter of fact that was at issue between us. One strongly Liberal critic, the late Moy Thomas, who had, in the teeth of a chorus of dissent, received my first play with the most generous encouragement, declared, when Arms and The Man was produced, that I had struck a wanton blow at the cause of liberty in the Balkan Peninsula by mentioning that it was not a matter of course for a Bulgarian in 1885 to wash his hands every day. He no doubt saw soon afterwards the squabble, reported all through Europe, between Stambouloff and an eminent lady of the Bulgarian court who took exception to his neglect of his fingernails. After that came the news of his ferocious assassination, with a description of the room prepared for the reception of visitors by his widow, who draped it with black, and decorated it with photographs of the mutilated body of her husband. Here was a sufficiently sensational confirmation of the accuracy of my sketch of the theatrical nature of the first apings of western civilization by spirited races just emerging from slavery. But it had no bearing on the real issue between my critic and myself, which was, whether the political and religious idealism which had inspired Gladstone to call for the rescue of these Balkan principalities from the despotism of the Turk, and converted miserably enslaved provinces into hopeful and gallant little States, will survive the general onslaught on idealism which is implicit, and indeed explicit, in Arms and The Man and the naturalist plays of the modern school. For my part I hope not; for idealism, which is only a flattering name for romance in politics and morals, is as obnoxious to me as romance in ethics or religion. In spite of a Liberal Revolution or two, I can no longer be satisfied with fictitious morals and fictitious good conduct, shedding fictitious glory on robbery, starvation, disease, crime, drink, war, cruelty, cupidity, and all the other commonplaces of civilization which drive men to the theatre to make foolish pretences that such things are progress, science, morals, religion, patriotism, imperial supremacy, national greatness and all the other names the newspapers call them. On the other hand, I see plenty of good in the world working itself out as fast as the idealists will allow it; and if they would only let it alone and learn to respect reality, which would include the beneficial exercise of respecting themselves, and incidentally respecting me, we should all get along much better and faster. At all events, I do not see moral chaos and anarchy as the alternative to romantic convention; and I am not going to pretend I do merely to please the people who are convinced that the world is held together only by the force of unanimous, strenuous, elo-quent, trumpet-tongued lying. To me the tragedy and comedy of life lie in the consequences, sometimes terrible, sometimes ludicrous, of our persistent attempts to found our institutions on the ideals suggested to our imaginations by our half-satisfied passions, instead of on a genuinely scientific natural history. And with that hint as to what I am driving at, I withdraw and ring up the curtain.

XXIX

THREE PLAYS FOR PURITANS

1900

WHY FOR PURITANS?

Since I gave my Plays, Pleasant and Unpleasant, to the world two years ago, many things have happened to me. I had then just entered on the fourth year of my activity as a critic of the London theatres. They very nearly killed me. I had survived seven years of London's music, four or five years of London's pictures, and about as much of its current literature, wrestling critically with them with all my force and skill. After that, the criticism of the theatre came to me as a huge relief in point of bodily exertion. The difference between the leisure of a Persian cat and the labor of a cockney cab horse is not greater than the difference between the official weekly or fortnightly playgoings of the theatre critic and the restless daily rushing to and fro of the music critic, from the stroke of three in the afternoon, when the concerts begin, to the stroke of twelve at night, when the opera ends. The pictures were nearly as bad. An Alpinist once, noticing the massive soles of my boots, asked me whether I climbed mountains. No, I replied: these boots are for the hard floors of the London galleries. Yet I once dealt with music and pictures together in the spare time of an active young revolutionist, and wrote plays and books and other toilsome things into the bargain. But the theatre struck me down like the veriest weakling. I sank under it like a baby fed on starch. My very bones began to perish, so that I had to get them planed and gouged by accomplished surgeons. I fell from heights and broke my limbs in pieces. The doctors said: This man has not eaten meat for twenty years: he must eat it or die. I said: This man has been going to the London

theatres for three years; and the soul of him has become inane and is feeding unnaturally on his body. And I was right. I did not change my diet; but I had myself carried up into a mountain where there was no theatre; and there I began to revive. Too weak to work, I wrote books and plays: hence the second and third plays in this volume. And now I am stronger than I have been at any moment since my feet first carried me as a critic across the fatal threshold of a London playhouse.

Why was this? What is the matter with the theatre, that a strong man can die of it? Well, the answer will make a long story; but it must be told. And, to begin, why have I just called the theatre a playhouse? The well-fed Englishman, though he lives and dies a schoolboy, cannot play. He cannot even play cricket or football: he has to work at them: that is why he beats the foreigner who plays at them. To him playing means playing the fool. He can hunt and shoot and travel and fight: he can, when special holiday festivity is suggested to him, eat and drink, dice and drab, smoke and lounge. But play he cannot. The moment you make his theatre a place of amusement instead of a place of edification, you make it, not a real playhouse, but a place of excitement for the sportsman and the sensualist.

However, this well-fed grown-up-schoolboy Englishman counts for little in the modern metropolitan audience. In the long lines of waiting playgoers lining the pavements outside our fashionable theatres every evening, the men are only the currants in the dumpling. Women are in the majority; and women and men alike belong to that least robust of all our social classes, the class which earns from eighteen to thirty shillings a week in sedentary employment, and lives in lonely lodgings or in drab homes with nagging relatives. These people preserve the innocence of the theatre: they have neither the philosopher's impatience to get to realities (reality being the one thing they want to escape from), nor the longing of the sportsman for violent action, nor the full-fed, experienced, disillusioned sensuality of the rich man, whether he be gentleman or sporting publican. They read a good deal, and are at home in the fool's paradise of popular romance. They love the pretty man and the pretty woman, and will have both of them fashionably dressed and exquisitely idle, posing against backgrounds of drawing room and dainty garden; in love, but sentimentally, romantically; always ladylike and gentlemanlike. Jejunely insipid, all this, to the stalls, which are paid for (when they *are* paid for) by people who have their own dresses and drawing rooms, and know them to be a mere masquerade behind which there is nothing romantic, and little that is interesting to most of the masqueraders except the clandestine play of natural licentiousness.

The stalls cannot be fully understood without taking into account the absence of the rich evangelical English merchant and his family, and the presence of the rich Jewish merchant and *his* family. I can see no validity whatever in the view that the influence of the rich Jews on the theatre is any worse than the influence of the rich of any other race. Other qualities being equal, men become rich in commerce in proportion to the intensity and exclusiveness of their desire for money. It may be a misfortune that the purchasing power of men who value money above art, philosophy, and the welfare of the whole community, should enable them to influence the theatre (and everything else in the market); but there is no reason to suppose that their influence is any nobler when they imagine themselves Christians than when they know themselves Jews. All that can fairly be said of the Jewish influence on the theatre is that it is exotic, and is not only a customer's influence but a financier's influence: so much so, that the way is smoothest for those plays and those performers that appeal specially to the Jewish taste. English influence on the theatre, as far as the stalls are concerned, does not exist, because the rich purchasing-powerful Englishman prefers politics and church-going: his soul is too stubborn to be purged by an avowed make-believe. When he wants sensuality he practises it: he does not play with voluptuous or romantic ideas. From the play of ideas—and the drama can never be anything more—he demands edification, and will not pay for anything else in that arena. Consequently the box office will never become an English influence until the theatre turns from the drama of romance and sensuality to the drama of edification.

Turning from the stalls to the whole auditorium, consider what is implied by the fact that the prices (all much too high, by the way) range from half a guinea to a shilling, the ages from eighteen to eighty, whilst every age, and nearly every price, represents a different taste. Is it not clear that this diversity in the audience makes it impossible to gratify every one of its units by the same luxury, since in that domain of infinite caprice, one man's meat is another man's poison, one age's longing another age's loathing? And yet that is just what the theatres kept trying to do almost all the time I was doomed to attend them. On the other hand, to interest people of divers ages, classes, and temperaments by some generally momentous subject of thought, as the politicians and preachers do, would seem the most obvious course in the world. And yet the theatres avoided that as a ruinous eccentricity. Their wiseacres persisted in

2 A

assuming that all men have the same tastes, fancies, and qualities of passion; that no two have the same interests; and that most playgoers have no interests at all. This being precisely contrary to the obvious facts, it followed that the majority of the plays produced were failures, recognizable as such before the end of the first act by the very wiseacres aforementioned, who, quite incapable of understanding the lesson, would thereupon set to work to obtain and produce a play applying their theory still more strictly, with proportionately more disastrous results. The sums of money I saw thus transferred from the pockets of theatrical speculators and syndicates to those of wigmakers, costumiers, scene painters, carpenters, doorkeepers, actors, theatre landlords, and all the other people for whose exclusive benefit most London theatres seem to exist, would have kept a theatre devoted exclusively to the highest drama open all the year round. If the Browning and Shelley Societies were fools, as the wiseacres said they were, for producing Strafford, Colombe's Birthday, and The Cenci; if the Independent Theatre, the New Century Theatre, and the Stage Society are impracticable faddists for producing the plays of Ibsen and Maeterlinck, then what epithet is contemptuous enough for the people who produce the would-be popular plays?

The actor-managers were far more successful, because they produced plays that at least pleased themselves, whereas Commerce, with a false theory of how to please everybody, produced plays that pleased nobody. But their occasional personal successes in voluptuous plays, and, in any case, their careful concealment of failure, confirmed the prevalent error, which was exposed fully only when the plays had to stand or fall openly by their own merits. Even Shakespear was played with his brains cut out. In 1896, when Sir Henry Irving was disabled by an accident at a moment when Miss Ellen Terry was too ill to appear, the theatre had to be closed after a brief attempt to rely on the attraction of a Shakespearean play performed by the stock company. This may have been Shakespear's fault: indeed Sir Henry later on complained that he had lost a princely sum by Shakespear. But Shakespear's reply to this, if he were able to make it, would be that the princely sum was spent, not on his dramatic poetry, but on a gorgeous stage ritualism superimposed on reckless mutilations of his text, the whole being addressed to a public as to which nothing is certain except that its natural bias is towards reverence for Shakespear and dislike and distrust of ritualism. No doubt the Irving ritual appealed to a far more cultivated sensuousness and imaginativeness than the musical farces in which our stage Abbots of Misrule pontificated (with the same financially disastrous result); but in both there was the same intentional brainlessness, founded on the same theory that the public did not want brains, did not want to think, did not want anything but pleasure at the theatre. Unfortunately, this theory happens to be true of a certain section of the public. This section, being courted by the theatres, went to them and drove the other people out. It then discovered, as any expert could have foreseen, that the theatre cannot compete in mere pleasuremongering either with the other arts or with matter-of-fact gallantry. Stage pictures are the worst pictures, stage music the worst music, stage scenery the worst scenery within reach of the Londoner. The leading lady or gentleman may be as tempting to the admirer in the pit as the dishes in a cookshop window are to the penniless tramp on the pavement; but people do not, I presume, go to the theatre to be merely tantalized.

The breakdown on the last point was conclusive. For when the managers tried to put their principle of pleasing everybody into practice, Necessity, ever ironical towards Folly, had driven them to seek a universal pleasure to appeal to. And since many have no ear for music or eye for color, the search for universality inevitably flung the managers back on the instinct of sex as the avenue to all hearts. Of course the appeal was a vapid failure. Speaking for my own sex, I can say that the leading lady was not to everybody's taste: her pretty face often became ugly when she tried to make it expressive; her voice lost its charm (if it ever had any) when she had nothing sincere to say; and the stalls, from racial prejudice, were apt to insist on more Rebecca and less Rowena than the pit cared for. It may seem strange, even monstrous, that a man should feel a constant attachment to the hideous witches in Macbeth, and yet yawn at the prospect of spending another evening in the contemplation of a beauteous young leading lady with voluptuous contours and longlashed eyes, painted and dressed to perfection in the latest fashions. But that is just what happened to me in the theatre.

I did not find that matters were improved by the lady pretending to be "a woman with a past," violently oversexed, or the play being called a problem play, even when the manager, and sometimes, I suspect, the very author, firmly believed the word problem to be the latest euphemism for what Justice Shallow called a bona roba, and certainly would not either of them have staked a farthing on the interest of a genuine problem. In fact these so-called problem plays invariably depended for their dramatic interest on foregone conclusions of the most heartwearying conventionality concerning sexual morality. The authors had no problematic views: all they wanted was to capture some of the fascination of Ibsen. It seemed to them that most of Ibsen's heroines were naughty ladies. And they tried to produce Ibsen plays by making their heroines naughty. But they took great care to make them pretty and expensively dressed. Thus the pseudo-Ibsen play was nothing but the ordinary sensuous ritual of the stage become as frankly pornographic as good manners allowed.

I found that the whole business of stage sensuousness, whether as Lyceum Shakespear, musical farce, or sham Ibsen, finally disgusted me, not because I was Pharisaical, or intolerantly refined, but because I was bored; and boredom is a condition which makes men as susceptible to disgust and irritation as headache makes them to noise and glare. Being a man, I have my share of the masculine silliness and vulgarity on the subject of sex which so astonishes women, to whom sex is a serious matter. I am not an archbishop, and do not pretend to pass my life on one plane or in one mood, and that the highest: on the contrary, I am, I protest, as accessible to the humors of The Rogue's Comedy or The Rake's Progress as to the pious decencies of The Sign of the Cross. Thus Falstaff, coarser than any of the men in our loosest plays, does not bore me: Doll Tearsheet, more abandoned than any of the women, does not shock me. I admit that Romeo and Juliet would be a duller play if it were robbed of the solitary fragment it has preserved for us of the conversation of the husband of Juliet's nurse. No: my disgust was not mere thinskinned prudery. When my moral sense revolted, as it often did to the very fibres, it was invariably at the nauseous compliances of the theatre with conventional virtue. If I despised the musical farces, it was because they never had the courage of their vices. With all their labored efforts to keep up an understanding of furtive naughtiness between the low comedian on the stage and the drunken undergraduate in the stalls, they insisted all the time on their virtue and patriotism and loyalty as pitifully as a poor girl of the pavement will pretend to be a clergyman's daughter. True, I may have been offended when a manager, catering for me with coarse frankness as a slave dealer caters for a Pasha, invited me to forget the common bond of humanity between me and his company by demanding nothing from them but a gloatably voluptuous appearance. But this extreme is never reached at our better theatres. The shop assistants, the typists, the clerks, who, as I have said, preserve the innocence of the theatre, would not dare to let themselves be pleased by it. Even if they did, they would not get it from our reputable managers, who, when faced with the only logical conclusion from their principle of making the theatre a temple of pleasure, indignantly refuse to change the theatrical profession for Mrs Warren's. For that is what all this demand for pleasure at the theatre finally comes to; and the answer to it is, not that people ought not to desire sensuous pleasure (they cannot help it) but that the theatre cannot give it to them, even to the extent permitted by the honor and conscience of the best managers, because a theatre is so far from being a pleasant or even a comfortable place that only by making us forget ourselves can it prevent us from realizing its inconveniences. A play that does not do this for the pleasure-seeker allows him to discover that he has chosen a disagreeable and expensive way of spending the evening. He wants to drink, to smoke, to change the spectacle, to get rid of the middle-aged actor and actress who are boring him, and to see shapely young dancing girls and acrobats doing more amusing things in a more plastic manner. In short, he wants the music hall; and he goes there, leaving the managers astonished at this unexpected but quite inevitable result of the attempt to please him. Whereas, had he been enthralled by the play, even with horror, instead of himself enthralling with the dread of his displeasure the manager, the author and the actors, all had been well. And so we must conclude that the theatre is a place which people can endure only when they forget themselves: that is, when their attention is entirely captured, their interest thoroughly aroused, their sympathies raised to the eagerest readiness, and their selfishness utterly annihilated. Imagine, then, the result of conducting theatres on the principle of appealing exclusively to the instinct of self-gratification in people without power of attention, without interests, without sympathy: in short, without brains or heart. That is how they were conducted whilst I was writing about them; and that is how they nearly killed me.

Yet the managers mean well. Their self-respect is in excess rather than in defect; for they are in full reaction against the Bohemianism of past generations of actors, and so bent on compelling social recognition by a blameless respectability, that the drama, neglected in the struggle, is only just beginning to stir feebly after standing still in England from Tom Robertson's time in the sixties until the first actor was knighted in the nineties. The manager may not want good plays; but he does not want bad plays: he wants nice ones. Nice plays, with nice dresses, nice drawing rooms and nice people, are indispensable: to be ungenteel is worse than to fail. I use the word ungenteel purposely; for the stage presents life on thirty pounds a day, not as it is, but as it is conceived by the earners of thirty shillings a week. The real thing would shock the audience exactly as the manners of the public school and university shock a Board of Guardians. In just the same way, the plays which constitute the genuine aristocracy of modern dramatic literature shock the reverence for gentility which governs our theatres today. For instance, the objection to Ibsen is not really an objection to his philosophy: it is a protest against the fact that his characters do not behave as ladies and gentlemen are popularly supposed to behave. If you adore Hedda Gabler in real life, if you envy her and feel that nothing but your poverty prevents you from being as exquisite a creature, if you know that the accident of matrimony (say with an officer of the guards who falls in love with you across the counter whilst you are reckoning the words in his telegram) may at any moment put you in her place, Ibsen's exposure of the worthlessness and meanness of her life is cruel and blasphemous to you. This point of view is not caught by the clever ladies of Hedda's own class, who recognize the portrait, applaud its painter, and think the fuss against Ibsen means nothing more than the conventional disapproval of her discussions of a *ménage à trois* with Judge Brack. A little experience of popular plays would soon convince these clever ladies that a heroine who atones in the last act by committing suicide may do all the things that Hedda only talked about, without a word of remonstrance from the press or the public. It is not murder, not adultery, not rapine that is objected to: quite the contrary. It is an unladylike attitude towards life: in other words, a disparagement of the social ideals of the poorer middle class and of the vast reinforcements it has had from the working class during the last twenty years. Let but the attitude of the author be gentlemanlike, and his heroines may do what they please. Mrs Tanqueray was received with delight by the public: Saint Teresa would have been hissed off the same stage for her contempt for the ideal represented by a carriage, a fashionable dressmaker, and a dozen servants.

Here, then, is a pretty problem for the manager. He is convinced that plays must depend for their dramatic force on appeals to the sex instinct; and yet he owes it to his own newly conquered social position that they shall be perfectly genteel plays, fit for churchgoers. The sex instinct must therefore proceed upon genteel assumptions. Impossible! you will exclaim. But you are wrong: nothing is more astonishing than the extent to which, in real life, the sex instinct does so proceed, even when the consequence is its lifelong starvation. Few of us have vitality enough to make any of our instincts imperious: we can be made to live on pretences, as the masterful minority well know. But the timid majority, if it rules nowhere else, at least rules in the theatre: fitly enough too, because on the stage pretence is all that can exist. Life has its realities behind its shows: the theatre has nothing but its shows. But can the theatre make a show of lovers' endearments? A thousand times no: perish the thought of such unladylike, ungentlemanlike exhibitions. You can have fights, rescues, conflagrations, trials-at-law, avalanches, murders and executions all directly simulated on the stage if you will. But any such realistic treatment of the incidents of sex is quite out of the question. The singer, the dramatic dancer, the exquisite declaimer of impassioned poesy, the rare artist who, bringing something of the art of all three to the ordinary work of the theatre, can enthral an audience by the expression of dramatic feeling alone, may take love for a theme on the stage; but the prosaic walking gentleman of our fashionable theatres, realistically simulating the incidents of life, cannot touch it without indecorum.

Can any dilemma be more complete? Love is assumed to be the only theme that touches all your audience infallibly, young and old, rich and poor. And yet love is the one subject that the drawing room drama dare not present.

Out of this dilemma, which is a very old one, has come the romantic play: that is, the play in which love is carefully kept off the stage, whilst it is alleged as the motive of all the actions presented to the audience. The result is, to me at least, an intolerable perversion of human conduct. There are two classes of stories that seem to me to be not only fundamentally false but sordidly base. One is the pseudo-religious story, in which the hero and heroine does good on strictly commercial grounds, reluctantly exercising a little virtue on earth in consideration of receiving in return an exorbitant payment in heaven: much as if an odalisque were to allow a cadi to whip her for a couple of millions in gold. The other is the romance in which the hero, also rigidly commercial, will do nothing except for the sake of the heroine. Surely this is as depressing as it is unreal. Compare with it the treatment of love, frankly indecent according to our notions, in oriental fiction. In The Arabian Nights we have a series of stories, some of them very good ones, in which no sort of decorum is observed. The result is that they are infinitely more instructive and enjoyable than our romances, because love is treated in them as naturally as any other passion. There is no cast iron convention as to its effects; no false association of general depravity of character with its corporealities or of general elevation with its sentimentalities; no pretence that a man or woman cannot be courageous and kind and friendly unless infatuatedly in love with somebody (is no poet manly enough to sing The Old Maids of England?): rather, indeed, an insistence on the blinding and narrowing power of lovesickness to make princely heroes unhappy and unfortunate. These tales expose, further, the delusion that the interest of this most capricious, most transient, most easily baffled of all instincts, is inexhaustible, and that the field of the English romancer has been cruelly narrowed by the restrictions under which he is permitted to deal with it. The Arabian storyteller, relieved of all such restrictions, heaps character on character, adventure on adventure, marvel on marvel; whilst the English novelist, like the starving tramp who can think of nothing but his hunger, seems to be unable to escape from the obsession of sex, and will rewrite the very gospels because the originals are not written in the sensuously ecstatic style. At the instance of Martin Luther we long ago gave up imposing celibacy on our priests; but we still impose it on our art, with the very undesirable and unexpected result that no editor, publisher, or manager, will now accept a story or produce a play without "love interest" in it. Take, for a recent example, Mr H. G. Wells's War of Two Worlds, a tale of the invasion of the earth by the inhabitants of the planet Mars: a capital story, not to be laid down until finished. Love interest is impossible on its scientific plane: nothing could be more impertinent and irritating. Yet Mr Wells has had to pretend that the hero is in love with a young lady manufactured for the purpose, and to imply that it is on her account alone that he feels concerned about the apparently inevitable destruction of the human race by the Martians. Another example. An American novelist, recently deceased, made a hit some years ago by compiling a Bostonian Utopia from the prospectuses of the little bands of devout Communists who have from time to time, since the days of Fourier and Owen, tried to establish millennial colonies outside our commercial civilization. Even in this economic Utopia we find the inevitable love affair. The hero, waking up in a distant future from a miraculous sleep, meets a Boston young lady, provided expressly for him to fall in love with. Women have by that time given up wearing skirts; but she, to spare his delicacy, gets one out of a museum of antiquities to wear in his presence until he is hardened to the customs of the new age. When I came to that touching incident, I became as Paolo and Francesca: "in that book I read no more." I will not multiply examples: if such unendurable follies occur in the sort of story made by working out a meteorological or economic hypothesis, the extent to which it is carried in sentimental romances needs no expatiation.

The worst of it is that since man's intellectual consciousness of himself is derived from the descriptions of him in books, a persistent misrepresentation of humanity in literature gets finally accepted and acted upon. If every mirror reflected our noses twice their natural size, we should live and die in the faith that we were all Punches; and we should scout a true mirror as the work of a fool, madman, or jester. Nay, I believe we should, by Lamarckian adaptation, enlarge our noses to the admired size; for I have noticed that when a certain type of feature appears in painting and is admired as beautiful, it presently becomes common in nature; so that the Beatrices and Francescas in the picture galleries of one generation, to whom minor poets address verses entitled To My Lady, come to life as the parlormaids and waitresses of the next. If the conventions of romance are only insisted on long enough and uniformly enough (a condition guaranteed by the uniformity of human folly and vanity), then, for the huge compulsorily schooled masses who read romance or nothing, these conventions will become the laws of personal honor. Jealousy, which is either an egotistical meanness or a specific mania, will become obligatory; and ruin, ostracism, breaking up of homes, duelling, murder, suicide and infanticide will be produced (often have been produced, in fact) by incidents which, if left to the operation of natural and right feeling, would produce nothing worse than an hour's soon-forgotten fuss. Men will be slain needlessly on the field of battle because officers conceive it to be their first duty to make romantic exhibitions of conspicuous gallantry. The squire who has never spared an hour from the hunting field to do a little public work on a parish council will be cheered as a patriot because he is willing to kill and get killed for the sake of conferring himself as an institution on other countries. In the courts cases will be argued, not on juridical but on romantic principles; and vindictive damages and vindictive sentences, with the acceptance of nonsensical, and the repudiation or suppression of sensible testimony, will destroy the very sense of law. Kaisers, generals, judges, and prime ministers will set the example of playing to the gallery. Finally the people, now that their compulsory literacy enables every penman to play on their romantic illusions, will be led by the nose far more completely than they ever were by playing on their former ignorance and superstition. Nay, why should I say will be? they *are*. Ten years of cheap reading have changed the English from the most stolid nation in Europe to the most theatrical and hysterical.

Is it clear now, why the theatre was insufferable to me; why it left its black mark on my bones as it has left its black mark on the character of the nation; why I call the Puritans to rescue it again as they rescued it before when its foolish pursuit of pleasure sunk it in "profaneness and immorality"? I have, I think, always been a Puritan in my attitude towards Art. I am as fond of fine music and handsome building as Milton was, or Cromwell, or Bunyan; but if I found that they were becoming the instruments of a systematic idolatry of sensuousness, I would hold it good statesmanship to blow every cathedral in the world to pieces with dynamite, organ and all, without the least heed to the screams of the art critics and cultured voluptuaries. And when I see that the nineteenth century has crowned the idolatry of Art with the deification of Love, so that every poet is supposed to have pierced to the holy of holies when he has announced that Love is the Supreme, or the Enough, or the All. I feel that Art was safer in the hands of the most fanatical of Cromwell's major generals than it will be if ever it gets into mine. The pleasures of the senses I can sympathize with and share; but the substitution of sensuous ecstasy for intellectual activity and honesty is the very devil. It has already brought us to Flogging Bills in Parliament, and, by reaction, to androgynous heroes on the stage; and if the infection spreads until the democratic attitude becomes thoroughly Romanticist, the country will become unbearable for all realists, Philistine or Platonic. When it comes to that, the brute force of the strong-minded Bismarckian man of action, impatient of humbug, will combine with the subtlety and spiritual energy of the man of thought whom shams cannot illude or interest. That combination will be on one side; and Romanticism will be on the other. In which event, so much the worse for Romanticism, which will come down even if it has to drag Democracy down with it. For all institutions have in the long run to live by the nature of things, and not by childish pretendings.

ON DIABOLONIAN ETHICS

There is a foolish opinion prevalent that an author should allow his works to speak for themselves, and that he who appends and prefixes explanations to them is likely to be as bad an artist as the painter cited by Cervantes, who wrote under his picture This is a Cock, lest there should be any mistake about it. The pat retort to this thoughtless comparison is that the painter invariably does so label his picture. What is a Royal Academy catalogue but a series of statements that This is The Vale of Rest, This The Shaving of Samson, This Chill October, This H.R.H. The Prince of Wales, and so on? The reason most playwrights do not publish their plays with prefaces is that they cannot write them, the business of intellectually conscious philosopher and skilled critic being no necessary part of their craft. Naturally, making a virtue of their incapacity, they either repudiate prefaces as shameful, or else, with a modest air, request some popular critic to supply one, as much as to say, Were I to tell the truth about myself I must needs seem vainglorious: were I to tell less than the truth I should do myself an injustice and deceive my readers. As to the critic thus called in from the outside, what can he do but imply that his friend's transcendent ability as a dramatist is surpassed only by his beautiful nature as a man? Now what I say is, why should I get another man to praise me when I can praise myself? I have no disabilities to plead: produce me your best critic, and I will criticize his head off. As to philosophy, I taught my critics the little they know in my Quintessence of Ibsenism; and now they turn their guns—the guns I loaded for them—on me, and proclaim that I write as if mankind had intellect without will, or heart, as they call it. Ingrates: who was it that directed your attention to the distinction between Will and Intellect? Not Schopenhauer, I think, but Shaw.

Again, they tell me that So-and-So, who does not write prefaces, is no charlatan. Well, I am. I first caught the ear of the British public on a cart in Hyde Park, to the blaring of brass bands, and this not at all as a reluctant sacrifice of my instinct of privacy to political necessity, but because, like all dramatists and mimes of genuine vocation, I am a natural-born mountebank. I am well aware that the ordinary British citizen requires a profession of shame from all mountebanks by way of homage to the sanctity of the ignoble private life to which he is condemned by his incapacity for public life. Thus Shakespear, after proclaiming that Not marble nor the gilded monuments of Princes should outlive his powerful rhyme, would apologize, in the approved taste, for making himself a motley to the view; and the British citizen has ever since quoted the apology and ignored the fanfare. When an actress writes her memoirs, she impresses on you in every chapter how cruelly it tried her feelings to exhibit her person to the public gaze; but she does not forget to decorate the book with a dozen portraits of herself. I really cannot respond to this demand for mock-modesty. I am ashamed neither of my work nor of the way it is done. I like explaining its merits to the huge majority who dont know good work from bad. It does them good; and it does me good, curing me of nervousness, laziness, and snobbishness. I write prefaces as Dryden did, and treatises as Wagner, because I *can*; and I would give half a dozen of Shakespear's plays for one of the prefaces he ought to have written. I leave the delicacies of retirement to those who are gentlemen first and literary workmen afterwards. The cart and trumpet for me.

This is all very well; but the trumpet is an instrument that grows on one; and sometimes my blasts have been so strident that even those who are most annoyed by them have mistaken the novelty of my shamelessness for novelty in my plays and opinions. Take, for instance, the play entitled The Devil's Disciple. It does not contain a single even passably novel incident. Every old patron of the Adelphi pit would, were he not beglamored in a way presently to be explained, recognize the reading of the will, the oppressed orphan finding a protector, the arrest, the heroic sacrifice, the court martial, the scaffold, the reprieve at the last moment, as he recognizes beefsteak pudding on the bill of fare at his restaurant. Yet when the play was produced in 1897 in New York by Mr Richard Mansfield, with a success that proves either that the melodrama was built on very safe old lines, or that the American public is composed exclusively of men of genius, the critics, though one said one thing and another another as to the play's merits, yet all agreed that it was novel—*original*, as they put it—to the verge of audacious eccentricity.

Now this, if it applies to the incidents, plot, construction, and general professional and technical qualities of the play, is nonsense; for the truth is, I am in these matters a very old-fashioned playwright. When a good deal of the same talk, both hostile and friendly, was provoked by my last volume of plays, Mr Robert Buchanan, a dramatist who knows what I know and remembers what I remember of the history of the stage, pointed out that the stage tricks by which I gave the younger generation of playgoers an exquisite sense of quaint unexpectedness, had done duty years ago in Cool as a Cucumber, Used Up, and many forgotten farces and comedies of the Byron-Robertson school, in which the imperturbably impudent comedian, afterwards shelved by the reaction to brainless sentimentality, was a stock figure. It is always so more or less: the novelties of one generation are only the resuscitated fashions of the generation before last.

But the stage tricks of The Devil's Disciple are not, like some of those of Arms and The Man, the forgotten ones of the sixties, but the hackneyed ones of our own time. Why, then, were they not recognized? Partly, no doubt, because of my trumpet and cartwheel declamation. The critics were the victims of the long course of hypnotic suggestion by which G.B.S. the journalist manufactured an unconventional reputation for Bernard Shaw the author. In England as elsewhere the spontaneous recognition of really original work begins with a mere

2 A 2

handful of people, and propagates itself so slowly that it has become a commonplace to say that genius, demanding bread, is given a stone after its possessor's death. The remedy for this is sedulous advertisement. Accordingly, I have advertized myself so well that I find myself, whilst still in middle life, almost as legendary a person as the Flying Dutchman. Critics, like other people, see what they look for, not what is actually before them. In my plays they look for my legendary qualities, and find originality and brilliancy in my most hackneyed claptraps. Were I to republish Buckstone's Wreck Ashore as my latest comedy, it would be hailed as a masterpiece of perverse paradox and scintillating satire. Not, of course, by the really able critics—for example, you, my friend, now reading this sentence. The illusion that makes *you* think me so original is far subtler than that. The Devil's Disciple has, in truth, a genuine novelty in it. Only, that novelty is not any invention of my own, but simply the novelty of the advanced thought of my day. As such, it will assuredly lose its gloss with the lapse of time, and leave The Devil's Disciple exposed as the threadbare popular melodrama it technically is.

Let me explain (for, as Mr A. B. Walkley has pointed out in his disquisitions on Frames of Mind, I am nothing if not explanatory). Dick Dudgeon, the devil's disciple, is a Puritan of the Puritans. He is brought up in a household where the Puritan religion has died, and become, in its corruption, an excuse for his mother's master passion of hatred in all its phases of cruelty and envy. This corruption has already been dramatized for us by Charles Dickens in his picture of the Clennam household in Little Dorrit: Mrs Dudgeon being a replica of Mrs Clennam with certain circumstantial variations, and perhaps a touch of the same author's Mrs Gargery in Great Expectations. In such a home the young Puritan finds himself starved of religion, which is the most clamorous need of his nature. With all his mother's indomitable selffulness, but with Pity instead of Hatred as his master passion, he pities the devil; takes his side; and champions him, like a true Covenanter, against the world. He thus becomes, like all genuinely religious men, a reprobate and an outcast. Once this is understood, the play becomes straightforwardly simple.

The Diabolonian position is new to the London playgoer of today, but not to lovers of serious literature. From Prometheus to the Wagnerian Siegfried, some enemy of the gods, unterrified champion of those oppressed by them, has always towered among the heroes of the loftiest poetry. Our newest idol, the Superman, celebrating the death of godhead, may be younger than the hills; but he is as old as the shepherds. Two and a half centuries ago our greatest English dramatizer of life, John Bunyan, ended one of his stories with the remark that there is a way to hell even from the gates of heaven, and so led us to the equally true proposition that there is a way to heaven even from the gates of hell. A century ago William Blake was, like Dick Dudgeon, an avowed Diabolonian: he called his angels devils and his devils angels. His devil is a Redeemer. Let those who have praised my originality in conceiving Dick Dudgeon's strange religion read Blake's Marriage of Heaven and Hell, and I shall be fortunate if they do not rail at me for a plagiarist. But they need not go back to Blake and Bunyan. Have they not heard the recent fuss about Nietzsche and his Good and Evil Turned Inside Out? Mr Robert Buchanan has actually written a long poem of which the Devil is the merciful hero, which poem was in my hands before a word of The Devil's Disciple was written. There never was a play more certain to be written than The Devil's Disciple at the end of the nineteenth century. The age was visibly pregnant with it.

I grieve to have to add that my old friends and colleagues the London critics for the most part shewed no sort of connoisseurship either in Puritanism or in Diabolonianism when the play was performed for a few weeks at a suburban theatre (Kennington) in October 1899 by Mr Murray Carson. They took Mrs Dudgeon at her own valuation as a religious woman because she was detestably disagreeable. And they took Dick as a blackguard on her authority, because he was neither detestable nor disagreeable. But they presently found themselves in a dilemma. Why should a blackguard save another man's life, and that man no friend of his, at the risk of his own? Clearly, said the critics, because he is redeemed by love. All wicked heroes are, on the stage: that is the romantic metaphysic. Unfortunately for this explanation (which I do not profess to understand) it turned out in the third act that Dick was a Puritan in this respect also: a man impassioned only for saving grace, and not to be led or turned by wife or mother, Church or State, pride of life or lust of the flesh. In the lovely home of the courageous, affectionate, practical minister who marries a pretty wife twenty years younger than himself, and turns soldier in an instant to save the man who has saved him, Dick looks round and understands the charm and the peace and the sanctity, but knows that such material comforts are not for him. When the woman nursed in that atmosphere falls in love with him and concludes (like the critics, who somehow always agree with my sentimental heroines) that he risked his life for her sake, he tells her the obvious truth that he would have done as much for any stranger—that the law of his own nature, and no interest nor lust whatsoever, forbad him to cry out that the hangman's noose should be taken off his neck only to be put on another man's.

But then, said the critics, where is the motive? *Why* did Dick save Anderson? On the stage, it appears, people do things for reasons. Off the stage they dont: that is why your penny-in-the-slot heroes, who only work when you drop a motive into them, are so oppressively automatic and uninteresting. The saving of life at the risk of the saver's own is not a common thing; but modern populations are so vast that even the most uncommon things are recorded once a week or oftener. Not one of my critics but has seen a hundred times in his paper how some policeman or fireman or nursemaid has received a medal, or the compliments of a magistrate, or perhaps a public funeral, for risking his or her life to save another's. Has he ever seen it added that the saved was the husband of the woman the saver loved, or was that woman herself, or was even known to the saver as much as by sight? Never. When we want to read of the deeds that are done for love, whither do we turn? To the murder column; and there we are rarely disappointed.

Need I repeat that the theatre critic's professional routine so discourages any association between real life and the stage, that he soon loses the natural habit of referring to the one to explain the other? The critic who discovered a romantic motive for Dick's sacrifice was no mere literary dreamer, but a clever barrister. He pointed out that Dick Dudgeon clearly did adore Mrs Anderson; that it was for her sake that he offered his life to save her beloved husband; and that his explicit denial of his passion was the splendid mendacity of a gentleman whose respect for a married woman, and duty to her absent husband, sealed his passion-palpitating lips. From the moment that this fatally plausible explanation was launched, my play became my critic's play, not mine. Thenceforth Dick Dudgeon every night confirmed the critic by stealing behind Judith, and mutely attesting his passion by surreptitiously imprinting a heart-broken kiss on a stray lock of her hair whilst he uttered the barren denial. As for me, I was just then wandering about the streets of Constantinople, unaware of all these doings. When I returned all was over. My personal relations with the critic and the actor forbad me to curse them. I had not even the chance of publicly forgiving them. They meant well by me; but if they ever write a play, may I be there to explain![1]

BETTER THAN SHAKESPEAR?

As to the other plays in the volume, the application of my title is less obvious, since neither Julius Cæsar, Cleopatra, nor Lady Cicely Waynflete have any external political connexion with Puritanism. The very name of Cleopatra suggests at once a tragedy of Circe, with the horrible difference that whereas the ancient myth rightly represents Circe as turning heroes into hogs, the modern romantic convention would represent her as turning hogs into heroes. Shakespear's Antony and Cleopatra must needs be as intolerable to the true Puritan as it is vaguely distressing to the ordinary healthy citizen, because, after giving a faithful picture of the soldier broken down by debauchery, and the typical wanton in whose arms such men perish, Shakespear finally strains all his huge command of rhetoric and stage pathos to give a theatrical sublimity to the wretched end of the business, and to persuade foolish spectators that the world was well lost

[1] As I pass these pages through the press (September 1900), the critics of Yorkshire are struggling, as against some unholy fascination, with the apparition of Dick Dudgeon on their stage in the person of Forbes Robertson. "A finished scoundrel" is the description which one of them gives of Dick. This is worth recording as an example of the extent to which the moral sense remains dormant in people who are content with the customary formulas for respectable conduct.

by the twain. Such falsehood is not to be borne except by the real Cleopatras and Antonys (they are to be found in every public house) who would no doubt be glad enough to be transfigured by some poet as immortal lovers. Woe to the poet who stoops to such folly! The lot of the man who sees life truly and thinks about it romantically is Despair. How well we know the cries of that despair! Vanity of vanities, all is vanity! moans the Preacher, when life has at last taught him that Nature will not dance to his moralist-made tunes. Thackeray, scores of centuries later, was still baying the moon in the same terms. Out, out, brief candle! cries Shakespear, in his tragedy of the modern literary man as murderer and witch consulter. Surely the time is past for patience with writers who, having to choose between giving up life in despair and discarding the trumpery moral kitchen scales in which they try to weigh the universe, superstitiously stick to the scales, and spend the rest of the lives they pretend to despise in breaking men's spirits. But even in pessimism there is a choice between intellectual honesty and dishonesty. Hogarth drew the rake and the harlot without glorifying their end. Swift, accepting our system of morals and religion, delivered the inevitable verdict of that system on us through the mouth of the king of Brobdingnag, and described Man as the Yahoo, shocking his superior the horse by his every action. Strindberg, the only genuinely Shakespearean modern dramatist, shews that the female Yahoo, measured by romantic standards, is viler than her male dupe and slave. I respect these resolute tragi-comedians: they are logical and faithful: they force you to face the fact that you must either accept their conclusions as valid (in which case it is cowardly to continue living) or admit that their way of judging conduct is absurd. But when your Shakespears and Thackerays huddle up the matter at the end by killing somebody and covering your eyes with the undertaker's handkerchief, duly onioned with some pathetic phrase, as The flight of angels sing thee to thy rest, or Adsum, or the like, I have no respect for them at all: such maudlin tricks may impose on tea-drunkards, not on me.

Besides, I have a technical objection to making sexual infatuation a tragic theme. Experience proves that it is only effective in the comic spirit. We can bear to see Mrs Quickly pawning her plate for love of Falstaff, but not Antony running away from the battle of Actium for love of Cleopatra. Let realism have its demonstration, comedy its criticism, or even bawdry its horse-laugh at the expense of sexual infatuation, if it must; but to ask us to subject our souls to its ruinous glamor, to worship it, deify it, and imply that it alone makes our life worth living, is nothing but folly gone mad erotically—a thing compared to which Falstaff's unbeglamored drinking and drabbing is respectable and rightminded. Whoever, then, expects to find Cleopatra a Circe and Cæsar a hog in these pages, had better lay down my book and be spared a disappointment.

In Cæsar, I have used another character with which Shakespear has been beforehand. But Shakespear, who knew human weakness so well, never knew human strength of the Cæsarian type. His Cæsar is an admitted failure: his Lear is a masterpiece. The tragedy of disillusion and doubt, of the agonized struggle for a foothold on the quicksand made by an acute observation striving to verify its vain attribution of morality and respectability to Nature, of the faithless will and the keen eyes that the faithless will is too weak to blind: all this will give you a Hamlet or a Macbeth, and win you great applause from literary gentlemen; but it will not give you a Julius Cæsar. Cæsar was not in Shakespear, nor in the epoch, now fast waning, which he inaugurated. It cost Shakespear no pang to write Cæsar

down for the merely technical purpose of writing Brutus up. And what a Brutus! A perfect Girondin, mirrored in Shakespear's art two hundred years before the real thing came to maturity and talked and stalked and had its head duly cut off by the coarser Antonys and Octaviuses of its time, who at least knew the difference between life and rhetoric.

It will be said that these remarks can bear no other construction than an offer of my Cæsar to the public as an improvement on Shakespear's. And in fact, that is their precise purport. But here let me give a friendly warning to those scribes who have so often exclaimed against my criticisms of Shakespear as blasphemies against a hitherto unquestioned Perfection and Infallibility. Such criticisms are no more new than the creed of my Diabolonian Puritan or my revival of the humors of Cool as a Cucumber. Too much surprise at them betrays an acquaintance with Shakespear criticism so limited as not to include even the prefaces of Dr. Johnson and the utterances of Napoleon. I have merely repeated in the dialect of my own time and in the light of its philosophy what they said in the dialect and light of theirs. Do not be misled by the Shakespear fanciers who, ever since his own time, have delighted in his plays just as they might have delighted in a particular breed of pigeons if they had never learnt to read. His genuine critics, from Ben Jonson to Mr Frank Harris, have always kept as far on this side idolatry as I.

As to our ordinary uncritical citizens, they have been slowly trudging forward these three centuries to the point which Shakespear reached at a bound in Elizabeth's time. Today most of them have arrived there or thereabouts, with the result that his plays are at last beginning to be performed as he wrote them; and the long line of disgraceful farces, melodramas, and stage pageants which actor-managers, from Garrick and Cibber to our own contemporaries, have hacked out of his plays as peasants have hacked huts out of the Coliseum, are beginning to vanish from the stage. It is a significant fact that the mutilators of Shakespear, who never could be persuaded that Shakespear knew his business better than they, have ever been the most fanatical of his worshippers. The late Augustin Daly thought no price too extravagant for an addition to his collection of Shakespear relics; but in arranging Shakespear's plays for the stage, he proceeded on the assumption that Shakespear was a botcher and he an artist. I am far too good a Shakespearean ever to forgive Henry Irving for producing a version of King Lear so mutilated that the numerous critics who had never read the play could not follow the story of Gloster. Both these idolaters of the Bard must have thought Forbes Robertson mad because he restored Fortinbras to the stage and played as much of Hamlet as there was time for instead of as little. And the instant success of the experiment probably altered their minds no further than to make them think the public mad. Mr Benson actually gives the play complete at two sittings, causing the aforesaid numerous critics to remark with naïve surprise that Polonius is a complete and interesting character. It was the age of gross ignorance of Shakespear and incapacity for his works that produced the indiscriminate eulogies with which we are familiar. It was the revival of serious attention to those works that coincided with the movement for giving genuine instead of spurious and silly representations of his plays. So much for Bardolatry!

It does not follow, however, that the right to criticize Shakespear involves the power of writing better plays. And in fact —do not be surprised at my modesty—I do not profess to write better plays. The writing of practicable stage plays does not present an infinite scope to human talent;

and the playwrights who magnify its difficulties are humbugs. The summit of their art has been attained again and again. No man will ever write a better tragedy than Lear, a better comedy than Le Festin de Pierre or Peer Gynt, a better opera than Don Giovanni, a better music drama than The Niblung's Ring or, for the matter of that, better fashionable plays and melodramas than are now being turned out by writers whom nobody dreams of mocking with the word immortal. It is the philosophy, the outlook on life, that changes, not the craft of the playwright. A generation that is thoroughly moralized and patriotized, that conceives virtuous indignation as spiritually nutritious, that murders the murderer and robs the thief, that grovels before all sorts of ideals, social, military, ecclesiastical, royal and divine, may be, from my point of view, steeped in error; but it need not want for as good plays as the hand of man can produce. Only, those plays will be neither written nor relished by men in whose philosophy guilt and innocence, and consequently revenge and idolatry, have no meaning. Such men must rewrite all the old plays in terms of their own philosophy; and that is why, as Stuart-Glennie has pointed out, there can be no new drama without a new philosophy. To which I may add that there can be no Shakespear or Goethe without one either, nor two Shakespears in one philosophic epoch, since, as I have said, the first great comer in that epoch reaps the whole harvest and reduces those who come after to the rank of mere gleaners, or, worse than that, fools who go laboriously through all the motions of the reaper and binder in an empty field. What is the use of writing plays or painting frescoes if you have nothing more to say or shew than was said and shewn by Shakespear, Michael Angelo, and Raphael? If these had not seen things differently, for better or worse, from the dramatic poets of the Townley mysteries, or from

Giotto, they could not have produced their works: no, not though their skill of pen and hand had been double what it was. After them there was no need (and *need* alone nerves men to face the persecution in the teeth of which new art is brought to birth) to redo the already done, until in due time, when their philosophy wore itself out, a new race of nineteenth century poets and critics, from Byron to William Morris, began, first to speak coldly of Shakespear and Raphael, and then to rediscover, in the medieval art which these Renascence masters had superseded, certain forgotten elements which were germinating again for the new harvest. What is more, they began to discover that the technical skill of the masters was by no means superlative. Indeed, I defy anyone to prove that the great epoch makers in fine art have owed their position to their technical skill. It is true that when we search for examples of a prodigious command of language and of graphic line, we can think of nobody better than Shakespear and Michael Angelo. But both of them laid their arts waste for centuries by leading later artists to seek greatness in copying their technique. The technique was acquired, refined on, and elaborated over and over again; but the supremacy of the two great exemplars remained undisputed. As a matter of easily observable fact, every generation produces men of extraordinary special faculty, artistic, mathematical and linguistic, who for lack of new ideas, or indeed of any ideas worth mentioning, achieve no distinction outside music halls and class rooms, although they can do things easily that the great epoch makers did clumsily or not at all. The contempt of the academic pedant for the original artist is often founded on a genuine superiority of technical knowledge and aptitude: he is sometimes a better anatomical draughtsman than Raphael, a better hand at triple counterpoint than Beethoven, a better versifier than Byron. Nay, this is true not merely of pedants, but of men who have produced works of art of some note. If technical facility were the secret of greatness in art, Swinburne would be greater than Browning and Byron rolled into one, Stevenson greater than Scott or Dickens, Mendelssohn than Wagner, Maclise than Madox Brown. Besides, new ideas make their technique as water makes its channel; and the technician without ideas is as useless as the canal constructor without water, though he may do very skilfully what the Mississippi does very rudely. To clinch the argument, you have only to observe that the epoch maker himself has generally begun working professionally before his new ideas have mastered him sufficiently to insist on constant expression by his art. In such cases you are compelled to admit that if he had by chance died earlier, his greatness would have remained unachieved, although his technical qualifications would have been well enough established. The early imitative works of great men are usually conspicuously inferior to the best works of their forerunners. Imagine Wagner dying after composing Rienzi, or Shelley after Zastrozzi! Would any competent critic then have rated Wagner's technical aptitude as high as Rossini's, Spontini's, or Meyerbeer's; or Shelley's as high as Moore's? Turn the problem another way: does anyone suppose that if Shakespear had conceived Goethe's or Ibsen's ideas, he would have expressed them any worse than Goethe or Ibsen? Human faculty being what it is, is it likely that in our time any advance, except in external conditions, will take place in the arts of expression sufficient to enable an author, without making himself ridiculous, to undertake to say what he has to say better than Homer or Shakespear? But the humblest author, and much more a rather arrogant one like myself, may profess to have something to say by this time that neither

Homer nor Shakespear said. And the play-goer may reasonably ask to have historical events and persons presented to him in the light of his own time, even though Homer and Shakespear have already shewn them in the light of their time. For example, Homer presented Achilles and Ajax as heroes to the world in the Iliads. In due time came Shakespear, who said, virtually: I really cannot accept this spoilt child and this brawny fool as great men merely because Homer flattered them in playing to the Greek gallery. Consequently we have, in Troilus and Cressida, the verdict of Shakespear's epoch (our own) on the pair. This did not in the least involve any pretence on Shakespear's part to be a greater poet than Homer.

When Shakespear in turn came to deal with Henry V and Julius Cæsar, he did so according to his own essentially knightly conception of a great statesman-commander. But in the XIX century comes the German historian Mommsen, who also takes Cæsar for his hero, and explains the immense difference in scope between the perfect knight Vercingetorix and his great conqueror Julius Cæsar. In this country, Carlyle, with his vein of peasant inspiration, apprehended the sort of greatness that places the true hero of history so far beyond the mere *preux chevalier*, whose fanatical personal honor, gallantry, and self-sacrifice, are founded on a passion for death born of inability to bear the weight of a life that will not grant ideal conditions to the liver. This one ray of perception became Carlyle's whole stock-in-trade; and it sufficed to make a literary master of him. In due time, when Mommsen is an old man, and Carlyle dead, come I, and dramatize the by-this-time familiar distinction in Arms and The Man, with its comedic conflict between the knightly Bulgarian and the Mommsenite Swiss captain. Whereupon a great many playgoers who have not yet read Cervantes, much less Mommsen and

Carlyle, raise a shriek of concern for their knightly ideal as if nobody had ever questioned its sufficiency since the middle ages. Let them thank me for educating them so far. And let them allow me to set forth Cæsar in the same modern light, taking the platform from Shakespear as he from Homer, and with no thought of pretending to express the Mommsenite view of Cæsar any better than Shakespear expressed a view which was not even Plutarchian, and must, I fear, be referred to the tradition in stage conquerors established by Marlowe's Tamerlane as much as to the chivalrous conception of heroism dramatized in Henry V.

For my own part, I can avouch that such powers of invention, humor and stage ingenuity as I have been able to exercise in Plays Pleasant and Unpleasant, and in Three Plays for Puritans, availed me not at all until I saw the old facts in a new light. Technically, I do not find myself able to proceed otherwise than as former playwrights have done. True, my plays have the latest mechanical improvements: the action is not carried on by impossible soliloquys and asides; and my people get on and off the stage without requiring four doors to a room which in real life would have only one. But my stories are the old stories; my characters are the familiar harlequin and columbine, clown and pantaloon (note the harlequin's leap in the third act of Cæsar and Cleopatra); my stage tricks and suspenses and thrills and jests are the ones in vogue when I was a boy, by which time my grandfather was tired of them. To the young people who make their acquaintance for the first time in my plays, they may be as novel as Cyrano's nose to those who have never seen Punch; whilst to older playgoers the unexpectedness of my attempt to substitute natural history for conventional ethics and romantic logic may so transfigure the eternal stage puppets and their inevitable dilemmas as to make their identification impossible for the moment. If so, so much the better for me: I shall perhaps enjoy a few years of immortality. But the whirligig of time will soon bring my audiences to my own point of view; and then the next Shakespear that comes along will turn these petty tentatives of mine into masterpieces final for their epoch. By that time my twentieth century characteristics will pass unnoticed as a matter of course, whilst the eighteenth century artificiality that marks the work of every literary Irishman of my generation will seem antiquated and silly. It is a dangerous thing to be hailed at once, as a few rash admirers have hailed me, as above all things original: what the world calls originality is only an unaccustomed method of tickling it. Meyerbeer seemed prodigiously original to the Parisians when he first burst on them. Today, he is only the crow who followed Beethoven's plough. I am a crow who have followed many ploughs. No doubt I seem prodigiously clever to those who have never hopped, hungry and curious, across the fields of philosophy, politics, and art. Karl Marx said of Stuart Mill that his eminence was due to the flatness of the surrounding country. In these days of Free Schools, universal reading, cheap newspapers, and the inevitable ensuing demand for notabilities of all sorts, literary, military, political, and fashionable, to write paragraphs about, that sort of eminence is within the reach of very moderate ability. Reputations are cheap nowadays. Even were they dear, it would still be impossible for any public-spirited citizen of the world to hope that his reputation might endure; for this would be to hope that the flood of general enlightenment may never rise above his miserable high-watermark. I hate to think that Shakespear has lasted 300 years, though he got no further than Koheleth the Preacher, who died many centuries before him; or that Plato, more than 2000 years old, is still ahead of our voters. We must hurry on: we must get rid of reputations: they are weeds in the soil of ignorance. Cultivate that soil, and they will flower more beautifully, but only as annuals. If this preface will at all help to get rid of mine, the writing of it will have been well worth the pains.

XXX

THE DARK LADY OF THE SONNETS

1910

HOW THE PLAY CAME TO BE WRITTEN

I had better explain why, in this little *pièce d'occasion*, written for a performance in aid of the funds of the project of establishing a National Theatre as a memorial to Shakespear, I have identified the Dark Lady with Mistress Mary Fitton. First, let me say that I do not contend that the Dark Lady was Mary Fitton, because when the case in Mary's favor (or against her, if you please to consider that the Dark Lady was no better than she ought to have been) was complete, a portrait of Mary came to light and turned out to be that of a fair lady, not of a dark one. That settles the question, if the portrait is authentic, which I see no reason to doubt, and the lady's hair undyed, which is perhaps less certain. Shakespear rubbed in the lady's complexion in his sonnets mercilessly; for in his day black hair was as unpopular as red hair was in the early days of Queen Victoria. Any tinge lighter than raven black must be held fatal to the strongest claim to be the Dark Lady. And so, unless it can be shewn that Shakespear's sonnets exasperated Mary Fitton into dyeing her hair and getting painted in false colors, I must give up all pretence that my play is historical. The later suggestion of Mr Acheson that the Dark Lady, far from being a maid of honor, kept a tavern in Oxford, and was the mother of Davenant the poet, is the one I should have adopted had I wished to be up to date. Why, then, did I introduce the Dark Lady as Mistress Fitton?

Well, I had two reasons. The play was not to have been written by me at all, but by Dame Edith Lyttelton; and it was she who suggested a scene of jealousy between Queen Elizabeth and the Dark Lady at the expense of the unfortunate Bard. Now this, if the Dark Lady was a maid of honor, was quite easy. If she were a tavern landlady, it would have strained all probability. So I stuck to Mary Fitton. But I had another and more personal reason. I was, in a manner, present at the birth of the Fitton theory. Its parent and I had become acquainted; and he used to consult me on obscure passages in the sonnets, on which, as far as I can remember, I never succeeded in throwing the faintest light, at a time when nobody else thought my opinion, on that or any other subject, of the slightest importance. I thought it would be friendly to immortalize him, as the silly literary saying is, much as Shakespear immortalized Mr W. H., as he said he would, simply by writing about him.

Let me tell the story formally.

THOMAS TYLER

Throughout the eighties at least, and probably for some years before, the British Museum reading room was used daily by a gentleman of such astonishing and crushing ugliness that no one who had once seen him could ever thereafter forget him. He was of fair complexion, rather golden red than sandy; aged between forty-five and sixty; and dressed in frock coat and tall hat of presentable but never new appearance. His figure was rectangular, waistless, neckless, ankleless, of middle height, looking shortish because, though he was not particularly stout, there was nothing slender about him. His ugliness was not unamiable: it was accidental, external, excrescential. Attached to his face from the left ear to the point of his chin was a monstrous goitre, which hung down to his collar bone, and was very inadequately balanced by a smaller one on his right eyelid. Nature's malice was so overdone in his case that it somehow failed to produce the effect of repulsion it seemed to have aimed at. When you first met Thomas Tyler you could think of nothing else but whether surgery could really do nothing for him. But after a very brief acquaintance you never thought of his disfigurements at all, and talked to him as you might to Romeo or Lovelace; only, so many people, especially women, would not risk the preliminary ordeal, that he remained a man apart and a bachelor all his days. I am not to be frightened or prejudiced by a tumor; and I struck up a cordial acquaintance with him, in the course of which he kept me pretty closely on the track of his work at the Museum, in which I was then, like himself, a daily reader.

He was by profession a man of letters of an uncommercial kind. He was a specialist in pessimism; had made a translation of Ecclesiastes of which eight copies a year were sold; and followed up the pessimism of Shakespear and Swift with keen interest. He delighted in a hideous conception which he called the theory of the cycles, according to which the history of mankind and the universe keeps eternally repeating itself without the slightest variation throughout all eternity; so that he had lived and died and had his goitre before and would live and die and have it again and again and again. He liked to believe that nothing that happened to him was completely novel: he was persuaded that he often had some recollection of its previous occurrence in the last cycle. He hunted out allusions to this favorite theory in his three favorite pessimists. He tried his hand occasionally at deciphering ancient inscriptions, reading them as people seem to read the stars, by discovering bears and bulls and swords and goats where, as it seems to me, no sane human being can see anything but stars higgledy-piggledy. Next to the translation of Ecclesiastes, his *magnum opus* was his work on Shakespear's Sonnets, in which he accepted a previous identification of Mr W. H., the "onlie begetter" of the sonnets, with the Earl of Pembroke (William Herbert), and promulgated his own identification of Mistress Mary Fitton with the Dark Lady. Whether he was right or wrong about the Dark Lady did not matter urgently to me: she might have been Maria Tompkins for all I cared. But Tyler would have it that she was Mary Fitton; and he tracked Mary down from the first of her marriages in her teens to her tomb in Cheshire, whither he made a pilgrimage and whence returned in triumph with a picture of her statue, and the news that he was convinced she was a dark lady by traces of paint still discernible.

In due course he published his edition of the Sonnets, with the evidence he had collected. He lent me a copy of the book, which I never returned. But I reviewed it in the Pall Mall Gazette on the 7th of January 1886, and thereby let loose the Fitton theory in a wider circle of readers than the book could reach. Then Tyler died, sinking unnoted like a stone in the sea. I observe that Mr Acheson, Mrs Davenant's champion, calls him Reverend. It may very well be that he got his knowledge of Hebrew in reading for the Church; and there was always something of the clergyman or the schoolmaster in his dress and air. Possibly he may actually have been ordained. But he never told me that or anything else about his affairs; and his black pessimism would have shot him violently out of any church at present established in the West. We never talked about affairs: we talked about Shakespear, and the Dark Lady, and Swift, and Koheleth, and the cycles, and the mysterious moments when a feeling came over us that this had happened to us before, and about the forgeries of the Pentateuch which were offered for sale to the British Museum, and about literature and things of the spirit generally. He always came to my desk at the Museum and spoke to me about something or other, no doubt finding that people who were keen on this sort of conversation were rather scarce. He remains a vivid spot of memory in the void of my forgetfulness, a quite considerable and dignified soul in a grotesquely disfigured body.

FRANK HARRIS

To the review in the Pall Mall Gazette I attribute, rightly or wrongly, the introduction of Mary Fitton to Mr Frank Harris. My reason for this is that Mr Harris wrote a play about Shakespear and Mary Fitton; and when I, as a pious duty to Tyler's ghost, reminded the world that it was to Tyler we owed the Fitton theory, Frank Harris, who clearly had not a notion of what had first put Mary into his head, believed, I think, that I had invented Tyler expressly for his discomfiture; for the stress I laid on Tyler's claims must have seemed unaccountable and perhaps malicious on the assumption that he was to me a mere name among the thousands of names in the British Museum catalogue. Therefore I make it clear that I had and have personal reasons for remembering Tyler, and for regarding myself as in some sort charged with the duty of reminding the world of his work. I am sorry for his sake that Mary's portrait is fair, and that Mr W. H. has veered round again from Pembroke to Southampton; but even so his work was not wasted: it is by exhausting all the hypotheses that we reach the verifiable one; and after all, the wrong road always leads somewhere.

Frank Harris's play was written long before mine. I read it in manuscript before the Shakespear Memorial National Theatre was mooted; and if there is anything except the Fitton theory (which is Tyler's property) in my play which is also in Mr Harris's it was I who annexed it from him and not he from me. It does not matter anyhow, because this play of mine is a brief trifle, and full of manifest impossibilities at that; whilst Mr Harris's play is serious both in size, intention, and quality. But there could not in the nature of things be much resemblance, because Frank conceives Shakespear to have been a broken-hearted, melancholy, enormously sentimental person, whereas I am convinced that he was very like myself: in fact, if I had been born in 1556 instead of in 1856, I should have taken to blank verse and given Shakespear a harder run for his money than all the other Elizabethans put together. Yet the success of Frank Harris's book on Shakespear gave me great delight.

To those who know the literary world of London there was a sharp stroke of ironic comedy in the irresistible verdict in its favor. In critical literature there is one prize that is always open to competition, one blue ribbon that always carries the highest critical rank with it. To win, you must write the best book of your generation on Shakespear. It is felt on all sides that to do this a certain fastidious refinement, a delicacy of taste, a correctness of manner and tone, and high academic distinction in addition to the indispensable scholarship and literary reputation, are needed; and men who pretend to these qualifications are constantly looked to with a gentle expectation that presently they will achieve the great feat. Now if there is a man on earth who is the utter contrary of everything that this description implies; whose very existence is an insult to the ideal it realizes; whose eye disparages, whose resonant voice denounces, whose cold shoulder jostles every decency, every delicacy, every amenity, every dignity, every sweet usage of that quiet life of mutual admiration in which perfect Shakespearean appreciation is expected to arise, that man is Frank Harris. Here is one who is extraordinarily qualified, by a range of sympathy and understanding that extends from the ribaldry of a buccaneer to the shyest tendernesses of the most sensitive poetry, to be all things to all men, yet whose proud humor it is to be to every man, provided the man is eminent and pretentious, the champion of his enemies. To the Archbishop he is an atheist, to the atheist a Catholic mystic, to the Bismarckian Imperialist an Anacharsis Klootz, to Anacharsis Klootz a Washington, to Mrs Proudie a Don Juan, to Aspasia a John Knox: in short, to everyone his complement rather than his counterpart, his antagonist rather than his fellow-creature. Always provided, however, that the persons thus affronted are respectable persons. Sophie Perovskaia, who perished on the scaffold for blowing Alexander II to fragments, may perhaps have echoed Hamlet's

Oh God, Horatio, what a wounded name—
Things standing thus unknown—I leave
    behind!

but Frank Harris, in his Sonia, has rescued her from that injustice, and enshrined her among the saints. He has lifted the Chicago anarchists out of their infamy, and shewn that, compared with the Capitalism that killed them, they were heroes and martyrs. He has done this with the most unusual power of conviction. The story, as he tells it, inevitably and irresistibly displaces all the vulgar, mean, purblind, spiteful versions. There is a precise realism and an unsmiling, measured, determined sincerity which gives a strange dignity to the work of one whose fixed practice and ungovernable impulse it is to kick conventional dignity whenever he sees it.

HARRIS "DURCH MITLEID WISSEND"

Frank Harris is everything except a humorist, not, apparently, from stupidity, but because scorn overcomes humor in him. Nobody ever dreamt of reproaching Milton's Lucifer for not seeing the comic side of his fall; and nobody who has read Mr Harris's stories desires to have them lightened by chapters from the hand of Artemus Ward. Yet he knows the taste and the value of humor. He was one of the few men of letters who really appreciated Oscar Wilde, though he did not rally fiercely to Wilde's side until the world deserted Oscar in his ruin. I myself was present at a curious meeting between the two, when Harris, on the eve of the Queensberry trial, prophesied to Wilde with miraculous precision exactly what immediately afterwards happened to him, and warned him to leave the country. It was the first time within my knowledge that such a forecast proved true. Wilde, though under no illusion as to the folly of the quite unselfish suit-at-law he had been persuaded to begin, nevertheless so miscalculated the force of the social vengeance he was unloosing on himself that he fancied it could be stayed by putting up the editor of The Saturday Review (as Mr Harris then was) to declare that he considered Dorian Grey a highly moral book, which it certainly is. When Harris foretold him the truth, Wilde denounced him as a faint-hearted friend who was failing him in his hour of need, and left the room in anger. Harris's idiosyncratic power of pity saved him from feeling or shewing the smallest resentment; and events presently proved to Wilde how insanely he had been advised in taking the action, and how accurately Harris had gauged the situation.

The same capacity for pity governs

Harris's study of Shakespear, whom, as I have said, he pities too much; but that he is not insensible to humor is shewn not only by his appreciation of Wilde, but by the fact that the group of contributors who made his editorship of The Saturday Review so remarkable, and of whom I speak none the less highly because I happened to be one of them myself, were all, in their various ways, humorists.

"SIDNEY'S SISTER: PEMBROKE'S MOTHER"

And now to return to Shakespear. Though Mr Harris followed Tyler in identifying Mary Fitton as the Dark Lady, and the Earl of Pembroke as the addressee of the other sonnets and the man who made love successfully to Shakespear's mistress, he very characteristically refuses to follow Tyler on one point, though for the life of me I cannot remember whether it was one of the surmises which Tyler published, or only one which he submitted to me to see what I would say about it, just as he used to submit difficult lines from the sonnets.

This surmise was that "Sidney's sister: Pembroke's mother" set Shakespear on to persuade Pembroke to marry, and that this was the explanation of those earlier sonnets which so persistently and unnaturally urged matrimony on Mr W. H. I take this to be one of the brightest of Tyler's ideas, because the persuasions in the sonnets are unaccountable and out of character unless they were offered to please somebody whom Shakespear desired to please, and who took a motherly interest in Pembroke. There is a further temptation in the theory for me. The most charming of all Shakespear's old women, indeed the most charming of all his women, young or old, is the Countess of Rousillon in All's Well That Ends Well. It has a certain individuality among them which suggests a portrait. Mr Harris will have it that all Shakespear's nice old women are drawn from his beloved mother; but I see no evidence whatever that Shakespear's mother was a particularly nice woman or that he was particularly fond of her. That she was a simple incarnation of extravagant maternal pride like the mother of Coriolanus in Plutarch, as Mr Harris asserts, I cannot believe: she is quite as likely to have borne her son a grudge for becoming "one of these harlotry players" and disgracing the Ardens. Anyhow, as a conjectural model for the Countess of Rousillon, I prefer that one of whom Jonson wrote

> Sidney's sister: Pembroke's mother:
> Death ere thou has slain another,
> Learned and fair and good as she,
> Time shall throw a dart at thee.

But Frank will not have her at any price, because his ideal Shakespear is rather like a sailor in a melodrama; and a sailor in a melodrama must adore his mother. I do not at all belittle such sailors. They are the emblems of human generosity; but Shakespear was not an emblem; he was a man and the author of Hamlet, who had no illusions about his mother. In weak moments one almost wishes he had.

SHAKESPEAR'S SOCIAL STANDING

On the vexed question of Shakespear's social standing Mr Harris says that Shakespear "had not had the advantage of a middle-class training." I suggest that Shakespear missed this questionable advantage, not because he was socially too low to have attained to it, but because he conceived himself as belonging to the upper class from which our public school boys are now drawn. Let Mr Harris survey for a moment the field of contemporary journalism. He will see there some men who have the very characteristics from which he infers that Shakespear was at a social disadvantage through his lack of middle-class training. They are rowdy, ill-mannered, abusive, mischievous, fond of quoting obscene schoolboy anecdotes, adepts in that sort of blackmail which consists in mercilessly libelling and insulting every writer whose opinions are sufficiently heterodox to make it almost impossible for him to risk perhaps five years of a slender income by an appeal to a prejudiced orthodox jury; and they see nothing in all this cruel blackguardism but an uproariously jolly rag, although they are by no means without genuine literary ability, a love of letters, and even some artistic conscience. But he will find not one of the models of this type (I say nothing of mere imitators of it) below the rank that looks at the middle class, not humbly and enviously from below, but insolently from above. Mr Harris himself notes Shakespear's contempt for the tradesman and mechanic, and his incorrigible addiction to smutty jokes. He does us the public service of sweeping away the familiar plea of the Bardolatrous ignoramus, that Shakespear's coarseness was part of the manners of his time, putting his pen with precision on the one name, Spenser, that is necessary to expose such a libel on Elizabethan decency. There was nothing whatever to prevent Shakespear from being as decent as More was before him, or Bunyan after him, and as self-respecting as Raleigh or Sidney, except the tradition of his class, in which education or statesmanship may no doubt be acquired by those who have a turn for them, but in which insolence, derision, profligacy, obscene jesting, debt contracting, and rowdy mischievousness, give continual scandal to the pious, serious, industrious, solvent bourgeois. No other class is infatuated enough to believe that gentlemen are born and not made by a very elaborate process of culture. Even kings are taught and coached and drilled from their earliest boyhood to play their part. But the man of family (I am convinced that Shakespear took that view of himself) will plunge into society without a lesson in table manners, into politics without a lesson in history, into the city without a lesson in business, and into the army without a lesson in honor.

It has been said, with the object of proving Shakespear a laborer, that he could hardly write his name. Why? Because he "had not the advantage of a middle-class training." Shakespear himself tells us, through Hamlet, that gentlemen purposely wrote badly lest they should be mistaken for scriveners; but most of them, then as now, wrote badly because they could not write any better. In short, the whole range of Shakespear's foibles: the snobbishness, the naughtiness, the contempt for tradesmen and mechanics, the assumption that witty conversation can only mean smutty conversation, the flunkeyism towards social superiors and insolence towards social inferiors, the easy ways with servants which is seen not only between The Two Gentlemen of Verona and their valets, but in the affection and respect inspired by a great servant like Adam: all these are the characteristics of Eton and Harrow, not of the public elementary or private adventure school. They prove, as everything we know about Shakespear suggests, that he thought of the Shakespears and Ardens as families of consequence, and regarded himself as a gentleman under a cloud through his father's ill luck in business, and never for a moment as a man of the people. This is at once the explanation of and excuse for his snobbery. He was not a parvenu trying to cover his humble origin with a purchased coat of arms: he was a gentleman resuming what he conceived to be his natural position as soon as he gained the means to keep it up.

THIS SIDE IDOLATRY

There is another matter which I think Mr Harris should ponder. He says that

Shakespear was but "little esteemed by his own generation." He even describes Jonson's description of his "little Latin and less Greek" as a sneer, whereas it occurs in an unmistakeably sincere eulogy of Shakespear, written after his death, and is clearly meant to heighten the impression of Shakespear's prodigious natural endowments by pointing out that they were not due to scholastic acquirements. Now there is a sense in which it is true enough that Shakespear was too little esteemed by his own generation, or, for the matter of that, by any subsequent generation. The bargees on the Regent's Canal do not chant Shakespear's verses as the gondoliers in Venice are said to chant the verses of Tasso (a practice which was suspended for some reason during my stay in Venice: at least no gondolier ever did it in my hearing). Shakespear is no more a popular author than Rodin is a popular sculptor or Richard Strauss a popular composer. But Shakespear was certainly not such a fool as to expect the Toms, Dicks, and Harrys of his time to be any more interested in dramatic poetry than Newton, later on, expected them to be interested in fluxions. And when we come to the question whether Shakespear missed that assurance which all great men have had from the more capable and susceptible members of their generation that they were great men, Ben Jonson's evidence disposes of so improbable a notion at once and for ever. "I loved the man," says Ben, "this side idolatry, as well as any." Now why in the name of common sense should he have made that qualification unless there had been, not only idolatry, but idolatry fulsome enough to irritate Jonson into an express disavowal of it? Jonson, the bricklayer, must have felt sore sometimes when Shakespear spoke and wrote of bricklayers as his inferiors. He must have felt it a little hard that being a better scholar, and perhaps a braver and

tougher man physically than Shakespear, he was not so successful or so well liked. But in spite of this he praised Shakespear to the utmost stretch of his powers of eulogy: in fact, notwithstanding his disclaimer, he did not stop "this side idolatry." If, therefore, even Jonson felt himself forced to clear himself of extravagance and absurdity in his appreciation of Shakespear, there must have been many people about who idolized Shakespear as American ladies idolize Paderewski, and who carried Bardolatry, even in the Bard's own time, to an extent that threatened to make his reasonable admirers ridiculous.

SHAKESPEAR'S PESSIMISM

I submit to Mr Harris that by ruling out this idolatry, and its possible effect in making Shakespear think that his public would stand anything from him, he has ruled out a far more plausible explanation of the faults of such a play as Timon of Athens than his theory that Shakespear's passion for the Dark Lady "cankered and took on proud flesh in him, and tortured him to nervous breakdown and madness." In Timon the intellectual bankruptcy is obvious enough: Shakespear tried once too often to make a play out of the cheap pessimism which is thrown into despair by a comparison of actual human nature with theoretical morality, actual law and administration with abstract justice, and so forth. But Shakespear's perception of the fact that all men, judged by the moral standard which they apply to others and by which they justify their punishment of others, are fools and scoundrels, does not date from the Dark Lady complication: he seems to have been born with it. If in The Comedy of Errors and A Midsummer Night's Dream the persons of the drama are not quite so ready for treachery and murder as Laertes and even Hamlet himself (not to mention the procession of ruffians who pass through the latest plays) it is certainly not because they have any more regard for law or religion. There is only one place in Shakespear's plays where the sense of shame is used as a human attribute; and that is where Hamlet is ashamed, not of anything he himself has done, but of his mother's relations with his uncle. This scene is an unnatural one: the son's reproaches to his mother, even the fact of his being able to discuss the subject with her, is more repulsive than her relations with her deceased husband's brother.

Here, too, Shakespear betrays for once his religious sense by making Hamlet, in his agony of shame, declare that his mother's conduct makes "sweet religion a rhapsody of words." But for that passage we might almost suppose that the feeling of Sunday morning in the country which Orlando describes so perfectly in As You Like It was the beginning and end of Shakespear's notion of religion. I say almost, because Isabella in Measure for Measure has religious charm, in spite of the conventional theatrical assumption that female religion means an inhumanly ferocious chastity. But for the most part Shakespear differentiates his heroes from his villains much more by what they do than by what they are. Don Juan in Much Ado is a true villain: a man with a malicious will; but he is too dull a duffer to be of any use in a leading part; and when we come to the great villains like Macbeth, we find, as Mr Harris points out, that they are precisely identical with the heroes: Macbeth is only Hamlet incongruously committing murders and engaging in hand-to-hand combats. And Hamlet, who does not dream of apologizing for the three murders he commits, is always apologizing because he has not yet committed a fourth, and finds, to his great bewilderment, that he does not want to commit it. "It cannot be," he says, "but I am pigeon-livered, and lack gall

to make oppression bitter; else, ere this, I should have fatted all the region kites with this slave's offal." Really one is tempted to suspect that when Shylock asks "Hates any man the thing he would not kill?" he is expressing the natural and proper sentiments of the human race as Shakespear understood them, and not the vindictiveness of a stage Jew.

GAIETY OF GENIUS

In view of these facts, it is dangerous to cite Shakespear's pessimism as evidence of the despair of a heart broken by the Dark Lady. There is an irrepressible gaiety of genius which enables it to bear the whole weight of the world's misery without blenching. There is a laugh always ready to avenge its tears of discouragement. In the lines which Mr Harris quotes only to declare that he can make nothing of them, and to condemn them as out of character, Richard III, immediately after pitying himself because

> There is no creature loves me
> And if I die no soul will pity me,

adds, with a grin,

> Nay, wherefore should they, since that I myself
> Find in myself no pity for myself?

Let me again remind Mr Harris of Oscar Wilde. We all dreaded to read De Profundis: our instinct was to stop our ears, or run away from the wail of a broken, though by no means contrite, heart. But we were throwing away our pity. De Profundis was de profundis indeed: Wilde was too good a dramatist to throw away so powerful an effect; but none the less it was de profundis in excelsis. There was more laughter between the lines of that book than in a thousand farces by men of no genius. Wilde, like Richard and Shakespear, found in himself no pity for himself. There is nothing that marks the born dramatist more unmistakeably than this discovery of comedy in his own misfortunes almost in proportion to the pathos with which the ordinary man announces their tragedy. I cannot for the life of me see the broken heart in Shakespear's latest works. "Hark, hark! the lark at heaven's gate sings" is not the lyric of a broken man; nor is Cloten's comment that if Imogen does not appreciate it, "it is a vice in her ears which horse hairs, and cats' guts, and the voice of unpaved eunuch to boot, can never amend," the sally of a saddened one. Is it not clear that to the last there was in Shakespear an incorrigible divine levity, an inexhaustible joy that derided sorrow? Think of the poor Dark Lady having to stand up to this unbearable power of extracting a grim fun from everything. Mr Harris writes as if Shakespear did all the suffering and the Dark Lady all the cruelty. But why does he not put himself in the Dark Lady's place for a moment as he has put himself so successfully in Shakespear's? Imagine her reading the hundred and thirtieth sonnet!

My mistress' eyes are nothing like the sun;
Coral is far more red than her lips' red;
If snow be white, why then her breasts are
    dun;
If hairs be wire, black wires grow on her
    head;
I have seen roses damasked, red and white,
But no such roses see I in her cheeks;
And in some perfumes is there more delight
Than in the breath that from my mistress
    reeks.
I love to hear her speak; yet well I know
That music hath a far more pleasing sound.
I grant I never saw a goddess go:
My mistress, when she walks, treads on the
    ground.
  And yet, by heaven, I think my love as
    rare
  As any she belied with false compare.

Take this as a sample of the sort of compliment from which she was never for a moment safe with Shakespear. Bear in mind that she was not a comedian; that the Elizabethan fashion of treating brunettes as ugly women must have made her rather sore on the subject of her complexion; that no human being, male or female, can conceivably enjoy being chaffed on that point in the fourth couplet about the perfumes; that Shakespear's revulsions, as the sonnet immediately preceding shews, were as violent as his ardors, and were expressed with the realistic power and horror that makes Hamlet say that the heavens got sick when they saw the queen's conduct; and then ask Mr Harris whether any woman could have stood it for long, or have thought the "sugred" compliment worth the cruel wounds, the cleaving of the heart in twain, that seemed to Shakespear as natural and amusing a reaction as the burlesquing of his heroics by Pistol, his sermons by Falstaff, and his poems by Cloten and Touchstone.

JUPITER AND SEMELE

This does not mean that Shakespear was cruel: evidently he was not; but it was not cruelty that made Jupiter reduce Semele to ashes: it was the fact that he could not help being a god nor she help being a mortal. The one thing Shakespear's passion for the Dark Lady was not, was what Mr Harris in one passage calls it: idolatrous. If it had been, she might have been able to stand it. The man who dotes "yet doubts; suspects, yet strongly loves," is tolerable even by a spoilt and tyrannical mistress; but what woman could possibly endure a man who dotes without doubting; who *knows* and who is hugely amused at the absurdity of his infatuation for a woman of whose mortal imperfections not one escapes him: a man always exchanging grins with Yorick's skull, and inviting "my lady" to laugh at the sepulchral humor of the fact that though she paint an inch thick (which the Dark Lady may have done), to Yorick's favor she must come at last. To the Dark Lady he must sometimes have seemed cruel beyond description: an intellectual Caliban. True, a Caliban who could say

Be not afeard: the isle is full of noises,
Sounds and sweet airs that give delight and
  hurt not.
Sometimes a thousand twangling instru-
  ments
Will hum about mine ears; and sometimes
  voices,
That, if I then had waked after long sleep,
Will make me sleep again; and then, in
  dreaming,
The clouds, methought, would open and
  shew riches
Ready to drop on me: that when I wak'd
I cried to dream again,

which is very lovely; but the Dark Lady may have had that vice in her ears which Cloten dreaded: she may not have seen the beauty of it, whereas there can be no doubt at all that of "My mistress' eyes are nothing like the sun," &c., not a word was lost on her.

And is it to be supposed that Shakespear was too stupid or too modest not to see at last that it was a case of Jupiter and Semele? Shakespear was most certainly not modest in that sense. The timid cough of the minor poet was never heard from him.

Not marble, nor the gilded monuments
Of princes, shall outlive this powerful rhyme

is only one out of a dozen passages in which he (possibly with a keen sense of the fun of scandalizing the modest coughers) proclaimed his place and his power in "the wide world dreaming of things to come." The Dark Lady most likely thought this side of him insufferably conceited; for there is no reason to suppose that she liked his plays any better than Minna Wagner liked Richard's music dramas: as likely as not, she thought The Spanish Tragedy worth six Hamlets. He was not stupid either: if his class limitations and a profession that cut him off from actual participation in

great affairs of State had not confined his opportunities of intellectual and political training to private conversation and to the Mermaid Tavern, he would probably have become one of the ablest men of his time instead of being merely its ablest playwright. One might surmise that Shakespear found out that the Dark Lady's brains could no more keep pace with his than Anne Hathaway's, if there were any evidence that their friendship ceased when he stopped writing sonnets to her. As a matter of fact the consolidation of a passion into an enduring intimacy generally puts an end to sonnets.

That the Dark Lady broke Shakespear's heart, as Mr Harris will have it she did, is an extremely unShakespearean hypothesis. "Men have died from time to time, and worms have eaten them; but not for love," says Rosalind. Richard of Gloster, into whom Shakespear put all his own impish superiority to vulgar sentiment, exclaims

And this word "love," which greybeards
  call divine,
Be resident in men like one another
And not in me: I am myself alone.

Hamlet has not a tear for Ophelia: her death moves him to fierce disgust for the sentimentality of Laertes by her grave; and when he discusses the scene with Horatio immediately after, he utterly forgets her, though he is sorry he forgot himself, and jumps at the proposal of a fencing match to finish the day with. As against this view Mr Harris pleads Romeo, Orsino, and even Antonio; and he does it so penetratingly that he convinces you that Shakespear did betray himself again and again in these characters; but self-betrayal is one thing; and self-portrayal, as in Hamlet and Mercutio, is another. Shakespear never "saw himself," as actors say, in Romeo or Orsino or Antonio. In Mr Harris's own play Shakespear is presented with the most pathetic tenderness. He is tragic, bitter, pitiable, wretched and broken among a robust crowd of Jonsons and Elizabeths; but to me he is not Shakespear because I miss the Shakespearean irony and the Shakespearean gaiety. Take these away and Shakespear is no longer Shakespear: all the bite, the impetus, the strength, the grim delight in his own power of looking terrible facts in the face with a chuckle, is gone; and you have nothing left but that most depressing of all things: a victim. Now who can think of Shakespear as a man with a grievance? Even in that most thoroughgoing and inspired of all Shakespear's loves: his love of music (which Mr Harris has been the first to appreciate at anything like its value), there is a dash of mockery. "Spit in the hole, man; and tune again." "Divine air! Now is his soul ravished. Is it not strange that sheep's guts should hale the souls out of men's bodies?" "An he had been a dog that should have howled thus, they would have hanged him." There is just as much Shakespear here as in the inevitable quotation about the sweet south and the bank of violets.

I lay stress on this irony of Shakespear's, this impish rejoicing in pessimism, this exultation in what breaks the hearts of common men, not only because it is diagnostic of that immense energy of life which we call genius, but because its omission is the one glaring defect in Mr Harris's otherwise extraordinary penetrating book. Fortunately, it is an omission that does not disable the book as (in my judgment) it disabled the hero of the play, because Mr Harris left himself out of his play, whereas he pervades his book, mordant, deep-voiced, and with an unconquerable style which is the man.

THE IDOL OF THE BARDOLATERS

There is even an advantage in having a book on Shakespear with the Shakespearean irony left out of account. I do not say that the missing chapter should not be added in the next edition: the hiatus is too great: it leaves the reader too uneasy before this touching picture of a writhing worm substituted for the invulnerable giant. But it is none the less probable that in no other way could Mr Harris have got at his man as he has. For, after all, what is the secret of the hopeless failure of the academic Bardolaters to give us a credible or even interesting Shakespear, and the easy triumph of Mr Harris in giving us both? Simply that Mr Harris has assumed that he was dealing with a man, whilst the others have assumed that they were writing about a god, and have therefore rejected every consideration of fact, tradition, or interpretation, that pointed to any human imperfection in their hero. They thus leave themselves with so little material that they are forced to begin by saying that we know very little about Shakespear. As a matter of fact, with the plays and sonnets in our hands, we know much more about Shakespear than we know about Dickens or Thackeray: the only difficulty is that we deliberately suppress it because it proves that Shakespear was not only very unlike the conception of a god current in Clapham, but was not, according to the same reckoning, even a respectable man. The academic view starts with a Shakespear who was not scurrilous; therefore the verses about "lousy Lucy" cannot have been written by him, and the cognate passages in the plays are either strokes of character-drawing or gags interpolated by the actors. This ideal Shakespear was too well behaved to get drunk; therefore the tradition that his death was hastened by a drinking bout with Jonson and Drayton must be rejected, and the remorse of Cassio treated as a thing observed, not experienced: nay, the disgust of Hamlet at the drinking customs of Denmark is taken to establish Shakespear as the superior of Alexander in self-control, and the greatest of teetotalers.

Now this system of inventing your great man to start with, and then rejecting all the materials that do not fit him, with the ridiculous result that you have to declare that there are no materials at all (with your waste-paper basket full of them), ends in leaving Shakespear with a much worse character than he deserves. For though it does not greatly matter whether he wrote the lousy Lucy lines or not, and does not really matter at all whether he got drunk when he made a night of it with Jonson and Drayton, the sonnets raise an unpleasant question which does matter a good deal; and the refusal of the academic Bardolaters to discuss or even mention this question has had the effect of producing a silent verdict against Shakespear. Mr Harris tackles the question openly, and has no difficulty whatever in convincing us that Shakespear was a man of normal constitution sexually, and was not the victim of that most cruel and pitiable of all the freaks of nature: the freak which transposes the normal aim of the affections. Silence on this point means condemnation; and the condemnation has been general throughout the present generation, though it only needed Mr Harris's fearless handling of the matter to sweep away what is nothing but a morbid and very disagreeable modern fashion. There is always some stock accusation brought against eminent persons. When I was a boy every well-known man was accused of beating his wife. Later on, for some unexplained reason, he was accused of psychopathic derangement. And this fashion is retrospective. The cases of Shakespear and Michael Angelo are cited as proving that every genius of the first magnitude was a sufferer; and both here and in Germany there are circles in which such derangement is grotesquely reverenced as part of the stigmata of heroic powers. All of which is gross nonsense. Unfortunately, in

Shakespear's case, prudery, which cannot prevent the accusation from being whispered, does prevent the refutation from being shouted. Mr Harris, the deep-voiced, refuses to be silenced. He dismisses with proper contempt the stupidity which places an outrageous construction on Shakespear's apologies in the sonnets for neglecting that "perfect ceremony" of love which consists in returning calls and making protestations and giving presents and paying the trumpery attentions which men of genius always refuse to bother about, and to which touchy people who have no genius attach so much importance. No reader who had not been tampered with by the psychopathic monomaniacs could ever put any construction but the obvious and innocent one on these passages. But the general vocabulary of the sonnets to Pembroke (or whoever "Mr W. H." really was) is so overcharged according to modern ideas that a reply on the general case is necessary.

SHAKESPEAR'S ALLEGED SYCOPHANCY AND PERVERSION

That reply, which Mr Harris does not hesitate to give, is twofold: first, that Shakespear was, in his attitude towards earls, a sycophant; and, second, that the normality of Shakespear's sexual constitution is only too well attested by the excessive susceptibility to the normal impulse shewn in the whole mass of his writings. This latter is the really conclusive reply. In the case of Michael Angelo, for instance, one must admit that if his works are set beside those of Titian or Paul Veronese, it is impossible not to be struck by the absence in the Florentine of that susceptibility to feminine charm which pervades the pictures of the Venetians. But, as Mr Harris points out (though he does not use this particular illustration) Paul Veronese is an anchorite compared to Shakespear. The language of the sonnets addressed to Pembroke, extravagant as it now seems, is the language of compliment and fashion, transfigured no doubt by Shakespear's verbal magic, and hyperbolical, as Shakespear always seems to people who cannot conceive so vividly as he, but still unmistakeable for anything else than the expression of a friendship delicate enough to be wounded, and a manly loyalty deep enough to be outraged. But the language of the sonnets to the Dark Lady is the language of passion: their cruelty shews it. There is no evidence that Shakespear was capable of being unkind in cold blood. But in his revulsions from love, he was bitter, wounding, even ferocious; sparing neither himself nor the unfortunate woman whose only offence was that she had reduced the great man to the common human denominator.

In seizing on these two points Mr Harris has made so sure a stroke, and places his evidence so featly that there is nothing left for me to do but to plead that the second is sounder than the first, which is, I think, marked by the prevalent mistake as to Shakespear's social position, or, if you prefer it, the confusion between his actual social position as a penniless tradesman's son taking to the theatre for a livelihood, and his own conception of himself as a gentleman of good family. I am prepared to contend that though Shakespear was undoubtedly sentimental in his expressions of devotion to Mr W. H. even to a point which nowadays makes both ridiculous, he was not sycophantic if Mr W. H. was really attractive and promising, and Shakespear deeply attached to him. A sycophant does not tell his patron that his fame will survive, not in the renown of his own actions, but in the sonnets of his sycophant. A sycophant, when his patron cuts him out in a love affair, does not tell his patron exactly what he thinks of him. Above all, a sycophant does not write to his patron

precisely as he feels on all occasions; and this rare kind of sincerity is all over the sonnets. Shakespear, we are told, was "a very civil gentleman." This must mean that his desire to please people and be liked by them, and his reluctance to hurt their feelings, led him into amiable flattery even when his feelings were not strongly stirred. If this be taken into account along with the fact that Shakespear conceived and expressed all his emotions with a vehemence that sometimes carried him into ludicrous extravagance, making Richard offer his kingdom for a horse and Othello declare of Cassio that

Had all his hairs been lives, my great revenge
Had stomach for them all,

we shall see more civility and hyperbole than sycophancy even in the earlier and more coldblooded sonnets.

SHAKESPEAR AND DEMOCRACY

Now take the general case pled against Shakespear as an enemy of democracy by Tolstoy, the late Ernest Crosbie and others, and endorsed by Mr Harris. Will it really stand fire? Mr Harris emphasizes the passages in which Shakespear spoke of mechanics and even of small master tradesmen as base persons whose clothes were greasy, whose breath was rank, and whose political imbecility and caprice moved Coriolanus to say to the Roman Radical who demanded at least "good words" from him

He that will give good words to thee will flatter
   Beneath abhorring.

But let us be honest. As political sentiments these lines are an abomination to every democrat. But suppose they are not political sentiments! Suppose they are merely a record of observed fact. John Stuart Mill told our British workmen that they were mostly liars. Carlyle told us all that we are mostly fools. Matthew Arnold and Ruskin were more circumstantial and more abusive. Everybody, including the workers themselves, know that they are dirty, drunken, foul-mouthed, ignorant, gluttonous, prejudiced: in short, heirs to the peculiar ills of poverty and slavery, as well as co-heirs with the plutocracy to all the failings of human nature. Even Shelley admitted, 200 years after Shakespear wrote Coriolanus, that universal suffrage was out of the question. Surely the real test, not of Democracy, which was not a live political issue in Shakespear's time, but of impartiality in judging classes, which is what one demands from a great human poet, is not that he should flatter the poor and denounce the rich, but that he should weigh them both in the same balance. Now whoever will read Lear and Measure for Measure will find stamped on his mind such an appalled sense of the danger of dressing man in a little brief authority, such a merciless stripping of the purple from the "poor, bare, forked animal" that calls itself a king and fancies itself a god, that one wonders what was the real nature of the mysterious restraint that kept "Eliza and our James" from teaching Shakespear to be civil to crowned heads, just as one wonders why Tolstoy was allowed to go free when so many less terrible levellers went to the galleys or Siberia. From the mature Shakespear we get no such scenes of village snobbery as that between the stage country gentleman Alexander Iden and the stage Radical Jack Cade. We get the shepherd in As You Like It, and many honest, brave, human, and loyal servants, beside the inevitable comic ones. Even in the Jingo play, Henry V, we get Bates and Williams drawn with all respect and honor as normal rank and file men. In Julius Cæsar, Shakespear went to work with a will when he took his cue from Plutarch in glorifying regicide and transfiguring the republicans. Indeed hero-worshippers have never forgiven him for belittling

Cæsar and failing to see that side of his assassination which made Goethe denounce it as the most senseless of crimes. Put the play beside the Charles I of Wills, in which Cromwell is written down to a point at which the Jack Cade of Henry VI becomes a hero in comparison; and then believe, if you can, that Shakespear was one of them that "crook the pregnant hinges of the knee where thrift may follow fawning." Think of Rosencrantz, Guildenstern, Osric, the fop who annoyed Hotspur, and a dozen passages concerning such people! If such evidence can prove anything (and Mr Harris relies throughout on such evidence) Shakespear loathed courtiers.

If, on the other hand, Shakespear's characters are mostly members of the leisured classes, the same thing is true of Mr Harris's own plays and mine. Industrial slavery is not compatible with that freedom of adventure, that personal refinement and intellectual culture, that scope of action, which the higher and subtler drama demands. Even Cervantes had finally to drop Don Quixote's troubles with innkeepers demanding to be paid for his food and lodging, and make him as free of economic difficulties as Amadis de Gaul. Hamlet's experiences simply could not have happened to a plumber. A poor man is useful on the stage only as a blind man is: to excite sympathy. The poverty of the apothecary in Romeo and Juliet produces a great effect, and even points the sound moral that a poor man cannot afford to have a conscience; but if all the characters of the play had been as poor as he, it would have been nothing but a melodrama of the sort that the Sicilian players gave us here; and that was not the best that lay in Shakespear's power. When poverty is abolished, and leisure and grace of life become general, the only plays surviving from our epoch which will have any relation to life as it will be lived then will be those in which none of the persons represented are troubled with want of money or wretched drudgery. Our plays of poverty and squalor, now the only ones that are true to the life of the majority of living men, will then be classed with the records of misers and monsters, and read only by historical students of social pathology.

Then consider Shakespear's kings and lords and gentlemen! Would even John Ball or Jeremiah complain that they are flattered? Surely a more mercilessly exposed string of scoundrels never crossed the stage. The very monarch who paralyses a rebel by appealing to the divinity that hedges a king, is a drunken and sensual assassin, and is presently killed contemptuously before our eyes in spite of his hedge of divinity. I could write as convincing a chapter on Shakespear's Dickensian prejudice against the throne and the nobility and gentry in general as Mr Harris or Ernest Crosbie on the other side. I could even go so far as to contend that one of Shakespear's defects is his lack of an intelligent comprehension of feudalism. He had of course no prevision of democratic Collectivism. He was, except in the commonplaces of war and patriotism, a privateer through and through. Nobody in his plays, whether king or citizen, has any civil public business or conception of such a thing, except in the method of appointing constables, to the abuses in which he called attention quite in the vein of the Fabian Society. He was concerned about drunkenness and about the idolatry and hypocrisy of our judicial system; but his implied remedy was personal sobriety and freedom from idolatrous illusion in so far as he had any remedy at all, and did not merely despair of human nature. His first and last word on parliament was "Get thee glass eyes, and, like a scurvy politician, seem to see the thing thou dost not." He had no notion of the feel-ing with which the land nationalizers of today regard the fact that he was a party to the enclosure of common lands at Wellcome. The explanation is, not a general deficiency in his mind, but the simple fact that in his day what English land needed was individual appropriation and cultivation, and what the English Constitution needed was the incorporation of Whig principles of individual liberty.

SHAKESPEAR AND THE BRITISH PUBLIC

I have rejected Mr. Harris's view that Shakespear died broken-hearted of "the pangs of love despised." I have given my reasons for believing that Shakespear died game, and indeed in a state of levity which would have been considered unbecoming in a bishop. But Mr Harris's evidence does prove that Shakespear had a grievance and a very serious one. He might have been jilted by ten dark ladies and been none the worse for it; but his treatment by the British Public was another matter. The idolatry which exasperated Ben Jonson was by no means a popular movement; and, like all such idolatries, it was excited by the magic of Shakespear's art rather than by his views. He was launched on his career as a successful playwright by the Henry VI trilogy, a work of no originality, depth, or subtlety except the originality, depth, and subtlety of the feelings and fancies of the common people. But Shakespear was not satisfied with this. What is the use of being Shakespear if you are not allowed to express any notions but those of Autolycus? Shakespear did not see the world as Autolycus did: he saw it, if not exactly as Ibsen did (for it was not quite the same world), at least with much of Ibsen's power of penetrating its illusions and idolatries, and with all Swift's horror of its cruelty and uncleanliness.

Now it happens to some men with these powers that they are forced to impose their fullest exercise on the world because they cannot produce popular work. Take Wagner and Ibsen for instance! Their earlier works are no doubt much cheaper than their later ones; still, they were not popular when they were written. The alternative of doing popular work was never really open to them: had they stooped they would have picked up less than they snatched from above the people's heads. But Handel and Shakespear were not held to their best in this way. They could turn out anything they were asked for, and even heap up the measure. They reviled the British Public, and never forgave it for ignoring their best work and admiring their splendid commonplaces; but they produced the commonplaces all the same, and made them sound magnificent by mere brute faculty for their art. When Shakespear was forced to write popular plays to save his theatre from ruin, he did it mutinously, calling the plays As *You* Like It, and Much Ado About Nothing. All the same, he did it so well that to this day these two genial vulgarities are the main Shakespearean stock-in-trade of our theatres. Later on Burbage's power and popularity as an actor enabled Shakespear to free himself from the tyranny of the box office, and to express himself more freely in plays consisting largely of monologue to be spoken by a great actor from whom the public would stand a good deal. The history of Shakespear's tragedies has thus been the history of a long line of famous actors, from Burbage and Betterton to Forbes Robertson; and the man of whom we are told that "when he would have said that Richard died, and cried A horse! A horse! he Burbage cried" was the father of nine generations of Shakespearean playgoers, all speaking of Garrick's Richard, and Kean's Othello, and Irving's Shylock, and Forbes Robertson's Hamlet without knowing or caring how much these had to do with Shakespear's Richard and Othello and so forth. And the plays which were written without great and predominant parts, such as Troilus and Cressida, All's Well That Ends Well, and Measure for Measure, have dropped on our stage as dead as the second part of Goethe's Faust or Ibsen's Emperor or Galilean.

Here, then, Shakespear had a real grievance; and though it is a sentimental exaggeration to describe him as a broken-hearted man in the face of the passages of reckless jollity and serenely happy poetry in his latest plays, yet the discovery that his most serious work could reach success only when carried on the back of a very fascinating actor who was enormously overcharging his part, and that the serious plays which did not contain parts big enough to hold the overcharge were left on the shelf, amply accounts for the evident fact that Shakespear did not end his life in a glow of enthusiastic satisfaction with mankind and with the theatre, which is all that Mr Harris can allege in support of his broken-heart theory. But even if Shakespear had had no failures, it was not possible for a man of his powers to observe the political and moral conduct of his contemporaries without perceiving that they were incapable of dealing with the problems raised by their own civilization, and that their attempts to carry out the codes of law and to practise the religions offered to them by great prophets and law-givers were and still are so foolish that we now call for The Superman, virtually a new species, to rescue the world from mismanagement. This is the real sorrow of great men; and in the face of it the notion that when a great man speaks bitterly or looks melancholy he must be troubled by a disappointment in love seems to me sentimental trifling.

If I have carried the reader with me thus far, he will find that trivial as this little play of mine is, its sketch of Shakespear is more complete than its levity suggests. Alas! its appeal for a National Theatre as a monument to Shakespear failed to touch the very stupid people who cannot see that a National Theatre is worth having for the sake of the National Soul. I had unfortunately represented Shakespear as treasuring and using (as I do myself) the jewels of unconsciously musical speech which common people utter and throw away every day; and this was taken as a disparagement of Shakespear's "originality." Why was I born with such contemporaries? Why is Shakespear made ridiculous by such a posterity?

POSTSCRIPT 1933. The recent death of Frank Harris has refreshed the interest of the sketch of him in this preface, especially as he died in the act of finishing a curious biography of me which has attracted a good deal of notice, and which is truthful as to its record of bare facts, though its critical side is badly lamed through Frank's having lost touch with me before the end of the nineteenth century, and never reconsidered his estimates in the light of my later exploits.

The appeal for a national theatre with which the play concludes, and for the sake of which it was written, elicited applause but no subscriptions. Two years ago a great Shakespear Memorial Theatre was completed at Stratford-upon-Avon through the efforts of Sir Archibald Flower, replacing the old Shakespear theatre which owed its existence to his family; but Sir Archibald had wasted no time in appealing to Shakespear's countrymen: he had turned to America and received a noble response. The attempt to establish a National Theatre in London to commemorate Shakespear's exploits in that old city, now expanded into a concentration camp much too big for any civic consciousness, was and still is a complete failure, though there is enough money (not English money, of course) available to carry out the project if the Government would provide a site, and the municipality forgo its rates, as foreign Governments and municipalities do.

XXXI

THE ADMIRABLE BASHVILLE

1909

It may be asked why I wrote The Admirable Bashville in blank verse. My answer is that the operation of the copyright law of that time (now happily superseded) left me only a week to write it in. Blank verse is so childishly easy and expeditious (hence, by the way, Shakespear's copious output) that by adopting it I was enabled to do within the week what would have cost me a month in prose.

Besides, I am fond of blank verse. Not nineteenth century blank verse, of course, nor indeed, with a very few exceptions, any post-Shakespearean blank verse. Nay not Shakespearean blank verse itself later than the histories. I am quite sure that anyone who is to recover the charm of blank verse must go back frankly to its beginnings, and start a literary pre-Raphaelite Brotherhood. I like the melodious singsong, the clear simple one-line and two-line sayings, and the occasional rhymed tags, like the half closes in an eighteenth century symphony, in Peele, Kyd, Greene, and the histories of Shakespear. Accordingly, I poetasted The Admirable Bashville in the primitive Elizabethan style. And lest the literary connoisseurs should declare that there was not a single correct line in all my three acts, I stole or paraphrased a few from Marlowe and Shakespear (not to mention Henry Carey); so that if any man dared quote me derisively, he should do so in peril of inadvertently lighting on a purple patch from Hamlet or Faustus.

I also endeavored in this little play to prove that I was not the heartless creature some of my critics took me for. I observed the established laws of stage popularity and probability. I simplified the character of the heroine, and summed up her sweetness in the one sacred word: Love. I gave consistency to the heroism of Cashel. I paid to Morality, in the final scene, the tribute of poetic justice. I restored to Patriotism its usual place on the stage, and gracefully acknowledged The Throne as the fountain of social honor. I paid particular attention to the construction of the play, which will be found equal in this respect to the best contemporary models.

And the result was that the British playgoer, to whom Elizabethan English is a dead language, only half understood nine-tenths of the play, and applauded the other tenth (the big speeches) with a seriousness that was far funnier than any burlesque.

The play, by the way, should be performed on an Elizabethan stage, with traverses for the indoor scenes, and with only one interval after the second act.

*　　*　　*　　*　　*

On reading over the above after a lapse of thirty years I am not quite so sure as I was that Elizabethan English may not again become a living language to the ordinary playgoer. To people who never read anything but newspapers and popular magazines, a good deal of Shakespear's more euphuistic blank verse is hardly more intelligible than classical Greek. Even actors may be heard repeating it by rote with an air that persuades the public that they understand what they are saying; but it cannot impose any such illusion on a professionally skilled listener.

Then there are the people who do not go to Protestant churches nor read anything at all, and consequently understand no English except modern vernacular English. This class is by no means a negligible one even in the theatre; for it includes a large body of intelligent manual and open air workers and sportsmen who, though after their day's exertions they fall asleep in less than a minute if they sit down with an open book in their hands, can be kept awake and alert very effectually in the theatre by a play. Only, it must be a play in the vernacular. Otherwise it does not exist for them except as an incomprehensible bore.

There was a time when not only the theatres but the newspapers addressed themselves to the literate alone. Hunt up an old melodrama (say Sweeny Todd the Demon Barber of Fleet Street) or an old newspaper file; and you will at once see that the writers of the play and of the contemporary leading articles, though they may have been the seediest of Bohemians, had learnt Latin grammar and read books written by persons similarly schooled. They had literally the benefit of clergy, and wrote accordingly. With the advent of compulsory education sixty years ago, and the creation thereby of a class which could read and write, but had no Latin and less Greek, newspapers and plays alike soon came to be written by illiterate masters of the vernacular; and I myself welcomed the change and discarded my early very classical style for a vernacular one. Nowadays, when I read typewritten plays by young authors, as I sometimes have occasion to do, I find in them such illiteracies as He exits, She exits, They exit, etc. etc. Chapman, who wrote all his stage directions in Latin, or Ben Jonson, who deplored the slenderness of Shakespear's classical education, would have risen up and roared for a birchrod to castigate such execrable solecisms. By the end of the nineteenth century the press and the theatre had lost all their Latinity; and this was why, whenever The Admirable Bashville was performed, men of letters like Maurice Hewlett would chuckle delightedly over it almost line by line, whilst the ordinary playgoers would listen with a puzzled and troubled stare, wondering what on earth it was all about and how they ought to take it, and the unfortunate persons who had been forced to "get up Shakespear" as part of an academic course on English literature, sat with a scowl of malignant hatred that poisoned the atmosphere. When Bashville was followed by a piece in the vernacular the relief of the audience was so great that there was always a burst of applause at the very first sentence.

And yet, whenever the meaning of the words was clear, the listeners shewed unmistakeably that they liked hyperbolical rhetoric and deliberately artificial language. My parodies of the Elizabethan mannerism, and funny echoes of pet lines from the Elizabethan playwrights were, as such, quite lost on them; but Ben Webster brought down the house with Cashel Byron's declamatory repudiation of the name of gentleman, and James Hearn's lamentation over the tragedy of Cetewayo came off, not as a mockery, but as genuine tragedy, which indeed it also is. It was the literary fun that proved a mere puzzle, in spite of the acting of casts which included such accomplished comedians as Charles Quatermaine, William Wyes, Lennox Pawle, Henrietta Watson, Marie Lohr, and Fanny Brough.

Another significant fact pointed in the same direction. In no country is the worship of the old authorized version of the Bible carried to greater lengths than in the United States of America. To alter a single word of it was, it was believed, to incur the curse in the last chapter of Revelations. Even in England the very timid official revision of 1885 shocked our native Fundamentalists (a ridiculous but convenient name not then invented). Yet it was in the United States that the ministers of religion first found themselves compelled to produce versions in modern vernacular and journalese under stress of the flat fact that their flocks often could not understand the old authorized version, and always found the style so artificial that though it could produce an unintelligent reverence it brought no intimate conviction to the reader.

Sometimes, however, the simple and direct passages were not sentimental enough to satisfy people whose minds were steeped in modern literary sob stuff. For instance, such bald statements about Barabbas as that he was a robber, or that he had killed a certain man in a sedition, quite failed to interest anyone in him; but when Marie Corelli expanded this concise information into a novel in her own passionate and richly colored style it sold like hot cakes.

I must make a personal confession in this matter. Though I was saturated with the Bible and with Shakespear before I was ten years old, and the only grammar I ever learned was Latin grammar, so that Elizabethan English became a mother tongue to me, yet when I first read such vivid and unaffected modern versions as Dr James Moffatt's New Translation of the New Testament I at once got from them so many lights on the Bible narratives which I had missed in the authorized version that I said to myself "Some day I will translate Hamlet into modern vernacular English." But indeed if the alienation of our young from Elizabethan English continues it will be necessary to produce revised versions not only of Shakespear but of Sir Walter Scott and even of my own early novels.

Still, a revival of Elizabethan literature may be possible. If I, as an Irish child in the eighteen-sixties, could without enforced study become so familiar with it that I had some difficulty as a journalist later on in getting rid of it, it must be possible for the same thing to occur to an English child in the nineteen-sixties. The Elizabethan style has many charms for imaginative children. It is bloody, bombastic, violent, senselessly pretentious, barbarous and childish in its humor, and full of music. In short, the taste for it, as anyone can observe at the Old Vic or the Stratford Festivals, is essentially half childish, half musical. To acquire it, all that is necessary is access to it. Now the opportunities for such access are enormously wider than they used to be. Of course as long as we persist in stuffing Shakespear and the Bible down our children's throats with threats of condign punishment if they fail to answer silly questions about them, they will continue to be loathed as they very largely are at present. But if our children, when they have been simply taught to read, have plenty of dramatically illustrated Bibles and Shakespears left in their way, with the illustrated passages printed under the pictures, it will soon be possible to find a general audience which can laugh at The Admirable Bashville as heartily as Maurice Hewlett did, and for repertory theatres to amuse themselves and their congregations with occasional performances of Carey's Chrononhotonthologos, Fielding's Tom Thumb, and even Bombastes Furioso.

I shall not here raise the question of whether such a revival is desirable. It would carry me too far and plunge me too deep for a volume of trifles and tomfooleries. But as the Elizabethan style is unquestionably both musical and powerful, I may at least say that it is better to have a sense of it and a fancy for it than to have no sense of style or literary fancy at all.

XXXII

OUR THEATRES IN THE NINETIES

1906

THE AUTHOR'S APOLOGY

In justice to many well-known public persons who are handled rather recklessly in the following pages, I beg my readers not to mistake my journalistic utterances for final estimates of their worth and achievements as dramatic artists and authors. It is not so much that the utterances are unjust; for I have never claimed for myself the divine attribute of justice. But as some of them are hardly even reasonably fair I must honestly warn the reader that what he is about to study is not a series of judgments aiming at impartiality, but a siege laid to the theatre of the XIXth Century by an author who had to cut his own way into it at the point of the pen, and throw some of its defenders into the moat.

Pray do not conclude from this that the things hereinafter written were not true, or not the deepest and best things I knew how to say. Only, they must be construed in the light of the fact that all through I was accusing my opponents of failure because they were not doing what I wanted, whereas they were often succeeding very brilliantly in doing what they themselves wanted. I postulated as desirable a certain kind of play in which I was destined ten years later to make my mark (as I very well foreknew in the depth of my own unconsciousness); and I brought everybody: authors, actors, managers and all, to the one test: were they coming my way or staying in the old grooves?

Sometimes I made allowances for the difference in aim, especially in the case of personal friends. But as a rule I set up my own standard of what the drama should be and how it should be presented; and I used all my art to make every deviation in aiming at this standard, every recalcitrance in approaching it, every refusal to accept it seem ridiculous and old-fashioned. In this, however, I only did what all critics do who are worth their salt. The critics who attacked Ibsen and defended Shakespear whilst I was defending Ibsen and attacking Shakespear; or who were acclaiming the reign of Irving at the Lyceum Theatre as the Antonine age of the Shakespearean drama whilst I was battering at it in open preparation for its subsequent downfall, were no more impartial than I. And when my own turn came to be criticized, I also was attacked because I produced what I wanted to produce and not what some of my critics wanted me to produce.

Dismissing, then, the figment of impartiality as attainable only through an indifference which would have prevented me from writing about the theatre at all, or even visiting it, what merit have these essays to justify their republication? Well, they contain something like a body of doctrine, because when I criticized I really did know definitely what I wanted. Very few journalistic critics do. When they attack a new man as Ibsen was attacked, they are for the most part only resisting a change which upsets their habits, the proof being that when they get the sort of play they blame the innovator for not producing, they turn up their noses at it, yawn over it, even recommend the unfortunate author to learn from the newcomer how to open his eyes and use his brains. Weariness of the theatre is the prevailing note of London criticism. Only the ablest critics believe that the theatre is really important: in my time none of them would claim for it, as

I claimed for it, that it is as important as the Church was in the Middle Ages and much more important than the Church was in London in the years under review. A theatre to me is a place "where two or three are gathered together." The apostolic succession from Eschylus to myself is as serious and as continuously inspired as that younger institution, the apostolic succession of the Christian Church.

Unfortunately this Christian Church, founded gaily with a pun, has been so largely corrupted by rank Satanism that it has become the Church where you must not laugh; and so it is giving way to that older and greater Church to which I belong: the Church where the oftener you laugh the better, because by laughter only can you destroy evil without malice, and affirm good fellowship without mawkishness. When I wrote, I was well aware of what an unofficial census of Sunday worshippers presently proved: that churchgoing in London has been largely replaced by playgoing. This would be a very good thing if the theatre took itself seriously as a factory of thought, a prompter of conscience, an elucidator of social conduct, an armory against despair and dullness, and a temple of the Ascent of Man. I took it seriously in that way, and preached about it instead of merely chronicling its news and alternately petting and snubbing it as a licentious but privileged form of public entertainment. This, I believe, is why my sermons gave so little offence, and created so much interest. The artists of the theatre, led by Sir Henry Irving, were winning their struggle to be considered ladies and gentlemen, qualified for official honors. Now for their gentility and knighthoods I cared very little: what lay at the root of my criticism was their deeper claim to be considered, not merely actors and actresses, but men and women, not hired buffoons and posturers, however indulged, but hierophants of a cult as eternal and sacred as any professed religion in the world. And so, consciously or unconsciously, I was forgiven when many of my colleagues, less severe because less in earnest on the subject, gave deadly offence.

POSTSCRIPT, 1931. The foregoing was prefaced to a reprint of a selection from my criticisms entitled Dramatic Opinions and Essays, edited in America by the late James Huneker. Let me add now what I should have added then: that a certain correction should be made, especially in reading my onslaught on Shakespear, but also in valuing my vigorous slating of my contemporaries, for the devastating effect produced in the nineties by the impact of Ibsen on the European theatre. Until then Shakespear had been conventionally ranked as a giant among psychologists and philosophers. Ibsen dwarfed him so absurdly in those aspects that it became impossible for the moment to take him seriously as an intellectual force. And if this was Shakespear's fate what could the others expect? The appearance of a genius of the first order is always hard on his competitors. Salieri said of Mozart "If this young man goes on what is to become of us?" and was actually accused of poisoning him. And certainly no one has since been just to Salieri. If my head had not been full of Ibsen and Wagner in the nineties I should have been kinder and more reasonable in my demands. Also, perhaps, less amusing. So forgive; but make the necessary allowances.

XXXIII

ELLEN TERRY AND BERNARD SHAW
A CORRESPONDENCE

1931

In allowing everybody who cares about Ellen Terry to read this correspondence, I must warn them not to judge it according to the code of manners which regulates polite letter writing in cathedral country towns. As a correspondence between a churchwarden and a deaconess its implications would make its publication impossible. But the theatre, behind the scenes, has an emotional freemasonry of its own, certainly franker and arguably wholesomer than the stiffnesses of suburban society outside. The difference is less than it used to be; for actors, like the members of the other professions, have made their way into the general body of society and been accepted as ladies and gentlemen of the professional class rather than as players; and just as it was becoming difficult fifty years ago to imagine a medical baronet or a vicar or a prosperous solicitor or stockbroker accepting a position of social inferiority in a Bloomsbury mansion or a country house, which they had nevertheless had to do within living memory of that time, it is difficult now to imagine an actor being at any disadvantage in ordinary professional society in respect of his occupation, however he may happen to be disqualified in point of education and social habits. If there is nothing wrong with his table manners, his dress, and his accent, nobody will venture to snub or patronize an actor merely because he is an actor; and if he is not qualified in these respects he is at all events no worse off than any other professional man who has not taken the trouble to make himself presentable.

This social acceptance of the actor did not become quite unquestionable until Henry Irving insisted on its official recognition, even at the cost to his singular eminence of a much disrelished knighthood for himself, in 1895. The theatre into which Ellen Terry was born in 1848 enjoyed no such general consideration. Actors, like Jews, were a race apart; and like all segregated races they preserved manners and customs peculiar to themselves. My first youthful contacts with the stage were in connection with certain amateur enterprises; and I well remember the puzzled mixture of amusement and indignation with which a company of ladies and gentlemen of considerable social position who had engaged a professional London stage manager (the modern Producer had not then been invented) to direct their operations, found themselves addressed by him, all the ladies as Darling and all the gentlemen as Old Boy. No modern Producer says Old Boy; and Darling survives only as an elderly joke to turn away the wrath of irritable stars at critical moments; but to the stage manager of that day they were as conventional as the Sir and Madam of a well trained shop assistant.

But though that stage manager's Darling did not mean what it would have meant if it had been addressed to the same ladies by a Dean, it is none the less significant that the convention of the stage should have been one of personal endearment whilst in other professions it was one of cold politeness. That difference still exists, and will exist as long as acting remains an art. When I was a boy, interested much more in music than in literature, I managed to get admitted to the stage once or twice during an opera performance, and learned thereby that this is quite the worst way to enjoy it, and that anyone behind the scenes who has no business there is as great a nuisance, and is as little considered by those who have some business there, as Mr Pickwick at the Chatham review. But what is more to the present purpose is that, the opera being Donizetti's Lucrezia Borgia, and Maffio Orsini and his comrades having overwhelmed Lucrezia with their exposure of her infamies in the exciting finale to the first act, the curtain had no sooner descended and Maffio ceased to be Maffio and become Trebelli, and Lucrezia ceased to be Lucrezia and become Tietjens, than the two hurled themselves frantically into one another's arms in a transport of some emotion that was certainly not any of the emotions of ordinary life outside the theatre, but something peculiar to their work that insisted on the most rapturous expression they could give it. It cannot be explained by what people called the Italian temperament: Trebelli was a Frenchwoman and Tietjens a German. It was something *sui generis* that nobody who has not experienced it can credit, and that soon becomes second nature in those who have experienced it. The Initiates never resent its expression. When they say "he (or she) is one of us," they mean that the happy person is privileged to express any extremity of affection for an artist who achieves a fine piece of acting, and any extremity of disgust at one who wilfully acts basely. The measured public judgments of the critics cannot express this impulse or satisfy this need. The stage is not one fairyland but two: one for the public when the curtain rises, and another, which the public never discovers, for the theatre folk when the curtain falls. In that secret paradise genius excites a flush of adoration in the properly tuned recipient and is satisfied with nothing less. I adored Ellen Terry accordingly, and did not tell her so by halves. And it never occurred to her to say "Sir: how dare you insult a respectable female by such expressions?" *Honi soit qui mal y pense.*

Genius, I may add, is not commoner on the stage than elsewhere; but there, as elsewhere, it produces extravagance of language. The epithet beautiful is used by surgeons to describe operations which their patients describe as ghastly, by physicists to describe methods of measurement which leave sentimentalists cold, by lawyers to describe cases which ruin all the parties to them, and by lovers to describe the objects of their infatuation, however unattractive they may appear to the unaffected spectators. Within the magnetic field of the theatrical profession such hyperbole became conventional, and was finally used by the rank and file who had never felt the emotion until at last every actress was every stage manager's darling and every actor his old boy.

There is another peculiarity of the stage to be borne in mind. An actress is not a lady: at least when she is she is not an actress. Let me explain. A lady is—or in Ellen Terry's generation was—a person trained to the utmost attainable degree in the art and habit of concealing her feelings and maintaining an imperturbable composure under the most trying circumstances. An actress is a person trained even more severely in the art and habit of displaying her feelings so demonstratively that every occupant of the back row in a remote gallery can read them in her face and see them in her gestures. What to the lady is an emergency in which dissimulation is her first duty is to the actress an opportunity for explosive self-expression, however skilled her guidance of the explosion may be. Modern frankness has reduced this difference; but it remains, and is accentuated by the slovenliness of modern middle class speech, which contrasts strongly with the distinct articulation of the actress who knows her business. Ellen Terry escaped the trials of our young actresses, who find themselves between silly producers who tell them that they must not articulate because it is not natural and not ladylike, and despairing authors who warn them that nobody in the theatre will know what they are saying unless they articulate very distinctly. When the author is experienced and wily, the lesson takes the form of a conversational remark that slovenly speech is middle class, and that great ladies owe much of their distinction to their scrupulous articulation, of which Queen Victoria, one of the most perfect speakers of her day, was a conspicuous example. To tell a young woman that if she speaks well she will be mistaken for an actress may spoil her for the stage; but there is a ready antidote in telling her that she may also be mistaken for a member of the royal family. Ellen Terry's articulation was perfect. Her slightly veiled voice reached the remotest listener in the theatre without apparent effort, though the nervous athleticism behind it was of championship quality.

Howbeit the fact remains that an actress, having to exaggerate to get her effects on the stage (on the film, by the way, the contrary is the case: an unnatural quietude and delicacy is the trade mark of the Movie Star), finally from mere habit exaggerates to get her effects off it; and the greater the actress the greater is her power of seizing on every emotional impulse and not only amplifying it as a microphone or a thermionic valve amplifies a sound, but uttering it with a muscular articulation which gives it an impressive driving power. The story of Mrs Siddons terrifying the shop assistant by the intensity with which she asked "Will it wash?" is quite probable. And the playwright, supplying the verbal material for this skilled speech, develops the same quality in his writing. The reader of this budget of intimate letters must therefore not be surprised, and certainly not scandalized, by the reckless way in which the two correspondents express their delight in one another. I do not mean that they were insincere: all that the writers set down they felt at the moment. But their profession freed them from many of the inhibitions to which people outside that profession have to submit; and their language must be interpreted without the inferences which would be drawn from the same language on the part of a governess corresponding with a divinity student.

Possibly a little allowance should be made also for the very objectionable tradition of eighteenth century gallantry into which I, as an Irishman, was born. "Remember" said the most attractive of my aunts to me by way of improving my young mind "that the least plain girl in a house is the family beauty." An English actress once expressed contemptuous impatience with women who want to be placed on a pedestal and worshipped. An Irish actress who was present exclaimed indignantly "I would not *look* at a man who did not place me on a pedestal." It was her right, by Irish tradition. Now I claim that no male writer born in the nineteenth century outside Norway and Sweden did more to knock Woman off her pedestal and plant her on the solid earth than I. But as, like all reactionaries, I was steeped in the tendency against which I was reacting, it was part of my conventional manners to concede a pedestal to every woman as such; and naturally in approaching a woman so goddesslike as Ellen Terry I did not pause to consider whether this attitude would have earned the approval of Ibsen or Strindberg. I do not justify it: it is really a relic of relations between men and women which are not only happily outmoded but insufferable. Still, there it was for what it was worth.

It must be borne in mind too, that we were both comedians, each acting as audience to the other, and each desiring to please and amuse the other without ulterior motives or what matchmaking mothers call intentions. A word, however, must be said about Ellen Terry's ethical position. She once said that what had supported her through all her trials was the consciousness that she had never done anything wrong; and this entirely sincere claim was quoted to me as an audacious hypocrisy. Ellen Terry was never called an advanced woman, the reason being that she was born, as Nietzsche put it, on the far side of good and evil as defined by the Victorian code. Such a play as Ibsen's Ghosts had no mission for her, because she had not had to break Mrs Alving's chains, never having worn them. She did not fight prejudices nor argue with them: like Mrs Stetson's heroine she walked through them as if they were not there, as indeed for her they were not. This was partly individual character; but it must be remembered that in the old segregated theatre religion and morality were homemade: the actress did not live in ordinary society and go out to her work like a doctor or lawyer or clergyman or man of business: she belonged to a little world apart, with morals of its own; and though actors, being human beings, necessarily had the same morals as other people to the extent of, say, nine tenths, yet there was a difference in the other tenth. For instance, in the outside world ladies were not economically independent; and in the rare instances where a lady was paid for working she never dreamt of being paid as much as a gentleman, and felt herself heavily compromised socially by being paid at all. On the stage not only was the actress self-supporting, but if, as often happened, she attracted the public more than her male colleagues, she was paid more. Consequently the trade union view of marriage, from which the unmarried woman who is not a celibate must at all

costs be boycotted as a blackleg, had no meaning in the theatre. Outside it women were held to a strict licitness in their sexual relations on penalty of ostracism, loss of employment, and every other injury that could express total reprobation by all decent people. In fact, a woman incurring this penalty used to be described as "ruined" until Ibsen set us laughing at the epithet by applying it to a man. In the theatre illicit relations *as such* involved no penalty whatever. But please remark the italicized limitation. The notion that actors can behave wickedly without incurring the reprobation of their colleagues and being passed over and replaced by better conducted substitutes when any are available is a vulgar error. But the wickedness must be real wickedness, not mere disregard of the law. The result is that the standard of morals on the stage is in some important aspects higher than it is outside the theatre, where married couples regard the legal tie between them as justifying them in treating each other much worse than they dare treat an independent stranger. In the very important matter of sexual temperance a marriage licence is held to dispense with it as completely as is humanly possible. But it is impossible to keep in training for stage work on such terms. Behind the scenes self-preservation unites with lay opinion to make the life of the theatrical performer in many respects a model which might be followed in the most straitlaced suburb with considerable advantage to its matrimonial morals.

When a late well-known Roman Catholic critic declared that no woman could be an actress and "a good woman," he was perhaps sufficiently answered by Robert Buchanan, who exclaimed "What! No good women on the stage! There are thousands of them—and only about six actresses." When Dumas *fils* publicly assured a young lady of good family who wanted to become an actress that it was quite out of the question for a person in her social position, and when Charles Dickens, himself an incorrigible actor, imposed the same prohibition on his daughter, they were expressing a class prejudice, not a moral one; for the stage is socially quite promiscuous. As no extra money is attracted to the payboxes by the social standing of the performers, talent is everything and pedigree nothing. You must rub shoulders there with persons of every degree, accepting an order of precedence in which a person born in a caravan may be paid and estimated more highly than one born in a palace. It takes a revolution to produce such a state of things outside the theatre: inside it is readymade and inevitable from the nature of the institution.

All this has to be grasped before the lay reader can understand how Ellen Terry could be a woman of very exceptional virtue without having the smallest respect for the law. She did not care enough about it to have even a prejudice against it. If the man of her choice was free, she married him. If the marriage was not a success, she left him. She had many enduring friendships, some transient fancies, and five domestic partnerships of which two were not legalized, though they would have been if the English marriage law had been decently reasonable. She was not in the least what is called a *grande amoureuse*. In the ordering of her life there was nothing of the infatuations and extravagances, the reckless expenditure, the fantastic equipment, the debts, the jewels, the caprices, the menagerie of strange pet animals and reptiles, and all the other affectations and fictions by which actresses' press agents advertize their mostly sober honest industrious economical and monogamous principals. Ellen Terry did not know what an actress's press agent was. And she was no fool: she lived and died within her means. She was certainly no skinflint: she would

have run through her money too generously if she had not given it to business-like friends to keep for her; but she died solvent, an honest woman with no vices.

Emotionally she was not quite so fortunate. She ran through her husbands, and ended as her own mistress and no man's housemate, though she retained the affection of her first husband, who was much older than herself, and of her last, who was much younger. One may say that her marriages were adventures and her friendships enduring. And all these friendships had the character of innocent love affairs: her friends were her lovers in every sense except the technical one; and she was incapable of returning their regard coolly: she felt either warmly or not at all. And yet she was critical, and never lost her head when it was necessary to keep it. Her soft side was her mothering side, her sensitive pity. She was drawn to men of brains because they interested her, and because she was very conscious of the holes left in her mind by the curious patchiness of theatrical culture and the ladylike ignorance of her day; yet she could not resist men who were so helplessly outside the world of intellect that their devotion to her was childlike and their distress at being repulsed by her more than she could bear unless they were personally repulsive to her. She seemed a mass of incalculable contradictions to people who had no analytic sense of character, and expected to find people either All Whites or All Blacks. But she was really as consistent off the stage as she was competent on it.

It must be noted also that she was not stage-struck. Her parents were actors. Like her famous contemporary Madge Robertson (Dame Madge Kendal) she found it as impossible to keep off the stage as it is for many stage-struck outsiders to get on it. You cannot say that Ellen Terry, like Garrick or Irving, was a player by irresistible vocation. She was a player by force of circumstances. I am not sure that she would have become a professional actress if she had not been born with a property spoon in her mouth. Her natural taste was for pictorial art, not for histrionics. Her first husband was a great painter. She left the stage without hesitation for the best years of her youth to keep house on £3 a week with Edward William Godwin, a distinguished architect with a craze for stage pictures and pageantry, and was induced to return to it only by an offer of £40 when she had two children to provide for. Although she was soundly skilled in the technique of her profession she never needed to perform any remarkable feat of impersonation: the spectators would have resented it: they did not want Ellen Terry to be Olivia Primrose: they wanted Olivia Primrose to be Ellen Terry. Her combination of beauty with sensitive intelligence was unique: a disguise would have been intolerable. Her instinct was for beauty and for sincerity: she had only to play a part "straight," as actors say, to transfigure it into something much better than its raw self. But she could take this transfiguration home with her and fascinate her friends with it. She was not the sort of actress who is a genius on the stage and a nobody off it. She could do without the stage both as artist and woman. In her letters she often speaks of wanting work and having to earn some money; but there is no trace of the desperate need to be acting at any cost felt by those who are so completely specialized for the stage that they hardly exist except in fictitious characters.

This is almost a family characteristic. Her sister Kate, when she was in the first rank of London actresses, retired after marriage apparently without hesitation or regret. Miss Phyllis Neilson Terry, Ellen Terry's niece, does not follow up her successes, though she seems to have every qualification for a repetition of the career of her aunt. Ellen Terry's son, Edward Gordon Craig, who succeeded with the greatest ease as an actor, cared so little for acting or for the drama that he gave up acting whilst he was still a juvenile, and engaged in a lifelong struggle to use the stage as a frame for the pictorial architecture in which his father delighted.

I must now say a word about my own theatrical antecedents, as they explain the grudge against the old Lyceum Theatre, against Irving, and even against Ellen herself, which comes out so strongly in our correspondence, as it did publicly and in presentably measured terms through the series of my criticisms in The Saturday Review which ran alongside the correspondence during its main period.

From my birth in 1856 to my Hegira to London in 1876, I lived in Dublin, where the theatre had hardly altered, except for its illumination by coal gas, since the eighteenth century. There were two theatres: the Queen's, which was then not respectable (I visited it, at most, twice, perhaps only once), and the old Theatre Royal, since unhappily burnt down, which maintained a stock company to support the stars who came to Dublin on their touring circuits, and to perform the Christmas pantomime and keep the house open in the occasional weeks left unfilled by the stars. As nobody nowadays has the least notion of what the old stock companies were like, and as my own plays are written largely for the feats of acting they aimed at, and as moreover both Ellen Terry and Irving were rooted like myself in that phase of the evolution of the theatre, I may as well say a word or two about them.

To begin with, the playgoers of their towns grew so desperately tired of them, and so hopelessly unable to imagine them to be any but their too familiar selves, that they performed in an atmosphere of hatred and derision which few of their members had talent or charm enough to

conciliate. The modern practice of selecting for the performances actors and actresses suited to the parts they had to play
was impossible: the stock company was a
readymade cast that had to fit all plays,
from Hamlet down to the latest burlesque; and as it never fitted any of them
completely, and seldom fitted at all, the
casts were more or less grotesque misfits.
This system did not develop versatility:
it destroyed it. Every member of the company except the utilities, as they called the
worst actors who got parts that did not
matter, had his or her specialty or "line."
Thus there were leading juveniles with
an age limit of fifty. There were walking
gentlemen, first and second light comedians, first and second low comedians, first
and second old men, heavies who played
all the villains, and, as aforeaid, utilities.
There were leading ladies and walking ladies, singing chambermaids (sou-
brettes), heavies to whom Lady Macbeth
was all in the night's work, a pair of old
women of whom one played the great
ladies and the other the comic landladies,
and, of course, female utilities. Each
claimed as of right the part which came
nearest to his or her specialty; and each
played all his or her parts in exactly the
same way. The low comedian was traditionally cast for Roderigo; and Roderigo
consequently was presented, not as a
foolish Venetian gentleman about town,
but as a clown. The king in Hamlet and
Ham Peggotty might have been twins
except for the costume, because the heavy
man had to play Ham, the juveniles being
used up for Copperfield and Steerforth.
On no other terms could stock actors
play all the parts that had to be, not
studied, but "swallowed"; for the stars
and other travelling attractions came and
went week after week, and had not only
to be "supported," but eked out by farces
to fill up what the playgoers of that time
demanded as a sufficient program. At my
first visit to the theatre I saw on the same
evening Tom Taylor's three-act drama
Plot and Passion followed by a complete
Christmas pantomime, with a couple of
farces as hors-d'œuvre. Tom Taylor's Joan
of Arc had Massinger's New Way to Pay
Old Debts as a curtain raiser. Under such
circumstances serious character study was
impossible; and the intensive elaboration
of an impersonation which an actor can
achieve when he can repeat his performance without having anything else to do
in the theatre was out of the question.
The actress learnt, not how to interpret
plays, but how to appear sweet and
gentle, or jealous and wicked, or funny,
or matronly, or deaf and palsied, and how
to make up her face and wear wigs. The
actor learnt how to appear sprightly, or
romantic, or murderous, or bucolic, or
doddering, and to make funny faces. In
addition he had one step dance, which he
displayed annually in the pantomime, and
one combat, which served for all stage
duels.

These qualifications are not to be despised. In the modern cases in which they
have been lost without being replaced by
any discoverable technical qualifications
at all they may well be sincerely regretted.
The stock actor, with his conscientiously
articulated elocution which reached the
back row of the pit effectively (it is really
more satisfactory to hear an actor say
meechee-yah-eeld and know that he
means my child than to hear him say
msha and wonder what on earth the fellow thinks he is mumbling), his pompous
entrance which invited and seized the
attention of the audience, his momentous
exit on the last word of his last speech
(your modern novice as often as not
finishes in the middle of the stage and
stops the play until the audience has
enjoyed the spectacle of his walking to
the door), could plead that he knew the
routine of his business and did not need
a producer to teach him the A.B.C. of it.
But only those who have seen him, as

I have, in his native element, and lived to witness the effect of entrusting to his skilled hands a part in a play by Ibsen, can imagine how completely he could kill the dramatic illusion of a modern play.

The truth is, the style of work at which he aimed was wholly rhetorical and hyperbolical. Actors of gigantic or intense personalities could carry it off; but it made commonplace actors ridiculous, though commonplace actors could with ordinary diligence under good teachers acquire its technique only too easily. The teaching could give them style; but it could not give them taste or good sense or power, without which style is an affectation and an impertinence. The invariable effectiveness of the stock actor was a worse offence than the ineffectiveness of the generation which supplanted him, because it enabled and even obliged him to substitute himself for his part in and out of season. His blatant force, when he had any, was less impressive than the so-called "reserved force" of his comparatively impotent successor, who made a merit of either having no force to reserve or not knowing how to use it. When he was thrown on the world in the long interval between the break-up of the stock system in the latter half of the nineteenth century and the beginnings of the local repertory theatres in the twentieth, his plea that he knew his business, far from recommending him to the managers with whom he sought employment, only sealed his fate as a plague to be shunned at all hazards.

Conceive me then, a future playwright, with no conscious prevision of that destiny, gathering my practical knowledge of the stage from a company of such actors as I have just described playing round a star on tour. Of the English-speaking stars incomparably the greatest was Barry Sullivan, who was in his prime when I was in my teens, the last of the race of heroic figures which had domin-ated the stage since the palmy Siddons-Kemble days. Ellen Terry shrank from his acting as from a display of pugilism in which his trembling supporters had no part except to give him his cues and be played off the stage by him. His stage fights in Richard III and Macbeth appealed irresistibly to a boy spectator like myself: I remember one delightful evening when two inches of Macbeth's sword, a special fighting sword carried in that scene only, broke off and whizzed over the heads of the cowering pit (there were no stalls then) to bury itself deep in the front of the dress circle after giving those who sat near its trajectory more of a thrill than they had bargained for. Barry Sullivan was a tall powerful man with a cultivated resonant voice: his stage walk was the perfection of grace and dignity; and his lightning swiftness of action, as when in the last scene of Hamlet he shot up the stage and stabbed the king four times before you could wink, all provided a physical exhibition which attracted audiences quite independently of the play. To John Coleman and T. C. King and other provincial stars with whom he has been sometimes ignorantly classed by London stage historians he was as Hyperion to a very thirdrate satyr. He was as proud as Lucifer, and as imposing; but he was the only actor I ever heard come before the curtain at the end of a play to apologize for having acted badly. He had opened on Monday night in Hamlet (he was at his best in Hamlet and Richelieu) after a very rough passage from Holyhead. Certainly some of the usual charm was lacking; but only very sensitive Barry Sullivan connoisseurs could have noticed it. With an unanswerable dignity he informed the applauding Dublin playgoers that he had done justice neither to them nor to himself, and begged their indulgence. They were awestruck; and then their applause had a note of bewilderment; for most of them had thought it all very splendid.

Yet this great actor—for such of his kind and in his prime he was—had no notion of what we now require as artistic production. He went into a provincial theatre as into a rag and bottle shop; made them drag out the old scenes that the people of the town had seen hundreds of times in all sorts of plays; and, by summary methods that involved a good deal of swearing and bullying, drilled the stock company in a day's rehearsal into giving him his cues and playing up to his strokes of stage business that night. At first he brought with him nothing but his costumes and swords. Later on, he travelled with a fairly good looking young leading lady (possibly in consequence of an experience with a local Ophelia who reduced me to such paroxysms of laughter that I narrowly escaped ejection from the theatre) and an old actor, Cathcart, who had supported Charles Kean, and who, as Richmond or Macduff, got the worst of all the stage fights except the final fatal thrust under the arm, and who relieved the star of the worst drudgery of rehearsal when advancing age compelled him to husband his still mighty forces. In spite of this relief and of his haughty sobriety and irreproachable private life Barry Sullivan died paralysed, exhausted by the impossible task of being superhuman for six nights in every week; for, clever as he was technically, he revelled in his work too keenly to keep within the limits of that passionless science of acting which enabled Salvini to make his audiences imagine him a volcano in eruption when he was in sober fact hardly moving, and Coquelin, without turning a hair, to get through a night's work that would have worn most of our actors to rags or driven them to stimulants to pull them through.

Had I passed my boyhood in London I should have seen nothing of the very important side of stage art represented by Barry Sullivan's acting. He had appeared there with Helen Faucit as Hamlet at the Haymarket Theatre, and been hailed by The Times as the leading legitimate actor of the British stage. But when he found, as Irving found later, that this meant being skinned alive by the London landlords, he shook the dust of London off his feet, and, first in Australia and then in the English provinces and in Ireland and Scotland, set to work with a fixed determination that, however scanty the audience, whoever once saw him act would come again. He soon secured crowded houses every night, and died leaving £100,000 at about the age at which Irving had to abandon his London theatre penniless and fall back on America and the provinces. Had Barry Sullivan produced Shakespear's plays as handsomely as Irving did at the Lyceum they would not have drawn an extra farthing (for a theatre can be no more than full) and he would have had to spend much more money on them.

I certainly learnt nothing from Barry Sullivan's exploits of how far the grand style in acting can be carried by women. Most fortunately for me, however, a visit was paid to Dublin by Adelaide Ristori, who completed my education in this respect, besides convincing me that an Italian stock company, when the novelty of its foreign conventions wears off, can become even more unbearably stale than an English one. The nearest English approach to a tragic actress was Ada Cavendish, whose performance as Wilkie Collins's New Magdalen made an extraordinary impression; but she only flashed across the sky and vanished, leaving no successor until Janet Achurch arrived fifteen years later and inaugurated the Ibsen movement. Both of them, like Edmund Kean, Robson, and many others, called to their aid powers that destroyed them. Ellen Terry did not visit Dublin, and was only a name to me when I came to London in 1876; but everything that the perfection of technical accomplishment could do with youth, cleverness, wit, and irresistible charm in drawing-room drama was demonstrated by Madge Robertson, who came with Buckstone and the entire Haymarket company from London, and struck the first shattering blow at our poor old stock company.

The stock company was hard enough to bear when there was no alternative; but when the London successes began touring through the provinces and the Irish and Scottish capitals, and were performed there not as now by secondrate companies giving a mechanical imitation of the original London production, but by the London cast which had created the success, the stock companies fell dead at their impact. To say that they perished unwept, unhonored, and unsung would be to give only the faintest idea of their death and damnation. When we who had seen them scrambling anyhow through all sorts of plays in the way I have tried to describe first saw finished acting, careful production, thorough identification of the performers with parts for which they had been carefully selected as suitable, with new faces, new voices, new clothes, and new scenery, a return to the stock company was impossible.

And now I come to the link between all this theatrical history and the present volume. Among these London successes which brought London productions unchanged to Dublin was a play called The Two Roses, by Albery. One of the characters was a selfish old humbug named Digby Grant. It made the success of the piece by a certain egotistical intensity, sinister and yet dignified in its indignity, which was not in the play but in the actor: an actor with a tall thin figure, which if it could not be convicted of grotesqueness was certainly indescribably peculiar, and a voice which was dependent so much on the resonance of a cavernous nose that it was, compared to the powerful and musi-

cal chest voice of Barry Sullivan, a highly cultivated neigh. His name was Henry Irving. I instinctively felt that a new drama inhered in this man, though I had then no conscious notion that I was destined to write it; and I perceive now that I never forgave him for baffling the plans I made for him (always, be it remembered, unconsciously). His stage disguise was so perfect that I did not even know that he was still a young man: indeed the one effect he never could produce on the stage was a youthful effect: his Romeo was no younger than his Digby Grant. He was utterly unlike anyone else: he could give importance and a noble melancholy to any sort of drivel that was put into his mouth; and it was this melancholy, bound up with an impish humor, which forced the spectator to single him out as a leading figure with an inevitability that I never saw again in any other actor until it rose from Irving's grave in the person of a nameless cinema actor who afterwards became famous as Charlie Chaplin. Here, I felt, is something that leaves the old stage and its superstitions and staleness completely behind, and inaugurates a new epoch in the theatre.

The theatrical system to which the stock company belonged decomposed and broke up; and when I came to London it seemed to recede into a remote provincial past. I hastened to the famous little theatre off Tottenham Court Road, where the Scala Theatre now stands, to see the Cup and Saucer drama of Robertson handled by the Bancrofts. The play I hit on was Ours; and in it I saw Ellen Terry for the first time. She left on me an impression of waywardness: of not quite fitting into her part and not wanting to; and she gave no indication of her full power, for which the part afforded no scope. As her portraits had prepared me to find her interesting and singular (I have never been susceptible to mere prettiness) I was less struck than I should have been if she had been quite new to me. It was not until I saw her in New Men and Old Acres, which was made a success by her performance as The Two Roses had been made a success by Irving's, that I was completely conquered and convinced that here was the woman for the new drama which was still in the womb of Time, waiting for Ibsen to impregnate it. If ever there were two artists apparently marked out by Nature to make a clean break with an outworn past and create a new stage world they were Ellen Terry and Henry Irving. Nobody can really understand my correspondence with Ellen Terry twenty years later without grasping this situation.

What actually happened was an anticlimax which in its public aspect was a glorious success for both of them. Irving fascinated London in a play called The Bells under an oldfashioned management. His success was so great and so entirely personal that he was able to lift the theatre out of the grip of his manager and take its professional destiny into his own hands with all shackles cast off from his art, in the position as head of the English stage which he held almost unchallenged for thirty years. The earliest notable use he made of his freedom was to engage Ellen Terry as his leading lady. It was his first and last enlightened stroke of policy. For he immediately turned back to the old Barry Sullivan repertory of mutilated Shakespear and Bulwer Lytton, to which he actually added The Iron Chest of the obsolete Colman. From the public point of view he never looked back: from my point of view he never looked forward. As far as the drama was concerned he was more oldfashioned than the oldest of his predecessors, and apparently more illiterate than the most ignorant of them. The taste and judgment which enabled him to achieve so much beauty and dignity in scenery and costume and to rid his theatre of all the old vulgarities when he had Ellen Terry to reveal such possibilities to

him did not extend to literature. He seemed the most pedantic of elocutionists, because his peculiar nasal method of securing resonance obliged him to pronounce our English diphthongs as vowels; and though he delivered Shakespear's lines (what he left of them) like one who had a sense of their music he would cut a purple passage even out of his own parts quite callously. If any doubts remain as to whether an actor who could look so profoundly and venerably scholarly did not know the difference between Colman and Shakespear, much less between Shakespear's poetry and Shakespear's verbiage, a glance at his acting version of King Lear will dispel them. His henchmen Bram Stoker and L. F. Austin wrote his letters for him; for he did not know how much more creditable to him were his own simple and natural compositions than their displays of cleverness. He took no interest in the drama as such: a play was to him a length of stuff necessary to his appearance on the stage, but so entirely subordinate to that consummation that it could be cut to his measure like a roll of cloth. Of the theatre at large he knew almost nothing; for he never left his own stage. I am exaggerating when I say that he regarded an author as a person whose business it was to provide plays at five shillings an act, and, in emergencies, to write the fifth act whilst the fourth was being performed; and yet, in spite of his intercourse with Tennyson, Traill, Wills, and Comyns Carr, I believe that this caricature of his attitude gives a juster impression of it than any statement of the sober facts. He composed his acting with extraordinary industry and minuteness: his Matthias in The Bells and his Charles I were wonderful mosaics of bits of acting thought out touch by touch. His Macaire and Louis XI will hardly be surpassed: they were limit achievements in their *genre*. Even in his Shakespearean impostures (for such they were) there were unforgettable moments. But he composed his parts not only without the least consideration for the play as a whole, or even for the character as portrayed by the author (he always worked out some fancy of his own), but without any for the unfortunate actors whom he employed to support him. A great deal of that absence of vulgarity which I have noted as characteristic of his management was secured by the simple method of not allowing his company to act. He worked hard to make them do what he wanted for his own effects; but if they tried to make independent effects of their own, he did not hesitate to spoil them by tricks of stage management. In this way he threw on himself the enormous burden of attracting the public single-handed. He achieved the celebrated feat of performing Hamlet with the part of Hamlet omitted and all the other parts as well, substituting for it and for them the fascinating figure of Henry Irving, which for many years did not pall on his audience, and never palled on himself. If those present could have remembered Barry Sullivan's Hamlet in the eighteen-sixties or foreseen Forbes-Robertson's Hamlet of the eighteen-nineties some of them might have said that Irving's Hamlet was neither skilled classic acting nor Shakespear's Hamlet, and that compared to Sullivan he was a limp duffer and compared to Robertson a freak; but most of them would have paid their money none the less to enjoy the performance as an avatar of Henry Irving.

When I use the word duffer I mean that when he began to play heroic parts he had neither the physique nor the technique needed for this sort of work, in which the actor must persuade the audience that he is sustaining bodily and vocal exertions which are, as a matter of fact, physically impossible. When Salvini electrified London with his Othello, Irving had a golden opportunity of finding out how this can be done by a study of the Italian actor's very scientific methods; but he flatly refused to avail himself of it, whereat Salvini was somewhat shocked. International courtesy apart, Irving was probably right in classing himself with the unteachables who have to find and go their own way rather than with the apprehensive geniuses who learn from everything and everybody.

I, being interested in the technique of acting, and having learned from Barry Sullivan, Ristori, and Salvini, what could be done in the grand school, was very conscious of Irving's technical shortcomings, and greatly relieved when, on his production of The Lady of Lyons, I found that he had at last learnt the limitations of the stage and of human faculty on it. Except for an occasional relapse into whinnying, he was maintaining his dignity and allowing the imagination of the audience to do its proper share of the work. Later on I saw him as Macbeth, his first assumption of which had provoked something like a storm of derision from the unconverted. I found it a performance of refined beauty. It was not any conceivable historical Macbeth; but then neither is Shakespear's. And I have not the faintest recollection of any other figure in the play, from which I infer that Ellen Terry cannot have played Lady Macbeth on that occasion, nor of any particular scene except the banquet scene, in which the violence of Macbeth's defiance of Banquo's ghost was rather ridiculously beyond the actor's resources; but still his performance was a fine piece of work within its limits. Mr Gordon Craig's idolatrous memoir of Irving, though its judgments are invalidated by the misfortune that the author had no external standards except those set him by Irving himself, gives the most vivid extant pen-portrait of him both as actor and man.

To me, however, Irving's thirty years at the Lyceum, though a most imposing episode in the history of the English theatre, were an exasperating waste of the talent of the two artists who had seemed to me peculiarly fitted to lift the theatre out of its old ruts and head it towards unexplored regions of drama. With Lyceum Shakespear I had no patience. Shakespear, even in his integrity, could not satisfy the hungry minds whose spiritual and intellectual appetites had been whetted and even created by Ibsen; and Shakespear in his integrity was then unknown in the theatre, and remained so until William Poel and Harley Granville-Barker rediscovered and revived him. The shreds and patches which Irving and his predecessors tore out of his plays and tacked crudely together for performances which were interrupted four or five times by intolerable intervals, during which the women in the audience sat in silent boredom whilst the men wandered about the corridors and refreshment bars, were endurable only by people who, knowing no better, thought they were assisting at a very firstrate solemnization, and were helped by that illusion to persuade themselves that they were enjoying the best that a great institution and two great performers could do for them. I knew better. Irving, wasting his possibilities in costly Bardicide, was wasting Ellen Terry's as well. Her only rival as a Shakespearean actress was the great Ada Crehan (who by a printer's error became famous as Ada C. Rehan); and her genius too was being wasted by Augustin Daly, another master-mutilator of the unfortunate playwright whom he professed to adore. But as Daly did not himself act, his hackings and hewings were very largely addressed to the object of taking all the good lines out of the other parts and adding them to Ada Rehan's; and she spoke them so harmoniously that when listening to her it was impossible to care much about anything but the mere music of her voice and Shakespear's, whereas at the Lyceum Irving's peculiarities were the first con-

sideration. To him professionally Ellen Terry was only the chief ornament of his theatre. Besides, his method was so slow that it was almost impossible to act with him. She had to stop too often and wait too long to sustain her part continuously when he was on the stage.

All this enraged me. I can keep my temper as well as most people; for my double training as a critic of highly sensitive living persons and a propagandist of seditious, not to say subversive, political views, kept me constantly on my guard against letting my temper get the better of me or my manners the worse of me: in short, against the least indulgence of personal malice. Besides, I am tolerant in matters of morals which provoke most people to censoriousness; for to me a great deal of current morality is unsound and mischievous. But when questions of art are concerned I am really malicious. Retrogressive art and wasted or unworthily used talent (the theatre is full of both) make me aware that I am capable of something as near to hatred as any emotion can be that has no taint of fear in it. This correspondence shews how, because Irving would not put his peculiar talent at the service of the new and intensely interesting development of the drama which had begun with Ibsen, and because he wasted not only his own talent but Ellen's, I destroyed her belief in him and gave shape and consciousness to her sense of having her possibilities sterilized by him. Then her position became unbearable; and she broke loose from the Ogre's castle, as I called it, only to find that she had waited too long for his sake, and that her withdrawal was rather a last service to him than a first to herself.

The castle did not long survive her departure. Irving, himself poorer and the landlords of the Lyceum Theatre richer than when he entered it, went to the provinces to exploit his great reputation and retrieve his fortunes as Barry Sullivan had built his up. When he died, he was buried as a prince of the theatre, in Westminster Abbey, with only one dissenting voice, which I, by good luck, succeeded in silencing. His singleness of interest and purpose, his industry, his imagination, and his intensity had triumphed over his ignorance and self-sought isolation, and almost made qualities of them, forcing his audiences to attribute to him every talent, every dignity, and every accomplishment. Those who understood the art of the theatre and knew his limitations could challenge him on every point except one; and that one was his eminence. Even to call him eminent belittles his achievement: he was pre-eminent. He was not pre-eminent in or for this, that, or the other talent or faculty: his pre-eminence was abstract and positive: a quality in itself and in himself so powerful that it carried him to Westminster Abbey. Unlike Macready, Forbes-Robertson, and many of the best actors, he was stagestruck, and cared for nothing but acting: a craze and a limitation if you will, but one which saved him from being half ashamed of his profession, as Shakespear (the actor as distinct from the author) was, and thus enabled him finally to extort from the Government for his art the same official recognition which was accorded as a matter of course to painting and music.

Ellen Terry, not at all stagestruck, was extremely unlike Irving. She had had her professional technique hammered into her in her childhood by Mrs Charles Kean, who would sit in the gallery and see to it that every word of Ellen's reached her there. Thus she had skill at the back of her beauty and charm. Success came to her without the asking. She never had to struggle, like Irving, against derision and dislike. The few and insignificant attempts that were made to caricature her were hopeless misfires, whereas caricature alone could give a truthful impression of Irving. The posthumous statue of him outside the National Portrait Gallery in London, though possibly quite accurate in its measurements, gives no notion of what he was like; and even the portrait by Millais is only Irving carefully drest up to be as unlike himself as possible, the ghostly impression of his Philip II by Whistler being more suggestive of him than either. Artists were so eager to do Ellen Terry justice, and found it so difficult, that they had neither the time nor the desire to mock her. All this smoothing of her path had its disadvantages. She was not hardened and given the grim but invaluable quality of tenacity by having to struggle with an implacable resistance. Her value was so promptly and easily admitted that she did not realize it herself at all fully. I have already said that she trifled with her career by leaving the stage for years to devote herself to Godwin, an eminent architect in full practice outside the theatre. Irving would not have left the stage for a night to spend it with Helen of Troy. She squandered herself on all sorts of people and all sorts of interests until she lost the habit and power of mental concentration to such an extent that the slightest distraction made her forget her lines on the stage. She told me once that her memory was all right, but that if on the stage she saw the smallest thing (she instanced a matchbox) that had not been in exactly the same place the night before, it interested her so much that everything else at once went out of her head. Her sister Kate told me impatiently that Ellen could learn her parts well enough if she chose, but preferred to scatter her mind before the girls who crowded up to her to adore her. She was physically restless: when I reproached her for fidgeting she said "Do you know, I have no weight on the stage: unless I have heavy robes I cant keep on the ground." She literally did not think enough of herself: that was why her greatest self-squandering of all, her devotion of herself to the support of Irving at the Lyceum Theatre, did not until it was too late present itself to her otherwise than as a quite eligible professional opportunity.

And so, in the end, my early vision of the two as ideal instruments for a new drama did not come true.

When reading the letters which follow it must be borne in mind that long and intimate correspondence can occur only between people who never meet one another. Swift's journal to Stella would not have been written if they had met every day as Ellen Terry and Irving did, instead of living in separate islands. Ellen and I lived within twenty minutes of each other's doorstep, and yet lived in different worlds: she in a theatre that was a century behind the times, and I in a political society (the Fabian) a century ahead of them. We were both too busy to have any personal intercourse except with the people we were working with. Our correspondence began when I was a professional critic of music through a move she made to help a young musician in whom she was interested. Now critics, like dentists, are a good deal occupied in hurting sensitive people in sensitive places; and as they have to do it in an entertaining manner, which no doubt gives them an air of enjoying it, they produce an impression of Sadism. And so I, being a critic, and, I hope, an entertaining one, had been classed by Ellen Terry as an unamiable person. This was fortunate for me, because instead of having to live up to an exalted estimate of my merits I had only to be commonly civil and helpful to produce a surprised and pleased reaction in my favor. Finding her delightful as a correspondent, and having some gifts in that way myself, I improved the opportunity to such purpose that we presently became occupied with one another in a paper courtship, which is perhaps the pleasantest, as it is the most enduring, of all courtships. We both felt instinctively that a meeting might spoil it, and would certainly alter it and bring it into conflict with other personal relationships. And so I hardly ever saw her, except across the footlights, until the inevitable moment at last arrived when we had to meet daily at the rehearsals of the play I wrote for her: Captain Brassbound's Conversion. By that time Irving had passed out of her life, and indeed out of his own; and Ellen's heart was for the moment vacant. I could not help speculating as to the possibility of my filling the vacancy. But Providence had other views. At our first serious meeting in the rehearsal room at the Court Theatre, Ellen and I were talking together before business began when the door opened, and a young American actor, James Carew, who had been engaged to play the part of Captain Hamlin Kearney, came in. "Who is that?" said Ellen, looking at him with quick interest. "That's the American captain" I answered. Without an instant's hesitation she sailed across the room; put Mr Carew in her pocket (so to speak); and married him. The lucky captive naturally made no resistance; and some of the letters in this volume shew how far the marriage was successful, though I cannot believe that James had any choice of his own in the matter. I was awestruck; for I had not believed it possible for even the most wonderful of women to choose her man at a single glance and bear him off before he had time to realize who she was. Shooting a lion at sight is child's play in comparison, because it does not matter which lion it happens to be: if you do not kill it, it may kill you; so—bang! But it matters very much which man it is when marriage is in question; and so swift a decision by a huntress who, far from being promiscuous in her attachments, was highly fastidious, made me marvel and say to myself "There, but for the grace of God, goes Bernard Shaw."

After the play was disposed of our

meetings were few, and all accidental. One of these chance meetings was on a summer day in the country near Elstree, where I came upon a crowd of people at work on a cinema film. Ellen Terry was there, acting the heroine. She was astonishingly beautiful. She had passed through that middle phase, so trying to handsome women, of matronly amplitude, and was again tall and slender, with a new delicacy and intensity in her saddened expression. She was always a little shy in speaking to me; for talking, hampered by material circumstances, is awkward and unsatisfactory after the perfect freedom of writing between people who *can* write. She asked me why I did not give her some work in the theatre. "I do not expect leading parts" she said: "I am too old. I am quite willing to play a charwoman. I should like to play a charwoman." "What would become of the play?" I said. "Imagine a scene in which the part of a canal barge was played by a battleship! What would happen to my play, or to anyone else's, if whenever the charwoman appeared the audience forgot the hero and heroine, and could think of nothing but the wonderful things the charwoman was going to say and do?" It was unanswerable; and we both, I think, felt rather inclined to cry.

She became a legend in her old age; but of that I have nothing to say; for we did not meet, and, except for a few broken letters, did not write; and she never was old to me.

Let those who may complain that it was all on paper remember that only on paper has humanity yet achieved glory, beauty, truth, knowledge, virtue, and abiding love.

AYOT ST LAWRENCE
26th June 1929

XXXIV

THE AUTOBIOGRAPHY OF A SUPERTRAMP

1907

I hasten to protest at the outset that I have no personal knowledge of the incorrigible Supertramp who wrote this amazing book. If he is to be encouraged and approved, then British morality is a mockery, British respectability an imposture, and British industry a vice. Perhaps they are: I have always kept an open mind on the subject; but still one may ask some better ground for pitching them out of window than the caprice of a tramp.

I hope these expressions will not excite unreasonable expectations of a thrilling realistic romance, or a scandalous chronicle, to follow. Mr Davies' autobiography is not a bit sensational: it might be the Post Office Directory for the matter of that. A less simple minded supertramp would not have thought it worth writing at all; for it mentions nothing that might not have happened to any of us. As to scandal, I, though a most respectable author, have never written half so proper a book. These pudent pages are unstained with the frightful language, the debased dialect, of the fictitious proletarians of Mr Rudyard Kipling and other genteel writers. In them the patrons of the casual ward and the dosshouse argue with the decorum of Socrates, and narrate in the style of Tacitus. They have that pleasant combination of childish freshness with scrupulous literary conscientiousness only possible to people for whom speech, spoken or written, but especially written, is still a feat to be admired and shewn off for its own sake. Not for the life of me could I capture that boyish charm and combine it with the *savoir vivre* of an experienced man of the world, much less of an experienced tramp. The innocence of the author's manner and the perfection of his delicacy is such, that you might read his book aloud in an almshouse without shocking the squeamishness of old age. As for the young, nothing shocks the young. The immorality of the matter is stupendous; but it is purely an industrial immorality. As to the sort of immorality that is most dreaded by schoolmistresses and duennas, there is not a word in the book to suggest that tramps know even what it means. On the contrary, I can quite believe that the author would die of shame if he were asked to write such books as Adam Bede or David Copperfield.

The manuscript came into my hands under the following circumstances. In the year 1905 I received by post a volume of poems by one William H. Davies, whose address was The Farm House, Kennington, S.E. I was surprised to learn that there was still a farmhouse left in Kennington; for I did not then suspect that the Farmhouse, like the Shepherdess Walks and Nightingale Lanes and Whetstone Parks of Bethnal Green and Holborn, is so called nowadays in irony, and is, in fact, a dosshouse, or hostelry where single men can have a night's lodging for, at most, sixpence.

I was not surprised at getting the poems. I get a gift of minor poetry once a week or so; and yet, hardened as I am to it, I still, knowing how much these little books mean to their authors, can seldom throw them aside without a twinge of compunction which I allay by a glance at one of the pages in the faint but inextinguishable hope of finding something valuable there. Sometimes a letter accompanies the book; and then I get a rapid impression, from the handwriting and notepaper as well as from the binding and type in the book, or even from the reputation of the publisher, of the class and type of the author. Thus I guess Cambridge or Oxford or Maida Vale or West Kensington or Exeter or the lakes or the east coast; or a Newdigate prizeman, a romantic Jew, a maiden lady, a shy country parson or whom not, what not, where not. When Mr Davies' book came to hand my imagination failed me. I could not place him. There were no author's compliments, no publisher's compliments, indeed no publisher in the ordinary channel of the trade in minor poetry. The author, as far as I could guess, had walked into a printer's or stationer's shop; handed in his manuscript; and ordered his book as he might have ordered a pair of boots. It was marked "price half a crown." An accompanying letter asked me very civilly if I required a half-crown book of verses; and if so, would I please send the author the half crown: if not, would I return the book. This was attractively simple and sensible. Further, the handwriting was remarkably delicate and individual: the sort of handwriting one might expect from Shelley or George Meredith. I opened the book, and was more puzzled than ever; for before I had read three lines I perceived that the author was a real poet. His work was not in the least strenuous or modern: there was in it no sign that he had ever read anything later than Cowper or Crabbe, not even Byron, Shelley or Keats, much less Morris, Swinburne, Tennyson, or Henley and Kipling. There was indeed no sign of his ever having read anything otherwise than as a child reads. The result was a freedom from literary vulgarity which was like a draught of clear water in a desert. Here, I saw, was a genuine innocent, writing odds and ends of verse about odds and ends of things, living quite out of the world in which such things are usually done, and knowing no better (or rather no worse) than to get his book made by the appropriate craftsman and hawk it round like any other ware.

Evidently, then, a poor man. It horrified me to think of a poor man spending his savings in printing something that nobody buys: poetry, to wit. I thought of Browning threatening to leave the country when the Surveyor of Taxes fantastically assessed him for an imaginary income derived from his poems. I thought of Morris, who, even after The Earthly Paradise, estimated his income as a poet at a hundred a year. I saw that this man might well be simple enough to suppose that he could go into the verse business and make a living at it as one makes a living by auctioneering or shopkeeping. So instead of throwing the book away as I have thrown so many, I wrote him a letter telling him that he could not live by poetry. Also, I bought some spare copies, and told him to send them to such critics and verse fanciers as he knew of, wondering whether they would recognize a poet when they met one.

And they actually did. I presently saw in a London newspaper an enthusiastic notice of the poems, and an account of an interview with the author, from which I learnt that he was a tramp; that "the farm house" was a dosshouse; and that he was cut off from ordinary industrial pursuits by two circumstances: first, that he had mislaid one of his feet somewhere on his trampings, and now had to make shift as best he could with the other; second, that he was a man of independent means—a *rentier*—in short, a gentleman.

The exact amount of his independent income was ten shillings a week. Finding this too much for his needs, he devoted twenty per cent of it to pensioning necessitous friends in his native place; saved a further percentage to print verses with; and lived modestly on the remainder. My purchase of eight copies of the book enabled him, I gathered, to discard all economy for about three months. It also moved him to offer me the privilege (for such I quite sincerely deem it) of reading his autobiography in manuscript. The following pages will enable the world at large to read it in print.

All I have to say by way of recommendation of the book is that I have read it through from beginning to end, and would have read more of it had there been any more to read. It is a placid narrative, unexciting in matter and unvarnished in manner, of the commonplaces of a tramp's life. It is of a very curious quality. Were not the author an approved poet of remarkable sensibility and delicacy I should put down the extraordinary quietness of his narrative to a monstrous callousness. Even as it is, I ask myself with some indignation whether a man should lose a limb with no more to-do than a lobster loses a claw or a lizard his tail, as if he could grow a new one at his next halting place! If such a thing happened to me, I should begin the chapter describing it with "I now come to the event which altered the whole course of my life, and blighted, etc. etc." In Mr Davies' pages the thing happens as unexpectedly as it did in real life, and with an effect on the reader as appalling as if he were an actual spectator. Fortunately it only happened once: half a dozen such shocks would make any book unbearable by a sensitive soul.

I do not know whether I should describe our supertramp as a lucky man or an unlucky one. In making him a poet, Fortune gave him her supremest gift; but such high gifts are hardly personal assets: they are often terrible destinies and crushing burdens. Also, he chanced upon an independent income: enough to give him reasonable courage, and not enough to bring him under the hoof of suburban convention, lure him into a premature marriage, or deliver him into the hands of the doctors. Still, not quite enough to keep his teeth in proper repair and his feet dry in all weathers.

Some flat bad luck he has had. I suppose every imaginative boy is a criminal, stealing and destroying for the sake of being great in the sense in which greatness is presented to him in the romance of history. But very few get caught. Mr Davies unfortunately was seized by the police; haled before the magistrate; and made to expiate by stripes the bygone crimes of myself and some millions of other respectable citizens. That was hard luck, certainly. It gives me a feeling of moral superiority to him; for I never fell into the hands of the police—at least they did not go on with the case (one of incendiarism), because the gentleman whose property I burnt had a strong sense of humor and a kindly nature, and let me off when I made him a precocious speech— the first I ever delivered—on the thoughtlessness of youth. It is remarkable what a difference it makes, this matter of the police; though it is obviously quite beside the ethical question. Mr Davies tells us, with his inimitable quiet modesty, that he begged, stole, and drank. Now I have begged and stolen; and if I never drank, that was only an application of the principle of division of labor to the Shaw clan; for several members of it drank enough for ten. But I have always managed to keep out of the casual ward and the police court; and this gives me an ineffable sense of superior respectability when I read the deplorable confessions of Mr Davies, who is a true poet in his disregard for appearances, and is quite at home in tramp wards.

Another effect of this book on me is to make me realize what a slave of convention I have been all my life. When I think of the way I worked tamely for my living during all those years when Mr Davies, a free knight of the highway, lived like a pet bird on titbits, I feel that I have been duped out of my natural liberty. Why had I not the luck, at the outset of my career, to meet that tramp who came to Mr Davies, like Evangelist to Christian, on the first day of his American pilgrim's progress, and saved him on the very brink of looking for a job, by bidding him to take no thought for the morrow; to ask and it should be given to him; to knock and it should be opened to him; and to free himself from the middle-class assumption that only through taking a ticket can one take a train. Let every youth into whose hands this book falls ponder its lesson well, and, when next his parents and guardians attempt to drive him into some inhuman imprisonment and drudgery under the pretext that he should earn his own living, think of the hospitable countrysides of America, with their farmhouses overflowing with milk and honey for the tramp, and their offers of adoption for every day laborer with a dash of poetry in him.

And then, how much did I know about hotels until I read this book! I have often wondered how the poor travel; for it is plain that the Ritzes and Metropoles, and even the hotels noted by Baedeker as "unpretending," are not for them. Where does the man with sixpence in his pocket stay? Mr Davies knows. Read and learn.

It is to be noted that Mr Davies is no propagandist of the illusions of the middle-class tramp fancier. You never suspect him of having read Lavengro, or got his notions of nomads from Mr Theodore Watts Dunton. He does not tell you that there is honor among tramps: on the contrary, he makes it clear that only by being too destitute to be worth robbing and murdering can a tramp insure himself against being robbed and murdered by his comrade of the road. The tramp is fastidious and accomplished, audacious and self-possessed; but he is free from divine exploitation: he has no orbit: he has the endless trouble of doing what he likes with himself, and the endless discountenance of being passed by as useless by the Life Force that finds superselfish work for other men. That, I suppose, is why Mr Davies tramps no more, but writes verses and saves money to print them out of eight shillings a week. And this, too, at a moment when the loss of a limb has placed within his reach such success in begging as he had never before dared to dream of!

Mr Davies is now a poet of established reputation. He no longer prints his verses and hawks them: he is regularly published and reviewed. Whether he finds the change a lucrative one I venture to doubt. That the verses in The Soul's Destroyer and in his New Poems will live is beyond question; but whether Mr Davies can live if anything happens to his eight shillings a week (unless he takes to the road again) is another matter. That is perhaps why he has advised himself to write and print his autobiography, and try his luck with it as Man of Letters in a more general sense. Though it is only in verse that he writes exquisitely, yet this book, which is printed as it was written, without any academic corrections from the point of view of the Perfect Commercial Letter Writer, is worth reading by literary experts for its style alone. And since his manner is so quiet, it has been thought well by his friends and his publishers to send a trumpeter before him the more effectually to call attention to him before he begins. I have volunteered for that job for the sake of his poems. Having now done it after my well-known manner, I retire and leave the stage to him.

XXXV

THE SANITY OF ART

1907

The re-publication of this open letter to Mr Benjamin Tucker places me, not for the first time, in the difficulty of the journalist whose work survives the day on which it was written. What the journalist writes about is what everybody is thinking about (or ought to be thinking about) at the moment of writing. To revive his utterances when everybody is thinking about something else; when the tide of public thought and imagination has turned; when the front of the stage is filled with new actors; when many lusty crowers have either survived their vogue or perished with it; when the little men you patronized have become great, and the great men you attacked have been sanctified and pardoned by popular sentiment in the tomb: all these inevitables test the quality of your journalism very severely. Nevertheless, journalism can claim to be the highest form of literature; for all the highest literature is journalism. The writer who aims at producing the platitudes which are "not for an age, but for all time" has his reward in being unreadable in all ages; whilst Plato and Aristophanes trying to knock some sense into the Athens of their day, Shakespear peopling that same Athens with Elizabethan mechanics and Warwickshire hunts, Ibsen photographing the local doctors and vestrymen of a Norwegian parish, Carpaccio painting the life of St Ursula exactly as if she were a lady living in the next street to him, are still alive and at home everywhere among the dust and ashes of many thousands of academic, punctilious, most archæologically correct men of letters and art who spent their lives haughtily avoiding the journalist's vulgar obsession with the ephemeral. I also am a journalist, proud of it, deliber-ately cutting out of my works all that is not journalism, convinced that nothing that is not journalism will live long as literature, or be of any use whilst it does live. I deal with all periods; but I never study any period but the present, which I have not yet mastered and never shall; and as a dramatist I have no clue to any historical or other personage save that part of him which is also myself, and which may be nine tenths of him or ninety-nine hundredths, as the case may be (if, indeed, I do not transcend the creature), but which, anyhow, is all that can ever come within my knowledge of his soul. The man who writes about himself and his own time is the only man who writes about all people and about all time. The other sort of man, who believes that he and his period are so distinct from all other men and periods that it would be immodest and irrelevant to allude to them or assume that they could illustrate anything but his own private circumstances, is the most infatuated of all the egotists, and consequently the most unreadable and negligible of all the authors. And so, let others cultivate what they call literature: journalism for me!

The following remnant of the journalism of 1895 will, I hope, bear out these preliminary remarks, which are none the less valid because they are dragged in here to dismount the critics who ride the high horse of Letters at me. It was undertaken under the following circumstances. In 1893 Doctor Max Nordau, one of those remarkable cosmopolitan Jews who go forth against modern civilization as David went against the Philistines or Charles Martel against the Saracens, smiting it hip and thigh without any sense of common humanity with it, trumped up an indictment of its men of genius as depraved lunatics, and pled it (in German) before the bar of Europe under the title Entartung. It was soon translated for England and America as Degeneration. Like all rigorous and thorough-going sallies of special pleading, it had its value; for the way to get at the merits of a case is not to listen to the fool who imagines himself impartial, but to get it argued with reckless bias for and against. To understand a saint, you must hear the devil's advocate; and the same is true of the artist. Nordau had briefed himself as devil's advocate against the great artistic reputations of the XIX century; and he did his duty as well as it could be done at the price, incidentally saying many more true and important things than most of the counsel on the other side were capable of.

Indeed counsel on the other side mostly threw up their briefs in consternation, and began to protest that they entirely agreed with Dr Nordau, and that though they had perhaps dallied a little with Rossetti, Wagner, Ibsen, Tolstoy, Nietzsche, and the rest of the degenerates before their true character had been exposed, yet they had never really approved of them. Even those who stood to their guns had not sufficient variety of culture to contradict the cosmopolitan doctor on more than one or two points, being often not champions of Art at large, but merely jealous fanciers of some particular artist. Thus the Wagnerians were ready to give up Ibsen; the Ibsenites were equally suspicious of Wagner; the Tolstoyans gave up both; the Nietzscheans were only too glad to see Tolstoy catching it; and the connoisseurs of Impressionism in painting, though fairly impartial in music and literature, could not handle the technics of the case for the defence. Yet Dr Nordau knew so little, and his technical handling of painting and music was so like Captain Lemuel Gulliver's nautical observations, that I, being familiar with

all the arts, and as accustomed as any Jew to the revolutionary cosmopolitan climate, looked on at his triumph much as Napoleon looked on at the massacre of the Swiss, thinking how easy it would be to change the rout into the cheapest of victories. However, none of our silly editors had the gumption to offer me the command; so, like Napoleon, I went home and left them to be cut to pieces.

But Destiny will not allow her offers to be completely overlooked. In the Easter of 1895, when Nordau was master of the field, and the newspaper champions of modern Literature and Art were on their knees before him, weeping and protesting their innocence, I was staying in the wooden hotel on Beachy Head, with a select party of Fabians, politicians, and philosophers, diligently trying to ride a bicycle for the first time in my life. My efforts set the coastguards laughing as no audience had ever laughed at my plays. I made myself ridiculous with such success that I felt quite ready to laugh at somebody else. Just then there arrived a proposal from Mr Benjamin Tucker, philosophic Anarchist, and Editor of an American paper called Liberty, which, as it was written valiantly up to its title, was having a desperate struggle for existence in a country where every citizen is free to suppress liberty, and usually does so in such moments as he cares to spare from the pursuit of money. Mr Tucker, seeing that nobody had answered Dr Nordau, and perceiving with the penetration of an unterrified common sense that a doctor who had written manifest nonsense must be answerable technically by anybody who could handle his weapons, was of opinion that I was the man to do it. Accordingly, said Mr Tucker, I invite you, Shaw, to ascertain the highest price that has ever been paid to any man, even to Gladstone, for a magazine article; and I will pay you that price for a review of Degeneration in the columns of Liberty.

This was really great editing. Mr Tucker got his review, as he deserved, and sent a copy of the number of Liberty containing it (now a collector's treasure) to every paper in the United States. There was a brisk and quick sale of copies in London among the cognoscenti. And Degeneration was never heard of again. It is open to the envious to contend that this was a mere coincidence—that the Degeneration boom was exhausted at that moment; but I naturally prefer to believe that Mr Tucker and I slew it. I may add that the slaughter incidentally ruined Mr Tucker, as a circulation among cognoscenti does not repay the cost of a free distribution to the Philistines; but Mr Tucker was always ruining himself for Liberty and always retrieving the situation by his business ability. I saw him this year in London, as prosperous looking a man as I could desire to dine with, thirsting for fresh struggles with the courts and public departments of the United States.

I have left the essay substantially as it first appeared, the main alteration being an expansion of the section dealing with the importance of that mass of law which lies completely outside morals and religion, and is really pure convention: the point being, not that the course prescribed by such law is ethically right, or indeed better in any sense than its direct opposite (as in the rule of the road, for example), but that it is absolutely necessary for economy and smoothness of social action that everybody should do the same thing and be able to count on everybody else doing it. I have appropriated this from Mr Aylmer Maude's criticism of Tolstoyan Anarchism, on which I am unable to improve.

I have also, with the squeamishness of advancing years, softened one or two expressions which now shock me as uncivil to Dr Nordau. In doing so I am not offering him the insult of an attempt to spare his feelings: I am simply trying to mend my own manners.

Finally, let me say that though I think this essay of mine did dispose of Dr Nordau's special pleadings, neither the pleadings nor the criticism dispose of the main question as to how far genius is a morbid symptom. I should rather like Dr Nordau to try again; for I do not see how any observant student of genius from the life can deny that the Arts have their criminals and lunatics as well as their sane and honest men (they are more or less the same men too, just as our ordinary criminals are in the dock by the accident of a single transaction and not by a difference in nature between them and the judge and jury), and that the gratuitous delusion that the great poet and artist can do no wrong is much more mischievous than the necessary convention that the King can do no wrong and that the Pope is infallible.

In my play called The Doctor's Dilemma I have recognized this by dramatizing a rascally genius, with the disquieting result that several highly intelligent and sensitive persons have passionately defended him, on the ground, apparently, that high artistic faculty and an ardent artistic imagination entitle a man to be recklessly dishonest about money and recklessly selfish about women, just as kingship in an African tribe entitles a man to kill whom he pleases on the most trifling provocation. I know no harder practical question than how much selfishness one ought to stand from a gifted person for the sake of his gifts or on the chance of his being right in the long run. The Superman will certainly come like a thief in the night, and be shot at accordingly; but we cannot leave our property wholly undefended on that account. On the other hand, we cannot ask the Superman simply to add a higher set of virtues to current respectable morals; for he is undoubtedly going to empty a good deal of respectable morality out like so much dirty water, and replace it by new and strange customs, shedding old obligations and accepting new and heavier ones. Every step of his progress must horrify conventional people; and if it were possible for even the most superior man to march ahead all the time, every pioneer of the march towards the Superman would be crucified. Fortunately what actually happens is that your geniuses are for the most part keeping step and marking time with the rest, an occasional stumble forward being the utmost they can accomplish, often visibly against their own notions of propriety. The greatest possible difference in conduct between a genius and his contemporaries is so small that it is always difficult to persuade the people who are in daily contact with the gifted one that he is anybody in particular: all the instances to the contrary (Gorki scandalizing New York, for example) being cases in which the genius is in conflict, not with contemporary feeling in his own class, but with some institution which is far behind the times, like the institution of marriage in Russia (to put it no nearer home). In really contemporary situations, your genius is ever 1 part genius and 99 parts Tory.

Still, especially when we turn from conduct to the expression of opinion—from what the man of genius dares do to what he dares advocate—it is necessary for the welfare of society that genius should be privileged to utter sedition, to blaspheme, to outrage good taste, to corrupt the youthful mind, and, generally, to scandalize one's uncles. But such licence is accordable only on the assumption that men of genius are saner, sounder, farther sighted and deeper fathoming than the uncles; and it is idle to demand unlimited toleration of apparently outrageous conduct on the plea that the offender is a genius, even if by the abnormal development of some specific talent he may be highly skilled as an artist. Andrea del Sarto was a better draughtsman and fresco painter than Raphael; but he was a swindler all the same; and no honorable artist would plead on his behalf that misappropriating trust money is one of the superiorities of that very loosely defined diathesis which we call the artistic temperament. If Dr Nordau would make a serious attempt to shew us exactly where we are in this matter by ascertaining the real stigmata of genius; so that we may know whom to crucify, and whom to put above the law, he would place the civilization he attacks under an obligation which would wipe out the marks of all the wounds (mostly thoroughly deserved) he has dealt it.

MISCELLANEOUS

XXXVI

PYGMALION

1912

A PROFESSOR OF PHONETICS

As will be seen later on, Pygmalion needs, not a preface, but a sequel, which I have supplied in its due place.

The English have no respect for their language, and will not teach their children to speak it. They spell it so abominably that no man can teach himself what it sounds like. It is impossible for an Englishman to open his mouth without making some other Englishman hate or despise him. German and Spanish are accessible to foreigners: English is not accessible even to Englishmen. The reformer England needs today is an energetic phonetic enthusiast: that is why I have made such a one the hero of a popular play. There have been heroes of that kind crying in the wilderness for many years past. When I became interested in the subject towards the end of the eighteen-seventies, the illustrious Alexander Melville Bell, the inventor of Visible Speech, had emigrated to Canada, where his son invented the telephone; but Alexander J. Ellis was still a London patriarch, with an impressive head always covered by a velvet skull cap, for which he would apologize to public meetings in a very courtly manner. He and Tito Pagliardini, another phonetic veteran, were men whom it was impossible to dislike. Henry Sweet, then a young man, lacked their sweetness of character: he was about as conciliatory to conventional mortals as Ibsen or Samuel Butler. His great ability as a phonetician (he was, I think, the best of them all at his job) would have entitled him to high official recognition, and perhaps enabled him to popularize his subject, but for his Satanic contempt for all academic dignitaries and persons in general who thought more of

Greek than of phonetics. Once, in the days when the Imperial Institute rose in South Kensington, and Joseph Chamberlain was booming the Empire, I induced the editor of a leading monthly review to commission an article from Sweet on the imperial importance of his subject. When it arrived, it contained nothing but a savagely derisive attack on a professor of language and literature whose chair Sweet regarded as proper to a phonetic expert only. The article, being libellous, had to be returned as impossible; and I had to renounce my dream of dragging its author into the limelight. When I met him afterwards, for the first time for many years, I found to my astonishment that he, who had been a quite tolerably presentable young man, had actually managed by sheer scorn to alter his personal appearance until he had become a sort of walking repudiation of Oxford and all its traditions. It must have been largely in his own despite that he was squeezed into something called a Readership of phonetics there. The future of phonetics rests probably with his pupils, who all swore by him; but nothing could bring the man himself into any sort of compliance with the university to which he nevertheless clung by divine right in an intensely Oxonian way. I daresay his papers, if he has left any, include some satires that may be published without too destructive results fifty years hence. He was, I believe, not in the least an illnatured man: very much the opposite, I should say; but he would not suffer fools gladly.

Those who knew him will recognize in my third act the allusion to the patent shorthand in which he used to write postcards, and which may be acquired from a four and sixpenny manual published by the Clarendon Press. The postcards which Mrs Higgins describes are such as I have received from Sweet. I would decipher a sound which a cockney would represent by *ӡerr*, and a Frenchman by *seu*, and then write demanding with some heat what on earth it meant. Sweet, with boundless contempt for my stupidity, would reply that it not only meant but obviously was the word Result, as no other word containing that sound, and capable of making sense with the context, existed in any language spoken on earth. That less expert mortals should require fuller indications was beyond Sweet's patience. Therefore, though the whole point of his 'Current Shorthand' is that it can express every sound in the language perfectly, vowels as well as consonants, and that your hand has to make no stroke except the easy and current ones with which you write m, n, and u, l, p, and q, scribbling them at whatever angle comes easiest to you, his unfortunate determination to make this remarkable and quite legible script serve also as a shorthand reduced it in his own practice to the most inscrutable of cryptograms. His true objective was the provision of a full, accurate, legible script for our noble but ill-dressed language; but he was led past that by his contempt for the popular Pitman system of shorthand, which he called the Pitfall system. The triumph of Pitman was a triumph of business organization: there was a weekly paper to persuade you to learn Pitman: there were cheap textbooks and exercise books and transcripts of speeches for you to copy, and schools where experienced teachers coached you up to the necessary proficiency. Sweet could not organize his market in that fashion. He might as well have been the Sybil who tore up the leaves of prophecy that nobody would attend to. The four and sixpenny manual, mostly in his lithographed handwriting, that was never vulgarly advertized, may perhaps some day be taken up by a syndicate and pushed upon the public as The Times pushed the Encyclopædia Britannica; but until then it will certainly not prevail against Pitman. I have bought three copies of it during my lifetime; and I am informed by the publishers that its cloistered existence is still a steady and healthy one. I actually learned the system two several times; and yet the shorthand in which I am writing these lines is Pitman's. And the reason is, that my secretary cannot transcribe Sweet, having been perforce taught in the schools of Pitman. Therefore, Sweet railed at Pitman as vainly as Thersites railed at Ajax: his raillery, however it may have eased his soul, gave no popular vogue to Current Shorthand.

Pygmalion Higgins is not a portrait of Sweet, to whom the adventure of Eliza Doolittle would have been impossible; still, as will be seen, there are touches of Sweet in the play. With Higgins's physique and temperament Sweet might have set the Thames on fire. As it was, he impressed himself professionally on Europe to an extent that made his comparative personal obscurity, and the failure of Oxford to do justice to his eminence, a puzzle to foreign specialists in his subject. I do not blame Oxford, because I think Oxford is quite right in demanding a certain social amenity from its nurslings (heaven knows it is not exorbitant in its requirements!); for although I well know how hard it is for a man of genius with a seriously underrated subject to maintain serene and kindly relations with the men who underrate it, and who keep all the best places for less important subjects which they profess without originality and sometimes without much capacity for them, still, if he overwhelms them with wrath and disdain, he cannot expect them to heap honors on him.

Of the later generations of phoneticians I know little. Among them towers the Poet Laureate [Robert Bridges], to whom perhaps Higgins may owe his Miltonic sympathies, though here again I must disclaim all portraiture. But if the play makes the public aware that there are such people as phoneticians, and that they are among the most important people in England at present, it will serve its turn.

I wish to boast that Pygmalion has been an extremely successful play all over Europe and North America as well as at home. It is so intensely and deliberately didactic, and its subject is esteemed so dry, that I delight in throwing it at the heads of the wiseacres who repeat the parrot cry that art should never be didactic. It goes to prove my contention that art should never be anything else.

Finally, and for the encouragement of people troubled with accents that cut them off from all high employment, I may add that the change wrought by Professor Higgins in the flower-girl is neither impossible nor uncommon. The modern concierge's daughter who fulfils her ambition by playing the Queen of Spain in Ruy Blas at the Théâtre Français is only one of many thousands of men and women who have sloughed off their native dialects and acquired a new tongue. But the thing has to be done scientifically, or the last state of the aspirant may be worse than the first. An honest and natural slum dialect is more tolerable than the attempt of a phonetically untaught person to imitate the vulgar dialect of the golf club; and I am sorry to say that in spite of the efforts of our Royal Academy of Dramatic Art, there is still too much sham golfing English on our stage, and too little of the noble English of Forbes Robertson.

XXXVII

GREAT CATHERINE

1913

THE AUTHOR'S APOLOGY FOR GREAT CATHERINE

Exception has been taken to the title of this seeming tomfoolery on the ground that the Catherine it represents is not Great Catherine, but the Catherine whose gallantries provide some of the lightest pages of modern history. Great Catherine, it is said, was the Catherine whose diplomacy, whose campaigns and conquests, whose plans of Liberal reform, whose correspondence with Grimm and Voltaire enabled her to cut such a magnificent figure in the XVIII century. In reply, I can only confess that Catherine's diplomacy and her conquests do not interest me. It is clear to me that neither she nor the statesmen with whom she played this mischievous kind of political chess had any notion of the real history of their own times, or of the real forces that were moulding Europe. The French Revolution, which made such short work of Catherine's Voltairean principles, surprised and scandalized her as much as it surprised and scandalized any provincial governess in the French chateaux.

The main difference between her and our modern Liberal Governments was that whereas she talked and wrote quite intelligently about Liberal principles before she was frightened into making such talking and writing a flogging matter, our Liberal ministers take the name of Liberalism in vain without knowing or caring enough about its meaning even to talk and scribble about it, and pass their flogging Bills, and institute their prosecutions for sedition and blasphemy and so forth, without the faintest suspicion that such proceedings need any apology from the Liberal point of view.

It was quite easy for Patiomkin to humbug Catherine as to the condition of Russia by conducting her through sham cities run up for the occasion by scenic artists; but in the little world of European court intrigue and dynastic diplomacy which was the only world she knew she was more than a match for him and for all the rest of her contemporaries. In such intrigue and diplomacy, however, there was no romance, no scientific political interest, nothing that a sane mind can now retain even if it can be persuaded to waste time in reading it up. But Catherine as a woman, with plenty of character and (as we should say) no morals, still fascinates and amuses us as she fascinated and amused her contemporaries. They were great sentimental comedians, these Peters, Elizabeths, and Catherines who played their Tsarships as eccentric character parts, and produced scene after scene of furious harlequinade with the monarch as clown, and of tragic relief in the torture chamber with the monarch as pantomime demon committing real atrocities, not forgetting the indispensable love interest on an enormous and utterly indecorous scale. Catherine kept this vast Guignol Theatre open for nearly half a century, not as a Russian, but as a highly domesticated German lady whose household routine was not at all so unlike that of Queen Victoria as might be expected from the difference in their notions of propriety in sexual relations.

In short, if Byron leaves you with an impression that he said very little about Catherine, and that little not what was best worth saying, I beg to correct your impression by assuring you that what Byron said was all there really is to say that is worth saying. His Catherine is my Catherine and everybody's Catherine. The young man who gains her favor is a Spanish nobleman in his version. I have made him an English country gentleman, who gets out of his rather dangerous scrape by simplicity, sincerity, and the courage of these qualities. By this I have given some offence to the many Britons who see themselves as heroes: what they mean by heroes being theatrical snobs of superhuman pretensions which, though quite groundless, are admitted with awe by the rest of the human race. They say I think an Englishman a fool. When I do, they have themselves to thank.

I must not, however, pretend that historical portraiture was the motive of a play that will leave the reader as ignorant of Russian history as he may be now before he has turned the page. Nor is the sketch of Catherine complete even idiosyncratically, leaving her politics out of the question. For example, she wrote bushels of plays. I confess I have not yet read any of them. The truth is, this play grew out of the relations which inevitably exist in the theatre between authors and actors. If the actors have sometimes to use their skill as the author's puppets rather than in full self-expression, the author has sometimes to use his skill as the actors' tailor, fitting them with parts written to display the virtuosity of the performer rather than to solve problems of life, character, or history. Feats of this kind may tickle an author's technical vanity; but he is bound on such occasions to admit that the performer for whom he writes is "the onlie begetter" of his work, which must be regarded critically as an addition to the debt dramatic literature owes to the art of acting and its exponents. Those who have seen Miss Gertrude Kingston play the part of Catherine will have no difficulty in believing that it was her talent rather than mine that brought the play into existence. I once recommended Miss Kingston professionally to play queens. Now in the modern drama there were no queens for her to play; and as to the older literature of our stage, did it not provoke the veteran actress in Sir Arthur Pinero's Trelawny of the Wells to declare that, as parts, queens are not worth a tinker's oath? Miss Kingston's comment on my suggestion, though more elegantly worded, was to the same effect; and it ended in my having to make good my advice by writing Great Catherine. History provided no other queen capable of standing up to our joint talents.

In composing such bravura pieces, the author limits himself only by the range of the virtuoso, which by definition far transcends the modesty of nature. If my Russians seem more Muscovite than any Russian, and my English people more insular than any Briton, I will not plead, as I honestly might, that the fiction has yet to be written that can exaggerate the reality of such subjects; that the apparently outrageous Patiomkin is but a timidly bowdlerized ghost of the original; and that Captain Edstaston is no more than a miniature that might hang appropriately on the walls of nineteen out of twenty English country houses to this day. An artistic presentment must not condescend to justify itself by a comparison with crude nature; and I prefer to admit that in this kind my *dramatis personæ* are, as they should be, of the stage stagey, challenging the actor to act up to them or beyond them, if he can. The more heroic the overcharging, the better for the performance.

In dragging the reader thus for a moment behind the scenes, I am departing from a rule which I have hitherto imposed on myself so rigidly that I never permit myself, even in a stage direction, to let slip a word that could bludgeon the imagination of the reader by reminding him of the boards and the footlights and the sky borders and the rest of the theatrical scaffolding, for which nevertheless I have to plan as carefully as if I were the head carpenter as well as the author. But even at the risk of talking shop, an honest playwright should take at least one opportunity of acknowledging that his art is not only limited by the art of the actor, but often stimulated and developed by it. No sane and skilled author writes plays that present impossibilities to the actor or to the stage engineer. If, as occasionally happens, he asks them to do things that they have never done before and cannot conceive as presentable or possible (as Wagner and Thomas Hardy have done, for example), it is always found that the difficulties are not really insuperable, the author having foreseen unsuspected possibilities both in the actor and in the audience, whose will-to-make-believe can perform the quaintest miracles. Thus may authors advance the arts of acting and of staging plays. But the actor also may enlarge the scope of the drama by displaying powers not previously discovered by the author. If the best available actors are only Horatios, the authors will have to leave Hamlet out, and be content with Horatios for heroes. Some of the difference between Shakespear's Orlandos and Bassanios and Bertrams and his Hamlets and Macbeths must have been due not only to his development as a dramatic poet, but to the development of Burbage as an actor. Playwrights do not write for ideal actors when their livelihood is at stake: if they did, they would write parts for heroes with twenty arms like an Indian god. Indeed the actor often influences the author too much; for I can remember a time (I am not implying that it is yet wholly past) when the art of writing a fashionable play had become very largely the art of writing it "round" the personalities of a group of fashionable performers of whom Burbage would certainly have said that their parts needed no acting. Everything has its abuse as well as its use.

It is also to be considered that great plays live longer than great actors, though little plays do not live nearly so long as the worst of their exponents. The consequence is that the great actor, instead of putting pressure on contemporary authors to supply him with heroic parts, falls back on the Shakespearean repertory, and takes what he needs from a dead hand. In the nineteenth century, the careers of Kean, Macready, Barry Sullivan, and Irving ought to have produced a group of heroic plays comparable in intensity to those of Æschylus, Sophocles, and Euripides; but nothing of the kind happened: these actors played the works of dead authors, or, very occasionally, of live poets who were hardly regular professional playwrights. Sheridan Knowles, Bulwer Lytton, Wills, and Tennyson produced a few glaringly artificial high horses for the great actors of their time; but the playwrights proper, who really kept the theatre going, and were kept going by the theatre, did not cater for the great actors: they could not afford to compete with a bard who was not of an age but for all time, and who had, moreover, the overwhelming attraction for the actor-managers of not charging author's fees. The result was that the playwrights and the great actors ceased to think of themselves as having any concern with one another: Tom Robertson, Ibsen, Pinero, and Barrie might as well have belonged to a different solar system as far as Irving was concerned; and the same was true of their respective predecessors.

Thus was established an evil tradition; but I at least can plead that it does not always hold good. If Forbes Robertson had not been there to play Cæsar, I should not have written Cæsar and Cleopatra. If Ellen Terry had never been born, Captain Brassbound's conversion would never have been effected. The Devil's Disciple, with which I won my *cordon bleu* in America as a potboiler, would have had a different sort of hero if Richard

Mansfield had been a different sort of actor, though the actual commission to write it came from an English actor, William Terriss, who was assassinated before he recovered from the dismay into which the result of his rash proposal threw him. For it must be said that the actor or actress who inspires or commissions a play as often as not regards it as a Frankenstein's monster, and will none of it. That does not make him or her any the less parental in the fecundity of the playwright.

To an author who has any feeling of his business there is a keen and whimsical joy in divining and revealing a side of an actor's genius overlooked before, and unsuspected even by the actor himself. When I snatched Mr Louis Calvert from Shakespear, and made him wear a frock coat and silk hat on the stage for perhaps the first time in his life, I do not think he expected in the least that his performance would enable me to boast of his Tom Broadbent as a genuine stage classic. Mrs Patrick Campbell was famous before I wrote for her, but not for playing illiterate cockney flowermaidens. And in the case which is provoking me to all these impertinences, I am quite sure that Miss Gertrude Kingston, who first made her reputation as an impersonator of the most delightfully feather-headed and inconsequent ingenues, thought me more than usually mad when I persuaded her to play the Helen of Euripides, and then launched her on a queenly career as Catherine of Russia.

It is not the whole truth that if we take care of the actors the plays will take care of themselves; nor is it any truer that if we take care of the plays the actors will take care of themselves. There is both give and take in the business. I have seen plays written for actors that made me exclaim, "How oft the sight of means to do ill deeds makes deeds ill done!" But Burbage may have flourished the prompt copy of Hamlet under Shakespear's nose at the tenth rehearsal and cried, "How oft the sight of means to do great deeds makes playwrights great!" I say the tenth because I am convinced that at the first he denounced his part as a rotten one; thought the ghost's speech ridiculously long; and wanted to play the king. Anyhow, whether he had the wit to utter it or not, the boast would have been a valid one. The best conclusion is that every actor should say, "If I create the hero in myself, God will send an author to write his part." For in the long run the actors will get the authors, and the authors the actors, they deserve.

INDEX

THE END